850

SPANISH·ENGLISH
ENGLISH·SPANISH
DICTIONARY

DICCIONARIO
ESPAÑOL·INGLÉS
INGLÉS·ESPAÑOL

COLLINS
GEM
DICTIONARY

SPANISH·ENGLISH
ENGLISH·SPANISH

ESPAÑOL·INGLÉS
INGLÉS·ESPAÑOL

Mike Gonzalez

HarperCollinsPublishers

grijalbo

first published in this edition 1982
revised edition 1989

© William Collins Sons & Co. Ltd. 1982, 1989

latest reprint 1992

ISBN 0 00 458544 5

contributors/con la colaboración de
Margaret Tejerizo, John Forry,
Carmen Billinghurst, Liam Kane, Pat Feehan,
Soledad Pérez-López, José Ramón Parrondo

editorial staff/redacción
Claire Evans, Jeremy Butterfield, Irene Lakhani

Ediciones Grijalbo, S.A.
Aragón 385, Barcelona 08013

ISBN 84-253-2111-5

Printed in Great Britain by
HarperCollins Manufacturing, Glasgow

INTRODUCCIÓN

Quien desee leer y entender el inglés encontrará en este diccionario un extenso léxico moderno que abarca una amplia gama de locuciones de uso corriente. Igualmente encontrará, en su debido orden alfabético, las abreviaturas, las siglas, los nombres geográficos más conocidos y, además, las principales formas de verbo irregulares, donde se le referirá a las respectivas formas de base, hallándose allí la traducción.

Quien aspire comunicarse y expresarse en lengua extranjera, hallará aquí una clara y detallada explicación de las palabras básicas, empleándose un sistema de indicadores que le remitirán a la traducción más apta y le señalarán su correcto uso.

INTRODUCTION

The user whose aim is to read and understand Spanish will find a comprehensive and up-to-date wordlist including numerous phrases in current use. He will also find listed alphabetically the main irregular forms with a cross-reference to the basic form where a translation is given, as well as some of the most common abbreviations, acronyms and geographical names.

The user who wishes to communicate and to express himself in the foreign language will find clear and detailed treatment of all the basic words, with numerous indicators pointing to the appropriate translation, and helping him to use it correctly.

ABREVIATURAS		ABBREVIATIONS
adjetivo, locución adjetiva	**a**	adjective, adjectival phrase
abreviatura	**ab(b)r**	abbreviation
adverbio, locución adverbial	**ad**	adverb, adverbial phrase
administración, lengua administrativa	**ADMIN**	administration
agricultura	**AGR**	agriculture
América Latina	**AM**	Latin America
anatomía	**ANAT**	anatomy
arquitectura	**ARQ, ARCH**	architecture
astrología, astronomía	**ASTRO**	astrology, astronomy
el automóvil	**AUT(O)**	the motor car and motoring
aviación, viajes aéreos	**AVIAT**	flying, air travel
biología	**BIO(L)**	biology
botánica, flores	**BOT**	botany
inglés británico	**Brit**	British English
química	**CHEM**	chemistry
lengua familiar	**col**	colloquial usage
comercio, finanzas, banca	**COM(M)**	commerce, finance, banking
informática	**COMPUT**	computers
conjunción	**conj**	conjunction
construcción	**CONSTR**	building
compuesto	**cpd**	compound element
cocina	**CULIN**	cookery
economía	**ECON**	economics
electricidad, electrónica	**ELEC**	electricity, electronics
enseñanza, sistema escolar y universitario	**ESCOL**	schooling, schools and universities
España	**Esp**	Spain
especialmente	**esp**	especially
exclamación, interjección	**excl**	exclamation, interjection
femenino	**f**	feminine
lengua familiar	**fam**	colloquial usage
ferrocarril	**FERRO**	railways
uso figurado	**fig**	figurative use
fotografía	**FOTO**	photography
(verbo inglés) del cual la partícula es inseparable	**fus**	(phrasal verb) where the particle is inseparable
generalmente	**gen**	generally
geografía, geología	**GEO**	geography, geology
geometría	**GEOM**	geometry

ABREVIATURAS		ABBREVIATIONS
infinitivo	**inf**	infinitive
informática	**INFORM**	computers
invariable	**inv**	invariable
irregular	**irg**	irregular
lo jurídico	**JUR**	law
América Latina	**LAm**	Latin America
gramática, lingüística	**LING**	grammar, linguistics
masculino	**m**	masculine
matemáticas	**MAT(H)**	mathematics
medicina	**MED**	medical term, medicine
masculino/femenino	**m/f**	masculine/feminine
lo militar, ejército	**MIL**	military matters
música	**MUS**	music
sustantivo, nombre	**n**	noun
navegación, náutica	**NAUT**	sailing, navigation
sustantivo numérico	**num**	numeral noun
complemento	**obj**	(grammatical) object
	o.s.	oneself
peyorativo	**pey, pej**	derogatory, pejorative
fotografía	**PHOT**	photography
fisiología	**PHYSIOL**	physiology
plural	**pl**	plural
política	**POL**	politics
participio de pasado	**pp**	past participle
prefijo	**pref**	prefix
preposición	**prep**	preposition
pronombre	**pron**	pronoun
psicología, psiquiatría	**PSICO,**	psychology, psychiatry
	PSYCH	
tiempo pasado	**pt**	past tense
sustantivo no empleado en el plural	**q**	collective (uncountable) noun, not used in plural
química	**QUIM**	chemistry
ferrocarril	**RAIL**	railways
religión, lo eclesiástico	**REL**	religion, church service
	sb	somebody
enseñanza, sistema escolar y universitario	**SCOL**	schooling, schools and universities
singular	**sg**	singular
España	**Sp**	Spain
	sth	something
sujeto	**su(b)j**	(grammatical) subject
subjuntivo	**subjun**	subjunctive
sufijo	**suff**	suffix

ABREVIATURAS		ABBREVIATIONS
tauromaquia	**TAUR**	bullfighting
también	**tb**	also
técnica, tecnología	**TEC(H)**	technical term, technology
telecomunicaciones	**TELEC, TEL**	telecommunications
televisión	**TV**	television
imprenta, tipografía	**TIP, TYP**	typography, printing
inglés norteamericano	**US**	American English
verbo	**vb**	verb
verbo intransitivo	**vi**	intransitive verb
verbo pronominal	**vr**	reflexive verb
verbo transitivo	**vt**	transitive verb
zoología, animales	**ZOOL**	zoology
marca registrada	®	registered trademark
indica un equivalente cultural	≈	introduces a cultural equivalent

SPANISH PRONUNCIATION

Consonants

c	[k]	caja	c before *a*, *o* or *u* is pronounced as in c*a*t
ce, ci	[θe, θi]	cero cielo	c before *e* or *i* is pronounced as in *th*in
ch	[tʃ]	chiste	ch is pronounced as ch in *ch*air
d	[d, ð]	danés ciudad	at the beginning of a phrase or after *l* or *n*, d is pronounced as in English. In any other position it is pronounced like *th* in *the*
g	[g, ɤ]	gafas paga	g before *a*, *o* or *u* is pronounced as in *g*ap, if at the beginning of a phrase or after *n*. In other positions the sound is softened
ge, gi	[xe, xi]	gente girar	g before *e* or *i* is pronounced similar to *ch* in Scottish lo*ch*
h		haber	h is always silent in Spanish
j	[x]	jugar	j is pronounced similar to *ch* in Scottish lo*ch*
ll	[ʎ]	talle	ll is pronounced like the *lli* in mi*lli*on
ñ	[ɲ]	niño	ñ is pronounced like the *ni* in o*ni*on
q	[k]	que	q is pronounced as *k* in *k*ing
r, rr	[r, rr]	quitar garra	r is always pronounced in Spanish, unlike the silent *r* in dan*cer*. rr is trilled, like a Scottish *r*
s	[s]	quizás isla	s is usually pronounced as in pa*ss*, but before *b*, *d*, *g*, *l*, *m* or *n* it is pronounced as in ro*s*e
v	[b, ß]	vía dividir	v is pronounced something like *b*. At the beginning of a phrase or after *m* or *n* it is pronounced as *b* in *b*oy. In any other position the sound is softened
z	[θ]	tenaz	z is pronounced as *th* in *th*in

b, f, k, l, m, n, p, t and x are pronounced as in English.

Vowels

a	[a]	p*a*t*a*	not as long as *a* in f*a*r. When followed by a consonant in the same syllable (i.e. in a closed syllable), as in am*a*nte, the *a* is short, as in b*a*t
e	[e]	m*e*	like *e* in th*e*y. In a closed syllable, as in g*e*nte, the *e* is short as in p*e*t
i	[i]	p*i*no	as in m*ea*n or mach*i*ne
o	[o]	l*o*	as in l*o*cal. In a closed syllable, as in c*o*ntrol, the *o* is short as in c*o*t
u	[u]	l*u*nes	as in r*u*le. It is silent after *q*, and in *gue*, *gui*, unless marked *güe*, *güi* e.g. antigüedad

Diphthongs

ai, ay	[ai]	b*ai*le	as *i* in r*i*de
au	[au]	*au*to	as *ou* in sh*ou*t
ei, ey	[ei]	bu*ey*	as *ey* in gr*ey*
eu	[eu]	d*eu*da	both elements pronounced independently [e] + [u]
oi, oy	[oi]	h*oy*	as *oy* in t*oy*

Stress

The rules of stress in Spanish are as follows:
(a) when a word ends in a vowel or in *n* or *s*, the second last syllable is stressed: pat*a*ta, pat*a*tas, com*e*, com*e*n
(b) when a word ends in a consonant other than *n* or *s*, the stress falls on the last syllable: par*e*d, habl*a*r
(c) when the rules set out in a and b are not applied, an acute accent appears over the stressed vowel: com*ún*, geograf*í*a, ingl*é*s

In the phonetic transcription, the symbol ['] precedes the syllable on which the stress falls.

PRONUNCIACIÓN INGLESA

Vocales y diptongos

	Ejemplo inglés	*Ejemplo español/explicación*
ɑː	f*a*ther	Entre *a* de p*a*dre y *o* de n*o*che
ʌ	b*u*t, c*o*me	*a* muy breve
æ	m*a*n, c*a*t	Se mantienen los labios en la posición de *e* en p*e*na y luego se pronuncia el sonido *a*
ə	father, *a*go	Sonido indistinto parecido a una *e* u *o* casi mudas
əː	b*i*rd, h*ea*rd	Entre *e* abierta, y *o* cerrada, sonido alargado
ɛ	g*e*t, b*e*d	como en p*e*rro
ɪ	*i*t, b*i*g	Más breve que en s*í*
iː	t*ea*, s*ee*	Como en f*i*no
ɔ	h*o*t, w*a*sh	Como en t*o*rre
ɔː	s*aw*, *a*ll	Como en p*o*r
u	p*u*t, b*oo*k	Sonido breve, más cerrado que b*u*rro
uː	t*oo*, y*ou*	Sonido largo, como en *u*no
aɪ	fl*y*, h*i*gh	Como en fr*ai*le
au	h*ow*, h*ou*se	Como en p*au*sa
ɛə	th*ere*, b*ear*	Casi como en v*ea*, pero el sonido *a* se mezcla con el indistinto [ə]
eɪ	d*ay*, ob*ey*	*e* cerrada seguida por una *i* débil
ɪə	h*ere*, h*ear*	Como en man*ía*, mezclándose el sonido *a* con el indistinto [ə]
əu	g*o*, n*o*te	[ə] seguido por una breve *u*
ɔɪ	b*oy*, *oi*l	Como en v*oy*
uə	p*oor*, s*ure*	*u* bastante larga más el sonido indistinto [ə]

Consonantes

	Ejemplo inglés	Ejemplo español/explicación
d	men**d**ed	Como en con**d**e, an**d**ar
g	**g**o, **g**et, bi**g**	Como en **g**rande, **g**ol
dʒ	**g**in, **j**udge	Como en la **ll** andaluza y en **G**eneralitat (catalán)
ŋ	si**ng**	Como en ví**n**culo
h	**h**ouse, **h**e	Como la jota hispanoamericana
j	**y**oung, **y**es	Como en **y**a
k	**c**ome, mo**ck**	Como en **c**aña, Es**c**ocia
r	**r**ed, t**r**ead	Se pronuncia con la punta de la lengua hacia atrás y sin hacerla vibrar
s	**s**and, ye**s**	Como en ca**s**a, **s**e**s**ión
z	ro**s**e, **z**ebra	Como en de**s**de, mi**s**mo
ʃ	**sh**e, ma**ch**ine	Como en **ch**ambre (francés), ro**x**o (portugués)
tʃ	**ch**in, ri**ch**	Como en **ch**ocolate
v	**v**alley	Como en f, pero se retiran los dientes superiores vibrándolos contra el labio inferior
w	**w**ater, **wh**ich	Como en la **u** de h**u**evo, p**u**ede
ʒ	vi**si**on	Como en **j**ournal (francés)
θ	**th**ink, my**th**	Como en re**c**eta, **z**apato
ð	**th**is, **th**e	Como en la **d** de habla**d**o, ver**d**ad

b, p, f, m, n, l, t iguales que en español
El signo * indica que la r final escrita apenas se pronuncia en inglés británico cuando la palabra siguiente empieza con vocal. El signo ['] indica la sílaba acentuada.

ESPAÑOL - INGLÉS
SPANISH - ENGLISH
A

PALABRA CLAVE

---

a [a] *prep* (*a + el = al*) **1** (*dirección*): to; **fueron ~ Madrid/Grecia** they went to Madrid/Greece; **me voy ~ casa** I'm going home
2 (*distancia*): **está ~ 15 km de aquí** it's 15 kms from here
3 (*posición*): **estar ~ la mesa** to be at table; **al lado de** next to, beside; *ver tb* **puerta**
4 (*tiempo*): **~ las 10/~ medianoche** at 10/midnight; **~ la mañana siguiente** the following morning; **~ los pocos días** after a few days; **estamos ~ 9 de julio** it's the ninth of July; **~ los 24 años** at the age of 24; **al año/~ la semana** (*AM*) a year/week later
5 (*manera*): **~ la francesa** the French way; **~ caballo** on horseback; **~ oscuras** in the dark
6 (*medio, instrumento*): **~ lápiz** in pencil; **~ mano** by hand; **cocina ~ gas** gas stove
7 (*razón*): **~ 30 ptas el kilo** at 30 pesetas a kilo; **~ más de 50 km/h** at more than 50 kms an hour
8 (*dativo*): **se lo di ~ él** I gave it to him; **vi al policía** I saw the policeman; **se lo compré ~ él** I bought it from him
9 (*tras ciertos verbos*): **voy ~ verle** I'm going to see him; **empezó ~ trabajar** he started working *o* to work
10 (*+ infinitivo*): **al verle, le reconocí inmediatamente** when I saw him I recognized him at once; **el camino ~ recorrer** the distance we (*etc*) have to travel; **¡~ callar!** keep quiet!; **¡~ comer!** let's eat!

abad, esa [a'βað, 'ðesa] *nm/f* abbot/

abbess; **~ía** *nf* abbey.
abajo [a'βaxo] *ad* (*situación*) (down) below, underneath; (*en edificio*) downstairs; (*dirección*) down, downwards; **~ de** *prep* below, under; **el piso de ~** the downstairs flat; **la parte de ~** the lower part; **¡~ el gobierno!** down with the government!; **cuesta/río ~** downhill/downstream; **de arriba ~** from top to bottom; **el ~ firmante** the undersigned; **más ~** lower *o* further down.
abalorios [aβa'lorjos] *nmpl* (*chucherías*) trinkets.
abalanzarse [aβalan'θarse] *vr*: **~ sobre** *o* **contra** to throw o.s. at.
abanderado [aβande'raðo] *nm* standard bearer.
abandonado, a [aβando'naðo, a] *a* derelict; (*desatendido*) abandoned; (*desierto*) deserted; (*descuidado*) neglected.
abandonar [aβando'nar] *vt* to leave; (*persona*) to abandon, desert; (*cosa*) to abandon, leave behind; (*descuidar*) to neglect; (*renunciar*) to give up; (*INFORM*) to quit; **~se** *vr*: **~se a** to abandon o.s. to; **abandono** *nm* (*acto*) desertion, abandonment; (*estado*) abandon, neglect; (*renuncia*) withdrawal, retirement; **ganar por ~** to win by default.
abanicar [aβani'kar] *vt* to fan; **abanico** *nm* fan; (*NAUT*) derrick.
abaratar [aβara'tar] *vt* to lower the price of // **~se** *vr* to go *o* come down in price.
abarcar [aβar'kar] *vt* to include, embrace; (*AM*) to monopolize.
abarrotado, a [aβarro'taðo, a] *a* packed.
abarrote [aβa'rrote] *nm* packing; **~s** *nmpl* (*AM*) groceries, provisions;

~ro, a *nm/f (AM)* grocer.

abastecer [aβaste'θer] *vt* to supply; **abastecimiento** *nm* supply.

abasto [a'βasto] *nm* supply; (*abundancia*) abundance; **no dar ~ a** to be unable to cope with.

abatido, a [aβa'tiðo, a] *a* dejected, downcast.

abatimiento [aβati'mjento] *nm* (*depresión*) dejection, depression.

abatir [aβa'tir] *vt* (*muro*) to demolish; (*pájaro*) to shoot *o* bring down; (*fig*) to depress; **~se** *vr* to get depressed; **~se sobre** to swoop *o* pounce on.

abdicación [aβðika'θjon] *nf* abdication.

abdicar [aβði'kar] *vi* to abdicate.

abdomen [aβ'ðomen] *nm* abdomen.

abecedario [aβeθe'ðarjo] *nm* alphabet.

abedul [aβe'ðul] *nm* birch.

abeja [a'βexa] *nf* bee.

abejorro [aβe'xorro] *nm* bumblebee.

aberración [aβerra'θjon] *nf* aberration.

abertura [aβer'tura] *nf* = **apertura**.

abeto [a'βeto] *nm* fir.

abierto, a [a'βjerto, a] *pp de* **abrir** // *a* open; (*AM*) generous.

abigarrado, a [aβiɣa'rraðo, a] *a* multi-coloured.

abismal [aβis'mal] *a* (*fig*) vast, enormous.

abismar [aβis'mar] *vt* to humble, cast down; **~se** *vr* to sink; **~se en** (*fig*) to be plunged into.

abismo [a'βismo] *nm* abyss.

abjurar [aβxu'rar] *vi*: **~ de** to abjure, forswear.

ablandar [aβlan'dar] *vt* to soften // *vi*, **~se** *vr* to get softer.

abnegación [aβneɣa'θjon] *nf* self-denial.

abnegado, a [aβne'ɣaðo, a] *a* self-sacrificing.

abocado, a [aβo'kaðo, a] *a*: **verse ~ al desastre** to be heading for disaster.

abochornar [aβotʃor'nar] *vt* to

embarrass; **~se** *vr* to get flustered; (*BOT*) to wilt.

abofetear [aβofete'ar] *vt* to slap (in the face).

abogacía [aβoɣa'θia] *nf* legal profession; (*ejercicio*) practice of the law.

abogado, a [aβo'ɣaðo, a] *nm/f* lawyer; (*notario*) solicitor; (*en tribunal*) barrister (*Brit*), attorney (*US*); **~ defensor** defence lawyer *o* attorney (*US*).

abogar [aβo'ɣar] *vi*: **~ por** to plead for; (*fig*) to advocate.

abolengo [aβo'lengo] *nm* ancestry, lineage.

abolición [aβoli'θjon] *nf* abolition.

abolir [aβo'lir] *vt* to abolish; (*cancelar*) to cancel.

abolladura [aβoʎa'ðura] *nf* dent.

abollar [aβo'ʎar] *vt* to dent.

abominable [aβomi'naβle] *a* abominable.

abominación [aβomina'θjon] *nf* abomination.

abonado, a [aβo'naðo, a] *a* (*deuda*) paid(-up) // *nm/f* subscriber.

abonar [aβo'nar] *vt* (*deuda*) to settle; (*terreno*) to fertilize; (*idea*) to endorse; **~se** *vr* to subscribe; **abono** *nm* payment; fertilizer; subscription.

abordar [aβor'ðar] *vt* (*barco*) to board; (*asunto*) to broach.

aborigen [aβo'rixen] *nm/f* aborigine.

aborrecer [aβorre'θer] *vt* to hate, loathe.

abortar [aβor'tar] *vi* (*malparir*) to have a miscarriage; (*deliberadamente*) to have an abortion; **aborto** *nm* miscarriage; abortion.

abotagado, a [aβota'ɣaðo, a] *a* swollen.

abotonar [aβoto'nar] *vt* to button (up), do up.

abovedado, a [aβoβe'ðaðo, a] *a* vaulted, domed.

abrasar [aβra'sar] *vt* to burn (up); (*AGR*) to dry up, parch.

abrazadera [aβraθa'ðera] *nf* bracket.

abrazar [aβra'θar] *vt* to embrace,

hug.

abrazo [aˈβraθo] nm embrace, hug; un ~ (en carta) with best wishes.

abrebotellas [aβreβoˈteʎas] nm inv bottle opener.

abrecartas [aβreˈkartas] nm inv letter opener.

abrelatas [aβreˈlatas] nm inv tin (Brit) o can opener.

abreviar [aβreˈβjar] vt to abbreviate; (texto) to abridge; (plazo) to reduce; **abreviatura** nf abbreviation.

abridor [aβriˈðor] nm bottle opener; (de latas) tin (Brit) o can opener.

abrigar [aβriˈɣar] vt (proteger) to shelter; (suj: ropa) to keep warm; (fig) to cherish.

abrigo [aˈβriɣo] nm (prenda) coat, overcoat; (lugar protegido) shelter.

abril [aˈβril] nm April.

abrillantar [aβriʎanˈtar] vt to polish.

abrir [aˈβrir] vt to open (up) // vi to open; ~se vr to open (up); (extenderse) to open out; (cielo) to clear; ~se paso to find o force a way through.

abrochar [aβroˈtʃar] vt (con botones) to button (up); (zapato, con broche) to do up.

abrumar [aβruˈmar] vt to overwhelm; (sobrecargar) to weigh down.

abrupto, a [aˈβrupto, a] a abrupt; (empinado) steep.

absceso [aβsˈθeso] nm abscess.

absentismo [aβsenˈtismo] nm absenteeism.

absolución [aβsoluˈθjon] nf (REL) absolution; (JUR) acquittal.

absoluto, a [aβsoˈluto, a] a absolute; en ~ ad not at all.

absolver [aβsolˈβer] vt to absolve; (JUR) to pardon; (: acusado) to acquit.

absorbente [aβsorˈβente] a absorbent; (interesante) absorbing.

absorber [aβsorˈβer] vt to absorb; (embeber) to soak up.

absorción [aβsorˈθjon] nf absorption; (COM) takeover.

absorto, a pp de **absorber** //

[aβˈsorto, a] a absorbed, engrossed.

abstemio, a [aβsˈtemjo, a] a teetotal.

abstención [aβstenˈθjon] nf abstention.

abstenerse [aβsteˈnerse] vr: ~ (de) to abstain o refrain (from).

abstinencia [aβstiˈnenθja] nf abstinence; (ayuno) fasting.

abstracción [aβstrakˈθjon] nf abstraction.

abstracto, a [aβsˈtrakto, a] a abstract.

abstraer [aβstraˈer] vt to abstract; ~se vr to be o become absorbed.

abstraído, a [aβstraˈiðo, a] a absent-minded.

absuelto [aβˈswelto] pp de **absolver**.

absurdo, a [aβˈsurðo, a] a absurd.

abuelo, a [aˈβwelo, a] nm/f grandfather/mother; ~s nmpl grandparents.

abulia [aˈβulja] nf lethargy.

abultado, a [aβulˈtaðo, a] a bulky.

abultar [aβulˈtar] vt to enlarge; (aumentar) to increase; (fig) to exaggerate // vi to be bulky.

abundancia [aβunˈdanθja] nf: una ~ de plenty of; **abundante** a abundant, plentiful; **abundar** vi to abound, be plentiful.

aburguesarse [aβurɣeˈsarse] vr to become middle-class.

aburrido, a [aβuˈrriðo, a] a (hastiado) bored; (que aburre) boring; **aburrimiento** nm boredom, tedium.

aburrir [aβuˈrrir] vt to bore; ~se vr to be bored, get bored.

abusar [aβuˈsar] vi to go too far; ~ de to abuse; **abuso** nm abuse.

abusivo, a [aβuˈsiβo, a] a (precio) exorbitant.

abyecto, a [aβˈjekto, a] a wretched, abject.

A.C. abr (= Año de Cristo) A.D.

a/c abr (= al cuidado de) c/o.

acá [aˈka] ad (lugar) here; ¿de cuándo ~? since when?

acabado, a [aka'βaðo, a] *a* finished, complete; *(perfecto)* perfect; *(agotado)* worn out; *(fig)* masterly // *nm* finish.

acabar [aka'βar] *vt (llevar a su fin)* to finish, complete; *(consumir)* to use up; *(rematar)* to finish off // *vi* to finish, end; ~**se** *vr* to finish, stop; *(terminarse)* to be over; *(agotarse)* to run out; ~ **con** to put an end to; ~ **de llegar** to have just arrived; ~ **por hacer** to end (up) by doing; **¡se acabó!** it's all over!; *(¡basta!)* that's enough!

acabóse [aka'βose] *nm*: **esto es el** ~ this is the last straw.

academia [aka'ðemja] *nf* academy; **académico, a** *a* academic.

acaecer [akae'θer] *vi* to happen, occur.

acalorado, a [akalo'raðo, a] *a (discusión)* heated.

acalorarse [akalo'rarse] *vr (fig)* to get heated.

acampar [akam'par] *vi* to camp.

acanalar [akana'lar] *vt* to groove; *(ondular)* to corrugate.

acantilado [akanti'laðo] *nm* cliff.

acaparar [akapa'rar] *vt* to monopolize; *(acumular)* to hoard.

acariciar [akari'θjar] *vt* to caress; *(esperanza)* to cherish.

acarrear [akarre'ar] *vt* to transport; *(fig)* to cause, result in.

acaso [a'kaso] *ad* perhaps, maybe // *nm* chance; **(por) si** ~ (just) in case.

acatamiento [akata'mjento] *nm* respect; *(de la ley)* observance.

acatar [aka'tar] *vt* to respect, obey.

acatarrarse [akata'rrarse] *vr* to catch a cold.

acaudalado, a [akauða'laðo, a] *a* well-off.

acaudillar [akauði'ʎar] *vt* to lead, command.

acceder [akθe'ðer] *vi*: ~ **a** *(petición etc)* to agree to; *(tener acceso a)* to have access to; *(INFORM)* to access.

accesible [akθe'siβle] *a* accessible.

acceso [ak'θeso] *nm* access, entry; *(camino)* access, approach; *(MED)* attack, fit.

accesorio, a [akθe'sorjo, a] *a, nm* accessory.

accidentado, a [akθiðen'taðo, a] *a* uneven; *(montañoso)* hilly; *(azaroso)* eventful // *nm/f* accident victim.

accidental [akθiðen'tal] *a* accidental; **accidentarse** *vr* to have an accident.

accidente [akθi'ðente] *nm* accident.

acción [ak'θjon] *nf* action; *(acto)* action, act; *(COM)* share; *(JUR)* action, lawsuit; ~ **ordinaria/preferente** ordinary/preference share; **accionar** *vt* to work, operate; *(INFORM)* to drive.

accionista [akθjo'nista] *nm/f* shareholder, stockholder.

acebo [a'θeβo] *nm* holly; *(árbol)* holly tree.

acechanza [aθe'tʃanθa] *nf* = **acecho**.

acechar [aθe'tʃar] *vt* to spy on; *(aguardar)* to lie in wait for; **acecho** *nm*: **estar al acecho (de)** to lie in wait (for).

aceitar [aθei'tar] *vt* to oil, lubricate.

aceite [a'θeite] *nm* oil; *(de oliva)* olive oil; ~**ra** *nf* oilcan; **aceitoso, a** *a* oily.

aceituna [aθei'tuna] *nf* olive.

acelerador [aθelera'ðor] *nm* accelerator.

acelerar [aθele'rar] *vt* to accelerate.

acelga [a'θelɣa] *nf* chard, beet.

acento [a'θento] *nm* accent; *(acentuación)* stress.

acentuar [aθen'twar] *vt* to accent; to stress; *(fig)* to accentuate.

acepción [aθep'θjon] *nf* meaning.

aceptable [aθep'taβle] *a* acceptable.

aceptación [aθepta'θjon] *nf* acceptance; *(aprobación)* approval.

aceptar [aθep'tar] *vt* to accept; *(aprobar)* to approve.

acequia [a'θekja] *nf* irrigation ditch.

acera [a'θera] *nf* pavement (Brit), sidewalk (US).

acerado, a [aθe'raðo, a] *a* steel; *(afilado)* sharp; *(fig: duro)* steely; (: *mordaz)* biting.

acerbo, a [a'θerβo, a] *a* bitter; *(fig)* harsh.

acerca [a'θerka]: ~ **de** *ad* about, concerning.

acercar [aθer'kar] *vt* to bring o move nearer; ~**se** *vr* to approach, come near.

acerico [aθe'riko] *nm* pincushion.

acero [a'θero] *nm* steel.

acérrimo, a [a'θerrimo, a] *a (partidario)* staunch; *(enemigo)* bitter.

acertado, a [aθer'taðo, a] *a* correct; *(apropiado)* apt; *(sensato)* sensible.

acertar [aθer'tar] *vt (blanco)* to hit; *(solución)* to get right; *(adivinar)* to guess // *vi* to get it right, be right; ~ **a** to manage to; ~ **con** to happen o hit on.

acertijo [aθer'tixo] *nm* riddle, puzzle.

acervo [a'θerβo] *nm* heap; ~ **común** undivided estate.

aciago, a [a'θjaɣo, a] *a* ill-fated, fateful.

acicalar [aθika'lar] *vt* to polish; *(persona)* to dress up; ~**se** *vr* to get dressed up.

acicate [aθi'kate] *nm* spur.

acidez [aθi'ðeθ] *nf* acidity.

ácido, a ['aθiðo, a] *a* sour, acid // *nm* acid.

acierto [a'θjerto] *etc vb ver* **acertar** // *nm* success; *(buen paso)* wise move; *(solución)* solution; *(habilidad)* skill, ability.

aclamación [aklama'θjon] *nf* acclamation; *(aplausos)* applause.

aclamar [akla'mar] *vt* to acclaim; *(aplaudir)* to applaud.

aclaración [aklara'θjon] *nf* clarification, explanation.

aclarar [akla'rar] *vt* to clarify, explain; *(ropa)* to rinse // *vi* to clear up; ~**se** *vr (explicarse)* to understand; ~ **se la garganta** to clear one's throat.

aclaratorio, a [aklara'torjo, a] *a* explanatory.

aclimatación [aklimata'θjon] *nf* acclimatization; **aclimatar** *vt* to acclimatize; **aclimatarse** *vr* to become acclimatized.

acné [ak'ne] *nm* acne.

acobardar [akoβar'ðar] *vt* to intimidate.

acodarse [ako'ðarse] *vr*: ~ **en** to lean on.

acogedor, a [akoxe'ðor, a] *a* welcoming; *(hospitalario)* hospitable.

acoger [ako'xer] *vt* to welcome; *(abrigar)* to shelter; ~**se** *vr* to take refuge.

acogida [ako'xiða] *nf* reception; refuge.

acolchar [akol'tʃar] *vt* to pad; *(fig)* to cushion.

acometer [akome'ter] *vt* to attack; *(emprender)* to undertake; **acometida** *nf* attack, assault.

acomodado, a [akomo'ðaðo, a] *a (persona)* well-to-do.

acomodador, a [akomoða'ðor, a] *nm/f* usher(ette).

acomodar [akomo'ðar] *vt* to adjust; *(alojar)* to accommodate; ~**se** *vr* to conform; *(instalarse)* to install o.s.; *(adaptarse)*: ~**se (a)** to adapt to.

acomodaticio, a [akomoða'tiθjo, a] *a (pey)* accommodating, obliging; *(manejable)* pliable.

acompañar [akompa'ɲar] *vt* to accompany; *(documentos)* to enclose.

acondicionar [akondiθjo'nar] *vt* to arrange, prepare; *(pelo)* to condition.

acongojar [akoŋgo'xar] *vt* to distress, grieve.

aconsejar [akonse'xar] *vt* to advise, counsel; ~**se** *vr*: ~**se con** to consult.

acontecer [akonte'θer] *vi* to happen, occur; **acontecimiento** *nm* event.

acopio [a'kopjo] *nm* store, stock.

acoplamiento [akopla'mjento] *nm* coupling, joint; **acoplar** *vt* to fit; *(ELEC)* to connect; *(vagones)* to couple.

acorazado, a [akora'θaðo, a] *a* armour-plated, armoured // *nm* battleship.

acordar [akor'ðar] vt (*resolver*) to agree, resolve; (*recordar*) to remind; ~se vr to agree; ~se (de algo) to remember sth; **acorde** a (MUS) harmonious; ~ con (*medidas etc*) in keeping with // nm chord.

acordeón [akorðe'on] nm accordion.

acordonado, a [akorðo'naðo, a] a (*calle*) cordoned-off.

acorralar [akorra'lar] vt to round up, corral.

acortar [akor'tar] vt to shorten; (*duración*) to cut short; (*cantidad*) to reduce; ~se vr to become shorter.

acosar [ako'sar] vt to pursue relentlessly; (*fig*) to hound, pester.

acostar [akos'tar] vt (*en cama*) to put to bed; (*en suelo*) to lay down; (*barco*) to bring alongside; ~se vr to go to bed; to lie down.

acostumbrado, a [akostum'braðo, a] a usual; ~ a used to.

acostumbrar [akostum'brar] vt: ~ **a uno a algo** to get sb used to sth // vi: ~ **(a) hacer** to be in the habit of doing; ~se vr: ~se a to get used to.

acotación [akota'θjon] nf marginal note; (GEO) elevation mark; (de límite) boundary mark; (TEATRO) stage direction.

ácrata ['akrata] a, nm/f anarchist.

acre ['akre] a (*sabor*) sharp, bitter; (*olor*) acrid; (*fig*) biting // nm acre.

acrecentar [akreθen'tar] vt to increase, augment.

acreditar [akreði'tar] vt (*garantizar*) to vouch for, guarantee; (*autorizar*) to authorize; (*dar prueba de*) to prove; (COM: *abonar*) to credit; (*embajador*) to accredit; ~se vr to become famous.

acreedor, a [akree'ðor, a] a: ~ **a** worthy of // nm/f creditor.

acribillar [akriβi'ʎar] vt: ~ **a balazos** to riddle with bullets.

acrimonia [akri'monja], **acritud** [akri'tuð] nf acrimony.

acróbata [a'kroβata] nm/f acrobat.

acta ['akta] nf certificate; (*de comi-*

sión) minutes pl, record; ~ **de nacimiento/de matrimonio** birth/marriage certificate; ~ **notarial** affidavit.

actitud [akti'tuð] nf attitude; (*postura*) posture.

activar [akti'βar] vt to activate; (*acelerar*) to speed up.

actividad [aktiβi'ðað] nf activity.

activo, a [ak'tiβo, a] a active; (*vivo*) lively // nm (COM) assets pl.

acto ['akto] nm act, action; (*ceremonia*) ceremony; (TEATRO) act; **en el ~** immediately.

actor [ak'tor] nm actor; (JUR) plaintiff // a: **parte ~a** prosecution.

actriz [ak'triθ] nf actress.

actuación [aktwa'θjon] nf action; (*comportamiento*) conduct, behaviour; (JUR) proceedings pl; (*desempeño*) performance.

actual [ak'twal] a present(-day), current; ~**idad** nf present time; ~**idades** nfpl news sg; **en la ~idad** at present; (*hoy día*) nowadays.

actualizar [aktwali'θar] vt to update, modernize.

actualmente [aktwal'mente] ad at present; (*hoy día*) nowadays.

actuar [ak'twar] vi (*obrar*) to work, operate; (*actor*) to act, perform // vt to work, operate; ~ **de** to act as.

actuario, a [ak'twarjo, a] nm/f clerk; (COM) actuary.

acuarela [akwa'rela] nf watercolour.

acuario [a'kwarjo] nm aquarium; A~ Aquarius.

acuartelar [akwarte'lar] vt (MIL: *disciplinar*) to confine to barracks.

acuático, a [a'kwatiko, a] a aquatic.

acuciar [aku'θjar] vt to urge on.

acuclillarse [akukli'ʎarse] vr to crouch down.

acuchillar [akutʃi'ʎar] vt (TEC) to plane (down), smooth.

acudir [aku'ðir] vi (*asistir*) to attend; (*ir*) to go; ~ **a** (*fig*) to turn to; ~ **en ayuda de** to go to the aid of.

acuerdo etc vb ver **acordar** // [a'kwerðo] nm agreement; **¡de ~!**

agreed!; **de ~ con** (*persona*) in agreement with; (*acción, documento*) in accordance with; **estar de ~ to** be agreed, agree.

acumular [akumu'lar] *vt* to accumulate, collect.

acuñar [aku'ɲar] *vt* (*moneda*) to mint; (*frase*) to coin.

acuoso, a [a'kwoso, a] *a* watery.

acurrucarse [akurru'karse] *vr* to crouch; (*ovillarse*) to curl up.

acusación [akusa'θjon] *nf* accusation; **acusar** *vt* to accuse; (*revelar*) to reveal; (*denunciar*) to denounce.

acuse [a'kuse] *nm*: **~ de recibo** acknowledgement of receipt.

acústico, a [a'kustiko, a] *a* acoustic // *nf* (*de una sala etc*) acoustics *pl*.

achacar [atʃa'kar] *vt* to attribute.

achacoso, a [atʃa'koso, a] *a* sickly.

achantar [atʃan'tar] *vt* (*fam*) to scare, frighten; **~se** *vr* to back down.

achaque *etc vb ver* **achacar** // [a'tʃake] *nm* ailment.

achicar [atʃi'kar] *vt* to reduce; (*humillar*) to humiliate; (*NAUT*) to bale out.

achicoria [atʃi'korja] *nf* chicory.

achicharrar [atʃitʃa'rrar] *vt* to scorch, burn.

adagio [a'ðaxjo] *nm* adage; (*MUS*) adagio.

adaptación [aðapta'θjon] *nf* adaptation.

adaptador [aðapta'ðor] *nm* (*ELEC*) adapter.

adaptar [aðap'tar] *vt* to adapt; (*acomodar*) to fit.

adecuado, a [aðe'kwaðo, a] *a* (*apto*) suitable; (*oportuno*) appropriate.

adecuar [aðe'kwar] *vt* to adapt; to make suitable.

a. de J.C. *abr* (= *antes de Jesucristo*) B.C.

adelantado, a [aðelan'taðo, a] *a* advanced; (*reloj*) fast; **pagar por ~** to pay in advance.

adelantamiento [aðelanta'mjento]

nm advance, advancement; (*AUTO*) overtaking.

adelantar [aðelan'tar] *vt* to move forward; (*avanzar*) to advance; (*acelerar*) to speed up; (*AUTO*) to overtake // *vi*, **~se** *vr* to go forward, advance.

adelante [aðe'lante] *ad* forward(s), ahead // *excl* come in!; **de hoy en ~** from now on; **más ~** later on; (*más allá*) further on.

adelanto [aðe'lanto] *nm* advance; (*mejora*) improvement; (*progreso*) progress.

adelgazar [aðelxa'θar] *vt* to thin (down) // *vi* to get thin; (*con régimen*) to slim down, lose weight.

ademán [aðe'man] *nm* gesture; **ademanes** *nmpl* manners; **en ~ de as** if to.

además [aðe'mas] *ad* besides; (*por otra parte*) moreover; (*también*) also; **~ de** besides, in addition to.

adentrarse [aðen'trarse] *vr*: **~ en** to go into, get inside; (*penetrar*) to penetrate (into).

adentro [a'ðentro] *ad* inside, in; **mar ~** out at sea; **tierra ~** inland.

adepto, a [a'ðepto, a] *nm/f* supporter.

aderezar [aðere'θar] *vt* (*ensalada*) to dress; (*comida*) to season; **aderezo** *nm* dressing; seasoning.

adeudar [aðeu'ðar] *vt* to owe; **~se** *vr* to run into debt.

adherirse [aðe'rirse] *vr*: **~ a** to adhere to; (*partido*) to join.

adhesión [aðe'sjon] *nf* adhesion; (*fig*) adherence.

adición [aði'θjon] *nf* addition.

adicionar [aðiθjo'nar] *vt* to add.

adicto, a [a'ðikto, a] *a*: **~ a** addicted to; (*dedicado*) devoted to // *nm/f* supporter, follower; (*toxicómano etc*) addict.

adiestrar [aðjes'trar] *vt* to train, teach; (*conducir*) to guide, lead; **~se** *vr* to practise; (*enseñarse*) to train o.s.

adinerado, a [aðine'raðo, a] *a*

wealthy.

adiós [a'ðjos] *excl* (*para despedirse*) goodbye!, cheerio!; (*al pasar*) hello!

aditivo [aði'tiβo] *nm* additive.

adivinanza [aðiβi'nanθa] *nf* riddle; **adivinar** *vt* to prophesy; (*conjeturar*) to guess; **adivino, a** *nm/f* fortune-teller.

adj *abr* (= *adjunto*) encl.

adjetivo [aðxe'tiβo] *nm* adjective.

adjudicación [aðxuðika'θjon] *nf* award; adjudication.

adjudicar [aðxuði'kar] *vt* to award; **~se** *vr*: **~ se algo** to appropriate sth.

adjuntar [aðxun'tar] *vt* to attach, enclose; **adjunto, a** *a* attached, enclosed // *nm/f* assistant.

administración [aðministra'θjon] *nf* administration; (*dirección*) management; **administrador, a** *nm/f* administrator; manager(ess).

administrar [aðminis'trar] *vt* to administer; **administrativo, a** *a* administrative.

admirable [aðmi'raβle] *a* admirable.

admiración [aðmira'θjon] *nf* admiration; (*asombro*) wonder; (*LING*) exclamation mark.

admirar [aðmi'rar] *vt* to admire; (*extrañar*) to surprise; **~se** *vr* to be surprised.

admisible [aðmi'siβle] *a* admissible.

admisión [aðmi'sjon] *nf* admission; (*reconocimiento*) acceptance.

admitir [aðmi'tir] *vt* to admit; (*aceptar*) to accept.

admonición [aðmoni'θjon] *nf* warning.

adobar [aðo'βar] *vt* (*CULIN*) to season.

adobe [a'ðoβe] *nm* adobe, sun-dried brick.

adoctrinar [aðoktri'nar] *vt*: **~ en** to indoctrinate with.

adolecer [aðole'θer] *vi*: **~ de** to suffer from.

adolescente [aðoles'θente] *nm/f* adolescent, teenager.

adonde [a'ðonde] *conj* (to) where.

adónde [a'ðonde] *ad* = **dónde**.

adopción [aðop'θjon] *nf* adoption.

adoptar [aðop'tar] *vt* to adopt.

adoptivo, a [aðop'tiβo, a] *a* (*padres*) adoptive; (*hijo*) adopted.

adoquín [aðo'kin] *nm* paving stone.

adorar [aðo'rar] *vt* to adore.

adormecer [aðorme'θer] *vt* to put to sleep; **~se** *vr* to become sleepy; (*dormirse*) to fall asleep.

adornar [aðor'nar] *vt* to adorn.

adorno [a'ðorno] *nm* adornment; (*decoración*) decoration.

adosado, a [aðo'saðo, a] *a*: **casa adosada** semi-detached house.

adquiero *etc vb ver* **adquirir**.

adquirir [aðki'rir] *vt* to acquire, obtain.

adquisición [aðkisi'θjon] *nf* acquisition.

adrede [a'ðreðe] *ad* on purpose.

adscribir [aðskri'βir] *vt* to appoint.

adscrito *pp de* **adscribir**.

aduana [a'ðwana] *nf* customs *pl*.

aduanero, a [aðwa'nero, a] *a* customs *cpd* // *nm/f* customs officer.

aducir [aðu'θir] *vt* to adduce; (*dar como prueba*) to offer as proof.

adueñarse [aðwe'narse] *vr*: **~ de** to take possession of.

adulación [aðula'θjon] *nf* flattery.

adular [aðu'lar] *vt* to flatter.

adulterar [aðulte'rar] *vt* to adulterate // *vi* to commit adultery.

adulterio [aðul'terjo] *nm* adultery.

adúltero, a [a'ðultero, a] *a* adulterous // *nm/f* adulterer/adulteress.

adulto, a [a'ðulto, a] *a*, *nm/f* adult.

adusto, a [a'ðusto, a] *a* (*severo*) stern; (*austero*) austere.

advenedizo, a [aðβene'ðiθo, a] *nm/f* upstart.

advenimiento [aðβeni'mjento] *nm* arrival; (*al trono*) accession.

adverbio [að'βerβjo] *nm* adverb.

adversario, a [aðβer'sarjo, a] *nm/f* adversary.

adversidad [aðβersi'ðað] *nf* adversity; (*contratiempo*) setback.

adverso, a [að'βerso, a] *a* adverse.

advertencia [aðβer'tenθja] *nf* warning.

ing; (*prefacio*) preface, foreword.

advertir [aðβer'tir] *vt* to notice; (*avisar*): ~ **a uno de** to warn sb about o of.

Adviento [að'βjento] *nm* Advent.

advierto *etc*, **advirtiendo** *etc vb ver* **advertir**.

adyacente [aðja'θente] *a* adjacent.

aéreo, a [a'ereo, a] *a* aerial.

aerobic [ae'roβik] *nm* aerobics *sg*.

aerodeslizador [aeroðesliθa'ðor], **aerodeslizante** [aeroðesli'θante] *nm* hovercraft.

aeromozo, a [aero'moθo, a] *nm/f* (*AM*) air steward(ess).

aeronáutica [aero'nautika] *nf* aeronautics *sg*.

aeronave [aero'naβe] *nm* spaceship.

aeroplano [aero'plano] *nm* aeroplane.

aeropuerto [aero'pwerto] *nm* airport.

aerosol [aero'sol] *nm* aerosol.

afabilidad [afaβili'ðað] *nf* friendliness; **afable** *a* affable.

afamado, a [afa'maðo, a] *a* famous.

afán [a'fan] *nm* hard work; (*deseo*) desire.

afanar [afa'nar] *vt* to harass; (*fam*) to pinch; ~**se** *vr*: ~**se por hacer** to strive to do; **afanoso, a** *a* (*trabajo*) hard; (*trabajador*) industrious.

afear [afe'ar] *vt* to disfigure.

afección [afek'θjon] *nf* (*MED*) disease.

afectación [afekta'θjon] *nf* affectation; **afectado, a** *a* affected; **afectar** *vt* to affect.

afectísimo, a [afek'tisimo, a] *a* affectionate; ~ **suyo** yours truly.

afectivo, a [afek'tiβo, a] *a* (*problema etc*) emotionally.

afecto [a'fekto] *nm* affection; **tenerle** ~ **a uno** to be fond of sb.

afectuoso, a [afek'twoso, a] *a* affectionate.

afeitar [afei'tar] *vt* to shave; ~**se** *vr* to shave.

afeminado, a [afemi'naðo, a] *a* effeminate.

aferrado, a [afe'rraðo, a] *a* stubborn.

aferrar [afe'rrar] *vt* to grasp; (*barco*) to moor // *vi* to moor.

Afganistán [afxanis'tan] *nm* Afghanistan.

afianzamiento [afjanθa'mjento] *nm* strengthening; security; **afianzar** *vt* to strengthen; to secure; **afianzarse** *vr* to become established.

afición [afi'θjon] *nf* fondness, liking; **la** ~ **the fans** *pl*; **pinto por** ~ I paint as a hobby; **aficionado, a** *a* keen, enthusiastic; (*no profesional*) amateur; **ser** ~ **a algo** to be very keen on o fond of sth // *nm/f* enthusiast, fan; amateur.

aficionar [afiθjo'nar] *vt*: ~ **a uno a algo** to make sb like sth; ~**se** *vr*: ~**se a algo** to grow fond of sth.

afiche [a'fitʃe] *nm* (*AM*) poster.

afilado, a [afi'laðo, a] *a* sharp.

afilar [afi'lar] *vt* to sharpen.

afiliarse [afi'ljarse] *vr* to affiliate.

afín [a'fin] *a* (*parecido*) similar; (*conexo*) related.

afinar [afi'nar] *vt* (*TEC*) to refine; (*MUS*) to tune // *vi* to play/sing in tune.

afincarse [afin'karse] *vr* to settle.

afinidad [afini'ðað] *nf* affinity; (*parentesco*) relationship; **por** ~ by marriage.

afirmación [afirma'θjon] *nf* affirmation; **afirmar** *vt* to affirm, state; (*reforzar*) to strengthen; **afirmativo, a** *a* affirmative.

aflicción [aflik'θjon] *nf* affliction; (*dolor*) grief.

afligir [afli'xir] *vt* to afflict; (*apenar*) to distress; ~**se** *vr* to grieve.

aflojar [aflo'xar] *vt* to slacken; (*desatar*) to loosen, undo; (*relajar*) to relax // *vi* to drop; (*bajar*) to go down; ~**se** *vr* to relax.

aflorar [aflo'rar] *vi* to come to the surface, emerge.

afluente [aflu'ente] *a* flowing // *nm* tributary.

afluir [aflu'ir] *vi* to flow.

afmo, a abr (= afectísimo(a) suyo(a)) Yours.

afónico, a [a'foniko, a] a: **estar ~** to have a sore throat; to have lost one's voice.

aforo [a'foro] nm (de teatro etc) capacity.

afortunado, a [afortu'naðo, a] a fortunate, lucky.

afrancesado, a [afranθe'saðo, a] a francophile; (pey) Frenchified.

afrenta [a'frenta] nf affront, insult; (deshonra) dishonour, shame.

África ['afrika] nf Africa; **~ del Sur** South Africa; **africano, a** a, nm/f African.

afrontar [afron'tar] vt to confront; (poner cara a cara) to bring face to face.

afuera [a'fwera] ad out, outside; **~s** nfpl outskirts.

agachar [aɣa'tʃar] vt to bend, bow; **~se** vr to stoop, bend.

agalla [a'ɣaʎa] nf (ZOOL) gill; **~s** nfpl (MED) tonsillitis sg; (ANAT) tonsils; **tener ~s** (fam) to have guts.

agarradera [aɣarra'ðera] nf (AM), **agarradero** [aɣarra'ðero] nm handle; **~s** npl pull sg, influence sg.

agarrado, a [aɣa'rraðo, a] a mean, stingy.

agarrar [aɣa'rrar] vt to grasp, grab; (AM) to take, catch; (recoger) to pick up // vi (planta) to take root; **~se** vr to hold on (tightly).

agarrotar [aɣarro'tar] vt (lío) to tie tightly; (persona) to squeeze tightly; (reo) to garrotte; **~se** vr (motor) to seize up; (MED) to stiffen.

agasajar [aɣasa'xar] vt to treat well, fête.

agencia [a'xenθja] nf agency; **~ inmobiliaria** estate (Brit) o real estate (US) agent's (office); **~ matrimonial** marriage bureau; **~ de viajes** travel agency.

agenciarse [axen'θjarse] vr to obtain, procure.

agenda [a'xenda] nf diary.

agente [a'xente] nm agent; (de

policía policeman; **~ femenino** policewoman; **~ inmobiliario** estate agent (Brit), realtor (US); **~ de bolsa** stockbroker; **~ de seguros** insurance agent.

ágil ['axil] a agile, nimble; **agilidad** nf agility, nimbleness.

agitación [axita'θjon] nf (de mano etc) shaking, waving; (de líquido etc) stirring; (fig) agitation.

agitar [axi'tar] vt to wave, shake; (líquido) to stir; (fig) to stir up, excite; **~se** vr to get excited; (inquietarse) to get worried o upset.

aglomeración [aɣlomera'θjon] nf: **~ de tráfico/gente** traffic jam/mass of people.

aglomerar [aɣlome'rar] vt, **aglomerarse** vr to crowd together.

agnóstico, a [aɣ'nostiko, a] a, nm/f agnostic.

agobiar [aɣo'βjar] vt to weigh down; (oprimir) to oppress; (cargar) to burden.

agolparse [aɣol'parse] vr to crowd together.

agonía [aɣo'nia] nf death throes pl; (fig) agony, anguish.

agonizante [aɣoni'θante] a dying.

agonizar [aɣoni'θar] vi (tb: estar agonizando) to be dying.

agosto [a'ɣosto] nm August.

agotado, a [aɣo'taðo, a] a (persona) exhausted; (libros) out of print; (acabado) finished; (COM) sold out.

agotador, a [aɣota'ðor, a] a exhausting.

agotamiento [aɣota'mjento] nm exhaustion.

agotar [aɣo'tar] vt to exhaust; (consumir) to drain; (recursos) to use up, deplete; **~se** vr to be exhausted; (acabarse) to run out; (libro) to go out of print.

agraciado, a [aɣra'θjaðo, a] a (atractivo) attractive; (en sorteo etc) lucky.

agraciar [aɣra'θjar] vt (JUR) to pardon; (con premio) to reward.

agradable [aɣra'ðaßle] *a* pleasant, nice.

agradar [aɣra'ðar] *vt*: él me agrada I like him.

agradecer [aɣraðe'θer] *vt* to thank; (*favor etc*) to be grateful for; **agradecido, a** *a* grateful; **¡muy ~!** thanks a lot!; **agradecimiento** *nm* thanks *pl*; gratitude.

agradezco *etc vb ver* **agradecer**.

agrado [a'ɣraðo] *nm*: **ser de tu** *etc* **agrado** to be to your *etc* liking.

agrandar [aɣran'dar] *vt* to enlarge; (*fig*) to exaggerate; **~se** *vr* to get bigger.

agrario, a [a'ɣrarjo, a] *a* agrarian, land *cpd*; (*política*) agricultural, farming.

agravante [aɣra'ßante] *a* aggravating // *nf*: **con la ~ de que ...** with the further difficulty that ...

agravar [aɣra'ßar] *vt* (*pesar sobre*) to make heavier; (*irritar*) to aggravate; **~se** *vr* to worsen, get worse.

agraviar [aɣra'ßjar] *vt* to offend; (*ser injusto con*) to wrong; **~se** *vr* to take offence; **agravio** *nm* offence; wrong; (*JUR*) grievance.

agredir [aɣre'ðir] *vt* to attack.

agregado [aɣre'ɣaðo] *nm* aggregate; (*persona*) attaché.

agregar [aɣre'ɣar] *vt* to gather; (*añadir*) to add; (*persona*) to appoint.

agresión [aɣre'sjon] *nf* aggression.

agresivo, a [aɣre'sißo, a] *a* aggressive.

agriar [a'ɣrjar] *vt* to (turn) sour; **~se** *vr* to turn sour.

agrícola [a'ɣrikola] *a* farming *cpd*, agricultural.

agricultor, a [aɣrikul'tor, a] *nm/f* farmer.

agricultura [aɣrikul'tura] *nf* agriculture, farming.

agridulce [aɣri'ðulθe] *a* bittersweet; (*CULIN*) sweet and sour.

agrietarse [aɣrje'tarse] *vr* to crack; (*piel*) to chap.

agrimensor, a [aɣrimen'sor, a] *nm/f* surveyor.

agrio, a [a'ɣrjo, a] *a* bitter.

agronomía [aɣrono'mia] *nf* agronomy, agriculture.

agropecuario, a [aɣrope'kwarjo, a] *a* farming *cpd*, agricultural.

agrupación [aɣrupa'θjon] *nf* group; (*acto*) grouping.

agrupar [aɣru'par] *vt* to group.

agua ['aɣwa] *nf* water; (*NAUT*) wake; (*ARQ*) slope of a roof; **~s** *nfpl* (*de piedra*) water *sg*, sparkle *sg*; (*MED*) water *sg*, urine *sg*; (*NAUT*) waters; **~s abajo/arriba** downstream/upstream; **~ bendita/destilada/potable** holy/distilled/drinking water; **~ caliente** hot water; **~ corriente** running water; **~ de colonia** eau de cologne; **~ mineral (con/sin gas)** (fizzy/non-fizzy) mineral water; **~s jurisdiccionales** territorial waters; **~s mayores** excrement *sg*.

aguacate [aɣwa'kate] *nm* avocado pear.

aguacero [aɣwa'θero] *nm* (heavy) shower, downpour.

aguado, a [a'ɣwaðo, a] *a* watery, watered down // *nf* (*AGR*) watering place; (*NAUT*) water supply; (*ARTE*) watercolour.

aguafiestas [aɣwa'fjestas] *nm/f inv* spoilsport, killjoy.

aguafuerte [aɣwa'fwerte] *nm o f* etching.

aguamanil [aɣwama'nil] *nm* (*jofaina*) washbasin.

aguanieve [aɣwa'njeße] *nf* sleet.

aguantar [aɣwan'tar] *vt* to bear, put up with; (*sostener*) to hold up // *vi* to last; **~se** *vr* to restrain o.s.; **aguante** *nm* (*paciencia*) patience; (*resistencia*) endurance.

aguar [a'ɣwar] *vt* to water down.

aguardar [aɣwar'ðar] *vt* to wait for.

aguardiente [aɣwar'ðjente] *nm* brandy, liquor.

aguarrás [aɣwa'rras] *nm* turpentine.

agudeza [aɣu'ðeθa] *nf* sharpness;

(ingenio) wit.

agudizar [ayuði'θar] *vt (crisis)* to make worse; **~se** *vr* to get worse.

agudo, a [a'yuðo, a] *a* sharp; *(voz)* high-pitched, piercing; *(dolor, enfermedad)* acute.

agüero [a'ywero] *nm*: **buen/mal ~** good/bad omen.

aguijar [ayi'xar] *vt* to goad; *(incitar)* to urge on // *vi* to hurry along.

aguijón [ayi'xon] *nm* sting; *(fig)* spur; **aguijonear** *vt* = **aguijar**.

águila ['axila] *nf* eagle; *(fig)* genius.

aguileño, a [ayi'leɲo, a] *a (nariz)* aquiline; *(rostro)* sharp-featured.

aguinaldo [ayi'naldo] *nm* Christmas box.

aguja [a'yuxa] *nf* needle; *(de reloj)* hand; *(ARQ)* spire; *(TEC)* firing-pin; **~s** *nfpl (ZOOL)* ribs; *(FERRO)* points.

agujerear [ayuxere'ar] *vt* to make holes in.

agujero [ayu'xero] *nm* hole.

agujetas [ayu'xetas] *nfpl* stitch *sg*; *(rigidez)* stiffness *sg*.

aguzar [ayu'θar] *vt* to sharpen; *(fig)* to incite.

ahí [a'i] *ad* there; **de ~ que** so that, with the result that; **~ llega** here he comes; **por ~** that way; *(allá)* over there; **200 o por ~** 200 or so.

ahijado, a [ai'xaðo, a] *nm/f* godson/daughter.

ahínco [a'inko] *nm* earnestness.

ahíto, a [a'ito, a] *a*: **estoy ~** I'm full up.

ahogar [ao'yar] *vt* to drown; *(asfixiar)* to suffocate, smother; *(fuego)* to put out; **~se** *vr (en el agua)* to drown; *(por asfixia)* to suffocate.

ahogo [a'oyo] *nm* breathlessness; *(fig)* financial difficulty.

ahondar [aon'dar] *vt* to deepen, make deeper; *(fig)* to study thoroughly // *vi*: **~ en** to study thoroughly.

ahora [a'ora] *ad* now; *(hace poco)* a moment ago, just now; *(dentro de poco)* in a moment; **~ voy** I'm coming; **~ mismo** right now; **~ bien** now then; **por ~** for the present.

ahorcar [aor'kar] *vt* to hang; **~se** *vr* to hang o.s.

ahorita [ao'rita] *ad (fam)* right now.

ahorrar [ao'rrar] *vt (dinero)* to save; *(esfuerzos)* to save, avoid; **ahorro** *nm (acto)* saving; *(frugalidad)* thrift; **ahorros** *nmpl* savings.

ahuecar [awe'kar] *vt* to hollow (out); *(voz)* to deepen; **~se** *vr* to give o.s. airs.

ahumar [au'mar] *vt* to smoke, cure; *(llenar de humo)* to fill with smoke // *vi* to smoke; **~se** *vr* to fill with smoke.

ahuyentar [aujen'tar] *vt* to drive off, frighten off; *(fig)* to dispel.

airado, a [ai'raðo, a] *a* angry; **airar** *vt* to anger; **airarse** *vr* to get angry.

aire ['aire] *nm* air; *(viento)* wind; *(corriente)* draught; *(MUS)* tune; **~s** *nmpl*: **darse ~s** to give o.s. airs; **al ~ libre** in the open air; **~ acondicionado** air conditioning; **airoso, a** *a* windy; draughty; *(fig)* graceful.

aislado, a [ais'laðo, a] *a* isolated; *(incomunicado)* cut-off; *(ELEC)* insulated.

aislar [ais'lar] *vt* to isolate; *(ELEC)* to insulate.

ajar [a'xar] *vt* to spoil; *(fig)* to abuse.

ajardinado, a [axarði'naðo, a] *a* landscaped.

ajedrez [axe'ðreθ] *nm* chess.

ajeno, a [a'xeno, a] *a (que pertenece a otro)* somebody else's; **~ a** foreign to; **~ de** free from, devoid of.

ajetreado, a [axetre'aðo, a] *a* busy.

ajetreo [axe'treo] *nm* bustle.

ají [a'xi] *nm* chili, red pepper; *(salsa)* chili sauce.

ajo ['axo] *nm* garlic.

ajorca [a'xorka] *nf* bracelet.

ajuar [a'xwar] *nm* household furnishings *pl*; *(de novia)* trousseau; *(de niño)* layette.

ajustado, a [axus'taðo, a] *a*

(*tornillo*) tight; (*cálculo*) right; (*ropa*) tight(-fitting); (*DEPORTE*: re-sultado*) close.

ajustar [axus'tar] *vt* (*adaptar*) to adjust; (*encajar*) to fit; (*TEC*) to engage; (*IMPRENTA*) to make up; (*apretar*) to tighten; (*concertar*) to agree (on); (*reconciliar*) to reconcile; (*cuenta*) to settle // *vi* to fit.

ajuste [a'xuste] *nm* adjustment; (*COSTURA*) fitting; (*acuerdo*) compromise; (*de cuenta*) settlement.

al [al] = **a + el**, ver **a**.

ala ['ala] *nf* wing; (*de sombrero*) brim; (*futbolista*) winger.

alabanza [ala'βanθa] *nf* praise.

alabar [ala'βar] *vt* to praise.

alacena [ala'θena] *nf* cupboard (*Brit*), closet (*US*).

alacrán [ala'kran] *nm* scorpion.

alado, a [a'laðo, a] *a* winged.

alambique [alam'bike] *nm* still.

alambrada [alam'braða] *nf*, **alambrado** [alam'braðo] *nm* wire fence; (*red*) wire netting.

alambre [a'lambre] *nm* wire; ~ **de púas** barbed wire; **alambrista** *nm/f* tightrope walker.

alameda [ala'meða] *nf* (*plantío*) poplar grove; (*lugar de paseo*) avenue, boulevard.

álamo ['alamo] *nm* poplar; ~ **temblón** aspen.

alano [a'lano] *nm* mastiff.

alarde [a'larðe] *nm* show, display; **hacer** ~ **de** to boast of.

alargador [alarva'ðor] *nm* (*ELEC*) extension lead.

alargar [alar'var] *vt* to lengthen, extend; (*paso*) to hasten; (*brazo*) to stretch out; (*cuerda*) to pay out; (*conversación*) to spin out; ~**se** *vr* to get longer.

alarido [ala'riðo] *nm* shriek.

alarma [a'larma] *nf* alarm.

alarmante [alar'mante] *a* alarming.

alazán [ala'θan] *nm* sorrel.

alba ['alβa] *nf* dawn.

albacea [alβa'θea] *nm/f* executor/executrix.

albahaca [al'βaka] *nf* basil.

Albania [al'βanja] *nf* Albania.

albañal [alβa'nal] *nm* drain, sewer.

albañil [alβa'nil] *nm* bricklayer; (*cantero*) mason.

albarán [alβa'ran] *nm* (*COM*) delivery note, invoice.

albaricoque [alβari'koke] *nm* apricot.

albedrío [alβe'ðrio] *nm*: **libre** ~ free will.

alberca [al'βerka] *nf* reservoir; (*AM*) swimming pool.

albergar [alβer'var] *vt* to shelter.

albergue etc *vb* ver **albergar** // [al'βerve] *nm* shelter, refuge; ~ **de juventud** youth hostel.

albóndiga [al'βondiva] *nf* meatball.

albor [al'βor] *nm* whiteness; (*amanecer*) dawn; ~**ada** *nf* dawn; (*diana*) reveille; ~**ear** *vi* to dawn.

albornoz [alβor'noθ] *nm* (*de los árabes*) burnous; (*para el baño*) bathrobe.

alborotar [alβoro'tar] *vi* to make a row // *vt* to agitate, stir up; ~**se** *vr* to get excited; (*mar*) to get rough; **alboroto** *nm* row, uproar.

alborozar [alβoro'θar] *vt* to gladden; ~**se** *vr* to rejoice.

alborozo [alβo'roθo] *nm* joy.

albricias [al'βriθjas] *nfpl*: ¡~! good news!

álbum ['alβum] (*pl* ~**s**, ~**es**) *nm* album; ~ **de recortes** scrapbook.

albumen [al'βumen] *nm* egg white, albumen.

alcachofa [alka'tʃofa] *nf* artichoke.

alcalde, esa [al'kalde, esa] *nm/f* mayor(ess).

alcaldía [alkal'dia] *nf* mayoralty; (*lugar*) mayor's office.

alcance etc *vb* ver **alcanzar** // [al'kanθe] *nm* reach; (*COM*) adverse balance.

alcancía [alkan'θia] *nf* money box.

alcantarilla [alkanta'riʎa] *nf* (*de aguas cloacales*) sewer; (*en la calle*) gutter.

alcanzar [alkan'θar] *vt* (*algo*: con la*

mano, el pie) to reach; (*alguien: en el camino etc*) to catch up with; (*autobús*) to catch; (*suj: bala*) to hit, strike // *vi* (*ser suficiente*) to be enough; ~ **a hacer** to manage to do.

alcaparra [alka'parra] *nf* caper.

alcatraz [alka'traθ] *nm* gannet.

alcayata [alka'jata] *nf* hook.

alcázar [al'kaθar] *nm* fortress; (*NAUT*) quarter-deck.

alcoba [al'koβa] *nf* bedroom.

alcohol [al'kol] *nm* alcohol; ~ **metílico** methylated spirits *pl* (*Brit*), wood alcohol (*US*); **alcohólico, a** *a, nm/f* alcoholic.

alcoholímetro [alko'limetro] *nm* Breathalyser ® (*Brit*), drunkometer (*US*).

alcoholismo [alko'lismo] *nm* alcoholism.

alcornoque [alkor'noke] *nm* cork tree; (*fam*) idiot.

aldaba [al'daβa] *nf* (door) knocker.

aldea [al'dea] *nf* village; ~**no, a** *nm/f* village cpd // *nm/f* villager.

ale ['ale] *excl* come on!, let's go!

aleación [alea'θjon] *nf* alloy.

aleatorio, a [alea'torjo, a] *a* random.

aleccionar [alekθjo'nar] *vt* to instruct; (*adiestrar*) to train.

alegación [aleva'θjon] *nf* allegation; **alegar** [ale'var] *vt* to allege; (*JUR*) to plead // *vi* (*AM*) to argue.

alegato [ale'vato] *nm* (*JUR*) allegation; (*AM*) argument.

alegoría [alevo'ria] *nf* allegory.

alegrar [ale'vrar] *vt* (*causar alegría*) to cheer (up); (*fuego*) to poke; (*fiesta*) to liven up; ~**se** *vr* (*fam*) to get merry o tight; ~**se de** to be glad about.

alegre [a'levre] *a* happy, cheerful; (*fam*) merry, †**tight**; (*chiste*) risqué, blue; **alegría** *nf* happiness; merriment.

alejamiento [alexa'mjento] *nm* removal; (*distancia*) remoteness.

alejar [ale'xar] *vt* to remove; (*fig*) to estrange; ~**se** *vr* to move away.

alemán, ana [ale'man, ana] *a, nm/f* German // *nm* (*LING*) German.

Alemania [ale'manja] *nf*: ~ **Occidental/Oriental** West/East Germany.

alentador, a [alenta'ðor, a] *a* encouraging.

alentar [alen'tar] *vt* to encourage.

alergia [a'lerxja] *nf* allergy.

alero [a'lero] *nm* (*de tejado*) eaves *pl*; (*de carruaje*) mudguard.

alerta [a'lerta] *a, nm* alert.

aleta [a'leta] *nf* (*de pez*) fin; (*de ave*) wing; (*de foca, DEPORTE*) flipper; (*AUTO*) mudguard.

aletargar [aletar'var] *vt* to make drowsy; (*entumecer*) to make numb; ~**se** *vr* to grow drowsy; to become numb.

aletear [alete'ar] *vi* to flutter.

alevín [ale'βin], **alevino** [ale'βino] *nm* fry, young fish.

alevosía [aleβo'sia] *nf* treachery.

alfabeto [alfa'βeto] *nm* alphabet.

alfalfa [al'falfa] *nf* alfalfa, lucerne.

alfarería [alfare'ria] *nf* pottery; (*tienda*) pottery shop; **alfarero, a** *nm/f* potter.

alféizar [al'feiθar] *nm* window-sill.

alférez [al'fereθ] *nm* (*MIL*) second lieutenant; (*NAUT*) ensign.

alfil [al'fil] *nm* (*AJEDREZ*) bishop.

alfiler [alfi'ler] *nm* pin; (*broche*) clip; (*pinza*) clothes peg.

alfiletero [alfile'tero] *nm* needlecase.

alfombra [al'fombra] *nf* carpet; (*más pequeña*) rug; **alfombrar** *vt* to carpet; **alfombrilla** *nf* rug, mat.

alforja [al'forxa] *nf* saddlebag.

alforza [al'forθa] *nf* pleat.

algas ['alvas] *nfpl* seaweed.

algarabía [alvara'βia] *nf* (*fam*) gibberish.

algarrobo [alva'rroβo] *nm* carob tree.

algazara [alva'θara] *nf* din, uproar.

álgebra ['alxeβra] *nf* algebra.

álgido, a [al'xiðo] *a* icy, chilly; (*momento etc*) crucial, decisive.

algo ['alvo] *pron* something; anything

// ad somewhat, rather; ¿~ más? anything else?; (en tienda) is that all?; **por ~ será** there must be some reason for it.

algodón [alɣo'ðon] nm cotton; (planta) cotton plant; ~ **de azúcar** candy floss (Brit), cotton candy (US); ~ **hidrófilo** cotton wool (Brit), absorbent cotton (US).

algodonero, a [alɣoðo'nero, a] a cotton cpd // nm/f cotton grower // nm cotton plant.

alguacil [alɣwa'θil] nm bailiff; (TAUR) mounted official.

alguien ['alɣjen] pron someone, somebody; (en frases interrogativas) anyone, anybody.

alguno, a, [al'ɣuno, a] a (delante de nm: **algún**) some; (después de n): **no tiene talento alguno** he has no talent, he doesn't have any talent // pron (alguien) someone, somebody; **algún que otro libro** some book or other; **algún día iré** I'll go one o some day; **sin interés** ~ without the slightest interest; ~ **que otro** an occasional one; ~**s piensan** some (people) think.

alhaja [a'laxa] nf jewel; (tesoro) precious object, treasure.

alhelí [ale'li] nm wallflower, stock.

aliado, a [a'ljaðo, a] a allied.

alianza [a'ljanθa] nf alliance; (anillo) wedding ring.

aliar [a'ljar] vt to ally; ~**se** vr to form an alliance.

alias ['aljas] ad alias.

alicates [ali'kates] nmpl pliers; ~ **de uñas** nail clippers.

aliciente [ali'θjente] nm incentive; (atracción) attraction.

alienación [aljena'θjon] nf alienation.

aliento [a'ljento] nm breath; (respiración) breathing; **sin** ~ breathless.

aligerar [alixe'rar] vt to lighten; (reducir) to shorten; (aliviar) to alleviate; (mitigar) to ease; (paso) to quicken.

alimaña [ali'maɲa] nf pest.

alimentación [alimenta'θjon] nf (comida) food; (acción) feeding; (tienda) grocer's (shop).

alimentador nm: **alimentador de papel** sheet-feeder; **alimentar** vt to feed; (nutrir) to nourish; **alimentarse** vr to feed.

alimenticio, a [alimen'tiθjo, a] a food cpd; (nutritivo) nourishing, nutritious.

alimento [ali'mento] nm food; (nutrición) nourishment; ~**s** nmpl (JUR) alimony sg.

alineación [alinea'θjon] nf alignment; (DEPORTE) line-up.

alinear [aline'ar] vt to align; ~**se** vr (DEPORTE) to line up; ~**se en** to fall in with.

aliñar [ali'ɲar] vt (CULIN) to season; **aliño** nm (CULIN) dressing.

alisar [ali'sar] vt to smooth.

aliso [a'liso] nm alder.

alistarse [alis'tarse] vr to enlist; (inscribirse) to enrol.

aliviar [ali'βjar] vt (carga) to lighten; (persona) to relieve; (dolor) to relieve, alleviate.

alivio [a'liβjo] nm alleviation, relief.

aljibe [al'xiβe] nm cistern.

alma ['alma] nf soul; (persona) person; (TEC) core.

almacén [alma'θen] nm (depósito) warehouse, store; (MIL) magazine; (AM) shop; (grandes) **almacenes** nmpl department store sg; **almacenaje** nm storage; **almacenaje secundaria** (INFORM) backing storage.

almacenar [almaθe'nar] vt to store, put in storage; (proveerse) to stock up with; **almacenero** nm warehouseman; (AM) shopkeeper.

almanaque [alma'nake] nm almanac.

almeja [al'mexa] nf clam.

almendra [al'mendra] nf almond; **almendro** nm almond tree.

almiar [al'mjar] nm haystack.

almíbar [al'miβar] nm syrup.

almidón [almi'ðon] nm starch.

almidonar *vt* to starch.

almirantazgo [almiran'taθνo] *nm* admiralty.

almirante [almi'rante] *nm* admiral.

almirez [almi'reθ] *nm* mortar.

almizcle [al'miθkle] *nm* musk.

almohada [almo'aða] *nf* pillow; *(funda)* pillowcase; **almohadilla** *nf* cushion; *(TEC)* pad; *(AM)* pincushion.

almohadón [almoa'ðon] *nm* large pillow; bolster.

almorranas [almo'rranas] *nfpl* piles, haemorrhoids.

almorzar [almor'θar] *vt*: ~ **una tortilla** to have an omelette for lunch // *vi* to (have) lunch.

almuerzo *etc vb ver* **almorzar** // [al'mwerθo] *nm* lunch.

alocado, a [alo'kaðo, a] *a* crazy.

alojamiento [aloxa'mjento] *nm* lodging(s) *(pl)*; *(viviendas)* housing.

alojar [alo'xar] *vt* to lodge; ~**se** *vr* to lodge, stay.

alondra [a'londra] *nf* lark, skylark.

alpargata [alpar'vata] *nf* rope-soled sandal, espadrille.

Alpes ['alpes] *nmpl*: **los** ~ the Alps.

alpinismo [alpi'nismo] *nm* mountaineering, climbing; **alpinista** *nmf* mountaineer, climber.

alpiste [al'piste] *nm* birdseed.

alquería [alke'ria] *nf* farmhouse.

alquilar [alki'lar] *vt* *(suj: propietario: inmuebles)* to let, rent (out); *(: coche)* to hire out; *(: TV)* to rent (out); *(suj: alquilador: inmuebles, TV)* to rent; *(: coche)* to hire; '**se alquila casa**' 'house to let *(Brit)* o to rent' *(US)*.

alquiler [alki'ler] *nm* renting; letting; hiring; *(arriendo)* rent; hire charge; ~ **de automóviles** car hire; **de** ~ for hire.

alquimia [al'kimja] *nf* alchemy.

alquitrán [alki'tran] *nm* tar.

alrededor [alreðe'ðor] *ad* around, about; ~**es** *nmpl* surroundings; ~ **de** *prep* around, about; **mirar a su** ~ to look (round) one about.

alta ['alta] *nf ver* **alto**.

altanería [altane'ria] *nf* haughtiness, arrogance; **altanero, a** *a* arrogant, haughty.

altar [al'tar] *nm* altar.

altavoz [alta'βoθ] *nm* loudspeaker; *(amplificador)* amplifier.

alteración [altera'θjon] *nf* alteration; *(alboroto)* disturbance.

alterar [alte'rar] *vt* to alter; to disturb; ~**se** *vr* *(persona)* to get upset.

altercado [alter'kaðo] *nm* argument.

alternar [alter'nar] *vt* to alternate // *vi*, ~**se** *vr* to alternate; *(turnar)* to take turns; ~ **con** to mix with; **alternativo, a** *a* alternative; *(alterno)* alternating // *alternative*; *(elección)* choice; **alterno, a** *a* alternate; *(ELEC)* alternating.

Alteza [al'teθa] *nf* *(tratamiento)* Highness.

altibajos [alti'βaxos] *nmpl* ups and downs.

altiplanicie [altipla'niθje] *nf*, **altiplano** [alti'plano] *nm* high plateau.

altisonante [altiso'nante] *a* high-flown, high-sounding.

altitud [alti'tuð] *nf* height; *(AVIAT, GEO)* altitude.

altivez [alti'βeθ] *nf* haughtiness, arrogance; **altivo, a** *a* haughty, arrogant.

alto, a ['alto, a] *a* high; *(persona)* tall; *(sonido)* high, sharp; *(noble)* high, lofty // *ad* *(estar)* high; *(hablar)* high, loudly // *nm* *(MUS)* alto; *(GEO)* hill; *(AM)* pile // *ad* *(de sitio)* high; *(de sonido)* loud, loudly // *nf* *(certificate of)* discharge // *excl* halt!; **la pared tiene 2 metros de** ~ the wall is 2 metres high; **en alta mar** on the high seas; **en voz alta** in a loud voice; **las altas horas de la noche** the small o wee hours; **en lo** ~ **de** at the top of; **pasar por** ~ to overlook; **dar de alta** to discharge.

altoparlante [altopar'lante] *nm* *(AM)* loudspeaker.

altura [al'tura] *nf* height; *(NAUT)* depth; *(GEO)* latitude; **la pared**

tiene 1.80 de ~ the wall is 1 metre 80cm high; a estas ~s at this stage; a esta ~ del año at this time of the year.

alubia [a'lußja] *nf* French bean, kidney bean.

alucinación [aluθina'θjon] *nf* hallucination; **alucinar** *vi* to hallucinate // to deceive; (*fascinar*) to fascinate.

alud [a'luð] *nm* avalanche; (*fig*) flood.

aludir [alu'ðir] *vi*: ~ a to allude to; **darse por aludido** to take the hint.

alumbrado [alum'braðo] *nm* lighting; **alumbramiento** *nm* lighting; (*MED*) childbirth, delivery.

alumbrar [alum'brar] *vt* to light (up) // *vi* (*MED*) to give birth.

aluminio [alu'minjo] *nm* aluminium (*Brit*), aluminum (*US*).

alumno, a [a'lumno, a] *nm/f* pupil, student.

alunizar [aluni'θar] *vi* to land on the moon.

alusión [alu'sjon] *nf* allusion.

alusivo, a [alu'sißo, a] *a* allusive.

aluvión [alu'ßjon] *nm* alluvium; (*fig*) flood.

alverja [al'ßerxa] *nf* (*AM*) pea.

alza [al'θa] *nf* rise; (*MIL*) sight.

alzada [al'θaða] *nf* (*de caballos*) height; (*JUR*) appeal.

alzamiento [alθa'mjento] *nm* (*aumento*) rise, increase; (*acción*) lifting, raising; (*mejor postura*) higher bid; (*rebelión*) rising; (*COM*) fraudulent bankruptcy.

alzar [al'θar] *vt* to lift (up); (*precio, muro*) to raise; (*cuello de abrigo*) to turn up; (*AGR*) to gather in; (*IMPRENTA*) to gather; ~se *vr* to get up, rise; (*rebelarse*) to revolt; (*COM*) to go fraudulently bankrupt; (*JUR*) to appeal.

allá [a'ʎa] *ad* (*lugar*) there; (*por ahí*) over there; (*tiempo*) then; ~ **abajo** down there; **más** ~ further on; **más** ~ **de** beyond; **¡**~ **tú!** that's your problem!

allanamiento [aʎana'mjento] *nm*: ~ **de morada** burglary.

allanar [aʎa'nar] *vt* to flatten, level (out); (*igualar*) to smooth (out); (*fig*) to subdue; (*JUR*) to burgle, break into; ~se *vr* to fall down; ~se a to submit to, accept.

allegado, a [aʎe'ɣaðo, a] *a* near, close // *nm/f* relation.

allí [a'ʎi] *ad* there; ~ **mismo** right there; **por** ~ over there; (*por ese camino*) that way.

ama [ama] *nf* lady of the house; (*dueña*) owner; (*institutriz*) governess; (*madre adoptiva*) foster mother; ~ **de casa** housewife; ~ **de cría** o **de leche** wet-nurse; ~ **de llaves** housekeeper.

amabilidad [amaßili'ðað] *nf* kindness; (*simpatía*) niceness; **amable** *a* kind; nice; **es Vd muy** ~ that's very kind of you.

amaestrado, a [amaes'traðo, a] *a* (*animal: en circo etc*) performing.

amaestrar [amaes'trar] *vt* to train.

amagar [ama'ɣar] *vt, vi* to threaten; (*DEPORTE, MIL*) to feint; **amago** *nm* threat; (*gesto*) threatening gesture; (*MED*) symptom.

amalgama [amal'ɣama] *nf* amalgam; **amalgamar** *vt* to amalgamate; (*combinar*) to combine, mix.

amamantar [amaman'tar] *vt* to suckle, nurse.

amanecer [amane'θer] *vi* to dawn // *nm* dawn; **el niño amaneció afiebrado** the child woke up with a fever.

amanerado, a [amane'raðo, a] *a* affected.

amansar [aman'sar] *vt* to tame; (*persona*) to subdue; ~se *vr* (*persona*) to calm down.

amante [a'mante] *a*: ~ **de** fond of // *nm/f* lover.

amapola [ama'pola] *nf* poppy.

amar [a'mar] *vt* to love.

amarar [ama'rar] *vi* (*avión*) to land (on the sea).

amargado, a [amar'ɣaðo, a] *a*

bitter.

amargar [amar'γar] *vt* to make bitter; *(fig)* to embitter; ~**se** *vr* to become embittered.

amargo, a [a'marγo, a] *a* bitter; **amargura** *nf* bitterness.

amarillento, a [amari'ʎento, a] *a* yellowish; *(tez)* sallow; **amarillo, a** *a, nm* yellow.

amarrar [ama'rrar] *vt* to moor; *(sujetar)* to tie up.

amarras [a'marras] *nfpl:* **soltar ~** to set sail.

amartillar [amarti'ʎar] *vt (fusil)* to cock.

amasar [ama'sar] *vt (masa)* to knead; *(mezclar)* to mix, prepare; *(confeccionar)* to concoct; **amasijo** *nm* kneading; mixing; *(fig)* hotchpotch.

amateur ['amatur] *nm/f* amateur.

amatista [ama'tista] *nf* amethyst.

amazona [ama'θona] *nf* horsewoman; **A~s** *nm:* **el A~s** the Amazon.

ambages [am'baxes] *nmpl:* **sin ~** in plain language.

ámbar ['ambar] *nm* amber.

ambición [ambi'θjon] *nf* ambition; **ambicionar** *vt* to aspire to; **ambicioso, a** *a* ambitious.

ambidextro, a [ambi'ðekstro, a] *a* ambidextrous.

ambientación [ambjenta'θjon] *nf (CINE, TEATRO etc)* setting; *(RADIO)* sound effects.

ambiente [am'bjente] *nm (tb fig)* atmosphere; *(medio)* environment.

ambigüedad [ambiɣwe'ðað] *nf* ambiguity; **ambigüo, a** *a* ambiguous.

ámbito ['ambito] *nm (campo)* field; *(fig)* scope.

ambos, as ['ambos, as] *apl, pron pl* both.

ambulancia [ambu'lanθja] *nf* ambulance.

ambulante [ambu'lante] *a* travelling *cpd*, itinerant.

ambulatorio [ambula'torio] *nm* state health-service clinic.

ameba [a'meßa] *nf* amoeba.

amedrentar [ameðren'tar] *vt* to scare.

amén [a'men] *excl* amen; **~ de** besides.

amenaza [ame'naθa] *nf* threat.

amenazar [amena'θar] *vt* to threaten // *vi:* **~ con hacer** to threaten to do.

amenguar [amen'ɣwar] *vt* to diminish; *(fig)* to dishonour.

amenidad [ameni'ðað] *nf* pleasantness.

ameno, a [a'meno, a] *a* pleasant.

América [a'merika] *nf* America; **~ del Norte/del Sur** North/South America; **~ Central/Latina** Central/Latin America; **americano, a** *a, nm/f* American // *nf* coat, jacket.

amerizar [ameri'θar] *vi (avión)* to land (on the sea).

ametralladora [ametraʎa'ðora] *nf* machine gun.

amianto [a'mjanto] *nm* asbestos.

amigable [ami'vaßle] *a* friendly.

amígdala [a'miχðala] *nf* tonsil; **amigdalitis** *nf* tonsillitis.

amigo, a [a'miɣo, a] *a* friendly // *nm/f* friend; *(amante)* lover; **ser ~ de algo** to be fond of sth; **ser muy ~s** to be close friends.

amilanar [amila'nar] *vt* to scare; **~se** *vr* to get scared.

aminorar [amino'rar] *vt* to diminish; *(reducir)* to reduce; **~ la marcha** to slow down.

amistad [amis'tað] *nf* friendship; **~es** *nfpl* friends; **amistoso, a** *a* friendly.

amnesia [am'nesja] *nf* amnesia.

amnistía [amnis'tia] *nf* amnesty.

amo ['amo] *nm* owner; *(jefe)* boss.

amodorrarse [amoðo'rrarse] *vr* to get sleepy.

amolar [amo'lar] *vt (perseguir)* to annoy.

amoldar [amol'dar] *vt* to mould; *(adaptar)* to adapt.

amonestación [amonesta'θjon] *nf* warning; **amonestaciones** *nfpl* marriage banns.

amonestar [amones'tar] *vt* to warn; (*REL*) to publish the banns of.

amontonar [amonto'nar] *vt* to collect, pile up; **~se** *vr* to crowd together; (*acumularse*) to pile up.

amor [a'mor] *nm* love; (*amante*) lover; **hacer el ~** to make love.

amoratado, a [amora'taðo, a] *a* purple.

amordazar [amorða'θar] *vt* to muzzle; (*fig*) to gag.

amorfo, a [a'morfo, a] *a* amorphous, shapeless.

amorío [amo'rio] *nm* (*fam*) love affair.

amoroso, a [amo'roso, a] *a* affectionate, loving.

amortajar [amorta'xar] *vt* to shroud.

amortiguador [amortigwa'ðor] *nm* shock absorber; (*parachoques*) bumper; **~es** *nmpl* (*AUTO*) suspension *sg*.

amortiguar [amorti'ɣwar] *vt* to deaden; (*ruido*) to muffle; (*color*) to soften.

amortización [amortiθa'θjon] *nf* (*de deuda*) repayment; (*de bono*) redemption.

amotinar [amoti'nar] *vt* to stir up, incite (to riot); **~se** *vr* to mutiny.

amparar [ampa'rar] *vt* to protect; **~se** *vr* to seek protection; (*de la lluvia etc*) to shelter; **amparo** *nm* help, protection; **al ~ de** under the protection of.

amperio [am'perjo] *nm* ampère, amp.

ampliación [amplja'θjon] *nf* enlargement; (*extensión*) extension; **ampliar** *vt* to enlarge; to extend.

amplificación [amplifika'θjon] *nf* enlargement; **amplificador** *nm* amplifier.

amplificar [amplifi'kar] *vt* to amplify.

amplio, a [am'pljo, a] *a* spacious; (*de falda etc*) full; (*extenso*) extensive; (*ancho*) wide; **amplitud** *nf* spaciousness; extent; (*fig*)

amplitude.

ampolla [am'poʎa] *nf* blister; (*MED*) ampoule.

ampuloso, a [ampu'loso, a] *a* bombastic, pompous.

amputar [ampu'tar] *vt* to cut off, amputate.

amueblar [amwe'βlar] *vt* to furnish.

amurallar [amura'ʎar] *vt* to wall up *o* in.

anacronismo [anakro'nismo] *nm* anachronism.

ánade ['anaðe] *nm* duck.

anadear [anaðe'ar] *vi* to waddle.

anales [a'nales] *nmpl* annals.

analfabetismo [analfaβe'tismo] *nm* illiteracy; **analfabeto, a** *a, nm/f* illiterate.

analgésico [anal'xesiko] *nm* painkiller, analgesic.

análisis [a'nalisis] *nm inv* analysis.

analista [ana'lista] *nm/f* (*gen*) analyst.

analizar [anali'θar] *vt* to analyse.

analogía [analo'xia] *nf* analogy.

analógico, a [ana'loxiko, a] *a* (*INFORM*) analog; (*reloj*) analogue (*Brit*), analog (*US*).

análogo, a [a'naloɣo, a] *a* analogous, similar (*a* to).

ananá(s) [ana'na(s)] *nm* pineapple.

anaquel [ana'kel] *nm* shelf.

anarquía [anar'kia] *nf* anarchy; **anarquismo** *nm* anarchism; **anarquista** *nm/f* anarchist.

anatomía [anato'mia] *nf* anatomy.

anca ['anka] *nf* rump, haunch; **~s** *nfpl* (*fam*) behind *sg*.

anciano, a [an'θjano, a] *a* old, aged // *nm/f* old man/woman // *nm/f* elder.

ancla ['ankla] *nf* anchor; **~dero** *nm* anchorage; **anclar** *vi* to (drop) anchor.

ancho, a [an'tʃo, a] *a* wide; (*falda*) full; (*fig*) liberal // *nm* width; (*FERRO*) gauge; **ponerse ~** to get conceited; **estar a sus anchas** to be at one's ease.

anchoa [an'tʃoa] *nf* anchovy.

anchura [an'tʃura] *nf* width; (*exten-*

sión) wideness.

andaderas [anda'ðeras] *nfpl* baby walker *sg*.

andadura [anda'ðura] *nf* gait; (*de caballo*) pace.

Andalucía [andalu'θia] *nf* Andalusia; **andaluz, a** *a, nm/f* Andalusian.

andamio [an'damjo], **andamiaje** [anda'mjaxe] *nm* scaffold(ing).

andar [an'dar] *vt* to go, cover, travel // *vi* to go, walk, travel; (*funcionar*) to go, work; (*estar*) to be // *nm* walk, gait, pace; ~**se** *vr* to go away; ~ **a pie/a caballo/en bicicleta** to go on foot/on horseback/by bicycle; ~ **haciendo algo** to be doing sth; **¡anda!**, (*sorpresa*) go on!; **anda por** *o* **en los 40** he's about 40.

andariego, a [anda'rjeɣo, a] *a* (*itinerante*) wandering.

andén [an'den] *nm* (FERRO) platform; (NAUT) quayside; (AM: *de la calle*) pavement (Brit), sidewalk (US).

Andes ['andes] *nmpl*: **los ~ the** Andes.

Andorra [an'dorra] *nf* Andorra.

andrajo [an'draxo] *nm* rag; ~**so, a** *a* ragged.

andurriales [andu'rrjales] *nmpl* wilds *npl*.

anduve, anduviera *etc vb ver* **andar**.

anécdota [a'nekðota] *nf* anecdote, story.

anegar [ane'xar] *vt* to flood; (*ahogar*) to drown; ~**se** *vr* to drown; (*hundirse*) to sink.

anejo, a [a'nexo, a] *a, nm* = **anexo**.

anemia [a'nemja] *nf* anaemia.

anestésico [anes'tesiko] *nm* anaesthetic.

anexar [anek'sar] *vt* to annex; (*documento*) to attach; **anexión** *nf*, **anexionamiento** *nm* annexation; **anexo, a** *a* attached // *nm* annexe.

anfibio, a [an'fiβjo, a] *a* amphibious // *nm* amphibian.

anfiteatro [anfite'atro] *nm* amphitheatre; (TEATRO) dress

circle.

anfitrión, ona [anfi'trjon, ona] *nm/f* host(ess).

ángel ['anxel] *nm* angel; ~ **de la guarda** guardian angel; **tener** ~ to be charming; **angélico, a**, **angelical** *a* angelic(al).

angina [an'xina] *nf* (MED) inflammation of the throat; ~ **de pecho** angina; **tener** ~**s** to have tonsillitis.

anglicano, a [angli'kano, a] *a, nm/f* Anglican.

angosto, a [an'gosto, a] *a* narrow.

anguila [an'gila] *nf* eel; ~**s** *nfpl* (NAUT) slipway *sg*.

angula [an'gula] *nf* elver, baby eel.

ángulo ['angulo] *nm* angle; (*esquina*) corner; (*curva*) bend.

angustia [an'gustja] *nf* anguish; **angustiar** *vt* to distress, grieve.

anhelante [ane'lante] *a* eager; (*deseoso*) longing.

anhelar [ane'lar] *vt* to be eager for; to long for, desire // *vi* to pant, gasp; **anhelo** *nm* eagerness; desire.

anidar [ani'ðar] *vi* to nest.

anillo [a'niλo] *nm* ring; ~ **de boda** wedding ring.

Angelus ['anxelus] *nm*: **las** ~**s** the Angelus (bell) *sg*.

animación [anima'θjon] *nf* liveliness; (*vitalidad*) life; (*actividad*) activity; bustle.

animado, a [ani'maðo, a] *a* lively; (*vivaz*) animated; **animador, a** *nm/f* (TV) host(ess), compère; (DEPORTE) cheerleader.

animadversión [animaðßer'sjon] *nf* ill-will, antagonism.

animal [ani'mal] *a* animal; (*fig*) stupid // *nm* animal; (*fig*) fool; (*bestia*) brute.

animar [ani'mar] *vt* (BIO) to animate, give life to; (*fig*) to liven up, brighten up, cheer up; (*estimular*) to stimulate; ~**se** *vr* to cheer up; to feel encouraged; (*decidirse*) to make up one's mind.

ánimo ['animo] *nm* (*alma*) soul; (*mente*) mind; (*valentía*) courage //

excl cheer up!

animoso, a [ani'moso, a] *a* brave; (*vivo*) lively.

aniquilar [aniki'lar] *vt* to annihilate, destroy.

anís [a'nis] *nm* aniseed; (*licor*) anisette.

aniversario [aniβer'sarjo] *nm* anniversary.

anoche [a'notʃe] *ad* last night; **antes de ~** the night before last.

anochecer [anotʃe'θer] *vi* to get dark // *nm* nightfall, dark; **al ~** at nightfall.

anodino, a [ano'ðino, a] *a* dull, anodyne.

anomalía [anoma'lia] *nf* anomaly.

anonimato [anoni'mato] *nm* anonymity.

anónimo, a [a'nonimo, a] *a* anonymous; (*COM*) limited // *nm* (*carta*) anonymous letter; (: *maliciosa*) poison-pen letter.

anormal [anor'mal] *a* abnormal.

anotación [anota'θjon] *nf* note; annotation.

anotar [ano'tar] *vt* to note down; (*comentar*) to annotate.

anquilosamiento [ankilosa'mjento] *nm* (*fig*) paralysis; stagnation.

ansia ['ansja] *nf* anxiety; (*añoranza*) yearning; **ansiar** *vt* to long for.

ansiedad [ansje'ðað] *nf* anxiety.

ansioso, a [an'sjoso, a] *a* anxious; (*anhelante*) eager; **~ de** o **por algo** greedy for sth.

antagónico, a [anta'yoniko, a] *a* antagonistic; (*opuesto*) contrasting; **antagonista** *nm/f* antagonist.

antaño [an'taɲo] *ad* long ago, formerly.

Antártico, a [an'tartiko] *nm*: **el ~** the Antarctic.

ante ['ante] *prep* before, in the presence of; (*encarado con*) faced with // *nm* (*piel*) suede; **~ todo** above all.

anteanoche [antea'notʃe] *ad* the night before last.

anteayer [antea'jer] *ad* the day before yesterday.

antebrazo [ante'βraθo] *nm* forearm.

antecedente [anteθe'ðente] *a* previous // *nm* antecedent; **~s** *nmpl* record *sg*; background *sg*.

anteceder [anteθe'ðer] *vt* to precede, go before.

antecesor, a [anteθe'sor, a] *nm/f* predecessor.

antedicho, a [ante'ðitʃo, a] *a* aforementioned.

antelación [antela'θjon] *nf*: **con ~** in advance.

antemano [ante'mano]: **de ~** *ad* beforehand, in advance.

antena [an'tena] *nf* antenna; (*de televisión etc*) aerial.

anteojo [ante'oxo] *nm* eyeglass; **~s** *nmpl* (*AM*) glasses, spectacles.

antepasados [antepa'saðos] *nmpl* ancestors.

antepecho [ante'petʃo] *nm* guardrail, parapet; (*repisa*) ledge, sill.

anteponer [antepo'ner] *vt* to place in front; (*fig*) to prefer.

anteproyecto [antepro'jekto] *nm* preliminary sketch; (*fig*) blueprint.

anterior [ante'rjor] *a* preceding, previous; **~idad** *nf*: **con ~idad a** prior to, before.

antes ['antes] *ad* (*con prioridad*) before // *prep*: **~ de** before // *conj*: **~ de ir/de que te vayas** before going/before you go; **~ bien** (but) rather; **dos días ~** two days before o previously; **no quiso venir ~** she didn't want to come any earlier; **tomo el avión ~ que el barco** I take the plane rather than the boat; **~ que** yo before me; **lo ~ posible** as soon as possible; **cuanto ~ mejor** the sooner the better.

antesala [ante'sala] *nf* anteroom.

antiaéreo, a [antia'ereo, a] *a* anti-aircraft.

antibalas [anti'βalas] *a inv*: **chaleco ~** bullet-proof jacket.

antibiótico [anti'βjotiko] *nm* antibiotic.

anticiclón [antiθi'klon] *nm* anti-

anticyclone.

anticipación [antiθipa'θjon] *nf* anticipation; **con 10 minutos de ~** 10 minutes early.

anticipado, a [antiθi'paðo, a] *a* (in) advance.

anticipar [antiθi'par] *vt* to anticipate; (*adelantar*) to bring forward; (*COM*) to advance; **~se** *vr*: **~se a su época** to be ahead of one's time.

anticipo [anti'θipo] *nm* (*COM*) advance.

anticonceptivo, a [antikonθep'tiβo, a] *a, nm* contraceptive.

anticongelante [antikonxe'lante] *nm* antifreeze.

anticuado, a [anti'kwaðo, a] *a* out-of-date, old-fashioned; (*desusado*) obsolete.

anticuario [anti'kwarjo] *nm* antique dealer.

anticuerpo [anti'kwerpo] *nm* (*MED*) antibody.

antidoto [an'tiðoto] *nm* antidote.

antiestético, a [anties'tetiko, a] *a* unsightly.

antifaz [anti'faθ] *nm* mask; (*velo*) veil.

antigualla [anti'ɣwaʎa] *nf* antique; (*reliquia*) relic.

antiguamente [antiɣwa'mente] *ad* formerly; (*hace mucho tiempo*) long ago.

antigüedad [antiɣwe'ðað] *nf* antiquity; (*artículo*) antique; (*rango*) seniority.

antiguo, a [an'tiɣwo, a] *a* old, ancient; (*que fue*) former.

antílope [an'tilope] *nm* antelope.

antillano, a [anti'ʎano, a] *a, nm/f* West Indian.

Antillas [an'tiʎas] *nfpl*: **las ~** the West Indies.

antinatural [antinatu'ral] *a* unnatural.

antipatía [antipa'tia] *nf* antipathy, dislike; **antipático, a** *a* disagreeable, unpleasant.

antirrobo [anti'rroβo] *a inv* (*alarma etc*) anti-theft.

antisemita [antise'mita] *a* anti-Semitic // *nm/f* anti-Semite.

antiséptico, a [anti'septiko, a] *a* antiseptic // *nm* antiseptic.

antítesis [an'titesis] *nf inv* antithesis.

antojadizo, a [antoxa'ðiθo, a] *a* capricious.

antojarse [anto'xarse] *vr* (*desear*): **se me antoja comprarlo** I have a mind to buy it; (*pensar*): **se me antoja que** I have a feeling that.

antojo [an'toxo] *nm* caprice, whim; (*rosa*) birthmark; (*lunar*) mole.

antología [antolo'xia] *nf* anthology.

antorcha [an'tortʃa] *nf* torch.

antro ['antro] *nm* cavern.

antropófago, a [antro'pofaxo, a] *a, nm/f* cannibal.

antropología [antropolo'xia] *nf* anthropology.

anual [a'nwal] *a* annual; **~idad** [anwali'ðað] *nf* annuity.

anuario [a'nwarjo] *nm* yearbook.

anudar [anu'ðar] *vt* to knot, tie; (*unir*) to join; **~se** *vr* to get tied up.

anulación [anula'θjon] *nf* annulment; (*cancelación*) cancellation.

anular [anu'lar] *vt* (*contrato*) to annul, cancel; (*ley*) to revoke, repeal; (*suscripción*) to cancel // *nm* ring finger.

anunciación [anunθja'θjon] *nf* announcement; **A~** (*REL*) Annunciation.

anunciante [anun'θjante] *nm/f* (*COM*) advertiser.

anunciar [anun'θjar] *vt* to announce; (*proclamar*) to proclaim; (*COM*) to advertise.

anuncio [a'nunθjo] *nm* announcement; (*señal*) sign; (*COM*) advertisement; (*cartel*) poster.

anzuelo [an'θwelo] *nm* hook; (*para pescar*) fish hook.

añadidura [aɲaði'ðura] *nf* addition, extra; **por ~** besides, in addition.

añadir [aɲa'ðir] *vt* to add.

añejo, a [a'ɲexo, a] *a* old; (*vino*) mellow.

añicos [a'ɲikos] *nmpl*: **hacer ~** to

smash, shatter.

añil [a'ɲil] *nm* (*BOT, color*) indigo.

año ['aɲo] *nm* year; ¡Feliz A~ Nuevo! Happy New Year!; tener 15 ~s to be 15 (years old); los ~s 80 the eighties; ~ **bisiesto/escolar** leap/school year; el ~ **que viene** next year.

añoranza [aɲo'ranθa] *nf* nostalgia; (*anhelo*) longing.

apabullar [apaβu'ʎar] *vt* (*tb fig*) to crush, squash.

apacentar [apaθen'tar] *vt* to pasture, graze.

apacible [apa'θiβle] *a* gentle, mild.

apaciguar [apaθi'ɣwar] *vt* to pacify, calm (down).

apadrinar [apaðri'nar] *vt* to sponsor, support; (*REL*) to be godfather to.

apagado, a [apa'ɣaðo, a] *a* (*volcán*) extinct; (*color*) dull; (*voz*) quiet; (*sonido*) muted, muffled; (*persona*) apático) listless; **estar** ~ (*fuego, luz*) to be out; (*RADIO, TV etc*) to be off.

apagar [apa'ɣar] *vt* to put out; (*ELEC, RADIO, TV*) to turn off; (*sonido*) to silence, muffle; (*sed*) to quench.

apagón [apa'ɣon] *nm* blackout; power cut.

apalabrar [apala'βrar] *vt* to agree to; (*contratar*) to engage.

apalear [apale'ar] *vt* to beat, thrash; (*AGR*) to winnow.

apañar [apa'ɲar] *vt* to pick up; (*asir*) to take hold of, grasp; (*reparar*) to mend, patch up; ~**se** *vr* to manage, get along.

aparador [apara'ðor] *nm* sideboard; (*escaparate*) shop window.

aparato [apa'rato] *nm* apparatus; (*máquina*) machine; (*doméstico*) appliance; (*boato*) ostentation; ~ **de facsímil** facsimile (machine), fax; ~**so, a** *a* showy, ostentatious.

aparcamiento [aparka'mjento] *nm* car park (*Brit*), parking lot (*US*).

aparcar [apar'kar] *vt, vi* to park.

aparear [apare'ar] *vt* (*objetos*) to

pair, match; (*animales*) to mate; ~**se** *vr* to make a pair; to mate.

aparecer [apare'θer] *vi*, **aparecerse** *vr* to appear.

aparejado, a [apare'xaðo, a] *a* fit, suitable; **llevar o traer** ~ to involve.

aparejo [apa'rexo] *nm* preparation; harness; rigging; (*de poleas*) block and tackle.

aparentar [aparen'tar] *vt* (*edad*) to look; (*fingir*): ~ **tristeza** to pretend to be sad.

aparente [apa'rente] *a* apparent; (*adecuado*) suitable.

aparezco *etc vb ver* **aparecer**.

aparición [apari'θjon] *nf* appearance; (*de libro*) publication; (*espectro*) apparition.

apariencia [apa'rjenθja] *nf* (*outward*) appearance; **en** ~ outwardly, seemingly.

apartado, a [apar'taðo, a] *a* separate; (*lejano*) remote // *nm* (*tipográfico*) paragraph; ~ **(de correos)** post office box.

apartamento [aparta'mento] *nm* apartment, flat (*Brit*).

apartamiento [aparta'mjento] *nm* separation; (*aislamiento*) remoteness, isolation; (*AM*) apartment, flat (*Brit*).

apartar [apar'tar] *vt* to separate; (*quitar*) to remove; (*MINE-ROLOGÍA*) to extract; ~**se** *vr* to separate, part; (*irse*) to move away; to keep away.

aparte [a'parte] *ad* (*separadamente*) separately; (*además*) besides // *nm* aside; (*tipográfico*) new paragraph.

apasionado, a [apasjo'naðo, a] *a* passionate; biassed, prejudiced.

apasionar [apasjo'nar] *vt* to excite; **le apasiona el fútbol** she's crazy about football; ~**se** *vr* to get excited.

apatía [apa'tia] *nf* apathy.

apático, a [a'patiko, a] *a* apathetic.

apátrida [a'patriða] *a* stateless.

Apdo *abr* (= **Apartado** (*de Correos*)) PO Box.

apeadero [apea'ðero] nm halt, stop, stopping place.

apearse [ape'arse] vr (jinete) to dismount; (bajarse) to get down o out; (AUTO, FERRO) to get off o out.

apechugar [apetʃu'ɣar] vr: ~ con algo to face up to sth.

apedrear [apeðre'ar] vt to stone.

apegarse [ape'ɣarse] vr: ~se a to become attached to; **apego** nm attachment, devotion.

apelación [apela'θjon] nf appeal.

apelar [ape'lar] vi to appeal; ~ a (fig) to resort to.

apellidar [apeʎi'ðar] vt to call, name; ~se vr: se apellida Pérez her (sur)name's Pérez.

apellido [ape'ʎiðo] nm surname.

apenar [ape'nar] vt to grieve, trouble; (AM: avergonzar) to embarrass; ~se vr to grieve; (AM) to be embarrassed.

apenas [a'penas] ad scarcely, hardly // conj as soon as, no sooner.

apéndice [a'pendiθe] nm appendix; **apendicitis** nf appendicitis.

apercibirse [aperθi'βirse] vr: ~ de to notice.

aperitivo [aperi'tiβo] nm (bebida) aperitif; (comida) appetizer.

apero [a'pero] nm (AGR) implement; ~s nmpl farm equipment sg.

apertura [aper'tura] nf opening; (POL) liberalization.

apesadumbrar [apesaðum'brar] vt to grieve, sadden; ~se vr to distress o.s.

apestar [apes'tar] vt to infect // vi: ~ (a) to stink (of).

apetecer [apete'θer] vt: ¿te apetece una tortilla? do you fancy an omelette?; **apetecible** a desirable; (comida) appetizing.

apetito [ape'tito] nm appetite; ~so, a a appetizing; (fig) tempting.

apiadarse [apja'ðarse] vr: ~ de to take pity on.

ápice ['apiθe] nm apex; (fig) whit, iota.

apilar [api'lar] vt to pile o heap up;

~se vr to pile up.

apiñarse [api'narse] vr to crowd o press together.

apio ['apjo] nm celery.

apisonadora [apisona'ðora] nf (máquina) steamroller.

aplacar [apla'kar] vt to placate; ~se vr to calm down.

aplanar [apla'nar] vt to smooth, level; (allanar) to roll flat, flatten.

aplastar [aplas'tar] vt to squash (flat); (fig) to crush.

aplatanarse [aplata'narse] vr to get lethargic.

aplaudir [aplau'ðir] vt to applaud.

aplauso [a'plauso] nm applause; (fig) approval, acclaim.

aplazamiento [aplaθa'mjento] nm postponement.

aplazar [apla'θar] vt to postpone, defer.

aplicación [aplika'θjon] nf application; (esfuerzo) effort.

aplicado, a [apli'kaðo, a] a diligent, hard-working.

aplicar [apli'kar] vt (ejecutar) to apply; ~se vr to apply o.s.

aplique etc vb ver **aplicar** // [a'plike] nm wall light.

aplomo [a'plomo] nm aplomb, self-assurance.

apocado, a [apo'kaðo, a] a timid.

apocamiento [apoka'mjento] nm timidity; (depresión) depression.

apocarse [apo'karse] vr to feel small o humiliated.

apodar [apo'ðar] vt to nickname.

apoderado [apoðe'raðo] nm agent, representative.

apoderar [apoðe'rar] vt to authorize, empower; (JUR) to grant (a) power of attorney to; ~se vr: ~se de to take possession of.

apodo [a'poðo] nm nickname.

apogeo [apo'xeo] nm peak, summit.

apolillarse [apoli'ʎarse] vr to get moth-eaten.

apología [apolo'xia] nf eulogy; (defensa) defence.

apoltronarse [apoltro'narse] vr

get lazy.

apoplejía [apople'xia] *nf* apoplexy, stroke.

apoquinar [apoki'nar] *vt* (*fam*) to fork out, cough up.

aporrear [aporre'ar] *vt* to beat (up).

aportar [apor'tar] *vt* to contribute // *vi* to reach port; ~**se** *vr* (*AM*) to arrive, come.

aposentar [aposen'tar] *vt* to lodge, put up; **aposento** *nm* lodging; (*habitación*) room.

apósito [a'posito] *nm* (*MED*) dressing.

apostar [apos'tar] *vt* to bet, stake; (*tropas etc*) to station, post // *vi* to bet.

apostilla [apos'tiʎa] *nf* note, comment.

apóstol [a'postol] *nm* apostle.

apóstrofo [a'postrofo] *nm* apostrophe.

apostura [apos'tura] *nf* neatness; (*elegancia*) elegance.

apoyar [apo'jar] *vt* to lean, rest; (*fig*) to support, back; ~**se** *vr*: ~**se en** to lean on; **apoyo** *nm* (*gen*) support; backing, help.

apreciable [apre'θjaβle] *a* considerable; (*fig*) esteemed.

apreciación [apreθja'θjon] *nf* appreciation; (*COM*) valuation.

apreciar [apre'θjar] *vt* to evaluate, assess; (*COM*) to appreciate, value.

aprecio [a'preθjo] *nm* valuation, estimate; (*fig*) appreciation.

aprehender [apreen'der] *vt* to apprehend, detain; **aprehensión** *nf* detention, capture.

apremiante [apre'mjante] *a* urgent, pressing.

apremiar [apre'mjar] *vt* to compel, force // *vi* to be urgent, press; **apremio** *nm* urgency.

aprender [apren'der] *vt*, *vi* to learn.

aprendiz, a [apren'diθ, a] *nm/f* apprentice; (*principiante*) learner; ~**aje** *nm* apprenticeship.

aprensión [apren'sjon] *nm* apprehension, fear; **aprensivo, a** *a*

apprehensive.

apresar [apre'sar] *vt* to seize; (*capturar*) to capture.

aprestar [apres'tar] *vt* to prepare, get ready; (*TEC*) to prime; size; ~**se** *vr* to get ready.

apresurado, a [apresu'raðo, a] *a* hurried, hasty; **apresuramiento** *nm* hurry, haste.

apresurar [apresu'rar] *vt* to hurry, accelerate; ~**se** *vr* to hurry, make haste.

apretado, a [apre'taðo, a] *a* tight; (*escritura*) cramped.

apretar [apre'tar] *vt* to squeeze; (*TEC*) to tighten; (*presionar*) to press together, pack // *vi* to be too tight.

apretón [apre'ton] *nm* squeeze; ~ **de manos** handshake.

aprieto [a'prjeto] *nm* squeeze; (*dificultad*) difficulty, jam; **estar en** ~ to be in a fix.

aprisa [a'prisa] *ad* quickly, hurriedly.

aprisionar [aprisjo'nar] *vt* to imprison.

aprobación [aproβa'θjon] *nf* approval.

aprobar [apro'βar] *vt* to approve (of); (*examen, materia*) to pass // *vi* to pass.

apropiación [apropja'θjon] *nf* appropriation.

apropiado, a [apro'pjaðo, a] *a* appropriate.

apropiarse [apro'pjarse] *vr*: ~ **de** to appropriate.

aprovechado, a [aproβe'tʃaðo, a] *a* industrious, hardworking; (*económico*) thrifty; (*pey*) unscrupulous; **aprovechamiento** *nm* use; exploitation.

aprovechar [aproβe'tʃar] *vt* to use; (*explotar*) to exploit; (*experiencia*) to profit from; (*oferta, oportunidad*) to take advantage of // *vi* to progress, improve; ~**se** *vr*: ~**se de** to make use of; to take advantage of; **¡que aproveche!** enjoy your meal!

aproximación [aproksima'θjon] *nf*

approximation; (*de lotería*) consolation prize; **aproximado, a** *a* approximate.

aproximar [aproksi'mar] *vt* to bring nearer; **~se** *vr* to come near, approach.

apruebo *etc vb ver* **aprobar**.

aptitud [apti'tuð] *nf* aptitude.

apto, a ['apto, a] *a* suitable.

apuesto, a [a'pwesto, a] *a* neat, elegant // *nf* bet, wager.

apuntador [apunta'ðor] *nm* prompter.

apuntalar [apunta'lar] *vt* to prop up.

apuntar [apun'tar] *vt* (*con arma*) to aim at; (*con dedo*) to point at o to; (*anotar*) to note (down); (*TEATRO*) to prompt; **~se** *vr* (*DEPORTE: tanto, victoria*) to score; (*ESCOL*) to enrol.

apunte [a'punte] *nm* note.

apuñalar [apuɲa'lar] *vt* to stab.

apurado, a [apu'raðo, a] *a* needy; (*difícil*) difficult; (*peligroso*) dangerous; (*AM*) hurried, rushed.

apurar [apu'rar] *vt* (*agotar*) to drain; (*recursos*) to use up; (*molestar*) to annoy; **~se** *vr* (*preocuparse*) to worry; (*darse prisa*) to hurry.

apuro [a'puro] *nm* (*aprieto*) fix, jam; (*escasez*) want, hardship; (*vergüenza*) embarrassment; (*AM*) haste, urgency.

aquejado, a [ake'xaðo, a] *a*: ~ de (*MED*) afflicted by.

aquel, aquella, aquellos, as [a'kel, a'keʎa, a'keʎos, as] *a* that; (*pl*) those.

aquél, aquélla, aquéllos, as [a'kel, a'keʎa, a'keʎos, as] *pron* that (one); (*pl*) those (ones).

aquello [a'keʎo] *pron* that, that business.

aquí [a'ki] *ad* (*lugar*) here; (*tiempo*) now; ~ arriba up here; ~ mismo right here; ~ yace here lies; de ~ a ocho días a week from now.

aquietar [akje'tar] *vt* to quieten (down), calm (down).

ara ['ara] *nf*: en ~s de for the sake of.

árabe ['araße] *a, nm/f* Arab // *nm* (*LING*) Arabic.

Arabia [a'raßja] *nf*: ~ Saudí o Saudita Saudi Arabia.

arado [a'raðo] *nm* plough.

Aragón [ara'von] *nm* Aragon; **aragonés, esa** *a, nm/f* Aragonese.

arancel [aran'θel] *nm* tariff, duty; ~ de aduanas customs (duty).

arandela [aran'dela] *nf* (*TEC*) washer.

araña [a'raɲa] *nf* (*ZOOL*) spider; (*lámpara*) chandelier.

arañar [ara'ɲar] *vt* to scratch.

arañazo [ara'ɲaθo] *nm* scratch.

arar [a'rar] *vt* to plough, till.

arbitraje [arßi'traxe] *nm* arbitration.

arbitrar [arßi'trar] *vt* to arbitrate in; (*DEPORTE*) to referee // *vi* to arbitrate.

arbitrariedad [arßitrarje'ðað] *nf* arbitrariness; (*acto*) arbitrary act; **arbitrario, a** *a* arbitrary.

arbitrio [ar'ßitrjo] *nm* free will; (*JUR*) adjudication, decision.

árbitro ['arßitro] *nm* arbitrator; (*DEPORTE*) referee; (*TENIS*) umpire.

árbol ['arßol] *nm* (*BOT*) tree; (*NAUT*) mast; (*TEC*) axle, shaft; **arbolado, a** *a* wooded; (*camino etc*) tree-lined // *nm* woodland.

arboladura [arßola'ðura] *nf* rigging.

arbolar [arßo'lar] *vt* to hoist, raise.

arboleda [arßo'leða] *nf* grove, plantation.

arbusto [ar'ßusto] *nm* bush, shrub.

arca ['arka] *nf* chest, box.

arcada [ar'kaða] *nf* arcade; (*de puente*) arch, span; ~s *nfpl* retching *sg*.

arcaico, a [ar'kaiko, a] *a* archaic.

arce ['arθe] *nm* maple tree.

arcén [ar'θen] *nm* (*de autopista*) hard shoulder; (*de carretera*) verge.

arcilla [ar'θiʎa] *nf* clay.

arco ['arko] *nm* arch; (*MAT*) arc; (*MIL, MUS*) bow; ~ **iris** rainbow.

archipiélago [artʃi'pjelaʁo] *nm*

archipelago.

archivador [artʃiβa'ðor] *nm* filing cabinet.

archivar [artʃi'βar] *vt* to file (away); **archivo** *nm* file, archive(s) (*pl*).

arder [ar'ðer] *vi* to burn; **estar que arde** (*persona*) to fume.

ardid [ar'ðið] *nm* ploy, trick.

ardiente [ar'ðjente] *a* burning, ardent.

ardilla [ar'ðiʎa] *nf* squirrel.

ardor [ar'ðor] *nm* (*calor*) heat; (*fig*) ardour; ~ **de estómago** heartburn.

arduo, a ['arðwo, a] *a* arduous.

área ['area] *nf* area; (*DEPORTE*) penalty area.

arena [a'rena] *nf* sand; (*de una lucha*) arena.

arenal [are'nal] *nm* (*arena movediza*) quicksand.

arengar [aren'gar] *vt* to harangue.

arenisca [are'niska] *nf* sandstone; (*cascajo*) grit.

arenoso, a [are'noso, a] *a* sandy.

arenque [a'renke] *nm* herring.

arete [a'rete] *nm* earring.

argamasa [arya'masa] *nf* mortar, plaster.

Argel [ar'xel] *nm* Algiers; **~ia** [ar'xelia] *nf* Algeria; **argelino, a** *a*, *nm/f* Algerian.

Argentina [arxen'tina] *nf*: **(la) A~** Argentina.

argentino, a [arxen'tino, a] *a* Argentinian; (*de plata*) silvery // *nm/f* Argentinian.

argolla [ar'voʎa] *nf* (large) ring.

argot [ar'xo] (*pl* ~**s**) *nm* slang.

argucia [ar'xuθja] *nf* subtlety, sophistry.

argüir [ar'xwir] *vt* to deduce; (*discutir*) to argue; (*indicar*) to indicate, imply; (*censurar*) to reproach // *vi* to argue.

argumentación [arvumenta'θjon] *nf* (line of) argument.

argumentar [arvumen'tar] *vt*, *vi* to argue.

argumento [arvu'mento] *nm* argument; (*razonamiento*) reasoning; (*de* *novela etc*) plot; (*CINE, TV*) storyline.

aria ['arja] *nf* aria.

aridez [ari'ðeθ] *nf* aridity, dryness.

árido, a ['ariðo, a] *a* arid, dry; **~s** *nmpl* dry goods.

Aries ['arjes] *nm* Aries.

ariete [a'rjete] *nm* battering ram.

ario, a ['arjo, a] *a* Aryan.

arisco, a [a'risko, a] *a* surly; (*insociable*) unsociable.

aristócrata [aris'tokrata] *nm/f* aristocrat.

aritmética [arit'metika] *nf* arithmetic.

arma ['arma] *nf* arm; **~s** *nfpl* arms; **~ blanca** blade, knife; (*espada*) sword; **~ de fuego** firearm; **~s cortas** small arms.

armadillo [arma'ðiʎo] *nm* armadillo.

armado, a [ar'maðo, a] *a* armed; (*TEC*) reinforced // armada *nf* (*flota*) fleet.

armadura [arma'ðura] *nf* (*MIL*) armour; (*TEC*) framework; (*ZOOL*) skeleton; (*FISICA*) armature.

armamento [arma'mento] *nm* armament; (*NAUT*) fitting-out.

armar [ar'mar] *vt* (*soldado*) to arm; (*máquina*) to assemble; (*navio*) to fit out; **~la, ~ un lío** to start a row, kick up a fuss.

armario [ar'marjo] *nm* wardrobe.

armatoste [arma'toste] *nm* (*mueble*) monstrosity; (*máquina*) contraption.

armazón [arma'θon] *nf o m* body, chassis; (*de mueble etc*) frame; (*ARQ*) skeleton.

armería [arme'ria] *nf* (*museo*) military museum; (*tienda*) gunsmith's.

armiño [ar'miɲo] *nm* stoat; (*piel*) ermine.

armisticio [armis'tiθjo] *nm* armistice.

armonía [armo'nia] *nf* harmony.

armónica [ar'monika] *nf* harmonica.

armonioso, a [armo'njoso, a] *a* harmonious.

armonizar [armoni'θar] *vt* to

harmonize; (*diferencias*) to reconcile // *vi:* ~ **con** (*fig*) to be in keeping with; (*colores*) to tone in with, blend.

arnés [ar'nes] *nm* armour; **arneses** *nmpl* harness *sg.*

aro ['aro] *nm* ring; (*tejo*) quoit; (*AM: pendiente*) earring.

aroma [a'roma] *nm* aroma, scent.

aromático, a [aro'matiko, a] *a* aromatic.

arpa ['arpa] *nf* harp.

arpía [ar'pia] *nf* shrew.

arpillera [arpiˈʎera] *nf* sacking, sackcloth.

arpón [ar'pon] *nm* harpoon.

arquear [arke'ar] *vt* to arch, bend; ~**se** *vr* to arch, bend; **arqueo** *nm* (*gen*) arching; (*NAUT*) tonnage.

arqueología [arkeolo'xia] *nf* archaeology; **arqueólogo, a** *nm/f* archaeologist.

arquero [ar'kero] *nm* archer, bowman.

arquetipo [arke'tipo] *nm* archetype.

arquitecto [arki'tekto] *nm* architect; **arquitectura** *nf* architecture.

arrabal [arra'βal] *nm* suburb; (*AM*) slum; ~**es** *nmpl* outskirts.

arraigado, a [arrai'ɣaðo, a] *a* deep-rooted; (*fig*) established.

arraigar [arrai'ɣar] *vt* to establish // *vi,* ~**se** *vr* to take root; (*persona*) to settle.

arrancar [arran'kar] *vt* (*sacar*) to extract, pull out; (*arrebatar*) to snatch (away); (*INFORM*) to boot; (*fig*) to extract // *vi* (*AUTO, máquina*) to start; (*ponerse en marcha*) to get going; ~ **de** to stem from.

arranque *etc vb ver* **arrancar** // [a'rranke] *nm* sudden start; (*AUTO*) start; (*fig*) fit, outburst.

arras ['arras] *nfpl* pledge *sg*, security *sg.*

arrasar [arra'sar] *vt* (*aplanar*) to level, flatten; (*destruir*) to demolish.

arrastrado, a [arras'traðo, a] *a* poor, wretched; (*AM*) servile.

arrastrar [arras'trar] *vt* to drag

(along); (*fig*) to drag down, degrade; (*suj: agua, viento*) to carry away // *vi* to drag, trail on the ground; ~**se** *vr* to crawl; (*fig*) to grovel; **llevar algo arrastrado** to drag sth along.

arrastre [a'rrastre] *nm* drag, dragging.

arrayán [arra'jan] *nm* myrtle.

arre ['arre] *excl* gee up!

arrear [arre'ar] *vt* to drive on, urge on // *vi* to hurry along.

arrebatado, a [arreβa'taðo, a] *a* rash, impetuous; (*repentino*) sudden, hasty.

arrebatar [arreβa'tar] *vt* to snatch (away), seize; (*fig*) to captivate; ~**se** *vr* to get carried away, get excited.

arrebato [arre'βato] *nm* fit of rage, fury; (*éxtasis*) rapture.

arreglado, a [arre'ɣlaðo, a] *a* (*ordenado*) neat, orderly; (*moderado*) moderate, reasonable.

arreglar [arre'ɣlar] *vt* (*poner orden*) to tidy up; (*algo roto*) to fix, repair; (*problema*) to solve; ~**se** *vr* to reach an understanding; **arreglárselas** (*fam*) to get by, manage.

arreglo [a'rreɣlo] *nm* settlement; (*orden*) order; (*acuerdo*) agreement; (*MUS*) arrangement, setting.

arremangar [arreman'gar] *vt* to roll up, turn up; ~**se** *vr* to roll up one's sleeves.

arremeter [arreme'ter] *vt* to attack, assault.

arrendador, a [arrenda'ðor, a] *nm/f* landlord/lady.

arrendamiento [arrenda'mjento] *nm* letting; (*alquiler*) hiring; (*contrato*) lease; (*alquiler*) rent; **arrendar** *vt* to let, lease; to rent; **arrendatario, a** *nm/f* tenant.

arreo [a'rreo] *nm* adornment; ~**s** *nmpl* harness *sg*, trappings.

arrepentimiento [arrepenti'mjento] *nm* regret, repentance.

arrepentirse [arrepen'tirse] *vr* to repent; ~ **de** to regret.

arrestar [arres'tar] *vt* to arrest; (*encarcelar*) to imprison; **arresto** *nm* arrest; (MIL) detention; (audacia) boldness, daring; **arresto domiciliario** house arrest.

arriar [a'rrjar] vt (velas) to haul down; (bandera) to lower, strike; (un cable) to pay out.

PALABRA CLAVE

arriba [a'rriβa] ◆ 1 ad (posición) above; desde ~ from above; ~ de todo at the very top, right on top; Juan está ~ Juan is upstairs; lo ~ mencionado the aforementioned
2 (dirección): calle ~ up the street
3: de ~ abajo from top to bottom; mirar a uno de ~ abajo to look sb up and down
4: para ~: de 5000 pesetas para ~ from 5000 pesetas up(wards)
◆ a: de ~: el piso de ~ the upstairs flat (Brit) o apartment; la parte de ~ the top o upper part
◆ prep: ~ de (AM) above; ~ de 200 pesetas more than 200 pesetas
◆ excl: ¡~! up!; ¡manos ~! hands up!; ¡~ España! long live Spain!

arribar [arri'βar] vi to put into port; (llegar) to arrive.

arribista [arri'βista] nm/f parvenu(e), upstart.

arriendo etc vb ver **arrendar** // [a'rrjendo] nm = **arrendamiento**.

arriero [a'rrjero] nm muleteer.

arriesgado, a [arrjes'γaðo, a] a (peligroso) risky; (audaz) bold, daring.

arriesgar [arrjes'γar] vt to risk; (poner en peligro) to endanger; ~se vr to take a risk.

arrimar [arri'mar] vt (acercar) to bring close; (poner de lado) to set aside; ~se vr to come close o closer; ~se a to lean on.

arrinconar [arrinko'nar] vt (colocar) to put in a corner; (enemigo) to corner; (fig) to put on one side; (abandonar) to push aside.

arrobado, a [arro'βaðo, a] a en-tranced, enchanted.

arrodillarse [arroði'Aarse] vr to kneel (down).

arrogancia [arro'γanθja] nf arrogance; **arrogante** a arrogant.

arrojar [arro'xar] vt to throw, hurl; (humo) to emit, give out; (COM) to yield, produce; ~se vr to throw o hurl o.s.

arrojo [a'rroxo] nm daring.

arrollador, a [arroAa'ðor, a] a crushing, overwhelming.

arrollar [arro'Aar] vt (AUTO etc) to run over, knock down; (DEPORTE) to crush.

aropar [arro'par] vt to cover, wrap up; ~se vr to wrap o.s. up.

arrostrar [arros'trar] vt to face (up to); ~se vr: ~se con uno to face up to sb.

arroyo [a'rrojo] nm stream; (de la calle) gutter.

arroz [a'rroθ] nm rice; ~ con leche rice pudding.

arruga [a'rruxa] nf fold; (de cara) wrinkle; (de vestido) crease.

arrugar [arru'xar] vt to fold; to wrinkle; to crease; ~se vr to get creased.

arruinar [arrwi'nar] vt to ruin, wreck; ~se vr to be ruined, go bank-rupt.

arrullar [arru'Aar] vi to coo // vt to lull to sleep.

arrumaco [arru'mako] nm (caricia) caress; (halago) piece of flattery.

arsenal [arse'nal] nm naval dock-yard; (MIL) arsenal.

arsénico [ar'seniko] nm arsenic.

arte ['arte] nm (gen m en sg y siempre f en pl) art; (maña) skill, guile; ~s nfpl arts.

artefacto [arte'fakto] nm appliance; (ARQUEOLOGÍA) artefact.

arteria [ar'terja] nf artery.

artesanía [artesa'nia] nf craftsman-ship; (artículos) handicrafts pl; **artesano, a** nm/f artisan, craftsman/woman.

ártico, a ['artiko, a] a Arctic // nm: **el Á~** the Arctic.

articulación [artikula'θjon] nf articulation; (MED, TEC) joint; **articulado, a** a articulated; jointed.

articular [artiku'lar] vt to articulate; to join together.

artículo [ar'tikulo] nm article; (cosa) thing, article; ~s nmpl goods.

artífice [ar'tifiθe] nm/f artist, craftsman/woman; (fig) architect.

artificial [artifi'θjal] a artificial.

artificio [artiˈfiθjo] nm art, skill; (artesanía) craftsmanship; (astucia) cunning.

artillería [artiʎeˈria] nf artillery.

artillero [artiˈʎero] nm artilleryman, gunner.

artimaña [artiˈmaɲa] nf trap, snare; (astucia) cunning.

artista [ar'tista] nm/f (pintor) artist, painter; (TEATRO) artist, artiste; **artístico, a** a artistic.

artritis [ar'tritis] nf arthritis.

arveja [ar'βexa] nf (AM) pea.

arzobispo [arθo'βispo] nm archbishop.

as [as] nm ace.

asa ['asa] nf handle; (fig) lever.

asado [a'saðo] nm roast (meat); (AM) barbecue.

asador [asa'ðor] nm spit.

asadura [asa'ðura] nf entrails pl, offal.

asalariado, a [asala'rjaðo, a] a paid, salaried // nm/f wage earner.

asaltador, a [asalta'ðor, a], **asaltante** [asal'tante] nm/f assailant.

asaltar [asal'tar] vt to attack, assault; (fig) to assail; **asalto** nm attack, assault; (DEPORTE) round.

asamblea [asam'blea] nf assembly; (reunión) meeting.

asar [a'sar] vt to roast.

asbesto [as'βesto] nm asbestos.

ascendencia [asθen'denθja] nf ancestry; (AM) ascendancy; **de ~ francesa** of French origin.

ascender [asθen'der] vi (subir) to ascend, rise; (ser promovido) to gain promotion // vt to promote; **~ a** to amount to; **ascendiente** nm in-fluence // nm/f ancestor.

ascensión [asθen'sjon] nf ascent; **la A~** (REL) the Ascension.

ascenso [as'θenso] nm ascent; (promoción) promotion.

ascensor [asθen'sor] nm lift (Brit), elevator (US).

ascético, a [as'θetiko, a] a ascetic.

asco ['asko] nm: ¡qué ~! how revolting o disgusting; **el ajo me da ~** I hate o loathe garlic; **estar hecho un ~** to be filthy.

ascua ['askwa] nf ember; **estar en ~s** to be on tenterhooks.

aseado, a [ase'aðo, a] a clean; (arreglado) tidy; (pulcro) smart.

asear [ase'ar] vt to clean, wash; to tidy (up).

asediar [ase'ðjar] vt (MIL) to besiege, lay siege to; (fig) to chase, pester; **asedio** nm siege; (COM) run.

asegurado, a [aseɣu'raðo, a] a insured; **asegurador, a** nm/f insurer.

asegurar [aseɣu'rar] vt (consolidar) to secure, fasten; (dar garantía de) to guarantee; (preservar) to safeguard; (afirmar, dar por cierto) to assure, affirm; (tranquilizar) to reassure; (tomar un seguro) to insure; **~se** vr to assure o.s., make sure.

asemejarse [aseme'xarse] vr to be alike; **~ a** to be like, resemble.

asentado, a [asen'taðo, a] a established, settled.

asentar [asen'tar] vt (sentar) to seat, sit down; (poner) to place, establish; (alisar) to level, smooth down o out; (anotar) to note down // vi to be suitable, suit.

asentir [asen'tir] vi to assent, agree; **~ con la cabeza** to nod (one's head).

aseo [a'seo] nm cleanliness; **~s** nmpl toilet sg (Brit), cloakroom sg (Brit), restroom sg (US).

aséptico, a [a'septiko, a] a germfree, free from infection.

asequible [aseˈkiβle] a (precio) reasonable; (meta) attainable;

(*persona*) approachable.

aserradero [aserra'ðero] *nm* saw-mill; **aserrar** *vt* to saw.

aserrín [ase'rrin] *nm* sawdust.

asesinar [asesi'nar] *vt* to murder; (*POL*) to assassinate; **asesinato** *nm* murder; assassination.

asesino, a [ase'sino, a] *nm/f* murderer, killer; (*POL*) assassin.

asesor, a [ase'sor, a] *nm/f* adviser, consultant.

asesorar [aseso'rar] *vt* (*JUR*) to advise, give legal advice to; (*COM*) to act as consultant to; **~se** *vr*: **~se con o de** to take advice from, consult; **~ía** *nf* (*cargo*) consultancy; (*oficina*) consultant's office.

asestar [ases'tar] *vt* (*golpe*) to deal, strike; (*arma*) to aim; (*tiro*) to fire.

asfalto [as'falto] *nm* asphalt.

asfixia [as'fiksja] *nf* asphyxia, suffocation.

asfixiar [asfik'sjar] *vt* to asphyxiate, suffocate; **~se** *vr* to be asphyxiated, suffocate.

asgo *etc vb ver* **asir**.

así [a'si] *ad* (*de esta manera*) in this way, like this; thus; (*aunque*) although; (*tan pronto como*) as soon as; **~ que** so; **~ como** as well as; **~ y todo** even so; **¿no es ~?** isn't it?, didn't you? *etc*; **~ de grande** this big.

Asia ['asja] *nf* Asia; **asiático, a** *a, nm/f* Asian, Asiatic.

asidero [asi'ðero] *nm* handle.

asiduidad [asiðwi'ðað] *nf* assiduousness; **asiduo, a** *a* assiduous; (*frecuente*) frequent // *nm/f* regular (*customer*).

asiento [a'sjento] *nm* (*mueble*) seat, chair; (*de coche, en tribunal etc*) seat; (*localidad*) seat, place; (*fundamento*) site; **~ delantero/trasero** front/back seat.

asignación [asiɣna'θjon] *nf* (*atribución*) assignment; (*reparto*) allocation; (*sueldo*) salary; **~ (semanal)** pocket money.

asignar [asiɣ'nar] *vt* to assign,

allocate.

asignatura [asiɣna'tura] *nf* subject; course.

asilado, a [asi'laðo, a] *nm/f* inmate; (*POL*) refugee.

asilo [a'silo] *nm* (*refugio*) asylum, refuge; (*establecimiento*) home, institution; **~ político** political asylum.

asimilación [asimila'θjon] *nf* assimilation.

asimilar [asimi'lar] *vt* to assimilate.

asimismo [asi'mismo] *ad* in the same way, likewise.

asir [a'sir] *vt* to seize, grasp.

asistencia [asis'tenθja] *nf* audience; (*MED*) attendance; (*ayuda*) assistance; **asistente** *nm/f* assistant; **los ~s** those present.

asistido, a [asis'tiðo, a] *a*: **~ por ordenador** computer-assisted.

asistir [asis'tir] *vt* to assist, help // *vi*: **~ a** to attend, be present at.

asma ['asma] *nf* asthma.

asno ['asno] *nm* donkey; (*fig*) ass.

asociación [asoθja'θjon] *nf* association; (*COM*) partnership; **asociado, a** *a* associate // *nm/f* associate; (*COM*) partner.

asociar [aso'θjar] *vt* to associate.

asolar [aso'lar] *vt* to destroy.

asolear [asole'ar] *vt* to put in the sun; **~se** *vr* to sunbathe.

asomar [aso'mar] *vt* to show, stick out // *vi* to appear; **~se** *vr* to appear, show up; **~ la cabeza por la ventana** to put one's head out of the window.

asombrar [asom'brar] *vt* to amaze, astonish; **~se** *vr* (*sorprenderse*) to be amazed; (*asustarse*) to get a fright; **asombro** *nm* amazement, astonishment; (*susto*) fright; **asombroso, a** *a* astonishing, amazing.

asomo [a'somo] *nm* hint, sign.

aspa ['aspa] *nf* (*cruz*) cross; (*de molino*) sail; **en ~** X-shaped.

aspaviento [aspa'βjento] *nm* exaggerated display of feeling; (*fam*) fuss.

aspecto [as'pekto] *nm* (*apariencia*)

look, appearance; (*fig*) aspect.

aspereza [aspe'reθa] *nf* roughness; (*agrura*) sourness; (*de carácter*) surliness; **áspero, a** *a* rough; bitter, sour; harsh.

aspersión [asper'sjon] *nf* sprinkling.

aspiración [aspira'θjon] *nf* breath, inhalation; (*MUS*) short pause; **aspiraciones** *nfpl* aspirations.

aspiradora [aspira'ðora] *nf* vacuum cleaner, Hoover ®.

aspirante [aspi'rante] *nm/f* (*candidato*) candidate; (*DEPORTE*) contender.

aspirar [aspi'rar] *vt* to breathe in // *vi*: ~ a to aspire to.

aspirina [aspi'rina] *nf* aspirin.

asquear [aske'ar] *vt* to sicken // *vi* to be sickening; ~**se** *vr* to feel disgusted; **asqueroso, a** *a* disgusting, sickening.

asta ['asta] *nf* lance; (*arpón*) spear; (*mango*) shaft, handle; (*ZOOL*) horn; **a media ~** at half mast.

astado, a [as'taðo, a] *a* horned // *nm* bull.

asterisco [aste'risko] *nm* asterisk.

astilla [as'tiʎa] *nf* splinter; (*pedacito*) chip; ~**s** *nfpl* firewood *sg*.

astillero [asti'ʎero] *nm* shipyard.

astringente [astrin'xente] *a, nm* - astringent.

astro ['astro] *nm* star.

astrología [astrolo'xia] *nf* astrology; **astrólogo, a** *nm/f* astrologer.

astronauta [astro'nauta] *nm/f* astronaut.

astronave [astro'naβe] *nm* spaceship.

astronomía [astrono'mia] *nf* astronomy; **astrónomo, a** *nm/f* astronomer.

astucia [as'tuθja] *nf* astuteness; (*ardid*) clever trick; **astuto, a** *a* astute; (*taimado*) cunning.

asueto [a'sweto] *nm* holiday; (*tiempo libre*) time off *q*.

asumir [asu'mir] *vt* to assume.

asunción [asun'θjon] *nf* assumption; (*REL*) **A~** Assumption.

asunto [a'sunto] *nm* (*tema*) matter, subject; (*negocio*) business.

asustar [asus'tar] *vt* to frighten; ~**se** *vr* to become frightened.

atacar [ata'kar] *vt* to attack.

atadura [ata'ðura] *nf* bond, tie.

atajo [a'taxo] *nm* short cut; (*DEPORTE*) tackle.

atañer [ata'ɲer] *vi*: ~ a to concern.

ataque *etc vb ver* **atacar** // [a'take] *nm* attack; ~ **cardíaco** heart attack.

atar [a'tar] *vt* to tie, tie up.

atardecer [atarðe'θer] *vi* to get dark // *nm* evening; (*crepúsculo*) dusk.

atareado, a [atare'aðo] *a* busy.

atascar [atas'kar] *vt* to clog up; (*obstruir*) to jam; (*fig*) to hinder; ~**se** *vr* to stall; (*cañería*) to get blocked up; **atasco** *nm* obstruction; (*AUTO*) traffic jam.

ataúd [ata'uð] *nm* coffin.

ataviar [ata'βjar] *vt* to deck, array; ~**se** *vr* to dress up.

atavío [ata'βio] *nm* attire, dress; ~**s** *nmpl* finery *sg*.

atemorizar [atemori'θar] *vt* to frighten, scare; ~**se** *vr* to get scared.

Atenas [a'tenas] *n* Athens.

atención [aten'θjon] *nf* attention; (*bondad*) kindness // *excl* (be) careful!, look out!

atender [aten'der] *vt* to attend to, look after // *vi* to pay attention.

atenerse [ate'nerse] *vr*: ~ a to abide by, adhere to.

atentado [aten'taðo] *nm* crime, illegal act; (*asalto*) assault; ~ **contra la vida de uno** attempt on sb's life.

atentamente [atenta'mente] *ad*: Le saluda ~ Yours faithfully.

atentar [aten'tar] *vi*: ~ a *o* contra to commit an outrage against.

atento, a [a'tento, a] *a* attentive, observant; (*cortés*) polite, thoughtful.

atenuante [ate'nwante] *a* attenuating, extenuating.

atenuar [ate'nwar] *vt* to attenuate; (*disminuir*) to lessen, minimize.

ateo, a [a'teo, a] *a* atheistic // *nm/f*

atheist.

aterciopelado, a [aterθjope'laðo, a] *a* velvety.

aterido, a [ate'riðo, a] *a*: ~ **de frío** frozen stiff.

aterrador, a [aterra'ðor, a] *a* frightening.

aterrar [ate'rrar] *vt* to frighten; to terrify; ~**se** *vr* to be frightened; to be terrified.

aterrizaje [aterri'θaxe] *nm* (AVIAT) landing.

aterrizar [aterri'θar] *vi* to land.

aterrorizar [aterrori'θar] *vt* to terrify.

atesorar [ateso'rar] *vt* to hoard, store up.

atestado, a [ates'taðo, a] *a* packed // *nm* (JUR) affidavit.

atestar [ates'tar] *vt* to pack, stuff; (JUR) to attest, testify to.

atestiguar [atesti'ɣwar] *vt* to testify to, bear witness to.

atiborrar [atiβo'rrar] *vt* to fill, stuff; ~**se** *vr* to stuff o.s.

ático ['atiko] *nm* attic; ~ **de lujo** penthouse (flat (Brit) o apartment).

atildar [atil'dar] *vt* to criticize; ~**se** *vr* to spruce o.s. up.

atinado, a [ati'naðo, a] *a* (sensato) wise; (correcto) right, correct.

atisbar [atis'βar] *vt* to spy on; (echar una ojeada) to peep at.

atizar [ati'θar] *vt* to poke; (horno etc) to stoke; (fig) to stir up, rouse.

atlántico, a [at'lantiko, a] *a* Atlantic // *nm*: **el (océano) A~** the Atlantic (Ocean).

atlas ['atlas] *nm* atlas.

atleta [at'leta] *nm* athlete; **atlético, a** *a* athletic; **atletismo** *nm* athletics *sg*.

atmósfera [at'mosfera] *nf* atmosphere.

atolondramiento [atolondra'mjento] *nm* bewilderment; (insensatez) silliness.

atollar [ato'ʎar] *vi*, **atollarse** *vr* to get stuck; (fig) to get into a jam.

atómico, a [a'tomiko, a] *a* atomic.

atomizador [atomiθa'ðor] *nm* atomizer; (de perfume) spray.

átomo ['atomo] *nm* atom.

atónito, a [a'tonito, a] *a* astonished, amazed.

atontado, a [aton'taðo, a] *a* stunned; (bobo) silly, daft.

atontar [aton'tar] *vt* to stun; ~**se** *vr* to become confused.

atormentar [atormen'tar] *vt* to torture; (molestar) to torment; (acosar) to plague, harass.

atornillar [atorni'ʎar] *vt* to screw on o down.

atracador, a [atraka'ðor, a] *nm/f* robber.

atracar [atra'kar] *vt* (NAUT) to moor; (robar) to hold up, rob // *vi* to moor; ~**se** *vr*: ~**se (de)** to stuff o.s. (with).

atracción [atrak'θjon] *nf* attraction.

atraco [a'trako] *nm* holdup, robbery.

atractivo, a [atrak'tiβo, a] *a* attractive // *nm* attraction; (belleza) attractiveness.

atraer [atra'er] *vt* to attract.

atragantarse [atraɣan'tarse] *vr*: ~ **(con)** to choke (on); **se me ha atragantado el chico** I can't stand the boy.

atrancar [atran'kar] *vt* (puerta) to bar, bolt.

atrapar [atra'par] *vt* to trap; (resfriado etc) to catch.

atrás [a'tras] *ad* (movimiento) back(wards); (lugar) behind; (tiempo) previously; **ir hacia** ~ to go back(wards); **to go to the rear; estar** ~ to be behind o at the back.

atrasado, a [atra'saðo, a] *a* slow; (pago) overdue, late; (país) backward.

atrasar [atra'sar] *vi* to be slow; ~**se** *vr* to remain behind; (tren) to be o run late; **atraso** *nm* slowness; lateness, delay; (de país) backwardness; **atrasos** *nmpl* arrears.

atravesar [atraβe'sar] *vt* (cruzar) to cross (over); (traspasar) to pierce; to go through; (poner al través) to lay o put across; **~se** *vr* to come in between; (*intervenir*) to interfere.

atravieso *etc vb ver* **atravesar**.

atrayente [atra'jente] *a* attractive.

atreverse [atre'βerse] *vr* to dare; (*insolentarse*) to be insolent; **atrevido, a** *a* daring; insolent; **atrevimiento** *nm* daring; insolence.

atribución [atriβu'θjon] *nf:* **atribuciones** (*POL*) powers; (*ADMIN*) responsibilities.

atribuir [atriβu'ir] *vt* to attribute; (*funciones*) to confer.

atribular [atriβu'lar] *vt* to afflict, distress.

atributo [atri'βuto] *nm* attribute.

atrocidad [atroθi'ðað] *nf* atrocity, outrage.

atropellar [atrope'ʎar] *vt* (*derribar*) to knock over o down; (*empujar*) to push (aside); (*AUTO*) to run over, run down; (*agraviar*) to insult; **~se** *vr* to act hastily; **atropello** *nm* (*AUTO*) accident; (*empujón*) push; (*agravio*) wrong; (*atrocidad*) outrage.

atroz [a'troθ] *a* atrocious, awful.

atto, a *abr* = **atento**.

atuendo [a'twendo] *nm* attire.

atún [a'tun] *nm* tuna.

aturdir [atur'ðir] *vt* to stun; (*de ruido*) to deafen; (*fig*) to dumbfound, bewilder.

atusar [atu'sar] *vt* to smooth (down).

audacia [au'ðaθja] *nf* boldness, audacity; **audaz** *a* bold, audacious.

audible [au'ðiβle] *a* audible.

audición [auði'θjon] *nf* hearing; (*TEATRO*) audition.

audiencia [au'ðjenθja] *nf* audience; A~ (*JUR*) High Court.

auditor [auði'tor] *nm* (*JUR*) judge-advocate; (*COM*) auditor.

auditorio [auði'torjo] *nm* audience; (*sala*) auditorium.

auge ['auxe] *nm* boom; (*clímax*) climax.

augurar [auɣu'rar] *vt* to predict; (*presagiar*) to portend.

augurio [au'ɣurjo] *nm* omen.

aula ['aula] *nf* classroom; (*en universidad etc*) lecture room.

aullar [au'ʎar] *vi* to howl, yell.

aullido [au'ʎiðo] *nm* howl, yell.

aumentar [aumen'tar] *vt* to increase; (*precios*) to put up; (*producción*) to step up; (*con microscopio, anteojos*) to magnify // *vi*, **~se** *vr* to increase, be on the increase; **aumento** *nm* increase; rise.

aun [a'un] *ad* even; **~ así** even so; **~ más** even o more.

aún [a'un] *ad:* **~ está aquí** he's still here; **~ no lo sabemos** we don't know yet; **¿no ha venido ~?** hasn't she come yet?

aunque [a'unke] *conj* though, although, even though.

aúpa [a'upa] *excl* come on!

aureola [aure'ola] *nf* halo.

auricular [auriku'lar] *nm* (*TEL*) earpiece, receiver; **~es** *nmpl* headphones.

aurora [au'rora] *nf* dawn.

auscultar [auskul'tar] *vt* (*MED: pecho*) to listen to, sound.

ausencia [au'senθja] *nf* absence.

ausentarse [ausen'tarse] *vr* to go away; (*por poco tiempo*) to go out.

ausente [au'sente] *a* absent.

auspicios [aus'piθjos] *nmpl* auspices; (*protección*) protection *sg*.

austeridad [austeri'ðað] *nf* austerity; **austero, a** *a* austere.

austral [aus'tral] *a* southern // *nm* monetary unit of Argentina.

Australia [aus'tralja] *nf* Australia; **australiano, a** *a, nm/f* Australian.

Austria ['austrja] *nf* Austria; **austríaco, a** *a, nm/f* Austrian.

autenticar [autenti'kar] *vt* to authenticate; **auténtico, a** *a* authentic.

auto ['auto] *nm* (*JUR*) edict, decree; (: *orden*) writ; (*AUTO*) car; **~s** *nmpl* (*JUR*) proceedings; (: *acta*) court record *sg*.

autoadhesivo [autoaðe'siβo] *a* self-adhesive; (*sobre*) self-sealing.

autobiografía [autoβjoɣra'fia]

autobiography.

autobús [auto'βus] nm bus.

autocar [auto'kar] nm coach (Brit), (passenger) bus (US).

autóctono, a [au'toktono, a] a native, indigenous.

autodefensa [autoðe'fensa] nf self-defence.

autodeterminación [autoðetermina'θjon] nf self-determination.

autoescuela [autoes'kwela] nf driving school.

autógrafo [au'toɣrafo] nm autograph.

automación [automa'θjon] nf = **automatización.**

autómata [au'tomata] nm automaton.

automático, a [auto'matiko, a] a automatic // nm press stud.

automatización [automatiθa'θjon] nf automation.

automotor, triz [automo'tor, 'triθ] a self-propelled // nm diesel train.

automóvil [auto'moßil] nm (motor) car (Brit), automobile (US); **automovilismo** nm (actividad) motoring; (DEPORTE) (sports)car racing; **automovilista** nm/f motorist, driver; **automovilístico, a** a (industria) car cpd.

autonomía [autono'mia] nf autonomy; **autonómico, a**, **autónomo, a** a (Esp POL) autonomous.

autopista [auto'pista] nf motorway (Brit), freeway (US).

autopsia [au'topsja] nf autopsy, post-mortem.

autor, a [au'tor, a] nm/f author.

autoridad [autori'ðað] nf authority; **autoritario, a** a authoritarian.

autorización [autoriθa'θjon] nf authorization; **autorizado, a** a authorized; (aprobado) approved.

autorizar [autori'θar] vt to authorize; (aprobar) to approve.

autorretrato [autorre'trato] nm self-portrait.

autoservicio [autoser'βiβjo] nm

(tienda) self-service shop (Brit) o store (US); (restaurante) self-service restaurant.

autostop [auto'stop] nm hitch-hiking; **hacer** ~ to hitch-hike; ~**ista** nm/f hitch-hiker.

autosuficiencia [autosufi'θjenθja] nf self-sufficiency.

autovía [auto'βia] nf = A-road (Brit), state highway (US).

auxiliar [auksi'ljar] vt to help // nm/f assistant; **auxilio** nm assistance, help; **primeros auxilios** first aid sg.

Av abr (= Avenida) Av(e).

aval [a'βal] nm guarantee; (persona) guarantor.

avalancha [aβa'lantʃa] nf avalanche.

avance [a'βanθe] nm advance; (pago) advance payment; (CINE) trailer.

avanzar [aβan'θar] vt, vi to advance.

avaricia [aβa'riθja] nf avarice, greed; **avaricioso, a** a a avaricious, greedy.

avaro, a [a'βaro, a] a miserly, mean // nm/f miser.

avasallar [aβasa'ʎar] vt to subdue, subjugate.

Avda abr (= Avenida) Av(e).

ave ['aβe] nf bird; ~ **de rapiña** bird of prey.

avecinarse [aβeθi'narse] vr (tormenta, fig) to be on the way.

avellana [aβe'ʎana] nf hazelnut; **avellano** nm hazel tree.

avemaría [aβema'ria] nm Hail Mary, Ave Maria.

avena [a'βena] nf oats pl.

avenida [aβe'niða] nf (calle) avenue.

avenir [aβe'nir] vt to reconcile; ~**se** vr to come to an agreement, reach a compromise.

aventajado, a [aβenta'xaðo, a] a outstanding.

aventajar [aβenta'xar] vt (sobrepasar) to surpass, outstrip.

aventar [aβen'tar] vt to fan, blow; (grano) to winnow.

aventura [aβen'tura] nf adventure; **aventurado, a** a risky; **aventurero, a** a adventurous.

avergonzar [aβerɣon'θar] *vt* to shame; (*desconcertar*) to embarrass; ~**se** *vr* to be ashamed; to be embarrassed.

avería [aβe'ria] *nf* (*TEC*) breakdown, fault.

averiado, a [aβe'rjaðo, a] *a* broken down; '~' 'out of order'.

averiguación [aβeriwa'θjon] *nf* investigation; (*descubrimiento*) ascertainment.

averiguar [aβeri'ɣwar] *vt* to investigate; (*descubrir*) to find out, ascertain.

aversión [aβer'sjon] *nf* aversion, dislike.

avestruz [aβes'truθ] *nm* ostrich.

aviación [aβja'θjon] *nf* aviation; (*fuerzas aéreas*) air force.

aviador, a [aβja'ðor, a] *nm/f* aviator, airman/woman.

aviar [a'βjar] *vt* to prepare; **estar aviado** (*fig*) to be in a mess.

avicultura [aβikul'tura] *nf* poultry farming.

avidez [aβi'ðeθ] *nf* avidity, eagerness; **ávido, a** *a* avid, eager.

avinagrado, a [aβina'xraðo, a] *a* sour, acid.

avinagrarse [aβina'xrarse] *vr* to go o turn sour.

avío [a'βio] *nm* preparation; ~**s** *nmpl* gear *sg*, kit *sg*.

avión [a'βjon] *nm* aeroplane; (*ave*) martin; ~ **de reacción** jet (plane).

avioneta [aβjo'neta] *nf* light aircraft.

avisar [aβi'sar] *vt* (*advertir*) to warn, notify; (*informar*) to tell; (*aconsejar*) to advise, counsel; **aviso** *nm* warning; (*noticia*) notice.

avispa [a'βispa] *nf* wasp.

avispado, a [aβis'paðo, a] *a* sharp, clever.

avispero [aβis'pero] *nm* wasp's nest.

avispón [aβis'pon] *nm* hornet.

avistar [aβis'tar] *vt* to sight, spot.

avituallar [aβitwa'ʎar] *vt* to supply with food.

avivar [aβi'βar] *vt* to strengthen, intensify; ~**se** *vr* to revive, acquire new life.

axila [ak'sila] *nf* armpit.

axioma [ak'sjoma] *nm* axiom.

ay [ai] *excl* (*dolor*) ow!, ouch!; (*aflicción*) oh!, oh dear!; ¡~ **de mí!** poor me!

aya ['aja] *nf* governess; (*niñera*) nanny.

ayer [a'jer] *ad*, *nm* yesterday; **antes de** ~ the day before yesterday.

ayo ['ajo] *nm* tutor.

ayote [a'jote] *nm* (*AM*) pumpkin.

ayuda [a'juða] *nf* help, assistance // *nm* page; **ayudante, a** *nm/f* assistant, helper; (*ESCOL*) assistant; (*MIL*) adjutant.

ayudar [aju'ðar] *vt* to help, assist.

ayunar [aju'nar] *vi* to fast; **ayunas** *nfpl*: **estar en ayunas** (*no haber comido*) to be fasting; (*ignorar*) to be in the dark; **ayuno** *nm* fasting.

ayuntamiento [ajunta'mjento] *nm* (*consejo*) town o city council; (*edificio*) town o city hall.

azabache [aθa'βatʃe] *nm* jet.

azada [a'θaða] *nf* hoe.

azafata [aθa'fata] *nf* air stewardess.

azafrán [aθa'fran] *nm* saffron.

azahar [aθa'ar] *nm* orange/lemon blossom.

azar [a'θar] *nm* (*casualidad*) chance, fate; (*desgracia*) misfortune, accident; **por** ~ by chance; **al** ~ at random.

azogue [a'θoxe] *nm* mercury.

azoramiento [aθora'mjento] *nm* alarm; (*confusión*) confusion.

azorar [aθo'rar] *vt* to alarm; ~**se** *vr* to get alarmed.

Azores [a'θores] *nmpl*: **los** ~ the Azores.

azotar [aθo'tar] *vt* to whip, beat; (*pegar*) to spank; **azote** *nm* (*látigo*) whip; (*latigazo*) lash, stroke; (*en las nalgas*) spank; (*calamidad*) calamity.

azotea [aθo'tea] *nf* (flat) roof.

azteca [aθ'teka] *a*, *nm/f* Aztec.

azúcar [a'θukar] *nm* sugar; **azucarado, a** *a* sugary, sweet.

azucarero, a [aθuka'rero, a] *a* sugar *cpd* // *nm* sugar bowl.

azucena [aθu'θena] *nf* white lily.

azufre [a'θufre] *nm* sulphur.

azul [a'θul] *a, nm* blue.

azulejo [aθu'lexo] *nm* tile.

azuzar [aθu'θar] *vt* to incite, egg on.

B

B.A. *abr* (= *Buenos Aires*) B.A.

baba ['baβa] *nf* spittle, saliva; **babear** *vi* to drool, slaver.

babel [ba'βel] *nm o f* bedlam.

babero [ba'βero] *nm* bib.

babor [ba'βor] *nm* port (side).

baboso, a [ba'βoso, a] *a* (*AM fam*) silly.

babucha [ba'βutʃa] *nf* slipper.

baca ['baka] *nf* (*AUTO*) luggage *o* roof rack.

bacalao [baka'lao] *nm* cod(fish).

bacinica [baθi'nika] *nf*, **bacinilla** [baθi'niʎa] *nf* chamber pot.

bacteria [bak'terja] *nf* bacterium, germ.

báculo ['bakulo] *nm* stick, staff.

bache ['batʃe] *nm* pothole, rut; (*fig*) bad patch.

bachillerato [batʃiʎe'rato] *nm* (*ESCOL*) school-leaving examination (*Brit*), bachelor's degree (*US*), baccalaureate (*US*).

bagaje [ba'xaxe] *nm* baggage, luggage.

bagatela [baxa'tela] *nf* trinket, trifle.

Bahama [ba'ama]: **las (Islas)** ~ the Bahamas.

bahía [ba'ia] *nf* bay.

bailar [bai'lar] *vt, vi* to dance; ~**ín, ina** *nm/f* (ballet) dancer; **baile** *nm* dance; (*formal*) ball.

baja ['baxa] *nf ver* **bajo**.

bajada [ba'xaða] *nf* descent; (*camino*) slope (*de aguas*) ebb.

bajamar [baxa'mar] *nf* low tide.

bajar [ba'xar] *vi* to go down, come down; (*temperatura, precios*) to drop, fall // *vt* (*cabeza*) to bow, bend;

(*escalera*) to go down, come down; (*precio, voz*) to lower; (*llevar abajo*) to take down; ~**se** *vr* to get out of; to get off; ~ **de** (*coche*) to get out of; (*autobus*) to get off.

bajeza [ba'xeθa] *nf* baseness *q*; (*una* ~) vile deed.

bajío [ba'xio] *nm* shoal, sandbank; (*AM*) lowlands *pl*.

bajo, a ['baxo, a] *a* (*mueble, número, precio*) low; (*piso*) ground; (*de estatura*) small, short; (*color*) pale; (*sonido*) faint, soft, low; (*voz: en tono*) deep; (*metal*) base; (*humilde*) low, humble // *ad* (*hablar*) softly, quietly; (*volar*) low // *prep* under, below, underneath // *nm* (*MUS*) bass // *nf* drop, fall; (*MIL*) casualty; **la lluvia en baja** in the rain; **dar de baja** (*soldado*) to discharge; (*empleado*) to dismiss, sack.

bajón [ba'xon] *nm* fall, drop.

bala ['bala] *nf* bullet.

baladí [bala'ði] *a* trivial.

baladronada [balaðro'naða] *nf* (*dicho*) boast, brag; (*hecho*) piece of bravado.

balance [ba'lanθe] *nm* (*COM*) balance; (: *libro*) balance sheet; (: *cuenta general*) stocktaking.

balancear [balanθe'ar] *vt* to balance // *vi*, ~**se** *vr* to swing (to and fro); (*vacilar*) to hesitate; **balanceo** *nm* swinging.

balanza [ba'lanθa] *nf* scales *pl*, balance; ~ **comercial** balance of trade; ~ **de pagos** balance of payments; (*ASTROLOGIA*) B~ Libra.

balar [ba'lar] *vi* to bleat.

balaustrada [balaus'traða] *nf* balustrade; (*pasamanos*) banisters *pl*.

balazo [ba'laθo] *nm* (*golpe*) shot; (*herida*) bullet wound.

balbucear [balβuθe'ar] *vi, vt* to stammer, stutter; **balbuceo** *nm* stammering, stuttering.

balbucir [balβu'θir] *vi, vt* to stammer, stutter.

balcón [bal'kon] *nm* balcony.

baldar [bal'dar] *vt* to cripple.

balde ['balde] *nm* bucket, pail; de ~
ad (for) free, for nothing; en ~ ad in
vain.

baldío, a [bal'dio, a] *a* uncultivated;
(*terreno*) waste // *nm* waste land.

baldosa [bal'dosa] *nf* (*azulejo*) floor
tile; (*grande*) flagstone.

Baleares [bale'ares] *nfpl*: las (Islas)
~ the Balearic Islands.

balido [ba'liðo] *nm* bleat, bleating.

balín [ba'lin] *nm* pellet; **balines** *nmpl*
buckshot *sg*.

balística [ba'listika] *nf* ballistics *pl*.

baliza [ba'liθa] *nf* (*AVIAT*) beacon;
(*NAUT*) buoy.

balneario, a [balne'arjo, a] *a*:
estación balnearia (bathing) resort
// *nm* spa, health resort.

balón [ba'lon] *nm* ball.

baloncesto [balon'θesto] *nm* basket-
ball.

balonmano [balom'mano] *nm* hand-
ball.

balonvolea [balombo'lea] *nm* volleyball.

balsa ['balsa] *nf* raft; (*BOT*) balsa
wood.

bálsamo ['balsamo] *nm* balsam,
balm.

baluarte [ba'lwarte] *nm* bastion,
bulwark.

ballena [ba'ʎena] *nf* whale.

ballesta [ba'ʎesta] *nf* crossbow;
(*AUTO*) spring.

ballet [ba'le] *nm* ballet.

bambolear [bambole'ar] *vi*,
bambolearse *vr* to swing, sway;
(*silla*) to wobble; **bamboleo** *nm*
swinging, swaying; wobbling.

bambú [bam'bu] *nm* bamboo.

banana [ba'nana] *nf* (*AM*) banana;
banano *nm* (*AM*) banana tree.

banca ['banka] *nf* (*asiento*) bench;
(*COM*) banking.

bancario, a [ban'karjo, a] *a* banking
cpd, bank *cpd*.

bancarrota [banka'rrota] *nf* bankruptcy; **hacer** ~ to go bankrupt.

banco ['banko] *nm* bench; (*ESCOL*)

desk; (*COM*) bank; (*GEO*) stratum;
~ **de crédito/de ahorros** credit/
savings bank; ~ **de arena** sandbank; ~ **de hielo** iceberg.

banda ['banda] *nf* band; (*pandilla*)
gang; (*NAUT*) side, edge; **la B~**
Oriental Uruguay; ~ **sonora** sound-
track.

bandada [ban'daða] *nf* (*de pájaros*)
flock; (*de peces*) shoal.

bandeja [ban'dexa] *nf* tray.

bandera [ban'dera] *nf* (*de tela*) flag;
(*estandarte*) banner.

banderilla [bande'riʎa] *nf* banderilla.

banderín [bande'rin] *nm* pennant,
small flag.

banderola [bande'rola] *nf* banderole;
(*MIL*) pennant.

bandido [ban'diðo] *nm* bandit.

bando ['bando] *nm* (*edicto*) edict,
proclamation; (*facción*) faction; **los**
~**s** the banns.

bandolero [bando'lero] *nm* bandit,
brigand.

banquero [ban'kero] *nm* banker.

banqueta [ban'keta] *nf* stool; (*AM*:
en la calle) pavement (*Brit*), sidewalk (*US*).

banquete [ban'kete] *nm* banquet;
(*para convidados*) formal dinner.

banquillo [ban'kiʎo] *nm* (*JUR*) dock,
prisoner's bench; (*banco*) bench;
(*para los pies*) footstool.

bañador [bana'ðor] *nm* swimming
costume (*Brit*), bathing suit (*US*).

bañar [ba'nar] *vt* to bathe, bathe;
(*objeto*) to dip; (*de barniz*) to cover;
~**se** *vr* (*en el mar*) to bathe, swim;
(*en la bañera*) to bath, have a bath.

bañera [ba'nera] *nf* bath(tub).

bañero [ba'nero] *nm* lifeguard.

bañista [ba'nista] *nm/f* bather.

baño ['bano] *nm* (*en bañera*) bath;
(*en río*) dip, swim; (*cuarto*) bathroom; (*bañera*) bath(tub); (*capa*)
coating.

baptista [bap'tista] *nm/f* Baptist.

baqueta [ba'keta] *nf* (*MUS*) drum-
stick.

bar [bar] *nm* bar.

barahúnda [bara'unda] *nf* uproar, hubbub.

baraja [ba'raxa] *nf* pack (of cards).

barajar *vt* (*naipes*) to shuffle; (*fig*) to jumble up.

baranda [ba'randa], **barandilla** [baran'diʎa] *nf* rail, railing.

baratija [bara'tixa] *nf* trinket.

baratillo [bara'tiʎo] *nm* (*tienda*) junkshop; (*subasta*) bargain sale; (*conjunto de cosas*) secondhand goods *pl*.

barato, a [ba'rato, a] *a* cheap // *ad* cheap, cheaply.

baraúnda [bara'unda] *nf* = **barahúnda**.

barba ['barβa] *nf* (*mentón*) chin; (*pelo*) beard.

barbacoa [barβa'koa] *nf* (*parrilla*) barbecue; (*carne*) barbecued meat.

barbaridad [barβari'ðað] *nf* barbarity; (*acto*) barbarism; (*atrocidad*) outrage; **una ~** (*fam*) loads *pl*; **¡qué ~!** (*fam*) how awful!

barbarie [bar'βarje] *nf*, **barbarismo** [barβa'rismo] *nm* barbarism, savagery; (*crueldad*) barbarity.

bárbaro, a ['barβaro, a] *a* barbarous, cruel; (*grosero*) rough, uncouth // *nm/f* barbarian // *ad*: **lo pasamos ~** (*fam*) we had a great time; **¡qué ~!** (*fam*) how marvellous!; **un éxito ~** (*fam*) a terrific success; **es un tipo ~** (*fam*) he's a great bloke.

barbecho [bar'βetʃo] *nm* fallow land.

barbero [bar'βero] *nm* barber, hairdresser.

barbilampiño [barβilam'piɲo] *a* clean-shaven, smooth-faced; (*fig*) inexperienced.

barbilla [bar'βiʎa] *nf* chin, tip of the chin.

barbo ['barβo] *nm*: **~ de mar** red mullet.

barbotar [barβo'tar], **barbotear** [barβote'ar] *vt, vi* to mutter, mumble.

barbudo, a [bar'βuðo, a] *a* bearded.

barca ['barka] *nf* (*small*) boat; **~ pesquera** fishing boat; **~ de pasaje** ferry; **~za** *nf* barge; **~za de desembarco** landing craft.

Barcelona [barθe'lona] *nf* Barcelona.

barcelonés, esa [barθelo'nes, esa] *a* of *o* from Barcelona.

barco ['barko] *nm* boat; (*buque*) ship; **~ de carga** cargo boat.

barítono [ba'ritono] *nm* baritone.

barman ['barman] *nm* barman.

Barna. *abr* = **Barcelona.**

barniz [bar'niθ] *nm* varnish; (*en la loza*) glaze; (*fig*) veneer; **~ar** *vt* to varnish; (*loza*) to glaze.

barómetro [ba'rometro] *nm* barometer.

barquero [bar'kero] *nm* boatman.

barquillo [bar'kiʎo] *nm* cone, cornet.

barra ['barra] *nf* bar, rod; (*de un bar, café*) bar; (*de pan*) French loaf; (*palanca*) lever; **~ de carmín** *o* **de labios** lipstick.

barraca [ba'rraka] *nf* hut, cabin.

barranca [ba'rranka] *nf* ravine, gully; **barranco** *nm* ravine; (*fig*) difficulty.

barrena [ba'rrena] *nf* drill; **barrenar** *vt* to drill (*through*); bore; **barreno** *nm* large drill.

barrer [ba'rrer] *vt* to sweep; (*quitar*) to sweep away.

barrera [ba'rrera] *nf* barrier.

barriada [ba'rrjaða] *nf* quarter, district.

barricada [barri'kaða] *nf* barricade.

barrido [ba'rriðo] *nm*, **barrida** [ba'rriða] *nf* sweep, sweeping.

barriga [ba'rriɣa] *nf* belly; (*panza*) paunch; **barrigón, ona, barrigudo, a** *a* potbellied.

barril [ba'rril] *nm* barrel, cask.

barrio ['barrjo] *nm* (*vecindad*) area, neighborhood (*US*); (*en las afueras*) suburb; **~ chino** red-light district.

barro ['barro] *nm* (*lodo*) mud; (*objetos*) earthenware; (*MED*) pimple.

barroco, a [ba'rroko, a] *a, nm* baroque.

barrote [ba'rrote] *nm* (*de ventana*) bar.

barruntar [barrun'tar] vt (conjeturar) to guess; (presentir) to suspect; **barrunto** nm guess; suspicion.

bartola [bar'tola]: **a la ~ ad**: tirarse a la ~ to take it easy, be lazy.

bártulos ['bartulos] nmpl things, belongings.

barullo [ba'ruʎo] nm row, uproar.

basamento [basa'mento] nm base, plinth.

basar [ba'sar] vt to base; ~se vr: ~se en to be based on.

basca ['baska] nf nausea.

báscula ['baskula] nf (platform) scales pl.

base ['base] nf base; **a ~ de** on the basis of; (mediante) by means of; ~ **de datos** (INFORM) database.

básico, a ['basiko, a] a basic.

basílica [ba'silika] nf basilica.

PALABRA CLAVE

bastante [bas'tante] ♦ a **1** (suficiente) enough; ~ **dinero** enough o sufficient money; ~s **libros** enough books

2 (valor intensivo): ~ **gente** quite a lot of people; **tener ~ calor** to be rather hot

♦ ad: ~ **bueno/malo** quite good/ rather bad; ~ **rico** pretty rich; (lo) ~ **inteligente** (como) **para hacer algo** clever enough o sufficiently clever to do sth.

---

bastar [bas'tar] vi to be enough o sufficient; ~se vr to be self-sufficient; ~ **para** to be enough to; **¡basta!** (that's) enough!

bastardilla [bastar'ðiʎa] nf italics pl.

bastardo, a [bas'tarðo, a] a, nm/f bastard.

bastidor [basti'ðor] nm frame; (de coche) chassis; (TEATRO) wing; **entre ~es** (fig) behind the scenes.

basto, a ['basto, a] a coarse, rough; ~s nmpl (NAIPES) ≈ clubs.

bastón [bas'ton] nm stick, staff; (para pasear) walking stick.

basura [ba'sura] nf rubbish (Brit), garbage (US).

basurero [basu'rero] nm (hombre) dustman (Brit), garbage man (US); (lugar) dump; (cubo) (rubbish) bin (Brit), trash can (US).

bata ['bata] nf (gen) dressing gown; (cubretodo) smock, overall; (MED, TEC etc) lab(oratory) coat.

batalla [ba'taʎa] nf battle; **de ~** for everyday use.

batallar [bata'ʎar] vi to fight.

batallón [bata'ʎon] nm battalion.

batata [ba'tata] nf (AM) sweet potato.

bate ['bate] nm bat; ~**ador** nm (AM) batter, batsman.

batería [bate'ria] nf battery; (MUS) drums pl; ~ **de cocina** kitchen utensils pl.

batido, a [ba'tiðo, a] a (camino) beaten, well-trodden // nm (CULIN) batter; ~ **(de leche)** milk shake.

batidora [bati'ðora] nf beater, mixer; ~ **eléctrica** food mixer, blender.

batir [ba'tir] vt to beat, strike; (vencer) to beat, defeat; (revolver) to beat, mix; ~se vr to fight; ~ **palmas** to clap, applaud.

batuta [ba'tuta] nf baton; **llevar la ~** (fig) to be the boss, be in charge.

baúl [ba'ul] nm trunk; (AUTO) boot (Brit), trunk (US).

bautismo [bau'tismo] nm baptism, christening.

bautizar [bauti'θar] vt to baptize, christen; (fam: diluir) to water down; **bautizo** nm baptism, christening.

bayeta [ba'jeta] nf floorcloth.

bayo, a ['bajo, a] a bay // nf berry.

bayoneta [bajo'neta] nf bayonet.

baza ['baθa] nf trick; **meter ~** to butt in.

bazar [ba'θar] nm bazaar.

bazofia [ba'θofja] nf pigswill (Brit), hogwash (US); (libro etc) trash.

beato, a [be'ato, a] a blessed; (piadoso) pious.

bebé [be'βe] nm baby.

bebedero [beβe'ðero] nm (para animales) drinking trough.

bebedizo, a [beβe'ðiθo, a] a drinkable // nm potion.

bebedor, a [beβe'ðor, a] a hard-drinking.

beber [be'βer] vt, vi to drink.

bebida [be'βiða] nf drink.

beca ['beka] nf grant, scholarship.

befarse [be'farse] vr: ~ de algo to scoff at sth.

beldad [bel'dað] nf beauty.

Belén [be'len] nm Bethlehem; **b~** nm (de navidad) nativity scene, crib.

belga ['belɣa] a, nm/f Belgian.

Bélgica ['belxika] nf Belgium.

Belice [be'liθe] nm Belize.

bélico, a ['beliko] a (actitud) war-like; **belicoso, a** (guerrero) war-like; (agresivo) aggressive, bellicose.

beligerante [belixe'rante] a belligerent.

bellaco, a [be'ʎako, a] a sly, cunning // nm villain, rogue; **bellaquería** nf (acción) dirty trick; (calidad) wickedness.

belleza [be'ʎeθa] nf beauty.

bello, a ['beʎo, a] a beautiful, lovely; Bellas Artes Fine Art.

bellota [be'ʎota] nf acorn.

bemol [be'mol] nm (MUS) flat; esto tiene ~es (fam) this is a tough one.

bencina [ben'θina] nf (AM: gasolina) petrol (Brit), gasoline (US).

bendecir [bende'θir] vt to bless.

bendición [bendi'θjon] nf blessing.

bendito, a [ben'dito, a] pp de **bendecir** // a holy; (afortunado) lucky; (feliz) happy; (sencillo) simple // nm/f simple soul.

benedictino, a [beneðik'tino, a] a, nm Benedictine.

beneficencia [benefi'θenθja] nf charity.

beneficiar [benefi'θjar] vt to benefit, be of benefit to; ~se vr to benefit, profit; ~io, a nm/f beneficiary.

beneficio [bene'fiθjo] nm (bien) benefit, advantage; (ganancia) profit, gain; ~so, a a beneficial.

benéfico, a [be'nefiko, a] a charitable.

beneplácito [bene'plaθito] nm approval, consent.

benevolencia [beneβo'lenθja] nf benevolence, kindness; **benévolo, a** a benevolent, kind.

benigno, a [be'niɣno, a] a kind; (suave) mild; (MED: tumor) benign, non-malignant.

beodo, a [be'oðo, a] a drunk.

berenjena [beren'xena] nf aubergine (Brit), eggplant (US).

Berlín [ber'lin] n Berlin; **berlinés, esa** a of o from Berlin // nm/f Berliner.

bermejo, a [ber'mexo, a] a red.

berrear [berre'ar] vi to bellow, low.

berrido [be'rriðo] nm bellow(ing).

berrinche [be'rrintʃe] nm (fam) temper, tantrum.

berro ['berro] nm watercress.

berza ['berθa] nf cabbage.

besamel [besa'mel] nf (CULIN) white sauce, bechamel sauce.

besar [be'sar] vt to kiss; (fig: tocar) to graze; ~se vr to kiss (one another); **beso** nm kiss.

bestia ['bestja] nf beast, animal; (fig) idiot; ~ de carga beast of burden.

bestial [bes'tjal] a bestial; (fam) terrific; ~idad nf bestiality; (fam) stupidity.

besugo [be'suɣo] nm sea bream; (fam) idiot.

besuquear [besuke'ar] vt to cover with kisses; ~se vr to kiss and cuddle.

betún [be'tun] nm shoe polish; (QUIMICA) bitumen.

biberón [biβe'ron] nm feeding bottle.

Biblia ['biβlja] nf Bible.

bibliografía [biβljoɣra'fia] nf bibliography.

biblioteca [biβljo'teka] nf library; (mueble) bookshelves pl; ~ de consulta reference library; ~rio, a nm/f librarian.

B.I.C. nf abr (= Brigada de Investigación Criminal) CID (Brit), FBI (US).

bicarbonato [bikar'βo'nato] *nm* bicarbonate.

bici ['biθi] *nf (fam)* bike.

bicicleta [biθi'kleta] *nf* bicycle, cycle.

bicho ['bitʃo] *nm (animal)* small animal; *(sabandija)* bug, insect; *(TAUR)* bull.

bidé [bi'ðe] *nm* bidet.

PALABRA CLAVE

bien [bjen] ◆ *nm* 1 *(bienestar)* good; **te lo digo por tu ~** I'm telling you for your own good; **el ~ y el mal** good and evil

2 *(posesión)*: **~es** goods; **~es de consumo** consumer goods; **~es inmuebles o raíces/~es muebles** real estate *sg*/personal property *sg*

◆ *ad* 1 *(de manera satisfactoria, correcta etc)* well; **trabaja/come ~** she works/eats well; **contestó ~** he answered correctly; **me siento ~** I feel fine; **no me siento ~** I don't feel very well; **se está ~ aquí** it's nice here

2 *(frases)*: **hiciste ~ en llamarme** you were right to call me

3 *(valor intensivo)* very; **un cuarto ~ caliente** a nice warm room; **~ se ve que ...** it's quite clear that ...

4: **estar ~**: **estoy muy bien aquí** I feel very happy here; **está bien que vengan** it's alright for them to come; **¡está bien! lo haré oh** alright, I'll do it

5 *(de buena gana)*: **yo ~ que iría pero ...** I'd gladly go but ...

◆ *excl*: **¡~!** *(aprobación)* O.K!; **¡muy ~!** well done!

◆ *a inv (matiz despectivo)*: **niño ~** rich kid; **gente ~** posh people

◆ *conj* 1: **~ ... o ...** either ... or ...; **~ en coche ~ en tren** either by car or by train

2: **no ~** *(esp AM)*: **no ~ llegue te llamaré** as soon as I arrive I'll call you

3: **si ~** even though; *ver tb* **más.**

---

bienal [bje'nal] *a* biennial.

bienaventurado, a [bjenaβentu-'raðo, a] *a (feliz)* happy, fortunate.

bienestar [bjenes'tar] *nm* well-being, welfare.

bienhechor, a [bjene'tʃor, a] *a* beneficent // *nm/f* benefactor/benefactress.

bienvenida [bjembe'niða] *nf* welcome; **dar la ~ a uno** to welcome sb.

bienvenido [bjembe'niðo] *excl* welcome!

bife ['bife] *nm (AM)* steak.

bifurcación [bifurka'θjon] *nf* fork.

bigamia [bi'yamja] *nf* bigamy; **bígamo, a** *a* bigamous // *nm/f* bigamist.

bigote [bi'yote] *nm* moustache; **bigotudo, a** *a* with a big moustache.

bikini [bi'kini] *nm* bikini; *(CULIN)* toasted ham and cheese sandwich.

bilingüe [bi'lingwe] *a* bilingual.

billar [bi'ʎar] *nm* billiards *sg*; *(lugar)* billiard hall; *(mini-casino)* amusement arcade.

billete [bi'ʎete] *nm* ticket; *(de banco)* banknote *(Brit)*, bill *(US)*; *(carta)* note; **~ sencillo, ~ de ida solamente/de ida y vuelta** single *(Brit)* o one-way *(US)* ticket/return *(Brit)* o round-trip *(US)* ticket; **~ de 20 libras** £20 note.

billetera [biʎe'tera] *nf*, **billetero** [biʎe'tero] *nm* wallet.

billón [bi'ʎon] *nm* billion.

bimensual [bimen'swal] *a* twice monthly.

bimotor [bimo'tor] *a* twin-engined // *nm* twin-engined plane.

binóculo [bi'nokulo] *nm* pince-nez.

biografía [bjoyra'fia] *nf* biography; **biógrafo, a** *nm/f* biographer.

biología [bjolo'xia] *nf* biology; **biológico, a** *a* biological; **biólogo, a** *nm/f* biologist.

biombo ['bjombo] *nm* (folding) screen.

biopsia [bi'opsja] *nf* biopsy.

birlar [bir'lar] *vt (fam)* to pinch.

Birmania [bir'manja] *nf* Burma.

bis [bis] *excl* encore! // *ad*: **viven en el 27 ~** they live at 27a.

bisabuelo, a [bisa'βwelo, a] *nm/f* great-grandfather/mother.

bisagra [bi'saɣra] *nf* hinge.

bisbisar [bisβi'sar], **bisbisear** [bisβise'ar] *vt* to mutter, mumble.

bisiesto [bi'sjesto] *a*: **año ~** leap year.

bisnieto, a [bis'njeto, a] *nm/f* great-grandson/daughter.

bisonte [bi'sonte] *nm* bison.

bistec [bis'tek], **bisté** [bis'te] *nm* steak.

bisturí [bistu'ri] *nm* scalpel.

bisutería [bisute'ria] *nf* imitation *o* costume jewellery.

bit [bit] *nm* (INFORM) bit.

bizcar [biθ'kar] *vi* to squint.

bizco, a ['biθko, a] *a* cross-eyed.

bizcocho [biθ'kotʃo] *nm* (CULIN) sponge cake.

bizquear [biθke'ar] *vi* to squint.

blanco, a ['blanko, a] *a* white // *nm/f* white man/woman, white // *nm* (color) white; (en texto) blank; (MIL, fig) target // *nf* (MUS) minim; **en ~** blank; **noche en ~** sleepless night; **estar sin ~** to be broke.

blancura [blan'kura] *nf* whiteness.

blandir [blan'dir] *vt* to brandish.

blando, a ['blando, a] *a* soft; (tierno) tender, gentle; (carácter) mild; (fam) cowardly; **blandura** *nf* softness; tenderness; mildness.

blanquear [blanke'ar] *vt* to whiten; (fachada) to whitewash; (paño) to bleach // *vi* to turn white; **blanquecino, a** *a* whitish.

blasfemar [blasfe'mar] *vi* to blaspheme, curse; **blasfemia** *nf* blasphemy.

blasón [bla'son] *nm* coat of arms; (fig) honour; **blasonar** *vt* to emblazon // *vi* to boast, brag.

bledo ['bleðo] *nm*: **me importa un ~** I couldn't care less.

blindado, a [blin'daðo, a] *a* (MIL) armour-plated; (antibala) bullet-proof; **coche** (Esp) *o* **carro** (AM) ~

armoured car.

blindaje [blin'daxe] *nm* armour, armour-plating.

bloc [blok] (*pl* ~s) *nm* writing pad.

bloque ['bloke] *nm* block; (POL) bloc; **~ de cilindros** cylinder block.

bloquear [bloke'ar] *vt* to blockade; **bloqueo** *nm* blockade; (COM) freezing, blocking.

blusa ['blusa] *nf* blouse.

boato [bo'ato] *nm* show, ostentation.

bobada [bo'βaða], **bobería** [boβe'ria] *nf* foolish action; foolish statement; **decir bobadas** to talk nonsense.

bobina [bo'βina] *nf* (TEC) bobbin; (FOTO) spool; (ELEC) coil.

bobo, a ['boβo, a] *a* (tonto) daft, silly; (cándido) naive // *nm/f* fool, idiot // *nm* (TEATRO) clown, funny man.

boca ['boka] *nf* mouth; (de crustáceo) pincer; (de cañón) muzzle; (entrada) mouth, entrance; **~s** *nfpl* (de río) mouth *sg*; **~ abajo/arriba** face down/up; **a ~jarro** point-blank; **se me hace agua la ~** my mouth is watering.

bocacalle [boka'kaʎe] *nf* (entrance to a) street; **la primera ~** the first turning *o* street.

bocadillo [boka'ðiʎo] *nm* sandwich.

bocado [bo'kaðo] *nm* mouthful, bite; (de caballo) bridle; **~ de Adán** Adam's apple.

bocanada [boka'naða] *nf* (de vino) mouthful, swallow; (de aire) gust, puff.

bocazas [bo'kaθas] *nm inv* (fam) bigmouth.

boceto [bo'θeto] *nm* sketch, outline.

bocina [bo'θina] *nf* (MUS) trumpet; (AUTO) horn; (para hablar) megaphone.

bocha ['botʃa] *nf* bowl; **~s** *nfpl* bowls *sg*.

bochinche [bo'tʃintʃe] *nm* (fam) uproar.

bochorno [bo'tʃorno] *nm* (vergüenza) embarrassment;

(calor): **hace ~** it's very muggy; **~so, a** muggy; embarrassing.

boda [ˈboða] nf (tb: **~s**) wedding, marriage; (fiesta) wedding reception; **~s de plata/de oro** silver/golden wedding.

bodega [boˈðeɣa] nf (de vino) (wine) cellar; (depósito) storeroom; (de barco) hold.

bodegón [boðeˈɣon] nm (ARTE) still life.

bofe [ˈbofe] nm (tb: **~s**: **de res**) lights.

bofetada [bofeˈtaða] nf, **bofetón** [bofeˈton] nm slap (in the face).

boga [ˈboɣa] nf: **en ~** (fig) in vogue.

bogar [boˈɣar] vi (remar) to row; (navegar) to sail.

Bogotá [boɣoˈta] n Bogotá; **bogotano, a** a o of from Bogotá.

bohemio, a [boˈemjo, a] a, nm/f Bohemian.

boicot [boiˈkot] (pl **~s**) nm boycott; **~ear** vt to boycott; **~eo** nm boycott.

boina [ˈboina] nf beret.

bola [ˈbola] nf ball; (canica) marble; (NAIPES) (grand) slam; (betún) shoe polish; (mentira) tale, story; **~s** nfpl (AM) bolas sg; **~ de billar** billiard ball; **~ de nieve** snowball.

bolchevique [boltʃeˈβike] a, nm/f Bolshevik.

boleadoras [bolea'ðoras] nfpl (AM) bolas sg.

bolera [boˈlera] nf skittle o bowling alley.

boleta [boˈleta] nf (AM: billete) ticket; (: permiso) pass, permit.

boletería [bolete'ria] nf (AM) ticket office.

boletín [bole'tin] nm bulletin; (periódico) journal, review; **~ escolar** (Esp) school report; **~ de noticias** news bulletin; **~ de pedido** application form; **~ de precios** price list; **~ de prensa** press release.

boleto [bo'leto] nm ticket.

boli [ˈboli] nm (fam) Biro ®, pen.

boliche [bo'litʃe] nm (bola) jack; (juego) bowls sg; (lugar) bowling alley.

bolígrafo [bo'liɣrafo] nm ball-point pen, Biro ®.

bolívar [bo'liβar] nm monetary unit of Venezuela.

Bolivia [bo'liβja] nf Bolivia; **boliviano, a** a, nm/f Bolivian.

bolo [ˈbolo] nm skittle; (píldora) (large) pill; (juego de) **~s** nmpl skittles sg.

bolsa [ˈbolsa] nf (cartera) purse; (saco) bag; (AM) pocket; (ANAT) cavity, sac; (COM) stock exchange; (MINERÍA) pocket; **~ de agua caliente** hot water bottle; **~ de aire** air pocket; **~ de papel** paper bag; **~ de plástico** plastic bag.

bolsillo [bol'siʎo] nm pocket; (cartera) purse; **de ~** pocket(-size).

bolsista [bol'sista] nm/f stockbroker.

bolso [ˈbolso] nm (bolsa) bag; (de mujer) handbag.

bollo [ˈboʎo] nm (pan) roll; (bulto) bump, lump; (abolladura) dent.

bomba [ˈbomba] nf (MIL) bomb; (TEC) pump // a (fam): **noticia ~** bombshell // ad (fam): **pasarlo ~** to have a great time; **~ atómica/de humo/de retardo** atomic/smoke/time bomb; **~ de gasolina** petrol pump.

bombardear [bombarðe'ar] vt to bombard; (MIL) to bomb; **bombardeo** nm bombardment; bombing.

bombardero [bombar'ðero] nm bomber.

bombear [bombe'ar] vt (agua) to pump (out o up); (MIL) to bomb; **~se** vr to warp.

bombero [bom'bero] nm fireman.

bombilla [bom'biʎa] nf (Esp) (light) bulb.

bombín [bom'bin] nm bowler hat.

bombo [ˈbombo] nm (MUS) bass drum; (TEC) drum.

bombón [bom'bon] nm chocolate.

bonachón, ona [bona'tʃon, ona] a good-natured, easy-going.

bonaerense [bonae'rense] *a* of *o* from Buenos Aires.

bonanza [bo'nanθa] *nf* (*NAUT*) fair weather; (*fig*) bonanza; (*MINERIA*) rich pocket *o* vein.

bondad [bon'daθ] *nf* goodness, kindness; **tenga la ~ de** (please) be good enough to; **~oso, a** *a* good, kind.

bonito, a [bo'nito, a] *a* pretty; (*agradable*) nice // *nm* (*atún*) tuna (fish).

bono ['bono] *nm* voucher; (*FINANZAS*) bond.

bonobús [bono'βus] *nm* (*Esp*) bus pass.

boquear [boke'ar] *vi* to gasp.

boquerón [boke'ron] *nm* (*pez*) (kind of) anchovy; (*agujero*) large hole.

boquete [bo'kete] *nm* gap, hole.

boquiabierto, a [bokia'βjerto, a] *a*: **quedar ~** to be amazed *o* flabbergasted.

boquilla [bo'kiʎa] *nf* (*para riego*) nozzle; (*para cigarro*) cigarette holder; (*MUS*) mouthpiece.

borbollar [borβo'ʎar], **borbollear** [borβoʎe'ar], **borbotar** [borβo'tar] *vi* to bubble.

borbotón [borβo'ton] *nm*: **salir a borbotones** to gush out.

bordado [bor'daθo] *nm* embroidery.

bordar [bor'dar] *vt* to embroider.

borde ['borθe] *nm* edge, border; (*de camino etc*) side; (*en la costura*) hem; **al ~ de** (*fig*) on the verge *o* brink of; **ser ~** (*Esp: fam*) to be a pain (in the neck); **~ar** *vt* to border.

bordillo [bor'diʎo] *nm* kerb (*Brit*), curb (*US*).

bordo ['borθo] *nm* (*NAUT*) side; **a ~** on board.

borinqueño, a [borin'kenjo, a] *a*, *nm/f* Puerto Rican.

borra ['borra] *nf* (*pelusa*) fluff; (*sedimento*) sediment.

borrachera [borra'tʃera] *nf* (*ebriedad*) drunkenness; (*orgía*) spree, binge.

borracho, a [bo'rratʃo, a] *a* drunk //

nm/f (*que bebe mucho*) drunkard, drunk; (*temporalmente*) drunk man/woman.

borrador [borra'δor] *nm* (*escritura*) first draft, rough sketch; (*cuaderno*) scribbling pad; (*goma*) rubber (*Brit*), eraser.

borrajear [borraxe'ar] *vt*, *vi* to scribble.

borrar [bo'rrar] *vt* to erase, rub out.

borrasca [bo'rraska] *nf* storm.

borrico, a [bo'rriko, a] *nm/f* donkey; she-donkey; (*fig*) stupid man/woman.

borrón [bo'rron] *nm* (*mancha*) stain.

borroso, a [bo'rroso, a] *a* vague, unclear; (*escritura*) illegible.

bosque ['boske] *nm* wood; (*grande*) forest.

bosquejar [boske'xar] *vt* to sketch.

bosquejo *nm* sketch.

bosta ['bosta] *nf* dung; (*abono*) manure.

bostezar [boste'θar] *vi* to yawn.

bostezo *nm* yawn.

bota ['bota] *nf* (*calzado*) boot; (*saco*) leather wine bottle.

botánico, a [bo'taniko, a] *a* botanical // *nm/f* botanist // *nf* botany.

botar [bo'tar] *vt* to throw, hurl; (*NAUT*) to launch; (*fam*) to throw out // *vi* to bounce.

bote ['bote] *nm* (*salto*) bounce; (*golpe*) thrust; (*vasija*) tin, can; (*embarcación*) boat; **de ~ en ~** packed, jammed full; **~ salvavidas** lifeboat; **~ de la basura** (*AM*) dustbin (*Brit*), trashcan (*US*).

botella [bo'teʎa] *nf* bottle.

botica [bo'tika] *nf* chemist's (shop) (*Brit*), pharmacy; **~rio, a** *nm/f* chemist (*Brit*), pharmacist.

botijo [bo'tixo] *nm* (earthenware) jug.

botín [bo'tin] *nm* (*calzado*) half boot; (*polaina*) spat; (*MIL*) booty.

botiquín [boti'kin] *nm* (*armario*) medicine cabinet; (*portátil*) first-aid kit.

botón [bo'ton] *nm* button; (*BOT*)

bud; *(de florete)* tip; ~ **de oro** buttercup.

botones [bo'tones] *nm inv* bellboy (*Brit*), bellhop (*US*).

bóveda [bo'βeða] *nf* (*ARQ*) vault.

boxeador [boksea'ðor] *nm* boxer.

boxeo [bok'seo] *nm* boxing.

boya ['boja] *nf* (*NAUT*) buoy; *(flotador)* float.

bozal [bo'θal] *nm* *(de caballo)* halter; *(de perro)* muzzle.

bracear [braθe'ar] *vi* *(agitar los brazos)* to wave one's arms.

bracero [bra'θero] *nm* labourer; *(en el campo)* farmhand.

bracete [bra'θete]: **de ~** *ad* arm in arm.

braga ['braɣa] *nf* *(cuerda)* sling, rope; *(de bebé)* nappy (*Brit*), diaper (*US*); **~s** *nfpl* *(de mujer)* panties, knickers (*Brit*).

bragueta [bra'ɣeta] *nf* fly, flies *pl*.

braille [breil] *nm* braille.

bramar [bra'mar] *vi* to bellow, roar; **bramido** *nm* bellow, roar.

brasa ['brasa] *nf* live o hot coal.

brasero [bra'sero] *nm* brazier.

Brasil [bra'sil] *nm*: (el) ~ Brazil; **brasileño, a** *a*, *nm/f* Brazilian.

bravata [bra'βata] *nf* boast.

braveza [bra'βeθa] *nf* *(valor)* bravery; *(ferocidad)* ferocity.

bravío, a [bra'βio, a] *a* wild; *(feroz)* fierce.

bravo, a [braβo, a] *a* *(valiente)* brave; *(bueno)* fine, splendid; *(feroz)* ferocious; *(salvaje)* wild; *(mar etc)* rough, stormy // *excl* bravo!; **bravura** *nf* bravery; ferocity; *(pey)* boast.

braza ['braθa] *nf* fathom; **nadar a la ~** to swim the breast-stroke.

brazada [bra'θaða] *nf* stroke.

brazado [bra'θaðo] *nm* armful.

brazalete [braθa'lete] *nm* *(pulsera)* bracelet; *(banda)* armband.

brazo ['braθo] *nm* arm; (*ZOOL*) foreleg; (*BOT*) limb, branch; **luchar a ~ partido** to fight hand-to-hand; **ir del ~** to walk arm in arm.

brea ['brea] *nf* pitch, tar.

brebaje [bre'βaxe] *nm* potion.

brecha ['bretʃa] *nf* *(hoyo, vacío)* gap, opening; (*MIL, fig*) breach.

brega ['breɣa] *nf* *(lucha)* struggle; *(trabajo)* hard work.

breve ['breβe] *a* short, brief // *nf* (*MUS*) breve; **~dad** *nf* brevity, shortness.

brezal [bre'θal] *nm* moor(land), heath; **brezo** *nm* heather.

bribón, ona [bri'βon, ona] *a* idle, lazy // *nm/f* *(vagabundo)* vagabond; *(pícaro)* rascal, rogue.

bricolaje [briko'laxe] *nm* do-it-yourself, DIY.

brida ['briða] *nf* bridle, rein; (*TEC*) clamp; **a toda ~** at top speed.

bridge [britʃ] *nm* bridge.

brigada [bri'ɣaða] *nf* *(unidad)* brigade; *(trabajadores)* squad, gang // *nm* ~ staff-sergeant, sergeant-major.

brillante [bri'ʎante] *a* brilliant // *nm* diamond.

brillar [bri'ʎar] *vi* *(tb fig)* to shine; *(joyas)* to sparkle.

brillo ['briʎo] *nm* shine; *(brillantez)* brilliance; *(fig)* splendour; **sacar ~ a** to polish.

brincar [brin'kar] *vi* to skip about, hop about, jump about; **está que brinca** he's hopping mad.

brinco ['brinko] *nm* jump, leap.

brindar [brin'dar] *vi*: **~ a o por** to drink (a toast) to // *vt* to offer, present.

brindis ['brindis] *nm* toast; (*TAUR*) (ceremony of) dedication.

brío ['brio] *nm* spirit, dash; **brioso, a** *a* spirited, dashing.

brisa ['brisa] *nf* breeze.

británico, a [bri'taniko, a] *a* British // *nm/f* Briton, British person.

brocal [bro'kal] *nm* rim.

brocha ['brotʃa] *nf* *(large)* paint-brush; **~ de afeitar** shaving brush.

broche ['brotʃe] *nm* brooch.

broma ['broma] *nf* joke; **en ~** in fun, as a joke; **bromear** *vi* to joke.

bromista [bro'mista] a fond of joking // nm/f joker, wag.

bronca ['bronka] nf row; **echar una ~ a uno** to tick sb off.

bronce ['bronθe] nm bronze; ~**ado, a** a bronze; (por el sol) tanned // nm (sun)tan; (TEC) bronzing.

broncearse [bronθe'arse] vr to get a suntan.

bronco, a ['bronko, a] a (manera) rude, surly; (voz) harsh.

bronquitis [bron'kitis] nf bronchitis.

brotar [bro'tar] vi (BOT) to sprout; (aguas) to gush (forth); (MED) to break out.

brote ['brote] nm (BOT) shoot; (MED, fig) outbreak.

bruces ['bruθes]: **de ~ ad: caer o dar de ~** to fall headlong, fall flat.

bruja ['bruxa] nf witch; **brujería** nf witchcraft.

brujo ['bruxo] nm wizard, magician.

brújula ['bruxula] nf compass.

bruma ['bruma] nf mist; **brumoso, a** a misty.

bruñido [bru'niðo] nm polish; **bruñir** vt to polish.

brusco, a ['brusko, a] a (súbito) sudden; (áspero) brusque.

Bruselas [bru'selas] n Brussels.

brutal [bru'tal] a brutal.

brutalidad [brutali'ðað] nf brutality.

bruto, a ['bruto, a] a (idiota) stupid; (bestial) brutish; (peso) gross; **en ~** raw, unworked.

Bs.As. abr (= Buenos Aires) B.A.

bucal [bu'kal] a oral; **por vía ~** orally.

bucear [buθe'ar] vi to dive // vt to explore; **buceo** nm diving; (fig) investigation.

bucle ['bukle] nm curl.

budismo [bu'ðismo] nm Buddhism.

buen [bwen] am ver **bueno**.

buenamente [bwena'mente] ad (fácilmente) easily; (voluntariamente) willingly.

buenaventura [bwenaßen'tura] nf (suerte) good luck; (adivinación) fortune.

bueno, a ['bweno, a] ♦ a (antes de nmsg: buen) 1 (excelente etc) es un libro ~ o es un buen libro it's a good book; hace ~, hace buen tiempo the weather is o it is fine; el ~ de Paco good old Paco; fue muy ~ conmigo he was very nice o kind to me

2 (apropiado): ser bueno/a para to be good for; creo que vamos por buen camino I think we're on the right track

3 (irónico): le di un buen rapapolvo I gave him a good o real ticking off; ¡buen conductor estás hecho! some o a fine driver you are!; ¡estaría ~ que...! a fine thing it would be if ...!

4 (atractivo, sabroso): está bueno este bizcocho this sponge is delicious; Carmen está muy buena Carmen is looking good

5 (saludos): ¡buen día!, ¡buenos días! good morning!; ¡buenas (tardes)! good afternoon!; (más tarde) good evening!; ¡buenas noches! good night!

6 (otras locuciones): estar de buenas to be in a good mood; por las buenas o por las malas by hook or by crook; de buenas a primeras all of a sudden

♦ excl: ¡~! all right!; ~, ¿y qué? well, so what?

Buenos Aires nm Buenos Aires.

buey [bwei] nm ox.

búfalo ['bufalo] nm buffalo.

bufanda [bu'fanda] nf scarf.

bufar [bu'far] vi to snort.

bufete [bu'fete] nm (despacho de abogado) lawyer's office.

buffer ['bufer] nm (INFORM) buffer.

bufón [bu'fon, ona] nm clown.

buhardilla [buar'ðiʎa] nf (desván) attic.

búho ['buo] nm owl; (fig) hermit, recluse.

buhonero [buo'nero] *nm* pedlar.

buitre ['bwitre] *nm* vulture.

bujía [bu'xia] *nf* (*vela*) candle; (*ELEC*) candle (power); (*AUTO*) spark plug.

bula ['bula] *nf* (*papal*) bull.

bulbo ['bulβo] *nm* bulb.

bulevar [bule'βar] *nm* boulevard.

Bulgaria [bul'xarja] *nf* Bulgaria; **búlgaro, a** *a*, *nm/f* Bulgarian.

bulto ['bulto] *nm* (*paquete*) package; (*fardo*) bundle; (*tamaño*) size, bulkiness; (*MED*) swelling, lump; (*silueta*) vague shape; (*estatua*) bust, statue.

bulla ['buλa] *nf* (*ruido*) uproar; (*de gente*) crowd.

bullicio [bu'λiθjo] *nm* (*ruido*) uproar; (*movimiento*) bustle.

bullir [bu'λir] *vi* (*hervir*) to boil; (*burbujear*) to bubble; (*mover*) to move, stir.

buñuelo [bu'nwelo] *nm* ≈ doughnut (*Brit*), donut (*US*); (*fruta de sartén*) fritter.

BUP [bup] *nm abr* (*Esp = Bachillerato Unificado Polivalente*) secondary education and leaving certificate for 14–17 age group.

buque ['buke] *nm* ship, vessel.

burbuja [bur'βuxa] *nf* bubble; **burbujear** *vi* to bubble.

burdel [bur'ðel] *nm* brothel.

burdo, a ['burðo, a] *a* coarse, rough.

burgués, esa [bur'ves, esa] *a* middle-class, bourgeois; **burguesía** *nf* middle class, bourgeoisie.

burla ['burla] *nf* (*mofa*) gibe; (*broma*) joke; (*engaño*) trick.

burladero [burla'ðero] *nm* (bullfighter's) refuge.

burlador, a [burla'ðor, a] *a* mocking // *nm/f* (*bromista*) joker // *nm* (*libertino*) seducer.

burlar [bur'lar] *vt* (*engañar*) to deceive; (*seducir*) to seduce // *vi*, **~se** *vr* to joke; **~se de** to make fun of.

burlesco, a [bur'lesko, a] *a* burlesque.

burlón, ona [bur'lon, ona] *a* mocking.

burocracia [buro'kraθja] *nf* civil service; (*pey*) bureaucracy.

burócrata [bu'rokrata] *nm/f* civil servant; (*pey*) bureaucrat.

buromática [buro'matika] *nf* office automation.

burro, a ['burro] *nm/f* donkey/she-donkey; (*fig*) ass, idiot.

bursátil [bur'satil] *a* stock-exchange *cpd*.

bus [bus] *nm* bus.

busca ['buska] *nf* search, hunt // *nm* (*TEL*) bleeper; **en ~ de** in search of.

buscapleitos [buska'pleitos] *nm/f inv* troublemaker.

buscar [bus'kar] *vt* to look for, search for, seek // *vi* to look, search, seek; **se busca secretaria** secretary wanted.

buscón, ona [bus'kon, ona] *a* thieving // *nm* petty thief // *nf* whore.

busilis [bu'silis] *nm* (*fam*) snag.

busque *etc vb ver* **buscar**.

búsqueda ['buskeða] *nf* = **busca**.

busto ['busto] *nm* (*ANAT, ARTE*) bust.

butaca [bu'taka] *nf* armchair; (*de cine, teatro*) stall, seat.

butano [bu'tano] *nm* butane (gas).

buzo ['buθo] *nm* diver.

buzón [bu'θon] *nm* (*en puerta*) letter box; (*en la calle*) pillar box.

C

C. *abr* (= *centígrado*) C; (= *compañía*) Co.

c. *abr* (= *capítulo*) ch.

C/ *abr* (= *calle*) St.

c.a. *abr* (= *corriente alterna*) AC.

cabal [ka'βal] *a* (*exacto*) exact; (*correcto*) right, proper; (*acabado*) finished, complete; **~es** *nmpl*: **estar en sus ~es** to be in one's right mind.

cabalgadura [kaβalva'ðura] *nf* mount, horse.

cabalgar [kaßal'ɣar] *vt, vi* to ride.
cabalgata [kaßal'ɣata] *nf* procession.
caballa [ka'ßaʎa] *nf* mackerel.
caballeresco, a [kaßaʎe'resko, a] *a* noble, chivalrous.
caballería [kaßaʎe'ria] *nf* mount; (MIL) cavalry.
caballeriza [kaßaʎe'riθa] *nf* stable; **caballerizo** *nm* groom, stableman.
caballero [kaßa'ʎero] *nm* (hombre galante) gentleman; (de la orden de caballería) knight; (trato directo) sir.
caballerosidad [kaßaʎerosi'ðað] *nf* chivalry.
caballete [kaßa'ʎete] *nm* (ARTE) easel; (TEC) trestle.
caballito [kaßa'ʎito] *nm* (caballo pequeño) small horse, pony; ~s *nmpl* (en verbena) roundabout sg, merry-go-round.
caballo [ka'ßaʎo] *nm* horse; (AJEDREZ) knight; (NAIPES) queen; ~ **de vapor** o **de fuerza** horse-power.
cabaña [ka'ßaɲa] *nf* (casita) hut, cabin.
cabaré, cabaret [kaßa're] (pl **cabarés, cabarets**) *nm* cabaret.
cabecear [kaßeθe'ar] *vt, vi* to nod.
cabecera [kaße'θera] *nf* head; (de distrito) chief town; (IMPRENTA) headline.
cabecilla [kaße'θiʎa] *nm/f* ringleader.
cabellera [kaße'ʎera] *nf* (head of) hair; (de cometa) tail.
cabello [ka'ßeʎo] *nm* (tb: ~s) hair sg.
caber [ka'ßer] *vi* (entrar) to fit, go; **caben 3 más** there's room for 3 more.
cabestrillo [kaßes'triʎo] *nm* sling.
cabestro [ka'ßestro] *nm* halter.
cabeza [ka'ßeθa] *nf* head; (POL) chief, leader; ~**da** *nf* (golpe) butt; **dar** ~**das** to nod off.
cabida [ka'ßiða] *nf* space.
cabildo [ka'ßildo] *nm* (de iglesia) chapter; (POL) town council.
cabina [ka'ßina] *nf* cabin; (de

camión) cab; ~ **telefónica** telephone box (Brit) o booth.
cabizbajo, a [kaßiθ'ßaxo, a] *a* crestfallen, dejected.
cable ['kaßle] *nm* cable.
cabo ['kaßo] *nm* (de objeto) end, extremity; (MIL) corporal; (NAUT) rope, cable; (GEO) cape; **al** ~ **de 3 días** after 3 days.
cabra ['kaßra] *nf* goat.
cabré etc *vb ver* **caber.**
cabrío, a [ka'ßrio, a] *a* goatish; **macho** ~ (he-) goat, billy goat.
cabriola [ka'ßrjola] *nf* caper.
cabritilla [kaßri'tiʎa] *nf* kid, kidskin.
cabrito [ka'ßrito] *nm* kid.
cabrón [ka'ßron] *nm* cuckold; (fam!) bastard (!).
cacahuete [kaka'wete] *nm* (Esp) peanut.
cacao [ka'kao] *nm* cocoa; (BOT) cacao.
cacarear [kakare'ar] *vi* (persona) to boast; (gallina) to crow.
cacería [kaθe'ria] *nf* hunt.
cacerola [kaθe'rola] *nf* pan, saucepan.
cacique [ka'θike] *nm* chief, local ruler; (POL) local party boss; **caciquismo** *nm* system of dominance by the local boss.
caco ['kako] *nm* pickpocket.
cacto ['kakto] *nm*, **cactus** ['kaktus] *nm inv* cactus.
cacharro [ka'tʃarro] *nm* earthenware pot; ~s *nmpl* pots and pans.
cachear [katʃe'ar] *vt* to search, frisk.
cachemir [katʃe'mir] *nm* cashmere.
cacheo [ka'tʃeo] *nm* searching, frisking.
cachete [ka'tʃete] *nm* (ANAT) cheek; (bofetada) slap (in the face).
cachimba [ka'tʃimba] *nf* pipe.
cachiporra [katʃi'porra] *nf* truncheon.
cachivache [katʃi'ßatʃe] *nm* (trasto) piece of junk; ~s *nmpl* junk sg.
cacho ['katʃo, a] *nm* (small) bit; (AM: cuerno) horn.
cachondeo [katʃon'deo] *nm* (fam)

farce, joke.

cachondo, a [ka'tʃondo, a] *a* (*ZOOL*) on heat; (*fam*) randy, sexy; (*gracioso*) funny.

cachorro, a [ka'tʃorro, a] *nm/f* (*perro*) pup, puppy; (*león*) cub.

cada ['kaða] *a inv* each; (*antes de número*) every; ~ *día* each day, every day; ~ **dos días** every other day; ~ **uno/a** each one, every one; ~ **vez más** more and more; **uno de** ~ **diez** one out of every ten.

cadalso [ka'ðalso] *nm* scaffold.

cadáver [ka'ðaβer] *nm* (dead) body, corpse.

cadena [ka'ðena] *nf* chain; (*TV*) channel; **trabajo en** ~ assembly line work.

cadencia [ka'ðenθja] *nf* cadence, rhythm.

cadera [ka'ðera] *nf* hip.

cadete [ka'ðete] *nm* cadet.

caducar [kaðu'kar] *vi* to expire; **caduco, a** *a* expired; (*persona*) very old.

C.A.E. *abr* (= *cóbrese al entregar*) COD.

caer [ka'er] *vi*, **caerse** *vr* to fall (down); **me cae bien/mal** I get on well with him/I can't stand him; ~ **en la cuenta** to catch on; **su cumpleaños cae en viernes** his birthday falls on a Friday.

café [ka'fe] (*pl* ~s) *nm* (*bebida, planta*) coffee; (*lugar*) café // *a* (*color*) brown; ~ **con leche** white coffee; ~ **solo** black coffee; **cafetal** *nm* coffee plantation.

cafetería [kafete'ria] *nf* (*gen*) café.

cafetero, a [kafe'tero, a] *a* coffee *cpd*; **ser muy** ~ to be a coffee addict // *nf* coffee pot.

cagar [ka'ɣar] *vt* (*fam!*) to shit (!); to bungle, mess up // *vi* to fall; (*declive*) slope; (*disminución*) fall, drop.

caiga *etc vb ver* **caer**.

caimán [kai'man] *nm* alligator.

caja ['kaxa] *nf* box; (*para reloj*) case;

(*de ascensor*) shaft; (*COM*) cashbox; (*donde se hacen los pagos*) cashdesk; (: *en supermercado*) checkout, till; ~ **de ahorros** savings bank; ~ **de cambios** gearbox; ~ **fuerte**, ~ **de caudales** safe, strongbox.

cajero, a [ka'xero, a] *nm/f* cashier.

cajetilla [kaxe'tiʎa] *nf* (*de cigarrillos*) packet.

cajón [ka'xon] *nm* big box; (*de mueble*) drawer.

cal [kal] *nf* lime.

cala [ka'la] *nf* (*GEO*) cove, inlet; (*de barco*) hold.

calabacín [kalaβa'θin] *nm* (*BOT*) baby marrow; (: *más pequeño*) courgette (*Brit*), zucchini (*US*).

calabacita [kalaβa'θita] *nf* (*AM*) courgette (*Brit*), zucchini (*US*).

calabaza [kala'βaθa] *nf* (*BOT*) pumpkin.

calabozo [kala'βoθo] *nm* (*cárcel*) prison; (*celda*) cell.

calado, a [ka'laðo, a] *a* (*prenda*) lace *cpd* // *nm* (*NAUT*) draught // *nf* (*de cigarrillo*) puff.

calamar [kala'mar] *nm* squid.

calambre [ka'lambre] *nm* (*tb*: ~s) cramp.

calamidad [kalami'ðað] *nf* calamity, disaster.

calamina [kala'mina] *nf* calamine.

calaña [ka'lana] *nf* model, pattern.

calar [ka'lar] *vt* to soak, drench; (*penetrar*) to pierce, penetrate; (*comprender*) to see through; (*vela, red*) to lower; ~**se** *vr* (*AUTO*) to stall; ~**se las gafas** to stick one's glasses on.

calavera [kala'βera] *nf* skull.

calcañal [kalka'nal], **calcañar** [kalka'nar], **calcaño** [kal'kaɲo] *nm* heel.

calcar [kal'kar] *vt* (*reproducir*) to trace; (*imitar*) to copy.

calceta [kal'θeta] *nf* (knee-length) stocking; **hacer** ~ to knit.

calcetín [kalθe'tin] *nm* sock.

calcinar [kalθi'nar] *vt* to burn, blacken.

calcio ['kalθjo] nm calcium.

calco ['kalko] nm tracing.

calcomanía [kalkoma'nia] nf transfer.

calculadora [kalkula'ðora] nf calculator.

calcular [kalku'lar] vt (MAT) to calculate, compute; **~ que ...** to reckon that ...; **cálculo** nm calculation.

caldear [kalde'ar] vt to warm (up), heat (up).

caldera [kal'dera] nf boiler.

calderilla [kalde'riʎa] nf (moneda) small change.

caldero [kal'dero] nm small boiler.

caldo ['kaldo] nm stock; (consomé) consommé.

calefacción [kalefak'θjon] nf heating; **~ central** central heating.

calendario [kalen'darjo] nm calendar.

calentador [kalenta'ðor] nm heater.

calentar [kalen'tar] vt to heat (up); **~se** vr to heat up, warm up; (fig: discusión etc) to get heated.

calentura [kalen'tura] nf (MED) fever, (high) temperature.

calibrar [kali'βrar] vt to gauge, measure; **calibre** nm (de cañón) calibre, bore; (diámetro) diameter; (fig) calibre.

calidad [kali'ðað] nf quality; **de ~** quality cpd; **en ~ de** in the capacity of, as.

cálido, a ['kaliðo, a] a hot; (fig) warm.

caliente etc vb ver **calentar** // [ka'ljente] a hot; (fig) fiery; (disputa) heated; (fam: cachondo) randy.

calificación [kalifika'θjon] nf qualification; (de alumno) grade, mark.

calificar [kalifi'kar] vt to qualify; (alumno) to grade, mark; **~ de** to describe as.

calizo, a [ka'liθo, a] a lime cpd // nf limestone.

calma ['kalma] nf calm; (pachorra) slowness.

calmante [kal'mante] nm sedative, tranquillizer.

calmar [kal'mar] vt to calm, calm down // vi (tempestad) to abate; (mente etc) to become calm.

calmoso, a [kal'moso, a] a calm, quiet.

calor [ka'lor] nm heat; (~ agradable) warmth.

caloría [kalo'ria] nf calorie.

calorífero, a [kalo'rifero, a] a heat-producing, heat-giving // nm heating system.

calumnia [ka'lumnja] nf calumny, slander; **calumnioso, a** a slanderous.

caluroso, a [kalu'roso, a] a hot; (sin exceso) warm; (fig) enthusiastic.

calvario [kal'βarjo] nm stations of the cross.

calvicie [kal'βiθje] nf baldness.

calvo, a ['kalβo, a] a bald; (terreno) bare, barren; (tejido) threadbare // nf bald patch; (en bosque) clearing.

calza ['kalθa] nf wedge, chock.

calzado, a [kal'θaðo, a] a shod // nm footwear // nf roadway, highway.

calzador [kalθa'ðor] nm shoehorn.

calzar [kal'θar] vt (zapatos etc) to wear; (un mueble) to put a wedge under; **~se** vr: **~se los zapatos** to put on one's shoes; **¿qué (número) calza?** what size do you take?

calzón [kal'θon] nm (tb: **calzones** nmpl) shorts pl; (AM: de hombre) pants, (: de mujer) panties.

calzoncillos [kalθon'θiʎos] nmpl underpants.

callado, a [ka'ʎaðo, a] a quiet.

callar [ka'ʎar] vt (asunto delicado) to keep quiet about, say nothing about; (persona, oposición) to silence // vi, **~se** vr to keep quiet, to be silent; **¡cállate!** be quiet!, shut up!

calle ['kaʎe] nf street; (DEPORTE) lane; **~ arriba/abajo** up/down the street; **~ de un solo sentido** one-way street.

calleja [ka'ʎexa] nf alley, narrow street; **callejear** vi to wander (about) the streets; **callejero, a** a street *cpd* // *nm* street map; **callejón** *nm* alley, passage; **callejón sin salida** cul-de-sac; **callejuela** *nf* side-street, alley.

callista [kaˈʎista] *nm/f* chiropodist.

callo [ˈkaʎo] *nm* callus; (*en el pie*) corn; ~**s** *nmpl* (*CULIN*) tripe *sg*; ~**so, a** a horny, rough.

cama [ˈkama] *nf* bed; (*GEO*) stratum; ~ **individual/de matrimonio** single/double bed.

camada [kaˈmaða] *nf* litter; (*de personas*) gang, band.

camafeo [kamaˈfeo] *nm* cameo.

cámara [ˈkamara] *nf* chamber; (*habitación*) room; (*sala*) hall; (*CINE*) cine camera; (*fotográfica*) camera; ~ **de aire** inner tube.

camarada [kamaˈraða] *nm* comrade, companion.

camarera [kamaˈrera] *nf* (*en restaurante*) waitress; (*en casa, hotel*) maid.

camarero [kamaˈrero] *nm* waiter.

camarilla [kamaˈriʎa] *nf* (*clan*) clique; (*POL*) lobby.

camarín [kamaˈrin] *nm* dressing room.

camarón [kamaˈron] *nm* shrimp.

camarote [kamaˈrote] *nm* cabin.

cambiable [kamˈbjaβle] a (*variable*) changeable, variable; (*intercambiable*) interchangeable.

cambiante [kamˈbjante] a variable.

cambiar [kamˈbjar] *vt* to change; (*dinero*) to change // *vi* to change; ~**se** *vr* (*mudarse*) to move; (*de ropa*) to change; ~ **de idea** to change one's mind; ~ **de ropa** to change (one's clothes).

cambiazo [kamˈbjaθo] *nm*: **dar el** ~ **a** uno to swindle sb.

cambio [ˈkambjo] *nm* change; (*trueque*) exchange; (*COM*) rate of exchange; (*oficina*) bureau de change; (*dinero menudo*) small change; **en** ~ on the other hand; (*en lugar de*) instead; ~ **de divisas** foreign exchange; ~ **de velocidades**

gear lever; ~ **de vía** points *pl*.

cambista [kamˈbista] *nm* (*COM*) exchange broker.

camelar [kameˈlar] *vt* (*con mujer*) to flirt with; (*persuadir*) to cajole.

camello [kaˈmeʎo] *nm* camel; (*fam: traficante*) pusher.

camilla [kaˈmiʎa] *nf* (*MED*) stretcher.

caminante [kamiˈnante] *nm/f* traveller.

caminar [kamiˈnar] *vi* (*marchar*) to walk, go; (*viajar*) to travel, journey // *vt* (*recorrer*) to cover, travel.

caminata [kamiˈnata] *nf* long walk; (*por el campo*) hike.

camino [kaˈmino] *nm* way, road; (*sendero*) track; **a medio** ~ halfway (there); **en el** ~ on the way, en route; ~ **de** on the way to; ~ **particular** private road.

camión [kaˈmjon] *nm* lorry (*Brit*), truck (*US*); **camionero, a** *nm/f* lorry o truck driver.

camioneta [kamjoˈneta] *nf* van, light truck.

camisa [kaˈmisa] *nf* shirt; (*BOT*) skin; ~ **de dormir** nightdress; ~ **de fuerza** straitjacket; **camisería** *nf* outfitter's (shop).

camiseta [kamiˈseta] *nf* (*prenda*) tee-shirt; (: *ropa interior*) vest; (*de deportista*) top.

camisón [kamiˈson] *nm* nightdress, nightgown.

camorra [kaˈmorra] *nf*: **armar** o **buscar** ~ to look for trouble, kick up a fuss.

campamento [kampaˈmento] *nm* camp.

campana [kamˈpana] *nf* bell; ~**da** *nf* peal; ~**rio** *nm* belfry.

campanilla [kampaˈniʎa] *nf* small bell.

campaña [kamˈpaɲa] *nf* (*MIL, POL*) campaign.

campechano, a [kampeˈtʃano, a] a (*franco*) open.

campeón, ona [kampeˈon, ona] *nm/f* champion; **campeonato** *nm* championship.

campesino, a [kampe'sino, a] *a* country *cpd*, rural; *(gente)* peasant *cpd* // *nm/f* countryman/woman; *(agricultor)* farmer.

campestre [kam'pestre] *a* country *cpd*, rural.

camping ['kampin] *nm* camping; *(lugar)* campsite; **ir de o hacer ~** to go camping.

campiña [kam'piɲa] *nf* countryside.

campo ['kampo] *nm* *(fuera de la ciudad)* country, countryside; *(AGR, ELEC)* field; *(de fútbol)* pitch; *(de golf)* course; *(MIL)* camp.

camposanto [kampo'santo] *nm* cemetery.

camuflaje [kamu'flaxe] *nm* camouflage.

cana ['kana] *nf ver* **cano**.

Canadá [kana'ða] *nm* Canada; **canadiense** *a, nm/f* Canadian // *nf* fur-lined jacket.

canal [ka'nal] *nm* canal; *(GEO)* channel, strait; *(de televisión)* channel; *(de tejado)* gutter; **~ de Panamá** Panama Canal; **~izar** *vt* to channel.

canalón [kana'lon] *nm* *(conducto vertical)* drainpipe; *(del tejado)* gutter.

canalla [ka'naʎa] *nf* rabble, mob // *nm* swine.

canapé [kana'pe] *(pl* **~s**) *nm* sofa, settee; *(CULIN)* canapé.

Canarias [ka'narjas] *nfpl*: **(las Islas) ~** the Canary Islands, the Canaries.

canario, a [ka'narjo, a] *a, nm/f* *(native)* of the Canary Isles // *nm* *(ZOOL)* canary.

canasta [ka'nasta] *nf* *(round)* basket; **canastilla** [-'tiʎa] *nf* small basket; *(de niño)* layette.

canasto [ka'nasto] *nm* large basket.

cancela [kan'θela] *nf* gate.

cancelación [kanθela'θjon] *nf* cancellation.

cancelar [kanθe'lar] *vt* to cancel; *(una deuda)* to write off.

cáncer ['kanθer] *nm* *(MED)* cancer;

C~ *(ASTROLOGÍA)* Cancer.

canciller [kanθi'ʎer] *nm* chancellor.

canción [kan'θjon] *nf* song; **~ de cuna** lullaby; **cancionero** *nm* song book.

cancha ['kantʃa] *nf* *(de baloncesto, tenis etc)* court; *(AM: de fútbol)* pitch.

candado [kan'daðo] *nm* padlock.

candela [kan'dela] *nf* candle.

candelero [kande'lero] *nm* *(para vela)* candlestick; *(de aceite)* oil lamp.

candente [kan'dente] *a* red-hot; *(fig: tema)* burning.

candidato, a [kandi'ðato, a] *nm/f* candidate.

candidez [kandi'ðeθ] *nf* *(sencillez)* simplicity; *(simpleza)* naiveté; **cándido, a** *a* simple; naive.

candil [kan'dil] *nm* oil lamp; **~ejas** [-'lexas] *nfpl* *(TEATRO)* footlights.

candor [kan'dor] *nm* *(sinceridad)* frankness; *(inocencia)* innocence.

canela [ka'nela] *nf* cinnamon.

cangrejo [kan'grexo] *nm* crab.

canguro [kan'guro] *nm* kangaroo; **hacer de ~** to babysit.

caníbal [ka'nißal] *a, nm/f* cannibal.

canica [ka'nika] *nf* marble.

canijo, a [ka'nixo, a] *a* frail, sickly.

canino, a [ka'nino, a] *a* canine // *nm* canine (tooth).

canjear [kanxe'ar] *vt* to exchange.

cano, a ['kano, a] *a* grey-haired, white-haired // *nf* white *o* grey hair; **tener canas** to be going grey.

canoa [ka'noa] *nf* canoe.

canon ['kanon] *nm* canon; *(pensión)* rent; *(COM)* tax.

canónigo [ka'noniχo] *nm* canon.

canonizar [kanoni'θar] *vt* to canonize.

cansado, a [kan'saðo, a] *a* tired, weary; *(tedioso)* tedious, boring.

cansancio [kan'sanθjo] *nm* tiredness, fatigue.

cansar [kan'sar] *vt* *(fatigar)* to tire, tire out; *(aburrir)* to bore; *(fastidiar)* to bother; **~se** *vr* to tire, get tired; (*aburrirse*) to get bored.

cantábrico, a [kan'taβriko, a] *a* Cantabrian; **mar C~** ≈ Bay of Biscay.

cantante [kan'tante] *a* singing // *nm/f* singer.

cantar [kan'tar] *vt* to sing // *vi* to sing; (*insecto*) to chirp; (*rechinar*) to squeak // *nm* (*acción*) singing; (*canción*) song; (*poema*) poem.

cántara [kantara] *nf* large pitcher.

cántaro ['kantaro] *nm* pitcher, jug; **llover a ~s** to rain cats and dogs.

cante ['kante] *nm*: ~ **jondo** flamenco singing.

cantera [kan'tera] *nf* quarry.

cantidad [kanti'ðað] *nf* quantity, amount.

cantilena [kanti'lena] *nf* = **cantinela**.

cantimplora [kantim'plora] *nf* (*frasco*) water bottle, canteen.

cantina [kan'tina] *nf* canteen; (*de estación*) buffet.

cantinela [kanti'nela] *nf* ballad, song.

canto ['kanto] *nm* singing; (*canción*) song; (*borde*) edge, rim; (*de un cuchillo*) back; ~ **rodado** boulder.

cantor, a [kan'tor, a] *nm/f* singer.

canturrear [kanturre'ar] *vi* to sing softly.

canuto [ka'nuto] *nm* (*tubo*) small tube; (*fam: droga*) joint.

caña ['kaɲa] *nf* (*BOT: tallo*) stem, stalk; (*carrizo*) reed; (*vaso*) tumbler; (*de cerveza*) glass of beer; (*ANAT*) shinbone; ~ **de azúcar** sugar cane; ~ **de pescar** fishing rod.

cañada [ka'ɲaða] *nf* (*entre dos montañas*) gully, ravine; (*camino*) cattle track.

cáñamo ['kaɲamo] *nm* hemp.

caño ['kaɲo] *nm* (*tubo*) tube, pipe; (*de albañal*) sewer; (*MUS*) pipe; (*de fuente*) jet.

cañón [ka'ɲon] *nm* (*MIL*) cannon; (*de fusil*) barrel; (*GEO*) canyon, gorge.

cañonera [kaɲo'nera] *nf* (*tb: lancha ~*) gunboat.

caoba [ka'oβa] *nf* mahogany.

caos ['kaos] *nm* chaos.

cap. *abr* (= *capítulo*) ch.

capa ['kapa] *nf* cloak, cape; (*GEO*) layer, stratum; **so ~ de** under the pretext of.

capacidad [kapaθi'ðað] *nf* (*medida*) capacity; (*aptitud*) capacity, ability.

capacitación [kapaθita'θjon] *nf* training.

capar [ka'par] *vt* to castrate, geld.

caparazón [kapara'θon] *nm* shell.

capataz [kapa'taθ] *nm* foreman.

capaz [ka'paθ] *a* able, capable; (*amplio*) capacious, roomy.

capcioso, a [kap'θjoso, a] *a* wily, deceitful.

capellán [kape'ʎan] *nm* chaplain; (*sacerdote*) priest.

caperuza [kape'ruθa] *nf* hood.

capilla [ka'piʎa] *nf* chapel.

capital [kapi'tal] *a* capital // *nm* (*COM*) capital // *nf* (*ciudad*) capital; ~ **social** share capital.

capitalismo [kapita'lismo] *nm* capitalism; **capitalista** *a, nm/f* capitalist.

capitalizar [kapitali'θar] *vt* to capitalize.

capitán [kapi'tan] *nm* captain.

capitanear [kapitane'ar] *vt* to captain.

capitolio [kapi'toljo] *nm* capitol.

capitulación [kapitula'θjon] *nf* (*rendición*) capitulation, surrender; (*acuerdo*) agreement, pact; **capitulaciones (matrimoniales)** *nfpl* marriage contract *sg*.

capitular [kapitu'lar] *vi* to come to terms, make an agreement.

capítulo [ka'pitulo] *nm* chapter.

capó [ka'po] *nm* (*AUTO*) bonnet.

capón [ka'pon] *nm* (*gallo*) capon.

caporal [kapo'ral] *nm* chief, leader.

capota [ka'pota] *nf* (*de mujer*) bonnet; (*AUTO*) hood (*Brit*), top (*US*).

capote [ka'pote] *nm* (*abrigo: de militar*) greatcoat; (: *de torero*) cloak.

Capricornio [kapri'kornjo] *nm* Capricorn.

capricho [ka'pritʃo] *nm* whim, caprice; ~**so, a** *a* capricious.

cápsula ['kapsula] *nf* capsule.

captar [kap'tar] *vt* (*comprender*) to understand; (*RADIO*) to pick up; (*atención, apoyo*) to attract.

captura [kap'tura] *nf* capture; (*JUR*) arrest; **capturar** *vt* to capture; to arrest.

capucha [ka'putʃa] *nf* hood, cowl.

capullo [ka'puʎo] *nm* (*BOT*) bud; (*ZOOL*) cocoon; (*fam*) idiot.

caqui ['kaki] *nm* khaki.

cara ['kara] *nf* (*ANAT, de moneda*) face; (*aspecto*) appearance; (*de disco*) side; (*fig*) boldness; ~ **a** *ad* facing; **de** ~ opposite, facing; **dar la** ~ to face the consequences; ¿~ **o** **cruz?** heads or tails?; ¡**qué** ~ **más dura!** what a nerve!

carabina [kara'βina] *nf* carbine, rifle; (*persona*) chaperone.

Caracas [ka'rakas] *n* Caracas.

caracol [kara'kol] *nm* (*ZOOL*) snail; (*concha*) (sea) shell.

caracolear [karakole'ar] *vi* (*caballo*) to prance about.

carácter [ka'rakter] (*pl* **caracteres**) *nm* character; **tener buen/mal** ~ to be good natured/bad tempered.

característico, a [karakte'ristiko, a] *a* characteristic // *nf* characteristic.

caracterizar [karakteri'θar] *vt* (*distinguir*) to characterize, typify; (*honrar*) to confer a) distinction on.

caradura [kara'ðura] *nm/f*: **es un** ~ he's got a nerve.

carajo [ka'raxo] *nm* (*fam!*): ¡~! shit! (!).

caramba [ka'ramba] *excl* good gracious!

carámbano [ka'rambano] *nm* icicle.

caramelo [kara'melo] *nm* (*dulce*) sweet; (*azúcar fundida*) caramel.

carapacho [kara'patʃo] *nm* shell, carapace.

caraqueño, a [kara'keɲo, a] *a, nm/f*

of o from Caracas.

carátula [ka'ratula] *nf* (*careta, máscara*) mask; (*TEATRO*): **la** ~ the stage.

caravana [kara'βana] *nf* caravan; (*fig*) group; (*AUTO*) tailback.

carbón [kar'βon] *nm* coal; **papel** ~ carbon paper; **carboncillo** *nm* (*ARTE*) charcoal; **carbonero, a** *nm/f* coal merchant; **carbonilla** [-'niʎa] *nf* coal dust.

carbonizar [karβoni'θar] *vt* to carbonize; (*quemar*) to char.

carbono [kar'βono] *nm* carbon.

carburador [karβura'ðor] *nm* carburettor.

carcajada [karka'xaða] *nf* (loud) laugh, guffaw.

cárcel ['karθel] *nf* prison, jail; (*TEC*) clamp; **carcelero, a** *a* prison *cpd* // *nm/f* warder.

carcomer [karko'mer] *vt* to bore into, eat into; (*fig*) to undermine; ~**se** *vr* to become worm-eaten; (*fig*) to decay; **carcomido, a** *a* worm-eaten; (*fig*) rotten.

cardenal [karðe'nal] *nm* (*REL*) cardinal; (*MED*) bruise.

cárdeno, a ['karðeno, a] *a* purple; (*lívido*) livid.

cardíaco, a [kar'ðiako, a] *a* cardiac, heart *cpd*.

cardinal [karði'nal] *a* cardinal.

cardo ['karðo] *nm* thistle.

carear [kare'ar] *vt* to bring face to face; (*comparar*) to compare; ~**se** *vr* to come face to face, meet.

carecer [kare'θer] *vi*: ~ **de** to lack, be in need of.

carencia [ka'renθja] *nf* lack; (*escasez*) shortage; (*MED*) deficiency.

carente [ka'rente] *a*: ~ **de** lacking in, devoid of.

carestía [kares'tia] *nf* (*escasez*) scarcity, shortage; (*COM*) high cost.

careta [ka'reta] *nf* mask.

carga ['karva] *nf* (*peso, ELEC*) load; (*de barco*) cargo, freight; (*MIL*) charge; (*obligación, responsabilidad*) duty, obligation.

cargado, a [kar'γaðo, a] *a* loaded; (*ELEC*) live; (*café, té*) strong; (*cielo*) overcast.

cargamento [karγa'mento] *nm* (*acción*) loading; (*mercancías*) load, cargo.

cargar [kar'γar] *vt* (*barco, arma*) to load; (*ELEC*) to charge; (*COM: en cuenta*) to charge; (*INFORM*) to load // *vi* (*MIL: enemigo*) to attack; (*AUTO*) to load (up); (*inclinarse*) to lean; ~ **con** to pick up, carry away; (*peso, fig*) to shoulder, bear; ~**se** *vr* (*fam: estropear*) to break; (: *matar*) to bump off.

cargo ['karγo] *nm* (*puesto*) post, office; (*responsabilidad*) duty, obligation; (*fig*) weight, burden; (*JUR*) charge; **hacerse** ~ **de** to take charge of o responsibility for.

carguero [kar'γero] *nm* freighter, cargo boat; (*avión*) freight plane.

Caribe [ka'riβe] *nm*: **el** ~ the Caribbean; **del** ~ Caribbean.

caribeño, a [kari'βeɲo, a] *a* Caribbean.

caricatura [karika'tura] *nf* caricature.

caricia [ka'riθja] *nf* caress.

caridad [kari'ðað] *nf* charity.

caries ['karjes] *nf inv* (*MED*) tooth decay.

cariño [ka'riɲo] *nm* affection, love; (*caricia*) caress; (*en carta*) love...; ~**so, a** *a* affectionate.

caritativo, a [karita'tiβo, a] *a* charitable.

cariz [ka'riθ] *nm*: **tener** o **tomar buen/mal** ~ to look good/bad.

carmesí [karme'si] *a, nm* crimson.

carmín [kar'min] *nm* lipstick.

carnal [kar'nal] *a* carnal; **primo** ~ first cousin.

carnaval [karna'βal] *nm* carnival.

carne ['karne] *nf* flesh; (*CULIN*) meat; ~ **de cerdo/cordero/ternera/vaca** pork/lamb/veal/beef.

carné [kar'ne] *nm*: ~ **de conducir** driving licence (*Brit*), driver's

license (*US*); ~ **de identidad** identity card.

carnero [kar'nero] *nm* sheep, ram; (*carne*) mutton.

carnet [kar'ne(t)] *nm* = **carné.**

carnicería [karniθe'ria] *nf* butcher's (shop); (*fig: matanza*) carnage, slaughter.

carnicero, a [karni'θero, a] *a* carnivorous // *nm/f* (*tb fig*) butcher; (*carnívoro*) carnivore.

carnívoro, a [kar'niβoro, a] *a* carnivorous.

carnoso, a [kar'noso, a] *a* beefy, fat.

caro, a ['karo, a] *a* (*COM*) dear, expensive // *ad* dear, dearly.

carpa ['karpa] *nf* (*pez*) carp; (*de circo*) big top; (*AM: de camping*) tent.

carpeta [kar'peta] *nf* folder, file.

carpintería [karpinte'ria] *nf* carpentry, joinery; **carpintero** *nm* carpenter.

carraspera [karras'pera] *nf* hoarseness.

carrera [ka'rrera] *nf* (*acción*) run(ning); (*espacio recorrido*) run; (*certamen*) race; (*trayecto*) course; (*profesión*) career; (*ESCOL*) course.

carreta [ka'rreta] *nf* wagon, cart.

carrete [ka'rrete] *nm* reel, spool; (*TEC*) coil.

carretera [karre'tera] *nf* (*main*) road, highway; ~ **de circunvalación** ring road; ~ **nacional** ≈ A road (*Brit*), state highway (*US*).

carretilla [karre'tiλa] *nf* trolley; (*AGR*) (wheel)barrow.

carril [ka'rril] *nm* furrow; (*de autopista*) lane; (*FERRO*) rail.

carrillo [ka'rriλo] *nm* (*ANAT*) cheek; (*TEC*) pulley.

carrizo [ka'rriθo] *nm* reed.

carro ['karro] *nm* cart, wagon; (*MIL*) tank; (*AM: coche*) car.

carrocería [karroθe'ria] *nf* bodywork, coachwork.

carroña [ka'rroɲa] *nf* carrion *q.*

carrusel [karru'sel] *nm* merry-go-round, roundabout.

carta ['karta] nf letter; (CULIN) menu; (naipe) card; (mapa) map; (JUR) document; ~ **de crédito** credit card; ~ **certificada** registered letter; ~ **marítima** chart; ~ **verde** (AUTO) green card.

cartel [kar'tel] nm (anuncio) poster, placard; (ESCOL) wall chart; (COM) cartel; ~**era** nf hoarding, billboard; (en periódico etc) entertainments guide; '**en ~era**' 'showing'.

cartera [kar'tera] nf (de bolsillo) wallet; (de colegial, cobrador) satchel; (de señora) handbag; (para documentos) briefcase; (COM) portfolio; **ocupa la ~ de Agricultura** she is Minister of Agriculture.

carterista [karte'rista] nm/f pickpocket.

cartero [kar'tero] nm postman.

cartilla [kar'tiʎa] nf primer, first reading book; ~ **de ahorros** savings book.

cartón [kar'ton] nm cardboard.

cartucho [kar'tutʃo] nm (MIL) cartridge.

casa ['kasa] nf house; (hogar) home; (edificio) building; (COM) firm, company; ~ **consistorial** town hall; ~ **de huéspedes** boarding house; ~ **de socorro** first aid post.

casadero, a [kasa'ðero, a] a of marrying age.

casado, a [ka'saðo, a] a married // nm/f married man/woman.

casamiento [kasa'mjento] nm marriage, wedding.

casar [ka'sar] vt to marry; (JUR) to quash, annul; ~**se** vr to marry, get married.

cascabel [kaska'ßel] nm (small) bell.

cascada [kas'kaða] nf waterfall.

cascanueces [kaska'nweθes] nm inv nutcrackers.

cascar [kas'kar] vt, **cascarse** vr to crack, split, break (open).

cáscara ['kaskara] nf (de huevo, fruta seca) shell; (de fruta) skin; (de limón) peel.

casco ['kasko] nm (de bombero, soldado) helmet; (NAUT: de barco) hull; (ZOOL: de caballo) hoof; (botella) empty bottle; (de ciudad): **el ~ antiguo** the old part; **el ~ urbano** the town centre.

cascote [kas'kote] nm rubble.

caserío [kase'rio] nm hamlet; (casa) country house.

casero, a [ka'sero, a] a (pan etc) home-made // nm/f (propietario) landlord/lady; (COM) house agent; **ser muy ~** to be home-loving; '**comida casera**' 'home cooking'.

caseta [ka'seta] nf hut; (para bañista) cubicle; (de feria) stall.

casete [ka'sete] nm o f cassette.

casi ['kasi] ad almost, nearly; ~ **nada** hardly anything; ~ **nunca** hardly ever, almost never; ~ **te caes** you almost fell.

casilla [ka'siʎa] nf (casita) hut, cabin; (TEATRO) box office; (AJEDREZ) square; (para cartas) pigeonhole.

casino [ka'sino] nm club; (de juego) casino.

caso ['kaso] nm case; en ~ de... in case of...; **el ~ es que** the fact is that; **en ese ~** in that case; **hacer ~ a** to pay attention to; **hacer o venir al ~** to be relevant.

caspa ['kaspa] nf dandruff.

cassette [ka'sete] nm o f = **casete**.

casta ['kasta] nf caste; (raza) breed; (linaje) lineage.

castañetear [kastaɲete'ar] vi (dientes) to chatter.

castaño, a [kas'taɲo, a] a chestnut(-coloured), brown // nm chestnut tree.

castañuelas [kasta'ɲwelas] nfpl castanets.

castellano, a [kaste'ʎano, a] a Castilian // nm (LING) Castilian, Spanish.

castidad [kasti'ðað] nf chastity, purity.

castigar [kasti'ɣar] vt to punish; (DEPORTE) to penalize; (aﬂigir) to afflict; **castigo** nm punishment; (DEPORTE) penalty.

Castilla [kas'tiʎa] nf Castile.

castillo [kas'tiʎo] nm castle.

castizo, a [kas'tiθo, a] a (LING) pure; (de buena casta) purebred, pedigree.

casto, a ['kasto, a] a chaste, pure.

castor [kas'tor] nm beaver.

castrar [kas'trar] vt to castrate.

casual [ka'swal] a chance, accidental; **~idad** nf chance, accident; (combinación de circunstancias) coincidence; ¡qué ~idad! what a coincidence!

cataclismo [kata'klismo] nm cataclysm.

catador, a [kata'ðor, a] nm/f wine taster.

catalán, ana [kata'lan, ana] a, nm/f Catalan // nm (LING) Catalan.

catalizador [kataliθa'ðor] nm catalyst.

catálogo [ka'taloɣo] nm catalogue.

Cataluña [kata'luɲa] nf Catalonia.

catar [ka'tar] vt to taste, sample.

catarata [kata'rata] nf (GEO) waterfall; (MED) cataract.

catarro [ka'tarro] nm catarrh; (constipado) cold.

catástrofe [ka'tastrofe] nf catastrophe.

catedral [kate'ðral] nf cathedral.

catedrático, a [kate'ðratiko, a] nm/f professor.

categoría [kateɣo'ria] nf category; (rango) rank, standing; (calidad) quality; de ~ (hotel) top-class.

categórico, a [kate'ɣoriko, a] a categorical.

catolicismo [katoli'θismo] nm Catholicism.

católico, a [ka'toliko, a] a, nm/f Catholic.

catorce [ka'torθe] num fourteen.

cauce ['kauθe] nm (de río) riverbed; (fig) channel.

caución [kau'θjon] nf bail;

caucionar vt (JUR) to bail, go bail for.

caucho ['kautʃo] nm rubber; (AM: llanta) tyre.

caudal [kau'ðal] nm (de río) volume, flow; (fortuna) wealth; (abundancia) abundance; **~oso, a** a (río) large; (persona) wealthy, rich.

caudillo [kau'ðiʎo] nm leader, chief.

causa ['kausa] nf cause; (razón) reason; (JUR) lawsuit, case; a ~ de because of.

causar [kau'sar] vt to cause.

cautela [kau'tela] nf caution, cautiousness; **cauteloso, a** a cautious, wary.

cautivar [kauti'βar] vt to capture; (fig) to captivate.

cautiverio [kauti'βerjo] nm, **cautividad** [kautiβi'ðað] nf captivity.

cautivo, a [kau'tiβo, a] a, nm/f captive.

cauto, a ['kauto, a] a cautious, careful.

cava ['kaβa] nm champagne-type wine.

cavar [ka'βar] vt to dig.

caverna [ka'βerna] nf cave, cavern.

cavidad [kaβi'ðað] nf cavity.

cavilar [kaβi'lar] vt to ponder.

cayado [ka'jaðo] nm (de pastor) crook; (de obispo) crozier.

cayendo etc vb ver **caer**.

caza ['kaθa] nf (acción: gen) hunting; (: con fusil) shooting; (una ~) hunt, chase; (animales) game // nm (AVIAT) fighter.

cazador, a [kaθa'ðor, a] nm/f hunter // nf jacket.

cazar [ka'θar] vt to hunt; (perseguir) to chase; (prender) to catch.

cazo [ka'θo] nm saucepan.

cazuela [ka'θwela] nf (vasija) pan; (guisado) casserole.

cebada [θe'βaða] nf barley.

cebar [θe'βar] vt (animal) to fatten (up); (anzuelo) to bait; (MIL, TEC) to prime.

cebo ['θeβo] nm (para animales) feed, food; (para peces, fig) bait; (de *arma*) charge.

cebolla [θe'βoʎa] *nf* onion; **cebollín** *nm* spring onion.

cebra ['θeβra] *nf* zebra.

cecear [θeθe'ar] *vi* to lisp; **ceceo** *nm* lisp.

cedazo [θe'θaðo] *nm* sieve.

ceder [θe'ðer] *vt* to hand over, give up, part with // *vi* (*renunciar*) to give in, yield; (*disminuir*) to diminish, decline; (*romperse*) to give way.

cedro ['θeðro] *nm* cedar.

cédula ['θeðula] *nf* certificate, document.

CEE *nf abr* (= *Comunidad Económica Europea*) EEC.

cegar [θe'ɣar] *vt* to blind; (*tubería etc*) to block up, stop up // *vi* to go blind; **~se** *vr*: **~ (de)** to be blinded (by).

ceguera [θe'ɣera] *nf* blindness.

ceja ['θexa] *nf* eyebrow.

cejar [θe'xar] *vi* (*fig*) to back down.

celada [θe'laða] *nf* ambush, trap.

celador, a [θela'ðor, a] *nm/f* (*de edificio*) watchman; (*de museo etc*) attendant.

celda ['θelda] *nf* cell.

celebración [θeleβra'θjon] *nf* celebration.

celebrar [θele'βrar] *vt* to celebrate; (*alabar*) to praise // *vi* to be glad; **~se** *vr* to occur, take place.

célebre ['θeleβre] *a* famous.

celebridad [θeleβri'ðað] *nf* fame; (*persona*) celebrity.

celeste [θe'leste] *a* sky-blue; (*ASTRO*) celestial, heavenly.

celestial [θeles'tjal] *a* celestial, heavenly.

celibato [θeli'βato] *nm* celibacy.

célibe ['θeliβe] *a, nm/f* celibate.

celo ['θelo] *nm* zeal; (*REL*) fervour; (*ZOOL*): **en ~** on heat; **~s** *nmpl* jealousy *sg*.

celofán [θelo'fan] *nm* cellophane.

celoso, a [θe'loso, a] *a* (*envidioso*) jealous; (*trabajador*) zealous; (*desconfiado*) suspicious.

celta ['θelta] *a* Celtic // *nm/f* Celt.

célula ['θelula] *nf* cell.

celuloide [θelu'loiðe] *nm* celluloid.

cementerio [θemen'terjo] *nm* cemetery, graveyard.

cemento [θe'mento] *nm* cement; (*hormigón*) concrete; (*AM*: *cola*) glue.

cena ['θena] *nf* evening meal, dinner.

cenagal [θena'val] *nm* bog, quagmire.

cenar [θe'nar] *vt* to have for dinner // *vi* to have dinner.

cenicero [θeni'θero] *nm* ashtray.

cenit [θe'nit] *nm* zenith.

ceniza [θe'niθa] *nf* ash, ashes *pl*.

censo ['θenso] *nm* census; **~ electoral** electoral roll.

censura [θen'sura] *nf* (*POL*) censorship; (*moral*) censure.

censurar [θensu'rar] *vt* (*idea*) to censure; (*cortar: película*) to censor.

centella [θen'teʎa] *nf* spark.

centellear [θenteʎe'ar] *vi* (*metal*) to gleam; (*estrella*) to twinkle; (*fig*) to sparkle; **centelleo** *nm* gleam(ing); twinkling; sparkling.

centenar [θente'nar] *nm* hundred.

centenario, a [θente'narjo, a] *a* centenary; hundred-year-old // *nm* centenary.

centésimo, a [θen'tesimo, a] *a* hundredth.

centígrado [θen'tiɣraðo] *a* centigrade.

centímetro [θen'timetro] *nm* centimetre (*Brit*), centimeter (*US*).

céntimo [θentimo] *nm* cent.

centinela [θenti'nela] *nm* sentry, guard.

centollo [θen'toʎo] *nm* spider crab.

central [θen'tral] *a* central // *nf* head office; (*TEC*) plant; (*TEL*) exchange; **~ nuclear** nuclear power station.

centralización [θentraliθa'θjon] *nf* centralization.

centralizar [θentrali'θar] *vt* to centralize.

centrar [θen'trar] *vt* to centre.

céntrico, a ['θentriko, a] *a* central.

centrista [θen'trista] *a* centre *cpd*.

centro ['θentro] nm centre; ~ comercial shopping centre; ~ juvenil youth club.

centroamericano, a [θentroameri'kano, a] a, nm/f Central American.

ceñir [θe'nir] vt (rodear) to encircle, surround; (ajustar) to fit (tightly); (apretar) to tighten.

ceño ['θeɲo] nm frown, scowl; fruncir el ~ to frown, knit one's brow.

CEOE nf abr (Esp = Confederación Española de Organizaciones Empresariales) ≈ CBI (Brit), employers' organization.

cepillar [θepi'ʎar] vt to brush; (madera) to plane (down).

cepillo [θe'piʎo] nm brush; (para madera) plane.

cera ['θera] nf wax.

cerámica [θe'ramika] nf ceramics pl, pottery.

cerca ['θerka] nf fence // ad near, nearby, close; ~s nmpl foreground sg; ~ de prep near, close to.

cercanía [θerka'nia] nf nearness, closeness; ~s nfpl outskirts, suburbs.

cercano, a [θer'kano, a] a close, near.

cercar [θer'kar] vt to fence in; (rodear) to surround.

cerciorar [θerθjo'rar] vt (asegurar) to assure; ~se vr (descubrir) to find out; (asegurarse) to make sure.

cerco ['θerko] nm (AGR) enclosure; (AM) fence; (MIL) siege.

cerdo ['θerðo] nm pig.

cereal [θere'al] nm cereal; ~es nmpl cereals, grain sg.

cerebro [θe'reβro] nm brain; (fig) brains pl.

ceremonia [θere'monja] nf ceremony; **ceremonial** a, nm ceremonial; **ceremonioso, a** a ceremonious; (cumplido) formal.

cereza [θe'reθa] nf cherry.

cerilla [θe'riʎa] nf (fósforo) match.

cernerse [θer'nerse] vr to hover.

cernidor [θerni'ðor] nm sieve.

cero ['θero] nm nothing, zero.

cerrado, a [θe'rraðo, a] a closed, shut; (con llave) locked; (tiempo) cloudy, overcast; (curva) sharp; (acento) thick, broad.

cerradura [θerra'ðura] nf (acción) closing; (mecanismo) lock.

cerrajero [θerra'xero] nm locksmith.

cerrar [θe'rrar] vt to close, shut; (paso, carretera) to close; (grifo) to turn off; (cuenta, negocio) to close // vi to close, shut; (la noche) to come down; ~se vr to close, shut; ~ con llave to lock; ~ un trato to strike a bargain.

cerro ['θerro] nm hill.

cerrojo [θe'rroxo] nm (herramienta) bolt; (de puerta) latch.

certamen [θer'tamen] nm competition, contest.

certero, a [θer'tero, a] a (gen) accurate.

certeza [θer'teθa], **certidumbre** [θerti'ðumbre] nf certainty.

certificado [θertifi'kaðo] nm certificate.

certificar [θertifi'kar] vt (asegurar, atestar) to certify.

cervatillo [θerβa'tiʎo] nm fawn.

cervecería [θerβeθe'ria] nf (fábrica) brewery; (bar) public house, pub.

cerveza [θer'βeθa] nf beer.

cesación [θesa'θjon] nf cessation, suspension.

cesante [θe'sante] a redundant.

cesantía [θesan'tia] nf unemployment.

cesar [θe'sar] vi to cease, stop // vt (funcionario) to remove from office.

cese ['θese] nm (de trabajo) dismissal; (de pago) suspension.

césped ['θespeð] nm grass, lawn.

cesta ['θesta] nf basket.

cesto ['θesto] nm (large) basket, hamper.

cetro ['θetro] nm sceptre.

cfr abr (= confróntese) cf.

ch... ver bajo la letra CH, después de C.

Cía abr (= compañía) Co.

cianuro [θja'nuro] nm cyanide.

cicatriz [θika'triθ] nf scar; **~ar** vt to heal; **~arse** vr to heal (up), form a scar.

ciclismo [θi'klismo] nm cycling.

ciclo [θi'klo] nm cycle.

ciclón [θi'klon] nm cyclone.

ciego, a [θj'eɣo, a] a blind // nm/f blind man/woman.

cielo [θj'elo] nm sky; (REL) heaven; **¡~s!** good heavens!

ciempiés [θjem'pjes] nm inv centipede.

cien [θjen] num ver **ciento**.

ciénaga [θj'enaɣa] nf marsh, swamp.

ciencia [θj'enθja] nf science; **~s** nfpl (ESCOL) science sg; **~-ficción** nf science fiction.

cieno [θj'eno] nm mud, mire.

científico, a [θjen'tifiko, a] a scientific // nm/f scientist.

ciento [θj'ento], **cien** num hundred; **pagar al 10 por ~** to pay at 10 per cent.

cierne [θj'erne] nm: **en ~** in blossom.

cierre etc vb ver **cerrar** // [θj'erre] nm closing, shutting; (con llave) locking; **~ de cremallera** zip (fastener).

cierro etc vb ver **cerrar**.

cierto, a [θj'erto, a] a sure, certain; (un tal) a certain; (correcto) right, correct; **~ hombre** a certain man; **ciertas personas** certain o some people; **sí, es ~** yes, that's correct.

ciervo [θj'erβo] nm (ZOOL) deer; (: macho) stag.

cierzo [θj'erθo] nm north wind.

cifra [θj'ifra] nf number, numeral; (cantidad) number, quantity; (secreta) code.

cifrar [θi'frar] vt to code, write in code; (resumir) to abridge.

cigala [θi'vala] nf Norway lobster.

cigarra [θi'yarra] nf cicada.

cigarrera [θiɣa'rrera] nf cigar case.

cigarrillo [θiɣa'rriʎo] nm cigarette.

cigarro [θi'yarro] nm cigarette; (puro) cigar.

cigüeña [θi'ɣweɲa] nf stork.

cilíndrico, a [θi'lindriko, a] a cylindrical.

cilindro [θi'lindro] nm cylinder.

cima [θj'ima] nf (de montaña) top, peak; (de árbol) top; (fig) height.

címbalo [θj'imbalo] nm cymbal.

cimbrar [θim'brar], **cimbrear** [θim-bre'ar] vt to brandish; **~se** vr to sway.

cimentar [θimen'tar] vt to lay the foundations of; (fig: fundar) to found.

cimiento [θi'mjento] nm foundation.

cinc [θink] nm zinc.

cincel [θin'θel] nm chisel; **~ar** vt to chisel.

cinco [θj'inko] num five.

cincuenta [θin'kwenta] num fifty.

cine [θj'ine] nm cinema.

cineasta [θine'asta] nm/f (director de cine) film director.

cinematográfico, a [θinemato-'yrafiko, a] a cine-, film cpd.

cínico, a [θj'iniko, a] a cynical // nm/f cynic.

cinismo [θi'nismo] nm cynicism.

cinta [θj'inta] nf band, strip; (de tela) ribbon; (película) reel; (de máquina de escribir) ribbon; **~ adhesiva** sticky tape; **~ magnetofónica** tape; **~ métrica** tape measure.

cinto [θj'into] nm belt.

cintura [θin'tura] nf waist.

cinturón [θintu'ron] nm belt; **~ de seguridad** safety belt.

ciprés [θi'pres] nm cypress (tree).

circo [θj'irko] nm circus.

circuito [θir'kwito] nm circuit.

circulación [θirkula'θjon] nf circulation; (AUTO) traffic.

circular [θirku'lar] a, nf circular // vi, vt to circulate // vi (AUTO) to drive; **'circule por la derecha'** 'keep (to the) right'.

círculo [θj'irkulo] nm circle.

circuncidar [θirkunθi'dar] vt to circumcise.

circundar [θirkun'dar] vt to surround.

circunferencia [θirkunfe'renθja] nf circumference.

circunscribir [θirkunskri'βir] *vt* to circumscribe; **~se** *vr* to be limited.

circunscripción [θirkunskrip'θjon] *nf* division; (*POL*) constituency.

circunspecto, a [θirkuns'pekto, a] *a* circumspect, cautious.

circunstancia [θirkuns'tanθja] *nf* circumstance.

circunstante [θirkuns'tante] *nm/f* onlooker, bystander.

cirio ['θirjo] *nm* (wax) candle.

ciruela [θi'rwela] *nf* plum; **~ pasa** prune.

cirugía [θiru'xia] *nf* surgery; **~ estética** o **plástica** plastic surgery.

cirujano [θiru'xano] *nm* surgeon.

cisne ['θisne] *nm* swan.

cisterna [θis'terna] *nf* cistern, tank.

cita ['θita] *nf* appointment, meeting; (*de novios*) date; (*referencia*) quotation.

citación [θita'θjon] *nf* (*JUR*) summons *sg*.

citar [θi'tar] *vt* (*gen*) to make an appointment with; (*JUR*) to summons; (*un autor, texto*) to quote; **~se** *vr*: **se citaron en el cine** they arranged to meet at the cinema.

cítricos ['θitrikos] *nmpl* citrus fruit(s).

ciudad [θju'ðað] *nf* town; (*más grande*) city; **~anía** *nf* citizenship; **~ano, a** *nm/f* citizen.

cívico, a ['θiβiko, a] *a* civic.

civil [θi'βil] *a* civil // *nm* (*guardia*) policeman.

civilización [θiβiliθa'θjon] *nf* civilization.

civilizar [θiβili'θar] *vt* to civilize.

civismo [θi'βismo] *nm* public spirit.

cizaña [θi'θaɲa] *nf* (*fig*) discord.

cl. *abr* (= *centilitro*) cl.

clamar [kla'mar] *vt* to clamour for, cry out for // *vi* to cry out, clamour.

clamor [kla'mor] *nm* (*grito*) cry, shout; (*fig*) clamour, protest.

clandestino, a [klandes'tino, a] *a* clandestine; (*POL*) underground.

clara ['klara] *nf* (*de huevo*) egg white.

claraboya [klara'βoja] *nf* skylight.

clarear [klare'ar] *vi* (*el día*) to dawn; (*el cielo*) to clear up, brighten up; **~se** *vr* to be transparent.

clarete [kla'rete] *nm* rosé (wine).

claridad [klari'ðað] *nf* (*del día*) brightness; (*de estilo*) clarity.

clarificar [klarifi'kar] *vt* to clarify.

clarín [kla'rin] *nm* bugle.

clarinete [klari'nete] *nm* clarinet.

clarividencia [klariβi'ðenθja] *nf* clairvoyance; (*fig*) far-sightedness.

claro, a ['klaro, a] *a* clear; (*luminoso*) bright; (*color*) light; (*evidente*) clear, evident; (*poco espeso*) thin // *nm* (*en bosque*) clearing // *ad* clearly // *excl* of course!

clase ['klase] *nf* class; **~ alta/media/obrera** upper/middle/working class.

clásico, a ['klasiko, a] *a* classical; (*fig*) classic.

clasificación [klasifika'θjon] *nf* classification; (*DEPORTE*) league (table).

clasificar [klasifi'kar] *vt* to classify.

claudia ['klauðja] *nf* greengage.

claudicar [klauði'kar] *vi* (*fig*) to back down.

claustro ['klaustro] *nm* cloister.

cláusula ['klausula] *nf* clause.

clausura [klau'sura] *nf* closing, closure; **clausurar** *vt* (*congreso etc*) to bring to a close.

clavar [kla'βar] *vt* (*clavo*) to hammer in; (*cuchillo*) to stick, thrust; (*tablas etc*) to nail (together).

clave ['klaβe] *nf* key; (*MUS*) clef.

clavel [kla'βel] *nm* carnation.

clavícula [kla'βikula] *nf* collar bone.

clavija [kla'βixa] *nf* peg, dowel, pin; (*ELEC*) plug.

clavo ['klaβo] *nm* (*de metal*) nail; (*BOT*) clove.

claxon ['klakson] (*pl* **~s**) *nm* horn.

clemencia [kle'menθja] *nf* mercy, clemency.

cleptómano, a [klep'tomano, a] *nm/f* kleptomaniac.

clerical [kleri'kal] *a* clerical.

clérigo ['klerivo] *nm* clergyman.

clero ['klero] nm clergy.

cliché [kli't∫e] nm cliché; (FOTO) negative.

cliente, a [kljente, a] nm/f client, customer.

clientela [kljen'tela] nf clientele, customers pl.

clima ['klima] nm climate.

climatizado, a [klimati'θaðo, a] a air-conditioned.

clínica ['klinika] nf clinic; (particular) private hospital.

clip [klip] (pl ~s) nm paper clip.

clorhídrico, a [klo'riðriko, a] a hydrochloric.

club [klub] (pl ~s o ~es) nm club; ~ de jóvenes youth club.

cm abr (= centímetro, centímetros) cm.

C.N.T. abr (Esp) = Confederación Nacional de Trabajo.

coacción [koak'θjon] nf coercion, compulsion.

coagular [koaɣu'lar] vt, **coagularse** vr (leche, sangre) to clot; **coágulo** nm clot.

coalición [koali'θjon] nf coalition.

coartada [koar'taða] nf alibi.

coartar [koar'tar] vt to limit, restrict.

coba ['koβa] nf: dar ~ a uno to soft-soap sb.

cobarde [ko'βarðe] a cowardly // nm coward; **cobardía** nf cowardice.

cobaya [ko'βaja] nf, **cobayo** [ko'βajo] nm guinea pig.

cobertizo [koβer'tiθo] nm shelter.

cobertor [koβer'tor] nm bedspread.

cobertura [koβer'tura] nf cover.

cobija [ko'βixa] nf (AM) blanket.

cobijar [koβi'xar] vt (cubrir) to cover; (abrigar) to shelter; **cobijo** nm shelter.

cobra [ko'βra] nf cobra.

cobrador, a [koβra'ðor, a] nm/f (de autobús) conductor/conductress; (de impuestos, gas) collector.

cobrar [ko'βrar] vt (cheque) to cash; (sueldo) to collect, draw; (objeto) to recover; (precio) to charge; (deuda) to collect // vi to draw one's pay; ~se

vr to recover, get well; **cóbrese al entregar** cash on delivery (COD).

cobre [ko'βre] nm copper; ~s nmpl brass instruments.

cobro [ko'βro] nm (de cheque) cashing; (pago) payment; **presentar al ~** to cash.

Coca-Cola ['koka'kola] nf ® Coca-Cola ®.

cocaína [koka'ina] nf cocaine.

cocción [kok'θjon] nf (CULIN) cooking; (: el hervir) boiling.

cocear [koθe'ar] vi to kick.

cocer [ko'θer] vt, vi to cook; (en agua) to boil; (en horno) to bake.

cocido [ko'θiðo] nm stew.

cocina [ko'θina] nf kitchen; (aparato) cooker, stove; (acto) cookery; ~ eléctrica/de gas electric/gas cooker; ~ francesa French cuisine; **cocinar** vt, vi to cook.

cocinero, a [koθi'nero, a] nm/f cook.

coco ['koko] nm coconut; ~tero nm coconut palm.

cocodrilo [koko'ðrilo] nm crocodile.

coche ['kot∫e] nm (AUTO) car (Brit), automobile (US); (de tren, de caballos) coach, carriage; (para niños) pram (Brit), baby carriage (US); ~ celular Black Maria, prison van; ~ fúnebre hearse; **coche-cama** (pl coches-camas) nm (FERRO) sleeping car, sleeper.

cochera [ko't∫era] nf garage; (de autobuses, trenes) depot.

coche restaurante nm (pl coches restaurantes) nm (FERRO) dining car, diner.

cochino, a [ko't∫ino, a] a filthy, dirty // nm/f pig.

codazo [ko'ðaθo] nm: dar un ~ a uno to nudge sb.

codear [koðe'ar] vi to elbow, nudge; ~se vr: ~se con to rub shoulders with.

codicia [ko'ðiθja] nf greed; (fig) lust; **codiciar** vt to covet; **codicioso, a** a covetous.

código [ko'ðiɣo] nm code; ~ de barras bar code; ~ civil common law.

codillo [ko'ðiʎo] nm (ZOOL) knee; (TEC) elbow (joint).

codo [ko'ðo] nm (ANAT, de tubo) elbow; (ZOOL) knee.

codorniz [koðor'niθ] nf quail.

coerción [koer'θjon] nf coercion.

coetáneo, a [koe'taneo, a] nm/f contemporary.

coexistir [koe(k)sis'tir] vi to coexist.

cofradía [kofra'ðia] nf brotherhood, fraternity.

coger [ko'xer] vt (Esp) to take (hold of); (objeto caído) to pick up; (frutas) to pick, harvest; (resfriado, ladrón, pelota) to catch // vi: ~ por el buen camino to take the right road; ~se vt (el dedo) to catch; ~se a algo to get hold of sth.

cogollo [ko'ɣoʎo] nm (de lechuga) heart.

cogote [ko'ɣote] nm back o nape of the neck.

cohabitar [koaβi'tar] vi to live together, cohabit.

cohecho [ko'etʃo] nm (acción) bribery; (soborno) bribe.

coherente [koe'rente] a coherent.

cohesión [koe'sjon] nm cohesion.

cohete [ko'ete] nm rocket.

cohibido, a [koi'βiðo, a] a (PSICO) inhibited; (tímido) shy.

cohibir [koi'βir] vt to restrain, restrict.

coima [ko'ima] nf (AM) bribe.

coincidencia [koinθi'ðenθja] nf coincidence.

coincidir [koinθi'ðir] vi (en idea) to coincide, agree; (en lugar) to coincide.

coito ['koito] nm intercourse, coitus.

coja etc vb ver **coger**.

cojear [koxe'ar] vi (persona) to limp, hobble; (mueble) to wobble, rock.

cojera [ko'xera] nf lameness; (andar cojo) limp.

cojín [ko'xin] nm cushion; **cojinete** nm small cushion, pad; (TEC) ball bearing.

cojo, a etc vb ver **coger** // ['koxo, a] a (que no puede andar) lame,

crippled; (mueble) wobbly // nm/f lame person, cripple.

cojón [ko'xon] nm: ¡cojones! (fam!) shit! (!); **cojonudo, a** a (fam) great, fantastic.

col [kol] nf cabbage; ~es de Bruselas Brussels sprouts.

cola ['kola] nf tail; (de gente) queue; (lugar) end, last place; (para pegar) glue, gum; hacer ~ to queue (up).

colaborador, a [kolaβora'ðor, a] nm/f collaborator.

colaborar [kolaβo'rar] vi to collaborate.

colada [ko'laða] nf: hacer la ~ to do the washing.

colador [kola'ðor] nm (de té) strainer; (para verduras etc) colander.

colapso [ko'lapso] nm collapse; ~ nervioso nervous breakdown.

colar [ko'lar] vt (líquido) to strain off; (metal) to cast // vi to ooze, seep (through); ~se vr to jump the queue; ~se en to get into without paying; (fiesta) to gatecrash.

colateral [kolate'ral] nm collateral.

colcha ['koltʃa] nf bedspread.

colchón [kol'tʃon] nm mattress.

colchoneta [koltʃo'neta] nf (en gimnasio) mattress.

colear [kole'ar] vi (perro) to wag its tail.

colección [kolek'θjon] nf collection; **coleccionar** vt to collect; **coleccionista** nm/f collector.

colecta [ko'lekta] nf collection.

colectivo, a [kolek'tiβo, a] a collective, joint // nm (AM) (small) bus.

colector [kolek'tor] nm collector; (sumidero) sewer.

colega [ko'leɣa] nm/f colleague.

colegial, a [kole'xjal, a] nm/f schoolboy/girl.

colegio [ko'lexjo] nm college; (escuela) school; (de abogados etc) association.

colegir [kole'xir] vt (juntar) to collect, gather; (deducir) to infer, conclude.

cólera ['kolera] nf (ira) anger; (MED) cholera; **colérico, a** [ko'leriko, a] a angry, furious.

colesterol [koleste'rol] nm cholesterol.

coleta [ko'leta] nf pigtail.

colgante [kol'vante] a hanging // nm (joya) pendant.

colgar [kol'var] vt to hang (up); (ropa) to hang out // vi to hang; (teléfono) to hang up.

coliflor [koli'flor] nf cauliflower.

colilla [ko'liʎa] nf cigarette end, butt.

colina [ko'lina] nf hill.

colindante [kolin'dante] a adjacent, neighbouring.

colindar [kolin'dar] vi to adjoin, be adjacent.

colisión [koli'sjon] nf collision; ~ **de frente** head-on crash.

colmado, a [kol'maðo, a] a full.

colmar [kol'mar] vt to fill to the brim; (fig) to fulfil, realize.

colmena [kol'mena] nf beehive.

colmillo [kol'miʎo] nm (diente) eye tooth; (de elefante) tusk; (de perro) fang.

colmo ['kolmo] nm height, summit; ¡es el ~! it's the limit!

colocación [koloka'θjon] nf (acto) placing; (empleo) job, position; (situación) place, position.

colocar [kolo'kar] vt to place, put, position; (dinero) to invest; (poner en empleo) to find a job for; ~**se** vr to get a job.

Colombia [ko'lombja] nf Colombia; **colombiano, a** a a, nm/f Colombian.

colonia [ko'lonja] nf colony; (de casas) housing estate; (agua de ~) cologne.

colonización [koloniθa'θjon] nf colonization; **colonizador, a** [koloniθa'ðor, a] a colonizing // nm/f colonist, settler.

colonizar [koloni'θar] vt to colonize.

coloquio [ko'lokjo] nm conversation; (congreso) conference.

color [ko'lor] nm colour.

colorado, a [kolo'raðo, a] a (rojo) red; (chiste) rude.

colorante [kolo'rante] nm colouring.

colorar [kolo'rar] vt to colour; (teñir) to dye.

colorear [kolore'ar] vt to colour.

colorete [kolo'rete] nm blusher.

colorido [kolo'riðo] nm colouring.

columna [ko'lumna] nf column; (pilar) pillar; (apoyo) support.

columpiar [kolum'pjar] vt, **columpiarse** vr to swing; **columpio** nm swing.

collar [ko'ʎar] nm necklace; (de perro) collar.

coma ['koma] nf comma // nm (MED) coma.

comadre [ko'maðre] nf (madrina) godmother; (vecina) neighbour; (chismosa) gossip; **~ar** vi to gossip.

comandancia [koman'danθja] nf command.

comandante [koman'dante] nm commandant.

comandar [koman'dar] vt to command.

comarca [ko'marka] nf region.

comba ['komba] nf (curva) curve; (cuerda) skipping rope; **saltar a la ~** to skip.

combar [kom'bar] vt to bend, curve.

combate [kom'bate] nm fight; (fig) battle; **combatiente** nm combatant.

combatir [komba'tir] vt to fight, combat.

combinación [kombina'θjon] nf combination; (QUIMICA) compound; (bebida) cocktail; (plan) scheme, setup; (prenda) slip.

combinar [kombi'nar] vt to combine.

combustible [kombus'tiβle] nm fuel.

combustión [kombus'tjon] nf combustion.

comedia [ko'meðja] nf comedy; (TEATRO) play, drama.

comediante [kome'ðjante] nm/f (comic) actor/actress.

comedido, a [kome'ðiðo, a] a moderate.

comedor, a [kome'ðor, a] nm/f (persona) glutton // nm (habitación) dining room; (*restaurante*) restaurant; (*cantina*) canteen.

comensal [komen'sal] *nm/f* fellow guest (*o* diner).

comentar [komen'tar] *vt* to comment on; (*fam*) to discuss.

comentario [komen'tarjo] *nm* comment, remark; ' (*literario*) commentary; ~s *nmpl* gossip *sg*.

comentarista [komenta'rista] *nm/f* commentator.

comenzar [komen'θar] *vt*, *vi* to begin, start, commence; ~ a hacer algo to begin *o* start doing sth.

comer [ko'mer] *vt* to eat; (*DAMAS, AJEDREZ*) to take, capture // *vi* to eat; (*almorzar*) to have lunch; ~se *vr* to eat up.

comercial [komer'θjal] *a* commercial; (*relativo al negocio*) business *cpd*.

comerciante [komer'θjante] *nm/f* trader, merchant.

comerciar [komer'θjar] *vi* to trade, do business.

comercio [ko'merθjo] *nm* commerce, trade; (*negocio*) business; (*fig*) dealings *pl*.

comestible [komes'tißle] *a* eatable, edible; ~s *nmpl* food *sg*, foodstuffs.

cometa [ko'meta] *nm* comet // *nf* kite.

cometer [kome'ter] *vt* to commit.

cometido [kome'tiðo] *nm* (*misión*) task, assignment; (*deber*) commitment.

comezón [kome'θon] *nf* itch, itching.

comicios [ko'miθjos] *nmpl* elections.

cómico, a ['komiko, a] *a* comic(al) // *nm/f* comedian; (*de teatro*) (comic) actor/actress.

comida [ko'miða] *nf* (*alimento*) food; (*almuerzo*, *cena*) meal; (*de mediodía*) lunch.

comidilla [komi'ðiʎa] *nf*: ser la ~ de la ciudad to be the talk of the town.

comienzo *etc vb ver* **comenzar** // [ko'mjenθo] *nm* beginning, start.

comilona [komi'lona] *nf* (*fam*)

blow-out.

comillas [ko'miʎas] *nfpl* quotation marks.

comino [ko'mino] *nm*: (no) me importa un ~ I don't give a damn.

comisaría [komisa'ria] *nf* (*de policía*) police station; (*MIL*) commissariat.

comisario [komi'sarjo] *nm* (*MIL etc*) commissary; (*POL*) commissar.

comisión [komi'sjon] *nf* commission.

comité [komi'te] (*pl* ~s) *nm* committee.

como ['komo] *ad* as; (*tal* ~) like; (*aproximadamente*) about, approximately // *conj* (*ya que, puesto que*) as, since; (*en cuanto*) as soon as; ¡~ no! of course!; ~ no lo haga hoy unless he does it today; ~ si as if; es tan alto ~ ancho it is as high as it is wide.

cómo ['komo] *ad* how?, why? // *excl* what?, I beg your pardon? // *nm*: el ~ y el porqué the whys and wherefores.

cómoda ['komoða] *nf* chest of drawers.

comodidad [komoði'ðað] *nf* comfort; venga a su ~ come at your convenience.

comodín [komo'ðin] *nm* joker.

cómodo, a ['komoðo, a] *a* comfortable; (*práctico, de fácil uso*) convenient.

compacto, a [kom'pakto, a] *a* compact.

compadecer [kompaðe'θer] *vt* to pity, be sorry for; ~se *vr*: ~se de to pity, be sorry *o* feel sorry for.

compadre [kom'paðre] *nm* (*padrino*) godfather; (*amigo*) friend, pal.

compañero, a [kompa'ɲero, a] *nm/f* companion; (*novio*) boy/girlfriend; ~ de clase classmate.

compañía [kompa'ɲia] *nf* company.

comparación [kompara'θjon] *nf* comparison; en ~ con in comparison with.

comparar [kompa'rar] *vt* to

compare.

comparativo, a [kompara'tiβo, a] *a* comparative.

comparecer [kompare'θer] *vi* to appear (in court).

comparsa [kom'parsa] *nm/f* (*TEATRO*) extra.

compartimiento [komparti'mjento] *nm* (*FERRO*) compartment.

compartir [kompar'tir] *vt* to divide (up), share (out).

compás [kom'pas] *nm* (*MUS*) beat, rhythm; (*MAT*) compasses *pl*; (*NAUT etc*) compass.

compasión [kompa'sjon] *nf* compassion, pity.

compasivo, a [kompa'siβo, a] *a* compassionate.

compatibilidad [kompatiβili'ðað] *nf* compatibility.

compatible [kompa'tiβle] *a* compatible.

compatriota [kompa'trjota] *nm/f* compatriot, fellow countryman/woman.

compendiar [kompen'djar] *vt* to summarize; (*libro*) to abridge; **compendio** *nm* summary; abridgement.

compensación [kompensa'θjon] *nf* compensation.

compensar [kompen'sar] *vt* to compensate.

competencia [kompe'tenθja] *nf* (*incumbencia*) domain, field; (*JUR, habilidad*) competence; (*rivalidad*) competition.

competente [kompe'tente] *a* (*JUR, persona*) competent; (*conveniente*) suitable.

competición [kompeti'θjon] *nf* competition.

competir [kompe'tir] *vi* to compete.

compilar [kompi'lar] *vt* to compile.

complacencia [kompla'θenθja] *nf* (*placer*) pleasure; (*tolerancia excesiva*) complacency.

complacer [kompla'θer] *vt* to please; **~se** *vr* to be pleased.

complaciente [kompla'θjente] *a* kind, obliging, helpful.

complejo, a [kom'plexo, a] *a, nm* complex.

complementario, a [komplemen-'tarjo, a] *a* complementary.

completar [komple'tar] *vt* to complete.

completo, a [kom'pleto, a] *a* complete; (*perfecto*) perfect; (*lleno*) full // *nm* full complement.

complicado, a [kompli'kaðo, a] *a* complicated; **estar ~ en** to be mixed up in.

complicar [kompli'kar] *vt* to complicate.

cómplice ['kompliθe] *nm/f* accomplice.

complot [kom'plo(t)] (*pl* ~**s**) *nm* plot; (*conspiración*) conspiracy.

componer [kompo'ner] *vt* to make up, put together; (*MUS, LITERATURA, IMPRENTA*) to compose; (*algo roto*) to mend, repair; (*arreglar*) to arrange; **~se** *vr*: **~se de** to consist of; **componérselas para hacer algo** to manage to do sth.

comportamiento [komporta-'mjento] *nm* behaviour, conduct.

comportarse [kompor'tarse] *vr* to behave.

composición [komposi'θjon] *nf* composition.

compositor, a [komposi'tor, a] *nm/f* composer.

compostura [kompos'tura] *nf* (*composición*) composition; (*reparación*) mending, repair; (*acuerdo*) agreement; (*actitud*) composure.

compra ['kompra] *nf* purchase; **~s** *nfpl* purchases, shopping *sg*; **ir de ~s** to go shopping; **comprador, a** *nm/f* buyer, purchaser.

comprar [kom'prar] *vt* to buy, purchase.

comprender [kompren'der] *vt* to understand; (*incluir*) to comprise, include.

comprensión [kompren'sjon] *nf* understanding; (*totalidad*) comprehensiveness; **comprensivo,**

a *a* comprehensive; (*actitud*) understanding.

compresa [kom'presa] *nf*: ~ higiénica sanitary towel (*Brit*) o napkin (*US*).

comprimido, a [kompri'miðo, a] *a* compressed // *nm* (*MED*) pill, tablet.

comprimir [kompri'mir] *vt* to compress; (*fig*) to control.

comprobante [kompro'ßante] *nm* proof; (*COM*) voucher; ~ **de recibo** receipt.

comprobar [kompro'ßar] *vt* to check; (*probar*) to prove; (*TEC*) to check, test.

comprometer [komprome'ter] *vt* to compromise; (*exponer*) to endanger; **~se** *vr* to compromise o.s.; (*involucrarse*) to get involved.

compromiso [kompro'miso] *nm* (*obligación*) obligation; (*cometido*) commitment; (*convenio*) agreement; (*dificultad*) awkward situation.

compuesto, a [kom'pwesto, a] *a*: ~ **de** composed of, made up of // *nm* compound.

computador [komputa'ðor] *nm*, **computadora** [komputa'ðora] *nf* computer; ~ **central** mainframe computer; ~ **personal** personal computer.

cómputo ['komputo] *nm* calculation.

comulgar [komul'var] *vi* to receive communion.

común [ko'mun] *a* common // *nm*: **el** ~ the community.

comunicación [komunika'θjon] *nf* communication; (*informe*) report.

comunicado [komuni'kaðo] *nm* announcement; ~ **de prensa** press release.

comunicar [komuni'kar] *vt, vi*, **comunicarse** *vr* to communicate; **está comunicando** (*TEL*) the line's engaged (*Brit*) o busy (*US*); **comunicativo, a** *a* communicative.

comunidad [komuni'ðað] *nf* community.

comunión [komu'njon] *nf* communion.

comunismo [komu'nismo] *nm* communism; **comunista** *a, nm/f* communist.

con [kon] ♦ *prep* **1** (*medio, compañía*) with; **comer** ~ **cuchara** to eat with a spoon; **atar algo** ~ **cuerda** to tie sth up with string; **pasear** ~ **uno** to go for a walk with sb

2 (*a pesar de*): ~ **todo, merece nuestros respetos** all the same, he deserves our respect

3 (*para* ~): **es muy bueno para** ~ **los niños** he's very good with (the) children

4 (*infin*): ~ **llegar tan tarde se quedó sin comer** by arriving so late he missed out on eating

♦ *conj*: ~ **que**: **será suficiente** ~ **que le escribas** it will be sufficient if you write to her.

conato [ko'nato] *nm* attempt; ~ **de robo** attempted robbery.

concebir [konθe'ßir] *vt, vi* to conceive.

conceder [konθe'ðer] *vt* to concede.

concejal, a [konθe'xal, a] *nm/f* town councillor.

concejo [kon'θexo] *nm* council.

concentración [konθentra'θjon] *nf* concentration.

concentrar [konθen'trar] *vt*, **concentrarse** *vr* to concentrate.

concepción [konθep'θjon] *nf* conception.

concepto [kon'θepto] *nm* concept.

concertar [konθer'tar] *vt* (*MUS*) to harmonize; (*acordar*: *precio*) to agree; (: *tratado*) to conclude; (*trato*) to arrange, fix up; (*combinar*: *esfuerzos*) to combine; (*reconciliar*: *personas*) to reconcile // *vi* to harmonize, be in tune.

concesión [konθe'sjon] *nf* concession.

concesionario [konθesjo'narjo] *nm* (licensed) dealer, agent.

conciencia [kon'θjenθja] nf conscience; **tener/tomar ~ de** to be/become aware of; **tener la ~ limpia/tranquila** to have a clear conscience.

concienciar [konθjen'θjar] vt to make aware; **~se** vr to become aware.

concienzudo, a [konθjen'θuðo, a] a conscientious.

concierto etc vb ver **concertar** // [kon'θjerto] nm concert; (obra) concerto.

conciliar [konθi'ljar] vt to reconcile.

concilio [kon'θiljo] nm council.

conciso, a [kon'θiso, a] a concise.

conciudadano, a [konθjuða'ðano, a] nm/f fellow citizen.

concluir [konklu'ir] vt, vi, **concluirse** vr to conclude.

conclusión [konklu'sjon] nf conclusion.

concluyente [konklu'jente] a (prueba, información) conclusive.

concordar [konkor'ðar] vt to reconcile // vi to agree, tally.

concordia [kon'korðja] nf harmony.

concretar [konkre'tar] vt to make concrete, make more specific; **~se** vr to become more definite.

concreto, a [kon'kreto, a] a, nm (AM) concrete; **en ~** (en resumen) to sum up; (específicamente) specifically; **no hay nada en ~** there's nothing definite.

concurrencia [konku'rrenθja] nf turnout.

concurrido, a [konku'rriðo, a] a (calle) busy; (local, reunión) crowded.

concurrir [konku'rrir] vi (juntarse: ríos) to meet, come together; (: personas) to gather, meet.

concursante [konkur'sante] nm/f competitor.

concurso [kon'kurso] nm (de público) crowd; (ESCOL, DEPORTE, competencia) competition; (ayuda) help, cooperation.

concha ['kontʃa] nf shell.

conde ['konde] nm count; **condal** a: **la ciudad condal** Barcelona.

condecoración [kondekora'θjon] nf (MIL) medal.

condecorar [kondeko'rar] vt (MIL) to decorate.

condena [kon'dena] nf sentence.

condenación [kondena'θjon] nf condemnation; (REL) damnation.

condenar [konde'nar] vt to condemn; (JUR) to convict; **~se** vr (JUR) to confess (one's guilt); (REL) to be damned.

condensar [konden'sar] vt to condense.

condesa [kon'desa] nf countess.

condescender [kondesθen'der] vi to acquiesce, comply.

condición [kondi'θjon] nf condition; **condicional** a conditional.

condicionar [kondiθjo'nar] vt (acondicionar) to condition; **~ algo a** to make sth conditional on.

condimento [kondi'mento] nm seasoning.

condolerse [kondo'lerse] vr to sympathize.

condón [kon'don] nm condom.

conducir [kondu'θir] vt to take, convey; (AUTO) to drive // vi to drive; (fig) to lead; **~se** vr to behave.

conducta [kon'dukta] nf conduct, behaviour.

conducto [kon'dukto] nm pipe, tube; (fig) channel.

conductor, a [konduk'tor, a] a leading, guiding // nm (FISICA) conductor; (de vehículo) driver.

conduje etc vb ver **conducir**.

conduzco etc vb ver **conducir**.

conectado, a [konek'taðo, a] a (INFORM) on-line.

conectar [konek'tar] vt to connect (up); (enchufar) plug in.

conejo [ko'nexo] nm rabbit.

conexión [konek'sjon] nf connection.

confección [konfe(k)'θjon] nf preparation; (industria) clothing industry.

confeccionar [konfekθjo'nar] vt to

make (up).

confederación [konfeðera'θjon] *nf* confederation.

conferencia [konfe'renθja] *nf* conference; *(lección)* lecture; *(TEL)* call.

conferir [konfe'rir] *vt* to award.

confesar [konfe'sar] *vt* to confess, admit.

confesión [konfe'sjon] *nf* confession.

confesionario [konfesjo'narjo] *nm* confessional.

confeti [kon'feti] *nm* confetti.

confiado, a [kon'fjaðo, a] *a (crédulo)* trusting; *(seguro)* confident; *(presumido)* conceited, vain.

confianza [kon'fjanθa] *nf* trust; *(aliento, confidencia)* confidence; *(familiaridad)* intimacy, familiarity; *(pey)* vanity, conceit.

confiar [kon'fjar] *vt* to entrust // *vi* to trust.

confidencia [konfi'ðenθja] *nf* confidence.

confidencial [konfiðen'θjal] *a* confidential.

confidente [konfi'ðente] *nm/f* confidant/e; *(policía)* informer.

configurar [konfiɣu'rar] *vt* to shape, form.

confín [kon'fin] *nm* limit; ~**es** *nmpl* confines, limits.

confinar [konfi'nar] *vi* to confine; *(desterrar)* to banish.

confirmar [konfir'mar] *vt* to confirm.

confiscar [konfis'kar] *vt* to confiscate.

confite [kon'fite] *nm* sweet *(Brit)*, candy *(US)*.

confitería [konfite'ria] *nf* confectionery; *(tienda)* confectioner's *(shop)*.

confitura [konfi'tura] *nf* jam.

conflictivo, a [konflik'tiβo, a] *a (asunto, propuesta)* controversial; *(país, situación)* troubled.

conflicto [kon'flikto] *nm* conflict; *(fig)* clash.

confluir [kon'fluir] *vi (ríos)* to meet; *(gente)* to gather.

conformar [konfor'mar] *vt* to shape,

fashion // *vi* to agree; ~**se** *vr* to conform; *(resignarse)* to resign o.s.

conforme [kon'forme] *a* alike, similar; *(de acuerdo)* agreed, in agreement // *ad* as // *excl* agreed! // *nm* agreement // *prep:* ~ **a** in accordance with.

conformidad [konformi'ðað] *nf (semejanza)* similarity; *(acuerdo)* agreement; *(resignación)* resignation; **conformista** *a, nm/f* conformist.

confortable [konfor'taβle] *a* comfortable.

confortar [konfor'tar] *vt* to comfort.

confrontar [konfron'tar] *vt* to confront; *(dos personas)* to bring face to face; *(cotejar)* to compare // *vi* to border.

confundir [konfun'dir] *vt (borrar)* to blur; *(equivocar)* to mistake, confuse; *(mezclar)* to mix; *(turbar)* to confuse; ~**se** *vr (hacerse borroso)* to become blurred; *(turbarse)* to get confused; *(equivocarse)* to make a mistake; *(mezclarse)* to mix.

confusión [konfu'sjon] *nf* confusion.

confuso, a [kon'fuso, a] *a* confused.

congelado, a [konxe'laðo, a] *a* frozen; ~**s** *nmpl* frozen food(s); **congelador** *nm*, **congeladora** *nf (aparato)* freezer, deep freeze.

congelar [konxe'lar] *vt* to freeze; ~**se** *vr (sangre, grasa)* to congeal.

congeniar [konxe'njar] *vi* to get on *(Brit)* o along *(US)* well.

congestionar [konxestjo'nar] *vt* to congest; ~**se** *vr:* **se le congestionó la cara** his face became flushed.

congoja [kon'goxa] *nf* distress, grief.

congraciarse [kongra'θjarse] *vr* to ingratiate o.s.

congratular [kongratu'lar] *vt* to congratulate.

congregación [kongreɣa'θjon] *nf* congregation.

congregar [kongre'ɣar] *vt*, **congregarse** *vr* to gather together.

congresista [kongre'sista] *nm/f* delegate, congressman/woman.

congreso [kon'greso] nm congress.

conjetura [konxe'tura] nf guess; **conjeturar** vt to guess.

conjugar [konxu'var] vt to combine, fit together; (LING) to conjugate.

conjunción [konxun'θjon] nf conjunction.

conjunto, a [kon'xunto, a] a joint, united // nm whole; (MUS) band; ~ as a whole.

conjurar [konxu'rar] vt (REL) to exorcise; (fig) to ward off // vi to plot.

conmemoración [konmemora'θjon] nf commemoration.

conmemorar [konmemo'rar] vt to commemorate.

conmigo [kon'mivo] pron with me.

conminar [konmi'nar] vt to threaten.

conmoción [konmo'θjon] nf shock; (fig) upheaval; ~ **cerebral** (MED) concussion.

conmovedor, a [konmoβe'ðor, a] a touching, moving; (emocionante) exciting.

conmover [konmo'βer] vt to shake, disturb; (fig) to move.

conmutador [konmuta'ðor] nm switch; (AM TEL: centralita) switchboard; (: central) telephone exchange.

cono ['kono] nm cone.

conocedor, a [konoθe'ðor, a] a expert, knowledgeable // nm/f expert.

conocer [kono'θer] vt to know; (por primera vez) to meet, get to know; (entender) to know about; (reconocer) to recognize; ~se vi (una persona) to know o.s.; (dos personas) to know each other.

conocido, a [kono'θiðo, a] a (well-)known // nm/f acquaintance.

conocimiento [konoθi'mjento] nm knowledge; (MED) consciousness; ~s nmpl (personas) acquaintances; (saber) knowledge sg.

conozco etc vb ver **conocer**.

conque ['konke] conj and so, so then.

conquista [kon'kista] nf conquest;

conquistador, a a conquering // nm conqueror.

conquistar [konkis'tar] vt to conquer.

consagrar [konsa'vrar] vt (REL) to consecrate; (fig) to devote.

consciente [kons'θjente] a conscious.

consecución [konseku'θjon] nf acquisition; (de fin) attainment.

consecuencia [konse'kwenθja] nf consequence, outcome; (firmeza) consistency.

consecuente [konse'kwente] a consistent.

consecutivo, a [konseku'tiβo, a] a consecutive.

conseguir [konse'vir] vt to get, obtain; (sus fines) to attain.

consejero [konse'xero] a nm/f adviser, consultant; (POL) councillor.

consejo [kon'sexo] nm advice; (POL) council.

consenso [kon'senso] nm consensus.

consentimiento [konsenti'mjento] nm consent.

consentir [konsen'tir] vt (permitir, tolerar) to consent to; (mimar) to pamper, spoil; (aguantar) to put up with // vi to agree, consent; ~ **que uno haga algo** to allow sb to do sth.

conserje [kon'serxe] nm caretaker; (portero) porter.

conservación [konserβa'θjon] nf conservation; (de alimentos, vida) preservation.

conservador, a [konserβa'ðor, a] a (POL) conservative // nm/f conservative.

conservante [konser'βante] nm preservative.

conservar [konser'βar] vt to conserve, keep; (alimentos, vida) to preserve; ~se vr to survive.

conservas [kon'serβas] nfpl canned food(s).

conservatorio [konserβa'torjo] nm (MUS) conservatoire.

considerable [konsiðe'raβle] a considerable.

consideración [konsiðera'θjon] nf consideration; *(estimación)* respect.

considerado, a [konsiðe'raðo, a] a *(atento)* considerate; *(respetado)* respected.

considerar [konsiðe'rar] vt to consider.

consigna [kon'siɣna] nf *(orden)* order, instruction; *(para equipajes)* left-luggage office.

consigo etc vb ver **conseguir //** [kon'siɣo] pron (m) with him; *(f)* with her; *(Vd.)* with you; *(reflexivo)* with o.s.

consiguiendo etc vb ver **conseguir.**

consiguiente [konsi'ɣjente] a consequent; **por ~** and so, therefore, consequently.

consistente [konsis'tente] a consistent; *(sólido)* solid, firm; *(válido)* sound.

consistir [konsis'tir] vi: ~ **en** *(componerse de)* to consist of; *(ser resultado de)* to be due to.

consola [kon'sola] nf control panel.

consolación [konsola'θjon] nf consolation.

consolar [konso'lar] vt to console.

consolidar [konsoli'ðar] vt to consolidate.

consomé [konso'me] nm *(pl ~s)* nm consommé, clear soup.

consonante [konso'nante] a consonant, harmonious // nf consonant.

consorcio [kon'sorθjo] nm consortium.

conspiración [konspira'θjon] nf conspiracy.

conspirador, a [konspira'ðor, a] nm/f conspirator.

conspirar [konspi'rar] vi to conspire.

constancia [kons'tanθja] nf constancy; **dejar ~ de** to put on record.

constante [kons'tante] a, nf constant.

constar [kons'tar] vi *(evidenciarse)* to be clear o evident; ~ **de** to consist of.

constatar [konsta'tar] vt *(controlar)* to check; *(observar)* to note.

consternación [konsterna'θjon] nf consternation.

constipado, a [konsti'paðo, a] a: **estar ~** to have a cold // nm cold.

constitución [konstitu'θjon] nf constitution; **constitucional** a constitutional.

constituir [konstitu'ir] vt *(formar, componer)* to constitute, make up; *(fundar, erigir, ordenar)* to constitute, establish.

constitutivo, a [konstitu'tiβo, a] a constitutive, constituent.

constituyente [konstitu'jente] a constituent.

constreñir [konstre'ɲir] vt *(restringir)* to restrict.

construcción [konstruk'θjon] nf construction, building.

constructor, a [konstruk'tor, a] nm/f builder.

construir [konstru'ir] vt to build, construct.

construyendo etc vb ver **construir.**

consuelo [kon'swelo] nm consolation, solace.

cónsul ['konsul] nm consul; **consulado** nm consulate.

consulta [kon'sulta] nf consultation; *(MED)*: **horas de ~** surgery hours.

consultar [konsul'tar] vt to consult.

consultorio [konsul'torjo] nm *(MED)* surgery.

consumar [konsu'mar] vt to complete, carry out; *(crimen)* to commit; *(sentencia)* to carry out.

consumición [konsumi'θjon] nf consumption; *(bebida)* drink; *(comida)* food; ~ **mínima** cover charge.

consumidor, a [konsumi'ðor, a] nm/f consumer.

consumir [konsu'mir] vt to consume; ~**se** vr to be consumed; *(persona)* to waste away.

consumismo [konsu'mismo] nm consumerism.

consumo [kon'sumo] nm consumption.

contabilidad [kontaβili'ðað] *nf* accounting, book-keeping; *(profesión)* accountancy; **contable** *nmf* accountant.

contacto [kon'takto] *nm* contact; *(AUTO)* ignition.

contado, a [kon'taðo, a] *a*: ~s *(escasos)* numbered, scarce, few // *nm*: **pagar al** ~ to pay (in) cash.

contador [konta'ðor] *nm (aparato)* meter; *(AM: contante)* accountant.

contagiar [konta'xjar] *vt (enfermedad)* to pass on, transmit; *(persona)* to infect; **~se** *vr* to become infected.

contagio [kon'taxjo] *nm* infection; **contagioso, a** *a* infectious; *(fig)* catching.

contaminación [kontamina'θjon] *nf* contamination; *(polución)* pollution.

contaminar [kontami'nar] *vt* to contaminate; *(aire, agua)* to pollute.

contante [kon'tante] *a*: **dinero** ~ **(y sonante)** cash.

contar [kon'tar] *vt (páginas, dinero)* to count; *(anécdota, chiste etc)* to tell // *vi* to count; ~ **con** to rely on, count on.

contemplación [kontempla'θjon] *nf* contemplation.

contemplar [kontem'plar] *vt* to contemplate; *(mirar)* to look at.

contemporáneo, a [kontempo-'raneo, a] *a, nmf* contemporary.

contendiente [konten'djente] *nmf* contestant.

contenedor [kontene'ðor] *nm* container.

contener [konte'ner] *vt* to contain, hold; *(retener)* to hold back, contain; **~se** *vr* to control o restrain o.s.

contenido, a [konte'niðo, a] *a (moderado)* restrained; *(risa etc)* suppressed // *nm* contents, content.

contentar [konten'tar] *vt (satisfacer)* to satisfy; *(complacer)* to please; **~se** *vr* to be satisfied.

contento, a [kon'tento, a] *a* contented, content; *(alegre)* pleased;

(feliz) happy.

contestación [kontesta'θjon] *nf* answer, reply.

contestador [kontesta'ðor] *nm*: ~ **automático** answering machine.

contestar [kontes'tar] *vt* to answer, reply; *(JUR)* to corroborate, confirm.

contexto [kon'te(k)sto] *nm* context.

contienda [kon'tjenda] *nf* contest.

contigo [kon'tivo] *pron* with you.

contiguo, a [kon'tivwo, a] *a (de al lado)* next; *(vecino)* adjacent, adjoining.

continente [konti'nente] *a, nm* continent.

contingencia [kontin'xenθja] *nf* contingency; *(riesgo)* risk; **contingente** *a, nm* contingent.

continuación [kontinwa'θjon] *nf* continuation; **a** ~ then, next.

continuar [konti'nwar] *vt* to continue, go on with // *vi* to continue, go on; ~ **hablando** to continue talking *o* to talk.

continuidad [kontinwi'ðað] *nf* continuity.

continuo, a [kon'tinwo, a] *a (sin interrupción)* continuous; *(acción perseverante)* continual.

contorno [kon'torno] *nm* outline; *(GEO)* contour; ~**s** *nmpl* neighbourhood *sg*, surrounding area *sg*.

contorsión [kontor'sjon] *nf* contortion.

contra ['kontra] *prep, ad* against // *nm inv* con // *nf*: **la C~** *(Nicaragua)* the Contras *pl*.

contraataque [kontraa'take] *nm* counter-attack.

contrabajo [kontra'βaxo] *nm* double bass.

contrabandista [kontraβan'dista] *nmf* smuggler.

contrabando [kontra'βando] *nm (acción)* smuggling; *(mercancías)* contraband.

contracción [kontrak'θjon] *nf* contraction.

contrachapado [kontratʃa'paðo] *nm* plywood.

contradecir [kontraðe'θir] vt to contradict.

contradicción [kontraðik'θjon] nf contradiction.

contradictorio, a [kontraðik'torjo, a] a contradictory.

contraer [kontra'er] vt to contract; (limitar) to restrict; ~se vr to contract; (limitarse) to limit o.s.

contragolpe [kontra'volpe] nm backlash.

contraluz [kontra'luθ] nf: a ~ against the light.

contramaestre [kontrama'estre] nm foreman.

contrapartida [kontrapar'tiða] nf: como ~ (de) in return (for).

contrapelo [kontra'pelo] a ~ al the wrong way.

contrapesar [kontrape'sar] vt to counterbalance; (fig) to offset; **contrapeso** nm counterweight.

contraproducente [kontraproðu-'θente] a counterproductive.

contrariar [kontra'rjar] vt (oponerse) to oppose; (poner obstáculo) to impede; (enfadar) to vex.

contrariedad [kontrarje'ðað] nf (oposición) opposition; (obstáculo) obstacle, setback; (disgusto) vexation, annoyance.

contrario, a [kon'trarjo, a] a contrary; (persona) opposed; (sentido, lado) opposite // nm/f enemy, adversary; (DEPORTE) opponent; al/por el ~ on the contrary; de lo ~ otherwise.

contrarrestar [kontrarres'tar] vt to counteract.

contrasentido [kontrasen'tiðo] nm: es un ~ que él ... it doesn't make sense for him to ....

contraseña [kontra'seɲa] nf (INFORM) password.

contrastar [kontras'tar] vt to resist // vi to contrast.

contraste [kon'traste] nm contrast.

contratar [kontra'tar] vt (firmar un acuerdo para) to contract for; (empleados, obreros) to hire, engage;

~se vr to sign on.

contratiempo [kontra'tjempo] nm setback.

contratista [kontra'tista] nm/f contractor.

contrato [kon'trato] nm contract.

contravenir [kontraβe'nir] vi: ~ a to contravene, violate.

contraventana [kontraβen'tana] nf shutter.

contribución [kontriβu'θjon] nf (municipal etc) tax; (ayuda) contribution.

contribuir [kontriβu'ir] vt, vi to contribute; (COM) to pay (in taxes).

contribuyente [kontriβu'jente] nm/f (COM) taxpayer; (que ayuda) contributor.

control [kon'trol] nm control; (inspección) inspection, check; ~ador, a nm/f controller; **controlador aéreo** air-traffic controller.

controlar [kontro'lar] vt to control; (inspeccionar) to inspect, check.

controversia [kontro'βersja] nf controversy.

contundente [kontun'dente] a (instrumento) blunt; (argumento, derrota) overwhelming.

contusión [kontu'sjon] nf bruise.

convalecencia [konβale'θenθja] nf convalescence.

convalecer [konβale'θer] vi to convalesce, get better.

convaleciente [konβale'θjente] a, nm/f convalescent.

convalidar [konβali'ðar] vt (título) to recognize.

convencer [konβen'θer] vt to convince; (persuadir) to persuade.

convencimiento [konβenθi'mjento] nm (acción) convincing; (persuasión) persuasion; (certidumbre) conviction.

convención [konβen'θjon] nf convention.

conveniencia [konβe'njenθja] nf suitability; (conformidad) agreement; (utilidad, provecho) usefulness; ~s nfpl conventions; (COM) property sg.

conveniente [konβe'njente] a suitable; (*útil*) useful.

convenio [kon'βenjo] nm agreement, treaty.

convenir [konβe'nir] vi (*estar de acuerdo*) to agree; (*ser conveniente*) to suit, be suitable.

convento [kon'βento] nm convent.

convenza etc vb ver **convencer**.

converger [konβer'xer], **convergir** [konβer'xir] vi to converge.

conversación [konβersa'θjon] nf conversation.

conversar [konβer'sar] vi to talk, converse.

conversión [konβer'sjon] nf conversion.

convertir [konβer'tir] vt to convert.

convicción [konβik'θjon] nf conviction.

convicto, a [kon'βikto, a] a convicted, found guilty; (*condenado*) condemned.

convidado, a [konβi'ðaðo, a] nm/f guest.

convidar [konβi'ðar] vt to invite.

convincente [konβin'θente] a convincing.

convite [kon'βite] nm invitation; (*banquete*) banquet.

convivencia [konβi'βenθja] nf coexistence, living together.

convocar [konβo'kar] vt to summon, call (together).

convulsión [konβul'sjon] nf convulsion.

conyugal [konju'yal] a conjugal; **cónyuge** [kon'juye] nm/f spouse.

coñac [ko'nak] (pl ~s) nm cognac, brandy.

coño [ko'no] excl (*fam!: enfado*) shit! (!); (: *sorpresa*) bloody hell! (!).

cooperación [koopera'θjon] nf cooperation.

cooperar [koope'rar] vi to cooperate.

cooperativa [koopera'tiβa] nf cooperative.

coordinadora [koorðina'ðora] nf (*comité*) coordinating committee.

coordinar [koorði'nar] vt to coordinate.

copa ['kopa] nf cup; (*vaso*) glass; (*de árbol*) top; (*de sombrero*) crown; ~s nfpl (NAIPES) = hearts; (**tomar una**) ~ (to have a) drink.

copia ['kopja] nf copy; ~ **de respaldo** *o* **seguridad** (INFORM) back-up copy; **copiar** vt to copy.

copioso, a [ko'pjoso, a] a copious, plentiful.

copla ['kopla] nf verse; (*canción*) (popular) song.

copo ['kopo] nm: ~ **de nieve** snowflake; ~**s de maíz** cornflakes.

copropietarios [kopropje'tarjos] nmpl joint owners.

coqueta [ko'keta] a flirtatious, coquettish; **coquetear** vi to flirt.

coraje [ko'raxe] nm courage; (*ánimo*) spirit; (*ira*) anger.

coral [ko'ral] a choral // nf (MUS) choir // nm (ZOOL) coral.

coraza [ko'raθa] nf (*armadura*) armour; (*blindaje*) armour-plating.

corazón [kora'θon] nm heart.

corazonada [koraθo'naða] nf impulse; (*presentimiento*) hunch.

corbata [kor'βata] nf tie.

corchete [kor'tʃete] nm catch, clasp.

corcho ['kortʃo] nm cork; (PESCA) float.

cordel [kor'ðel] nm cord, line.

cordero [kor'ðero] nm lamb.

cordial [kor'ðjal] a cordial; ~**idad** nf warmth, cordiality.

cordillera [korði'ʎera] nf range (of mountains).

Córdoba ['korðoβa] n Cordova.

cordón [kor'ðon] nm (*cuerda*) cord, string; (*de zapatos*) lace; (MIL etc) cordon.

corneta [kor'neta] nf bugle.

coro ['koro] nm chorus; (*conjunto de cantores*) choir.

corona [ko'rona] nf crown; (*de flores*) garland; ~**ción** nf coronation; **coronar** vt to crown.

coronel [koro'nel] nm colonel.

coronilla [koro'niʎa] nf (ANAT)

crown (of the head).

corporación [korpora'θjon] *nf* corporation.

corporal [korpo'ral] *a* corporal, bodily.

corpulento, a [korpu'lento] a] *a* (*persona*) heavily-built.

corral [ko'rral] *nm* farmyard.

correa [ko'rrea] *nf* strap; (*cinturón*) belt; (*de perro*) lead, leash.

corrección [korrek'θjon] *nf* correction; (*reprensión*) rebuke; **correccional** *nm* reformatory.

correcto, a [ko'rrekto, a] *a* correct; (*persona*) well-mannered.

corredizo, a [korre'ðiθo, a] *a* (*puerta etc*) sliding.

corredor, a [korre'ðor, a] *a* running // (*pasillo*) corridor; (*balcón corrido*) gallery; (*COM*) agent, broker // *nm/f* (*DEPORTE*) runner.

corregir [korre'xir] *vt* (*error*) to correct; (*amonestar, reprender*) to rebuke, reprimand; **~se** *vr* to reform.

correo [ko'rreo] *nm* post, mail; (*persona*) courier; **C~s** Post Office *sg*; ~ **aéreo** airmail.

correr [ko'rrer] *vt* to run; (*viajar*) to cover, travel; (*cortinas*) to draw; (*cerrojo*) to shoot // *vi* to run; (*líquido*) to run, flow; **~se** *vr* to slide, move; (*colores*) to run.

correspondencia [korrespon-'denθja] *nf* correspondence; (*FERRO*) connection.

corresponder [korrespon'der] *vi* to correspond; (*convenir*) to be suitable; (*pertenecer*) to belong; (*tocar*) to concern; **~se** *vr* (*por escrito*) to correspond; (*amarse*) to love one another.

correspondiente [korrespon'djente] *a* corresponding.

corresponsal [korrespon'sal] *nm/f* correspondent.

corrido, a [ko'rriðo, a] *a* (*avergonzado*) abashed // *nf* (*de toros*) bullfight; **3 noches corridas** 3 nights running; **un kilo ~** a good

kilo.

corriente [ko'rrjente] *a* (*agua*) running; (*fig*) flowing; (*dinero etc*) current; (*común*) ordinary, normal // *nf* current // *nm* current month; ~ **eléctrica** electric current.

corrija *etc vb ver* **corregir**.

corrillo [ko'rriʎo] *nm* ring, circle (of people); (*fig*) clique.

corro ['korro] *nm* ring, circle (of people).

corroborar [korroβo'rar] *vt* to corroborate.

corroer [korro'er] *vt* to corrode; (*GEO*) to erode.

corromper [korrom'per] *vt* (*madera*) to rot; (*fig*) to corrupt.

corrosivo, a [korro'siβo, a] *a* corrosive.

corrupción [korrup'θjon] *nf* rot, decay; (*fig*) corruption.

corsé [kor'se] *nm* corset.

cortacésped [korta'θespeð] *nm* lawn mower.

cortado, a [kor'taðo, a] *a* (*gen*) cut; (*leche*) sour; (*confuso*) confused; (*desconcertado*) embarrassed // *nm* coffee (with a little milk).

cortar [kor'tar] *vt* to cut; (*suministro*) to cut off; (*un pasaje*) to cut out // *vi* to cut; **~se** *vr* (*turbarse*) to become embarrassed; (*leche*) to turn, curdle; **~se el pelo** to have one's hair cut.

cortauñas [korta'uɲas] *nm inv* nail clippers *pl*.

corte ['korte] *nm* cut, cutting; (*de tela*) piece, length; **las C~s** the Spanish Parliament; ~ **y confección** dressmaking; ~ **de luz** power cut.

cortedad [korte'ðað] *nf* shortness; (*fig*) bashfulness, timidity.

cortejar [korte'xar] *vt* to court.

cortejo [kor'texo] *nm* entourage; ~ **fúnebre** funeral procession.

cortés [kor'tes] *a* courteous, polite.

cortesía [korte'sia] *nf* courtesy.

corteza [kor'teθa] *nf* (*de árbol*) bark; (*de pan*) crust.

cortina [kor'tina] *nf* curtain.

corto, a ['korto, a] *a* (*breve*) short; (*tímido*) bashful; **~ de luces** not very bright; **~ de vista** shortsighted; **estar ~ de fondos** to be short of funds; **~circuito** *nm* short circuit.

corvo, a ['korβo, a] *a* curved.

cosa ['kosa] *nf* thing; (*asunto*) affair; **~ de** about; **eso es ~ mía** that's my business.

cosecha [ko'setʃa] *nf* (AGR) harvest; (*de vino*) vintage.

cosechar [kose'tʃar] *vt* to harvest, gather (in).

coser [ko'ser] *vt* to sew.

cosmético, a [kos'metiko, a] *a, nm* cosmetic.

cosquillas [kos'kiʎas] *nfpl:* **hacer ~** to tickle; **tener ~** to be ticklish.

costa ['kosta] *nf* (GEO) coast; **C~ Brava** Costa Brava; **C~ Cantábrica** Cantabrian Coast; **C~ del Sol** Costa del Sol; **a toda ~** at any price.

costado [kos'taðo] *nm* side.

costal [kos'tal] *nm* sack.

costar [kos'tar] *vt* (*valer*) to cost; (*necesitar*) to require, need; **me cuesta hablarle** I find it hard to talk to him.

Costa Rica *nf* Costa Rica; **costarricense, costarriqueño** *a* a, *nm/f* Costa Rican.

coste ['koste] *nm* = **costo**.

costear [koste'ar] *vt* to pay for.

costilla [kos'tiʎa] *nf* rib; (CULIN) cutlet.

costo ['kosto] *nm* cost, price; **~ de la vida** cost of living; **~so, a** *a* costly, expensive.

costra ['kostra] *nf* (*corteza*) crust; (MED) scab.

costumbre [kos'tumbre] *nf* custom, habit.

costura [kos'tura] *nf* sewing, needlework; (*zurcido*) seam.

costurera [kostu'rera] *nf* dressmaker.

costurero [kostu'rero] *nm* sewing box *o* case.

cotejar [kote'xar] *vt* to compare.

cotidiano, a [koti'ðjano, a] *a* daily, day to day.

cotización [kotiθa'θjon] *nf* (COM) quotation, price; (*de club*) dues pl.

cotizar [koti'θar] *vt* (COM) to quote, price; **~se** *vr:* **~se a** to sell at, fetch; (BOLSA) to stand at, be quoted at.

coto ['koto] *nm* (*terreno cercado*) enclosure; (*de caza*) reserve.

cotorra [ko'torra] *nf* parrot.

COU [kou] *nm abr* (*Esp*) = *Curso de Orientación Universitaria*.

coyote [ko'jote] *nm* coyote, prairie wolf.

coyuntura [kojun'tura] *nf* (ANAT) joint; (*fig*) juncture, occasion.

coz [koθ] *nf* kick.

cráneo ['kraneo] *nm* skull, cranium.

cráter ['krater] *nm* crater.

creación [krea'θjon] *nf* creation.

creador, a [krea'ðor, a] *a* creative // *nm/f* creator.

crear [kre'ar] *vt* to create, make.

crecer [kre'θer] *vi* to grow; (*precio*) to rise.

creces ['kreθes]: **con ~** *ad* amply, fully.

crecido, a [kre'θiðo, a] *a* (*persona, planta*) full-grown; (*cantidad*) large.

creciente [kre'θjente] *a* growing; (*cantidad*) increasing; (*luna*) crescent // *nm* crescent.

crecimiento [kreθi'mjento] *nm* growth; (*aumento*) increase.

credenciales [kreðen'θjales] *nfpl* credentials.

crédito ['kreðito] *nm* credit.

credo ['kreðo] *nm* creed.

crédulo, a ['kreðulo, a] *a* credulous.

creencia [kre'enθja] *nf* belief.

creer [kre'er] *vt, vi* to think, believe; **~se** *vr* to believe o.s. (to be); **~ en** to believe in; **¡ya lo creo!** I should think so!

creíble [kre'iβle] *a* credible, believable.

creído, a [kre'iðo, a] *a* (*engreído*) conceited.

crema ['krema] *nf* cream; (*natillas*)

custard.

cremallera [krema'ʎera] nf zip (fastener).

crepitar [krepi'tar] vi to crackle.

crepúsculo [kre'puskulo] nm twilight, dusk.

crespo, a ['krespo, a] a (pelo) curly.

crespón [kres'pon] nm crêpe.

cresta ['kresta] nf (GEO, ZOOL) crest.

creyendo vb ver **creer**.

creyente [kre'jente] nm/f believer.

creyó etc vb ver **creer**.

crezco etc vb ver **crecer**.

cría etc vb ver **criar** // ['kria] nf (de animales) rearing; breeding; (animal) young; ver tb **crío**.

criadero [kria'ðero] nm nursery; (ZOOL) breeding place.

criado, a [kri'aðo, a] nm servant // nf servant, maid.

criador [kria'ðor] nm breeder.

crianza [kri'anθa] nf rearing, breeding; (fig) breeding.

criar [kri'ar] vt (amamantar) to suckle, feed; (educar) to bring up; (producir) to grow, produce; (animales) to breed.

criatura [kria'tura] nf creature; (niño) baby, (small) child.

criba ['kriβa] nf sieve; **cribar** vt to sieve.

crimen ['krimen] nm crime.

criminal [krimi'nal] a, nm/f criminal.

crin [krin] nf (tb: ~es nfpl) mane.

crío, a ['krio, a] nm/f (fam) kid.

crisis ['krisis] nf inv crisis; ~ **nerviosa** nervous breakdown.

crispar [kris'par] vt (músculo) to tense (up); (nervios) to set on edge.

cristal [kris'tal] nm crystal; (de ventana) glass, pane; (lente) lens; ~**ino, a** [-'lino, a] a crystalline; (fig) clear // nm lens of the eye; ~**izar** vt, vi to crystallize.

cristiandad [kristjan'daθ] nf Christianity.

cristianismo [kristja'nismo] nm Christianity.

cristiano, a [kris'tjano, a] a, nm/f

Christian.

Cristo ['kristo] nm (Dios) Christ; (crucifijo) crucifix.

criterio [kri'terjo] nm criterion; (juicio) judgement.

criticar [kriti'kar] vt to criticize.

crítico, a ['kritiko, a] a critical // nm/f critic // nf criticism.

croar [kro'ar] vi to croak.

cromo ['kromo] nm chrome.

crónico, a ['kroniko, a] a chronic // nf chronicle, account.

cronómetro [kro'nometro] nm (DEPORTE) stopwatch.

cruce etc vb ver **cruzar** // ['kruθe] nm crossing; (de carreteras) crossroads.

crucificar [kruθifi'kar] vt to crucify.

crucifijo [kruθi'fixo] nm crucifix.

crucigrama [kruθi'γrama] nm crossword (puzzle).

crudo, a ['kruðo, a] a raw; (no maduro) unripe; (petróleo) crude; (rudo, cruel) cruel // nm crude (oil).

cruel [krwel] a cruel; ~**dad** nf cruelty.

crujido [kru'xiðo] nm (de madera etc) creak.

crujiente [kru'xjente] a (galleta etc) crunchy.

crujir [kru'xir] vi (madera etc) to creak; (dedos) to crack; (dientes) to grind; (nieve, arena) to crunch.

cruz [kruθ] nf cross; (de moneda) tails sg.

cruzado, a [kru'θaðo, a] a crossed // nm crusader // nf crusade.

cruzar [kru'θar] vt to cross; ~**se** vr (líneas etc) to cross; (personas) to pass each other.

Cruz Roja nf Red Cross.

cuaderno [kwa'ðerno] nm notebook; (de escuela) exercise book; (NAUT) logbook.

cuadra ['kwaðra] nf (caballeriza) stable; (AM) block.

cuadrado, a [kwa'ðraðo, a] a square // nm (MAT) square.

cuadrar [kwa'ðrar] vt to square // vi: ~ **con** to square with, tally with;

~se *vr* (*soldado*) to stand to attention.

cuadrilátero [kwaðri'latero] *nm* (*DEPORTE*) boxing ring; (*GEOM*) quadrilateral.

cuadrilla [kwa'ðriʎa] *nf* party, group.

cuadro ['kwaðro] *nm* square; (*ARTE*) painting; (*TEATRO*) scene; (*diagrama*) chart; (*DEPORTE, MED*) team; (*POL*) executive; **tela a ~s** checked (*Brit*) o chequered (*US*) material.

cuádruplo, a ['kwaðruplo, a], **cuádruple** ['kwaðruple] *a* quadruple.

cuajar [kwa'xar] *vt* to thicken; (*leche*) to curdle; (*sangre*) to congeal; (*adornar*) to adorn; (*CULIN*) to set; ~**se** *vr* to curdle; to congeal; to set; (*llenarse*) to fill up.

cual [kwal] *ad* like, as // *pron*: **el ~** *etc* which; (*persona: sujeto*) who; (: *objeto*) whom // *a* such as; **cada ~** each one; **tal ~** just as it is.

cuál [kwal] *pron interr* which (one).

cualesquiera(a) [kwales'kjer(a)] *pl de* **cualquier(a)**.

cualidad [kwali'ðað] *nf* quality.

cualquier [kwal'kjer], *pl* **cualesquier(a)** *a* (*indefinido*) any; ~ **día de éstos** any day now; (*después de n*: ~**a**): **no es un hombre** ~**a** he isn't an ordinary man, he isn't just anybody; *pron*: ~**a**: **eso** ~**a lo sabe hacer** anybody can do that; **es un** ~**a** he's a nobody.

cuando ['kwando] *ad* when; (*aún si*) if, even if // *conj* (*puesto que*) since // *prep*: **yo,** ~ **niño...** when I was a child...; ~ **no sea así** even if it is not so; ~ **más** at (the) most; ~ **menos** at least; ~ **no** if not, otherwise; **de** ~ **en** ~ from time to time.

cuándo ['kwando] *ad* when; **¿desde** ~?, **¿de** ~ **acá?** since when?

cuantioso, a [kwan'tjoso, a] *a* substantial.

PALABRA CLAVE

cuanto, a ['kwanto, a] ♦ *a* **1** (*todo*): **tiene todo** ~ **desea** he's got every-
thing he wants; **le daremos** ~**s ejemplares necesite** we'll give him as many copies *o* as *o* all the copies he needs; ~**s hombres la ven** all the men who see her

2: **unos** ~**s**: **había unos** ~**s periodistas** there were (quite) a few journalists

3 (+ *más*): ~ **más vino bebes peor te sentirás** the more wine you drink the worse you'll feel

♦ *pron*: **tiene** ~ **desea** he has everything he wants; **tome** ~/~**s quiera** take as much/many as you want

♦ *ad*: **en** ~: **en** ~ **profesor** as a teacher; **en** ~ **a mí** as for me; *ver tb* **antes**

♦ *conj* **1**: ~ **más gana menos gasta** the more he earns the less he spends; ~ **más joven se es más se es confiado** the younger you are the more trusting you are

2: **en** ~: **en** ~ **llegue/llegué** as soon as I arrive/arrived

cuánto, a ['kwanto, a] *a* (*exclamación*) what a lot of; (*interr: sg*) how much?; (: *pl*) how many? // *pron, ad* how; (*interr: sg*) how much?; (: *pl*) how many?; **¡~a gente!** what a lot of people!; **¿~ cuesta?** how much does it cost?; **¿a** ~ **estamos?** what's the date?; **Señor no sé** ~**s** Mr. So-and-So.

cuarenta [kwa'renta] *num* forty.

cuarentena [kwaren'tena] *nf* quarantine.

cuaresma [kwa'resma] *nf* Lent.

cuartear [kwarte'ar] *vt* to quarter; (*dividir*) to divide up; ~**se** *vr* to crack, split.

cuartel [kwar'tel] *nm* (*de ciudad*) quarter, district; (*MIL*) barracks *pl*; ~ **general** headquarters *pl*.

cuarteto [kwar'teto] *nm* quartet.

cuarto, a ['kwarto, a] *a* fourth // *nm* (*MAT*) quarter, fourth; (*habitación*) room // *nf* (*MAT*) quarter, fourth; (*palmo*) span; ~ **de baño** bathroom;

~ **de estar** living room; ~ **de hora** quarter (of an) hour; ~ **de kilo** quarter kilo.

cuatro ['kwatro] num four.

cuba ['kuβa] nf cask, barrel.

Cuba ['kuβa] nf Cuba; **cubano, a** a, nm/f Cuban.

cúbico, a ['kuβiko, a] a cubic.

cubierto, a [ku'βjerto, a] pp de **cubrir** // nm cover; (en la mesa) place; ~s nmpl cutlery sg // nf cover, covering; (neumático) tyre; (NAUT) deck; **a** ~ **de** covered with o in.

cubil [ku'βil] nm den; ~**ete** nm (en juegos) cup.

cubo ['kuβo] nm cube; (balde) bucket, tub; (TEC) drum.

cubrecama [kuβre'kama] nm bedspread.

cubrir [ku'βrir] vt to cover; ~**se** vr (cielo) to become overcast.

cucaracha [kuka'ratʃa] nf cockroach.

cuco, a ['kuko, a] a pretty; (astuto) sharp // nm cuckoo.

cucurucho [kuku'rutʃo] nm cornet.

cuchara [ku'tʃara] nf spoon; (TEC) scoop; ~**da** nf spoonful; ~**dita** nf teaspoonful.

cucharita [kutʃa'rita] nf teaspoon.

cucharón [kutʃa'ron] nm ladle.

cuchichear [kutʃitʃe'ar] vi to whisper.

cuchilla [ku'tʃiʎa] nf (large) knife; (de arma blanca) blade; ~ **de afeitar** razor blade.

cuchillo [ku'tʃiʎo] nm knife.

cuchitril [kutʃi'tril] nm hovel; (habitación etc) pigsty.

cuello ['kweʎo] nm (ANAT) neck; (de vestido, camisa) collar.

cuenca ['kwenka] nf (ANAT) eye socket; (GEO) bowl, deep valley.

cuenta etc vb ver **contar** // ['kwenta] nf (cálculo) count, counting; (en café, restaurante) bill; (COM) account; (de collar) bead; (fig) account; **a fin de** ~s in the end; **caer en la** ~ to catch on; **darse** ~ **de** to realize; **tener en** ~

to bear in mind; echar ~s to take stock; ~ **corriente/de ahorros** current/savings account; ~ **kilómetros** nm inv = milometer; (de velocidad) speedometer.

cuento etc vb ver **contar** // ['kwento] nm story.

cuerda ['kwerða] nf rope; (hilo) string; (de reloj) spring; **dar** ~ **a un reloj** to wind up a clock.

cuerdo, a ['kwerðo, a] a sane; (prudente) wise, sensible.

cuerno ['kwerno] nm horn.

cuero ['kwero] nm (ZOOL) skin, hide; (TEC) leather; **en** ~s stark naked; ~ **cabelludo** scalp.

cuerpo ['kwerpo] nm body.

cuervo ['kwerβo] nm crow.

cuesta etc vb ver **costar** // ['kwesta] nf slope; (en camino etc) hill; ~ **arriba/abajo** uphill/downhill; **a** ~s on one's back.

cueste etc vb ver **costar.**

cuestión [kwes'tjon] nf matter, question, issue; (riña) quarrel, dispute.

cueva ['kweβa] nf cave.

cuidado [kwi'ðaðo] nm care, carefulness; (preocupación) care, worry // excl careful!, look out!

cuidadoso, a [kwiða'ðoso, a] a careful; (preocupado) anxious.

cuidar [kwi'ðar] vt (MED) to care for; (ocuparse de) to take care of, look after // vi: ~ **de** to take care of, look after; ~**se** vr to look after o.s.; ~**se de hacer algo** to take care to do sth.

culata [ku'lata] nf (de fusil) butt.

culebra [ku'leβra] nf snake.

culinario, a [kuli'narjo, a] a culinary, cooking cpd.

culminación [kulmina'θjon] nf culmination.

culo ['kulo] nm bottom, backside; (de vaso, botella) bottom.

culpa ['kulpa] nf fault; (JUR) guilt; **por** ~ **de** because of, through; **tener la** ~ (**de**) to be to blame (for); ~**bilidad** nf guilt; ~**ble** a guilty // nm/f culprit.

culpar [kul'par] *vt* to blame; (*acusar*) to accuse.

cultivar [kulti'ßar] *vt* to cultivate.

cultivo [kul'tißo] *nm* (*acto*) cultivation; (*plantas*) crop.

culto, a ['kulto, a] *a* (*cultivado*) cultivated; (*que tiene cultura*) cultured, educated // *nm* (*homenaje*) worship; (*religión*) cult.

cultura [kul'tura] *nf* culture.

cumbre ['kumbre] *nf* summit, top.

cumpleaños [kumple'anos] *nm inv* birthday.

cumplido, a [kum'pliðo, a] *a* complete, perfect; (*abundante*) plentiful; (*cortés*) courteous // *nm* compliment; **visita de ~** courtesy call.

cumplidor, a [kumpli'ðor, a] *a* reliable.

cumplimentar [kumplimen'tar] *vt* to congratulate.

cumplimiento [kumpli'mjento] *nm* (*de un deber*) fulfilment; (*acabamiento*) completion.

cumplir [kum'plir] *vt* (*orden*) to carry out, obey; (*promesa*) to carry out, fulfil; (*condena*) to serve; (*años*) to reach, attain // *vi*: **~ con** (*deberes*) to carry out, fulfil; **~se** *vr* (*plazo*) to expire; **hoy cumple dieciocho años** he is eighteen today.

cúmulo ['kumulo] *nm* heap.

cuna ['kuna] *nf* cradle, cot.

cundir [kun'dir] *vi* (*noticia, rumor, pánico*) to spread; (*rendir*) to go a long way.

cuneta [ku'neta] *nf* ditch.

cuña ['kuna] *nf* wedge.

cuñado, a [ku'naðo, a] *nm/f* brother/sister-in-law.

cuota ['kwota] *nf* (*parte proporcional*) share; (*cotización*) fee, dues *pl*.

cupe, cupiera *etc vb ver* **caber.**

cupo *vb ver* **caber** // ['kupo] *nm* quota.

cupón [ku'pon] *nm* coupon.

cúpula ['kupula] *nf* dome.

cura ['kura] *nf* (*curación*) cure;

(*método curativo*) treatment // *nm* priest.

curación [kura'θjon] *nf* cure; (*acción*) curing.

curar [ku'rar] *vt* (*MED: herida*) to treat, dress; (: *enfermo*) to cure; (*CULIN*) to cure, salt; (*cuero*) to tan // *vi*, **~se** *vr* to get well, recover.

curiosear [kurjose'ar] *vt* to glance at, look over // *vi* to look round, wander round; (*explorar*) to poke about.

curiosidad [kurjosi'ðað] *nf* curiosity.

curioso, a [ku'rjoso, a] *a* curious // *nm/f* bystander, onlooker.

currante [ku'rrante] *nm/f* (*fam*) worker.

currar [ku'rrar], **currelar** [kurre'lar] *vi* (*fam*) to work; **curro** *nm* (*fam*) work, job.

currículo [ku'rrikolo], **currículum** [ku'rrikulum] *nm* curriculum vitae.

cursi ['kursi] *a* (*fam*) pretentious; (: *amanerado*) affected.

cursiva [kur'sißa] *nf* italics *pl*.

curso ['kurso] *nm* course; **en ~** (*año*) current; (*proceso*) going on, under way.

cursor [kur'sor] *nm* (*INFORM*) cursor.

curtido, a [kur'tiðo, a] *a* (*cara etc*) weather-beaten; (*fig: persona*) experienced.

curtir [kur'tir] *vt* (*cuero etc*) to tan.

curvo, a ['kurßo, a] *a* (*gen*) curved; (*torcido*) bent // *nf* (*gen*) curve, bend.

cúspide ['kuspiðe] *nf* (*GEO*) peak; (*fig*) top.

custodia [kus'toðja] *nf* safekeeping; custody; **custodiar** *vt* (*conservar*) to take care of; (*vigilar*) to guard.

custodio [kus'toðjo] *nm* guardian, keeper.

cutícula [ku'tikula] *nf* cuticle.

cutis ['kutis] *nm inv* skin, complexion.

cutre ['kutre] *a* (*fam: lugar*) grotty; (: *persona*) naff.

cuyo, a ['kujo, a] *pron* (*de quien*) whose; (*de que*) whose, of which; **en**

~ **caso** in which case.

C.V. *abr* (= *caballos de vapor*) H.P.

CH

chabacano, a [tʃaβa'kano, a] *a* vulgar, coarse.

chabola [tʃa'βola] *nf* shack; ~**s** *nfpl* shanty town *sg*.

chacal [tʃa'kal] *nm* jackal.

chacra ['tʃakra] *nf* (*AM*) smallholding.

chacha ['tʃatʃa] *nf* (*fam*) maid.

cháchara ['tʃatʃara] *nf* chatter; **estar de** ~ to chatter away.

chafar [tʃa'far] *vt* (*aplastar*) to crush; (*arruinar*) to ruin.

chal [tʃal] *nm* shawl.

chalado, a [tʃa'lado, a] *a* (*fam*) crazy.

chalé, chalet [tʃa'le] (*pl* **chalés, chalets**) *nm* villa, ≈ detached house.

chaleco [tʃa'leko] *nm* waistcoat, vest (*US*); ~ **salvavidas** life jacket.

chalupa [tʃa'lupa] *nf* launch, boat.

champán [tʃam'pan], **champaña** [tʃam'paɲa] *nm* champagne.

champiñón [tʃampi'ɲon] *nm* mushroom.

champú [tʃam'pu] (*pl* **champúes, champús**) *nm* shampoo.

chamuscar [tʃamus'kar] *vt* to scorch, sear, singe.

chance ['tʃanθe] *nm* (*AM*) chance.

chancho, a ['tʃantʃo, a] *nm/f* (*AM*) pig.

chanchullo [tʃan'tʃuʎo] *nm* (*fam*) fiddle.

chantaje [tʃan'taxe] *nm* blackmail.

chapa ['tʃapa] *nf* (*de metal*) plate, sheet; (*de madera*) board, panel; (*AM AUTO*) number (*Brit*) *o* license (*US*) plate.

chaparrón [tʃapa'rron] *nm* downpour, cloudburst.

chapotear [tʃapote'ar] *vt* to sponge down // *vi* (*fam*) to splash about.

chapucero, a [tʃapu'θero, a] *a* rough, crude // *nm/f* bungler.

chapurrear [tʃapurre'ar] *vt* (*idioma*) to speak badly.

chapuza [tʃa'puθa] *nf* botched job.

chaqueta [tʃa'keta] *nf* jacket.

charca ['tʃarka] *nf* pond, pool.

charco ['tʃarko] *nm* pool, puddle.

charcutería [tʃarkute'ria] *nf* (*tienda*) shop selling chiefly pork meat products; (*productos*) cooked pork meats *pl*.

charla ['tʃarla] *nf* talk, chat; (*conferencia*) lecture.

charlar [tʃar'lar] *vi* to talk, chat.

charlatán, ana [tʃarla'tan, ana] *nm/f* chatterbox; (*estafador*) trickster.

charol [tʃa'rol] *nm* varnish; (*cuero*) patent leather.

chascarrillo [tʃaska'rriʎo] *nm* (*fam*) funny story.

chasco ['tʃasko] *nm* (*broma*) trick, joke; (*desengaño*) disappointment.

chasis ['tʃasis] *nm inv* chassis.

chasquear [tʃaske'ar] *vt* (*látigo*) to crack; (*lengua*) to click; **chasquido** *nm* (*de lengua*) click; (*de látigo*) crack.

chatarra [tʃa'tarra] *nf* scrap (metal).

chato, a ['tʃato, a] *a* flat; (*nariz*) snub.

chaval, a [tʃa'βal, a] *nm/f* kid, lad/lass.

checo(e)slovaco, a [tʃeko(e)slo-'βako, a] *a, nm/f* Czech, Czechoslovak.

Checo(e)slovaquia [tʃeko(e)slo-'βakja] *nf* Czechoslovakia.

cheque ['tʃeke] *nm* cheque (*Brit*), check (*US*); ~ **de viajero** traveller's cheque (*Brit*), traveler's check (*US*).

chequeo [tʃe'keo] *nm* (*MED*) checkup; (*AUTO*) service.

chequera [tʃe'kera] *nf* (*AM*) chequebook (*Brit*), checkbook (*US*).

chicano, a [tʃi'kano, a] *a, nm/f* chicano.

chicle ['tʃikle] *nm* chewing gum.

chico, a ['tʃiko, a] *a* small, little // *nm/f* (*niño*) child; (*muchacho*) boy/girl.

chícharo ['tʃitʃaro] *nm* (*AM*) pea.

chicharrón [tʃitʃa'rron] nm (pork) crackling.

chichón [tʃi'tʃon] nm bump, lump.

chiflado, a [tʃi'flaðo, a] a crazy.

chiflar [tʃi'flar] vt to hiss, boo.

chile ['tʃile] nm chilli pepper.

Chile ['tʃile] nm Chile; **chileno, a** [tʃi'leno, a] a, nm/f Chilean.

chillar [tʃi'ʎar] vi (persona) to yell, scream; (animal salvaje) to howl; (cerdo) to squeal; (puerta) to creak.

chillido [tʃi'ʎiðo] nm (de persona) yell, scream; (de animal) howl; (de frenos) screech(ing).

chillón, ona [tʃi'ʎon, ona] a (niño) noisy; (color) loud, gaudy.

chimenea [tʃime'nea] nf chimney; (hogar) fireplace.

China ['tʃina] nf: **(la)** ~ China.

chinche ['tʃintʃe] nf (insecto) (bed)bug; (TEC) drawing pin (Brit), thumbtack (US) // nm/f nuisance, pest.

chincheta [tʃin'tʃeta] nf drawing pin (Brit), thumbtack (US).

chino, a ['tʃino, a] a, nm/f Chinese // nm (LING) Chinese.

Chipre ['tʃipre] nf Cyprus; **chipriota, chipriote** a, nm/f Cypriot.

chiquito, a [tʃi'kito, a] a very small, tiny // nm/f kid.

chiripa [tʃi'ripa] nf fluke.

chirriar [tʃi'rrjar] vi (goznes etc) to creak, squeak; (pájaros) to chirp, sing.

chirrido [tʃi'rriðo] nm creak(ing), squeak(ing); (de pájaro) chirp(ing).

chis [tʃis] excl sh!

chisme ['tʃisme] nm (habladurías) piece of gossip; (fam: objeto) thingummyjig.

chismoso, a [tʃis'moso, a] a gossiping // nm/f gossip.

chispa ['tʃispa] nf spark; (fig) sparkle; (ingenio) wit; (fam) drunkenness.

chispeante [tʃispe'ante] a sparkling.

chispear [tʃispe'ar] vi to spark; (lloviznar) to drizzle.

chisporrotear [tʃisporrote'ar] vi

(fuego) to throw out sparks; (leña) to crackle; (aceite) to hiss, splutter.

chiste ['tʃiste] nm joke, funny story.

chistoso, a [tʃis'toso, a] a (gracioso) funny, amusing; (bromista) witty.

chivo, a ['tʃiβo, a] nm/f (billy-/nanny-)goat; ~ **expiatorio** scapegoat.

chocante [tʃo'kante] a startling; (extraño) odd; (ofensivo) shocking.

chocar [tʃo'kar] vi (coches etc) to collide, crash // vt to shock; (sorprender) to startle; ~ **con** to collide with; (fig) to run into, run up against; **¡chócala!** (fam) put it there!

chocolate [tʃoko'late] a, nm chocolate.

chochear [tʃotʃe'ar] vi to dodder, be senile.

chocho, a ['tʃotʃo, a] a doddering, senile; (fig) soft, doting.

chollo ['tʃoʎo] nm (fam) bargain, snip.

choque etc vb ver **chocar** // ['tʃoke] nm (impacto) impact; (golpe) jolt; (AUTO) crash; (fig) conflict.

chorizo [tʃo'riθo] nm hard pork sausage, (type of) salami.

chorrear [tʃorre'ar] vi to gush (out), spout (out); (gotear) to drip, trickle.

chorro ['tʃorro] nm jet; (fig) stream.

choza ['tʃoθa] nf hut, shack.

chubasco [tʃu'βasko] nm squall.

chuleta [tʃu'leta] nf chop, cutlet.

chulo ['tʃulo] nm (pícaro) rascal; (rufián) pimp.

chupado, a [tʃu'paðo, a] a (delgado) skinny, gaunt.

chupete [tʃu'pete] nm dummy (Brit), pacifier (US).

chupar [tʃu'par] vt to suck; (absorber) to absorb; ~**se** vr to grow thin.

churro ['tʃurro, a] a coarse // nm (type of) fritter.

chusco, a ['tʃusko, a] a funny.

chusma ['tʃusma] *nf* rabble, mob.

chutar [tʃu'tar] *vi* (*DEPORTE*) to shoot (at goal).

D

D. *abr* (= *Don*) Esq.

Da. *abr* = **Doña.**

dactilógrafo, a [dakti'loɣrafo, a] *nm/f* typist.

dádiva ['daðiβa] *nf* (*donación*) donation; (*regalo*) gift; **dadivoso, a** *a* generous.

dado, a ['daðo, a] *pp* de **dar** // *nm* die; ~s *nmpl* dice; ~ **que** *conj* given that.

daltónico, a [dal'toniko, a] *a* colour-blind.

dama ['dama] *nf* (*gen*) lady; (*AJEDREZ*) queen; ~s *nfpl* (*juego*) draughts.

damasco [da'masko] *nm* damask.

damnificar [damnifi'kar] *vt* to harm; (*persona*) to injure.

danés, esa [da'nes, esa] *a* Danish // *nm/f* Dane.

danzar [dan'θar] *vt, vi* to dance.

dañar [da'ɲar] *vt* (*objeto*) to damage; (*persona*) to hurt; ~**se** *vr* (*objeto*) to get damaged.

dañino, a [da'ɲino, a] *a* harmful.

daño ['daɲo] *nm* (*a un objeto*) damage; (*a una persona*) harm, injury; ~**s y perjuicios** (*JUR*) damages; **hacer** ~ **a** to damage; (*persona*) to hurt, injure; **hacerse** ~ to hurt o.s.

dar [dar] ♦ *vt* **1** (*gen*) to give; (*obra de teatro*) to put on; (*film*) to show; (*fiesta*) to hold; ~ **algo a uno** to give sb sth o sth to sb; ~ **de beber a uno** to give sb a drink

2 (*producir: intereses*) to yield; (*fruta*) to produce

3 (*locuciones + n*): **da gusto escucharle** it's a pleasure to listen to him; *ver tb* **paseo** y *otros n*

4 (+ *n*: = *perifrasis de verbo*): **me**

da pena/asco it frightens/sickens me

5 (*considerar*): ~ **algo por descontado/entendido** to take sth for granted/as read; ~ **algo por concluido** to consider sth finished

6 (*hora*): **el reloj dio las 6** the clock struck 6 (o'clock)

7: **me da lo mismo** it's all the same to me; *ver tb* **igual, más**

♦ *vi* **1**: ~ **con: dimos con él dos horas más tarde** we came across him two hours later; **al final di con la solución** I eventually came up with the answer

2: ~ **en:** ~ **en** (*blanco, suelo*) to hit; **el sol me da en la cara** the sun is shining (right) on my face

3: ~ **de sí** (*zapatos etc*) to stretch, give

♦ ~**se** *vr* **1**: ~**se por vencido** to give up

2 (*ocurrir*): **se han dado muchos casos** there have been a lot of cases

3: ~**se a:** **se ha dado a la bebida** he's taken to drinking

4: **se me dan bien/mal las ciencias** I'm good/bad at science

5: **dárselas de: se las da de experto** he fancies himself *o* poses as an expert.

dardo ['darðo] *nm* dart.

dársena ['darsena] *nf* dock.

datar [da'tar] *vi*: ~ **de** to date from.

dátil ['datil] *nm* date.

dato ['dato] *nm* fact, piece of information.

dcha. *abr* (= *derecha*) r.h.

d. de J.C. *abr* (= *después de Jesucristo*) A.D.

de [de] *prep* (*de + el = del*) **1** (*posesión*) of; **la casa** ~ **Isabel/mis padres** Isabel's/my parents' house; **es** ~ **ellos** it's theirs

2 (*origen, distancia, con números*) from; **soy** ~ **Gijón** I'm from Gijón; ~ **8 a 20** from 8 to 20; **salir del cine** to go out of *o* leave the cinema; ~ ...

en ... from ... to ...; ~ 2 en 2 2 by 2, 2 at a time
3 (*valor descriptivo*): una copa ~ vino a glass of wine; la mesa ~ la cocina the kitchen table; un billete ~ 1000 pesetas a 1000 peseta note; un niño ~ tres años a three-year-old (child); una máquina ~ coser a sewing machine; ir vestido ~ gris to be dressed in grey; la niña del vestido azul the girl in the blue dress; trabaja ~ profesora she works as a teacher; ~ lado sideways; ~ atrás/delante rear/front
4 (*hora, tiempo*): a las 8 ~ la mañana at 8 o'clock in the morning; ~ día/noche by day/night; ~ hoy en ocho días a week from now; ~ niño era gordo as a child he was fat
5 (*comparaciones*): más/menos ~ cien personas more/less than a hundred people; el más caro ~ la tienda the most expensive in the shop; menos/más ~ lo pensado less/more than expected
6 (*causa*): del calor from the heat; ~ puro tonto out of sheer stupidity
7 (*tema*) about; clases ~ inglés English classes; ¿sabes algo ~ él? do you know anything about him?; un libro ~ física a physics book
8 (*adjetivo + de + infin*): fácil ~ entender easy to understand
9 (*oraciones pasivas*): fue respetado ~ todos he was loved by all
10 (*condicional + infin*) if; ~ ser posible if possible; ~ no terminarlo hoy if I *etc* don't finish it today.

dé *vb ver* **dar.**
deambular [deambu'lar] *vi* to stroll, wander.
debajo [de'βaxo] *ad* underneath; ~ de below, under; por ~ de beneath.
debate [de'βate] *nm* debate; **debatir** *vt* to debate.
deber [de'βer] *nm* duty // *vt* to owe // *vi*: **debe** (**de**) it must, it should;

~es *nmpl* (*ESCOL*) homework; **debo** hacerlo I must do it; **debe de** ir he should go; ~se *vr*: ~se a to be owing *o* due to.
debido, a [de'βiðo, a] *a* proper, just; ~ a a due to, because of.
débil ['deβil] *a* (*persona, carácter*) weak; (*luz*) dim; **debilidad** *nf* weakness; dimness.
debilitar [deβili'tar] *vt* to weaken; ~se *vr* to grow weak.
debutar [deβu'tar] *vi* to make one's debut.
década ['dekaða] *nf* decade.
decadencia [deka'ðenθja] *nf* (*estado*) decadence; (*proceso*) decline, decay.
decaer [deka'er] *vi* (*declinar*) to decline; (*debilitarse*) to weaken.
decaído, a [deka'iðo, a] *a*: **estar** ~ (*abatido*) to be down.
decaimiento [dekai'mjento] *nm* (*declinación*) decline; (*desaliento*) discouragement; (*MED*: *estado débil*) weakness.
decano [de'kano, a] *nm/f* (*de universidad etc*) dean.
decapitar [dekapi'tar] *vt* to behead.
decena [de'θena] *nf*: **una** ~ ten (or so).
decencia [de'θenθja] *nf* (*modestia*) modesty; (*honestidad*) respectability.
decente [de'θente] *a* (*correcto*) seemly, proper; (*honesto*) respectable.
decepción [deθep'θjon] *nf* disappointment.
decepcionar [deθepθjo'nar] *vt* to disappoint.
decidir [deθi'ðir] *vt* (*persuadir*) to convince, persuade; (*resolver*) to decide // *vi* to decide; ~se *vr*: ~se a to make up one's mind to.
décimo, a ['deθimo, a] *a* tenth // *nm* tenth.
decir [de'θir] *vt* (*expresar*) to say; (*contar*) to tell; (*hablar*) to speak // *nm* saying; ~se *vr*: **se dice que** it is said that; ~ **para** *o* **entre sí** to say to o.s.; **querer** ~ to mean;

¡dígame! (TEL) hello!; (en tienda) can I help you?

decisión [deθi'sjon] nf (resolución) decision; (firmeza) decisiveness.

decisivo, a [deθi'siβo, a] a decisive.

declamar [dekla'mar] vt, vi to declaim.

declaración [deklara'θjon] nf (manifestación) statement; (explicación) explanation.

declarar [dekla'rar] vt to declare, state; to explain // vi to declare; (JUR) to testify; ~se vr to propose.

declinar [dekli'nar] vt (gen) to decline; (JUR) to reject // vi (el día) to draw to a close.

declive [de'kliβe] nm (cuesta) slope; (fig) decline.

decolorarse [dekolo'rarse] vr to become discoloured.

decoración [dekora'θjon] nf decoration.

decorado [deko'raðo] nm (CINE, TEATRO) scenery, set.

decorar [deko'rar] vt to decorate; **decorativo, a** a ornamental, decorative.

decoro [de'koro] nm (respeto) respect; (dignidad) decency; (recato) propriety; ~so, a a (decente) decent; (modesto) modest; (digno) proper.

decrecer [dekre'θer] vi to decrease, diminish.

decrépito, a [de'krepito, a] a decrepit.

decretar [dekre'tar] vt to decree; **decreto** nm decree.

dedal [de'ðal] nm thimble.

dedicación [deðika'θjon] nf dedication; **dedicar** vt (libro) to dedicate; (tiempo, dinero) to devote; (palabras: decir, consagrar) to dedicate, devote; **dedicatoria** nf (de libro) dedication.

dedo ['deðo] nm finger; ~ del pie toe; ~ pulgar thumb; ~ índice index finger; ~ mayor o cordial middle finger; ~ anular ring finger; ~ meñique little finger; hacer ~

(fam) to hitch (a lift).

deducción [deðuk'θjon] nf deduction.

deducir [deðu'θir] vt (concluir) to deduce, infer; (COM) to deduct.

defecto [de'fekto] nm defect, flaw; **defectuoso, a** a defective, faulty.

defender [defen'der] vt to defend.

defensa [de'fensa] nf defence // nm (DEPORTE) defender, back; **defensivo, a** a defensive // nf: **a la defensiva** on the defensive.

defensor, a [defen'sor, a] a defending // nmf (abogado ~) defending counsel; (protector) protector.

deficiencia [defi'θjenθja] nf deficiency.

deficiente [defi'θjente] a (defectuoso) defective; ~ en lacking o deficient in; **ser un** ~ **mental** to be mentally handicapped.

déficit ['defiθit] (pl ~s) nm deficit.

definir [defi'nir] vt (determinar) to determine, establish; (decidir) to define; (aclarar) to clarify; **definitivo, a** a definitive; **en definitiva** definitively; (en resumen) in short.

deformación [deforma'θjon] nf (alteración) deformation; (RADIO etc) distortion.

deformar [defor'mar] vt (gen) to deform; ~se vr to become deformed; **deforme** a (informe) deformed; (feo) ugly; (malhecho) misshapen.

defraudar [defrau'ðar] vt (decepcionar) to disappoint; (estafar) to cheat; to defraud.

defunción [defun'θjon] nf death, demise.

degeneración [dexenera'θjon] nf (de las células) degeneration; (moral) degeneracy.

degenerar [dexene'rar] vi to degenerate.

degollar [devo'ʎar] vt to behead; (fig) to slaughter.

degradar [devra'ðar] vt to debase, degrade; ~se vr to demean o.s.

degustación [deɣusta'θjon] *nf* sampling, tasting.

deificar [deifi'kar] *vt* (*persona*) to deify.

dejadez [dexa'ðeθ] *nf* (*negligencia*) neglect; (*descuido*) untidiness, carelessness; **dejado, a** *a* (*negligente*) careless; (*indolente*) lazy.

dejar [de'xar] *vt* to leave; (*permitir*) to allow, let; (*abandonar*) to abandon, forsake; (*beneficios*) to produce, yield // *vi*: ~ **de** (*parar*) to stop; (*no hacer*) to fail to; **no dejes de comprar un billete** make sure you buy a ticket; ~ **a un lado** to leave o set aside.

dejo ['dexo] *nm* (*LING*) accent.

del [del] = **de** + **el**, *see* **de.**

delantal [delan'tal] *nm* apron.

delante [de'lante] *ad* in front, (*enfrente*) opposite; (*adelante*) ahead; ~ **de** in front of, before.

delantero, a [delan'tero, a] *a* front // *nm* (*DEPORTE*) forward, striker // *nf* (*de vestido, casa etc*) front part; (*DEPORTE*) forward line; **llevar la delantera (a uno)** to be ahead of (*sb*).

delatar [dela'tar] *vt* to inform on o against, betray; **delator, a** *nm/f* informer.

delegación [deleɣa'θjon] *nf* (*acción, delegados*) delegation; (*COM: oficina*) office, branch; ~ **de policía** police station.

delegado, a [dele'ɣaðo, a] *nm/f* delegate; (*COM*) agent.

delegar [dele'ɣar] *vt* to delegate.

deletrear [deletre'ar] *vt* to spell (out).

deleznable [deleθ'naβle] *a* brittle; (*excusa, idea*) feeble.

delfín [del'fin] *nm* dolphin.

delgadez [delɣa'ðeθ] *nf* thinness, slimness.

delgado, a [del'ɣaðo, a] *a* thin; (*persona*) slim, thin; (*tierra*) poor; (*tela etc*) light, delicate.

deliberación [deliβera'θjon] *nf* deliberation.

deliberar [deliβe'rar] *vt* to debate, discuss.

delicadeza [delika'ðeθa] *nf* (*gen*) delicacy; (*refinamiento, sutileza*) refinement.

delicado, a [deli'kaðo, a] *a* (*gen*) delicate; (*sensible*) sensitive; (*quisquilloso*) touchy.

delicia [de'liθja] *nf* delight.

delicioso, a [deli'θjoso, a] *a* (*gracioso*) delightful; (*exquisito*) delicious.

delincuencia [delin'kwenθja] *nf* delinquency; **delincuente** *nm/f* delinquent; (*criminal*) criminal.

delineante [deline'ante] *nm/f* draughtsman/woman.

delinear [deline'ar] *vt* (*dibujo*) to draw; (*fig, contornos*) to outline.

delinquir [delin'kir] *vi* to commit an offence.

delirante [deli'rante] *a* delirious.

delirar [deli'rar] *vi* to be delirious, rave.

delirio [de'lirjo] *nm* (*MED*) delirium; (*palabras insensatas*) ravings *pl.*.

delito [de'lito] *nm* (*gen*) crime; (*infracción*) offence.

demacrado, a [dema'kraðo, a] *a*: **estar** ~ to look pale and drawn, be wasted away.

demagogo, a [dema'ɣoɣo, a] *nm/f* demagogue.

demanda [de'manda] *nf* (*pedido, COM*) demand; (*petición*) request; (*JUR*) action, lawsuit.

demandante [deman'dante] *nm/f* claimant.

demandar [deman'dar] *vt* (*gen*) to demand; (*JUR*) to sue, file a lawsuit against.

demarcación [demarka'θjon] *nf* (*de terreno*) demarcation.

demás [de'mas] *a*: **los** ~ **niños** the other children, the remaining children // *pron*: **los/las** ~ the others, the rest (of them); **lo** ~ the rest of it.

demasía [dema'sia] *nf* (*exceso*) excess, surplus; **comer en** ~ to eat to excess.

demasiado, a [dema'sjaðo, a] *a* too, too much; ~s too many // *ad* too, too much; ¡es ~! it's too much!; ¡qué ~! (*fam*) great!

demencia [de'menθja] *nf* (*locura*) madness; **demente** *nmf* lunatic // *a* mad, insane.

democracia [demo'kraθja] *nf* democracy.

demócrata [de'mokrata] *nm/f* democrat; **democrático, a** *a* democratic.

demoler [demo'ler] *vt* to demolish; **demolición, a** *a* demolition.

demonio [de'monjo] *nm* devil, demon; ¡~s! hell!, damn!; ¿cómo ~s? how the hell?

demora [de'mora] *nf* delay; **demorar** *vt* (*retardar*) to delay, hold back; (*detener*) to hold up // *vi* to linger, stay on; ~se *vr* to be delayed.

demos *vb ver* **dar**.

demostración [demostra'θjon] *nf* (*de teorema*) demonstration; (*de afecto*) show, display.

demostrar [demos'trar] *vt* (*probar*) to prove; (*mostrar*) to show; (*manifestar*) to demonstrate; **demostrativo, a** *a* demonstrative.

demudado, a [demu'ðaðo, a] *a* (*rostro*) pale.

den *vb ver* **dar**.

denegar [dene'var] *vt* (*rechazar*) to refuse; (*JUR*) to reject.

denigrar [deni'vrar] *vt* (*desacreditar, infamar*) to denigrate; (*injuriar*) to insult.

denominación [denomina'θjon] *nf* (*clase*) denomination.

denotar [deno'tar] *vt* (*indicar*) to indicate; (*significar*) to denote.

densidad [densi'ðað] *nf* (*FÍSICA*) density; (*fig*) thickness.

denso, a [ˈdenso, a] *a* (*apretado*) solid; (*espeso, pastoso*) thick; (*fig*) heavy.

dentadura [denta'ðura] *nf* (*set of*) teeth *pl*; ~ **postiza** false teeth *pl*.

dentera [den'tera] *nf* (*sensación desagradable*) the shivers *pl*.

dentífrico, a [den'tifriko, a] *a* dental // *nm* toothpaste.

dentista [den'tista] *nm/f* dentist.

dentro [ˈdentro] *ad* inside // *prep*: ~ **de**, in, inside, within; **mirar por** ~ to look inside; ~ **de tres meses** within three months.

denuncia [de'nunθja] *nf* (*delación*) denunciation; (*acusación*) accusation; (*de accidente*) report; **denunciar** *vt* to report; (*delatar*) to inform on *o* against.

departamento [departa'mento] *nm* (*sección administrativa*) department, section; (*AM*: *piso*) flat (*Brit*), apartment.

departir [depar'tir] *vi* to converse.

dependencia [depen'denθja] *nf* dependence; (*POL*) dependency; (*COM*) office, section.

depender [depen'der] *vi*: ~ **de** to depend on.

dependienta [depen'djenta] *nf* saleswoman, shop assistant.

dependiente [depen'djente] *a* dependent // *nm* salesman, shop assistant.

depilar [depi'lar] *vt* (*con cera*) to wax; (*cejas*) to pluck; **depilatorio** *nm* hair remover.

deplorable [deplo'raßle] *a* deplorable.

deplorar [deplo'rar] *vt* to deplore.

deponer [depo'ner] *vt* to lay down // *vi* (*JUR*) to give evidence; (*declarar*) to make a statement.

deportar [depor'tar] *vt* to deport.

deporte [de'porte] *nm* sport; **deportista** *a* sports *cpd* // *nm/f* sportsman/woman; **deportivo, a** *a* (*club, periódico*) sports *cpd* // *nm* sports car.

depositante [deposi'tante], **depositador, a** [deposita'ðor, a] *nm/f* depositor.

depositar [deposi'tar] *vt* (*dinero*) to deposit; (*mercaderías*) to put away, store; (*persona*) to confide; ~se *vr* to settle; ~io, a *nm/f* trustee.

depósito [de'posito] *nm* (*gen*)

deposit; (de mercaderías) ware-house, store; (de agua, gasolina etc) tank.

depravar [depra'βar] vt to deprave, corrupt; ~se vr to become depraved.

depreciar [depre'θjar] vt to depreciate, reduce the value of; ~se vr to depreciate, lose value.

depredador, a [depreða'ðor, a] a (ZOOL) predatory // nm (ZOOL) pre-dator.

depresión [depre'sjon] nf depression.

deprimido, a [depri'miðo, a] a depressed.

deprimir [depri'mir] vt to depress; ~se vr (persona) to become depressed.

deprisa [de'prisa] ad quickly, hur-riedly.

depuración [depura'θjon] nf pur-ification; (POL) purge; **depurar** vt to purify; (purgar) to purge.

derecha [de'retʃa] nf right(-hand) side; (POL) right; **a la ~** (estar) on the right; (torcer etc) (to the) right.

derecho, a [de'retʃo, a] a right, right-hand // nm (privilegio) right; (lado) right(-hand) side; (leyes) law // ad straight, directly; ~s nmpl (de aduana) duty sg; (de autor) royalties; **tener ~ a** to have a right to.

deriva [de'riβa] nf: **ir o estar a la ~** to drift, be adrift.

derivado [deri'βaðo] nm (COM) by-product.

derivar [deri'βar] vt to derive; (desviar) to direct // vi, ~se vr to derive, be derived; (NAUT) to drift.

derramamiento [derrama'mjento] nm (de sangre) shedding; (disper-sión) spilling.

derramar [derra'mar] vt to spill; (verter) to pour out; (esparcir) to scatter; ~se vr to pour out; ~ **lágri-mas** to weep.

derrame [de'rrame] nm (de líquido) spilling; (de sangre) shedding; (de tubo etc) overflow; (pérdida) leak-age; (MED) discharge; (declive)

slope.

derredor [derre'ðor] ad: **al o en ~ de** around, about.

derretido, a [derre'tiðo, a] a (metal) molten.

derretir [derre'tir] vt (gen) to melt; (nieve) to thaw; (fig) to squander; ~se vr to melt.

derribar [derri'βar] vt to knock down; (construcción) to demolish; (persona, gobierno, político) to bring down.

derrocar [derro'kar] vt (gobierno) to bring down, overthrow.

derrochar [derro'tʃar] vt to squander; **derroche** nm (despilfarro) waste, squandering.

derrota [de'rrota] nf (NAUT) course; (MIL, DEPORTE etc) defeat, rout; **derrotar** vt (gen) to defeat; **der-rotero** nm (rumbo) course.

derrumbar [derrum'bar] vt to throw down; ~se vr to collapse.

des vb ver **dar**.

desabotonar [desaβoto'nar] vt to unbutton, undo // vi (flores) to bloom; ~se vr to come undone.

desabrido, a [desa'βriðo, a] a (comida) insipid, tasteless; (persona) rude, surly; (respuesta) sharp; (tiempo) unpleasant.

desabrochar [desaβro'tʃar] vt (botones, broches) to undo, unfasten; ~se vr (ropa etc) to come undone.

desacato [desa'kato] nm (falta de respeto) disrespect; (JUR) contempt.

desacertado, a [desaθer'taðo, a] a (equivocado) mistaken; (inoportuno) unwise.

desacierto [desa'θjerto] nm mistake, error.

desaconsejado, a [desakonse'xaðo, a] a ill-advised.

desaconsejar [desakonse'xar] vt to advise against.

desacorde [desa'korðe] a dis-cordant; **estar ~ con algo** to dis-agree with sth.

desacreditar [desakreði'tar] vt (de-sprestigiar) to discredit, bring into disrepute; (*denigrar*) to run down.

desacuerdo [desaˈkwerðo] *nm* (*conflicto*) disagreement, discord; (*error*) error, blunder.

desafiar [desaˈfjar] *vt* (*retar*) to challenge; (*enfrentarse a*) to defy.

desafilado, a [desafiˈlaðo, a] *a* blunt.

desafinado, a [desafiˈnaðo, a] *a*: estar ~ to be out of tune.

desafinarse [desafiˈnarse] *vr* to go out of tune.

desafío *etc vb ver* **desafiar** // [desaˈfio] *nm* (*reto*) challenge; (*combate*) duel; (*resistencia*) defiance.

desaforado, a [desafoˈraðo, a] *a* (*grito*) ear-splitting; (*comportamiento*) outrageous.

desafortunadamente [desafortunaðaˈmente] *ad* unfortunately.

desafortunado, a [desafortuˈnaðo, a] *a* (*desgraciado*) unfortunate, unlucky.

desagradable [desaɣraˈðaβle] *a* (*fastidioso, enojoso*) unpleasant; (*irritante*) disagreeable.

desagradar [desaɣraˈðar] *vi* (*disgustar*) to displease; (*molestar*) to bother.

desagradecido, a [desaɣraðeˈθiðo, a] *a* ungrateful.

desagrado [desaˈɣraðo] *nm* (*disgusto*) displeasure; (*contrariedad*) dissatisfaction.

desagraviar [desaɣraˈβjar] *vt* to make amends to; **desagravio** *nm* (*satisfacción*) amends; (*compensación*) compensation.

desagüe [desˈaɣwe] *nm* (*de un líquido*) drainage; (*cañería*) drainpipe; (*salida*) outlet, drain.

desaguisado, a [desaɣiˈsaðo, a] *a* illegal // *nm* outrage.

desahogado, a [desaoˈɣaðo, a] *a* (*holgado*) comfortable; (*espacioso*) roomy, large.

desahogar [desaoˈɣar] *vt* (*aliviar*) to ease, relieve; (*ira*) to vent; ~se *vr* (*relajarse*) to relax; (*desfogarse*) to

let off steam.

desahogo [desaˈoɣo] *nm* (*alivio*) relief; (*comodidad*) comfort, ease.

desahuciar [desauˈθjar] *vt* (*enfermo*) to give up hope for; (*inquilino*) to evict; **desahucio** *nm* eviction.

desairar [desaiˈrar] *vt* (*menospreciar*) to slight, snub; (*cosa*) to disregard.

desaire [desˈaire] *nm* (*menosprecio*) slight; (*falta de garbo*) unattractiveness.

desajustar [desaxusˈtar] *vt* (*desarreglar*) to disarrange; (*desconcertar*) to throw off balance; ~se *vr* to get out of order; (*aflojarse*) to loosen.

desajuste [desaˈxuste] *nm* (*de máquina*) disorder; (*situación*) imbalance.

desalentador, a [desalentaˈðor, a] *a* disheartening.

desalentar [desalenˈtar] *vt* (*desanimar*) to discourage.

desaliento *etc vb ver* **desalentar** // [desaˈljento] *nm* discouragement.

desaliño [desaˈliɲo] *nm* (*negligencia*) slovenliness.

desalmado, a [desalˈmaðo, a] *a* (*cruel*) cruel, heartless.

desalojar [desaloˈxar] *vt* (*expulsar, echar*) to eject; (*abandonar*) to move out of // *vi* to move out.

desamarrar [desamaˈrrar] *vt* to untie; (*NAUT*) to cast off.

desamor [desaˈmor] *nm* (*frialdad*) indifference; (*odio*) dislike.

desamparado, a [desampaˈraðo, a] *a* (*persona*) helpless; (*lugar: expuesto*) exposed; (*desierto*) deserted.

desamparar [desampaˈrar] *vt* (*abandonar*) to desert, abandon; (*JUR*) to leave defenceless; (*barco*) to abandon.

desandar [desanˈdar] *vt*: ~ lo andado *o* el camino to retrace one's steps.

desangrar [desanˈgrar] *vt* to bleed; (*fig: persona*) to bleed dry; ~se *vr* to lose a lot of blood.

desanimado, a [desani'maðo, a] *a* (*persona*) downhearted; (*espectáculo, fiesta*) dull.

desanimar [desani'mar] *vt* (*desalentar*) to discourage; (*deprimir*) to depress; ~se *vr* to lose heart.

desapacible [desapa'θiβle] *a* (*gen*) unpleasant.

desaparecer [desapare'θer] *vi* (*gen*) to disappear; (*el sol, la luz*) to vanish; **desaparecido, a** *a* missing; **desaparecidos** *nmpl* (*en accidente*) people missing; **desaparición** *nf* disappearance.

desapasionado, a [desapasjo'naðo, a] *a* dispassionate, impartial.

desapego [desa'peɣo] *nm* (*frialdad*) coolness; (*distancia*) detachment.

desapercibido, a [desaperθi'βiðo, a] *a* (*desprevenido*) unprepared; **pasar** ~ to go unnoticed.

desaplicado, a [desapli'kaðo, a] *a* slack, lazy.

desaprensivo, a [desapren'siβo, a] *a* unscrupulous.

desaprobar [desapro'βar] *vt* (*reprobar*) to disapprove of; (*condenar*) to condemn; (*no consentir*) to reject.

desaprovechado, a [desaproβe-'tʃaðo, a] *a* (*oportunidad, tiempo*) wasted; (*estudiante*) slack.

desaprovechar [desaproβe'tʃar] *vt* to waste.

desarmar [desar'mar] *vt* (*MIL, fig*) to disarm; (*TEC*) to take apart, dismantle; **desarme** *nm* disarmament.

desarraigar [desarrai'ɣar] *vt* to uproot; **desarraigo** *nm* uprooting.

desarreglado, a [desarre'ɣlaðo, a] *a* (*desordenado*) disorderly, untidy.

desarreglar [desarre'ɣlar] *vt* (*desordenar*) to disarrange; (*trastocar*) to upset, disturb.

desarreglo [desa'rreɣlo] *nm* (*de casa, persona*) untidiness; (*desorden*) disorder.

desarrollar [desarro'ʎar] *vt* (*gen*) to develop; (*extender*) to unfold; ~se

vr to develop; (*extenderse*) to open (out); (*FOTO*) to develop; **desarrollo** *nm* development.

desarticular [desartiku'lar] *vt* (*hueso*) to dislocate; (*objeto*) to take apart, (*fig*) to break up.

desaseo [desa'seo] *nm* (*suciedad*) slovenliness; (*desarreglo*) untidiness.

desasir [desa'sir] *vt* to loosen; ~se *vr* to extricate o.s.; ~se de to let go, give up.

desasosegar [desasose'ɣar] *vt* (*inquietar*) to disturb, make uneasy; ~se *vr* to become uneasy.

desasosiego *etc vb ver* **desasosegar** // [desaso'sjeɣo] *nm* (*intranquilidad*) uneasiness, restlessness; (*ansiedad*) anxiety.

desastrado, a [desas'traðo, a] *a* (*desaliñado*) shabby; (*sucio*) dirty.

desastre [de'sastre] *nm* disaster; **desastroso, a** *a* disastrous.

desatado, a [desa'taðo, a] *a* (*desligado*) untied; (*violento*) violent, wild.

desatar [desa'tar] *vt* (*nudo*) to untie; (*paquete*) to undo; (*separar*) to detach; ~se *vr* (*zapatos*) to come untied; (*tormenta*) to break.

desatascar [desatas'kar] *vt* (*cañería*) to unblock, clear.

desatender [desaten'der] *vt* (*no prestar atención a*) to disregard; (*abandonar*) to neglect.

desatento, a [desa'tento, a] *a* (*distraído*) inattentive; (*descortés*) discourteous.

desatinado, a [desati'naðo, a] *a* foolish, silly; **desatino** *nm* (*idiotez*) foolishness, folly; (*error*) blunder.

desatornillar [desatorni'ʎar] *vt* to unscrew.

desautorizado, a [desautori'θaðo, a] *a* unauthorized.

desautorizar [desautori'θar] *vt* (*oficial*) to deprive of authority; (*informe*) to deny.

desavenencia [desaβe'nenθja] *nf* (*desacuerdo*) disagreement; (*discrepancia*) quarrel.

desaventajado, a [desaßenta'xaðo, a] *a* (*inferior*) inferior; (*poco ventajoso*) disadvantageous.

desayunar [desaju'nar] *vi* to have breakfast // *vt* to have for breakfast; **desayuno** *nm* breakfast.

desazón [desa'θon] *nf* (*angustia*) anxiety; (*fig*) annoyance.

desazonar [desaθo'nar] *vt* (*fig*) to annoy, upset; ~**se** *vr* (*enojarse*) to be annoyed; (*preocuparse*) to worry, be anxious.

desbandarse [desßan'darse] *vr* (*MIL*) to disband; (*fig*) to flee in disorder.

desbarajuste [desßara'xuste] *nm* confusion, disorder.

desbaratar [desßara'tar] *vt* (*deshacer, destruir*) to ruin.

desbloquear [desßloke'ar] *vt* (*negociaciones, tráfico*) to get going again; (*COM: cuenta*) to unfreeze.

desbocado, a [desßo'kaðo, a] *a* (*caballo*) runaway.

desbordar [desßor'ðar] *vt* (*sobrepasar*) to go beyond; (*exceder*) to exceed // *vi*, ~**se** *vr* (*río*) to overflow; (*entusiasmo*) to erupt.

descabalgar [deskaßal'var] *vi* to dismount.

descabellado, a [deskaße'Áaðo, a] *a* (*disparatado*) wild, crazy.

descabellar [deskaße'Áar] *vt* to ruffle; (*TAUR: toro*) to give the coup de grace to.

descafeinado, a [deskafei'naðo, a] *a* decaffeinated // *nm* decaffeinated coffee.

descalabro [deska'laßro] *nm* blow; (*desgracia*) misfortune.

descalificar [deskalifi'kar] *vt* to disqualify; (*desacreditar*) to discredit.

descalzar [deskal'θar] *vt* (*zapato*) to take off; **descalzo, a** *a* barefoot(ed); (*fig*) destitute.

descambiar [deskam'bjar] *vt* to exchange.

descaminado, a [deskami'naðo, a] *a* (*equivocado*) on the wrong road; (*fig*) misguided.

descampado [deskam'paðo] *nm* open space.

descansado, a [deskan'saðo, a] *a* (*gen*) rested; (*que tranquiliza*) restful.

descansar [deskan'sar] *vt* (*gen*) to rest // *vi* to rest, have a rest; (*echarse*) to lie down.

descansillo [deskan'siÁo] *nm* (*de escalera*) landing.

descanso [des'kanso] *nm* (*reposo*) rest; (*alivio*) relief; (*pausa*) break; (*DEPORTE*) interval, half time.

descapotable [deskapo'taßle] *nm* (*tb:* **coche** ~) convertible.

descarado, a [deska'raðo, a] *a* (*sin vergüenza*) shameless; (*insolente*) cheeky.

descarga [des'karva] *nf* (*ARQ, ELEC, MIL*) discharge; (*NAUT*) unloading.

descargar [deskar'var] *vt* to unload; (*golpe*) to let fly; ~**se** *vr* to unburden o.s.; **descargo** *nm* (*COM*) receipt; (*JUR*) evidence.

descarnado, a [deskar'naðo, a] *a* scrawny; (*fig*) bare.

descaro [des'karo] *nm* nerve.

descarriar [deska'rrjar] *vt* (*descaminar*) to misdirect; (*fig*) to lead astray; ~**se** *vr* (*perderse*) to lose one's way; (*separarse*) to stray; (*pervertirse*) to err, go astray.

descarrilamiento [deskarrila-'mjento] *nm* (*de tren*) derailment.

descarrilar [deskarri'lar] *vi* to be derailed.

descartar [deskar'tar] *vt* (*rechazar*) to reject; (*eliminar*) to rule out; ~**se** *vr* (*NAIPES*) to discard; ~**se de** to shirk.

descascarillado, a [deskaskari-'Áaðo, a] *a* (*paredes*) peeling.

descendencia [desðen'denθja] *nf* (*origen*) origin, descent; (*hijos*) offspring.

descender [desðen'der] *vt* (*bajar: escalera*) to go down // *vi* to descend; (*temperatura, nivel*) to fall, drop; ~ **de** to be descended from.

descendiente [desθen'djente] *nm/f* descendant.

descenso [des'θenso] *nm* descent; (*de temperatura*) drop.

descifrar [desθi'frar] *vt* to decipher; (*mensaje*) to decode.

descolgar [deskol'ɣar] *vt* (*bajar*) to take down; (*teléfono*) to pick up; ~**se** *vr* to let o.s. down.

descolorido, a [deskolo'riðo, a] *a* (*pálido*) pale. = faded;

descompaginar [deskompaxi'nar] *vt* (*desordenar*) to disarrange, mess up.

descompasado, a [deskompa'saðo, a] *a* (*sin proporción*) out of all proportion; (*excesivo*) excessive.

descomponer [deskompo'ner] *vt* (*desordenar*) to disarrange, disturb; (*TEC*) to put out of order; (*dividir*) to break down (into parts); (*fig*) to provoke; ~**se** *vr* (*corromperse*) to rot, decompose; (*el tiempo*) to change (for the worse); (*TEC*) to break down.

descomposición [deskomposi'θjon] *nf* (*gen*) breakdown; (*de fruta etc*) decomposition.

descompostura [deskompos'tura] *nf* (*TEC*) breakdown; (*desorganización*) disorganization; (*desorden*) untidiness.

descompuesto, a [deskom'pwesto, a] *a* (*corrompido*) decomposed; (*roto*) broken.

descomunal [deskomu'nal] *a* (*enorme*) huge.

desconcertado, a [deskonθer'taðo, a] *a* disconcerted, bewildered.

desconcertar [deskonθer'tar] *vt* (*confundir*) to baffle; (*incomodar*) to upset, put out; ~**se** *vr* (*turbarse*) to be upset.

desconchado, a [deskon'tʃaðo, a] *a* (*pintura*) peeling.

desconcierto *etc vb ver* **desconcertar** // [deskon'θjerto] *nm* (*gen*) disorder; (*desorientación*) uncertainty; (*inquietud*) uneasiness.

desconectar [deskonek'tar] *vt* to disconnect.

desconfianza [deskon'fjanθa] *nf* distrust.

desconfiar [deskon'fjar] *vi* to be distrustful; ~ **de** to distrust, suspect.

descongelar [deskonxe'lar] *vt* to defrost; (*COM, POL*) to unfreeze.

descongestionar [deskonxestjo'nar] *vt* (*cabeza, tráfico*) to clear.

desconocer [deskono'θer] *vt* (*ignorar*) not to know, be ignorant of; (*no aceptar*) to deny; (*repudiar*) to disown.

desconocido, a [deskono'θiðo, a] *a* unknown // *nm/f* stranger.

desconocimiento [deskonoθi'mjento] *nm* (*falta de conocimientos*) ignorance; (*repudio*) disregard.

desconsiderado, a [deskonsiðe'raðo, a] *a* (*descuidado*) inconsiderate; (*insensible*) thoughtless.

desconsolar [deskonso'lar] *vt* to distress; ~**se** *vr* to despair.

desconsuelo *etc vb ver* **desconsolar** // [deskon'swelo] *nm* (*tristeza*) distress; (*desesperación*) despair.

descontado, a [deskon'taðo, a] *a*: **dar por** ~ **(que)** to take (it) for granted (that).

descontar [deskon'tar] *vt* (*deducir*) to take away, deduct; (*rebajar*) to discount.

descontento, a [deskon'tento, a] *a* dissatisfied // *nm* dissatisfaction, discontent.

descorazonar [deskoraθo'nar] *vt* to discourage, dishearten.

descorchar [deskor'tʃar] *vt* to uncork.

descorrer [desko'rrer] *vt* (*cortinas, cerrojo*) to draw back.

descortés [deskor'tes] *a* (*mal educado*) discourteous; (*grosero*) rude.

descoser [desko'ser] *vt* to unstitch; ~**se** *vr* to come apart (at the seams).

descosido, a [desko'siðo, a] *a* a

(*COSTURA*) unstitched; (*desordenado*) disjointed.

descrédito [des'kreðito] nm discredit.

descreído, a [deskre'iðo, a] a (*incrédulo*) incredulous; (*falto de fe*) unbelieving.

descremado, a [deskre'maðo, a] a skimmed.

describir [deskri'βir] vt to describe; **descripción** [deskrip'θjon] nf description.

descrito [des'krito] pp de **describir**.

descuartizar [deskwarti'θar] vt (*animal*) to cut up.

descubierto, a pp de **descubrir** // [desku'βjerto, a] a uncovered, bare; (*persona*) bareheaded // nm (*bancario*) overdraft; **al ~** in the open.

descubrimiento [deskuβri'mjento] nm (*hallazgo*) discovery; (*revelación*) revelation.

descubrir [desku'βrir] vt to discover, find; (*inaugurar*) to unveil; (*vislumbrar*) to detect; (*revelar*) to reveal, show; (*destapar*) to uncover; **~se** vr to reveal o.s.; (*quitarse sombrero*) to take off one's hat; (*confesar*) to confess.

descuento etc vb ver **descontar** // [des'kwento] nm discount.

descuidado, a [deskwi'ðaðo, a] a (*sin cuidado*) careless; (*desordenado*) untidy; (*olvidadizo*) forgetful; (*dejado*) neglected; (*desprevenido*) unprepared.

descuidar [deskwi'ðar] vt (*dejar*) to neglect; (*olvidar*) to overlook // vi, **~se** vr (*distraerse*) to be careless; (*estar desaliñado*) to let o.s. go; (*desprevenirse*) to drop one's guard; **¡descuida!** don't worry!; **descuido** nm (*dejadez*) carelessness; (*olvido*) negligence.

---

desde ['desðe] ◆ prep 1 (*lugar*) from; ~ Burgos hasta mi casa hay 30 km it's 30 kms from Burgos to my house

2 (*posición*): hablaba ~ el balcón she was speaking from the balcony

3 (*tiempo*: + ad, n): ~ ahora from now on; ~ la boda since the wedding; ~ niño since I etc was a child; ~ 3 años atrás since 3 years ago

4 (*tiempo*: + vb) since; for; nos conocemos ~ 1978/hace 20 años we've known each other since 1978/for 20 years; no le veo ~ 1983/hace 5 años I haven't seen him since 1983/for 5 years

5 (*gama*): ~ los más lujosos hasta los más económicos from the most luxurious to the most reasonably priced

6: ~ luego (que no) of course (not)
◆ conj: ~ que: ~ que recuerdo for as long as o ever since I can remember; ~ que llegó no ha salido he hasn't been out since he arrived.

---

desdecirse [desðe'θirse] vr to retract; ~ de to go back on.

desdén [des'ðen] nm scorn.

desdeñar [desðe'nar] vt (*despreciar*) to scorn.

desdicha [des'ðitʃa] nf (*desgracia*) misfortune; (*infelicidad*) unhappiness; **desdichado, a** a (*sin suerte*) unlucky; (*infeliz*) unhappy.

desdoblar [desðo'βlar] vt (*extender*) to spread out; (*desplegar*) to unfold.

desear [dese'ar] vt to want, desire, wish for.

desecar [dese'kar] vt, **desecarse** vr to dry up.

desechar [dese'tʃar] vt (*basura*) to throw out o away; (*ideas*) to reject, discard; **desechos** nmpl rubbish sg, waste sg.

desembalar [desemba'lar] vt to unpack.

desembarazado, a [desembara'θaðo, a] a (*libre*) clear, free; (*desenvuelto*) free and easy.

desembarazar [desembara'θar] vt (*desocupar*) to clear; (*desenredar*) to free; **~se** vr: **~se de** to free o.s. of, get rid of.

desembarcar [desembar'kar] vt (mercancías etc) to unload // vi, ~se vr to disembark.

desembocadura [desemboka'ðura] nf (de río) mouth; (de calle) opening.

desembocar [desembo'kar] vi to flow into; (fig) to result in.

desembolso [desem'bolso] nm payment.

desembragar [desembra'var] vi to declutch.

desemejanza [deseme'xanθa] nf dissimilarity.

desempatar [desempa'tar] vi to replay, hold a play-off; **desempate** nm (FÚTBOL) replay, play-off; (TENIS) tie-break(er).

desempeñar [desempe'ɲar] vt (cargo) to hold; (papel) to perform; (lo empeñado) to redeem; ~se vr to get out of debt; ~ un papel (fig) to play (a role).

desempeño [desem'peɲo] nm redeeming; (de cargo) occupation.

desempleado, a [desemple'aðo, a] nm/f unemployed person; **desempleo** nm unemployment.

desempolvar [desempol'ßar] vt (muebles etc) to dust; (lo olvidado) to revive.

desencadenar [desenkaðe'nar] vt to unchain; (ira) to unleash; ~se vr to break loose; (tormenta) to burst; (guerra) to break out.

desencajar [desenka'xar] vt (hueso) to put out of joint; (mandíbula) to dislocate; (mecanismo, pieza) to disconnect, disengage.

desencanto [desen'kanto] nm disillusionment.

desenchufar [desentʃu'far] vt to unplug.

desenfadado, a [desenfa'ðaðo, a] a (desenvuelto) uninhibited; (descarado) forward; **desenfado** nm (libertad) freedom; (comportamiento) free and easy manner; (descaro) forwardness.

desenfocado, a [desenfo'kaðo, a] a

(FOTO) out of focus.

desenfrenado, a [desenfre'naðo, a] a (descontrolado) uncontrolled; (inmoderado) unbridled; **desenfreno** nm (vicio) wildness; (de las pasiones) lack of self-control.

desenganchar [desengan'tʃar] vt (gen) to unhook; (FERRO) to uncouple.

desengañar [desenga'ɲar] vt to disillusion; ~se vr to become disillusioned; **desengaño** nm disillusionment; (decepción) disappointment.

desenlace [desen'laθe] nm outcome.

desenmarañar [desenmara'ɲar] vt (fig) to unravel.

desenmascarar [desenmaska'rar] vt to unmask.

desenredar [desenre'ðar] vt (pelo) to untangle; (problema) to sort out.

desentenderse [desenten'derse] vr: ~ de to pretend not to know about; (apartarse) to have nothing to do with.

desenterrar [desente'rrar] vt to exhume; (tesoro, fig) to unearth, dig up.

desentonar [desento'nar] vi (MUS) to sing (o play) out of tune; (color) to clash.

desentrañar [desentra'ɲar] vt (misterio) to unravel.

desentumecer [desentume'θer] vt (pierna etc) to stretch; (DEPORTE) to loosen up.

desenvoltura [desenßol'tura] nf (libertad, gracia) ease; (descaro) free and easy manner.

desenvolver [desenßol'ßer] vt (paquete) to unwrap; (fig) to develop; ~se vr (desarrollarse) to unfold, develop; (arreglárselas) to cope.

deseo [de'seo] nm desire, wish; ~**so, a** a: estar ~so de to be anxious to.

desequilibrado, a [desekili'ßraðo, a] a unbalanced.

desertar [deser'tar] vi to desert.

desértico, a [de'sertiko, a] a desert

cpd.

desesperación [desespera'θjon] nf (impaciencia) desperation; (irritación) fury.

desesperar [desespe'rar] vt to drive to despair; (exasperar) to drive to distraction // vi: ~ **de** to despair of; ~**se** vr to despair, lose hope.

desestabilizar [desestaβili'θar] vt to destabilize.

desestimar [desesti'mar] vt (menospreciar) to have a low opinion of; (rechazar) to reject.

desfachatez [desfatʃa'teθ] nf (insolencia) impudence; (descaro) rudeness.

desfalco [des'falko] nm embezzlement.

desfallecer [desfaλe'θer] vi (perder las fuerzas) to become weak; (desvanecerse) to faint.

desfasado, a [desfa'saðo, a] a (anticuado) old-fashioned; **desfase** nm (diferencia) gap.

desfavorable [desfaβo'raβle] a unfavourable.

desfigurar [desfiɣu'rar] vt (cara) to disfigure; (cuerpo) to deform.

desfiladero [desfila'ðero] nm gorge.

desfilar [desfi'lar] vi to parade; **desfile** nm procession.

desfogarse [desfo'ɣarse] vr (fig) to let off steam.

desgajar [desɣa'xar] vt (arrancar) to tear off; (romper) to break off; ~**se** vr to come off.

desgana [des'ɣana] nf (falta de apetito) loss of appetite; (renuncia) unwillingness; ~**do, a** a: **estar** ~ (sin apetito) to have no appetite; (sin entusiasmo) to have lost interest.

desgarrador, a [desɣarra'ðor, a] a (fig) heartrending.

desgarrar [desɣa'rrar] vt to tear (up); (fig) to shatter; **desgarro** nm (en tela) tear; (aflicción) grief; (descaro) impudence.

desgastar [desɣas'tar] vt (deteriorar) to wear away o down; (estropear) to spoil; ~**se** vr to get

worn out; **desgaste** nm wear (and tear).

desgracia [des'ɣraθja] nf misfortune; (accidente) accident; (vergüenza) disgrace; (contratiempo) setback; **por** ~ unfortunately.

desgraciado, a [desɣra'θjaðo, a] a (sin suerte) unlucky, unfortunate; (miserable) wretched; (infeliz) miserable.

desgreñado, a [desɣre'naðo, a] a dishevelled.

deshabitado, a [desaβi'taðo, a] a uninhabited.

deshacer [desa'θer] vt (casa) to break up; (TEC) to take apart; (enemigo) to defeat; (diluir) to melt; (contrato) to break; (intriga) to solve; ~**se** vr (disolverse) to dissolve; (despedazarse) to come apart o undone; ~**se de** to get rid of; ~**se en lágrimas** to burst into tears.

deshecho, a [des'etʃo, a] a undone; (roto) smashed; **estar** ~ (persona) to be shattered.

desheredar [desere'ðar] vt to disinherit.

deshidratar [desiðra'tar] vt to dehydrate.

deshielo [des'jelo] nm thaw.

deshonesto, a [deso'nesto, a] a indecent.

deshonra [des'onra] nf (deshonor) dishonour; (vergüenza) shame; **deshonrar** vt to dishonour.

deshora [des'ora]: **a** ~ ad at the wrong time.

deshuesar [deswe'sar] vt (carne) to bone; (fruta) to stone.

desierto, a [de'sjerto, a] a (casa, calle, negocio) deserted // nm desert.

designar [desiɣ'nar] vt (nombrar) to designate; (indicar) to fix.

designio [de'siɣnjo] nm plan.

desigual [desi'ɣwal] a (terreno) uneven; (lucha etc) unequal.

desilusión [desilu'sjon] nf disillusionment; (decepción) disappointment; **desilusionar** vt to disillusion; to disappoint; **desilusionarse** vr to become disillusioned.

desinfectar [desinfek'tar] vt to disinfect.

desinflar [desin'flar] vt to deflate.

desintegración [desinteɣra'θjon] nf disintegration.

desinterés [desinte'res] nm (objetividad) disinterestedness; (altruismo) unselfishness.

desistir [desis'tir] vi (renunciar) to stop, desist.

desleal [desle'al] a (infiel) disloyal; (COM: competencia) unfair; **~tad** nf disloyalty.

desleír [desle'ir] vt (líquido) to dilute; (sólido) to dissolve.

deslenguado, a [deslen'gwaðo, a] a (grosero) foul-mouthed.

desligar [desli'ɣar] vt (desatar) to untie, undo; (separar) to separate; **~se** vr (de un compromiso) to extricate o.s.

desliz [des'liθ] nm (fig) lapse; **~ar** vt to slip, slide; **~arse** vr (escurrirse: persona) to slip, slide; (coche) to skid; (aguas mansas) to flow gently; (error) to creep in.

deslucido, a [deslu'θiðo, a] a dull; (torpe) awkward, graceless; (deslustrado) tarnished.

deslumbrar [deslum'brar] vt to dazzle.

desmán [des'man] nm (exceso) outrage; (abuso de poder) abuse.

desmandarse [desman'darse] vr (portarse mal) to behave badly; (excederse) to get out of hand; (caballo) to bolt.

desmantelar [desmante'lar] vt (deshacer) to dismantle; (casa) to strip.

desmaquillador [desmakiʎa'ðor] nm make-up remover.

desmayado, a [desma'jaðo, a] a (sin sentido) unconscious; (carácter) dull; (débil) faint, weak.

desmayar [desma'jar] vi to lose heart; **~se** vr (MED) to faint; **desmayo** nm (MED: acto) faint; (: estado) unconsciousness; (depresión)

dejection.

desmedido, a [desme'ðiðo, a] a excessive.

desmejorar [desmexo'rar] vt (dañar) to impair, spoil; (MED) to weaken.

desmembrar [desmem'brar] vt (MED) to dismember; (fig) to separate.

desmemoriado, a [desmemo'rjaðo, a] a forgetful.

desmentir [desmen'tir] vt (contradecir) to contradict; (refutar) to deny // vi: **~ de** to refute; **~se** vr to contradict o.s.

desmenuzar [desmenu'θar] vt (deshacer) to crumble; (carne) to chop; (examinar) to examine closely.

desmerecer [desmere'θer] vt to be unworthy of // vi (deteriorarse) to deteriorate.

desmesurado, a [desmesu'raðo, a] a disproportionate.

desmontar [desmon'tar] vt (deshacer) to dismantle; (tierra) to level // vi to dismount.

desmoralizar [desmorali'θar] vt to demoralize.

desmoronar [desmoro'nar] vt to wear away, erode; **~se** vr (edificio, dique) to fall into disrepair; (economía) to decline.

desnatado, a [desna'taðo, a] a skimmed.

desnivel [desni'βel] nm (de terreno) unevenness.

desnudar [desnu'ðar] vt (desvestir) to undress; (despojar) to strip; **~se** vr (desvestirse) to get undressed; **desnudo, a** a naked // nm/f nude; desnudo de devoid o bereft of.

desnutrición [desnutri'θjon] nf malnutrition; **desnutrido, a** a undernourished.

desobedecer [desoβeðe'θer] vt, vi to disobey; **desobediencia** nf disobedience.

desocupado, a [desoku'paðo, a] a at leisure; (desempleado) unemployed; (deshabitado) empty, vacant.

desocupar [desoku'par] vt to vacate.

desodorante [desoðo'rante] nm deodorant.

desolación [desola'θjon] nf (lugar) desolation; (fig) grief.

desolar [deso'lar] vt to ruin, lay waste.

desorden [des'orðen] nm confusion; (politico) disorder, unrest.

desorganizar [desorvani'θar] vt (desordenar) to disorganize.

desorientar [desorjen'tar] vt (extraviar) to mislead; (confundir, desconcertar) to confuse; ~se vr (perderse) to lose one's way.

desovar [deso'βar] vi (peces) to spawn; (insectos) to lay eggs.

despabilado, a [despaßi'laðo, a] a (despierto) wide-awake; (fig) alert, sharp.

despabilar [despaβi'lar] vt (el ingenio) to sharpen // vi, ~se vr to wake up; (fig) to get a move on.

despacio [des'paθjo] ad slowly.

despachar [despa't∫ar] vt (negocio) to do, complete; (enviar) to send, dispatch; (vender) to sell, deal in; (billete) to issue; (mandar ir) to send away.

despacho [des'pat∫o] nm (oficina) office; (de paquetes) dispatch; (venta) sale; (comunicación) message.

desparpajo [despar'paxo] nm self-confidence; (pey) nerve.

desparramar [desparra'mar] vt (esparcir) to scatter; (liquido) to spill.

despavorido, a [despaßo'riðo, a] a terrified.

despectivo, a [despek'tiβo, a] a (despreciativo) derogatory; (LING) pejorative.

despecho [des'pet∫o] nm spite; a ~ de in spite of.

despedazar [despeða'θar] vt to tear to pieces.

despedida [despe'ðiða] nf (adiós) farewell; (de obrero) sacking.

despedir [despe'ðir] vt (visita) to see off, show out; (empleado) to dismiss; (inquilino) to evict; (objeto) to hurl; (olor etc) to give out o off; ~se vr: ~se de to say goodbye to.

despegar [despe'xar] vt to unstick // vi (avión) to take off; ~se vr to come loose, come unstuck; **despego** nm detachment.

despegue etc vb ver **despegar** //
[des'peɣe] nm takeoff.

despeinado, a [despei'naðo, a] a dishevelled, unkempt.

despejado, a [despe'xaðo, a] a (lugar) clear, free; (cielo) clear; (persona) wide-awake; bright.

despejar [despe'xar] vt (gen) to clear; (misterio) to clear up // vi (el tiempo) to clear; ~se vr (tiempo, cielo) to clear (up); (misterio) to become clearer; (cabeza) to clear.

despellejar [despeʎe'xar] vt (animal) to skin.

despensa [des'pensa] nf larder.

despeñadero [despeɲa'ðero] nm (GEO) cliff, precipice.

desperdicio [desper'ðiθjo] nm (despilfarro) squandering; ~s nmpl (basura) rubbish sg (Brit), garbage sg (US); (residuos) waste sg.

desperezarse [despere'θarse] vr to stretch (o.s.).

desperfecto [desper'fekto] nm (deterioro) slight damage; (defecto) flaw, imperfection.

despertador [desperta'ðor] nm alarm clock.

despertar [desper'tar] vt (persona) to wake up; (recuerdos) to revive; (sentimiento) to arouse // vi, ~se vr to awaken, wake up // nm awakening.

despiadado, a [despja'ðaðo, a] a (ataque) merciless; (persona) heartless.

despido etc vb ver **despedir** //
[des'piðo] nm dismissal, sacking.

despierto, a etc vb ver **despertar**
// [des'pjerto, a] a awake; (fig) sharp, alert.

despilfarro [despil'farro] nm

(derroche) squandering; *(lujo desmedido)* extravagance.

despistar [despis'tar] *vt* to throw off the track *o* scent; *(fig)* to mislead, confuse; ~**se** *vr* to take the wrong road; *(fig)* to become confused.

desplazamiento [desplaθa'mjento] *nm* displacement.

desplazar [despla'θar] *vt* to move; *(NAUT)* to displace; *(INFORM)* to scroll; *(fig)* to oust; *(persona)* to travel.

desplegar [desple'xar] *vt (tela, papel)* to unfold, open out; *(bandera)* to unfurl; **despliegue** *vb etc ver* **desplegar** // [des'pljexe] *nm* display.

desplomarse [desplo'marse] *vr (edificio, gobierno, persona)* to collapse.

desplumar [desplu'mar] *vt (ave)* to pluck; *(fam: estafar)* to fleece.

despoblado, a [despo'βlaðo, a] *a (sin habitantes)* uninhabited.

despojar [despo'xar] *vt (alguien: de sus bienes)* to divest of, deprive of; *(casa)* to strip, leave bare; *(alguien: de su cargo)* to strip of.

despojo [des'poxo] *nm (acto) plundering)* plunder, loot; ~**s** *nmpl (de ave, res)* offal *sg.*

desposado, a [despo'saðo, a] *a, nm/f* newly-wed.

desposeer [despose'er] *vt:* ~ **a uno de** *(puesto, autoridad)* to strip sb of.

déspota ['despota] *nm/f* despot.

despreciar [despre'θjar] *vt (desdeñar)* to despise, scorn; *(afrentar)* to slight; **desprecio** *nm* scorn, contempt; slight.

desprender [despren'der] *vt (separar)* to separate; *(desatar)* to unfasten; *(olor)* to give off; ~**se** *vr (botón: caerse)* to fall off; *(abrirse)* to unfasten; *(olor, perfume)* to be given off; *(fig)* to follow from; **se desprende que** it transpires that.

desprendimiento [desprendi'mjento] *nm (gen)* loosening; *(generosidad)* disinterestedness; *(indifer-*

encia) detachment; *(de gas)* leak; *(de tierra, rocas)* landslide.

despreocupado, a [despreoku-'paðo, a] *a (sin preocupación)* unworried, nonchalant; *(negligente)* careless.

despreocuparse [despreoku'parse] *vr* to be carefree; ~ **de** to have no interest in.

desprestigiar [despresti'xjar] *vt (criticar)* to run down; *(desacreditar)* to discredit.

desprevenido, a [despreβe'niðo, a] *a (no preparado)* unprepared, unready.

desproporcionado, a [despropor-θjo'naðo, a] *a* disproportionate, out of proportion.

después [des'pwes] *ad* afterwards, later; *(próximo paso)* next; ~ **de comer** after lunch; **un año** ~ a year later; ~ **se debatió el tema** next the matter was discussed; ~ **de corregido el texto** after the text had been corrected; ~ **de todo** after all.

desquite [des'kite] *nm (satisfacción)* satisfaction; *(venganza)* revenge.

destacar [desta'kar] *vt* to emphasize, point up; *(MIL)* to detach, detail // *vi,* ~**se** *vr (resaltarse)* to stand out; *(persona)* to be outstanding *o* exceptional.

destajo [des'taxo] *nm:* **trabajar a** ~ to do piecework.

destapar [desta'par] *vt (botella)* to open; *(cacerola)* to take the lid off; *(descubrir)* uncover; ~**se** *vr (revelarse)* to reveal one's true character.

destartalado, a [destarta'laðo, a] *a (desordenado)* untidy; *(ruinoso)* tumbledown.

destello [des'teʎo] *nm (de estrella)* () twinkle; *(de faro)* signal light.

destemplado, a [destem'plaðo, a] *a (MUS)* out of tune; *(voz)* harsh; *(MED)* out of sorts; *(tiempo)* unpleasant, nasty.

desteñir [deste'nir] *vt* to fade // *vi,* ~**se** *vr* to fade; **esta tela no des-**

tiñe this fabric will not run.

desternillarse [destɛrni'ʎarse] vr: ~ **de risa** to split one's sides laughing.

desterrar [deste'rrar] vt (exilar) to exile; (fig) to banish, dismiss.

destetar [deste'tar] vt to wean.

destierro etc vb ver **desterrar** // [des'tjɛrro] nm exile.

destilar [desti'lar] vt to distil; **destilería** nf distillery.

destinar [desti'nar] vt (funcionario) to appoint, assign; (fondos) to set aside (a for).

destinatario, a [destina'tarjo, a] nm/f addressee.

destino [des'tino] nm (suerte) destiny; (de avión, viajero) destination.

destituir [destitu'ir] vt to dismiss.

destornillador [destorniʎa'ðor] nm screwdriver.

destornillar [destorni'ʎar] vt, **destornillarse** vr (tornillo) to unscrew.

destreza [des'treθa] nf (habilidad) skill; (maña) dexterity.

destrozar [destro'θar] vt (romper) to smash, break (up); (estropear) to ruin; (nervios) to shatter.

destrozo [des'troθo] nm (acción) destruction; (desastre) smashing; ~s nmpl (pedazos) pieces; (daños) havoc sg.

destrucción [destruk'θjon] nf destruction.

destruir [destru'ir] vt to destroy.

desuso [des'uso] nm disuse; **caer en ~** to become obsolete.

desvalido, a [desβa'liðo, a] a (desprotegido) destitute; (sin fuerzas) helpless.

desvalijar [desβali'xar] vt (persona) to rob; (casa, tienda) to burgle; (coche) to break into.

desván [des'βan] nm attic.

desvanecer [desβane'θer] vt (disipar) to dispel; (borrar) to blur; ~se vr (humo etc) to vanish, disappear; (color) to fade; (recuerdo, sonido) to fade away; (MED) to pass out; (duda) to be dispelled.

desvanecimiento [desβaneθi'mjento] nm (desaparición) disappearance; (de colores) fading; (evaporación) evaporation; (MED) fainting fit.

desvariar [desβa'rjar] vi (enfermo) to be delirious; **desvarío** nm delirium.

desvelar [desβe'lar] vt to keep awake; ~se vr (no poder dormir) to stay awake; (vigilar) to be vigilant o watchful.

desvencijado, a [desβenθi'xaðo, a] a (silla) rickety; (máquina) broken-down.

desventaja [desβen'taxa] nf disadvantage.

desventura [desβen'tura] nf misfortune.

desvergonzado, a [desβergon-'θaðo, a] a shameless.

desvergüenza [desβer'ɣwenθa] nf (descaro) shamelessness; (insolencia) impudence; (mala conducta) effrontery.

desvestir [desβes'tir] vt, **desvestirse** vr to undress.

desviación [desβja'θjon] nf deviation; (AUTO) diversion, detour.

desviar [desβi'ar] vt to turn aside; (río) to alter the course of; (navío) to divert, re-route; (conversación) to sidetrack; ~se vr (apartarse del camino) to turn aside; (: barco) to go off course.

desvío etc vb ver **desviar** // [des'βio] nm (desviación) detour, diversion; (fig) indifference.

desvirtuar [desβir'twar] vt, **desvirtuarse** vr to spoil.

desvivirse [desβi'βirse] vr: ~ **por** (anhelar) to long for, crave for; (hacer lo posible por) to do one's utmost for.

detallar [deta'ʎar] vt to detail.

detalle [de'taʎe] nm (fig) gesture, token; **al ~** in detail; (COM) retail.

detallista [deta'ʎista] nm/f retailer.

detener [dete'ner] vt (gen) to stop;

(JUR) to arrest; (objeto) to keep; ~se vr to stop; (demorarse): ~se en to delay over, linger over.

detenidamente [deteniða'mente] ad (minuciosamente) carefully; (extensamente) at great length.

detenido, a [dete'niðo, a] a (arrestado) under arrest; (minucioso) detailed // nm/f person under arrest, prisoner.

detergente [deter'xente] nm detergent.

deteriorar [deterjo'rar] vt to spoil, damage; ~se vr to deteriorate; **deterioro** nm deterioration.

determinación [determina'θjon] nf (empeño) determination; (decisión) decision.

determinar [determi'nar] vt (plazo) to fix; (precio) to settle; ~se vr to decide.

detestar [detes'tar] vt to detest.

detonar [deto'nar] vi to detonate.

detrás [de'tras] ad behind; (atrás) at the back; ~ de behind.

detrimento [detri'mento] nm: en ~ de to the detriment of.

deuda ['deuða] nf (condición) indebtedness, debt; (cantidad) debt.

deudor, a [deu'ðor, a] nm/f debtor.

devaluación [deβalwa'θjon] nf devaluation.

devastar [deβas'tar] vt (destruir) to devastate.

devengar [deβen'gar] vt (COM) to accrue, earn.

devoción [deβo'θjon] nf devotion.

devolución [deβolu'θjon] nf (reenvío) return, sending back; (reembolso) repayment; (JUR) devolution.

devolver [deβol'βer] vt to return; (lo extraviado, lo prestado) to give back; (carta al correo) to send back; (COM) to repay, refund; (visita, la palabra) to return // vi (fam) to be sick.

devorar [deβo'rar] vt to devour.

devoto, a [de'βoto, a] a devout // nm/f admirer.

devuelto, devuelva etc vb ver **devolver**.

di vb ver **dar**; **decir**.

día ['dia] nm day; ¿qué ~ es? what's the date?; **estar/poner al ~** to be/keep up to date; **el ~ de hoy/de mañana** today/tomorrow; **al ~ siguiente** (on) the following day; **vivir al ~** to live from hand to mouth; **de ~** by day, in daylight; **en pleno ~** in full daylight; **~ festivo** (Esp) o **feriado** (AM) holiday; **~ libre** day off.

diablo ['djaβlo] nm devil; **diablura** nf prank.

diafragma [dja'fraxma] nm diaphragm.

diagnosis [djav'nosis] nf inv, **diagnóstico** [djav'nostiko] nm diagnosis.

diagrama [dja'xrama] nm diagram; **~ de flujo** flowchart.

dialecto [dja'lekto] nm dialect.

dialogar [djalo'xar] vi: **~ con** (POL) to hold talks with.

diálogo ['djaloxo] nm dialogue.

diamante [dja'mante] nm diamond.

diana ['djana] nf (MIL) reveille; (de blanco) centre, bull's-eye.

diapositiva [djaposi'tiβa] nf (FOTO) slide, transparency.

diario, a [dj'arjo, a] a daily // nm newspaper; **a ~** daily; **de ~** everyday.

diarrea [dja'rrea] nf diarrhoea.

dibujar [diβu'xar] vt to draw, sketch; **dibujo** nm drawing; **dibujos animados** cartoons.

diccionario [dikθjo'narjo] nm dictionary.

dice etc vb ver **decir**.

diciembre [di'θjembre] nm December.

dictado [dik'taðo] nm dictation.

dictador [dikta'ðor] nm dictator; **dictadura** nf dictatorship.

dictamen [dik'tamen] nm (opinión) opinion; (juicio) judgment; (informe) report.

dictar [dik'tar] vt (carta) to dictate;

(*JUR*: *sentencia*) to pronounce; (*decreto*) to issue; (*AM*: *clase*) to give.

dicho, a ['ditʃo, a] *pp de* **decir** // *a*: en ~s países in the aforementioned countries // *nm* saying.

diecinueve [djeθi'nweβe] *num* nineteen.

dieciocho [dje'θi'otʃo] *num* eighteen.

dieciséis [djeθi'seis] *num* sixteen.

diecisiete [djeθi'sjete] *num* seventeen.

diente ['djente] *nm* (*ANAT, TEC*) tooth; (*ZOOL*) fang; (: *de elefante*) tusk; (*de ajo*) clove; **hablar entre ~s** to mutter, mumble.

diera, dieron *etc vb ver* **dar**.

diesel ['disel] *a*: **motor ~** diesel engine.

dieta ['djeta] *nf* diet.

diez [djeθ] *num* ten.

difamar [difa'mar] *vt* (*JUR*: *hablando*) to slander; (: *por escrito*) to libel.

diferencia [dife'renθja] *nf* difference; **diferenciar** *vt* to differentiate between // *vi* to differ; **diferenciarse** *vr* to differ, be different; (*distinguirse*) to distinguish o.s.

diferente [dife'rente] *a* different.

diferido [dife'riðo] *nm*: **en ~** (*TV etc*) recorded.

difícil [di'fiθil] *a* difficult.

dificultad [difikul'taθ] *nf* difficulty; (*problema*) trouble; (*objeción*) objection.

dificultar [difikul'tar] *vt* (*complicar*) to complicate, make difficult; (*estorbar*) to obstruct.

difundir [difun'dir] *vt* (*calor, luz*) to diffuse; (*RADIO, TV*) to broadcast; **~ una noticia** to spread a piece of news; **~se** *vr* to spread (out).

difunto, a [di'funto, a] *a* dead, deceased // *nm/f* deceased (person).

diga *etc vb ver* **decir**.

digerir [dixe'rir] *vt* to digest; (*fig*) to absorb.

digital [dixi'tal] *a* (*INFORM*) digital.

dignarse [diɣ'narse] *vr* to deign to.

digno, a ['diɣno, a] *a* worthy.

digo *etc vb ver* **decir**.

dije *etc vb ver* **decir**.

dilatado, a [dila'taðo, a] *a* dilated; (*período*) long drawn-out; (*extenso*) extensive.

dilatar [dila'tar] *vt* (*cuerpo*) to dilate; (*prolongar*) to prolong; (*aplazar*) to delay.

dilema [di'lema] *nm* dilemma.

diligencia [dili'xenθja] *nf* diligence; (*ocupación*) errand, job; **~s** *nfpl* (*JUR*) formalities; **diligente** *a* diligent.

diluir [dilu'ir] *vt* to dilute.

diluvio [di'luβjo] *nm* deluge, flood.

dimensión [dimen'sjon] *nf* dimension.

diminuto, a [di'minuto, a] *a* tiny, diminutive.

dimitir [dimi'tir] *vi* to resign.

dimos *vb ver* **dar**.

Dinamarca [dina'marka] *nf* Denmark; **dinamarqués, esa** *a* Danish // *nm/f* Dane.

dinámico, a [di'namiko, a] *a* dynamic.

dinamita [dina'mita] *nf* dynamite.

dinamo ['dinamo] *nf* dynamo.

dineral [dine'ral] *nm* large sum of money, fortune.

dinero [di'nero] *nm* money; **~ contante**, **~ efectivo** cash, ready cash.

dio *vb ver* **dar**.

dios [djos] *nm* god; **¡D~ mío!** (oh,) my God!

diosa [di'josa] *nf* goddess.

diploma [di'ploma] *nm* diploma.

diplomacia [diplo'maθja] *nf* diplomacy; (*fig*) tact.

diplomado, a [diplo'maðo, a] *a* qualified.

diplomático, a [diplo'matiko, a] *a* diplomatic // *nm/f* diplomat.

diputado, a [dipu'taðo, a] *nm/f* delegate; (*POL*) ≈ member of parliament (*Brit*), ≈ representative (*US*).

dique ['dike] *nm* dyke.

diré *etc vb ver* **decir**.

dirección [direk'θjon] *nf* direction; (*señas*) address; (*AUTO*) steering; (*gerencia*) management; (*POL*) leadership; ~ **única/prohibida** one-way street/no entry.

directo, a [di'rekto, a] *a* direct; (*RADIO, TV*) live; **transmitir en** ~ to broadcast live.

director, a [direk'tor, a] *a* leading // *nm/f* director; (*ESCOL*) head(teacher) (*Brit*), principal (*US*); (*gerente*) manager(ess); (*PRENSA*) editor; ~ **de cine** film director; ~ **general** managing director.

dirigir [diri'xir] *vt* to direct; (*carta*) to address; (*obra de teatro, film*) to direct; (*MUS*) to conduct; (*comercio*) to manage; ~**se** *vr*: ~**se a** to go towards, make one's way towards; (*hablar con*) to speak to.

dirija *etc* vb *ver* **dirigir**.

discernir [disθer'nir] *vt* (*distinguir, discriminar*) to discern.

disciplina [disθi'plina] *nf* discipline.

discípulo, a [dis'θipulo, a] *nm/f* disciple.

disco ['disko] *nm* disc; (*DEPORTE*) discus; (*TEL*) dial; (*AUTO: semáforo*) light; (*MUS*) record; ~ **compacto/de larga duración** compact disc/long-playing record (L.P.); ~ **de freno** brake disc; (*INFORM*): ~ **flexible/rígido** floppy/hard disk.

disconforme [diskon'forme] *a* differing; **estar** ~ **(con)** to be in disagreement (with).

discordia [dis'korðja] *nf* discord.

discoteca [disko'teka] *nf* disco(theque).

discreción [diskre'θjon] *nf* discretion; (*reserva*) prudence; **comer a** ~ to eat as much as one wishes; **discrecional** *a* (*facultativo*) discretionary.

discrepancia [diskre'panθja] *nf* (*diferencia*) discrepancy; (*desacuerdo*) disagreement.

discreto, a [dis'kreto, a] *a* (*diplomático*) discreet; (*sensato*)

sensible; (*reservado*) quiet; (*sobrio*) sober.

discriminación [diskrimina'θjon] *nf* discrimination.

disculpa [dis'kulpa] *nf* excuse; (*pedir perdón*) apology; **pedir** ~**s a/por** to apologize to/for; **disculpar** *vt* to excuse, pardon; **disculparse** *vr* to excuse o.s.; to apologize.

discurrir [disku'rrir] *vi* (*pensar, reflexionar*) to think, meditate; (*recorrer*) to roam, wander; (*el tiempo*) to pass, flow by.

discurso [dis'kurso] *nm* speech.

discutir [disku'tir] *vt* (*debatir*) to discuss; (*pelear*) to argue about; (*contradecir*) to argue against // *vi* to discuss; (*disputar*) to argue.

disecar [dise'kar] *vt* (*conservar: animal*) to stuff; (: *planta*) to dry.

diseminar [disemi'nar] *vt* to disseminate, spread.

diseño [di'seɲo] *nm* design; (*ARTE*) drawing.

disfraz [dis'fraθ] *nm* (*máscara*) disguise; (*excusa*) pretext; ~**ar** *vt* to disguise; ~**arse** *vr*: ~**arse de** to disguise o.s. as.

disfrutar [disfru'tar] *vt* to enjoy // *vi* to enjoy o.s.; ~ **de** to enjoy, possess.

disgustar [disɣus'tar] *vt* (*no gustar*) to displease; (*contrariar, enojar*) to annoy, upset; ~**se** *vr* to be annoyed; (*dos personas*) to fall out.

disgusto [dis'ɣusto] *nm* (*repugnancia*) disgust; (*contrariedad*) annoyance; (*tristeza*) grief; (*riña*) quarrel; (*avería*) misfortune.

disidente [disi'ðente] *nm* dissident.

disimular [disimu'lar] *vt* (*ocultar*) to hide, conceal // *vi* to dissemble.

disipar [disi'par] *vt* to dispel; (*fortuna*) to squander; ~**se** *vr* (*nubes*) to vanish; (*indisciplinarse*) to dissipate.

disminución [disminu'θjon] *nf* diminution.

disminuir [disminu'ir] *vt* (*acortar*) to decrease; (*achicar*) to diminish; (*estrechar*) to lessen.

disolver [disol'βer] *vt* (*gen*) to dissolve; **~se** *vr* to dissolve; (*COM*) to go into liquidation.

disparar [dispa'rar] *vt, vi* to shoot, fire.

disparate [dispa'rate] *nm* (*tontería*) foolish remark; (*error*) blunder; **decir ~s** to talk nonsense.

disparo [dis'paro] *nm* shot.

dispensar [dispen'sar] *vt* to dispense; (*disculpar*) to excuse.

dispersar [disper'sar] *vt* to disperse; **~se** *vr* to scatter.

disponer [dispo'ner] *vt* (*arreglar*) to arrange; (*ordenar*) to put in order; (*preparar*) to prepare, get ready // *vi*: **~ de** to have, own; **~se** *vr*: **~se para** to prepare to, prepare for.

disponible [dispo'niβle] *a* available.

disposición [disposi'θjon] *nf* arrangement, disposition; (*aptitud*) aptitude; (*INFORM*) layout; **a la ~ de** at the disposal of.

dispositivo [disposi'tiβo] *nm* device, mechanism.

dispuesto, a *pp de* **disponer** // [dis'pwesto] *a* (*arreglado*) arranged; (*preparado*) disposed.

disputar [dispu'tar] *vt* (*discutir*) to dispute, question; (*contender*) to contend for // *vi* to argue.

disquete [dis'kete] *nm* floppy disk, diskette.

distancia [dis'tanθja] *nf* distance.

distanciar [distan'θjar] *vt* to space out; **~se** *vr* to become estranged.

distante [dis'tante] *a* distant.

diste, disteis *vb ver* **dar**.

distinción [distin'θjon] *nf* distinction; (*elegancia*) elegance; (*honor*) honour.

distinguido, a [distin'giðo, a] *a* distinguished.

distinguir [distin'gir] *vt* to distinguish; (*escoger*) to single out; **~se** *vr* to be distinguished.

distinto, a [dis'tinto, a] *a* different; (*claro*) clear.

distracción [distrak'θjon] *nf* distraction; (*pasatiempo*) hobby, pastime; (*olvido*) absent-mindedness, distrac-

tion.

distraer [distra'er] *vt* (*atención*) to distract; (*divertir*) to amuse; (*fondos*) to embezzle; **~se** *vr* (*entretenerse*) to amuse o.s.; (*perder la concentración*) to allow one's attention to wander.

distraído, a [distra'iðo, a] *a* (*gen*) absent-minded; (*entretenido*) amusing.

distribuir [distriβu'ir] *vt* to distribute.

distrito [dis'trito] *nm* (*sector, territorio*) region; (*barrio*) district.

disturbio [dis'turβjo] *nm* disturbance; (*desorden*) riot.

disuadir [diswa'ðir] *vt* to dissuade.

disuelto [di'swelto] *pp de* **disolver**.

DIU *nm abr* (= *dispositivo intrauterino*) IUD.

diurno, a ['djurno, a] *a* day *cpd*.

divagar [diβa'xar] *vi* (*desviarse*) to digress.

diván [di'βan] *nm* divan.

divergencia [diβer'xenθja] *nf* divergence.

diversidad [diβersi'ðaθ] *nf* diversity, variety.

diversificar [diβersifi'kar] *vt* to diversify.

diversión [diβer'sjon] *nf* (*gen*) entertainment; (*actividad*) hobby, pastime.

diverso, a [di'βerso, a] *a* diverse; **~s** *nmpl* sundries; **~s libros** several books.

divertido, a [diβer'tiðo, a] *a* (*chiste*) amusing; (*fiesta etc*) enjoyable.

divertir [diβer'tir] *vt* (*entretener, recrear*) to amuse; **~se** *vr* (*pasarlo bien*) to have a good time; (*distraerse*) to amuse o.s.

dividir [diβi'ðir] *vt* (*gen*) to divide; (*separar*) to separate; (*distribuir*) to distribute, share out.

divierta *etc vb ver* **divertir**.

divino, a [di'βino, a] *a* divine.

divirtiendo *etc vb ver* **divertir**.

divisa [di'βisa] *nf* (*emblema, moneda*) emblem, badge; **~s** *nfpl* foreign exchange *sg*.

divisar [diβi'sar] vt to make out, distinguish.

división [diβi'sjon] nf (gen) division; (de partido) split; (de país) partition.

divorciar [diβor'θjar] vt to divorce; ~se vr to get divorced; **divorcio** nm divorce.

divulgar [diβul'γar] vt (desparramar) to spread; (hacer circular) to divulge, circulate; ~se vr to leak out.

DNI nm abr (Esp: = Documento Nacional de Identidad) national identity card.

dobladillo [doβla'ðiʎo] nm (de vestido) hem; (de pantalón: vuelta) turn-up (Brit), cuff (US).

doblar [do'βlar] vt to double; (papel) to fold; (caño) to bend; (la esquina) to turn, go round; (film) to dub // vi to turn; (campana) to toll; ~se vr (plegarse) to fold (up), crease; (encorvarse) to bend.

doble ['doβle] a double; (de dos aspectos) dual; (fig) two-faced // double; ~s nmpl (DEPORTE) doubles sg // nm/f (TEATRO) double, stand-in; **con sentido** ~ with a double meaning.

doblegar [doβle'γar] vt to fold, crease; ~se vr to yield.

doce ['doθe] num twelve; **~na** nf dozen.

docente [do'θente] a: **centro/personal** ~ teaching establishment/staff.

dócil ['doθil] a (pasivo) docile; (obediente) obedient.

doctor, a [dok'tor, a] nm/f doctor.

doctrina [dok'trina] nf doctrine, teaching.

documentación [dokumenta'θjon] nf documentation, papers pl.

documento [doku'mento] nm (certificado) document; **documental** a, nm documentary.

dólar ['dolar] nm dollar.

doler [do'ler] vt, vi to hurt; (fig) to grieve; ~se vr (de su situación) to grieve, feel sorry; (de las desgracias

ajenas) to sympathize; **me duele el brazo** my arm hurts.

dolor [do'lor] nm pain; (fig) grief, sorrow; ~ **de cabeza** headache; ~ **de estómago** stomachache.

domar [do'mar], **domesticar** [domesti'kar] vt to tame.

domiciliación [domiθilia'θjon] nf: ~ **de pagos** (COM) standing order.

domicilio [domi'θiljo] nm home; **particular** private residence; ~ **social** (COM) head office; **sin** ~ **fijo** of no fixed abode.

dominante [domi'nante] a dominant; (persona) domineering.

dominar [domi'nar] vt (gen) to dominate; (idiomas) to be fluent in // vi to dominate, prevail; ~se vr to control o.s.

domingo [do'mingo] nm Sunday.

dominio [do'minjo] nm (tierras) domain; (autoridad) power, authority; (de las pasiones) grip, hold; (de varios idiomas) command.

don [don] nm (talento) gift; ~ **Juan Gómez** Mr Juan Gomez o Juan Gomez Esq.

donaire [do'naire] nm charm.

donar [do'nar] vt to donate.

doncella [don'θeʎa] nf (criada) maid.

donde ['donde] ad where // prep: **el coche está allí** ~ **el farol** the car is over there by the lamppost o where the lamppost is; **por** ~ through which; **en** ~ where, in which.

dónde ['donde] ad interr where?; ¿a ~ **vas?** where are you going (to)?; ¿de ~ **vienes?** where have you come from?; ¿por ~? where?, whereabouts?

dondequiera [donde'kjera] ad anywhere; **por** ~ everywhere, all over the place // conj: ~ **que** wherever.

doña ['dona] nf: ~ **Alicia** Alicia; ~ **Victoria Benito** Mrs Victoria Benito.

dorado, a [do'raðo, a] a (color) golden; (TEC) gilt.

dormir [dor'mir] vt: ~ **la siesta por**

la tarde to have an afternoon nap //
vi to sleep; **~se** vr to fall asleep.
dormitar [dormi'tar] vi to doze.
dormitorio [dormi'torjo] nm bedroom; **~ común** dormitory.
dorsal [dor'sal] nm (DEPORTE)
number.
dos [dos] núm two.
dosis ['dosis] nf inv dose, dosage.
dotado, a [do'taðo, a] a gifted; **~ de** endowed with.
dotar [do'tar] vt to endow; **dote** nf
dowry; **dotes** nfpl (talentos) gifts.
doy vb ver **dar**.
drama ['drama] nm drama.
dramaturgo [drama'turyo] nm
dramatist, playwright.
droga ['droya] nf drug.
drogadicto, a [droya'ðikto, a] nm/f
drug addict.
droguería [droye'ria] nf hardware
shop (Brit) o store (US).
ducha ['dutʃa] nf (baño) shower;
(MED) douche; **ducharse** vr to take
a shower.
duda ['duða] nf doubt; **dudar** vt, vi
to doubt; **dudoso, a** [du'ðoso, a] a
(incierto) hesitant; (sospechoso)
doubtful.
duela etc vb ver **doler**.
duelo vb ver **doler** // ['dwelo] nm
(combate) duel; (luto) mourning.
duende ['dwende] nm imp, goblin.
dueño, a ['dweɲo, a] nm/f
(propietario) owner; (de pensión,
taberna) landlord/lady; (empresario)
employer.
duermo etc vb ver **dormir**.
dulce ['dulθe] a sweet // ad gently,
softly // nm sweet; **~ría** nf (AM)
confectioner's.
dulzura [dul'θura] nf sweetness;
(ternura) gentleness.
duplicar [dupli'kar] vt (hacer el
doble de) to duplicate; **~se** vr to
double.
duque ['duke] nm duke; **~sa** nf
duchess.
duración [dura'θjon] nf duration.
duradero, a [dura'ðero, a] a (tela)

hard-wearing; (fe, paz) lasting.
durante [du'rante] ad during.
durar [du'rar] vi (permanecer) to
last; (recuerdo) to remain.
durazno [du'raθno] nm (AM: fruta)
peach; (: árbol) peach tree.
durex ['dureks] nm (AM: tira
adhesiva) Sellotape ® (Brit), Scotch
tape ® (US).
dureza [du'reθa] nf (calidad) hardness.
durmiente [dur'mjente] nm/f
sleeper.
duro, a ['duro, a] a hard; (carácter)
tough // ad hard // nm (moneda) five
peseta coin o piece.

E

e [e] conj and.
E abr (= este) E.
ebanista [eβa'nista] nm/f cabinetmaker.
ébano ['eβano] nm ebony.
ebrio, a ['eβrjo, a] a drunk.
ebullición [eβuʎi'θjon] nf boiling.
eccema [ek'θema] nf (MED) eczema.
eclesiástico, a [ekle'sjastiko, a] a
ecclesiastical.
eclipse [e'klipse] nm eclipse.
eco ['eko] nm echo; **tener ~** to catch
on.
ecología [ekolo'ria] nf ecology.
economato [ekono'mato] nm cooperative store.
economía [ekono'mia] nf (sistema)
economy; (cualidad) thrift.
económico, a [eko'nomiko, a] a
(barato) cheap, economical;
(persona) thrifty; (COM: año etc)
financial; (: situación) economic.
economista [ekono'mista] nm/f
economist.
ecuador [ekwa'ðor] nm equator;
(el) E~ Ecuador.
ecuánime [e'kwanime] a (carácter)
level-headed; (estado) calm.
ecuatoriano, a [ekwato'rjano, a] a,
nm/f Ecuadorian.

ecuestre [e'kwestre] *a* equestrian.

echar [e'tʃar] *vt* to throw; *(agua, vino)* to pour (out); *(empleado: despedir)* to fire, sack; *(hojas)* to sprout; *(cartas)* to post; *(humo)* to emit, give out // *vi:* ~ **a correr/llorar** to run off/burst into tears; ~**se** *vr* to lie down; ~ **llave a** to lock (up); ~ **abajo** *(gobierno)* to overthrow; *(edificio)* to demolish; ~ **mano a** to lay hands on; ~ **una mano a uno** *(ayudar)* to give sb a hand; ~ **de menos** to miss.

edad [e'ðað] *nf* age; **¿qué ~ tienes?** how old are you?; **tiene ocho años de** ~ he is eight (years old); **de ~ mediana/avanzada** middle-aged/advanced in years; **la E~ Media** the Middle Ages.

edición [eði'θjon] *nf (acto)* publication; *(ejemplar)* edition.

edicto [e'ðikto] *nm* edict, proclamation.

edificio [eði'fiθjo] *nm* building; *(fig)* edifice, structure.

Edimburgo [eðim'burɣo] *nm* Edinburgh.

editar [eði'tar] *vt (publicar)* to publish; *(preparar textos)* to edit.

editor, a [eði'tor, a] *nm/f (que publica)* publisher; *(redactor)* editor // *a:* **casa** ~**a** a publishing house, publisher; ~**ial** *a* editorial // *nm* leading article, editorial; **casa** ~**ial** publishing house, publisher.

educación [eðuka'θjon] *nf* education; *(crianza)* upbringing; *(modales)* (good) manners *pl*.

educar [eðu'kar] *vt* to educate; *(criar)* to bring up; *(voz)* to train.

EE. UU. *nmpl abr* = **Estados Unidos.**

efectista [efek'tista] *a* sensationalist.

efectivamente [efektiβa'mente] *ad (como respuesta)* exactly, precisely; *(verdaderamente)* really; *(de hecho)* in fact.

efectivo, a [efek'tiβo, a] *a (real)* actual, real // *nm:* **pagar en** ~ to pay (in) cash; **hacer** ~ **un**

cheque to cash a cheque.

efecto [e'fekto] *nm* effect, result; ~**s** *nmpl (~s personales)* effects; *(bienes)* goods; *(COM)* assets; **en** ~ in fact; *(respuesta)* exactly, indeed.

efectuar [efek'twar] *vt* to carry out; *(viaje)* to make.

eficacia [efi'kaθja] *nf (de persona)* efficiency; *(de medicamento etc)* effectiveness.

eficaz [efi'kaθ] *a (persona)* efficient; *(acción)* effective.

efusivo, a [efu'siβo, a] *a* effusive; **mis más efusivas gracias** my warmest thanks.

EGB *nf abr (Esp ESCOL)* = **Educación General Básica.**

egipcio, a [e'xipθjo, a] *a, nm/f* Egyptian.

Egipto [e'xipto] *nm* Egypt.

egoísmo [exo'ismo] *nm* egoism.

egoísta [exo'ista] *a* egoistical, selfish // *nm/f* egoist.

egregio, a [e'xrexjo, a] *a* eminent, distinguished.

Eire ['eire] *nm* Eire.

ej. *abr (= ejemplo)* eg.

eje ['exe] *nm (GEO, MAT)* axis; *(de rueda)* axle; *(de máquina)* shaft, spindle.

ejecución [exeku'θjon] *nf* execution; *(cumplimiento)* fulfilment; *(actuación)* performance; *(JUR: embargo de deudor)* attachment.

ejecutar [exeku'tar] *vt* to execute, carry out; *(matar)* to execute; *(cumplir)* to fulfil; *(MUS)* to perform; *(JUR: embargar)* to attach, distrain (on).

ejecutivo, a [exeku'tiβo, a] *a* executive; **el** *(poder)* ~ the executive (power).

ejemplar [exem'plar] *a* exemplary // *nm* example; *(ZOOL)* specimen; *(de libro)* copy; *(de periódico)* number, issue.

ejemplo [e'xemplo] *nm* example; **por** ~ for example.

ejercer [exer'θer] *vt* to exercise; *(influencia)* to exert; *(un oficio)* to practise // vi (practicar) to practise (de as); (tener oficio) to hold office.

ejercicio [exer'θiθjo] nm exercise; (periodo) tenure; ~ **comercial** financial year.

ejército [e'xerθito] nm army; **entrar en el** ~ to join the army, join up.

ejote [e'xote] nm (AM) green bean.

PALABRA CLAVE

el, la, los, las, lo [el, la, los, las, lo] ♦ *artículo definido* **1** the; **el libro/la mesa/los estudiantes** the book/table/students

2 (con n abstracto: no se traduce): **el amor/la juventud** love/youth

3 (posesión: se traduce a menudo por a posesivo): **romperse el brazo** to break one's arm; **levantó la mano** he put his hand up; **se puso el sombrero** she put her hat on

4 (valor descriptivo): **tener la boca grande/los ojos azules** to have a big mouth/blue eyes

5 (con días) on; **me iré el viernes** I'll leave on Friday; **los domingos suelo ir a nadar** on Sundays I generally go swimming

6 (lo + adj): **lo difícil/caro** what is difficult/expensive; (= cuán): **no se da cuenta de lo pesado que es** he doesn't realise how boring he is

♦ *pron demostrativo* **1:** **mi libro y el de usted** my book and yours; **las de Pepe son mejores** Pepe's are better; **no las** (o **la**) **blancas sino la(s) gris(es)** not the white ones but the grey one(s)

2: lo de: lo de ayer what happened yesterday; **lo de las facturas** that business about the invoices

♦ *pron relativo:* **que** etc **1** (indefinido): **el** (**los**) **que quiera(n)** anyone who wants to can leave; **llévese el que más le guste** take the one you like best

2 (definido): **el que compré ayer** the one I bought yesterday; **los que se van** those who leave

3: lo que: lo que pienso yo/más

me gusta what I think/like most

♦ *conj*: **el que: el que lo diga** the fact that he says so; **el que sea tan vago** *m* **molesta** his being so lazy bothers me

♦ *excl*: **¡el susto que me diste!** what a fright you gave me!

♦ *pron personal* **1** (persona: m) him; (: f) her; (: pl) them; **lo/las veo** I can see him/them

2 (animal, cosa: sg) it; (: pl) them; **lo** (o **la**) **veo** I can see it; **los** (o **las**) **veo** I can see them

3: lo (como sustituto de frase): **no lo sabía** I didn't know; **ya lo entiendo** I understand now.

él [el] pron (persona) he; (cosa) it; (después de prep: persona) him; (: cosa) it.

elaborar [elaβo'rar] vt (producto) to make, manufacture; (preparar) to prepare; (madera, metal etc) to work; (proyecto etc) to work on o out.

elasticidad [elastiθi'ðað] nf elasticity.

elástico, a [e'lastiko, a] a elastic; (flexible) flexible // nm elastic; (un ~) elastic band.

elección [elek'θjon] nf election; (selección) choice, selection.

electorado [elekto'raðo] nm electorate, voters pl.

electricidad [elektriθi'ðað] nf electricity.

electricista [elektri'θista] nmf electrician.

eléctrico, a [e'lektriko, a] a electric.

electrizar [elektri'θar] vt to electrify.

electro... [elektro] pref electro...; **~cución** nf electrocution; **~cutar** vt to electrocute; **electrodo** nm electrode; **~domésticos** nmpl (electrical) household appliances; **~imán** nm electromagnet; **~magnético, a** a electromagnetic.

electrónico, a [elek'troniko, a] a electronic // nf electronics sg.

electrotecnia [elektro'teknja] nf

electrical engineering; **elec-trotécnico, a** *nm/f* electrical engineer.`

electrotermo [elektro'termo] *nm* immersion heater.

elefante [ele'fante] *nm* elephant.

elegancia [ele'γanθja] *nf* elegance, grace; (*estilo*) stylishness.

elegante [ele'γante] *a* elegant, graceful; (*estiloso*) stylish, fashionable.

elegía [ele'xia] *nf* elegy.

elegir [ele'xir] *vt* (*escoger*) to choose, select; (*optar*) to opt for; (*presidente*) to elect.

elemental [elemen'tal] *a* (*claro, obvio*) elementary; (*fundamental*) elemental, fundamental.

elemento [ele'mento] *nm* element; (*fig*) ingredient; ~s *nmpl* elements, rudiments.

elevación [eleβa'θjon] *nf* elevation; (*acto*) raising, lifting; (*de precios*) rise; (GEO *etc*) height, altitude; (*de persona*) loftiness.

elevar [ele'βar] *vt* to raise, lift (up); (*precio*) to put up; ~se *vr* (*edificio*) to rise; (*precios*) to go up; (*transportarse, enajenarse*) to get carried away.

eligiendo *etc vb ver* **elegir**.

elija *etc vb ver* **elegir**.

eliminar [elimi'nar] *vt* to eliminate, remove.

eliminatoria [elimina'torja] *nf* heat, preliminary (round).

elite [e'lite] *nf* elite.

elocuencia [elo'kwenθja] *nf* eloquence.

elogiar [elo'xjar] *vt* to praise, eulogize; **elogio** *nm* praise.

elote [e'lote] *nm* (AM) corn on the cob.

eludir [elu'ðir] *vt* (*evitar*) to avoid, evade; (*escapar*) to escape, elude.

ella ['eʎa] *pron* (*persona*) she; (*cosa*) it; (*después de prep*: *persona*) her; (: *cosa*) it.

ellas ['eʎas] *pron* (*personas y cosas*) they; (*después de prep*) them.

ello ['eʎo] *pron* it.

ellos ['eʎos] *pron* they; (*después de prep*) them.

emanar [ema'nar] *vi*: ~ **de** to emanate from, come from; (*derivar de*) to originate in.

emancipar [emanθi'par] *vt* to emancipate; ~se *vr* to become emancipated, free o.s.

embadurnar [embaður'nar] *vt* to smear.

embajada [emba'xaða] *nf* embassy.

embajador, a [embaxa'ðor, a] *nm/f* ambassador/ambassadress.

embalar [emba'lar] *vt* (*envolver*) to parcel, wrap (up); (*envasar*) to package // *vi* to sprint.

embalsamar [embalsa'mar] *vt* to embalm.

embalse [em'balse] *nm* (*presa*) dam; (*lago*) reservoir.

embarazada [embara'θaða] *a* pregnant // *nf* pregnant woman.

embarazar [embara'θar] *vt* to obstruct, hamper; ~se *vr* (*aturdirse*) to become embarrassed; (*confundirse*) to get into a mess.

embarazo [emba'raθo] *nm* (*de mujer*) pregnancy; (*impedimento*) obstacle, obstruction; (*timidez*) embarrassment.

embarcación [embarka'θjon] *nf* (*barco*) boat, craft; (*acto*) embarkation, boarding.

embarcadero [embarka'ðero] *nm* pier, landing stage.

embarcar [embar'kar] *vt* (*cargamento*) to ship, stow; (*persona*) to embark, put on board; ~se *vr* to embark, go on board.

embargar [embar'var] *vt* (JUR) to seize, impound.

embarque *etc vb ver* **embarcar** // [em'barke] *nm* shipment, loading.

embaucar [embau'kar] *vt* to trick, fool.

embeber [embe'βer] *vt* (*absorber*) to absorb, soak up; (*empapar*) to saturate // *vi* to shrink; ~se *vr*: ~se **en la lectura** to be engrossed o absorbed in a book.

embellecer [embeʎe'θer] vt to embellish, beautify.

embestida [embes'tiða] nf attack, onslaught; (carga) charge; **embestir** vt to attack, assault; to charge, attack // vi to attack.

emblema [em'blema] nm emblem.

embobado, a [embo'βaðo, a] a (atontado) stunned, bewildered.

émbolo ['embolo] nm (AUTO) piston.

embolsar [embol'sar] vt to pocket, put in one's pocket.

emborrachar [emborra'tʃar] vt to make drunk, intoxicate; ~se vr to get drunk.

emboscada [embos'kaða] nf (celada) ambush.

embotar [embo'tar] vt to blunt, dull; ~se vr (adormecerse) to go numb.

embotellamiento [emboteʎa-'mjento] nm (AUTO) traffic jam.

embotellar [embote'ʎar] vt to bottle; ~se vr (circulación) to get into a jam.

embrague [em'braβe] nm (tb: pedal de ~) clutch.

embriagar [embrja'ɣar] vt (emborrachar) to make drunk; (alegrar) to delight; ~se vr (emborracharse) to get drunk.

embriaguez [embrja'veθ] nf (borrachera) drunkenness.

embrión [em'brjon] nm embryo.

embrollar [embro'ʎar] vt (el asunto) to confuse, complicate; (persona) to involve, embroil; ~se vr (confundirse) to get into a muddle o mess.

embrollo [em'broʎo] nm (enredo) muddle, confusion; (aprieto) jam.

embromar [embro'mar] vt (burlarse de) to tease, make fun of.

embrujado, a [embru'xaðo, a] a bewitched; **casa embrujada** haunted house.

embrutecer [embrute'θer] vt (atontar) to stupefy; ~se vr to be stupefied.

embudo [em'buðo] nm funnel.

embuste [em'buste] nm trick; (mentira) lie; (hum) fib; ~ro, a a lying, deceitful // nm/f (tramposo) cheat; (mentiroso) liar; (hum) fibber.

embutido [embu'tiðo] nm (CULIN) sausage; (TEC) inlay.

embutir [embu'tir] vt (TEC) to inlay; (llenar) to pack tight, cram.

emergencia [emer'xenθja] nf emergency; (surgimiento) emergence.

emerger [emer'xer] vi to emerge, appear.

emigración [emixra'θjon] nf emigration; (de pájaros) migration.

emigrar [emi'xrar] vi (personas) to emigrate; (pájaros) to migrate.

eminencia [emi'nenθja] nf eminence; **eminente** a eminent, distinguished; (elevado) high.

emisario [emi'sarjo] nm emissary.

emisión [emi'sjon] nf (acto) emission; (COM etc) issue; (RADIO, TV: acto) broadcasting; (: programa) broadcast, programme (Brit), program (US).

emisora [emi'sora] nf radio o broadcasting station.

emitir [emi'tir] vt (olor etc) to emit, give off; (moneda etc) to issue; (opinión) to express; (RADIO) to broadcast.

emoción [emo'θjon] nf emotion; (excitación) excitement; (sentimiento) feeling.

emocionante [emoθjo'nante] a (excitante) exciting, thrilling.

emocionar [emoθjo'nar] vt (excitar) to excite, thrill; (conmover) to move, touch; (impresionar) to impress.

emotivo, a [emo'tiβo, a] a emotional.

empacar [empa'kar] vt (gen) to pack; (en caja, crate) to crate.

empacho [em'patʃo] nm (MED) indigestion; (fig) embarrassment.

empadronarse [empaðro'narse] vr (POL: como elector) to register.

empalagoso, a [empala'ɣoso, a] *a* cloying; *(fig)* tiresome.

empalmar [empal'mar] *vt* to join, connect // *vi (dos caminos)* to meet, join; **empalme** *nm* joint, connection; junction; *(de trenes)* connection.

empanada [empa'naða] *nf* pie, pasty.

empantanarse [empanta'narse] *vr* to get swamped; *(fig)* to get bogged down.

empañarse [empa'ɲarse] *vr (nublarse)* to get misty, steam up.

empapar [empa'par] *vt (mojar)* to soak, saturate; *(absorber)* to soak up, absorb; ~**se** *vr:* ~**se de** to soak up.

empapelar [empape'lar] *vt (paredes)* to paper.

empaquetar [empake'tar] *vt* to pack, parcel up.

emparedado [empare'ðaðo] *nm* sandwich.

empastar [empas'tar] *vt (embadurnar)* to paste; *(diente)* to fill.

empaste [em'paste] *nm (de diente)* filling.

empatar [empa'tar] *vi* to draw, tie; **empate** *nm* draw, tie.

empecé, empecemos *vb ver* **empezar.**

empedernido, a [empeðer'niðo, a] *a* hard, heartless; *(fijado)* hardened, inveterate.

empedrado, a [empe'ðraðo, a] *a* paved // *nm* paving.

empedrar [empe'ðrar] *vt* to pave.

empeine [em'peine] *nm (de pie, zapato)* instep.

empeñado, a [empe'ɲaðo, a] *a (persona)* determined; *(objeto)* pawned.

empeñar [empe'ɲar] *vt (objeto)* to pawn, pledge; *(persona)* to compel; ~**se** *vr (obligarse)* to bind o.s., pledge o.s.; *(endeudarse)* to get into debt; ~**se en** to be set on, be determined to.

empeño [em'peɲo] *nm (determinación, insistencia)* determination, insistence; *(cosa prendada)* pledge; **casa de** ~**s** pawnshop.

empeorar [empeo'rar] *vt* to make worse, worsen // *vi* to get worse, deteriorate.

empequeñecer [empekeɲe'θer] *vt* to dwarf; *(fig)* to belittle.

emperador [empera'ðor] *nm* emperor.

emperatriz [empera'triθ] *nf* empress.

empezar [empe'θar] *vt, vi* to begin, start.

empiece *etc vb ver* **empezar.**

empiezo *etc vb ver* **empezar.**

empinar [empi'nar] *vt* to raise; ~**se** *vr (persona)* to stand on tiptoe; *(animal)* to rear up; *(camino)* to climb steeply.

empírico, a [em'piriko, a] *a* empirical.

emplasto [em'plasto], **emplaste** [em'plaste] *nm (MED)* plaster.

emplazamiento [emplaθa'mjento] *nm* site, location; *(JUR)* summons *sg.*

emplazar [empla'θar] *vt (ubicar)* to site, place, locate; *(JUR)* to summons; *(convocar)* to summon.

empleado, a [emple'aðo, a] *nm/f (gen)* employee; *(de banco etc)* clerk.

emplear [emple'ar] *vt (usar)* to use, employ; *(dar trabajo a)* to employ; ~**se** *vr (conseguir trabajo)* to be employed; *(ocuparse)* to occupy o.s.

empleo [em'pleo] *nm (puesto)* job; *(puestos: colectivamente)* employment; *(uso)* use, employment.

empobrecer [empoβre'θer] *vt* to impoverish; ~**se** *vr* to become poor o impoverished.

empollar [empo'ʎar] *vt, vi (fam)* to swot (up); **empollón, ona** *nm/f (fam)* swot.

emporio [em'porjo] *nm* emporium, trading centre; *(AM: gran almacén)* department store.

empotrado, a [empo'traðo, a] *a*

(armario etc) built-in.

emprender [empren'der] *vt*
(empezar) to begin, embark on;
(acometer) to tackle, take on.

empresa [em'presa] *nf (de espíritu
etc)* enterprise; *(COM)* company,
firm; ~**rio, a** *nm (COM)* manager.

empréstito [em'prestito] *nm* (public) loan.

empujar [empu'xar] *vt* to push,
shove; **empuje** *nm* thrust; *(presión)*
pressure; *(fig)* vigour, drive.

empujón [empu'xon] *nm* push,
shove.

empuñar [empu'ɲar] *vt (asir)* to
grasp, take (firm) hold of.

emular [emu'lar] *vt* to emulate;
(rivalizar) to rival.

EN [en] *prep* **1** *(posición)* in; (: *sobre)*
on; **está ~ el cajón** it's in the
drawer; **~ Argentina/La Paz** in
Argentina/La Paz; **~ la oficina/el
colegio** at the office/school; **está ~
el suelo/quinto piso** it's on the
floor/the fifth floor
2 *(dirección)* into; **entró ~ el aula**
she went into the classroom; **meter
algo ~ el bolso** to put sth into one's
bag
3 *(tiempo)* in; on; **~ 1605/3
semanas/invierno** in 1605/3 weeks/
winter; **~ (el mes de) enero** in
(the month of) January; **~ aquella
ocasión/aquella época** on that
occasion/at that time
4 *(precio)* for; **lo vendió ~ 20
dólares** he sold it for 20 dollars
5 *(diferencia)* by; **reducir/
aumentar ~ una tercera parte/un
20 por ciento** to reduce/increase by
a third/20 per cent
6 *(manera)*: **~ avión/autobús** by
plane/bus; **escrito ~ inglés** written
in English
7 *(después de vb que indica gastar
etc)* on; **han cobrado demasiado ~
dietas** they've charged too much to
expenses; **se le va la mitad del**

sueldo ~ comida he spends half his
salary on food
8 *(tema, ocupación)*: **experto ~ la
materia** expert on the subject;
trabaja ~ la construcción he
works in the building industry
9 *(a ~ + infinitivo)*: **lento ~
reaccionar** slow to react.

---

enajenación [enaxena'θjon] *nf*,
enajenamiento [enaxena'mjento]
nm alienation; *(fig: distracción)*
absent-mindedness; (: *embelesa-
miento)* rapture, trance.

enajenar [enaxe'nar] *vt* to alienate;
(fig) to carry away.

enamorado, a [enamo'raðo, a] *a* in
love // *nm/f* lover.

enamorar [enamo'rar] *vt* to win the
love of; ~**se** *vr*: ~**se de alguien** to
fall in love with sb.

enano, a [e'nano, a] *a* tiny // *nm/f*
dwarf.

enardecer [enarðe'θer] *vt (pasiones)*
to fire, inflame; *(persona)* to fill with
enthusiasm; ~**se** *vr*: ~ **por** to get
excited about; *(entusiasmarse)* to get
enthusiastic about.

encabezamiento [enkaβeθa'mjento]
nm (de carta) heading; *(de periódico)* headline; *(preámbulo)* foreword,
preface.

encabezar [enkaβe'θar] *vt
(movimiento, revolución)* to lead,
head; *(lista)* to head, be at the top
of; *(carta)* to put a heading to; *(libro)* to entitle.

encadenar [enkaðe'nar] *vt* to chain
(together); *(poner grilletes a)* to
shackle.

encajar [enka'xar] *vt (ajustar)*: ~
(en) to fit (into); *(fam: golpe)* to
give, deal; *(entrometer)* to insert // *vi*
to fit (well); *(fig: corresponder a)* to
match; ~**se** *vr*: ~**se en un sillón** to
squeeze into a chair.

encaje [en'kaxe] *nm (labor)* lace.

encalar [enka'lar] *vt (pared)* to
whitewash.

encallar [enka'ʎar] *vi (NAUT)* to run

aground.

encaminar [enkami'nar] vt to direct, send; ~se vr: ~se a to set out for.

encandilar [enkandi'lar] vt to dazzle.

encantado, a [enkan'taðo, a] a (hechizado) bewitched; (muy contento) delighted; ¡~! how do you do!, pleased to meet you.

encantador, a [enkãnta'ðor, a] a charming, lovely // nm/f magician, enchanter/enchantress.

encantar [enkan'tar] vt to charm, delight; (hechizar) to bewitch, cast a spell on; **encanto** nm (magia) spell, charm; (fig) charm, delight.

encarcelar [enkarθe'lar] vt to imprison, jail.

encarecer [enkare'θer] vt to put up the price of // vi, ~se vr to get dearer.

encarecimiento [enkareθi'mjento] nm price increase.

encargado, a [enkar'γaðo, a] a in charge // nm/f agent, representative; (responsable) person in charge.

encargar [enkar'γar] vt to entrust; (recomendar) to urge, recommend; ~se vr: ~se de to look after, take charge of.

encargo [en'karγo] nm (pedido) assignment, job; (responsabilidad) responsibility; (recomendación) recommendation; (COM) order.

encariñarse [enkari'narse] vr: ~ con to grow fond of, get attached to.

encarnación [enkarna'θjon] nf incarnation, embodiment.

encarnizado, a [enkarni'θaðo, a] a (lucha) bloody, fierce.

encarrilar [enkarri'lar] vt (tren) to put back on the rails; (fig) to correct, put on the right track.

encasillar [enkasi'Aar] vt (tb: fig) to pigeonhole; (actor) to typecast.

encauzar [enkau'θar] vt to channel.

encendedor [enθende'ðor] nm lighter.

encender [enθen'der] vt (con fuego) to light; (incendiar) to set fire to; (luz, radio) to put on, switch on;

(avivar: pasiones) to inflame; ~se vr to catch fire; (excitarse) to get excited; (de cólera) to flare up; (el rostro) to blush.

encendido [enθen'diðo] nm (AUTO) ignition.

encerado [enθe'raðo] nm (ESCOL) blackboard.

encerar [enθe'rar] vt (suelo) to wax, polish.

encerrar [enθe'rrar] vt (confinar) to shut in, shut up; (comprender, incluir) to include, contain.

encía [en'θia] nf gum.

encienda etc vb ver **encender**.

encierro etc vb ver **encerrar** // [en'θjerro] nm shutting in, shutting up; (calabozo) prison.

encima [en'θima] ad (sobre) above, over; (además) besides; ~ **de** (en) on, on top of; (sobre) above, over; (además de) besides, on top of; **por** ~ **de** over; ¿llevas dinero ~? have you (got) any money on you?; **se me vino** ~ it got on top of me.

encinta [en'θinta] a pregnant.

enclenque [en'klenke] a weak, sickly.

encoger [enko'xer] vt to shrink, contract; (fig: asustar) to scare; ~se vr to shrink, contract; (fig) to cringe; ~se **de hombros** to shrug one's shoulders.

encolar [enko'lar] vt (engomar) to glue, paste; (pegar) to stick down.

encolerizar [enkoleri'θar] vt to anger, provoke; ~se vr to get angry.

encomendar [enkomen'dar] vt to entrust, commend; ~se vr: ~se **a** to put one's trust in.

encomiar [enko'mjar] vt to praise, pay tribute to.

encomienda etc vb ver **encomendar** // [enko'mjenda] nf (encargo) charge, commission; (elogio) tribute; ~ **postal** (AM) parcel post.

encono [en'kono] nm (rencor) rancour, spite.

encontrado, a [enkon'traðo, a] a

(*contrario*) contrary, conflicting; (*hostil*) hostile.

encontrar [enkon'trar] *vt* (*hallar*) to find; (*inesperadamente*) to meet, run into; ~**se** *vr* to meet (each other); (*situarse*) to be (situated); (*entrar en conflicto*) to crash, collide; ~**se con** o meet; ~**se bien** (**de salud**) to feel well.

encorvar [enkor'βar] *vt* to curve; (*inclinar*) to bend (down); ~**se** *vr* to bend down, bend over.

encrespar [enkres'par] *vt* (*cabellos*) to curl; (*fig*) to anger, irritate; ~**se** *vr* (*el mar*) to get rough; (*fig*) to get cross, get irritated.

encrucijada [enkruθi'xaða] *nf* crossroads *sg*; (*empalme*) junction.

encuadernación [enkwaðerna'θjon] *nf* binding.

encuadernador, a [enkwaðerna-'ðor, a] *nm/f* bookbinder.

encuadrar [enkwa'ðrar] *vt* (*retrato*) to frame; (*ajustar*) to fit, insert; (*encerrar*) to contain.

encubrir [enku'βrir] *vt* (*ocultar*) to hide, conceal; (*criminal*) to harbour, shelter.

encuentro *etc vb ver* **encontrar** // [en'kwentro] *nm* (*de personas*) meeting; (*AUTO etc*) collision, crash; (*DEPORTE*) match, game; (*MIL*) encounter.

encuesta [en'kwesta] *nf* inquiry, investigation; (*sondeo*) (public) opinion poll; ~ **judicial** post mortem.

encumbrado, a [enkum'braðo, a] *a* eminent, distinguished.

encumbrar [enkum'brar] *vt* (*persona*) to exalt; ~**se** *vr* (*fig*) to become conceited.

encharcado, a [entʃar'kaðo, a] *a* (*terreno*) flooded.

enchufar [entʃu'far] *vt* (*ELEC*) to plug in; (*TEC*) to connect, fit together; **enchufe** *nm* (*ELEC*: *clavija*) plug; (: *toma*) socket; (*de dos tubos*) joint, connection; (*fam*: *influencia*) contact, connection; (: *puesto*) cushy job.

endeble [en'deβle] *a* (*argumento*, *excusa*, *persona*) weak.

endemoniado, a [endemo'njaðo, a] *a* possessed (of the devil); (*travieso*) devilish.

enderezar [endere'θar] *vt* (*poner derecho*) to straighten (out); (*verticalmente*) to set upright; (*fig*) to straighten o sort out; (*dirigir*) to direct; ~**se** *vr* to straighten up.

endeudarse [endeu'ðarse] *vr* to get into debt.

endiablado, a [endja'βlaðo, a] *a* devilish, diabolical; (*hum*) mischievous.

endilgar [endil'γar] *vt* (*fam*): ~**le algo a uno** to lumber sb with sth; ~**le un sermón a uno** to lecture sb.

endomingarse [endomin'garse] *vr* to dress up, put on one's best clothes.

endosar [endo'sar] *vt* (*cheque etc*) to endorse.

endulzar [endul'θar] *vt* to sweeten; (*suavizar*) to soften.

endurecer [endure'θer] *vt* to harden; ~**se** *vr* to harden, grow hard.

endurecido, a [endure'θiðo, a] *a* (*duro*) hard; (*fig*) hardy, tough; **estar ~ a algo** to be hardened o used to sth.

enemigo, a [ene'miɣo, a] *a* enemy, hostile // *nm/f* enemy.

enemistad [enemis'tað] *nf* enmity.

enemistar [enemis'tar] *vt* to make enemies of, cause a rift between; ~**se** *vr* to become enemies; (*amigos*) to fall out.

energía [ener'xia] *nf* (*vigor*) energy, drive; (*empuje*) push; (*TEC*, *ELEC*) energy, power.

enérgico, a [e'nerxiko, a] *a* (*gen*) energetic; (*voz*, *modales*) forceful.

energúmeno, a [ener'xumeno, a] *nm/f* (*fig fam*) madman/woman.

enero [e'nero] *nm* January.

enfadado, a [enfa'ðaðo, a] *a* angry, annoyed.

enfadar [enfa'ðar] *vt* to anger, annoy; ~**se** *vr* to get angry o annoyed.

enfado [en'faðo] *nm* (*enojo*) anger, annoyance; (*disgusto*) trouble, bother.

énfasis ['enfasis] *nm* emphasis, stress.

enfático, a [en'fatiko, a] *a* emphatic.

enfermar [enfer'mar] *vt* to make ill // *vi* to fall ill, be taken ill.

enfermedad [enferme'ðað] *nf* illness; ~ **venérea** venereal disease.

enfermera [enfer'mera] *nf* nurse.

enfermería [enferme'ria] *nf* infirmary; (*de colegio etc*) sick bay.

enfermero [enfer'mero] *nm* male nurse.

enfermizo, a [enfer'miθo, a] *a* (*persona*) sickly, unhealthy; (*fig*) unhealthy.

enfermo, a [en'fermo, a] *a* ill, sick // *nm/f* invalid, sick person; (*en hospital*) patient.

enflaquecer [enflake'θer] *vt* (*adelgazar*) to make thin; (*debilitar*) to weaken.

enfocar [enfo'kar] *vt* (*foto etc*) to focus; (*problema etc*) to consider, look at.

enfoque *etc vb ver* **enfocar** [en'foke] *nm* focus.

enfrentar [enfren'tar] *vt* (*peligro*) to face (up to), confront; (*oponer, carear*) to put face to face; ~**se** *vr* (*dos personas*) to face o confront each other; (*DEPORTE: dos equipos*) to meet; ~**se** *a o con* to face up to, confront.

enfrente [en'frente] *ad* opposite; la casa de ~ the house opposite, the house across the street; ~ **de** *prep* opposite, facing.

enfriamiento [enfria'mjento] *nm* chilling, refrigeration; (*MED*) cold, chill.

enfriar [enfri'ar] *vt* (*alimentos*) to cool, chill; (*algo caliente*) to cool down; (*habitación*) to air, freshen; ~**se** *vr* to cool down; (*MED*) to catch a chill; (*amistad*) to cool.

enfurecer [enfure'θer] *vt* to enrage, madden; ~**se** *vr* to become furious,

fly into a rage; (*mar*) to get rough.

engalanar [engala'nar] *vt* (*adornar*) to adorn; (*ciudad*) to decorate; ~**se** *vr* to get dressed up.

enganchar [engan'tʃar] *vt* to hook; (*ropa*) to hang up; (*dos vagones*) to hitch up; (*TEC*) to couple, connect; (*MIL*) to recruit; (*fam: persona*) to rope in; ~**se** *vr* (*MIL*) to enlist, join up.

enganche [en'gantʃe] *nm* hook; (*TEC*) coupling, connection; (*acto*) hooking (up); (*MIL*) recruitment, enlistment; (*AM: depósito*) deposit.

engañar [enga'ɲar] *vt* to deceive; (*estafar*) to cheat, swindle; ~**se** *vr* (*equivocarse*) to be wrong; (*disimular la verdad*) to deceive o kid o.s.

engaño [en'gaɲo] *nm* deceit; (*estafa*) trick, swindle; (*error*) mistake, misunderstanding; (*ilusión*) delusion; ~**so, a** *a* (*tramposo*) crooked; (*mentiroso*) dishonest, deceitful; (*aspecto*) deceptive; (*consejo*) misleading.

engarzar [engar'θar] *vt* (*joya*) to set, mount; (*fig*) to link, connect.

engatusar [engatu'sar] *vt* (*fam*) to coax.

engendrar [enxen'drar] *vt* to breed; (*procrear*) to beget; (*fig*) to cause, produce; **engendro** *nm* (*BIO*) foetus; (*fig*) monstrosity; (*idea*) brainchild.

englobar [englo'βar] *vt* (*incluir*) to include, comprise.

engomar [engo'mar] *vt* to glue, stick.

engordar [engor'ðar] *vt* to fatten // *vi* to get fat, put on weight.

engorroso, a [engo'rroso, a] *a* bothersome, trying.

engranaje [engra'naxe] *nm* (*AUTO*) gear.

engrandecer [engrande'θer] *vt* to enlarge, magnify; (*alabar*) to praise, speak highly of; (*exagerar*) to exaggerate.

engrasar [engra'sar] *vt* (*TEC: poner*

grasa) to grease; (: *lubricar*) to lubricate, oil; (*manchar*) to make greasy.

engreído, a [engre'iðo, a] *a* vain, conceited.

engrosar [engro'sar] *vt* (*ensanchar*) to enlarge; (*aumentar*) to increase; (*hinchar*) to swell.

enhebrar [ene'βrar] *vt* to thread.

enhorabuena [enora'βwena] *nf* congratulations *pl* // *ad* well and good.

enigma [e'niɣma] *nm* enigma; (*problema*) puzzle; (*misterio*) mystery.

enjabonar [enxaβo'nar] *vt* to soap; (*fam: adular*) to soft-soap; (: *regañar*) to tick off.

enjambre [en'xambre] *nm* swarm.

enjaular [enxau'lar] *vt* to (put in a) cage; (*fam*) to jail, lock up.

enjuagar [enxwa'ɣar] *vt* (*ropa*) to rinse (out).

enjuague *etc vb ver* **enjuagar** // [en'xwaɣe] *nm* (MED) mouthwash; (*de ropa*) rinse, rinsing.

enjugar [enxu'ɣar] *vt* to wipe (off); (*lágrimas*) to dry; (*déficit*) to wipe out.

enjuiciar [enxwi'θjar] *vt* (JUR: *procesar*) to prosecute, try; (*fig*) to judge.

enjuto, a [en'xuto, a] *a* dry, dried up; (*fig*) lean, skinny.

enlace [en'laθe] *nm* link, connection; (*relación*) relationship; (*tb*: ~ **matrimonial**) marriage; (*de carretera, trenes*) connection; ~ **sindical** shop steward.

enlazar [enla'θar] *vt* (*unir con lazos*) to bind together; (*atar*) to tie; (*conectar*) to link, connect; (*AM*) to lasso.

enlodar [enlo'ðar] *vt* to cover in mud; (*fig: manchar*) to stain; (: *rebajar*) to debase.

enloquecer [enloke'θer] *vt* to drive mad // *vi*, ~**se** *vr* to go mad.

enlutado, a [enlu'taðo, a] *a* (*persona*) in mourning.

enmarañar [enmara'par] *vt* (*en-*

redar) to tangle (up), entangle; (*complicar*) to complicate; (*confundir*) to confuse; ~**se** *vr* (*enredarse*) to become entangled; (*confundirse*) to get confused.

enmarcar [enmar'kar] *vt* (*cuadro*) to frame.

enmascarar [enmaska'rar] *vt* to mask; ~**se** *vr* to put on a mask.

enmendar [enmen'dar] *vt* to emend, correct; (*constitución etc*) to amend; (*comportamiento*) to reform; ~**se** *vr* to reform, mend one's ways; **enmienda** *nf* correction; amendment; reform.

enmohecerse [enmoe'θerse] *vr* (*metal*) to rust, go rusty; (*muro, plantas*) to get mouldy.

enmudecer [enmuðe'θer] *vi*, **enmudecerse** *vr* (*perder el habla*) to fall silent; (*guardar silencio*) to remain silent.

ennegrecer [ennevre'θer] *vt* (*poner negro*) to blacken; (*oscurecer*) to darken; ~**se** *vr* to turn black; (*oscurecerse*) to get dark, darken.

ennoblecer [ennoβle'θer] *vt* to ennoble.

enojadizo, a [enoxa'ðiθo, a] *a* irritable, short-tempered.

enojar [eno'xar] *vt* (*encolerizar*) to anger; (*disgustar*) to annoy, upset; ~**se** *vr* to get angry; to get annoyed.

enojo [e'noxo] *nm* (*cólera*) anger; (*irritación*) annoyance; ~**so, a** *a* annoying.

enorgullecerse [enorɣuʎe'θerse] *vr* to be proud; ~ **de** to pride o.s. on, be proud of.

enorme [e'norme] *a* enormous, huge; (*fig*) monstrous; **enormidad** *nf* hugeness, immensity.

enraizar [enrai'θar] *vi* to take root.

enredadera [enreða'ðera] *nf* (BOT) creeper, climbing plant.

enredar [enre'ðar] *vt* (*cables, hilos etc*) to tangle (up), entangle; (*situación*) to complicate, confuse; (*meter cizaña*) to sow discord among o between; (*implicar*) to embroil, implicate; ~se *vr* to get entangled, get tangled (up); (*situación*) to get complicated; (*persona*) to get embroiled; (*AM: fam*) to meddle.

enredo [en'reðo] *nm* (*maraña*) tangle; (*confusión*) mix-up, confusion; (*intriga*) intrigue.

enrevesado, a [enreβe'saðo, a] *a* (*asunto*) complicated, involved.

enriquecer [enrike'θer] *vt* to make rich, enrich; ~se *vr* to get rich.

enrojecer [enroxe'θer] *vt* to redden // *vi*, ~se *vr* (*persona*) to blush.

enrolar [enro'lar] *vt* (*MIL*) to enlist; (*reclutar*) to recruit; ~se *vr* (*MIL*) to join up; (*afiliarse*) to enrol.

enrollar [enro'ʎar] *vt* to roll (up), wind (up).

enroscar [enros'kar] *vt* (*torcer, doblar*) to coil (round), wind; (*tornillo, rosca*) to screw in; ~se *vr* to coil, wind.

ensalada [ensa'laða] *nf* salad; **ensaladilla (rusa)** *nf* Russian salad.

ensalzar [ensal'θar] *vt* (*alabar*) to praise, extol; (*exaltar*) to exalt.

ensambladura [ensambla'ðura] *nf*, **ensamblaje** [ensam'blaxe] *nm* assembly; (*TEC*) joint.

ensamblar [ensam'blar] *vt* to assemble.

ensanchar [ensan'tʃar] *vt* (*hacer más ancho*) to widen; (*agrandar*) to enlarge, expand; (*COSTURA*) to let out; ~se *vr* to get wider, expand; (*pey*) to give o.s. airs; **ensanche** *nm* (*de calle*) widening; (*de negocio*) expansion.

ensangrentar [ensangren'tar] *vt* to stain with blood.

ensañar [ensa'ɲar] *vt* to enrage; ~se *vr*: ~se con to treat brutally.

ensartar [ensar'tar] *vt* (*cuentas, perlas etc*) to string (together).

ensayar [ensa'jar] *vt* to test, try (out); (*TEATRO*) to rehearse.

ensayista [ensa'jista] *nm/f* essayist.

ensayo [en'sajo] *nm* test, trial; (*QUÍMICA*) experiment; (*TEATRO*) rehearsal; (*DEPORTE*) try; (*ESCOL,*

(*LITERATURA*) essay.

ensenada [ense'naða] *nf* inlet, cove.

enseñanza [ense'ɲanθa] *nf* (*educación*) education; (*acción*) teaching; (*doctrina*) teaching, doctrine.

enseñar [ense'ɲar] *vt* (*educar*) to teach; (*instruir*) to teach, instruct; (*mostrar, señalar*) to show.

enseres [en'seres] *nmpl* belongings.

ensillar [ensi'ʎar] *vt* to saddle (up).

ensimismarse [ensimis'marse] *vr* (*abstraerse*) to become lost in thought; (*estar absorto*) to be lost in thought; (*AM*) to become conceited.

ensordecer [ensorðe'θer] *vt* to deafen // *vi* to go deaf.

ensortijado, a [ensorti'xaðo, a] (*pelo*) curly.

ensuciar [ensu'θjar] *vt* (*manchar*) to dirty, soil; (*fig*) to defile; ~se *vr* (*mancharse*) to get dirty; (*fig*) to dirty o.s., wet o.s.

ensueño [en'sweɲo] *nm* (*sueño*) dream, fantasy; (*ilusión*) illusion; (*soñando despierto*) daydream.

entablado [enta'βlaðo] *nm* (*piso*) floorboards *pl*; (*armazón*) boarding.

entablar [enta'βlar] *vt* (*recubrir*) to board (up); (*AJEDREZ, DAMAS*) to set up; (*conversación*) to strike up; (*JUR*) to file // *vi* to draw.

entablillar [entaβli'ʎar] *vt* (*MED*) to (put in a) splint.

entallar [enta'ʎar] *vt* (*traje*) to tailor // *vi*: **el traje entalla bien** the suit fits well.

ente ['ente] *nm* (*organización*) body, organization; (*fam: persona*) odd character.

entender [enten'der] *vt* (*comprender*) to understand; (*darse cuenta*) to realize; (*querer decir*) to mean // *vi* to understand; (*creer*) to think, believe; ~ **de** to know all about; ~ **algo de** to know a little about; ~ **en** to deal with, have to do with; ~se *vr* (*comprenderse*) to be understood; (*2 personas*) to get on together; (*ponerse de acuerdo*) to agree, reach an agreement; ~se mal (2 personas) to get on badly.

entendido, a [enten'diðo, a] *a* (*comprendido*) understood; (*hábil*) skilled; (*inteligente*) knowledgeable // *nmf* (*experto*) expert // *excl* agreed!

entendimiento *nm* (*comprensión*) understanding; (*inteligencia*) mind, intellect; (*juicio*) judgement.

enterado, a [ente'raðo, a] *a* a well-informed; **estar ~ de** to know about, be aware of.

enteramente [entera'mente] *ad* entirely, completely.

enterar [ente'rar] *vt* (*informar*) to inform, tell; **~se** *vr* to find out, get to know.

entereza [ente'reθa] *nf* (*totalidad*) entirety; (*fig*: *carácter*) strength of mind; (*: honradez*) integrity.

enternecer [enterne'θer] *vt* (*ablandar*) to soften; (*apiadar*) to touch, move; **~se** *vr* to be touched, be moved.

entero, a [en'tero, a] *a* (*total*) whole, entire; (*fig*: *recto*) honest; (*: firme*) firm, resolute // *nm* (*COM*: *punto*) point; (*AM*: *pago*) payment.

enterrador [enterra'ðor] *nm* gravedigger.

enterrar [ente'rrar] *vt* to bury.

entibiar [enti'βjar] *vt* (*enfriar*) to cool; (*calentar*) to warm; **~se** *vr* (*fig*) to cool.

entidad [enti'ðað] *nf* (*empresa*) firm, company; (*organismo*) body; (*sociedad*) society; (FILOSOFÍA) entity.

entiendo *etc vb ver* **entender.**

entierro [en'tjerro] *nm* (*acción*) burial; (*funeral*) funeral.

entomología [entomolo'xia] *nf* entomology.

entonación [entona'θjon] *nf* (LING) intonation; (*fig*) conceit.

entonar [ento'nar] *vt* (*canción*) to intone; (*colores*) to tone; (MED) to tone up // *vi* to be in tune; **~se** *vr* (*engreírse*) to give o.s. airs.

entonces [en'tonθes] *ad* then, at that time; **desde ~** since then; **en aquel**

~ at that time; (pues) ~ and so.

entornar [entor'nar] *vt* (*puerta, ventana*) to half close, leave ajar; (*los ojos*) to screw up.

entorpecer [entorpe'θer] *vt* (*entendimiento*) to dull; (*impedir*) to obstruct, hinder; (*: tránsito*) to slow down, delay.

entrada [en'traða] *nf* (*acción*) entry, access; (*sitio*) entrance, way in; (INFORM) input; (COM) receipts *pl*, takings *pl*; (CULIN) entrée; (DEPORTE) innings *sg*; (TEATRO) house, audience; (*para el cine etc*) ticket; (COM): **~s y salidas** income and expenditure; (TEC): **~ de aire** intake *o* inlet; **de ~** from the outset.

entrado, a [en'traðo, a] *a*: **~ en años** elderly; **una vez ~ el verano** in the summer(time), when summer comes.

entrante [en'trante] *a* next, coming; **mes/año ~** next month/year.

entraña [en'traŋa] *nf* (*fig*: *centro*) heart, core; (*raíz*) root; **~s** *nfpl* (ANAT) entrails; (*fig*) heart *sg*; **entrañable** *a* close, intimate.

entrar [en'trar] *vt* (*introducir*) to bring in; (INFORM) to input // *vi* (*meterse*) to go in, come in, enter; (*comenzar*): **~ diciendo** to begin by saying; **no me entra** I can't get the hang of it.

entre ['entre] *prep* (*dos*) between; (*más de dos*) among(st).

entreabrir [entrea'βrir] *vt* to half-open, open halfway.

entrecejo [entre'θexo] *nm*: **fruncir el ~** to frown.

entrecortado, a [entrekor'taðo, a] *a* (*respiración*) difficult; (*habla*) faltering.

entredicho [entre'ðitʃo] *nm* (JUR) injunction; **poner en ~** to cast doubt on; **estar en ~** to be banned.

entrega [en'treɣa] *nf* (*de mercancías*) delivery; (*de novela etc*) instalment.

entregar [entre'ɣar] *vt* (*dar*) to hand (over), deliver; **~se** *vr* (*rendirse*) to surrender, give in, submit; (*dedicarse*) to devote o.s.

entrelazar [entrela'θar] vt to entwine.

entremeses [entre'meses] nmpl hors d'œuvres.

entremeter [entreme'ter] vt to insert, put in; ~**se** vr to meddle, interfere; **entremetido**, a a meddling, interfering.

entremezclar [entremeθ'klar] vt, **entremezclarse** vr to intermingle.

entrenador, a [entrena'ðor, a] nm/f trainer, coach.

entrenarse [entre'narse] vr to train.

entrepierna [entre'pjerna] nf crotch.

entresacar [entresa'kar] vt to pick out, select.

entresuelo [entre'swelo] nm mezzanine, entresol.

entretanto [entre'tanto] ad meanwhile, meantime.

entretejer [entrete'xer] vt to interweave.

entretener [entrete'ner] vt (*divertir*) to entertain, amuse; (*detener*) to hold up, delay; (*mantener*) to maintain; ~**se** vr (*divertirse*) to amuse o.s.; (*retrasarse*) to delay, linger; **entretenido**, a a entertaining, amusing; **entretenimiento** nm entertainment, amusement; (*mantenimiento*) upkeep, maintenance.

entrever [entre'βer] vt to glimpse, catch a glimpse of.

entrevista [entre'βista] nf interview; **entrevistar** vt to interview; **entrevistarse** vr to have an interview.

entristecer [entriste'θer] vt to sadden, grieve; ~**se** vr to grow sad.

entrometer [entrome'ter] vt etc = **entremeter** etc.

entroncar [entron'kar] vi to be connected o related.

entumecer [entume'θer] vt to numb, benumb; ~**se** vr (*por el frío*) to go o become numb; **entumecido**, a a numb, stiff.

enturbiar [entur'βjar] vt (*el agua*) to

make cloudy; (*fig*) to confuse; ~**se** vr (*oscurecerse*) to become cloudy; (*fig*) to get confused, become obscure.

entusiasmar [entusjas'mar] vt to excite, fill with enthusiasm; (*gustar mucho*) to delight; ~**se** vr: (*~se con o por* to get enthusiastic o excited about.

entusiasmo [entu'sjasmo] nm enthusiasm; (*excitación*) excitement.

entusiasta [entu'sjasta] a enthusiastic // nm/f enthusiast.

enumerar [enume'rar] vt to enumerate.

enunciación [enunθja'θjon] nf, **enunciado** [enun'θjaðo] nm enunciation; (*declaración*) declaration, statement.

envainar [enβai'nar] vt to sheathe.

envalentonar [enβalento'nar] vt to give courage to; ~**se** vr (*pey: jactarse*) to boast, brag.

envanecer [enβane'θer] vt to make conceited; ~**se** vr to grow conceited.

envasar [enβa'sar] vt (*empaquetar*) to pack, wrap; (*enfrascar*) to bottle; (*enlatar*) to can; (*embolsar*) to pocket.

envase [en'βase] nm (*en paquete*) packing, wrapping; (*en botella*) bottling; (*en lata*) canning; (*recipiente*) container; (*paquete*) package; (*botella*) bottle; (*lata*) tin (*Brit*), can.

envejecer [enβexe'θer] vt to make old, age // vi, ~**se** vr (*volverse viejo*) to grow old; (*parecer viejo*) to age.

envenenar [enβene'nar] vt to poison; (*fig*) to embitter.

envergadura [enβerɣa'ðura] nf (*fig*) scope, compass.

envés [en'βes] nm (*de tela*) back, wrong side.

enviar [en'βjar] vt to send.

envidia [en'βiðja] nf (*deseo ferviente*) envy; (*celos*) jealousy; **envidiar** vt (*desear*) to envy; (*tener celos de*) to be jealous of.

envío [en'βio] nm (*acción*) sending;

(de mercancías) consignment; *(de dinero)* remittance.

enviudar [enβju'ðar] *vi* to be widowed.

envoltura [enßol'tura] *nf (cobertura)* cover; *(embalaje)* wrapper, wrapping.

envolver [enßol'ßer] *vt* to wrap (up); *(cubrir)* to cover; *(enemigo)* to surround; *(implicar)* to involve, implicate.

envuelto [en'ßwelto] *pp* de **envolver**.

enyesar [enje'sar] *vt (pared)* to plaster; *(MED)* to put in plaster.

épico, a ['epiko, a] *a* epic // *nf* epic.

epidemia [epi'ðemja] *nf* epidemic.

epilepsia [epi'lepsja] *nf* epilepsy.

epílogo [e'piloɣo] *nm* epilogue.

episodio [epi'soðjo] *nm* episode.

epístola [e'pistola] *nf* epistle.

época ['epoka] *nf* period, time; *(HISTORIA)* age, epoch; **hacer ~** to be epoch-making.

equidad [eki'ðað] *nf* equity.

equilibrar [ekili'βrar] *vt* to balance; **equilibrio** *nm* balance, equilibrium; **equilibrista** *nm/f (funámbulo)* tightrope walker; *(acróbata)* acrobat.

equipaje [eki'paxe] *nm* luggage; *(avíos)* equipment, kit; **~ de mano** hand luggage.

equipar [eki'par] *vt (proveer)* to equip.

equipararse [ekipa'rarse] *vr*: **~ con** to be on a level with.

equipo [e'kipo] *nm (conjunto de cosas)* equipment; *(DEPORTE, grupo)* team; (: *de obreros)* shift.

equis ['ekis] *nf inv* (the letter) X.

equitación [ekita'θjon] *nf (acto)* riding; *(arte)* horsemanship.

equitativo, a [ekita'tiβo, a] *a* equitable, fair.

equivalente [ekiβa'lente] *a, nm* equivalent.

equivaler [ekiβa'ler] *vi* to be equivalent o equal.

equivocación [ekiβoka'θjon] *nf* mistake, error.

equivocado, a [ekiβo'kaðo, a] *a* wrong, mistaken.

equivocarse [ekiβo'karse] *vr* to be wrong, make a mistake; **~ de camino** to take the wrong road.

equívoco, a [e'kiβoko, a] *a (dudoso)* suspect; *(ambiguo)* ambiguous // *nm* ambiguity; *(malentendido)* misunderstanding.

era *vb ver* **ser** // ['era] *nf* era, age.

erais *vb ver* **ser**.

éramos *vb ver* **ser**.

eran *vb ver* **ser**.

erario [e'rarjo] *nm* exchequer *(Brit)*, treasury.

eras *vb ver* **ser**.

eres *vb ver* **ser**.

erguir [er'vir] *vt* to raise, lift; *(poner derecho)* to straighten; **~se** *vr* to straighten up.

erigir [eri'xir] *vt* to erect, build; **~se** *vr*: **~se en** to set o.s. up.

erizado, a [eri'θaðo, a] *a* bristly.

erizarse [eri'θarse] *vr (pelo: de perro)* to bristle; (: *de persona)* to stand on end.

erizo [e'riθo] *nm (ZOOL)* hedgehog; *(tb:* **~ de mar**) sea-urchin.

ermitaño, a [ermi'taɲo, a] *nm/f* hermit.

erosionar [erosjo'nar] *vt* to erode.

erótico, a [e'rotiko, a] *a* erotic; **erotismo** *nm* eroticism.

erradicar [erraði'kar] *vt* to eradicate.

errante [e'rrante] *a* wandering, errant.

errar [e'rrar] *vi (vagar)* to wander, roam; *(equivocarse)* to be mistaken // *vt*: **~ el camino** to take the wrong road; **~ el tiro** to miss.

erróneo, a [e'rroneo, a] *a (equivocado)* wrong, mistaken; *(falso)* false, untrue.

error [e'rror] *nm* error, mistake; *(INFORM)* bug; **~ de imprenta** misprint.

eructar [eruk'tar] *vt* to belch, burp.

erudito, a [eru'ðito, a] *a* erudite, learned.

erupción [erup'θjon] *nf* eruption;

(MED) rash.

es vb ver **ser**.

esa, esas a demostrativo ver **ese**.

ésa, ésas pron ver **ése**.

esbelto, a [es'βelto, a] a slim, slender.

esbozo [es'βoθo] nm sketch, outline.

escabeche [eska'βetʃe] nm brine; (de aceitunas etc) pickle; **en ~** pickled.

escabroso, a [eska'βroso, a] a (accidentado) rough, uneven; (fig) tough, difficult; (: atrevido) risqué.

escabullirse [eskaβu'ʎirse] vr to slip away, to clear out.

escafandra [eska'fandra] nf (buzo) diving suit; (~ espacial) space suit.

escala [es'kala] nf (proporción, MUS) scale; (de mano) ladder; (AVIAT) stopover; **hacer ~ en** to stop o call in at.

escalafón [eskala'fon] nm (escala de salarios) salary scale, wage scale.

escalar [eska'lar] vt to climb, scale.

escalera [eska'lera] nf stairs pl, staircase; (escala) ladder; (NAIPES) run; **~ mecánica** escalator; **~ de caracol** spiral staircase.

escalfar [eskal'far] vt (huevos) to poach.

escalinata [eskali'nata] nf staircase.

escalofrío [eskalo'frio] nm (MED) chill; **~s** nmpl (fig) shivers; **escalofriante** a chilling.

escalón [eska'lon] nm step, stair; (de escalera) rung.

escalope [eska'lope] nm (CULIN) escalope.

escama [es'kama] nf (de pez, serpiente) scale; (de jabón) flake; (fig) resentment.

escamotear [eskamote'ar] vt (fam: robar) to lift, swipe; (hacer desaparecer) to make disappear.

escampar [eskam'par] vb impersonal to stop raining.

escandalizar [eskandali'θar] vt to scandalize, shock; **~se** vr to be shocked; (ofenderse) to be offended.

escándalo [es'kandalo] nm scandal;

(alboroto, tumulto) row, uproar; **escandaloso, a** a scandalous, shocking.

escandinavo, a [eskandi'naβo, a] a, nm/f Scandinavian.

escaño [es'kaɲo] nm bench; (POL) seat.

escapar [eska'par] vi (gen) to escape, run away; (DEPORTE) to break away; **~se** vr to escape, get away; (agua, gas) to leak (out).

escaparate [eskapa'rate] nm shop window.

escape [es'kape] nm (de agua, gas) leak; (de motor) exhaust; (de persona) escape.

escarabajo [eskara'βaxo] nm beetle.

escaramuza [eskara'muθa] nf skirmish; (fig) brush.

escarbar [eskar'βar] vt (gallina) to scratch; (fig) to inquire into, investigate.

escarcha [es'kartʃa] nf frost.

escarlata [eskar'lata] a inv scarlet; **escarlatina** nf scarlet fever.

escarmentar [eskarmen'tar] vt to punish severely // vi to learn one's lesson.

escarmiento etc vb ver **escarmentar** // [eskar'mjento] nm (ejemplo) lesson; (castigo) punishment.

escarnio [es'karnjo] nm mockery; (injuria) insult.

escarola [eska'rola] nf endive.

escarpado, a [eskar'paðo, a] a (pendiente) sheer, steep; (rocas) craggy.

escasear [eskase'ar] vi to be scarce.

escasez [eska'seθ] nf (falta) shortage, scarcity; (pobreza) poverty.

escaso, a [es'kaso, a] a (poco) scarce; (raro) rare; (ralo) thin, sparse; (limitado) limited.

escatimar [eskati'mar] vt (limitar) to skimp (on), be sparing with.

escena [es'θena] nf scene.

escenario [esθe'narjo] nm (TEATRO) stage; (CINE) set; (fig) scene; **escenografía** nf set design.

escepticismo [esθepti'θismo] *nm* scepticism; **escéptico, a** *a* sceptical // *nm/f* sceptic.

esclarecer [esklare'θer] *vt* (*iluminar*) to light up, illuminate; (*misterio, problema*) to shed light on.

esclavitud [esklaβi'tuð] *nf* slavery.

esclavizar [esklaβi'θar] *vt* to enslave.

esclavo, a [es'klaβo, a] *nm/f* slave.

esclusa [es'klusa] *nf* (*de canal*) lock; (*compuerta*) floodgate.

escoba [es'koβa] *nf* broom.

escocer [esko'θer] *vt* to burn, sting; ~**se** *vr* to chafe, get chafed.

escocés, esa [esko'θes, esa] *a* Scottish // *nm/f* Scotsman/woman, Scot.

Escocia [es'koθja] *nf* Scotland.

escoger [esko'xer] *vt* to choose, pick, select; **escogido, a** *a* chosen, selected; (*calidad*) choice, select.

escolar [esko'lar] *a* school *cpd* // *nm/f* schoolboy/girl, pupil.

escolta [es'kolta] *nf* escort; **escoltar** *vt* to escort.

escombros [es'kombros] *nmpl* (*basura*) rubbish *sg*; (*restos*) debris *sg*.

esconder [eskon'der] *vt* to hide, conceal; ~**se** *vr* to hide; **escondite** *nm* hiding place; (*juego*) hide-and-seek; **escondrijo** *nm* hiding place, hideout.

escopeta [esko'peta] *nf* shotgun.

escoria [es'korja] *nf* (*de alto horno*) slag; (*fig*) scum, dregs *pl*.

Escorpio [es'korpjo] *nm* Scorpio.

escorpión [eskor'pjon] *nm* scorpion.

escotado, a [esko'taðo, a] *a* low-cut.

escote [es'kote] *nm* (*de vestido*) low neck; **pagar a** ~ to share the expenses.

escotilla [esko'tiʎa] *nf* (*NAUT*) hatch(way).

escozor [esko'θor] *nm* (*dolor*) sting(ing).

escribano, a [eskri'βano, a], **escribiente** [eskri'βjente] *nm/f* clerk.

escribir [eskri'βir] *vt*, *vi* to write; ~ **a máquina** to type; ¿cómo se es-

cribe? how do you spell it?

escrito, a [es'krito, a] *pp de* **escribir** // *nm* (*documento*) document; (*manuscrito*) text, manuscript; **por** ~ in writing.

escritor, a [eskri'tor, a] *nm/f* writer.

escritorio [eskri'torjo] *nm* desk; (*oficina*) office.

escritura [eskri'tura] *nf* (*acción*) writing; (*caligrafía*) (hand)writing; (*JUR: documento*) deed.

escrúpulo [es'krupulo] *nm* scruple; (*minuciosidad*) scrupulousness; **escrupuloso, a** *a* scrupulous.

escrutar [eskru'tar] *vt* to scrutinize, examine; (*votos*) to count.

escrutinio [eskru'tinjo] *nm* (*examen atento*) scrutiny; (*POL: recuento de votos*) count(ing).

escuadra [es'kwaðra] *nf* (*MIL etc*) squad; (*NAUT*) squadron; (*de coches etc*) fleet; **escuadrilla** *nf* (*de aviones*) squadron; (*AM: de obreros*) gang.

escuadrón [eskwa'ðron] *nm* squadron.

escuálido, a [es'kwaliðo, a] *a* skinny, scraggy; (*sucio*) squalid.

escuchar [esku'tʃar] *vt* to listen to // *vi* to listen.

escudilla [esku'ðiʎa] *nf* bowl, basin.

escudo [es'kuðo] *nm* shield.

escudriñar [eskuðri'ɲar] *vt* (*examinar*) to investigate, scrutinize; (*mirar de lejos*) to scan.

escuela [es'kwela] *nf* school; ~ **de artes y oficios** (*Esp*) ≈ technical college; ~ **normal** teacher training college.

escueto, a [es'kweto, a] *a* plain; (*estilo*) simple.

escuincle [es'kwinkle] *nm/f* (*AM fam*) kid.

esculpir [eskul'pir] *vt* to sculpt; (*grabar*) to engrave; (*tallar*) to carve; **escultor, a** *nm/f* sculptor/tress; **escultura** *nf* sculpture.

escupidera [eskupi'ðera] *nf* spittoon.

escupir [esku'pir] *vt*, *vi* to spit (out).

escurreplatos [eskurre'platos]

inv plate rack.

escurridizo, a [eskurri'ðiθo, a] *a* slippery.

escurrir [esku'rrir] *vt* (*ropa*) to wring out; (*verduras, platos*) to drain // *vi* (*los líquidos*) to drip; **~se** *vr* (*secarse*) to drain; (*resbalarse*) to slip, slide; (*escaparse*) to slip away.

ese, esa, esos, esas ['ese, 'esa, 'esos, 'esas] *a demostrativo* (*sg*) that; (*pl*) those.

ése, ésa, ésos, ésas ['ese, 'esa, 'esos, 'esas] *pron* (*sg*) that (one); (*pl*) those (ones); **~... éste** the former... the latter...; **no me vengas con ésas** don't give me any more of that nonsense.

esencia [e'senθja] *nf* essence; **esencial** *a* essential.

esfera [es'fera] *nf* sphere; (*de reloj*) face; **esférico, a** *a* spherical.

esforzado, a [esfor'θaðo, a] *a* (*enérgico*) energetic, vigorous.

esforzarse [esfor'θarse] *vr* to exert o.s., make an effort.

esfuerzo *etc vb ver* **esforzar** // [es'fwerθo] *nm* effort.

esfumarse [esfu'marse] *vr* (*apoyo, esperanzas*) to fade away.

esgrima [es'rrima] *nf* fencing.

esguince [es'ɣinθe] *nm* (MED) sprain.

eslabón [esla'βon] *nm* link.

esmaltar [esmal'tar] *vt* to enamel; **esmalte** *nm* enamel; **esmalte de uñas** nail varnish *o* polish.

esmerado, a [esme'raðo, a] *a* careful, neat.

esmeralda [esme'ralda] *nf* emerald.

esmerarse [esme'rarse] *vr* (*aplicarse*) to take great pains, exercise great care; (*afanarse*) to work hard.

esmero [es'mero] *nm* (great) care.

esnob [es'nob] *a inv* (*persona*) snobbish; (*coche etc*) posh (*pl ~s*) *nm/f* snob; **~ismo** *nm* snobbery.

eso ['eso] *pron* that, that thing *o* matter; **~ de su coche** that business about his car; **~ de ir al cine** all

that about going to the cinema; **a ~ de las cinco** at about five o'clock; **en ~** thereupon, at that point; **~ es** that's it; **¡~ sí que es vida!** now that is really living!; **por ~ te lo dije** that's why I told you; **y ~ que llovía** in spite of the fact it was raining.

esos ['esos] *a demostrativo ver* **ese**.

ésos ['esos] *pron ver* **ése**.

espabilar [espaβi'lar] *vt*, **espabilarse** *vr* = **despabilar**.

espacial [espa'θjal] *a* (*del espacio*) space *cpd*.

espaciar [espa'θjar] *vt* to space (out).

espacio [es'paθjo] *nm* space; (MUS) interval; (RADIO, TV) programme (*Brit*), program (*US*); **el ~** space; **~so, a** a spacious, roomy.

espada [es'paða] *nf* sword; **~s** *nfpl* (NAIPES) spades.

espaguetis [espa'ɣetis] *nmpl* spaghetti *sg*.

espalda [es'palda] *nf* (*gen*) back; **~s** *nfpl* (*hombros*) shoulders; **a ~s de uno** behind sb's back; **tenderse de ~s** to lie (down) on one's back; **volver la ~ a alguien** to cold-shoulder sb.

espaldilla [espal'ðiλa] *nf* shoulder blade.

espantadizo, a [espanta'ðiθo, a] *a* timid, easily frightened.

espantajo [espan'taxo] *nm*, **espantapájaros** [espanta'paxaros] *nm inv* scarecrow.

espantar [espan'tar] *vt* (*asustar*) to frighten, scare; (*ahuyentar*) to frighten off; (*asombrar*) to horrify, appal; **~se** *vr* to get frightened *o* scared; to be appalled.

espanto [es'panto] *nm* (*susto*) fright; (*terror*) terror; (*asombro*) astonishment; **~so, a** *a* frightening; terrifying; astonishing.

España [es'paɲa] *nf* Spain; **español, a** *a* Spanish // *nm/f* Spaniard // *nm* (LING) Spanish.

esparadrapo [espara'ðrapo] *nm* (sticking) plaster (*Brit*), adhesive tape (US).

esparcimiento [esparθi'mjento] nm (dispersión) spreading; (derramamiento) scattering; (fig) cheerfulness.

esparcir [espar'θir] vt to spread; (derramar) to scatter; ~se vr to spread (out); to scatter; (divertirse) to enjoy o.s.

espárrago [es'parraɣo] nm asparagus.

espasmo [es'pasmo] nm spasm.

espátula [es'patula] nf spatula.

especia [es'peθja] nf spice.

especial [espe'θjal] a special; ~idad nf speciality (Brit), specialty (US).

especie [es'peθje] nf (BIO) species; (clase) kind, sort; en ~ in kind.

especificar [espeθifi'kar] vt to specify; **específico, a** a specific.

espécimen [es'peθimen] (pl **especímenes**) nm specimen.

espectáculo [espek'takulo] nm (gen) spectacle; (TEATRO etc) show.

espectador, a [espekta'ðor, a] nm/f spectator.

espectro [es'pektro] nm ghost; (fig) spectre.

especular [espeku'lar] vt, vi to speculate.

espejismo [espe'xismo] nm mirage.

espejo [es'pexo] nm mirror; (fig) model; ~ **retrovisor** rear-view mirror.

espeluznante [espeluθ'nante] a horrifying, hair-raising.

espera [es'pera] nf (pausa, intervalo) wait; (JUR: plazo) respite; en ~ de waiting for; (con expectativa) expecting.

esperanza [espe'ranθa] nf (confianza) hope; (expectativa) expectation; hay pocas ~s de que venga there is little prospect of his coming; **esperanzar** vt to give hope to.

esperar [espe'rar] vt (aguardar) to wait for; (tener expectativa de) to expect; (desear) to hope for // vi to wait; to expect; to hope.

esperma [es'perma] nf sperm.

espesar [espe'sar] vt to thicken; ~se vr to thicken, get thicker.

espeso, a [es'peso, a] a thick; **espesor** nm thickness.

espía [es'pia] nm/f spy; **espiar** vt (observar) to spy on // vi: ~ **para** to spy for.

espiga [es'piɣa] nf (BOT: de trigo etc) ear.

espina [es'pina] nf thorn; (de pez) bone; ~ **dorsal** (ANAT) spine.

espinaca [espi'naka] nf spinach.

espinazo [espi'naθo] nm spine, backbone.

espinilla [espi'niʎa] nf (ANAT: tibia) shin(bone); (grano) blackhead.

espino [es'pino] nm hawthorn.

espinoso, a [espi'noso, a] a (planta) thorny, prickly; (fig) difficult.

espionaje [espjo'naxe] nm spying, espionage.

espiral [espi'ral] a, nf spiral.

espirar [espi'rar] vt to breathe out, exhale.

espiritista [espiri'tista] a, nm/f spiritualist.

espíritu [es'piritu] nm spirit; **espiritual** a spiritual.

espita [es'pita] nf tap.

espléndido, a [es'plendiðo, a] a (magnífico) magnificent, splendid; (generoso) generous.

esplendor [esplen'dor] nm splendour.

espolear [espole'ar] vt to spur on.

espoleta [espo'leta] nf (de bomba) fuse.

espolvorear [espolβore'ar] vt to dust, sprinkle.

esponja [es'ponxa] nf sponge; (fig) sponger; **esponjoso, a** a spongy.

espontaneidad [espontanei'ðað] nf spontaneity; **espontáneo, a** a spontaneous.

esposa [es'posa] nf wife; ~s nfpl handcuffs; **esposar** vt to handcuff.

esposo [es'poso] nm husband.

espuela [es'pwela] nf spur.

espuma [es'puma] nf foam; (de cerveza) froth, head; (de jabón) lather; **espumoso, a** a frothy, foamy; (vino) sparkling.

esqueje [es'kexe] nm (de planta) cutting.

esqueleto [eske'leto] nm skeleton.

esquema [es'kema] nm (diagrama) diagram; (dibujo) plan; (plan) scheme; (FILOSOFÍA) schema.

esquí [es'ki] (pl ~s) nm (objeto) ski; (DEPORTE) skiing; ~ **acuático** water-skiing; **esquiar** vi to ski.

esquilar [eski'lar] vt to shear.

esquimal [eski'mal] a, nm/f Eskimo.

esquina [es'kina] nf corner.

esquirol [eski'rol] nm blackleg.

esquivar [eski'βar] vt to avoid; (evadir) to dodge, elude.

esquivo, a [es'kiβo, a] a (altanero) aloof; (desdeñoso) scornful, disdainful.

esta ['esta] a demostrativo ver **este**.

ésta ['esta] pron ver **éste**.

está vb ver **estar**.

estabilidad [estaβili'ðað] nf stability; **estable** a stable.

establecer [estaβle'θer] vt to establish; ~**se** vr to establish o.s.; (echar raíces) to settle (down); **establecimiento** nm establishment.

estaca [es'taka] nf stake, post; (de tienda de campaña) peg.

estacada [esta'kaða] nf (cerca) fence, fencing; (palenque) stockade.

estación [esta'θjon] nf station; (del año) season; ~ **de autobuses** bus station; ~ **balnearia** seaside resort; ~ **de servicio** service station.

estacionamiento [estaθjona-'mjento] nm (AUTO) parking; (MIL) stationing.

estacionar [estaθjo'nar] vt (AUTO) to park; (MIL) to station; ~**io, a** a stationary; (COM: mercado) slack.

estadio [es'taðjo] nm (fase) stage, phase; (DEPORTE) stadium.

estadista [esta'ðista] nm (POL) statesman; (ESTADÍSTICA) statistician.

estadística [esta'ðistika] nf (una ~) figure, statistic; (ciencia) statistics

sg.

estado [es'taðo] nm (POL: condición) state; ~ **de cuenta** bank statement; ~ **civil** marital status; ~ **mayor** staff; **estar en** ~ to be pregnant; **E~ Unidos** (EE.UU.) nmpl United States of (America) (USA) sg.

estadounidense [estaðouni'ðense] a United States cpd, American // nm/f American.

estafa [es'tafa] nf swindle, trick; **estafar** vt to swindle, defraud.

estafeta [esta'feta] nf (oficina de correos) post office; ~ **diplomática** diplomatic bag.

estáis vb ver **estar**.

estallar [esta'ʎar] vi to burst; (bomba) to explode, go off; (epidemia, guerra, rebelión) to break out; ~ **en llanto** to burst into tears; **estallido** nm explosion; (fig) outbreak.

estampa [es'tampa] nf (impresión, imprenta) print, engraving; (imagen, figura: de persona) appearance.

estampado, a [estam'paðo, a] a printed // nm (impresión: acción) printing; (: efecto) print; (marca) stamping.

estampar [estam'par] vt (imprimir) to print; (marcar) to stamp; (metal) to engrave; (poner sello en) to stamp; (fig) to stamp, imprint.

estampida [estam'piða] nf stampede.

estampido [estam'piðo] nm bang, report.

estampilla [estam'piʎa] nf stamp.

están vb ver **estar**.

estancado, a [estan'kaðo, a] a stagnant.

estancar [estan'kar] vt (aguas) to hold up, hold back; (COM) to monopolize; (fig) to block, hold up; ~**se** vr to stagnate.

estancia [es'tanθja] nf (permanencia) stay; (sala) room; (AM) farm, ranch; **estanciero** nm (AM) farmer, rancher.

estanco, a [es'tanko, a] *a* watertight // *nm* tobacconist's (shop).

estándar [es'tandar] *a, nm* standard; **estandarizar** *vt* to standardize.

estandarte [estan'darte] *nm* banner, standard.

estanque [es'tanke] *nm* (*lago*) pool, pond; (*AGR*) reservoir.

estanquero, a [estan'kero, a] *nm/f* tobacconist.

estante [es'tante] *nm* (*armario*) rack, stand; (*biblioteca*) bookcase; (*anaquel*) shelf; (*AM*) prop; **estantería** *nf* shelving, shelves *pl*.

estaño [es'tapo] *nm* tin.

PALABRA CLAVE

---

estar [es'tar] ♦ *vi* 1 (*posición*) to be; **está en la plaza** it's in the square; **¿está Juan?** is Juan in?; **estamos a 30 km de Junín** we're 30 kms from Junín
2 (+ *adjetivo: estado*) to be; ~ **enfermo** to be ill; **está muy elegante** he's looking very smart; **¿cómo estás?** how are you keeping?
3 (+ *gerundio*) to be; **estoy leyendo** I'm reading
4 (*uso pasivo*): **está condenado a muerte** he's been condemned to death; **está envasado en ...** it's packed in ...
5 (*con fechas*): **¿a cuántos estamos?** what's the date today?; **estamos a 5 de mayo** it's the 5th of May
6 (*locuciones*): **¿estamos?** (*¿de acuerdo?*) okay?; (*¿listo?*) ready?; **¡ya está bien!** that's enough!
7: ~ **de**: ~ **de vacaciones/viaje** to be on holiday/away *o* on a trip; **está de camarero** he's working as a waiter
8: ~ **para**: **está para salir** he's about to leave; **no estoy para bromas** I'm not in the mood for jokes
9: ~ **por** (*propuesta etc*) to be in favour of; (*persona etc*) to support, side with; **está por limpiar** it still

has to be cleaned
10: ~ **sin**: ~ **sin dinero** to have no money; **está sin terminar** it isn't finished yet
♦ *vr*: ~**se**: **se estuvo en la cama toda la tarde** he stayed in bed all afternoon.

---

estas ['estas] *a ver* **este**.

éstas ['estas] *pron ver* **éste**.

estatal [esta'tal] *a* state *cpd*.

estático, a [es'tatiko, a] *a* static.

estatua [es'tatwa] *nf* statue.

estatura [esta'tura] *nf* stature, height.

estatuto [esta'tuto] *nm* (*JUR*) statute; (*de ciudad*) bye-law; (*de comité*) rule.

este ['este] *nm* east.

este, esta, estos, estas ['este, 'esta, 'estos, 'estas] *a demostrativo* (*sg*) this; (*pl*) these.

éste, ésta, éstos, éstas ['este, 'esta, 'estos, 'estas] *pron* (*sg*) this (one); (*pl*) these (ones); **ése... ~...** the former... the latter...

esté *etc vb ver* **estar**.

estela [es'tela] *nf* wake, wash; (*fig*) trail.

estén *etc vb ver* **estar**.

estenografía [estenoxra'fia] *nf* shorthand.

estera [es'tera] *nf* mat(ting).

estéreo [es'tereo] *a inv, nm* stereo; **estereotipo** *nm* stereotype.

estéril [es'teril] *a* sterile, barren; (*fig*) vain, futile.

esterlina [ester'lina] *a*: **libra** ~ pound sterling.

estés *etc vb ver* **estar**.

estético, a [es'tetiko, a] *a* aesthetic // *nf* aesthetics *sg*.

estiércol [es'tjerkol] *nm* dung, manure.

estigma [es'tivma] *nm* stigma.

estilar [esti'lar] *vi*, **estilarse** *vr* (*estar de moda*) to be in fashion; (*usarse*) to be used.

estilo [es'tilo] *nm* style; (*TEC*) stylus; (*NATACIÓN*) stroke; **algo por**

el ~ something along those lines.

estima [es'tima] nf esteem, respect.

estimación [estima'θjon] nf (evaluación) estimation; (aprecio, afecto) esteem, regard.

estimar [esti'mar] vt (evaluar) to estimate; (valorar) to value; (apreciar) to esteem, respect; (pensar, considerar) to think, reckon.

estimulante [estimu'lante] a stimulating // nm stimulant.

estimular [estimu'lar] vt to stimulate; (excitar) to excite.

estímulo [es'timulo] nm stimulus; (ánimo) encouragement.

estío [es'tio] nm summer.

estipulación [estipula'θjon] nf stipulation, condition; **estipular** [estipu'lar] vt to stipulate.

estirado, a [esti'raðo, a] a (tenso) (stretched o drawn) tight; (fig: persona) stiff, pompous.

estirar [esti'rar] vt to stretch; (dinero, suma etc) to stretch out; ~se vr to stretch.

estirón [esti'ron] nm pull, tug; (crecimiento) spurt, sudden growth; **dar un ~** (niño) to shoot up.

estirpe [es'tirpe] nf stock, lineage.

estival [esti'ßal] a summer cpd.

esto ['esto] pron this, this thing o matter; ~ **de la boda** this business about the wedding.

Estocolmo [esto'kolmo] nm Stockholm.

estofa [es'tofa] nf: **de baja ~** poor-quality.

estofado [esto'faðo] nm (CULIN) stew.

estofar [esto'far] vt (CULIN) to stew.

estómago [es'tomavo] nm stomach; **tener ~** to be thick-skinned.

estorbar [estor'ßar] vt to hinder, obstruct; (fig) to bother, disturb // vi to be in the way; **estorbo** nm (molestia) bother, nuisance; (obstáculo) hindrance, obstacle.

estornudar [estornu'ðar] vi to sneeze.

estos ['estos] a demostrativo ver **este**.

éstos ['estos] pron ver **éste**.

estoy vb ver **estar**.

estrafalario, a [estrafa'larjo, a] a odd, eccentric; (desarreglado) slovenly, sloppy.

estrago [es'travo] nm ruin, destruction; **hacer ~s en** to wreak havoc among.

estragón [estra'von] nm tarragon.

estrangulador, a [estrangula'ðor, a] nm/f strangler // nm (TEC) throttle; (AUTO) choke.

estrangulamiento [estrangula-'mjento] nm (AUTO) bottleneck.

estrangular [estrangu'lar] vt (persona) to strangle; (MED) to strangulate.

estraperlo [estra'perlo] nm black market.

estratagema [estrata'xema] nf (MIL) stratagem; (astucia) cunning.

estrategia [estra'texja] nf strategy; **estratégico, a** a strategic.

estratificar [estratifi'kar] vt to stratify.

estrato [es'trato] nm stratum, layer.

estrechar [estre'tʃar] vt (reducir) to narrow; (COSTURA) to take in; (persona) to hug, embrace; ~se vr (reducirse) to narrow, grow narrow; (2 personas) to embrace; ~ **la mano** to shake hands.

estrechez [estre'tʃeθ] nf narrowness; (de ropa) tightness; (intimidad) intimacy; (COM) want o shortage of money; **estrecheces** nfpl financial difficulties.

estrecho, a [es'tretʃo, a] a narrow; (apretado) tight; (íntimo) close, intimate; (miserable) mean // nm strait; ~ **de miras** narrow-minded.

estrella [es'treʎa] nf star.

estrellar [estre'ʎar] vt (hacer añicos) to smash (to pieces); (huevos) to fry; ~se vr to smash; (chocarse) to crash; (fracasar) to fail.

estremecer [estreme'θer] vt to shake; ~se vr to shake, tremble; **estremecimiento** nm (temblor) trembling, shaking.

estrenar [estre'nar] *vt* (*vestido*) to wear for the first time; (*casa*) to move into; (*película, obra de teatro*) to present for the first time; ~se *vr* (*persona*) to make one's début; **estreno** *nm* (*primer uso*) first use; (*CINE etc*) première.

estreñido, a [estre'niðo, a] *a* constipated.

estreñimiento [estreni'mjento] *nm* constipation.

estrépito [es'trepito] *nm* noise, racket; (*fig*) fuss; **estrepitoso, a** *a* noisy; (*fiesta*) rowdy.

estría [es'tria] *nf* groove.

estribar [estri'ßar] *vi*: ~ en to rest on, be supported by.

estribillo [estri'ßiʎo] *nm* (*LITERATURA*) refrain; (*MUS*) chorus.

estribo [es'trißo] *nm* (*de jinete*) stirrup; (*de coche, tren*) step; (*de puente*) support; (*GEO*) spur; perder los ~s to fly off the handle.

estribor [estri'ßor] *nm* (*NAUT*) starboard.

estricnina [estrik'nina] *nf* strychnine.

estricto, a [es'trikto, a] *a* (*riguroso*) strict; (*severo*) severe.

estropajo [estro'paxo] *nm* scourer.

estropear [estrope'ar] *vt* (*arruinar*) to spoil; (*dañar*) to damage; ~se *vr* (*objeto*) to get damaged; (*persona: la piel etc*) to be ruined.

estructura [estruk'tura] *nf* structure.

estruendo [es'trwendo] *nm* (*ruido*) racket, din; (*fig: alboroto*) uproar, turmoil.

estrujar [estru'xar] *vt* (*apretar*) to squeeze; (*aplastar*) to crush; (*fig*) to drain, bleed.

estuario [es'twarjo] *nm* estuary.

estuche [es'tutʃe] *nm* box, case.

estudiante [estu'ðjante] *nm/f* student; **estudiantil** *a* student *cpd*.

estudiar [estu'ðjar] *vt* to study.

estudio [es'tuðjo] *nm* study; (*CINE, ARTE, RADIO*) studio; ~s *nmpl* studies; (*erudición*) learning *sg*; ~so, a *a* studious.

estufa [es'tufa] *nf* heater, fire.

estupefaciente [estupefa'θjente] *nm* drug, narcotic.

estupefacto, a [estupe'fakto, a] *a* speechless, thunderstruck.

estupendo, a [estu'pendo, a] *a* wonderful, terrific; (*fam*) great; ¡~! that's great!; fantastic!

estupidez [estupi'ðeθ] *nf* (*torpeza*) stupidity; (*acto*) stupid thing (to do).

estúpido, a [es'tupiðo, a] *a* stupid, silly.

estupor [estu'por] *nm* stupor; (*fig*) astonishment, amazement.

estupro [es'tupro] *nm* rape.

estuve *etc vb ver* **estar**.

esvástica [es'ßastika] *nf* swastika.

ETA ['eta] *nf abr* (*Esp*) ETA.

etapa [e'tapa] *nf* (*de viaje*) stage; (*DEPORTE*) leg; (*parada*) stopping place; (*fig*) stage, phase.

etarra [e'tarra] *nm/f* member of ETA.

etc. *abr* (= *etcétera*) etc.

etcétera [et'θetera] *ad* etcetera.

eternidad [eterni'ðað] *nf* eternity; **eterno, a** *a* eternal, everlasting.

ético, a ['etiko, a] *a* ethical // *nf* ethics *pl*.

etiqueta [eti'keta] *nf* (*modales*) etiquette; (*rótulo*) label, tag.

Eucaristía [eukaris'tia] *nf* Eucharist.

eufemismo [eufe'mismo] *nm* euphemism.

euforia [eu'forja] *nf* euphoria.

eunuco [eu'nuko] *nm* eunuch.

Europa [eu'ropa] *nf* Europe; **europeo, a** *a, nm/f* European.

éuscaro, a ['euskaro, a] *a* Basque // *nm* (*LING*) Basque.

Euskadi [eus'kaði] *nm* the Basque Country *o* Provinces *pl*.

euskera [eus'kera] *nm* (*LING*) Basque.

evacuación [eßakwa'θjon] *nf* evacuation; **evacuar** *vt* to evacuate.

evadir [eßa'ðir] *vt* to evade, avoid; ~se *vr* to escape.

evaluar [eßa'lwar] *vt* to evaluate.

evangélico, a [eßan'xeliko, a] *a* evangelic(al).

evangelio [eßan'xeljo] *nm* gospel.

evaporar [eβapo'rar] vt to evaporate; **~se** vr to vanish.

evasión [eβa'sjon] nf escape, flight; (fig) evasion.

evasivo, a [eβa'siβo, a] a evasive, non-committal // nf (pretexto) excuse.

evento [e'βento] nm event.

eventual [eβen'twal] a possible, conditional (upon circumstances); (trabajador) casual, temporary.

evidencia [eβi'ðenθja] nf evidence, proof; **evidenciar** vt (hacer patente) to make evident; (probar) to prove, show; **evidenciarse** vr to be evident.

evidente [eβi'ðente] a obvious, clear, evident.

evitar [eβi'tar] vt (evadir) to avoid; (impedir) to prevent.

evocar [eβo'kar] vt to evoke, call forth.

evolución [eβolu'θjon] nf (desarrollo) evolution, development; (cambio) change; (MIL) manoeuvre; **evolucionar** vi to evolve; to manoeuvre.

ex [eks] a ex-; **el ~ ministro** the former minister, the ex-minister.

exacerbar [eksaθer'βar] vt to irritate, annoy.

exactamente [eksakta'mente] ad exactly.

exactitud [eksakti'tuð] nf exactness; (precisión) accuracy; (puntualidad) punctuality; **exacto, a** a exact; accurate; punctual; **¡exacto!** exactly!

exageración [eksaxera'θjon] nf exaggeration; **exagerar** vt, vi to exaggerate.

exaltado, a [eksal'taðo, a] a (apasionado) over-excited, worked-up; (exagerado) extreme.

exaltar [eksal'tar] vt to exalt, glorify; **~se** vr (excitarse) to get excited o worked-up.

examen [ek'samen] nm examination.

examinar [eksami'nar] vt to examine; **~se** vr to be examined, take an examination.

exasperar [eksaspe'rar] vt to exasperate; **~se** vr to get exasperated, lose patience.

Exca. abr = **Excelencia**.

excavadora [ekskaβa'ðora] nf excavator.

excavar [ekska'βar] vt to excavate.

excedente [eksθe'ðente] a, nm excess, surplus.

exceder [eksθe'ðer] vt to exceed, surpass; **~se** vr (extralimitarse) to go too far; (sobrepasarse) to excel o.s.

excelencia [eksθe'lenθja] nf excellence; **E~** Excellency; **excelente** a excellent.

excelso, a [eks'θelso, a] a lofty, sublime.

excentricidad [eksθentriθi'ðað] nf eccentricity; **excéntrico, a** a, nm/f eccentric.

excepción [eksθep'θjon] nf exception; **excepcional** a exceptional.

excepto [eks'θepto] ad excepting, except (for).

exceptuar [eksθep'twar] vt to except, exclude.

excesivo, a [eksθe'siβo, a] a excessive.

exceso [eks'θeso] nm (gen) excess; (COM) surplus; **~ de equipaje/peso** excess luggage/weight.

excitación [eksθita'θjon] nf (sensación) excitement; (acción) excitation.

excitado, a [eksθi'taðo, a] a excited; (emociones) aroused.

excitar [eksθi'tar] vt to excite; (incitar) to urge; **~se** vr to get excited.

exclamación [eksklama'θjon] nf exclamation; **exclamar** vi to exclaim.

excluir [eksklu'ir] vt to exclude; (dejar fuera) to shut out; (descartar) to reject; **exclusión** nf exclusion.

exclusiva [eksklu'siβa] nf (PRENSA) exclusive, scoop; (COM) sole right.

exclusivo, a [eksklu'siβo, a] a exclusive; **derecho ~ sole** exclusive right.

Excmo. abr = **excelentísimo**.

excomulgar [ekskomul'xar] vt (REL) to excommunicate.

excomunión [ekskomu'njon] nf excommunication.

excursión [ekskur'sjon] nf excursion,

outing; **excursionista** nm/f (turista) sightseer.

excusa [eks'kusa] nf excuse; (disculpa) apology.

excusar [eksku'sar] vt to excuse; (evitar) to avoid, prevent; ~**se** vr (disculparse) to apologize.

exento, a [ek'sento, a] a exempt.

exequias [ek'sekjas] nfpl funeral rites.

exhalar [eksa'lar] vt to exhale, breathe out; (olor etc) to give off; (suspiro) to breathe, heave.

exhausto, a [ek'sausto, a] a exhausted.

exhibición [eksiβi'θjon] nf exhibition, display, show.

exhibir [eksi'βir] vt to exhibit, display, show.

exhortación [eksorta'θjon] nf exhortation; **exhortar** vt: exhortar a to exhort to.

exigencia [eksi'xenθja] nf demand, requirement; **exigente** a demanding.

exigir [eksi'xir] vt (gen) to demand, require; ~ **el pago** to demand payment.

exiliado, a [eksi'ljaðo, a] a exiled // nm/f exile.

exilio [ek'siljo] nm exile.

eximio, a [ek'simjo, a] a (eminente) distinguished, eminent.

eximir [eksi'mir] vt to exempt.

existencia [eksis'tenθja] nf existence; ~**s** nfpl stock(s) (pl).

existir [eksis'tir] vi to exist, be.

éxito ['eksito] nm (resultado) result, outcome; (triunfo) success; (MUS etc) hit; **tener** ~ to be successful.

exonerar [eksone'rar] vt to exonerate; ~ **de una obligación** to free from an obligation.

exorcizar [eksorθi'θar] vt to exorcize.

exótico, a [ek'sotiko, a] a exotic.

expandir [ekspan'dir] vt to expand.

expansión [ekspan'sjon] nf expansion.

expatriarse [ekspa'trjarse] vr to emigrate; (POL) to go into exile.

expectativa [ekspekta'tiβa] nf (espera) expectation; (perspectiva) prospect.

expedición [ekspeði'θjon] nf (excursión) expedition.

expediente [ekspe'ðjente] nm expedient; (JUR: procedimiento) action, proceedings pl; (: papeles) dossier, file, record.

expedir [ekspe'ðir] vt (despachar) to send, forward; (pasaporte) to issue.

expedito, a [ekspe'ðito, a] a (libre) clear, free.

expendedor, a [ekspende'ðor, a] nm/f (vendedor) dealer; (aparato) (vending) machine; ~ **de cigarrillos** cigarette machine.

expendeduría [ekspendeðu'ria] nf (estanco) tobacconist's (shop).

expensas [eks'pensas] nfpl: **a** ~ **de** at the expense of.

experiencia [ekspe'rjenθja] nf experience.

experimentado, a [eksperimen'taðo, a] a experienced.

experimentar [eksperimen'tar] vt (en laboratorio) to experiment with; (probar) to test, try out; (notar, observar) to experience; (deterioro, pérdida) to suffer; **experimento** nm experiment.

experto, a [eks'perto, a] a expert, skilled // nm/f expert.

expiar [ekspi'ar] vt to atone for.

expirar [ekspi'rar] vi to expire.

explayarse [ekspla'jarse] vr (en discurso) to speak at length; ~ **con uno** to confide in sb.

explicación [eksplika'θjon] nf explanation; **explicar** vt to explain; explicarse vr to explain (o.s.).

explícito, a [eks'pliθito, a] a explicit.

explique etc vb ver **explicar**.

explorador, a [eksplora'ðor, a] nm/f (pionero) explorer; (MIL) scout // nm (MED) probe; (TEC) (radar) scanner.

explorar [eksplo'rar] vt to explore; (MED) to probe; (radar) to scan.

explosión [eksplo'sjon] nf explosion; **explosivo, a** a explosive.

explotación [eksplota'θjon] nf exploitation; (de planta etc) running.

explotar [eksplo'tar] vt to exploit; to run, operate // vi to explode.

exponer [ekspo'ner] vt to expose; (cuadro) to display; (vida) to risk; (idea) to explain; ~se vr: ~se a (hacer) algo to run the risk of (doing) sth.

exportación [eksporta'θjon] nf (acción) export; (mercancías) exports pl; **exportar** vt to export.

exposición [eksposi'θjon] nf (gen) exposure; (de arte) show, exhibition; (explicación) explanation; (narración) account, statement.

expresar [ekspre'sar] vt to express; **expresión** nf expression.

expreso, a pp de **expresar** // [eks'preso, a] a (explícito) express; (claro) specific, clear; (tren) fast // nm: **mandar** ~ to send by express (delivery).

express [eks'pres] ad (AM): **enviar algo** ~ to send sth special delivery.

exprimidor [eksprimi'ðor] nm squeezer.

exprimir [ekspri'mir] vt (fruta) to squeeze; (zumo) to squeeze out.

expropiar [ekspro'pjar] vt to expropriate.

expuesto, a [eks'pwesto, a] a exposed; (cuadro etc) on show, on display.

expulsar [ekspul'sar] vt (echar) to eject, throw out; (alumno) to expel; (despedir) to sack, fire; (DEPORTE) to send off; **expulsión** nf expulsion; sending-off.

exquisito, a [ekski'sito, a] a exquisite; (comida) delicious.

éxtasis [ekstasis] nm ecstasy.

extender [eksten'der] vt to extend; (los brazos) to stretch out, hold out; (mapa, tela) to spread (out), open (out); (mantequilla) to spread; (certificado) to issue; (cheque, recibo) to make out; (documento) to

draw up; ~se vr (gen) to extend; (persona: en el suelo) to stretch out; (epidemia) to spread; **extendido, a** a (abierto) spread out, open; (brazos) outstretched; (prevaleciente) widespread.

extensión [eksten'sjon] nf (de terreno, mar) expanse, stretch; (de tiempo) length, duration; (TEL) extension; en toda la ~ de la palabra in every sense of the word.

extenso, a [eks'tenso, a] a extensive.

extenuar [ekste'nwar] vt (debilitar) to weaken.

exterior [ekste'rjor] a (de fuera) external; (afuera) outside, exterior; (apariencia) outward; (deuda, relaciones) foreign // nm (gen) exterior, outside; (aspecto) outward appearance; (DEPORTE) wing(er); (países extranjeros) abroad; **en el** ~ abroad; **al** ~ outwardly, on the surface.

exterminar [ekstermi'nar] vt to exterminate; **exterminio** nm extermination.

externo, a [eks'terno, a] a (exterior) external, outside; (superficial) outward // nm/f day pupil.

extinguir [ekstin'gir] vt (fuego) to extinguish, put out; (raza, población) to wipe out; ~se vr (fuego) to go out; (BIO) to die out, become extinct.

extinto, a [eks'tinto, a] a extinct.

extintor [ekstin'tor] nm (fire) extinguisher.

extra ['ekstra] a inv (tiempo) extra; (chocolate, vino) good-quality // nm/f extra // nm extra; (bono) bonus.

extracción [ekstrak'θjon] nf extraction; (en lotería) draw.

extracto [eks'trakto] nm extract.

extraer [ekstra'er] vt to extract, take out.

extralimitarse [ekstralimi'tarse] vr to go too far.

extranjero, a [ekstran'xero, a] a foreign // nm/f foreigner // nm foreign countries pl; **en el** ~ abroad.

extrañar [ekstra'nar] vt (sorprender) to find strange o odd; (echar de menos) to miss; ~se vr (sorprenderse) to be amazed, be surprised; (distanciarse) to become estranged, grow apart.

extrañeza [ekstra'neθa] nf (rareza) strangeness, oddness; (asombro) amazement, surprise.

extraño, a [eks'trapo, a] a (extranjero) foreign; (raro, sorprendente) strange, odd.

extraordinario, a [ekstraorði'narjo, a] a extraordinary; (edición, número) special // nm (de periódico) special edition; **horas extraordinarias** overtime sg.

extrarradio [ekstra'rraðjo] nm poor suburban area.

extravagancia [ekstraβa'vanθja] nf oddness; outlandishness; **extravagante** a (excéntrico) eccentric; (estrafalario) outlandish.

extraviado, a [ekstra'βjaðo, a] a lost, missing.

extraviar [ekstra'βjar] vt (persona: desorientar) to mislead, misdirect; (perder) to lose, misplace; ~se vr to lose one's way, get lost; **extravío** nm loss; (fig) deviation.

extremar [ekstre'mar] vt to carry to extremes; ~se vr to do one's utmost, make every effort.

extremaunción [ekstremaun'θjon] nf extreme unction.

extremidad [ekstremi'ðað] nf (punta) extremity; (fila) edge; ~es nfpl (ANAT) extremities.

extremo, a [eks'tremo, a] a extreme; (último) last // nm end; (límite, grado sumo) extreme; **en último** ~ as a last resort.

extrovertido, a [ekstroβer'tiðo, a] a, nm/f extrovert.

exuberancia [eksuβe'ranθja] nf exuberance; **exuberante** a exuberant; (fig) luxuriant, lush.

eyacular [ejaku'lar] vt, vi to ejaculate.

F

f.a.b. abr (= franco a bordo) f.o.b.

fábrica ['faβrika] nf factory; **marca de ~** trademark; **precio de ~** factory price.

fabricación [faβrika'θjon] nf (manufactura) manufacture; (producción) production; **de ~ casera** home-made; **~ en serie** mass production.

fabricante [faβri'kante] nm/f manufacturer.

fabricar [faβri'kar] vt (manufacturar) to manufacture, make; (construir) to build; (cuento) to fabricate, devise.

fábula ['faβula] nf (cuento) fable; (chisme) rumour; (mentira) fib.

facción [fak'θjon] nf (POL) faction; **facciones** nfpl (del rostro) features.

fácil ['faθil] a (simple) easy; (probable) likely.

facilidad [faθili'ðað] nf (capacidad) ease; (sencillez) simplicity; (de palabra) fluency; ~es nfpl facilities.

facilitar [faθili'tar] vt (hacer fácil) to make easy; (proporcionar) to provide.

fácilmente ['faθilmente] ad easily.

facsímil [fak'simil] nm facsimile, fax.

factible [fak'tiβle] a feasible.

factor [fak'tor] nm factor.

factura [fak'tura] nf (cuenta) bill; (hechura) manufacture; **facturar** vt (COM) to invoice, charge for; (equipaje) to register (Brit), check (US).

facultad [fakul'tað] nf (aptitud, ESCOL etc) faculty; (poder) power.

facha ['fatʃa] nf (fam: aspecto) look; (: cara) face.

fachada [fa'tʃaða] nf (ARQ) façade, front.

faena [fa'ena] nf (trabajo) work; (quehacer) task, job.

fagot [fa'vot] (pl ~es) [fa'vot] nm (MUS) bassoon.

faisán [fai'san] nm pheasant.

faja ['faxa] nf (para la cintura) sash;

(de mujer) corset; *(de tierra)* strip.

fajo ['faxo] *nm (de papeles)* bundle; *(de billetes)* wad.

Falange [fa'lanxe] *nf (POL)* Falange.

falda ['falda] *nf (prenda de vestir)* skirt.

falo ['falo] *nm* phallus.

falsedad [false'ðað] *nf* falseness; *(hipocresía)* hypocrisy; *(mentira)* falsehood.

falsificar [falsifi'kar] *vt (firma etc)* to forge; *(voto etc)* to rig; *(moneda)* to counterfeit.

falso, a ['falso, a] *a* false; *(erróneo)* mistaken; *(documento, moneda etc)* fake; **en ~** falsely.

falta ['falta] *nf (defecto)* fault, flaw; *(privación)* lack, want; *(ausencia)* absence; *(carencia)* shortage; *(equivocación)* mistake; *(DEPORTE)* foul; **echar en ~** to miss; **hacer ~ hacer** algo to be necessary to do sth; **me hace falta una pluma** I need a pen.

faltar [fal'tar] *vi (escasear)* to be lacking, be wanting; *(ausentarse)* to be absent, be missing; **faltan 2 horas para llegar** there are 2 hours to go till arrival; **~ el respeto a uno** to be disrespectful to sb; **¡no faltaba más!** that's the last straw!

falto, a ['falto, a] *a (desposeído)* deficient, lacking; *(necesitado)* poor, wretched.

falla ['faʎa] *nf (defecto)* fault, flaw.

fallar [fa'ʎar] *vt (JUR)* to pronounce sentence on // *vi (memoria)* to fail; *(motor)* to miss.

fallecer [faʎe'θer] *vi* to pass away, die; **fallecimiento** *nm* decease, demise.

fallido, a [fa'ʎiðo] *a (gen)* frustrated, unsuccessful.

fallo ['faʎo] *nm (JUR)* verdict, ruling; *(fracaso)* failing.

fama ['fama] *nf (renombre)* fame; *(reputación)* reputation.

famélico, a [fa'meliko, a] *a* starving.

familia [fa'milja] *nf* family.

familiar [fami'ljar] *a (relativo a*

familia) family cpd; *(conocido, informal)* familiar // *nm* relative, relation; **~idad** *nf (gen)* familiarity; *(informalidad)* homeliness; **~izarse** *vr*: **~izarse con** to familiarize o.s. with.

famoso, a [fa'moso, a] *a (renombrado)* famous.

fanático, a [fa'natiko, a] *a* fanatical // *nm/f* fanatic; *(CINE, DEPORTE)* fan; **fanatismo** *nm* fanaticism.

fanfarrón, ona [fanfa'rron, ona] *a* boastful; *(pey)* showy.

fango ['fango] *nm* mud; **~so, a** *a* muddy.

fantasía [fanta'sia] *nf* fantasy, imagination; **joyas de ~** imitation jewellery *sg*.

fantasma [fan'tasma] *nm (espectro)* ghost, apparition // *(presumido)* show-off.

fantástico, a [fan'tastiko, a] *a (irreal, fam)* fantastic.

farmacéutico, a [farma'θeutiko, a] *a* pharmaceutical // *nm/f* chemist *(Brit)*, pharmacist.

farmacia [far'maθja] *nf* chemist's (shop) *(Brit)*, pharmacy; **~ de turno** duty chemist.

fármaco ['farmako] *nm* drug.

faro ['faro] *nm (NAUT: torre)* lighthouse; *(AUTO)* headlamp; *(foco)* floodlight; **~s antiniebla** fog lamps; **~s delanteros/traseros** headlights/ rear lights.

farol [fa'rol] *nm* lantern, lamp.

farola [fa'rola] *nf* street lamp *(Brit)* o light *(US)*.

farsa ['farsa] *nf (gen)* farce.

farsante [far'sante] *nm/f* fraud, fake.

fascículo [fas'θikulo] *nm (de revista)* part, instalment.

fascinar [fasθi'nar] *vt (gen)* to fascinate.

fascismo [fas'θismo] *nm* fascism; **fascista** *a, nm/f* fascist.

fase ['fase] *nf* phase.

fastidiar [fasti'ðjar] *vt (disgustar)* to annoy, bother; *(estropear)* to spoil; **~se** *vr (disgustarse)* to get annoyed

o cross; **¡que se fastidie!** (*fam*)
he'll have to put up with it!

fastidio [fas'tiðjo] *nm* (*disgusto*)
annoyance; **~so, a** *a* (*molesto*)
annoying.

fatal [fa'tal] *a* (*gen*) fatal; (*desgraciado*) ill-fated; (*fam: malo,
pésimo*) awful; **~idad** *nf* (*destino*)
fate; (*mala suerte*) misfortune.

fatiga [fa'tiɣa] *nf* (*cansancio*) fatigue,
weariness.

fatigar [fati'ɣar] *vt* to tire, weary;
~se *vr* to get tired.

fatigoso, a [fati'ɣoso, a] *a*
(*cansador*) tiring.

fatuo, a [ˈfatwo, a] *a* (*vano*) fatuous;
(*presuntuoso*) conceited.

fauces [ˈfauθes] *nfpl* jaws, mouth *sg*.

favor [faˈβor] *nm* favour; **estar a ~
de** to be in favour of; **haga el ~
de...** would you be so good as to...,
kindly...; **por ~** please; **~able** *a*
favourable.

favorecer [faβoreˈθer] *vt* to favour;
(*vestido etc*) to become, flatter; **este
peinado le favorece** this hairstyle
suits him.

favorito, a [faβoˈrito, a] *a, nm/f*
favourite.

faz [faθ] *nf* face; **la ~ de la tierra**
the face of the earth.

fe [fe] *nf* (*REL*) faith; (*confianza*)
belief; (*documento*) certificate; **estar ~ a** to believe, credit; **actuar
con buena/mala ~** to act in good/
bad faith; **dar ~ de** to bear witness
to.

fealdad [fealˈdað] *nf* ugliness.

febrero [feˈβrero] *nm* February.

fecundar [fekunˈdar] *vt* (*generar*) to
fertilize, make fertile; **fecundo, a** *a*
(*fértil*) fertile; (*fig*) prolific;
(*productivo*) productive.

fecha [ˈfetʃa] *nf* date; **~ de
caducidad, ~ límite de venta** (*de
producto alimenticio*) sell-by date; **en
~ próxima** soon; **hasta la ~** so
far; **poner a ~** to date; **fechar** *vt* to date.

federación [federaˈθjon] *nf* federa-

tion.

federal [feðeˈral] *a* federal.

felicidad [feliθiˈðað] *nf* (*satisfacción,
contento*) happiness; **~es** *nfpl* best
wishes, congratulations.

felicitación [feliθitaˈθjon] *nf*: **¡felicitaciones!** congratulations!

felicitar [feliθiˈtar] *vt* to congratulate.

feligrés, esa [feliˈɣres, esa] *nm/f*
parishioner.

feliz [feˈliθ] *a* (*contento*) happy;
(*afortunado*) lucky.

felpudo [felˈpuðo] *nm* doormat.

femenino, a [femeˈnino, a] *a, nm*
feminine.

feminista [femiˈnista] *a, nm/f* feminist.

fenómeno [feˈnomeno] *nm*
phenomenon; (*fig*) freak, accident // *a*
great // *excl* great!, marvellous!

feo, a [ˈfeo, a] *a* (*gen*) ugly; (*desagradable*) bad, nasty.

féretro [ˈferetro] *nm* (*ataúd*) coffin;
(*sarcófago*) bier.

feria [ˈferja] *nf* (*gen*) fair; (*descanso*)
holiday, rest day; (*AM: mercado*)
village market; (*c: cambio*) loose or
small change.

fermentar [fermenˈtar] *vi* to ferment.

ferocidad [feroθiˈðað] *nf* fierceness,
ferocity.

feroz [feˈroθ] *a* (*cruel*) cruel;
(*salvaje*) fierce.

férreo, a [ˈferreo, a] *a* iron.

ferretería [ferreteˈria] *nf* (*tienda*) ironmonger's (*shop*) (*Brit*), hardware
store.

ferrocarril [ferrokaˈrril] *nm* railway.

ferroviario, a [ferroˈβjarjo, a] *a* rail
cpd.

fértil [ˈfertil] *a* (*productivo*) fertile;
(*rico*) rich; **fertilidad** *nf* (*gen*)
fertility; (*productividad*) fruitfulness.

fertilizar [fertiliˈθar] *vt* to fertilize.

fervor [ferˈβor] *nm* fervour; **~oso, a**
a fervent.

festejar [festeˈxar] *vt* (*agasajar*) to
wine and dine; (*galantear*) to court;
(*celebrar*) to celebrate; **festejo** *nm*
(*diversión*) entertainment; (*galanteo*)

festividad [festiβi'ðað] *nf* festivity.

festivo, a [fes'tiβo, a] *a* (*de fiesta*) festive; (*fig*) witty; (*CINE, LITERATURA*) humorous; *día* ~ holiday.

fétido, a [ˈfetiðo, a] *a* (*hediondo*) foul-smelling.

feto [ˈfeto] *nm* foetus.

fiable [ˈfjaβle] *a* (*persona*) trustworthy; (*máquina*) reliable.

fiador, a [fjaˈðor, a] *nm/f* (*JUR*) surety, guarantor; (*COM*) backer; **salir ~ por alguien** to stand bail for sb.

fiambre [ˈfjambre] *nm* cold meat.

fianza [ˈfjanθa] *nf* surety; (*JUR*): **libertad bajo** ~ release on bail.

fiar [fiˈar] *vt* (*salir garante de*) to guarantee; (*vender a crédito*) to sell on credit; (*secreto*) to confide (a to) // *vi* to trust; ~se *vr* to trust (in), rely on; ~se de uno to rely on sb.

fibra [ˈfiβra] *nf* fibre; ~ **óptica** optical fibre.

ficción [fikˈθjon] *nf* fiction.

ficticio, a [fikˈtiθjo, a] *a* (*imaginario*) fictitious; (*falso*) fabricated.

ficha [ˈfitʃa] *nf* (*TEL*) token; (*en juegos*) counter, marker; (*tarjeta*) (index) card; **fichar** *vt* (*archivar*) to file, index; (*DEPORTE*) to sign; **estar fichado** to have a record; **fichero** *nm* box file; (*INFORM*) file.

fidelidad [fiðeliˈðað] *nf* (*lealtad*) fidelity, loyalty; **alta** ~ high fidelity, hi-fi.

fideos [fiˈðeos] *nmpl* noodles.

fiebre [ˈfjeβre] *nf* (*MED*) fever; (*fig*) fever, excitement; ~ **amarilla/del heno** yellow/hay fever; ~ **palúdica** malaria; **tener** ~ to have a temperature.

fiel [fjel] *a* (*leal*) faithful, loyal; (*fiable*) reliable; (*exacto*) accurate, faithful // *nm*: **los** ~s the faithful.

fieltro [ˈfjeltro] *nm* felt.

fiero, a [ˈfjero, a] *a* (*cruel*) cruel; (*feroz*) fierce; (*duro*) harsh // *nf* (*animal feroz*) wild animal o beast; (*fig*) dragon // *nm/f* (*fig*) fiend.

fiesta [ˈfjesta] *nf* party; (*de pueblo*)

festival; (*vacaciones, tb*: ~s) holiday *sg*; (*REL*): ~ **de guardar** day of obligation.

figura [fiˈɣura] *nf* (*gen*) figure; (*forma, imagen*) shape, form; (*NAIPES*) face card.

figurar [fiɣuˈrar] *vt* (*representar*) to represent; (*fingir*) to figure // *vi* to figure; ~se *vr* (*imaginarse*) to imagine; (*suponer*) to suppose.

fijador [fixaˈðor] *nm* (*FOTO etc*) fixative; (*de pelo*) gel.

fijar [fiˈxar] *vt* (*gen*) to fix; (*estampilla*) to affix, stick (on); (*fig*) to settle (on), decide; ~se *vr*: ~se **en** to notice.

fijo, a [ˈfixo, a] *a* (*gen*) fixed; (*firme*) firm; (*permanente*) permanent // *ad*: **mirar** ~ to stare.

fila [ˈfila] *nf* row; (*MIL*) rank; (*cadena*) line; **ponerse en** ~ to line up, get into line.

filántropo, a [fiˈlantropo, a] *nm/f* philanthropist.

filatelia [filaˈtelja] *nf* philately, stamp collecting.

filete [fiˈlete] *nm* (*carne*) fillet steak; (*pescado*) fillet.

filial [fiˈljal] *a* filial // *nf* subsidiary.

Filipinas [filiˈpinas] *nfpl*: **las** ~ the Philippines; **filipino, a, ** *nm/f* Philippine.

filmar [filˈmar] *vt* to film, shoot.

filo [ˈfilo] *nm* (*gen*) edge; **sacar** ~ a to sharpen; **al** ~ **del mediodía** at about midday; **de doble** ~ double-edged.

filón [fiˈlon] *nm* (*MINERÍA*) vein, lode; (*fig*) goldmine.

filosofía [filosoˈfia] *nf* philosophy; **filósofo, a** *nm/f* philosopher.

filtrar [filˈtrar] *vt, vi* to filter, strain; ~se *vr* to filter; (*fig*: *dinero*) to dwindle; **filtro** *nm* (*TEC, utensilio*) filter.

fin [fin] *nm* end; (*objetivo*) aim, purpose; **al** ~ **y al cabo** when all's said and done; **a** ~ **de** in order to; **por** ~ finally; **en** ~ in short; ~ **de semana** weekend.

final [fi'nal] *a* final // *nm* end, conclusion // *nf* final; ~**idad** *nf* (*propósito*) purpose, intention; ~**ista** *nmf* finalist; ~**izar** *vt* to end, finish; (*INFORM*) to log out o off // *vi* to end, come to an end.

financiar [finan'θjar] *vt* to finance; **financiero, a** *a* financial // *nm/f* financier.

finca ['finka] *nf* country estate; (*AM*) farm.

fingir [fin'xir] *vt* (*simular*) to simulate, feign; (*pretextar*) to sham, fake // *vi* (*aparentar*) to pretend; ~**se** *vr* to pretend to be.

finlandés, esa [finlan'des, esa] *a* Finnish // *nm/f* Finn // *nm* (*LING*) Finnish.

Finlandia [fin'landja] *nf* Finland.

fino, a ['fino, a] *a* fine; (*delgado*) slender; (*de buenas maneras*) polite, refined; (*jerez*) fino, dry.

firma ['firma] *nf* signature; (*COM*) firm, company; **firmar** *vt* to sign.

firme ['firme] *a* firm; (*estable*) stable; (*sólido*) solid; (*constante*) steady; (*decidido*) resolute // *nm* road (surface); ~**mente** *ad* firmly; ~**za** *nf* firmness; (*constancia*) steadiness; (*solidez*) solidity.

fiscal [fis'kal] *a* fiscal // *nm/f* public prosecutor; **año** ~ tax o fiscal year.

fisco ['fisko] *nm* (*hacienda*) treasury, exchequer (*Brit*).

fisgar [fis'xar] *vt* to pry into.

físico, a ['fisiko, a] *a* physical // *nm* physique // *nm/f* physicist // *nf* physics *sg.*

flaco, a ['flako, a] *a* (*muy delgado*) skinny, thin; (*débil*) weak, feeble.

flagrante [fla'xrante] *a* flagrant.

flamante [fla'mante] *a* (*fam*) brilliant; (: *nuevo*) brand-new.

flamenco, a [fla'menko, a] *a* (*de Flandes*) Flemish; (*baile, música*) flamenco // *nm* (*baile, música*) flamenco.

flan [flan] *nm* creme caramel.

flaqueza [fla'keθa] *nf* (*delgadez*) thinness, leanness; (*fig*) weakness.

flash [flaʃ] (*pl* ~s o ~es) *nm* (*FOTO*) flash.

flauta ['flauta] *nf* (*MUS*) flute.

fleco ['fleko] *nm* fringe.

flecha ['fletʃa] *nf* arrow.

flema ['flema] *nm* phlegm.

flequillo [fle'kiʎo] *nm* (*pelo*) fringe.

flete ['flete] *nm* (*carga*) freight; (*alquiler*) charter; (*precio*) freight-age.

flexible [flek'sißle] *a* flexible.

flipper ['fliper] *nm* pinball (machine).

flojera [flo'xera] *nf* (*AM fam*): me da ~ I can't be bothered.

flojo, a ['floxo, a] *a* (*gen*) loose; (*sin fuerzas*) limp; (*débil*) weak.

flor [flor] *nf* flower; (*piropo*) compliment; **a** ~ **de** on the surface of; ~**ecer** *vi* (*BOT*) to flower, bloom; (*fig*) to flourish; ~**eciente** *a* (*BOT*) in flower, flowering; (*fig*) thriving; ~**ero** *nm* vase; ~**ista** *nm/f* florist.

flota ['flota] *nf* fleet.

flotador [flota'ðor] *nm* (*gen*) float; (*para nadar*) rubber ring.

flotar [flo'tar] *vi* (*gen*) to float; **flote** *nm*: **a flote** afloat; **sacar a flote** (*fig*) to get back on one's feet.

fluctuar [fluk'twar] *vi* (*oscilar*) to fluctuate.

fluidez [flui'ðeθ] *nf* fluidity; (*fig*) fluency.

fluído, a [flu'iðo, a] *a, nm* fluid.

fluir [flu'ir] *vi* to flow.

flujo ['fluxo] *nm* flow; ~ **y reflujo** ebb and flow; ~ **de sangre** (*MED*) loss of blood; ~**grama** *nm* flowchart.

foca ['foka] *nf* seal.

foco ['foko] *nm* focus; (*ELEC*) floodlight; (*AM*) (light) bulb.

fogón [fo'xon] *nm* (*de cocina*) ring, burner.

fogoso, a [fo'xoso, a] *a* spirited.

follaje [fo'ʎaxe] *nm* foliage.

folleto [fo'ʎeto] *nm* pamphlet.

follón [fo'ʎon] *nm* (*fam*: *lio*) mess; (: *conmoción*) fuss; **armar un** ~ to kick up a row.

fomentar [fomen'tar] *vt* (*MED*) to

foment; **fomento** nm (promoción) promotion.

fonda ['fonda] nf inn.

fondo ['fondo] nm (de mar) bottom; (de coche, sala) back; (ARTE etc) background; (reserva) fund; ~s nmpl (COM) funds, resources; **una investigación a** ~ a thorough investigation; **en el** ~ at bottom, deep down.

fono ['fono] nm (AM) telephone number.

fontanería [fontane'ria] nf plumbing; **fontanero, a** nm/f plumber.

forastero, a [foras'tero, a] nm/f stranger.

forcejear [forθexe'ar] vi (luchar) to struggle.

forjar [for'xar] vt to forge.

forma ['forma] nf (figura) form, shape; (molde) mould, pattern; (MED) fitness; (método) way, means; **las** ~s the conventions; **estar en** ~ to be fit.

formación [forma'θjon] nf (gen) formation; (educación) education; ~ **profesional** vocational training.

formal [for'mal] a (gen) formal; (fig: persona) serious; (: de fiar) reliable; ~**idad** nf formality; seriousness; ~**izar** vt (JUR) to formalize; (situación) to put in order, regularize; ~**izarse** vr (situación) to be put in order, be regularized.

formar [for'mar] vt (componer) to form, shape; (constituir) to make up, constitute; (ESCOL) to train, educate; ~**se** vr (ESCOL) to be trained, educated; (cobrar forma) to form, take form; (desarrollarse) to develop.

formatear [formate'ar] vt to format.

formidable [formi'ðaßle] a (temible) formidable; (asombroso) tremendous.

formulario [formu'larjo] nm form.

fornido, a [for'niðo, a] a well-built.

foro ['foro] nm (gen) forum; (JUR) court.

forrar [fo'rrar] vt (abrigo) to line; (li-

bro) to cover; **forro** nm (de cuaderno) cover; (COSTURA) lining; (de sillón) upholstery.

fortalecer [fortale'θer] vt to strengthen.

fortaleza [forta'leθa] nf (MIL) fortress, stronghold; (fuerza) strength; (determinación) resolution.

fortuito, a [for'twito, a] a accidental.

fortuna [for'tuna] nf (suerte) fortune, (good) luck; (riqueza) fortune, wealth.

forzar [for'θar] vt (puerta) to force (open); (compeler) to compel.

forzoso, a [for'θoso, a] a necessary.

fosa ['fosa] nf (sepultura) grave; (en tierra) pit; (ANAT) cavity.

fósforo ['fosforo] nm (QUÍMICA) phosphorus; (cerilla) match.

foso ['foso] nm ditch; (TEATRO) pit; (AUTO): ~ **de reconocimiento** inspection pit.

foto ['foto] nf photo, snap(shot); **sacar una** ~ to take a photo o picture.

fotocopia [foto'kopja] nf photocopy; ~**copiadora** nf photocopier; ~**copiar** vt to photocopy.

fotografía [fotoɣra'fia] nf (ARTE) photography; (una ~) photograph; **fotografiar** vt to photograph.

fotógrafo, a [fo'toɣrafo, a] nm/f photographer.

fracaso [fra'kaso] nm (desgracia, revés) failure; **fracasar** vi (gen) to fail.

fracción [frak'θjon] nf fraction; (POL) faction; **fraccionamiento** nm (AM) housing estate.

fractura [frak'tura] nf fracture, break.

fragancia [fra'ɣanθja] nf (olor) fragrance, perfume.

frágil ['fraxil] a (débil) fragile; (COM) breakable.

fragmento [fraɣ'mento] nm (pedazo) fragment.

fragua ['fraɣwa] nf forge; **fraguar** vt to forge; (fig) to concoct // vi to harden.

fraile ['fraile] *nm* (REL) friar; (: *monje*) monk.

frambuesa [fram'bwesa] *nf* raspberry.

francés, esa [fran'θes, esa] *a* French // *nm/f* Frenchman/woman // *nm* (LING) French.

Francia ['franθja] *nf* France.

franco, a ['franko, a] *a* (*cándido*) frank, open; (COM: *exento*) free // *nm* (*moneda*) franc.

francotirador, a [frankotira'ðor, a] *nm/f* sniper.

franela [fra'nela] *nf* flannel.

franja ['franxa] *nf* fringe.

franquear [franke'ar] *vt* (*camino*) to clear; (*carta, paquete postal*) to frank, stamp; (*obstáculo*) to overcome.

franqueo [fran'keo] *nm* postage.

franqueza [fran'keθa] *nf* (*candor*) frankness.

frasco ['frasko] *nm* bottle, flask; ~ al vacío (vacuum) flask.

frase ['frase] *nf* sentence; ~ hecha set phrase.

fraude ['frauðe] *nm* (*cualidad*) dishonesty; (*acto*) fraud; **fraudulento, a** *a* fraudulent.

frazada [fra'saða] *nf* (AM) blanket.

frecuencia [fre'kwenθja] *nf* frequency; **con** ~ frequently, often.

fregadero [freɣa'ðero] *nm* (kitchen) sink.

fregar [fre'ɣar] *vt* (*frotar*) to scrub; (*platos*) to wash (up); (AM) to annoy.

fregona [fre'ɣona] *nf* (*utensilio*) mop; (*pey: sirvienta*) skivvy.

freír [fre'ir] *vt* to fry.

frenar [fre'nar] *vt* to brake; (*fig*) to check.

frenesí [frene'si] *nm* frenzy; **frenético, a** *a* frantic.

freno ['freno] *nm* (TEC, AUTO) brake; (*de cabalgadura*) bit; (*fig*) check.

frente ['frente] *nm* (ARQ, POL) front; (*de objeto*) front part // *nf* fore-head, brow; ~ a in front of; (*en situación opuesta de*) opposite; **al** ~ **de** (*fig*) at the head of; **chocar de** ~ to crash head-on; **hacer** ~ a to face up to.

fresa ['fresa] *nf* (Esp) strawberry.

fresco, a ['fresko, a] *a* (*nuevo*) fresh; (*frío*) cool // *nm* (*aire*) fresh air; (ARTE) fresco; (AM: *jugo*) fruit drink // *nm/f* (*fam*) shameless person; (*persona insolente*) impudent person; **tomar el** ~ to get some fresh air; **frescura** *nf* freshness; (*descaro*) cheek, nerve; (*calma*) calmness.

frialdad [frial'daθ] *nf* (*gen*) coldness; (*indiferencia*) indifference.

fricción [frik'θjon] *nf* (*gen*) friction; (*acto*) rub(bing); (MED) massage.

frigidez [frixi'ðeθ] *nf* frigidity.

frigorífico [friɣo'rifiko] *nm* refrigerator.

frijol [fri'xol] *nm* kidney bean.

frío, a etc *vb ver* freír // ['frio, a] *a* cold; (*indiferente*) indifferent // *nm* cold; indifference.

frito, a ['frito, a] *a* fried; **me trae** ~ **ese hombre** I'm sick and tired of that man.

frívolo, a ['friβolo, a] *a* frivolous.

frontera [fron'tera] *nf* frontier; **fronterizo, a** *a* frontier *cpd*; (*contiguo*) bordering.

frontón [fron'ton] *nm* (DEPORTE: *cancha*) pelota court; (: *juego*) pelota.

frotar [fro'tar] *vt* to rub; ~se *vr*: ~se las manos to rub one's hands.

fructífero, a [fruk'tifero, a] *a* fruitful.

frugal [fru'ɣal] *a* frugal.

fruncir [frun'θir] *vt* to pucker; (COSTURA) to pleat; ~ **el ceño** to knit one's brow.

frustrar [frus'trar] *vt* to frustrate.

fruta ['fruta] *nf* fruit; **frutería** *nf* fruit shop; **frutero, a** *a* fruit *cpd* // *nm/f* fruiterer // *nm* fruit bowl.

frutilla [fru'tiʎa] *nf* (AM) strawberry.

fue *vb ver* ser, ir.

fuego ['fweɣo] nm (gen) fire; a ~ lento on a low flame o gas; ¿tienes ~? have you (got) a light?

fuente ['fwente] nf fountain; (manantial, fig) spring; (origen) source; (plato) large dish.

fuera etc vb ver **ser**, **ir** // ['fwera] ad out(side); (en otra parte) away; (excepto, salvo) except, save // prep: ~ de outside; (fig) besides; ~ de sí beside o.s.

fuerte ['fwerte] a strong; (golpe) hard; (ruido) loud; (comida) rich; (lluvia) heavy; (dolor) intense // ad strongly; hard; loud(ly).

fuerza etc vb ver **forzar** // ['fwerθa] nf (fortaleza) strength; (TEC, ELEC) power; (coacción) force; (MIL: tb: ~s) forces pl; a ~ de by dint of; cobrar ~s to recover one's strength; tener ~s para to have the strength to; a la ~ forcibly, by force; por ~ of necessity.

fuga ['fuɣa] nf (huida) flight, escape; (de gas etc) leak.

fugarse [fu'ɣarse] vr to flee, escape.

fugaz [fu'ɣaθ] a fleeting.

fugitivo, a [fuxi'tiβo, a] a, nm/f fugitive.

fui vb ver **ser**, **ir**.

fulano, a [fu'lano, a] nm/f so-and-so, what's-his-name/what's-her-name.

fulgor [ful'ɣor] nm brilliance.

fumador, a [fuma'ðor, a] nm/f smoker.

fumar [fu'mar] vt, vi to smoke; ~se vr (disipar) to squander; ~ en pipa to smoke a pipe.

funambulista [funambu'lista] nm/f tightrope walker.

función [fun'θjon] nf function; (de puesto) duties pl; (espectáculo) show; entrar en funciones to take up one's duties.

funcionar [funθjo'nar] vi (gen) to function; (máquina) to work; 'no funciona' 'out of order'.

funcionario, a [funθjo'narjo, a] nm/f official; (público) civil servant.

funda ['funda] nf (gen) cover; (de almohada) pillowcase.

fundación [funda'θjon] nf foundation.

fundamental [fundamen'tal] a fundamental, basic.

fundamentar [fundamen'tar] vt (poner base) to lay the foundations of; (establecer) to found; (fig) to base; **fundamento** nm (base) foundation.

fundar [fun'dar] vt to found; ~se vr: ~se en to be founded on.

fundición [fundi'θjon] nf fusing; (fábrica) foundry.

fundir [fun'dir] vt (gen) to fuse; (metal) to smelt, melt down; (nieve etc) to melt; (COM) to merge; (estatua) to cast; ~se vr (colores etc) to merge, blend; (unirse) to fuse together; (ELEC: fusible, lámpara etc) to fuse, blow; (nieve etc) to melt.

fúnebre ['funeβre] a funeral cpd, funereal.

funeral [fune'ral] nm funeral.

furgón [fur'ɣon] nm wagon; **furgoneta** nf (AUTO, COM) (transit) van (Brit), pick-up (truck) (US).

furia ['furja] nf (ira) fury; (violencia) violence; **furibundo, a** a furious; **furioso, a** a (iracundo) furious; (violento) violent; **furor** nm (cólera) rage.

furúnculo [fu'runkulo] nm boil.

fusible [fu'siβle] nm fuse.

fusil [fu'sil] nm rifle; ~ar vt to shoot.

fusión [fu'sjon] nf (gen) melting; (unión) fusion; (COM) merger.

fusta ['fusta] nf (látigo) riding crop.

fútbol ['futβol] nm football; **futbolista** nm footballer.

fútil ['futil] a trifling; **futilidad** nf triviality.

futuro, a [fu'turo, a] a, nm future.

G

gabán [ga'βan] nm overcoat.

gabardina [gaβar'ðina] nf raincoat,

gabardine.

gabinete [gaßi'nete] *nm* (*POL*) cabinet; (*estudio*) study; (*de abogados etc*) office.

gaceta [ga'θeta] *nf* gazette.

gachas ['gatʃas] *nfpl* porridge *sg*.

gafar [ga'far] *vt* to jinx.

gafas ['gafas] *nfpl* glasses; ~ **de sol** sunglasses.

gafe ['gafe] *nm* jinx.

gaita ['gaita] *nf* bagpipes *pl*.

gajes ['gaxes] *nmpl*: los ~ **del oficio** occupational hazards.

gajo ['gaxo] *nm* (*de naranja*) segment.

gala ['gala] *nf* (*traje de etiqueta*) full dress; (*fig: flor*) cream, flower; ~**s** *nfpl* finery *sg*; **estar de** ~ to be in one's best clothes; **hacer** ~ **de** to display, show off.

galán [ga'lan] *nm* lover; (*Don Juan*) ladies' man; (*TEATRO*): **primer** ~ leading man.

galante [ga'lante] *a* gallant; **galantear** *vt* (*hacer la corte a*) to court, woo; **galantería** *nf* (*caballerosidad*) gallantry; (*cumplido*) politeness; (*comentario*) compliment.

galápago [ga'lapaγo] *nm* (*ZOOL*) turtle.

galaxia [ga'laksja] *nf* galaxy.

galera [ga'lera] *nf* (*nave*) galley; (*carro*) wagon; (*IMPRENTA*) galley.

galería [gale'ria] *nf* (*gen*) gallery; (*balcón*) veranda(h); (*pasillo*) corridor.

Gales ['gales] *nm* (*tb*: **País de** ~) Wales; **galés, esa** *a* Welsh // *nm/f* Welshman/woman // *nm* (*LING*) Welsh.

galgo, a ['galγo, a] *nm/f* greyhound.

galimatías [galima'tias] *nmpl* (*lenguaje*) gibberish *sg*, nonsense *sg*.

galón [ga'lon] *nm* (*MIL*) stripe; (*COSTURA*) braid; (*medida*) gallon.

galopar [galo'par] *vi* to gallop.

gallardía [gaʎar'ðia] *nf* (*galantería*) dash; (*valor*) bravery; (*elegancia*) elegance.

gallego, a [ga'ʎeɣo, a] *a, nm/f* Galician.

galleta [ga'ʎeta] *nf* biscuit (*Brit*), cookie (*US*).

gallina [ga'ʎina] *nf* hen // *nm/f* (*fam: cobarde*) chicken.

gallo ['gaʎo] *nm* cock, rooster.

gama ['gama] *nf* (*fig*) range.

gamba ['gamba] *nf* (*de*) prawn (*Brit*), shrimp (*US*).

gamberro, a [gam'berro, a] *nm/f* hooligan, lout.

gamuza [ga'muθa] *nf* chamois.

gana ['gana] *nf* (*deseo*) desire, wish; (*apetito*) appetite; (*voluntad*) will; (*añoranza*) longing; **de buena** ~ willingly; **de mala** ~ reluctantly; **me da** ~**s de** I feel like, I want to; **no me da la** ~ I don't feel like it; **tener** ~**s de** to feel like.

ganadería [ganaðe'ria] *nf* (*ganado*) livestock; (*ganado vacuno*) cattle *pl*; (*cría, comercio*) cattle raising.

ganado [ga'naðo] *nm* livestock; ~ **lanar** sheep *pl*; ~ **mayor** cattle *pl*; ~ **porcino** pigs *pl*.

ganador, a [gana'ðor, a] *a* winning // *nm/f* winner.

ganancia [ga'nanθja] *nf* (*lo ganado*) gain; (*aumento*) increase; (*beneficio*) profit; ~**s** *nfpl* (*ingresos*) earnings; (*beneficios*) profit *sg*, winnings.

ganar [ga'nar] *vt* (*obtener*) to get, obtain; (*sacar ventaja*) to gain; (*salario etc*) to earn; (*DEPORTE, premio*) to win; (*derrotar a*) to beat; (*alcanzar*) to reach // *vi* (*DEPORTE*) to win; ~**se** *vr*: ~**se la vida** to earn one's living.

gancho ['gantʃo] *nm* (*gen*) hook; (*colgador*) hanger.

gandul, a [gan'dul, a] *a, nm/f* good-for-nothing, layabout.

ganga ['ganga] *nf* (*cosa buena y barata*) bargain; (*buena situación*) cushy job.

gangrena [gan'grena] *nf* gangrene.

gansada [gan'saða] *nf* (*fam*) stupid thing to do.

ganso, a ['ganso, a] *nm/f* (*ZOOL*) goose; (*fam*) idiot.

ganzúa [gan'θua] *nf* skeleton key.

garabatear [garaβate'ar] *vi, vt (al escribir)* to scribble, scrawl.

garabato [gara'βato] *nm (escritura)* scrawl, scribble.

garaje [ga'raxe] *nm* garage.

garante [ga'rante] *a* responsible // *nm/f* guarantor.

garantía [garan'tia] *nf* guarantee.

garantizar [garanti'θar] *vt (hacerse responsable de)* to vouch for; *(asegurar)* to guarantee.

garbanzo [gar'βanθo] *nm* chickpea *(Brit)*, garbanzo *(US)*.

garbo ['garβo] *nm* grace, elegance.

garfio ['garfjo] *nm* grappling iron.

garganta [gar'γanta] *nf (ANAT)* throat; *(de botella)* neck; **gargantilla** *nf* necklace.

gárgaras ['garγaras] *nfpl*: **hacer ~** to gargle.

garita [ga'rita] *nf* cabin, hut; *(MIL)* sentry box.

garito [ga'rito] *nm (lugar)* gambling house *o* den.

garra ['garra] *nf (de gato, TEC)* claw; *(de ave)* talon; *(fam)* hand, paw.

garrafa [ga'rrafa] *nf* carafe, decanter.

garrapata [garra'pata] *nf* tick.

garrapatear [garrapate'ar] *vi, vt* = **garabatear**.

garrote [ga'rrote] *nm (palo)* stick; *(porra)* cudgel; *(suplicio)* garrotte.

garúa [ga'rua] *nf (AM)* drizzle.

garza ['garθa] *nf* heron.

gas [gas] *nm* gas.

gasa ['gasa] *nf* gauze.

gaseoso, a [gase'oso, a] *a* gassy, fizzy // *nf* lemonade, pop *(Brit)*.

gasfitero [gasfi'tero] *nm (AM)* plumber.

gasoil [ga'soil], **gasóleo** [ga'soleo] *nm* diesel (oil).

gasolina [gaso'lina] *nf* petrol, gas(oline) *(US)*; **gasolinera** *nf* petrol *(Brit) o* gas *(US)* station.

gastado, a [gas'taðo, a] *a (rendido)* spent; *(raído)* worn out; *(usado: frase etc)* trite.

gastar [gas'tar] *vt (dinero, tiempo)* to spend; *(fuerzas)* to use up;

(desperdiciar) to waste; *(llevar)* to wear; **~se** *vr* to wear out; *(estropearse)* to waste; **~ bromas** to crack jokes; **¿qué número gastas?** what size (shoe) do you take?

gasto ['gasto] *nm (desembolso)* expenditure, spending; *(consumo, uso)* use; **~s** *nmpl (desembolsos)* expenses; *(cargos)* charges, costs.

gatear [gate'ar] *vi (andar a gatas)* to go on all fours.

gatillo [ga'tiʎo] *nm (de arma de fuego)* trigger; *(de dentista)* forceps.

gato, a ['gato, a] *nm/f* cat // *nm (TEC)* jack; **andar a gatas** to go on all fours.

gaveta [ga'βeta] *nf* drawer.

gaviota [ga'βjota] *nf* seagull.

gay [ge] *a inv, nm* gay, homosexual.

gazapo [ga'θapo] *nm* young rabbit.

gazpacho [gaθ'patʃo] *nm* gazpacho.

gelatina [xela'tina] *nf* jelly; *(polvos etc)* gelatine.

gema ['xema] *nf* gem.

gemelo, a [xe'melo, a] *a, nm/f* twin; **~s** *nmpl (de camisa)* cufflinks; **~s de campo** field glasses, binoculars.

Géminis ['xeminis] *nm* Gemini.

gemido [xe'miðo] *nm (quejido)* moan, groan; *(aullido)* howl.

gemir [xe'mir] *vi (quejarse)* to moan, groan; *(aullar)* to howl.

generación [xenera'θjon] *nf* generation.

general [xene'ral] *a* general // *nm* general; **por lo** *o* **en ~** in general; **G~itat** *nf* Catalan parliament; **~izar** *vt* to generalize; **~izarse** *vr* to become generalized, spread; **~mente** *ad* generally.

generar [xene'rar] *vt* to generate.

género ['xenero] *nm (clase)* kind, sort; *(tipo)* type; *(BIO)* genus; *(LING)* gender; *(COM)* material; **~ humano** human race.

generosidad [xenerosi'ðað] *nf* generosity; **generoso, a** *a* generous.

genial [xe'njal] *a (inspirado)* inspired; *(idea)* brilliant; *(afable)* genial.

genio ['xenjo] *nm (carácter)* nature,

disposition; *(humor)* temper; *(facultad creadora)* genius; **de mal ~** bad-tempered.

genitales [xeni'tales] *nmpl* genitals.

gente ['xente] *nf (personas)* people *pl*; *(raza)* race; *(nación)* nation; *(parientes)* relatives *pl*.

gentil [xen'til] *a (elegante)* graceful; *(encantador)* charming; **~eza** *nf* grace; charm; *(cortesía)* courtesy.

gentío [xen'tio] *nm* crowd, throng.

genuino, a [xe'nwino, a] *a* genuine.

geografía [xeoɣra'fia] *nf* geography.

geología [xeolo'xia] *nf* geology.

geometría [xeome'tria] *nf* geometry.

gerencia [xe'renθja] *nf* management; **gerente** *nm/f (supervisor)* manager; *(jefe)* director.

geriatría [xerja'tria] *nf (MED)* geriatrics *sg*.

germen ['xermen] *nm* germ.

germinar [xermi'nar] *vi* to germinate.

gesticulación [xestikula'θjon] *nf* gesticulation; *(mueca)* grimace.

gestión [xes'tjon] *nf* management; *(diligencia, acción)* negotiation; **gestionar** *vt (lograr)* to try to arrange; *(llevar)* to manage.

gesto ['xesto] *nm (mueca)* grimace; *(ademán)* gesture.

Gibraltar [xiβral'tar] *nm* Gibraltar; **gibraltareño, a** *a*, *nm/f* Gibraltarian.

gigante [xi'ɣante] *a*, *nm/f* giant.

gilipollas [xili'poʎas] *(fam)* *a inv* daft // *nm/f inv* wally.

gimnasia [xim'nasja] *nf* gymnastics *pl*; **gimnasio** *nm* gymnasium; **gimnasta** *nm/f* gymnast.

gimotear [ximote'ar] *vi* to whine, whimper.

ginebra [xi'neβra] *nf* gin.

ginecólogo, a [xine'koloɣo, a] *nm/f* gynecologist.

gira ['xira] *nf* tour, trip.

girar [xi'rar] *vt (dar la vuelta)* to turn (around); (: *rápidamente)* to spin; *(COM: giro postal)* to draw; *(comerciar: letra de cambio)* to issue

// *vi* to turn (round); *(rápido)* to spin; *(COM)* to draw.

girasol [xira'sol] *nm* sunflower.

giratorio, a [xira'torjo, a] *a (gen)* revolving; *(puente)* swing.

giro ['xiro] *nm (movimiento)* turn, revolution; *(LING)* expression; *(COM)* draft; **~ bancario/postal** bank giro/postal order.

gis [xis] *nm (AM)* chalk.

gitano, a [xi'tano, a] *a*, *nm/f* gypsy.

glacial [gla'θjal] *a* icy, freezing.

glaciar [gla'θjar] *nm* glacier.

glándula ['glandula] *nf* gland.

globo ['gloβo] *nm (esfera)* globe, sphere; *(aerostato, juguete)* balloon.

glóbulo ['gloβulo] *nm* globule; *(ANAT)* corpuscle.

gloria ['glorja] *nf* glory.

glorieta [glo'rjeta] *nf (de jardín)* bower, arbour; *(plazoleta)* roundabout *(Brit)*, traffic circle *(US)*.

glorificar [glorifi'kar] *vt (enaltecer)* to glorify, praise.

glorioso, a [glo'rjoso, a] *a* glorious.

glosa ['glosa] *nf* comment; **glosar** *vt (comentar)* to comment on.

glosario [glo'sarjo] *nm* glossary.

glotón, ona [glo'ton, ona] *a* gluttonous, greedy // *nm/f* glutton.

gobernación [goβerna'θjon] *nf* government, governing; **G~** *(AM ADMIN)* Ministry of the Interior; **gobernador, a** *a* governing // *nm/f* governor; **gobernante** *a* governing.

gobernar [goβer'nar] *vt (dirigir)* to guide, direct; *(POL)* to rule, govern // *vi* to govern; *(NAUT)* to steer.

gobierno *etc vb ver* **gobernar** // [go'βjerno] *nm (POL)* government; *(dirección)* guidance; direction; *(NAUT)* steering.

goce *etc vb ver* **gozar** // ['goθe] *nm* enjoyment.

gol [gol] *nm* goal.

golf [golf] *nm* golf.

golfo, a ['golfo, a] *nm (GEO)* gulf // *nm/f (fam: niño)* urchin; *(: pillo)* lout // *nf (: mujer)* slut, whore.

golondrina [golon'drina] *nf* swallow.

golosina [golo'sina] nf titbit; (dulce) sweet; **goloso, a** a sweet-toothed.

golpe ['golpe] nm blow; (de puño) punch; (de mano) smack; (de manera) stroke; (fig: choque) 'clash; **no dar ~ to be bone idle; de un ~ with one blow; de ~ suddenly; de ~ (de estado) coup (d'état); golpear [golpe'ar] vt, vi to strike, knock; (asestar) to beat; (de puño) to punch; (golpetear) to tap.

goma ['goma] nf (caucho) rubber; (elástico) elastic; (una ~) elastic band; ~ espuma foam rubber; ~ de pegar gum, glue.

gordo, a ['gorðo, a] a (gen) fat; (persona) plump; (fam) enormous; el (premio) ~ (en lotería) first prize; **gordura** nf fat; (corpulencia) fatness, stoutness.

gorila [go'rila] nm gorilla.

gorjear [gorxe'ar] vi to twitter, chirp.

gorra ['gorra] nf cap; (de niño) bonnet; (militar) bearskin; **entrar de ~** (fam) to gatecrash; **ir de ~** to sponge.

gorrión [go'rrjon] nm sparrow.

gorro ['gorro] nm (gen) cap; (de niño, mujer) bonnet.

gorrón, ona [go'rron, ona] nm/f scrounger.

gota ['gota] nf (gen) drop; (de sudor) bead; (MED) gout; **gotear** vi to drip; (lloviznar) to drizzle; **gotera** nf leak.

gozar [go'θar] vi to enjoy o.s.; ~ de (disfrutar) to enjoy; (poseer) to possess.

gozne ['goθne] nm hinge.

gozo ['goθo] nm (alegría) joy; (placer) pleasure.

gr. abr (= gramo, gramos) g.

grabación [graβa'θjon] nf recording.

grabado [gra'βaðo] nm print, engraving.

grabadora [graβa'ðora] nf tape-recorder.

grabar [gra'βar] vt to engrave; (discos, cintas) to record.

gracia ['graθja] nf (encanto) grace,
gracefulness; (humor) humour, wit; **¡(muchas) ~s!** thanks (very much)!; ~s a thanks to; **tener ~** (chiste etc) to be funny; **no me hace ~ I am not keen; gracioso, a** (divertido) funny, amusing; (cómico) comical // nm/f (TEATRO) comic character.

grada ['graða] nf (de escalera) step; (de anfiteatro) tier, row; ~s nfpl (DEPORTE: de estadio) terraces.

gradación [graða'θjon] nf gradation.

gradería [graðe'ria] nf (gradas) (flight of) steps pl; (de anfiteatro) tiers pl, rows pl; (DEPORTE: de estadio) terraces pl; ~ **cubierta** covered stand.

grado ['graðo] nm degree; (de aceite, vino) grade; (grada) step; (MIL) rank; **de buen ~** willingly.

graduación [graðwa'θjon] nf (del alcohol) proof, strength; (ESCOL) graduation; (MIL) rank.

gradual [gra'ðwal] a gradual.

graduar [gra'ðwar] vt (gen) to graduate; (MIL) to commission; ~**se** vr to graduate; ~**se la vista** to have one's eyes tested.

gráfico, a ['grafiko, a] a graphic // nm diagram // nf graph; ~**s** nmpl (INFORM) graphics.

grajo ['graxo] nm rook.

Gral abr (= General) Gen.

gramática [gra'matika] nf grammar.

gramo ['gramo] nm gramme (Brit), gram (US).

gran [gran] a ver **grande.**

grana ['grana] nf (BOT) seedling; (color, tela) scarlet.

granada [gra'naða] nf pomegranate; (MIL) grenade.

Gran Bretaña [-bre'taɲa] nf Great Britain.

grande ['grande] (antes de nmsg: **gran**) a (de tamaño) big, large; (alto) tall; (distinguido) great; (impresionante) grand // nm grandee; **grandeza** nf greatness.

grandioso, a [gran'djoso, a] a magnificent, grand.

granel [gra'nel]: **a ~ ad** (COM) in bulk.

granero [gra'nero] nm granary, barn.

granito [gra'nito] nm (AGR) small grain; (roca) granite.

granizado [grani'θaðo] nm iced drink.

granizar [grani'θar] vi to hail; **granizo** nm hail.

granja ['granxa] nf (gen) farm; **granjero, a** nm/f farmer.

grano ['grano] nm grain; (semilla) seed; (baya) berry; (MED) pimple, spot; ~**s** nmpl cereals.

granuja [gra'nuxa] nm/f rogue; (golfillo) urchin.

grapa ['grapa] nf staple; (TEC) clamp.

grasa ['grasa] nf (gen) grease; (de cocina) fat, lard; (sebo) suet; (mugre) filth; **grasiento, a** a greasy; (de aceite) oily.

gratificación [gratifika'θjon] nf (propina) tip; (bono) bonus; (recompensa) reward; **gratificar** vt to tip; to reward.

gratis ['gratis] ad free.

gratitud [grati'tuð] nf gratitude.

grato, a ['grato, a] a (agradable) pleasant, agreeable; (bienvenido) welcome.

gratuito, a [gra'twito, a] a (gratis) free; (sin razón) gratuitous.

gravamen [gra'βamen] nm (carga) burden; (impuesto) tax.

gravar [gra'βar] vt to burden; (COM) to tax.

grave ['graβe] a heavy; (serio) grave, serious; ~**dad** nf gravity.

gravilla [gra'βiʎa] nf gravel.

gravitar [graβi'tar] vi to gravitate; ~ **sobre** to rest on.

gravoso, a [gra'βoso, a] a (pesado) burdensome; (costoso) costly.

graznar [graθ'nar] vi (cuervo) to squawk; (pato) to quack; (hablar ronco) to croak.

Grecia ['greθja] nf Greece.

gremio ['gremjo] nm (asociación) trade, industry.

greña ['greña] nf (cabellos) shock of hair; (maraña) tangle.

gresca ['greska] nf uproar.

griego, a ['grjeɣo, a] a, nm/f Greek.

grieta ['grjeta] nf crack.

grifo ['grifo] nm tap; (AM AUTO) petrol (Brit) o gas (US) station.

grilletes [gri'ʎetes] nmpl fetters.

grillo ['griʎo] nm (ZOOL) cricket; (BOT) shoot.

gripe ['gripe] nf flu, influenza.

gris [gris] a (color) grey.

gritar [gri'tar] vt, vi to shout, yell; **grito** nm shout, yell; (de horror) scream.

grosella [gro'seʎa] nf (red)currant; ~ **negra** blackcurrant.

grosería [grose'ria] nf (actitud) rudeness; (comentario) vulgar comment; **grosero, a** a (poco cortés) rude, bad-mannered; (ordinario) vulgar, crude.

grosor [gro'sor] nm thickness.

grúa ['grua] nf (TEC) crane; (de petróleo) derrick.

grueso, a ['grweso, a] a thick; (persona) stout // nm bulk; **el ~ de** the bulk of.

grulla ['gruʎa] nf crane.

grumo ['grumo] nm clot, lump.

gruñido [gru'ɲiðo] nm grunt; (fig) grumble; **gruñir** (vi animal) to growl; (fam) to grumble.

grupa ['grupa] nf (ZOOL) rump.

grupo ['grupo] nm group; (TEC) unit, set.

gruta ['gruta] nf grotto.

guadaña [gwa'ðaɲa] nf scythe.

guagua [gwa'rwa] nf (AM: niño) baby; (: bus) bus.

guante ['gwante] nm glove.

guapo, a ['gwapo, a] a (good-looking, attractive; (hombre) handsome; (elegante) smart.

guarda ['gwarða] nm/f (persona) guard, keeper // nf (acto) guarding; (custodia) custody; ~**bosques** nm inv gamekeeper; ~**costas** nm inv coastguard vessel; ~**dor, a** a protective // nm/f guardian, protector; **~espaldas** nm/f inv bodyguard; **~meta** nm/f goalkeeper; **~polvo** nm dust cover; (prenda de vestir) overalls pl; **guardar** vt (gen) to keep; (vigilar) to guard, watch over; (dinero: ahorrar) to save; **~ cama** to stay in bed; **guardarse** vr (preservarse) to protect o.s.; (evitar) to avoid; **guardarropa** nm (armario) wardrobe; (en establecimiento público) cloakroom.

guardería [gwarðe'ria] nf nursery.

guardia ['gwarðja] nf (MIL) guard; (cuidado) care, custody // nm/f guard; (policía) policeman/woman; **estar de ~** to be on guard; **montar ~** to mount guard; **G~** Civil Civil Guard; **G~ Nacional** National Guard.

guardián, ana [gwar'ðjan, ana] nm/f (gen) guardian, keeper.

guardilla [gwar'ðiʎa] nf attic.

guarecer [gware'θer] vt (proteger) to protect; (abrigar) to shelter; **~se** vr to take refuge.

guarida [gwa'riða] nf (de animal) den, lair; (refugio) refuge.

guarnecer [gwarne'θer] vt (equipar) to provide; (adornar) to adorn; (TEC) to reinforce; **guarnición** nf (de vestimenta) trimming; (de piedra) mount; (CULIN) garnish; (arneses) harness; (MIL) garrison.

guarro, a ['gwarro, a] nm/f pig.

guasa ['gwasa] nf joke; **guasón, ona** a (bromista) joking // nm/f wit; joker.

Guatemala [gwate'mala] nf Guatemala.

gubernativo, a [guβerna'tiβo, a] a governmental.

guerra ['gerra] nf war; (pelea) struggle; **~ civil** civil war; **~ fría** cold war; **dar ~** to annoy; **guerrear** vi to wage war; **guerrero, a** a fighting; (carácter) warlike // nm/f warrior.

guerrilla [ge'rriʎa] nf guerrilla warfare; (tropas) guerrilla band o group.

guía etc vb ver **guiar** // ['gia] nm/f (persona) guide // nf (libro) guidebook; **~ de ferrocarriles** railway timetable; **~ telefónica** telephone directory.

guiar [gi'ar] vt to guide, direct; (AUTO) to steer; **~se** vr: **~se por** to be guided by.

guijarro [gi'xarro] nm pebble.

guinda ['ginda] nf morello cherry.

guindilla [gin'diʎa] nf chilli pepper.

guiñapo [gi'ɲapo] nm (harapo) rag; (persona) reprobate, rogue.

guiñar [gi'ɲar] vi to wink.

guión [gi'on] nm (LING) hyphen, dash; (CINE) script; **guionista** nm/f scriptwriter.

guirnalda [gir'nalda] nf garland.

guisa ['gisa] nf: **a ~ de** as, like.

guisado [gi'saðo] nm stew.

guisante [gi'sante] nm pea.

guisar [gi'sar] vt, vi to cook; **guiso** nm cooked dish.

guitarra [gi'tarra] nf guitar.

gula ['gula] nf gluttony, greed.

gusano [gu'sano] nm maggot; (lombriz) earthworm.

gustar [gus'tar] vt to taste, sample // vi to please, be pleasing; **~ de** algo to like o enjoy sth; **me gustan las uvas** I like grapes; **le gusta nadar** she likes o enjoys swimming.

gusto ['gusto] nm (sentido, sabor) taste; (placer) pleasure; **tiene ~ a menta** it tastes of mint; **tener buen ~** to have good taste; **sentirse a ~** to feel at ease; **mucho ~ (en conocerle)** pleased to meet you; **el ~ es mío** the pleasure is mine; **con ~** willingly, gladly; **~so, a** a (sabroso) tasty; (agradable) pleasant.

gutural [gutu'ral] a guttural.

H

ha vb ver **haber**.

haba ['aβa] nf bean.

Habana [a'βana] nf: **la ~** Havana.

habano [a'βano] nm Havana cigar.

habéis *vb ver* **haber**.

haber [a'βer] ♦ *vb auxiliar* **1** (*tiempos compuestos*) to have; **he/ había comido** I have/had eaten; **antes/después de ~lo visto** before seeing/after seeing *o* having seen it

2 : **¡~lo dicho antes!** you should have said so before!

3 : **~ de**: **he de hacerlo** I have to do it; **ha de llegar mañana** it should arrive tomorrow

♦ *vb impersonal* (*existencia*: *sg*) there is; (: *pl*) there are; **hay un hermano/dos hermanos** there is one brother/there are two brothers; **¿cuánto hay de aquí a Sucre?** how far is it from here to Sucre?

2 (*obligación*): **hay que hacer algo** something must be done; **hay que apuntarlo para acordarse** you have to write it down to remember

3 : **¡hay que ver!** well I never!

4 : **¡no hay de** *o* **qué!** don't mention it!, not at all!

5 : **¿qué hay?** (*¿qué pasa?*) what's up?, what's the matter?; (*¿qué tal?*) how's it going?

♦ *vr*: **habérselas con uno** to have it out with sb

♦ *vt*: **he aquí unas sugerencias** here are some suggestions; **no hay cintas blancas pero sí las hay rojas** there aren't any white ribbons but there are some red ones

♦ *nm* (*en cuenta*) credit side; **~es** *nmpl* assets; **¿cuánto tengo en el ~?** how much do I have in my account?; **tiene varias novelas en su ~** he has several novels to his credit.

habichuela [aβi'tʃwela] *nf* kidney bean.

hábil ['aβil] *a* (*listo*) clever, smart; (*capaz*) fit, capable; (*experto*) expert; **día ~** working day; **habilidad** *nf* (*gen*) skill, ability; (*inteligencia*) cleverness.

habilitar [aβili'tar] *vt* (*capacitar*) to enable; (*dar instrumentos*) to equip; (*financiar*) to finance.

hábilmente [aβil'mente] *ad* skilfully, expertly.

habitación [aβita'θjon] *nf* (*cuarto*) room; (*casa*) dwelling, abode; (*BIO*: *morada*) habitat; **~ sencilla** *o* **individual** single room; **~ doble** *o* **de matrimonio** double room.

habitante [aβi'tante] *nm/f* inhabitant.

habitar [aβi'tar] *vt* (*residir en*) to inhabit; (*ocupar*) to occupy // *vi* to live.

hábito ['aβito] *nm* habit.

habituar [aβi'twar] *vt* to accustom; **~se** *vr*: **~se a** to get used to.

habla ['aβla] *nf* (*capacidad de hablar*) speech; (*idioma*) language; (*dialecto*) dialect; **perder el ~** to become speechless; **de ~ francesa** French-speaking; **estar al ~** to be in contact; (*TEL*) to be on the line; **¡González al ~!** (*TEL*) González speaking!

hablador, a [aβla'ðor, a] *a* talkative // *nm/f* chatterbox.

habladuría [aβlaðu'ria] *nf* rumour; **~s** *nfpl* gossip *sg*.

hablante [a'βlante] *a* speaking // *nm/f* speaker.

hablar [a'βlar] *vt* to speak, talk // *vi* to speak; **~se** *vr* to speak to each other; **~ con** to speak to; **~ de** to speak of *o* about; **'se habla inglés'** 'English spoken here'.

habré *etc vb ver* **haber**.

hacedor, a [aθe'ðor, a] *nm/f* maker.

hacendado [asen'daðo] *nm* (*AM*) large landowner.

hacendoso, a [aθen'doso, a] *a* industrious.

hacer [a'θer] ♦ *vt* **1** (*fabricar, producir*) to make; (*construir*) to build; **~ una película/un ruido** to make a film/noise; **el guisado lo hice yo** I made *o* cooked the stew

2 (*ejecutar: trabajo etc*) to do; **la**

colada to do the washing; ~ **la comida** to do the cooking; **¿qué haces?** what are you doing?; ~ **el malo** o **el papel del malo** (TEAT) to play the villain

3 (estudios, algunos deportes) to do; ~ **español/económicas** to do o study Spanish/Economics; ~ **yoga/ gimnasia** to do yoga/go to gym

4 (transformar, incidir en): **esto lo hará más difícil** this will make it more difficult; **salir te hará sentir mejor** going out will make you feel better

5 (cálculo): **2 y 2 hacen 4** 2 and 2 make 4; **éste hace 100** this one makes 100

6 (+ subjun): **esto hará que ganemos** this will make us win; **harás que no quiera venir** you'll stop him wanting to come

7 (como sustituto de vb) to do; **él bebió y yo hice lo mismo** he drank and I did likewise

8: no hace más que criticar al he does is criticize

♦ vb semi-auxiliar: ~ + infinitivo **1** (directo): **les hice venir** I made o had them come; ~ **trabajar a los demás** to get others to work

2 (por intermedio de otros): ~ **reparar algo** to get sth repaired

♦ vi **1: haz como que no lo sabes** act as if you don't know

2 (ser apropiado): **si os hace** if it's alright with you

3: ~ **de:** ~ **de madre para uno** to be like a mother to sb; (TEATRO): ~ **de Otelo** to play Othello

♦ vb impersonal **1: hace calor/ frío** it's hot/cold; ver tb **bueno, sol, tiempo**

2 (tiempo): **hace 3 años** 3 years ago; **hace un mes que voy/no voy** I've been going/I haven't been for a month

4: ¿cómo has hecho para llegar tan rápido? how did you manage to get here so quickly?

♦ vr **1** (volverse) to become; **se**

hicieron amigos they became friends

2 (acostumbrarse): ~**se a** to get used to

3: se hace con huevos y leche it's made out of eggs and milk; **eso no se hace** that's not done

4 (obtener): ~**se de** o **con algo** to get hold of sth

5 (fingirse): ~**se el sueco** to turn a deaf ear.

hacia [ˈaθja] prep (en dirección de) towards; (cerca de; near): (actitud) towards; ~ **arriba/abajo** up(wards)/ down(wards); ~ **mediodía** about noon.

hacienda [aˈθjenda] nf (propiedad) property; (finca) farm; (AM) ranch; ~ **pública** public finance; (Ministerio de) **H~** Exchequer (Brit), Treasury Department (US).

hacha [ˈatʃa] nf axe; (antorcha) torch.

hada [ˈaða] nf fairy.

hago etc vb ver **hacer**.

Haití [aiˈti] nm Haiti.

halagar [alaˈɣar] vt (lisonjear) to flatter.

halago [aˈlaɣo] nm (adulación) flattery; **halagüeño, a** a flattering.

halcón [alˈkon] nm falcon, hawk.

hálito [ˈalito] nm breath.

halterofilia [alteroˈfilja] nf weight-lifting.

hallar [aˈʎar] vt (gen) to find; (descubrir) to discover; (toparse con) to run into; ~**se** vr to be (situated); **hallazgo** nm discovery; (cosa) find.

hamaca [aˈmaka] nf hammock.

hambre [ˈambre] nf hunger; (carencia) famine; (fig) longing; **tener** ~ **to** be hungry; **hambriento, a** a hungry, starving.

hamburguesa [amburˈɣesa] nf hamburger.

hampón [amˈpon] nm thug.

han vb ver **haber**.

haragán, ana [araˈɣan, ana] a, nm/f good-for-nothing.

harapiento, a [ara'pjento, a] *a* tattered, in rags; **harapo** nm rag.

haré etc vb ver **hacer**.

harina [a'rina] nf flour.

hartar [ar'tar] vt to satiate, glut; (*fig*) to tire, sicken; ~se vr (*de comida*) to fill o.s., gorge o.s.; (*cansarse*) to get fed up (de with); **hartazgo** nm surfeit, glut; **harto, a** *a* (*lleno*) full; (*cansado*) fed up // *ad* (*bastante*) enough; (*muy*) very; **estar harto de** to be fed up with; **hartura** nf (*exceso*) surfeit; (*abundancia*) abundance; (*satisfacción*) satisfaction.

has vb ver **haber**.

hasta ['asta] *ad* even // *prep* (*alcanzando a*) as far as, up to, down to; (*de tiempo: a tal hora*) till, until; (*antes de*) before // *conj*: ~ **que** until; ~ **luego/el sábado** see you soon/ on Saturday.

hastiar [as'tjar] vt (*gen*) to weary; (*aburrir*) to bore; ~se vr: ~**se de** to get fed up with; **hastío** nm weariness; boredom.

hatillo [a'tiʎo] nm belongings pl, kit; (*montón*) bundle, heap.

hay vb ver **haber**.

Haya ['aja] nf: **la** ~ The Hague.

haya etc vb ver **haber** // ['aja] nf beech tree.

haz vb ver **hacer** // [aθ] nm bundle, bunch; (*rayo: de luz*) beam.

hazaña [a'θaɲa] nf feat, exploit.

hazmerreír [aθmerre'ir] nm inv laughing stock.

he vb ver **haber**.

hebilla [e'βiʎa] nf buckle, clasp.

hebra ['eβra] nf thread; (*BOT: fibra*) fibre, grain.

hebreo, a [e'βreo, a] *a, nm/f* Hebrew // nm (*LING*) Hebrew.

hectárea [ek'tarea] nf hectare.

hechizar [etʃi'θar] vt to cast a spell on, bewitch.

hechizo [e'tʃiθo] nm witchcraft, magic; (*acto de magia*) spell, charm.

hecho, a *pp de* **hacer** // ['etʃo, a] *a* complete; (*maduro*) mature; (*COSTURA*) ready-to-wear // nm

deed, act; (*dato*) fact; (*cuestión*) matter; (*suceso*) event // *excl* agreed!, done!; **¡bien** ~! well done!; **de** ~ in fact, as a matter of fact.

hechura [e'tʃura] nf making, creation; (*producto*) product; (*forma*) form, shape; (*de persona*) build; (*TEC*) craftsmanship.

heder [e'ðer] vi to stink, smell; (*fig*) to be unbearable.

hediondo, a [e'ðjondo, a] *a* stinking.

hedor [e'ðor] nm stench.

heladera [ela'ðera] nf (*AM: refrigerador*) refrigerator.

helado, a [e'laðo, a] *a* frozen; (*glacial*) icy; (*fig*) chilly, cold // nm ice cream // nf frost.

helar [e'lar] vt to freeze, ice (up); (*dejar atónito*) to amaze; (*desalentar*) to discourage // vi, ~se vr to freeze.

helecho [e'letʃo] nm fern.

hélice ['eliθe] nf spiral; (*TEC*) propeller.

helicóptero [eli'koptero] nm helicopter.

hembra ['embra] nf (*BOT, ZOOL*) female; (*mujer*) woman; (*TEC*) nut.

hemorroides [emo'rroiðes] nfpl haemorrhoids, piles.

hemos vb ver **haber**.

hendidura [endi'ðura] nf crack, split; (*geo*) fissure.

heno ['eno] nm hay.

herbicida [erβi'θiða] nm weedkiller.

heredad [ere'ðað] nf landed property; (*granja*) farm.

heredar [ere'ðar] vt to inherit; **heredero, a** nm/f heir/heiress.

hereje [e'rexe] nm/f heretic.

herencia [e'renθja] nf inheritance.

herido, a [e'riðo, a] *a* injured, wounded // nm/f casualty // nf wound, injury.

herir [e'rir] vt to wound, injure; (*fig*) to offend.

hermanastro, a [erma'nastro, a] nm/f stepbrother/sister.

hermandad [erman'daθ] *nf* brotherhood.

hermano, a [er'mano, a] *nm/f* brother/sister; ~ **gemelo** twin brother; ~ **político** brother-in-law; **hermana política** sister-in-law.

hermético, a [er'metiko, a] *a* hermetic; (*fig*) watertight.

hermoso, a [er'moso, a] *a* beautiful, lovely; (*estupendo*) splendid; (*guapo*) handsome; **hermosura** *nf* beauty.

héroe ['eroe] *nm* hero.

heroína [ero'ina] *nf* (*mujer*) heroine; (*droga*) heroin.

heroísmo [ero'ismo] *nm* heroism.

herradura [erra'ðura] *nf* horseshoe.

herramienta [erra'mjenta] *nf* tool.

herrería [erre'ria] *nf* smithy; (*TEC*) forge; **herrero** *nm* blacksmith.

herrumbre [e'rrumbre] *nf* rust.

hervidero [erßi'ðero] *nm* (*fig*) swarm; (*POL etc*) hotbed.

hervir [er'ßir] *vi* to boil; (*burbujear*) to bubble; (*fig*): ~ **de** to teem with; ~ **a fuego lento** to simmer; **hervor** *nm* boiling; (*fig*) ardour, fervour.

hice *etc vb ver* **hacer**.

hidratante [iðra'tante] *a*: **crema** ~ moisturizing cream, moisturizer.

hidráulico, a [i'ðrauliko, a] *a* hydraulic // *nf* hydraulics *sg*.

hidro... [iðro] *pref* hydro-, water-...; ~**eléctrico, a** a hydroelectric; ~**fobia** *nf* hydrophobia, rabies; **hidrógeno** *nm* hydrogen.

hiedra ['jeðra] *nf* ivy.

hiel [jel] *nf* gall, bile; (*fig*) bitterness.

hiela *etc vb ver* **helar**.

hielo ['jelo] *nm* (*gen*) ice; (*escarcha*) frost; (*fig*) coldness, reserve.

hiena ['jena] *nf* hyena.

hierba ['jerßa] *nf* (*pasto*) grass; (*CULIN, MED*: *planta*) herb; **mala** ~ weed; (*fig*) evil influence; ~**buena** *nf* mint.

hierro ['jerro] *nm* (*metal*) iron; (*objeto*) iron object.

hígado ['iɣaðo] *nm* liver.

higiene [i'xjene] *nf* hygiene; **higiénico, a** *a* hygienic.

higo ['iɣo] *nm* fig; **higuera** *nf* fig tree.

hijastro, a [i'xastro, a] *nm/f* stepson/daughter.

hijo, a ['ixo, a] *nm/f* son/daughter, child; ~**s** *nmpl* children, sons and daughters; ~ **de papá/mamá** daddy's/mummy's boy; ~ **de puta** (*fam!*) bastard (!), son of a bitch (!).

hilar [i'lar] *vt* to spin; ~ **fino** to split hairs.

hilera [i'lera] *nf* row, file.

hilo ['ilo] *nm* thread; (*BOT*) fibre; (*metal*) wire; (*de agua*) trickle, thin stream; (*de luz*) beam, ray.

hilvanar [ilßa'nar] *vt* (*COSTURA*) to tack (*Brit*), baste (*US*); (*fig*) to do hurriedly.

himno ['imno] *nm* hymn; ~ **nacional** national anthem.

hincapié [inka'pje] *nm*: **hacer** ~ **en** to emphasize.

hincar [in'kar] *vt* to drive (in), thrust (in); ~**se** *vr*: ~**se de rodillas** to kneel down.

hincha ['intʃa] *nm/f* (*fam*) fan.

hinchado, a [in'tʃaðo, a] *a* (*gen*) swollen; (*persona*) pompous.

hinchar [in'tʃar] *vt* (*gen*) to swell; (*inflar*) to blow up, inflate; (*fig*) to exaggerate; ~**se** *vr* (*inflarse*) to swell up; (*fam*: *llenarse*) to stuff o.s.; **hinchazón** *nf* (*MED*) swelling; (*altivez*) arrogance.

hinojo [i'noxo] *nm* fennel.

hipermercado [ipermer'kaðo] *nm* hypermarket, superstore.

hipnotismo [ipno'tismo] *nm* hypnotism; **hipnotizar** *vt* to hypnotize.

hipo ['ipo] *nm* hiccups *pl*.

hipocresía [ipokre'sia] *nf* hypocrisy; **hipócrita** *a* hypocritical // *nm/f* hypocrite.

hipódromo [i'poðromo] *nm* racetrack.

hipopótamo [ipo'potamo] *nm* hippopotamus.

hipoteca [ipo'teka] *nf* mortgage.

hipótesis [i'potesis] *nf inv* hypothesis.

hiriente [i'rjente] *a* offensive, wounding.

hispánico, a [is'paniko, a] *a* Hispanic.

hispano, a [is'pano, a] *a* Hispanic, Spanish, Hispano- // *nm/f* Spaniard; **H~américa** *nf* Spanish *o* Latin America; **~americano, a** *a, nm/f* Spanish *o* Latin American.

histeria [is'terja] *nf* hysteria.

historia [is'torja] *nf* history; (*cuento*) story, tale; **~s** *nfpl* (*chismes*) gossip *sg*; **dejarse de ~s** to come to the point; **pasar a la ~** to go down in history; **~dor, a** *nm/f* historian; **historiar** *vt* to chronicle, write the history of; **histórico, a** *a* historical; (*fig*) historic.

historieta [isto'rjeta] *nf* tale, anecdote; (*dibujos*) comic strip.

hito ['ito] *nm* (*fig*) landmark; (*objetivo*) goal, target.

hizo *vb ver* **hacer**.

Hnos *abr* (= *Hermanos*) Bros.

hocico [o'θiko] *nm* snout; (*fig*) grimace.

hockey ['xoki] *nm* hockey; **~ sobre hielo** ice hockey.

hogar [o'ɣar] *nm* fireplace, hearth; (*casa*) home; (*vida familiar*) home life; **~eño, a** *a* home; (*persona*) home-loving.

hoguera [o'ɣera] *nf* (*gen*) bonfire.

hoja ['oxa] *nf* (*gen*) leaf; (*de flor*) petal; (*de papel*) sheet; (*página*) page; **~ de afeitar** razor blade.

hojalata [oxa'lata] *nf* tin(plate).

hojaldre [o'xaldre] *nm* (*CULIN*) puff pastry.

hojear [oxe'ar] *vt* to leaf through, turn the pages of.

hola ['ola] *excl* hello!

Holanda [o'landa] *nf* Holland; **holandés, esa** *a* Dutch // *nm/f* Dutchman/woman // *nm* (*LING*) Dutch.

holgado, a [ol'ɣaðo, a] *a* loose, baggy; (*rico*) well-to-do.

holgar [ol'ɣar] *vi* (*descansar*) to

rest; (*sobrar*) to be superfluous; **huelga decir que** it goes without saying that.

holgazán, ana [olɣa'θan, ana] *a* idle, lazy // *nm/f* loafer.

holgura [ol'ɣura] *nf* looseness, bagginess; (*TEC*) play, free movement; (*vida*) comfortable living, luxury.

hollín [o'ʎin] *nm* soot.

hombre ['ombre] *nm* (*gen*) man; (*raza humana*): **el ~** man(kind); (*uno*) man // *excl*: **¡sí ~!** (*claro*) of course!; (*para énfasis*) man, old boy; **~ de negocios** businessman; **~rana** frogman; **~ de pro** honest man.

hombrera [om'brera] *nf* shoulder strap.

hombro ['ombro] *nm* shoulder.

hombruno, a [om'bruno, a] *a* mannish.

homenaje [ome'naxe] *nm* (*gen*) homage; (*tributo*) tribute.

homicida [omi'θiða] *a* homicidal // *nm/f* murderer; **homicidio** *nm* murder, homicide.

homosexual [omosek'swal] *a, nm/f* homosexual.

hondo, a ['ondo, a] *a* deep; **lo ~** the depth(s) (*pl*), the bottom; **~nada** *nf* hollow, depression; (*cañón*) ravine; (*GEO*) lowland; **hondura** *nf* depth, profundity.

Honduras [on'duras] *nf* Honduras.

hondureño, a [ondu'reɲo, a] *a, nm/f* Honduran.

honestidad [onesti'ðað] *nf* purity, chastity; (*decencia*) decency; **honesto, a** *a* chaste; decent, honest; (*justo*) just.

hongo ['ongo] *nm* (*BOT*: *gen*) fungus; (: *comestible*) mushroom; (: *venenoso*) toadstool.

honor [o'nor] *nm* (*gen*) honour; (*gloria*) glory; **en ~ a la verdad** to be fair; **~able** *a* honourable.

honorario, a [ono'rarjo, a] *a* honorary; **~s** *nmpl* fees.

honra ['onra] *nf* (*gen*) honour; (*renombre*) good name; **~dez** *nf* honesty; (de persona) integrity; **~do, a** a honest, upright.

honrar [on'rar] vt to honour; **~se** vr: ~se con algo/de hacer algo to be honoured by sth/to do sth.

honroso, a [on'roso, a] a (honrado) honourable; (respetado) respectable.

hora ['ora] nf (una ~) hour; (tiempo) time; ¿qué ~ es? what time is it?; ¿a qué ~? at what time?; **media ~** half an hour; **a la ~ de recreo** at playtime; **a primera ~** first thing (in the morning); **a última ~** at the last moment; **a altas ~s** in the small hours; **¡a buena ~s!** about time, too!; **dar la ~** to strike the hour; **~s de oficina/de trabajo** office/working hours; **~s de visita** visiting times; **~s extras** o **extraordinarias** overtime sg; **~s punta** rush hours.

horadar [ora'ðar] vt to drill, bore.

horario, a [o'rarjo, a] a hourly, hour cpd // nm timetable; **~ comercial** business hours pl.

horca ['orka] nf gallows sg.

horcajadas [orka'xaðas]: **a ~** ad astride.

horchata [or'tʃata] nf cold drink made from tiger nuts and water, tiger nut milk.

horda ['orða] nf horde.

horizontal [oriθon'tal] a horizontal.

horizonte [ori'θonte] nm horizon.

horma ['orma] nf mould.

hormiga [or'miɣa] nf ant; **~s** nfpl (MED) pins and needles.

hormigón [ormi'ɣon] nm concrete; **~ armado/pretensado** reinforced/prestressed concrete.

hormigueo [ormi'ɣeo] nm (comezón) itch; (fig) uneasiness.

hormona [or'mona] nf hormone.

hornada [or'naða] nf batch (of loaves etc).

hornillo [or'niʎo] nm (cocina) portable stove.

horno ['orno] nm (CULIN) oven; (TEC) furnace; **alto ~** blast furnace.

horóscopo [o'roskopo] nm horo-

scope.

horquilla [or'kiʎa] nf hairpin; (AGR) pitchfork.

horrendo, a [o'rrendo, a] a horrendous, frightful.

horrible [o'rriβle] a horrible, dreadful.

horripilante [orripi'lante] a hairraising, horrifying.

horror [o'rror] nm horror, dread; (atrocidad) atrocity; **¡qué ~!** (fam) oh, my God!; **~izar** vt to horrify, frighten; **~izarse** vr to be horrified; **~oso, a** a horrifying, ghastly.

hortaliza [orta'liθa] nf vegetable.

hortelano, a [orte'lano, a] nm/f (market) gardener.

hosco, a ['osko, a] a dark; (persona) sullen, gloomy.

hospedar [ospe'ðar] vt to put up; **~se** vr to stay, lodge.

hospital [ospi'tal] nm hospital.

hospitalario, a [ospita'larjo, a] a (acogedor) hospitable; **hospitalidad** nf hospitality.

hostal [os'tal] nm small hotel.

hostelería [ostele'ria] nf hotel business o trade.

hostelero, a [oste'lero, a] nm/f innkeeper, landlord/lady.

hostia ['ostja] nf (REL) host, consecrated wafer; (fam: golpe) whack, punch // excl: **¡~(s)!** (fam!) damn!

hostigar [osti'ɣar] vt to whip; (fig) to harass, pester.

hostil [os'til] a hostile; **~idad** nf hostility.

hotel [o'tel] nm hotel; **~ero, a** a hotel cpd // nm/f hotelier.

hoy [oi] ad (este día) today; (la actualidad) now(adays) // nm present time; **~ (en) día** now(adays).

hoyo ['ojo] nm hole, pit; **hoyuelo** nm dimple.

hoz [oθ] nf sickle.

hube etc vb ver **haber**.

hucha ['utʃa] nf money box.

hueco, a ['weko, a] a (vacío) hollow, empty; (resonante) booming // nm hollow, cavity.

huelga *etc vb ver* **holgar** // ['welɣa] *nf* strike; **declararse en** ~ **to go on** strike, come out on strike; ~ **de hambre** hunger strike.

huelgo *etc vb ver* **holgar**.

huelguista [wel'ɣista] *nmf* striker.

huelo *etc vb ver* **oler**.

huella ['weʎa] *nf* (*acto de pisar, pisada*) tread(ing); (*marca del paso*) footprint, footstep; (: *de animal, máquina*) track; ~ **digital** fingerprint.

huérfano, a ['werfano, a] *a* orphan(ed) // *nmf* orphan.

huerta ['werta] *nf* market garden; (*en Murcia y Valencia*) irrigated region.

huerto ['werto] *nm* kitchen garden; (*de árboles frutales*) orchard.

hueso ['weso] *nm* (ANAT) bone; (*de fruta*) stone.

huésped, a ['wespeð, a] *nmf* (*invitado*) guest; (*habitante*) resident; (*anfitrión*) host(ess).

huesudo, a [we'suðo, a] *a* bony, big-boned.

huevera [we'ßera] *nf* eggcup.

huevo ['weßo] *nm* egg; ~ **duro/ escalfado/frito** (*Esp*) *o* **estrellado** (AM)/**pasado por agua** hard-boiled/ poached/fried/soft-boiled egg; ~**s revueltos** scrambled eggs.

huida [u'iða] *nf* escape, flight.

huidizo, a [ui'ðiße, a] *a* (*tímido*) shy; (*pasajero*) fleeting.

huir [u'ir] *vi* (*escapar*) to flee, escape; (*evadir*) to avoid; ~**se** *vr* (*escaparse*) to escape.

hule ['ule] *nm* (*encerado*) oilskin.

humanidad [umani'ðað] *nf* (*género humano*) man(kind); (*cualidad*) humanity.

humano, a [u'mano, a] *a* (*gen*) human; (*humanitario*) humane // *nm* human; **ser** ~ human being.

humareda [uma'reða] *nf* cloud of smoke.

humedad [ume'ðað] *nf* (*del clima*) humidity; (*de pared etc*) dampness; **a prueba de** ~ damp-proof;

humedecer *vt* to moisten, wet; **humedecerse** *vr* to get wet.

húmedo, a ['umeðo, a] *a* (*mojado*) damp, wet; (*tiempo etc*) humid.

humildad [umil'dað] *nf* humility, humbleness; **humilde** *a* humble, modest.

humillación [umiʎa'θjon] *nf* humiliation; **humillante** *a* humiliating.

humillar [umi'ʎar] *vt* to humiliate; ~**se** *vr* to humble o.s., grovel.

humo ['umo] *nm* (*de fuego*) smoke; (*gas nocivo*) fumes *pl*; (*vapor*) steam, vapour; ~**s** *nmpl* (*fig*) conceit *sg*.

humor [u'mor] *nm* (*disposición*) mood, temper; (*lo que divierte*) humour; **de buen/mal** ~ in a good/ bad mood; ~**ismo** *nm* humour; ~**ista** *nmf* comic; ~**ístico, a** *a* funny, humorous.

hundimiento [undi'mjento] *nm* (*gen*) sinking; (*colapso*) collapse.

hundir [un'dir] *vt* to sink; (*edificio, plan*) to ruin, destroy; ~**se** *vr* to sink, collapse.

húngaro, a ['ungaro, a] *a, nmf* Hungarian.

Hungría [un'gria] *nf* Hungary.

huracán [ura'kan] *nm* hurricane.

huraño, a [u'raɲo, a] *a* shy; (*antisocial*) unsociable.

hurgar [ur'ɣar] *vt* to poke, jab; (*remover*) to stir (up); ~**se** *vr*: ~ (**las narices**) to pick one's nose.

hurón, ona [u'ron, ona] *nm* (ZOOL) ferret.

hurtadillas [urta'ðiʎas]: **a** ~ *ad* stealthily, on the sly.

hurtar [ur'tar] *vt* to steal; **hurto** *nm* theft, stealing.

husmear [usme'ar] *vt* (*oler*) to sniff out, scent; (*fam*) to pry into // *vi* to smell bad.

huyo *etc vb ver* **huir**.

I

iba *etc vb ver* **ir.**

ibérico, a [i'βeriko, a] *a* Iberian.

iberoamericano, a [iβeroameri-'kano, a] *a, nm/f* Latin American.

íbice ['iβiθe] *nm* ibex.

Ibiza [i'βiθa] *nf* Ibiza.

iceberg [iθe'βer] *nm* iceberg.

ícono ['ikono] *nm* ikon, icon.

iconoclasta [ikono'klasta] *a* iconoclastic // *nm/f* iconoclast.

ictericia [ikte'riθja] *nf* jaundice.

ida ['iδa] *nf* going, departure; ~ y vuelta round trip, return.

idea [i'δea] *nf* idea; no tengo la menor ~ I haven't a clue.

ideal [iδe'al] *a, nm* ideal; ~**ista** *nm/f* idealist; ~**izar** *vt* to idealize.

idear [iδe'ar] *vt* to think up; (*aparato*) to invent; (*viaje*) to plan.

ídem ['iδem] *pron* ditto.

idéntico, a [i'δentiko, a] *a* identical.

identidad [iδenti'δaδ] *nf* identity.

identificación [iδentifika'θjon] *nf* identification.

identificar [iδentifi'kar] *vt* to identify; ~**se** *vr*: ~**se con** to identify with.

ideología [iδeolo'xia] *nf* ideology.

idioma [i'δjoma] *nm* (*gen*) language.

idiota [i'δjota] *a* idiotic // *nm/f* idiot; **idiotez** *nf* idiocy.

ídolo ['iδolo] *nm* (*tb: fig*) idol.

idóneo, a [i'δoneo, a] *a* suitable.

iglesia [i'vlesja] *nf* church.

ignominia [ivno'minja] *nf* ignominy.

ignorancia [ivno'ranθja] *nf* ignorance; **ignorante** *a* ignorant, uninformed // *nm/f* ignoramus.

ignorar [ivno'rar] *vt* not to know, be ignorant of; (*no hacer caso a*) to ignore.

igual [i'ywal] *a* (*gen*) equal; (*similar*) like, similar; (*mismo*) (the) same; (*constante*) constant; (*temperatura*) even // *nm/f* equal; ~ que like, the same as; me da o es ~ I don't

care; **son** ~**es** they're the same; **al** ~ **que** *prep, conj* like, just like.

igualada [ivwa'laδa] *nf* equaliser.

igualar [ivwa'lar] *vt* to equalize, make equal; (*allanar, nivelar*) to level (off), even (out); ~**se** *vr* (*platos de balanza*) to balance out.

igualdad [ivwal'daδ] *nf* equality; (*similaridad*) sameness; (*uniformidad*) uniformity.

igualmente [ivwal'mente] *ad* equally; (*también*) also, likewise // *excl* the same to you!

ikurriña [iku'rriɲa] *nf* Basque flag.

ilegal [ile'val] *a* illegal.

ilegítimo, a [ile'xitimo, a] *a* illegitimate.

ileso, a [i'leso, a] *a* unhurt.

ilícito, a [i'liθito] *a* illicit.

ilimitado, a [ilimi'taδo, a] *a* unlimited.

ilógico, a [i'loxiko, a] *a* illogical.

iluminación [ilumina'θjon] *nf* illumination; (*alumbrado*) lighting.

iluminar [ilumi'nar] *vt* to illuminate, light (up); (*fig*) to enlighten.

ilusión [ilu'sjon] *nf* illusion; (*quimera*) delusion; (*esperanza*) hope; **hacerse ilusiones** to build up one's hopes; **ilusionado, a** *a* excited.

ilusionista [ilusjo'nista] *nm/f* conjurer.

iluso, a [i'luso, a] *a* easily deceived // *nm/f* dreamer.

ilusorio, a [ilu'sorjo, a] *a* (*de ilusión*) illusory, deceptive; (*esperanza*) vain.

ilustración [ilustra'θjon] *nf* illustration; (*saber*) learning, erudition; **la I~** the Enlightenment; **ilustrado, a** *a* illustrated; learned.

ilustrar [ilus'trar] *vt* to illustrate; (*instruir*) to instruct; (*explicar*) to explain, make clear; ~**se** *vr* to acquire knowledge.

ilustre [i'lustre] *a* famous, illustrious.

imagen [i'maxen] *nf* (*gen*) image; (*dibujo*) picture.

imaginación [imaxina'θjon]

imagination.

imaginar [imaxi'nar] *vt* (*gen*) to imagine; (*idear*) to think up; (*suponer*) to suppose; **~se** *vr* to imagine; **~io, a** *a* imaginary; **imaginativo, a** *a* imaginative.

imán [i'man] *nm* magnet.

imbécil [im'beθil] *nm/f* imbecile, idiot.

imbuir [imbu'ir] *vt* to imbue.

imitación [imita'θjon] *nf* imitation.

imitar [imi'tar] *vt* to imitate; (*parodiar, remedar*) to mimic, ape.

impaciencia [impa'θjenθja] *nf* impatience; **impaciente** *a* impatient; (*nervioso*) anxious.

impacto [im'pakto] *nm* impact.

impar [im'par] *a* odd.

imparcial [impar'θjal] *a* impartial, fair; **~idad** *nf* impartiality, fairness.

impartir [impar'tir] *vt* to impart, give.

impasible [impa'siβle] *a* impassive.

impávido, a [im'paβiðo, a] *a* fearless, intrepid.

impecable [impe'kaβle] *a* impeccable.

impedimento [impeði'mento] *nm* impediment, obstacle.

impedir [impe'ðir] *vt* (*obstruir*) to impede, obstruct; (*estorbar*) to prevent.

impeler [impe'ler] *vt* to drive, propel; (*fig*) to impel.

impenetrable [impene'traβle] *a* impenetrable; (*fig*) incomprehensible.

imperar [impe'rar] *vi* (*reinar*) to rule, reign; (*fig*) to prevail, reign; (*precio*) to be current.

imperativo, a [impera'tiβo, a] *a* (*persona*) imperious; (*urgente, LING*) imperative.

imperceptible [imperθep'tiβle] *a* imperceptible.

imperdible [imper'ðiβle] *nm* safety pin.

imperdonable [imperðo'naβle] *a* unforgivable, inexcusable.

imperfección [imperfek'θjon] *nf* imperfection.

imperfecto, a [imper'fekto, a] *a* imperfect.

imperial [impe'rjal] *a* imperial; **~ismo** *nm* imperialism.

imperio [im'perjo] *nm* empire; (*autoridad*) rule, authority; (*fig*) pride, haughtiness; **~so, a** *a* imperious; (*urgente*) urgent; (*imperativo*) imperative.

impermeable [imperme'aβle] *a* (*a prueba de agua*) waterproof // *nm* raincoat.

impersonal [imperso'nal] *a* impersonal.

impertérrito, a [imper'territo, a] *a* undaunted.

impertinencia [imperti'nenθja] *nf* impertinence; **impertinente** *a* impertinent.

imperturbable [impertur'βaβle] *a* imperturbable.

ímpetu ['impetu] *nm* (*impulso*) impetus, impulse; (*impetuosidad*) impetuosity; (*violencia*) violence.

impetuoso, a [impe'twoso, a] *a* impetuous; (*río*) rushing; (*acto*) hasty.

impío, a [im'pio, a] *a* impious, ungodly.

implacable [impla'kaβle] *a* implacable.

implicar [impli'kar] *vt* to implicate, involve; (*entrañar*) to imply.

implícito, a [im'pliθito, a] *a* (*tácito*) implicit; (*sobreentendido*) implied.

implorar [implo'rar] *vt* to beg, implore.

imponente [impo'nente] *a* (*impresionante*) impressive, imposing; (*solemne*) grand.

imponer [impo'ner] *vt* (*gen*) to impose; (*exigir*) to exact, command; **~se** *vr* to assert o.s.; (*prevalecer*) to prevail; **imponible** *a* (*COM*) taxable.

impopular [impopu'lar] *a* unpopular.

importación [importa'θjon] *nf* (*acto*) importing; (*mercancías*) imports *pl*.

importancia [impor'tanθja] *nf* importance; (*valor*) value, significance; (*extensión*) size, magnitude; **importante** *a* important; valuable, significant.

importar [impor'tar] *vt* (*del extranjero*) to import; (*valer*) to amount to, be worth // *vi* to be important, matter; **me importa un rábano** I don't give a damn; **no importa** it doesn't matter; **¿le importa que fume?** do you mind if I smoke?

importe [im'porte] *nm* (*total*) amount; (*valor*) value.

importunar [importu'nar] *vt* to bother, pester.

imposibilidad [imposißili'ðað] *nf* impossibility; **imposibilitar** *vt* to make impossible, prevent.

imposible [impo'sißle] *a* (*gen*) impossible; (*insoportable*) unbearable, intolerable.

imposición [imposi'θjon] *nf* imposition; (COM: *impuesto*) tax; (: *inversión*) deposit.

impostor, a [impos'tor, a] *nm/f* impostor.

impotencia [impo'tenθja] *nf* impotence; **impotente** *a* impotent, powerless.

impracticable [imprakti'kaßle] *a* (*irrealizable*) impracticable; (*intransitable*) impassable.

imprecar [impre'kar] *vi* to curse.

impreciso, a [impre'θiso, a] *a* imprecise, vague.

impregnar [impreɣ'nar] *vt* to impregnate; **~se** *vr* to become impregnated.

imprenta [im'prenta] *nf* (*acto*) printing; (*aparato*) press; (*casa*) printer's; (*letra*) print.

imprescindible [impresθin'dißle] *a* essential, vital.

impresión [impre'sjon] *nf* (*gen*) impression; (IMPRENTA) printing; (*edición*) edition; (FOTO) print; (*marca*) imprint; **~ digital** fingerprint.

impresionable [impresjo'naßle] *a* (*sensible*) impressionable.

impresionante [impresjo'nante] *a* impressive; (*tremendo*) tremendous; (*maravilloso*) great, marvellous.

impresionar [impresjo'nar] *vt* (*conmover*) to move; (*afectar*) to impress, strike; (*película fotográfica*) to expose; **~se** *vr* to be impressed; (*conmoverse*) to be moved.

impreso, a *pp de* **imprimir** // [im'preso, a] *a* printed **~s** *nmpl*: printed matter; **impresora** *nf* printer.

imprevisto, a [impre'ßisto, a] *a* (*gen*) unforeseen; (*inesperado*) unexpected **~s** *nmpl*: (*gastos*) unforeseen expenses.

imprimir [impri'mir] *vt* to imprint, impress, stamp; (*textos*) to print; (INFORM) to output, print out.

improbable [impro'ßaßle] *a* improbable; (*inverosímil*) unlikely.

improcedente [improθe'ðente] *a* inappropriate.

improductivo, a [improðuk'tißo, a] *a* unproductive.

improperio [impro'perjo] *nm* insult.

impropiedad [impropje'ðað] *nf* impropriety (of language).

impropio, a [im'propjo, a] *a* improper.

improvisación [improßisa'θjon] *nf* improvisation; **improvisado, a** *a* improvised.

improvisar [improßi'sar] *vt* to improvise.

improviso, a [impro'ßiso, a] *a*: **de ~** unexpectedly, suddenly.

imprudencia [impru'ðenθja] *nf* imprudence; (*indiscreción*) indiscretion; (*descuido*) carelessness; **imprudente** *a* imprudent; indiscreet; (*irreflexivo*) unwise.

impúdico, a [im'puðiko, a] *a* shameless; (*lujurioso*) lecherous.

impudor [impu'ðor] *nm* shamelessness; (*lujuria*) lechery.

impuesto, a [im'pwesto, a] *a* imposed // *nm* tax; **~ sobre el valor añadido (IVA)** value added tax (VAT).

impugnar [impuɣ'nar] *vt* to oppose, contest; (*refutar*) to refute, impugn.

impulsar [impul'sar] *vt* = **impeler**.

impulso [im'pulso] *nm* impulse; (*fuerza, empuje*) thrust, drive; (*fig: sentimiento*) urge, impulse.

impune [im'pune] *a* unpunished; **impunidad** *nf* impunity.

impureza [impu'reθa] *nf* impurity; (*fig*) lewdness; **impuro, a** *a* impure; lewd.

imputar [impu'tar] *vt* (*atribuir*) to attribute to; (*cargar*) to impute to.

inacabable [inaka'βaβle] *a* (*infinito*) endless; (*interminable*) interminable.

inaccesible [inakθe'siβle] *a* inaccessible.

inacción [inak'θjon] *nf* (*gen*) inaction; (*desocupación*) inactivity.

inaceptable [inaθep'taβle] *a* unacceptable.

inactividad [inaktiβi'ðað] *nf* inactivity; (*COM*) dullness; **inactivo, a** *a* inactive.

inadaptación [inaðapta'θjon] *nf* maladjustment.

inadecuado, a [inaðe'kwaðo, a] *a* (*insuficiente*) inadequate; (*inapto*) unsuitable.

inadmisible [inaðmi'siβle] *a* inadmissible.

inadvertido, a [inaðβer'tiðo, a] *a* (*no visto*) unnoticed.

inagotable [inaɣo'taβle] *a* inexhaustible.

inaguantable [inaɣwan'taβle] *a* unbearable.

inalterable [inalte'raβle] *a* immutable, unchangeable.

inanición [inani'θjon] *nf* starvation.

inanimado, a [inani'maðo, a] *a* inanimate.

inapto, a [in'apto] *a* unsuited.

inaudito, a [inau'ðito, a] *a* unheard-of.

inauguración [inauɣura'θjon] *nf* inauguration; (*de exposición*) opening; **inaugurar** *vt* to inaugurate; to open.

I.N.B. *abr* (*Esp* = *Instituto Nacional de Bachillerato*) ≈ comprehensive

school (*Brit*), ≈ high school (*US*).

inca ['inka] *nm/f* Inca; **~ico, a** *a* Inca *cpd*.

incalculable [inkalku'laβle] *a* incalculable.

incandescente [inkandes'θente] *a* incandescent.

incansable [inkan'saβle] *a* tireless, untiring.

incapacidad [inkapaθi'ðað] *nf* incapacity; (*incompetencia*) incompetence; **~ física/mental** physical/mental disability.

incapacitar [inkapaθi'tar] *vt* (*inhabilitar*) to incapacitate, render unfit; (*descalificar*) to disqualify.

incapaz [inka'paθ] *a* incapable.

incautación [inkauta'θjon] *nf* confiscation.

incautarse [inkau'tarse] *vr*: **~ de** to seize, confiscate.

incauto, a [in'kauto, a] *a* (*imprudente*) incautious, unwary.

incendiar [inθen'djar] *vt* to set fire to; (*fig*) to inflame; **~se** *vr* to catch fire; **~io, a** *a* incendiary.

incendio [in'θendjo] *nm* fire.

incentivo [inθen'tiβo] *nm* incentive.

incertidumbre [inθerti'ðumbre] *nf* (*inseguridad*) uncertainty; (*duda*) doubt.

incesante [inθe'sante] *a* incessant.

incesto [in'θesto] *nm* incest.

incidencia [inθi'ðenθja] *nf* (*MAT*) incidence.

incidente [inθi'ðente] *nm* incident.

incidir [inθi'ðir] *vi* (*influir*) to influence; (*afectar*) to affect; **~ en un error** to fall into error.

incienso [in'θjenso] *nm* incense.

incierto, a [in'θjerto, a] *a* uncertain.

incineración [inθinera'θjon] *nf* incineration; (*de cadáveres*) cremation.

incinerar [inθine'rar] *vt* to burn; (*cadáveres*) to cremate.

incipiente [inθi'pjente] *a* incipient.

incisión [inθi'sjon] *nf* incision.

incisivo, a [inθi'siβo, a] *a* sharp, cutting; (*fig*) incisive.

incitar [inθi'tar] vt to incite, rouse.

incivil [inθi'βil] a rude, uncivil.

inclemencia [inkle'menθja] nf (severidad) harshness, severity; (del tiempo) inclemency.

inclinación [inklina'θjon] nf (gen) inclination; (de tierras) slope, incline; (de cabeza) nod, bow; (fig) leaning, bent.

inclinar [inkli'nar] vt to incline; (cabeza) to nod, bow; (tierras) to slope; ~se vr to bow; (encorvarse) to stoop; ~se a to take after, resemble; ~se ante to bow down to; me inclino a pensar que I'm inclined to think that.

incluir [inklu'ir] vt to include; (incorporar) to incorporate; (meter) to enclose.

inclusive [inklu'siβe] ad inclusive // prep including.

incluso, a [in'kluso, a] a included // ad inclusively; (hasta) even.

incógnito [in'koɣnito] nm: de ~ incognito.

incoherente [inkoe'rente] a incoherent.

incoloro, a [inko'loro, a] a colourless.

incólume [in'kolume] a (gen) safe; (indemne) unhurt, unharmed.

incomodar [inkomo'ðar] vt to inconvenience; (molestar) to bother, trouble; (fastidiar) to annoy; ~se vr to put o.s. out; (fastidiarse) to get annoyed.

incomodidad [inkomoði'ðað] nf inconvenience; (fastidio, enojo) annoyance; (de vivienda) discomfort.

incómodo, a [in'komoðo, a] a (incomfortable) uncomfortable; (molesto) annoying; (inconveniente) inconvenient.

incomparable [inkompa'raβle] a incomparable.

incompatible [inkompa'tiβle] a incompatible.

incompetencia [inkompe'tenθja] nf incompetence; **incompetente** a incompetent.

incompleto, a [inkom'pleto, a] a incomplete, unfinished.

incomprensible [inkompren'siβle] a incomprehensible.

incomunicado, a [inkomuni'kaðo, a] a (aislado) cut off, isolated; (confinado) in solitary confinement.

inconcebible [inkonθe'βiβle] a inconceivable.

inconcluso, a [inkon'kluso, a] a (inacabado) unfinished.

incondicional [inkondiθjo'nal] a unconditional; (apoyo) wholehearted; (partidario) staunch.

inconexo, a [inko'nekso, a] a (gen) unconnected; (desunido) disconnected.

inconfundible [inkonfun'diβle] a unmistakable.

incongruente [inkon'grwente] a incongruous.

inconmensurable [inkonmensu'raβle] a immeasurable, vast.

inconsciencia [inkons'θjenθja] nf unconsciousness; (fig) thoughtlessness; **inconsciente** a unconscious; thoughtless.

inconsecuente [inkonse'kwente] a inconsistent.

inconsiderado, a [inkonsiðe'raðo, a] a inconsiderate.

inconsistente [inkonsis'tente] a weak; (tela) flimsy.

inconstancia [inkon'stanθja] nf (veleidad) inconstancy; (inestabilidad) unsteadiness; **inconstante** a inconstant.

incontable [inkon'taβle] a countless, innumerable.

incontestable [inkontes'taβle] a unanswerable; (innegable) undeniable.

incontinencia [inkonti'nenθja] nf incontinence.

inconveniencia [inkonβe'njenθja] nf unsuitability, inappropriateness; (descortesía) impoliteness; **inconveniente** a unsuitable; impolite // nm obstacle; (desventaja) disadvantage; **el inconveniente es que...** the trouble is that...

incorporación [inkorpora'θjon] *nf* incorporation.

incorporar [inkorpo'rar] *vt* to incorporate; **~se** *vr* to sit/stand up.

incorrección [inkorrek'θjon] *nf* (*gen*) incorrectness, inaccuracy; (*descortesía*) bad-mannered behaviour; **incorrecto, a** *a* (*gen*) incorrect, wrong; (*comportamiento*) bad-mannered.

incorregible [inkorre'xiβle] *a* incorrigible.

incredulidad [inkreðuli'ðað] *nf* incredulity; (*escepticismo*) scepticism; **incrédulo, a** *a* incredulous, unbelieving; sceptical.

increíble [inkre'iβle] *a* incredible.

incremento [inkre'mento] *nm* increment; (*aumento*) rise, increase.

increpar [inkre'par] *vt* to reprimand.

incruento, a [in'krwento, a] *a* bloodless.

incrustar [inkrus'tar] *vt* to incrust; (*piedras: en joya*) to inlay.

incubar [inku'βar] *vt* to incubate; (*fig*) to hatch.

inculcar [inkul'kar] *vt* to inculcate.

inculpar [inkul'par] *vt* (*acusar*) to accuse; (*achacar, atribuir*) to charge, blame.

inculto, a [in'kulto, a] *a* (*persona*) uneducated; (*grosero*) uncouth // *nm/f* ignoramus.

incumplimiento [inkumpli'mjento] *nm* non-fulfilment; **~ de contrato** breach of contract.

incurrir [inku'rrir] *vi*: **~ en** to incur; (*crimen*) to commit; **~ en un error** to fall into error.

indagación [indaɣa'θjon] *nf* investigation; (*búsqueda*) search; (*JUR*) inquest.

indagar [inda'ɣar] *vt* to investigate; to search for; (*averiguar*) to ascertain.

indecente [inde'θente] *a* indecent, improper; (*lascivo*) obscene.

indecible [inde'θiβle] *a* unspeakable; (*indescriptible*) indescribable.

indeciso, a [inde'θiso, a] *a* (*por decidir*) undecided; (*vacilante*) hesitant.

indefenso, a [inde'fenso, a] *a* defenceless.

indefinido, a [indefi'niðo, a] *a* indefinite; (*vago*) vague, undefined.

indeleble [inde'leβle] *a* indelible.

indemne [in'demne] *a* (*objeto*) undamaged; (*persona*) unharmed, unhurt.

indemnizar [indemni'θar] *vt* to indemnify; (*compensar*) to compensate.

independencia [indepen'denθja] *nf* independence.

independiente [indepen'djente] *a* (*libre*) independent; (*autónomo*) self-sufficient.

indeterminado, a [indetermi'naðo, a] *a* indefinite; (*desconocido*) determinate.

India ['indja] *nf*: **la ~** India.

indicación [indika'θjon] *nf* indication; (*señal*) sign; (*sugerencia*) suggestion, hint.

indicador [indika'ðor] *nm* indicator; (*TEC*) gauge, meter.

indicar [indi'kar] *vt* (*mostrar*) to indicate, show; (*termómetro etc*) to read, register; (*señalar*) to point to.

índice ['indiθe] *nm* index; (*catálogo*) catalogue; (*ANAT*) index finger, forefinger.

indicio [in'diθjo] *nm* indication, sign; (*pista*) clue.

indiferencia [indife'renθja] *nf* indifference; (*apatía*) apathy; **indiferente** *a* indifferent.

indígena [in'dixena] *a* indigenous, native // *nm/f* native.

indigencia [indi'xenθja] *nf* poverty, need.

indigestión [indixes'tjon] *nf* indigestion.

indigesto, a [indi'xesto, a] *a* undigested; (*indigestible*) indigestible; (*fig*) turgid.

indignación [indiɣna'θjon] *nf* indignation.

indignar [indiɣ'nar] *vt* to anger, make indignant; **~se** *vr*: **~se por** to get indignant about.

indigno, a [in'diɣno, a] a (*despreciable*) low, contemptible; (*innerecido*) unworthy.

indio, a ['indjo, a] a, nmf Indian.

indirecta [indi'rekta] nf insinuation, innuendo; (*sugerencia*) hint.

indirecto, a [indi'rekto, a] a indirect.

indiscreción [indiskre'θjon] nf (*imprudencia*) indiscretion; (*irreflexión*) tactlessness; (*acto*) gaffe, faux pas.

indiscreto, a [indis'kreto, a] a indiscreet.

indiscutible [indisku'tiβle] a indisputable, unquestionable.

indispensable [indispen'saβle] a indispensable, essential.

indisponer [indispo'ner] vt to spoil, upset; (*salud*) to make ill; ~**se** vr to fall ill; ~**se con uno** to fall out with sb.

indisposición [indisposi'θjon] nf indisposition.

indistinto, a [indis'tinto, a] a distinct; (*vago*) vague.

individual [indiβi'ðwal] a individual; (*habitación*) single // nm (DEPORTE) singles sg.

individuo, a [indi'βiðwo, a] a individual // nm individual.

índole ['indole] nf (*naturaleza*) nature; (*clase*) sort, kind.

indolencia [indo'lenθja] nf indolence, laziness.

indómito, a [in'domito, a] a indomitable.

inducir [indu'θir] vt to induce; (*inferir*) to infer; (*persuadir*) to persuade.

indudable [indu'ðaβle] a undoubted; (*incuestionable*) unquestionable.

indulgencia [indul'xenθja] nf indulgence.

indultar [indul'tar] vt (*perdonar*) to pardon, reprieve; (*librar de pago*) to exempt: **indulto** nm pardon; exemption.

industria [in'dustrja] nf industry; (*habilidad*) skill; **industrial** a industrial // nm industrialist.

inédito, a [in'eðito, a] a (*libro*) unpublished; (*fig*) new.

inefable [ine'faβle] a ineffable, indescribable.

ineficaz [inefi'kaθ] a (*inútil*) ineffective; (*ineficiente*) inefficient.

ineludible [inelu'ðiβle] a inescapable, unavoidable.

ineptitud [inepti'tuð] nf ineptitude, incompetence; **inepto, a** a inept, incompetent.

inequívoco, a [ine'kiβoko, a] a unequivocal; (*inconfundible*) unmistakable.

inercia [in'erθja] nf inertia; (*pasividad*) passivity.

inerme [in'erme] a (*sin armas*) unarmed; (*indefenso*) defenceless.

inerte [in'erte] a inert; (*inmóvil*) motionless.

inesperado, a [inespe'raðo, a] a unexpected, unforeseen.

inestable [ines'taβle] a unstable.

inevitable [ineβi'taβle] a inevitable.

inexactitud [ineksakti'tuð] nf inaccuracy; **inexacto, a** a inaccurate; (*falso*) untrue.

inexperto, a [inek'sperto, a] a (*novato*) inexperienced.

infalible [infa'liβle] a infallible; (*plan*) foolproof.

infame [in'fame] a infamous; (*horrible*) dreadful; **infamia** nf infamy; (*deshonra*) disgrace.

infancia [in'fanθja] nf infancy, childhood.

infante [in'fante] nm (*hijo del rey*) infante, prince; (MIL) infantryman.

infantería [infante'ria] nf infantry.

infantil [infan'til] a (*pueril, aniñado*) infantile; (*cándido*) childlike; (*literatura, ropa etc*) children's.

infarto [in'farto] nm (tb: ~ **de miocardio**) heart attack.

infatigable [infati'xaβle] a tireless, untiring.

infección [infek'θjon] nf infection; **infeccioso, a** a infectious.

infectar [infek'tar] vt to infect; ~**se**

vr to become infected.

infeliz [infe'liθ] *a* unhappy, wretched // *nm/f* wretch.

inferior [infe'rjor] *a* inferior; (*situación*) lower // *nm/f* inferior, subordinate.

inferir [infe'rir] *vt* (*deducir*) to infer, deduce; (*causar*) to cause.

infestar [infes'tar] *vt* (*apestar*) to infest; (*fig*) to harass.

infidelidad [infiðeli'ðað] *nf* (*gen*) infidelity, unfaithfulness.

infiel [in'fjel] *a* unfaithful, disloyal; (*erróneo*) inaccurate // *nm/f* infidel, unbeliever.

infierno [in'fjerno] *nm* hell.

ínfimo, a ['infimo, a] *a* (*más bajo*) lowest; (*despreciable*) vile, mean.

infinidad [infini'ðað] *nf* infinity; (*abundancia*) great quantity.

infinito, a [infi'nito, a] *a, nm* infinite.

inflación [infla'θjon] *nf* (*hinchazón*) swelling; (*monetaria*) inflation; (*fig*) conceit; **inflacionario, a** *a* inflationary.

inflamar [infla'mar] *vt* to set on fire; (*MED*) to inflame; ~**se** *vr* to catch fire; (*fig*) to become inflamed.

inflar [in'flar] *vt* (*hinchar*) to inflate, blow up; (*fig*) to exaggerate; ~**se** *vr* to swell (up); (*fig*) to get conceited.

inflexible [inflek'sißle] *a* inflexible; (*fig*) unbending.

infligir [infli'xir] *vt* to inflict.

influencia [influ'enθja] *nf* influence; **influenciar** *vt* to influence.

influir [influ'ir] *vt* to influence.

influjo [in'fluxo] *nm* influence.

influya *etc vb ver* **influir**.

influyente [influ'jente] *a* influential.

información [informa'θjon] *nf* information; (*noticias*) news *sg*; (*JUR*) inquiry; **I~** (*oficina*) Information Office; (*mostrador*) Information Desk; (*TEL*) Directory Enquiries.

informal [infor'mal] *a* (*gen*) informal.

informante [infor'mante] *nm/f* informant.

informar [infor'mar] *vt* (*gen*) to in-

form; (*revelar*) to reveal, make known // *vi* (*JUR*) to plead; (*denunciar*) to inform; (*dar cuenta de*) to report on; ~**se** *vr* to find out; ~**se de** to inquire into.

informática [infor'matika] *nf* computer science, information technology.

informe [in'forme] *a* shapeless // *nm* report.

infortunio [infor'tunjo] *nm* misfortune.

infracción [infrak'θjon] *nf* infraction, infringement.

infranqueable [infranke'aßle] *a* impassable; (*fig*) insurmountable.

infringir [infrin'xir] *vt* to infringe, contravene.

infructuoso, a [infruk'twoso, a] *a* fruitless, unsuccessful.

infundado, a [infun'daðo, a] *a* groundless, unfounded.

infundir [infun'dir] *vt* to infuse, instil.

infusión [infu'sjon] *nf* infusion; ~ **de manzanilla** camomile tea.

ingeniar [inxe'njar] *vt* to think up, devise; ~**se** *vr*: ~**se para** to manage to.

ingeniería [inxenje'ria] *nf* engineering; **ingeniero, a** *nm/f* engineer; **ingeniero de caminos/de sonido** civil engineer/sound engineer.

ingenio [in'xenjo] *nm* (*talento*) talent; (*agudeza*) wit; (*habilidad*) ingenuity, inventiveness; (*TEC*): ~ **azucarero** sugar refinery.

ingenioso, a [inxe'njoso, a] *a* ingenious, clever; (*divertido*) witty.

ingenuidad [inxenwi'ðað] *nf* ingenuousness; (*sencillez*) simplicity; **ingenuo, a** *a* ingenuous.

ingerir [inxe'rir] *vt* to ingest; (*tragar*) to swallow; (*consumir*) to consume.

Inglaterra [ingla'terra] *nf* England.

ingle ['ingle] *nf* groin.

inglés, esa [in'gles, esa] *a* English // *nm/f* Englishman/woman // *nm* (*LING*) English.

ingratitud [ingrati'tuð] *nf* ingratitude; **ingrato, a** *a* (*gen*) ungrateful.

ingrediente [ingre'ðjente] *nm* ingredient.

ingresar [ingre'sar] *vt* (*dinero*) to deposit // *vi* to come in; ~ **en un club** to join a club; ~ **en el hospital** to go into hospital.

ingreso [in'greso] *nm* (*entrada*) entry; (: *en hospital etc*) admission; ~**s** *nmpl* (*dinero*) income *sg*; (: *COM*) takings *pl*.

inhabitable [inaβi'taßle] *a* uninhabitable.

inhalar [ina'lar] *vt* to inhale.

inherente [ine'rente] *a* inherent.

inhibir [ini'βir] *vt* to inhibit; (*REL*) to restrain.

inhumano, a [inu'mano, a] *a* inhuman.

INI ['ini] *nm abr* (*Esp = Instituto Nacional de Industria*) ≈ NEB (*Brit*).

inicial [ini'θjal] *a, nf* initial.

iniciar [ini'θjar] *vt* (*persona*) to initiate; (*empezar*) to begin, commence; (*conversación*) to start up.

iniciativa [iniθja'tiβa] *nf* initiative; **la ~ privada** private enterprise.

inicuo, a [in'ikwo, a] *a* iniquitous.

ininterrumpido, a [ininterrum-'piðo, a] *a* uninterrupted.

injerencia [inxe'renθja] *nf* interference.

injertar [inxer'tar] *vt* to graft; **injerto** *nm* graft.

injuria [in'xurja] *nf* (*agravio, ofensa*) offence; (*insulto*) insult; **injuriar** *vt* to insult; **injurioso, a** *a* offensive, insulting.

injusticia [inxus'tiθja] *nf* injustice.

injusto, a [in'xusto, a] *a* unjust, unfair.

inmadurez [inmaðu'reθ] *nf* immaturity.

inmediaciones [inmeðja'θjones] *nfpl* neighbourhood *sg*, environs.

inmediato, a [inme'ðjato, a] *a* immediate; (*contiguo*) adjoining;

(*rápido*) prompt; (*próximo*) neighbouring, next; **de ~** immediately.

inmejorable [inmexo'raßle] *a* unsurpassable; (*precio*) unbeatable.

inmenso, a [in'menso, a] *a* immense, huge.

inmerecido, a [inmere'θiðo, a] *a* undeserved.

inmigración [inmixra'θjon] *nf* immigration.

inmiscuirse [inmisku'irse] *vr* to interfere, meddle.

inmobiliario, a [inmoβi'ljarjo, a] *a* real-estate *cpd*, property *cpd* // *nf* estate agency.

inmolar [inmo'lar] *vt* to immolate, sacrifice.

inmoral [inmo'ral] *a* immoral.

inmortal [inmor'tal] *a* immortal; **~izar** *vt* to immortalize.

inmóvil [in'moβil] *a* immobile.

inmueble [in'mweβle] *a*: **bienes ~s** real estate, landed property // *nm* property.

inmundicia [inmun'diθja] *nf* filth; **inmundo, a** *a* filthy.

inmunidad [inmuni'ðað] *nf* immunity.

inmutarse [inmu'tarse] *vr* to turn pale; **no se inmutó** he didn't turn a hair.

innato, a [in'nato, a] *a* innate.

innecesario, a [inneθe'sarjo, a] *a* unnecessary.

innoble [in'noßle] *a* ignoble.

innovación [innoβa'θjon] *nf* innovation.

innovar [inno'βar] *vt* to introduce.

inocencia [ino'θenθja] *nf* innocence.

inocentada [inoθen'taða] *nf* practical joke.

inocente [ino'θente] *a* (*ingenuo*) naive, innocent; (*inculpable*) innocent; (*sin malicia*) harmless // *nm/f* simpleton.

inodoro [ino'ðoro] *nm* toilet, lavatory (*Brit*).

inofensivo, a [inofen'siβo, a] *a* inoffensive, harmless.

inolvidable [inolβi'ðaβle] *a* unforgettable.

inoperante [inope'rante] *a* ineffective.

inopinado, a [inopi'naðo. a] *a* unexpected.

inoportuno, a [inopor'tuno. a] *a* untimely; (*molesto*) inconvenient.

inoxidable [inoksi'ðaβle] *a*: **acero ~** stainless steel.

inquebrantable [inkeβran'taβle] *a* unbreakable.

inquietar [inkje'tar] *vt* to worry, trouble; **~se** *vr* to worry, get upset; **inquieto, a** *a* anxious, worried; **inquietud** *nf* anxiety, worry.

inquilino, a [inki'lino. a] *nm/f* tenant.

inquirir [inki'rir] *vt* to enquire into, investigate.

insaciable [insa'θjaβle] *a* insatiable.

insalubre [insa'luβre] *a* unhealthy.

inscribir [inskri'βir] *vt* to inscribe; (*lista*) to list; (*censo*) to register; **~se** *vr* to register; (*ESCOL etc*) to enrol.

inscripción [inskrip'θjon] *nf* inscription; (*ESCOL etc*) enrolment; (*censo*) registration.

insecticida [insekti'θiða] *nm* insecticide.

insecto [in'sekto] *nm* insect.

inseguridad [inseɣuri'ðað] *nf* insecurity.

inseguro, a [inse'ɣuro. a] *a* insecure; (*inconstante*) unsteady; (*incierto*) uncertain.

insensato, a [insen'sato. a] *a* foolish, stupid.

insensibilidad [insensiβili'ðað] *nf* (*gen*) insensitivity; (*dureza de corazón*) callousness.

insensible [insen'siβle] *a* (*gen*) insensitive; (*movimiento*) imperceptible; (*sin sentido*) numb.

insertar [inser'tar] *vt* to insert.

inservible [inser'βiβle] *a* useless.

insidioso, a [insi'ðjoso. a] *a* insidious.

insignia [in'siɣnja] *nf* (*señal dis-* *tintiva*) badge; (*estandarte*) flag.

insignificante [insiɣnifi'kante] *a* insignificant.

insinuar [insi'nwar] *vt* to insinuate, imply; **~se** *vr*: **~se con uno** to ingratiate o.s. with sb.

insípido, a [in'sipiðo. a] *a* insipid.

insistencia [insis'tenθja] *nf* insistence.

insistir [insis'tir] *vi* to insist; **~ en algo** to insist on sth; (*enfatizar*) to stress sth.

insolación [insola'θjon] *nf* (*MED*) sunstroke.

insolencia [inso'lenθja] *nf* insolence; **insolente** *a* insolent.

insólito, a [in'solito. a] *a* unusual.

insoluble [inso'luβle] *a* insoluble.

insolvencia [insol'βenθja] *nf* insolvency.

insomnio [in'somnjo] *nm* insomnia.

insondable [inson'daβle] *a* bottomless; (*fig*) impenetrable.

insonorizado, a [insonori'θaðo. a] *a* (*cuarto etc*) soundproof.

insoportable [insopor'taβle] *a* unbearable.

insospechado, a [insospe'tʃaðo. a] *a* (*inesperado*) unexpected.

inspección [inspek'θjon] *nf* inspection, check; **inspeccionar** *vt* (*examinar*) to inspect, examine; (*controlar*) to check.

inspector, a [inspek'tor. a] *nm/f* inspector.

inspiración [inspira'θjon] *nf* inspiration.

inspirar [inspi'rar] *vt* to inspire; (*MED*) to inhale; **~se** *vr*: **~se en** to be inspired by.

instalación [instala'θjon] *nf* (*equipo*) fittings *pl*, equipment; **~ eléctrica** wiring.

instalar [insta'lar] *vt* (*establecer*) to install; (*erguir*) to set up, erect; **~se** *vr* to establish o.s.; (*en una vivienda*) to move into.

instancia [ins'tanθja] *nf* (*JUR*) petition; (*ruego*) request; **en última ~** as a last resort.

instantáneo, a [instan'taneo, a] *a* instantaneous // *nf* snap(shot); **café ~** instant coffee.

instante [ins'tante] *nm* instant, moment.

instar [ins'tar] *vt* to press, urge.

instigar [insti'ɣar] *vt* to instigate.

instinto [ins'tinto] *nm* instinct; **por ~** instinctively.

institución [institu'θjon] *nf* institution, establishment.

instituir [institu'ir] *vt* to establish; *(fundar)* to found; **instituto** *nm* *(gen)* institute; **Instituto Nacional de Enseñanza** *(Esp)* ≈ comprehensive *(Brit)* o high *(US)* school.

institutriz [institu'triθ] *nf* governess.

instrucción [instruk'θjon] *nf* instruction.

instructivo, a [instruk'tiβo, a] *a* instructive.

instruir [instru'ir] *vt* *(gen)* to instruct; *(enseñar)* to teach, educate.

instrumento [instru'mento] *nm* *(gen)* instrument; *(herramienta)* tool, implement.

insubordinarse [insuβorði'narse] *vr* to rebel.

insuficiencia [insufi'θjenθja] *nf* *(carencia)* lack; *(inadecuación)* inadequacy; **insuficiente** *a* *(gen)* insufficient; *(ESCOL: calificación)* unsatisfactory.

insufrible [insu'friβle] *a* insufferable.

insular [insu'lar] *a* insular.

insultar [insul'tar] *vt* to insult; **insulto** *nm* insult.

insuperable [insupe'raβle] *a* *(excelente)* unsurpassable; *(arduo)* insurmountable.

insurgente [insur'xente] *a, nmf* insurgent.

insurrección [insurrek'θjon] *nf* insurrection, rebellion.

intacto, a [in'takto, a] *a* intact.

intachable [inta'tʃaβle] *a* irreproachable.

integral [inte'ɣral] *a* integral; *(completo)* complete; **pan ~** whole-

meal *(Brit)* o wholewheat *(US)* bread.

integrar [inte'ɣrar] *vt* to make up, compose; *(MAT, fig)* to integrate.

integridad [inteɣri'ðað] *nf* wholeness; *(carácter)* integrity; **íntegro, a** *a* whole, entire; *(honrado)* honest.

intelectual [intelek'twal] *a, nmf* intellectual.

inteligencia [inteli'xenθja] *nf* intelligence; *(ingenio)* ability; **inteligente** *a* intelligent.

inteligible [inteli'xiβle] *a* intelligible.

intemperie [intem'perje] *nf*: **a la ~** out in the open, exposed to the elements.

intempestivo, a [intempes'tiβo, a] *a* untimely.

intención [inten'θjon] *nf* *(gen)* intention, purpose; **con segundas intenciones** maliciously; **con ~** deliberately.

intencionado, a [intenθjo'naðo, a] *a* deliberate; **bien/mal ~** well-meaning/ill-disposed, hostile.

intensidad [intensi'ðað] *nf* *(gen)* intensity; *(ELEC, TEC)* strength; **llover con ~** to rain hard.

intenso, a [in'tenso, a] *a* intense; *(sentimiento)* profound, deep.

intentar [inten'tar] *vt* *(tratar)* to try, attempt; **intento** *nm* *(intención)* intention, purpose; *(tentativa)* attempt.

intercalar [interka'lar] *vt* to insert.

intercambio [inter'kambjo] *nm* exchange, swap.

interceder [interθe'ðer] *vi* to intercede.

interceptar [interθep'tar] *vt* to intercept.

intercesión [interθe'sjon] *nf* intercession.

interés [inte'res] *nm* *(gen)* interest; *(parte)* share, part; *(pey)* self-interest; **intereses creados** vested interests.

interesado, a [intere'saðo, a] *a* interested; *(prejuiciado)* prejudiced; *(pey)* mercenary, self-seeking.

interesante [intere'sante] *a* interesting.

interesar [intere'sar] *vt, vi* to interest, be of interest to; **~se** *vr:* **~se en** *o* **por** to take an interest in.

interface [inter'faθe], **interfase** ['-fase] *nm* (INFORM) interface.

interferir [interfe'rir] *vt* to interfere with; (TEL) to jam // *vi* to interfere.

interfono [inter'fono] *nm* intercom.

interino, a [inte'rino, a] *a* temporary // *nm/f* temporary holder of a post; (MED) locum; (ESCOL) supply teacher.

interior [inte'rjor] *a* inner, inside; (COM) domestic, internal // *nm* interior, inside; (fig) soul, mind; **Ministerio del I~** ≈ Home Office (Brit), ≈ Department of the Interior (US).

interjección [interxek'θjon] *nf* interjection.

interlocutor, a [interloku'tor, a] *nm/f* speaker.

intermediario, a [interme'ðjarjo, a] *nm/f* intermediary.

intermedio, a [inter'meðjo, a] *a* intermediate // *nm* interval.

interminable [intermi'naβle] *a* endless.

intermitente [intermi'tente] *a* intermittent // *nm* (AUTO) indicator.

internacional [internaθjo'nal] *a* international.

internado [inter'naðo] *nm* boarding school.

internar [inter'nar] *vt* to intern; (en un manicomio) to commit; **~se** *vr* (penetrar) to penetrate.

interno, a [in'terno, a] *a* internal, interior; (POL etc) domestic // *nm/f* (alumno) boarder.

interponer [interpo'ner] *vt* to interpose, put in; **~se** *vr* to intervene.

interpretación [interpreta'θjon] *nf* interpretation.

interpretar [interpre'tar] *vt* to interpret; (TEATRO, MUS) to perform, play; **intérprete** *nm/f* (LING) interpreter, translator; (MUS, TEATRO) performer, artist(e).

interrogación [interroɣa'θjon] *nf* interrogation; (LING: tb: **signo de ~**) question mark.

interrogar [interro'ɣar] *vt* to interrogate, question.

interrumpir [interrum'pir] *vt* to interrupt.

interrupción [interrup'θjon] *nf* interruption.

interruptor [interrup'tor] *nm* (ELEC) switch.

intersección [intersek'θjon] *nf* intersection.

interurbano, a [interur'βano, a] *a:* **llamada interurbana** long-distance call.

intervalo [inter'βalo] *nm* interval; (descanso) break; **a ~s** at intervals, every now and then.

intervenir [interβe'nir] *vt* (controlar) to control, supervise; (MED) to operate on // *vi* (participar) to take part, participate; (mediar) to intervene.

interventor, a [interβen'tor, a] *nm/f* inspector; (COM) auditor.

interviú [inter'βju] *nf* interview.

intestino [intes'tino] *nm* intestine.

intimar [inti'mar] *vi* to become friendly.

intimidad [intimi'ðað] *nf* intimacy; (familiaridad) familiarity; (vida privada) private life; (JUR) privacy.

íntimo, a [i'ntimo, a] *a* intimate.

intolerable [intole'raβle] *a* intolerable, unbearable.

intranquilizarse [intrankili'θarse] *vr* to get worried *o* anxious; **intranquilo, a** *a* worried.

intransigente [intransi'xente] *a* intransigent.

intransitable [intransi'taβle] *a* impassable.

intrepidez [intrepi'ðeθ] *nf* courage, bravery; **intrépido, a** *a* intrepid.

intriga [in'triɣa] *nf* intrigue; (plan) plot; **intrigar** *vt, vi* to intrigue.

intrincado, a [intrin'kaðo, a] *a* intricate.

intrínseco, a [in'trinseko, a] *a* intrinsic.

introducción [introðuk'θjon] *nf* introduction.

introducir [introðu'θir] *vt* (*gen*) to introduce; (*moneda etc*) to insert; (*INFORM*) to input, enter.

intromisión [intromi'sjon] *nf* interference, meddling.

introvertido, a [introβer'tiðo, a] *a, nm/f* introvert.

intruso, a [in'truso, a] *a* intrusive // *nm/f* intruder.

intuición [intwi'θjon] *nf* intuition.

inundación [inunda'θjon] *nf* flood(ing); **inundar** *vt* to flood; (*fig*) to swamp, inundate.

inusitado, a [inusi'taðo, a] *a* unusual, rare.

inútil [in'util] *a* useless; (*esfuerzo*) vain, fruitless; **inutilidad** *nf* uselessness.

inutilizar [inutili'θar] *vt* to make *o* render useless; **~se** *vr* to become useless.

invadir [inβa'ðir] *vt* to invade.

inválido, a [in'βaliðo, a] *a* invalid // *nm/f* invalid.

invariable [inβa'rjaβle] *a* invariable.

invasión [inβa'sjon] *nf* invasion.

invasor, a [inβa'sor, a] *a* invading // *nm/f* invader.

invención [inβen'θjon] *nf* invention.

inventar [inβen'tar] *vt* to invent.

inventario [inβen'tarjo] *nm* inventory.

inventiva [inβen'tiβa] *nf* inventiveness.

inventor, a [inβen'tor, a] *nm/f* inventor.

invernadero [inβerna'ðero] *nm* greenhouse.

inverosímil [inβero'simil] *a* implausible.

inversión [inβer'sjon] *nf* (*COM*) investment.

inverso, a [in'βerso, a] *a* inverse, opposite; **en el orden ~** in reverse order; **a la inversa** inversely, the other way round.

inversor, a [inβer'sor, a] *nm/f* (*COM*) investor.

invertir [inβer'tir] *vt* (*COM*) to invest; (*volcar*) to turn upside down; (*tiempo etc*) to spend.

investigación [inβestiɣa'θjon] *nf* investigation; (*ESCOL*) research; **~ de mercado** market research.

investigar [inβesti'ɣar] *vt* to investigate; (*ESCOL*) to do research into.

invicto, a [in'βikto, a] *a* unconquered.

invierno [in'βjerno] *nm* winter.

invisible [inβi'siβle] *a* invisible.

invitado, a [inβi'taðo, a] *nm/f* guest.

invitar [inβi'tar] *vt* to invite; (*incitar*) to entice; (*pagar*) to buy, pay for.

invocar [inβo'kar] *vt* to invoke, call on.

inyección [injek'θjon] *nf* injection.

inyectar [injek'tar] *vt* to inject.

PALABRA CLAVE

ir [ir] ◆ *vi* **1** to go; (*a pie*) to walk; (*viajar*) to travel; **~ caminando** to walk; **fui en tren** I went *o* travelled by train; **¡(ahora) voy!** (I'm just) coming!

2: ~ (a) por: **~ (a) por el médico** to fetch the doctor

3 (*progresar: persona, cosa*) to go; **el trabajo va muy bien** work is going very well; **¿cómo te va?** how are things going?; **me va muy bien** I'm getting on very well; **le fue fatal** it went awfully badly for him

4 (*funcionar*): **el coche no va muy bien** the car isn't running very well

5: **te va estupendamente ese color** that colour suits you fantastically well

6 (*locuciones*): **¿vino? - ¡que va!** did he come? - of course not!; **vamos, no llores** come on, don't cry; **¡vaya coche!** what a car!, that's some car!

7: no vaya a ser: tienes que correr, no vaya a ser que pierdas el tren you'll have to run so as not to miss the train

8 (+ *pp*): **iba vestido muy bien** he was very well dressed

9: no me *etc* va ni me viene I *etc* don't care

◆ *vb auxiliar* **1**: ~ **a**: voy/iba a hacerlo hoy I am/was going to do it today

2 (+ *gerundio*): iba anocheciendo it was getting dark; todo se me iba aclarando everything was gradually becoming clearer to me

3 (+ *pp = pasivo*): van vendidos 300 ejemplares 300 copies have been sold so far

◆ ~se *vr* **1**: ¿por dónde se va al zoológico? which is the way to the zoo?

2 (*marcharse*) to leave; ya se habrán ido they must already have left o gone.

ira ['ira] *nf* anger, rage.
iracundo, a [ira'kundo, a] *a* irascible.
Irak [i'rak] *nm* = **Iraq**.
Irán [i'ran] *nm* Iran; **iraní** *a*, *nm/f* Iranian.
Iraq [i'rak], **Irak** *nm* Iraq; **iraquí** [ira'ki] *a*, *nm/f* Iraqi.
iris ['iris] *nm* (*arco* ~) rainbow; (*ANAT*) iris.
Irlanda [ir'landa] *nf* Ireland; **irlandés, esa** *a* Irish // *nm/f* Irishman/woman; los **irlandeses** the Irish.
ironía [iro'nia] *nf* irony; **irónico, a** *a* ironic(al).
irreal [irre'al] *a* unreal.
irrecuperable *a* [irrekupe'raßle] irrecoverable, irretrievable.
irreflexión [irreflek'sjon] *nf* thoughtlessness.
irregular [irrexu'lar] *a* (*gen*) irregular; (*situación*) abnormal.
irremediable *a* [irreme'ðjaßle] irremediable; (*vicio*) incurable.
irresoluto, a [irreso'luto, a] *a* irresolute, hesitant.
irrespetuoso, a [irrespe'twoso, a] *a* disrespectful.
irresponsable [irrespon'saßle] *a* irresponsible.

irrigar [irri'var] *vt* to irrigate.
irrisorio, a [irri'sorjo, a] *a* derisory, ridiculous.
irritar [irri'tar] *vt* to irritate, annoy.
irrupción [irrup'θjon] *nf* irruption; (*invasión*) invasion.
isla ['isla] *nf* island.
islandés, esa [islan'des, esa] *a* Icelandic // *nm/f* Icelander.
Islandia [is'landja] *nf* Iceland.
isleño, a [is'leɲo, a] *a* island *cpd* // *nm/f* islander.
Israel [isra'el] *nm* Israel; **israelí** *a*, *nm/f* Israeli.
istmo ['istmo] *nm* isthmus.
Italia [i'talja] *nf* Italy; **italiano, a** *a*, *nm/f* Italian.
itinerario [itine'rarjo] *nm* itinerary, route.
IVA ['iβa] *nm abr ver* **impuesto**.
izar [i'θar] *vt* to hoist.
izdo, a *abr* (= *izquierdo, a*) l.
izquierda [iθ'kjerda] *nf* left; (*POL*) left (wing); **a la ~** (*estar*) on the left; (*torcer etc*) to the left.
izquierdista [iθkjer'ðista] *nm/f* leftwinger, leftist.
izquierdo, a [iθ'kjerðo, a] *a* left.

J

jabalí [xaβa'li] *nm* wild boar.
jabalina [xaβa'lina] *nf* javelin.
jabón [xa'βon] *nm* soap; **jabonar** *vt* to soap.
jaca ['xaka] *nf* pony.
jacinto [xa'θinto] *nm* hyacinth.
jactarse [xak'tarse] *vr* to boast, brag.
jadear [xaðe'ar] *vi* to pant, gasp for breath; **jadeo** *nm* panting, gasping.
jaguar [xa'ywar] *nm* jaguar.
jalbegue [xal'βexe] *nm* (*pintura*) whitewash.
jalea [xa'lea] *nf* jelly.
jaleo [xa'leo] *nm* racket, uproar; armar un ~ to kick up a racket.
jalón [xa'lon] *nm* (*AM*) tug.
Jamaica [xa'maika] *nf* Jamaica.
jamás [xa'mas] *ad* never; (*sin nega-*

ción) ever.

jamón [xa'mon] *nm* ham; ~ **dulce**, ~ **de York** cooked ham; ~ **serrano** cured ham.

Japón [xa'pon] *nm*: **el** ~ Japan; **japonés, esa** *a, nm/f* Japanese.

jaque [xake] *nm*: ~ **mate** checkmate.

jaqueca [xa'keka] *nf* (very bad) headache, migraine.

jarabe [xa'raße] *nm* syrup.

jarcia ['xarθja] *nf* (*NAUT*) ropes *pl*, rigging.

jardín [xar'ðin] *nm* garden; ~ **de (la) infancia** (*Esp*) o **de niños** (*AM*) nursery (school); **jardinería** *nf* gardening; **jardinero, a** *nm/f* gardener.

jarra ['xarra] *nf* jar; (*jarro*) jug.

jarro ['xarro] *nm* jug.

jaula ['xaula] *nf* cage.

jauría [xau'ria] *nf* pack of hounds.

J. C. *abr* (= *Jesucristo*) J.C.

jefa ['xefa] *nf* woman head *o* boss.

jefatura [xefa'tura] *nf*: ~ **de policía** police headquarters *sg*.

jefe ['xefe] *nm* (*gen*) chief, head; (*patrón*) boss; ~ **de camareros** head waiter; ~ **de cocina** chef; ~ **de estación** stationmaster; ~ **de estado** head of state; ~ **supremo** commander-in-chief; **ser el** ~ (*fig*) to be the boss.

jengibre [xen'xißre] *nm* ginger.

jeque ['xeke] *nm* sheik.

jerarquía [xerar'kia] *nf* (*orden*) hierarchy; (*rango*) rank; **jerárquico, a** *a* hierarchic(al).

jerez [xe'reθ] *nm* sherry.

jerga ['xerɣa] *nf* (*tela*) coarse cloth; (*lenguaje*) jargon.

jerigonza [xeri'ɣonθa] *nf* (*jerga*) jargon, slang; (*galimatías*) nonsense, gibberish.

jeringa [xe'riŋga] *nf* syringe; (*AM*) annoyance, bother; ~ **de engrase** grease gun; **jeringar** *vt* (*AM*) to annoy, bother.

jeroglífico [xero'ɣlifiko] *nm* hieroglyphic.

jersé, jersey [xer'sei] (*pl* **jerseys**) *nm* jersey, pullover, jumper.

Jerusalén [xerusa'len] *nf* Jerusalem.

Jesucristo [xesu'kristo] *nm* Jesus Christ.

jesuita [xe'swita] *a, nm* Jesuit.

Jesús [xe'sus] *nm* Jesus; ¡~! good heavens!; (*al estornudar*) bless you!

jet ['jet] (*pl* ~**s**) *nm* jet (plane).

jícara [xikara] *nf* small cup.

jinete, a [xi'nete, a] *nm/f* horseman/woman, rider.

jipijapa [xipi'xapa] *nm* (*AM*) straw hat.

jirafa [xi'rafa] *nf* giraffe.

jirón [xi'ron] *nm* rag, shred.

jocoso [xo'koso, a] *a* humorous, jocular.

jofaina [xo'faina] *nf* washbasin.

jornada [xor'naða] *nf* (*viaje de un día*) day's journey; (*camino o viaje entero*) journey; (*día de trabajo*) working day.

jornal [xor'nal] *nm* (day's) wage; ~**ero** *nm* (day) labourer.

joroba [xo'roßa] *nf* hump, hunched back; ~**do, a** *a* hunchbacked // *nm/f* hunchback.

jota ['xota] *nf* (the letter) J; (*danza*) Aragonese dance; (*fam*) jot, iota; **no saber ni** ~ to have no idea.

joven ['xoßen] *a* (*pl* **jóvenes**) *a* young // *nm* young man, youth // *nf* young woman, girl.

jovial [xo'ßjal, a] *a* cheerful, jolly; ~**idad** *nf* cheerfulness, jolliness.

joya ['xoja] *nf* jewel, gem; (*fig: persona*) gem; **joyería** (*joyas*) jewellery; (*tienda*) jeweller's (shop); **joyero** (*persona*) jeweller; (*caja*) jewel case.

juanete [xwa'nete] *nm* (*del pie*) bunion.

jubilación [xußila'θjon] *nf* (*retiro*) retirement.

jubilado, a [xußi'laðo, a] *a* retired // *nm/f* pensioner (*Brit*), senior citizen.

jubilar [xußi'lar] *vt* to pension off, retire; (*fam*) to discard; ~**se** *vr* to retire.

jubileo [xuβi'leo] *nm* jubilee.

júbilo ['xuβilo] *nm* joy, rejoicing; **jubiloso, a** *a* jubilant.

judía [xu'δia] *nf* Jewess; (*CULIN*) bean; ~ **verde** French bean.

judicial [xuδi'θjal] *a* judicial.

judío, a [xu'δio, a] *a* Jewish // *nm/f* Jew(ess).

judo ['juδo] *nm* judo.

juego *etc vb ver* **jugar** // ['xweɣo] *nm* (*gen*) play; (*pasatiempo, partido*) game; (*en casino*) gambling; (*conjunto*) set; **fuera de** ~ (*DEPORTE: persona*) offside; (: *pelota*) out of play; **J~s Olímpicos** Olympic Games.

juerga ['xwerɣa] *nf* binge; (*fiesta*) party; **ir de** ~ to go out on a binge.

jueves ['xweβes] *nm inv* Thursday.

juez [xweθ] *nm/f* judge; ~ **de línea** linesman; ~ **de salida** starter.

jugada [xu'ɣaδa] *nf* play; **buena** ~ good move/shot/stroke *etc*.

jugador, a [xuɣa'δor, a] *nm/f* player; (*en casino*) gambler.

jugar [xu'ɣar] *vt, vi* to play; (*en casino*) to gamble; (*apostar*) to bet; ~ **al fútbol** to play football; ~se *vr* to gamble (away).

juglar [xu'ɣlar] *nm* minstrel.

jugo ['xuɣo] *nm* (*BOT*) juice; (*fig*) essence, substance; ~ **de fruta** (*AM*) fruit juice; **~so, a** *a* juicy; (*fig*) substantial, important.

juguete [xu'ɣete] *nm* toy; **~ar** *vi* to play; **~ría** *nf* toyshop.

juguetón, ona [xuɣe'ton, ona] *a* playful.

juicio ['xwiθjo] *nm* judgement; (*razón*) sanity, reason; (*opinión*) opinion; **estar fuera de** ~ to be out of one's mind; **~so, a** *a* wise, sensible.

julio ['xuljo] *nm* July.

junco ['xunko] *nm* rush, reed.

jungla ['xungla] *nf* jungle.

junio ['xunjo] *nm* June.

junta ['xunta] *nf ver* **junto**.

juntar [xun'tar] *vt* to join, unite; (*maquinaria*) to assemble, put

together; (*dinero*) to collect; ~se *vr* to join, meet; (*reunirse: personas*) to meet, assemble; (*arrimarse*) to approach, draw closer; ~se **con uno** to join sb.

junto, a ['xunto, a] *a* joined; (*unido*) united; (*anexo*) near, close; (*contiguo, próximo*) next, adjacent; ~s together // *ad*: **todo** ~ all at once // *nf* (*asamblea*) meeting, assembly; (*comité, consejo*) board, council, committee; (*articulación*) joint; ~ **a** near (to), next to.

jurado [xu'raδo] *nm* (*JUR: individuo*) juror; (: *grupo*) jury; (*de concurso: grupo*) panel of judges); (: *individuo*) member of a panel.

juramento [xura'mento] *nm* oath; (*maldición*) oath, curse; **prestar** ~ to take the oath; **tomar** ~ **a** to swear in, administer the oath to.

jurar [xu'rar] *vt, vi* to swear; ~ **en falso** to commit perjury; **jurársela a uno** to have it in for sb.

jurídico, a [xu'riδiko, a] *a* legal.

jurisdicción [xurisδik'θjon] *nf* (*poder, autoridad*) jurisdiction; (*territorio*) district.

jurisprudencia [xurispru'δenθja] *nf* jurisprudence.

jurista [xu'rista] *nm/f* jurist.

justamente [xusta'mente] *ad* justly, fairly; (*precisamente*) just, exactly.

justicia [xus'tiθja] *nf* justice; (*equidad*) fairness, justice; **justiciero, a** *a* just, righteous.

justificación [xustifika'θjon] *nf* justification; **justificar** *vt* to justify.

justo, a ['xusto, a] *a* (*equitativo*) just, fair, right; (*preciso*) exact, correct; (*ajustado*) tight // *ad* (*precisamente*) exactly, precisely; (*AM*: apenas a tiempo*) just in time.

juvenil [xuβe'nil] *a* youthful.

juventud [xuβen'tuδ] *nf* (*adolescencia*) youth; (*jóvenes*) young people *pl*.

juzgado [xuθ'ɣaδo] *nm* tribunal; (*JUR*) court.

juzgar [xuθ'ɣar] *vt* to judge; **a** ~

por... to judge by..., judging by... .

K

kg abr (= *kilogramo*) kg.
kilo ['kilo] nm kilo // pref: ~**gramo** nm kilogramme; ~**metraje** nm distance in kilometres, ≈ mileage; **kilómetro** nm kilometre; ~**vatio** nm kilowatt.
kiosco ['kjosko] nm = **quiosco**.
km abr (= *kilómetro*) km.
kv abr (= *kilovatio*) kw.

L

l abr (= *litro*) l.
la [la] *artículo definido* the // *pron* her; (*Ud.*) you; (*cosa*) it // nm (*MUS*) la; ~ **del sombrero rojo** the girl in the red hat; *tb ver* **el**.
laberinto [laβe'rinto] nm labyrinth.
labia ['laβja] nf fluency; (*pey*) glib tongue.
labial [la'βjal] a labial.
labio ['laβjo] nm lip.
labor [la'βor] nf labour; (*AGR*) farm work; (*tarea*) job, task; (*COSTURA*) needlework; ~**able** a (*AGR*) workable; **día** ~**able** working day; ~ **vi** to work.
laboratorio [laβora'torjo] nm laboratory.
laborioso, a [laβo'rjoso, a] a (*persona*) hard-working; (*trabajo*) tough.
laborista [laβo'rista] a: **Partido L~** Labour Party.
labrado, a [la'βraðo, a] a worked; (*madera*) carved; (*metal*) wrought // nm (*AGR*) cultivated field.
labrador, a [laβra'ðor, a] a farming cpd // nm/f farmer.
labranza [la'βranθa] nf (*AGR*) cultivation.
labrar [la'βrar] vt (*gen*) to work; (*madera etc*) to carve; (*fig*) to cause, bring about.
labriego, a [la'βrjeɣo, a] nm/f

peasant.
laca ['laka] nf lacquer.
lacayo [la'kajo] nm lackey.
lacerar [laθe'rar] vt to lacerate.
lacio, a ['laθjo, a] a (*pelo*) lank, straight.
lacónico, a [la'koniko, a] a laconic.
lacrar [la'krar] vt (*cerrar*) to seal (with sealing wax); **lacre** nm sealing wax.
lacrimoso, a [lakri'moso, a] a tearful.
lactar [lak'tar] vt, vi to suckle.
lácteo, a ['lakteo, a] a: **productos** ~**s** dairy products.
ladear [laðe'ar] vt to tip, tilt // vi to tilt; ~**se** vr to lean.
ladera [la'ðera] nf slope.
ladino, a [la'ðino, a] a cunning.
lado ['laðo] nm (*gen*) side; (*fig*) protection; (*MIL*) flank; **al** ~ **de** beside; **poner de** ~ to put on its side; **poner a un** ~ to put aside; **por todos** ~**s** on all sides, all round (*Brit*).
ladrar [la'ðrar] vi to bark; **ladrido** nm bark, barking.
ladrillo [la'ðriʎo] nm (*gen*) brick; (*azulejo*) tile.
ladrón, ona [la'ðron, ona] nm/f thief.
lagar [la'var] nm (*wine/oil*) press.
lagartija [laɣar'tixa] nf (*small*) lizard.
lagarto [la'ɣarto] nm (*ZOOL*) lizard.
lago ['laɣo] nm lake.
lágrima ['laɣrima] nf tear.
laguna [la'ɣuna] nf (*lago*) lagoon; (*hueco*) gap.
laico, a ['laiko, a] a lay.
lamentable [lamen'taβle] a lamentable, regrettable; (*miserable*) pitiful.
lamentar [lamen'tar] vt (*sentir*) to regret; (*deplorar*) to lament; **lo lamento mucho** I'm very sorry; ~**se** vr to lament; **lamento** nm lament.
lamer [la'mer] vt to lick.
lámina ['lamina] nf (*plancha*

delgada) sheet; *(para estampar, estampa)* plate; **laminar** *vt (en libro)* to laminate.

lámpara ['lampara] *nf* lamp; ~ de alcohol/gas spirit/gas lamp; ~ de pie standard lamp.

lamparón [lampa'ron] *nm* grease spot.

lampiño [lam'pino] *a* clean-shaven.

lana ['lana] *nf* wool.

lance *vt ver* **lanzar** // ['lanθe] *nm (golpe)* stroke; *(suceso)* event, incident.

lancha ['lantʃa] *nf* launch; ~ de pesca fishing boat; ~ salvavidas/torpedera lifeboat/torpedo boat.

lanero, a [la'nero, a] *a* woollen.

langosta [lan'gosta] *nf (insecto)* locust; *(crustáceo)* lobster; **~ plaga** plague; **langostino** *nm* king prawn *(Brit)*, crayfish *(US)*.

languidecer [langiðe'θer] *vi* to languish; **languidez** *nf* langour; **lánguido, a** *a (gen)* languid; *(sin energía)* listless.

lanilla [la'niʎa] *nf* nap.

lanudo, a [la'nuðo, a] *a* woolly.

lanza ['lanθa] *nf (arma)* lance, spear.

lanzadera [lanθa'ðera] *nf* shuttle.

lanzamiento [lanθa'mjento] *nm (gen)* throwing; *(NAUT, COM)* launch, launching; ~ de peso putting the shot.

lanzar [lan'θar] *vt (gen)* to throw; *(DEPORTE: pelota)* to bowl; *(NAUT, COM)* to launch; *(JUR)* to evict; ~ *vr* to throw o.s.

lapa ['lapa] *nf* limpet.

lapicero [lapi'θero] *nm* propelling *(Brit) o* mechanical *(US)* pencil; *(AM: bolígrafo)* Biro ®.

lápida ['lapiða] *nf* stone; ~ mortuoria headstone; ~ conmemorativa memorial stone; **lapidar** *vt* to stone; **lapidario, a** *a, nm* lapidary.

lápiz ['lapiθ] *nm* pencil; ~ de color coloured pencil; ~ de labios lipstick.

lapón, ona [la'pon, ona] *nm/f* Lap-

lander, Lapp.

Laponia [la'ponja] *nf* Lapland.

lapso ['lapso] *nm (de tiempo)* interval; *(error)* error.

lapsus ['lapsus] *nm inv* error, mistake.

largar [lar'var] *vt (soltar)* to release; *(aflojar)* to loosen; *(fam)* to let fly; *(velas)* to unfurl; *(AM)* to throw; ~ *se vr (fam)* to beat it; ~ **se a** *(AM)* to start to.

largo, a ['larvo, a] *a (longitud)* long; *(tiempo)* lengthy; *(fig)* generous // *nm (longh)*; *(MUS)* largo // *ad* widely; **dos años** ~s two long years; **tiene 9 metros de** ~ it is 9 metres long; **a lo** ~ de along; *(tiempo)* all through, throughout.

laringe [la'rinxe] *nf* larynx; **laringitis** *nf* laryngitis.

larva ['larßa] *nf* larva.

las [las] *artículo definido* the // *pron* them; ~ que cantan the ones/women/girls who sing; *tb ver* **el**.

lascivo, a [las'θißo, a] *a* lewd.

láser ['laser] *nm* laser.

lástima ['lastima] *nf (pena)* pity; **dar** ~ to be pitiful; **es una** ~ **que** it's a pity that; **¡qué** ~! what a pity!; **ella está hecha una** ~ she looks pitiful.

lastimar [lasti'mar] *vt (herir)* to wound; *(ofender)* to offend; ~ **se** *vr* to hurt o.s.; **lastimero, a** *a* pitiful, pathetic.

lastre ['lastre] *nm (TEC, NAUT)* ballast; *(fig)* dead weight.

lata ['lata] *nf (metal)* tin; *(caja)* tin *(Brit)*, can; *(fam)* nuisance; **en** ~ tinned *(Brit)*, canned; **dar (la)** ~ to be a nuisance.

latente [la'tente] *a* latent.

lateral [late'ral] *a* side *cpd*, lateral // *nm (TEATRO)* wings.

latido [la'tiðo] *nm (del corazón)* beat.

latifundio [lati'fundjo] *nm* large estate; **latifundista** *nm/f* owner of a large estate.

latigazo [lati'ɣaθo] *nm (golpe)* lash; *(sonido)* crack.

látigo ['lativo] *nm* whip.

latín [la'tin] *nm* Latin.

latino, a [la'tino, a] *a* Latin; **~americano, a** *a, nmf* Latin-American.

latir [la'tir] *vi (corazón, pulso)* to beat.

latitud [lati'tuð] *nf (GEO)* latitude.

latón [la'ton] *nm* brass.

latoso, a [la'toso, a] *a (molesto)* annoying; *(aburrido)* boring.

laúd [la'uð] *nm* lute.

laureado, a [laure'aðo, a] *a* honoured // *nm* laureate.

laurel [lau'rel] *nm (BOT)* laurel; *(CULIN)* bay.

lava ['laβa] *nf* lava.

lavabo [la'βaβo] *nm (jofaina)* washbasin; *(tb: ~s)* toilet.

lavadero [laβa'ðero] *nm* laundry.

lavado [la'βaðo] *nm* washing; *(de ropa)* laundry; *(ARTE)* wash; **~ de cerebro** brainwashing; **~ en seco** dry-cleaning.

lavadora [laβa'ðora] *nf* washing machine.

lavanda [la'βanda] *nf* lavender.

lavandería [laβande'ria] *nf* laundry; **~ automática** launderette.

lavaplatos [laβa'platos] *nm inv* dishwasher.

lavar [la'βar] *vt* to wash; *(borrar)* to wipe away; **~se** *vr* to wash o.s.; **~se las manos** to wash one's hands; **~y marcar** *(pelo)* to shampoo and set; **~ en seco** to dry-clean.

lavavajillas [laβaβa'xiʎas] *nm inv* dishwasher.

laxante [lak'sante] *nm* laxative.

lazada [la'θaða] *nf* bow.

lazarillo [laθa'riʎo] *nm:* **perro ~** guide dog.

lazo ['laθo] *nm* knot; *(lazada)* bow; *(para animales)* lasso; *(trampa)* snare; *(vínculo)* tie.

le [le] *pron (directo)* him; *(: usted)* you; *(indirecto)* to him; *(: usted)* to you.

leal [le'al] *a* loyal; **~tad** *nf* loyalty.

lebrel [le'βrel] *nm* greyhound.

lección [lek'θjon] *nf* lesson.

lector, a [lek'tor, a] *nmf* reader.

lectura [lek'tura] *nf* reading.

leche ['letʃe] *nf* milk; **tener mala ~** *(fam!)* to be nasty; **~ condensada** *(en polvo)* condensed/powdered milk; **~ desnatada** skimmed milk; **~ra** *nf (vendedora)* milkmaid; *(recipiente)* milk churn; *(AM)* cow; **~ría** *nf* dairy; **~ro, a** *a* dairy.

lecho ['letʃo] *nm (cama, de río)* bed; *(GEO)* layer.

lechón [le'tʃon] *nm* sucking *(Brit)* o suckling *(US)* pig.

lechoso, a [le'tʃoso, a] *a* milky.

lechuga [le'tʃuɣa] *nf* lettuce.

lechuza [le'tʃuθa] *nf* owl.

leer [le'er] *vt* to read.

legado [le'ɣaðo] *nm (don)* bequest; *(herencia)* legacy; *(enviado)* legate.

legajo [le'ɣaxo] *nm* file.

legal [le'ɣal] *a (gen)* legal; *(persona)* trustworthy; **~idad** *nf* legality; **~izar** *vt* to legalize; *(documento)* to authenticate.

legaña [le'ɣaɲa] *nf* sleep *(in eyes)*.

legar [le'ɣar] *vt* to bequeath, leave.

legendario, a [lexen'darjo, a] *a* legendary.

legión [le'xjon] *nf* legion; **legionario, a** *a* legionary // *nm* legionnaire.

legislación [lexisla'θjon] *nf* legislation; **legislar** *vt* to legislate.

legitimar [lexiti'mar] *vt* to legitimize; **legítimo, a** *a (genuino)* authentic; *(legal)* legitimate.

lego, a ['leɣo, a] *a (REL)* secular; *(ignorante)* ignorant // *nm* layman.

legua ['leɣwa] *nf* league.

legumbres [le'ɣumbres] *nfpl* pulses.

leído, a [le'iðo, a] *a* well-read.

lejanía [lexa'nia] *nf* distance; **lejano, a** *a* far-off; *(en el tiempo)* distant; *(fig)* remote.

lejía [le'xia] *nf* bleach.

lejos ['lexos] *ad* far, far away; **a lo ~** in the distance; **de o desde ~** from afar; **~ de** *prep* far from.

lelo, a ['lelo, a] *a* silly // *nmf* idiot.

lema ['lema] *nm* motto; *(POL)*

slogan.

lencería [lenθe'ria] nf linen, drapery.

lengua ['lengwa] nf tongue; (LING) language; **morderse la ~** to hold one's tongue.

lenguado [len'gwaðo] nm sole.

lenguaje [len'gwaxe] nm language.

lengüeta [len'gweta] nf (ANAT) epiglottis; (zapatos, MUS) tongue.

lente ['lente] nf lens; (lupa) magnifying glass; **~s** nfpl glasses; **~ s de contacto** contact lenses.

lenteja [len'texa] nf lentil; **lentejuela** nf sequin.

lentilla [len'tiʎa] nf contact lens.

lentitud [lenti'tuð] nf slowness; **con ~** slowly.

lento, a [a 'lento, a] a slow.

leña ['leɲa] nf firewood; **~dor, a** nm/f woodcutter.

leño ['leɲo] nm (trozo de árbol) log; (madera) timber; (fig) blockhead.

Leo ['leo] nm Leo.

león [le'on] nm lion; **~ marino** sea lion; **leonino, a** a leonine.

leopardo [leo'parðo] nm leopard.

leotardos [leo'tarðos] nmpl tights.

lepra ['lepra] nf leprosy; **leproso, a** nm/f leper.

lerdo, a [a 'lerðo, a] a (lento) slow; (patoso) clumsy.

les [les] pron (directo) them; (: ustedes) you; (indirecto) to them; (: ustedes) to you.

lesbiana [les'bjana] a, nf lesbian.

lesión [le'sjon] nf wound, lesion; (DEPORTE) injury; **lesionado, a** a injured // nm/f injured person.

letal [le'tal] a lethal.

letanía [leta'nia] nf litany.

letargo [le'tarɣo] nm lethargy.

letra ['letra] nf letter; (escritura) handwriting; (MUS) lyrics pl; **~ de cambio** bill of exchange; **~ de imprenta** print; **~do, a** a learned; (fam) pedantic // nm lawyer; **letrero** nm (cartel) sign; (etiqueta) label.

letrina [le'trina] nf latrine.

leucemia [leu'θemja] nf leukaemia.

levadizo [leβa'ðiθo] a: **puente ~**

drawbridge.

levadura [leβa'ðura] nf (para el pan) yeast; (de la cerveza) brewer's yeast.

levantamiento [leβanta'mjento] nm raising, lifting; (rebelión) revolt, rising; **~ de pesos** weight-lifting.

levantar [leβan'tar] vt (gen) to raise; (del suelo) to pick up; (hacia arriba) to lift (up); (plan) to make, draw up; (mesa) to clear away; (campamento) to strike; (fig) to cheer up, hearten; **~se** vr to get up; (enderezarse) to straighten up; (rebelarse) to rebel; **~ el ánimo** to cheer up.

levante [le'βante] nm east coast; **el L~** region of Spain extending from Castellón to Murcia.

levar [le'βar] vt to weigh anchor.

leve ['leβe] a light; (fig) trivial; **~dad** nf lightness.

levita [le'βita] nf frock coat.

léxico ['leksiko] nm (vocabulario) vocabulary.

ley [lei] nf (gen) law; (metal) standard.

leyenda [le'jenda] nf legend.

leyó etc vb ver **leer**.

liar [li'ar] vt to tie (up); (unir) to bind; (envolver) to wrap up; (enredar) to confuse; (cigarrillo) to roll; **~se** vr (fam) to get involved; **~se a palos** to get involved in a fight.

Líbano ['liβano] nm: **el ~** the Lebanon.

libar [li'βar] vt to suck.

libelo [li'βelo] nm satire, lampoon; (JUR) petition.

libélula [li'βelula] nf dragonfly.

liberación [liβera'θjon] nf liberation; (de la cárcel) release.

liberal [liβe'ral] a, nm/f liberal; **~idad** nf liberality, generosity.

liberar [liβe'rar] vt to liberate.

libertad [liβer'tað] nf liberty, freedom; **~ de culto/de comercio/de prensa/de** freedom of worship/of trade; **~ condicional** probation; **~ bajo palabra** parole; **~**

bajo fianza bail.

libertar [liβer'tar] vt (preso) to set free; (de una obligación) to release; (eximir) to exempt.

libertino, a [liβer'tino, a] a permissive // nm/f permissive person.

libra ['liβra] nf pound sterling; L~ (ASTROLOGIA) Libra; ~ esterlina pound sterling.

librador, a [liβra'ðor, a] nm/f drawer.

libramiento [liβra'mjento] nm rescue; (COM) delivery.

libranza [li'βranθa] nf (COM) draft; (letra de cambio) bill of exchange.

librar [li'βrar] vt (de peligro) to save; (batalla) to wage, fight; (de impuestos) to exempt; (cheque) to make out; (JUR) to exempt; ~se vr: ~se de to escape from, free o.s. from.

libre ['liβre] a free; (lugar) unoccupied; (asiento) vacant; (de deudas) free of debts; ~ de impuestos free of tax; tiro ~ free kick; los 100 metros ~ the 100 metres free-style (race); al aire ~ in the open air.

librería [liβre'ria] nf (tienda) bookshop; **librero, a** nm/f bookseller.

libreta [li'βreta] nf notebook; ~ de ahorros savings book.

libro ['liβro] nm book; ~ de bolsillo paperback; ~ de caja cashbook; ~ de cheques chequebook (Brit), checkbook (US); ~ de texto textbook.

Lic. abr = **licenciado, a.**

licencia [li'θenθja] nf (gen) licence; (permiso) permission; ~ por enfermedad/con goce de sueldo sick leave/paid leave; ~ de caza game licence; ~do, a a licensed // nm/f graduate; **licenciar** vt (empleado) to dismiss; (permitir) to permit, allow; (soldado) to discharge; (estudiante) to confer a degree upon; **licenciarse** vr: **licenciarse en letras** to graduate in arts.

licencioso, a [liθen'θjoso, a] a licentious.

liceo [li'θeo] nm (high) school.

licitar [liθi'tar] vt to bid for; (AM) to sell by auction.

lícito, a ['liθito, a] a (legal) lawful; (justo) fair, just; (permisible) permissible.

licor [li'kor] nm spirits pl (Brit), liquor (US); (de frutas etc) liqueur.

licuadora [likwa'ðora] nf blender.

licuar [li'kwar] vt to liquidize.

lid [lið] nf combat; (fig) controversy.

líder ['liðer] nm/f leader; **liderato, liderazgo** nm leadership.

lidia ['liðja] nf bullfighting; (una ~) bullfight; **toros de ~** fighting bulls; **lidiar** vt, vi to fight.

liebre ['ljeβre] nf hare.

lienzo ['ljenθo] nm linen; (ARTE) canvas; (ARQ) wall.

liga ['liɣa] nf (de medias) garter, suspender; (AM: gomita) rubber band; (confederación) league.

ligadura [liɣa'ðura] nf bond, tie; (MED, MUS) ligature.

ligamento [liɣa'mento] nm (ANAT) ligament; (atadura) tie; (unión) bond.

ligar [li'ɣar] vt (atar) to tie; (unir) to join; (MED) to bind up; (MUS) to slur // vi to mix, blend; (fam) to pick up; ~se vr to commit o.s.

ligereza [lixe'reθa] nf lightness; (rapidez) swiftness; (agilidad) agility; (superficialidad) flippancy.

ligero, a [li'xero, a] a (de peso) light; (tela) thin; (rápido) swift, quick; (ágil) agile, nimble; (de importancia) slight; (de carácter) flippant, superficial // ad: **a la ligera** superficially.

liguero [li'xero] nm suspender (Brit) o garter (US) belt.

lija ['lixa] nf (ZOOL) dogfish; (papel de) ~ sandpaper.

lila ['lila] nf lilac.

lima ['lima] nf file; (BOT) lime; ~ de uñas nailfile; L~ n (GEO) Lima; **limar** vt to file.

limitación [limita'θjon] nf limitation,

limit; ~ **de velocidad** speed limit.
limitar [limi'tar] vt to limit; (reducir) to reduce, cut down // vi: ~ **con** to border on; ~**se** vr: ~**se a** to limit o.s. to.
límite ['limite] nm (gen) limit; (fin) end; (frontera) border; ~ **de velocidad** speed limit.
limítrofe [li'mitrofe] a bordering, neighbouring.
limón [li'mon] nm lemon // a: **amarillo** ~ lemon-yellow; **limonada** nf lemonade; **limonero** nm lemon tree.
limosna [li'mosna] nf alms pl; **vivir de** ~ to live on charity.
limpiabotas [limpja'βotas] nm/f inv bootblack (Brit), shoeshine boy/girl.
limpiaparabrisas [limpjapara'βrisas] nm inv windscreen (Brit) o windshield (US) wiper.
limpiar [lim'pjar] vt to clean; (con trapo) to wipe; (quitar) to wipe away; (zapatos) to shine, polish; (fig) to clean up.
limpieza [lim'pjeθa] nf (estado) cleanliness; (acto) cleaning; (: de las calles) cleansing; (: de zapatos) polishing; (habilidad) skill; (fig: POLICIA) clean-up; (pureza) purity; ~ **en seco** dry cleaning.
limpio, a ['limpjo, a] a clean; (moralmente) pure; (COM) clear, net; (fam) honest // ad: **jugar** ~ to play fair // nm: **pasar a** (Esp) o **en** (AM) ~ to make a fair copy.
linaje [li'naxe] nm lineage, family.
linaza [li'naθa] nf linseed.
lince [li'nθe] nm lynx.
linchar [lin'tʃar] vt to lynch.
lindar [lin'dar] vi to adjoin; ~ **con** to border on; **linde** nm o f boundary; **lindero, a** a adjoining // nm boundary.
lindo, a ['lindo, a] a pretty, lovely // ad: **nos divertimos de lo** ~ we had a marvellous time; **canta muy** ~ (AM) he sings beautifully.
línea ['linea] nf (gen) line; en ~ (INFORM) on line; ~ **aérea** airline; ~

de meta goal line; (de carrera) finishing line; ~ **recta** straight line.
lingote [lin'gote] nm ingot.
lingüista [lin'gwista] nm/f linguist; **lingüística** nf linguistics sg.
linimento [lini'mento] nm liniment.
lino ['lino] nm linen; (BOT) flax.
linóleo [li'noleo] nm lino, linoleum.
linterna [lin'terna] nf lantern, lamp; ~ **eléctrica** o **a pilas** torch (Brit), flashlight (US).
lio ['lio] nm bundle; (fam) fuss; (desorden) muddle, mess; **armar un** ~ to make a fuss.
liquen ['liken] nm lichen.
liquidación [likiða'θjon] nf liquidation; **venta de** ~ clearance sale.
liquidar [liki'ðar] vt (mercancías) to liquidate; (deudas) to pay off; (empresa) to wind up.
líquido, a ['likiðo, a] a liquid; (ganancia) net // nm liquid; ~ **imponible** net taxable income.
lira ['lira] nf (MUS) lyre; (moneda) lira.
lírico, a ['liriko, a] a lyrical.
lirio ['lirjo] nm (BOT) iris.
lirón [li'ron] nm (ZOOL) dormouse; (fig) sleepyhead.
Lisboa [lis'βoa] n Lisbon.
lisiado, a [li'sjaðo, a] a injured // nm/f cripple.
lisiar [li'sjar] vt to maim; ~**se** vr to injure o.s.
liso, a ['liso, a] a (terreno) flat; (cabello) straight; (superficie) even; (tela) plain.
lisonja [li'sonxa] nf flattery; **lisonjear** vt to flatter; (fig) to please; **lisonjero, a** a flattering; (agradable) gratifying, pleasing // nm/f flatterer.
lista ['lista] nf list; (de alumnos) school register; (de libros) catalogue; (de platos) menu; (de precios) price list; **pasar** ~ to call the roll; ~ **de correos** poste restante; ~ **de espera** waiting list; **tela a** ~**s** striped material.
listado, a [lis'taðo, a] a striped.

listo, a ['listo, a] a (perspicaz) smart, clever; (preparado) ready.
listón [lis'ton] nm (tela) ribbon; (de madera, metal) strip.
litera [li'tera] nf (en barco, tren) berth; (en dormitorio) bunk, bunk bed.
literal [lite'ral] a literal.
literario, a [lite'rarjo, a] a literary.
literato, a [lite'rato, a] a literary // nm/f writer.
literatura [litera'tura] nf literature.
litigar [liti'var] vt to fight // vi (JUR) to go to law; (fig) to dispute, argue.
litigio [li'tixjo] nm (JUR) lawsuit; (fig): **en ~ con** in dispute with.
litografía [litovra'fia] nf lithography; (una ~) lithograph.
litoral [lito'ral] a coastal // nm coast, seaboard.
litro ['litro] nm litre.
liviano, a [li'βjano, a] a (persona) fickle; (cosa, objeto) trivial.
lívido, a ['liβiðo, a] a livid.
ll... ver bajo la letra LL, después de L.
lo [lo] artículo definido neutro; **~ bello** the beautiful, what is beautiful, that which is beautiful // pron (persona) him; (cosa) it; tb ver **el**.
loa ['loa] nf praise; **loable** a praiseworthy; **loar** vt to praise.
lobato [lo'βato] nm (ZOOL) wolf cub.
lobo ['loβo] nm wolf; **~ de mar** (fig) sea dog; **~ marino** seal.
lóbrego, a ['loβreyo, a] a dark; (fig) gloomy.
lóbulo ['loβulo] nm lobe.
local [lo'kal] a local // nm place, site; (oficinas) premises pl; **~idad** nf (barrio) locality; (lugar) location; (TEATRO) seat, ticket; **~izar** vt (ubicar) to locate, find; (restringir) to localize; (situar) to place.
loción [lo'θjon] nf lotion.
loco, a ['loko, a] a mad // nm/f lunatic, mad person.
locomoción [lokomo'θjon] nf locomotion.

locomotora [lokomo'tora] nf engine, locomotive.
locuaz [lo'kwaθ] a loquacious.
locución [loku'θjon] nf expression.
locura [lo'kura] nf madness; (acto) crazy act.
locutor, a [loku'tor, a] nm/f (RADIO) announcer; (comentarista) commentator; (TV) newsreader.
locutorio [loku'torjo] nm (en telefónica) telephone booth.
lodo ['loðo] nm mud.
lógico, a ['loxiko, a] a logical // nf logic.
logística [lo'xistika] nf logistics pl.
lograr [lo'vrar] vt to achieve; (obtener) to get, obtain; **~ hacer** to manage to do; **~ que uno venga** to manage to get sb to come.
logro ['lovro] nm achievement, success.
loma ['loma] nf hillock (Brit), small hill.
lombriz [lom'briθ] nf worm.
lomo ['lomo] nm (de animal) back; (CULIN: de cerdo) pork loin; (: de vaca) rib steak; (de libro) spine.
lona ['lona] nf canvas.
loncha ['lontʃa] nf = **lonja**.
lonche ['lontʃe] nm (AM) lunch; **~ría** nf (AM) snack bar, diner (US).
Londres ['londres] n London.
longaniza [longa'niθa] nf pork sausage.
longitud [lonxi'tuð] nf length; (GEO) longitude; **tener 3 metros de ~** to be 3 metres long; **~ de onda** wavelength.
lonja ['lonxa] nf slice; (de tocino) rasher; **~ de pescado** fish market.
loro ['loro] nm parrot.
los [los] artículo definido the // pron them; (ustedes) you; **mis libros y ~ de Ud** my books and yours; tb ver **el**.
losa ['losa] nf stone; **~ sepulcral** gravestone.
lote ['lote] nm portion; (COM) lot.
lotería [lote'ria] nf lottery; (juego) lotto.

loza [ˈloθa] nf crockery.

lozanía [loθaˈnia] nf (lujo) luxuriance; **lozano, a** a luxuriant; (animado) lively.

lubricante [luβriˈkante] nm lubricant.

lubricar [luβriˈkar] vt to lubricate.

lucero [luˈθero] nm bright star; (fig) brilliance.

lucidez [luθiˈðeθ] nf lucidity; **lúcido, a** a lucid.

luciérnaga [luˈθjernaɣa] nf glowworm.

lucimiento [luθiˈmjento] nm (brillo) brilliance; (éxito) success.

lucir [luˈθir] vt to illuminate, light (up); (ostentar) to show off // vi (brillar) to shine; **~se** vr (irónico) to make a fool of o.s.

lucro [ˈlukro] nm profit, gain.

lucha [ˈlutʃa] nf fight, struggle; **~ de clases** class struggle; **~ libre** wrestling; **luchar** vi to fight.

luego [ˈlweɣo] ad (después) next; (más tarde) later, afterwards; **desde ~** of course.

lugar [luˈɣar] nm place; (sitio) spot; **en ~ de** instead of; **hacer ~** to make room; **fuera de ~** out of place; **tener ~** to take place; **~ común** commonplace.

lugareño, a [luɣaˈreɲo, a] a village cpd // nm/f villager.

lugarteniente [luɣarteˈnjente] nm deputy.

lúgubre [ˈluɣuβre] a mournful.

lujo [ˈluxo] nm luxury; (fig) profusion, abundance; **~so, a** a luxurious.

lujuria [luˈxurja] nf lust.

lumbre [ˈlumbre] nf (gen) light.

lumbrera [lumˈbrera] nf luminary.

luminoso, a [lumiˈnoso, a] a luminous, shining.

luna [ˈluna] nf moon; (de un espejo) glass; (de gafas) lens; (fig) crescent; **~ llena/nueva** full/new moon; **estar en la ~** to have one's head in the clouds; **~ de miel** honeymoon.

lunar [luˈnar] a lunar // nm (ANAT)

mole; **tela a ~es** spotted material.

lunes [ˈlunes] nm inv Monday.

lupa [ˈlupa] nf magnifying glass.

lustrar [lusˈtrar] vt (mueble) to polish; (zapatos) to shine; **lustre** nm polish; (fig) lustre; **dar lustre a** to polish; **lustroso, a** a shining.

luterano, a [luteˈrano, a] a Lutheran.

luto [ˈluto] nm mourning; (congoja) grief, sorrow; **llevar el o vestirse de ~** to be in mourning.

Luxemburgo [luksemˈburɣo] nm Luxembourg.

luz [luθ] (pl **luces**) nf light; **dar a ~ un niño** to give birth to a child; **sacar a la ~** to bring to light; (ELEC): **dar o encender** (Esp) o **prender** (AM)/**apagar la ~** to switch the light on/off; **a todas luces** by any reckoning; **hacer la ~ sobre** to shed light on; **tener pocas luces** to be dim o stupid; **~ roja/verde** red/green light; (AUTO): **~ de freno** brake light; **luces de tráfico** traffic lights; **traje de luces** bullfighter's costume.

LL

llaga [ˈʎaɣa] nf wound.

llama [ˈʎama] nf flame; (ZOOL) llama.

llamada [ʎaˈmaða] nf call; **~ al orden** call to order; **~ a pie de página** reference note.

llamamiento [ʎamaˈmjento] nm call.

llamar [ʎaˈmar] vt to call; (atención) to attract // vi (por teléfono) to telephone; (a la puerta) to knock/ring; (por señas) to beckon; (MIL) to call up; **~se** vr to be called, be named; **¿cómo se llama usted?** what's your name?

llamarada [ʎamaˈraða] nf (llamas) blaze; (rubor) flush; (fig) flare-up.

llamativo, a [ʎamaˈtiβo, a] a showy; (color) loud.

llamear [ʎame'ar] vi to blaze.

llano, a [ʎano, a] a (superficie) flat; (persona) straightforward; (estilo) clear // nm plain, flat ground.

llanta [ʎanta] nf (wheel) rim; (AM): ~ de goma tyre; (: cámara) inner (tube).

llanto [ʎanto] nm weeping.

llanura [ʎa'nura] nf plain.

llave [ʎaβe] nf key; (del agua) tap; (MECANICA) spanner; (de la luz) switch; (MUS) key; ~ inglesa monkey wrench; ~ maestra master key; ~ de contacto (AUTO) ignition key; ~ de paso stopcock; echar a to lock up; ~ro nm keyring; **llavín** nm latchkey.

llegada [ʎe'ɣaða] nf arrival.

llegar [ʎe'ɣar] vi to arrive; (alcanzar) to reach; (bastar) to be enough; ~se vr: ~se a to approach; ~ a to manage to, succeed in; ~ a saber to find out; ~ a ser to become; ~ a las manos de to come into the hands of.

llenar [ʎe'nar] vt to fill; (espacio) to cover; (formulario) to fill in o up; (fig) to heap.

lleno, a [ʎeno, a] a full, filled; (repleto) full up // nm (abundancia) abundance; (TEATRO) full house; dar de ~ contra un muro to hit a wall head-on.

llevadero, a [ʎeβa'ðero, a] a bearable, tolerable.

llevar [ʎe'βar] vt to take; (ropa) to wear; (cargar) to carry; (quitar) to take away; (conducir a alguien) to drive; (transportar) to transport; (traer: dinero) to carry; (conducir) to lead; (MAT) to carry; ~se vr to carry off, take away; **llevamos dos días aquí** we have been here for two days; **él me lleva 2 años** he's 2 years older than me; (COM): ~ los libros to keep the books; ~se bien to get on well (together).

llorar [ʎo'rar] vt, vi to cry, weep; ~ de risa to cry with laughter.

lloriquear [ʎorike'ar] vi to snivel,

whimper.

lloro [ʎoro] nm crying, weeping; **llorón, ona** a tearful // nm/f crybaby; ~ **sa** a (gen) weeping, tearful; (triste) sad, sorrowful.

llover [ʎo'βer] vi to rain.

llovizna [ʎo'βiθna] nf drizzle; **lloviznar** vi to drizzle.

llueve etc vb ver **llover**.

lluvia [ʎuβja] nf rain; ~ **radioactiva** radioactive fallout; **lluvioso, a** a rainy.

M

m abr (= metro) m; (= minuto) m.

macarrones [maka'rrones] nmpl macaroni sg.

macedonia [maθe'ðonja] nf: ~ de frutas fruit salad.

macerar [maθe'rar] vt to macerate.

maceta [ma'θeta] nf (de flores) pot of flowers; (para plantas) flowerpot.

macizo, a [ma'θiθo, a] a (grande) massive; (fuerte, sólido) solid // nm mass, chunk.

mácula [makula] nf stain, blemish.

machacar [matʃa'kar] vt to crush, pound // vi (insistir) to go on, keep on.

machete [ma'tʃete] nm (AM) machete, (large) knife.

machista [ma'tʃista] a, nm sexist.

macho [matʃo] a male; (fig) virile // nm male; (fig) he-man.

machucar [matʃu'kar] vt to pound.

madeja [ma'ðexa] nf (de lana) skein, hank; (de pelo) mass, mop.

madera [ma'ðera] nf wood; (fig) nature, character; **una ~** a piece of wood.

madero [ma'ðero] nm beam; (fig) ship.

madrastra [ma'ðrastra] nf stepmother.

madre [maðre] a mother cpd; (AM) tremendous // nf mother; (de vino etc) dregs pl; ~ **politica/soltera** mother-in-law/unmarried mother.

madreperla [maðre'perla] nf
mother-of-pearl.

madreselva [maðre'selβa] nf
honeysuckle.

Madrid [ma'ðrið] n Madrid.

madriguera [maðri'veɾa] nf burrow.

madrileño, a [maðri'leɲo, a] a of o
from Madrid // nm/f native of Madrid.

madrina [ma'ðrina] nf godmother;
(ARQ) prop, shore; (TEC) brace; ~
de boda bridesmaid.

madrugada [maðru'vaða] nf early
morning; (alba) dawn, daybreak.

madrugador, a [maðruva'ðor, a] a
early-rising.

madrugar [maðru'var] vi to get up
early; (fig) to get ahead.

madurar [maðu'rar] vt, vi (fruta) to
ripen; (fig) to mature; **madurez** nf
ripeness; maturity; **maduro, a** a
ripe; mature.

maestra [ma'estra] nf ver **maestro**.

maestría [maes'tria] nf mastery;
(habilidad) skill, expertise.

maestro, a [ma'estro, a] a
masterly; (perito) skilled, expert;
(principal) main; (educado) trained
// nm/f master/mistress; (profesor)
teacher // nm (autoridad) authority;
(MUS) maestro; (AM) skilled work-
man; ~ **albañil** master mason.

magia ['maxja] nf magic; **mágico, a**
a magic(al) // nm/f magician.

magisterio [maxis'terjo] nm (enseñanza) teaching; (profesión) teaching profession; (maestros) teachers
pl.

magistrado [maxis'traðo] nm
magistrate.

magistral [maxis'tral] a magisterial;
(fig) masterly.

magnánimo, a [mav'nanimo, a] a
magnanimous.

magnate [mav'nate] nm magnate,
tycoon.

magnético, a [mav'netiko, a] a
magnetic; **magnetizar** vt to
magnetize.

magnetofón [mavneto'fon] **mag-
netófono** [mavne'tofono] nm tape

recorder; **magnetofónico, a** a:
cinta magnetofónica recording
tape.

magnífico, a [mav'nifiko, a] a
splendid, magnificent.

magnitud [mavni'tuð] nf magnitude.

mago, a ['mavo, a] nm/f magician;
los Reyes M~s the Magi, the Three
Wise Men.

magro, a ['mavro, a] a (persona)
thin, lean; (carne) lean.

maguey [ma'vei] nm agave.

magullar [mavu'ʎar] vt (amoratar)
to bruise; (dañar) to damage; (fam:
golpear) to bash, beat.

mahometano, a [maome'tano, a] a
Mohammedan.

mahonesa [mao'nesa] nf =
mayonesa.

maíz [ma'iθ] nm maize (Brit), corn
(US); sweet corn.

majadero, a [maxa'ðero, a] a silly,
stupid.

majestad [maxes'tað] nf majesty;
majestuoso, a a majestic.

majo, a ['maxo, a] a nice; (guapo)
attractive, good-looking; (elegante)
smart.

mal [mal] ad badly; (equi-
vocadamente) wrongly; (con
dificultad) with difficulty // a = **malo**
// nm evil; (desgracia) misfortune;
(daño) harm, damage; (MED) illness; **¡menos ~!** just as well!; ~
que bien rightly or wrongly.

malabarismo [malaβa'rismo] nm
juggling; **malabarista** nm/f juggler.

malaconsejado, a [malakonse-
'xaðo, a] a ill-advised.

malaria [ma'larja] nf malaria.

malcriado, a [mal'krjaðo, a] a (con-
sentido) spoiled.

maldad [mal'dað] nf evil, wickedness.

maldecir [malde'θir] vt to curse // vi:
~ **de** to speak ill of.

maldición [maldi'θjon] nf curse.

maldito, a [mal'dito, a] a (condenado) damned; (perverso) wicked;
¡~ sea! damn it!

maleante [male'ante] *a* wicked // *nm/f* malefactor.

malecón [male'kon] *nm* pier, jetty.

maledicencia [maleδi'θenθja] *nf* slander, scandal.

maleducado, a [maleδu'kaδo, a] *a* bad-mannered, rude.

maleficio [male'fiθjo] *nm* curse, spell.

malestar [males'tar] *nm* (*gen*) discomfort; (*fig: inquietud*) uneasiness; (*POL*) unrest.

maleta [ma'leta] *nf* case, suitcase; (*AUTO*) boot (*Brit*), trunk (*US*); **maletera** *nf* (*AM AUTO*) = **maletero**; **maletero** *nm* (*AUTO*) boot (*Brit*), trunk (*US*); **maletín** *nm* small case, bag.

malévolo, a [ma'leβolo, a] *a* malicious, spiteful.

maleza [ma'leθa] *nf* (*hierbas malas*) weeds *pl*; (*arbustos*) thicket.

malgastar [malɣas'tar] *vt* (*tiempo, dinero*) to waste; (*salud*) to ruin.

malhechor, a [male'tʃor, a] *nm/f* malefactor; (*criminal*) criminal.

malhumorado, a [malumo'raδo, a] *a* bad-tempered, cross.

malicia [ma'liθja] *nf* (*maldad*) wickedness; (*astucia*) slyness, guile; (*mala intención*) malice, spite; (*carácter travieso*) mischievousness; **malicioso, a** *a* wicked, evil; sly, crafty; malicious, spiteful; mischievous.

maligno, a [ma'liɣno, a] *a* evil; (*malévolo*) malicious; (*MED*) malignant.

malo, a ['malo, a] *a* bad; (*falso*) false // *nm/f* villain // *nm* spell of bad luck; **estar** ~ to be ill; **estar de malas** (*de mal humor*) to be in a bad mood.

malograr [malo'ɣrar] *vt* to spoil; (*plan*) to upset; (*ocasión*) to waste; **~se** *vr* (*plan etc*) to fail, come to grief; (*persona*) to die before one's time.

malparado, a [malpa'raδo, a] *a*: **salir** ~ to come off badly.

malparir [malpa'rir] *vi* to have a miscarriage.

malsano, a [mal'sano, a] *a* unhealthy.

Malta ['malta] *nf* Malta.

malteada [malte'aδa] *nf* (*AM*) milk shake.

maltratar [maltra'tar] *vt* to ill-treat, mistreat.

maltrecho, a [mal'tretʃo, a] *a* battered, damaged.

malvado, a [mal'βaδo, a] *a* evil, villainous.

malvavisco [malβa'βisko] *nm* marshmallow.

malversar [malβer'sar] *vt* to embezzle, misappropriate.

Malvinas [mal'βinas]: **Islas** ~ *nfpl* Falkland Islands.

malla ['maʎa] *nf* (*red*) mesh; (*de baño*) swimsuit; (*de ballet, gimnasia*) leotard; ~**s** *nfpl* tights; ~ **de alambre** wire mesh.

Mallorca [ma'ʎorka] *nf* Majorca.

mama ['mama] *nf* (*de animal*) teat; (*de mujer*) breast.

mamá [ma'ma] *nf* (*pl* ~**s**) *nf* (*fam*) mum, mummy.

mamar [ma'mar] *vt* (*pecho*) to suck; (*fig*) to absorb, assimilate // *vi* to suck.

mamarracho [mama'rratʃo] *nm* sight, mess.

mamífero [ma'mifero] *nm* mammal.

mampara [mam'para] *nf* (*entre habitaciones*) partition; (*biombo*) screen.

mampostería [mamposte'ria] *nf* masonry.

mamut [ma'mut] (*pl* ~**s**) *nm* mammoth.

manada [ma'naδa] *nf* (*ZOOL*) herd; (: *de leones*) pride; (: *de lobos*) pack.

Managua [ma'naɣwa] *nf* Managua.

manantial [manan'tjal] *nm* spring; (*fuente*) fountain; (*fig*) source.

manar [ma'nar] *vt* to run with, flow with // *vi* to run, flow; (*abundar*) to abound.

mancilla [man'θiʎa] *nf* stain, blemish.

manco, a ['manko, a] *a (de un brazo)* one-armed; *(de una mano)* one-handed; *(fig)* defective, faulty.

mancomunar [mankomu'nar] *vt* to unite, bring together; *(recursos)* to pool; *(JUR)* to make jointly responsible; **mancomunidad** *nf* union, association; *(comunidad)* community; *(JUR)* joint responsibility.

mancha ['mantʃa] *nf* stain, mark; *(ZOOL)* patch; *(boceto)* sketch, outline; **manchar** *vt (gen)* to stain, mark; *(ensuciar)* to soil.

manchego, a [man'tʃeɣo, a] *a* of o from La Mancha.

mandado [man'daðo] *nm (orden)* order; *(comisión)* commission, errand.

mandamiento [manda'mjento] *nm (orden)* order, command; *(REL)* commandment; ~ **judicial** warrant.

mandar [man'dar] *vt (ordenar)* to order; *(dirigir)* to lead, command; *(enviar)* to send; *(pedir)* to order, ask for // *vi* to be in charge; *(pey)* to be bossy; ¿**mande**? pardon?, excuse me?; ~ **hacer un traje** to have a suit made.

mandarín [manda'rin] *nm* mandarin.

mandarina [manda'rina] *nf (fruta)* tangerine, mandarin (orange).

mandatario, a [manda'tarjo, a] *nm/f (representante)* agent; *(AM: líder)* leader.

mandato [man'dato] *nm (orden)* order; *(INFORM)* command; *(POL: período)* term of office; *(: territorio)* mandate; ~ **judicial** (search) warrant.

mandíbula [man'diβula] *nf* jaw.

mandil [man'dil] *nm (delantal)* apron.

mando ['mando] *nm (MIL)* command; *(de país)* rule; *(el primer lugar)* lead; *(POL)* term of office; *(TEC)* control; ~ **a la izquierda** left-hand drive.

mandolina [mando'lina] *nf* mandolin(e).

mandón, ona [man'don, ona] *a* bossy, domineering.

manejable [mane'xaβle] *a* manageable.

manejar [mane'xar] *vt* to manage; *(máquina)* to work, operate; *(caballo etc)* to handle; *(casa)* to run, manage; *(AM: AUTO)* to drive; ~**se** *vr (comportarse)* to act, behave; *(arreglárselas)* to manage; **manejo** *nm* management; handling; running; driving; *(facilidad de trato)* ease, confidence; **manejos** *nmpl* intrigues.

manera [ma'nera] *nf* way, manner, fashion; ~**s** *nfpl (modales)* manners; **su** ~ **de ser** the way he is; *(aire)* his manner; **de ninguna** ~ no way, by no means; **de otra** ~ otherwise; **de todas** ~**s** at any rate; **no hay** ~ **de persuadirle** there's no way of convincing him.

manga ['manga] *nf (de camisa)* sleeve; *(de riego)* hose.

mangana [man'gana] *nf* lasso.

mango ['mango] *nm* handle; *(BOT)* mango.

mangonear [mangone'ar] *vi (meterse)* to meddle, interfere; *(ser mandón)* to boss people about.

manguera [man'gera] *nf (de riego)* hose; *(tubo)* pipe.

maní [ma'ni] *nm (AM)* peanut.

manía [ma'nia] *nf (MED)* mania; *(fig: moda)* rage, craze; *(disgusto)* dislike; *(malicia)* spite; **maníaco, a** *a* maniac(al) // *nm/f* maniac.

maniatar [manja'tar] *vt* to tie the hands of.

maniático, a [ma'njatiko, a] *a* maniac(al) // *nm/f* maniac.

manicomio [mani'komjo] *nm* mental hospital *(Brit)*, insane asylum *(US)*.

manicura [mani'kura] *nf* manicure.

manifestación [manifesta'θjon] *nf (declaración)* statement, declaration; *(de emoción)* show, display; *(POL: desfile)* demonstration; *(: concentración)* mass meeting.

manifestar [manifes'tar] *vt* to show, manifest; (*declarar*) to state, declare; **manifiesto, a** *a* clear, manifest // *nm* manifesto.

manija [ma'nixa] *nf* handle.

maniobra [ma'njoβra] *nf* manœuvring; (*manejo*) handling; (*fig*) manœuvre; (*estratagema*) stratagem; ~**s** *nfpl* manœuvres; **maniobrar** *vt* to manœuvre; (*manejar*) to handle.

manipulación [manipula'θjon] *nf* manipulation; **manipular** *vt* to manipulate; (*manejar*) to handle.

maniquí [mani'ki] *nm* dummy // *nm/f* model.

manirroto, a [mani'rroto, a] *a* lavish, extravagant // *nm/f* spendthrift.

manivela [mani'βela] *nf* crank.

manjar [man'xar] *nm* (tasty) dish.

mano ['mano] *nf* hand; (*ZOOL*) foot, paw; (*de pintura*) coat; (*serie*) lot, series; **a** ~ by hand; **a** ~ **derecha/izquierda** on the right(-hand side)/left(-hand side); **de primera** ~ (at) first hand; **de segunda** ~ (at) second hand; **robo a** ~ **armada** armed robbery; ~ **de obra** labour, manpower; **estrechar la** ~ **a uno** to shake sb's hand.

manojo [ma'noxo] *nm* handful, bunch; ~ **de llaves** bunch of keys.

manopla [ma'nopla] *nf* (*guante*) glove; (*paño*) face cloth.

manoseado, a [mano'seaðo, a] *a* well-worn; **manosear** *vt* (*tocar*) to handle, touch; (*desordenar*) to mess up, rumple; (*insistir en*) to overwork; (*AM*) to caress, fondle.

manotazo [mano'taðo] *nm* slap, smack.

mansalva [man'salβa]: **a** ~ *ad* indiscriminately.

mansedumbre [manse'ðumbre] *nf* gentleness, meekness.

mansión [man'sjon] *nf* mansion.

manso, a ['manso, a] *a* gentle, mild; (*animal*) tame.

manta ['manta] *nf* blanket; (*AM*: *poncho*) poncho.

manteca [man'teka] *nf* fat; ~ **de cacahuete/cacao** peanut/cocoa butter; ~ **de cerdo** lard.

mantecado [mante'kaðo] *nm* (*AM*) ice cream.

mantel [man'tel] *nm* tablecloth.

mantendré *etc vb ver* **mantener.**

mantener [mante'ner] *vt* to support, maintain; (*alimentar*) to sustain; (*conservar*) to keep; (*TEC*) to maintain, service; ~**se** *vr* (*seguir de pie*) to be still standing; (*no ceder*) to hold one's ground; (*subsistir*) to sustain o.s., keep going; **mantenimiento** *nm* maintenance; sustenance; (*sustento*) support.

mantequilla [mante'kiʎa] *nf* butter.

mantilla [man'tiʎa] *nf* mantilla; ~**s** *nfpl* baby clothes.

manto ['manto] *nm* (*capa*) cloak; (*de ceremonia*) robe, gown.

mantón [man'ton] *nm* shawl.

mantuve, mantuviera *etc vb ver* **mantener.**

manual [ma'nwal] *a* manual // *nm* manual, handbook.

manufactura [manufak'tura] *nf* manufacture; (*fábrica*) factory.

manuscrito, a [manus'krito, a] *a* handwritten // *nm* manuscript.

manutención [manuten'θjon] *nf* maintenance; (*sustento*) support.

manzana [man'θana] *nf* apple; (*ARQ*) block (of houses).

manzanilla [manθa'niʎa] *nf* (*planta*) camomile; (*infusión*) camomile tea; (*vino de jerez*) manzanilla sherry.

manzano [man'θano] *nm* apple tree.

maña ['mana] *nf* (*gen*) skill, dexterity; (*pey*) guile; (*costumbre*) habit; (*destreza*) trick, knack.

mañana [ma'nana] *ad* tomorrow // *nm* future // *nf* morning; **de** *o* **por la** ~ **in the morning;** **¡hasta** ~! see you tomorrow!; ~ **por la** ~ tomorrow morning; **mañanero, a** *a* early-rising.

mañoso, a [ma'noso, a] *a* (*hábil*) skilful; (*astuto*) smart, clever.

mapa ['mapa] *nm* map.

maqueta [ma'keta] nf (scale) model.

maquillaje [maki'ʎaxe] nm make-up; (acto) making up.

maquillar [maki'ʎar] vt to make up; ~se vr to put on (some) make-up.

máquina ['makina] nf machine; (de tren) locomotive, engine; (FOTO) camera; (fig) machinery; (: proyecto) plan, project; escrito a ~ typewritten; ~ de escribir typewriter; ~ de coser/lavar sewing/washing machine.

maquinación [makina'θjon] nf machination, plot.

maquinal [maki'nal] a (fig) mechanical, automatic.

maquinaria [maki'narja] nf (máquinas) machinery; (mecanismo) mechanism, works pl.

maquinilla [maki'niʎa] nf: ~ de afeitar razor.

maquinista [maki'nista] nm/f (de tren) engine driver; (TEC) operator; (NAUT) engineer.

mar [mar] nm o f sea; ~ adentro o afuera out at sea; en alta ~ on the high seas; la ~ de (fam) lots of; el M~ Negro/Báltico the Black/Baltic Sea.

maraña [ma'raɲa] nf (maleza) thicket; (confusión) tangle.

maravilla [mara'βiʎa] nf marvel, wonder; (BOT) marigold; **maravillar** vt to astonish, amaze; **maravillarse** vr to be astonished, be amazed; **maravilloso, a** a wonderful, marvellous.

marca ['marka] nf (gen) mark; (sello) stamp; (COM) make, brand; de ~ excellent, outstanding; ~ de fábrica trademark; ~ registrada registered trademark.

marcado, a [mar'kaðo, a] a marked, strong.

marcador [marka'ðor] nm (DEPORTE) scoreboard; (: persona) scorer.

marcar [mar'kar] vt to mark; (número de teléfono) to dial; (gol) to score; (números) to record, keep a tally of; (pelo) to set // vi

(DEPORTE) to score; (TEL) to dial.

marcial [mar'θjal] a martial, military.

marciano, a [mar'θjano, a] a Martian.

marco ['marko] nm frame; (DEPORTE) goal-posts pl; (moneda) mark; (fig) framework; ~ de chimenea mantelpiece.

marcha ['martʃa] nf march; (TEC) running, working; (AUTO) gear; (velocidad) speed; (fig) progress; (dirección) course; poner en ~ to put into gear; (fig) to set in motion, get going; dar ~ atrás to reverse, put into reverse; estar en ~ to be under way, be in motion.

marchar [mar'tʃar] vi (ir) to go; (funcionar) to work, go; ~se vr to go (away), leave.

marchitar [martʃi'tar] vt to wither, dry up; ~se vr (BOT) to wither; (fig) to fade away; **marchito, a** a withered, faded; (fig) in decline.

marea [ma'rea] nf tide; (llovizna) drizzle.

marear [mare'ar] vt (fig) to annoy, upset; (MED): ~ a uno to make sb feel sick; ~se vr (tener náuseas) to feel sick; (desvanecerse) to feel faint; (aturdirse) to feel dizzy; (fam: emborracharse) to get tipsy.

maremoto [mare'moto] nm tidal wave.

mareo [ma'reo] nm (náusea) sick feeling; (aturdimiento) dizziness; (fam: lata) nuisance.

marfil [mar'fil] nm ivory.

margarina [marɣa'rina] nf margarine.

margarita [marɣa'rita] nf (BOT) daisy; (rueda) ~ daisywheel.

margen ['marxen] nm (borde) edge, border; (fig) margin, space // nf (de río etc) bank; dar ~ para to give an opportunity for; mantenerse al ~ to keep out (of things).

marica [ma'rika] nm (fam) sissy.

maricón [mari'kon] nm (fam) queer.

marido [ma'riðo] nm husband.

mariguana [mari'ɣwana], **mariuana** [mari'wana] nf marijuana, cannabis.

marimacho [mari'matʃo] nm (fam) mannish woman.

marina [ma'rina] nf navy; ~ **mercante** merchant navy.

marinero, a [mari'nero, a] a sea cpd; (barco) seaworthy // nm sailor, seaman.

marino, a [ma'rino, a] a sea cpd, marine // nm sailor.

marioneta [marjo'neta] nf puppet.

mariposa [mari'posa] nf butterfly.

mariquita [mari'kita] nf ladybird (Brit), ladybug (US).

mariscos [ma'riskos] nmpl shellfish inv, seafood(s).

marisma [ma'risma] nf marsh, swamp.

marítimo, a [ma'ritimo, a] a sea cpd, maritime.

marmita [mar'mita] nf pot.

mármol ['marmol] nm marble.

marqués, esa [mar'kes, esa] nm/f marquis/marchioness.

marrón [ma'rron] a brown.

marroquí [marro'ki] a, nm/f Moroccan // nm Morocco (leather).

Marruecos [ma'rrwekos] nm Morocco.

martes ['martes] nm inv Tuesday.

martillar [marti'ʎar] vt to hammer.

martillo [mar'tiʎo] nm hammer; ~ **neumático** pneumatic drill (Brit), jackhammer.

mártir ['martir] nm/f martyr; **martirio** nm martyrdom; (fig) torture, torment.

marxismo [mark'sismo] nm Marxism; **marxista** a, nm/f Marxist.

marzo ['marθo] nm March.

mas [mas] conj but.

PALABRA CLAVE

más [mas] ◆ a, ad 1: ~ (que, de) (comparativo) more (than), ...+ est (than); ~ **grande/inteligente** bigger/more intelligent; **trabaja ~ (que yo)** he works more (than me); ver tb **cada**

2 (superlativo): **el ~** the most, ...+ est; **el ~ grande/inteligente (de)** the biggest/most intelligent (in)

3 (negativo): **no tengo ~ dinero** I haven't got any more money; **no viene ~ por aquí** he doesn't come round here any more

4 (adicional): **no le veo ~ solución que ...** I see no other solution than to ...; **¿quién ~?** anybody else?

5 (+ a: valor intensivo): **¡qué perro ~ sucio!** what a filthy dog!; **¡es ~ tonto!** he's so stupid!

6 (locuciones): ~ **o menos** more or less; **los ~** most people; **es ~** furthermore; **¡ni ~ ni menos!** no less!; **¡qué ~ da!** what does it matter!; ver tb **no**

7: **por ~: por ~ que te esfuerces** no matter how hard you try; **por ~ que quisiera ...** much as I should like to ...

8: **de ~: veo que aquí estoy de ~** I can see I'm not needed here; **tenemos uno de ~** we've got one extra

◆ prep: **2 ~ 2 son 4** 2 and 2 plus 2 are 4

◆ nm: **este trabajo tiene sus ~ y sus menos** this job's got its good points and its bad points.

---

masa ['masa] nf (mezcla) dough; (volumen) volume, mass; (FÍSICA) mass; **en ~** en masse; **las ~s** (POL) the masses.

masacre [ma'sakre] nf massacre.

masaje [ma'saxe] nm massage.

mascar [mas'kar] vt to chew; (fig) to mumble, mutter.

máscara ['maskara] nf (gen) mask // nm/f masked person; **mascarada** nf masquerade; **mascarilla** nf (de belleza, MED) mask.

masculino, a [masku'lino, a] a masculine; (BIO) male.

mascullar [masku'ʎar] vt to mumble, mutter.

masilla [ma'siʎa] nf putty.

masivo, a [ma'siβo, a] a (en masa) mass, en masse.

masón [ma'son] *nm* (free)mason.

masoquista [maso'kista] *nmf* masochist.

masticar [masti'kar] *vt* to chew; (*fig*) to ponder.

mástil ['mastil] *nm* (*de navío*) mast; (*de guitarra*) neck.

mastín [mas'tin] *nm* mastiff.

masturbación [masturβa'θjon] *nf* masturbation; **masturbarse** *vr* to masturbate.

mata ['mata] *nf* (*arbusto*) bush, shrub; (*de hierba*) tuft.

matadero [mata'ðero] *nm* slaughterhouse, abattoir.

matador, a [mata'ðor, a] *a* killing // *nm/f* killer // *nm* (*TAUR*) matador, bullfighter.

matamoscas [mata'moskas] *nm inv* (*palo*) fly swat.

matanza [ma'tanθa] *nf* (*de personas*) slaughter, killing; (*de animales*) slaughter(ing).

matar [ma'tar] *vt, vi* to kill; **~se** *vr* (*suicidarse*) to kill o.s., commit suicide; (*morir*) to be o get killed; **~ el hambre** to stave off hunger.

matasellos [mata'seʎos] *nm inv* postmark.

mate ['mate] *a* (*sin brillo: color*) dull, matt // *nm* (*en ajedrez*) (check)mate; (*AM: hierba*) maté; (: *vasija*) gourd.

matemáticas [mate'matikas] *nfpl* mathematics; **matemático, a** *a* mathematical // *nm/f* mathematician.

materia [ma'terja] *nf* (*gen*) matter; (*TEC*) material; (*ESCOL*) subject; **en ~ de** on the subject of; **~ prima** raw material; **material** *a* material; (*dolor*) physical // *nm* material; (*TEC*) equipment; **materialismo** *nm* materialism; **materialista** *a* materialist(ic); **materialmente** *ad* materially; (*fig*) absolutely.

maternal [mater'nal] *a* motherly, maternal.

maternidad [materni'ðað] *nf* motherhood, maternity; **materno, a** *a* maternal; (*lengua*) mother *cpd*.

matinal [mati'nal] *a* morning *cpd*.

matiz [ma'tiθ] *nm* shade; **~ar** *vt* (*dar tonos de*) to tinge, tint; (*variar*) to vary; (*ARTE*) to blend.

matón [ma'ton] *nm* bully.

matorral [mato'rral] *nm* thicket.

matraca [ma'traka] *nf* rattle.

matrícula [ma'trikula] *nf* (*registro*) register; (*AUTO*) registration number; (: *placa*) number plate; **matricular** *vt* to register, enrol.

matrimonial [matrimo'njal] *a* matrimonial.

matrimonio [matri'monjo] *nm* (*pareja*) (married) couple; (*unión*) marriage.

matriz [ma'triθ] *nf* (*ANAT*) womb; (*TEC*) mould; **casa ~** (*COM*) head office.

matrona [ma'trona] *nf* (*persona de edad*) matron.

maullar [mau'ʎar] *vi* to mew, miaow.

mausoleo [mauso'leo] *nm* mausoleum.

maxilar [maksi'lar] *nm* jaw(bone).

máxima ['maksima] *ver* **máximo**.

máxime ['maksime] *ad* especially.

máximo, a ['maksimo, a] *a* maximum; (*más alto*) highest; (*más grande*) greatest // *nm* maximum // *nf* maxim.

mayo ['majo] *nm* May.

mayonesa [majo'nesa] *nf* mayonnaise.

mayor [ma'jor] *a* main, chief; (*adulto*) adult; (*de edad avanzada*) elderly; (*MUS*) major; (*comparativo: de tamaño*) bigger; (: *de edad*) older; (*superlativo: de tamaño*) biggest; (: *de edad*) oldest // *nm* chief, boss; (*adulto*) adult; **al por ~** wholesale; **~ de edad** adult; **~es** *nmpl* (*antepasados*) ancestors.

mayoral [majo'ral] *nm* foreman.

mayordomo [major'ðomo] *nm* butler.

mayoría [majo'ria] *nf* majority, greater part.

mayorista [majo'rista] *nm/f* wholesaler.

mayúsculo, a [ma'juskulo, a] *a* (*fig*) big, tremendous // *nf* capital (letter).

mazapán [maθa'pan] *nm* marzipan.

mazo ['maθo] *nm* (*martillo*) mallet; (*de flores*) bunch; (*DEPORTE*) bat.

me [me] *pron* (*directo*) me; (*indirecto*) (to) me; (*reflexivo*) (to) myself; **¡dámelo!** give it to me!

mear [me'ar] *vi* (*fam*) to pee, piss.

mecánico, a [me'kaniko, a] *a* mechanical // *nmf* mechanic // *nf* (*estudio*) mechanics *sg*; (*mecanismo*) mechanism.

mecanismo [meka'nismo] *nm* mechanism; (*marcha*) gear.

mecanografía [mekanoɣra'fia] *nf* typewriting; **mecanógrafo, a** *nmf* typist.

mecate [me'kate] *nm* (*AM*) rope.

mecedora [meθe'ðora] *nf* rocking chair.

mecer [me'θer] *vt* (*cuna*) to rock; **~se** *vr* to rock; (*ramo*) to sway.

mecha ['metʃa] *nf* (*de vela*) wick; (*de bomba*) fuse.

mechero [me'tʃero] *nm* (cigarette) lighter.

mechón [me'tʃon] *nm* (*gen*) tuft; (*manojo*) bundle; (*de pelo*) lock.

medalla [me'ðaʎa] *nf* medal.

media ['meðja] *nf* ver **medio**.

mediado, a [me'ðjaðo, a] *a* half-full; (*trabajo*) half-complete; **a ~s de** in the middle of, halfway through.

mediano, a [me'ðjano, a] *a* (*regular*) medium, average; (*mediocre*) mediocre.

medianoche [meðja'notʃe] *nf* midnight.

mediante [me'ðjante] *ad* by (means of), through.

mediar [me'ðjar] *vi* (*interceder*) to mediate, intervene.

medicación [meðika'θjon] *nf* medication, treatment.

medicamento [meðika'mento] *nm* medicine, drug.

medicina [meði'θina] *nf* medicine.

medición [meði'θjon] *nf* measurement.

médico, a ['meðiko, a] *a* medical // *nmf* doctor.

medida [me'ðiða] *nf* measure; (*medición*) measurement; (*prudencia*) moderation, prudence; **en cierta/gran ~** up to a point/to a great extent; **un traje a ~** made-to-measure suit; **~ de cuello** collar size; **a ~ de** in proportion to; (*de acuerdo con*) in keeping with; **a ~ que** (*conforme*) as.

medio, a ['meðjo, a] *a* half (a); (*punto*) mid, middle; (*promedio*) average // *ad* half // *nm* (*centro*) middle, centre; (*promedio*) average; (*método*) means, way; (*ambiente*) environment // *nf* (*Esp: prenda de vestir*) stocking; (*AM: prenda de vestir*) sock; (*promedio*) average; **~s** *nmpl* means, resources; **~ litro** half a litre; **las tres y media** half past three; **M~ Oriente** Middle East; **a ~ terminar** half finished; **pagar a medias** to share the cost.

mediocre [me'ðjokre] *a* middling, average; (*pey*) mediocre.

mediodía [meðjo'ðia] *nm* midday, noon.

medir [me'ðir] *vt, vi* (*gen*) to measure.

meditar [meði'tar] *vt* to ponder, think over, meditate (on); (*planear*) to think out.

mediterráneo, a [meðite'rraneo, a] *a* Mediterranean // *nm*: **el M~** the Mediterranean.

médula ['meðula] *nf* (*ANAT*) marrow; **~ espinal** spinal cord.

medusa [me'ðusa] *nf* (*Esp*) jellyfish.

megáfono [me'ɣafono] *nm* megaphone.

megalómano, a [meɣa'lomano, a] *nm/f* megalomaniac.

mejicano, a [mexi'kano, a] *a, nm/f* Mexican.

Méjico ['mexiko] *nm* Mexico.

mejilla [me'xiʎa] *nf* cheek.

mejillón [mexi'ʎon] *nm* mussel.

mejor [me'xor] *a, ad* (*comparativo*) better; (*superlativo*) best; **a lo ~**

probably; (*quizá*) maybe; ~ **dicho**
rather; **tanto** ~ so much the better.

mejora [me'xora] *nf* improvement.

mejorar *vt* to improve, make better
// *vi*, **mejorarse** *vr* to improve, get
better.

melancólico, a [melan'koliko, a] *a*
(*triste*) sad, melancholy; (*soñador*)
dreamy.

melena [me'lena] *nf* (*de persona*)
long hair; (*ZOOL*) mane.

melocotón [meloko'ton] (*Esp*)
peach.

melodía [melo'ðia] *nf* melody, tune.

melodrama [melo'ðrama] *nm*
melodrama; **melodramático, a** *a*
melodramatic.

melón [me'lon] *nm* melon.

meloso, a [me'loso, a] *a* honeyed,
sweet.

mellizo, a [me'ʎiθo, a] *a, nm/f* twin;
~**s** *nmpl* (*AM*) cufflinks.

membrete [mem'brete] *nm* letter-
head.

membrillo [mem'briʎo] *nm* quince;
carne de ~ quince jelly.

memorable [memo'raßle] *a* memorable.

memorándum [memo'randum] (*pl*
~**s**) *nm* (*libro*) notebook; (*comunicación*) memorandum.

memoria [me'morja] *nf* (*gen*)
memory; ~**s** *nfpl* (*de carácter*)
memoirs; ~ **intermedia** (*INFORM*)
buffer; **memorizar** *vt* to memorize.

menaje [me'naxe] *nm*: ~ **de cocina**
kitchenware.

mencionar [menθjo'nar] *vt* to mention.

mendigar [mendi'yar] *vt* to beg
(for).

mendigo, a [men'diyo, a] *nm/f*
beggar.

mendrugo [men'druyo] *nm* crust.

menear [mene'ar] *vt* to move; (*fig*)
to handle; ~**se** *vr* to shake;
(*balancearse*) to sway; (*moverse*) to
move; (*fig*) to get a move on.

menester [menes'ter] *nm* (*necesidad*) necessity; ~**es** *nmpl* (*de-*

beres) duties; **es** ~ it is necessary.

menestra [me'nestra] *nf*: ~ **de
verduras** vegetable stew.

menguante [men'gwante] *a* decreas-
ing, diminishing; **menguar** *vt* to
lessen, diminish; (*fig*) to discredit //
vi to diminish, decrease; (*fig*) to decline.

menopausia [meno'pausja] *nf*
menopause.

menor [me'nor] *a* (*más pequeño*:
comparativo) smaller; (: *superlativo*) smallest; (*más joven*:
comparativo) younger; (: *superlativo*) youngest; (*MUS*) minor // *nm/f*
(*joven*) young person, juvenile; **no
tengo la** ~ **idea** I haven't the faint-
est idea; **al por** ~ retail; ~ **de edad**
person under age.

Menorca [me'norka] *nf* Minorca.

menoría [meno'ria] *nf*: **a** ~ (*AM*)
retail.

menos [menos] ♦ *a* 1: ~ (**que, de**)
(*comparativo*: *cantidad*) less (than);
(: *número*) fewer (than); **con** ~
entusiasmo with less enthusiasm; ~
gente fewer people; *ver tb* **cada**
2 (*superlativo*): **es el que** ~ **culpa**
tiene he is the least to blame
♦ *ad* 1 (*comparativo*): ~ (**que, de**)
less (than); **me gusta** ~ **que el
otro** I like it less than the other one
2 (*superlativo*): **es la** ~ **lista** (**de
su clase**) she's the least bright in
her class; **de todas ellas es la que**
~ **me agrada** out of all of them
she's the one I like least; (**por**) **lo** ~
at (the very) least
3 (*locuciones*): **no quiero verle y** ~
visitarle I don't want to see him let
alone visit him; **tenemos 7 de** ~
we're seven short
♦ *prep* except; (*cifras*) minus;
todos ~ **él** everyone except (for)
him; **5** ~ **2 5 minus 2**
♦ *conj*: **a** ~ **que: a** ~ **que venga
mañana** unless he comes tomorrow.

menoscabar [menoska'βar] *vt* (*estropear*) to damage, harm; (*fig*) to discredit.

menospreciar [menospre'θjar] *vt* to underrate, undervalue; (*despreciar*) to scorn, despise.

mensaje [men'saxe] *nm* message; **~ro, a** *nm/f* messenger.

menstruación [menstrua'θjon] *nf* menstruation.

menstruar [mens'trwar] *vi* to menstruate.

mensual [men'swal] *a* monthly; **1000 ptas ~es** 1000 ptas a month; **~idad** *nf* (*salario*) monthly salary; (*COM*) monthly payment, monthly instalment.

menta ['menta] *nf* mint.

mental [men'tal] *a* mental; **~idad** *nf* mentality.

mentar [men'tar] *vt* to mention, name.

mente ['mente] *nf* mind.

mentecato, a [mente'kato, a] *a* silly, stupid // *nm/f* fool, idiot.

mentir [men'tir] *vi* to lie.

mentira [men'tira] *nf* (*una*) lie; (*acto*) lying; (*invención*) fiction; **parece ~ que...** it seems incredible that..., I can't believe that....

mentiroso, a [menti'roso, a] *a* lying // *nm/f* liar.

menú [me'nu] (*pl* **~s**) *nm* menu; (*AM*) set meal.

menudo, a [me'nuðo, a] *a* (*pequeño*) small, tiny; (*sin importancia*) petty, insignificant; **¡~ negocio!** (*fam*) some deal!; **a ~** often, frequently.

meñique [me'ɲike] *nm* little finger.

meollo [me'oʎo] *nm* (*fig*) core.

mercadería [merkaðe'ria] *nf* commodity; **~s** *nfpl* goods, merchandise *sg*.

mercado [mer'kaðo] *nm* market; **M~ Común** Common Market.

mercancía [merkan'θia] *nf* commodity; **~s** *nfpl* goods, merchandise *sg*.

mercantil [merkan'til] *a* mercantile,

commercial.

mercenario, a [merθe'narjo, a] *a*, *nm* mercenary.

mercería [merθe'ria] *nf* haberdashery (*Brit*), notions (*US*); (*tienda*) haberdasher's (*Brit*), notions store (*US*); (*AM*) drapery.

mercurio [mer'kurjo] *nm* mercury.

merecer [mere'θer] *vt* to deserve, merit // *vi* to be deserving, be worthy; **merece la pena** it's worthwhile; **merecido, a** *a* (*well*) deserved; **llevar su merecido** to get one's deserts.

merendar [meren'dar] *vt* to have for tea // *vi* to have tea; (*en el campo*) to have a picnic.

merengue [me'renge] *nm* meringue.

meridiano [meri'ðjano] *nm* (*GEO*) meridian.

merienda [me'rjenda] *nf* (*light*) tea, afternoon snack; (*de campo*) picnic.

mérito ['merito] *nm* merit; (*valor*) worth, value.

merluza [mer'luθa] *nf* hake.

merma ['merma] *nf* decrease; (*pérdida*) wastage; **mermar** *vt* to reduce, lessen // *vi* to decrease, dwindle.

mermelada [merme'laða] *nf* jam.

mero, a ['mero, a] *a* mere; (*AM*: *fam*) very.

mes [mes] *nm* month; (*salario*) month's pay.

mesa ['mesa] *nf* table; (*de trabajo*) desk; (*GEO*) plateau; (*ARQ*) landing; **~ directiva** board; **~ redonda** (*reunión*) round table; **poner/quitar la ~** to lay/clear the table; **mesero, a** *nm/f* (*AM*) waiter/waitress.

meseta [me'seta] *nf* (*GEO*) meseta, tableland; (*ARQ*) landing.

mesilla [me'siʎa], **mesita** [me'sita] *nf*: **~ (de noche)** bedside table.

mesón [me'son] *nm* inn.

mestizo, a [mes'tiθo, a] *a* half-caste, of mixed race; (*ZOOL*) crossbred // *nm/f* half-caste.

mesura [me'sura] *nf* (*moderación*) moderation, restraint; (*cortesía*) courtesy.

meta ['meta] *nf* goal; (*de carrera*) finish.

metáfora [me'tafora] *nf* metaphor.

metal [me'tal] *nm* (*materia*) metal; (*MUS*) brass; **metálico, a** *a* metallic; (*de metal*) metal // (*dinero contante*) cash.

metalurgia [meta'lurxja] *nf* metallurgy.

meteoro [mete'oro] *nm* meteor.

meter [me'ter] *vt* (*colocar*) to put, place; (*introducir*) to put in, insert; (*involucrar*) to involve; (*causar*) to make, cause; ~**se** *vr*: ~**se en** to go into, enter; (*fig*) to interfere in, meddle in; ~**se a** to start; ~**se a escritor** to become a writer; ~**se con uno** to provoke sb, pick a quarrel with sb.

meticuloso, a [metiku'loso, a] *a* meticulous, thorough.

metódico, a [me'toðiko, a] *a* methodical.

metodismo [meto'ðismo] *nm* Methodism.

método ['metoðo] *nm* method.

metralleta [metra'ʎeta] *nf* submachine-gun.

métrico, a ['metriko, a] *a* metric.

metro ['metro] *nm* metre; (*tren*) underground (*Brit*), subway (*US*).

México ['mexiko] *nm* Mexico; **Ciudad de ~** Mexico City.

mezcla ['meθkla] *nf* mixture; **mezclar** *vt* to mix (up); **mezclarse** *vr* to mix, mingle; **mezclarse en** to get mixed up in, get involved in.

mezquino, a [meθ'kino, a] *a* (*cicatero*) mean.

mezquita [meθ'kita] *nf* mosque.

mg. *abr* (= *miligramo*) mg.

mi [mi] *adjetivo posesivo* my // *nm* (*MUS*) E.

mí [mi] *pron* me; myself.

miaja ['mjaxa] *nf* crumb.

micro ['mikro] *nm* (*AM*) minibus.

microbio [mi'kroβjo] *nm* microbe.

microbús [mikro'βus] *nm* minibus.

micrófono [mi'krofono] *nm* micro-

phone.

microordenador [mikro(o)rðena-'ðor] *nm* microcomputer.

microscopio [mikro'skopjo] *nm* microscope.

miedo ['mjeðo] *nm* fear; (*nerviosismo*) apprehension, nervousness; **tener ~** to be afraid; **de ~** wonderful, marvellous; **hace un frío de ~** (*fam*) it's terribly cold; ~**so, a** *a* fearful, timid.

miel [mjel] *nf* honey.

miembro ['mjembro] *nm* limb; (*socio*) member; ~ **viril** penis.

mientras ['mjentras] *conj* while; (*duración*) as long as // *ad* meanwhile; ~ **tanto** meanwhile; ~ **más tiene, más quiere** the more he has, the more he wants.

miércoles ['mjerkoles] *nm inv* Wednesday.

mierda ['mjerða] *nf* (*fam!*) shit (!).

miga ['miɣa] *nf* crumb; (*fig: meollo*) essence; **hacer buenas ~s** (*fam*) to get on well.

migración [miɣra'θjon] *nf* migration.

mil [mil] *num* thousand; **dos ~ libras** two thousand pounds.

milagro [mi'laɣro] *nm* miracle; ~**so, a** *a* miraculous.

mili ['mili] *nf*: **hacer la ~** (*fam*) to do one's military service.

milicia [mi'liθja] *nf* militia; (*servicio militar*) military service.

milímetro [mi'limetro] *nm* millimetre.

militante [mili'tante] *a* militant.

militar [mili'tar] *a* (*del ejército*) military // *nmf* soldier // *vi* to serve in the army; (*fig*) to be a member of a party.

milla ['miʎa] *nf* mile.

millar [mi'ʎar] *nm* thousand.

millón [mi'ʎon] *num* million; **millonario, a** *nm/f* millionaire.

mimar [mi'mar] *vt* (*gen*) to spoil, pamper.

mimbre ['mimbre] *nm* wicker.

mímica ['mimika] *nf* (*para comunicarse*) sign language; (*imitación*) mimicry.

mimo ['mimo] nm (caricia) caress; (de niño) spoiling; (TEATRO) mime; (: actor) mime artist.

mina ['mina] nf mine; **minar** vt to mine; (fig) to undermine.

mineral [mine'ral] a mineral // nm (GEO) mineral; (mena) ore.

minero, a [mi'nero, a] a mining cpd // nm/f miner.

miniatura [minja'tura] a inv, nf miniature.

minifalda [mini'falda] nf miniskirt.

mínimo, a ['minimo, a] a, nm minimum.

minino, a [mi'nino, a] nm/f (fam) puss, pussy.

ministerio [minis'terjo] nm Ministry; M~ de Hacienda/del Exterior Treasury (Brit), Treasury Department (US)/Foreign Office (Brit), State Department (US).

ministro, a [mi'nistro, a] nm/f minister.

minoría [mino'ria] nf minority.

minucioso, a [minu'θjoso, a] a thorough, meticulous; (prolijo) very detailed.

minúsculo, a [mi'nuskulo, a] a tiny, minute // nf small letter.

minusválido, a [minus'βaliðo, a] a (physically) handicapped // nm/f (physically) handicapped person.

minuta [mi'nuta] nf (de comida) menu.

minutero [minu'tero] nm minute hand.

minuto [mi'nuto] nm minute.

mío, a ['mio, a] pron: el ~ mine; un amigo ~ a friend of mine; lo ~ what is mine.

miope [mi'ope] a short-sighted.

mira ['mira] nf (de arma) sight(s) (pl); (fig) aim, intention.

mirada [mi'raða] nf look, glance; (expresión) look, expression; clavar la ~ en to stare at; echar una ~ a to glance at.

mirado, a [mi'raðo, a] a (sensato) sensible; (considerado) considerate;

bien/mal ~ well/not well thought of; bien ~ ad all things considered.

mirador [mira'ðor] nm viewpoint, vantage point.

mirar [mi'rar] vt to look at; (observar) to watch; (considerar) to consider, think over; (vigilar, cuidar) to watch, look after // vi to look; (ARQ) to face; ~se vr (dos personas) to look at each other; ~ bien/mal to think highly of/have a poor opinion of; ~se al espejo to look at o.s. in the mirror.

mirilla [mi'riʎa] nf (agujero) spyhole, peephole.

mirlo ['mirlo] nm blackbird.

misa ['misa] nf mass.

miserable [mise'raβle] a (avaro) mean, stingy; (nimio) miserable, paltry; (lugar) squalid; (fam) vile, despicable // nm (perverso) rotter (Brit).

miseria [mi'serja] nf misery; (pobreza) poverty; (tacañería) meanness, stinginess; (condiciones) squalor; una ~ a pittance.

misericordia [miseri'korðja] nf (compasión) compassion, pity; (piedad) mercy.

misil [mi'sil] nm missile.

misión [mi'sjon] nf mission; **misionero, a** nm/f missionary.

mismo, a ['mismo, a] a (semejante) same; (después de pronombre) -self; (para énfasis) very; el ~ traje the same suit; en ese ~ momento at that very moment; vino el ~ Ministro the minister himself came; yo ~ lo vi I saw it myself; lo ~ the same (thing); da lo ~ it's all the same; quedamos en las mismas we're no further forward // ad: aquí/hoy ~ right here/this very day; ahora ~ right now // conj: lo ~ que just like, just as; por lo ~ for the same reason.

misterio [mis'terjo] nm (gen) mystery; (lo secreto) secrecy; ~so, a a mysterious.

mitad [mi'tað] nf (medio) half; (cen-

tro) middle; **a ~ de precio** (at) half-price; **en o a ~ del camino** halfway along the road; **cortar por la ~** to cut through the middle.

mitigar [miti'var] *vt* to mitigate; (*dolor*) to ease; (*sed*) to quench.

mitin ['mitin] (*pl* **mítines**) *nm* meeting.

mito ['mito] *nm* myth.

mixto, a ['miksto, a] *a* mixed.

ml. *abr* (= *mililitro*) ml.

mm. *abr* (= *milímetro*) mm.

mobiliario [moßi'ljarjo] *nm* furniture.

moción [mo'θjon] *nf* motion.

mocos ['mokos] *nmpl* mucus *sg*; (*fam*) snot *sg*.

mochila [mo'tʃila] *nf* rucksack (*Brit*), back-pack.

moda ['moða] *nf* fashion; (*estilo*) style; **a la o de ~** in fashion, fashionable; **pasado de ~** out of fashion.

modales [mo'ðales] *nmpl* manners.

modalidad [moðali'ðað] *nf* kind, variety.

modelar [moðe'lar] *vt* to model.

modelo [mo'ðelo] *a inv*, *nm/f* model.

moderado, a [moðe'raðo, a] *a* moderate.

moderar [moðe'rar] *vt* to moderate; (*violencia*) to restrain, control; (*velocidad*) to reduce; **~se** *vr* to restrain o.s., control o.s.

modernizar [moðerni'θar] *vt* to modernize.

moderno, a [mo'ðerno, a] *a* modern; (*actual*) present-day.

modestia [mo'ðestja] *nf* modesty; **modesto, a** *a* modest.

módico, a ['moðiko, a] *a* moderate, reasonable.

modificar [moðifi'kar] *vt* to modify.

modista [mo'ðista] *nm/f* dressmaker.

modo ['moðo] *nm* (*manera, forma*) way, manner; (*MUS*) mode; **~s** *nmpl* manners; **de ningún ~** in no way; **de todos ~s** at any rate; **~ de empleo** directions *pl* (for use).

modorra [mo'ðorra] *nf* drowsiness.

modular [moðu'lar] *vt* to modulate.

mofa ['mofa] *nf*: **hacer ~ de** to mock; **mofarse** *vr*: **mofarse de** to mock, scoff at.

moho ['moo] *nm* (*BOT*) mould, mildew; (*en metal*) rust; **~so, a** *a* mouldy; rusty.

mojar [mo'xar] *vt* to wet; (*humedecer*) to damp(en), moisten; (*calar*) to soak; **~se** *vr* to get wet.

mojón [mo'xon] *nm* (*en un camino*) boundary stone.

molde ['molde] *nm* mould; (*COSTURA*) pattern; (*fig*) model; **~ar** *vt* to mould.

mole ['mole] *nf* mass, bulk; (*edificio*) pile.

moler [mo'ler] *vt* to grind, crush; (*cansar*) to tire out, exhaust.

molestar [moles'tar] *vt* to bother; (*fastidiar*) to annoy; (*incomodar*) to inconvenience, put out // *vi* to be a nuisance; **~se** *vr* to bother; (*incomodarse*) to go to trouble; (*ofenderse*) to take offence.

molestia [mo'lestja] *nf* bother, trouble; (*incomodidad*) inconvenience; (*MED*) discomfort; **es una ~** it's a nuisance; **molesto, a** *a* (*que fastidia*) annoying; (*incómodo*) inconvenient; (*inquieto*) uncomfortable, ill at ease; (*enfadado*) annoyed.

molinillo [moli'niʎo] *nm*: **~ de carne/café** mincer/coffee grinder.

molino [mo'lino] *nm* (*edificio*) mill; (*máquina*) grinder.

momentáneo, a [momen'taneo, a] *a* momentary.

momento [mo'mento] *nm* (*gen*) moment; (*TEC*) momentum; **de ~** at the moment, for the moment.

momia ['momja] *nf* mummy.

monarca [mo'narka] *nm/f* monarch, ruler; **monarquía** *nf* monarchy; **monárquico, a** *nm/f* royalist, monarchist.

monasterio [monas'terjo] *nm* monastery.

mondadientes [monda'ðjentes] *nm inv* toothpick.

mondar [mon'dar] *vt* (*limpiar*) to

clean; (*pelar*) to peel; ~**se** *vr*: ~**se de risa** (*fam*) to split one's sides laughing.

moneda [mo'neða] *nf* (*tipo de dinero*) currency, money; (*pieza*) coin; **una** ~ **de 5 pesetas** a 5 peseta piece; **monedero** *nm* purse; **monetario, a** *a* monetary, financial.

monja ['monxa] *nf* nun.

monje ['monxe] *nm* monk.

mono, a ['mono, a] *a* (*bonito*) lovely, pretty; (*gracioso*) nice, charming // *nm/f* monkey, ape // *nm* dungarees *pl*; (*overoles*) overalls *pl*.

monopolio [mono'poljo] *nm* monopoly; **monopolizar** *vt* to monopolize.

monotonía [monoto'nia] *nf* (*sonido*) monotone; (*fig*) monotony.

monótono, a [mo'notono, a] *a* monotonous.

monstruo ['monstrwo] *nm* monster // *a inv* fantastic; ~**so, a** *a* monstrous.

monta ['monta] *nf* total, sum; **de poca** ~ unimportant, of little account.

montaje [mon'taxe] *nm* assembly; (*TEATRO*) décor; (*CINE*) montage.

montaña [mon'taɲa] *nf* (*monte*) mountain; (*sierra*) mountains *pl*, mountainous area; (*AM: selva*) forest; ~ **rusa** roller coaster; **montañés, esa** *a* mountain *cpd* // *nm/f* highlander.

montar [mon'tar] *vt* (*subir a*) to mount, get on; (*TEC*) to assemble, put together; (*negocio*) to set up; (*arma*) to cock; (*colocar*) to lift on to; (*CULIN*) to beat // *vi* to mount, get on; (*sobresalir*) to overlap; ~ **en cólera** to get angry; ~ **a caballo** to ride, go horseriding.

montaraz [monta'raθ] *a* mountain *cpd*, highland *cpd*; (*salvaje*) wild, untamed; (*pey*) uncivilized.

monte ['monte] *nm* (*montaña*) mountain; (*bosque*) woodland; (*área sin cultivar*) wild area, wild country; **M~ de Piedad** pawnshop.

Montevideo [monteβi'ðeo] *n* Mon-

tevideo.

monto ['monto] *nm* total, amount.

montón [mon'ton] *nm* heap, pile; (*fig*): **un** ~ **de** heaps of, lots of.

monumento [monu'mento] *nm* monument.

monzón [mon'θon] *nm* monsoon.

moño ['moɲo] *nm* bun.

mora ['mora] *nf* blackberry.

morado, a [mo'raðo, a] *a* purple, violet // *nm* bruise // *nf* (*casa*) dwelling, abode.

moral [mo'ral] *a* moral // *nf* (*ética*) ethics *pl*; (*moralidad*) morals *pl*, morality; (*ánimo*) morale.

moraleja [mora'lexa] *nf* moral.

moralizar [morali'θar] *vt* to moralize.

morboso, a [mor'βoso, a] *a* morbid.

morcilla [mor'θiʎa] *nf* blood sausage, ≈ black pudding (*Brit*).

mordaz [mor'ðaθ] *a* (*crítica*) biting, scathing.

mordaza [mor'ðaθa] *nf* (*para la boca*) gag; (*TEC*) clamp.

morder [mor'ðer] *vt* to bite; (*mordisquear*) to nibble; (*fig: consumir*) to eat away, eat into; **mordisco** *nm* bite.

moreno, a [mo'reno, a] *a* (*color*) (dark) brown; (*de tez*) dark; (*de pelo* ~) dark-haired; (*negro*) black.

moretón [more'ton] *nm* (*fam*) bruise.

morfina [mor'fina] *nf* morphine.

moribundo, a [mori'βundo, a] *a* dying.

morir [mo'rir] *vi* to die; (*fuego*) to die down; (*luz*) to go out; (*fig*) to die; (*fig*) to be dying; **fue muerto en un accidente** he was killed in an accident; ~**se por algo** to be dying for sth.

moro, a ['moro, a] *a* Moorish // *nm/f* Moor.

moroso, a [mo'roso, a] *a* *nm/f* (*COM*) bad debtor, defaulter.

morral [mo'rral] *nm* haversack.

morro ['morro] *nm* (*ZOOL*) snout, nose; (*AUTO, AVIAT*) nose.

morsa ['morsa] nf walrus.

mortaja [mor'taxa] nf shroud.

mortal [mor'tal] a mortal; (golpe) deadly; **~idad**, **mortandad** nf mortality.

mortero [mor'tero] nm mortar.

mortífero, a [mor'tifero, a] a deadly, lethal.

mortificar [mortifi'kar] vt to mortify.

mosca ['moska] nf fly.

Moscú [mos'ku] n Moscow.

mosquearse [moske'arse] vr (fam: enojarse) to get cross; (: ofenderse) to take offence.

mosquitero [moski'tero] nm mosquito net.

mosquito [mos'kito] nm mosquito.

mostaza [mos'taθa] nf mustard.

mostrador [mostra'ðor] nm (de tienda) counter; (de café) bar.

mostrar [mos'trar] vt to show; (exhibir) to display, exhibit; (explicar) to explain; **~se** vr: **~se amable** to be kind; to prove to be kind; **no se muestra muy inteligente** he doesn't seem (to be) very intelligent.

mota ['mota] nf speck, tiny piece; (en diseño) dot.

mote ['mote] nm (apodo) nickname.

motín [mo'tin] nm (del pueblo) revolt, rising; (del ejército) mutiny.

motivar [moti'βar] vt (causar) to cause, motivate; (explicar) to explain, justify; **motivo** nm motive, reason.

moto ['moto] (fam), **motocicleta** [motoθi'kleta] nf motorbike (Brit), motorcycle.

motor [mo'tor] nm motor, engine; **~ a chorro** o **de reacción/de explosión** jet engine/internal combustion engine.

motora [mo'tora] nf, **motorbote** [motor'βote] nm motorboat.

motosierra [moto'sjerra] nf mechanical saw.

movedizo, a [moβe'ðiθo, a] a (inseguro) unsteady; (fig) unsettled, changeable; (persona) fickle.

mover [mo'βer] vt to move; (cabeza) to shake; (accionar) to drive; (fig) to cause, provoke; **~se** vr to move; (fig) to get a move on.

móvil ['moβil] a mobile; (pieza de máquina) moving; (mueble) movable // nm motive; **movilidad** nf mobility; **movilizar** vt to mobilize.

movimiento [moβi'mjento] nm movement; (TEC) motion; (actividad) activity.

mozo, a ['moθo, a] a (joven) young // nm/f (joven) youth, young man/girl; (camarero) waiter; (camarera) waitress.

muchacho, a [mu'tʃatʃo, a] nm/f (niño) boy/girl; (criado) servant; (criada) maid.

muchedumbre [mutʃe'ðumbre] nf crowd.

PALABRA CLAVE

---

mucho, a ['mutʃo, a] ♦ a 1 (cantidad) a lot of, much; (número) lots of, a lot of, many; **~ dinero** a lot of money; **hace ~ calor** it's very hot; **muchas amigas** lots o a lot of friends

2 (sg: grande): **ésta es mucha casa para él** this house is much too big for him

♦ pron: **tengo ~ que hacer** I've got a lot to do; **~s dicen que ...** a lot of people say that ...; ver tb **tener**

♦ ad 1: **me gusta ~** I like it a lot; **lo siento ~** I'm very sorry; **come ~** he eats a lot; **¿te vas a quedar ~?** are you going to be staying long?

2 (respuesta) very; **¿estás cansado? –¡~!** are you tired? – very!

3 (locuciones): **como ~** at (the) most; **con ~** el mejor **con ~** by far the best; **ni ~ menos**: **no es rico ni ~ menos** he's far from being rich

4: **por ~ que**: **por ~ que le creas** no matter how o however much you believe her.

muda ['muða] *nf* change of clothes.

mudanza [mu'ðanθa] *nf* (*cambio*) change; (*de casa*) move.

mudar [mu'ðar] *vt* to change; (*ZOOL*) to shed // *vi* to change; ~se *vr* (*la ropa*) to change; ~se de casa to move house.

mudo, a ['muðo, a] *a* dumb; (*callado*, *CINE*) silent.

mueble ['mweβle] *nm* piece of furniture; ~s *nmpl* furniture *sg*.

mueca ['mweka] *nf* face, grimace; hacer ~s a to make faces at.

muela ['mwela] *nf* (*diente*) tooth; (: *de atrás*) molar.

muelle ['mweʎe] *nm* spring; (*NAUT*) wharf; (*malecón*) pier.

muero *etc vb ver* **morir**.

muerte ['mwerte] *nf* death; (*homicidio*) murder; **dar** ~ **a** to kill.

muerto, a *pp de* **morir** // ['mwerto, a] *a* dead; (*color*) dull // *nm/f* dead man/woman; (*difunto*) deceased; (*cadáver*) corpse; **estar** ~ **de cansancio** to be dead tired.

muestra ['mwestra] *nf* (*señal*) indication, sign; (*demostración*) demonstration; (*prueba*) proof; (*estadística*) sample; (*modelo*) model, pattern; (*testimonio*) token.

muestreo [mwes'treo] *nm* sample, sampling.

muestro *etc vb ver* **mostrar**.

muevo *etc vb ver* **mover**.

mugir [mu'xir] *vi* (*vaca*) to moo.

mugre ['muɣre] *nf* dirt, filth; **mugriento, a** *a* dirty, filthy.

mujer [mu'xer] *nf* woman; (*esposa*) wife; ~**iego** *nm* womanizer.

mula ['mula] *nf* mule.

mulato, a [mu'lato, a] *a*, *nm/f* mulatto.

muleta [mu'leta] *nf* (*para andar*) crutch; (*TAUR*) stick with red cape attached.

multa ['multa] *nf* fine; **multar** *vt* to fine.

multicopista [multiko'pista] *nm* duplicator.

múltiple ['multiple] *a* multiple; (*pl*)

many, numerous.

multiplicar [multipli'kar] *vt* (*MAT*) to multiply; (*fig*) to increase; ~se *vr* (*BIO*) to multiply; (*fig*) to be everywhere at once.

multitud [multi'tuð] *nf* (*muchedumbre*) crowd; ~ **de** lots of.

mullido, a [mu'ʎiðo, a] *a* (*cama*) soft; (*hierba*) soft, springy.

mundano, a [mun'dano, a] *a* worldly; (*de moda*) fashionable.

mundial [mun'djal] *a* world-wide, universal; (*guerra*, *récord*) world *cpd*.

mundo ['mundo] *nm* world; **todo el** ~ everybody; **tener** ~ to be experienced, know one's way around.

munición [muni'θjon] *nf* (*MIL*: *provisiones*) stores *pl*, supplies *pl*; (: *balas*) ammunition.

municipio [muni'θipjo] *nm* (*ayuntamiento*) town council, corporation; (*territorio administrativo*) town, municipality.

muñeca [mu'ɲeka] *nf* (*ANAT*) wrist; (*juguete*) doll.

muñeco [mu'ɲeko] *nm* (*figura*) figure; (*marioneta*) puppet; (*fig*) puppet, pawn.

mural [mu'ral] *a* mural, wall *cpd* // *nm* mural.

muralla [mu'raʎa] *nf* (city) wall(s) (*pl*).

murciélago [mur'θjelaɣo] *nm* bat.

murmullo [mur'muʎo] *nm* murmur(ing); (*cuchicheo*) whispering; (*de arroyo*) murmur, rippling.

murmuración [murmura'θjon] *nf* gossip; **murmurar** *vi* to murmur, whisper; (*criticar*) to criticize; (*cotillear*) to gossip.

muro ['muro] *nm* wall.

muscular [musku'lar] *a* muscular.

músculo ['muskulo] *nm* muscle.

museo [mu'seo] *nm* museum.

musgo ['musɣo] *nm* moss.

músico, a ['musiko, a] *a* musical // *nm/f* musician // *nf* music.

musitar [musi'tar] *vt*, *vi* to mutter, mumble.

muslo ['muslo] nm thigh.

mustio, a ['mustjo, a] a (persona) depressed, gloomy; (planta) faded, withered.

musulmán, ana [musul'man, ana] nm/f Moslem.

mutación [muta'θjon] nf (BIO) mutation; (: cambio) (sudden) change.

mutilar [muti'lar] vt to mutilate; (a una persona) to maim.

mutuamente [mutwa'mente] ad mutually.

mutuo, a ['mutwo, a] a mutual.

muy [mwi] ad very; (demasiado) too; M~ Señor mío Dear Sir; ~ de noche very late at night; eso es ~ de él that's just like him.

N

N abr (= norte) N.

n/ abr = nuestro, a.

nabo ['naβo] nm turnip.

nácar ['nakar] nm mother-of-pearl.

nacer [na'θer] vi to be born; (de huevo) to hatch; (vegetal) to sprout; (río) to rise; nací en Barcelona i was born in Barcelona; nació una sospecha en su mente a suspicion formed in her mind; **nacido, a** a born; **recién nacido** newborn; **naciente** a new, emerging; (sol) rising; **nacimiento** nm birth; (fig) birth, origin; (de Navidad) Nativity; (linaje) descent, family; (de río) source.

nación [na'θjon] nf nation; **nacional** a national; **nacionalismo** nm nationalism; **nacionalista** nm/f nationalist; **nacionalizar** vt to nationalize; **nacionalizarse** vr (persona) to become naturalized.

nada ['naða] pron nothing // ad not at all, in no way; no decir ~ to say nothing, not to say anything; de ~ don't mention it.

nadador, a [naða'ðor, a] nm/f swimmer.

nadar [na'ðar] vi to swim.

nadie ['naðje] pron nobody, no-one; ~ habló nobody spoke; no había ~ there was nobody there, there wasn't anybody there.

nado ['naðo]: a ~ ad: pasar a ~ to swim across.

nafta ['nafta] nf (AM) petrol (Brit), gas (US).

naipe ['naipe] nm (playing card); ~s nmpl cards.

nalgas ['nalɣas] nfpl buttocks.

nana ['nana] nf lullaby.

naranja [na'ranxa] a inv, nf orange; media ~ (fam) better half; **naranjada** nf orangeade; **naranjo** nm orange tree.

narciso [nar'θiso] nm narcissus.

narcótico, a [nar'kotiko, a] a, nm narcotic; **narcotizar** vt to drug.

nardo ['narðo] nm lily.

narigón, ona [nari'ɣon, ona] a, **narigudo, a** [nari'ɣuðo, a] a big-nosed.

nariz [na'riθ] nf nose; **narices** nfpl nostrils; delante de las narices de uno under one's (very) nose.

narración [narra'θjon] nf narration; **narrador, a** nm/f narrator.

narrar [na'rrar] vt to narrate, recount; **narrativa** nf narrative, story.

nata ['nata] nf cream.

natación [nata'θjon] nf swimming.

natal [na'tal] a: ciudad ~ home town; **natalicio** nm birthday; **~idad** nf birth rate.

natillas [na'tiʎas] nfpl custard sg.

natividad [natiβi'ðað] nf nativity.

nativo, a [na'tiβo, a] a, nm/f native // nm (disposición) nature.

naturaleza [natura'leθa] nf (género) nature, kind; ~ **muerta** still life.

naturalidad [naturali'ðað] nf naturalness.

naturalización [naturaliθa'θjon]

naturalization.

naturalizarse [naturali'θarse] *vr* to become naturalized; (*aclimatarse*) to become acclimatized.

naturalmente [natural'mente] *ad* (*de modo natural*) in a natural way; ¡~! of course!

naufragar [naufra'ɣar] *vi* to sink; **naufragio** *nm* shipwreck; **náufrago, a** *nm/f* castaway, shipwrecked person.

nauseabundo, a [nausea'βundo, a] *a* nauseating, sickening.

náuseas ['nauseas] *nfpl* nausea; **me da ~** it makes me feel sick.

náutico, a ['nautiko, a] *a* nautical.

navaja [na'βaxa] *nf* (*cortaplumas*) clasp knife (Brit), penknife; (*de barbero, peluquero*) razor.

Navarra [na'βarra] *nf* Navarre.

nave ['naβe] *nf* (*barco*) ship, vessel; (ARQ) nave; ~ **espacial** spaceship.

navegación [naβeɣa'θjon] *nf* navigation; (*viaje*) sea journey; ~ **aérea** air traffic; ~ **costera** coastal shipping; **navegante** *nm/f* navigator; **navegar** *vi* (*barco*) to sail; (*avión*) to fly // *vt* to sail; to fly; (*dirigir el rumbo*) to navigate.

navidad [naβi'ðað] *nf* Christmas; ~es *nfpl* Christmas time; **navideño, a** *a* Christmas *cpd*.

navío [na'βjo] *nm* ship.

nazca *etc vb ver* **nacer.**

nazi ['naθi] *a*, *nm/f* Nazi.

NE *abr* (= *nor(d)este*) NE.

neblina [ne'βlina] *nf* mist.

nebuloso, a [neβu'loso, a] *a* foggy; (*calinoso*) misty; (*indefinido*) nebulous, vague // *nf* nebula.

necedad [neθe'ðað] *nf* foolishness; (*una ~*) foolish act.

necesario, a [neθe'sarjo, a] *a* necessary.

neceser [neθe'ser] *nm* toilet bag; (*bolsa grande*) holdall.

necesidad [neθesi'ðað] *nf* need; (*lo inevitable*) necessity; (*miseria*) poverty, need; **en caso de ~** in case of need *o* emergency; **hacer sus**

~es to relieve o.s.

necesitado, a [neθesi'taðo, a] *a* needy, poor; ~ **de** in need of.

necesitar [neθesi'tar] *vt* to need, require // *vi*: ~ **de** to have need of.

necio, a ['neθjo, a] *a* foolish.

necrología [nekrolo'xja] *nf* obituary.

necrópolis [ne'kropolis] *nf inv* cemetery.

nectarina [nekta'rina] *nf* nectarine.

nefasto, a [ne'fasto, a] *a* ill-fated, unlucky.

negación [neɣa'θjon] *nf* negation; (*rechazo*) refusal, denial.

negar [ne'ɣar] *vt* (*renegar, rechazar*) to refuse; (*prohibir*) to refuse; deny; (*desmentir*) to deny; ~**se** *vr*: ~**se a** to refuse to.

negativo, a [neɣa'tiβo, a] *a*, *nm* negative // *nf* (*gen*) negative; (*rechazo*) refusal, denial.

negligencia [neɣli'xenθja] *nf* negligence; **negligente** *a* negligent.

negociable [neɣo'θjaβle] *a* (COM) negotiable.

negociado [neɣo'θjaðo] *nm* department, section.

negociante [neɣo'θjante] *nm/f* businessman/woman.

negociar [neɣo'θjar] *vt*, *vi* to negotiate; ~ **en** to deal in, trade in.

negocio [ne'ɣoθjo] *nm* (COM) business; (*asunto*) affair, business; (*operación comercial*) deal, transaction; (AM) firm; (*lugar*) place of business; **los ~s** business *sg*; **hacer ~** to do business.

negro, a ['neɣro, a] *a* black; (*suerte*) awful // *nm* black // *nm/f* Negro/Negress, Black // *nf* (MUS) crotchet; **negrura** *nf* blackness.

nene, a ['nene, a] *nm/f* baby, small child.

nenúfar [ne'nufar] *nm* water lily.

neologismo [neolo'xismo] *nm* neologism.

neoyorquino, a [neojor'kino, a] *a* (of) New York.

nepotismo [nepo'tismo] *nm* nepotism.

nervio ['nerβjo] *nm* (ANAT) nerve; (: *tendón*) tendon; (*fig*) vigour; **nerviosismo** *nm* nervousness, nerves *pl*; ~**so, a, nervudo, a** *a* nervous.

neto, a ['neto, a] *a* clear; (*limpio*) clean; (COM) net.

neumático, a [neu'matiko, a] *a* pneumatic // *nm* (*Esp*) tyre (*Brit*), tire (*US*); ~ **de recambio** spare tyre.

neurastenia [neuras'tenja] *nf* (MED) neurasthenia; (*fig*) excitability.

neurólogo, a [neu'roloγo, a] *nm/f* neurologist.

neutral [neu'tral] *a* neutral; ~**izar** *vt* to neutralize; (*contrarrestar*) to counteract.

neutro, a ['neutro, a] *a* (BIO) neuter; (LING) neuter.

neutrón [neu'tron] *nm* neutron.

nevada [ne'βaða] *nf* snowstorm; (*caída de nieve*) snowfall.

nevar [ne'βar] *vi* to snow.

nevera [ne'βera] *nf* (*Esp*) refrigerator (*Brit*), icebox (*US*).

nevería [neβe'ria] *nf* (AM) ice-cream parlour.

nevisca [ne'βiska] *nf* flurry of snow.

nexo ['nekso] *nm* link, connection.

ni [ni] *conj* nor, neither; (*tb:* ~ **siquiera**) not ... even; ~ **que no** not even if; ~ **blanco** ~ **negro** neither white nor black.

Nicaragua [nika'raγwa] *nf* Nicaragua; **nicaragüense** *a, nm/f* Nicaraguan.

nicotina [niko'tina] *nf* nicotine.

nicho ['nitʃo] *nm* niche.

nido ['niðo] *nm* nest; (*fig*) hiding place.

niebla ['njeβla] *nf* fog; (*neblina*) mist.

niego *etc vb ver* **negar**.

nieto, a ['njeto, a] *nm/f* grandson/daughter; ~**s** *nmpl* grandchildren.

nieve *etc vb ver* **nevar** // ['njeβe] *nf* snow; (AM) icecream.

nigromancia [niγro'manθja] *nf* necromancy, black magic.

Nilo ['nilo] *nm*: **el** ~ the Nile.

nimiedad [nimje'ðað] *nf* smallmindedness; (*trivialidad*) triviality.

nimio, a ['nimjo, a] *a* trivial, insignificant.

ninfa ['ninfa] *nf* nymph.

ninfómana [nin'fomana] *nf* nymphomaniac.

ninguno, a [nin'guno, a], **ningún** [nin'gun] *a* no // *pron* (*nadie*) nobody; (*ni uno*) none, not one; (*ni uno ni otro*) neither; **de ninguna manera** by no means, not at all.

niña ['nina] *nf ver* **niño**.

niñera [ni'nera] *nf* nursemaid, nanny; **niñería** *nf* childish act.

niñez [ni'neθ] *nf* childhood; (*infancia*) infancy.

niño, a ['nino, a] *a* (*joven*) young; (*inmaduro*) immature // *nm* (*chico*) boy, child // *nf* (*chica*) girl, child; (ANAT) pupil.

nipón, ona [ni'pon, ona] *a, nm/f* Japanese.

níquel ['nikel] *nm* nickel; **niquelar** *vt* (TEC) to nickel-plate.

níspero ['nispero] *nm* medlar.

nitidez [niti'ðeθ] *nf* (*claridad*) clarity; (: *de atmósfera*) brightness; (: *de imagen*) sharpness; **nítido, a** *a* clear; sharp.

nitrato [ni'trato] *nm* nitrate.

nitrógeno [ni'troxeno] *nm* nitrogen.

nitroglicerina [nitroγliθe'rina] *nf* nitroglycerine.

nivel [ni'βel] *nm* (GEO) level; (*norma*) level, standard; (*altura*) height; ~ **de aceite** oil level; ~ **de aire** spirit level; ~ **de vida** standard of living; ~**ar** *vt* to level out; (*fig*) to even up; (COM) to balance.

NN. UU. *nfpl abr* (= *Naciones Unidas*) U.N. *sg.*

NO *abr* (= *noroeste*) NW.

no [no] *ad* no; not; (*con verbo*) not // *excl* no!; ~ **tengo nada** I don't have anything, I have nothing; ~ **es el mío** it's not mine; **ahora** ~ not now; **¿**~ **lo sabes?** don't you know? ~

mucho not much; ~ bien termine, lo entregaré as soon as I finish I'll hand it over; ¡a que ~ lo sabes! I bet you don't know!; ¡cómo ~! of course!; los paises ~ alineados the non-aligned countries; la ~ intervención non-intervention.

noble ['noβle] a nmf noble; ~za nf nobility.

noción [no'θjon] nf notion.

nocivo, a [no'θiβo, a] a harmful.

noctámbulo, a [nok'tambulo, a] nmf sleepwalker.

nocturno, a [nok'turno, a] a (de la noche) nocturnal, night cpd; (de la tarde) evening cpd // nm nocturne.

noche ['notʃe] nf night, night-time; (la tarde) evening; (fig) darkness; de ~, por la ~ at night.

nochebuena [notʃe'βwena] nf Christmas Eve.

nochevieja [notʃe'βjexa] nf New Year's Eve.

nodriza [no'ðriθa] nf wet nurse; buque o nave ~ supply ship.

nogal [no'ɣal] nm walnut tree.

nómada ['nomaða] a nomadic // nmf nomad.

nombramiento [nombra'mjento] nm naming; (a un empleo) appointment.

nombrar [nom'brar] vt (designar) to name; (mencionar) to mention; (dar puesto a) to appoint.

nombre ['nombre] nm name; (sustantivo) noun; (fama) renown; ~ y apellidos name in full; ~ común/propio common/proper noun; ~ de pila/de soltera Christian/maiden name.

nomenclatura [nomenkla'tura] nf nomenclature.

nomeolvides [nomeol'βiðes] nm inv forget-me-not.

nómina ['nomina] nf (lista) list; (COM) payroll.

nominal [nomi'nal] a nominal.

nominar [nomi'nar] vt to nominate.

nominativo, a [nomina'tiβo, a] a (COM): cheque ~ a X cheque made

out to X.

non [non] a odd, uneven // nm odd number.

nono, a ['nono, a] a ninth.

nordeste [nor'ðeste] a north-east, north-eastern, north-easterly // nm north-east.

nórdico, a ['norðiko, a] a (del norte) northern, northerly; (escandinavo) Nordic.

noreste [no'reste] a, nm = **nordeste**.

noria ['norja] nf (AGR) waterwheel; (de carnaval) big (Brit) o Ferris (US) wheel.

normal [nor'mal] a (corriente) normal; (habitual) usual, natural; (gasolina) ~ two-star petrol; **~idad** nf normality; restablecer la **~idad** to restore order; **~izar** vt (reglamentar) to normalize; (TEC) to standardize; **~izarse** vr to return to normal.

normando, a [nor'mando, a] a, nmf Norman.

noroeste [noro'este] a north-west, north-western, north-westerly // nm north-west.

norte ['norte] a north, northern, northerly // nm north; (fig) guide.

norteamericano, a [norteameri-'kano, a] a, nmf (North) American.

Noruega [no'rweɣa] nf Norway.

noruego, a [no'rweɣo, a] a, nmf Norwegian.

nos [nos] pron (directo) us; (indirecto) us; to us; for us; from us; (reflexivo) (to) ourselves; (recíproco) (to) each other; ~ levantamos a las 7 we get up at 7.

nosotros, as [no'sotros, as] pron (sujeto) we; (después de prep) us.

nostalgia [nos'talxja] nf nostalgia.

nota ['nota] nf note; (ESCOL) mark.

notable [no'taβle] a notable; (ESCOL) outstanding // nmf notable.

notar [no'tar] vt to notice, note; ~se vr to be obvious; se nota que ... one observes that ....

notarial [nota'rjal] a: acta

affidavit.

notario [no'tarjo] *nm* notary.

noticia [no'tiθja] *nf* (*información*) piece of news; **las ~s** the news *sg*; **tener ~s de alguien** to hear from sb.

noticiario [noti'θjarjo] *nm* (*CINE*) newsreel; (*TV*) news bulletin.

noticiero [noti'θjero] *nm* (*AM*) news bulletin.

notificación [notifika'θjon] *nf* notification; **notificar** *vt* to notify, inform.

notoriedad [notorje'ðað] *nf* fame, renown; **notorio, a** *a* (*público*) well-known; (*evidente*) obvious.

novato, a [no'βato, a] *a* inexperienced // *nm/f* beginner, novice.

novecientos, as [noβe'θjentos, as] *a, num* nine hundred.

novedad [noβe'ðað] *nf* (*calidad de nuevo*) newness; (*noticia*) piece of news; (*cambio*) change, (new) development.

novedoso, a [noβe'ðoso, a] *a* novel.

novel [no'βel] *a* new; (*inexperto*) inexperienced // *nm/f* beginner.

novela [no'βela] *nf* novel.

novelero, a [noβe'lero, a] *a* highly imaginative.

novelesco, a [noβe'lesko, a] *a* fictional; (*romántico*) romantic; (*fantástico*) fantastic.

noveno, a [no'βeno, a] *a* ninth.

noventa [no'βenta] *num* ninety.

novia ['noβja] *nf* ver **novio**.

noviazgo [no'βjaθ ɣo] *nm* engagement.

novicio, a [no'βiθjo, a] *nm/f* novice.

noviembre [no'βjembre] *nm* November.

novilla [no'βiʎa] *nf* heifer; **~da** *nf* (*TAUR*) bullfight with young bulls; **novillero** *nm* novice bullfighter; **novillo** *nm* young bull, bullock; **hacer novillos** (*fam*) to play truant.

novio, a [no'βjo, a] *nm/f* boyfriend/girlfriend; (*prometido*) fiancé/fiancée; (*recién casado*) bridegroom/bride; **los ~s** the newly-weds.

N. S. *abr = Nuestro Señor.*

nubarrón [nuβa'rron] *nm* storm cloud.

nube ['nuβe] *nf* cloud.

nublado, a [nu'βlaðo, a] *a* cloudy // *nm* storm cloud; **nublar** *vt* (*oscurecer*) to darken; (*confundir*) to cloud; **nublarse** *vr* to grow dark.

nuca ['nuka] *nf* nape of the neck.

nuclear [nukle'ar] *a* nuclear.

núcleo ['nukleo] *nm* (*centro*) core; (*FÍSICA*) nucleus.

nudillo [nu'ðiʎo] *nm* knuckle.

nudo ['nuðo] *nm* knot; (*unión*) bond; (*de problema*) crux; **~so, a** *a* knotty.

nuera ['nwera] *nf* daughter-in-law.

nuestro, a ['nwestro, a] *adjetivo posesivo* our // *pron* ours; **~ padre** our father; **un amigo ~** a friend of ours; **es el ~** it's ours.

nueva ['nweβa] *nf, ver* **nuevo**.

nuevamente [nweβa'mente] *ad* (*otra vez*) again; (*de nuevo*) anew.

nueve ['nweβe] *num* nine.

nuevo, a ['nweβo, a] *a* (*gen*) new // *nf* piece of news; **de ~** again; **Nueva York** *n* New York; **Nueva Zelandia** *nf* New Zealand.

nuez [nweθ] *nf* (*fruto*) nut; (*de nogal*) walnut; **~ de Adán** Adam's apple; **~ moscada** nutmeg.

nulidad [nuli'ðað] *nf* (*incapacidad*) incompetence; (*abolición*) nullity.

nulo, a ['nulo, a] *a* (*inepto, torpe*) useless; (*inválido*) (null and) void; (*DEPORTE*) drawn, tied.

núm. *abr = (número)* no.

numeración [numera'θjon] *nf* (*cifras*) numbers *pl*; (*arábiga, romana etc*) numerals *pl*.

numeral [nume'ral] *nm* numeral.

numerar [nume'rar] *vt* to number.

numérico, a [nu'meriko, a] *a* numerical.

número ['numero] *nm* (*gen*) number; (*tamaño: de zapato*) size; (*ejemplar: de diario*) number, issue; **sin ~** numberless, unnumbered; **~ de matrícula/de teléfono**

registration/telephone number; ~
atrasado back number.
numeroso, a [nume'roso, a] *a*
numerous.
nunca ['nunka] *ad* (*jamás*) never; ~
lo pensé I never thought it; **no
viene** ~ he never comes; ~ **más**
never again.
nuncio ['nunθjo] *nm* (*REL*) nuncio.
nupcias ['nupθjas] *nfpl* wedding *sg*,
nuptials.
nutria ['nutrja] *nf* otter.
nutrición [nutri'θjon] *nf* nutrition.
nutrido, a [nu'triðo, a] *a*
(*alimentado*) nourished; (*fig:
grande*) large; (*abundante*)
abundant.
nutrir [nu'trir] *vt* (*alimentar*) to nourish; (*dar de comer*) to feed; (*fig*) to
strengthen; **nutritivo, a** *a* nourishing, nutritious.
nylon [ni'lon] *nm* nylon.

Ñ

ñato, a ['nato, a] *a* (*AM*) snub-
nosed.
ñoñería [none'ria], **ñoñez** [no'neθ]
nf insipidness.
ñoño, a ['nono, a] *a* (*AM: tonto*)
silly, stupid; (*soso*) insipid;
(*persona*) spineless.

O

o [o] *conj* or.
O *abr* (= *oeste*) W.
o/ *abr* (= *orden*) O.
oasis [o'asis] *nm inv* oasis.
obcecar [oβθe'kar] *vt* to blind.
obedecer [oβeðe'θer] *vt* to obey;
obediencia *nf* obedience;
obediente *a* obedient.
obertura [oβer'tura] *nf* overture.
obesidad [oβesi'ðað] *nf* obesity;
obeso, a *a* obese.
obispo [o'βispo] *nm* bishop.
objeción [oβxe'θjon] *nf* objection.

objetar [oβxe'tar] *vt, vi* to object.
objetivo, a [oβxe'tiβo, a] *a, nm*
objective.
objeto [oβ'xeto] *nm* (*cosa*) object;
(*fin*) aim.
objetor, a [oβxe'tor, a] *nm/f* objec-
tor.
oblicuo, a [o'βlikwo, a] *a* oblique;
(*mirada*) sidelong.
obligación [oβliγa'θjon] *nf* obligation; (*COM*) bond.
obligar [oβli'γar] *vt* to force; ~**se** *vr*
to bind o.s.; **obligatorio, a** *a*
compulsory, obligatory.
oboe [o'βoe] *nm* oboe.
obra ['oβra] *nf* work; (*hechura*) piece
of work; (*ARQ*) construction, building; (*TEATRO*) play; ~ **maestra**
masterpiece; **o~s públicas** public
works; **por** ~ **de** thanks to (the
efforts of); **obrar** *vt* to work; (*tener
efecto*) to have an effect on // *vi* to
act, behave; (*tener efecto*) to have
an effect; **la carta obra en su
poder** the letter is in his/her possession.
obrero, a [o'βrero, a] *a* (*clase*)
working; (*movimiento*) labour *cpd*;
clase obrera working class // *nm/f*
(*gen*) worker; (*sin oficio*) labourer.
obscenidad [oβsθeni'ðað] *nf* obscen-
ity; **obsceno, a** *a* obscene.
obscu... = oscu... .
obsequiar [oβse'kjar] *vt* (*ofrecer*) to
present with; (*agasajar*) to make a
fuss of, lavish attention on;
obsequio *nm* (*regalo*) gift;
(*cortesía*) courtesy, attention;
obsequioso, a *a* attentive.
observación [oβserβa'θjon] *nf*
observation; (*reflexión*) remark.
observador, a [oβserβa'ðor, a] *nm/f*
observer.
observancia [oβser'βanθja] *nf*
observance.
observar [oβser'βar] *vt* to observe;
(*anotar*) to notice; ~**se** *vr* to keep to,
observe.
obsesión [oβse'sjon] *nf* obsession;
obsesionar *vt* to obsess.

obsesionar *vt* to obsess.

obstaculizar [oβstakuli'θar] *vt* (*dificultar*) to hinder, hamper.

obstáculo [oβ'stakulo] *nm* (*gen*) obstacle; (*impedimento*) hindrance, drawback.

obstante [oβ'stante]: **no ~** *ad* nevertheless // *prep* in spite of.

obstetricia [oβste'triθja] *nf* obstetrics *sg*; **obstétrico, a** *a* obstetric // *nmf* obstetrician.

obstinado, a [oβsti'naðo, a] *a* (*gen*) obstinate, stubborn.

obstinarse [oβsti'narse] *vr* to be obstinate; **~ en** to persist in.

obstrucción [oβstruk'θjon] *nf* obstruction; **obstruir** [oβs'truir] *vt* to obstruct.

obtener [oβte'ner] *vt* (*conseguir*) to obtain; (*ganar*) to gain.

obturador [oβtura'ðor] *nm* (*FOTO*) shutter.

obtuso, a [oβ'tuso, a] *a* (*filo*) blunt; (*MAT, fig*) obtuse.

obviar [oβ'βjar] *vt* to obviate, remove.

obvio, a [oβjo, a] *a* obvious.

ocasión [oka'sjon] *nf* (*oportunidad*) opportunity, chance; (*momento*) occasion, time; (*causa*) cause; **de ~** secondhand; **ocasionar** *vt* to cause.

ocaso [o'kaso] *nm* (*fig*) decline.

occidente [okθi'ðente] *nm* west.

océano [o'θeano] *nm* ocean; **el ~ Indico** the Indian Ocean.

OCDE *nf abr* (= *Organización de Cooperación y Desarrollo Económico*) OECD.

ocio [o'θjo] *nm* (*tiempo*) leisure; (*pey*) idleness; **~sidad** *nf* idleness; **~so, a** *a* (*inactivo*) idle; (*inútil*) useless.

octanaje [okta'naxe] *nm*: **de alto ~** high octane; **octano** *nm* octane.

octavilla [okta'viʎa] *nf* leaflet, pamphlet.

octavo, a [ok'taβo, a] *a* eighth.

octogenario, a [oktoxe'narjo, a] *a* octogenarian.

octubre [ok'tuβre] *nm* October.

ocular [oku'lar] *a* ocular, eye *cpd*;

testigo ~ eyewitness.

oculista [oku'lista] *nmf* oculist.

ocultar [okul'tar] *vt* (*esconder*) to hide; (*callar*) to conceal; **oculto, a** *a* hidden; (*fig*) secret.

ocupación [okupa'θjon] *nf* occupation.

ocupado, a [oku'paðo, a] *a* (*persona*) busy; (*plaza*) occupied, taken; (*teléfono*) engaged; **ocupar** *vt* (*gen*) to occupy; **ocuparse** *vr*: **ocuparse de o en** (*gen*) to concern o.s. with; (*cuidar*) to look after.

ocurrencia [oku'rrenθja] *nf* (*suceso*) incident, event; (*idea*) bright idea.

ocurrir [oku'rrir] *vi* to happen; **~se** *vr*: **se me ocurrió que...** it occurred to me that... .

ochenta [o'tʃenta] *num* eighty.

ocho [o'tʃo] *num* eight; **~ días** a week.

odiar [o'ðjar] *vt* to hate; **odio** *nm* (*gen*) hate, hatred; (*disgusto*) dislike; **odioso, a** *a* (*gen*) hateful; (*malo*) nasty.

odontólogo, a [oðon'toloɣo, a] *nmf* dentist, dental surgeon.

OEA *nf abr* (= *Organización de Estados Americanos*) OAS.

oeste [o'este] *nm* west; **una película del ~** a western.

ofender [ofen'der] *vt* (*agraviar*) to offend; (*insultar*) to insult; **~se** *vr* to take offence; **ofensa** *nf* offence; **ofensivo, a** *a* (*insultante*) insulting; (*MIL*) offensive // *a* offensive.

oferta [o'ferta] *nf* offer; (*propuesta*) proposal; **la ~ y la demanda** supply and demand; **artículos en ~** goods on offer.

oficial [ofi'θjal] *a* official // *nm* official; (*MIL*) officer.

oficina [ofi'θina] *nf* office; **~ de correos** post office; **~ de turismo** tourist office; **oficinista** *nmf* clerk.

oficio [o'fiθjo] *nm* (*profesión*) profession; (*puesto*) post; (*REL*) service; **ser del ~** to be an old hand; **tener mucho ~** to have a lot of experience; **~ de difuntos** funeral service; **de ~** officially.

oficioso, a [ofi'θjoso, a] *a* (*pey*) officious; (*no oficial*) unofficial, informal.

ofimática [ofi'matika] *nf* office automation.

ofrecer [ofre'θer] *vt* (*dar*) to offer; (*proponer*) to propose; **~se** *vr* (*persona*) to offer o.s., volunteer; (*situación*) to present itself; **¿qué se le ofrece?**, **¿se le ofrece algo?** what can I do for you?, can I get you anything?

ofrecimiento [ofreθi'mjento] *nm* offer, offering.

ofrendar [ofren'dar] *vt* to offer, contribute.

oftalmólogo, a [oftal'molovo, a] *nm/f* ophthalmologist.

ofuscación [ofuska'θjon] *nf*, **ofuscamiento** [ofuska'mjento] *nm* (*fig*) bewilderment.

ofuscar [ofus'kar] *vt* (*confundir*) to bewilder; (*enceguecer*) to dazzle, blind.

oída [o'iða] *nf*: **de ~s** by hearsay.

oído [o'iðo] *nm* (*ANAT*) ear; (*sentido*) hearing.

oigo *etc* **vb** *ver* **oír**.

oír [o'ir] *vt* (*gen*) to hear; (*atender a*) to listen to; **¡oiga!** listen!; **~ misa** to attend mass.

OIT *nf abr* (= *Organización Internacional del Trabajo*) ILO.

ojal [o'xal] *nm* buttonhole.

ojalá [oxa'la] *excl* if only (it were so)!, some hope! // *conj* if only...!, would that...!; **~ que venga hoy** I hope he comes today.

ojeada [oxe'aða] *nf* glance.

ojera [o'xera] *nf*: **tener ~s** to have bags under one's eyes.

ojeriza [oxe'riθa] *nf* ill-will.

ojeroso, a [oxe'roso, a] *a* haggard.

ojete [o'xete] *nm* eyelet.

ojo [o'xo] *nm* eye; (*de puente*) span; (*de cerradura*) keyhole // *excl* careful!; **tener ~ para** to have an eye for; **~ de buey** porthole.

ola [o'la] *nf* wave.

olé [o'le] *excl* bravo!, olé!

oleada [ole'aða] *nf* big wave, swell; (*fig*) wave.

oleaje [ole'axe] *nm* swell.

óleo [o'leo] *nm* oil; **oleoducto** [oleo'ðukto] *nm* (oil) pipeline.

oler [o'ler] *vt* (*gen*) to smell; (*inquirir*) to pry into; (*fig: sospechar*) to sniff out // *vi* to smell; **~ a** to smell of.

olfatear [olfate'ar] *vt* to smell; (*fig: sospechar*) to sniff out; (*inquirir*) to pry into; **olfato** *nm* sense of smell.

oligarquía [olivar'kia] *nf* oligarchy.

olimpíada [olim'piaða] *nf*: **las O~s** the Olympics.

oliva [o'liβa] *nf* (*aceituna*) olive; **aceite de ~** olive oil; **olivo** *nm* olive tree.

olmo [o'lmo] *nm* elm (tree).

olor [o'lor] *nm* smell; **~oso, a** *a* scented.

olvidadizo, a [olβiða'ðiθo, a] *a* (*desmemoriado*) forgetful; (*distraído*) absent-minded.

olvidar [olβi'ðar] *vt* to forget; (*omitir*) to omit; **~se** *vr* (*fig*) to forget o.s.; **se me olvidó** I forgot.

olvido [ol'βiðo] *nm* oblivion; (*despiste*) forgetfulness.

olla [o'λa] *nf* pan; (*comida*) stew; **~ a presión** *o* **exprés** pressure cooker; **~ podrida** *type of Spanish stew*.

ombligo [om'blivo] *nm* navel.

ominoso, a [omi'noso, a] *a* ominous.

omisión [omi'sjon] *nf* (*abstención*) omission; (*descuido*) neglect.

omiso, a [o'miso, a] *a*: **hacer caso ~ de** to ignore, pass over.

omitir [omi'tir] *vt* to omit.

omnipotente [omnipo'tente] *a* omnipotent.

omnívoro, a [om'niβoro, a] *a* omnivorous.

omóplato [o'moplato] *nm* shoulder blade.

OMS *nf abr* (= *Organización Mundial de la Salud*) WHO.

once [ˈonθe] *num* eleven; **~s** *nmpl*

(AM) tea break.

onda ['onda] *nf* wave; ~ **corta/ larga/media** short/long/medium wave; **ondear** *vt, vi* to wave; *(tener ondas)* to be wavy; *(agua)* to ripple; **ondearse** *vr* to swing, sway.

ondulación [ondula'θjon] *nf* undulation; **ondulado, a** *a* wavy // *nm* wave; **ondulante** *a* undulating.

ondular [ondu'lar] *vt (el pelo)* to wave // *vi, ~se vr* to undulate.

oneroso, a [one'roso, a] *a* onerous.

ONU ['onu] *nf abr (= Organización de las Naciones Unidas)* UNO.

opaco, a [o'pako, a] *a* opaque; *(fig)* dull.

ópalo ['opalo] *nm* opal.

opción [op'θjon] *nf (gen)* option; *(derecho)* right, option.

OPEP ['opep] *nf abr (= Organización de Países Exportadores de Petróleo)* OPEC.

ópera ['opera] *nf* opera; ~ **bufa** *o* **cómica** comic opera.

operación [opera'θjon] *nf (gen)* operation; *(COM)* transaction, deal.

operador, a [opera'ðor, a] *nm/f* operator; *(CINE: proyección)* projectionist; *(: rodaje)* cameraman.

operante [ope'rante] *a* operating.

operar [ope'rar] *vt (producir)* to produce, bring about; *(MED)* to operate on // *vi (COM)* to operate, deal; ~**se** *vr* to occur; *(MED)* to have an operation.

opereta [ope'reta] *nf* operetta.

opinar [opi'nar] *vt (estimar)* to think // *vi (enjuiciar)* to give one's opinion; **opinión** *nf (creencia)* belief; *(criterio)* opinion.

opio ['opjo] *nm* opium.

oponente [opo'nente] *nm/f* opponent.

oponer [opo'ner] *vt (resistencia)* to put up, offer; *(negativa)* to raise; ~**se** *vr (objetar)* to object; *(estar frente a frente)* to be opposed; *(dos personas)* to oppose each other; ~ **A a B** to set A against B; **me opongo a pensar que...** I refuse to believe *o*

think that... .

oportunidad [oportuni'ðað] *nf (ocasión)* opportunity; *(posibilidad)* chance.

oportunismo [oportu'nismo] *nm* opportunism; **oportunista** *nm/f* opportunist.

oportuno, a [opor'tuno, a] *a (en su tiempo)* opportune, timely; *(respuesta)* suitable; **en el momento ~** at the right moment.

oposición [oposi'θjon] *nf* opposition; **oposiciones** *nfpl* public examinations.

opositor, a [oposi'tor, a] *nm/f (adversario)* opponent; *(candidato)* candidate.

opresión [opre'sjon] *nf* oppression; **opresivo, a** *a* oppressive; **opresor, a** *nm/f* oppressor.

oprimir [opri'mir] *vt* to squeeze; *(fig)* to oppress.

oprobio [o'proβjo] *nm (infamia)* ignominy; *(descrédito)* shame.

optar [op'tar] *vi (elegir)* to choose; ~ **a** *o* **por** to opt for; **optativo, a** *a* optional.

óptico, a ['optiko, a] *a* optic(al) // *nm/f* optician.

optimismo [opti'mismo] *nm* optimism; **optimista** *nm/f* optimist.

óptimo, a ['optimo, a] *a (el mejor)* very best.

opuesto, a [o'pwesto, a] *a (contrario)* opposite; *(antagónico)* opposing.

opulencia [opu'lenθja] *nf* opulence; **opulento, a** *a* opulent.

oración [ora'θjon] *nf (discurso)* speech; *(REL)* prayer; *(LING)* sentence.

oráculo [o'rakulo] *nm* oracle.

orador, a [ora'ðor, a] *nm/f (conferenciante)* speaker, orator.

oral [o'ral] *a* oral.

orangután [orangu'tan] *nm* orangutan.

orar [o'rar] *vi (REL)* to pray.

oratoria [ora'torja] *nf* oratory.

órbita ['orβita] *nf* orbit.

orden ['orðen] *nm (gen)* order //

ordenado (*gen*) order; (*INFORM*) command; ~ **del día agenda**; **de primer** ~ first-rate; **en** ~ **de prioridad** in order of priority.

ordenado, a [orðe'naðo, a] *a* (*metódico*) methodical; (*arreglado*) orderly.

ordenador [orðena'ðor] *nm* computer; ~ **central** mainframe computer.

ordenanza [orðe'nanθa] *nf* ordinance.

ordenar [orðe'nar] *vt* (*mandar*) to order; (*poner orden*) to put in order, arrange; ~**se** *vr* (*REL*) to be ordained.

ordeñar [orðe'ɲar] *vt* to milk.

ordinario, a [orði'narjo, a] *a* (*común*) ordinary, usual; (*vulgar*) vulgar, common.

orégano [o'reɣano] *nm* oregano.

oreja [o'rexa] *nf* ear; (*MECÁNICA*) lug, flange.

orfanato [orfa'nato] *nm* orphanage.

orfandad [orfan'dað] *nf* orphanhood.

orfebrería [orfeβre'ria] *nf* gold/silver work.

orgánico, a [or'ɣaniko, a] *a* organic.

organigrama [orɣani'ɣrama] *nm* flow chart.

organismo [orɣa'nismo] *nm* (*BIO*) organism; (*POL*) organization.

organista [orɣa'nista] *nm/f* organist.

organización [orɣaniθa'θjon] *nf* organization; **organizar** *vt* to organize.

órgano [or'ɣano] *nm* organ.

orgasmo [or'ɣasmo] *nm* orgasm.

orgía [or'xia] *nf* orgy.

orgullo [or'ɣuʎo] *nm* (*altanería*) pride; (*autorespeto*) self-respect; **orgulloso, a** *a* (*gen*) proud; (*altanero*) haughty.

orientación [orjenta'θjon] *nf* (*posición*) position; (*dirección*) direction.

orientar [orjen'tar] *vt* (*situar*) to orientate; (*señalar*) to point; (*dirigir*) to guide; ~**se** *vr* to get one's bearings; (*decidirse*) to decide on a course of action.

oriente [o'rjente] *nm* east; **Cercano/Medio/Lejano O~** Near/Middle/Far East.

origen [o'rixen] *nm* origin; (*nacimiento*) lineage, birth.

original [orixi'nal] *a* (*nuevo*) original; (*extraño*) odd, strange; ~**idad** *nf* originality.

originar [orixi'nar] *vt* to start, cause; ~**se** *vr* to originate; ~**io, a** *a* (*nativo*) native; (*primordial*) original.

orilla [o'riʎa] *nf* (*borde*) border; (*de río*) bank; (*de bosque, tela*) edge; (*de mar*) shore.

orín [o'rin] *nm* rust.

orina [o'rina] *nf* urine; **orinal** *nm* (*chamber*) pot; **orinar** *vi* to urinate; **orinarse** *vr* to wet o.s.; **orines** *nmpl* urine *sg*.

oriundo, a [o'rjundo, a] *a*: ~ **de** native of.

ornamento [orna'mento] *nm* ornament.

ornar [or'nar] *vt* to adorn.

ornitología [ornitolo'xia] *nf* ornithology, bird-watching.

oro ['oro] *nm* gold; ~**s** *nmpl* (*NAIPES*) hearts.

oropel [oro'pel] *nm* tinsel.

orquesta [or'kesta] *nf* orchestra; ~ **de cámara/sinfónica** chamber/symphony orchestra.

orquídea [or'kiðea] *nf* orchid.

ortiga [or'tiɣa] *nf* nettle.

ortodoxo, a [orto'ðokso, a] *a* orthodox.

ortografía [ortoɣra'fia] *nf* spelling.

ortopedia [orto'peðja] *nf* orthopaedics *sg*.

oruga [o'ruɣa] *nf* caterpillar.

orzuelo [or'θwelo] *nm* (*MED*) stye.

os [os] *pron* (*gen*) you; (*a vosotros*) to you.

osa ['osa] *nf* (she-)bear; **O~ Mayor/Menor** Great/Little Bear.

osadía [osa'ðia] *nf* daring.

osar [o'sar] *vi* to dare.

oscilación [osθila'θjon] *nf* (*movimiento*) oscillation; (*fluctua-*

ción) fluctuation; (vacilación) hesitation; (columpio) swinging, movement to and fro.

oscilar [osθi'lar] vi to oscillate; to fluctuate; to hesitate.

oscurecer [oskure'θer] vt to darken // vi to grow dark; **~se** vr to grow o get dark.

oscuridad [oskuri'ðað] nf obscurity; (tinieblas) darkness.

oscuro, a [os'kuro, a] a dark; (fig) obscure; a **oscuras** in the dark.

óseo, a [l'oseo, a] a bony.

oso [l'oso] nm bear; **~ de peluche** teddy bear; **~ hormiguero** anteater.

ostensible [osten'siβle] a obvious.

ostentación [ostenta'θjon] nf (gen) ostentation; (acto) display.

ostentar [osten'tar] vt (gen) to show; (pey) to flaunt, show off; (poseer) to have, possess; **ostentoso, a** a ostentatious, showy.

ostra [l'ostra] nf oyster.

OTAN [l'otan] nf abr (= Organización del Tratado del Atlántico Norte) NATO.

otear [ote'ar] vt to observe; (fig) to look into.

otitis [o'titis] nf earache.

otoñal [oto'nal] a autumnal.

otoño [o'tono] nm autumn.

otorgamiento [otorɣa'mjento] nm conferring, granting; execution.

otorgar [otor'ɣar] vt (conceder) to concede; (dar) to grant.

otorrino, a [oto'rrino, a], **otorrinolaringólogo, a** [otorrinolarin'ɣolovo, a] nm/f ear, nose and throat specialist.

PALABRA CLAVE

otro, a [l'otro, a] ◆ a 1 (distinto: sg) another; (: pl) other; **con ~s amigos** with other o different friends 2 (adicional): **tráigame ~ café** (más), **por favor** can I have another coffee please; **~s 10 días más** another ten days
◆ pron 1: **el ~** the other one; (los) **~s** (the) others; **de ~** somebody

else's; **que lo haga ~** let somebody else do it

2 (recíproco): **se odian (la) una a (la) otra** they hate one another o each other

3: **~ tanto: comer ~ tanto** to eat the same o as much again; **recibió una docena de telegramas y otras tantas llamadas** he got about ten telegrams and as many calls.

---

ovación [oβa'θjon] nf ovation.

oval [o'βal], **ovalado, a** [oβa'laðo, a] a oval; **óvalo** nm oval.

oveja [o'βexa] nf sheep.

overol [oβe'rol] nm (AM) overalls pl.

ovillo [o'βiλo] nm (de lana) ball of wool; **hacerse un ~** to curl up.

OVNI [l'oβni] nm abr (= objeto volante no identificado) UFO.

ovulación [oβula'θjon] nf ovulation; **óvulo** nm ovum.

oxidación [oksiða'θjon] nf rusting.

oxidar [oksi'ðar] vt to rust; **~se** vr to go rusty.

óxido [l'oksiðo] nm oxide.

oxigenado, a [oksixe'naðo, a] a (QUIMICA) oxygenated; (pelo) bleached.

oxígeno [ok'sixeno] nm oxygen.

oyente [o'jente] nm/f listener, hearer.

oyes, oyó etc vb ver **oír**.

P

P abr (= padre) Fr.

pabellón [paβe'λon] nm bell tent; (ARQ) pavilion; (de hospital etc) block, section; (bandera) flag.

pábilo [l'paβilo] nm wick.

pacer [pa'θer] vi to graze.

paciencia [pa'θjenθja] nf patience.

paciente [pa'θjente] a, nm/f patient.

pacificación [paθifika'θjon] nf pacification.

pacificar [paθifi'kar] vt to pacify; (tranquilizar) to calm.

pacífico, a [pa'θifiko, a] a (persona)

peaceable; (*existencia*) peaceful; el (*océano*) P~ the Pacific (Ocean).

pacifismo [paθi'fismo] *nm* pacifism; **pacifista** *nmf* pacifist.

pacotilla [pako'tiʎa] *nf*: **de** ~ (*actor, escritor*) third-rate; (*mueble etc*) cheap.

pactar [pak'tar] *vt* to agree to *o* on // *vi* to come to an agreement.

pacto ['pakto] *nm* (*tratado*) pact; (*acuerdo*) agreement.

padecer [paðe'θer] *vt* (*sufrir*) to suffer; (*soportar*) to endure, put up with; (*engaño, error*) to be a victim of; **padecimiento** *nm* suffering.

padrastro [pa'ðrastro] *nm* step-father.

padre ['paðre] *nm* father // *a* (*fam*): **un éxito** ~ a tremendous success; ~**s** *nmpl* parents.

padrino [pa'ðrino] *nm* (*REL*) godfather; (*tb*: ~ **de boda**) best man; (*fig*) sponsor, patron; ~**s** *nmpl* godparents.

padrón [pa'ðron] *nm* (*censo*) census, roll; (*de socios*) register.

paella [pa'eʎa] *nf* paella, dish of rice with meat, shellfish etc.

pág(s). *abr* (= *página(s)*) p(p).

paga ['paɣa] *nf* (*pago*) payment; (*sueldo*) pay, wages *pl*.

pagadero, a [paɣa'ðero, a] *a* payable; ~ **a plazos** payable in instalments.

pagano, a [pa'ɣano, a] *a*, *nmf* pagan, heathen.

pagar [pa'ɣar] *vt* to pay; (*las compras, crimen*) to pay for; (*fig: favor*) to repay // *vi* to pay; ~ **al contado/a plazos** to pay (in) cash/in instalments.

pagaré [paɣa're] *nm* I.O.U.

página ['paxina] *nf* page.

pago ['paɣo] *nm* (*dinero*) payment; (*fig*) return; **estar** ~ to be even *o* quits; ~ **anticipado/a cuenta/contra reembolso/en especie** advance payment/payment on account/cash on delivery/payment in kind.

pague *etc vb ver* **pagar**.

país [pa'is] *nm* (*gen*) country; (*región*) land; **los P~es Bajos** the Low Countries; **el P~ Vasco** the Basque Country.

paisaje [pai'saxe] *nm* countryside, scenery.

paisano, a [pai'sano, a] *a* of the same country // *nmf* (*compatriota*) fellow countryman/woman; **vestir de** ~ (*soldado*) to be in civvies; (*guardia*) to be in plain clothes.

paja ['paxa] *nf* straw; (*fig*) rubbish (*Brit*), trash (*US*).

pájara ['paxara] *nf* hen (bird).

pajarita [paxa'rita] *nf* (*corbata*) bow tie.

pájaro ['paxaro] *nm* bird; ~ **carpintero** woodpecker.

pajita [pa'xita] *nf* (drinking) straw.

pala ['pala] *nf* spade, shovel; (*raqueta etc*) bat; (: **de tenis**) racquet; (*CULIN*) slice; ~ **matamoscas** fly swat.

palabra [pa'laβra] *nf* word; (*facultad*) (power of) speech; (*derecho de hablar*) right to speak; **tomar la** ~ (*en mitin*) to take the floor.

palabrota [pala'βrota] *nf* swearword.

palacio [pa'laθjo] *nm* palace; (*mansión*) mansion, large house; ~ **de justicia** courthouse; ~ **municipal** town/city hall.

paladar [pala'ðar] *nm* palate; **paladear** *vt* to taste.

palanca [pa'lanka] *nf* lever; (*fig*) pull, influence.

palangana [palan'gana] *nf* wash-basin.

palco ['palko] *nm* box.

Palestina [pales'tina] *nf* Palestine; **palestino, a** *nmf* Palestinian.

paleta [pa'leta] *nf* (*de pintor*) palette; (*de albañil*) trowel; (*de ping-pong*) bat; (*AM*) ice lolly.

paliar [pa'ljar] *vt* (*mitigar*) to mitigate, alleviate; **paliativo** *nm* palliative.

palidecer [paliðe'θer] *vi* to turn pale;

palidez nf paleness; **pálido, a** a pale.

palillo [pa'liʎo] nm small stick; (mondadientes) toothpick.

paliza [pa'liθa] nf beating, thrashing.

palma ['palma] nf (ANAT) palm; (árbol) palm tree; **batir** o **dar** ~**s** to clap, applaud; ~**da** nf slap; ~**s** nfpl clapping sg, applause sg.

palmear [palme'ar] vi to clap.

palmo ['palmo] nm (medida) span; (fig) small amount; ~ **a** ~ inch by inch.

palmotear [palmote'ar] vi to clap, applaud; **palmoteo** nm clapping, applause.

palo ['palo] nm stick; (poste) post, pole; (mango) handle, shaft; (golpe) blow, hit; (de golf) club; (de béisbol) bat; (NAUT) mast; (NAIPES) suit.

paloma [pa'loma] nf dove, pigeon.

palomilla [palo'miʎa] nf moth; (TEC: tuerca) wing nut; (: hierro) angle iron.

palomitas [palo'mitas] nfpl popcorn sg.

palpar [pal'par] vt to touch, feel.

palpitación [palpita'θjon] nf palpitation.

palpitante [palpi'tante] a palpitating; (fig) burning.

palpitar [palpi'tar] vi to palpitate; (latir) to beat.

palta ['palta] nf (AM) avocado (pear).

palúdico, a [pa'luðiko, a] a marshy.

paludismo [palu'ðismo] nm malaria.

pampa ['pampa] nf (AM) pampa(s), prairie.

pan [pan] nm bread; (una barra) loaf; ~ **integral** wholemeal (Brit) o wholewheat (US) bread; ~ **rallado** breadcrumbs pl.

pana ['pana] nf corduroy.

panadería [panaðe'ria] nf baker's (shop); **panadero, a** nm/f baker.

Panamá [pana'ma] nm Panama; **panameño, a** a Panamanian.

pancarta [pan'karta] nf placard, banner.

panda ['panda] nm (ZOOL) panda.

pandereta [pande'reta] nf tambourine.

pandilla [pan'diʎa] nf set, group; (de criminales) gang; (pey: camarilla) clique.

panecillo [pane'θiʎo] nm (bread) roll.

panel [pa'nel] nm panel.

panfleto [pan'fleto] nm pamphlet.

pánico [panico] nm panic.

panorama [pano'rama] nm panorama; (vista) view.

pantalón [panta'lon] nm, **pantalones** [panta'lones] nmpl trousers.

pantalla [pan'taʎa] nf (de cine) screen; (de lámpara) lampshade.

pantano [pan'tano] nm (ciénaga) marsh, swamp; (depósito: de agua) reservoir; (fig) jam, difficulty.

panteón [pante'on] nm: ~ **familiar** family tomb.

pantera [pan'tera] nf panther.

pantomima [panto'mima] nf pantomime.

pantorrilla [panto'rriʎa] nf calf (of the leg).

pantufla [pan'tufla] nf slipper.

panza ['panθa] nf belly, paunch; **panzón, ona, panzudo, a** a fat, potbellied.

pañal [pa'ɲal] nm nappy (Brit), diaper (US); ~**es** nmpl (fig) early stages, infancy sg.

pañería [paɲe'ria] nf drapery.

paño ['paɲo] nm (tela) cloth; (pedazo de tela) (piece of) cloth; (trapo) duster, rag; ~ **higiénico** sanitary towel; ~**s menores** underclothes.

pañuelo [pa'ɲwelo] nm handkerchief, hanky (fam); (para la cabeza) (head)scarf.

papa ['papa] nf (AM) potato // nm: el P~ the Pope.

papá [pa'pa] (pl ~**s**) nm (fam) dad(dy), pa (US).

papagayo [papa'yajo] nm parrot.

papanatas [papa'natas] nm inv (fam) simpleton.

paparrucha [papaˈrrutʃa] *nf* piece of nonsense.

papaya [paˈpaja] *nf* papaya.

papel [paˈpel] *nm* paper; (*hoja de ~*) sheet of paper; (*TEATRO, fig*) role; **~ de calco/carbón/de cartas** tracing paper/carbon paper/stationery; **~ de envolver/pintado** wrapping paper/wallpaper; **~ de aluminio/higiénico** aluminium (*Brit*) *o* aluminum (*US*) foil/toilet paper; **~ de lija** sandpaper; **~ moneda** paper money; **~ secante** blotting paper.

papeleo [papeˈleo] *nm* red tape.

papelera [papeˈlera] *nf* wastepaper basket; (*escritorio*) desk.

papelería [papeleˈria] *nf* stationer's (shop).

papeleta [papeˈleta] *nf* (*pedazo de papel*) slip of paper; (*POL*) ballot paper; (*ESCOL*) report.

paperas [paˈperas] *nfpl* mumps.

papilla [paˈpiʎa] *nf* (*para niños*) baby food.

paquete [paˈkete] *nm* (*de cigarrillos etc*) packet; (*CORREOS etc*) parcel; (*AM*) package tour; (: *fam*) nuisance, bore.

par [par] *a* (*igual*) like, equal; (*MAT*) even // *nm* equal; (*de guantes*) pair; (*de veces*) couple; (*POL*) peer; (*GOLF, COM*) par; **abrir** *o* **~ en ~** to open wide.

para ['para] *prep* for; **no es ~ comer** it's not for eating; **decir ~ sí** to say to o.s.; **¿~ qué lo quieres?** what do you want it for?; **se casaron ~ separarse otra vez** they married only to separate again; **lo tendré ~ mañana** I'll have it (for) tomorrow; **ir ~ casa** to go home, head for home; **~ profesor es muy estúpido** he's very stupid for a teacher; **¿quién es usted ~ gritar así?** who are you to shout like that?; **tengo bastante ~ vivir** I have enough to live on.

parabién [paraˈβjen] *nm* congratulations *pl*.

parábola [paˈraβola] *nf* parable;

(*MAT*) parabola.

parabrisas [paraˈβrisas] *nm inv* windscreen (*Brit*), windshield (*US*).

paracaídas [parakaˈiðas] *nm inv* parachute; **paracaidista** *nm/f* parachutist; (*MIL*) paratrooper.

parachoques [paraˈtʃokes] *nm inv* (*AUTO*) bumper; (*MECÁNICA etc*) shock absorber.

parada [paˈraða] *nf* stop; (*acto*) stopping; (*de industria*) shutdown, stoppage; (*lugar*) stopping place; **~ de autobús** bus stop.

paradero [paraˈðero] *nm* stopping-place; (*situación*) whereabouts.

parado, a [paˈraðo, a] *a* (*persona*) motionless, standing still; (*fábrica*) closed, at a standstill; (*coche*) stopped; (*AM*) standing (up); (*sin empleo*) unemployed, idle.

paradoja [paraˈðoxa] *nf* paradox.

parador [paraˈðor] *nm* parador, state-owned hotel.

paráfrasis [paˈrafrasis] *nf inv* paraphrase.

paraguas [paˈraɣwas] *nm inv* umbrella.

Paraguay [paraˈɣwai] *nm*: **el ~** Paraguay; **paraguayo, a** *a, nm/f* Paraguayan.

paraíso [paraˈiso] *nm* paradise, heaven.

paraje [paˈraxe] *nm* place, spot.

paralelo, a [paraˈlelo, a] *a* parallel.

parálisis [paˈralisis] *nf inv* paralysis; **paralítico, a** *a, nm/f* paralytic.

paralizar [paraliˈθar] *vt* to paralyse; **~se** *vr* to become paralysed; (*fig*) to come to a standstill.

paramilitar [paramiliˈtar] *a* paramilitary.

páramo ['paramo] *nm* bleak plateau.

parangón [paranˈgon] *nm*: **sin ~** incomparable.

paranoico, a [paraˈnoiko, a] *nm/f* paranoiac.

parapléjico, a [paraˈplexiko, a] *a, nm/f* paraplegic.

parar [paˈrar] *vt* to stop; (*golpe*) to ward off // *vi* to stop; **~se** *vr* to stop;

(*AM*) to stand up; **ha parado de llover** it has stopped raining; **van a ~ en la comisaría** they're going to end up in the police station; **~se en** to pay attention to.

parásito, a [pa'rasito, a] *nm/f* parasite.

parasol [para'sol] *nm* parasol, sunshade.

parcela [par'θela] *nf* plot, piece of ground.

parcial [par'θjal] *a* (*pago*) part-; (*eclipse*) partial; (*JUR*) prejudiced, biased; (*POL*) partisan; **~idad** *nf* (*prejuicio*) prejudice, bias.

parco, a [parko, a] *a* (*moderado*) moderate.

parche [partʃe] *nm* (*gen*) patch.

parear [pare'ar] *vt* (*juntar, hacer par*) to match, put together; (*BIO*) to mate, pair.

parecer [pare'θer] *nm* (*opinión*) opinion, view; (*aspecto*) looks *pl* // *vi* (*tener apariencia*) to seem, look; (*asemejarse*) to look o seem like; (*aparecer, llegar*) to appear; **~se** *vr* to look alike, resemble each other; **~se a** to look like, resemble; **según o a lo que parece** evidently, apparently; **me parece que I** think (that), it seems to me that.

parecido, a [pare'θiðo, a] *a* similar // *nm* similarity, likeness, resemblance; **bien ~** good-looking, nice-looking.

pared [pa'reð] *nf* wall.

parejo, a [pa'rexo, a] *a* (*igual*) equal; (*liso*) smooth, even // *nf* (*par*) pair; (*dos personas*) couple; (*otro: de un par*) other one (of a pair); (*persona*) partner.

parentela [paren'tela] *nf* relations *pl*.

parentesco [paren'tesko] *nm* relationship.

paréntesis [pa'rentesis] *nm inv* parenthesis; (*digresión*) digression (*en escrito*) bracket.

parezco *etc vb ver* **parecer**.

pariente, a [pa'rjente, a] *nm/f* relative, relation.

parir [pa'rir] *vt* to give birth to // *vi* (*mujer*) to give birth, have a baby.

París [pa'ris] *n* Paris.

parking [parkin] *nm* car park (*Brit*), parking lot (*US*).

parlamentar [parlamen'tar] *vi* (*negociar*) to parley.

parlamentario, a [parlamen'tarjo, a] *a* parliamentary // *nm/f* member of parliament.

parlamento [parla'mento] *nm* (*POL*) parliament.

parlanchín, ina [parlan'tʃin, ina] *a* indiscreet // *nm/f* chatterbox.

paro [paro] *nm* (*huelga*) stoppage (of work), strike; (*desempleo*) unemployment; **subsidio de ~** unemployment benefit; **hay ~ en la industria** work in the industry is at a standstill.

parodia [pa'roðja] *nf* parody; **parodiar** *vt* to parody.

parpadear [parpaðe'ar] *vi* (*ojos*) to blink; (*luz*) to flicker.

párpado [parpaðo] *nm* eyelid.

parque [parke] *nm* (*lugar verde*) park; **~ de atracciones/infantil/zoológico** fairground/playground/zoo.

parquímetro [par'kimetro] *nm* parking meter.

parra [parra] *nf* (*grape*)vine.

párrafo [parrafo] *nm* paragraph; **echar un ~** (*fam*) to have a chat.

parranda [pa'rranda] *nf* (*fam*) spree, binge.

parrilla [pa'rriʎa] *nf* (*CULIN*) grill; (*de coche*) grille; (*carne a la*) **~** barbecue; **~da** *nf* barbecue.

párroco [parroko] *nm* parish priest.

parroquia [pa'rrokja] *nf* parish; (*iglesia*) parish church; (*COM*) clientele, customers *pl*; **~no, a** *nm/f* parishioner; client, customer.

parte [parte] *nm* message; (*informe*) report // *nf* part; (*lado, cara*) side; (*de reparto*) share; (*JUR*) party; **en alguna ~ de Europa** somewhere in Europe; **en/por todas ~s** everywhere; **en gran ~** to a large extent; **la mayor ~ de los españoles** most

Spaniards; **de un tiempo a esta ~** for some time past; **de ~ de alguien** on sb's behalf; **¿de ~ de quién?** (*TEL*) who is speaking?; **por ~ de** on the part of; **yo por mí ~** I for my part; **por otra ~** on the other hand; **dar ~** to inform; **tomar ~** to take part.

partera [par'tera] *nf* midwife.

partición [parti'θjon] *nf* division, sharing-out; (*POL*) partition.

participación [partiθipa'θjon] *nf* (*acto*) participation, taking part; (*parte*, *COM*) share; (*de lotería*) shared prize; (*aviso*) notice, notification.

participante [partiθi'pante] *nm/f* participant.

participar [partiθi'par] *vt* to notify, inform // *vi* to take part, participate.

partícipe [par'tiθipe] *nm/f* participant.

particular [partiku'lar] *a* (*especial*) particular, special; (*individual*, *personal*) private, personal // *nm* (*punto*, *asunto*) particular, point; (*individuo*) individual; **tiene coche ~** he has a car of his own; **~izar** *vt* to distinguish; (*especificar*) to specify; (*detallar*) to give details about.

partida [par'tiða] *nf* (*salida*) departure; (*COM*) entry, item; (*juego*) game; (*grupo de personas*) band, group; **mala ~** dirty trick; **~ de nacimiento/matrimonio/defunción** birth/marriage/death certificate.

partidario, a [parti'ðarjo] *a*] partisan // *nm/f* supporter, follower.

partido [par'tiðo] *nm* (*POL*) party; (*DEPORTE*: *encuentro*) game, match; (*: equipo*) team; (*apoyo*) support; **sacar ~ de** to profit o benefit from; **tomar ~** to take sides.

partir [par'tir] *vt* (*dividir*) to split, divide; (*compartir*, *distribuir*) to share (out), distribute; (*romper*) to break open, split open; (*rebanada*) to cut (off) // *vi* (*ponerse en camino*) to set off o out; (*comenzar*) to start (off

o out); **~se** *vr* to crack *o* split *o* break in two *etc*); **a ~ de** (*starting*) from.

parto [parto] *nm* birth; (*fig*) product, creation; **estar de ~** to be in labour.

parvulario [parβu'larjo] *nm* nursery school, kindergarten.

pasa ['pasa] *nf* raisin; **~ de Corinto/de Esmirna** currant/sultana.

pasada [pa'saða] *af, nf ver* **pasado**.

pasadizo [pasa'ðiθo] *nm* (*pasillo*) passage, corridor; (*callejuela*) alley.

pasado, a [pa'saðo, a] *a* past; (*malo: comida, fruta*) bad; (*muy cocido*) overdone; (*anticuado*) out of date // *nm* past *nf* passing, passage; **~ mañana** the day after tomorrow; **el mes ~** last month; **de pasada** in passing, incidentally; **una mala pasada** a dirty trick.

pasador [pasa'ðor] *nm* (*gen*) bolt; (*de pelo*) hair slide; (*horquilla*) grip.

pasaje [pa'saxe] *nm* (*pago de viaje*) fare; (*los pasajeros*) passengers *pl*; (*pasillo*) passageway.

pasajero, a [pasa'xero, a] *a* passing // *nm/f* passenger.

pasamanos [pasa'manos] *nm inv* (*hand*)rail; (*de escalera*) banisters *pl*.

pasamontañas [pasamon'taɲas] *nm inv* balaclava helmet.

pasaporte [pasa'porte] *nm* passport.

pasar [pa'sar] *vt* to pass; (*tiempo*) to spend; (*desgracias*) to suffer, endure; (*noticia*) to give, pass on; (*río*) to cross; (*barrera*) to pass through; (*falta*) to overlook, tolerate; (*contrincante*) to surpass, do better than; (*coche*) to overtake; (*CINE*) to show; (*enfermedad*) to give, infect with // *vi* (*gen*) to pass; (*terminarse*) to be over; (*ocurrir*) to happen; **~se** *vr* (*flores*) to fade; (*comida*) to go bad o off; (*fig*) to overdo it, go too far; **~ de** to go beyond, exceed; **~ por** (*AM*) to fetch; **¡lo bien/mal** to have a good/bad time; **¡pase!** come in!; **~se al enemigo** to go over to the enemy; **se me pasó** I forgot; **no se le pasa nada** he misses nothing; **pase lo que pase** come what may.

pasarela [pasa'rela] *nf* footbridge; *(en barco)* gangway.

pasatiempo [pasa'tjempo] *nm* pastime, hobby.

Pascua ['paskwa] *nf*: ~ **(de Resurrección)** Easter; ~ **de Navidad** Christmas; **~s** *nfpl* Christmas (time); **¡felices ~s!** Merry Christmas!

pase ['pase] *nm* pass; *(CINE)* performance, showing.

pasear [pase'ar] *vt* to take for a walk; *(exhibir)* to parade, show off // *vi*, **~se** *vr* to walk, go for a walk; **~ en coche** to go for a drive; **paseo** *nm (avenida)* avenue; *(distancia corta)* walk, stroll; **dar un o ir de paseo** to go for a walk.

pasillo [pa'siλo] *nm* passage, corridor.

pasión [pa'sjon] *nf* passion.

pasivo, a [pa'siβo, a] *a* passive; *(inactivo)* inactive // *nm (COM)* liabilities *pl*, debts *pl*; *(LING)* passive.

pasmar [pas'mar] *vt (asombrar)* to amaze, astonish; **pasmo** *nm* amazement, astonishment; *(resfriado)* chill; *(fig)* wonder, marvel; **pasmoso, a** *a* amazing, astonishing.

paso, a ['paso, a] *a* dried // *nm* step; *(modo de andar)* walk; *(huella)* footprint; *(rapidez)* speed, pace, rate; *(camino accesible)* way through, passage; *(cruce)* crossing; *(pasaje)* passing, passage; *(GEO)* pass; *(estrecho)* strait; ~ **de peatones** pedestrian crossing; **a ese** ~ *(fig)* at that rate; **salir al** ~ **de o** a to waylay; **estar de** ~ to be passing through; ~ **elevado** flyover; **prohibido el** ~ no entry; **ceda el** ~ give way.

pasota [pa'sota] *a, nmf (fam)* = dropout; **ser un (tipo)** ~ to be a bit of a dropout; *(ser indiferente)* not to care about anything.

pasta ['pasta] *nf* paste; *(CULIN: masa)* dough; (: *de bizcochos etc)* pastry; *(fam)* dough; **~s** *nfpl (bizcochos)* pastries, small cakes; *(fideos, espaguetis etc)* pasta; ~ **de dientes o dentífrica** toothpaste.

pastar [pas'tar] *vt, vi* to graze.

pastel [pas'tel] *nm (dulce)* cake; ~ **de carne** meat pie; *(ARTE)* pastel; **~ería** *nf* cake shop.

pasteurizado, a [pasteuri'θaðo, a] *a* pasteurized.

pastilla [pas'tiλa] *nf (de jabón, chocolate)* bar; *(píldora)* tablet, pill.

pasto ['pasto] *nm (hierba)* grass; *(lugar)* pasture, field.

pastor, a [pas'tor, a] *nm/f* shepherd/ess // *nm (REL)* clergyman, pastor.

pata ['pata] *nf (pierna)* leg; *(pie)* foot; *(de muebles)* leg; **~s arriba** upside down; **meter la** ~ to put one's foot in it; *(TEC)*: ~ **de cabra** crowbar; **tener buena/mala** ~ to be lucky/unlucky; **~da** *nf* kick; *(en el suelo)* stamp.

patalear [patale'ar] *vi (en el suelo)* to stamp one's feet.

patata [pa'tata] *nf* potato; **~s fritas o a la española** chips, French fries; **~s fritas (de bolsa)** crisps.

paté [pa'te] *nm* pâté.

patear [pate'ar] *vt (pisar)* to stamp on, trample (on); *(pegar con el pie)* to kick // *vi* to stamp (with rage), stamp one's feet.

patente [pa'tente] *a* obvious, evident; *(COM)* patent // *nf* patent.

paternal [pater'nal] *a* fatherly, paternal; **paterno, a** *a* paternal.

patético, a [pa'tetiko, a] *a* pathetic, moving.

patillas [pa'tiλas] *nfpl* sideburns.

patín [pa'tin] *nm* skate; *(de trineo)* runner; **patinaje** *nm* skating; **patinar** *vi* to skate; *(resbalarse)* to skid, slip; *(fam)* to slip up, blunder.

patio ['patjo] *nm (de casa)* patio, courtyard; ~ **de recreo** playground.

pato ['pato] *nm* duck; **pagar el** ~ *(fam)* to take the blame, carry the can.

patológico, a [pato'loxiko, a] *a* pathological.

patoso, a [pa'toso, a] *a* (*fam*) clumsy.

patraña [pa'traɲa] *nf* story, fib.

patria ['patrja] *nf* native land, mother country.

patrimonio [patri'monjo] *nm* inheritance; (*fig*) heritage.

patriota [pa'trjota] *nm/f* patriot; **patriotismo** *nm* patriotism.

patrocinar [patroθi'nar] *vt* to sponsor; (*apoyar*) to back, support; **patrocinio** *nm* sponsorship; backing, support.

patrón, ona [pa'tron, ona] *nm/f* (*jefe*) boss, chief, master/mistress; (*propietario*) landlord/lady; (*REL*) patron saint // *nm* (*TEC, COSTURA*) pattern.

patronal [patro'nal] *a*: **la clase ~** management.

patronato [patro'nato] *nm* sponsorship; (*acto*) patronage; (*fundación benéfica*) trust, foundation.

patrulla [pa'truʎa] *nf* patrol.

pausa ['pausa] *nf* pause, break.

pausado, a [pau'saðo, a] *a* slow, deliberate.

pauta ['pauta] *nf* line, guide line.

pavimento [paβi'mento] *nm* (*con losas*) pavement, paving.

pavo ['paβo] *nm* turkey; **~ real** peacock.

pavor [pa'βor] *nm* dread, terror.

payaso, a [pa'jaso, a] *nm/f* clown.

payo, a ['pajo] *nm/f* (*para gitanos*) non-gipsy.

paz [paθ] *nf* peace; (*tranquilidad*) peacefulness, tranquillity; **hacer las paces** to make peace; (*fig*) to make up; **La P~ n** (*GEO*) La Paz.

PC *abr* = **Partido Comunista.**

P.D. *abr* (= *posdata*) PS, ps.

peaje [pe'axe] *nm* toll.

peatón [pea'ton] *nm* pedestrian.

peca ['peka] *nf* freckle.

pecado [pe'kaðo] *nm* sin; **pecador, a** *a* sinful // *nm/f* sinner.

pecaminoso, a [pekami'noso, a] *a* sinful.

pecar [pe'kar] *vi* (*REL*) to sin; (*fig*): **peca de generoso** he is generous to a fault.

peculiar [peku'ljar] *a* special, peculiar; (*característico*) typical, characteristic; **~idad** *nf* peculiarity; special feature, characteristic.

pecho ['petʃo] *nm* (*ANAT*) chest; (*de mujer*) breast(s) (*pl*), bosom; (*fig*: *corazón*) heart, breast; (: *valor*) courage, spirit; **dar el ~ a** to breast-feed; **tomar algo a ~** to take sth to heart.

pechuga [pe'tʃuɣa] *nf* breast.

pedal [pe'ðal] *nm* pedal; **~ear** *vi* to pedal.

pédalo ['peðalo] *nm* pedal boat.

pedante [pe'ðante] *a* pedantic // *nm/f* pedant; **~ría** *nf* pedantry.

pedazo [pe'ðaθo] *nm* piece, bit; **hacerse ~s** (*romperse*) to smash, shatter.

pedernal [peðer'nal] *nm* flint.

pediatra [pe'ðjatra] *nm/f* paediatrician.

pedicuro, a [peði'kuro, a] *nm/f* chiropodist.

pedido [pe'ðiðo] *nm* (*COM*: *mandado*) order; (*petición*) request.

pedir [pe'ðir] *vt* to ask for, request; (*comida, COM*: *mandar*) to order; (*exigir: precio*) to ask; (*necesitar*) to need, demand, require // *vi* to ask; **me pidió que cerrara la puerta** he asked me to shut the door; **¿cuánto piden por el coche?** how much are they asking for the car?

pegadizo, a [peɣa'ðiθo, a] *a* (*MUS*) catchy.

pegajoso, a [peɣa'xoso, a] *a* sticky, adhesive.

pegamento [peɣa'mento] *nm* gum, glue.

pegar [pe'ɣar] *vt* (*papel, sellos*) to stick (on); (*cartel*) to stick up; (*coser*) to sew (on); (*unir: partes*) to join, fix together; (*MED*) to give, infect with; (*dar: golpe*) to give, deal // *vi* *vi (adherirse)* to stick, adhere; *(ir juntos: colores)* to match, go together; *(golpear)* to match; *(quemar: el sol)* to strike hot, burn *(fig)*; ~se *vr (gen)* to stick; *(dos personas)* to hit each other, fight; *(fam)*: ~ **un grito** to let out a yell; ~ **un salto** to jump (with fright); ~ **en** to touch; ~**se un tiro** to shoot o.s.

pegatina [peɣa'tina] *nf* sticker.

peinado [pei'naðo] *nm (en peluqueria)* hairdo; *(estilo)* hair style.

peinar [pei'nar] *vt* to comb; *(hacer estilo)* to style; ~se *vr* to comb one's hair.

peine ['peine] *nm* comb; ~**ta** *nf* ornamental comb.

p.ej. *abr (= por ejemplo)* eg.

Pekín [pe'kin] *n* Pekin(g).

pelado, a [pe'laðo, a] *a (fruta, patata etc)* peeled; *(cabeza)* shorn; *(campo)* bare; *(fam: sin dinero)* broke.

pelaje [pe'laxe] *nm (ZOOL)* fur, coat; *(fig)* appearance.

pelambre [pe'lambre] *nm (pelo largo)* long hair, mop.

pelar [pe'lar] *vt (fruta, patatas etc)* to peel; *(cortar el pelo a)* to cut the hair of; *(quitar la piel: animal)* to skin; ~se *vr (la piel)* to peel off; **voy a ~me** I'm going to get my hair cut.

peldaño [pel'daɲo] *nm* step.

pelea [pe'lea] *nf (lucha)* fight; *(discusión)* quarrel, row.

peleado, a [pele'aðo, a] *a*: **estar ~ (con uno)** to have fallen out (with sb).

pelear [pele'ar] *vi* to fight; ~se *vr* to fight; *(reñirse)* to fall out, quarrel.

peletería [pelete'ria] *nf* furrier's, fur shop.

pelícano [pe'likano] *nm* pelican.

película [pe'likula] *nf* film; *(cobertura ligera)* thin covering; *(FOTO: rollo)* roll o reel of film.

peligro [pe'liɣro] *nm* danger; *(riesgo)* risk; **correr ~ de** to run the risk of; ~**so, a** *a* dangerous; risky.

pelirrojo, a [peli'rroxo, a] *a* red-haired, red-headed // *nm/f* redhead.

pelma ['pelma] *nm/f*, **pelmazo** [pel'maθo] *nm (fam)* pain (in the neck).

pelo ['pelo] *nm (cabellos)* hair; *(de barba, bigote)* whisker; *(de animal: pellejo)* hair, fur, coat; **al ~** just right; **venir al ~** to be exactly what one needs; **un hombre de ~ en pecho** a brave man; **por los ~s** by the skin of one's teeth; **no tener ~s en la lengua** to be outspoken, not mince words; **tomar el ~ a uno** to pull sb's leg.

pelón, ona [pe'lon, ona] *a* hairless, bald.

pelota [pe'lota] *nf* ball; *(fam: cabeza)* nut; **en ~** stark naked; **hacer la ~ (a uno)** *(fam)* to creep (to sb); ~ **vasca** pelota.

pelotari [pelo'tari] *nm* pelota player.

pelotón [pelo'ton] *nm (MIL)* squad, detachment.

peluca [pe'luka] *nf* wig.

peluche [pe'lutʃe] *nm*: **oso/muñeco de ~** teddy bear/soft toy.

peludo, a [pe'luðo, a] *a* hairy, shaggy.

peluquería [peluke'ria] *nf* hairdresser's; *(para hombres)* barber's *(shop)*; **peluquero, a** *nm/f* hairdresser; barber.

pelusa [pe'lusa] *nf (BOT)* down; *(COSTURA)* fluff.

pellejo [pe'ʎexo] *nm (de animal)* skin, hide.

pellizcar [peʎiθ'kar] *vt* to pinch, nip.

pena ['pena] *nf (congoja)* grief, sadness; *(remordimiento)* regret; *(dificultad)* trouble; *(dolor)* pain; *(JUR)* sentence; **merecer o valer la ~** to be worthwhile; **a duras ~s** with great difficulty; ~ **de muerte** death penalty; ~ **pecuniaria** fine; **¡qué ~!** what a shame!

penal [pe'nal] *a* penal // *nm (cárcel)* prison.

penalidad [penali'ðað] *nf (problema, dificultad)* trouble, hardship; *(JUR)* penalty, punishment.

penalti, penalty [pe'nalti] (*pl* **penaltis, penaltý(e)s, penalties**) *nm* penalty (kick).

penar [pe'nar] *vt* to penalize; (*castigar*) to punish // *vi* to suffer.

pendiente [pen'djente] *a* pending, unsettled // *nm* earring // *nf* hill, slope.

pene ['pene] *nm* penis.

penetración [penetra'θjon] *nf* (*acto*) penetration; (*agudeza*) sharpness, insight.

penetrante [pene'trante] *a* (*herida*) deep; (*persona, arma*) sharp; (*sonido*) penetrating, piercing; (*mirada*) searching; (*viento, ironía*) biting.

penetrar [pene'trar] *vt* to penetrate, pierce; (*entender*) to grasp // *vi* to penetrate, go in; (*entrar*) to enter, go in; (*líquido*) to soak in; (*fig*) to pierce.

penicilina [peniθi'lina] *nf* penicillin.

península [pe'ninsula] *nf* peninsula; **peninsular** *a* peninsular.

penique [pe'nike] *nm* penny.

penitencia [peni'tenθja] *nf* (*remordimiento*) penitence; (*castigo*) penance; **~ría** *nf* prison, penitentiary.

penoso, a [pe'noso, a] *a* (*difícil*) arduous, difficult.

pensador, a [pensa'ðor, a] *nm/f* thinker.

pensamiento [pensa'mjento] *nm* thought; (*mente*) mind; (*idea*) idea.

pensar [pen'sar] *vt* to think; (*considerar*) to think over, think out; (*proponerse*) to intend, plan; (*imaginarse*) to think up, invent // *vi* to think; **~ en** to aim at, aspire to; **pensativo, a** *a* thoughtful, pensive.

pensión [pen'sjon] *nf* (*casa*) boarding *o* guest house; (*dinero*) pension; (*cama y comida*) board and lodging; **~ completa** full board; **pensionista** *nm/f* (*jubilado*) (old-age) pensioner; (*huésped*) lodger.

penúltimo, a [pe'nultimo, a] *a*

penultimate, last but one.

penumbra [pe'numbra] *nf* half-light.

penuria [pe'nurja] *nf* shortage, want.

peña ['pena] *nf* (*roca*) rock; (*cuesta*) cliff, crag; (*grupo*) group, circle; (*AM: club*) folk club.

peñasco [pe'nasko] *nm* large rock, boulder.

peñón [pe'non] *nm* wall of rock; **el P~** the Rock (of Gibraltar).

peón [pe'on] *nm* labourer; (*AM*) farm labourer, farmhand; (*AJEDREZ*) pawn.

peonza [pe'onθa] *nf* spinning top.

peor [pe'or] *a* (*comparativo*) worse; (*superlativo*) worst // *ad* worse; worst; **de mal en ~** from bad to worse.

pepinillo [pepi'niλo] *nm* gherkin.

pepino [pe'pino] *nm* cucumber; (**no**) **me importa un ~** I don't care one bit.

pepita [pe'pita] *nf* (*BOT*) pip; (*MINERÍA*) nugget.

pequeñez [peke'neθ] *nf* smallness, littleness; (*trivialidad*) trifle, triviality.

pequeño, a [pe'keno, a] *a* small, little.

pera ['pera] *nf* pear; **peral** *nm* pear tree.

percance [per'kanθe] *nm* setback, misfortune.

percatarse [perka'tarse] *vr*: **~ de** to notice, take note of.

percepción [perθep'θjon] *nf* (*vista*) perception; (*idea*) notion, idea.

perceptible [perθep'tiβle] *a* perceptible, noticeable; (*COM*) payable, receivable.

percibir [perθi'βir] *vt* to perceive, notice; (*COM*) to earn, get.

percusión [perku'sjon] *nf* percussion.

percha [pertʃa] *nf* (*ganchos*) coat hooks *pl*; (*colgador*) coat hanger; (*de ave*) perch.

perdedor, a [perðe'ðor, a] *a* losing // *nm/f* loser.

perder [per'ðer] *vt* to lose; (*tiempo, palabras*) to waste; (*oportunidad*) to lose, miss; *(tren)* to miss // *vi* to lose; **~se** *vr (extraviarse)* to get lost; *(desaparecer)* to disappear, be lost to view; *(arruinarse)* to be ruined; **echar a ~** *(comida)* to spoil, ruin; *(oportunidad)* to waste.

perdición [perði'θjon] *nf* perdition, ruin.

pérdida ['perðiða] *nf* loss; *(de tiempo)* waste; **~s** *nfpl (COM)* losses.

perdido, a [per'ðiðo, a] *a* lost.

perdiz [per'ðiθ] *nf* partridge.

perdón [per'ðon] *nm (disculpa)* pardon, forgiveness; *(clemencia)* mercy; **¡~!** sorry!, I beg your pardon!; **perdonar** *vt* to pardon, forgive; *(la vida)* to spare; *(excusar)* to exempt, excuse; **¡perdone (usted)!** sorry!, I beg your pardon!

perdurable [perðu'raßle] *a* lasting; *(eterno)* everlasting.

perdurar [perðu'rar] *vi (resistir)* to last, endure; *(seguir existiendo)* to stand, still exist.

perecedero, a [pereθe'ðero, a] *a (COM etc)* perishable.

perecer [pere'θer] *vi (morir)* to perish, die; *(objeto)* to shatter.

peregrinación [pereɣrina'θjon] *nf (REL)* pilgrimage.

peregrino, a [pere'ɣrino, a] *a (idea)* strange, absurd // *nm/f* pilgrim.

perejil [pere'xil] *nm* parsley.

perenne [pe'renne] *a* everlasting, perennial.

perentorio, a [peren'torjo, a] *a (urgente)* urgent, peremptory; *(fijo)* set, fixed.

pereza [pe'reθa] *nf* laziness, idleness; **perezoso, a** *a* lazy, idle.

perfección [perfek'θjon] *nf* perfection; **perfeccionar** *vt* to perfect; *(mejorar)* to improve; *(acabar)* to complete, finish.

perfectamente [perfekta'mente] *ad* perfectly.

perfecto, a [per'fekto, a] *a (gen)* perfect; *(terminado)* complete, finished.

perfidia [per'fiðja] *nf* perfidy,

treachery.

perfil [per'fil] *nm* profile; *(contorno)* silhouette, outline; *(ARQ) (cross)* section; **~es** *nmpl* features; *(fig)* social graces; **~ado, a** *a (bien formado)* well-shaped; *(largo: cara)* long; **~ar** *vt (trazar)* to outline; *(fig)* to shape, give character to.

perforación [perfora'θjon] *nf* perforation; *(con taladro)* drilling; **perforadora** *nf* punch.

perforar [perfo'rar] *vt* to perforate; *(agujero)* to drill, bore; *(papel)* to punch a hole in // *vi* to drill, bore.

perfume [per'fume] *nm* perfume, scent.

pericia [pe'riθja] *nf* skill, expertise.

periferia [peri'ferja] *nf* periphery; *(de ciudad)* outskirts *pl*.

periférico [peri'feriko] *nm (AM)* ring road *(Brit)*, beltway *(US)*.

perímetro [pe'rimetro] *nm* perimeter.

periódico, a [pe'rjoðiko, a] *a* periodic(al) // *nm* newspaper.

periodismo [perjo'ðismo] *nm* journalism; **periodista** *nm/f* journalist.

periodo [pe'rjoðo], **período** [pe'rioðo] *nm* period.

periquito [peri'kito] *nm* budgerigar, budgie.

perito, a [pe'rito, a] *a (experto)* expert; *(diestro)* skilled, skilful // *nm/f* expert; skilled worker; *(técnico)* technician.

perjudicar [perxuði'kar] *vt (gen)* to damage, harm; **perjudicial** *a* damaging, harmful; *(en detrimento)* detrimental; **perjuicio** *nm* damage, harm.

perjurar [perxu'rar] *vi* to commit perjury.

perla ['perla] *nf* pearl; **me viene de ~** it suits me fine.

permanecer [permane'θer] *vi (quedarse)* to stay, remain; *(seguir)* to continue to be.

permanencia [perma'nenθja] *nf* permanence; *(estancia)* stay.

permanente [perma'nente] *a*

permanent, constant // nf perm.

permisible [permi'siβle] a permissible, allowable.

permiso [per'miso] nm permission; (*licencia*) permit, licence; **con ~** excuse me; **estar de ~** (*MIL*) to be on leave; **~ de conducir** driving licence (*Brit*), driver's license (*US*).

permitir [permi'tir] vt to permit, allow.

pernera [per'nera] nf trouser leg.

pernicioso, a [perni'θjoso, a] a (*maligno, MED*) pernicious; (*persona*) wicked.

pernio [per'njo] nm hinge.

perno ['perno] nm bolt.

pero ['pero] conj but; (*aún*) yet // nm (*defecto*) flaw, defect; (*reparo*) objection.

perol [pe'rol] nm, **perola** [pe'rola] nf (large metal) pan.

perpendicular [perpendiku'lar] a perpendicular.

perpetrar [perpe'trar] vt to perpetrate.

perpetuar [perpe'twar] vt to perpetuate; **perpetuo, a** a perpetual.

perplejo, a [per'plexo, a] a perplexed, bewildered.

perra ['pera] nf (*ZOOL*) bitch; (*fam: dinero*) money; **estar sin una ~** to be flat broke.

perrera [pe'rrera] nf kennel.

perro ['pero] nm dog.

persa ['persa] a, nm/f Persian.

persecución [perseku'θjon] nf pursuit, chase; (*REL, POL*) persecution.

perseguir [perse'xir] vt to pursue, hunt; (*cortejar*) to chase after; (*molestar*) to pester, annoy; (*REL, POL*) to persecute.

perseverante [perseβe'rante] a persevering, persistent.

perseverar [perseβe'rar] vi to persevere, persist; **~ en** to persevere in, persist with.

persiana [per'sjana] nf (Venetian) blind.

persignarse [persiɣ'narse] vr to cross o.s.

persistente [persis'tente] a persistent.

persistir [persis'tir] vi to persist.

persona [per'sona] nf person; **~ mayor** elderly person; **10 ~s** 10 people.

personaje [perso'naxe] nm important person, celebrity; (*TEATRO etc*) character.

personal [perso'nal] a (*particular*) personal; (*para una persona*) single, for one person // nm personnel, staff; **~idad** nf personality.

personarse [perso'narse] vr to appear in person.

personificar [personifi'kar] vt to personify.

perspectiva [perspek'tiβa] nf perspective; (*vista, panorama*) view, panorama; (*posibilidad futura*) outlook, prospect.

perspicacia [perspi'kaθja] nf (*fig*) discernment, perspicacity.

perspicaz [perspi'kaθ] a shrewd.

persuadir [perswa'ðir] vt (*gen*) to persuade; (*convencer*) to convince; **~se** vr to become convinced; **persuasión** nf persuasion; **persuasivo, a** a persuasive; convincing.

pertenecer [pertene'θer] vi to belong; (*fig*) to concern; **pertenencia** nf ownership; **pertenencias** nfpl possessions, property sg; **perteneciente** a: **perteneciente a** belonging to.

pertenezca etc vb ver **pertenecer**.

pértiga [pertiɣa] nf: **salto de ~** pole vault.

pertinaz [perti'naθ] a (*persistente*) persistent; (*terco*) obstinate.

pertinente [perti'nente] a relevant, pertinent; (*apropiado*) appropriate; **~ a** concerning, relevant to.

perturbación [perturβa'θjon] nf (*POL*) disturbance; (*MED*) upset, disturbance.

perturbado, a [pertur'βaðo, a] a mentally unbalanced.

perturbador, a [perturβa'ðor, a] a perturbing, disturbing; (*subversivo*) subversive.

perturbar [pertur'βar] vt (el orden) to disturb; (MED) to upset, disturb; (mentalmente) to perturb.

Perú [pe'ru] nm: **el ~** Peru; **peruano, a** a, nm/f Peruvian.

perversión [perβer'sjon] nf perversion; **perverso, a** a perverse; (depravado) depraved.

pervertido, a [perβer'tiðo, a] a perverted // nm/f pervert.

pervertir [perβer'tir] vt to pervert, corrupt.

pesa ['pesa] nf weight; (DEPORTE) shot.

pesadez [pesa'ðeθ] nf (peso) heaviness; (lentitud) slowness; (aburrimiento) tediousness.

pesadilla [pesa'ðiʎa] nf nightmare, bad dream.

pesado, a [pe'saðo, a] a heavy; (lento) slow; (difícil, duro) tough, hard; (aburrido) boring, tedious; (tiempo) sultry.

pesadumbre [pesa'ðumbre] nf grief, sorrow.

pésame ['pesame] nm expression of condolence, message of sympathy; **dar el ~** to express one's condolences.

pesar [pe'sar] vt to weigh // vi to weigh; (ser pesado) to weigh a lot, be heavy; (fig: opinión) to carry weight; **no pesa mucho** it doesn't weigh much // nm (arrepentimiento) regret; (pena) grief, sorrow; **a ~ de o pese a (que)** in spite of, despite.

pesario [pe'sarjo] nm pessary.

pesca ['peska] nf (acto) fishing; (lo pescado) catch; **ir de ~** to go fishing.

pescadería [peskaðe'ria] nf fish shop, fishmonger's (Brit).

pescado [pes'kaðo] nm fish.

pescador, a [peska'ðor, a] nm/f fisherman/woman.

pescar [pes'kar] vt (tomar) to catch; (intentar tomar) to fish for; (conseguir: trabajo) to manage to get // vi to fish, go fishing.

pescuezo [pes'kweθo] nm (ZOOL) neck.

pesebre [pe'seβre] nm manger.

peseta [pe'seta] nf peseta.

pesimista [pesi'mista] a pessimistic // nm/f pessimist.

pésimo, a ['pesimo, a] a awful, dreadful.

peso ['peso] nm weight; (balanza) scales pl; (moneda) peso; **~ bruto/neto** gross/net weight; **vender a ~** to sell by weight.

pesquero, a [pes'kero, a] a fishing cpd.

pesquisa [pes'kisa] nf inquiry, investigation.

pestaña [pes'taɲa] nf (ANAT) eyelash; (borde) rim; **pestañear** vi to blink.

peste ['peste] nf plague; (mal olor) stink, stench.

pesticida [pesti'θiða] nm pesticide.

pestilencia [pesti'lenθja] nf (mal olor) stink, stench.

pestillo [pes'tiʎo] nm (cerrojo) bolt; (picaporte) doorhandle.

petaca [pe'taka] nf (AM) suitcase.

pétalo ['petalo] nm petal.

petardo [pe'tardo] nm firework, firecracker.

petición [peti'θjon] nf (pedido) request, plea; (memorial) petition; (JUR) plea.

petrificar [petrifi'kar] vt to petrify.

petróleo [pe'troleo] nm oil, petroleum; **petrolero, a** a petroleum cpd // nm (COM: persona) oil man; (buque) (oil) tanker.

peyorativo, a [pejora'tiβo, a] a pejorative.

pez [peθ] nm fish.

pezón [pe'θon] nm teat, nipple.

pezuña [pe'θuɲa] nf hoof.

piadoso, a [pja'ðoso, a] a (devoto) pious, devout; (misericordioso) kind, merciful.

pianista [pja'nista] nm/f pianist.

piano ['pjano] nm piano.

piar [pjar] vi to cheep.

pibe, a ['piβe, a] nm/f (AM) boy/girl.

picadero [pika'ðero] *nm* riding school.

picadillo [pika'ðiʎo] *nm* mince, minced meat.

picado, a [pi'kaðo, a] *a* pricked, punctured; (*CULIN*) minced, chopped; (*mar*) choppy; (*diente*) bad; (*tabaco*) cut; (*enfadado*) cross.

picador [pika'ðor] *nm* (*TAUR*) picador; (*minero*) faceworker.

picadura [pika'ðura] *nf* (*pinchazo*) puncture; (*de abeja*) sting; (*de mosquito*) bite; (*tabaco picado*) cut tobacco.

picante [pi'kante] *a* hot; (*comentario*) racy, spicy.

picaporte [pika'porte] *nm* (*manija*) doorhandle; (*pestillo*) latch.

picar [pi'kar] *vt* (*agujerear, perforar*) to prick, puncture; (*abeja*) to bite; (*mosquito, serpiente*) to bite; (*CULIN*) to mince, chop; (*incitar*) to incite, goad; (*dañar, irritar*) to annoy, bother; (*quemar: lengua*) to burn, sting // *vi* (*pez*) to bite, take the bait; (*sol*) to burn, scorch; (*abeja, MED*) to sting; (*mosquito*) to bite; ~**se** *vr* (*agriarse*) to turn sour, go off; (*ofenderse*) to take offence.

picardía [pikar'ðia] *nf* villainy; (*astucia*) slyness, craftiness; (*una*) dirty trick; (*palabra*) rude/bad word *o* expression.

pícaro, a [pi'karo, a] *a* (*malicioso*) villainous; (*travieso*) mischievous // *nm* (*astuto*) crafty sort; (*sinvergüenza*) rascal, scoundrel.

pico [piko] *nm* (*de ave*) beak; (*punta*) sharp point; (*TEC*) pick, pickaxe; (*GEO*) peak, summit; **y ~** and a bit.

picotear [pikote'ar] *vt* to peck // *vi* to nibble, peck.

picudo, a [pi'kuðo, a] *a* pointed, with a point.

pichón [pi'tʃon] *nm* young pigeon.

pido, pidió *etc vb ver* pedir.

pie [pje] (*pl* ~**s**) *nm* foot; (*fig: motivo*) motive, basis; (*: fundamento*) foothold; **ir a ~** to go on foot, walk; **estar de ~** to be standing (up); **ponerse de ~** to stand up; **de ~ s a cabeza** from top to bottom; **al ~ de la letra** (*citar*) literally, verbatim; (*copiar*) exactly, word for word; **en ~ de guerra** on a war footing; **dar ~ a** to give cause for; **hacer ~** (*en el agua*) to touch the bottom.

piedad [pje'ðað] *nf* (*lástima*) pity, compassion; (*clemencia*) mercy; (*devoción*) piety, devotion.

piedra ['pjeðra] *nf* stone; (*roca*) rock; (*de mechero*) flint; (*METEOROLOGÍA*) hailstone.

piel [pjel] *nf* (*ANAT*) skin; (*ZOOL*) skin, hide, fur; (*cuero*) leather; (*BOT*) skin, peel.

pienso *etc vb ver* **pensar**.

pierdo *etc vb ver* **perder**.

pierna ['pjerna] *nf* leg.

pieza ['pjeθa] *nf* piece; (*habitación*) room; **~ de recambio *o* repuesto** spare (part).

pigmeo, a [piɣ'meo, a] *a, nm/f* pigmy.

pijama [pi'xama] *nm* pyjamas *pl*.

pila ['pila] *nf* (*ELEC*) battery; (*montón*) heap, pile; (*lavabo*) sink.

píldora ['pilðora] *nf* pill; **la ~ (anticonceptiva)** the (contraceptive) pill.

pileta [pi'leta] *nf* basin, bowl; (*AM*) swimming pool.

piloto [pi'loto] *nm* pilot; (*de aparato*) (pilot) light; (*AUTO: luz*) tail *o* rear light; (*: conductor*) driver.

pillaje [pi'ʎaxe] *nm* pillage, plunder.

pillar [pi'ʎar] *vt* (*saquear*) to pillage, plunder; (*fam: coger*) to catch; (*: agarrar*) to grasp, seize; (*: entender*) to grasp, catch on to; **~se** *vr*: **~se un dedo con la puerta** to catch one's finger in the door.

pillo, a ['piʎo, a] *a* villainous; (*astuto*) sly, crafty // *nm/f* rascal, rogue, scoundrel.

pimentón [pimen'ton] *nm* paprika.

pimienta [pi'mjenta] *nf* pepper.

pimiento [pi'mjento] *nm* pepper, pimiento.

pinacoteca [pinako'teka] *nf* art gallery.

pinar [pi'nar] *nm* pine forest (*Brit*), pine grove (*US*).

pincel [pin'θel] *nm* paintbrush.

pinchar [pin'tʃar] *vt* (*perforar*) to prick, pierce; (*neumático*) to puncture; (*fig*) to prod.

pinchazo [pin'tʃaθo] *nm* (*perforación*) prick; (*de neumático*) puncture; (*fig*) to prod.

pinchito [pin'tʃito] *nm* shish kebab.

pincho [pin'tʃo] *nm* savoury (snack); ~ **moruno** shish kebab; ~ **de tortilla** small slice of omelette.

ping-pong ['pin'pon] *nm* table tennis.

pingüino [pin'gwino] *nm* penguin.

pino ['pino] *nm* pine (tree).

pinta ['pinta] *nf* spot; (*de líquidos*) spot, drop; (*aspecto*) appearance, look(s) (*pl*); ~**do, a** *a* spotted; (*de muchos colores*) colourful.

pintar [pin'tar] *vt* to paint // *vi* to paint; (*fam*) to count, be important; ~**se** *vr* to put on make-up.

pintor, a [pin'tor, a] *nm/f* painter.

pintoresco, a [pinto'resko, a] *a* picturesque.

pintura [pin'tura] *nf* painting; ~ **a la acuarela** watercolour; ~ **al óleo** oil painting.

pinza ['pinθa] *nf* (*ZOOL*) claw; (*para colgar ropa*) clothes peg; (*TEC*) pincers *pl*; ~**s** *nfpl* (*para depilar etc*) tweezers *pl*.

piña ['pina] *nf* (*fruto del pino*) pine cone; (*fruta*) pineapple; (*fig*) group.

piñón [pi'non] *nm* (*fruto*) pine nut; (*TEC*) pinion.

pío, a ['pio, a] *a* (*devoto*) pious, devout; (*misericordioso*) merciful.

piojo ['pjoxo] *nm* louse.

pionero, a [pjo'nero, a] *a* pioneering // *nm/f* pioneer.

pipa ['pipa] *nf* pipe; (*BOT*) (edible) sunflower seed.

pipí [pi'pi] *nm* (*fam*): **hacer** ~ to have a wee(-wee) (*Brit*), have to go (wee-wee) (*US*).

pique ['pike] *nm* (*resentimiento*) pique, resentment; (*rivalidad*) rivalry, competition; **irse a** ~ to sink; (*esperanza, familia*) to be ruined.

piqueta [pi'keta] *nf* pick(axe).

piquete [pi'kete] *nm* (*agujerito*) small hole; (*MIL*) squad, party; (*de obreros*) picket.

piragua [pi'raywa] *nf* canoe; **piragüismo** *nm* canoeing.

pirámide [pi'ramiðe] *nf* pyramid.

pirata [pi'rata] *a, nm* pirate.

Pirineo(s) [piri'neo(s)] *nm(pl)* Pyrenees *pl*.

piropo [pi'ropo] *nm* compliment, (piece of) flattery.

pirueta [pi'rweta] *nf* pirouette.

pisada [pi'saða] *nf* (*paso*) footstep; (*huella*) footprint.

pisar [pi'sar] *vt* (*caminar sobre*) to walk on, tread on; (*apretar con el pie*) to press; (*fig*) to trample on, walk all over // *vi* to tread, step, walk.

piscina [pis'θina] *nf* swimming pool.

Piscis ['pisθis] *nm* Pisces.

piso ['piso] *nm* (*suelo, planta*) floor; (*apartamento*) flat (*Brit*), apartment; **primer** ~ (*Esp*) first floor; (*AM*) ground floor.

pisotear [pisote'ar] *vt* to trample (on o underfoot).

pista ['pista] *nf* track, trail; (*indicio*) clue; ~ **de aterrizaje** runway; ~ **de baile** dance floor; ~ **de tenis** tennis court; ~ **de hielo** ice rink.

pistola [pis'tola] *nf* pistol; (*TEC*) spray-gun; **pistolero, a** *nm/f* gunman/woman, gangster // *nf* holster.

pistón [pis'ton] *nm* (*TEC*) piston; (*MUS*) key.

pitar [pi'tar] *vt* (*silbato*) to blow; (*rechiflar*) to whistle at, boo // *vi* to whistle; (*AUTO*) to sound o toot one's horn; (*AM*) to smoke.

pitillo [pi'tiʎo] *nm* cigarette.

pito ['pito] *nm* whistle; (*de coche*) horn.

pitón [pi'ton] *nm* (*ZOOL*) python.

pitonisa [pito'nisa] *nf* fortune-teller.

pitorreo [pito'rreo] *nm* joke; **estar de ~** to be joking.

pizarra [pi'θarra] *nf* (*piedra*) slate; (*encerado*) blackboard.

pizca ['piθka] *nf* pinch, spot; (*fig*) spot, speck; **ni ~** not a bit.

placa ['plaka] *nf* plate; (*distintivo*) badge, insignia; **~ de matrícula** number plate.

placentero, a [plaθen'tero, a] *a* pleasant, agreeable.

placer [pla'θer] *nm* pleasure // *vt* to please.

plácido, a ['plaθiδo, a] *a* placid.

plaga ['plaγa] *nf* pest; (*MED*) plague; (*abundancia*) abundance; **plagar** *vt* to infest, plague; (*llenar*) to fill.

plagio ['plaxjo] *nm* plagiarism.

plan [plan] *nm* (*esquema, proyecto*) plan; (*idea, intento*) idea, intention; **tener ~** (*fam*) to have a date; **tener un ~** (*fam*) to have an affair; **en ~ económico** (*fam*) on the cheap; **vamos en ~ de turismo** we're going as tourists; **si te pones en ese ~...** if that's your attitude... .

plana ['plana] *nf ver* **plano**.

plancha ['plantʃa] *nf* (*para planchar*) iron; (*rótulo*) plate, sheet; (*NAUT*) gangway; **~do en** *nm* ironing; **planchar** *vt* to iron // *vi* to do the ironing.

planeador [planea'δor] *nm* glider.

planear [plane'ar] *vt* to plan // *vi* to glide.

planeta [pla'neta] *nm* planet.

planicie [pla'niθje] *nf* plain.

planificación [planifika'θjon] *nf* planning; **~ familiar** family planning.

plano, a ['plano, a] *a* flat, level, even // *nm* (*MAT, TEC, AVIAT*) plane; (*FOTO*) shot; (*ARQ*) plan; (*GEO*) map; (*de ciudad*) map, street plan // *nf* sheet (of paper), page; (*TEC*) trowel; **primer ~** close-up; **caer de ~** to fall flat; **en primera plana** on

the front page; **plana mayor** staff.

planta ['planta] *nf* (*BOT, TEC*) plant; (*ANAT*) sole of the foot, foot; (*piso*) floor; (*personal*) staff; **~ baja** ground floor.

plantación [planta'θjon] *nf* (*AGR*) plantation; (*acto*) planting.

plantar [plan'tar] *vt* (*BOT*) to plant; (*levantar*) to erect, set up; **~se** *vr* to stand firm; **~ a uno en la calle** to throw sb out; **dejar plantado a uno** (*fam*) to stand sb up.

plantear [plante'ar] *vt* (*problema*) to pose; (*dificultad*) to raise.

plantilla [plan'tiʎa] *nf* (*de zapato*) insole; (*personal*) personnel; **ser de ~** to be on the staff.

plantón [plan'ton] *nm* (*MIL*) guard, sentry; (*fam*) long wait; **dar (un) ~ a uno** to stand sb up.

plañir [pla'nir] *vi* to mourn.

plasmar [plas'mar] *vt* (*dar forma*) to mould, shape; (*representar*) to represent // *vi*: **~ en** to take the form of.

Plasticina ® [plasti'θina] *nf* Plasticine ®.

plástico, a ['plastiko, a] *a* plastic // *nm* plastic *nf* (*art of*) sculpture, modelling.

Plastilina ® [plasti'lina] *nf* (*AM*) Plasticine ®.

plata ['plata] *nf* (*metal*) silver; (*cosas hechas de ~*) silverware; (*AM*) cash, dough; **hablar en ~** to speak bluntly or frankly.

plataforma [plata'forma] *nf* platform; **~ de lanzamiento/perforación** launch(ing) pad/drilling rig.

plátano ['platano] *nm* (*fruta*) banana; (*árbol*) banana tree.

platea [pla'tea] *nf* (*TEATRO*) pit.

plateado, a [plate'aδo, a] *a* silver; (*TEC*) silver-plated.

plática ['platika] *nf* talk, chat; **platicar** *vi* to talk, chat.

platillo [pla'tiʎo] *nm* saucer; **~s** *nmpl* cymbals; **~ volador** *o* **volante** flying saucer.

platino [pla'tino] *nm* platinum; **~s**

nmpl (*AUTO*) contact points.

plato ['plato] *nm* plate, dish; (*parte de comida*) course; (*comida*) dish; **primer ~** first course.

playa ['plaja] *nf* beach; (*costa*) seaside; **~ de estacionamiento** (*AM*) car park.

playera [pla'jera] *nf* (*AM: camiseta*) T-shirt; **~s** *nfpl* (slip-on) canvas shoes.

plaza ['plaθa] *nf* square; (*mercado*) market(place); (*sitio*) room, space; (*en vehículo*) seat, place; (*colocación*) post, job; **~ de toros** bullring.

plazo ['plaθo] *nm* (*lapso de tiempo*) time, period; (*fecha de vencimiento*) expiry date; (*pago parcial*) instalment; **a corto/largo ~** short/long-term; **comprar a ~s** to buy on hire purchase, pay for in instalments.

plazoleta [plaθo'leta], **plazuela** [pla'θwela] *nf* small square.

pleamar [plea'mar] *nf* high tide.

plebe ['pleβe] *nf*: **la ~** the common people *pl*, the masses *pl*; (*pey*) the plebs *pl*; **~yo, a** *a* plebeian; (*pey*) coarse, common.

plebiscito [pleβis'θito] *nm* plebiscite.

plegable [ple'γaβle] *a* pliable; (*silla*) folding.

plegar [ple'γar] *vt* (*doblar*) to fold, bend; (*COSTURA*) to pleat; **~se** *vr* to yield, submit.

pleito ['pleito] *nm* (*JUR*) lawsuit, case; (*fig*) dispute, feud.

plenilunio [pleni'lunjo] *nm* full moon.

plenitud [pleni'tuð] *nf* plenitude, fullness; (*abundancia*) abundance.

pleno, a ['pleno, a] *a* full; (*completo*) complete // *nm* assembly; **en ~ día** in broad daylight; **en ~ verano** at the height of summer; **en plena cara** full in the face.

pleuresía [pleure'sia] *nf* pleurisy.

Plexiglás ® [pleksi'γlas] *nm* acrylic glass, Plexiglas (*US*).

pliego *etc vb ver* **plegar** // ['pljeγo] *nm* (*hoja*) sheet (of paper); (*carta*) sealed letter/document; **~ de**

condiciones details *pl*, specifications *pl*.

pliegue *etc vb ver* **plegar** // ['pljeγe] *nm* fold, crease; (*de vestido*) pleat.

plisado [pli'saðo] *nm* pleating.

plomero [plo'mero] *nm* (*AM*) plumber.

plomo ['plomo] *nm* (*metal*) lead; (*ELEC*) fuse.

pluma ['pluma] *nf* feather; (*para escribir*) pen.

plumero [plu'mero] *nm* (*quitapolvos*) feather duster.

plumón [plu'mon] *nm* (*AM: fino*) felt-tip pen; (: *ancho*) marker.

plural [plu'ral] *a* plural; **~idad** *nf* plurality; **una ~idad de votos** a majority of votes.

plus [plus] *nm* bonus; **~valía** *nf* (*COM*) appreciation.

plutocracia [pluto'kraθja] *nf* plutocracy.

población [poβla'θjon] *nf* population; (*pueblo, ciudad*) town, city.

poblado, a [po'βlaðo, a] *a* inhabited // *nm* (*aldea*) village; (*pueblo*) (small) town; **densamente ~** densely populated.

poblador, a [poβla'ðor, a] *nm/f* settler, colonist.

poblar [po'βlar] *vt* (*colonizar*) to colonize; (*fundar*) to found; (*habitar*) to inhabit.

pobre ['poβre] *a* poor // *nm/f* poor person; **¡~!** poor thing!; **~za** *nf* poverty.

pocilga [po'θilγa] *nf* pigsty.

pocillo [po'siʎo] *nm* (*AM*) coffee cup.

poción [po'θjon], **pócima** [po'θima] *nf* potion.

PALABRA CLAVE

---

poco, a ['poko, a] ◆ *a* **1** (*sg*) little, not much; **~ tiempo** little o not much time; **~ de interés** little interest, not very interesting; **poca cosa** not much

2 (*pl*) few, not many; **unos ~s a** few, some; **~s niños comen lo que**

les conviene few children eat what they should
♦ **ad** 1 little, not much; **cuesta** ~ it doesn't cost much
2 (+ a: = negativo, antónimo): ~ **amable/inteligente** not very nice/intelligent
3: **por** ~ **me caigo** I almost fell
4: **a** ~: **a** ~ **de haberse casado** shortly after getting married
5: ~ **a** ~ little by little
♦ **nm** a little, a bit; **un** ~ **triste/de dinero** a little sad/money.

podar [po'ðar] vt to prune.

PALABRA CLAVE

---

poder [po'ðer] ♦ vi 1 (capacidad) can, be able to; **no puedo hacerlo** I can't do it, I'm unable to do it
2 (permiso) can, may, be allowed to; **¿se puede?** may I (o we)?; **puedes irte ahora** you may go now; **no se puede fumar en este hospital** smoking is not allowed in this hospital
3 (posibilidad) may, might, could; **puede llegar mañana** he may o might arrive tomorrow; **pudiste haberte hecho daño** you might o could have hurt yourself; **¡podías habérmelo dicho antes!** you might have told me before!
4: **puede ser:** puede ser perhaps; **puede ser que lo sepa Tomás** Tomás may o might know
5: **¡no puedo más!** I've had enough!; **no pude menos que dejarlo** I couldn't help but leave it; **es tonto a más no** ~ he's as stupid as they come
6: ~ **con: no puedo con este crío** this kid's too much for me
♦ **nm** power; ~ **adquisitivo** purchasing power; **detentar** o **ocupar** o **estar en el** ~ to be in power.

podrido, a [po'ðriðo, a] a rotten, bad; (fig) rotten o corrupt.

---

podrir [po'ðrir] = **pudrir.**

poema [po'ema] nm poem.

poesía [poe'sia] nf poetry.

poeta [po'eta] nm poet; **poético, a** a poetic(al).

poetisa [poe'tisa] nf (woman) poet.

póker ['poker] nm poker.

polaco, a [po'lako, a] a Polish // nm/f Pole.

polar [po'lar] a polar; ~**idad** nf polarity; ~**izarse** vr to polarize.

polea [po'lea] nf pulley.

polémica [po'lemika] nf polemics sg; (una ~) controversy, polemic.

polen ['polen] nm pollen.

policía [poli'θia] nm/f policeman/woman // nf police; ~**co, a** a police cpd; **novela policíaca** detective story; **policial** a police cpd.

polideportivo [poliðepor'tiβo] nm sports centre o complex.

polietileno [polieti'leno] nm polythene (Brit), polyethylene (US).

poligamia [poli'yamja] nf polygamy.

polilla [po'liʎa] nf moth.

polio ['poljo] nf polio.

politécnico [poli'tekniko] nm polytechnic.

político, a [po'litiko, a] a political; (discreto) tactful; (de familia) -in-law // nm/f politician // nf politics sg; (económica, agraria etc) policy; **pa-dre** ~ father-in-law; **politicastro** nm (pey) politician, politico.

póliza ['poliθa] nf certificate, voucher; (impuesto) tax stamp; ~ **de seguros** insurance policy.

polizón [poli'θon] nm (en barco etc) stowaway.

polo ['polo] nm (GEO, ELEC) pole; (helado) ice lolly; (DEPORTE) polo; (suéter) polo-neck; ~ **Norte/Sur** North/South Pole.

Polonia [po'lonja] nf Poland.

poltrona [pol'trona] nf easy chair.

polución [polu'θjon] nf pollution.

polvera [pol'βera] nf powder compact.

polvo ['polβo] nm dust; (QUÍMICA, CULIN, MED) powder; ~**s** nmpl powder *sg*; ~ **de talco** talcum powder; **estar hecho** ~ (*fam*) to be worn out *o* exhausted.

pólvora [ˈpolβora] *nf* gunpowder; (*fuegos artificiales*) fireworks *pl*.

polvoriento, a [polβoˈrjento, a] *a* (*superficie*) dusty; (*sustancia*) powdery.

pollera [poˈʎera] *nf* (*AM*) skirt.

pollería [poʎeˈria] *nf* poulterer's (shop).

pollo [ˈpoʎo] *nm* chicken.

pomada [poˈmaða] *nf* (*MED*) cream, ointment.

pomelo [poˈmelo] *nm* grapefruit.

pómez [ˈpomeθ] *nf*: **piedra** ~ pumice stone.

pompa [ˈpompa] *nf* (*burbuja*) bubble; (*bomba*) pump; (*esplendor*) pomp, splendour; **pomposo, a** *a* splendid, magnificent; (*pey*) pompous.

pómulo [ˈpomulo] *nm* cheekbone.

pon [pon] *vb ver* **poner**.

ponche [ˈpontʃe] *nm* punch.

poncho [ˈpontʃo] *nm* (*AM*) poncho, cape.

ponderar [pondeˈrar] *vt* (*considerar*) to weigh up, consider; (*elogiar*) to praise highly, speak in praise of.

pondré *etc vb ver* **poner**.

PALABRA CLAVE

poner [poˈner] ♦ *vt* **1** (*colocar*) to put; (*telegrama*) to send; (*obra de teatro*) to put on; (*película*) to show; **ponlo más fuerte** turn it up; **¿qué ponen en el Excelsior?** what's on at the Excelsior?

2 (*tienda*) to open; (*instalar*: *gas etc*) to put in; (*radio, TV*) to switch *o* turn on

3 (*suponer*): **pongamos que ...** let's suppose that

4 (*contribuir*): **el gobierno ha puesto otro millón** the government has contributed another million

5 (*TELEC*): **póngame con el Sr. López** can you put me through to Mr. López

6: ~ **de**: **le han puesto de director general** they've appointed him general manager

7 (+ *a*) to make; **me estás poniendo nerviosa** you're making me nervous

8 (*dar nombre*): **al hijo le pusieron Diego** they called their son Diego

♦ *vi* (*gallina*) to lay

♦ ~**se** *vr* **1** (*colocarse*): **se puso a mi lado** he came and stood beside me; **tú ponte en esa silla** you go and sit on that chair

2 (*vestido, cosméticos*) to put on; **¿por qué no te pones el vestido nuevo?** why don't you put on *o* wear my new dress?

3: (+ *a*) to turn; to get, become: **se puso muy serio** he got very serious; **después de lavarla la tela se puso azul** after washing it the material turned blue

4: ~**se a**: **se puso a llorar** he started to cry; **tienes que** ~**te a estudiar** you must get down to studying

5: ~**se a bien con uno** to make it up with sb; ~**se a mal con uno** to get on the wrong side of sb.

---

pongo *etc vb ver* **poner**.

poniente [poˈnjente] *nm* (*occidente*) west; (*viento*) west wind.

pontificado [pontifiˈkaðo] *nm* papacy, pontificate; **pontífice** *nm* pope, pontiff.

pontón [ponˈton] *nm* pontoon.

ponzoña [ponˈθoɲa] *nf* poison, venom.

popa [ˈpopa] *nf* stern.

popular [popuˈlar] *a* popular; (*cultura*) of the people, folk *cpd*; ~**idad** *nf* popularity; ~**izarse** *vr* to become popular.

PALABRA CLAVE

por [por] ♦ *prep* **1** (*objetivo*) for; **luchar** ~ **la patria** to fight for one's country

2 (+ *infinitivo*): ~ **no llegar tarde**

so as not to arrive late; ~ **citar unos ejemplos** to give a few examples

3 (*causa*): **out of, because of;** ~ **escasez de fondos** through *o* for lack of funds

4 (*tiempo*): ~ **la mañana/noche** in the morning/at night; **se queda ~ una semana** she's staying (for) a week

5 (*lugar*): **pasar ~ Madrid** to pass through Madrid; **ir a Guayaquil ~ Quito** to go to Guayaquil via Quito; **caminar ~ la calle** to walk along the street; *ver tb* **todo**

6 (*cambio, precio*): **te doy uno nuevo ~ el que tienes** I'll give you a new one (in return) for the one you've got

7 (*valor distributivo*): **550 pesetas ~ hora/cabeza** 550 pesetas an *o* per hour/a *o* per head

8 (*modo, medio*) **by;** ~ **correo/avión** by post/air; **día ~ día** day by day; **entrar ~ la entrada principal** to go in through the main entrance

9: **10 ~ 10 son 100** 10 by 10 is 100

10 (*en lugar de*): **vino él ~ su jefe** he came instead of his boss

11: ~ **mí que revienten** as far as I'm concerned they can drop dead.

porcelana [porθe'lana] *nf* porcelain; (*china*) china.

porcentaje [porθen'taxe] *nm* percentage.

porción [por'θjon] *nf* (*parte*) portion, share; (*cantidad*) quantity, amount.

pordiosero, a [porðjo'sero, a] *nm/f* beggar.

porfía [por'fia] *nf* persistence; (*terquedad*) obstinacy.

porfiado, a [por'fjaðo, a] *a* persistent; obstinate.

porfiar [por'fjar] *vi* to persist, insist; (*disputar*) to argue stubbornly.

pormenor [porme'nor] *nm* detail, particular.

pornografía [pornovra'fia] *nf* pornography.

poro ['poro] *nm* pore; ~**so, a** *a* porous.

porque ['porke] *conj* (*a causa de*) because; (*ya que*) since; (*con el fin de*) so that, in order that.

porqué [por'ke] *nm* reason, cause.

porquería [porke'ria] *nf* (*suciedad*) filth, dirt; (*acción*) dirty trick; (*objeto*) small thing, trifle; (*fig*) rubbish.

porra ['porra] *nf* (*arma*) stick, club.

porrón [po'rron] *nm* glass wine jar with a long spout.

portada [por'taða] *nf* (*de revista*) cover.

portador, a [porta'ðor, a] *nm/f* carrier, bearer; (*COM*) bearer, payee.

portaequipajes [portaeki'paxes] *nm inv* (*AUTO*: *maletero*) boot; (: *baca*) luggage rack.

portal [por'tal] *nm* (*entrada*) vestibule, hall; (*portada*) porch, doorway; (*puerta de entrada*) main door; (*DEPORTE*) goal.

portaligas [porta'livas] *nm inv* suspender belt.

portamaletas [portama'letas] *nm inv* (*AUTO*: *maletero*) boot; (: *baca*) roof rack.

portamonedas [portamo'neðas] *nm inv* purse.

portarse [por'tarse] *vr* to behave, conduct o.s.

portátil [por'tatil] *a* portable.

porta(a)viones [porta'(a)βjones] *nm inv* aircraft carrier.

portavoz [porta'βoθ] *nm/f* (*persona*) spokesman/woman.

portazo [por'taðo] *nm*: **dar un ~** to slam the door.

porte ['porte] *nm* (*COM*) transport; (*precio*) transport charges *pl*.

portento [por'tento] *nm* marvel, wonder; ~**so, a** *a* marvellous, extraordinary.

porteño, a [por'teno, a] *a* of *o* from Buenos Aires.

portería [porte'ria] *nf* (*oficina*) porter's office; (*gol*) goal.

portero, a [por'tero, a] *nm/f* porter; *(conserje)* caretaker; *(ujier)* doorman; *(DEPORTE)* goalkeeper.

pórtico ['portiko] *nm (patio)* portico, porch; *(fig)* gateway; *(arcada)* arcade.

portilla [por'tiʎa] *nf,* **portillo** [por'tiʎo] *nm (cancela)* gate.

portorriqueño, a [portorri'keɲo, a] *a* Puerto Rican.

Portugal [portu'ɣal] *nm* Portugal; **portugués, esa** *a, nm/f* Portuguese // *nm (LING)* Portuguese.

porvenir [porβe'nir] *nm* future.

pos [pos] *prep:* **en ~ de** after, in pursuit of.

posada [po'saða] *nf (refugio)* shelter, lodging; *(mesón)* guest house; **dar ~ a** to give shelter to, take in.

posaderas [posa'ðeras] *nfpl* backside *sg,* buttocks.

posar [po'sar] *vt (en el suelo)* to lay down, put down; *(la mano)* to place, put gently // *vi* to sit, pose; **~se** *vr* to settle; *(pájaro)* to perch; *(avión)* to land, come down.

posdata [pos'ðata] *nf* postscript.

pose ['pose] *nf* pose.

poseedor, a [pose'eðor, a] *nm/f* owner, possessor; *(de récord, puesto)* holder.

poseer [pose'er] *vt* to possess, own; *(ventaja)* to enjoy; *(récord, puesto)* to hold; **poseído, a** *a* possessed.

posesión [pose'sjon] *nf* possession; **posesionarse** *vr:* **posesionarse de** to take possession of, take over.

posesivo, a [pose'siβo, a] *a* possessive.

posibilidad [posiβili'ðað] *nf* possibility; *(oportunidad)* chance; **posibilitar** *vt* to make possible; *(hacer realizable)* to make feasible.

posible [po'siβle] *a* possible; *(realizable)* feasible; **de ser ~** if possible; **en lo ~** as far as possible.

posición [posi'θjon] *nf* position; *(rango social)* status.

positivo, a [posi'tiβo, a] *a* positive // *nf (FOTO)* print.

poso ['poso] *nm* sediment; *(heces)* dregs *pl.*

posponer [pospo'ner] *vt* to put behind/below; *(aplazar)* to postpone.

posta ['posta] *nf:* **a ~ ad** deliberately, on purpose.

postal [pos'tal] *a* postal // *nf* postcard.

poste ['poste] *nm (de telégrafos etc)* post, pole; *(columna)* pillar.

póster ['poster] *(pl* **pósteres** *o* **posters)** *nm* poster.

postergar [poster'var] *vt* to postpone, delay.

posteridad [posteri'ðað] *nf* posterity.

posterior [poste'rjor] *a* back, rear; *(siguiente)* following, subsequent; *(más tarde)* later; **~idad** *nf:* **con ~idad** later, subsequently.

postizo, a [pos'tiθo, a] *a* false, artificial // *nm* hairpiece.

postor, a [pos'tor, a] *nm/f* bidder.

postrado, a [pos'traðo, a] *a* prostrate.

postre ['postre] *nm* sweet, dessert.

postrero, a [pos'trero, a] *a (delante de nmsg:* **postrer)** *(último)* last; *(que viene detrás)* rear.

postulado [postu'laðo] *nm* postulate.

póstumo, a ['postumo, a] *a* posthumous.

postura [pos'tura] *nf (del cuerpo)* posture, position; *(fig)* attitude, position.

potable [po'taβle] *a* drinkable; **agua ~** drinking water.

potaje [po'taxe] *nm* thick vegetable soup.

pote ['pote] *nm* pot, jar.

potencia [po'tenθja] *nf* power; **potenciar** *vt* to boost.

potencial [poten'θjal] *a, nm* potential.

potente [po'tente] *a* powerful.

potro, a ['potro, a] *nm/f (ZOOL)* colt/filly // *nm (de gimnasia)* vaulting horse.

pozo ['poθo] *nm* well; *(de río)* deep pool; *(de mina)* shaft.

P.P. *abr (= porte pagado)* CP.

p.p. *abr* (= *por poder*) p.p.

práctica ['praktika] *nf ver* **práctico**.

practicable [prakti'kaβle] *a* practicable; (*camino*) passable.

practicante [prakti'kante] *nm/f* (*MED: ayudante de doctor*) medical assistant; (: *enfermero*) male nurse; (*quien practica algo*) practitioner // *a* practising.

practicar [prakti'kar] *vt* to practise; (*DEPORTE*) to go in for (*Brit*) o out for (*US*), play; (*realizar*) to carry out, perform.

práctico, a ['praktiko, a] *a* practical; (*instruido: persona*) skilled, expert // *nf* practice; (*método*) method; (*arte, capacidad*) skill; **en la práctica** in practice.

practique *etc vb ver* **practicar**.

pradera [pra'ðera] *nf* meadow; (*US etc*) prairie.

prado ['praðo] *nm* (*campo*) meadow, field; (*pastizal*) pasture.

Praga ['praɣa] *n* Prague.

pragmático, a [praɣ'matiko, a] *a* pragmatic.

preámbulo [pre'ambulo] *nm* preamble, introduction.

precario, a [pre'karjo, a] *a* precarious.

precaución [prekau'θjon] *nf* (*medida preventiva*) preventive measure, precaution; (*prudencia*) caution, wariness.

precaver [preka'βer] *vt* to guard against; (*impedir*) to forestall; ~**se** *vr*: ~**se de** o **contra algo** to (be on one's) guard against sth; **precavido, a** *a* cautious, wary.

precedencia [preθe'ðenθja] *nf* precedence; (*prioridad*) priority; (*preeminencia*) greater importance, superiority; **precedente** *a* preceding; (*anterior*) former // *nm* precedent.

preceder [preθe'ðer] *vt, vi* to precede, go before, come before.

precepto [pre'θepto] *nm* precept.

preciado, a [pre'θjaðo, a] *a* (*estimado*) esteemed, valuable.

preciar [pre'θjar] *vt* to esteem, value; ~**se** *vr* to boast; ~**se de** to pride o.s. on, boast of being.

precinto [pre'θinto] *nm* (*tb*: ~ **de garantía**) seal.

precio ['preθjo] *nm* price; (*costo*) cost; (*valor*) value, worth; (*de viaje*) fare; ~ **al contado/de coste/de oportunidad** cash/cost/bargain price; ~ **al detalle** o **al por menor** retail price; ~ **tope** top price.

preciosidad [preθjosi'ðað] *nf* (*valor*) (high) value, (great) worth; (*encanto*) charm; (*cosa bonita*) beautiful thing; **es una** ~ it's lovely, it's really beautiful.

precioso, a [pre'θjoso, a] *a* precious; (*de mucho valor*) valuable; (*fam*) lovely, beautiful.

precipicio [preθi'piθjo] *nm* cliff, precipice; (*fig*) abyss.

precipitación [preθipita'θjon] *nf* haste; (*lluvia*) rainfall.

precipitado, a [preθipi'taðo, a] *a* (*conducta*) hasty, rash; (*salida*) hasty, sudden.

precipitar [preθipi'tar] *vt* (*arrojar*) to hurl down, throw; (*apresurar*) to hasten; (*acelerar*) to speed up, accelerate; ~**se** *vr* to throw o.s.; (*apresurarse*) to rush; (*actuar sin pensar*) to act rashly.

precisamente [preθisa'mente] *ad* precisely; (*exactamente*) precisely, exactly.

precisar [preθi'sar] *vt* (*necesitar*) to need, require; (*fijar*) to determine exactly, fix; (*especificar*) to specify.

precisión [preθi'sjon] *nf* (*exactitud*) precision.

preciso, a [pre'θiso, a] *a* (*exacto*) precise; (*necesario*) necessary, essential.

preconcebido, a [prekonθe'βiðo, a] *a* preconceived.

precoz [pre'koθ] *a* (*persona*) precocious; (*calvicie etc*) premature.

precursor, a [prekur'sor, a] *nm/f* predecessor, forerunner.

predecir [preðe'θir] *vt* to predict, forecast.

predestinado, a [preðesti'naðo, a] *a* predestined.

predeterminar [preðetermi'nar] *vt* to predetermine.

prédica ['preðika] *nf* sermon.

predicador, a [preðika'ðor, a] *nm/f* preacher.

predicar [preði'kar] *vt, vi* to preach.

predicción [preðik'θjon] *nf* prediction.

predilecto, a [preði'lekto, a] *a* favourite.

predisponer [preðispo'ner] *vt* to predispose; *(pey)* to prejudice; **predisposición** *nf* inclination; prejudice, bias.

predominante [preðomi'nante] *a* predominant.

predominar [preðomi'nar] *vt* to dominate // *vi* to predominate; *(prevalecer)* to prevail; **predominio** *nm* predominance; prevalence.

preescolar [pre(e)sko'lar] *a* preschool.

prefabricado, a [prefaßri'kaðo, a] *a* prefabricated.

prefacio [pre'faθjo] *nm* preface.

preferencia [prefe'renθja] *nf* preference; **de ~** preferably, for preference.

preferible [prefe'riße] *a* preferable.

preferir [prefe'rir] *vt* to prefer.

prefiero *etc vb ver* **preferir**.

prefigurar [prefiɣu'rar] *vt* to foreshadow, prefigure.

pregonar [preɣo'nar] *vt* to proclaim, announce.

pregunta [pre'ɣunta] *nf* question; **hacer una ~** to ask o put (forth (US)) a question.

preguntar [preɣun'tar] *vt* to ask; *(cuestionar)* to question // *vi* to ask; **~se** *vr* to wonder; **~ por alguien** to ask for sb.

preguntón, ona [preɣun'ton, ona] *a* inquisitive.

prehistórico, a [preis'toriko, a] *a* prehistoric.

prejuicio [pre'xwiθjo] *nm* *(acto)* prejudgement; *(idea preconcebida)* preconception; *(parcialidad)* prejudice, bias.

preliminar [prelimi'nar] *a* preliminary.

preludio [pre'luðjo] *nm* prelude.

prematuro, a [prema'turo, a] *a* premature.

premeditación [premeðita'θjon] *nf* premeditation.

premeditar [premeði'tar] *vt* to premeditate.

premiar [pre'mjar] *vt* to reward; *(en un concurso)* to give a prize to.

premio ['premjo] *nm* reward; prize; *(COM)* premium.

premonición [premoni'θjon] *nf* premonition.

premura [pre'mura] *nf* *(aprieto)* pressure; *(prisa)* haste, urgency.

prenatal [prena'tal] *a* antenatal, prenatal.

prenda ['prenda] *nf* *(ropa)* garment, article of clothing; *(garantía)* pledge; **~s** *nfpl* talents, gifts.

prendar [pren'dar] *vt* to captivate, enchant; **~se de uno** to fall in love with sb.

prendedor [prende'ðor] *nm* brooch.

prender [pren'der] *vt* *(captar)* to catch, capture; *(detener)* to arrest; *(COSTURA)* to pin, attach; *(sujetar)* to fasten // *vi* to catch; *(arraigar)* to take root; **~se** *vr* *(encenderse)* to catch fire.

prendido, a [pren'diðo, a] *a* *(AM: luz etc)* on.

prensa ['prensa] *nf* press; **la P~** the press; **prensar** *vt* to press.

preñado, a [pre'ɲaðo, a] *a* *(ZOOL)* pregnant; **~ de** pregnant with, full of; **preñez** *nf* pregnancy.

preocupación [preokupa'θjon] *nf* worry, concern; *(ansiedad)* anxiety.

preocupado, a [preoku'paðo, a] *a* worried, concerned; *(ansioso)* anxious.

preocupar [preoku'par] *vt* to worry; **~se** *vr* to worry; **~se de algo**

(*hacerse cargo*) to take care of sth.

preparación [prepara'θjon] nf (*acto*) preparation; (*estado*) readiness; (*entrenamiento*) training.

preparado, a [prepa'raðo, a] a (*dispuesto*) prepared; (*CULIN*) ready (to serve) // nm preparation.

preparador, a [prepara'ðor, a] nm/f trainer.

preparar [prepa'rar] vt (*disponer*) to prepare, get ready; (*TEC: tratar*) to prepare, process; (*entrenar*) to teach, train; **~se** vr: **~se a** o **para** to prepare to o for; get ready to o for; **preparativo, a** a preparatory, preliminary; **preparativos** nmpl preparations; **preparatorio, a** a preparatory // nf (*AM*) sixth-form college (*Brit*), senior high school (*US*).

prerrogativa [prerrova'tiβa] nf prerogative, privilege.

presa ['presa] nf (*cosa apresada*) catch; (*víctima*) victim; (*de animal*) prey; (*de agua*) dam.

presagiar [presa'xjar] vt to presage, forebode.

presbítero [pres'βitero] nm priest.

prescindir [presθin'dir] vi: ~ **de** (*privarse de*) to do without, go without; (*descartar*) to dispense with.

prescribir [preskri'βir] vt to prescribe; **prescripción** nf prescription.

presencia [pre'senθja] nf presence; **presencial** a: testigo presencial eyewitness; **presenciar** vt to be present at; (*asistir a*) to attend; (*ver*) to see, witness.

presentación [presenta'θjon] nf presentation; (*introducción*) introduction.

presentador, a [presenta'ðor, a] nm/f presenter, compère.

presentar [presen'tar] vt to present; (*ofrecer*) to offer; (*mostrar*) to show, display; (*a una persona*) to introduce; **~se** vr (*llegar inesperadamente*) to appear, turn up; (*ofrecerse como candidato*) to run, stand; (*aparecer*) to show, appear;

(*solicitar empleo*) to apply.

presente [pre'sente] a present // nm present; hacer ~ to state, declare; tener ~ to remember, bear in mind.

presentimiento [presenti'mjento] nm premonition, presentiment.

presentir [presen'tir] vt to have a premonition of.

preservación [preserβa'θjon] nf protection, preservation.

preservar [preser'βar] vt to protect, preserve; **preservativo** nm sheath, condom.

presidencia [presi'ðenθja] nf presidency; (*de comité*) chairmanship.

presidente [presi'ðente] nm/f president; (*de comité*) chairman/woman.

presidiario [presi'ðjarjo] nm convict.

presidio [pre'siðjo] nm prison, penitentiary.

presidir [presi'ðir] vt (*dirigir*) to preside at, preside over; (*: comité*) to take the chair at; (*dominar*) to dominate, rule // vi to preside, to take the chair.

presión [pre'sjon] nf pressure; **presionar** vt to press; (*fig*) to press, put pressure on // vi: **presionar para** to press for.

preso, a ['preso, a] nm/f prisoner; tomar o llevar **a** uno to arrest sb, take sb prisoner.

prestado, a [pres'taðo, a] a on loan; pedir ~ to borrow.

prestamista [presta'mista] nm/f moneylender.

préstamo ['prestamo] nm loan; ~ hipotecario mortgage.

prestar [pres'tar] vt to lend, loan; (*atención*) to pay; (*ayuda*) to give.

presteza [pres'teθa] nf speed, promptness.

prestigio [pres'tixjo] nm prestige; **~so, a** a (*honorable*) prestigious; (*famoso, renombrado*) renowned, famous.

presto, a ['presto, a] a (*rápido*) quick, prompt; (*dispuesto*) ready // ad at once, right away.

presumir [presu'mir] vt to presume //

vi (*tener aires*) to be conceited; **según cabe ~** as may be presumed, presumably; **presunción** *nf* presumption; **presunto, a** *a* (*supuesto*) supposed, presumed; (*así llamado*) so-called; **presuntuoso, a** *a* conceited, presumptuous.

presuponer [presupo'ner] *vt* to presuppose.

presupuesto *pp de* **presuponer** // [presu'pwesto] *nm* (*FINANZAS*) budget; (*estimación: de costo*) estimate.

presuroso, a *a* [presu'roso, a] *a* (*rápido*) quick, speedy; (*que tiene prisa*) hasty.

pretencioso, a [preten'θjoso, a] *a* pretentious.

pretender [preten'der] *vt* (*intentar*) to try to, seek to; (*reivindicar*) to claim; (*buscar*) to seek, try for; (*cortejar*) to woo, court; **~ que** to expect that; **pretendiente** *nm/f* (*candidato*) candidate, applicant; (*amante*) suitor; **pretensión** *nf* (*aspiración*) aspiration; (*reivindicación*) claim; (*orgullo*) pretension.

pretexto [pre'teksto] *nm* pretext; (*excusa*) excuse.

prevalecer [preβale'θer] *vi* to prevail.

prevención [preβen'θjon] *nf* (*preparación*) preparation; (*estado*) preparedness, readiness; (*el evitar*) prevention; (*previsión*) foresight, forethought; (*precaución*) precaution.

prevenido, a [preβe'niðo, a] *a* prepared, ready; (*cauteloso*) cautious.

prevenir [preβe'nir] *vt* (*impedir*) to prevent; (*prever*) to foresee, anticipate; (*predisponer*) to prejudice, bias; (*avisar*) to warn; (*preparar*) to prepare, get ready; **~se** *vr* to get ready, prepare; **~se contra** to take precautions against; **preventivo, a** *a* preventive, precautionary.

prever [pre'βer] *vt* to foresee.

previo, a *a* ['preβjo, a] *a* (*anterior*) previous; (*preliminar*) preliminary // *prep*: **~ acuerdo de los otros** subject to the agreement of the others.

previsión [preβi'sjon] *nf* (*perspicacia*) foresight; (*predicción*) forecast.

prima ['prima] *nf ver* **primo**.

primacía [prima'θia] *nf* primacy.

primario, a [pri'marjo, a] *a* primary.

primavera [prima'βera] *nf* spring(time).

primero, a [pri'mero, a] *a* (*delante de nmsg*: **primer**) first; (*principal*) prime // *ad* first; (*más bien*) sooner, rather // *nf* (*AUTO*) first gear; (*FERRO*: *tb*: **primera clase**) first class; **de primera** (*fam*) first-class, first-rate; **primera plana** front page.

primitivo, a [primi'tiβo, a] *a* primitive; (*original*) original.

primo, a *a* ['primo, a] *a* prime // *nm/f* cousin; (*fam*) fool, idiot // *nf* (*COM*) bonus; **~ de seguro** insurance premium; **~ hermano** first cousin; **materias primas** raw materials.

primogénito, a [primo'xenito, a] *a* first-born.

primordial [primor'ðjal] *a* basic, fundamental.

primoroso, a [primo'roso, a] *a* exquisite, delicate.

princesa [prin'θesa] *nf* princess.

principal [prinθi'pal] *a* principal, main // *nm* (*COM*) chief, principal.

príncipe ['prinθipe] *nm* prince.

principiante [prinθi'pjante] *nm/f* beginner.

principiar [prinθi'pjar] *vt* to begin.

principio [prin'θipjo] *nm* (*comienzo*) beginning, start; (*origen*) origin; (*primera etapa*) rudiment, basic idea; (*moral*) principle; **a ~s de** at the beginning of.

pringoso, a [prin'xoso, a] *a* (*grasiento*) greasy; (*pegajoso*) sticky.

pringue ['pringe] *nm* (*grasa*) grease, fat, dripping.

prioridad [priori'ðað] *nf* priority.

prisa ['prisa] *nf* (*apresuramiento*) hurry, haste; (*rapidez*) speed; (*urgencia*) (sense of) urgency; **a o**

de ~ quickly; correr ~ to be urgent; darse ~ to hurry up; estar de o tener ~ to be in a hurry.

prisión [pri'sjon] nf (cárcel) prison; (período de cárcel) imprisonment; **prisionero, a** nm/f prisoner.

prismáticos [pris'matikos] nmpl binoculars.

privación [priβa'θjon] nf deprivation; (falta) want, privation.

privado, a [pri'βaðo, a] a private.

privar [pri'βar] vt to deprive; **privativo, a** a exclusive.

privilegiado, a [priβile'xjaðo, a] a privileged; (memoria) very good.

privilegiar [priβile'xjar] vt to grant a privilege to; (favorecer) to favour.

privilegio [priβi'lexjo] nm privilege; (concesión) concession.

pro [pro] nm o f profit, advantage // prep: **asociación** ~ **ciegos** association for the blind // pref: ~ **soviético/americano** pro-Soviet/ American; **en** ~ **de** on behalf of, for; **los** ~**s y los contras** the pros and cons.

proa ['proa] nf bow, prow; de ~ bow cpd, fore.

probabilidad [proβaβili'ðað] nf probability, likelihood; (oportunidad, posibilidad) chance, prospect; **probable** a probable, likely.

probador [proβa'ðor] nm (en tienda) fitting room.

probar [pro'βar] vt (demostrar) to prove; (someter a prueba) to test, try out; (ropa) to try on; (comida) to taste // vi to try; ~**se un traje** to try on a suit.

probeta [pro'βeta] nf test tube.

problema [pro'βlema] nm problem.

procedente [proθe'ðente] a (razonable) reasonable; (conforme a derecho) proper, fitting; ~ **de** coming from, originating in.

proceder [proθe'ðer] vi (avanzar) to proceed; (actuar) to act; (ser correcto) to be right (and proper), be fitting; ~ **de** to come from, originate in // nm (comportamiento) behaviour;

conduct; **procedimiento** nm procedure; (proceso) process; (método) means pl, method.

procesado, a [proθe'saðo, a] nm/f accused.

procesador [proθesa'ðor] nm: ~ **de textos** word processor.

procesar [proθe'sar] vt to try, put on trial.

procesión [proθe'sjon] nf procession.

proceso [pro'θeso] nm process; (JUR) trial; (lapso) course (of time).

proclamar [prokla'mar] vt to proclaim.

procreación [prokrea'θjon] nf procreation.

procrear [prokre'ar] vt, vi to procreate.

procurador, a [prokura'ðor, a] nm/f attorney.

procurar [proku'rar] vt (intentar) to try, endeavour; (conseguir) to get, obtain; (asegurar) to secure; (producir) to produce.

prodigio [pro'ðixjo] nm prodigy; (milagro) wonder, marvel; ~**so, a** a prodigious, marvellous.

pródigo, a [pro'ðiɣo, a] a: **hijo** ~ prodigal son.

producción [proðuk'θjon] nf (gen) production; (producto) product; ~ **en serie** mass production.

producir [proðu'θir] vt to produce; (causar) to cause, bring about; ~**se** vr (cambio) to come about; (accidente) to take place; (problema etc) to arise; (hacerse) to be produced, be made; (estallar) to break out.

productividad [proðuktiβi'ðað] nf productivity; **productivo, a** a productive; (provechoso) profitable.

producto [pro'ðukto] nm product; (producción) production.

productor, a [proðuk'tor, a] a productive, producing // nm/f producer.

proeza [pro'eθa] nf exploit, feat.

profanar [profa'nar] vt to desecrate, profane; **profano, a** a profane //

nm/f layman/woman.

profecía [profe'θia] *nf* prophecy.

proferir [profe'rir] *vt* (*palabra, sonido*) to utter; (*injuria*) to hurl, let fly.

profesar [profe'sar] *vt* (*practicar*) to practise.

profesión [profe'sjon] *nf* profession; **profesional** *a* professional.

profesor, a [profe'sor, a] *nm/f* teacher; **~ado** *nm* teaching profession.

profeta [pro'feta] *nm/f* prophet; **profetizar** *vt, vi* to prophesy.

prófugo, a [pro'fuɣo, a] *nm/f* fugitive; (*MIL: desertor*) deserter.

profundidad [profundi'ðað] *nf* depth; **profundizar** *vt* (*fig*) to go deeply into; **profundo, a** *a* deep; (*misterio, pensador*) profound.

profusión [profu'sjon] *nf* (*abundancia*) profusion; (*prodigalidad*) extravagance.

progenitor [proxeni'tor] *nm* ancestor; **~es** *nmpl* (*padres*) parents.

programa [pro'ɣrama] *nm* programme (*Brit*), program (*US*); **~ción** *nf* programming; **~dor, a** *nm/f* programmer; **programar** *vt* to program.

progresar [proɣre'sar] *vi* to progress, make progress; **progresista** *a, nm/f* progressive; **progresivo, a** *a* progressive; (*gradual*) gradual; (*continuo*) continuous; **progreso** *nm* progress.

prohibición [proiβi'θjon] *nf* prohibition, ban.

prohibir [proi'βir] *vt* to prohibit, ban, forbid; **se prohíbe fumar**, **prohibido fumar** no smoking.

prójimo, a [pro'ximo, a] *nm/f* fellow man; (*vecino*) neighbour.

proletariado [proleta'rjaðo] *nm* proletariat.

proletario, a [prole'tarjo, a] *a, nm/f* proletarian.

proliferación [prolifera'θjon] *nf* proliferation.

proliferar [prolife'rar] *vi* to proliferate; **prolífico, a** *a* prolific.

prolijo, a [pro'lixo, a] *a* long-winded, tedious.

prólogo ['proloɣo] *nm* prologue.

prolongación [prolonɣa'θjon] *nf* extension; **prolongado, a** *a* (*largo*) long; (*alargado*) lengthy.

prolongar [prolonɣ'ar] *vt* to extend; (*reunión etc*) to prolong; (*calle, tubo*) to extend.

promedio [pro'meðjo] *nm* average; (*de distancia*) middle, mid-point.

promesa [pro'mesa] *nf* promise.

prometer [prome'ter] *vt* to promise // *vi* to show promise; **~se** *vr* (*novios*) to get engaged; **prometido, a** *a* promised; engaged // *nm/f* fiancé/fiancée.

prominente [promi'nente] *a* prominent.

promiscuo, a [pro'miskwo, a] *a* promiscuous.

promoción [promo'θjon] *nf* promotion.

promotor [promo'tor] *nm* promoter; (*instigador*) instigator.

promover [promo'βer] *vt* to promote; (*causar*) to cause; (*en stigar*) to instigate, stir up.

promulgar [promul'ɣar] *vt* to promulgate; (*fig*) to proclaim.

pronombre [pro'nombre] *nm* pronoun.

pronosticar [pronosti'kar] *vt* to predict, foretell, forecast; **pronóstico** *nm* prediction, forecast; **pronóstico del tiempo** weather forecast.

pronto, a ['pronto, a] *a* (*rápido*) prompt, quick; (*preparado*) ready // *ad* quickly, promptly; (*en seguida*) at once, right away; (*dentro de poco*) soon; (*temprano*) early // *nm*: **tener ~s de enojo** to be quick-tempered; **al ~** at first; **de ~** suddenly; **por lo ~** meanwhile, for the present.

pronunciación [pronunθja'θjon] *nf* pronunciation.

pronunciar [pronun'θjar] *vt* to pronounce; (*discurso*) to make, deliver; **~se** *vr* to revolt, rebel; (*declararse*) to declare o.s.

propagación [propaγa'θjon] nf propagation.

propaganda [propa'γanda] nf (política) propaganda; (comercial) advertising.

propagar [propa'γar] vt to propagate.

propensión [propen'sjon] nf inclination, propensity; **propenso, a** a inclined to; **ser propenso a** to be inclined to, have a tendency to.

propiamente [propja'mente] ad properly; (realmente) really, exactly.

propicio, a [pro'piθjo, a] a favourable, propitious.

propiedad [propje'ðað] nf property; (posesión) possession, ownership; ~ **particular** private property.

propietario, a [propje'tarjo, a] nm/f owner, proprietor.

propina [pro'pina] nf tip.

propio, a ['propjo, a] a own, of one's own; (característico) characteristic, typical; (debido) proper; (mismo) selfsame, very; **el ~ ministro** the minister himself; **¿tienes casa propia?** have you a house of your own?

proponer [propo'ner] vt to propose, put forward; (problema) to pose; ~**se** vr to propose, intend.

proporción [propor'θjon] nf proportion; (MAT) ratio; **proporciones** nfpl dimensions; (fig) size sg; **proporcionado, a** a proportionate; (regular) medium, middling; (justo) just right; **proporcionar** vt (dar) to give, supply, provide.

proposición [proposi'θjon] nf proposition; (propuesta) proposal.

propósito [pro'posito] nm purpose; (intento) aim, intention // ad: **a ~** by the way, incidentally; (a posta) on purpose, deliberately; **a ~ de** about, with regard to.

propuesta [pro'pwesta] vb ver **proponer** // nf proposal.

propulsar [propul'sar] vt to drive, propel; (fig) to promote, encourage; **propulsión** nf propulsion;

propulsión a chorro o **por reacción** jet propulsion.

prórroga ['prorroγa] nf extension; (JUR) stay; (COM) deferment; (DEPORTE) extra time; **prorrogar** vt (período) to extend; (decisión) to defer, postpone.

prorrumpir [prorrum'pir] vi to burst forth, break out.

prosa ['prosa] nf prose.

proscripción [proskrip'θjon] nf prohibition, ban; (destierro) banishment; (de un partido) proscription.

proscrito, a [pro'skrito, a] a (prohibido, desterrado) banned.

prosecución [proseku'θjon] nf continuation.

proseguir [prose'γir] vt to continue, carry on // vi to continue, go on.

prospección [prospek'θjon] nf exploration; (del oro) prospecting.

prospecto [pro'spekto] nm prospectus.

prosperar [prospe'rar] vi to prosper, thrive, flourish; **prosperidad** nf prosperity; (éxito) success; **próspero, a** a prosperous, flourishing; (que tiene éxito) successful.

prostíbulo [pros'tiβulo] nm brothel (Brit), house of prostitution (US).

prostitución [prostitu'θjon] nf prostitution.

prostituir [prosti'twir] vt to prostitute; ~**se** vr to prostitute o.s., become a prostitute.

prostituta [prosti'tuta] nf prostitute.

protagonista [protaγo'nista] nm/f protagonist.

protagonizar [protaγoni'θar] vt to take the chief rôle in.

protección [protek'θjon] nf protection.

protector, a [protek'tor, a] a protective, protecting // nm/f protector.

proteger [prote'xer] vt to protect; **protegido, a** nm/f protégé/protégée.

proteína [prote'ina] nf protein.

protesta [pro'testa] nf protest; (declaración) protestation.

protestante [protes'tante] a Protestant.

protestar [protes'tar] vt to protest, declare; (fe) to protest // vi to protest.

protocolo [proto'kolo] nm protocol.

prototipo [proto'tipo] nm prototype.

prov. abr (= provincia) prov.

provecho [pro'βetʃo] nm advantage, benefit; (FINANZAS) profit; (buen ~! bon appétit!; en ~ de to the benefit of; sacar ~ de to benefit from, profit by.

proveer [proβe'er] vt to provide, supply // vi: ~ a to provide for.

provenir [proβe'nir] vi: ~ de to come from, stem from.

proverbio [pro'βerβjo] nm proverb.

providencia [proβi'ðenθja] nf providence; (previsión) foresight.

provincia [pro'βinθja] nf province; ~no, a a provincial; (del campo) country cpd.

provisión [proβi'sjon] nf provision; (abastecimiento) provision, supply; (medida) measure, step.

provisional [proβisjo'nal] a a provisional.

provocación [proβoka'θjon] nf provocation.

provocar [proβo'kar] vt to provoke; (alentar) to tempt, invite; (causar) to bring about, lead to; (promover) to promote; (estimular) to rouse, stimulate; ¿te provoca un café? (AM) would you like a coffee?; **provocativo, a** a provocative.

próximamente [proksima'mente] ad shortly, soon.

proximidad [proksimi'ðað] nf closeness, proximity; **próximo, a** a near, close; (vecino) neighbouring; (siguiente) next.

proyectar [projek'tar] vt (objeto) to hurl, throw; (luz) to cast, shed; (CINE) to screen, show; (planear) to plan.

proyectil [projek'til] nm projectile, missile.

proyecto [pro'jekto] nm plan;

(estimación de costo) detailed estimate.

proyector [projek'tor] nm (CINE) projector.

prudencia [pru'ðenθja] nf (sabiduría) wisdom; (cuidado) care; **prudente** a sensible, wise; (conductor) careful.

prueba etc vb ver **probar** // ['prweβa] nf proof; (ensayo) test, trial; (degustación) tasting, sampling; (de ropa) fitting; a ~ on trial; a ~ de proof against; a ~ de agua/ fuego waterproof/fireproof; **someter** a ~ to put to the test.

prurito [pru'rito] nm itch; (de bebé) nappy (Brit) o diaper (US) rash.

psico... [siko] pref psycho...; **~análisis** nm inv psychoanalysis; **~logía** nf psychology; **~lógico, a** a psychological; **psicólogo, a** nm/f psychologist; **psicópata** nm/f psychopath; **~sis** nf inv psychosis.

psiquiatra [si'kjatra] nm/f psychiatrist; **psiquiátrico, a** a psychiatric.

psíquico, a ['sikiko, a] a psychic(al).

PSOE [pe'soe] nm abr = Partido Socialista Obrero Español.

pta(s) abr = **peseta(s)**.

pts abr = **pesetas**.

púa ['pua] nf sharp point; (BOT, ZOOL) prickle, spine; (para guitarra) plectrum (Brit), pick (US); alambre de ~ barbed wire.

pubertad [puβer'tað] nf puberty.

publicación [puβlika'θjon] nf publication.

publicar [puβli'kar] vt (editar) to publish; (hacer público) to publicize; (divulgar) to make public, divulge.

publicidad [puβliθi'ðað] nf publicity; (COM: propaganda) advertising; **publicitario, a** a publicity cpd; advertising cpd.

público, a ['puβliko, a] a public // nm public; (TEATRO etc) audience.

puchero [pu'tʃero] nm (CULIN: guiso) stew; (: olla) cooking pot; hacer ~s to pout.

pude *etc vb ver* **poder.**

púdico, a [a'puðiko, a] *a* modest.

pudiente [pu'ðjente] *a (rico)* wealthy, well-to-do.

pudiera *etc vb ver* **poder.**

pudor [pu'ðor] *nm* modesty.

pudrir [pu'ðrir] *vt* to rot; *(fam)* to upset, annoy; **~se** *vr* to rot, decay.

pueblo ['pweßlo] *nm* people; *(nación)* nation; *(aldea)* village.

puedo *etc vb ver* **poder.**

puente ['pwente] *nm* bridge; **~ aéreo** shuttle service; **~ colgante** suspension bridge; **hacer ~** *(fam)* to take an extra day off work between 2 public holidays; to take a long weekend.

puerco, a ['pwerko, a] *nm/f* pig/sow // *a (sucio)* dirty, filthy; *(obsceno)* disgusting; **~ de mar** porpoise; **~ marino** dolphin.

pueril [pwe'ril] *a* childish.

puerro ['pwerro] *nm* leek.

puerta ['pwerta] *nf* door; *(de jardín)* gate; *(portal)* doorway; *(fig)* gateway; *(portería)* goal; **a la ~** at the door; **a ~ cerrada** behind closed doors; **~ giratoria** revolving door.

puertaventana [pwertaßen'tana] *nf* shutter.

puerto ['pwerto] *nm* port; *(paso)* pass; *(fig)* haven, refuge.

Puerto Rico ['pwerto'riko] *nm* Puerto Rico; **puertorriqueño, a** *a, nm/f* Puerto Rican.

pues [pwes] *ad (entonces)* then; *(bueno)* well, well then; *(así que)* so // *conj (ya que)* since; **¡~!** *(sí)* yes!, certainly!

puesto, a ['pwesto, a] *pp de* **poner** // *a* dressed // *nm (lugar, posición)* place; *(trabajo)* post, job; *(COM)* stall // *conj:* **~ que** since, as // *nf (apuesta)* bet, stake; **puesta en marcha** starting; **puesta del sol** sunset.

púgil ['puxil] *nm* boxer.

pugna ['puγna] *nf* battle, conflict; **~cidad** *nf* pugnacity, aggressiveness; **pugnar** *vi (luchar)* to

struggle, fight; *(pelear)* to fight

pujar [pu'xar] *vi (en subasta)* to bid; *(esforzarse)* to struggle, strain.

pulcro ['pulkro, a] *a* neat, tidy; *(bello)* exquisite.

pulga ['pulγa] *nf* flea.

pulgada [pul'γaða] *nf* inch.

pulgar [pul'γar] *nm* thumb.

pulir [pu'lir], **pulimentar** [pulimen'tar] *vt* to polish; *(alisar)* to smooth; *(fig)* to polish up, touch up.

pulmón [pul'mon] *nm* lung; **pulmonía** *nf* pneumonia.

pulpa ['pulpa] *nf* pulp; *(de fruta)* flesh, soft part.

pulpería [pulpe'ria] *nf (AM: tienda)* small grocery store.

púlpito ['pulpito] *nm* pulpit.

pulpo ['pulpo] *nm* octopus.

pulsación [pulsa'θjon] *nf* beat, pulsation; *(ANAT)* throb(bing).

pulsador [pulsa'ðor] *nm* button, push button.

pulsar [pul'sar] *vt (tecla)* to touch, tap; *(MUS)* to play; *(botón)* to press, push // *vi* to pulsate; *(latir)* to beat, throb; *(MED):* **~ a uno** to take sb's pulse.

pulsera [pul'sera] *nf* bracelet.

pulso ['pulso] *nm (ANAT)* pulse; *(: muñeca)* wrist; *(fuerza)* strength; *(firmeza)* steadiness, steady hand; *(tacto)* tact, good sense.

pulverizador [pulßeriθa'ðor] *nm* spray, spray gun.

pulverizar [pulßeri'θar] *vt* to pulverize; *(líquido)* to spray.

pulla ['puʎa] *nf* cutting remark; *(expresión grosera)* obscene remark.

puna ['puna] *nf (AM MED)* mountain sickness.

pungir [pun'xir] *vt* to puncture, pierce; *(fig)* to cause suffering to.

punición [puni'θjon] *nf* punishment; **punitivo, a** *a* punitive.

punta ['punta] *nf* point, tip; *(extremidad)* end; *(fig)* touch, trace; **horas ~s** peak hours, rush hours; **sacar ~ a** to sharpen; **estar de ~** to be edgy.

puntada [pun'taða] nf (COSTURA) stitch.

puntal [pun'tal] nm prop, support.

puntapié [punta'pje] nm kick.

puntear [punte'ar] vt to tick, mark.

puntería [punte'ria] nf (de arma) aim, aiming; (destreza) marksmanship.

puntero, a [pun'tero, a] a leading // nm (palo) pointer.

puntiagudo, a [puntja'vuðo, a] a sharp, pointed.

puntilla [pun'tiʎa] nf (encaje) lace edging o trim; (andar) de ~s (to walk) on tiptoe.

punto ['punto] nm (gen) point; (señal diminuta) spot, dot; (COSTURA, MED) stitch; (lugar) spot, place; (momento) point, moment; a ~ ready; estar a ~ de to be on the point of o about to; en ~ on the dot; ~ muerto dead centre; (AUTO) neutral (gear); ~ final full stop (Brit), period (US); ~ y coma semicolon; ~ de interrogación question mark; hacer ~ (tejer) to knit.

puntuación [puntwa'θjon] nf punctuation; (puntos: en examen) mark(s) (pl); (: DEPORTE) score.

puntual [pun'twal] a (a tiempo) punctual; (exacto) exact, accurate; (seguro) reliable; ~idad nf punctuality; exactness, accuracy; reliability; ~izar vt to fix, specify.

punzante [pun'θante] a (dolor) shooting, sharp; (herramienta) sharp; **punzar** vt to prick, pierce // vi to shoot, stab.

puñado [pu'ɲaðo] nm handful.

puñal [pu'ɲal] nm dagger; ~ada nf stab.

puñetazo [puɲe'taθo] nm punch.

puño ['puɲo] nm (ANAT) fist; (cantidad) fistful, handful; (COSTURA) cuff; (de herramienta) handle.

pupila [pu'pila] nf pupil.

pupitre [pu'pitre] nm desk.

puré [pu're] nm puree; (sopa) (thick) soup; ~ de patatas mashed potatoes.

pureza [pu'reθa] nf purity.

purga ['purva] nf purge; **purgante** a, nm purgative; **purgar** vt to purge.

purgatorio [purva'torjo] nm purgatory.

purificar [purifi'kar] vt to purify; (refinar) to refine.

puritano, a [puri'tano, a] a (actitud) puritanical; (iglesia, tradición) puritan // nm/f puritan.

puro, a ['puro, a] a pure; (cielo) clear; (verdad) simple, plain // ad: de ~ cansado out of sheer tiredness // nm cigar.

púrpura ['purpura] nf purple; **purpúreo, a** a purple.

pus [pus] nm pus.

puse, pusiera etc vb ver **poner**.

pústula ['pustula] nf pimple, sore.

puta ['puta] nf whore, prostitute.

putrefacción [putrefak'θjon] nf rotting, putrefaction.

pútrido, a ['putriðo, a] a rotten.

PVP abr (Esp: = precio venta al público) RRP.

Q

q.e.p.d. abr (= que en paz descanse) R.I.P.

que [ke] ♦ conj 1 (con oración subordinada: muchas veces no se traduce) that; **dijo** ~ **vendría** he said (that) he would come; **espero** ~ **lo encuentres** I hope (that) you find it; ver tb **el**

2 (en oración independiente): ¡~ **entre!** send him in; ¡**que se mejore tu padre!** I hope your father gets better

3 (enfático): ¿**me quieres?** - ¡~ **sí!** do you love me? - of course!

4 (consecutivo: muchas veces no se traduce) that; **es tan grande** ~ **no**

lo puedo levantar it's so big (that) I can't lift it

5 (*comparaciones*) than; **yo ~ tú/él** if I were you/him; **ver tú más, menos, mismo**

6 (*valor disyuntivo*) ~ **le guste o no** whether he likes it or not; ~ **venga o ~ no venga** whether he comes or not

7 (*porque*): **no puedo, ~ tengo ~ quedarme en casa** I can't, I've got to stay in

♦ *pron* **1** (*cosa*) that, which; (+ *prep*) which; **el sombrero ~ te compraste** the hat (that o which) you bought; **la cama en ~ dormí** the bed (that o which) I slept in

2 (*persona: suj*) that, who; (: *objeto*) that, whom; **el amigo ~ me acompañó al museo** the friend that o who went to the museum with me; **la chica que invité** the girl (that o whom) I invited

qué [ke] *a* what?, which? // *pron* what?; **¡~ divertido!** how funny!; **¿~ edad tienes?** how old are you?; **¿de ~ me hablas?** what are you saying to me?; **¿~ tal?** how are you?, how are things?; **¿~ hay (de nuevo)?** what's new?

quebrada [ke'βraða] *nf ver* quebrado.

quebradizo, a [keβra'ðiθo, a] *a* fragile; (*persona*) frail.

quebrado, a [ke'βraðo, a] *a* (*roto*) broken // *nm* bankrupt // *nm* (MAT) fraction // *nm* ravine.

quebradura [keβra'ðura] *nf* (*fisura*) fissure; (GEO) gorge; (MED) rupture.

quebrantar [keβran'tar] *vt* (*infringir*) to violate, transgress; **~se** *vr* (*persona*) to fail in health.

quebranto [ke'βranto] *nm* damage, harm; (*decaimiento*) exhaustion; (*dolor*) grief, pain.

quebrar [ke'βrar] *vt* to break, smash // *vi* to go bankrupt; **~se** *vr* to break, get broken; (MED) to be ruptured.

quedar [ke'ðar] *vi* to stay, remain; (*encontrarse: sitio*) to be; (*restar*) to remain, be left; **~se** *vr* to remain, stay (behind); **~se con algo** to keep sth; **~ en** (*acordar*) to agree on/to; **~ en nada** to come to nothing; **~ por hacer** to be still to be done; **~ ciego/mudo** to be left blind/dumb; **no te queda bien ese vestido** that dress doesn't suit you; **eso queda muy lejos** that's a long way (away); **quedamos a las seis** we agreed to meet at six.

quedo, a [ˈkeðo, a] *a* still // *ad* softly, gently.

quehacer [kea'θer] *nm* task, job; **~es** (*domésticos*) *nmpl* household chores.

queja ['kexa] *nf* complaint; **quejarse** *vr* (*enfermo*) to moan, groan; (*protestar*) to complain; **quejarse de que** to complain (about the fact) that; **quejido** *nm* moan; **quejoso, a** *a* complaining.

quemado, a [ke'maðo, a] *a* burnt.

quemadura [kema'ðura] *nf* burn, scald.

quemar [ke'mar] *vt* to burn; (*fig: malgastar*) to burn up, squander // *vi* to be burning hot; **~se** *vr* (*consumirse*) to burn (up); (*del sol*) to get sunburnt.

quemarropa [kema'rropa]: **a ~** *ad* point-blank.

quemazón [kema'θon] *nf* burn; (*calor*) intense heat; (*sensación*) itch.

quepo *etc vb ver* **caber.**

querella [ke'reʎa] *nf* (JUR) charge; (*disputa*) dispute.

PALABRA CLAVE

---

querer [ke'rer] *vt* **1** (*desear*) to want; **quiero más dinero** I want more money; **quisiera o querría un té** I'd like a tea; **sin ~** unintentionally; **quiero ayudar/que vayas** I want to help/you to go

2 (*preguntas: para pedir algo*) **¿quiere abrir la ventana?** could you open the window?; ¿quieres **echarme una mano?** can you give me a hand?

3 (amar) to love; (tener cariño a) to be fond of; **quiere mucho a sus hijos** he's very fond of his children

4 (requerir): **esta planta quiere más luz** this plant needs more light

5: le pedí que me dejara ir pero no quiso I asked him to let me go but he refused.

querido, a [keˈriðo, a] a dear // nm/f darling; (amante) lover.

quesería [keseˈria] nf dairy; (fábrica) cheese factory.

queso [ˈkeso] nm cheese; ~ **crema** cream cheese.

quicio [ˈkiθjo] nm hinge; **sacar a uno de** ~ to get on sb's nerves.

quiebra [ˈkjeβra] nf break, split; (COM) bankruptcy; (ECON) slump.

quiebro [ˈkjeβro] nm (del cuerpo) swerve.

quien [kjen] pron who; **hay** ~ **piensa que** there are those who think that; **no hay** ~ **lo haga** no-one will do it.

quién [kjen] pron who, whom; ¿~ **es?** who's there?

quienquiera [kjenˈkjera] (pl **quienesquiera**) pron whoever.

quiero etc vb ver **querer**.

quieto, a [ˈkjeto, a] a still; (carácter) placid; **quietud** nf stillness.

quijada [kiˈxaða] nf jaw, jawbone.

quilate [kiˈlate] nm carat.

quilla [ˈkiʎa] nf keel.

quimera [kiˈmera] nf chimera; **quimérico, a** a fantastic.

químico, a [ˈkimiko, a] a chemical // nm/f chemist // nf chemistry.

quincalla [kinˈkaʎa] nf hardware, ironmongery (Brit).

quince [ˈkinθe] num fifteen; ~ **días** a fortnight; ~**añero, a** nm/f teenager; ~**na** nf fortnight; (pago) fortnightly pay; ~**nal** a fortnightly.

quiniela [kiˈnjela] nf football pools pl; ~**s** nfpl pools coupon sg.

quinientos, as [kiˈnjentos, as] a, num five hundred.

quinina [kiˈnina] nf quinine.

quinqui [ˈkinki] nm delinquent.

quinto, a [ˈkinto, a] a fifth // nf country house; (MIL) call-up, draft.

quiosco [ˈkjosko] nm (de música) bandstand; (de periódicos) news stand.

quirúrgico, a [kiˈrurxiko, a] a surgical.

quise, quisiera etc vb ver **querer**.

quisquilloso, a [kiskiˈʎoso, a] a (susceptible) touchy; (meticuloso) pernickety.

quiste [ˈkiste] nm cyst.

quitaesmalte [kitaesˈmalte] nm nail-polish remover.

quitamanchas [kitaˈmantʃas] nm inv stain remover.

quitanieves [kitaˈnjeβes] nm inv snowplough (Brit), snowplow (US).

quitar [kiˈtar] vt to remove, take away; (ropa) to take off; (dolor) to relieve; **¡quita de ahí!** get away!; ~**se** vr to withdraw; (ropa) to take off; **se quitó el sombrero** he took off his hat.

quitasol [kitaˈsol] nm sunshade (Brit), parasol.

quite [ˈkite] nm (esgrima) parry; (evasión) dodge.

Quito [ˈkito] n Quito.

quizá(s) [kiˈθa(s)] ad perhaps, maybe.

R

rábano [ˈraβano] nm radish; **me importa un** ~ I don't give a damn.

rabia [ˈraβja] nf (MED) rabies sg; (fig: ira) fury, rage; **rabiar** vi to have rabies; to rage, be furious; **rabiar por algo** to long for sth.

rabieta [raˈβjeta] nf tantrum, fit of temper.

rabino [raˈβino] nm rabbi.

rabioso, a [raˈβjoso, a] a rabid; (fig)

furious.

rabo ['raβo] *nm* tail.

racial [ra'θjal] *a* racial, race *cpd*.

racimo [ra'θimo] *nm* bunch.

raciocinio [raθjo'θinjo] *nm* reason.

ración [ra'θjon] *nf* portion; **raciones** *nfpl* rations.

racional [raθjo'nal] *a* (*razonable*) reasonable; (*lógico*) rational; **~izar** *vt* to rationalize.

racionar [raθjo'nar] *vt* to ration (out).

racismo [ra'θismo] *nm* racialism, racism; **racista** *a*, *nm/f* racist.

racha ['ratʃa] *nf* gust of wind: **buena/mala ~** (*fig*) spell of good/ bad luck.

radar [ra'ðar] *nm* radar.

radiactivo, a [raðiak'tiβo, a] *a* = **radioactivo**.

radiador [raðja'ðor] *nm* radiator.

radiante [ra'ðjante] *a* radiant.

radical [raði'kal] *a*, *nm/f* radical.

radicar [raði'kar] *vi* to take root; **~ en** to lie o consist in; **~se** *vr* to establish o.s., put down (one's) roots.

radio ['raðjo] *nf* radio; (*aparato*) radio (set) // *nm* (*MAT*) radius; (*QUÍMICA*) radium; **~activo, a** *a* radioactive; **~difusión** *nf* broadcasting; **~emisora** *nf* transmitter, radio station; **~escucha** *nm/f* listener; **~grafía** *nf* X-ray; **~grafiar** *vt* to X-ray; **~terapia** *nf* radiotherapy.

raer [ra'er] *vt* to scrape (off).

ráfaga ['rafaɣa] *nf* gust; (*de luz*) flash; (*de tiros*) burst.

raído, a [ra'iðo, a] *a* (*ropa*) threadbare.

raigambre [rai'ɣambre] *nf* (*BOT*) roots *pl*; (*fig*) tradition.

raíz [ra'iθ] *nf* root; **~ cuadrada** square root; **a ~ de** as a result of.

raja ['raxa] *nf* (*de melón etc*) slice; (*grieta*) crack; **rajar** *vt* to split; (*fam*) to slash; **rajarse** *vr* to split, crack; **rajarse de** to back out of.

rajatabla [raxa'taβla]: **a ~** *ad* (*estrictamente*) strictly, to the letter.

ralo, a ['ralo, a] *a* thin, sparse.

rallado, a [ra'ʎaðo, a] *a* grated; **rallador** *nm* grater.

rallar [ra'ʎar] *vt* to grate.

RAM [ram] *nf abr* (= *memoria de acceso aleatorio*) RAM.

rama ['rama] *nf* branch; **~je** *nm* branches *pl*, foliage; **ramal** *nm* (*de cuerda*) strand; (*FERRO*) branch line (*Brit*); (*AUTO*) branch (road) (*Brit*).

rambla ['rambla] *nf* (*avenida*) avenue.

ramera [ra'mera] *nf* whore.

ramificación [ramifika'θjon] *nf* ramification.

ramificarse [ramifi'karse] *vr* to branch out.

ramillete [rami'ʎete] *nm* bouquet.

ramo ['ramo] *nm* branch; (*sección*) department, section.

rampa ['rampa] *nf* ramp.

ramplón, ona [ram'plon, ona] *a* uncouth, coarse.

rana ['rana] *nf* frog; **salto de ~** leap-frog.

rancio, a ['ranθjo, a] *a* (*comestibles*) rancid; (*vino*) aged, mellow; (*fig*) ancient.

ranchero [ran'tʃero] *nm* (*AM*) rancher; smallholder.

rancho ['rantʃo] *nm* grub (*fam*); (*AM*: *grande*) ranch; (: *pequeño*) small farm.

rango ['rango] *nm* rank, standing.

ranura [ra'nura] *nf* groove; (*de teléfono etc*) slot.

rapar [ra'par] *vt* to shave; (*los cabellos*) to crop.

rapaz [ra'paθ] *a* (*ZOOL*) predatory // *nm/f* (*f*: **rapaza**) young boy/girl.

rape ['rape] *nm* quick shave; (*pez*) angler (fish); **al ~** cropped.

rapé [ra'pe] *nm* snuff.

rapidez [rapi'ðeθ] *nf* speed, rapidity; **rápido, a** *a* fast, quick // *ad* quickly // *nm* (*FERRO*) express; **rápidos** *nmpl* rapids.

rapiña [ra'piɲa] *nm* robbery; **ave de ~** bird of prey.

raptar [rap'tar] *vt* to kidnap; **rapto**

nm kidnapping; (*impulso*) sudden impulse; (*éxtasis*) ecstasy, rapture.

raqueta [ra'keta] *nf* racquet.

raquítico, a [ra'kitiko, a] *a* stunted; (*fig*) poor, inadequate; **raquitismo** *nm* rickets *sg*.

rareza [ra'reθa] *nf* rarity; (*fig*) eccentricity.

raro, a ['raro, a] *a* (*poco común*) rare; (*extraño*) odd, strange; (*excepcional*) remarkable.

ras [ras] *nm*: **a ~ de** level with; **a ~ de tierra** at ground level.

rasar [ra'sar] *vt* (*igualar*) to level.

rascacielos [raska'θjelos] *nm inv* skyscraper.

rascar [ras'kar] *vt* (*con las uñas etc*) to scratch; (*raspar*) to scrape; **~se** *vr* to scratch (o.s.).

rasgar [ras'ɣar] *vt* to tear, rip (up).

rasgo ['rasɣo] *nm* (*con pluma*) stroke; **~s** *nmpl* features, characteristics; **a grandes ~s** in outline, broadly.

rasguñar [rasɣu'nar] *vt* to scratch; **rasguño** *nm* scratch.

raso, a ['raso, a] *a* (*liso*) flat, level; (*a baja altura*) very low // *nm* satin; **cielo ~** clear sky.

raspadura [raspa'ðura] *nf* (*acto*) scrape, scraping; (*marca*) scratch; **~s** *nfpl* scrapings.

raspar [ras'par] *vt* to scrape; (*arañar*) to scratch; (*limar*) to file.

rastra ['rastra] *nf* (*AGR*) rake; **a ~s** by dragging; (*fig*) unwillingly.

rastreador [rastrea'ðor] *nm* tracker; **~ de minas** minesweeper.

rastrear [rastre'ar] *vt* (*seguir*) to track.

rastrero, a [ras'trero, a] *a* (*BOT, ZOOL*) creeping; (*fig*) despicable, mean.

rastrillar [rastri'ʎar] *vt* to rake; **rastrillo** *nm* rake.

rastro ['rastro] *nm* (*AGR*) rake; (*pista*) track, trail; (*vestigio*) trace; **el R~** the Madrid fleamarket.

rastrojo [ras'troxo] *nm* stubble.

rasurador [rasura'ðor] *nm*, **rasura-**

dora [rasura'ðora] *nf* (*AM*) electric shaver.

rasurarse [rasu'rarse] *vr* to shave.

rata ['rata] *nf* rat.

ratear [rate'ar] *vt* (*robar*) to steal.

ratería [rate'ria] *nf* petty theft.

ratero, a [ra'tero, a] *a* light-fingered // *nm* (*carterista*) pickpocket; (*AM*: *de casas*) burglar.

ratificar [ratifi'kar] *vt* to ratify.

rato ['rato] *nm* while, short time; **a ~s** from time to time; **hay para ~** there's still a long way to go; **al poco ~** soon afterwards; **pasar el ~** to kill time; **pasar un buen/mal ~** to have a good/rough time.

ratón [ra'ton] *nm* mouse; **ratonera** *nf* mousetrap.

raudal [rau'ðal] *nm* torrent; **a ~es** in abundance.

raya ['raja] *nf* line; (*marca*) scratch; (*en tela*) stripe; (*de pelo*) parting; (*límite*) boundary; (*pez*) ray; (*puntuación*) hyphen; **a ~s** striped; **pasarse de la ~** to go too far; **tener a ~** to keep in check; **rayar** *vt* to line; to scratch; (*subrayar*) to underline // *vi*: **rayar en** o **con** to border on.

rayo ['rajo] *nm* (*del sol*) ray, beam; (*de luz*) shaft; (*en una tormenta*) (flash of) lightning; **~s X** X-rays.

rayón [ra'jon] *nm* rayon.

raza ['raθa] *nf* race; **~ humana** human race.

razón [ra'θon] *nf* reason; (*justicia*) right, justice; (*razonamiento*) reasoning; (*motivo*) reason, motive; (*MAT*) ratio; **a ~ de 10 cada día** at the rate of 10 a day; **'~: ...'** 'inquiries to ...'; **en ~ de** with regard to; **dar ~ a uno** to agree that sb is right; **tener ~** to be right; **~ directa/inversa** direct/inverse proportion; **~ de ser** raison d'être; **razonable** *a* reasonable; (*justo, moderado*) fair; **razonamiento** *nm* (*juicio*) judgement; (*argumento*) reasoning; **razonar** *vt* to reason, argue // *vi* to reason, argue.

reacción [reak'θjon] *nf* reaction; avión a ~ jet plane; **~ en cadena** chain reaction; **reaccionar** *vi* to react; **reaccionario, a** *a* reactionary.

reacio, a [re'aθjo, a] *a* stubborn.

reactor [reak'tor] *nm* reactor.

readaptación [reaðapta'θjon] *nf*: ~ **profesional** industrial retraining.

reajuste [rea'xuste] *nm* readjustment.

real [re'al] *a* real; (*del rey, fig*) royal.

realce [re'alθe] *nm* (*TEC*) embossing; (*lustre, fig*) splendour; (*ARTE*) highlight; **poner de** ~ to emphasize.

realidad [reali'ðað] *nf* reality, fact; (*verdad*) truth.

realista [rea'lista] *nm/f* realist.

realización [realiθa'θjon] *nf* fulfilment; (*COM*) selling up (*Brit*), conversion into money (*US*).

realizador, a [realiθa'ðor, a] *nm/f* (*TV etc*) producer.

realizar [reali'θar] *vt* (*objetivo*) to achieve; (*plan*) to carry out; (*viaje*) to make, undertake; (*COM*) to sell up (*Brit*), convert into money (*US*); ~**se** *vr* to come about, come true.

realmente [real'mente] *ad* really, actually.

realquilar [realki'lar] *vt* (*subarrendar*) to sublet.

realzar [real'θar] *vt* (*TEC*) to raise; (*embellecer*) to enhance; (*acentuar*) to highlight.

reanimar [reani'mar] *vt* to revive; (*alentar*) to encourage; ~**se** *vr* to revive.

reanudar [reanu'ðar] *vt* (*renovar*) to renew; (*historia, viaje*) to resume.

reaparición [reapari'θjon] *nf* reappearance.

rearme [re'arme] *nm* rearmament.

rebaja [re'βaxa] *nf* (*COM*) reduction; (*menoscabo*) lessening; **~s** *nfpl* (*COM*) sale; **rebajar** *vt* (*bajar*) to lower; (*reducir*) to reduce; (*disminuir*) to lessen; (*humillar*) to humble.

rebanada [reβa'naða] *nf* slice.

rebaño [re'βaɲo] *nm* herd; (*de ovejas*) flock.

rebasar [reβa'sar] *vt* (*tb*: ~ **de**) to exceed.

rebatir [reβa'tir] *vt* to refute.

rebeca [re'βeka] *nf* cardigan.

rebelarse [reβe'larse] *vr* to rebel, revolt.

rebelde [re'βelde] *a* rebellious; (*niño*) unruly // *nm/f* rebel; **rebeldía** *nf* rebelliousness; (*desobediencia*) disobedience.

rebelión [reβe'ljon] *nf* rebellion.

reblandecer [reβlande'θer] *vt* to soften.

rebosante [reβo'sante] *a* overflowing.

rebosar [reβo'sar] *vi* (*líquido, recipiente*) to overflow; (*abundar*) to abound, be plentiful.

rebotar [reβo'tar] *vt* to bounce; (*rechazar*) to repel // *vi* (*pelota*) to bounce; (*bala*) to ricochet; **rebote** *nm* rebound; **de rebote** on the rebound.

rebozado, a [reβo'θaðo, a] *a* fried in batter *o* breadcrumbs.

rebozar [reβo'θar] *vt* to wrap up; (*CULIN*) to fry in batter *o* breadcrumbs.

rebuscado, a [reβus'kaðo, a] *a* (*amanerado*) affected; (*palabra*) recherché; (*idea*) far-fetched.

rebuznar [reβuθ'nar] *vi* to bray.

recabar [reka'βar] *vt* (*obtener*) to manage to get.

recado [re'kaðo] *nm* message; **tomar un** ~ (*TEL*) to take a message.

recaer [reka'er] *vi* to relapse; ~ **en** to fall to *o* on; (*criminal etc*) to fall back into, relapse into; **recaída** *nf* relapse.

recalcar [rekal'kar] *vt* (*fig*) to stress, emphasize.

recalcitrante [rekalθi'trante] *a* recalcitrant.

recalentar [rekalen'tar] *vt* (*volver a calentar*) to reheat; (*calentar demasiado*) to overheat.

recámara [re'kamara] *nf* (*AM*) bedroom.

recambio [re'kambjo] nm spare; (de pluma) refill.

recapacitar [rekapaθi'tar] vi to reflect.

recargado, a [rekar'γaðo, a] a overloaded.

recargar [rekar'γar] vt to overload; (batería) to recharge; **recargo** nm surcharge; (aumento) increase.

recatado, a [reka'taðo, a] a (modesto) modest, demure; (prudente) cautious.

recato [re'kato] nm (modestia) modesty, demureness; (cautela) caution.

recaudación [rekauða'θjon] nf (acción) collection; (cantidad) takings pl; (en deporte) gate; **recaudador, a** nm/f tax collector.

recelar [reθe'lar] vt: ~ que (sospechar) to suspect that; (temer) to fear that // vi: ~ de to distrust; **recelo** nm distrust, suspicion; **receloso, a** a distrustful, suspicious.

recepción [reθep'θjon] nf reception; **recepcionista** nm/f receptionist.

receptáculo [reθep'takulo] nm receptacle.

receptivo, a [reθep'tiβo, a] a receptive.

receptor, a [reθep'tor, a] nm/f recipient // nm (TEL) receiver.

recesión [reθe'sjon] nf (COM) recession.

receta [re'θeta] nf (CULIN) recipe; (MED) prescription.

recibidor [reθiβi'ðor, a] nm entrance hall.

recibimiento [reθiβi'mjento] nm reception, welcome.

recibir [reθi'βir] vt to receive; (dar la bienvenida) to welcome // vi to entertain; ~se vr: ~se de (AM) to qualify as; **recibo** nm receipt.

recién [re'θjen] ad recently, newly; los ~ casados the newly-weds; el ~ llegado the newcomer; el ~ nacido the newborn child.

reciente [re'θjente] a recent;

(fresco) fresh; ~**mente** ad recently.

recinto [re'θinto] nm enclosure; (área) area, place.

recio, a [re'θjo, a] a strong, tough; (voz) loud // ad hard; loud(ly).

recipiente [reθi'pjente] nm receptacle.

reciprocidad [reθiproθi'ðað] nf reciprocity; **recíproco, a** a reciprocal.

recital [reθi'tal] nm (MUS) recital; (LITERATURA) reading.

recitar [reθi'tar] vt to recite.

reclamación [reklama'θjon] nf claim, demand; (queja) complaint.

reclamar [rekla'mar] vt to claim, demand // vi: ~ contra to complain about; ~ a uno en justicia to take sb to court; **reclamo** nm (anuncio) advertisement; (tentación) attraction.

reclinar [rekli'nar] vt to recline, lean; ~se vr to lean back.

recluir [reklu'ir] vt to intern, confine.

reclusión [reklu'sjon] nf (prisión) prison; (refugio) seclusion; ~ perpetua life imprisonment.

recluta [re'kluta] nm/f recruit // nf recruitment.

reclutamiento [rekluta'mjento] nm recruitment.

recobrar [reko'βrar] vt (salud) to recover; (rescatar) to get back; ~se vr to recover.

recodo [re'koðo] nm (de río, camino) bend.

recoger [reko'xer] vt to collect; (AGR) to harvest; (levantar) to pick up; (juntar) to gather; (pasar a buscar) to come for, get; (dar asilo) to give shelter to; (faldas) to gather up; (pelo) to put up; ~se vr (retirarse) to retire; **recogido, a** a (lugar) quiet, secluded; (pequeño) small // nf (CORREOS) collection; (AGR) harvest.

recolección [rekolek'θjon] nf (AGR) harvesting; (colecta) collection.

recomendación [rekomenda'θjon] nf (sugerencia) suggestion, recommendation; (referencia) reference.

recomendar [rekomen'dar] *vt* to suggest, recommend; (*confiar*) to entrust.

recompensa [rekom'pensa] *nf* reward, recompense; **recompensar** *vt* to reward, recompense.

recomponer [rekompo'ner] *vt* to mend.

reconciliación [rekonθilja'θjon] *nf* reconciliation.

reconciliar [rekonθi'ljar] *vt* to reconcile; ~**se** *vr* to become reconciled.

recóndito, a [re'kondito, a] *a* (*lugar*) hidden, secret.

reconfortar [rekonfor'tar] *vt* to comfort.

reconocer [rekono'θer] *vt* to recognize; (*registrar*) to search; (*MED*) to examine; **reconocido, a** *a* recognized; (*agradecido*) grateful; **reconocimiento** *nm* recognition; search; examination; gratitude; (*confesión*) admission.

reconquista [rekon'kista] *nf* reconquest; **la R~** the Reconquest (of Spain).

reconstituyente [rekonstitu'jente] *nm* tonic.

reconstruir [rekonstru'ir] *vt* to reconstruct.

reconversión [rekonβer'sjon] *nf*: ~ **industrial** industrial rationalization.

recopilación [rekopila'θjon] *nf* (*resumen*) summary; (*compilación*) compilation; **recopilar** *vt* to compile.

récord ['rekorð] *a inv, nm* record.

recordar [rekor'ðar] *vt* (*acordarse de*) to remember; (*acordar a otro*) to remind // *vi* to remember.

recorrer [reko'rrer] *vt* (*país*) to cross, travel through; (*distancia*) to cover; (*registrar*) to search; (*repasar*) to look over; **recorrido** *nm* run, journey; **tren de largo recorrido** main-line train.

recortado, a [rekor'taðo, a] *a* uneven, irregular.

recortar [rekor'tar] *vt* to cut out; **recorte** *nm* (*acción, de prensa*) cutting; (*de telas, chapas*) trimming.

recostado, a [rekos'taðo, a] *a* leaning; **estar ~** to be lying down.

recostar [rekos'tar] *vt* to lean; ~**se** *vr* to lie down.

recoveco [reko'βeko] *nm* (*de camino, río etc*) bend; (*en casa*) cubby hole.

recreación [rekrea'θjon] *nf* recreation.

recrear [rekre'ar] *vt* (*entretener*) to entertain; (*volver a crear*) to re-create; **recreativo, a** *a* recreational; **recreo** *nm* recreation; (*ESCOL*) break, playtime.

recriminar [rekrimi'nar] *vt* to reproach // *vi* to recriminate; ~**se** *vr* to reproach each other.

recrudecer [rekruðe'θer] *vt, vi,* **recrudecerse** *vr* to worsen.

recrudecimiento [rekruðeθi'mjento] *nm* upsurge.

recta ['rekta] *nf* ver **recto**.

rectángulo, a [rek'tangulo, a] *a* rectangular // *nm* rectangle.

rectificar [rektifi'kar] *vt* to rectify; (*volverse recto*) to straighten // *vi* to correct o.s.

rectitud [rekti'tuð] *nf* straightness; (*fig*) rectitude.

recto, a ['rekto, a] *a* straight; (*persona*) honest, upright // *nm* rectum // *nf* straight line.

rector, a [rek'tor, a] *a* governing.

recua ['rekwa] *nf* mule train.

recuadro [re'kwaðro] *nm* box; (*TIPOGRAFÍA*) inset.

recuento [re'kwento] *nm* inventory; **hacer el ~ de** to count o reckon up.

recuerdo [re'kwerðo] *nm* souvenir; ~**s** *nmpl* memories; **¡~s a tu madre!** give my regards to your mother!

recular [reku'lar] *vi* to back down.

recuperable [rekupe'raßle] *a* recoverable.

recuperación [rekupera'θjon] *nf* recovery.

recuperar [rrkupe'rar] *vt* to recover; (*tiempo*) to make up; ~se *vr* to recuperate.

recurrir [reku'rrir] *vi* (JUR) to appeal; ~ a to resort to; (*persona*) to turn to; **recurso** *nm* resort; (*medios*) means *pl*, resources *pl*; (JUR) appeal.

recusar [rreku'sar] *vt* to reject, refuse.

rechazar [rretʃa'θar] *vt* to repel, drive back; (*idea*) to reject; (*oferta*) to turn down.

rechazo [rre'tʃaθo] *nm* (de fusil) recoil; (*rebote*) rebound; (*negación*) rebuff.

rechifla [rre'tʃifla] *nf* hissing, booing; (*fig*) derision.

rechiflar [rretʃi'flar] *vt* to hiss, boo.

rechinar [rretʃi'nar] *vi* to creak; (*dientes*) to grind.

rechistar [rretʃis'tar] *vi*: **sin ~** without a murmur.

rechoncho, a [rre'tʃontʃo, a] *a* (*fam*) thickset (Brit), heavy-set (US).

red [reð] *nf* net, mesh; (FERRO etc) network; (*trampa*) trap.

redacción [rreðak'θjon] *nf* (de acción) editing; (*personal*) editorial staff; (ESCOL) essay, composition.

redactar [rreðak'tar] *vt* to draw up, draft; (*periódico*) to edit.

redactor, a [rreðak'tor, a] *nm/f* editor.

redada [rre'ðaða] *nf*: ~ **policial** police raid, round-up.

rededor [rreðe'ðor] *nm*: **al o en ~** around, round about.

redención [rreðen'θjon] *nf* redemption; **redentor, a** *a* redeeming.

redescubrir [rreðesku'ßrir] *vt* to rediscover.

redicho, a [rre'ðitʃo, a] *a* affected.

redil [rre'ðil] *nm* sheepfold.

redimir [rreði'mir] *vt* to redeem.

rédito ['rreðito] *nm* interest, yield.

redoblar [rreðo'ßlar] *vt* to redouble // *vi* (*tambor*) to play a roll on the drums.

redomado, a [rreðo'maðo, a] *a* (*astuto*) sly, crafty; (*perfecto*) utter.

redonda [rre'ðonda] *nf ver* redondo.

redondear [rreðonde'ar] *vt* to round, round off.

redondel [rreðon'del] *nm* (*círculo*) circle; (TAUR) bullring, arena; (AUTO) roundabout.

redondo, a [rre'ðondo, a] *a* (*circular*) round; (*completo*) complete // *nf*: **a la redonda** around, round about.

reducción [rreðuk'θjon] *nf* reduction.

reducido, a [rreðu'θiðo, a] *a* reduced; (*limitado*) limited; (*pequeño*) small.

reducir [rreðu'θir] *vt* to reduce; to limit; ~se *vr* to diminish.

redundancia [rreðun'danθja] *nf* redundancy.

reembolsar [re(e)mbol'sar] *vt* (*persona*) to reimburse; (*dinero*) to repay, pay back; (*depósito*) to refund; **reembolso** *nm* reimbursement; refund.

reemplazar [re(e)mpla'θar] *vt* to replace; **reemplazo** *nm* replacement; **de reemplazo** (MIL) reserve.

referencia [rrefe'renθja] *nf* reference; **con ~** a with reference to.

referéndum [rrefe'rendum] (*pl* ~s) *nm* referendum.

referente [rrefe'rente] *a*: ~ a concerning, relating to.

referir [rrefe'rir] *vt* (*contar*) to tell, recount; (*relacionar*) to refer, relate; ~se *vr*: ~se a to refer to.

refilón [rrefi'lon]: **de ~** *ad* obliquely.

refinado, a [rrefi'naðo, a] *a* refined.

refinamiento [rrefina'mjento] *nm* refinement.

refinar [rrefi'nar] *vt* to refine; **refinería** *nf* refinery.

reflejar [rrefle'xar] *vt* to reflect; **reflejo, a** *a* reflected; (*movimiento*) reflex // *nm* reflection; (ANAT) reflex.

reflexión [rreflek'sjon] *nf* reflection; **reflexionar** *vt* to reflect on // *vi* to reflect; (*detenerse*) to pause (to think).

reflexivo, a [reflek'sißo, a] *a* thoughtful; (*LING*) reflexive.

reflujo [re'fluxo] *nm* ebb.

reforma [re'forma] *nf* reform; (*ARQ etc*) repair; ~ **agraria** agrarian reform.

reformar [refor'mar] *vt* to reform; (*modificar*) to change, alter; (*ARQ*) to repair; ~**se** *vr* to mend one's ways.

reformatorio [reforma'torjo] *nm* reformatory.

reforzar [refor'θar] *vt* to strengthen; (*ARQ*) to reinforce; (*fig*) to encourage.

refractario, a [refrak'tarjo, a] *a* (*TEC*) heat-resistant.

refrán [re'fran] *nm* proverb, saying.

refregar [refre'ɣar] *vt* to scrub.

refrenar [refre'nar] *vt* to check, restrain.

refrendar [refren'dar] *vt* (*firma*) to endorse, countersign; (*ley*) to approve.

refrescante [refres'kante] *a* refreshing, cooling.

refrescar [refres'kar] *vt* to refresh // *vi* to cool down; ~**se** *vr* to get cooler; (*tomar aire fresco*) to go out for a breath of fresh air; (*beber*) to have a drink.

refresco [re'fresko] *nm* soft drink, cool drink; '~**s**' 'refreshments'.

refriega [re'frjeɣa] *nf* scuffle, brawl.

refrigeración [refrixera'θjon] *nf* refrigeration; (*de sala*) air-conditioning.

refrigerador [refrixera'ðor] *nm*, **refrigeradora** [-a] *nf* (*AM*) refrigerator (*Brit*), icebox (*US*).

refrigerar [refrixe'rar] *vt* to refrigerate; (*sala*) to air-condition.

refuerzo [re'fwerθo] *nm* reinforcement; (*TEC*) support.

refugiado, a [refu'xjaðo, a] *nm/f* refugee.

refugiarse [refu'xjarse] *vr* to take refuge, shelter.

refugio [re'fuxjo] *nm* refuge; (*protección*) shelter.

refulgir [reful'xir] *vi* to shine, be dazzling.

refunfuñar [refunfu'ɲar] *vi* to grunt, growl; (*quejarse*) to grumble.

refutar [refu'tar] *vt* to refute.

regadera [reɣa'ðera] *nf* watering can.

regadío [reɣa'ðio] *nm* irrigated land.

regalado, a [reɣa'laðo, a] *a* comfortable, luxurious; (*gratis*) free, for nothing.

regalar [reɣa'lar] *vt* (*dar*) to give (as a present); (*entregar*) to give away; (*mimar*) to pamper, make a fuss of.

regalía [reɣa'lia] *nf* privilege, prerogative; (*COM*) bonus; (*de autor*) royalty.

regaliz [reɣa'liθ] *nm* liquorice.

regalo [re'ɣalo] *nm* (*obsequio*) gift, present; (*gusto*) pleasure; (*comodidad*) comfort.

regalón, ona [reɣa'lon, ona] *a* spoiled, pampered.

regañadientes [reɣaɲa'ðjentes]: **a ~ de** reluctantly.

regañar [reɣa'ɲar] *vt* to scold // *vi* to grumble; **regaño** *nm* scolding, telling-off; (*queja*) grumble.

regañón, ona *a* nagging.

regar [re'ɣar] *vt* to water, irrigate; (*fig*) to scatter, sprinkle.

regatear [reɣate'ar] *vt* (*COM*) to bargain over; (*escatimar*) to be mean with // *vi* to bargain, haggle; (*DEPORTE*) to dribble; **regateo** *nm* bargaining; (*del cuerpo*) swerve, dodge.

regazo [re'ɣaθo] *nm* lap.

regeneración [rexenera'θjon] *nf* regeneration.

regenerar [rexene'rar] *vt* to regenerate.

regentar [rexen'tar] *vt* to direct, manage; **regente** *nm* (*COM*) manager; (*POL*) regent.

régimen ['reximen] (*pl* **regímenes**) *nm* regime; (*MED*) diet.

regimiento [rexi'mjento] *nm* regiment.

regio, a ['rexjo, a] *a* royal; regal;

(*fig: suntuoso*) splendid; (*AM fam*) great, terrific.

región [re'xjon] *nf* region; **regionalista** *nm/f* regionalist.

regir [re'xir] *vt* to govern, rule; (*dirigir*) to manage, run // *vi* to apply, be in force.

registrador [rexistra'ðor] *nm* registrar, recorder.

registrar [rexis'trar] *vt* (*buscar*) to search; (: *en cajón*) to look through; (*inspeccionar*) to inspect; (*anotar*) to register, record; (*INFORM*) to log; **~se** *vr* to register; (*ocurrir*) to happen.

registro [re'xistro] *nm* (*acto*) registration; (*MUS, libro*) register; (*inspección*) inspection, search; **~ civil** registry office.

regla ['rexla] *nf* (*ley*) rule, regulation; (*de medir*) ruler, rule; (*MED: período*) period.

reglamentación [rexlamenta'θjon] *nf* (*acto*) regulation; (*lista*) rules *pl*.

reglamentar [rexlamen'tar] *vt* to regulate; **reglamentario, a** *a* statutory; **reglamento** *nm* rules *pl*, regulations *pl*.

reglar [re'xlar] *vt* (*acciones*) to regulate.

regocijarse [rexoθi'xarse] *vr* (*pasarlo bien*) to have a good time; (*alegrarse*) to rejoice; **regocijo** *nm* joy, happiness.

regodearse [rexoðe'arse] *vr* to be glad, be delighted; **regodeo** *nm* delight.

regresar [rexre'sar] *vi* to come back, go back, return; **regresivo, a** *a* backward; (*fig*) regressive; **regreso** *nm* return.

reguero [re'xero] *nm* (*de sangre etc*) trickle; (*de humo*) trail.

regulador [rexula'ðor] *nm* regulator; (*de radio etc*) knob, control.

regular [rexu'lar] *a* regular; (*normal*) normal, usual; (*común*) ordinary; (*organizado*) regular, orderly; (*mediano*) average; (*fam*) not bad, so-so // *ad* so-so, alright // *vt*

(*controlar*) to control, regulate; (*TEC*) to adjust; **por lo ~** as a rule; **~idad** *nf* regularity; **~izar** *vt* to regularize.

regusto [re'xusto] *nm* aftertaste.

rehabilitación [reaβilita'θjon] *nf* rehabilitation; (*ARQ*) restoration.

rehabilitar [reaβili'tar] *vt* to rehabilitate; (*ARQ*) to restore; (*reintegrar*) to reinstate.

rehacer [rea'θer] *vt* (*reparar*) to mend, repair; (*volver a hacer*) to redo, repeat; **~se** *vr* (*MED*) to recover.

rehén [re'en] *nm* hostage.

rehuir [reu'ir] *vt* to avoid, shun.

rehusar [reu'sar] *vt, vi* to refuse.

reina ['reina] *nf* queen; **~do** *nm* reign.

reinante [rei'nante] *a* (*fig*) prevailing.

reinar [rei'nar] *vi* to reign.

reincidir [reinθi'ðir] *vi* to relapse.

reincorporarse [reinkorpo'rarse] *vr*: **~ a** to rejoin.

reino ['reino] *nm* kingdom; **el R~ Unido** the United Kingdom.

reintegrar [reinte'xrar] *vt* (*reconstituir*) to reconstruct; (*persona*) to reinstate; (*dinero*) to refund, pay back; **~se** *vr*: **~ a** to return to.

reír [re'ir] *vi*, **reírse** *vr* to laugh; **~se de** to laugh at.

reiterar [reite'rar] *vt* to reiterate.

reivindicación [reißindika'θjon] *nf* (*demanda*) claim, demand; (*justificación*) vindication.

reivindicar [reißindi'kar] *vt* to claim.

reja ['rexa] *nf* (*de ventana*) grille, bars *pl*; (*en la calle*) grating.

rejilla [re'xiʎa] *nf* grating, grille; (*muebles*) wickerwork; (*de ventilación*) vent; (*de coche etc*) luggage rack.

rejoneador [rexonea'ðor] *nm* mounted bullfighter.

rejuvenecer [rexuβene'θer] *vt, vi* to rejuvenate.

relación [rela'θjon] *nf* relation, relationship; (*MAT*) ratio; (*narración*) report; **relaciones públicas** public relations; **con ~ a, en ~ con** in relation to; **relacionar** vt to relate, connect; **relacionarse** vr to be connected, be linked.

relajación [relaxa'θjon] nf relaxation.

relajado, a [rela'xaðo, a] a (disoluto) loose; (cómodo) relaxed; (MED) ruptured.

relajar [rela'xar] vt, **relajarse** vr to relax.

relamerse [rela'merse] vr to lick one's lips.

relamido, a [rela'miðo, a] a (pulcro) overdressed; (afectado) affected.

relámpago [re'lampaxo] nm flash of lightning; **visita/huelga ~** lightning visit/strike; **relampaguear** vi to flash.

relatar [rela'tar] vt to tell, relate.

relativo, a [rela'tiβo, a] a relative; **en lo ~ a** concerning.

relato [re'lato] nm (narración) story, tale.

relax [re'la(k)s] nm: **hacer ~** to relax.

relegar [rele'xar] vt to relegate.

relevante [rele'βante] a eminent, outstanding.

relevar [rele'βar] vt (sustituir) to relieve; **~se** vr to relay; **~ a uno de un cargo** to relieve sb of his post.

relevo [re'leβo] nm relief; **carrera de ~s** relay race.

relieve [re'ljeβe] nm (ARTE, TEC) relief; (fig) prominence, importance; **bajo ~** bas-relief.

religión [reli'xjon] nf religion; **religioso, a** a religious // nm/f monk/nun.

relinchar [relin'tʃar] vi to neigh; **relincho** nm neigh; (acto) neighing.

reliquia [re'likja] nf relic; **~ de familia** heirloom.

reloj [re'lo(x)] nm clock; **~ (de pulsera)** wristwatch; **~ despertador** alarm (clock); **poner el ~** to set one's watch (o the clock); **~ero, a** nm/f clockmaker; watchmaker.

reluciente [relu'θjente] a brilliant, shining.

relucir [relu'θir] vi to shine; (fig) to excel.

relumbrar [relum'brar] vi to dazzle, shine brilliantly.

rellano [re'ʎano] nm (ARQ) landing.

rellenar [reʎe'nar] vt (llenar) to fill up; (CULIN) to stuff; (COSTURA) to pad; **relleno, a** a full up; stuffed // nm stuffing; (de tapicería) padding.

remachar [rema'tʃar] vt to rivet; (fig) to hammer home, drive home; **remache** nm rivet.

remanente [rema'nente] nm remainder; (COM) balance; (de producto) surplus.

remangar [reman'gar] vt to roll up.

remanso [re'manso] nm pool.

remar [re'mar] vi to row.

rematado, a [rema'taðo, a] a complete, utter.

rematar [rema'tar] vt to finish off; (COM) to sell off cheap // vi to end, finish off; (DEPORTE) to shoot.

remate [re'mate] nm end, finish; (punta) tip; (DEPORTE) shot; (ARQ) top; (COM) auction sale; **de o para ~** to crown it all (Brit), to top it off.

remedar [reme'ðar] vt to imitate.

remediar [reme'ðjar] vt to remedy; (subsanar) to make good, repair; (evitar) to avoid.

remedio [re'meðjo] nm remedy; (alivio) relief, help; (JUR) recourse, remedy; **poner ~ a** to correct, stop; **no tener más ~** to have no alternative; **¡qué ~!** there's no choice!; **sin ~** hopeless.

remedo [re'meðo] nm imitation; (pey) parody.

remendar [remen'dar] vt to repair; (con parche) to patch.

remesa [re'mesa] nf remittance; (COM) shipment.

remiendo [re'mjendo] nm mend; (con parche) patch; (cosido) darn.

remilgado, a [remil'xaðo, a] a prim; (afectado) affected.

remilgo [re'milvo] nm primness.

(*afectación*) affectation.

reminiscencia [reminis'θenθja] *nf* reminiscence.

remiso, a [re'miso, a] *a* slack, slow.

remitir [remi'tir] *vt* to remit, send // *vi* to slacken; (*en carta*): **remite: X** sender: X; **remitente** *nm/f* sender.

remo ['remo] *nm* (*de barco*) oar; (*DEPORTE*) rowing.

remojar [remo'xar] *vt* to steep, soak; (*galleta etc*) to dip, dunk.

remojo [re'moxo] *nm*: **dejar la ropa en ~** to leave clothes to soak.

remolacha [remo'latʃa] *nf* beet, beetroot.

remolcador [remolka'ðor] *nm* (*NAUT*) tug; (*AUTO*) breakdown lorry.

remolcar [remol'kar] *vt* to tow.

remolino [remo'lino] *nm* eddy; (*de agua*) whirlpool; (*de viento*) whirlwind; (*de gente*) crowd.

remolque [re'molke] *nm* tow, towing; (*cuerda*) towrope; **llevar a ~** to tow.

remontar [remon'tar] *vt* to mend; **~se** *vr* to soar; **~se a** (*COM*) to amount to; **~ el vuelo** to soar.

remorder [remor'ðer] *vt* to distress, disturb; **~le la conciencia a uno** to have a guilty conscience; **remordimiento** *nm* remorse.

remoto, a [re'moto, a] *a* remote.

remover [remo'ßer] *vt* to stir; (*tierra*) to turn over; (*objetos*) to move round.

remozar [remo'θar] *vt* (*ARQ*) to refurbish.

remuneración [remunera'θjon] *nf* remuneration.

remunerar [remune'rar] *vt* to remunerate; (*premiar*) to reward.

renacer [rena'θer] *vi* to be reborn; (*fig*) to revive; **renacimiento** *nm* rebirth; **el Renacimiento** the Renaissance.

renacuajo [rena'kwaxo] *nm* (*ZOOL*) tadpole.

renal [re'nal] *a* renal, kidney *cpd*.

rencilla [ren'θiʎa] *nf* quarrel.

rencor [ren'kor] *nm* rancour, bitterness; **~oso, a** *a* spiteful.

rendición [rendi'θjon] *nf* surrender.

rendido, a [ren'diðo, a] *a* (*sumiso*) submissive; (*cansado*) worn-out, exhausted.

rendija [ren'dixa] *nf* (*hendedura*) crack, cleft.

rendimiento [rendi'mjento] *nm* (*producción*) output; (*TEC, COM*) efficiency.

rendir [ren'dir] *vt* (*vencer*) to defeat; (*producir*) to produce; (*dar beneficio*) to yield; (*agotar*) to exhaust // *vi* to pay; **~se** *vr* (*someterse*) to surrender; (*cansarse*) to wear o.s. out; **~ homenaje** *o* **culto a** to pay homage to.

renegado, a [rene'vaðo, a] *a, nm/f* renegade.

renegar [rene'var] *vi* (*renunciar*) to renounce; (*blasfemar*) to blaspheme; (*quejarse*) to complain.

RENFE ['renfe] *nf abr* (= Red Nacional de los Ferrocarriles Españoles) ≈ BR (*Brit*).

renglón [ren'glon] *nm* (*línea*) line; (*COM*) item, article; **a ~ seguido** immediately after.

renombrado, a [renom'braðo, a] *a* renowned.

renombre [re'nombre] *nm* renown.

renovación [renoßa'θjon] *nf* (*de contrato*) renewal; (*ARQ*) renovation.

renovar [reno'ßar] *vt* to renew; (*ARQ*) to renovate.

renta ['renta] *nf* (*ingresos*) income; (*beneficio*) profit; (*alquiler*) rent; **~ vitalicia** annuity; **rentable** *a* profitable; **rentar** *vt* to produce, yield.

rentista [ren'tista] *nm/f* (*accionista*) stockholder.

renuencia [re'nwenθja] *nf* reluctance.

renuncia [re'nunθja] *nf* resignation.

renunciar [renun'θjar] *vt* to renounce // *vi* to resign; **~ a hacer algo** to give up doing sth.

reñido, a [re'niðo, a] *a* (*batalla*) bitter, hard-fought; **estar ~ con uno**

to be on bad terms with sb.

reñir [re'ɲir] vt (regañar) to scold // vi (estar peleado) to quarrel, fall out; (combatir) to fight.

reo ['reo] nmf/ culprit, offender; ~ de muerte prisoner condemned to death.

reojo [re'oxo]: de ~ ad out of the corner of one's eye.

reparación [repara'θjon] nf (acto) mending, repairing; (TEC) repair; (fig) amends, reparation.

reparar [repa'rar] vt to repair; (fig) to make amends for; (observar) to observe // vi: ~ en (darse cuenta de) to notice; (prestar atención a) to pay attention to.

reparo [re'paro] nm (advertencia) observation; (duda) doubt; (dificultad) difficulty; poner ~s (a) to raise objections (to).

repartición [reparti'θjon] nf distribution; (división) division; repartidor, a nmf/ distributor.

repartir [repar'tir] vt to distribute, share out; (CORREOS) to deliver; reparto nm distribution; delivery; (TEATRO, CINE) cast; (AM: urbanización) housing estate (Brit), real estate development (US).

repasar [repa'sar] vt (ESCOL) to revise; (MECÁNICA) to check, overhaul; (COSTURA) to mend; repaso nm revision; overhaul, checkup; mending.

repatriar [repa'trjar] vt to repatriate.

repecho [re'petʃo] nm steep incline.

repelente [repe'lente] a repellent, repulsive.

repeler [repe'ler] vt to repel.

repensar [repen'sar] vt to reconsider.

repente [re'pente] nm: de ~ suddenly; ~ de ira fit of anger.

repentino, a [repen'tino, a] a sudden.

repercusión [reperku'sjon] nf repercussion.

repercutir [reperku'tir] vi (objeto) to rebound; (sonido) to echo; ~ en (fig) to have repercussions on.

repertorio [reper'torjo] nm list; (TEATRO) repertoire.

repetición [repeti'θjon] nf repetition.

repetir [repe'tir] vt to repeat; (plato) to have a second helping of // vi to repeat; (sabor) to come back; ~se (volver sobre un tema) to repeat o.s.

repicar [repi'kar] vt (campanas) to ring.

repique [re'pike] nm pealing, ringing; ~teo nm pealing; (de tambor) drumming.

repisa [re'pisa] nf ledge, shelf; (de ventana) windowsill; ~ de chimenea mantelpiece.

repito etc vb ver **repetir**.

replegarse [reple'xarse] vr to fall back, retreat.

repleto, a [re'pleto, a] a replete, full up.

réplica ['replika] nf answer; (ARTE) replica.

replicar [repli'kar] vi to answer; (objetar) to argue, answer back.

repliegue [re'pljexe] nm (MIL) withdrawal.

repoblación [repoβla'θjon] nf repopulation; (de río) restocking; ~ forestal reafforestation.

repoblar [repo'βlar] vt to repopulate; (con árboles) to reafforest.

repollo [re'poʎo] nm cabbage.

reponer [repo'ner] vt to replace, put back; (TEATRO) to revive; ~se vr to recover; ~ que to reply that.

reportaje [repor'taxe] nm report, article.

reportero, a [repor'tero, a] nmf/ reporter.

reposacabezas [reposaka'βeθas] nm inv headrest.

reposado, a [repo'saðo, a] a (descansado) restful; (tranquilo) calm.

reposar [repo'sar] vi to rest, repose.

reposición [reposi'θjon] nf replacement; (CINE) remake.

reposo [re'poso] nm rest.

repostar [repos'tar] vt to replenish; (AUTO) to fill up (with petrol (Brit) *o* gasoline (*US*)).

repostería [reposte'ria] *nf* confectioner's (shop); **repostero, a** *nm/f* confectioner.

reprender [repren'der] *vt* to reprimand.

represa [re'presa] *nf* dam; (*lago artificial*) lake, pool.

represalia [repre'salja] *nf* reprisal.

representación [representa'θjon] *nf* representation; (*TEATRO*) performance; **representante** *nm/f* representative; performer.

representar [represen'tar] *vt* to represent; (*TEATRO*) to perform; (*edad*) to look; ~**se** *vr* to imagine; **representativo, a** *a* representative.

represión [repre'sjon] *nf* repression.

reprimenda [repri'menda] *nf* reprimand, rebuke.

reprimir [repri'mir] *vt* to repress.

reprobar [repro'ßar] *vt* to censure, reprove.

réprobo, a ['reproßo, a] *nm/f* reprobate.

reprochar [repro'tʃar] *vt* to reproach; **reproche** *nm* reproach.

reproducción [reproðuk'θjon] *nf* reproduction.

reproducir [reproðu'θir] *vt* to reproduce; ~**se** *vr* to breed; (*situación*) to recur.

reproductor, a [reproðuk'tor, a] *a* reproductive.

reptil [rep'til] *nm* reptile.

república [re'pußlika] *nf* republic; **republicano, a** *a, nm/f* republican.

repudiar [repu'ðjar] *vt* to repudiate; (*fe*) to renounce; **repudio** *nm* de repudiation.

repuesto [re'pwesto] *nm* (*pieza de recambio*) spare (part); (*abastecimiento*) supply; **rueda de** ~ spare wheel.

repugnancia [repux'nanθja] *nf* repugnance; **repugnante** *a* repugnant, repulsive.

repugnar [repux'nar] *vt* to disgust.

repujar [repu'xar] *vt* to emboss.

repulsa [re'pulsa] *nf* rebuff.

repulsión [repul'sjon] *nf* repulsion, aversion; **repulsivo, a** *a* repulsive.

reputación [reputa'θjon] *nf* reputation.

reputar [repu'tar] *vt* to consider, deem.

requemado, a [reke'maðo, a] *a* (*quemado*) scorched; (*bronceado*) tanned.

requerimiento [rekeri'mjento] *nm* request; (*JUR*) summons.

requerir [reke'rir] *vt* (*pedir*) to ask, request; (*exigir*) to require; (*llamar*) to send for, summon.

requesón [reke'son] *nm* cottage cheese.

requete... [rekete] *pref* extremely.

réquiem ['rekjem] (*pl* ~**s**) *nm* requiem.

requisa [re'kisa] *nf* (*inspección*) survey, inspection; (*MIL*) inspection.

requisito [reki'sito] *nm* requirement, requisite.

res [res] *nf* beast, animal.

resabido, a [resa'ßiðo, a] *a*: **tener algo sabido y** ~ **to know sth perfectly well.**

resabio [re'saßjo] *nm* (*maña*) vice, bad habit; (*dejo*) (unpleasant) aftertaste.

resaca [re'saka] *nf* (*en el mar*) undertow, undercurrent; (*fig*) backlash; (*fam*) hangover.

resalado, a [resa'laðo, a] *a* (*fam*) lively.

resaltar [resal'tar] *vi* to project, stick out; (*fig*) to stand out.

resarcir [resar'θir] *vt* to compensate; ~**se** *vr* to make up for.

resbaladizo, a [resßala'ðiθo, a] *a* slippery.

resbalar [resßa'lar] *vi*, **resbalarse** *vr* to slip, slide; (*fig*) to slip (up); **resbalón** *nm* (*acción*) slip.

rescatar [reska'tar] *vt* (*salvar*) to save, rescue; (*objeto*) to get back, recover; (*cautivos*) to ransom.

rescate [res'kate] *nm* rescue; (*objeto*) recovery; **pagar un** ~ to pay a ransom.

rescindir [resθin'dir] vt to rescind.

rescisión [resθi'sjon] nf cancellation.

rescoldo [res'koldo] nm embers pl.

resecar [rese'kar] vt to dry thoroughly; (MED) to cut out, remove; ~se vr to dry up.

reseco, a [re'seko, a] a very dry; (fig) skinny.

resentido, a [resen'tiðo, a] a resentful.

resentimiento [resenti'mjento] nm resentment, bitterness.

resentirse [resen'tirse] vr (debilitarse: persona) to suffer; ~ de (consecuencias) to feel the effects of; ~ de (o por) algo to resent sth, be bitter about sth.

reseña [re'seɲa] nf (cuenta) account; (informe) report; (LITERATURA) review.

reseñar [rese'ɲar] vt to describe; (LITERATURA) to review.

reserva [re'serβa] nf reserve; (reservación) reservation; a ~ de que ... unless ...; con toda ~ in strictest confidence.

reservado, a [reser'βaðo, a] a reserved; (retraído) cold, distant // nm private room.

reservar [reser'βar] vt (guardar) to keep; (habitación, entrada) to reserve; ~se vr to save o.s.; (callar) to keep to o.s.

resfriado [resfri'aðo] nm cold; **resfriarse** vr to cool; (MED) to catch (a) cold.

resguardar [resɣwar'ðar] vt to protect, shield; ~se vr: ~se de to guard against; **resguardo** nm defence; (vale) voucher; (recibo) receipt, slip.

residencia [resi'ðenθja] nf residence; ~l (urbanización) housing estate.

residente [resi'ðente] a, nm/f resident.

residir [resi'ðir] vi to reside, live; ~ en to reside in, lie in.

residuo [re'siðwo] nm residue.

resignación [resiɣna'θjon] nf resignation; **resignarse** vr: **resignarse**

a o con to resign o.s. to, be resigned to.

resina [re'sina] nf resin.

resistencia [resis'tenθja] nf (dureza) endurance, strength; (oposición, ELEC) resistance; **resistente** a strong, hardy; resistant.

resistir [resis'tir] vt (soportar) to bear; (oponerse a) to resist, oppose; (aguantar) to put up with // vi to resist; (aguantar) to last, endure; ~se vr: ~se a to refuse to, resist.

resma ['resma] nf ream.

resol [re'sol] nm glare of the sun.

resolución [resolu'θjon] nf resolution; (decisión) decision; **resoluto, a** a resolute.

resolver [resol'βer] vt to resolve; (solucionar) to solve, resolve; (decidir) to decide, settle; ~se vr to make up one's mind.

resollar [reso'ʎar] vi to breathe noisily, wheeze.

resonancia [reso'nanθja] nf (del sonido) resonance; (repercusión) repercussion; **resonante** a resonant, resounding; (fig) tremendous.

resonar [reso'nar] vi to ring, echo.

resoplar [reso'plar] vi to snort; **resoplido** nm heavy breathing.

resorte [re'sorte] nm spring; (fig) lever.

respaldar [respal'dar] vt to back (up), support; ~se vr to lean back; ~se con o en (fig) to take one's stand on; **respaldo** nm (de sillón) back; (fig) support, backing.

respectivo, a [respek'tiβo, a] a respective; en lo ~ a with regard to.

respecto [res'pekto] nm: al ~ on this matter; con ~ a, ~ de with regard to, in relation to.

respetable [respe'taβle] a respectable.

respetar [respe'tar] vt to respect; **respeto** nm respect; (acatamiento) deference; **respetos** nmpl respects; **respetuoso, a** a respectful.

respingar [respin'gar] vi to shy; **respingo** nm start, jump.

respiración [respira'θjon] nf breathing; (MED) respiration; (ventilación) ventilation.

respirar [respi'rar] vi to breathe; **respiratorio, a** a respiratory; **respiro** nm breathing; (fig: descanso) respite.

resplandecer [resplande'θer] vi to shine; **resplandeciente** a resplendent, shining; **resplandor** nm brilliance, brightness; (de luz, fuego) blaze.

responder [respon'der] vt to answer // vi to answer; (fig) to respond; (pey) to answer back; ~ **de o por** to answer for; **respondón, ona** a cheeky.

responsabilidad, [responsaβili'ðað] nf responsibility.

responsabilizarse [responsaβili-'θarse] vr to make o.s. responsible, take charge.

responsable [respon'saβle] a responsible.

respuesta [res'pwesta] nf answer, reply.

resquebrajar [reskeβra'xar] vt, **resquebrajarse** vr to crack, split.

resquemor [reske'mor] nm resentment.

resquicio [res'kiθjo] nm chink; (hendedura) crack.

restablecer [restaβle'θer] vt to reestablish, restore; **~se** vr to recover.

restallar [resta'ʎar] vi to crack.

restante [res'tante] a remaining; lo ~ the remainder.

restar [res'tar] vt (MAT) to subtract; (fig) to take away // vi to remain, be left.

restauración [restaura'θjon] nf restoration.

restaurante [restau'rante] nm restaurant.

restaurar [restau'rar] vt to restore.

restitución [restitu'θjon] nf return, restitution.

restituir [restitu'ir] vt (devolver) to return, give back; (rehabilitar) to restore.

resto ['resto] nm (residuo) rest, remainder; (apuesta) stake; ~s nmpl remains.

restregar [restre'var] vt to scrub, rub.

restricción [restrik'θjon] nf restriction.

restrictivo, a [restrik'tiβo, a] a restrictive.

restringir [restrin'xir] vt to restrict, limit.

resucitar [resuθi'tar] vt, vi to resuscitate, revive.

resuelto, a pp de **resolver** // [re'swelto, a] a resolute, determined.

resuello [re'sweʎo] nm (aliento) breath; estar sin ~ to be breathless.

resultado [resul'taðo] nm result; (conclusión) outcome; **resultante** a resulting, resultant.

resultar [resul'tar] vi (ser) to be; (llegar a ser) to turn out to be; (salir bien) to turn out well; (COM) to amount to; ~ **de** to stem from; **me resulta difícil hacerlo** it's difficult for me to do it.

resumen [re'sumen] (pl **resúmenes**) nm summary, résumé; **en ~** in short.

resumir [resu'mir] vt to sum up; (cortar) to abridge, cut down; (condensar) to summarize.

resurgir [resur'xir] vi (reaparecer) to reappear.

resurrección [resurre(k)'θjon] nf resurrection.

retablo [re'taβlo] nm altarpiece.

retaguardia [reta'ɣwarðja] nf rearguard.

retahíla [reta'ila] nf series, string.

retal [re'tal] nm remnant.

retar [re'tar] vt to challenge; (desafiar) to defy, dare.

retardar [retar'ðar] vt (demorar) to delay; (hacer más lento) to slow down; (retener) to hold back; **retardo** nm delay.

retazo [re'taθo] nm snippet (Brit), fragment.

rete... [rete] pref very, extremely.

retener [rete'ner] *vt* (*intereses*) to withhold.

retina [re'tina] *nf* retina.

retintín [retin'tin] *nm* jangle, jingle.

retirada [reti'raða] *nf* (*MIL, refugio*) retreat; (*de dinero*) withdrawal; (*de embajador*) recall; **retirado, a** *a* (*lugar*) remote; (*vida*) quiet; (*jubilado*) retired.

retirar [reti'rar] *vt* to withdraw; (*quitar*) to remove; (*jubilar*) to retire, pension off; ~**se** *vr* to retreat, withdraw; to retire; (*acostarse*) to retire, go to bed; **retiro** *nm* retreat; retirement; (*pago*) pension.

reto ['reto] *nm* dare, challenge.

retocar [reto'kar] *vt* (*fotografía*) to touch up, retouch.

retoño [re'toɲo] *nm* sprout, shoot; (*fig*) offspring, child.

retoque [re'toke] *nm* retouching.

retorcer [retor'θer] *vt* to twist; (*manos, lavado*) to wring; ~**se** *vr* to become twisted; (*mover el cuerpo*) to writhe.

retorcimiento [retorθi'mjento] *nm* twist, twisting.

retórica [re'torika] *nf* rhetoric; (*pey*) affectedness.

retornar [retor'nar] *vt* to return, give back // *vi* to return, go/come back; **retorno** *nm* return.

retortijón [retorti'xon] *nm* twist, twisting.

retozar [reto'θar] *vi* (*juguetear*) to frolic, romp; (*saltar*) to gambol; **retozón, ona** *a* playful.

retracción [retrak'θjon] *nf* retraction.

retractarse [retrak'tarse] *vr* to retract; **me retracto** I take that back.

retraerse [retra'erse] *vr* to retreat, withdraw; **retraído, a** *a* shy, retiring; **retraimiento** *nm* retirement; (*timidez*) shyness.

retransmisión [retransmi'sjon] *nf* repeat (broadcast).

retransmitir [retransmi'tir] *vt* (*mensaje*) to relay; (*TV etc*) to repeat, retransmit; (: *en vivo*) to broadcast live.

retrasado, a [retra'saðo, a] *a* late; (*MED*) mentally retarded; (*país etc*) backward, underdeveloped.

retrasar [retra'sar] *vt* (*demorar*) to postpone, put off; (*retardar*) to slow down // *vi*, ~**se** *vr* (*atrasarse*) to be late; (*reloj*) to be slow; (*producción*) to fall (away); (*quedarse atrás*) to lag behind.

retraso [re'traso] *nm* (*demora*) delay; (*lentitud*) slowness; (*tardanza*) lateness; (*atraso*) backwardness; ~**s** *nmpl* arrears; **llegar con** ~ to arrive late; ~ **mental** mental deficiency.

retratar [retra'tar] *vt* (*ARTE*) to paint the portrait of; (*fotografiar*) to photograph; (*fig*) to depict, describe; ~**se** *vr* to have one's portrait painted; to have one's photograph taken; **retrato** *nm* portrait; (*fig*) likeness; **retrato-robot** *nm* identikit picture.

retreta [re'treta] *nf* retreat.

retrete [re'trete] *nm* toilet.

retribución [retriβu'θjon] *nf* (*recompensa*) reward; (*pago*) pay, payment.

retribuir [retri'βwir] *vt* (*recompensar*) to reward; (*pagar*) to pay.

retro... [retro] *pref* retro—.

retroactivo, a [retroak'tiβo, a] *a* retroactive, retrospective.

retroceder [retroθe'ðer] *vi* (*echarse atrás*) to move back(wards); (*fig*) to back down.

retroceso [retro'θeso] *nm* backward movement; (*MED*) relapse; (*fig*) backing down.

retrógrado, a [re'troɣraðo, a] *a* retrograde, retrogressive; (*POL*) reactionary.

retropropulsión [retropropul'sjon] *nf* jet propulsion.

retrospectivo, a [retrospek'tiβo, a] *a* retrospective.

retrovisor [retroβi'sor] *nm* rear-view mirror.

retumbar [retum'bar] *vi* to echo, resound.

reuma ['reuma], **reumatismo** [reuma'tismo] nm rheumatism.

reunificar [reunifi'kar] vt to reunify.

reunión [reu'njon] nf (asamblea) meeting; (fiesta) party.

reunir [reu'nir] vt (juntar) to reunite, join (together); (recoger) to gather (together); (personas) to get together; (cualidades) to combine; ~se vr (personas: en asamblea) to meet, gather.

revalidar [reβali'ðar] vt (ratificar) to confirm, ratify.

revalorar [reβalo'rar], **revalorizar** [reβalori'θar] vt to revalue, reassess.

revancha [re'βantʃa] nf revenge.

revelación [reβela'θjon] nf revelation.

revelado [reβe'laðo] nm developing.

revelar [reβe'lar] vt to reveal; (FOTO) to develop.

reventar [reβen'tar] vt to burst, explode.

reventón [reβen'ton] nm (AUTO) blow-out (Brit), flat (US).

reverberación [reβerβera'θjon] nf reverberation.

reverberar [reβerβe'rar] vi to reverberate.

reverencia [reβe'renθja] nf reverence; **reverenciar** vt to revere.

reverendo, a [reβe'rendo, a] a reverend.

reverente [reβe'rente] a reverent.

reverso [re'βerso] nm back, other side; (de moneda) reverse.

revertir [reβer'tir] vi to revert.

revés [re'βes] nm back, wrong side; (fig) reverse, setback; (DEPORTE) backhand; **al ~** the wrong way round; (de arriba abajo) upside down; (ropa) inside out; **volver algo al ~** to turn sth round; (ropa) to turn sth inside out.

revestir [reβes'tir] vt (poner) to put on; (cubrir) to cover, coat; **~ con o de** to invest with.

revisar [reβi'sar] vt (examinar) to check; (texto etc) to revise; **revisión** nf revision.

revisor, a [reβi'sor, a] nm/f inspector; (FERRO) ticket collector.

revista [re'βista] nf magazine, review; (TEATRO) revue; (inspección) inspection; **pasar ~ a** to review, inspect.

revivir [reβi'βir] vi to revive.

revocación [reβoka'θjon] nf repeal.

revocar [reβo'kar] vt to revoke.

revolcarse [reβol'karse] vr to roll about.

revolotear [reβolote'ar] vi to flutter.

revoltijo [reβol'tixo] nm mess, jumble.

revoltoso, a [reβol'toso, a] a (travieso) naughty, unruly.

revolución [reβolu'θjon] nf revolution; **revolucionar** vt to revolutionize; **revolucionario, a** a, nm/f revolutionary.

revolver [reβol'βer] vt (desordenar) to disturb, mess up; (mover) to move about; (POL) to stir up // vi: **~ en** to go through, rummage (about) in; **~se** vr (volver contra) to turn on o against.

revólver [re'βolβer] nm revolver.

revuelo [re'βwelo] nm fluttering; (fig) commotion.

revuelto, a [re'βwelto, a] pp de **revolver** // a (mezclado) mixed-up, in disorder // nf (motín) revolt; (agitación) commotion.

revulsivo [reβul'siβo] nm enema.

rey [rei] nm king; **Día R~es** Epiphany.

reyerta [re'jerta] nf quarrel, brawl.

rezagado, a [reθa'ɣaðo, a] nm/f straggler.

rezagar [reθa'ɣar] vt (dejar atrás) to leave behind; (retrasar) to delay, postpone.

rezar [re'θar] vi to pray; **~ con** (fam) to concern, have to do with; **rezo** nm prayer.

rezongar [reθon'ɡar] vi to grumble.

rezumar [reθu'mar] vt to ooze.

ría ['ria] nf estuary.

riada [ri'aða] nf flood.

ribera [ri'βera] nf (de río) bank;

(: *área*) riverside.

ribete [ri'βete] *nm* (*de vestido*) border; (*fig*) addition; **~ar** *vt* to edge, border.

ricino [ri'θino] *nm*: **aceite de ~** castor oil.

rico, a ['riko, a] *a* rich; (*adinerado*) wealthy, rich; (*lujoso*) luxurious; (*comida*) delicious; (*niño*) lovely, cute // *nm/f* rich person.

rictus ['riktus] *nm* (*mueca*) sneer, grin.

ridiculez [riðiku'leθ] *nf* absurdity.

ridiculizar [riðikuli'θar] *vt* to ridicule.

ridículo, a [ri'ðikulo, a] *a* ridiculous; **hacer el ~** to make a fool of o.s.; **poner a uno en ~** to make a fool of sb.

riego ['rjeɣo] *nm* (*aspersión*) watering; (*irrigación*) irrigation.

riel [rjel] *nm* rail.

rienda ['rjenda] *nf* rein; **dar ~ suelta a** to give free rein to.

riesgo ['rjesɣo] *nm* risk; **correr el ~ de** to run the risk of.

rifa ['rifa] *nf* (*lotería*) raffle; **rifar** *vt* to raffle.

rifle ['rifle] *nm* rifle.

rigidez [rixi'ðeθ] *nf* rigidity, stiffness; (*fig*) strictness; **rígido, a** *a* rigid, stiff; strict, inflexible.

rigor [ri'ɣor] *nm* strictness, rigour; (*inclemencia*) harshness; **de ~** de rigueur, essential; **riguroso, a** *a* rigorous; harsh; (*severo*) severe.

rimar [ri'mar] *vi* to rhyme.

rimbombante [rimbom'bante] *a* (*fig*) pompous.

rímel, rímmel ['rimel] *nm* mascara.

rincón [rin'kon] *nm* corner (*inside*).

rinoceronte [rinoθe'ronte] *nm* rhinoceros.

riña ['rina] *nf* (*disputa*) argument; (*pelea*) brawl.

riñón [ri'non] *nm* kidney; **tener riñones** to have guts.

río *etc vb ver* **reír** // ['rio] *nm* river; (*fig*) torrent, stream; **~ abajo/arriba** downstream/upstream; **~ de** la **Plata** River Plate.

rioja [ri'oxa] *nm* (*vino*) rioja (wine).

rioplatense [riopla'tense] *a* of o from the River Plate region.

riqueza [ri'keθa] *nf* wealth, riches *pl*; (*cualidad*) richness.

risa ['risa] *nf* laughter; (*una ~*) laugh; **¡qué ~!** what a laugh!

risco ['risko] *nm* crag, cliff.

risible [ri'siβle] *a* ludicrous, laughable.

risotada [riso'taða] *nf* guffaw, loud laugh.

ristra ['ristra] *nf* string.

risueño, a [ri'sweno, a] *a* (*sonriente*) smiling; (*contento*) cheerful.

ritmo ['ritmo] *nm* rhythm; **a ~ lento** slowly; **trabajar a ~ lento** to go slow.

rito ['rito] *nm* rite.

ritual [ri'twal] *a, nm* ritual.

rival [ri'βal] *a, nmf* rival; **~idad** *nf* rivalry; **~izar** *vi*: **~izar con** to rival, vie with.

rizado, a [ri'θaðo, a] *a* curly // *nm* curls *pl*.

rizar [ri'θar] *vt* to curl; **~se** *vr* (*pelo*) to curl; (*agua*) to ripple; **rizo** *nm* curl; ripple.

RNE *nf abr* = **Radio Nacional de España.**

robar [ro'βar] *vt* to rob; (*objeto*) to steal; (*casa etc*) to break into; (*NAIPES*) to draw.

roble ['roβle] *nm* oak; **~do, ~dal** *nm* oakwood.

robo ['roβo] *nm* robbery, theft.

robot [ro'βot] *nm* robot; **~ de cocina** food processor.

robustecer [roβuste'θer] *vt* to strengthen.

robusto, a [ro'βusto, a] *a* robust, strong.

roca ['roka] *nf* rock.

rocalla [ro'kaʎa] *nf* pebbles *pl*.

roce ['roθe] *nm* (*caricia*) brush; (*TEC*) friction; (*en la piel*) graze; **tener ~ con** to be in close contact with.

rociar [ro'θjar] vt to spray.

rocín [ro'θin] nm nag, hack.

rocío [ro'θio] nm dew.

rocoso, a [ro'koso, a] a rocky.

rodado, a [ro'ðaðo, a] a (con ruedas) wheeled // nf rut.

rodaja [ro'ðaxa] nf (raja) slice.

rodaje [ro'ðaxe] nm (CINE) shooting, filming; (AUTO): **en ~** running in.

rodar [ro'ðar] vt (vehículo) to wheel (along); (escalera) to roll down; (viajar por) to travel (over) // vi to roll; (coche) to go, run; (CINE) to shoot, film.

rodear [roðe'ar] vt to surround // vi to go round; **~se** vr: **~se de amigos** to surround o.s. with friends.

rodeo [ro'ðeo] nm (ruta indirecta) detour; (evasión) evasion; (AM) rodeo; **hablar sin ~s** to come to the point, speak plainly.

rodilla [ro'ðiʎa] nf knee; **de ~s** kneeling; **ponerse de ~s** to kneel (down).

rodillo [ro'ðiʎo] nm roller; (CULIN) rolling-pin.

rododendro [roðo'ðendro] nm rhododendron.

roedor, a [roe'ðor, a] a gnawing // nm rodent.

roer [ro'er] vt (masticar) to gnaw; (corroer, fig) to corrode.

rogar [ro'var] vt, vi (pedir) to ask for; (suplicar) to beg, plead; **se ruega no fumar** please do not smoke.

rojizo, a [ro'xiθo, a] a reddish.

rojo, a ['roxo, a] a, nm red; **al ~ vivo** red-hot.

rol [rol] nm list, roll; (AM: papel) role.

rollizo, a [ro'ʎiθo, a] a (objeto) cylindrical; (persona) plump.

rollo ['roʎo] nm roll; (de cuerda) coil; (madera) log; (fam) bore; **¡qué ~!** what a carry-on!

ROM [rom] nf abr (= memoria de sólo lectura) ROM.

Roma ['roma] n Rome.

romance [ro'manθe] nm (idioma castellano) Romance language; (LITERATURA) ballad; **hablar en ~** to speak plainly.

romanticismo [romanti'θismo] nm romanticism.

romántico, a [ro'mantiko, a] a romantic.

romería [rome'ria] nf (REL) pilgrimage; (excursión) trip, outing.

romero, a [ro'mero, a] nm/f pilgrim // nm rosemary.

romo, a ['romo, a] a blunt; (fig) dull.

rompecabezas [rompeka'βeθas] nm inv riddle, puzzle; (juego) jigsaw (puzzle).

rompehuelgas [rompe'welvas] nm inv strikebreaker, blackleg.

rompeolas [rompe'olas] nm inv breakwater.

romper [rom'per] vt to break; (hacer pedazos) to smash; (papel, tela etc) to tear, rip // vi (olas) to break; (sol, diente) to break through; **~ un contrato** to break a contract; **~ a** to start (suddenly) to; **~ a llorar** to burst into tears; **~ con uno** to fall out with sb.

rompimiento [rompi'mjento] nm (acto) breaking; (fig) break; (quiebra) crack.

ron [ron] nm rum.

roncar [ron'kar] vi to snore.

ronco, a ['ronko, a] a (afónico) hoarse; (áspero) raucous.

roncha ['rontʃa] nf weal; (contusión) bruise.

ronda ['ronda] nf (gen) round; (patrulla) patrol; **rondar** vt to patrol // vi to patrol; (fig) to prowl round.

ronquido [ron'kiðo] nm snore, snoring.

ronronear [ronrone'ar] vi to purr; **ronroneo** nm purr.

roña ['roɲa] nf (VETERINARIA) mange; (mugre) dirt, grime; (óxido) rust.

roñoso, a [ro'ɲoso, a] a (mugriento) filthy; (tacaño) mean.

ropa ['ropa] nf clothes pl, clothing; **~**

blanca linen; ~ **de cama** bed linen; ~ **interior** underwear; ~ **para lavar** washing; **~je** nm gown, robes pl; **~vejero, a** nm/f second-hand clothes dealer.

ropero [ro'pero] nm linen cupboard; (*guardarropa*) wardrobe.

rosa ['rosa] a *inv* pink // nf rose; (*ANAT*) red birthmark; ~ **de los vientos** the compass.

rosado, a [ro'saðo, a] a pink // nm rosé.

rosal [ro'sal] nm rosebush.

rosario [ro'sarjo] nm (*REL*) rosary; **rezar el** ~ to say the rosary.

rosca ['roska] nf (*de tornillo*) thread; (*de humo*) coil, spiral; (*pan, postre*) ring-shaped roll/pastry.

rosetón [rose'ton] nm rosette; (*ARQ*) rose window.

rosquilla [ros'kiʎa] nf doughnut-shaped fritter.

rostro ['rostro] nm (*cara*) face.

rotación [rota'θjon] nf rotation; ~ **de cultivos** crop rotation.

rotativo, a [rota'tiβo, a] a rotary.

roto, a pp **de romper** // ['roto, a] a broken.

rótula ['rotula] nf kneecap; (*TEC*) ball-and-socket joint.

rotulador [rotula'ðor] nm felt-tip pen.

rotular [rotu'lar] vt (*carta, documento*) to head, entitle; (*objeto*) to label; **rótulo** nm heading, title; label; (*letrero*) sign.

rotundo, a [ro'tundo, a] a round; (*enfático*) emphatic.

rotura [ro'tura] nf (*rompimiento*) breaking; (*MED*) fracture.

roturar [rotu'rar] vt to plough.

rozadura [roθa'ðura] nf abrasion, graze.

rozar [ro'θar] vt (*frotar*) to rub; (*arañar*) to scratch; (*tocar ligeramente*) to shave, touch lightly; ~**se** vr to rub (together); ~**se con** (*fam*) to rub shoulders with.

r.p.m. abr (= *revoluciones por minuto*) rpm.

rte. abr (= *remite, remitente*) sender.

RTVE nf abr = *Radiotelevisión Española*.

rubí [ru'βi] nm ruby; (*de reloj*) jewel.

rubicundo, a [ruβi'kundo, a] a ruddy.

rubio, a ['ruβjo, a] a fair-haired, blond(e) // nm/f blond/blonde; **tabaco** ~ Virginia tobacco.

rubor [ru'βor] nm (*sonrojo*) blush; (*timidez*) bashfulness; ~**izarse** vr to blush; ~**oso, a** a blushing.

rúbrica ['ruβrika] nf (*título*) title, heading; (*de la firma*) flourish; **rubricar** vt (*firmar*) to sign with a flourish; (*concluir*) to sign and seal.

rudeza [ru'ðeθa] nf (*tosquedad*) coarseness; (*sencillez*) simplicity.

rudimento [ruði'mento] nm rudiment.

rudo, a ['ruðo, a] a (*sin pulir*) unpolished; (*grosero*) coarse; (*violento*) violent; (*sencillo*) simple.

rueda ['rweða] nf wheel; (*círculo*) ring, circle; (*rodaja*) slice, round; ~ **delantera/trasera/de repuesto** front/back/spare wheel; ~ **de prensa** press conference.

ruedo ['rweðo] nm (*contorno*) edge, border; (*de vestido*) hem; (*círculo*) circle; (*TAUR*) arena, bullring.

ruego etc vb ver **rogar** // ['rwexo] nm request.

rufián [ru'fjan] nm scoundrel.

rugby ['ruxβi] nm rugby.

rugido [ru'xiðo] nm roar.

rugir [ru'xir] vi to roar.

rugoso, a [ru'xoso, a] a (*arrugado*) wrinkled; (*áspero*) rough; (*desigual*) ridged.

ruibarbo [rui'βarβo] nm rhubarb.

ruido ['rwiðo] nm noise; (*sonido*) sound; (*alboroto*) racket, row; (*escándalo*) commotion, rumpus; ~**so, a** a noisy, loud; (*fig*) sensational.

ruin [rwin] a contemptible, mean.

ruina ['rwina] nf ruin; (*colapso*) collapse; (*de persona*) ruin, downfall.

ruindad [rwin'dað] nf lowness, meanness; (acto) low o mean act.

ruinoso, a [rwi'noso, a] a ruinous; (destartalado) dilapidated, tumbledown; (COM) disastrous.

ruiseñor [rwise'ɲor] nm nightingale.

rula ['rula], **ruleta** [ru'leta] nf roulette.

rulo ['rulo] nm (para el pelo) curler.

rulota [ru'lota] nf caravan (Brit), trailer (US).

Rumania [ru'manja] nf Rumania.

rumba ['rumba] nf rumba.

rumbo ['rumbo] nm (ruta) route, direction; (ángulo de dirección) course, bearing; (fig) course of events: **ir con ~ a** to be heading for.

rumboso, a [rum'boso, a] a (generoso) generous.

rumiante [ru'mjante] nm ruminant.

rumiar [ru'mjar] vt to chew; (fig) to chew over // vi to chew the cud.

rumor [ru'mor] nm (ruido sordo) low sound; (murmuración) murmur, buzz: **rumorearse** vr: **se rumorea que** it is rumoured that.

runrún [run'run] nm (voces) murmur, sound of voices; (fig) rumour.

rupestre [ru'pestre] a rock cpd.

ruptura [rup'tura] nf rupture.

rural [ru'ral] a rural.

Rusia ['rusja] nf Russia; **ruso, a** a, nm/f Russian.

rústico, a [ru'stiko, a] a rustic; (ordinario) coarse, uncouth // nm/f yokel // nf: **libro en rústica** paperback.

ruta ['ruta] nf route.

rutina [ru'tina] nf routine; **~rio, a** a routine.

S

S abr (= santo, a) St; (= sur) S.

s. abr (= siglo) C.; (= siguiente) foll.

S.A. abr (= Sociedad Anónima) Ltd (Brit), Inc (US).

sábado ['saβaðo] nm Saturday.

sábana ['saβana] nf sheet.

sabandija [saβan'dixa] nf bug, insect.

sabañón [saβa'ɲon] nm chilblain.

sabelotodo [saβelo'toðo] nm/f inv know-all.

saber [sa'βer] vt to know; (llegar a conocer) to find out, learn; (tener capacidad de) to know how to // vi: ~ a to taste of, taste like // nm knowledge, learning; **a ~** namely; **¿sabes conducir/nadar?** can you drive/swim?; **¿sabes francés?** do you speak French?; **~ de memoria** to know by heart; **hacer ~ algo a uno** to inform sb of sth, let sb know sth.

sabiduría [saβiðu'ria] nf (conocimientos) wisdom; (instrucción) learning.

sabiendas [sa'βjendas]: **a ~** ad knowingly.

sabio, a [sa'βjo,a] a (docto) learned; (prudente) wise, sensible.

sabor [sa'βor] nm taste, flavour; **~ear** vt to taste, savour; (fig) to relish.

sabotaje [saβo'taxe] nm sabotage.

saboteador, a [saβotea'ðor, a] nm/f saboteur.

sabotear [saβote'ar] vt to sabotage.

sabré etc vb ver **saber**.

sabroso, a [sa'βroso, a] a tasty; (fig: fam) racy, salty.

sacacorchos [saka'kortʃos] nm inv corkscrew.

sacapuntas [saka'puntas] nm inv pencil sharpener.

sacar [sa'kar] vt to take out; (fig: extraer) to get (out); (quitar) to remove, get out; (hacer salir) to bring out; (conclusión) to draw; (novela etc) to publish, bring out; (ropa) to take off; (obra) to make; (premio) to receive; (entradas) to get; (TENIS) to serve; **~ adelante** (niño) to bring up; (negocio) to carry on, go on with; **~ a uno a bailar** to get sb up to dance; **~ una foto** to take a photo; **~ la lengua** to stick out one's tongue; **~ buenas/malas notas** to get good/bad marks.

sacarina [saka'rina] nf saccharin(e).

sacerdote [saθer'ðote] nm priest.

saco ['sako] nm bag; (grande) sack; (su contenido) bagful; (AM) jacket; ~ **de dormir** sleeping bag.

sacramento [sakra'mento] nm sacrament.

sacrificar [sakrifi'kar] vt to sacrifice; **sacrificio** nm sacrifice.

sacrilegio [sakri'leχjo] nm sacrilege; **sacrílego, a** a sacrilegious.

sacristía [sakris'tia] nf sacristy.

sacro, a ['sakro, a] a sacred.

sacudida [saku'ðiða] nf (agitación) shake, shaking; (sacudimiento) jolt, bump; ~ **eléctrica** electric shock.

sacudir [saku'ðir] vt to shake; (golpear) to hit.

sádico, a ['saðiko, a] a sadistic // nm/f sadist; **sadismo** nm sadism.

saeta [sa'eta] nf (flecha) arrow.

sagacidad [saɣaθi'ðað] nf shrewdness, cleverness; **sagaz** a shrewd, clever.

sagitario [saxi'tarjo] nm Sagittarius.

sagrado, a [sa'ɣraðo, a] a sacred, holy.

Sáhara ['saara] nm: **el** ~ the Sahara (desert).

sal vb ver **salir** // [sal] nf salt.

sala ['sala] nf (cuarto grande) large room; (~ **de estar**) living room; (TEATRO) house, auditorium; (de hospital) ward; ~ **de apelación** court; ~ **de espera** waiting room; ~ **de estar** living room; ~ **de fiestas** dance hall.

salado, a [sa'laðo, a] a salty; (fig) witty, amusing; **agua salada** salt water.

salar [sa'lar] vt to salt, add salt to.

salarial [sala'rjal] a (aumento, revisión) wage cpd, salary cpd.

salario [sa'larjo] nm wage, pay.

salchicha [sal'tʃitʃa] nf (pork) sausage; **salchichón** nm (salami-type) sausage.

saldar [sal'dar] vt to pay; (vender) to sell off; (fig) to settle, resolve; **saldo** nm (pago) settlement; (de una cuenta) balance; (lo restante) remnant(s) (pl), remainder; ~**s** mpl (en tienda) sale.

saldré etc vb ver **salir.**

salero [sa'lero] nm salt cellar.

salgo etc vb ver **salir.**

salida [sa'liða] nf (puerta etc) exit, way out; (acto) leaving, going out; (de tren, AVIAT) departure; (TEC) output, production; (fig) way out; (COM) opening; (GEO, válvula) outlet; (de gas) leak; **calle sin** ~ cul-de-sac; ~ **de incendios** fire escape.

saliente [sa'ljente] a (ARQ) projecting; (sol) rising; (fig) outstanding.

PALABRA CLAVE

---

salir [sa'lir] ♦ vi 1 (partir: tb: ~ **de**) to leave; **Juan ha salido** Juan is out; **salió de la cocina** he came out of the kitchen

2 (aparecer) to appear; (disco, libro) to come out; **anoche salió en la tele** she appeared o was on TV last night; **salió en todos los periódicos** it was in all the papers

3 (resultar): **la muchacha nos salió muy trabajadora** the girl turned out to be a very hard worker; **la comida te ha salido exquisita** the food was delicious; **sale muy caro** it's very expensive

4: ~ **a uno algo: la entrevista que hice me salió bien/mal** the interview I did went o turned out well/badly

5: ~ **adelante: no sé como haré para** ~ **adelante** I don't know how I'll get by

♦ ~**se** vr (líquido) to spill; (animal) to escape.

---

saliva [sa'liβa] nf saliva.

salmo ['salmo] nm psalm.

salmón [sal'mon] nm salmon.

salmuera [sal'mwera] nf pickle, brine.

salón [sa'lon] nm (de casa) living room, lounge; (muebles) lounge suite; ~ **de belleza** beauty parlour.

~ **de baile** dance hall.

salpicadero [salpika'ðero] nm (AUTO) dashboard.

salpicar [salpi'kar] vt (rociar) to sprinkle, spatter; (esparcir) to scatter.

salsa ['salsa] nf sauce; (con carne asada) gravy; (fig) spice.

saltado, a [sal'taðo, a] a (botón etc) missing; (ojos) bulging.

saltamontes [salta'montes] nm inv grasshopper.

saltar [sal'tar] vt to jump (over), leap (over); (dejar de lado) to skip, miss out // vi to jump, leap; (pelota) to bounce; (al aire) to fly up; (quebrarse) to break; (al agua) to dive; (fig) to explode, blow up.

saltear [salte'ar] vt (robar) to rob (in a holdup); (asaltar) to assault, attack; (CULIN) to sauté.

saltimbanqui [saltim'banki] nm/f acrobat.

salto ['salto] nm jump, leap; (al agua) dive; ~ **de agua** waterfall; ~ **de altura** high jump.

saltón, ona [sal'ton, ona] a (ojos) bulging, popping; (dientes) protruding.

salubre [sa'luβre] a healthy, salubrious.

salud [sa'luð] nf health; ¡(a su) ~! cheers!, good health!; ~**able** a (de buena ~) healthy; (provechoso) good, beneficial.

saludar [salu'ðar] vt to greet; (MIL) to salute; **saludo** nm greeting; **saludos** (en carta) best wishes, regards.

salva ['salβa] nf: ~ **de aplausos** ovation.

salvación [salβa'θjon] nf salvation; (rescate) rescue.

salvado [sal'βaðo] nm bran.

Salvador [salβa'ðor]: **El ~** El Salvador; **San ~** San Salvador; **s~eño, a** a, nm/f Salvadorian.

salvaguardar [salβaxwar'ðar] vt to safeguard.

salvaje [sal'βaxe] a wild; (tribu) sav-

age; **salvajismo** nm savagery.

salvar [sal'βar] vt (rescatar) to save, rescue; (resolver) to overcome, resolve; (cubrir distancias) to cover, travel; (hacer excepción) to except; (un barco) to salvage.

salvavidas [salβa'βiðas] a inv: **bote/chaleco/cinturón** ~ lifeboat/life jacket/life belt.

salvia ['salβja] nf sage.

salvo, a ['salβo, a] a safe // ad except (for), save; a ~ **out of danger**; ~ **que** unless; ~**conducto** nm safe-conduct.

san [san] a saint; ~ **Juan** St. John.

sanar [sa'nar] vt (herida) to heal; (persona) to cure // vi (persona) to get well, recover; (herida) to heal.

sanatorio [sana'torjo] nm sanatorium.

sanción [san'θjon] nf sanction; **sancionar** vt to sanction.

sandalia [san'dalja] nf sandal.

sandía [san'dia] nf watermelon.

sandwich ['sandwitʃ] (pl ~s, ~es) nm sandwich.

saneamiento [sanea'mjento] nm sanitation.

sanear [sane'ar] vt (terreno) to drain.

sangrar [san'grar] vt, vi to bleed; **sangre** nf blood.

sangría [san'gria] nf sangria, sweetened drink of red wine with fruit.

sangriento, a [san'grjento, a] a bloody.

sanguijuela [sangi'xwela] nf (ZOOL, fig) leech.

sanguinaria, a [sangi'narjo, a] a bloodthirsty.

sanguíneo, a [san'gineo, a] a blood cpd.

sanidad [sani'ðað] nf sanitation; (calidad de sano) health, healthiness; ~ **pública** public health.

sanitario [sani'tarjo, a] a sanitary; (de la salud) health; ~**s** nmpl toilets (Brit), washroom (US).

sano, a ['sano, a] a healthy; (sin daños) sound; (comida) wholesome;

(*entero*) whole, intact; ~ **y salvo** safe and sound.

Santiago [san'tjaɣo] *nm*: ~ **(de Chile)** Santiago.

santiamén [santja'men] *nm*: **en un** ~ in no time at all.

santidad [santi'ðað] *nf* holiness, sanctity; **santificar** *vt* to sanctify, make holy.

santiguarse [santi'ɣwarse] *vr* to make the sign of the cross.

santo, a ['santo, a] *a* holy; (*fig*) wonderful, miraculous // *nm/f* saint // *nm* saint's day; ~ **y seña** password.

santuario [san'twarjo] *nm* sanctuary, shrine.

saña ['saɲa] *nf* rage, fury.

sapo ['sapo] *nm* toad.

saque ['sake] *nm* (*TENIS*) service, serve; (*FÚTBOL*) throw-in; ~ **de esquina** corner (kick).

saquear [sake'ar] *vt* (*MIL*) to sack; (*robar*) to loot, plunder; (*fig*) to ransack; **saqueo** *nm* sacking; looting, plundering; ransacking.

sarampión [saram'pjon] *nm* measles *sg*.

sarcasmo [sar'kasmo] *nm* sarcasm; **sarcástico, a** *a* sarcastic.

sardina [sar'ðina] *nf* sardine.

sardónico, a [sar'ðoniko, a] *a* sardonic; (*irónico*) ironical, sarcastic.

sargento [sar'xento] *nm* sergeant.

sarna ['sarna] *nf* itch; (*MED*) scabies.

sarpullido [sarpu'ʎiðo] *nm* (*MED*) rash.

sartén [sar'ten] *nf* frying pan.

sastre ['sastre] *nm* tailor; **~ría** *nf* (*arte*) tailoring; (*tienda*) tailor's (shop).

Satanás [sata'nas] *nm* Satan.

satélite [sa'telite] *nm* satellite.

sátira ['satira] *nf* satire.

satisfacción [satisfak'θjon] *nf* satisfaction.

satisfacer [satisfa'θer] *vt* to satisfy; (*gastos*) to meet; (*pérdida*) to make good; **~se** *vr* to satisfy o.s., be satisfied; (*vengarse*) to take revenge;

satisfecho, a *a* satisfied; (*contento*) content(ed), happy; (*tb*: ~ **de sí mismo**) self-satisfied, smug.

saturar [satu'rar] *vt* to saturate.

sauce ['sauθe] *nm* willow; ~ **llorón** weeping willow.

sauna ['sauna] *nf* sauna.

savia ['saβja] *nf* sap.

saxofón [sakso'fon] *nm* saxophone.

sazonado, a [saθo'naðo, a] *a* (*fruta*) ripe; (*CULIN*) flavoured, seasoned.

sazonar [saθo'nar] *vt* to ripen; (*CULIN*) to flavour, season.

scotch [es'kotʃ] *nm* ® adhesive *o* sticky tape.

PALABRA CLAVE

---

se [se] *pron* **1** (*reflexivo*: *sg*: *m*) himself; (: *f*) herself; (: *pl*) themselves; (: *cosa*) itself; (: *de Vd*) yourself; (: *de Vds*) yourselves; **está preparando** she's preparing herself; **para usos léxicos del pronombre ver el vb en cuestión,** *p.ej.* **arrepentirse**

2 (*con complemento indirecto*) to him; to her; to them; to it; to you; a **usted** ~ **lo dije ayer** I told you yesterday; ~ **compró un sombrero** he bought himself a hat; ~ **rompió la pierna** he broke his leg

3 (*uso recíproco*) each other, one another; ~ **miraron (el uno al otro)** they looked at each other *o* one another

4 (*en oraciones pasivas*): **se han vendido muchos libros** a lot of books have been sold

5 (*impersonal*): ~ **dice que ...** people say that, it is said that; **allí** ~ **come muy bien** the food there is very good, you can eat very well there.

SE *abr* (= *sudeste*) SE.

sé *vb ver* **saber, ser.**

sea *etc vb ver* **ser.**

sebo ['seβo] *nm* fat, grease.

secador [seka'ðor] *nm*: ~ **de pelo**

hair-dryer.

secadora [seka'ðora] nf (ELEC) tumble dryer.

secar [se'kar] vt to dry; ~**se** vr to dry (off); (río, planta) to dry up.

sección [sek'θjon] nf section.

seco, a ['seko, a] a dry; (carácter) cold; (respuesta) sharp, curt; **habrá pan a secas** there will be just bread; **decir algo a secas** to say sth curtly; **parar en ~** to stop dead.

secretaría [sekreta'ria] nf secretariat.

secretario, a [sekre'tarjo, a] nm/f secretary.

secreto, a [se'kreto, a] a secret; (persona) secretive // nm secret; (calidad) secrecy.

secta ['sekta] nf sect; ~**rio, a** a sectarian.

sector [sek'tor] nm sector.

secuela [se'kwela] nf consequence.

secuencia [se'kwenθja] nf sequence.

secuestrar [sekwes'trar] vt to kidnap; (bienes) to seize, confiscate; **secuestro** nm kidnapping; seizure, confiscation.

secular [seku'lar] a secular.

secundar [sekun'dar] vt to second, support.

secundario, a [sekun'darjo, a] a secondary.

sed [seð] nf thirst; **tener ~** to be thirsty.

seda ['seða] nf silk.

sedal [se'ðal] nm fishing line.

sedante [se'ðante] nm sedative.

sede ['seðe] nf (de gobierno) seat; (de compañía) headquarters pl; **Santa S~** Holy See.

sediento, a [se'ðjento, a] a thirsty.

sedimentar [seðimen'tar] vt to deposit; ~**se** vr to settle; **sedimento** nm sediment.

sedoso, a [se'ðoso, a] a silky, silken.

seducción [seðuk'θjon] nf seduction.

seducir [seðu'θir] vt to seduce; (sobornar) to bribe; (cautivar) to charm, fascinate; (atraer) to attract;

seductor, a a seductive; charming, fascinating; attractive; (engañoso) deceptive, misleading // nm/f seducer.

segadora-trilladora [seɣa'ðora triʎa'ðora] nf combine harvester.

seglar [se'ɣlar] a secular, lay.

segregación [seɣreɣa'θjon] nf segregation. ~ **racial** racial segregation.

segregar [seɣre'ɣar] vt to segregate, separate.

seguido, a [se'ɣiðo, a] a (continuo) continuous, unbroken; (recto) straight; ~**s** consecutive, successive // ad (directo) straight (on); (después) after; (AM: a menudo) often // nf: **en seguida** at once, right away; **5 días** ~**s** 5 days running, 5 days in a row.

seguimiento [seɣi'mjento] nm chase, pursuit; (continuación) continuation.

seguir [se'ɣir] vt to follow; (venir después) to follow on, come after; (proseguir) to continue; (perseguir) to chase, pursue // vi (gen) to follow; (continuar) to continue, carry o go on; ~**se** vr to follow; **sigo sin comprender** I still don't understand; **sigue lloviendo** it's still raining.

según [se'ɣun] prep according to // ad according to circumstances; ~ **esté el tiempo** depending on the weather; **está ~ lo dejaste** it is just as you left it.

segundo, a [se'ɣundo, a] a second // nm (gen, medida de tiempo) second // nf second meaning; **segunda (clase)** second class; **segunda (marcha)** (AUTO) second (gear); **de segunda mano** second hand.

seguramente [seɣura'mente] ad surely; (con certeza) for sure, with certainty.

seguridad [seɣuri'ðað] nf safety; (del estado, de casa etc) security; (certidumbre) certainty; (confianza) confidence; (estabilidad) stability; ~ **social** social security.

seguro, a [se'ɣuro, a] a (cierto)

sure, certain; (*fiel*) trustworthy; (*libre del peligro*) safe; (*bien defendido, firme*) secure // *ad* for sure, certainly // *nm* (*COM*) insurance; ~ **contra terceros/a todo riesgo** third party/comprehensive insurance; ~**s sociales** social security *sg*.

seis [seis] *num* six.

seismo [se'ismo] *nm* tremor, earthquake.

selección [selek'θjon] *nf* selection; **seleccionar** *vt* to pick, choose, select.

selectividad [selektiβi'ðað] *nf* (*Esp*) university entrance examination.

selecto, a [se'lekto, a] *a* select, choice; (*escogido*) selected.

selva ['selβa] *nf* (*bosque*) forest, woods *pl*; (*jungla*) jungle.

sellar [se'ʎar] *vt* (*documento oficial*) to seal; (*pasaporte, visado*) to stamp; (*precinto*) seal.

sello ['seʎo] *nm* stamp; (*precinto*) seal.

semáforo [se'maforo] *nm* (*AUTO*) traffic lights *pl*; (*FERRO*) signal.

semana [se'mana] *nf* week; **entre** ~ during the week; **S~ Santa** Holy Week; **semanal** *a* weekly.

semblante [sem'blante] *nm* face; (*fig*) look.

sembrar [sem'brar] *vt* to sow; (*objetos*) to sprinkle, scatter about; (*noticias etc*) to spread.

semejante [seme'xante] *a* (*parecido*) similar; ~**s alike**, similar // *nm* fellow man, fellow creature; **nunca hizo cosa** ~ he never did any such thing; **semejanza** *nf* similarity, resemblance.

semejar [seme'xar] *vi* to seem like, resemble; ~**se** *vr* to look alike, be similar.

semen ['semen] *nm* semen; ~**tal** *nm* stud.

semestral [semes'tral] *a* half-yearly, bi-annual.

semicírculo [semi'θirkulo] *nm* semicircle.

semiconsciente [semikons'θjente] *a* semiconscious.

semifinal [semifi'nal] *nf* semifinal.

semilla [se'miʎa] *nf* seed.

seminario [semi'narjo] *nm* (*REL*) seminary; (*ESCOL*) seminar.

sémola ['semola] *nf* semolina.

sempiterno, a [sempi'terno, a] *a* everlasting.

Sena ['sena] *nm*: **el** ~ the (river) Seine.

senado [se'naðo] *nm* senate; **senador, a** *nm/f* senator.

sencillez [senθi'ʎeθ] *nf* simplicity; (*de persona*) naturalness; **sencillo, a** *a* simple; natural, unaffected.

senda ['senda] *nf*, **sendero** [sen'dero] *nm* path, track.

sendos, as ['sendos, as] *apl*: **les dio** ~ **golpes** he hit both of them.

senil [se'nil] *a* senile.

seno ['seno] *nm* (*ANAT*) bosom, bust; (*fig*) bosom; ~**s breasts**.

sensación [sensa'θjon] *nf* sensation; (*sentido*) sense; (*sentimiento*) feeling; **sensacional** *a* sensational.

sensato, a [sen'sato, a] *a* sensible.

sensible [sen'sible] *a* sensitive; (*apreciable*) perceptible, appreciable; (*pérdida*) considerable; ~**ro, a** *a* sentimental.

sensitivo, a [sensi'tiβo, a], **sensorial** [senso'rjal] *a* sense.

sensual [sen'swal] *a* sensual.

sentado, a [sen'taðo, a] *a* (*establecido*) settled; (*carácter*) sensible; **estar** ~ to sit, be sitting (down) // *nf* sitting; (*protesta*) sit-in; **dar por** ~ to take for granted, assume.

sentar [sen'tar] *vt* to sit, seat; (*fig*) to establish // *vi* (*vestido*) to suit; (*alimento*) to ~ **bien/mal a** to agree/disagree with; ~**se** *vr* (*persona*) to sit, sit down; (*el tiempo*) to settle (down); (*los depósitos*) to settle.

sentencia [sen'tenθja] *nf* (*máxima*) maxim, saying; (*JUR*) sentence; **sentenciar** *vt* to sentence.

sentido, a [sen'tiðo, a] *a* (*pérdida*) regrettable; (*carácter*) sensitive // *nm* sense; (*sentimiento*) feeling;

(*significado*) sense, meaning; (*dirección*) direction; **mi más ~ pésame** my deepest sympathy; **~ del humor** sense of humour; **~ único** one-way (street); **tener ~** to make sense.

sentimental [sentimen'tal] *a* sentimental; **vida ~** love life.

sentimiento [senti'mjento] *nm* (*emoción*) feeling, emotion; (*sentido*) sense; (*pesar*) regret, sorrow.

sentir [sen'tir] *vt* to feel; (*percibir*) to perceive, sense; (*lamentar*) to regret, be sorry for // *vi* (*tener la sensación*) to feel; (*lamentarse*) to feel sorry // *nm* opinion, judgement; **~se bien/mal** to feel well/ill; **lo siento** I'm sorry.

seña ['seɲa] *nf* sign; (*MIL*) password; **~s** *nfpl* address *sg*; **~s personales** personal description *sg*.

señal [se'ɲal] *nf* sign; (*síntoma*) symptom; (*FERRO, TELEC*) signal; (*marca*) mark; (*COM*) deposit; **en ~ de** as a token of, as a sign of; **~ar** *vt* to mark; (*indicar*) to point out, indicate; (*fijar*) to fix, settle.

señor [se'ɲor] *nm* (*hombre*) man; (*caballero*) gentleman; (*dueño*) owner, master; (*trato: antes de nombre propio*) sir; (*: hablando directamente*) sir; **muy ~ mío** Dear Sir; **el ~ alcalde/presidente** the mayor/president.

señora [se'ɲora] *nf* (*dama*) lady; (*trato: antes de nombre propio*) Mrs; (*: hablando directamente*) madam; (*esposa*) wife; **Nuestra S~** Our Lady.

señorita [seɲo'rita] *nf* (*con nombre y/o apellido*) Miss; (*mujer joven*) young lady.

señorito [seɲo'rito] *nm* young gentleman; (*pey*) rich kid.

señuelo [se'ɲwelo] *nm* decoy.

sepa *etc vb ver* **saber**.

separación [separa'θjon] *nf* separation; (*división*) division; (*distancia*) gap, distance.

separar [sepa'rar] *vt* to separate; (*dividir*) to divide; **~se** *vr* (*parte*) to

come away; (*partes*) to come apart; (*persona*) to leave, go away; (*matrimonio*) to separate; **separatismo** *nm* separatism.

sepia ['sepja] *nf* cuttlefish.

septiembre [sep'tjembre] *nm* September.

séptimo, a ['septimo, a] *a, nm* seventh.

sepultar [sepul'tar] *vt* to bury; **sepultura** *nf* (*acto*) burial; (*tumba*) grave, tomb; **sepulturero, a** *nm/f* gravedigger.

sequedad [seke'ðað] *nf* dryness; (*fig*) brusqueness, curtness.

sequía [se'kia] *nf* drought.

séquito ['sekito] *nm* (*de rey etc*) retinue; (*POL*) followers *pl*.

PALABRA CLAVE

ser [ser] ♦ *vi* **1** (*descripción*) to be; **es médica/muy alta** she's a doctor/very tall; **la familia es de Cuzco** his (*o her etc*) family is from Cuzco; **soy Anna** (*TELEC*) Anna speaking *o* here

2 (*propiedad*): **es de Joaquín** it's Joaquín's, it belongs to Joaquín

3 (*horas, fechas, números*): **es la una** it's one o'clock; **son las seis y media** it's half-past six; **es el 1 de junio** it's the first of June; **somos/son seis** there are six of us/them

4 (*en oraciones pasivas*): **ha sido descubierto ya** it's already been discovered

5: **es de esperar que** ... it is to be hoped *o* I *etc* hope that ...

6 (*locuciones con subjun*): **o sea** that is to say; **sea él sea su hermana** either him *or* his sister

7: **a no ~ por él** ... but for him ...

8: **a no ~ que** ... **o ~ que tenga uno ya** unless he's got one already

♦ *nm* being; **~ humano** human being.

---

serenarse [sere'narse] *vr* to calm down.

sereno, a [se'reno, a] *a* (*persona*)

calm, unruffled; (*el tiempo*) fine, settled; (*ambiente*) calm, peaceful // *nm* night watchman.

serial [ser'jal] *nm* serial.

serie ['serje] *nf* series; (*cadena*) sequence, succession; **fuera de** ~ out of order; (*fig*) special, out of the ordinary; **fabricación en** ~ mass production.

seriedad [serje'ðað] *nf* seriousness; (*formalidad*) reliability; (*de crisis*) gravity, seriousness; **serio, a** *a* serious; reliable, dependable; grave, serious; **en serio** *ad* seriously.

sermón [ser'mon] *nm* (REL) sermon.

serpentear [serpente'ar] *vi* to wriggle; (*camino, río*) to wind, snake.

serpentina [serpen'tina] *nf* streamer.

serpiente [ser'pjente] *nf* snake; ~ **boa** boa constrictor; ~ **de cascabel** rattlesnake.

serranía [serra'nia] *nf* mountainous area.

serrano, a [se'rrano] *a* highland *cpd*, hill *cpd* // *nm/f* highlander.

serrar [se'rrar] *vt* = aserrar.

serrín [se'rrin] *nm* = aserrín.

serrucho [se'rrutʃo] *nm* saw.

servicio [ser'βiθjo] *nm* service; ~s *nmpl* toilet(s); ~ **incluido** service charge included; ~ **militar** military service.

servidor, a [serβi'ðor, a] *nm/f* servant.

servidumbre [serβi'ðumbre] *nf* (*sujeción*) servitude; (*criados*) servants *pl*, staff.

servil [ser'βil] *a* servile.

servilleta [serβi'ʎeta] *nf* serviette, napkin.

servir [ser'βir] *vt* to serve // *vi* to serve; (*tener utilidad*) to be of use, be useful; ~**se** *vr* to serve *o* help o.s.; ~**se de algo** to make use of sth, use sth; **sírvase pasar** please come in.

sesenta [se'senta] *num* sixty.

sesgo ['sesɣo] *nm* slant; (*fig*) slant,

twist.

sesión [se'sjon] *nf* (POL) session, sitting; (*CINE*) showing.

seso ['seso] *nm* brain; **sesudo, a** *a* sensible, wise.

seta ['seta] *nf* mushroom; ~ **venenosa** toadstool.

setecientos, as [sete'θjentos, as] *a, num* seven hundred.

setenta [se'tenta] *num* seventy.

seudo... [seuðo] *pref* pseudo... .

seudónimo [seu'ðonimo] *nm* pseudonym.

severidad [seβeri'ðað] *nf* severity; **severo, a** *a* severe.

Sevilla [se'βiʎa] *n* Seville; **sevillano, a** *a* of *o* from Seville // *nm/f* native *o* inhabitant of Seville.

sexo ['sekso] *nm* sex.

sexto, a ['seksto, a] *a, nm* sixth.

sexual [sek'swal] *a* sexual; **vida** ~ sex life.

si [si] *conj* if; **me pregunto** ~... I wonder if *o* whether... .

sí [si] *ad* yes // *nm* consent *o* *pron* (*uso impersonal*) oneself; (*sg*: *m*) himself; (: *f*) herself; (: *de cosa*) itself; (*de usted*) yourself; (*pl*) themselves; (*de ustedes*) yourselves; (*recíproco*) each other; **él no quiere pero yo** ~ he doesn't want to but I do; **ella** ~ **vendrá** she will certainly come, she is sure to come; **claro que** ~ of course; **creo que** ~ I think so.

siamés, esa [sja'mes, esa] *a, nm/f* Siamese.

SIDA ['siða] *nm abr* (= *Síndrome de Inmuno-deficiencia Adquirida*) AIDS.

siderúrgico, a [siðe'rurxico, a] *a* iron and steel *cpd* // *nf*: **la siderúrgica** the iron and steel industry.

sidra ['siðra] *nf* cider.

siembra ['sjembra] *nf* sowing.

siempre ['sjempre] *ad* always; (*todo el tiempo*) all the time; ~ **que** *conj* (*cada vez*) whenever; (*dado que*) provided that; **como** ~ as usual; **para** ~ for ever.

sien [sjen] *nf* temple.

siento *etc vb ver* **sentar, sentir.**

sierra ['sjerra] *nf* (*TEC*) saw; (*cadena de montañas*) mountain range.

siervo, a ['sjerβo, a] *nm/f* slave.

siesta ['sjesta] *nf* siesta, nap; **echar la ~** to have an afternoon nap *o* a siesta.

siete ['sjete] *num* seven.

sífilis ['sifilis] *nf* syphilis.

sifón [si'fon] *nm* syphon; **whisky con ~** whisky and soda.

sigla ['siɣla] *nf* abbreviation; acronym.

siglo ['siɣlo] *nm* century; (*fig*) age.

significación [siɣnifika'θjon] *nf* significance.

significado, a [siɣnifi'kaðo] *nm* significance; (*de palabra etc*) meaning.

significar [siɣnifi'kar] *vt* to mean, signify; (*notificar*) to make known, express; **significativo, a** *a* significant.

signo ['siɣno] *nm* sign; **~ de admiración** *o* **exclamación** exclamation mark; **~ de interrogación** question mark.

sigo *etc vb ver* **seguir.**

siguiente [si'ɣjente] *a* next, following.

siguió *etc vb ver* **seguir.**

sílaba ['silaβa] *nf* syllable.

silbar [sil'βar] *vt, vi* to whistle; **silbato** *nm* whistle; **silbido** *nm* whistle, whistling.

silenciador [silenθja'ðor] *nm* silencer.

silenciar [silen'θjar] *vt* (*persona*) to silence; (*escándalo*) to hush up; **silencio** *nm* silence, quiet; **silencioso, a** *a* silent, quiet.

silicio [si'liθjo] *nm* silicon.

silueta [si'lweta] *nf* silhouette; (*de edificio*) outline; (*figura*) figure.

silvestre [sil'βestre] *a* (*BOT*) wild; (*fig*) rustic, rural.

silla ['siʎa] *nf* (*asiento*) chair; (*tb: ~ de montar*) saddle; **~ de ruedas** wheelchair.

sillón [si'ʎon] *nm* armchair, easy

chair.

simbólico, a [sim'boliko, a] *a* symbolic(al).

simbolizar [simboli'θar] *vt* to symbolize.

símbolo ['simbolo] *nm* symbol.

simetría [sime'tria] *nf* symmetry.

simiente [si'mjente] *nf* seed.

similar [simi'lar] *a* similar.

simio ['simjo] *nm* ape.

simpatía [simpa'tia] *nf* liking; (*afecto*) affection; (*amabilidad*) kindness; (*solidaridad*) mutual support, solidarity; **simpático, a** *a* nice, pleasant; kind.

simpatizante [simpati'θante] *nm/f* sympathizer.

simpatizar [simpati'θar] *vi*: **~ con** to get on well with.

simple ['simple] *a* simple; (*elemental*) simple, easy; (*mero*) mere; (*puro*) pure, sheer // *nm* simpleton; **~za** *nf* simpleness; (*necedad*) silly thing; **simplicidad** *nf* simplicity; **simplificar** *vt* to simplify.

simular [simu'lar] *vt* to simulate.

simultáneo, a [simul'taneo, a] *a* simultaneous.

sin [sin] *prep* without; **la ropa está ~ lavar** the clothes are unwashed; **~ que** (*con* without; **~ embargo** however, still.

sinagoga [sina'ɣoɣa] *nf* synagogue.

sinceridad [sinθeri'ðað] *nf* sincerity; **sincero, a** *a* sincere.

sincronizar [sinkroni'θar] *vt* to synchronize.

sindical [sindi'kal] *a* union *cpd*, trade-union *cpd*; **~ista** *a*, *nm/f* trade-unionist.

sindicato [sindi'kato] *nm* (*de trabajadores*) trade(s) union; (*de negociantes*) syndicate.

sinfín [sin'fin] *nm*: **un ~ de** a great many, no end of.

sinfonía [sinfo'nia] *nf* symphony.

singular [singu'lar] *a* singular; (*fig*) outstanding, exceptional; (*pey*) peculiar, odd; **~idad** *nf* singularity, peculiarity; **~izar** *vt* to single out;

~**izarse** vr to distinguish o.s., stand out.

siniestro, a [si'njestro, a] a left; (fig) sinister // nm (accidente) accident.

sinnúmero [sin'numero] nm = **sinfín.**

sino ['sino] nm fate, destiny // conj (pero) but; (salvo) except, save.

sinónimo, a [si'nonimo, a] a synonymous // nm synonym.

síntesis ['sintesis] nf synthesis; **sintético, a** a synthetic.

sintetizar [sinteti'θar] vt to synthesize.

sintió vb ver **sentir.**

síntoma ['sintoma] nm symptom.

sinvergüenza [simber'ɣwenθa] nm/f rogue, scoundrel; ¡es un ~! he's got a nerve!

sionismo [sjo'nismo] nm Zionism.

siquiera [si'kjera] conj even if, even though // ad at least; **ni** ~ not even.

sirena [si'rena] nf siren.

Siria ['sirja] nf Syria; **sirio, a** a, nm/f Syrian.

sirviente, a [sir'βjente, a] nm/f servant.

sirvo etc vb ver **servir.**

sisear [sise'ar] vt, vi to hiss.

sismógrafo [sis'moɣrafo] nm seismograph.

sistema [sis'tema] nm system; (método) method; **sistemático, a** a systematic.

sitiar [si'tjar] vt to beseige, lay seige to.

sitio ['sitjo] nm (lugar) place; (espacio) room, space; (MIL) siege.

situación [sitwa'θjon] nf situation, position; (estatus) position, standing.

situado, a [situ'aðo] a situated, placed.

situar [si'twar] vt to place, put; (edificio) to locate, situate.

slip [slip] nm pants pl, briefs pl.

smoking ['smokin, es'mokin] (pl ~s) nm dinner jacket (Brit), tuxedo (US).

snob [es'nob] = **esnob.**

so [so] prep under.

SO abr (= suroeste) SW.

sobaco [so'βako] nm armpit.

soberanía [soβera'nia] nf sovereignty; **soberano, a** a sovereign; (fig) supreme // nm/f sovereign.

soberbio, a [so'βerβjo, a] a (orgulloso) proud; (altivo) haughty, arrogant; (fig) magnificent, superb // nf pride; haughtiness, arrogance; magnificence.

sobornar [soβor'nar] vt to bribe; **soborno** nm bribe.

sobra ['soβra] nf excess, surplus; ~s nfpl left-overs; scraps; **de** ~ surplus, extra; **tengo de** ~ I've more than enough; ~**do, a** (más que suficiente) more than enough; (superfluo) excessive // ad too, exceedingly; **sobrante** a remaining, extra // nm surplus, remainder.

sobrar [so'βrar] vt to exceed, surpass // vi (tener de más) to be more than enough; (quedar) to remain, be left (over).

sobrasada [soβra'saða] nf pork sausage spread.

sobre ['soβre] prep (gen) on; (encima) on (top of); (por encima de, arriba de) over, above; (más que) more than; (además) in addition to, besides; (alrededor de, tratando de) about // nm envelope; ~ **todo** above all.

sobrecama [soβre'kama] nf bedspread.

sobrecargar [soβrekar'ɣar] vt (camión) to overload; (COM) to surcharge.

sobredosis [soβre'ðosis] nf inv overdose.

sobreentender [soβre(e)nten'der] vt (adivinar) to deduce, infer; ~**se** vr: se sobreentiende que ... it is implied that ....

sobrehumano, a [soβreu'mano, a] a superhuman.

sobrellevar [soβreʎe'βar] vt (fig) to bear, endure.

sobrenatural [soβrenatu'ral] a supernatural.

sobrepasar [soβrepa'sar] vt to exceed, surpass.

sobreponer [soβrepo'ner] vt (poner encima) to put on top; (añadir) to add; ~se vr: ~se a to win through, pull through.

sobresaliente [soβresa'ljente] a projecting; (fig) outstanding, excellent.

sobresalir [soβresa'lir] vi to project, jut out; (fig) to stand out, excel.

sobresaltar [soβresal'tar] vt (asustar) to scare, frighten; (sobrecoger) to startle; **sobresalto** nm (movimiento) start; (susto) scare; (turbación) sudden shock.

sobretodo [soβre'toðo] nm overcoat.

sobrevenir [soβreβe'nir] vi (ocurrir) to happen (unexpectedly); (resultar) to follow, ensue.

sobreviviente [soβreβi'βjente] a surviving // nmf survivor.

sobrevivir [soβreβi'βir] vi to survive.

sobrevolar [soβreβo'lar] vt to fly over.

sobriedad [soβrje'ðað] nf sobriety, soberness; (moderación) moderation, restraint.

sobrino, a [so'βrino, a] nm/f nephew/niece.

sobrio, a ['soβrjo, a] a (moderado) moderate, restrained.

socarrón, ona [soka'rron, ona] a (sarcástico) sarcastic, ironic(al).

socavón [soka'βon] nm (hoyo) hole.

sociable [so'θjaβle] a (persona) sociable, friendly; (animal) social.

social [so'θjal] a social; (COM) company cpd.

socialdemócrata [soθjalde'mokrata] nm/f social democrat.

socialista [soθja'lista] a, nm/f socialist.

socializar [soθjali'θar] vt to socialize.

sociedad [soθje'ðað] nf society; (COM) company; ~ anónima limited company; ~ de consumo consumer society.

socio, a ['soθjo, a] nm/f (miembro) member; (COM) partner.

sociología [soθjolo'xia] nf sociology.

sociólogo, a nm/f sociologist.

socorrer [soko'rrer] vt to help; **socorrista** nm/f first aider; (en piscina, playa) lifeguard; **socorro** nm (ayuda) help, aid; (MIL) relief; ¡socorro! help!

soda ['soða] nf (sosa) soda; (bebida) soda (water).

sofá [so'fa] (pl ~s) nm sofa, settee; ~-cama nm studio couch, sofa bed.

sofisticación [sofistika'θjon] nf sophistication.

sofocar [sofo'kar] vt to suffocate; (apagar) to smother, put out; ~se vr to suffocate; (fig) to blush, feel embarrassed; **sofoco** nm suffocation; embarrassment.

soga ['soɣa] nf rope.

sois vb ver **ser**.

soja ['soxa] nf soya.

sojuzgar [soxuθ'ɣar] vt to subdue, rule despotically.

sol [sol] nm sun; (luz) sunshine, sunlight; hace o hay ~ it is sunny.

solamente [sola'mente] ad only, just.

solapa [so'lapa] nf (de chaqueta) lapel; (de libro) jacket.

solar [so'lar] a solar, sun cpd.

solaz [so'laθ] nm recreation, relaxation; ~ar vt (divertir) to amuse.

soldada [sol'daða] nf pay.

soldado [sol'daðo] nm soldier; ~ raso private.

soldador [solda'ðor] nm soldering iron; (persona) welder.

soldar [sol'dar] vt to solder, weld; (unir) to join, unite.

soleado, a [sole'aðo, a] a sunny.

soledad [sole'ðað] nf solitude; (estado infeliz) loneliness.

solemne [so'lemne] a solemn; **solemnidad** nf solemnity.

soler [so'ler] vi to be in the habit of, be accustomed to; **suele salir a las ocho** she usually goes out at 8 o'clock.

solfeo [sol'feo] nm solfa.

solicitar [soliθi'tar] vt (permiso) to ask for, seek; (puesto) to apply for;

(*votos*) to canvass for; (*atención*) to attract; (*persona*) to pursue, chase after.

solícito, a [so'liθito, a] *a* (*diligente*) diligent; (*cuidadoso*) careful; **solicitud** *nf* (*calidad*) great care; (*petición*) request; (*a un puesto*) application.

solidaridad [soliðari'ðaθ] *nf* solidarity; **solidario, a** *a* (*participación*) joint, common; (*compromiso*) mutually binding.

solidez [soli'ðeθ] *nf* solidity; **sólido, a** *a* solid.

soliloquio [soli'lokjo] *nm* soliloquy.

solista [so'lista] *nm/f* soloist.

solitario, a [soli'tarjo, a] *a* (*persona*) lonely, solitary; (*lugar*) lonely, desolate // *nm/f* (*reclusa*) recluse; (*en la sociedad*) loner // *nm* solitaire.

solo, a ['solo, a] *a* (*único*) single, sole; (*sin compañía*) alone; (*solitario*) lonely; **hay una sola dificultad** there is just one difficulty; **a solas** alone, by o.s.

sólo ['solo] *ad* only, just.

solomillo [solo'miʎo] *nm* sirloin.

soltar [sol'tar] *vt* (*dejar ir*) to let go of; (*desprender*) to unfasten, loosen; (*librar*) to release, set free; (*risa etc*) to let out.

soltero, a [sol'tero, a] *a* single, unmarried // *nm* bachelor/single woman; **solterón, ona** *nm/f* old bachelor/spinster.

soltura [sol'tura] *nf* looseness, slackness; (*de los miembros*) agility, ease of movement; (*en el hablar*) fluency, ease.

soluble [so'luβle] *a* (*QUÍMICA*) soluble; (*problema*) solvable; ~ **en agua** soluble in water.

solución [solu'θjon] *nf* solution; **solucionar** *vt* (*problema*) to solve; (*asunto*) to settle, resolve.

solventar [solβen'tar] *vt* (*pagar*) to settle, pay; (*resolver*) to resolve.

sollozar [soʎo'θar] *vi* to sob; **sollozo** *nm* sob.

sombra ['sombra] *nf* shadow; (*como* protección) shade; ~**s** *nfpl* darkness *sg*, shadows; **tener buena/mala** ~ to be lucky/unlucky.

sombrero [som'brero] *nm* hat.

sombrilla [som'briʎa] *nf* parasol, sunshade.

sombrío, a [som'brio, a] *a* (*oscuro*) dark; (*fig*) sombre, sad; (*persona*) gloomy.

somero, a [so'mero, a] *a* superficial.

someter [some'ter] *vt* (*país*) to conquer; (*persona*) to subject to one's will; (*informe*) to present, submit; ~**se** *vr* to give in, yield, submit; ~ **a** to subject to.

somnífero [som'nifero] *nm* sleeping pill.

somos *vb ver* **ser**.

son *vb ver* **ser** // [son] *nm* sound; **en** ~ **de broma** as a joke.

sonajero [sona'xero] *nm* (*baby's*) rattle.

sonambulismo [sonambu'lismo] *nm* sleepwalking; **sonámbulo, a** *nm/f* sleepwalker.

sonar [so'nar] *vt* to ring // *vi* to sound; (*hacer ruido*) to make a noise; (*pronunciarse*) to be sounded, be pronounced; (*ser conocido*) to sound familiar; (*campana*) to ring; (*reloj*) to strike, chime; ~**se** *vr*: ~**se (las narices)** to blow one's nose; **me suena ese nombre** that name rings a bell.

sonda ['sonda] *nf* (*NAUT*) sounding; (*TEC*) bore, drill; (*MED*) probe.

sondear [sonde'ar] *vt* to sound; to bore (*into*), drill; to probe, sound; (*fig*) to sound out; **sondeo** *nm* sounding; boring, drilling; (*fig*) poll, enquiry.

sónico, a ['soniko, a] *a* sonic, sound *cpd*.

sonido [so'niðo] *nm* sound.

sonoro, a [so'noro, a] *a* sonorous; (*resonante*) loud, resonant.

sonreír [sonre'ir] *vi*, **sonreírse** *vr* to smile; **sonriente** *a* smiling; **sonrisa** *nf* smile.

sonrojo [son'roxo] *nm* blush.

soñador, a [soɲa'ðor, a] *nm/f* dreamer.

soñar [so'ɲar] *vt, vi* to dream; ~ **con** to dream about *o* of.

soñoliento, a [soɲo'ljento, a] *a* sleepy, drowsy.

sopa ['sopa] *nf* soup; **sopera** *nf* soup tureen.

soplar [so'plar] *vt (polvo)* to blow away, blow off; *(inflar)* to blow up; *(vela)* to blow out *o* / *vi* to blow; **soplo** *nm* blow, puff; *(de viento)* puff, gust.

soporífero [sopo'rifero] *nm* sleeping pill.

soportable [sopor'taβle] *a* bearable.

soportar [sopor'tar] *vt* to bear, carry; *(fig)* to bear, put up with; **soporte** *nm* support; *(fig)* pillar, support.

soprano [so'prano] *nf* soprano.

sorber [sor'ßer] *vt (chupar)* to sip; *(inhalar)* to inhale; *(tragar)* to swallow (up); *(absorber)* to soak up, absorb.

sorbete [sor'ßete] *nm* iced fruit drink.

sorbo ['sorßo] *nm (trago: grande)* gulp, swallow; *(: pequeño)* sip.

sordera [sor'ðera] *nf* deafness.

sórdido, a [sor'ðiðo, a] *a* dirty, squalid.

sordo, a ['sorðo, a] *a (persona)* deaf // *nm/f* deaf person; **~mudo, a** *a* deaf and dumb.

soroche [so'rotʃe] *nm (AM)* mountain sickness.

sorprendente [sorpren'dente] *a* surprising.

sorprender [sorpren'der] *vt* to surprise; **sorpresa** *nf* surprise.

sortear [sorte'ar] *vt* to draw lots for; *(rifar)* to raffle; *(dificultad)* to avoid; **sorteo** *nm (en lotería)* draw; *(rifa)* raffle.

sortija [sor'tixa] *nf* ring; *(rizo)* ringlet, curl.

sosegado, a [sose'ɣaðo, a] *a* quiet, calm.

sosegar [sose'ɣar] *vt* to quieten,

calm; *(el ánimo)* to reassure // *vi* to rest; **sosiego** *nm* quiet(ness), calm(ness).

soslayo [sos'lajo]: **de ~** *ad* obliquely, sideways.

soso, a ['soso, a] *a (CULIN)* tasteless; *(fig)* dull, uninteresting.

sospecha [sos'petʃa] *nf* suspicion; **sospechar** *vt* to suspect; **sospechoso, a** *a* suspicious; *(testimonio, opinión)* suspect // *nm/f* suspect.

sostén [sos'ten] *nm (apoyo)* support; *(sujetador)* bra; *(alimentación)* sustenance, food.

sostener [soste'ner] *vt* to support; *(mantener)* to keep up, maintain; *(alimentar)* to sustain, keep going; **~se** *vr* to support o.s.; *(seguir)* to continue, remain; **sostenido, a** *a* continuous, sustained; *(prolongado)* prolonged.

sótano ['sotano] *nm* basement.

soviético, a [so'ßjetiko, a] *a* Soviet; **los ~s** the Soviets.

soy [soj] *vb ver* **ser**.

Sr. *abr* (= *Señor*) Mr.

Sra. *abr* (= *Señora*) Mrs.

S.R.C. *abr* (= *se ruega contestación*) R.S.V.P.

Sres. *abr* (= *Señores*) Messrs.

Srta. *abr* (= *Señorita*) Miss.

Sta. *abr* (= *Santa*) St.

status ['status, e'status] *nm inv* status.

Sto. *abr* (= *Santo*) St.

su [su] *pron (de él)* his; *(de ella)* her; *(de una cosa)* its; *(de ellos, ellas)* their; *(de usted, ustedes)* your.

suave ['swaße] *a* gentle; *(superficie)* smooth; *(trabajo)* easy; *(música, voz)* soft, sweet; **suavidad** *nf* gentleness; smoothness; softness, sweetness; **suavizar** *vt* to soften; *(quitar la aspereza)* to smooth (out).

subalimentado, a [sußalimen'taðo, a] *a* undernourished.

subasta [su'ßasta] *nf* auction; **subastar** *vt* to auction (off).

subcampeón, ona [sußkampe'on, ona] *nm/f* runner-up.

subconsciente [suβkon'sθjente] a, nm subconscious.

subdesarrollado, a [suβðesarro-'λaðo, a] a underdeveloped.

subdesarrollo [suβðesa'rroλo] nm underdevelopment.

subdirector, a [suβðirek'tor, a] nm/f assistant director.

súbdito, a ['suβðito, a] nm/f subject.

subdividir [suβðiβi'ðir] vt to subdivide.

subestimar [suβesti'mar] vt to underestimate, underrate.

subido, a [su'βiðo, a] a (color) bright, strong; (precio) high // nf (de montaña etc) ascent, climb; (de precio) rise, increase; (pendiente) slope, hill.

subir [su'βir] vt (objeto) to raise, lift up; (cuesta, calle) to go up; (colina, montaña) to climb; (precio) to raise, put up // vi to go up, come up; (a un coche) to get in; (a un autobús, tren o avión) to get on, board; (precio) to rise, go up; (río, marea) to rise; ~se vr to get up, climb.

súbito, a ['suβito, a] a (repentino) sudden; (imprevisto) unexpected.

subjetivo, a [suβxe'tiβo, a] a subjective.

sublevación [suβleβa'θjon] nf revolt, rising.

sublevar [suβle'βar] vt to rouse to revolt; ~se vr to revolt, rise.

sublime [su'βlime] a sublime.

submarino, a [suβma'rino, a] a underwater // nm submarine.

subnormal [suβnor'mal] a subnormal // nm/f subnormal person.

subordinado, a [suβorði'naðo, a] a, nm/f subordinate.

subrayar [suβra'jar] vt to underline.

subrepticio, a [suβrep'tiθjo, a] a surreptitious.

subsanar [suβsa'nar] vt (reparar) to make good; (perdonar) to excuse; (sobreponerse a) to overcome.

subscribir [suβskri'βir] vt = suscribir.

subsidiario, a [suβsi'ðjarjo, a] a subsidiary.

subsidio [suβ'siðjo] nm (ayuda) aid, financial help; (subvención) subsidy, grant; (de enfermedad, paro etc) benefit, allowance.

subsistencia [suβsis'tenθja] nf subsistence.

subsistir [suβsis'tir] vi to subsist; (vivir) to live; (sobrevivir) to survive, endure.

subterráneo, a [suβte'rraneo, a] a underground, subterranean // nm underpass, underground passage.

suburbano, a [suβur'βano, a] a suburban.

suburbio [su'βurβjo] nm (barrio) slum quarter; (afueras) suburbs pl.

subvencionar [suββenθjo'nar] vt to subsidize.

subversión [suββer'sjon] nf subversion; **subversivo, a** a subversive.

subyugar [suβju'βar] vt (país) to subjugate, subdue; (enemigo) to overpower; (voluntad) to dominate.

succión [suk'θjon] nf suction.

sucedáneo, a [suθe'ðaneo, a] a substitute // nm substitute (food).

suceder [suθe'ðer] vt, vi to happen; (seguir) to succeed, follow; lo que sucede es que... the fact is that...; **sucesión** [suθe'sjon] nf succession; (serie) sequence, series.

sucesivamente [suθesiβa'mente] ad: y así ~ and so on.

sucesivo, a [suθe'siβo, a] a successive, following; en lo ~ in future, from now on.

suceso [su'θeso] nm (hecho) event, happening; (incidente) incident.

suciedad [suθje'ðað] nf (estado) dirtiness; (mugre) dirt, filth.

sucinto, a [su'θinto, a] a (conciso) succinct, concise.

sucio, a ['suθjo, a] a dirty.

Sucre ['sukre] n Sucre.

suculento, a [suku'lento, a] a succulent.

sucumbir [sukum'bir] vi to succumb.

sucursal [sukur'sal] nf branch (office).

Sudáfrica [suð'afrika] *nf* South Africa.

Sudamérica [suða'merika] *nf* South America; **sudamericano, a** *a, nm/f* South American.

sudar [su'ðar] *vt, vi* to sweat.

sudeste [su'ðeste] *nm* south-east.

sudoeste [suðo'este] *nm* south-west.

sudor [su'ðor] *nm* sweat; **~oso, a** *a* sweaty, sweating.

Suecia ['sweθja] *nf* Sweden; **sueco, a** *a* a Swedish // *nm/f* Swede.

suegro, a ['swevro, a] *nm/f* father-/mother-in-law.

suela ['swela] *nf* sole.

sueldo ['sweldo] *nm* pay, wage(s) (*pl*).

suele *etc vb ver* **soler.**

suelo ['swelo] *nm* (*tierra*) ground; (*de casa*) floor.

suelto, a ['swelto, a] *a* loose; (*libre*) free; (*separado*) detached; (*ágil*) quick, agile; (*corriente*) fluent, flowing // *nm* (*loose*) change, small change.

sueño *etc vb ver* **soñar** // ['sweɲo] *nm* sleep; (*somnolencia*) sleepiness, drowsiness; (*lo soñado*, *fig*) dream; **tener ~** to be sleepy.

suero ['swero] *nm* (*MED*) serum; (*de leche*) whey.

suerte ['swerte] *nf* (*fortuna*) luck; (*azar*) chance; (*destino*) fate, destiny; (*condición*) lot; (*género*) sort, kind; **tener ~** to be lucky; **de otra ~** otherwise, if not; **de ~ que** so that, in such a way that.

suéter ['sweter] *nm* sweater.

suficiente [sufi'θjente] *a* enough, sufficient // *nm* (*ESCOL*) pass.

sufragio [su'fraxjo] *nm* (*voto*) vote; (*derecho de voto*) suffrage.

sufrido, a [su'friðo, a] *a* (*persona*) tough; (*paciente*) long-suffering, patient.

sufrimiento [sufri'mjento] *nm* (*dolor*) suffering.

sufrir [su'frir] *vt* (*padecer*) to suffer; (*soportar*) to bear, put up with; (*apoyar*) to hold up, support // *vi* to suffer.

sugerencia [suxe'renθja] *nf* suggestion.

sugerir [suxe'rir] *vt* to suggest; (*sutilmente*) to hint.

sugestión [suxes'tjon] *nf* suggestion; (*sutil*) hint; **sugestionar** *vt* to influence.

sugestivo, a [suxes'tiβo, a] *a* stimulating; (*fascinante*) fascinating.

suicida [sui'θiða] *a* a suicidal // *nm/f* suicidal person; (*muerto*) suicide, person who has committed suicide; **suicidarse** *vr* to commit suicide, kill o.s.; **suicidio** *nm* suicide.

Suiza ['swiθa] *nf* Switzerland; **suizo, a** *a, nm/f* Swiss.

sujeción [suxe'θjon] *nf* subjection.

sujetador [suxeta'ðor] *nm* fastener, clip; (*sostén*) bra.

sujetar [suxe'tar] *vt* (*fijar*) to fasten; (*detener*) to hold down; (*fig*) to subject, subjugate; **~se** *vr* to subject o.s.; **sujeto, a** *a* fastened, secure // *nm* subject; (*individuo*) individual; **sujeto a** subject to.

suma ['suma] *nf* (*cantidad*) total, sum; (*de dinero*) sum; (*acto*) adding (up), addition; **en ~** in short.

sumamente [suma'mente] *ad* extremely, exceedingly.

sumar [su'mar] *vt* to add (up); (*reunir*) to collect, gather // *vi* to add up.

sumario, a [su'marjo, a] *a* brief, concise // *nm* summary.

sumergir [sumer'xir] *vt* to submerge; (*hundir*) to sink; (*bañar*) to immerse, dip.

sumidero [sumi'ðero] *nm* drain, sewer; (*TEC*) sump.

suministrar [sumini'strar] *vt* to supply, provide; **suministro** *nm* supply; (*acto*) supplying, providing.

sumir [su'mir] *vt* to sink, submerge; (*fig*) to plunge.

sumisión [sumi'sjon] *nf* (*acto*) submission; (*calidad*) submissiveness, docility; **sumiso, a** *a* submissive, docile.

sumo, a ['sumo, a] *a* great,

extreme; (*mayor*) highest, supreme.

suntuoso, a [sun'twoso, a] *a* sumptuous, magnificent.

supe *etc vb ver* **saber**.

super... [super] *pref* super..., over...; **~bueno** great, fantastic.

súper ['super] *nm* (*gasolina*) three-star (petrol).

superar [supe'rar] *vt* (*sobreponerse a*) to overcome; (*rebasar*) to surpass, do better than; (*pasar*) to go beyond; **~se** *vr* to excel o.s.

superávit [supe'raßit] *nm inv* surplus.

superficial [superfi'θjal] *a* superficial; (*medida*) surface *cpd*, of the surface.

superficie [super'fiθje] *nf* surface; (*área*) area.

superfluo, a [su'perflwo, a] *a* superfluous.

superintendente [superinten'dente] *nm/f* supervisor, superintendent.

superior [supe'rjor] *a* (*piso, clase*) upper; (*temperatura, número, nivel*) higher; (*mejor: calidad, producto*) superior, better // *nm/f* superior; **~idad** *nf* superiority.

supermercado [supermer'kaðo] *nm* supermarket.

supersónico, a [super'soniko, a] *a* supersonic.

superstición [supersti'θjon] *nf* superstition; **supersticioso, a** *a* superstitious.

supervisor, a [superßi'sor, a] *nm/f* supervisor.

supervivencia [superßi'ßenθja] *nf* survival.

superviviente [superßi'ßjente] *a* surviving.

supiera *etc vb ver* **saber**.

suplantar [suplan'tar] *vt* (*persona*) to supplant.

suplementario, a [suplemen'tarjo, a] *a* supplementary; **suplemento** *nm* supplement.

suplente [su'plente] *a, nm/f* substitute.

supletorio, a [suple'torjo, a] *a*

supplementary // *nm* supplement; **mesa supletoria** spare table.

súplica ['suplika] *nf* request; (*JUR*) petition.

suplicar [supli'kar] *vt* (*cosa*) to beg (for), plead for; (*persona*) to beg, plead with.

suplicio [su'pliθjo] *nm* torture.

suplir [su'plir] *vt* (*compensar*) to make good, make up for; (*reemplazar*) to replace, substitute // *vi*: **~ a** to take the place of, substitute for.

supo *etc vb ver* **saber**.

suponer [supo'ner] *vt* to suppose // *vi* to have authority; **suposición** *nf* supposition.

supremacía [suprema'θia] *nf* supremacy.

supremo, a [su'premo, a] *a* supreme.

supresión [supre'sjon] *nf* suppression; (*de derecho*) abolition; (*de dificultad*) removal; (*de palabra etc*) deletion; (*de restricción*) cancellation, lifting.

suprimir [supri'mir] *vt* to suppress; (*derecho, costumbre*) to abolish; (*dificultad*) to remove; (*palabra etc*) to delete; (*restricción*) to cancel, lift.

supuesto, a *a pp de* **suponer** // [su'pwesto, a] *a* (*hipotético*) supposed; (*falso*) false // *nm* assumption, hypothesis; **~ que** *conj* since; **por ~** of course.

sur [sur] *nm* south.

surcar [sur'kar] *vt* to plough; (*superficie*) to cut, score; **surco** *nm* (*en metal, disco*) groove; (*AGR*) furrow.

surgir [sur'xir] *vi* to arise, emerge; (*dificultad*) to come up, crop up.

surtido, a [sur'tiðo, a] *a* mixed, assorted // *nm* (*selección*) selection, assortment; (*abastecimiento*) supply, stock.

surtir [sur'tir] *vt* to supply, provide // *vi* to spout, spurt.

susceptible [susθep'tißle] *a* susceptible; (*sensible*) sensitive; **~ de** capable of.

suscitar [susθi'tar] vt to cause, provoke; (interés, sospechas) to arouse.

suscribir [suskri'βir] vt (firmar) to sign; (respaldar) to subscribe to, endorse; ~se vr to subscribe; **suscripción** nf subscription.

susodicho, a [suso'ðitʃo, a] a above-mentioned.

suspender [suspen'der] vt (objeto) to hang (up), suspend; (trabajo) to stop, suspend; (ESCOL) to fail; **suspensión** nf suspension; (fig) stoppage, suspension.

suspenso, a [sus'penso, a] a hanging, suspended; (ESCOL) failed // nm: **quedar** o **estar en ~** to be pending.

suspicacia [suspi'kaθja] nf suspicion, mistrust; **suspicaz** a suspicious, distrustful.

suspirar [suspi'rar] vi to sigh; **suspiro** nm sigh.

sustancia [sus'tanθja] nf substance.

sustentar [susten'tar] vt (alimentar) to sustain, nourish; (objeto) to hold up, support; (idea, teoría) to maintain, uphold; (fig) to sustain, keep going; **sustento** nm support; (alimento) sustenance, food.

sustituir [sustitu'ir] vt to substitute, replace; **sustituto, a** nmf substitute, replacement.

susto ['susto] nm fright, scare.

sustraer [sustra'er] vt to remove, take away; (MAT) to subtract.

susurrar [susu'rrar] vi to whisper; **susurro** nm whisper.

sutil [su'til] a (aroma, diferencia) subtle; (tenue) thin; (inteligencia, persona) sharp; **~eza** nf subtlety; thinness.

suyo, a ['sujo, a] a (con artículo o después del verbo ser: de él) his; (: de ella) hers; (: de ellos, ellas) theirs; (: de Ud, Uds) yours; **un amigo ~** a friend of his (o hers o theirs o yours).

T

taba ['taβa] nf (ANAT) anklebone; (juego) jacks sg.

tabacalero, a [taβaka'lero, a] nmf (vendedor) tobacconist // nf: **T~** Spanish state tobacco monopoly.

tabaco [ta'βako] nm tobacco; (fam) cigarettes pl: **tabaquería** nf tobacconist's (Brit), cigar store (US).

taberna [ta'βerna] nf bar, pub (Brit); **tabernero, a** nmf (encargado) publican; (camarero) barman/maid.

tabique [ta'βike] nm partition (wall).

tabla ['taβla] nf (de madera) plank; (estante) shelf; (de vestido) pleat; (ARTE) panel; **~s** nfpl: **estar o quedar en ~s** to draw; **~do** nm (plataforma) platform; (TEATRO) stage.

tablero [ta'βlero] nm (de madera) plank, board; (de ajedrez, damas) board; (AUTO) dashboard; **~ de anuncios** notice (Brit) o bulletin (US) board.

tableta [ta'βleta] nf (MED) tablet; (de chocolate) bar.

tablilla [ta'βliʎa] nf small board; (MED) splint.

tablón [ta'βlon] nm (de suelo) plank; (de techo) beam; **~ de anuncios** notice board (Brit), bulletin board (US).

tabú [ta'βu] nm taboo.

tabular [taβu'lar] vt to tabulate.

taburete [taβu'rete] nm stool.

tacaño, a [ta'kaɲo, a] a (avaro) mean.

tácito, a ['taθito, a] a tacit.

taciturno, a [taθi'turno, a] a (callado) silent; (malhumorado) sullen.

taco ['tako] nm (BILLAR) cue; (libro de billetes) book; (AM: de zapato) heel; (tarugo) peg; (palabrota) swear word.

tacón [ta'kon] nm heel; **de ~ alto**

high-heeled; **taconeo** nm (heel) stamping.

táctico, a [ˈtaktiko, a] a tactical // nf tactics pl.

tacto [ˈtakto] nm touch; (fig) tact.

tacha [ˈtatʃa] nf flaw; (TEC) stud; **tachar** vt (borrar) to cross out; **tachar de** to accuse of.

tafetán [tafeˈtan] nm taffeta.

tafilete [tafiˈlete] nm morocco leather.

tahona [taˈona] nf (panadería) bakery.

tahúr, a [taˈur, a] nm/f gambler; (pey) cheat.

taimado, a [taiˈmaðo, a] a (astuto) sly.

taita [ˈtaita] nm (fam) dad, daddy.

tajada [taˈxaða] nf slice.

tajante [taˈxante] a sharp.

tajar [taˈxar] vt to cut; **tajo** nm (corte) cut; (GEO) cleft.

tal [tal] a such; ~ **vez** perhaps // pron (persona) someone, such a one; (cosa) something, such a thing; ~ **como** such as; ~ **para cual** tit for tat; (dos iguales) two of a kind // ad: ~ **como** (igual) just as; ~ **cual** (como es) just as it is; ¿**qué** ~? how are things?; ¿**qué** ~ **te gusta?** how do you like it? // conj: **con** ~ **de que** provided that.

taladrar [talaˈðrar] vt to drill; **taladro** nm drill; (hoyo) drill hole.

talante [taˈlante] nm (humor) mood; (voluntad) will, willingness.

talar [taˈlar] vt to fell, cut down; (devastar) to devastate.

talco [ˈtalko] nm (polvos) talcum powder.

talego [taˈleɣo] nm, **talega** [taˈleɣa] nf sack.

talento [taˈlento] nm talent; (capacidad) ability.

TALGO [ˈtalɣo] nm abr (Esp = tren articulado ligero Goicoechea-Oriol) ≈ HST (Brit).

talismán [talisˈman] nm talisman.

talón [taˈlon] nm (ANAT) heel; (COM) counterfoil; (cheque) cheque

(Brit), check (US).

talonario [taloˈnarjo] nm (de cheques) chequebook (Brit), checkbook (US); (de billetes) book of tickets; (de recibos) receipt book.

talla [ˈtaʎa] nf (estatura, fig, MED) height, stature; (palo) measuring rod; (ARTE) carving; (medida) size.

tallado, a [taˈʎaðo, a] a carved // nf carving.

tallar [taˈʎar] vt (madera) to carve; (metal etc) to engrave; (medir) to measure.

tallarines [taʎaˈrines] nmpl noodles.

talle [ˈtaʎe] nm (ANAT) waist; (fig) appearance.

taller [taˈʎer] nm (TEC) workshop; (de artista) studio.

tallo [ˈtaʎo] nm (de planta) stem; (de hierba) blade; (brote) shoot.

tamaño, a [taˈmaɲo, a] a (tan grande) such a big; (tan pequeño) such a small // nm size; **de** ~ **natural** full-size.

tamarindo [tamaˈrindo] nm tamarind.

tambalearse [tambaleˈarse] vr (persona) to stagger; (vehículo) to sway.

también [tamˈbjen] ad (igualmente) also, too, as well; (además) besides.

tambor [tamˈbor] nm drum; (ANAT) eardrum; ~ **del freno** brake drum.

tamiz [taˈmiθ] nm sieve; **~ar** vt to sieve.

tampoco [tamˈpoko] ad nor, neither; **yo** ~ **lo compré** I didn't buy it either.

tampón [tamˈpon] nm tampon.

tan [tan] ad so; ~ **es así que** ... so much so that ...

tanda [ˈtanda] nf (gen) series; (turno) batch.

tangente [tanˈxente] nf tangent.

Tánger [ˈtanxer] n Tangier(s).

tangible [tanˈxiβle] a tangible.

tanque [ˈtanke] nm (cisterna, MIL) tank; (AUTO) tanker.

tantear [tanteˈar] vt (calcular) to reckon (up); (medir) to take the measure of; (*probar*) to test, try out; (*tomar la medida*: *persona*) to take the measurements of; (*situación*) to weigh up; (*persona*: *opinión*) to sound out // *vi* (*DEPORTE*) to score;

tanteo [tan'teo] *nm* (*cálculo*) (rough) calculation; (*prueba*) test, trial; (*DEPORTE*) scoring.

tanto, a ['tanto, a] *a* (*cantidad*) so much, as much; ~s so many, as many; 20 y ~s 20-odd // *ad* (*cantidad*) so much, as much; (*tiempo*) so long, as long; ~ tú como yo both you and I; ~ como eso it's not as bad as that; ~ más ... cuanto que it's all the more ... because; ~ mejor/peor so much the better/the worse; ~ si viene como si va whether he comes or whether he goes; ~ es así que so much so that; por o por lo ~ therefore; me he vuelto ronco de o con ~ hablar I have become hoarse with so much talking // *conj*: en ~ que while; hasta ~ (que) until such time as // *nm* (*suma*) certain amount; (*proporción*) so much; (*punto*) point; (*gol*) goal; un ~ perezoso somewhat lazy // *pron*: cada uno paga ~ each one pays so much; a ~s de agosto on such and such a day in August.

tapa ['tapa] *nf* (*de caja, olla*) lid; (*de botella*) top; (*de libro*) cover; (*comida*) snack.

tapadera [tapa'ðera] *nf* lid, cover.

tapar [ta'par] *vt* (*cubrir*) to cover; (*envolver*) to wrap o cover up; (*la vista*) to obstruct; (*persona, falta*) to conceal; (*AM*) to fill; ~se *vr* to wrap o.s. up.

taparrabo [tapa'rraβo] *nm* loincloth.

tapete [ta'pete] *nm* table cover.

tapia ['tapja] *nf* (*garden*) wall; **tapiar** *vt* to wall in.

tapicería [tapiθe'ria] *nf* tapestry; (*para muebles*) upholstery; (*tienda*) upholsterer's (shop).

tapiz [ta'piθ] *nm* (*alfombra*) carpet; (*tela tejida*) tapestry; ~**ar** *vt* (*muebles*) to upholster.

tapón [ta'pon] *nm* (*corcho*) stopper; (*TEC*) plug; ~ **de rosca** screw-top.

taquigrafía [takixra'fia] *nf* shorthand; **taquígrafo, a** *nm/f* shorthand writer, stenographer.

taquilla [ta'kiλa] *nf* (*donde se compra*) booking office; (*suma recogida*) takings *pl*; **taquillero, a** *a*: **función taquillera** box office success // *nm/f* ticket clerk.

tara ['tara] *nf* (*defecto*) defect; (*COM*) tare.

tarántula [ta'rantula] *nf* tarantula.

tararear [tarare'ar] *vi* to hum.

tardanza [tar'ðanθa] *nf* (*demora*) delay.

tardar [tar'ðar] *vi* (*tomar tiempo*) to take a long time; (*llegar tarde*) to be late; (*demorar*) to delay; ¿**tarda mucho el tren?** does the train take (very) long?; a más ~ at the latest; no tardes en venir come soon.

tarde [tar'ðe] *ad* late // *nf* (*de día*) afternoon; (*al anochecer*) evening; **de** ~ **en** ~ from time to time; ¡**buenas** ~**s!** good afternoon!; a o por la ~ in the afternoon, in the evening.

tardío, a [tar'ðio, a] *a* (*retrasado*) late; (*lento*) slow (to arrive).

tardo, a [tar'ðo, a] *a* (*lento*) slow; (*torpe*) dull.

tarea [ta'rea] *nf* task; (*ESCOL*) homework.

tarifa [ta'rifa] *nf* (*lista de precios*) price list; (*precio*) tariff.

tarima [ta'rima] *nf* (*plataforma*) platform.

tarjeta [tar'xeta] *nf* card; ~ **postal/de crédito/de Navidad** postcard/credit card/Christmas card.

tarro ['tarro] *nm* jar, pot.

tarta ['tarta] *nf* (*pastel*) cake; (*torta*) tart.

tartamudear [tartamuðe'ar] *vi* to stammer; **tartamudo, a** *a* stammering // *nm/f* stammerer.

tártaro, a ['tartaro, a] *a*: **salsa tártara** tartare sauce.

tasa ['tasa] *nf* (*precio*) (fixed) price,

rate; (*valoración*) valuation; (*medida, norma*) measure, standard; ~ **de cambio/interés** exchange/ interest rate; ~**ción** nf valuation; ~**dor, a** nm/f valuer.

tasar [ta'sar] vt (*arreglar el precio*) to fix a price for; (*valorar*) to value, assess.

tasca ['taska] nf (*fam*) pub.

tatarabuelo, a [tatara'βwelo, a] nm/f great-great-grandfather/mother.

tatuaje [ta'twaxe] nm (*dibujo*) tattoo; (*acto*) tattooing.

tatuar, a [tau'rino, a] vt to tattoo.

taurino, a [tau'rino, a] a a bullfighting cpd.

Tauro ['tauro] nm Taurus.

tauromaquia [tauro'makja] nf tauromachy, (art of) bullfighting.

taxi ['taksi] nm taxi.

taxista [tak'sista] nm/f taxi driver.

taza ['taθa] nf cup; (*de retrete*) bowl; ~ **para café** coffee cup; **tazón** nm (~ **grande**) mug, large cup; (*de fuente*) basin.

te [te] pron (*complemento de objeto*) you; (*complemento indirecto*) (to) you; (*reflexivo*) (to) yourself; *¿~ duele mucho el brazo?* does your arm hurt a lot?; ~ **equivocas** you're wrong; ¡**cálma**~! calm down!

té [te] nm tea.

tea ['tea] nf torch.

teatral [tea'tral] a a theatre cpd; (*fig*) theatrical.

teatro [te'atro] nm theatre; (*LITERATURA*) plays pl, drama.

tebeo [te'βeo] nm comic.

tecla ['tekla] nf key; ~**do** nm keyboard; **teclear** vi to strum; (*fig*) to drum; **tecleo** nm (*MUS: sonido*) strumming; (*fig*) drumming.

técnico, a ['tekniko, a] a technical // nm/f technician; (*experto*) expert // nf (*procedimientos*) technique; (*arte, oficio*) craft.

tecnócrata [tek'nokrata] nm/f technocrat.

tecnología [teknolo'xia] nf technology; **tecnológico, a** a a techno-

logical.

techo ['tetʃo] nm (*externo*) roof; (*interno*) ceiling; ~ **corredizo** sunroof.

tedio ['teðjo] nm boredom, tedium; ~**so, a** a a boring, tedious.

teja ['texa] nf (*azulejo*) tile; (*BOT*) lime (tree); ~**do** nm (tiled) roof.

tejanos [te'xanos] nmpl jeans.

tejemaneje [texema'nexe] nm (*lío*) fuss; (*intriga*) intrigue.

tejer [te'xer] vt to weave; (*hacer punto*) to knit; (*fig*) to fabricate; **tejido** nm (*tela*) material, fabric; (*telaraña*) web; (*ANAT*) tissue.

tel, teléf abr (= teléfono) tel.

tela ['tela] nf (*tejido*) material; (*telaraña*) web; (*en líquido*) skin; **telar** nm (*máquina*) loom; **telares** nmpl textile mill sg.

telaraña [tela'raɲa] nf cobweb.

tele ['tele] nf (*fam*) telly (*Brit*), tube (*US*).

tele... [tele] pref tele...; ~**comunicación** nf telecommunication; ~**control** nm remote control; ~**diario** nm television news; ~**difusión** nf (*television*) broadcast; ~**dirigido, a** a a remote-controlled.

telefax [tele'faks] nm inv fax; (*aparato*) fax (machine).

teleférico [tele'feriko] nm (*tren*) cable-railway; (*de esquí*) ski-lift.

telefonear [telefone'ar] vi to telephone.

telefónicamente [telefonika'mente] ad by (tele)phone.

telefónico, a [tele'foniko, a] a a telephone cpd.

telefonista [telefo'nista] nm/f telephonist.

teléfono [te'lefono] nm (tele)phone; *estar hablando al* ~ to be on the phone; *llamar a uno por* ~ to ring o phone sb up.

telegrafía [televra'fia] nf telegraphy.

telégrafo [te'levrafo] nm telegraph.

telegrama [tele'vrama] nm telegram.

tele: ~**impresor** nm teleprinter

(Brit), teletype (US); ~**objetivo** nm telephoto lens; ~**pático, a** a telepathic; ~**scópico, a** a telescopic; ~**scopio** nm telescope; ~**silla** nm chairlift; ~**spectador, a** nm/f viewer; ~**squí** nm ski-lift; ~**tipo** nm teletype.

televidente [teleβi'ðente] nm/f viewer.

televisar [teleβi'sar] vt to televise.

televisión [teleβi'sjon] nf television; ~ **en colores** colour television.

televisor [teleβi'sor] nm television set.

télex ['teleks] nm inv telex.

telón [te'lon] nm curtain; ~ **de acero** (POL) iron curtain; ~ **de fondo** backcloth, background.

tema ['tema] nm (asunto) subject, topic; (MUS) theme // nf (obsesión) obsession; **temático, a** a thematic.

temblar [tem'blar] vi to shake, tremble; (de frío) to shiver; **tembleque** nm shaking; **temblón, ona** a shaking; **temblor** nm trembling; (de tierra) earthquake; **tembloroso, a** a trembling.

temer [te'mer] vt to fear // vi to be afraid; **temo que llegue tarde** I am afraid he may be late.

temerario, a [teme'rarjo, a] a (descuidado) reckless; (irreflexivo) hasty; **temeridad** nf (imprudencia) rashness; (audacia) boldness.

temeroso, a [teme'roso, a] a (miedoso) fearful; (que inspira temor) frightful.

temible [te'mißle] a fearsome.

temor [te'mor] nm (miedo) fear; (duda) suspicion.

témpano ['tempano] nm: ~ **de hielo** ice-floe.

temperamento [tempera'mento] nm temperament.

temperatura [tempera'tura] nf temperature.

tempestad [tempes'tað] nf storm; **tempestuoso, a** a stormy.

templado, a [tem'plaðo, a] a (moderado) moderate; (: en el comer) frugal; (: en el beber) abstemious; (agua) lukewarm; (clima) mild; (MUS) well-tuned; **templanza** nf moderation; (abstemiousness); mildness.

templar [tem'plar] vt (moderar) to moderate; (furia) to restrain; (calor) to reduce; (afinar) to tune (up); (acero) to temper; (tuerca) to tighten up; **temple** nm (ajuste) tempering; (afinación) tuning; (clima) temperature; (pintura) tempera.

templete [tem'plete] nm bandstand.

templo ['templo] nm (iglesia) church; (pagano etc) temple.

temporada [tempo'raða] nf time, period; (estación) season.

temporal [tempo'ral] a (no permanente) temporary; (REL) temporal // nm storm.

tempranero, a [tempra'nero, a] a (BOT) early; (persona) early-rising.

temprano, a [tem'prano, a] a (demasiado pronto) too soon, too early.

ten vb ver **tener**.

tenaces [te'naθes] apl ver **tenaz**.

tenacidad [tenaθi'ðað] nf tenacity; (dureza) toughness; (terquedad) stubbornness.

tenacillas [tena'θiλas] nfpl tongs; (para el pelo) curling tongs (Brit) o iron (US); (MED) forceps.

tenaz [te'naθ] a (material) tough; (persona) tenacious; (creencia, resistencia) stubborn.

tenaza(s) [te'naθa(s)] nf(pl) (MED) forceps; (TEC) pliers; (ZOOL) pincers.

tendedero [tende'ðero] nm (para ropa) drying place; (cuerda) clothes line.

tendencia [ten'denθja] nf tendency; (proceso) trend; **tener ~ a** to tend to, have a tendency to; **tendencioso, a** a tendentious.

tender [ten'der] vt (extender) to spread out; (colgar) to hang out; (vía férrea, cable) to lay; (estirar) to stretch // vi: ~ **a** to tend to, have a tendency towards; ~**se** *vr* to lie down; ~ **la cama/la mesa** (*AM*) to make the bed/lay (*Brit*) o set (*US*) the table.

tenderete [tende'rete] *nm* (*puesto*) stall; (*exposición*) display of goods.

tendero, a [ten'dero, a] *nm/f* shop-keeper.

tendido, a [ten'diðo, a] *a* (*acostado*) lying down, flat; (*colgado*) hanging // *nm* (*TAUR*) front rows of seats; **a galope** ~ flat out.

tendón [ten'don] *nm* tendon.

tendré *etc vb ver* **tener**.

tenebroso, a [tene'βroso, a] *a* (*oscuro*) dark; (*fig*) gloomy; (*complot*) sinister.

tenedor [tene'ðor] *nm* (*CULIN*) fork; (*poseedor*) holder; ~ **de libros** book-keeper.

teneduría [teneðu'ria] *nf* keeping; ~ **de libros** book-keeping.

tenencia [te'nenθja] *nf* (*de casa*) tenancy; (*de oficio*) tenure; (*de propiedad*) possession.

PALABRA CLAVE

tener [te'ner] ♦ *vt* **1** (*poseer, gen*) to have; (*en la mano*) to hold; **¿tienes un boli?** have you got a pen?; **va a ~ un niño** she's going to have a baby; **¡ten** (o **tenga**)!, **¡aquí tienes** (o **tiene**)! here you are!

2 (*edad, medidas*) to be; **tiene 7 años** she's 7 (years old); **tiene 15 cm. de largo** it's 15 cms long; *ver* **calor, hambre** *etc*

3 (*considerar*): **lo tengo por brillante** I consider him to be brilliant; ~ **en mucho a uno** to think very highly of sb

4 (+ *pp*): = **pretérito**): **tengo terminada ya la mitad del trabajo** I've done half the work already

5: ~ **que hacer algo** to have to do sth; **tengo que acabar este trabajo hoy** I have to finish this job today

6: **¿qué tienes, estás enfermo?** what's the matter with you, are you ill?

♦ ~**se** *vr* **1**: ~**se en pie** to stand up

2: ~**se por**: to think o.s.; **se tiene por muy listo** he thinks himself very clever.

---

tengo *etc vb ver* **tener**.

tenia ['tenja] *nf* tapeworm.

teniente [te'njente] *nm* (*rango*) lieutenant; (*ayudante*) deputy.

tenis ['tenis] *nm* tennis; ~ **de mesa** table tennis; ~**ta** *nm/f* tennis player.

tenor [te'nor] *nm* (*sentido*) meaning; (*MUS*) tenor; **a** ~ **de** on the lines of.

tensar [ten'sar] *vt* to tauten; (*arco*) to draw.

tensión [ten'sjon] *nf* tension; (*TEC*) stress; (*MED*): ~ **arterial** blood pressure; **tener la** ~ **alta** to have high blood pressure.

tenso, a ['tenso, a] *a* tense.

tentación [tenta'θjon] *nf* temptation.

tentáculo [ten'takulo] *nm* tentacle.

tentador, a [tenta'ðor, a] *a* tempting // *nm/f* tempter/temptress.

tentar [ten'tar] *vt* (*tocar*) to touch, feel; (*seducir*) to tempt; (*atraer*) to attract; **tentativa** *nf* attempt; **tentativa de asesinato** attempted murder.

tentempié [tentem'pje] *nm* (*fam*) snack.

tenue ['tenwe] *a* (*delgado*) thin, slender; (*neblina*) light; (*lazo, vínculo*) slight.

teñir [te'nir] *vt* to dye; (*fig*) to tinge; ~**se** *vr* to dye; ~**se el pelo** to dye one's hair.

teología [teolo'xia] *nf* theology.

teorema [teo'rema] *nm* theorem.

teoría [teo'ria] *nf* theory; **en** ~ in theory; **teóricamente** *ad* theoretically; **teórico, a** *a* theoretic(al) // *nm/f* theoretician, theorist; **teorizar** *vi* to theorize.

terapéutico, a [tera'peutiko, a] *a* therapeutic.

terapia [te'rapja] *nf* therapy.

tercer [ter'θer] *a ver* **tercero**.

tercermundista [terθermun'dista] *a*

Third World *cpd.*

tercer(o), a [ter'θer(o), a] *a* third // *nm* (JUR) third party.

terceto [ter'θeto] *nm* trio.

terciado, a [ter'θjaðo, a] *a* slanting.

terciar [ter'θjar] *vt* (*llevar*) to wear (across the shoulder) // *vi* (*participar*) to take part; (*hacer de árbitro*) to mediate; ~**se** *vr* to come up; ~**io, a** *a* tertiary.

tercio ['terθjo] *nm* third.

terciopelo [terθjo'pelo] *nm* velvet.

terco, a ['terko, a] *a* obstinate.

tergiversar [terxiβer'sar] *vt* to distort.

termal [ter'mal] *a* thermal.

termas ['termas] *nfpl* hot springs.

terminación [termina'θjon] *nf* (*final*) end; (*conclusión*) conclusion, ending.

terminal [termi'nal] *a, nm, af* terminal.

terminante [termi'nante] *a* (*final*) final, definitive; (*tajante*) categorical.

terminar [termi'nar] *vt* (*completar*) to complete, finish; (*concluir*) to end // *vi* (*llegar a su fin*) to end; (*parar*) to stop; (*acabar*) to finish; ~**se** *vr* to come to an end; ~ **por hacer algo** to end up (by) doing sth.

término ['termino] *nm* end, conclusion; (*parada*) terminus; (*límite*) boundary; ~ **medio** average; (*fig*) middle way; **en último** ~ (*a fin de cuentas*) in the last analysis; (*como último recurso*) as a last resort; **en** ~**s de** in terms of.

terminología [terminolo'xia] *nf* terminology.

termodinámico, a [termoði'namiko, a] *a* thermodynamic.

termómetro [ter'mometro] *nm* thermometer.

termonuclear [termonukle'ar] *a* thermonuclear.

termo(s) ® ['termo(s)] *nm* Thermos ® (flask).

termostato [termo'stato] *nm* thermostat.

ternero, a [ter'nero, a] *nm/f* (*animal*) calf // *nf* (*carne*) veal.

terno ['terno] *nm* (AM) three-piece suit.

ternura [ter'nura] *nf* (*trato*) tenderness; (*palabra*) endearment; (*cariño*) fondness.

terquedad [terke'ðað] *nf* obstinacy; (*dureza*) harshness.

terrado [te'rraðo] *nm* terrace.

terraplén [terra'plen] *nm* (AGR) terrace; (*cuesta*) slope.

terrateniente [terrate'njente] *nm/f* landowner.

terraza [te'rraθa] *nf* (*balcón*) balcony; (*techo*) (flat) roof; (AGR) terrace.

terremoto [terre'moto] *nm* earthquake.

terrenal [terre'nal] *a* earthly.

terreno [te'rreno] *nm* (*tierra*) land; (*parcela*) plot; (*suelo*) soil; (*fig*) field; **un** ~ a piece of land.

terrestre [te'rrestre] *a* terrestrial; (*ruta*) land *cpd.*

terrible [te'rriβle] *a* terrible, awful.

territorio [terri'torjo] *nm* territory.

terrón [te'rron] *nm* (*de azúcar*) lump; (*de tierra*) clod, lump.

terror [te'rror] *nm* terror; ~**ífico, a** a terrifying; ~**ista** *a, nm/f* terrorist.

terroso, a [te'rroso, a] *a* earthy.

terruño [te'rruɲo] *nm* (*parcela*) plot; (*fig*) native soil.

terso, a ['terso, a] *a* (*liso*) smooth; (*pulido*) polished; **tersura** *nf* smoothness.

tertulia [ter'tulja] *nf* (*reunión informal*) social gathering; (*grupo*) group, circle.

tesis ['tesis] *nf inv* thesis.

tesón [te'son] *nm* (*firmeza*) firmness; (*tenacidad*) tenacity.

tesorero, a [teso'rero, a] *nm/f* treasurer.

tesoro [te'soro] *nm* treasure; (COM, POL) treasury.

testaferro [testa'ferro] *nm* figurehead.

testamentaría [testamenta'ria] *nf* execution of a will.

testamentario, a [testamen'tarjo,

al *a* testamentary // *nm/f* executor/ executrix.

testamento [testa'mento] *nm* will.

testar [tes'tar] *vi* to make a will.

testarudo, a [testa'ruðo, a] *a* a stubborn.

testículo [tes'tikulo] *nm* testicle.

testificar [testifi'kar] *vt* to testify; (*fig*) to attest // *vi* to give evidence.

testigo [tes'tiɣo] *nm/f* witness; ~ **de cargo/descargo** witness for the prosecution/defence; ~ **ocular** eye witness.

testimoniar [testimo'njar] *vt* to testify to; (*fig*) to show; **testimonio** *nm* testimony.

teta ['teta] *nf* (*de biberón*) teat; (*ANAT: pezón*) nipple; (: *fam*) breast.

tétanos ['tetanos] *nm* tetanus.

tetera [te'tera] *nf* teapot.

tetilla [te'tiʎa] *nf* (*ANAT*) nipple; (*de biberón*) teat.

tétrico, a ['tetriko, a] *a* gloomy, dismal.

textil [teks'til] *a* textile; ~**es** *nmpl* textiles.

texto ['teksto] *nm* text; **textual** *a* textual.

textura [teks'tura] *nf* (*de tejido*) texture.

tez [teθ] *nf* (*cutis*) complexion; (*color*) colouring.

ti [ti] *pron* you; (*reflexivo*) yourself.

tía ['tia] *nf* (*pariente*) aunt; (*fam*) chick, bird.

tibieza [ti'βjeθa] *nf* (*temperatura*) tepidness; (*fig*) coolness; **tibio, a** *a* lukewarm.

tiburón [tiβu'ron] *nm* shark.

tic [tik] *nm* (*ruido*) click; (*de reloj*) tick; (*MED*): ~ **nervioso** nervous tic.

tictac [tik'tak] *nm* (*de reloj*) tick tock.

tiempo ['tjempo] *nm* time; (*época, período*) age, period; (*METEOROLOGIA*) weather; (*LING*) tense; (*DEPORTE*) half; **a** ~ in time; **a un o al mismo** ~ at the same time; **al**

poco ~ very soon (after); **se quedó poco** ~ he didn't stay very long; **hace poco** ~ not long ago; **mucho** ~ a long time; **de** ~ **en** ~ from time to time; **hace buen/mal** ~ the weather is fine/bad; **estar a** ~ to be in time; **hace** ~ some time ago; **hacer** ~ to while away the time; **motor de 2** ~**s** two-stroke engine; **primer** ~ first half.

tienda ['tjenda] *nf* shop, store; ~ (**de campaña**) tent.

tienes *etc vb ver* **tener.**

tienta *etc vb ver* **tentar** // ['tjenta] *nf*: **andar a** ~**s** to grope one's way along.

tiento *vb ver* **tentar** // ['tjento] *nm* (*tacto*) touch; (*precaución*) wariness.

tierno, a ['tjerno, a] *a* (*blando*) tender; (*fresco*) fresh; (*amable*) sweet.

tierra ['tjerra] *nf* earth; (*suelo*) soil; (*mundo*) earth, world; (*país*) country, land; ~ **adentro** inland.

tieso, a ['tjeso, a] *a* (*rígido*) rigid; (*duro*) stiff; (*fam: orgulloso*) conceited.

tiesto ['tjesto] *nm* flowerpot.

tifoidea [tifoi'ðea] *nf* typhoid.

tifón [ti'fon] *nm* typhoon.

tifus ['tifus] *nm* typhus.

tigre ['tiɣre] *nm* tiger.

tijera [ti'xera] *nf* scissors *pl*; (*ZOOL*) claw; ~**s** *nfpl* scissors; (*para plantas*) shears.

tijereta [tixe'reta] *nf* earwig.

tijeretear [tixerete'ar] *vt* to snip.

tildar [til'dar] *vt*: ~ **de** to brand as.

tilde ['tilde] *nf* (*TIPOGRAFIA*) tilde.

tilín [ti'lin] *nm* tinkle.

tilo [ti'lo] *nm* lime tree.

timar [ti'mar] *vt* (*robar*) to steal; (*estafar*) to swindle.

timbal [tim'bal] *nm* small drum.

timbrar [tim'brar] *vt* to stamp.

timbre ['timbre] *nm* (*sello*) stamp; (*campanilla*) bell; (*tono*) timbre; (*COM*) stamp duty.

timidez [timi'ðeθ] *nf* shyness; **tímido, a** *a* shy.

timo ['timo] *nm* swindle.

timón [ti'mon] *nm* helm, rudder; **timonel** *nm* helmsman.

tímpano ['timpano] *nm* (ANAT) eardrum; (MUS) small drum.

tina ['tina] *nf* tub; (baño) bath(tub); **tinaja** *nf* large jar.

tinglado [tin'glaðo] *nm* (cobertizo) shed; (fig: truco) trick; (intriga) intrigue.

tinieblas [ti'njeβlas] *nfpl* darkness *sg*; (sombras) shadows.

tino ['tino] *nm* (habilidad) skill; (juicio) insight.

tinta ['tinta] *nf* ink; (TEC) dye; (ARTE) colour.

tinte ['tinte] *nm* (acto) dyeing.

tintero [tin'tero] *nm* inkwell.

tintinear [tintine'ar] *vt* to tinkle.

tinto, a ['tinto, a] *a* (teñido) dyed // *nm* red wine.

tintorería [tintore'ria] *nf* dry cleaner's.

tintura [tin'tura] *nf* (acto) dyeing; (QUIMICA) dye; (farmacéutico) tincture.

tío ['tio] *nm* (pariente) uncle; (fam: individuo) bloke (Brit), guy.

tiovivo [tio'βiβo] *nm* merry-go-round.

típico, a ['tipiko, a] *a* typical.

tiple ['tiple] *nm* soprano (voice) // *nmf* soprano.

tipo ['tipo] *nm* (clase) type, kind; (norma) norm; (patrón) pattern; (hombre) fellow; (ANAT: de hombre) build; (: de mujer) figure; (IMPRENTA) type; ~ **bancario/de descuento/de interés/de cambio** bank/discount/interest/exchange rate.

tipografía [tipoɣra'fia] *nf* (tipo) printing *cpd*; (lugar) printing press; **tipográfico, a** *a* printing *cpd*; **tipógrafo, a** *nm/f* printer.

tiquet ['tiket] (*pl* ~s) *nm* ticket; (en tienda) cash slip.

tiquismiquis [tikis'mikis] *nm inv* fussy person // *nmpl* (querellas) squabbling *sg*; (escrúpulos) silly scruples.

tira ['tira] *nf* strip; (fig) abundance;

~ **y afloja** give and take.

tirabuzón [tiraβu'θon] *nm* (rizo) curl.

tirachinas [tira'tʃinas] *nm inv* catapult.

tiradero [tira'ðero] *nm* rubbish dump.

tirado, a [ti'raðo, a] *a* (barato) dirtcheap; (fam: fácil) very easy // *nf* (acto) cast, throw; (distancia) distance; (serie) series; (TIPOGRAFIA) printing, edition; **de una tirada** at one go.

tirador [tira'ðor] *nm* (mango) handle.

tiranía [tira'nia] *nf* tyranny; **tirano, a** *a* tyrannical // *nm/f* tyrant.

tirante [ti'rante] *a* (cuerda etc) tight, taut; (relaciones) strained // *nm* (ARQ) brace; (TEC) stay; (correa) shoulder strap; ~**s** *nmpl* braces (Brit), suspenders (US); **tirantez** *nf* tightness; (fig) tension.

tirar [ti'rar] *vt* to throw; (dejar caer) to drop; (volcar) to upset; (derribar) to knock down *o* over; (jalar) to pull; (desechar) to throw out *o* away; (disipar) to squander; (imprimir) to print; (dar: golpe) to deal // *vi* (disparar) to shoot; (jalar) to pull; (fig) to draw; (fam: andar) to go; (tender a, buscar realizar) to tend to; (DEPORTE) to shoot; ~**se** *vr* to throw o.s.; (fig) to cheapen o.s.; ~ **abajo** to bring down, destroy; **tira más a su padre** he takes more after his father; **ir tirando** to manage; **a todo** ~ at the most.

tirita [ti'rita] *nf* (sticking) plaster (Brit), bandaid (US).

tiritar [tiri'tar] *vi* to shiver.

tiro ['tiro] *nm* (lanzamiento) throw; (disparo) shot; (disparar) shooting; (DEPORTE) shot; (GOLF, TENIS) drive; (alcance) range; (golpe) blow; (engaño) hoax; ~ **al blanco** target practice; **caballo de** ~ carthorse; **andar de** ~**s largos** to be all dressed up; **al** ~ (AM) at once.

tirón [ti'ron] *nm* (sacudida) pull, tug; **de un** ~ in one go, all at once.

tiroteo [tiro'teo] *nm* exchange of shots, shooting.

tísico, a ['tisiko, a] *a* consumptive.

tisis ['tisis] *nf inv* consumption, tuberculosis.

títere ['titere] *nm* puppet.

titilar [titi'lar] *vi* (*luz, estrella*) to twinkle; (*párpado*) to flutter.

titiritero, a [titiri'tero, a] *nm/f* puppeteer.

titubeante [tituβe'ante] *a* (*inestable*) shaky, tottering; (*farfullante*) stammering; (*dudoso*) hesitant.

titubear [tituβe'ar] *vi* to stagger; (*fig*) to hesitate; **titubeo** *nm* staggering; stammering; hesitation.

titulado, a [titu'laðo, a] *a* (*libro*) entitled; (*persona*) titled.

titular [titu'lar] *a* titular // *nm/f* occupant // *nm* headline // *vt* to title; **~se** *vr* to be entitled; **título** *nm* title; (*de diario*) headline; (*certificado*) professional qualification; (*universitario*) (university) degree; (*fig*) right; **a título de** in the capacity of.

tiza ['tiθa] *nf* chalk.

tiznar [tiθ'nar] *vt* to blacken; (*fig*) to tarnish.

tizón [ti'θon], **tizo** ['tiθo] *nm* brand; (*fig*) stain.

toalla [to'aʎa] *nf* towel.

tobillo [to'βiʎo] *nm* ankle.

tobogán [toβo'ɣan] *nm* toboggan; (*montaña rusa*) roller-coaster; (*resbaladilla*) chute, slide.

toca ['toka] *nf* headdress.

tocadiscos [toka'ðiskos] *nm inv* record player.

tocado, a [to'kaðo, a] *a* (*fam*) touched // *nm* headdress.

tocador [toka'ðor] *nm* (*mueble*) dressing table; (*cuarto*) boudoir; (*fam*) ladies' toilet (*Brit*) *o* room (*US*).

tocante [to'kante]: **~ a** *prep* with regard to.

tocar [to'kar] *vt* to touch; (*MUS*) to play; (*topar con*) to run into, strike;

(*referirse a*) to allude to; (*padecer*) to suffer // *vi* (*a la puerta*) to knock (on *o* at the door); (*ser de turno*) to fall to, be the turn of; (*ser hora*) to be due; (*barco, avión*) to call at; (*atañer*) to concern; **~se** *vr* (*cubrirse la cabeza*) to cover one's head; (*tener contacto*) to touch (each other); **por lo que a mí me toca** as far as I am concerned.

tocayo, a [to'kajo, a] *nm/f* namesake.

tocino [to'θino] *nm* bacon.

todavía [toða'βia] *ad* (*aun*) even; (*aún*) still; yet; **~ más** yet more; **~ no** not yet.

PALABRA CLAVE

todo, a ['toðo, a] ◆ *a* **1** (*con artículo sg*) all; **toda la carne** all the meat; **toda la noche** all night, the whole night; **~ el libro** the whole book; **toda una botella** a whole bottle; **~ lo contrario** quite the opposite; **está toda sucia** she's all dirty; **por ~ el país** throughout the whole country

2 (*con artículo pl*) all; every; **~s los libros** all the books; **todas las noches** every night; **~s los que quieran salir** all those who want to leave

◆ *pron* **1** everything, all; **~s** everyone, everybody; **lo sabemos ~** we know everything; **~s querían más tiempo** everybody *o* everyone wanted more time; **nos marchamos ~s** all of us left

2: **con ~: con ~ él me sigue gustando** even so I still like him

◆ *ad* all; **vaya ~ seguido** keep straight on *o* ahead

◆ *nm*: **como un ~** as a whole; **del ~: no me agrada del ~** I don't entirely like it.

---

todopoderoso, a [toðopoðe'roso, a] *a* all powerful; (*REL*) almighty.

toga ['toɣa] *nf* toga; (*ESCOL*) gown.

Tokio ['tokjo] *n* Tokyo.

toldo ['toldo] nm (para el sol) sunshade (Brit), parasol; (tienda) marquee.

tole ['tole] nm (fam) commotion.

tolerancia [tole'ranθja] nf tolerance.

tolerar [tole'rar] vt to tolerate; (resistir) to endure.

toma ['toma] nf (acto) taking; (MED) dose; ~ **(de corriente)** socket.

tomar [to'mar] vt to take; (aspecto) to take on; (beber) to drink // vi to take; (AM) to drink; ~**se** vr to take; ~**se por** to consider o.s. to be; ~ a **bien/a mal** to take well/badly; ~ **en serio** to take seriously; ~ **el pelo a alguien** to pull sb's leg; ~**la con uno** to pick a quarrel with sb.

tomate [to'mate] nm tomato; ~**ra** nf tomato plant.

tomavistas [toma'Bistas] nm inv movie camera.

tomillo [to'miʎo] nm thyme.

tomo ['tomo] nm (libro) volume.

ton [ton] abr = **tonelada** // nm: **sin ~ ni son** without rhyme or reason.

tonada [to'naða] nf tune.

tonalidad [tonali'ðað] nf tone.

tonel [to'nel] nm barrel.

tonelada [tone'laða] nf ton; **tonelaje** nm tonnage.

tonelero [tone'lero] nm cooper.

tónico, a ['toniko, a] a tonic // nm (MED) tonic // nf (MUS) tonic; (fig) keynote.

tonificar [tonifi'kar] vt to tone up.

tono ['tono] nm tone; **fuera de ~** inappropriate; **darse ~** to put on airs.

tontería [tonte'ria] nf (estupidez) foolishness; (cosa) stupid thing; (acto) foolish act; ~**s** nfpl rubbish sg, nonsense sg.

tonto, a ['tonto, a] a stupid, silly // nm/f fool; (payaso) clown.

topacio [to'paθjo] nm topaz.

topar [to'par] vt (tropezar) to bump into; (encontrar) to find, come across; (ZOOL) to butt // vi: ~ **contra o en** to run into; ~ **con** to run up against.

tope ['tope] a maximum // nm (fin) end; (límite) limit; (FERRO) buffer; (AUTO) bumper; **al ~** end to end.

tópico, a ['topiko, a] a topical // nm platitude.

topo ['topo] nm (ZOOL) mole; (fig) blunderer.

topografía [topoɣra'fia] nf topography; **topógrafo, a** nm/f topographer.

toque etc vb ver **tocar** // ['toke] nm touch; (MUS) beat; (de campana) peal; (fig) crux; **dar un ~ a** to test; ~ **de queda** curfew; ~**tear** vt to handle.

toqué vb ver **tocar.**

toquilla [to'kiʎa] nf (pañuelo) headscarf; (chal) shawl.

tórax ['toraks] nm thorax.

torbellino [torbe'ʎino] nm whirlwind; (fig) whirl.

torcedura [torθe'ðura] nf twist; (MED) sprain.

torcer [tor'θer] vt to twist; (la esquina) to turn; (MED) to sprain // vi (desviar) to turn off; ~**se** vr (ladearse) to bend; (desviarse) to go astray; (fracasar) to go wrong; **torcido, a** a twisted; (fig) crooked // nm curl.

tordo, a ['torðo, a] a dappled // nm thrush.

torear [tore'ar] vt (fig: evadir) to avoid; (jugar con) to tease // vi to fight bulls; **toreo** nm bullfighting; **torero, a** nm/f bullfighter.

tormenta [tor'menta] nf storm; (fig: confusión) turmoil.

tormento [tor'mento] nm torture; (fig) anguish.

tornar [tor'nar] vt (devolver) to return, give back; (transformar) to transform // vi to go back; ~**se** vr (ponerse) to become.

tornasolado, a [tornaso'laðo, a] a (brillante) iridescent; (reluciente) shimmering.

torneo [tor'neo] nm tournament.

tornillo [tor'niʎo] nm screw.

torniquete [torni'kete] nm (puerta)

turnstile; (MED) tourniquet.

torno ['torno] nm (TEC) winch; (tambor) drum; **en ~ (a)** round, about.

toro ['toro] nm bull; (fam) he-man; **los ~s** bullfighting.

toronja [to'ronxa] nf grapefruit.

torpe ['torpe] a (poco hábil) clumsy, awkward; (necio) dim; (lento) slow.

torpedo [tor'peðo] nm torpedo.

torpeza [tor'peθa] nf (falta de agilidad) clumsiness; (lentitud) slowness; (error) mistake.

torre ['torre] nf tower; (de petróleo) derrick.

torrefacto, a [torre'fakto, a] a roasted.

torrente [to'rrente] nm torrent.

tórrido, a ['torriðo, a] a torrid.

torrija [to'rrixa] nf French toast.

torsión [tor'sjon] nf twisting.

torso ['torso] nm torso.

torta ['torta] nf cake; (fam) slap.

tortícolis [tor'tikolis] nm inv stiff neck.

tortilla [tor'tiʎa] nf omelette; (AM) maize pancake; ~ **francesa/española** plain/potato omelette.

tórtola ['tortola] nf turtledove.

tortuga [tor'tuɣa] nf tortoise.

tortuoso, a [tor'twoso, a] a winding.

tortura [tor'tura] nf torture; **torturar** vt to torture.

tos [tos] nf cough; ~ **ferina** whooping cough.

tosco, a ['tosko, a] a coarse.

toser [to'ser] vi to cough.

tostado, a [tos'taðo, a] a toasted; (por el sol) dark brown; (piel) tanned.

tostador [tostaðor] nm toaster.

tostar [tos'tar] vt to toast; (café) to roast; (persona) to tan; ~**se** vr to get brown.

total [to'tal] a total // ad in short; (al fin y al cabo) when all is said and done // nm total; ~ **que** to cut (Brit) o make (US) a long story short.

totalidad [totali'ðað] nf whole.

totalitario, a [totali'tarjo, a] a

totalitarian.

tóxico, a ['toksiko, a] a toxic // nm poison; **toxicómano, a** nm/f drug addict.

tozudo, a [to'θuðo, a] a obstinate.

traba ['traβa] nf bond, tie; (cadena) shackle.

trabajador, a [traβaxa'ðor, a] a hard-working // nm/f worker.

trabajar [traβa'xar] vt to work; (AGR) to till; (empeñarse en) to work at; (empujar) persona) to push; (convencer) to persuade // vi to work; (esforzarse) to strive; **trabajo** nm work; (tarea) task; (POL) labour; (fig) effort; **tomarse el trabajo de** to take the trouble to; **trabajo por turno/a destajo** shift work/ piecework; **trabajoso, a** a hard.

trabalenguas [traβa'lenwas] nm inv tongue twister.

trabar [tra'βar] vt (juntar) to join, unite; (atar) to tie down, fetter; (agarrar) to seize; (amistad) to strike up; ~**se** vr to become entangled; **trabársele a uno la lengua** to be tongue-tied.

tracción [trak'θjon] nf traction; ~ **delantera/trasera** front-wheel/rear-wheel drive.

tractor [trak'tor] nm tractor.

tradición [traði'θjon] nf tradition; **tradicional** a traditional.

traducción [traðuk'θjon] nf translation.

traducir [traðu'θir] vt to translate; **traductor, a** nm/f translator.

traer [tra'er] vt to bring; (llevar) to carry; (ropa) to wear; (incluir) to carry; (fig) to cause; ~**se** vr: ~**se algo** to be up to sth.

traficar [trafi'kar] vi to trade.

tráfico ['trafiko] nm (COM) trade; (AUTO) traffic.

tragaluz [traɣa'luθ] nm skylight.

tragaperras [traɣa'perras] nm o f inv slot machine.

tragar [tra'ɣar] vt to swallow; (devorar) to devour, bolt down; ~**se** vr to swallow.

tragedia [tra'xeðja] *nf* tragedy; **trágico, a** *a* tragic.

trago ['trayo] *nm* (*líquido*) drink; (*bocado*) gulp; (*fam: de bebida*) swig; (*desgracia*) blow.

traición [trai'θjon] *nf* treachery; (*JUR*) treason; (*una* ~) act of treachery; **traicionar** *vt* to betray.

traicionero, a [traiθjo'nero, a] *a* treacherous.

traidor, a [trai'ðor, a] *a* treacherous // *nm/f* traitor.

traigo *etc vb ver* **traer.**

traje *vb ver* **traer** // ['traxe] *nm* (*de hombre*) suit; (*de mujer*) dress; (*vestido típico*) costume; ~ **de baño** swimsuit; ~ **de luces** bullfighter's costume.

trajera *etc vb ver* **traer.**

trajín [tra'xin] *nm* haulage; (*fam: movimiento*) bustle; **trajinar** *vi* (*llevar*) to carry, transport // *vi* (*moverse*) to bustle about; (*viajar*) to travel around.

trama ['trama] *nf* (*intriga*) plot; (*de tejido*) weft (*Brit*), woof (*US*); **tramar** *vt* to plot; (*TEC*) to weave.

tramitar [trami'tar] *vt* (*asunto*) to transact; (*negociar*) to negotiate; (*manejar*) to handle.

trámite ['tramite] *nm* (*paso*) step; (*JUR*) transaction; ~s *nmpl* (*burocracia*) procedure *sg*; (*JUR*) proceedings.

tramo ['tramo] *nm* (*de tierra*) plot; (*de escalera*) flight; (*de vía*) section.

tramoya [tra'moja] *nf* (*TEATRO*) piece of stage machinery; (*fig*) scheme; **tramoyista** *nm/f* scene shifter; (*fig*) trickster.

trampa ['trampa] *nf* trap; (*en el suelo*) trapdoor; (*engaño*) trick; (*fam*) fiddle; **trampear** *vt, vi* to cheat.

trampolín [trampo'lin] *nm* trampoline; (*de piscina etc*) diving board.

tramposo, a [tram'poso, a] *a* crooked, cheating // *nm/f* crook, cheat.

tranca ['tranka] *nf* (*palo*) stick; (*de puerta, ventana*) bar; **trancar** *vt* to bar.

trance ['tranθe] *nm* (*momento difícil*) difficult moment *o* juncture; (*estado hipnotizado*) trance.

tranco ['tranko] *nm* stride.

tranquilidad [trankili'ðað] *nf* (*calma*) calmness, stillness; (*paz*) peacefulness.

tranquilizar [trankili'θar] *vt* (*calmar*) to calm (down); (*asegurar*) to reassure; ~**se** *vr* to calm down; **tranquilo, a** *a* (*calmado*) calm; (*apacible*) peaceful; (*mar*) calm; (*mente*) untroubled.

transacción [transak'θjon] *nf* transaction.

transbordador [transβorða'ðor] *nm* ferry.

transbordar [transβor'ðar] *vt* to transfer; **transbordo** *nm* transfer; **hacer transbordo** to change (trains).

transcurrir [transku'rrir] *vi* (*tiempo*) to pass; (*hecho*) to turn out.

transcurso [trans'kurso] *nm*: ~ **del tiempo** lapse (of time).

transeúnte [transe'unte] *a* transient // *nm/f* passer-by.

transferencia [transfe'renθja] *nf* transference; (*COM*) transfer.

transferir [transfe'rir] *vt* to transfer.

transformador [transforma'ðor] *nm* (*ELEC*) transformer.

transformar [transfor'mar] *vt* to transform; (*convertir*) to convert.

tránsfuga ['transfuya] *nm/f* (*MIL*) deserter; (*POL*) turncoat.

transfusión [transfu'sjon] *nf* transfusion.

transición [transi'θjon] *nf* transition.

transido, a [tran'siðo, a] *a* overcome.

transigir [transi'xir] *vi* to compromise, make concessions.

transistor [transis'tor] *nm* transistor.

transitar [transi'tar] *vi* to go (from place to place); **tránsito** *nm* transit; (*AUTO*) traffic; **transitorio, a** *a* transitory.

transmisión [transmi'sjon] nf (TEC) transmission; (transferencia) transfer; **~ en directo/exterior** live/outside broadcast.

transmitir [transmi'tir] vt to transmit; (RADIO, TV) to broadcast.

transparencia [transpa'renθja] nf transparency; (claridad) clearness, clarity; (foto) slide.

transparentar [transparen'tar] vt to reveal // vi to be transparent; **transparente** a transparent; (claro) clear; (ligero) diaphanous.

transpirar [transpi'rar] vi to perspire, (fig) to transpire.

transponer [transpo'ner] vt to transpose; (cambiar de sitio) to change the place of.

transportar [transpor'tar] vt to transport; (llevar) to carry; **transporte** nm transport; (COM) haulage.

transversal [transßer'sal] a transverse, cross.

tranvía [tram'bia] nm tram.

trapecio [tra'peθjo] nm trapeze; **trapecista** nmf trapeze artist.

trapero, a [tra'pero, a] nm/f ragman.

trapicheo [trapi'tʃeo] nm (fam) scheme, fiddle.

trapo ['trapo] nm (tela) rag; (de cocina) cloth.

tráquea ['trakea] nf windpipe.

traqueteo [trake'teo] nm (golpeteo) rattling.

tras [tras] prep (detrás de) behind; (después) after; **~ besides.

trascendencia [trasθen'denθja] nf (importancia) importance; (FILOSOFÍA) transcendence.

trascendental [trasθenden'tal] a important; (FILOSOFÍA) transcendental.

trascender [trasθen'der] vi (noticias) to come out; (suceso) to have a wide effect.

trasegar [trase'var] vt (moverse) to move about; (vino) to decant.

trasero, a [tra'sero, a] a back, rear

// nm (ANAT) bottom.

trasfondo [tras'fondo] nm background.

trasgredir [trasvre'ðir] vt to contravene.

trashumante [trasu'mante] a (animales) migrating.

trasladar [trasla'ðar] vt to move; (persona) to transfer; (postergar) to postpone; (copiar) to copy; **~se vr** (mudarse) to move; **traslado** nm move; (mudanza) move, removal.

traslucir [traslu'θir] vt to show; **~se vr** to be translucent; (fig) to be revealed.

trasluz [tras'luθ] nm reflected light; **al ~** against o up to the light.

trasnochar [trasno'tʃar] vi (acostarse tarde) to stay up late; (no dormir) to have a sleepless night.

traspasar [traspa'sar] vt (bala etc) to pierce, go through; (propiedad) to sell, transfer; (calle) to cross over; (límites) to go beyond; (ley) to break; **traspaso** nm (venta) transfer, sale.

traspié [tras'pje] nm (tropezón) trip; (fig) blunder.

trasplantar [trasplan'tar] vt to transplant.

traste ['traste] nm (MUS) fret; **dar al ~ con algo** to ruin sth.

trastienda [tras'tjenda] nf backshop.

trasto ['trasto] nm (pey: cosa) piece of junk; (: persona) dead loss.

trastornado, a [trastor'naðo, a] a (loco) mad, crazy.

trastornar [trastor'nar] vt to overturn, upset; (fig: ideas) to confuse; (: nervios) to shatter; (: persona) to drive crazy; **~se vr** (volverse loco) to go mad o crazy; **trastorno** nm (acto) overturning; (confusión) confusion.

tratable [tra'taßle] a friendly.

tratado [tra'taðo] nm (POL) treaty; (COM) agreement.

tratamiento [trata'mjento] nm treatment.

tratar [tra'tar] vt (ocuparse de) to

treat; (*manejar*, *TEC*) to handle; (*MED*) to treat; (*dirigirse a*: *persona*) to address // *vi*: ~ de (*hablar sobre*) to deal with, be about; (*intentar*) to try to; ~ con (*COM*) to trade in; (*negociar*) to negotiate with; (*tener contactos*) to have dealings with; ~se *vr* to treat each other; ¿de qué se trata? what's it about?; **trato** *nm* dealings *pl*; (*relaciones*) relationship; (*comportamiento*) manner; (*COM*) agreement; (*título*) (form of) address.

trauma ['trauma] *nm* trauma.

través [tra'βes] *nm* (*fig*) reverse; al ~ ad across, crossways; a ~ de *prep* across; (*sobre*) over; (*por*) through.

travesaño [traβe'saɲo] *nm* (*ARQ*) crossbeam; (*DEPORTE*) crossbar.

travesía [traβe'sia] *nf* (*calle*) cross-street; (*NAUT*) crossing.

travesura [traβe'sura] *nf* (*broma*) prank; (*ingenio*) wit; **travieso, a** *a* (*niño*) naughty // *nf* (*ARQ*) crossbeam.

trayecto [tra'jekto] *nm* (*ruta*) road, way; (*viaje*) journey; (*tramo*) stretch; (*curso*) course; ~ria *nf* trajectory; (*fig*) path.

traza ['traθa] *nf* (*aspecto*) looks *pl*; (*señal*) sign; ~**do, a** *a*: **bien** ~**do** shapely, well-formed // *nm* (*ARQ*) plan, design; (*fig*) outline.

trazar [tra'θar] *vt* (*ARQ*) to plan; (*ARTE*) to sketch; (*fig*) to trace; (*plan*) to follow; **trazo** *nm* (*línea*) line; (*bosquejo*) sketch.

trébol ['treβol] *nm* (*BOT*) clover.

trece ['treθe] *num* thirteen.

trecho ['tretʃo] *nm* (*distancia*) distance; (*de tiempo*) while; (*fam*) piece; **de** ~ **en** ~ at intervals.

tregua ['trexwa] *nf* (*MIL*) truce; (*fig*) lull.

treinta ['treinta] *num* thirty.

tremendo, a [tre'mendo, a] *a* (*terrible*) terrible; (*imponente: cosa*) imposing; (*fam*: *fabuloso*) tremendous.

trémulo, a ['tremulo] *a* quivering.

tren [tren] *nm* train; ~ **de aterrizaje** undercarriage.

trenza ['trenθa] *nf* (*de pelo*) plait (*Brit*), braid (*US*); **trenzar** *vt* (*el pelo*) to plait; **trenzarse** *vr* (*AM*) to become involved with.

trepadora [trepa'ðora] *nf* (*BOT*) climber.

trepar [tre'par] *vt*, *vi* to climb.

trepidar [trepi'ðar] *vi* to shake, vibrate.

tres [tres] *num* three.

tresillo [tre'siʎo] *nm* three-piece suite; (*MUS*) triplet.

treta ['treta] *nf* (*COM etc*) gimmick; (*fig*) trick.

triángulo ['trjangulo] *nm* triangle.

tribu ['triβu] *nf* tribe.

tribuna [tri'βuna] *nf* (*plataforma*) platform; (*DEPORTE*) (grand)stand; (*fig*) public speaking.

tribunal [triβu'nal] *nm* (*JUR*) court; (*comisión*, *fig*) tribunal.

tributar [triβu'tar] *vt* (*gen*) to pay; **tributo** *nm* (*COM*) tax.

tricotar [triko'tar] *vi* to knit.

trigal [tri'val] *nm* wheat field.

trigo ['trivo] *nm* wheat.

trigueño, a [tri'veɲo, a] *a* (*pelo*) corn-coloured; (*piel*) olive-skinned.

trillado, a [tri'ʎaðo, a] *a* (*camino*) beaten; (*fig*) trite, hackneyed; **trilladora** *nf* threshing machine.

trillar [tri'ʎar] *vt* (*AGR*) to thresh.

trimestral [trimes'tral] *a* quarterly; (*ESCOL*) termly.

trimestre [tri'mestre] *nm* (*ESCOL*) term.

trinar [tri'nar] *vi* (*pájaros*) to sing; (*rabiar*) to fume, be angry.

trincar [trin'kar] *vt* (*atar*) to tie up; (*inmovilizar*) to pinion.

trinchar [trin'tʃar] *vt* to carve.

trinchera [trin'tʃera] *nf* (*fosa*) trench.

trineo [tri'neo] *nm* sledge.

trinidad [trini'ðað] *nf* trio; (*REL*): **la T~** the Trinity.

trino ['trino] *nm* trill.

tripa ['tripa] *nf* (*ANAT*) intestine; (*fam*: *tb*: ~s) insides *pl*.

triple ['triple] *a* triple.

triplicado, a [tripli'kaðo, a] *a*: **por ~** in triplicate.

tripulación [tripula'θjon] *nf* crew.

tripulante [tripu'lante] *nm/f* crewman/woman.

tripular [tripu'lar] *vt* (*barco*) to man; (*AUTO*) to drive.

triquiñuela [triki'nwela] *nf* trick.

tris [tris] *nm inv* crack; **en un ~** in an instant.

triste ['triste] *a* (*afligido*) sad; (*sombrío*) melancholy, gloomy; (*lamentable*) sorry, miserable; **~za** *nf* (*aflicción*) sadness; (*melancolía*) melancholy.

triturar [tritu'rar] *vt* (*moler*) to grind; (*mascar*) to chew.

triunfar [trjun'far] *vi* (*tener éxito*) to triumph; (*ganar*) to win; **triunfo** *nm* triumph.

trivial [tri'βjal] *a* trivial; **~izar** *vt* to minimize, play down.

triza ['triθa] *nf*: **hacer ~s** to smash to bits; (*papel*) to tear to shreds.

trizar [tri'θar] *vt* to smash to bits; (*papel*) to tear to shreds.

trocar [tro'kar] *vt* to exchange.

trocha ['trotʃa] *nf* short cut.

troche ['trotʃe]: **a ~ y moche** *ad* helter-skelter, pell-mell.

trofeo [tro'feo] *nm* (*premio*) trophy; (*éxito*) success.

tromba ['tromba] *nf* whirlwind.

trombón [trom'bon] *nm* trombone.

trombosis [trom'bosis] *nf inv* thrombosis.

trompa ['trompa] *nf* horn; (*trompo*) humming top; (*hocico*) snout; (*fam*): **cogerse una ~** to get tight.

trompeta [trom'peta] *nf* trumpet; (*clarín*) bugle.

trompo ['trompo] *nm* spinning top.

trompón [trom'pon] *nm* bump.

tronar [tro'nar] *vt* (*AM*) to shoot // *vi* to thunder; (*fig*) to rage.

tronco ['tronko] *nm* (*de árbol*, *ANAT*) trunk.

tronchar [tron'tʃar] *vt* (*árbol*) to chop down; (*fig*: *vida*) to cut short; (: *esperanza*) to shatter; (*persona*) to tire out; **~se** *vr* to fall down.

tronera [tro'nera] *nf* (*MIL*) loophole; (*ARQ*) small window.

trono ['trono] *nm* throne.

tropa ['tropa] *nf* (*MIL*) troop; (*soldados*) soldiers *pl*.

tropel [tro'pel] *nm* (*muchedumbre*) crowd.

tropelía [trope'lia] *nm* outrage.

tropezar [trope'θar] *vi* to trip, stumble; (*fig*) to slip up; **~ con** to run into; (*topar con*) to bump into; **tropezón** *nm* trip; (*fig*) blunder.

tropical [tropi'kal] *a* tropical.

trópico ['tropiko] *nm* tropic.

tropiezo *vb ver* **tropezar** // [tro'pjeθo] *nm* (*error*) slip, blunder; (*desgracia*) misfortune; (*obstáculo*) snag.

trotamundos [trota'mundos] *nm inv* globetrotter.

trotar [tro'tar] *vi* to trot; **trote** *nm* trot; (*fam*) travelling; **de mucho trote** hard-wearing.

trozo ['troθo] *nm* bit, piece.

truco ['truko] *nm* (*habilidad*) knack; (*engaño*) trick.

trucha ['trutʃa] *nf* trout.

trueno ['trweno] *nm* thunder; (*estampido*) bang.

trueque *etc vb ver* **trocar** // ['trweke] *nm* exchange; (*COM*) barter.

trufa ['trufa] *nf* (*BOT*) truffle.

truhán, ana [tru'an, ana] *nm/f* rogue.

truncar [trun'kar] *vt* (*cortar*) to truncate; (*fig*: *la vida etc*) to cut short; (: *el desarrollo*) to stunt.

tu [tu] *a* your.

tú [tu] *pron* you.

tubérculo [tu'βerkulo] *nm* (*BOT*) tuber.

tuberculosis [tußerku'losis] *nf inv* tuberculosis.

tubería [tuße'ria] *nf* pipes *pl*; (*con-*

ducto) pipeline.

tubo ['tuβo] _nm_ tube, pipe; ~ **de ensayo** test tube; ~ **de escape** exhaust (pipe).

tuerca ['twerka] _nf_ nut.

tuerto, a ['twerto, a] _a_ blind in one eye // _nm/f_ one-eyed person.

tuerza _etc vb ver_ **torcer.**

tuétano ['twetano] _nm_ marrow; _(BOT)_ pith.

tufo ['tufo] _nm_ vapour; _(fig: pey)_ stench.

tugurio [tu'ɣurjo] _nm_ slum.

tul [tul] _nm_ tulle.

tulipán [tuli'pan] _nm_ tulip.

tullido, a [tu'ʎiðo, a] _a_ crippled.

tumba ['tumba] _nf (sepultura)_ tomb.

tumbar [tum'bar] _vt_ to knock down; ~**se** _vr (echarse)_ to lie down; _(extenderse)_ to stretch out.

tumbo ['tumbo] _nm (caída)_ fall; _(de vehículo)_ jolt.

tumbona [tum'bona] _nf (butaca)_ easy chair; _(de playa)_ deckchair _(Brit),_ beach chair _(US)._

tumido, a [tu'miðo, a] _a_ swollen.

tumor [tu'mor] _nm_ tumour.

tumulto [tu'multo] _nm_ turmoil.

tuna ['tuna] _nf ver_ **tuno.**

tunante [tu'nante] _a_ rascally.

tunda ['tunda] _nf (golpeo)_ beating.

túnel ['tunel] _nm_ tunnel.

Túnez ['tuneθ] _nm_ Tunisia; _(ciudad)_ Tunis.

tuno, a ['tuno, a] _nm/f (fam)_ rogue // _nm_ member of student music group // _nf (BOT)_ prickly pear; _(MUS)_ student music group.

tuntún [tun'tun]: **al** ~ _ad_ thoughtlessly.

tupido, a [tu'piðo, a] _a (denso)_ dense; _(tela)_ close-woven; _(fig)_ dim.

turba ['turβa] _nf_ crowd.

turbación [turβa'θjon] _nf (molestia)_ disturbance; _(preocupación)_ worry; **turbado, a** _a (molesto)_ disturbed; _(preocupado)_ worried.

turbar [tur'βar] _vt (molestar)_ to disturb; _(incomodar)_ to upset; ~**se** _vr_ to be disturbed.

turbina [tur'βina] _nf_ turbine.

turbio, a ['turβjo, a] _a_ cloudy; _(tema etc)_ confused // _ad_ indistinctly.

turbulencia [turβu'lenθja] _nf_ turbulence; _(fig)_ restlessness; **turbulento, a** _a_ turbulent; _(fig: intranquilo)_ restless; _(: ruidoso)_ noisy.

turco, a ['turko, a] _a_ Turkish // _nm/f_ Turk.

turismo [tu'rismo] _nm_ tourism; _(coche)_ saloon car; **turista** _nm/f_ tourist; **turístico, a** _a_ tourist _cpd._

turnar [tur'nar] _vi,_ **turnarse** _vr_ to take (it in) turns; **turno** _nm (IN-DUSTRIA)_ shift; _(oportunidad, orden de prioridad)_ opportunity; _(juegos etc)_ turn.

turquesa [tur'kesa] _nf_ turquoise.

Turquía [tur'kia] _nf_ Turkey.

turrón [tu'rron] _nm (dulce)_ nougat.

tutear [tute'ar] _vt_ to address as familiar 'tú'; ~**se** _vr_ to be on familiar terms.

tutela [tu'tela] _nf (legal)_ guardianship; _(instrucción)_ guidance; **tutelar** _a_ tutelary // _vt_ to protect.

tutor, a [tu'tor, a] _nm/f (legal)_ guardian; _(ESCOL)_ tutor.

tuve, tuviera _etc vb ver_ **tener.**

tuyo, a ['tujo, a] _a_ yours, of yours // _pron_ yours; **los** ~**s** _(fam)_ your relations, your family.

TV ['te'βe] _nf abr (= televisión)_ TV.

TVE _nf abr = Televisión Española._

U

u [u] _conj_ or.

ubicar [uβi'kar] _vt_ to place, situate; _(: fig)_ to install in a post; _(AM: encontrar)_ to find; ~**se** _vr_ to be, be located.

ubre ['uβre] _nf_ udder.

UCD _nf abr = Unión del Centro Democrático._

Ud(s) _abr =_ **usted(es).**

ufanarse [ufa'narse] _vr_ to boast; ~ **de** to pride o.s. on; **ufano, a** _a (arrogante)_ arrogant; _(presumido)_ conceited.

UGT *nf abr* = *Unión General de Trabajadores.*

ujier [u'xjer] *nm* usher; (*portero*) doorkeeper.

úlcera [u'ulθera] *nf* ulcer.

ulcerar [ulθe'rar] *vt* to make sore; **~se** *vr* to ulcerate.

ulterior [ulte'rjor] *a* (*más allá*) farther, further; (*subsecuente, siguiente*) subsequent.

últimamente ['ultimamente] *ad* (*recientemente*) lately, recently.

ultimar [ulti'mar] *vt* to finish; (*finalizar*) to finalize; (*AM: rematar*) to finish off.

último, a ['ultimo, a] *a* last; (*más reciente*) latest, most recent; (*más bajo*) bottom; (*más alto*) top; (*fig*) final, extreme; **en las últimas** on one's last legs; **por ~** finally.

ultra ['ultra] *a* ultra // *nm/f* extreme right-winger.

ultrajar [ultra'xar] *vt* (*escandalizar*) to outrage; (*insultar*) to insult, abuse; **ultraje** *nm* outrage; insult.

ultramar [ultra'mar] *nm*: **de o en ~** abroad, overseas.

ultramarinos [ultrama'rinos] *nmpl* groceries; **tienda de ~** grocer's (shop).

ultranza [ul'tranθa]: **a ~** *ad* (*a todo trance*) at all costs; (*completo*) outright.

ultrasónico, a [ultra'soniko, a] *a* ultrasonic.

ultratumba [ultra'tumba] *nf*: **la vida de ~** the next life.

ulular [ulu'lar] *vi* to howl; (*búho*) to hoot.

umbral [um'bral] *nm* (*gen*) threshold.

umbroso, a [um'broso, a], **umbrío, a** [um'brio, a] *a* shady.

PALABRA CLAVE
---

un, una [un, 'una] ♦ *artículo definido* a; (*antes de vocal*) an; **una mujer/naranja** a woman/an orange

♦ *a*: **unos** (*o* **unas**): **hay unos**

regalos para ti there are some presents for you; **hay unas cervezas en la nevera** there are some beers in the fridge.

unánime [u'nanime] *a* unanimous; **unanimidad** *nf* unanimity.

unción [un'θjon] *nf* anointing; **extrema~** extreme unction.

undécimo, a [un'deθimo, a] *a* eleventh.

ungir [un'xir] *vt* to rub with ointment; (*REL*) to anoint.

ungüento [un'gwento] *nm* ointment; (*fig*) salve, balm.

únicamente ['unikamente] *ad* solely, only.

único, a ['uniko, a] *a* only, sole; (*sin par*) unique.

unidad [uni'ðað] *nf* unity; (*COM, TEC etc*) unit.

unido, a [u'niðo, a] *a* joined, linked; (*fig*) united.

unificar [unifi'kar] *vt* to unite, unify.

uniformar [unifor'mar] *vt* to make uniform, level up; (*persona*) to put into uniform.

uniforme [uni'forme] *a* uniform, equal; (*superficie*) even // *nm* uniform; **uniformidad** *nf* uniformity; (*llaneza*) levelness, evenness.

unilateral [unilate'ral] *a* unilateral.

unión [u'njon] *nf* union; (*acto*) uniting, joining; (*calidad*) unity; (*TEC*) joint; (*fig*) closeness, togetherness; **la U~ Soviética** the Soviet Union.

unir [u'nir] *vt* (*juntar*) to join, unite; (*atar*) to tie, fasten; (*combinar*) to combine; **~se** *vr* to join together, unite; (*empresas*) to merge.

unísono [u'nisono] *nm*: **al ~** in unison.

universal [uniβer'sal] *a* universal; (*mundial*) world *cpd*.

universidad [uniβersi'ðað] *nf* university.

universitario, a [uniβersi'tarjo, a] *a* university *cpd* // *nm/f* (*profesor*) lecturer; (*estudiante*) (university) student; (*graduado*) graduate.

universo [uni'ßerso] *nm* universe.

PALABRA CLAVE

uno, a ['uno, a] ◆ *a* one; **es todo** ~ it's all one and the same; **~s pocos** a few; **~s cien** about a hundred
◆ *pron* 1 one; **quiero** ~ **solo** I only want one; ~ **de ellos** one of them 2 *(alguien)* somebody, someone; **conozco a** ~ **que se te parece** I know somebody o someone who looks like you; ~ **mismo** oneself; ~s **querían quedarse** some (people) wanted to stay
3: **(los)** ~s ... **(los) otros** ... some ... others; each other, one another; **una y otra son muy agradables** they're both very nice
◆ *nf* one; **es la una** it's one o'clock
◆ *nm* (number) one.

untar [un'tar] *vt* to rub; *(engrasar)* to grease, oil; *(fig)* to bribe.

uña ['uɲa] *nf* (ANAT) nail; *(garra)* claw; *(casco)* hoof; *(arrancaclavos)* claw.

uranio [u'ranjo] *nm* uranium.

urbanidad [urßani'ðað] *nf* courtesy, politeness.

urbanismo [urßa'nismo] *nm* town planning.

urbanización [urßaniθa'θjon] *nf* *(barrio, colonia)* housing estate.

urbano, a [ur'ßano, a] *a* *(de ciudad)* urban; *(cortés)* courteous, polite.

urbe [ur'ße] *nf* large city.

urdimbre [ur'ðimbre] *nf* *(de tejido)* warp; *(intriga)* intrigue.

urdir [ur'ðir] *vt* to warp; *(fig)* to plot, contrive.

urgencia [ur'xenθja] *nf* urgency; *(prisa)* haste, rush; *(emergencia)* emergency; **servicios de** ~ emergency services; **urgente** *a* urgent.

urgir [ur'xir] *vi* to be urgent; **me urge** I'm in a hurry for it.

urinario, a [uri'narjo, a] *a* urinary // *nm* urinal.

urna ['urna] *nf* urn; *(POL)* ballot box.

urraca [u'rraka] *nf* magpie.

URSS *nf:* **la** ~ **the USSR**.

Uruguay [uru'ɣwai] *nm:* **el** ~ **Uruguay; uruguayo, a** *a, nm/f* Uruguayan.

usado, a [u'saðo, a] *a* used; *(ropa etc)* worn.

usanza [u'sanθa] *nf* custom, usage.

usar [u'sar] *vt* to use; *(ropa)* to wear; *(tener costumbre)* to be in the habit of; ~**se** *vr* to be used; **uso** *nm* use; wear; *(costumbre)* custom, usage; *(moda)* fashion; **al uso** in keeping with custom; **al uso de** in the style of.

usted [us'teð] *pron* *(sg)* you *sg*; *(pl)* ~s you *pl*.

usual [u'swal] *a* usual.

usuario, a [usu'arjo, a] *nm/f* user.

usufructo [usu'frukto] *nm* use.

usura [u'sura] *nf* usury; **usurero, a** *nm/f* usurer.

usurpar [usur'par] *vt* to usurp.

utensilio [uten'siljo] *nm* tool; *(CULIN)* utensil.

útero ['utero] *nm* uterus, womb.

útil ['util] *a* useful // *nm* tool; **utilidad** *nf* usefulness; *(COM)* profit; **utilizar** *vt* to use, utilize.

utopía [uto'pia] *nf* Utopia; **utópico, a** *a* Utopian.

uva ['ußa] *nf* grape.

V

v *abr* = **(voltio)** V.

va *vb ver* **ir**.

vaca ['baka] *nf* *(animal)* cow; **carne de** ~ beef.

vacaciones [baka'θjones] *nfpl* holidays.

vacante [ba'kante] *a* vacant, empty // *nf* vacancy.

vaciar [ba'θjar] *vt* to empty out; *(ahuecar)* to hollow out; *(moldear)* to cast // *vi* *(río)* to flow *(en* into*);* ~**se** *vr* to empty.

vaciedad [baθje'ðað] *nf* emptiness.

vacilación [baθila'θjon] *nf* hesitation.

vacilante [baθi'lante] *a* unsteady; *(habla)* faltering; *(fig)* hesitant.

vacilar [baθi'lar] *vi* to be unsteady; *(al hablar)* to falter; *(fig)* to hesitate, waver; *(memoria)* to fail.

vacío, a [ba'θio, a] *a* empty; *(puesto)* vacant; *(desocupado)* idle; *(vano)* vain // *nm* emptiness; *(FÍSICA)* vacuum; *(un ~)* (empty) space.

vacuna [ba'kuna] *nf* vaccine; **vacunar** *vt* to vaccinate.

vacuno, a [ba'kuno, a] *a* cow *cpd*; **ganado ~** cattle.

vacuo, a [ba'kwo, a] *a* empty.

vadear [baðe'ar] *vt* (*río*) to ford; **vado** *nm* ford.

vagabundo, a [baɣa'ßundo, a] *a* wandering; *(pey)* vagrant // *nm* tramp.

vagamente [baɣa'mente] *ad* vaguely.

vagancia [ba'ɣanθja] *nf* vagrancy.

vagar [ba'ɣar] *vi* to wander; *(no hacer nada)* to idle.

vagina [ba'xina] *nf* vagina.

vago, a [ba'ɣo, a] *a* vague; *(perezoso)* lazy; *(ambulante)* wandering // *nm/f* (*vagabundo*) tramp; *(flojo)* lazybones *sg*, idler.

vagón [ba'ɣon] *nm* (*FERRO: de pasajeros*) carriage; (: *de mercancías*) wagon.

vaguedad [baɣe'ðað] *nf* vagueness.

vaho ['bao] *nm* (*vapor*) vapour, steam; *(respiración)* breath.

vaina ['baina] *nf* sheath.

vainilla [bai'niʎa] *nf* vanilla.

vainita [bai'nita] *nf* (*AM*) green o French bean.

vais *vb ver* **ir**.

vaivén [bai'ßen] *nm* to-and-fro movement; *(de tránsito)* coming and going; **vaivenes** *nmpl* (*fig*) ups and downs.

vajilla [ba'xiʎa] *nf* crockery, dishes *pl*; **lavar la ~** to do the washing-up *(Brit)*, wash the dishes *(US)*.

valdré *etc vb ver* **valer**.

vale ['bale] *nm* voucher; *(recibo)* receipt; *(pagaré)* IOU.

valedero, a [bale'ðero, a] *a* valid.

valenciano, a [balen'θjano, a] *a* Valencian.

valentía [balen'tia] *nf* courage, bravery; *(acción)* heroic deed; **valentón, ona** *a* blustering.

valer [ba'ler] *vi* to be worth; *(costar)* to cost; *(ser útil)* to be useful; *(ser válido)* to be valid; **~se** *vr* to defend o.s.; **~se de** to make use of, take advantage of; **~ la pena** to be worthwhile; **¿vale?** *(Esp)* OK?

valeroso, a [bale'roso, a] *a* brave, valiant.

valgo *etc vb ver* **valer**.

valía [ba'lia] *nf* worth, value.

validar [bali'ðar] *vt* to validate; **validez** *nf* validity; **válido, a** *a* valid.

valiente [ba'ljente] *a* brave, valiant // *nm* hero.

valija [ba'lixa] *nf* suitcase; **~ diplomática** diplomatic bag.

valioso, a [ba'ljoso, a] *a* valuable; *(rico)* wealthy.

valor [ba'lor] *nm* value, worth; *(precio)* price; *(valentía)* valour, courage; *(importancia)* importance; **~es** *nmpl* (*COM*) securities; **~ación** *nf* valuation; **~ar** *vt* to value.

vals [bals] *nm* inv waltz.

válvula ['balßula] *nf* valve.

valla ['baʎa] *nf* fence; *(DEPORTE)* hurdle; *(fig)* barrier; **vallar** *vt* to fence in.

valle ['baʎe] *nm* valley.

vamos *vb ver* **ir**.

vampiro, resa [bam'piro, 'resa] *nm/f* vampire.

van *vb ver* **ir**.

vanagloriarse [banaɣlo'rjarse] *vr* to boast.

vándalo, a ['bandalo, a] *nm/f* vandal; **vandalismo** *nm* vandalism.

vanguardia [ban'gwarðja] *nf* vanguard; *(ARTE)* avant-garde.

vanidad [bani'ðað] *nf* vanity; **vanidoso, a** *a* vain, conceited.

vano, a ['bano, a] a (*irreal*) unreal, vain; (*inútil*) useless; (*persona*) vain, conceited; (*frívolo*) frivolous.

vapor [ba'por] nm vapour; (*vaho*) steam; **al ~** (CULIN) steamed; **~izador** nm atomizer; **~izar** vt to vaporize; **~oso, a** a vaporous.

vaquero, a [ba'kero, a] a (*ganado*) a cattle cpd // nm cowboy; **~s** nmpl jeans.

vara ['bara] nf (*palo*) (TEC) rod; **~ mágica** magic wand.

variable [ba'rjaβle] a, nf variable.

variación [barja'θjon] nf variation.

variar [bar'jar] vt to vary; (*modificar*) to modify; (*cambiar de posición*) to switch around // vi to vary.

varices [ba'riθes] nfpl varicose veins.

variedad [barje'ðað] nf variety.

varilla [ba'riʎa] nf (*palo*) stick; (TEC) rod; (*de rueda*) spoke.

vario, a ['barjo, a] a varied; **~s** various, several.

varón [ba'ron] nm male, man; **varonil** a manly, virile.

Varsovia [bar'soβja] n Warsaw.

vas vb ver **ir**.

vasco, a ['basko, a] a, nm/f Basque.

vascongado, a [baskon'gaðo, a], **vascuence** [bas'kwenθe] a Basque; **las Vascongadas** the Basque Country.

vaselina [base'lina] nf Vaseline ®.

vasija [ba'sixa] nf container, vessel.

vaso ['baso] nm glass, tumbler; (ANAT) vessel.

vástago ['bastaɣo] nm (BOT) shoot; (TEC) rod; (*fig*) offspring.

vasto, a ['basto, a] a vast, huge.

Vaticano [bati'kano] nm: **el ~** the Vatican.

vaticinio [bati'θinjo] nm prophecy.

vatio ['batjo] nm (ELEC) watt.

vaya etc vb ver **ir**.

Vd(s) abr = **usted(es)**.

ve vb ver **ver**, **ir**.

vecindad [beθin'dað] nf, **vecindario** [beθin'darjo] nm neighbourhood; (*habitantes*) residents pl.

vecino, a [be'θino, a] a neighbouring

// nm/f neighbour; (*residente*) resident.

veda ['beða] nf prohibition.

vedado [be'ðaðo] nm preserve.

vedar [be'ðar] vt (*prohibir*) to ban, prohibit; (*impedir*) to stop, prevent.

vegetación [bexeta'θjon] nf vegetation.

vegetariano, a [bexeta'rjano, a] a, nm/f vegetarian.

vegetal [bexe'tal] a, nm vegetable.

vehemencia [be(e)'menθja] nf (*insistencia*) vehemence; (*pasión*) passion; (*fervor*) fervour; (*violencia*) violence; **vehemente** a vehement; passionate; fervent.

vehículo [be'ikulo] nm vehicle; (MED) carrier.

veía etc vb ver **ver**.

veinte ['beinte] num twenty.

vejación [bexa'θjon] nf vexation; (*humillación*) humiliation.

vejar [be'xar] vt (*irritar*) to annoy, vex; (*humillar*) to humiliate.

vejez [be'xeθ] nf old age.

vejiga [be'xiɣa] nf (ANAT) bladder.

vela ['bela] nf (*de cera*) candle; (NAUT) sail; (*insomnio*) sleeplessness; (*vigilia*) vigil; (MIL) sentry duty; **estar a dos ~s** (*fam*) to be skint.

velado, a [be'laðo, a] a veiled; (*sonido*) muffled; (FOTO) blurred // nf soirée.

velador [bela'ðor] nm (*mesa*) pedestal table; (AM) lampshade.

velar [be'lar] vt (*vigilar*) to keep watch over // vi to stay awake; **~ por** to watch over, look after.

veleidad [belei'ðað] nf (*ligereza*) fickleness; (*capricho*) whim.

velero [be'lero] nm (NAUT) sailing ship; (AVIAT) glider.

veleta [be'leta] nf weather vane.

veliz [be'lis] nm (AM) suitcase.

velo ['belo] nm veil.

velocidad [beloθi'ðað] nf speed; (TEC, AUTO) gear.

velocímetro [belo'θimetro] nm speedometer.

veloz [be'loθ] a fast.

vello ['beλo] nm down, fuzz; **vellón** nm fleece; **~so,** a a fuzzy; **velludo,** a a shaggy.

ven vb ver **venir.**

vena ['bena] nf vein.

venado [be'naðo] nm deer.

vencedor, a [benθe'ðor, a] a victorious // nm/f victor, winner.

vencer [ben'θer] vt (dominar) to defeat, beat; (derrotar) to vanquish; (superar, controlar) to overcome, master // vi (triunfar) to win (through), triumph; (plazo) to expire; **vencido, a** (derrotado) defeated, beaten; (COM) due // ad: **pagar vencido** to pay in arrears; **vencimiento** nm (COM) maturity.

venda ['benda] nf bandage; **~je** nm bandage, dressing; **vendar** vt to bandage; **vendar los ojos** to blindfold.

vendaval [benda'βal] nm (viento) gale.

vendedor, a [bende'ðor, a] nm/f seller.

vender [ben'der] vt to sell; **~ al contado/al por mayor/al por menor** to sell for cash/wholesale/retail.

vendimia [ben'dimja] nf grape harvest.

vendré etc vb ver **venir.**

veneno [be'neno] nm poison; (de serpiente) venom; **~so,** a a poisonous; venomous.

venerable [bene'raβle] a venerable; **venerar** vt (respetar) to revere; (adorar) to worship.

venéreo, a [be'nereo, a] a: **enfermedad venérea** venereal disease.

venezolano, a [beneθo'lano, a] a Venezuelan.

Venezuela [bene'θwela] nf Venezuela.

venganza [ben'ganθa] nf vengeance, revenge; **vengar** vt to avenge; **vengarse** vr to take revenge; **vengativo, a** a (persona) vindic-

tive.

vengo etc vb ver **venir.**

venia ['benja] nf (perdón) pardon; (permiso) consent.

venial [be'njal] a venial.

venida [be'niða] nf (llegada) arrival; (regreso) return.

venidero, a [beni'ðero, a] a coming, future.

venir [be'nir] vi to come; (llegar) to arrive; (ocurrir) to happen; (fig): **~ de** to stem from; **~ bien/mal** to be suitable/unsuitable; **el año que viene** next year; **~se abajo** to collapse.

venta ['benta] nf (COM) sale; **~ a plazos** hire purchase; **~ al contado/al por mayor/al por menor** o **al detalle** cash sale/wholesale/retail; **~ con derecho a retorno** sale or return; **'en ~'** 'for sale'.

ventaja [ben'taxa] nf advantage; **ventajoso, a** a advantageous.

ventana [ben'tana] nf window; **~ de guillotina/salediza** sash/bay window; **ventanilla** nf (de taquilla) window (of booking office etc).

ventilación [bentila'θjon] nf ventilation; (corriente) draught; **ventilar** vt to ventilate; (para secar) to put out to dry; (fig) to air, discuss.

ventisca [ben'tiska] nf, **ventisquero** [bentis'kero] nm blizzard; (nieve amontonada) snowdrift.

ventoso, a a (día) windy.

ventrílocuo, a [ben'trilokwo, a] nm/f ventriloquist.

ventura [ben'tura] nf (felicidad) happiness; (buena suerte) luck; (destino) fortune; **a la (buena) ~** at random; **venturoso, a** a happy; (afortunado) lucky, fortunate.

veo etc vb ver **ver.**

ver [ber] vt to see; (mirar) to look at, watch; (entender) to understand; (investigar) to look into; // vi to see; to understand; **~se** vr (encontrarse) to meet; (dejarse ~) to be seen; (hallarse: en un apuro) to find o.s., be // *nm* looks *pl*, appearance; **a ~** let's see; **dejarse ~** to become apparent; **no tener nada que ~ con** to have nothing to do with; **a mi modo de ~** as I see it.

vera ['bera] *nf* edge, verge; *(de río)* bank.

veracidad [beraθi'ðað] *nf* truthfulness.

veranear [berane'ar] *vi* to spend the summer; **veraneo** *nm* summer holiday; **veraniego, a** *a* summer *cpd*.

verano [be'rano] *nm* summer.

veras ['beras] *nfpl* truth *sg*; **de ~** really, truly.

veraz [be'raθ] *a* truthful.

verbal [ber'βal] *a* verbal.

verbena [ber'βena] *nf* *(fiesta)* fair; *(baile)* open-air dance.

verbo ['berβo] *nm* verb; **~so, a** *a* verbose.

verdad [ber'ðað] *nf* truth; *(fiabilidad)* reliability; **de ~** a real, proper; **a decir ~** to tell the truth; **~ero, a** *a (veraz)* true, truthful; *(fiable)* reliable; *(fig)* real.

verde ['berðe] *a* green; *(chiste)* blue, dirty // *nm* green; **viejo ~** dirty old man; **~ar, ~cer** *vi* to turn green; **verdor** *nm (lo ~)* greenness; *(BOT)* verdure.

verdugo [ber'ðuɣo] *nm* executioner.

verdulero, a [berðu'lero, a] *nm/f* greengrocer.

verduras [ber'ðuras] *nfpl* *(CULIN)* greens.

vereda [be'reða] *nf* path; *(AM)* pavement *(Brit)*, sidewalk *(US)*.

veredicto [bere'ðikto] *nm* verdict.

vergonzoso, a [berɣon'θoso, a] *a* shameful; *(tímido)* timid, bashful.

vergüenza [ber'ɣwenθa] *nf* shame, sense of shame; *(timidez)* bashfulness; *(pudor)* modesty; **me da ~** I'm ashamed.

verídico, a [be'riðiko, a] *a* true, truthful.

verificar [berifi'kar] *vt* to check; *(corroborar)* to verify; *(llevar a cabo)* to carry out; **~se** *vr* to occur,

happen.

verja ['berxa] *nf* grating.

vermut [ber'mut] *(pl* **~s)** *nm* vermouth.

verosímil [bero'simil] *a* likely, probable; *(relato)* credible.

verruga [be'rruɣa] *nf* wart.

versado, a [ber'saðo, a] *a*: **~ en** versed in.

versátil [ber'satil] *a* versatile.

versión [ber'sjon] *nf* version.

verso ['berso] *nm* verse; **un ~** a line of poetry.

vértebra ['berteβra] *nf* vertebra.

verter [ber'ter] *vt (líquido; adrede)* to empty, pour (out); (: *sin querer)* to spill; *(basura)* to dump // *vi* to flow.

vertical [berti'kal] *a* vertical.

vértice ['bertiθe] *nm* vertex, apex.

vertiente [ber'tjente] *nf* slope; *(fig)* aspect.

vertiginoso, a [bertixi'noso, a] *a* giddy, dizzy.

vértigo ['bertiɣo] *nm* vertigo; *(mareo)* dizziness.

vesícula [be'sikula] *nf* blister.

vespertino, a [besper'tino, a] *a* evening *cpd*.

vestíbulo [bes'tiβulo] *nm* hall; *(de teatro)* foyer.

vestido [bes'tiðo] *pp de* **vestir**; **~ de azul/marinero** dressed in blue/as a sailor // *nm (ropa)* clothes *pl*, clothing; *(de mujer)* dress, frock.

vestigio [bes'tixjo] *nm (huella)* trace; **~s** *nmpl* remains.

vestimenta [besti'menta] *nf* clothing.

vestir [bes'tir] *vt (poner: ropa)* to put on; *(llevar: ropa)* to wear; *(proveer de ropa a)* to clothe; *(suj: sastre)* to make clothes for // *vi* to dress; *(verse bien)* to look good; **~se** *vr* to get dressed, dress o.s.

vestuario [bes'twarjo] *nm* clothes *pl*, wardrobe; *(TEATRO: cuarto)* dressing room; *(DEPORTE)* changing room.

veta ['beta] *nf (vena)* vein, seam; *(en*

carne) streak; *(de madera)* grain.

vetar [be'tar] *vt* to veto.

veterano, a [bete'rano, a] *a, nm* veteran.

veterinario, a [beteri'narjo, a] *nm/f* vet(erinary surgeon) // *nf* veterinary science.

veto ['beto] *nm* veto.

vetusto, a [be'tusto, a] *a* ancient.

vez [beθ] *nf* time; (*turno*) turn; a la ~ que at the same time as; a su ~ in its turn; otra ~ again; una ~ once; de una ~ in one go; de una ~ para siempre once and for all; en ~ de instead of; a o algunas veces sometimes; una y otra ~ repeatedly; de ~ en cuando from time to time; 7 veces 9 7 times 9; hacer las veces de to stand in for; tal ~ perhaps.

vía ['bia] *nf* track, route; (*FERRO*) line; *(fig)* way; *(ANAT)* passage, tube // *prep* via, by way of; por ~ judicial by legal means; por ~ oficial through official channels; en ~s de in the process of; ~ aérea airway; V~ Láctea Milky Way.

viaducto [bja'ðukto] *nm* viaduct.

viajante [bja'xante] *nm* commercial traveller.

viajar [bja'xar] *vi* to travel; **viaje** *nm* journey; (*gira*) tour; (*NAUT*) voyage; estar de viaje to be on a journey; **viaje de ida y vuelta** round trip; **viaje de novios** honeymoon; **viajero, a** *a* travelling; *(ZOOL)* migratory // *nm/f* (quien viaja) traveller; (*pasajero*) passenger.

vial [bjal] *a* road *cpd*, traffic *cpd*.

víbora ['biβora] *nf* viper; *(AM)* poisonous snake.

vibración [biβra'θjon] *nf* vibration; **vibrador** *nm* vibrator; **vibrante** *a* vibrant.

vibrar [bi'βrar] *vt, vi* to vibrate.

vicario [bi'karjo] *nm* curate.

vicegerente [biθexe'rente] *nm* assistant manager.

vicepresidente [biθepresi'ðente]

nm/f vice-president.

viceversa [biθe'βersa] *ad* vice versa.

viciado, a [bi'θjaðo, a] *a* *(corrompido)* corrupt; *(contaminado)* foul, contaminated; **viciar** *vt* *(pervertir)* to pervert; *(JUR)* to nullify; *(estropear)* to spoil; **viciarse** *vr* to become corrupted.

vicio ['biθjo] *nm* vice; (*mala costumbre*) bad habit; ~so, a *a* (*muy malo*) vicious; *(corrompido)* depraved // *nm/f* depraved person.

vicisitud [biθisi'tuð] *nf* vicissitude.

víctima ['biktima] *nf* victim.

victoria [bik'torja] *nf* victory; **victorioso, a** *a* victorious.

vicuña [bi'kuɲa] *nf* vicuna.

vid [bið] *nf* vine.

vida ['biða] *nf* (*gen*) life; *(duración)* lifetime; de por ~ for life; en la/mi ~ never; estar con ~ to be still alive; ganarse la ~ to earn one's living.

vídeo ['biðeo] *nm* video // *a inv*: **película ~** video film.

vidriero, a [bi'ðrjero, a] *nm/f* glazier // *nf* (*ventana*) stained-glass window; *(AM: de tienda)* shop window; *(puerta)* glass door.

vidrio ['biðrjo] *nm* glass; ~so, a *a* glassy.

vieira ['bjeira] *nf* scallop.

viejo, a ['bjexo, a] *a* old // *nm/f* old man/woman; **hacerse ~** to get old.

Viena ['bjena] *n* Vienna.

vienes *etc vb ver* **venir**.

vienés, esa [bje'nes, esa] *a* Viennese.

viento ['bjento] *nm* wind; **hacer ~** to be windy.

vientre ['bjentre] *nm* belly; (*matriz*) womb.

viernes ['bjernes] *nm inv* Friday; V~ Santo Good Friday.

Vietnam [bjet'nam] *nm*: el ~ Vietnam; **vietnamita** *a* Vietnamese.

viga ['biɣa] *nf* beam, rafter; *(de metal)* girder.

vigencia [bi'xenθja] *nf* validity; estar en ~ to be in force; **vigente**

a valid, in force; (*imperante*) prevailing.

vigésimo, a [bi'xesimo, a] *a* twentieth.

vigía [bi'xia] *nm* look-out // *nf* (*atalaya*) watchtower; (*acción*) watching.

vigilancia [bixi'lanθja] *nf*: **tener a uno bajo** ~ to keep watch on sb.

vigilar [bixi'lar] *vt* to watch over // *vi* (*gen*) to be vigilant; (*hacer guardia*) to keep watch; ~ **por** to take care of.

vigilia [vi'xilja] *nf* wakefulness, being awake; (*REL*) fast.

vigor [bi'vor] *nm* vigour, vitality; **en** ~ in force; **entrar/poner en** ~ to take/put into effect; ~**oso, a** *a* vigorous.

vil [bil] *a* vile, low; ~**eza** *nf* vileness; (*acto*) base deed.

vilipendiar [bilipen'djar] *vt* to vilify, revile.

vilo ['bilo]: **en** ~ *ad* in the air, suspended; (*fig*) on tenterhooks, in suspense.

villa ['biʎa] *nf* (*casa*) villa; (*pueblo*) small town; (*municipalidad*) municipality; ~ **miseria** (*AM*) shantytown.

villancico [biʎan'θiko] *nm* (Christmas) carol.

villorio [bi'ʎorjo] *nm* (*AM*) shantytown.

vinagre [bi'navre] *nm* vinegar; ~**ras** *nfpl* cruet *sg*.

vinagreta [bina'vreta] *nf* vinaigrette, French dressing.

vinculación [binkula'θjon] *nf* (*lazo*) link, bond; (*acción*) linking.

vincular [binku'lar] *vt* to link, bind; **vínculo** *nm* link, bond.

vine *etc vb ver* **venir**.

vinicultura [binikul'tura] *nf* wine growing.

viniera *etc vb ver* **venir**.

vino *vb ver* **venir** // *nm* wine; ~ **blanco/tinto** white/red wine.

viña ['biɲa] *nf*, **viñedo** [bi'ɲeðo] *nm* vineyard.

viola ['bjola] *nf* viola.

violación [bjola'θjon] *nf* violation; (*estupro*): ~ (**sexual**) rape.

violar [bjo'lar] *vt* to violate; (*cometer estupro*) to rape.

violencia [bjo'lenθja] *nf* (*fuerza*) violence, force; (*embarazo*) embarrassment; (*acto injusto*) unjust act; **violentar** *vt* to force; (*casa*) to break into; (*agredir*) to assault; (*violar*) to violate; **violento, a** *a* violent; (*furioso*) furious; (*situación*) embarrassing; (*acto*) forced, unnatural.

violeta [bjo'leta] *nf* violet.

violín [bjo'lin] *nm* violin.

violón [bjo'lon] *nm* double bass.

viraje [bi'raxe] *nm* turn; (*de vehículo*) swerve; (*de carretera*) bend; (*fig*) change of direction; **virar** *vi* to change direction.

virgen [bir'xen] *a, nf* virgin.

Virgo ['birvo] *nm* Virgo.

viril [bi'ril] *a* virile; ~**idad** *nf* virility.

virtualmente [birtwal'mente] *ad* virtually.

virtud [bir'tuð] *nf* virtue; **en** ~ **de** by virtue of; **virtuoso, a** *a* virtuous // *nm/f* virtuoso.

viruela [bi'rwela] *nf* smallpox; ~**s** *nfpl* pockmarks.

virulento, a [biru'lento, a] *a* virulent.

virus ['birus] *nm inv* virus.

visa ['bisa] *nf* (*AM*), **visado** [bi'saðo] *nm* visa.

viscoso, a [bis'koso, a] *a* viscous.

visera [bi'sera] *nf* visor.

visibilidad [bisiβili'ðað] *nf* visibility; **visible** *a* visible; (*fig*) obvious.

visillos [bi'siʎos] *nmpl* lace curtains.

visión [bi'sjon] *nf* (*ANAT*) vision, (eye)sight; (*fantasía*) fantasy; **visionario, a** *a* (*que prevé*) visionary; (*alucinado*) deluded // *nm/f* visionary.

visita [bi'sita] *nf* call, visit; (*persona*) visitor; **hacer una** ~ to pay a visit.

visitar [bisi'tar] *vt* to visit, call on.

vislumbrar [bislum'brar] *vt* to

glimpse, catch a glimpse of; **vislumbre** nf glimpse; (centelleo) gleam; (idea vaga) glimmer.

viso ['biso] nm (del metal) glint, gleam; (de tela) sheen; (aspecto) appearance.

visón [bi'son] nm mink.

visor [bi'sor] nm (FOTO) viewfinder.

víspera ['bispera] nf: **la ~ de** ... the day before ....

vista ['bista] nf sight, vision; (capacidad de ver) (eye)sight; (mirada) look(s) (pl) // nm customs officer; **a primera ~** at first glance; **hacer la ~ gorda** to turn a blind eye; **volver la ~** to look back; **está a la ~ que** it's obvious that; **en ~ de** in view of; **en ~ de que** in view of the fact that; **¡hasta la ~!** so long!, see you!; **con ~s a** with a view to; **~zo** nm glance; **dar o echar un ~zo a** to glance at.

visto, a pp de **ver** // vb **ver** tb **vestir** // ['bisto, a] a seen; (considerado) considered // nm: **bueno** approval; ' **~ bueno**' approved; **por lo ~** evidently; **está ~ que** it's clear that; **está bien/mal ~** it's acceptable/unacceptable; **~ que** since, considering that.

vistoso, a [bis'toso, a] a colourful.

vital [bi'tal] a life cpd, living cpd; (fig) vital; (persona) lively, vivacious; **~icio, a** a for life.

vitamina [bita'mina] nf vitamin.

viticultor, a [bitikul'tor, a] nm/f wine grower; **viticultura** nf wine growing.

vitorear [bitore'ar] vt to cheer, acclaim.

vítreo, a ['bitreo, a] a vitreous.

vitrina [bi'trina] nf show case; (AM) shop window.

vituperio [bitu'perjo] nm (condena) condemnation; (censura) censure; (insulto) insult.

viudo, a ['bjuðo, a] nm/f widower/widow; **viudez** nf widowhood.

vivacidad [biβaθi'ðað] nf (vigor) vigour; (vida) liveliness.

vivaracho, a [biβa'ratʃo, a] a jaunty, lively; (ojos) bright, twinkling.

vivaz [bi'βaθ] a lively.

víveres ['biβeres] nmpl provisions.

vivero [bi'βero] nm (para plantas) nursery; (para peces) fish farm; (fig) hotbed.

viveza [bi'βeθa] nf liveliness; (agudeza: mental) sharpness.

vivienda [bi'βjenda] nf housing; (una ~) house; (piso) flat (Brit), apartment (US).

viviente [bi'βjente] a living.

vivir [bi'βir] vt, vi to live // nm life, living.

vivo, a ['biβo, a] a living, alive; (fig: descripción) vivid; (persona: astuto) smart, clever; **en ~** (transmisión etc) live.

vocablo [bo'kaβlo] nm (palabra) word; (término) term.

vocabulario [bokaβu'larjo] nm vocabulary.

vocación [boka'θjon] nf vocation; **vocacional** nf (AM) ≈ technical college.

vocal [bo'kal] a vocal // nf vowel; **~izar** vi to vocalize.

vocear [boθe'ar] vt (para vender) to cry; (aclamar) to acclaim; (fig) to proclaim // vi to yell; **vocerío** nm, **vocería** nf shouting.

vocero [bo'θero] nm/f spokesman/woman.

voces [bo'θes] nfpl ver **voz**.

vociferar [boθife'rar] vt to shout // vi to yell.

vodka ['boðka] nm o f vodka.

vol abr = **volumen**.

volador, a [bola'ðor, a] a flying.

volandas [bo'landas]: **en ~** ad in the air; (fig) swiftly.

volante [bo'lante] a flying // nm (de coche) steering wheel; (de reloj) balance.

volar [bo'lar] vt (edificio) to blow up // vi to fly.

volátil [bo'latil] a volatile.

volcán [bol'kan] nm volcano; **~ico,**

a *a* volcanic.

volcar [bol'kar] *vt* to upset, overturn; (*tumbar, derribar*) to knock over; (*vaciar*) to empty out // *vi* to overturn; ~**se** *vr* to tip over.

voleíbol [bolei'βol] *nm* volleyball.

volqué, volquemos *etc vb ver* **volcar.**

volquete [bol'kete] *nm* (*carro*) tipcart; (*AUTO*) dumper.

voltaje [bol'taxe] *nm* voltage.

voltear [bolte'ar] *vt* to turn over; (*volcar*) to turn upside down.

voltereta [bolte'reta] *nf* somersault.

voltio ['boltjo] *nm* volt.

voluble [bo'luβle] *a* fickle.

volumen [bo'lumen] (*pl* **volúmenes**) *nm* volume; **voluminoso, a** *a* voluminous; (*enorme*) massive.

voluntad [bolun'tað] *nf* will; (*resolución*) willpower; (*deseo*) desire, wish.

voluntario, a [bolun'tarjo, a] *a* voluntary // *nm/f* volunteer.

voluntarioso, a [bolunta'rjoso, a] *a* headstrong.

voluptuoso, a [bolup'twoso, a] *a* voluptuous.

volver [bol'βer] *vt* (*gen*) to turn; (*dar vuelta a*) to turn (over); (*voltear*) to turn round, turn upside down; (*poner al revés*) to turn inside out; (*devolver*) to return // *vi* to return, go back, come back; ~**se** *vr* to turn round; ~ **la espalda** to turn one's back; ~ **triste** *etc* **a uno** to make sb sad *etc*; ~ **a hacer** to do again; ~ **en sí** to come to; ~**se insoportable/muy caro** to get o become unbearable/very expensive; ~**se loco** to go mad.

vomitar [bomi'tar] *vt, vi* to vomit; **vómito** *nm* (*acto*) vomiting; (*resultado*) vomit.

voraz [bo'raθ] *a* voracious.

vórtice ['bortiθe] *nm* whirlpool; (*de aire*) whirlwind.

vos [bos] *pron* (*AM*) you.

vosotros, as [bo'sotros, as] *pron* you; (*reflexivo*) **entre/para** ~ among/for yourselves.

votación [bota'θjon] *nf* (*acto*) voting; (*voto*) vote.

votar [bo'tar] *vi* to vote; **voto** *nm* vote; (*promesa*) vow; **votos** (*good*) wishes.

voy *vb ver* **ir.**

voz [boθ] *nf* voice; (*grito*) shout; (*chisme*) rumour; (*LING*) word; **dar voces** to shout, yell; **a media** ~ in a low voice; **a** ~ **en cuello o en grito** at the top of one's voice; **de viva** ~ verbally; **en** ~ **alta** aloud; ~ **de mando** command.

vuelco *vb ver* **volcar** // ['bwelko] *nm* spill, overturning.

vuelo *vb ver* **volar** // ['bwelo] *nm* flight; (*encaje*) lace, frill; **coger al** ~ to catch in flight; ~ **charter/regular** charter/regular flight.

vuelque *etc vb ver* **volcar.**

vuelta ['bwelta] *nf* (*gen*) turn; (*curva*) bend, curve; (*regreso*) return; (*revolución*) revolution; (*circuito*) lap; (*de papel, tela*) reverse; (*cambio*) change; **a la** ~ on one's return; **a** ~ **de correo** by return of post; **dar** ~**s** (*suj: cabeza*) to spin; **dar** ~**s a una idea** to turn over an idea (in one's head); **estar de** ~ to be back; **dar una** ~ to go for a walk; (*en coche*) to go for a drive.

vuelto *pp de* **volver.**

vuelvo *etc vb ver* **volver.**

vuestro, a ['bwestro, a] *a* your; **un amigo** ~ a friend of yours // *pron*: **el /la vuestra, los ~s/las vuestras** yours.

vulgar [bul'var] *a* (*ordinario*) vulgar; (*común*) common; ~**idad** *nf* commonness; (*acto*) vulgarity; (*expresión*) coarse expression; ~**idades** *nfpl* banalities; ~**izar** *vt* to popularize.

vulgo ['bulvo] *nm* common people.

vulnerable [bulne'raβle] *a* vulnerable.

W

wáter ['bater] nm toilet.

whisky ['wiski] nm whisky, whiskey.

X

xenofobia [kseno'foβja] nf xenophobia.

xilófono [ksi'lofono] nm xylophone.

Y

y [i] conj and.

ya [ja] ad (gen) already; (ahora) now; (en seguida) at once; (pronto) soon // excl all right! // conj (ahora que) now that; ~ lo sé I know; ~ que since.

yacer [ja'θer] vi to lie.

yacimiento [jaθi'mjento] nm deposit.

yanqui ['janki] a, nm/f Yankee.

yate ['jate] nm yacht.

yazco etc vb ver **yacer**.

yedra ['jeðra] nf ivy.

yegua ['jeɣwa] nf mare.

yema ['jema] nf (del huevo) yoke; (BOT) leaf bud; (fig) best part; ~ del dedo fingertip.

yergo etc vb ver **erguir**.

yermo, a ['jermo, a] a (despoblado) uninhabited; (estéril, fig) barren // nm wasteland.

yerno ['jerno] nm son-in-law.

yerro etc vb ver **errar**.

yerto, a ['jerto, a] a stiff.

yesca ['jeska] nf tinder.

yeso ['jeso] nm (GEO) gypsum; (ARQ) plaster.

yodo ['joðo] nm iodine.

yogur [jo'ɣur] nm yoghurt.

yugo ['juɣo] nm yoke.

Yugoslavia [juɣos'laβja] nf Yugoslavia.

yugular [juɣu'lar] a jugular.

yunque ['junke] nm anvil.

yunta ['junta] nf yoke; **yuntero** nm ploughman.

yute ['jute] nm jute.

yuxtaponer [jukstapo'ner] vt to juxtapose; **yuxtaposición** nf juxtaposition.

Z

zafar [θa'far] vt (soltar) to untie; (superficie) to clear; ~se vr (escaparse) to escape; (TEC) to slip off.

zafio, a ['θafjo, a] a coarse.

zafiro [θa'firo] nm sapphire.

zaga ['θaɣa] nf: a la ~ behind, in the rear.

zagal, a [θa'ɣal, a] nm/f boy/girl, lad/lass (Brit).

zaguán [θa'ɣwan] nm hallway.

zaherir [θae'rir] vt (criticar) to criticize.

zahorí [θao'ri] nm clairvoyant.

zaino, a ['θaino, a] a (color de caballo) chestnut.

zalamería [θalame'ria] nf flattery; **zalamero, a** a flattering; (relamido) suave.

zamarra [θa'marra] nf (piel) sheepskin; (chaqueta) sheepskin jacket.

zambullirse [θambu'Áirse] vr to dive; (ocultarse) to hide o.s.

zampar [θam'par] vt to gobble down // vi gobble (up).

zanahoria [θana'orja] nf carrot.

zancada [θan'kaða] nf stride.

zancadilla [θanka'ðiÁa] nf trip; (fig) stratagem.

zanco ['θanko] nm stilt.

zancudo, a [θan'kuðo, a] a longlegged // nm (AM) mosquito.

zángano ['θangano] nm drone.

zanja ['θanxa] nf ditch; **zanjar** vt (superar) to surmount; (resolver) to resolve.

zapata [θa'pata] nf half-boot; (MECÁNICA) shoe.

zapatear [θapate'ar] vi to tap with

zapatería 300 **zutano**

one's feet.

zapatería [θapate'ria] *nf* (*oficio*)
shoemaking; (*tienda*) shoe shop; (*fábrica*) shoe factory; **zapatero, a**
nm/f shoemaker.

zapatilla [θapa'tiʎa] *nf* slipper.

zapato [θa'pato] *nm* shoe.

zarandear [θarande'ar] *vt* (*fam*) to
shake vigorously.

zarpa ['θarpa] *nf* (*garra*) claw.

zarpar [θar'par] *vi* to weigh anchor.

zarza ['θarθa] *nf* (*BOT*) bramble;
zarzal *nm* (*matorral*) bramble
patch.

zarzamora [θarθa'mora] *nf* blackberry.

zarzuela [θar'θwela] *nf* Spanish light
opera.

zigzag [θiɣ'θaɣ] *nm* zigzag;
zigzaguear *vi* to zigzag.

zinc [θink] *nm* zinc.

zócalo ['θokalo] *nm* (*ARQ*) plinth,
base.

zona ['θona] *nf* zone; ~ **fronteriza**
border area.

zoo ['θoo] *nm* zoo.

zoología [θoolo'xia] *nf* zoology;
zoológico, a *a* zoological // *nm* zoo;
zoólogo, a *nm/f* zoologist.

zopenco, a [θo'penko, a] *nm/f* fool.

zopilote [θopi'lote] *nm* (*AM*)
buzzard.

zoquete [θo'kete] *nm* (*madera*)
block; (*fam*) blockhead.

zorro, a ['θorro, a] *a* crafty // *nm/f*
fox/vixen.

zozobra [θo'θoβra] *nf* (*fig*) anxiety;
zozobrar *vi* (*hundirse*) to capsize;
(*fig*) to fail.

zueco ['θweko] *nm* clog.

zumbar [θum'bar] *vt* (*golpear*) to hit
// *vi* to buzz; **zumbido** *nm* buzzing.

zumo ['θumo] *nm* juice.

zurcir [θur'θir] *vt* (*coser*) to darn.

zurdo, a ['θurðo, a] *a* (*mano*) left;
(*persona*) left-handed.

zurrar [θu'rrar] *vt* (*fam*) to wallop.

zurrón [θu'rron] *nm* pouch.

zutano, a [θu'tano, a] *nm/f* so-and-
so.

ENGLISH-SPANISH
INGLÉS-ESPAÑOL

A

A [eɪ] n (MUS) la m; (AUT): ~ **road** ≈ carretera nacional.

─── **KEYWORD** ───

a indefinite article (before vowel or silent h: **an**) [æ, ən] **1** un(a); ~ **book** un libro; **an apple** una manzana; **she's ~ doctor** (ella) es médica
2 (instead of the number 'one') un(a); ~**year ago** hace un año; ~ **hundred/thousand** etc **pounds** cien/mil etc libras
3 (in expressing ratios, prices etc): 3 ~ **day/week** 3 al día/a la semana; 10 **km an hour** 10 km por hora; £5 ~ **person** £5 por persona; 30p ~ **kilo** 30p el kilo.

A.A. n abbr (Brit = Automobile Association) ≈ RACE m (Sp); (= Alcoholics Anonymous) Alcohólicos Anónimos.

A.A.A. n abbr (US: = American Automobile Association) ≈ RACE m (Sp).

aback [ə'bæk] ad: to be taken ~ quedar desconcertado.

abandon [ə'bændən] vt abandonar; (renounce) renunciar a // n abandono; (wild behaviour): **with** ~ sin reparos.

abashed [ə'bæʃt] a avergonzado.

abate [ə'beɪt] vi (noise, pain) calmarse; (storm) amainar // vt reducir.

abattoir ['æbətwɑ:*] n (Brit) matadero.

abbey ['æbɪ] n abadía.

abbot ['æbət] n abad m.

abbreviate [ə'bri:vɪeɪt] vt abreviar; **abbreviation** [-'eɪʃən] n (short form) abreviatura f; (act) abreviación f.

abdicate ['æbdɪkeɪt] vt, vi abdicar;

abdication [-'keɪʃən] n abdicación f.

abdomen ['æbdəmən] n abdomen m.

abduct [æb'dʌkt] vt raptar, secuestrar.

aberration [æbə'reɪʃən] n aberración f.

abet [ə'bet] vt see **aid**.

abeyance [ə'beɪəns] n: **in** ~ (law) en desuso; (matter) en suspenso.

abhor [əb'hɔ:*] vt aborrecer, abominar (de).

abide [ə'baɪd] vt: **I can't** ~ **it/him** no lo/le puedo ver; **to** ~ **by** vt fus atenerse a.

ability [ə'bɪlɪtɪ] n habilidad f, capacidad f; (talent) talento.

abject ['æbdʒekt] a (poverty) miserable; (apology) rastrero.

ablaze [ə'bleɪz] a en llamas, ardiendo.

able ['eɪbl] a capaz; (skilled) hábil; **to be** ~ **to do sth** poder hacer algo; ~**-bodied** a sano; **ably** ad hábilmente.

abnormal [æb'nɔ:məl] a anormal.

aboard [ə'bɔ:d] ad a bordo // prep a bordo de.

abode [ə'bəud] n: **of no fixed** ~ sin domicilio fijo.

abolish [ə'bɔlɪʃ] vt suprimir, abolir; **abolition** [æbəu'lɪʃən] n supresión f, abolición f.

abominable [ə'bɔmɪnəbl] a abominable.

aborigine [æbə'rɪdʒɪnɪ] n aborigen m/f.

abort [ə'bɔ:t] vt abortar; ~**ion** [ə'bɔ:ʃən] n aborto (provocado); **to have an** ~**ion** abortarse, hacerse abortar; ~**ive** a malogrado.

abound [ə'baund] vi: **to** ~ (**in** or **with**) abundar (de or en).

KEYWORD

about [ə'baʊt] ◆ *ad* 1 (*approximately*) más o menos, aproximadamente; ~ **a hundred/thousand** *etc* unos(unas) cien/mil *etc*; **it takes ~ 10 hours** se tarda unas *or* más o menos 10 horas; **at ~ 2 o'clock** sobre las dos; **I've just ~ finished** casi he terminado

2 (*referring to place*) por todas partes; **to leave things lying ~** dejar las cosas (tiradas) por ahi; **to run ~** correr por todas partes; **to walk ~** pasearse, ir y venir

3: to be ~ to do sth estar a punto de hacer algo

◆ *prep* **1** (*relating to*) de, sobre, acerca de; **a book ~ London** un libro sobre *or* acerca de Londres; **what is it ~?** ¿de qué se trata?, ¿qué pasa?; **we talked ~ it** hablamos de eso *or* ello; **what** *or* **how ~ doing this?** ¿qué tal si hacemos esto?

2 (*referring to place*) por; **to walk ~ the town** caminar por la ciudad.

above [ə'bʌv] *ad* encima, por encima, arriba // *prep* encima de; **mentioned ~** susodicho; **~ all** sobre todo; **~ board** a legítimo.

abrasive [ə'breɪzɪv] *a* abrasivo.

abreast [ə'brest] *ad* de frente; **to keep ~** of mantenerse al corriente de.

abridge [ə'brɪdʒ] *vt* (*book*) abreviar.

abroad [ə'brɔːd] *ad* (*to be*) en el extranjero; (*to go*) al extranjero.

abrupt [ə'brʌpt] *a* (*sudden*) brusco; (*gruff*) áspero.

abruptly [ə'brʌptlɪ] *ad* (*leave*) repentinamente; (*speak*) bruscamente.

abscess ['æbsɪs] *n* absceso.

abscond [əb'skɒnd] *vi* fugarse.

absence ['æbsəns] *n* ausencia.

absent ['æbsənt] *a* ausente; **~ee** [-'tiː] *n* ausente *m/f*; **~eeism** [-'tiːɪzəm] *n* absentismo; **~-minded** *a* distraído.

absolute ['æbsəluːt] *a* absoluto; **~ly** [-'luːtlɪ] *ad* totalmente.

absolve [əb'zɒlv] *vt*: **to ~ sb** (**from**) absolver a alguien (de).

absorb [əb'zɔːb] *vt* absorber; **to be ~ed in a book** estar absorto en un libro; **~ent cotton** *n* (*US*) algodón *m* hidrófilo; **~ing** *a* absorbente.

absorption [əb'zɔːpʃən] *n* absorción *f*.

abstain [əb'steɪn] *vi*: **to ~** (**from**) abstenerse (de).

abstemious [əb'stiːmɪəs] *a* abstemio.

abstention [əb'stenʃən] *n* abstención *f*.

abstinence ['æbstɪnəns] *n* abstinencia.

abstract ['æbstrækt] *a* abstracto.

abstruse [æb'struːs] *a* oscuro.

absurd [əb'sɜːd] *a* absurdo.

abundance [ə'bʌndəns] *n* abundancia.

abuse [ə'bjuːs] *n* (*insults*) improperios *mpl*, injurias *fpl*; (*misuse*) abuso // *vt* [ə'bjuːz] (*ill-treat*) maltratar; (*take advantage of*) abusar de; **abusive** *a* ofensivo.

abysmal [ə'bɪzməl] *a* pésimo; (*ignorance*) supino.

abyss [ə'bɪs] *n* abismo.

AC *abbr* (= *alternating current*) corriente *f* alterna.

academic [ækə'demɪk] *a* académico, universitario; (*pej: issue*) puramente teórico // *n* estudioso/a; profesor(a) *m/f* universitario/a.

academy [ə'kædəmɪ] *n* (*learned body*) academia; (*school*) instituto, colegio; **~ of music** conservatorio.

accelerate [æk'seləreɪt] *vt* acelerar // *vi* acelerarse; **accelerator** *n* (*Brit*) acelerador *m*.

accent ['æksənt] *n* acento.

accept [ək'sept] *vt* aceptar; (*approve*) aprobar; (*concede*) admitir; **~able** *a* aceptable; admisible; **~ance** *n* aceptación *f*; aprobación *f*.

access ['æksɛs] *n* acceso; **to have ~ to** tener libre acceso a; **~ible**

[-'sɛsəbl] a accesible.

accessory [æk'sɛsərɪ] n accesorio;
toilet accessories artículos mpl de
tocador.

accident ['æksɪdənt] n accidente m;
(chance) casualidad f; by ~ (unintentionally) sin querer; (by coincidence) por casualidad; ~al [-'dɛntl]
a accidental, fortuito; ~ally
[-'dɛntlɪ] ad sin querer; por casualidad; ~-prone a propenso a los acci-
dentes.

acclaim [ə'kleɪm] vt aclamar, aplaudir // n aclamación f, aplausos mpl.

acclimatize [ə'klaɪmətaɪz], (US) **ac-
climate** [ə'klaɪmət] vt: to become
~d aclimatarse.

accolade ['ækəleɪd] n (prize) premio; (praise) alabanzas fpl.

accommodate [ə'kɔmədeɪt] vt alojar, hospedar; (oblige, help) complacer; **accommodating** a servicial,
complaciente.

accommodation [ə,kɔmə'deɪʃən], (US) **accom-
modations** npl [əkɔmə'deɪʃən(z)]
alojamiento.

accompany [ə'kʌmpənɪ] vt acompañar.

accomplice [ə'kʌmplɪs] n cómplice
m/f.

accomplish [ə'kʌmplɪʃ] vt (finish)
acabar; (aim) realizar; (task) llevar
a cabo; ~ed a experto, diestro;
~ment n (skill) talento; (feat) hazaña; (realization) realización f.

accord [ə'kɔːd] n acuerdo // vt conceder; of his own ~ espontáneamente;
~ance n: in ~ance with de acuerdo con; ~ing to prep según; (in accordance with) conforme a; ~ingly
ad (thus) por consiguiente.

accordion [ə'kɔːdɪən] n acordeón m.

accost [ə'kɔst] vt abordar, dirigirse
a.

account [ə'kaunt] n (COMM) cuenta,
factura; (report) informe m; ~s npl
(COMM) cuentas fpl; of little ~ de
poca importancia; on ~ a cuenta; on
no ~ bajo ningún concepto; on ~ of
a causa de, por motivo de; to take

into ~, take ~ of tener en cuenta;
to ~ for vt fus (explain) explicar;
~able a responsable.

accountancy [ə'kauntənsɪ] n contabilidad f.

accountant [ə'kauntənt] n contable
m/f, contador(a) m/f.

account number n (at bank etc)
número de cuenta.

accredited [ə'krɛdɪtɪd] a (agent etc)
autorizado.

accrue [ə'kruː] vi: ~d interest interés m acumulado.

accumulate [ə'kjuːmjuleɪt] vt acumular // vi acumularse.

accuracy ['ækjurəsɪ] n exactitud f,
precisión f.

accurate ['ækjurɪt] a (number) exacto; (answer) acertado; (shot) certero; ~ly ad (count, shoot, answer)
con precisión.

accusation [ækju'zeɪʃən] n acusación f.

accuse [ə'kjuːz] vt acusar; (blame)
echar la culpa a; ~d n acusado/a.

accustom [ə'kʌstəm] vt acostumbrar; ~ed a: ~ed to acostumbrado
a.

ace [eɪs] n as m.

acetate ['æsɪteɪt] n acetato.

ache [eɪk] n dolor m // vi doler; my
head ~s me duele la cabeza.

achieve [ə'tʃiːv] vt (reach) alcanzar;
(realize) realizar; (victory, success)
lograr, conseguir; ~ment n (completion) realización f; (success) éxito.

acid ['æsɪd] a ácido; (bitter) agrio // n
ácido; ~ rain n lluvia ácida.

acknowledge [ək'nɔlɪdʒ] vt (letter:
also: ~ receipt of) acusar recibo
de; (fact) reconocer; ~ment n acuse m de recibo; reconocimiento.

acne ['æknɪ] n acné m.

acorn ['eɪkɔːn] n bellota.

acoustic [ə'kuːstɪk] a acústico; ~s
n, npl acústica sg.

acquaint [ə'kweɪnt] vt: to ~ sb
with sth (inform) poner a uno al corriente de algo; to be ~ed with

(person) conocer; (fact) estar al corriente de; **~ance** n conocimiento; (person) conocido/a.

acquiesce [ækwɪ'es] vi: to ~ (in) consentir (en), conformarse (con).

acquire [ə'kwaɪə*] vt adquirir; **acquisition** [ækwɪ'zɪʃən] n adquisición f; **acquisitive** [ə'kwɪzɪtɪv] a codicioso.

acquit [ə'kwɪt] vt absolver, exculpar; to ~ o.s. well salir con éxito; **~tal** n absolución f, exculpación f.

acre ['eɪkə*] n acre m.

acrid ['ækrɪd] a acre.

acrimonious [ækrɪ'məʊnɪəs] a (remark) mordaz; (argument) reñido.

acrobat ['ækrəbæt] n acróbata m/f.

acronym ['ækrənɪm] n siglas fpl.

across [ə'krɒs] prep (on the other side of) al otro lado de, del otro lado de; (crosswise) a través de // ad de un lado a otro, de una parte a otra; a través, al través; to run/swim ~ atravesar corriendo/nadando; ~ from enfrente de.

acrylic [ə'krɪlɪk] a acrílico.

act [ækt] n acto, acción f; (THEATRE) acto; (in music hall etc) número; (LAW) decreto, ley f // vi (behave) comportarse; (THEATRE) actuar; (pretend) fingir; (take action) obrar // vt (part) hacer el papel de; to ~ as actuar o hacer de; **~ing** a suplente // n: to do some **~ing** hacer algo de teatro.

action ['ækʃən] n acción f, acto; (MIL) acción f, batalla; (LAW) proceso, demanda; **out of** ~ (person) fuera de combate; (thing) descompuesto; **to take** ~ tomar medidas; ~ **replay** n (TV) repetición f.

activate ['æktɪveɪt] vt activar.

active ['æktɪv] a activo, enérgico; (volcano) en actividad; **~ly** ad (participate) activamente; (discourage, dislike) enérgicamente; **activist** n activista m/f; **activity** [-'tɪvɪtɪ] n actividad f.

actor ['æktə*] n actor m.

actress ['æktrɪs] n actriz f.

actual ['æktjuəl] a verdadero, real; **~ly** ad realmente, en realidad.

acumen ['ækjumən] n perspicacia.

acute [ə'kjuːt] a agudo.

ad [æd] n abbr = advertisement.

A.D. ad abbr (= Anno Domini) A.C.

adamant ['ædəmənt] a firme, inflexible.

adapt [ə'dæpt] vt adaptar // vi: to ~ (to) adaptarse (a), ajustarse (a); **~able** a (device) adaptable; (person) que se adapta; **~er** or **~or** n (ELEC) adaptador m.

add [æd] vt añadir, agregar; (figures: also: ~ **up**) sumar // vi: to ~ to (increase) aumentar, acrecentar; **it doesn't ~ up** (fig) no tiene sentido.

adder ['ædə*] n víbora.

addict ['ædɪkt] n (to drugs etc) adicto/a; (enthusiast) entusiasta m/f; **~ed** [ə'dɪktɪd] a: to be **~ed** to ser adicto a; ser aficionado de; **~ion** [ə'dɪkʃən] n (dependence) hábito morboso; (enthusiasm) afición f; **~ive** [ə'dɪktɪv] a que causa adicción.

addition [ə'dɪʃən] n (adding up) adición f; (thing added) añadidura, añadido; **in** ~ además, por añadidura; **in** ~ **to** además de; **~al** a adicional.

additive ['ædɪtɪv] n aditivo.

address [ə'dres] n dirección f, señas fpl; (speech) discurso // vt (letter) dirigir; (speak to) dirigirse a, dirigir la palabra a.

adenoids ['ædənɔɪdz] npl vegetaciones fpl adenoideas.

adept ['ædɛpt] a: ~ **at** experto o hábil en.

adequate ['ædɪkwət] a (apt) adecuado; (enough) suficiente.

adhere [əd'hɪə*] vi: to ~ **to** pegarse a; (fig: abide by) observar.

adhesive [əd'hiːzɪv] a, n adhesivo; ~ **tape** n (Brit) cinta adhesiva; (US: MED) esparadrapo.

adjacent [ə'dʒeɪsənt] a: ~ **to** contiguo a, inmediato a.

adjective ['ædʒɛktɪv] n adjetivo.

adjoining [ə'dʒɔɪnɪŋ] a contiguo, vecino.

adjourn [ə'dʒəːn] vt aplazar // vi suspenderse.

adjudicate [ə'dʒuːdɪkeɪt] vi sentenciar.

adjust [ə'dʒʌst] vt (change) modificar; (machine) ajustar // vi: to ~ (to) adaptarse (a); ~**able** a ajustable; ~**ment** n modificación f; ajuste m.

adjutant ['ædʒətənt] n ayudante m.

ad-lib [æd'lɪb] vt, vi improvisar; **ad lib** ad a voluntad, a discreción.

administer [əd'mɪnɪstə*] vt proporcionar; (justice) administrar; ~**ion** [-'treɪʃən] n administración f; (government) gobierno; ~**ive** [-trətɪv] a administrativo.

admiral ['ædmərəl] n almirante m; **A~ty** n (Brit) Ministerio de Marina, Almirantazgo.

admiration [ædmə'reɪʃən] n admiración f.

admire [əd'maɪə*] vt admirar; ~**r** n admirador(a) m/f; (suitor) pretendiente m.

admission [əd'mɪʃən] n (exhibition, nightclub) entrada; (enrolment) ingreso; (confession) confesión f.

admit [əd'mɪt] vt dejar entrar, dar entrada a; (permit) admitir; (acknowledge) reconocer; **to ~ to** vt fus confesarse culpable de; ~**tance** n entrada; ~**tedly** ad de acuerdo que.

admonish [əd'mɒnɪʃ] vt amonestar.

ad nauseam [æd'nɔːsɪæm] ad hasta el cansancio.

ado [ə'duː] n: **without (any) more ~** sin más (ni más).

adolescence [ædəu'lɛsns] n adolescencia.

adolescent [ædəu'lɛsnt] a, n adolescente m/f.

adopt [ə'dɒpt] vt adoptar; ~**ed**, ~**ive** a adoptivo; ~**ion** [ə'dɒpʃən] n adopción f.

adore [ə'dɔː*] vt adorar.

adorn [ə'dɔːn] vt adornar.

Adriatic [eɪdrɪ'ætɪk] n: **the ~ (Sea)** el (Mar) Adriático.

adrift [ə'drɪft] ad a la deriva.

adult ['ædʌlt] n adulto/a.

adultery [ə'dʌltərɪ] n adulterio.

advance [əd'vɑːns] n adelanto, progreso; (money) anticipo, préstamo; (MIL) avance m // vt avanzar, adelantar; (money) anticipar // vi avanzar, adelantarse; **in ~** por adelantado; ~**d** a avanzado; (SCOL: studies) adelantado; ~**ment** n progreso; (in rank) ascenso.

advantage [əd'vɑːntɪdʒ] n (also TENNIS) ventaja; **to take ~ of** aprovecharse de; ~**ous** [ædvən'teɪdʒəs] a ventajoso, provechoso.

advent ['ædvənt] n advenimiento; **A~** Adviento.

adventure [əd'ventʃə*] n aventura; **adventurous** [-tʃərəs] a aventurero.

adverb ['ædvəːb] n adverbio.

adversary ['ædvəsərɪ] n adversario/a, contrario/a.

adverse ['ædvəːs] a adverso, contrario; ~ **to** adverso a.

adversity [əd'vəːsɪtɪ] n infortunio.

advert ['ædvəːt] n abbr (Brit) = **advertisement**.

advertise ['ædvətaɪz] vi hacer propaganda; (in newspaper etc) poner un anuncio; **to ~ for** (staff) buscar por medio de anuncios // vt anunciar; (publicize) dar publicidad a; ~**ment** [əd'vəːtɪsmənt] n (COMM) anuncio; ~**r** n anunciante m/f; **advertising** n publicidad f, propaganda; anuncios mpl.

advice [əd'vaɪs] n consejo, consejos mpl; (notification) aviso; **a piece of ~** un consejo; **to take legal ~** consultar con un abogado.

advisable [əd'vaɪzəbl] a aconsejable, conveniente.

advise [əd'vaɪz] vt aconsejar; (inform): **to ~ sb of sth** informar a uno de algo; **to ~ sb against sth/ doing sth** desaconsejar algo a uno/ aconsejar a uno que no haga algo;

~dly [əd'vaɪzɪdlɪ] *ad* (*deliberately*) deliberadamente; **~r** *n* consejero/a; (*business adviser*) asesor/a *m/f*; **advisory** *a* consultivo.

advocate ['ædvəkeit] *vt* (*argue for*) abogar por; (*give support to*) ser partidario de // *n* [-kɪt] abogado/a.

Aegean [iː'dʒiːən] *n*: the ~ (Sea) el (Mar) Egeo.

aerial ['eərɪəl] *n* antena *f* a aéreo.

aerobics [eə'rəubɪks] *n* aerobic *m.*

aerodrome ['eərədrəum] *n* (*Brit*) aeródromo.

aeroplane ['eərəpleɪn] *n* (*Brit*) avión *m.*

aerosol ['eərəsɔl] *n* aerosol *m.*

aesthetic [iːs'θetɪk] *a* estético.

afar [ə'fɑː*] *ad*: from ~ desde lejos.

affair [ə'feə*] *n* asunto; (*also*: love ~) relación *f* amorosa.

affect [ə'fekt] *vt* afectar, influir en; (*move*) conmover; **~ed** *a* afectado.

affection [ə'fekʃən] *n* afecto, cariño; **~ate** *a* afectuoso, cariñoso.

affirmation [æfə'meɪʃən] *n* afirmación *f.*

affix [ə'fɪks] *vt* (*signature*) estampar; (*stamp*) pegar.

afflict [ə'flɪkt] *vt* afligir.

affluence ['æfluəns] *n* opulencia, riqueza.

affluent ['æfluənt] *a* acaudalado.

afford [ə'fɔːd] *vt* (*provide*) dar, proporcionar; **can we ~ it/to buy it?** ¿tenemos bastante dinero para comprarlo?

affront [ə'frʌnt] *n* afrenta, ofensa.

Afghanistan [æf'gænɪstæn] *n* Afganistán *m.*

afield [ə'fiːld] *ad*: far ~ muy lejos.

afloat [ə'fləut] *ad* (*floating*) a flote; (*at sea*) en el mar.

afoot [ə'fut] *ad*: there is something ~ algo se está tramando.

afraid [ə'freɪd] *a*: to be ~ of (*person*) tener miedo a; (*thing*) tener miedo de; to be ~ to tener miedo de, temer; **I am ~ that** me temo que.

afresh [ə'freʃ] *ad* de nuevo, otra vez.

Africa ['æfrɪkə] *n* África; **~n** *a, n* africano/a *m/f.*

aft [ɑːft] *ad* (*to be*) en popa; (*to go*) a popa.

after ['ɑːftə*] *prep* (*time*) después de; (*place, order*) detrás de, tras // *ad* después // *conj* después (de) que; **who/who are you** ~? ¿qué/a quién busca usted?; ~ **having done/he left** después de haber hecho/después de que se marchó; **to ask** ~ **sb** preguntar por alguien; ~ **all** después de todo, al fin y al cabo; ~ **you!** ¡pase usted!; **~-effects** *npl* consecuencias *fpl*, efectos *mpl*; ~**life** *n* vida eterna; **~math** *n* consecuencias *fpl*, resultados *mpl*; **~noon** *n* tarde *f*; **~s** *n* (*col*: *dessert*) postre *m*; **~sales service** *n* (*Brit*: for car, washing machine etc) servicio de asistencia pos-venta; **~shave (lotion)** *n* aftershave *m*; **~thought** *n* ocurrencia (tardía); **~wards** *ad* después, más tarde.

again [ə'gen] *ad* otra vez, de nuevo; **to do sth** ~ volver a hacer algo; ~ **and** ~ una y otra vez.

against [ə'genst] *prep* (*opposed*) en contra de; (*close to*) contra, junto a.

age [eɪdʒ] *n* edad *f*; (*old* ~) vejez *f*; (*period*) época *f* // *vi* envejecer(se) // *vt* envejecer; **she is 20 years of** ~ tiene 20 años; **to come of** ~ llegar a la mayoría de edad; **it's been** ~**s since I saw you** hace siglos que no te veo; **~d** *a*: ~**d 10** de 10 años de edad; **the ~d** ['eɪdʒɪd] *npl* los ancianos; ~ **group** *n*: **to be in the same** ~ **group** tener la misma edad; ~ **limit** *n* edad *f* mínima/máxima.

agency ['eɪdʒənsɪ] *n* agencia; **through** *or* **by the** ~ **of** por medio de.

agenda [ə'dʒendə] *n* orden *m* del día.

agent ['eɪdʒənt] *n* (*gen*) agente *m/f*; (*representative*) representante *m/f*, delegado/a.

aggravate ['ægrəveɪt] *vt* agravar; (*annoy*) irritar.

aggregate ['ægrɪgɪt] n (whole) conjunto; (collection) agregado.

aggressive [ə'grɛsɪv] a agresivo; (vigorous) enérgico.

aggrieved [ə'griːvd] a ofendido, agraviado.

aghast [ə'gɑːst] a horrorizado.

agile ['ædʒaɪl] a ágil.

agitate ['ædʒɪteɪt] vt (shake) agitar; (trouble) inquietar; **to ~ for** hacer campaña pro or en favor de; **agitator** n agitador(a) m/f.

ago [ə'gəu] ad: **2 days ~** hace 2 días; **not long ~** hace poco; **how long ~?** ¿hace cuánto tiempo?

agog [ə'gɔg] a (anxious) ansiado; (excited) emocionado.

agonizing ['ægənaɪzɪŋ] a (pain) atroz; (suspense) angustioso.

agony ['ægənɪ] n (pain) dolor m agudo; (distress) angustia; **to be in ~** retorcerse de dolor.

agree [ə'griː] vt (price) acordar, quedar en // vi (statements etc) coincidir, concordar; **to ~ (with)** (person) estar de acuerdo (con), ponerse de acuerdo (con); **to ~ to do** aceptar hacer; **to ~ to sth** consentir en algo; **to ~ that** (admit) estar de acuerdo en que; **garlic doesn't ~ with me** el ajo no me sienta bien; **~able** a agradable; (person) simpático; (willing) de acuerdo, conforme; **~d** a (time, place) convenido; **~ment** n acuerdo; (COMM) contrato; **in ~ment** de acuerdo, conforme.

agricultural [ægrɪ'kʌltərəl] a agrícola.

agriculture ['ægrɪkʌltʃə*] n agricultura.

aground [ə'graund] ad: **to run ~** encallar, embarrancar.

ahead [ə'hɛd] ad delante; **~ of** delante de; (fig: schedule etc) antes de; **~ of time** antes de la hora; **to be ~ of** (fig) llevar la ventaja a alguien; **go right o straight ~** siga adelante; **they were (right) ~ of us** iban (justo) delante de nosotros.

aid [eɪd] n ayuda, auxilio // vt ayudar,

auxiliar; **in ~ of** a beneficio de; **to ~ and abet** (LAW) ser cómplice de.

aide [eɪd] n (POL) ayudante m/f.

AIDS [eɪdz] n abbr (= acquired immune deficiency syndrome) SIDA m.

ailing ['eɪlɪŋ] a (person, economy) enfermizo.

ailment ['eɪlmənt] n enfermedad f, achaque m.

aim [eɪm] n (gun, camera) apuntar; (missile, remark) dirigir; (blow) asestar // vi (also: **take ~**) apuntar // n puntería; (objective) propósito, meta; **to ~ at** (objective) aspirar a, pretender; **to ~ to do** tener la intención de hacer; **~less** a sin propósito, sin objeto; **~lessly** ad a la ventura, a la deriva.

ain't [eɪnt] (col) = **am not; aren't; isn't**.

air [ɛə*] n aire m; (appearance) aspecto // vt ventilar; (grievances, ideas) airear // cpd aéreo; **to throw sth into the ~** (ball etc) lanzar algo al aire; **by ~** (travel) en avión; **to be on the ~** (RADIO, TV) estar en antena; **~ bed** n (Brit) colchón m neumático; **~borne** a (in the air) en el aire; (MIL) aerotransportado; **~-conditioned** a climatizado; **~-conditioning** n aire acondicionado; **~craft** n, pl inv avión m; **~craft carrier** n portaa)viones m inv; **~-field** n campo de aviación; **~ force** n fuerzas fpl aéreas, aviación f; **~-freshener** n ambientador m; **~gun** n escopeta de aire comprimido; **~ hostess** (Brit) n azafata; **~ letter** n (Brit) carta aérea; **~lift** n puente m aéreo; **~line** n línea aérea; **~liner** n avión m de pasajeros; **~lock** n (in pipe) esclusa de aire; **~mail** n: **by ~mail** por avión; **~ mattress** n colchón m neumático; **~plane** n (US) avión m; **~port** n aeropuerto; **~ raid** n ataque m aéreo; **~sick** a: **to be ~sick** marearse (en avión); **~strip** n pista de aterrizaje; **~ terminal** n terminal f; **~tight** a hermético; **~ traffic con-**

troller n controlador(a) m/f aéreo/a;
~y a (room) bien ventilado; (manners) ligero.

aisle [ail] n (of church) nave f; (of theatre) pasillo.

ajar [ə'dʒɑːʳ] a entreabierto.

akin [ə'kɪn] a: **~ to** parecido a.

alacrity [ə'lækrɪtɪ] n: **with ~** con presteza.

alarm [ə'lɑːm] n alarma; (anxiety) inquietud f // vt asustar, inquietar; **~ (clock)** n despertador m.

alas [ə'læs] ad desgraciadamente.

albeit [ɔːl'biːɪt] conj aunque.

album ['ælbəm] n álbum m; (L.P.) elepé m.

alcohol ['ælkəhɔl] n alcohol m; **~ic** [-'hɔlɪk] a, alcohólico/a m/f.

alcove ['ælkəuv] n nicho, hueco.

alderman ['ɔːldəmən] n concejal m.

ale [eɪl] n cerveza.

alert [ə'lɜːt] a alerta; (sharp) despierto, despabilado // n alerta m, alarma // vt poner sobre aviso; **to be on the ~** estar alerta or sobre aviso.

algebra ['ældʒɪbrə] n álgebra.

Algeria [æl'dʒɪərɪə] n Argelia; **~n** a, n argelino/a m/f.

alias ['eɪlɪəs] ad alias, conocido por // n alias m.

alibi ['ælɪbaɪ] n coartada.

alien ['eɪlɪən] n (foreigner) extranjero/a // a: **~ to** ajeno a; **~ate** vt enajenar, alejar.

alight [ə'laɪt] a ardiendo // vi apearse, bajar.

align [ə'laɪn] vt alinear.

alike [ə'laɪk] a semejantes, iguales // ad igualmente, del mismo modo; **to look ~** parecerse.

alimony ['ælɪmənɪ] n (LAW) manutención f.

alive [ə'laɪv] a (gen) vivo; (lively) activo.

KEYWORD

all [ɔːl] ♦ a (singular) todo/a; (plural) todos/as; **~ day** todo el día; **~ night** toda la noche; **~ men** todos los hombres; **~ five came** vinieron los cinco; **~ the books** todos los libros; **~ his life** toda su vida

♦ pron 1 todo; I ate it **~**, I ate **~ of it** me lo comí todo; **~ of us went** fuimos todos; **~ the boys went** fueron todos los chicos; is that **~?** ¿eso es todo?, ¿algo más?; (in shop) ¿algo más?, ¿alguna cosa más?

2 (in phrases): **above ~** sobre todo; **above ~** por encima de todo; **after ~** después de todo; **at ~:** **not at ~** (in answer to question) en absoluto; (in answer to thanks) ¡de nada!, ¡no hay de qué!; **I'm not at ~ tired** no estoy nada cansado/a; **anything at ~ will do** cualquier cosa viene bien; **~ in ~** a fin de cuentas

♦ ad: **~ alone** completamente solo/a; **it's not as hard as ~ that** no es tan difícil como lo pintas; **the more/the better** tanto más/mejor; **~ but** casi; **the score is 2 ~** están empatados a 2.

allay [ə'leɪ] vt (fears) aquietar; (pain) aliviar.

all clear n (after attack etc) fin m de la alerta; (fig) luz f verde.

allegation [ælɪ'geɪʃən] n alegato.

allege [ə'ledʒ] vt pretender; **~dly** [ə'ledʒɪdlɪ] ad supuestamente, según se afirma.

allegiance [ə'liːdʒəns] n lealtad f.

allergy ['ælədʒɪ] n alergia.

alleviate [ə'liːvɪeɪt] vt aliviar.

alley ['ælɪ] n (street) callejuela; (in garden) paseo.

alliance [ə'laɪəns] n alianza.

allied ['ælaɪd] a aliado.

alligator ['ælɪɡeɪtəʳ] n caimán m.

all-in ['ɔːlɪn] a (Brit: also: ~ charge) todo incluido; **~ wrestling** n lucha libre.

all-night ['ɔːl'naɪt] a (café, shop) abierto toda la noche.

allocate ['æləkeɪt] vt (share out) repartir; (devote) asignar; **allocation** [-'keɪʃən] n (of money) cuota; (distribution) reparto.

allot [əˈlɔt] vt asignar; **~ment** n ración f; (garden) parcela.

all-out [ˈɔːlaut] a (effort etc) supremo; **all out** ad con todas las fuerzas.

allow [əˈlau] vt (permit) permitir, dejar; (a claim) admitir; (sum to spend etc, time estimated) dar, conceder; (concede): **to ~ that** reconocer que; **to ~ sb to do** permitir a alguien hacer; **he is ~ed to** ... se le permite ...; **to ~ for** vt fus tener en cuenta; **~ance** n concesión f; (payment) subvención f, pensión f; (discount) descuento, rebaja; **to make ~ances for** disculpar a; tener en cuenta.

alloy [ˈælɔɪ] n (mix) mezcla.

all: **~ right** ad (feel, work) bien; (as answer) ¡conforme!, ¡está bien!; **~-round** a completo; (view) amplio; **~-time** a (record) de todos los tiempos.

allude [əˈluːd] vi: **to ~ to** aludir a.

alluring [əˈljuərɪŋ] a seductor(a), atractivo.

allusion [əˈluːʒən] n referencia, alusión f.

ally [ˈælaɪ] n aliado/a.

almighty [ɔːlˈmaɪtɪ] a todopoderoso.

almond [ˈɑːmənd] n almendra.

almost [ˈɔːlməust] ad casi.

alms [ɑːmz] npl limosna sg.

aloft [əˈlɔft] ad arriba.

alone [əˈləun] a solo // ad sólo, solamente; **to leave sb ~** dejar a uno en paz; **to leave sth ~** no tocar algo, dejar algo sin tocar; **let ~** ... sin hablar de ...

along [əˈlɔŋ] prep a lo largo de, por // ad: **is he coming ~ with us?** ¿viene con nosotros?; **he was limping ~** iba cojeando; **~ with** junto con; **all ~** (all the time) desde un principio; **~side** prep al lado de // ad (NAUT) de costado.

aloof [əˈluːf] a reservado // ad: **to stand ~** mantenerse apartado.

aloud [əˈlaud] ad en voz alta.

alphabet [ˈælfəbet] n alfabeto; **~ical** [-ˈbetɪkəl] a alfabético.

alpine [ˈælpaɪn] a alpino, alpestre.

Alps [ælps] npl: **the ~** los Alpes.

already [ɔːlˈrɛdɪ] ad ya.

alright [ˈɔːlˈraɪt] ad (Brit) = **all right**.

Alsatian [ælˈseɪʃən] n (Brit: dog) pastor m alemán.

also [ˈɔːlsəu] ad también, además.

altar [ˈɔltə*] n altar m.

alter [ˈɔltə*] vt cambiar, modificar.

alternate [ɔlˈtəːnɪt] a alterno // vi [ˈɔltəːneɪt]: **to ~ (with)** alternar (con); **on ~ days** un día sí y otro no; **alternating** [-ˈneɪtɪŋ] a (current) alterno.

alternative [ɔlˈtəːnətɪv] a alternativo // n alternativa; **~ly** ad: **~ly one could...** por otra parte se podría...

alternator [ˈɔltəːneɪtə*] n (AUT) alternador m.

although [ɔːlˈðəu] conj aunque; (given that) si bien.

altitude [ˈæltɪtjuːd] n altitud f, altura.

alto [ˈæltəu] n (female) contralto f; (male) alto.

altogether [ɔːltəˈgɛðə*] ad completamente, del todo; (on the whole, in all) en total, en conjunto.

aluminium [æljuˈmɪnɪəm], (US) **aluminum** [əˈluːmɪnəm] n aluminio.

always [ˈɔːlweɪz] ad siempre.

am [æm] vb see **be**.

a.m. ad abbr (= ante meridiem) de la mañana.

amalgamate [əˈmælgəmeɪt] vi amalgamarse // vt amalgamar, unir.

amass [əˈmæs] vt amontonar, acumular.

amateur [ˈæmətə*] n aficionado/a, amateur m/f; **~ish** a (pej) torpe, inexperto.

amaze [əˈmeɪz] vt asombrar, pasmar; **to be ~d (at)** quedar pasmado (de); **~ment** n asombro, sorpresa; **amazing** a extraordinario, pasmoso.

Amazon [ˈæməzən] n (GEO) Amazonas m.

ambassador [æmˈbæsədə*] n embajador(a) m/f.

amber ['æmbə*] n ámbar m; **at ~** (Brit AUT) en el amarillo.

ambiguity [æmbɪ'gjuɪt] n ambigüedad f; (of meaning) doble sentido; **ambiguous** [-'bɪgjuəs] a ambiguo.

ambition [æm'bɪʃən] n ambición f; **ambitious** [-ʃəs] a ambicioso.

amble ['æmbl] vi (gen: ~ along) deambular, andar sin prisa.

ambulance ['æmbjuləns] n ambulancia; **~man/woman** n (Brit) ambulanciero/a.

ambush ['æmbuʃ] n emboscada // vt tender una emboscada a.

amenable [ə'miːnəbl] a: ~ **to** (advice etc) sensible a.

amend [ə'mɛnd] vt (law, text) enmendar; **to make ~s** enmendarlo; (apologize) dar cumplida satisfacción; **~ment** n enmienda.

amenities [ə'miːnɪtɪz] npl comodidades fpl.

America [ə'mɛrɪkə] n (North ~) América del norte; (USA) Estados mpl Unidos; **~n** a, n norteamericano/a m/f.

amiable ['eɪmɪəbl] a (kind) amable, simpático.

amicable ['æmɪkəbl] a amistoso, amigable.

amid(st) [ə'mɪd(st)] prep entre, en medio de.

amiss [ə'mɪs] ad: **to take sth ~** tomar algo a mal; **there's something ~** pasa algo.

ammonia [ə'məunɪə] n amoníaco.

ammunition [æmju'nɪʃən] n municiones fpl.

amnesia [æm'niːzɪə] n amnesia.

amnesty ['æmnɪstɪ] n amnistía.

amok [ə'mɔk] ad: **to run ~** enloquecerse, desbocarse.

among(st) [ə'mʌŋ(st)] prep entre, en medio de.

amoral [æ'mɔrəl] a amoral.

amorous ['æmərəs] a cariñoso.

amorphous [ə'mɔːfəs] a amorfo.

amount [ə'maunt] n (gen) cantidad f; (of bill etc) suma, importe m // vi:

to ~ to (total) sumar; (be same as) equivaler a, significar.

amp(ère) ['æmp(ɛə*)] n amperio.

amphibian [æm'fɪbɪən] n anfibio; **amphibious** [-bɪəs] a anfibio.

amphitheatre ['æmfɪθɪətə*] n anfiteatro.

ample ['æmpl] a (spacious) amplio; (abundant) abundante; (enough) bastante, suficiente.

amplifier ['æmplɪfaɪə*] n amplificador m.

amputate ['æmpjuteɪt] vt amputar.

amuse [ə'mjuːz] vt divertir; (distract) distraer, entretener; **~ment** n diversión f; (pastime) pasatiempo; (laughter) risa; **~ment arcade** n mini-casino.

an [æn, ən, n] indefinite article see **a**.

anaemia [ə'niːmɪə] n (Brit) anemia; **anaemic** [-mɪk] a anémico; (fig) soso, insípido.

anaesthetic [ænɪs'θɛtɪk] n (Brit) anestesia; **anaesthetist** [æ'niːsθɪtɪst] n anestesista m/f.

analog(ue) ['ænəlɔg] a (computer, watch) analógico.

analogy [ə'nælədʒɪ] n analogía.

analyse ['ænəlaɪz] vt (Brit) analizar; **analysis** [ə'nælɪsɪs], pl **-ses** [-siːz] n análisis m inv; **analyst** [-ʲst] n (political ~, psycho~) analista m/f; **analytic(al)** [-'lɪtɪk(əl)] a analítico.

analyze ['ænəlaɪz] vt (US) = **analyse**.

anarchist ['ænəkɪst] a, n anarquista m/f.

anarchy ['ænəkɪ] n anarquía; (fam) desorden m.

anathema [ə'næθɪmə] n: **that is ~ to him** eso es pecado para él.

anatomy [ə'nætəmɪ] n anatomía.

ancestor ['ænsɪstə*] n antepasado.

anchor ['æŋkə*] n ancla, áncora // vi (also: **to drop ~**) anclar // vt (fig) sujetar, afianzar; **to weigh ~** levar anclas; **~age** n ancladero.

anchovy ['æntʃəvɪ] n anchoa.

ancient ['eɪnʃənt] a antiguo.

ancillary ['æn'sɪlərɪ] a (*worker, staff*) auxiliar.

and [ænd] conj y; (*before i-, hi- + consonant*) e; men ~ women hombres y mujeres; father ~ son padre e hijo; trees ~ grass árboles y hierba; ~ so on etcétera, y así sucesivamente; try ~ come procura venir; he talked ~ talked habló sin parar; better ~ better cada vez mejor.

Andalusia [ændə'luːzɪə] n Andalucía.

Andes ['ændiːz] npl: the ~ los Andes.

anemia etc [ə'niːmɪə] n (US) = **anaemia** etc.

anesthetic etc [ænɪs'θetɪk] n (US) = **anaesthetic** etc.

anew [ə'njuː] ad de nuevo, otra vez.

angel ['eɪndʒəl] n ángel m.

anger ['æŋgə] n cólera // vt enojar, enfurecer.

angina [æn'dʒaɪnə] n angina (del pecho).

angle ['æŋgl] n ángulo; from their ~ desde su punto de vista.

angler ['æŋglə] n pescador(a) m/f (de caña).

Anglican ['æŋglɪkən] a, n anglicano/a m/f.

angling ['æŋglɪŋ] n pesca con caña.

Anglo... ['æŋgləu] pref anglo... .

angrily ['æŋgrɪlɪ] ad enojado, enfadado.

angry ['æŋgrɪ] a enfadado, enojado; to be ~ with sb/at sth estar enfadado con alguien/por algo; to get ~ enfadarse, enojarse.

anguish ['æŋgwɪʃ] n (*physical*) tormentos mpl; (*mental*) angustia.

angular ['æŋgjulə] a (*shape*) angular; (*features*) anguloso.

animal ['ænɪməl] n animal m, bestia f // a animal.

animate ['ænɪmeɪt] vt (*enliven*) animar; (*encourage*) estimular, alentar // a ['ænɪmɪt] vivo; ~d a vivo.

animosity [ænɪ'mɒsɪtɪ] n animosidad f, rencor m.

aniseed ['ænɪsiːd] n anís m.

ankle ['æŋkl] n tobillo m; ~ sock n calcetín m.

annex ['æneks] n (*also*: Brit: annexe) (*building*) edificio anexo // vt [æ'neks] (*territory*) anexar.

annihilate [ə'naɪɪleɪt] vt aniquilar.

anniversary [ænɪ'vɜːsərɪ] n aniversario.

announce [ə'nauns] vt (*gen*) anunciar; (*inform*) comunicar; ~ment n (*gen*) anuncio; (*declaration*) declaración f; ~r n (RADIO, TV) locutor(a) m/f.

annoy [ə'nɔɪ] vt molestar, fastidiar; don't get ~ed! ¡no se enfade!; ~ance n enojo; (*thing*) molestia; ~ing a molesto, fastidioso; (*person*) pesado.

annual ['ænjuəl] a anual // n (BOT) anual m; (*book*) anuario; ~ly ad anualmente, cada año.

annul [ə'nʌl] vt anular; (*law*) revocar; ~ment n anulación f.

annum ['ænəm] n see per.

anomaly [ə'nɒməlɪ] n anomalía.

anonymity [ænə'nɪmɪtɪ] n anonimato.

anonymous [ə'nɒnɪməs] a anónimo.

anorak ['ænəræk] n anorak m.

anorexia [ænə'reksɪə] n (MED) anorexia.

another [ə'nʌðə] a: ~ book (one more) otro libro; (a different one) un libro distinto // pron otro; see also one.

answer ['ɑːnsə] n (to question) contestación f, respuesta; (to problem) solución f // vt contestar, responder // vt (reply to) contestar a, responder a; (problem) resolver; to ~ the phone contestar el teléfono; in ~ to your letter contestando or en contestación a su carta; to ~ the door acudir a la puerta; to ~ back vi replicar, ser respondón/ona; to ~ for vt fus responder de or por; to ~ to vt fus (description) corresponder a; ~able a: ~able to sb for sth responsable ante uno de algo; ~ing machine n contestador m automático.

ant [ænt] n hormiga.

antagonism [ænˈtægənɪzm] n hostilidad f.

antagonize [ænˈtægənaɪz] vt provocar.

Antarctic [æntˈɑːktɪk] n: the ~ el Antártico.

antelope [ˈæntɪləʊp] n antílope m.

antenatal [ˈæntɪˈneɪtl] a antenatal, prenatal; ~ **clinic** n clínica prenatal.

antenna [ænˈtenə], pl ~**e** [-niː] n antena.

anthem [ˈænθəm] n: **national** ~ himno nacional.

anthology [ænˈθɒlədʒɪ] n antología.

anthropology [ænθrəˈpɒlədʒɪ] n antropología.

anti-aircraft [æntɪˈeəkrɑːft] a antiaéreo.

antibiotic [æntɪbaɪˈɒtɪk] a, n antibiótico.

antibody [ˈæntɪbɒdɪ] n anticuerpo.

anticipate [ænˈtɪsɪpeɪt] vt (foresee) prever; (expect) esperar, contar con; (forestall) anticiparse a, adelantarse a; **anticipation** [-ˈpeɪʃən] n previsión f; esperanza; anticipación f.

anticlimax [æntɪˈklaɪmæks] n decepción f.

anticlockwise [æntɪˈklɒkwaɪz] ad en dirección contraria a la de las agujas del reloj.

antics [ˈæntɪks] npl payasadas fpl; (of child) travesuras fpl.

anticyclone [æntɪˈsaɪkləʊn] n anticiclón m.

antidote [ˈæntɪdəʊt] n antídoto.

antifreeze [ˈæntɪfriːz] n anticongelante m.

antihistamine [æntɪˈhɪstəmɪn] n antihistamínico.

antipathy [ænˈtɪpəθɪ] n (between people) antipatía; (to person, thing) aversión f.

antiquated [ˈæntɪkweɪtɪd] a anticuado.

antique [ænˈtiːk] n antigüedad f // a antiguo; ~ **dealer** n anticuario/a; ~ **shop** n tienda de antigüedades.

antiquity [ænˈtɪkwɪtɪ] n antigüedad f.

anti-semitism [æntɪˈsemɪtɪzm] n antisemitismo.

antiseptic [æntɪˈseptɪk] a, n antiséptico.

antisocial [æntɪˈsəʊʃəl] a antisocial.

antlers [ˈæntləz] npl cuernas fpl.

anus [ˈeɪnəs] n ano.

anvil [ˈænvɪl] n yunque m.

anxiety [æɡˈzaɪətɪ] n (worry) inquietud f; (eagerness) ansia, anhelo.

anxious [ˈæŋkʃəs] a (worried) inquieto; (keen) deseoso.

KEYWORD

any [ˈenɪ] ♦ a **1** (in questions etc) algún/alguna; have you ~ butter/children? ¿tienes mantequilla/hijos?; **if there are** ~ **tickets left** si quedan billetes, si queda algún billete

2 (with negative): **I haven't** ~ money/books no tengo dinero/libros **3** (no matter which) cualquier; **excuse will do** valdrá o servirá cualquier excusa; **choose** ~ **book** you like escoge el libro que quieras; ~ **teacher** you ask will tell you cualquier profesor al que preguntes te lo dirá

4 (in phrases): **in** ~ **case** de todas formas, en cualquier caso; ~ **day now** cualquier día (de éstos); **at** ~ **moment** en cualquier momento, de un momento a otro; **at** ~ **rate** en todo caso; ~ **time: come (at)** ~ **time** venga cuando quieras; **he might come (at)** ~ **time** podría llegar de un momento a otro

♦ pron **1** (in questions etc): **have you got** ~? ¿tienes alguno/a?; **can** ~ **of you sing?** ¿sabéis/saben cantar alguno de vosotros/ustedes?

2 (with negative): **I haven't** ~ (of them) no tengo ninguno

3 (no matter which one(s)): **take** ~ **of those books (you like)** toma cualquier libro que quieras de ésos

♦ ad **1** (in questions etc): **do you want** ~ **more soup/sandwiches?** ¿quieres más sopa/bocadillos?; **are** you feeling ~ better? ¿te sientes algo mejor? **2** (*with negative*): I can't hear him ~ more ya no te oigo; don't wait ~ longer no esperes más.

anybody ['ɛnɪbɔdɪ] *pron* cualquiera; (*in interrogative sentences*) alguien; (*in negative sentences*): I don't see ~ no veo a nadie; if ~ should phone... si llama alguien....

anyhow ['ɛnɪhau] *ad* (*at any rate*) de todos modos, de todas formas; (*haphazard*): do it ~ you like hazlo como quieras; she leaves things just ~ deja las cosas como quiera *or* de cualquier modo; I shall go ~ de todos modos iré.

anyone ['ɛnɪwʌn] *pron* = **anybody**.

anything ['ɛnɪθɪŋ] *pron* (*in questions etc*) algo, alguna cosa; (*with negative*) nada; can you see ~? ¿ves algo?; if ~ happens to me... si algo me ocurre...; (*no matter what*): you can say ~ you like puedes decir lo que quieras; ~ will do vale todo *or* cualquier cosa; he'll eat ~ come de todo *or* lo que sea.

anyway ['ɛnɪweɪ] *ad* (*at any rate*) de todos modos, de todas formas; I shall go ~ de todos modos iré; (*besides*): ~, I couldn't come even if I wanted to además, no podría venir aunque quisiera; why are you phoning, ~? ¿entonces, por qué llamas?, ¿por qué llamas, pues?

anywhere ['ɛnɪwɛə*] *ad* (*in questions etc*): can you see him ~? ¿le ves por algún lado?; are you going ~? ¿vas a algún sitio?; (*with negative*): I can't see him ~ no le veo por ninguna parte; (*no matter where*): ~ in the world en cualquier parte (del mundo); put the books down ~ posa los libros donde quieras.

apart [ə'pɑːt] *ad* aparte, separadamente; 10 miles ~ separados por 10 millas; to take ~ desmontar; ~ from *prep* aparte de.

apartheid [ə'pɑːteɪt] *n* apartheid *m*.

apartment [ə'pɑːtmənt] *n* (US) piso, departamento (*LAm*), apartamento; (*room*) cuarto; ~ **house** *n* (US) casa de apartamentos.

apathetic [æpə'θɛtɪk] *a* apático, indiferente.

apathy ['æpəθɪ] *n* apatía, indiferencia.

ape [eɪp] *n* mono // *vt* remedar.

aperitif [ə'pɛrɪtɪf] *n* aperitivo.

aperture ['æpətʃjuə*] *n* rendija, resquicio; (*PHOT*) abertura.

apex ['eɪpɛks] *n* ápice *m*; (*fig*) cumbre *f*.

apiece [ə'piːs] *ad* cada uno.

aplomb [ə'plɔm] *n* aplomo.

apologetic [əpɔlə'dʒɛtɪk] *a* (*look, remark*) de disculpa.

apologize [ə'pɔlədʒaɪz] *vi*: to ~ (for sth to sb) disculparse (con alguien de algo).

apology [ə'pɔlədʒɪ] *n* disculpa, excusa.

apostle [ə'pɔsl] *n* apóstol *m/f*.

apostrophe [ə'pɔstrəfɪ] *n* apóstrofo *m*.

appal [ə'pɔːl] *vt* horrorizar, espantar; ~**ling** *a* espantoso; (*awful*) pésimo.

apparatus [æpə'reɪtəs] *n* aparato, (*in gymnasium*) aparatos *mpl*.

apparel [ə'pærəl] *n* (US) ropa.

apparent [ə'pærənt] *a* aparente; ~**ly** *ad* por lo visto, al parecer.

appeal [ə'piːl] *vi* (*LAW*) apelar // *n* (*LAW*) apelación *f*; (*request*) llamamiento; (*plea*) súplica; (*charm*) atractivo, encanto; to ~ for reclamar; to ~ to (*subj: person*) rogar a, suplicar a; (*subj: thing*) atraer, interesar; it doesn't ~ to me no me atrae, no me llama la atención; ~**ing** *a* (*nice*) atractivo; (*touching*) conmovedor(a), emocionante.

appear [ə'pɪə*] *vi* aparecer, presentarse; (*LAW*) comparecer; (*publication*) salir (a luz), publicarse; (*seem*) parecer; it would ~ that parecería que; ~**ance** *n* aparición *f*; (*look, as-*

pect) apariencia, aspecto.

appease [ə'pi:z] *vt* (*pacify*) apaciguar; (*satisfy*) satisfacer.

appendicitis [əpendɪ'saɪtɪs] *n* apendicitis *f*.

appendix [ə'pendɪks], *pl* **-dices** [-dɪsi:z] *n* apéndice *m*.

appetite ['æpɪtaɪt] *n* apetito; (*fig*) deseo, anhelo.

appetizer ['æpɪtaɪzə*] *n* (*drink*) aperitivo; (*food*) tapas *fpl* (*Sp*).

applaud [ə'plɔ:d] *vt, vi* aplaudir.

applause [ə'plɔ:z] *n* aplausos *mpl*.

apple ['æpl] *n* manzana; **~ tree** *n* manzano.

appliance [ə'plaɪəns] *n* aparato.

applicant ['æplɪkənt] *n* candidato/a; solicitante *m/f*.

application [æplɪ'keɪʃən] *n* aplicación *f*; (*for a job, a grant etc*) solicitud *f*, petición *f*; **~ form** *n* solicitud *f*.

applied [ə'plaɪd] *a* aplicado.

apply [ə'plaɪ] *vt*: **to ~ (to)** aplicar (a); (*fig*) emplear (para) // *vi*: **to ~ to** (*ask*) dirigirse a; (*be suitable for*) ser aplicable a; (*be relevant to*) tener que ver con; **~ for** (*permit, grant, job*) solicitar; **to ~ o.s. to** aplicarse a, dedicarse a.

appoint [ə'pɔɪnt] *vt* (*to post*) nombrar; (*date, place*) fijar, señalar; **~ment** *n* (*engagement*) cita; (*date*) compromiso; (*act*) nombramiento; (*post*) puesto.

appraisal [ə'preɪzl] *n* apreciación *f*.

appreciable [ə'pri:ʃəbl] *a* sensible.

appreciate [ə'pri:ʃɪeɪt] *vt* (*like*) apreciar, tener en mucho; (*be grateful for*) agradecer; (*be aware of*) comprender // *vi* (*COMM*) aumentar(se) en valor; **appreciation** [-'eɪʃən] *n* aprecio; reconocimiento, agradecimiento; aumento en valor.

appreciative [ə'pri:ʃɪətɪv] *a* apreciativo, agradecido.

apprehend [æprɪ'hend] *vt* percibir; (*arrest*) detener.

apprehension [æprɪ'henʃən] *n*

(*fear*) aprensión *f*; **apprehensive** [-'hensɪv] *a* aprensivo.

apprentice [ə'prentɪs] *n* aprendiz/a *m/f*; **~ship** *n* aprendizaje *m*.

approach [ə'prəutʃ] *vi* acercarse // *vt* acercarse a; (*be approximate*) aproximarse a; (*ask, apply to*) dirigirse a // *n* acercamiento; aproximación *f*; (*access*) acceso; (*proposal*) proposición *f*; **~able** *a* (*person*) abordable; (*place*) accesible.

appropriate [ə'prəuprɪɪt] *a* apropiado, conveniente // *vt* [-rɪeɪt] (*take*) apropiarse de; (*allot*): **to ~ sth for** destinar algo a.

approval [ə'pru:vəl] *n* aprobación *f*, visto bueno; **on ~** (*COMM*) a prueba.

approve [ə'pru:v] *vt* aprobar; **to ~ of** *vt fus* aprobar; **~d school** *n* (*Brit*) correccional *m*.

approximate [ə'prɒksɪmɪt] *a* aproximado; **~ly** *ad* aproximadamente, más o menos.

apricot ['eɪprɪkɒt] *n* albaricoque *m* (*Sp*), damasco (*LAm*).

April ['eɪprɪl] *n* abril *m*; **~ Fool's Day** *n* (*1 April*) = día *m* de los Inocentes (*28 December*).

apron ['eɪprən] *n* delantal *m*.

apt [æpt] *a* (*to the point*) acertado, oportuno; (*appropriate*) apropiado; (*likely*): **~ to do** propenso a hacer.

aqualung ['ækwəlʌŋ] *n* escafandra autónoma.

aquarium [ə'kweərɪəm] *n* acuario.

Aquarius [ə'kweərɪəs] *n* Acuario.

aquatic [ə'kwætɪk] *a* acuático.

aqueduct ['ækwɪdʌkt] *n* acueducto.

Arab ['ærəb] *n* árabe *m/f*.

Arabian [ə'reɪbɪən] *a* árabe.

Arabic ['ærəbɪk] *a* (*language, manuscripts*) árabe // *n* árabe *m*; **~ numerals** numeración *f* arábiga.

arable ['ærəbl] *a* cultivable.

Aragon ['ærəgən] *n* Aragón *m*.

arbitrary ['ɑ:bɪtrərɪ] *a* arbitrario.

arbitration [ɑ:bɪ'treɪʃən] *n* arbitraje *m*.

arcade [ɑ:'keɪd] *n* (*ARCH*) arcada;

(*round a square*) soportales *mpl*; (*shopping ~*) galería, pasaje *m*.

arch [ɑːtʃ] *n* arco; (*vault*) bóveda; (*of foot*) arco del pie // *vt* arquear.

archaeologist [ɑːkɪˈɔlədʒɪst] *n* arqueólogo/a.

archaeology [ɑːkɪˈɔlədʒɪ] *n* arqueología.

archaic [ɑːˈkeɪɪk] *a* arcaico.

archbishop [ɑːtʃˈbɪʃəp] *n* arzobispo.

arch-enemy [ɑːtʃˈɛnəmɪ] *n* enemigo jurado.

archeology *etc* [ɑːkɪˈɔlədʒɪ] (*US*) = **archaeology** *etc*.

archer [ˈɑːtʃə*] *n* arquero; **~y** *n* tiro al arco.

archipelago [ɑːkɪˈpelɪɡəu] *n* archipiélago.

architect [ˈɑːkɪtekt] *n* arquitecto/a; **~ural** [-ˈtektʃərəl] *a* arquitectónico; **~ure** *n* arquitectura.

archives [ˈɑːkaɪvz] *npl* archivo *sg*.

archway [ˈɑːtʃweɪ] *n* arco, arcada.

Arctic [ˈɑːktɪk] *a* ártico // *n*: **the** ~ el Ártico.

ardent [ˈɑːdənt] *a* (*desire*) ardiente; (*supporter, lover*) apasionado.

arduous [ˈɑːdjuəs] *a* (*gen*) arduo; (*journey*) penoso.

are [ɑː*] *vb see* **be**.

area [ˈɛərɪə] *n* área; (*MATH etc*) superficie *f*, extensión *f*; (*zone*) región *f*, zona; **~ code** *n* (*US TEL*) prefijo.

arena [əˈriːnə] *n* arena; (*of circus*) pista; (*for bullfight*) plaza, ruedo.

aren't [ɑːnt] = **are not**.

Argentina [ɑːdʒənˈtiːnə] *n* Argentina; **Argentinian** [-ˈtɪnɪən] *a*, *n* argentino/a *m/f*.

arguably [ˈɑːɡjuəblɪ] *ad* posiblemente.

argue [ˈɑːɡjuː] *vi* (*quarrel*) discutir, pelearse; (*reason*) razonar, argumentar; **to ~ that** sostener que.

argument [ˈɑːɡjumənt] *n* (*reasons*) argumento; (*quarrel*) discusión *f*, pelea; (*debate*) debate *m*, disputa; **~ative** [-ˈmentətɪv] *a* discutidor(a).

aria [ˈɑːrɪə] *n* (*MUS*) aria.

Aries [ˈɛərɪz] *n* Aries *m*.

arise [əˈraɪz], *pt* **arose**, *pp* **arisen** [əˈrɪzn] *vi* (*rise up*) levantarse, alzarse; (*emerge*) surgir, presentarse; **to ~ from** derivar de.

aristocrat [ˈærɪstəkræt] *n* aristócrata *m/f*.

arithmetic [əˈrɪθmətɪk] *n* aritmética.

ark [ɑːk] *n*: **Noah's A~** el Arca *f* de Noé.

arm [ɑːm] *n* (*ANAT*) brazo // *vt* armar; **~s** *npl* (*weapons*) armas *fpl*; (*HERALDRY*) escudo *sg*; **~ in ~** cogidos del brazo; **~s race** *n* carrera de armamentos.

armaments [ˈɑːməmənts] *npl* (*weapons*) armamentos *mpl*.

armchair [ˈɑːmtʃɛə*] *n* sillón *m*.

armed [ɑːmd] *a* armado; **~ robbery** *n* robo a mano armada.

armour, (*US*) **armor** [ˈɑːmə*] *n* armadura; **~ed car** *n* coche *m* or carro (*LAm*) blindado; **~y** *n* arsenal *m*.

armpit [ˈɑːmpɪt] *n* sobaco, axila.

armrest [ˈɑːmrest] *n* apoyabrazos *m inv*.

army [ˈɑːmɪ] *n* ejército.

aroma [əˈrəumə] *n* aroma *m*, fragancia.

arose [əˈrəuz] *pt of* **arise**.

around [əˈraund] *ad* alrededor; (*in the area*) a la redonda // *prep* alrededor de.

arouse [əˈrauz] *vt* despertar.

arrange [əˈreɪndʒ] *vt* arreglar, ordenar; (*programme*) organizar; **to ~ to do sth** quedar en hacer algo; **~ment** *n* arreglo; (*agreement*) acuerdo; **~ments** *npl* (*preparations*) preparativos *mpl*.

array [əˈreɪ] *n*: **~ of** (*things*) serie *f* de; (*people*) conjunto *m*.

arrears [əˈrɪəz] *npl* atrasos *mpl*; **to be in ~ with one's rent** estar retrasado en el pago del alquiler.

arrest [əˈrest] *vt* detener; (*sb's attention*) llamar // *n* detención *f*; **under ~** detenido.

arrival [əˈraɪvəl] *n* llegada; **new ~**

recién llegado/a.

arrive [ə'raɪv] *vi* llegar.

arrogant ['ærəgənt] *a* arrogante.

arrow ['ærəʊ] *n* flecha.

arse [ɑːs] *n* (*Brit col!*) culo, trasero.

arsenal ['ɑːsɪnl] *n* arsenal *m*.

arsenic ['ɑːsnɪk] *n* arsénico.

arson ['ɑːsn] *n* incendio premeditado.

art [ɑːt] *n* arte *m*; (*skill*) destreza; (*technique*) técnica; A~s *npl* (*SCOL*) Letras *fpl*.

artery ['ɑːtərɪ] *n* arteria.

artful ['ɑːtful] *a* (*cunning: person, trick*) mañoso.

art gallery *n* pinacoteca; (*saleroom*) galería de arte.

arthritis [ɑː'θraɪtɪs] *n* artritis *f*.

artichoke ['ɑːtɪtʃəuk] *n* alcachofa; Jerusalem ~ aguaturma.

article ['ɑːtɪkl] *n* artículo, (in *newspaper*) artículo; (*Brit LAW: training*): ~s *npl* contrato *sg* de aprendizaje; ~ of clothing prenda de vestir.

articulate [ɑː'tɪkjulɪt] *a* (*speech*) claro; (*person*) que se expresa bien // *vi* [-leɪt] articular; ~d lorry *n* (*Brit*) trailer *m*.

artificial [ɑːtɪ'fɪʃəl] *a* artificial; (*teeth etc*) postizo.

artillery [ɑː'tɪlərɪ] *n* artillería.

artisan ['ɑːtɪzæn] *n* artesano.

artist ['ɑːtɪst] *n* artista *m/f*; (*MUS*) intérprete *m/f*; ~ic [ɑː'tɪstɪk] *a* artístico; ~ry *n* arte *m*, habilidad *f* (artística).

artless ['ɑːtlɪs] *a* (*innocent*) natural, sencillo; (*clumsy*) torpe.

art school *n* escuela de bellas artes.

KEYWORD

as [æz] *conj* **1** (*referring to time*) cuando, mientras; a medida que; ~ the years went by con el paso de los años; he came in ~ I was leaving entró cuando me marchaba; ~ from tomorrow desde o a partir de mañana

2 (*in comparisons*): ~ big ~ tan grande como; twice ~ big ~ el doble de grande que; ~ much money/many books ~ tanto dinero/tantos libros como; ~ soon ~ en cuanto

3 (*since, because*) como, ya que; he left early ~ he had to be home by 10 se fue temprano como tenía que estar en casa a las 10

4 (*referring to manner, way*): do ~ you wish haz lo que quieras; ~ she said como dijo; he gave it to me ~ a present me lo dio de regalo

5 (*in the capacity of*): he works ~ a barman trabaja de barman; ~ chairman of the company, he... como presidente de la compañía, ...

6 (*concerning*): ~ for or to that por or en lo que respecta a eso

7: ~ if or though como si: he looked ~ if he was ill parecía como si estuviera enfermo, tenía aspecto de enfermo

see also long, such, well.

---

a.s.a.p. *abbr* (= as soon as possible) cuanto antes.

asbestos [æz'bestəs] *n* asbesto, amianto.

ascend [ə'send] *vt* subir; ~ancy *n* ascendiente *m*, dominio.

ascent [ə'sent] *n* subida; (*of plane*) ascenso.

ascertain [æsə'teɪn] *vt* averiguar.

ascribe [ə'skraɪb] *vt*: to ~ sth to atribuir algo a.

ash [æʃ] *n* ceniza; (*tree*) fresno; ~can *n* (*US*) cubo o bote *m* (*LAm*) de la basura.

ashamed [ə'ʃeɪmd] *a* avergonzado, apenado (*LAm*); to be ~ of avergonzarse de.

ashen ['æʃn] *a* pálido.

ashore [ə'ʃɔː*] *ad* en tierra.

ashtray ['æʃtreɪ] *n* cenicero.

Ash Wednesday *n* miércoles *m* de Cenizas.

Asia ['eɪʃə] *n* Asia; ~n, ~tic [eɪsɪ'ætɪk] *a, n* asiático/a *m/f*.

aside [ə'saɪd] *ad* a un lado.

ask [ɑːsk] *vt* (*question*) preguntar; (*demand*) pedir; (*invite*) invitar; to

~ **sb sth/to do sth** preguntar algo a alguien/pedir a alguien que haga algo; **to ~ sb about sth** preguntar algo a alguien; **to ~ (sb) a question** hacer una pregunta (a alguien); **to ~ sb out** to dinner invitar a cenar a uno; **to ~ after** sth fus preguntar por; **to ~ for** vt fus pedir.

askance [əˈskɑːns] ad: **to look ~** at sb mirar con recelo a uno.

askew [əˈskjuː] ad sesgado, ladeado.

asking price n precio inicial.

asleep [əˈsliːp] a dormido; **to fall ~** dormirse, quedarse dormido.

asparagus [əsˈpærəgəs] n espárragos mpl.

aspect [ˈæspekt] n aspecto, apariencia; (direction in which a building etc faces) orientación f.

aspersions [əsˈpəːʃənz] npl: **to cast ~ on** difamar a, calumniar a.

asphyxiation [æsˈfɪksɪˈeɪʃən] n asfixia.

aspirations [æspəˈreɪʃənz] npl anhelo sg, deseo sg; (ambition) ambición fsg.

aspire [əsˈpaɪə*] vi: **to ~** aspirar a, ambicionar.

aspirin [ˈæsprɪn] n aspirina.

ass [æs] n asno, burro; (col) imbécil m/f; (US col!) culo, trasero.

assailant [əˈseɪlənt] n asaltador/a m/f, agresor/a m/f.

assassin [əˈsæsɪn] n asesino/a; **~ate** vt asesinar; **~ation** [-ˈneɪʃən] n asesinato.

assault [əˈsɔːlt] n (gen: attack) asalto // vt asaltar, atacar; (sexually) violar.

assemble [əˈsembl] vt reunir, juntar; (TECH) montar // vi reunirse, juntarse.

assembly [əˈsembli] n (meeting) reunión f, asamblea; (construction) montaje m; **~ line** n cadena de montaje.

assent [əˈsent] n asentimiento, aprobación f // vi consentir, asentir.

assert [əˈsəːt] vt afirmar; (insist on) hacer valer.

assess [əˈses] vt valorar, calcular; (tax, damages) fijar; (property etc: for tax) gravar; **~ment** n valoración f; gravamen m; **~or** n asesor/a m/f; (of tax) tasador/a m/f.

asset [ˈæset] n posesión f; (quality) ventaja; **~s** npl (funds) activo sg, fondos mpl.

assign [əˈsaɪn] vt (date) fijar; (task) asignar; (resources) destinar; (property) traspasar; **~ment** n asignación f; (task) tarea.

assist [əˈsɪst] vt ayudar; **~ance** n ayuda, auxilio; **~ant** n ayudante m/f; (Brit: also: **shop ~ant**) dependiente/a m/f.

associate [əˈsəʊʃɪt] a asociado // n socio/a, colega m/f; (in crime) cómplice m/f; (member) miembro // vb [-ʃɪeɪt] vt asociar; (ideas) relacionar // vi: **to ~ with** sb tratar con alguien.

association [əsəʊsɪˈeɪʃən] n asociación f; (COMM) sociedad f.

assorted [əˈsɔːtɪd] a surtido, variado.

assortment [əˈsɔːtmənt] n surtido.

assume [əˈsjuːm] vt (suppose) suponer; (responsibilities etc) asumir; (attitude, name) adoptar, tomar; **~d name** n nombre m falso.

assumption [əˈsʌmpʃən] n (supposition) suposición f, presunción f; (act) asunción f.

assurance [əˈʃʊərəns] n garantía, promesa; (confidence) confianza, aplomo; (insurance) seguro.

assure [əˈʃʊə*] vt asegurar.

astern [əˈstəːn] ad a popa.

asthma [ˈæsmə] n asma.

astonish [əˈstɒnɪʃ] vt asombrar, pasmar; **~ment** n asombro, sorpresa.

astound [əˈstaund] vt asombrar, pasmar.

astray [əˈstreɪ] ad: **to go ~** extraviarse; **to lead ~** llevar por mal camino.

astride [əˈstraɪd] prep a caballo or horcajadas sobre.

astrology [æsˈtrɒlədʒɪ] n astrología.

astronaut ['æstrənɔːt] n astronauta m/f.

astronomical [æstrə'nɔmɪkəl] a astronómico.

astronomy [aes'trɔnəmɪ] n astronomía.

astute [əs'tjuːt] a astuto.

asylum [ə'saɪləm] n (refuge) asilo; (hospital) manicomio.

KEYWORD

---

at [æt] prep 1 (referring to position) en; (direction) a; ~ the top en lo alto; ~ home/school en casa/la escuela; to look ~ sth/sb mirar algo/a uno

2 (referring to time): ~ 4 o'clock a las 4; ~ night por la noche; ~ Christmas en Navidad; ~ times a veces

3 (referring to rates, speed etc): ~ £1 a kilo a una libra el kilo; two ~ a time de dos en dos; ~ 50 km/h a 50 km/h

4 (referring to manner): ~ a stroke de un golpe; ~ peace en paz

5 (referring to activity): to be ~ work estar trabajando; (in the office etc) estar en el trabajo; to play ~ cowboys jugar a los vaqueros; to be good ~ sth ser bueno en algo

6 (referring to cause): shocked/surprised/annoyed ~ sth asombrado/sorprendido/fastidiado por algo; I went ~ his suggestion fui a instancias suyas.

---

ate [eɪt] pt of **eat**.

atheist ['eɪθɪɪst] n ateo/a.

Athens ['æθɪnz] n Atenas f.

athlete ['æθliːt] n atleta m/f.

athletic [æθ'letɪk] a atlético; ~s n atletismo.

Atlantic [ət'læntɪk] a atlántico // n: the ~ (Ocean) el (Océano) Atlántico.

atlas ['ætləs] n atlas m.

atmosphere ['ætməsfɪə'] n atmósfera; (fig) ambiente m.

atom ['ætəm] n átomo; ~ic [ə'tɔmɪk]

a atómico; ~(ic) bomb n bomba atómica; ~izer ['ætəmaɪzə'] n atomizador m.

atone [ə'təun] vi: to ~ for expiar.

atrocious [ə'trəuʃəs] a atroz.

attach [ə'tætʃ] vt sujetar; (stick) pegar; (document, letter) adjuntar; to be ~ed to sb/sth (to like) tener cariño a alguien/algo.

attaché [ə'tæʃeɪ] n agregado/a; ~ case n (Brit) maletín m.

attachment [ə'tætʃmənt] n (tool) accesorio; (love): ~ (to) apego (a).

attack [ə'tæk] vt (MIL) atacar; (criminal) agredir, asaltar; (task etc) emprender // n ataque m, asalto; (on sb's life) atentado; heart ~ n infarto (de miocardio); ~er n agresor(a) m/f, asaltante m/f.

attain [ə'teɪn] vt (also: ~ to) alcanzar; (achieve) lograr, conseguir; ~ments npl (skill) talento sg.

attempt [ə'tempt] n tentativa, intento; (attack) atentado // vt intentar; ~ed a: ~ed burglary tentativa or intento de robo.

attend [ə'tend] vt asistir a; (patient) atender; to ~ to vt fus (needs, affairs etc) ocuparse de; (speech etc) prestar atención a; (customer) atender a; ~ance n asistencia, presencia; (people present) concurrencia; ~ant n sirviente/a m/f, mozo/a; (THEATRE) acomodador/a m/f // a concomitante.

attention [ə'tenʃən] n atención f // excl (MIL) ¡firme(s)!; for the ~ of... (ADMIN) atención... .

attentive [ə'tentɪv] a atento; (polite) cortés.

attest [ə'test] vi: to ~ to dar fe de.

attic ['ætɪk] n desván m.

attitude ['ætɪtjuːd] n (gen) actitud f; (disposition) disposición f.

attorney [ə'tɔːnɪ] n (lawyer) abogado/a; (having proxy) apoderado/a; A~ General n (Brit) = Presidente del Consejo del Poder Judicial (Sp); (US) = ministro de justicia.

attract [ə'trækt] vt atraer; (attention) llamar; ~**ion** [ə'trækʃən] n (gen) encanto; (amusements) diversiones fpl; (PHYSICS) atracción f; (fig: towards sth) atractivo m; ~**ive** a atractivo; (interesting) atrayente; (pretty) guapo, mono.

attribute ['ætrɪbjuːt] n atributo // a [ə'trɪbjuːt]: **to ~ sth** to atribuir algo a; (accuse) achacar algo a.

attrition [ə'trɪʃən] n: **war of ~** guerra de agotamiento.

aubergine ['əubəʒiːn] n (Brit) berenjena.

auburn ['ɔːbən] a color castaño rojizo.

auction ['ɔːkʃən] n (also: **sale by ~**) subasta // vt subastar; ~**eer** [-'ɪə*] n subastador/a m/f.

audacity [ɔː'dæsɪtɪ] n audacia, atrevimiento; (pej) descaro.

audience ['ɔːdɪəns] n auditorio; (gathering) público; (interview) audiencia.

audio-typist ['ɔːdɪəʊ'taɪpɪst] n mecanógrafo/a de dictáfono.

audio-visual ['ɔːdɪəʊ'vɪzjʊəl] a audiovisual; **~ aid** n ayuda audiovisual.

audit ['ɔːdɪt] vt revisar, intervenir.

audition [ɔː'dɪʃən] n audición f.

auditor ['ɔːdɪtə*] n interventor/a m/f, censor/a m/f de cuentas.

augment [ɔːg'ment] vt aumentar // vi aumentarse.

augur ['ɔːgə*] vi: **it ~s well** es de buen agüero.

August ['ɔːgəst] n agosto.

aunt [ɑːnt] n tía; ~**ie**, ~**y** n diminutive of **aunt**.

au pair ['əu'peə*] n (also: **~ girl**) au pair f.

aura ['ɔːrə] n aura; (atmosphere) ambiente m.

auspices ['ɔːspɪsɪz] npl: **under the ~ of** bajo los auspicios de.

auspicious [ɔːs'pɪʃəs] a propicio, de buen augurio.

austerity [ɔ'sterɪtɪ] n austeridad f.

Australia [ɔs'treɪlɪə] n Australia; ~**n** a, n australiano/a m/f.

Austria ['ɔstrɪə] n Austria; ~**n** a, n austríaco/a m/f.

authentic [ɔː'θentɪk] a auténtico.

author ['ɔːθə*] n autor/a m/f.

authoritarian [ɔːθɔrɪ'teərɪən] a autoritario.

authoritative [ɔː'θɔrɪtətɪv] a autorizado; (manner) autoritario.

authority [ɔː'θɔrɪtɪ] n autoridad f; **the authorities** npl las autoridades.

authorize ['ɔːθəraɪz] vt autorizar.

auto ['ɔːtəu] n (US) coche m, carro m, automóvil m.

autobiography [ɔːtəbaɪ'ɔgrəfɪ] n autobiografía.

autograph ['ɔːtəgrɑːf] n autógrafo // vt firmar; (photo etc) dedicar.

automated ['ɔːtəmeɪtɪd] a automatizado.

automatic [ɔːtə'mætɪk] a automático // n (gun) pistola automática; ~**ally** ad automáticamente.

automation [ɔːtə'meɪʃən] n reconversión f.

automaton [ɔː'tɔmətən], pl **-mata** [-tə] n autómata m/f.

automobile ['ɔːtəməbiːl] n (US) coche m, carro (LAm), automóvil m.

autonomy [ɔː'tɔnəmɪ] n autonomía.

autopsy ['ɔːtɔpsɪ] n autopsia.

autumn ['ɔːtəm] n otoño.

auxiliary [ɔːg'zɪlɪərɪ] a auxiliar.

Av. abbr = **avenue.**

avail [ə'veɪl] vt: **to ~ o.s. of** aprovechar(se), valerse de // n: **to no ~** en vano, sin resultado.

available [ə'veɪləbl] a disponible.

avalanche ['ævəlɑːnʃ] n alud m, avalancha.

avant-garde ['ævãŋˈgɑːd] a de vanguardia.

Ave. abbr = **avenue.**

avenge [ə'vendʒ] vt vengar.

avenue ['ævɪnjuː] n avenida; (fig) camino.

average ['ævərɪdʒ] n promedio, término medio // a (mean) medio, de término medio; (ordinary) regular, corriente // vt calcular el promedio de, prorratear; **on ~** por regla general; **to ~ out** vi: **to ~ out** salir en un promedio de.

averse [ə'vɜːs] a: **to be ~ to sth/ doing** sentir aversión or antipatía por algo/por hacer.

avert [ə'vɜːt] vt prevenir; (blow) desviar; (one's eyes) apartar.

aviary ['eɪvɪərɪ] n pajarera, avería.

avid ['ævɪd] a ávido, ansioso.

avocado [ævə'kɑːdəʊ] n (also: Brit: ~ **pear**) aguacate m, palta (LAm).

avoid [ə'vɔɪd] vt evitar, eludir.

avuncular [ə'vʌŋkjʊlə*] a paternal.

await [ə'weɪt] vt esperar, aguardar.

awake [ə'weɪk] a despierto // vb (pt **awoke**, pp **awoken** or **awaked**) vt despertar // vi despertarse: **to be ~** estar despierto; **~ning** el despertar.

award [ə'wɔːd] n (prize) premio; (medal) condecoración // (LAW) fallo, sentencia; (act) concesión // vt (prize) otorgar, conceder; (LAW: damages) adjudicar.

aware [ə'weə*] a consciente; (awake) despierto; (informed) enterado; **to become ~** of darse cuenta de, enterarse de; **~ness** n conciencia, conocimiento.

awash [ə'wɒʃ] a inundado.

away [ə'weɪ] ad (gen) fuera; (far ~) lejos; **two kilometres ~** a dos kilómetros de distancia; **two hours ~ by car** a dos horas en coche; **the holiday was two weeks ~** faltaba dos semanas para las vacaciones; **~ from** lejos de, fuera de; **he's ~ for a week** estará ausente una semana; **to work/pedal ~** seguir trabajando/ pedaleando; **to fade ~** desvanecerse; (sound) apagarse; **~ game** n (SPORT) partido de fuera.

awe [ɔː] n pavor m, respeto, temor m reverencial; **~inspiring**, **~some** a imponente, pasmoso.

awful ['ɔːful] a terrible, pasmoso; **~ly** ad (very) terriblemente.

awhile [ə'waɪl] ad (durante) un rato, algún tiempo.

awkward ['ɔːkwəd] a (clumsy) des-

mañado, torpe; (shape) incómodo; (problem) difícil; (embarrassing) delicado.

awning ['ɔːnɪŋ] n (of shop) toldo; (of window etc) marquesina.

awoke [ə'wəʊk], **awoken** [-kən] pt, pp of **awake**.

awry [ə'raɪ] ad: **to be ~** estar descolocado or atravesado; **to go ~** salir mal, fracasar.

axe, (US) **ax** [æks] n hacha // vt (employee) despedir; (project etc) cortar; (jobs) reducir.

axis ['æksɪs], pl **axes** [-siːz] n eje m.

axle ['æksl] n eje m, árbol m.

aye(e) [aɪ] excl (yes) sí; **the ayes** npl los que votan a favor.

B

B [biː] n (MUS) si m.

B.A. abbr = **Bachelor of Arts.**

babble ['bæbl] vi barbullar.

baby ['beɪbɪ] n bebé m/f; **~ carriage** n (US) cochecito; **~sit** vi hacer de canguro; **~sitter** n canguro/ a.

bachelor ['bætʃələ*] n soltero; **B~ of Arts/Science** (B.A./B.Sc.) licenciado/a en Filosofía y Letras/ Ciencias.

back [bæk] n (of person) espalda; (of animal) lomo; (of hand) dorso; (as opposed to front) parte f de atrás; (of room, car, etc) fondo; (of chair) respaldo; (of page) reverso; (FOOTBALL) defensa m // vt (candidate: also: ~ **up**) respaldar, apoyar; (horse: at races) apostar a; (car etc) dar marcha atrás or con // vi (car etc) dar marcha atrás // a (in compounds) de atrás; **~ seats/wheels** (AUT) asientos mpl/ruedas fpl de atrás; **~ payments** pagos mpl con efecto retroactivo; **~ rent** renta atrasada // ad (not forward) (hacia) atrás; (returned): **he's ~** está de vuelta, ha vuelto; **he ran ~** volvió corriendo; (restitution): **throw the**

ball ~ devuelve la pelota; **can I have it** ~? ¿me lo devuelve?; *(again)*: **he called** ~ llamó de nuevo; **to** ~ **down** *vi* echarse atrás; **to** ~ **out** *vi (of promise)* volverse atrás; **to** ~ **up** *vt (support: person)* apoyar, respaldar; *(: theory)* defender; *(car)* dar marcha atrás a; *(COMPUT)* hacer una copia preventiva *or* de reserva; **~bencher** *n (Brit)* miembro del parlamento sin portafolio; **~bone** *n* columna vertebral; **~cloth** *n* telón *m* de fondo; **~date** *vt (letter)* poner fecha atrasada a; **~ ~cloth**; **~fire** *vi (AUT)* petardear; *(plans)* fallar, salir mal; **~ground** *n* fondo; *(of events)* antecedentes *mpl*; *(basic knowledge)* bases *fpl*; *(experience)* conocimientos *mpl*, educación *f*; **family ~ground** origen *m*, antecedentes *mpl*; **~hand** *n (TENNIS: also:* **~hand stroke**) revés *m*; **~handed** *a (fig)* ambiguo, equívoco; **~hander** *n (Brit: bribe)* soborno; **~ing** *n (fig)* apoyo, respaldo; **~lash** *n* reacción *f*, resaca; **~log** *n:* **~log of work** atrasos *mpl*; **~ number** *n (of magazine etc)* número atrasado; **~pack** *n* mochila; **~pay** *n* pago atrasado; **~side** *n (col)* trasero, culo; **~stage** *ad* entre bastidores; **~stroke** *n* braza de espaldas; **~up** *a (train, plane)* suplementario; *(COMPUT: disk, file)* de reserva // *n (support)* apoyo; *(also:* **~up file**) copia preventiva *or* de reserva; **~- up lights** *npl (US)* luces *fpl* de marcha atrás; **~ward** *a (movement)* hacia atrás; *(person, country)* atrasado; *(shy)* tímido; **~wards** *ad (move, go)* hacia atrás; *(read a list)* al revés; *(fall)* de espaldas; **~ward** *n (fig)* lugar *m* atrasado *or* apartado; **~yard** *n* traspatío.

bacon ['beikən] *n* tocino, beicon *m*.

bad [bæd] *a* malo; *(serious)* grave; *(meat, food)* podrido, pasado; **his ~ leg** su pierna lisiada; **to go** ~ pasar-

se.

bade [bæd, beid] *pt of* **bid**.

badge [bædʒ] *n* insignia; *(metal ~)* chapa, placa.

badger ['bædʒə*] *n* tejón *m*.

badly ['bædli] *ad (work, dress etc)* mal; **~ wounded** gravemente herido; **he needs it** ~ le hace gran falta; **to be** ~ **off (for money)** andar mal de dinero.

badminton ['bædminton] *n* bádminton *m*.

bad-tempered ['bæd'tempəd] *a* de mal genio *or* carácter; *(temporary)* de mal humor.

baffle ['bæfl] *vt* desconcertar, confundir.

bag [bæg] *n* bolsa, saco; *(handbag)* bolso; *(satchel)* cartera; *(case)* maleta; *(of hunter)* caza // *vt (col: take)* coger *(Sp)*, agarrar *(LAm)*, pescar; **~s of** *(col: lots of)* un montón de; **~gage** *n* equipaje *m*; **~gy** *a (clothing)* amplio; **~pipes** *npl* gaita *sg*.

Bahamas [bə'hɑːməz] *npl:* **the ~** las Islas Bahama.

bail [beil] *n* fianza // *vt (prisoner: gen:* **grant ~ to)** poner en libertad bajo fianza; *(boat: also:* **~ out)** achicar; *on ~ (prisoner)* bajo fianza; **to ~ sb out** obtener la libertad de uno bajo fianza; **bail bond** fianza; *see also* **bale**.

bailiff ['beilif] *n* alguacil *m*.

bait [beit] *n* cebo // *vt* cebar.

bake [beik] *vt* cocer (al horno) // *vi (cook)* cocerse; *(be hot)* hacer un calor terrible; **~d beans** *npl* judías *fpl* en salsa de tomate; **~r** *n* panadero; **~ry** *n (for bread)* panadería; *(for cakes)* pastelería; **baking** *n (act)* amasar *m*; *(batch)* hornada; **baking powder** *n* levadura (en polvo).

balance ['bæləns] *n* equilibrio; *(COMM: sum)* balance *m*; *(remainder)* resto; *(scales)* balanza // *vt* equilibrar; *(budget)* nivelar; *(account)* saldar; *(compensate)* contrapesar; ~ **of trade/payments** balanza de comercio/pagos; ~**d** a (*personality, diet*) equilibrado; ~ **sheet** n balance m.

balcony ['bælkənı] n (*open*) balcón m; (*closed*) galería.

bald [bɔːld] a calvo; (*tyre*) liso.

bale [beıl] n (*AGR*) paca, fardo; **to ~ out** vi (*of a plane*) lanzarse en paracaídas.

Balearics [bælı'ærıks] npl: **the ~** las Baleares.

baleful ['beılful] a (*look*) triste; (*sinister*) funesto, siniestro.

ball [bɔːl] n (*sphere*) bola; (*football*) balón m; (*for tennis, golf etc*) pelota; (*dance*) baile m.

ballad ['bæləd] n balada, romance m.

ballast ['bæləst] n lastre m.

ball bearings npl cojinetes mpl de bolas.

ballerina [bælə'riːnə] n bailarina.

ballet ['bæleı] n ballet m; ~ **dancer** n bailarín/ina m/f.

ballistic [bə'lıstık] a balístico.

balloon [bə'luːn] n globo.

ballot ['bælət] n votación f.

ball-point (pen) ['bɔːlpɔınt-] n bolígrafo.

ballroom ['bɔːlrum] n salón m de baile.

balm [bɑːm] n (*also fig*) bálsamo.

Baltic ['bɔːltık] a báltico // n: **the ~** (*Sea*) el (Mar) Báltico.

balustrade [bæləstreıd] n barandilla.

bamboo [bæm'buː] n bambú m.

ban [bæn] n prohibición f, proscripción f // vt prohibir, proscribir.

banal [bə'nɑːl] a banal, vulgar.

banana [bə'nɑːnə] n plátano, banana (*LAm*).

band [bænd] n (*group*) banda; (*gang*) pandilla; (*strip*) faja, tira; (: *circular*) anillo; (*at a dance*) orquesta; (*MIL*) banda; **to ~ together** vi juntarse, asociarse.

bandage ['bændıdʒ] n venda, vendaje m // vt vendar.

bandaid ['bændeıd] n ® (*US*) tirita.

bandit ['bændıt] n bandido.

bandstand ['bændstænd] n quiosco.

bandwagon ['bændwægən] n: **to jump on the ~** (*fig*) subirse al carro.

bandy ['bændı] vt (*jokes, insults*) cambiar.

bandy-legged ['bændı'legd] a estevado.

bang [bæŋ] n estallido; (*of door*) portazo; (*blow*) golpe m // vt hacer estallar; (*door*) cerrar de golpe // vi estallar.

bangle ['bæŋgl] n ajorca.

bangs [bæŋz] npl (*US*) flequillo sg.

banish ['bænıʃ] vt desterrar.

banister(s) ['bænıstə(z)] n(pl) pasamanos m inv.

bank [bæŋk] n (*COMM*) banco; (*of river, lake*) ribera, orilla; (*of earth*) terraplén m // vi (*AVIAT*) ladearse; **to ~ on** vt fus contar con; ~ **account** n cuenta de banco; ~ **card** n tarjeta bancaria; ~**er** n banquero; ~**er's card** n (*Brit*) = ~ **card**; B~ **holiday** n (*Brit*) día m festivo; ~**ing** n banca; ~**note** n billete m de banco; ~ **rate** n tipo de interés bancario.

bankrupt ['bæŋkrʌpt] a quebrado, insolvente; **to go ~** hacer bancarrota; **to be ~** estar en quiebra; ~**cy** n quiebra, bancarrota.

bank statement n balance m or detalle m de cuenta.

banner ['bænə*] n bandera; (*in demonstration*) pancarta.

banns [bænz] npl amonestaciones fpl.

banquet ['bæŋkwıt] n banquete m.

baptism ['bæptızəm] n bautismo.

baptize [bæp'taız] vt bautizar.

bar [baː*] n barra; (*on door*) tranca; (*of window, cage*) reja; (*of soap*) pastilla; (*fig: hindrance*) obstáculo; (*prohibition*) proscripción f; (*pub*) bar m; (*counter: in pub*) mostrador m; (*MUS*) barra // vt (*road*) obstruir; (*window, door*) atrancar; (*person*) excluir; (*activity*) prohibir; **behind ~s** entre rejas; **the B~** (*LAW: pro-*

fession) la abogacía; (: _people_) el cuerpo de abogados; ~ **none** sin excepción.

barbaric [baːˈbærɪk] _a_ bárbaro.

barbarous [ˈbaːbərəs] _a_ bárbaro.

barbecue [ˈbaːbɪkjuː] _n_ barbacoa.

barbed wire [baːbd-] _n_ alambre _m_ de púas.

barber [ˈbaːbə*] _n_ peluquero, barbero.

bar code _n_ código de barras.

bare [bɛə*] _a_ desnudo; (_head_) descubierto // _vt_ desnudar; ~**back** _ad_ sin silla; ~**faced** _a_ descarado; ~**foot** _a, ad_ descalzo; ~**ly** _ad_ apenas.

bargain [ˈbaːgɪn] _n_ pacto, negocio; (_good buy_) ganga // _vi_ negociar; (_haggle_) regatear; **into** ~: **to** ~ además, encima, de añadidura; **to** ~ **for** _vt fus_: **he got more than he** ~**ed for** le resultó peor de lo que esperaba.

barge [baːdʒ] _n_ barcaza // **to** ~ **in** _vi_ irrumpir; (_conversation_) entrometerse; **to** ~ **into** _vt fus_ dar contra.

bark [baːk] _n_ (_of tree_) corteza; (_of dog_) ladrido // _vi_ ladrar.

barley [ˈbaːlɪ] _n_ cebada; ~ **sugar** _n_ azúcar _m_ cande.

barmaid [ˈbaːmeɪd] _n_ camarera.

barman [ˈbaːmən] _n_ camarero, barman _m_.

barn [baːn] _n_ granero.

barometer [bəˈrɒmɪtə*] _n_ barómetro.

baron [ˈbærən] _n_ barón _m_; ~**ess** _n_ baronesa.

barracks [ˈbærəks] _npl_ cuartel _m_.

barrage [ˈbæraːʒ] _n_ (_MIL_) descarga, bombardeo; (_dam_) presa; (_fig_: _of criticism etc_) lluvia, aluvión _m_.

barrel [ˈbærəl] _n_ tonel _m_, barril _m_; (_of gun_) cañón _m_.

barren [ˈbærən] _a_ estéril.

barricade [bærɪˈkeɪd] _n_ barricada // _vt_ cerrar con barricadas.

barrier [ˈbærɪə*] _n_ barrera.

barring [ˈbaːrɪŋ] _prep_ excepto, salvo.

barrister [ˈbærɪstə*] _n_ (_Brit_) abogado/a.

barrow [ˈbærəu] _n_ (_cart_) carretilla

(de mano).

bartender [ˈbaːtendə*] _n_ (_US_) camarero, barman _m_.

barter [ˈbaːtə*] _vt_: **to** ~ **sth for sth** trocar algo por algo.

base [beɪs] _n_ base _f_ // _vt_: **to** ~ **sth on** basar _or_ fundar algo en // _a_ bajo, infame.

baseball [ˈbeɪsbɔːl] _n_ béisbol _m_.

basement [ˈbeɪsmənt] _n_ sótano.

bases [ˈbeɪsiːz] _npl of_ **base**; [ˈbeɪsɪz] _npl of_ **basis**.

bash [bæʃ] _vt_ (_col_) golpear.

bashful [ˈbæʃful] _a_ tímido, vergonzoso.

basic [ˈbeɪsɪk] _a_ básico; ~**ally** _ad_ fundamentalmente, en el fondo.

basil [ˈbæzl] _n_ albahaca.

basin [ˈbeɪsn] _n_ (_vessel_) cuenco, tazón _m_; (_GEO_) cuenca; (_also_: **wash**~) palangana, jofaina.

basis [ˈbeɪsɪs], _pl_ **bases** [ˈbeɪsiːz] _n_ base _f_.

bask [baːsk] _vi_: **to** ~ **in the sun** tomar el sol.

basket [ˈbaːskɪt] _n_ cesta, cesto; (_with handle_) canasta; ~**ball** _n_ baloncesto.

Basque [bæsk] _a, n_ vasco/a _m/f_; ~ **Country** _n_ Euskadi _m_, País _m_ Vasco.

bass [beɪs] _n_ (_MUS_) contrabajo.

bassoon [bəˈsuːn] _n_ fagot _m_.

bastard [ˈbaːstəd] _n_ bastardo; (_col!_) hijo de puta (!).

bastion [ˈbæstɪən] _n_ baluarte _m_.

bat [bæt] _n_ (_ZOOL_) murciélago; (_for ball games_) palo; (_for cricket, baseball_) bate _m_; (_Brit_: _for table tennis_) pala; **he didn't** ~ **an eyelid** ni pestañeó.

batch [bætʃ] _n_ (_of bread_) hornada; (_of goods_) lote _m_.

bated [ˈbeɪtɪd] _a_: **with** ~ **breath** sin respirar.

bath [baːθ, _pl_ baːðz] _n_ (_action_) baño; (~**tub**) baño, bañera, tina (_LAm_); (_see also_ **baths**) piscina // _vt_ bañar; **to have a** ~ bañarse, tomar un baño; ~**chair** _n_ silla de ruedas.

bathe [beɪð] _vi_ bañarse // _vt_ bañar;

~r n bañista m/f.

bathing ['beɪðɪŋ] n el bañarse; ~ **cap** n gorro de baño; ~ **costume**, (US) ~ **suit** n traje m de baño; ~ **trunks** npl bañador m.

bath: ~ **robe** n (man's) batín m; (woman's); ~**room** n (cuarto de) baño.

baths [bɑːðz] npl piscina sg.

baton ['bætən] n (MUS) batuta.

battalion [bə'tælɪən] n batallón m.

batter ['bætə*] vt apalear, azotar // n batido; ~**ed** a (hat, pan) estropeado.

battery ['bætərɪ] n batería (of torch) pila.

battle ['bætl] n batalla; (fig) lucha // vi luchar; ~**field** n campo de batalla; ~**ship** n acorazado.

bawdy ['bɔːdɪ] a indecente; (joke) verde.

bawl [bɔːl] vi chillar, gritar.

bay [beɪ] n (GEO) bahía; (BOT) laurel m // vi aullar; B~ of Biscay = mar Cantábrico; **to hold sb at** ~ mantener a alguien a raya.

bay window n ventana salediza.

bazaar [bə'zɑː*] n bazar m.

b. & b., B. & B. abbr (= bed and breakfast) cama y desayuno.

BBC n abbr (= British Broadcasting Corporation) cadena de radio y televisión estatal británica.

B.C. ad abbr (= before Christ) a. de C.

KEYWORD

be [biː], pt **was, were,** pp **been** ◆ auxiliary vb **1** (with present participle: forming continuous tenses): **what are you doing?** ¿qué estás haciendo?, ¿qué haces?; **they're coming tomorrow** vienen mañana; **I've been waiting for you for hours** llevo horas esperándote

2 (with pp: forming passives) ser (but often replaced by active or reflective constructions); **to** ~ **murdered** ser asesinado; **the box had been opened** habían abierto la caja; **the thief was nowhere to** ~ **seen** no se veía al ladrón por ninguna parte

3 (in tag questions): **it was fun, wasn't it?** fue divertido, ¿no? or ¿verdad?; **he's good-looking, isn't he?** es guapo, ¿no te parece?; **she's back again, is she?** entonces, ¿ha vuelto?

4 (+ to + infinitive): **the house is to** ~ **sold** (necessity) hay que vender la casa; (future) van a vender la casa; **he's not to open it** no tiene que abrirlo

◆ vb + complement **1** (with noun or numeral complement, but see also 3, 4, 5 and impersonal vb below) ser; **he's a doctor** es médico; **2 and 2 are 4** 2 y 2 son 4

2 (with adjective complement: expressing permanent or inherent quality) ser; (: expressing state seen as temporary or reversible) estar; **I'm English** soy inglés/esa; **she's tall/pretty** es alta/bonita; **he's young** es joven; ~ **careful/quiet/good** ten cuidado/cállate/pórtate bien; **I'm tired** estoy cansado/a; **it's dirty** está sucio/a

3 (of health) estar; **how are you?** ¿cómo estás?; **he's very ill** está muy enfermo; **I'm better now** ya estoy mejor

4 (of age) tener; **how old are you?** ¿cuántos años tienes?; **I'm sixteen (years old)** tengo dieciséis años

5 (cost) costar; ser; **how much was the meal?** ¿cuánto fue or costó la comida?; **that'll** ~ **£5.75, please** son £5.75, por favor; **this shirt is £17.00** esta camisa cuesta £17.00

◆ vi **1** (exist, occur etc) existir, haber; **the best singer that ever was** el mejor cantante que existió jamás; **is there a God?** ¿hay un Dios?, ¿existe Dios?; ~ **that as it may** sea como sea; **so** ~ **it** así sea

2 (referring to place) estar; **I won't** ~ **here tomorrow** no estaré aquí mañana

3 (referring to movement): **where**

have you been? ¿dónde has estado? ◆ *impersonal vb* **1** (*referring to time*): **it's 5 o'clock** son las 5; **it's the 28th of April** estamos a 28 de abril

2 (*referring to distance*): **it's 10 km to the village** el pueblo está a 10 km **3** (*referring to the weather*): **it's too hot/cold** hace demasiado calor/frío; **it's windy today** hace viento hoy **4** (*emphatic*): **it's me** soy yo; **it was María who paid the bill** fue María la que pagó la cuenta.

beach [biːtʃ] *n* playa // *vt* varar.

beacon ['biːkən] *n* (*lighthouse*) faro; (*marker*) guía.

bead [biːd] *n* cuenta, abalorio; (*of sweat*) gota.

beak [biːk] *n* pico.

beaker ['biːkə*] *n* jarra.

beam [biːm] *n* (*ARCH*) viga, travesaño; (*of light*) rayo, haz *m* de luz // *vi* brillar; (*smile*) sonreír.

bean [biːn] *n* judía; **runner/broad ~** habichuela/haba; **coffee ~** grano de café; **~sprouts** *npl* brotes *mpl* de soja.

bear [bɛə*] *n* oso *m* // *vb* (*pt* bore, *pp* borne) *vt* (*weight etc*) llevar; (*cost*) pagar; (*responsibility*) tener; (*endure*) soportar, aguantar; (*stand up to*) resistir a; (*children*) parir // *vi*: **to ~ right/left** torcer a la derecha/izquierda; **to ~ out** *vt* (*suspicions*) corroborar, confirmar; (*person*) llevar; **to ~ up** *vi* (*person*) remain cheerful) animarse.

beard [bɪəd] *n* barba.

bearer ['bɛərə*] *n* (*of news, cheque*) portador(a) *m/f*.

bearing ['bɛərɪŋ] *n* porte *m*, comportamiento; (*connection*) relación *f*; (*ball*) **~s** *npl* cojinetes *mpl* a bolas; **to take a ~** = marcarse; **to find one's ~s** orientarse.

beast [biːst] *n* bestia; (*col*) bruto, salvaje *m*; **~ly** *a* bestial; (*awful*) horrible.

beat [biːt] *n* (*of heart*) latido *m*; (*MUS*)

ritmo, compás *m*; (*of policeman*) ronda *f* // *vb* (*pt* beat, *pp* beaten) *vt* (*hit*) golpear; (*eggs*) batir; (*defeat*) vencer, derrotar // *vi* (*heart*) sobrepasar; (*drum*) tocar; (*rhythm*) marcar // *vi* (*heart*) latir; **off the ~en track** aislado; **to ~ it** largarse; **to ~ off** *vt* rechazar; **to ~ up** *vt* (*col: person*) dar una paliza a; **~ing** *n* golpeo.

beautiful ['bjuːtɪful] *a* hermoso, bello; **~ly** *ad* maravillosamente.

beauty ['bjuːtɪ] *n* belleza, hermosura; (*person*) belleza; **~ salon** *n* salón *m* de belleza; **~ spot** *n* lunar *m* postizo; (*Brit TOURISM*) lugar *m* pintoresco.

beaver ['biːvə*] *n* castor *m*.

became [bɪ'keɪm] *pt of* become.

because [bɪ'kɔz] *conj* porque; **~ of** *prep* debido a, a causa de.

beck [bɛk] *n*: **to be at the ~ and call of** estar a disposición de.

beckon ['bɛkən] *vt* (*also*: **~ to**) llamar con señas.

become [bɪ'kʌm] (*irg: like come*) *vt* (*suit*) favorecer, sentar bien a // *vi* (+ *noun*) hacerse, llegar a ser; (+ *adj*) ponerse, volverse; **to ~ fat** engordar.

becoming [bɪ'kʌmɪŋ] *a* (*behaviour*) decoroso; (*clothes*) favorecedor(a).

bed [bɛd] *n* cama; (*of flowers*) macizo; (*of coal, clay*) capa; **to go to ~** acostarse; **~ and breakfast (b.&b.)** *n* (*place*) pensión *f*; (*terms*) cama y desayuno; **~clothes** *npl* ropa *sg* de cama; **~ding** *n* ropa *f* de cama.

bedlam ['bɛdləm] *n* confusión *f*.

bedraggled [bɪ'dræɡld] *a* mojado; desastrado.

bed: **~ridden** *a* postrado (en cama); **~room** *n* dormitorio, alcoba; **~side** *n*: **at sb's ~side** a la cabecera de alguien; **~sit(ter)** *n* (*Brit*) estudio, suite *m* (*LAm*); **~spread** *n* sobrecama *m*, colcha; **~time** *n* hora de acostarse.

bee [biː] *n* abeja.

beech [bi:tʃ] n haya.

beef [bi:f] n carne f de vaca; **roast ~** rosbif m; **~burger** n hamburguesa; **~ eater** n alabardero de la Torre de Londres.

bee: **~hive** n colmena; **~line** n: to make a **~line** for ir derecho a.

been [bi:n] pp of be.

beer [bɪəˀ] n cerveza.

beet [bi:t] n (US) remolacha.

beetle ['bi:tl] n escarabajo.

beetroot ['bi:tru:t] n (Brit) remolacha.

before [bɪ'fɔ:ˀ] prep (of time) antes de; (of space) delante de // conj antes (de) que // ad (time) antes, anteriormente; (space) delante, adelante; **~ going** antes de marcharse; **~ she** goes antes de que se vaya; **the week ~** la semana anterior; **I've never seen it ~** no lo he visto nunca; **~hand** ad de antemano, con anticipación.

beg [beg] vi pedir limosna // vt pedir, rogar; (entreat) suplicar.

began [bɪ'gæn] pt of begin.

beggar ['begəˀ] n mendigo/a.

begin [bɪ'gɪn], pt **began**, pp **begun** vt, vi empezar, comenzar; **to ~ doing** or **to do sth** empezar a hacer algo; **~ner** n principiante m/f; **~ning** n principio, comienzo.

begun [bɪ'gʌn] pp of begin.

behalf [bɪ'hɑ:f] n: **on ~ of** en nombre de, por.

behave [bɪ'heɪv] vi (person) portarse, comportarse; (thing) funcionar; (well: also: ~ o.s.) portarse bien; **behaviour**, (US) **behavior** n comportamiento, conducta.

behead [bɪ'hed] vt decapitar.

beheld [bɪ'held] pt, pp of behold.

behind [bɪ'haɪnd] prep detrás de // ad detrás, por detrás, atrás // n trasero; **to be ~** (schedule) ir retrasado; **~ the scenes** (fig) entre bastidores.

behold [bɪ'həʊld] vt (irg: like hold) contemplar.

beige [beɪʒ] a color beige.

being ['bi:ɪŋ] n ser m; **to come into ~** nacer, aparecer.

belated [bɪ'leɪtɪd] a atrasado, tardío.

belch [beltʃ] vi eructar // vt (also: ~ out: smoke etc) arrojar.

belfry ['belfrɪ] n campanario.

Belgian ['beldʒən] a, n belga m/f.

Belgium ['beldʒəm] n Bélgica.

belie [bɪ'laɪ] vt desmentir, contradecir.

belief [bɪ'li:f] n (opinion) opinión f; (trust, faith) fe f; (acceptance as true) creencia.

believe [bɪ'li:v] vt, vi creer; **to ~ in** creer en; **~r** n (in idea, activity) partidario/a; (REL) creyente m/f, fiel m/f.

belittle [bɪ'lɪtl] vt minimizar, despreciar.

bell [bel] n campana; (small) campanilla; (on door) timbre m; (animal's) cencerro; (on toy etc) cascabel m.

belligerent [bɪ'lɪdʒərənt] a (at war) beligerante, (fig) agresivo.

bellow ['beləʊ] vi bramar; (person) rugir.

bellows ['beləʊz] npl fuelle msg.

belly ['belɪ] n barriga, panza.

belong [bɪ'lɒŋ] vi: **to ~ to** pertenecer a; (club etc) ser socio de; **this book ~s here** este libro va aquí; **~ings** npl pertenencias fpl.

beloved [bɪ'lʌvɪd] a, n querido/a m/f, amado/a m/f.

below [bɪ'ləʊ] prep bajo, debajo de // ad abajo, (por) debajo; **see ~** véase más abajo.

belt [belt] n cinturón m; (TECH) correa, cinta // vt (thrash) golpear con correa; **~way** n (US AUT) carretera de circunvalación.

bemused [bɪ'mju:zd] a aturdido.

bench [bentʃ] n banco; **the B~** (LAW) tribunal m; (people) judicatura.

bend [bend], vb (pt, pp **bent**) vt doblar, inclinar; (leg, arm) torcer // vi inclinarse; (road) curvarse // n (Brit: in road, river) recodo; (in pipe) codo; **to ~ down** vi inclinarse, doblarse; **to ~ over** vi inclinarse.

beneath [bɪ'ni:θ] prep bajo, debajo de; (unworthy of) indigno de // ad abajo, (por) debajo.

benefactor ['bɛnɪfæktə*] n bienhechor m.

beneficial [bɛnɪ'fɪʃəl] a beneficioso.

benefit ['bɛnɪfɪt] n beneficio, provecho; (allowance of money) subsidio // vt beneficiar // vi: he'll ~ from it le sacará provecho.

benevolent [bɪ'nɛvələnt] a benévolo.

benign [bɪ'naɪn] a (person, MED) benigno; (smile) afable.

bent [bɛnt] pt, pp of bend // n inclinación f // a: to be ~ on estar empeñado en.

bequeath [bɪ'kwi:ð] vt legar.

bequest [bɪ'kwɛst] n legado.

bereaved [bɪ'ri:vd] npl: the ~ los afligidos mpl.

beret ['bɛreɪ] n boina.

Berlin [bɜː'lɪn] n Berlín m.

berm [bɜːm] n (US AUT) arcén m.

Bermuda [bə:'mju:də] n las Bermudas fpl.

berry ['bɛrɪ] n baya.

berserk [bə'sɜːk] a: to go ~ perder los estribos.

berth [bɜːθ] n (bed) litera; (cabin) camarote m; (for ship) amarradero // vi atracar, amarrar.

beseech [bɪ'si:tʃ], pt, pp besought [-'sɔ:t] vt suplicar.

beset [bɪ'sɛt], pt, pp beset vt (person) acosar.

beside [bɪ'saɪd] prep junto a, al lado de; to be ~ o.s. with anger estar fuera de sí; that's ~ the point eso no tiene nada que ver.

besides [bɪ'saɪdz] ad además // prep (as well as) además de; (except) excepto.

besiege [bɪ'si:dʒ] vt (town) sitiar; (fig) asediar.

besought [bɪ'sɔ:t] pt, pp of beseech.

best [bɛst] a (el/la) mejor // ad (el/la) mejor; the ~ part of (quantity) la mayor parte de; at ~ en el mejor de los casos; to make the ~ of sth sacar el mejor partido de algo; to do one's ~ hacer lo posible; to the ~ of my knowledge que yo sepa; to the ~ of my ability como mejor puedo; ~ man n padrino de boda.

bestow [bɪ'stəu] vt otorgar; (honour, praise) dispensar.

bestseller ['bɛst'sɛlə*] n éxito de librería, bestseller m.

bet [bɛt] n apuesta // vt, vi (pt, pp bet or betted) apostar (on a).

betray [bɪ'treɪ] vt traicionar; (inform on) delatar; ~al n traición f.

better ['bɛtə*] a mejor // ad mejor // vt mejorar; (record etc) superar // n: to get the ~ of sb quedar por encima de alguien; you had ~ do it más vale que lo hagas; he thought ~ of it cambió de parecer; to get ~ mejorar(se); (MED) reponerse; ~ off a más acomodado.

betting ['bɛtɪŋ] n juego, el apostar; ~ shop n (Brit) agencia de apuestas.

between [bɪ'twi:n] prep entre // ad (time) mientras tanto; (place) en medio.

beverage ['bɛvərɪdʒ] n bebida.

bevy ['bɛvɪ] n: a ~ of una bandada de.

beware [bɪ'wɛə*] vi: to ~ (of) tener cuidado (con) // excl ¡cuidado!

bewildered [bɪ'wɪldəd] a aturdido, perplejo.

bewitching [bɪ'wɪtʃɪŋ] a hechicero, encantador(a).

beyond [bɪ'jɔnd] prep más allá de; (exceeding) además de, fuera de; (above) superior a // ad más allá, más lejos; ~ doubt fuera de toda duda; ~ repair irreparable.

bias ['baɪəs] n (prejudice) prejuicio, (preference) predisposición f; ~(s)ed a parcial.

bib [bɪb] n babero.

Bible ['baɪbl] n Biblia.

bicarbonate of soda [baɪ'kɑ:bənɪt-] n bicarbonato de soda.

bicker ['bɪkə*] vi reñir.

bicycle ['baɪsɪkl] n bicicleta.

bid [bɪd] n (at auction) oferta, postura; (attempt) tentativa, conato // vi (pt, pp **bid**) hacer una oferta // vt (pt **bade** [bæd], pp **bidden** ['bɪdn]) mandar, ordenar; **to ~ sb good day** dar a uno los buenos días; **~der** n: **the highest ~der** el mejor postor; **~ding** n (at auction) ofertas fpl; (order) orden f, mandato.

bide [baɪd] vt: **to ~ one's time** esperar el momento adecuado.

bifocals [baɪ'fəʊklz] npl gafas fpl or anteojos mpl (LAm) bifocales.

big [bɪg] a grande.

bigamy ['bɪgəmɪ] n bigamia.

big dipper [-'dɪpə'] n montaña rusa.

bigheaded ['bɪg'hɛdɪd] a engreído.

bigot ['bɪgət] n fanático/a, intolerante m/f; **~ed** a fanático, intolerante; **~ry** n fanatismo, intolerancia.

big top n (circus) circo; (main tent) tienda principal.

bike [baɪk] n bici f.

bikini [bɪ'ki:nɪ] n bikini m.

bile [baɪl] n bilis f.

bilingual [baɪ'lɪŋgwəl] a bilingüe.

bill [bɪl] n (account) cuenta; (invoice) factura; (POL) proyecto de ley; (US: banknote) billete m; (of bird) pico; **'post no ~s'** 'prohibido fijar carteles'; **~board** n (US) cartelera.

billet ['bɪlɪt] n alojamiento.

billfold ['bɪlfəʊld] n (US) cartera.

billiards ['bɪljədz] n billar m.

billion ['bɪljən] n (Brit) billón m (millón de millones); (US) mil millones.

billy ['bɪlɪ] n (US) porra.

bin [bɪn] n (gen) cubo or bote m (LAm) de la basura; **litter ~** n (Brit) papelera.

bind [baɪnd], pt, pp **bound** vt atar, liar; (wound) vendar; (book) encuadernar; (oblige) obligar; **~ing** a (contract) obligatorio.

binge [bɪndʒ] n borrachera, juerga.

bingo ['bɪŋgəʊ] n bingo m.

binoculars [bɪ'nɔkjʊləz] npl prismáticos mpl.

bio... [baɪə'] pref: **~chemistry** n

bioquímica; **~graphy** [baɪ'ɔgrəfɪ] n biografía; **~logical** a biológico; **~logy** [baɪ'ɔlədʒɪ] n biología.

birch [bə:tʃ] n abedul m; (cane) vara.

bird [bə:d] n ave f, pájaro; (Brit col: girl) chica; **~'s eye view** vista de pájaro; **~ watcher** n ornitólogo/a.

Biro ['baɪrəʊ] n ® bolígrafo.

birth [bə:θ] n nacimiento; (MED) parto; **to give ~ to** parir, dar a luz; **~ certificate** n partida de nacimiento; **~ control** n control m de natalidad; (methods) métodos mpl anticonceptivos; **~day** n cumpleaños m inv; **~ rate** n (tasa de natalidad f.

biscuit ['bɪskɪt] n (Brit) galleta, bizcocho (LAm).

bisect [baɪ'sɛkt] vt bisecar.

bishop ['bɪʃəp] n obispo.

bit [bɪt] pt of **bite** // n trozo, pedazo, pedacito; (COMPUT) bit m, bitio; (for horse) freno, bocado; **a ~ of** un poco de; **a ~ mad** un poco loco; **~ by ~** poco a poco.

bitch [bɪtʃ] n (dog) perra; (col!) zorra (!).

bite [baɪt] (pt **bit**, pp **bitten**) vt, vi morder; (insect etc) picar // n mordedura; (insect ~) picadura; (mouthful) bocado; **to ~ one's nails** comerse las uñas; **let's have a ~ (to eat)** comamos algo.

biting ['baɪtɪŋ] a (wind) que traspasa los huesos; (criticism) mordaz.

bitten ['bɪtn] pp of **bite**.

bitter ['bɪtə'] a amargo; (wind, criticism) cortante, penetrante; (battle) encarnizado // n (Brit: beer) cerveza típica británica a base de lúpulos; **~ness** n amargura; (anger) rencor m.

bizarre [bɪ'za:'] a raro, estrafalario.

blab [blæb] vi chismear, soplar.

black [blæk] a (colour) negro; (dark) oscuro // n (colour) color m negro; (person): **B~** negro/a // vt (shoes) lustrar; (Brit: INDUSTRY) boicotear; **to give sb a ~ eye** ponerle a uno el ojo morado; ~ **and blue** a amoratado; **to be in the** ~ (*bank account*) estar en números negros; ~**berry** n zarzamora; ~**bird** n mirlo; ~**board** n pizarra; ~ **coffee** n café m solo; ~**currant** n grosella negra; ~ en vt ennegrecer; (*fig*) denigrar; ~**head** n espinilla; ~ **ice** n hielo invisible en la carretera; ~**jack** n (US) veintiuna; ~**leg** n (*Brit*) esquirol m, rompehuelgas m inv; ~**list** n lista negra; ~**mail** n chantaje m // vt chantajear; ~ **market** n mercado negro; ~**out** n apagón m; (*fainting*) desmayo, pérdida de conocimiento; **the B~ Sea** n el Mar Negro; ~ **sheep** n oveja negra; ~**smith** n herrero; ~ **spot** n (AUT) lugar m peligroso.

bladder ['blædə*] n vejiga.

blade [bleɪd] n hoja; (*cutting edge*) filo; **a ~ of grass** una brizna de hierba.

blame [bleɪm] n culpa // vt: **to ~ sb for sth** echar a uno la culpa de algo; **to be to ~** tener la culpa de; ~**less** a (*person*) inocente.

bland [blænd] a suave; (*taste*) soso.

blank [blæŋk] a en blanco; (*shot*) sin bala; (*look*) sin expresión // n blanco, espacio en blanco; cartucho sin bala or de fogueo; ~ **cheque** n cheque m en blanco.

blanket ['blæŋkɪt] n manta, cobija (LAm).

blare [blɛə*] vi resonar.

blasé ['blɑːzeɪ] a hastiado.

blasphemy ['blæsfɪmɪ] n blasfemia.

blast [blɑːst] n (of wind) ráfaga, soplo; (of whistle) toque m; (of explosive) carga explosiva; (force) choque m // vt (blow up) volar; (blow open) abrir con carga explosiva; ~**off** n (SPACE) lanzamiento.

blatant ['bleɪtənt] a descarado.

blaze [bleɪz] n (fire) fuego; (flames) llamarada; (fig) arranque m // vi (fire) arder en llamas; (fig) brillar // vt: **to ~ a trail** (fig) abrir (un) camino.

blazer ['bleɪzə*] n chaqueta de uni-

forme de colegial o de socio de club.

bleach [bliːtʃ] n (also: **household** ~) lejía // vt (linen) blanquear; ~**ed** a (hair) teñido de rubio; (clothes) descolorado; ~**ers** npl (US SPORT) gradas fpl al sol.

bleak [bliːk] a (countryside) desierto; (prospect) poco prometedor(a).

bleary-eyed ['blɪərˈaɪd] a: **to be ~** tener ojos de cansado.

bleat [bliːt] vi balar.

bleed [bliːd], pt, pp **bled** [bled] vt, vi sangrar.

bleeper ['bliːpə*] n (of doctor etc) busca m.

blemish ['blemɪʃ] n mancha, tacha.

blend [blend] n mezcla // vt mezclar // vi (colours etc) combinarse, mezclarse.

bless [bles], pt, pp **blessed** or **blest** [blest] vt bendecir; ~**ing** n bendición f; (advantage) beneficio, ventaja.

blew [bluː] pt of **blow.**

blight [blaɪt] vt (hopes etc) frustrar, arruinar.

blimey ['blaɪmɪ] excl (Brit col) ¡caray!

blind [blaɪnd] a ciego // n (for window) persiana // vt cegar; (dazzle) deslumbrar; ~ **alley** n callejón m sin salida; ~ **corner** n (Brit) esquina escondida; ~**ers** npl (US) anteojeras fpl; ~**fold** n venda // a, ad con los ojos vendados // vt vendar los ojos a; ~**ly** ad a ciegas, ciegamente; ~**ness** n ceguera; ~ **spot** n mácula.

blink [blɪŋk] vi parpadear, pestañear; (light) oscilar; ~**ers** npl (esp Brit) anteojeras fpl.

bliss [blɪs] n felicidad f.

blister ['blɪstə*] n (on skin) ampolla // vi (paint) ampollarse.

blithely ['blaɪðlɪ] ad alegremente.

blitz [blɪts] n bombardeo aéreo.

blizzard ['blɪzəd] n ventisca.

bloated ['bləʊtɪd] a hinchado.

blob [blɒb] n (drop) gota; (stain, spot) mancha.

bloc [blɒk] n (POL) bloque m.

block [blɔk] n bloque m; (in pipes) obstáculo; (of buildings) manzana, cuadra (LAm) // vt (gen) obstruir, cerrar; (progress) estorbar; ~**ade** [-'keid] n bloqueo // vt bloquear; ~**age** n estorbo, obstrucción f; ~**buster** n (book) bestseller m; (film) éxito de público; ~ **of flats** n (Brit) bloque m de pisos; ~ **letters** npl letras fpl de molde.

bloke [bləuk] n (Brit col) tipo, tío.

blond(e) [blɔnd] a, n rubio/a m/f.

blood [blʌd] n sangre f; ~ **donor** n donador(a) m/f de sangre; ~ **group** n grupo sanguíneo; ~**hound** n sabueso; ~ **poisoning** n envenenamiento de la sangre; ~ **pressure** n presión f sanguínea; ~**shed** n derramamiento de sangre; ~**shot** a inyectado en sangre; ~**stream** n corriente f sanguínea; ~ **test** n análisis m inv de sangre; ~**thirsty** a sanguinario; ~ **transfusion** n transfusión f de sangre; ~**y** a sangriento; (Brit col!): this ~**y**... este condenado o puñetero... (!) // ad: ~**y strong/good** (Brit col!) terriblemente fuerte/bueno; ~**y-minded** a (Brit col): **to be ~y-minded** ser un malasangre.

bloom [blu:m] n floración f; in ~ en flor // vi florecer; ~**ing** a (col): this ~**ing**... este condenado...

blossom ['blɔsəm] n flor f // vi (also fig) florecer; (person) realizarse.

blot [blɔt] n borrón m // vt (dry) secar; (stain) manchar; **to ~ out** vt (view) tapar; (memories) borrar.

blotchy ['blɔtʃi] a (complexion) lleno de manchas.

blotting paper ['blɔtiŋ-] n papel m secante.

blouse [blauz] n blusa.

blow [bləu] n golpe m // vb (pt **blew** [blu:], pp **blown** [bləun]) vi soplar; (fuse) fundirse // vt (glass) soplar; (fuse) quemar; (instrument) tocar; **to ~ one's nose** sonarse; **to ~ away** vt llevarse, arrancar; **to ~ down** vt derribar; **to ~ off** vt

arrebatar; **to ~ out** vi apagarse; **to ~ over** vi amainar; **to ~ up** vi estallar // vt volar; (tyre) inflar; (PHOT) ampliar; **blow-dry** n moldeado (con secador); ~**lamp** n (Brit) soplete m, lámpara de soldar; ~**-out** n (of tyre) pinchazo; ~**torch** n = ~**lamp**.

blubber ['blʌbə*] n grasa de ballena // vi (pej) lloriquear.

blue [blu:] a azul; ~ **film/joke** film/ chiste verde; **out of the ~** (fig)completamente inesperado; **to have the ~s** estar decaído; ~**bell** n campanilla, campánula azul; ~**bottle** n moscarda, mosca azul; ~**jeans** npl (pantalones m inv, vaqueros mpl; ~**print** n (fig) anteproyecto.

bluff [blʌf] vi hacer un bluff, farolear // n bluff m, farol m; **to call sb's ~** coger a uno en un renuncio.

blunder ['blʌndə*] n patinazo, metedura de pata // vi cometer un error, meter la pata.

blunt [blʌnt] a embotado, desafilado; (person) franco, directo // vt embotar, desafilar.

blur [blə:*] n aspecto borroso // vt (vision) enturbiar; (memory) empañar.

blurb [blə:b] n comentario de sobrecubierta.

blurt [blə:t] vt: **to ~ out** (say) descolgarse con, dejar escapar.

blush [blʌʃ] vi ruborizarse, ponerse colorado // n rubor m.

blustering ['blʌstəriŋ] a (person) fanfarrón/ona.

blustery ['blʌstəri] a (weather) tempestuoso, tormentoso.

boar [bɔ:*] n verraco, cerdo.

board [bɔ:d] n tabla, tablero; (on wall) tablón m; (for chess etc) tablero; (committee) junta, consejo; (in firm) mesa o junta directiva; (NAUT, AVIAT): **on ~** a bordo // vt (ship) embarcarse en; (train) subir a; **full ~** (Brit) pensión completa; **half ~** (Brit) media pensión; **to go by the ~** (fig) ser abandonado or olvidado; **to ~ up** vt (door) tapiar;

~ **and lodging** *n* casa y comida; ~**er** *n* huésped(a) *m/f*; (SCOL) interno/a; ~**ing card** *n* (Brit) tarjeta de embarque; ~**ing house** *n* casa de huéspedes; ~**ing pass** *n* (US) = ~**ing card**; ~**ing school** *n* internado; ~ **room** *n* sala de juntas.

boast [bəʊst] *vi*: to ~ (about or of) alardear (de) // *vt* ostentar // *n* alarde *m*, baladronada *f*.

boat [bəʊt] *n* barco, buque *m*; (small) barca, bote *m*; ~**er** *n* (hat) canotié *m*; ~**swain** ['bəʊsn] *n* contramaestre *m*.

bob [bɒb] *vi* (boat, cork on water: also: ~ **up and down**) menearse, balancearse // *n* (Brit col) = **shilling**; to ~ **up** *vi* (re)aparecer de repente.

bobby ['bɒbɪ] *n* (Brit col) poli *m*.

bobsleigh ['bɒbsleɪ] *n* bob *m*.

bode [bəʊd] *vi*: to ~ **well/ill (for)** ser prometedor/poco prometedor (para).

bodily ['bɒdɪlɪ] *a* corpóreo, corporal // *ad* (move: person) en peso; (: building) de una pieza.

body ['bɒdɪ] *n* cuerpo; (corpse) cadáver *m*; (of car) caja, carrocería; (fig: organization) organismo; (fig: quantity) masa; ~**building** *n* culturismo; ~**guard** *n* guardaespaldas *m inv*; ~**work** *n* carrocería.

bog [bɒg] *n* pantano, ciénaga // *vt*: to **get** ~**ged down** (fig) empantanarse, atascarse.

boggle ['bɒgl] *vi*: **the mind** ~**s**! ¡no puedo creerlo!

bogus ['bəʊgəs] *a* falso, fraudulento; (person) fingido.

boil [bɔɪl] *vt* cocer; (eggs) pasar por agua // *vi* hervir // *n* (MED) furúnculo, divieso; to **come to the** (Brit) or **a** (US) ~ comenzar a hervir; to ~ **down to** (fig) reducirse a; to ~ **over** *vi* rebosar; (anger etc) llegar al colmo; ~**ed egg** *n* huevo cocido (Sp) or pasado (LAm); ~**ed potatoes** *npl* patatas *fpl* or papas *fpl* (LAm) hervidas; ~**er** *n* caldera;

~**er suit** *n* (Brit) mono; ~**ing point** *n* punto de ebullición.

boisterous ['bɔɪstərəs] *a* (noisy) bullicioso; (excitable) exuberante; (crowd) tumultuoso.

bold [bəʊld] *a* (brave) valiente, audaz; (pej) descarado; (outline) grueso; (colour) llamativo.

Bolivia [bə'lɪvɪə] *n* Bolivia; ~**n** *a, n* boliviano/a *m/f*.

bollard ['bɒləd] *n* (Brit AUT) poste *m*.

bolster ['bəʊlstə*] *n* travesero, cabezal *m*; to ~ **up** *vt* reforzar.

bolt [bəʊlt] *n* (lock) cerrojo; (with nut) perno, tornillo // *ad*: ~ **upright** rígido, erguido // *vt* (door) echar el cerrojo a; (food) engullir // *vi* fugarse; (horse) desbocarse.

bomb [bɒm] *n* bomba // *vt* bombardear; ~**ard** [-'bɑːd] *vt* bombardear; (fig) asediar; ~**ardment** [-'bɑːdmənt] *n* bombardeo.

bombastic [bɒm'bæstɪk] *a* rimbombante; (person) farolero.

bomb: ~ **disposal** *n* desmontaje *m* de explosivos; ~**er** *n* (AVIAT) bombardero; ~**shell** *n* obús *m*, granada; (fig) bomba.

bona fide ['bəʊnə'faɪdɪ] *a* genuino, auténtico.

bond [bɒnd] *n* (binding promise) fianza; (FINANCE) bono; (link) vínculo, lazo; (COMM): **in** ~ en depósito bajo fianza.

bondage ['bɒndɪdʒ] *n* esclavitud *f*.

bone [bəʊn] *n* hueso; (of fish) espina // *vt* deshuesar; quitar las espinas a; ~-**dry** *a* completamente seco; ~**idle** *a* gandul.

bonfire ['bɒnfaɪə*] *n* hoguera, fogata.

bonnet ['bɒnɪt] *n* gorra; (Brit: of car) capó *m*.

bonus ['bəʊnəs] *n* sobrepaga, prima.

bony ['bəʊnɪ] *a* (arm, face, MED: tissue) huesudo; (meat) lleno de huesos; (fish) lleno de espinas.

boo [buː] *vt* abuchear, rechiflar.

booby trap ['buːbɪ-] *n* trampa explosiva.

book [buk] n libro m; (notebook) libreta; (of stamps etc) librito; (COMM) ~s cuentas fpl, contabilidad f // vt (ticket, seat, room) reservar; (driver) fichar; ~**case** n librería, estante m para libros; ~**ing office** n (Brit RAIL) despacho de billetes or boletos (LAm); (THEATRE) taquilla, boletería (LAm); ~**keeping** n contabilidad f; ~**let** n folleto; ~**maker** n corredor m de apuestas; ~**seller** n librero; ~**shop**, ~ **store** n librería.

boom [bu:m] n (noise) trueno, estampido; (in prices etc) alza rápida; (ECON) boom m, auge m // vi (cannon) hacer gran estruendo, retumbar; (ECON) estar en alza.

boon [bu:n] n favor m, beneficio.

boost [bu:st] n estímulo, empuje m // vt estimular, empujar; ~**er** n (MED) reinyección f.

boot [bu:t] n bota; (Brit: of car) maleta, maletero // vt dar un puntapié a; (COMPUT) arrancar; **to ~** (in addition) además, por añadidura.

booth [bu:ð] n (at fair) barraca; (telephone, voting ~) cabina.

booty ['bu:tɪ] n botín m.

booze [bu:z] n (col) bebida, trago // vi emborracharse.

border ['bɔ:də*] n borde m, margen m; (of a country) frontera // a fronterizo; the B~s región fronteriza entre Escocia e Inglaterra; **to ~ on** vt fus lindar con; (fig) rayar en; ~**line** n (fig) frontera.

bore [bɔ:*] pt of **bear** // vt (hole) hacer un agujero en; (well) perforar; (person) aburrir // n (person) pelmazo, pesado; (of gun) calibre m; ~**d** a aburrido; ~**dom** n aburrimiento.

boring ['bɔ:rɪŋ] a aburrido.

born [bɔ:n] a: **to be** ~ nacer; **I was** ~ **in** 1960 nací en 1960.

borne [bɔ:n] pp of **bear**.

borough ['bʌrə] n municipio.

borrow ['bɔrəu] vt: **to** ~ **sth** (from sb) tomar algo prestado (a alguien).

bosom ['buzəm] n pecho; (fig) seno.

boss [bɔs] n jefe/a m/f; (employer)

patrón/ona m/f; (political etc) cacique m // vt (also: ~ **about** or **around**) mangonear; ~**y** a mandón/ona.

bosun ['bəusn] n contramaestre m.

botany ['bɔtənɪ] n botánica.

botch [bɔtʃ] vt (also: ~ **up**) arruinar, estropear.

both [bəuθ] a, pron ambos/as, los/las dos; ~ **of us went, we** ~ **went** fuimos los dos, ambos fuimos // ad: ~ **A and B** tanto A como B.

bother ['bɔðə*] vt (worry) preocupar; (disturb) molestar, fastidiar // vi (also: ~ **o.s.**) molestarse // n: **what a** ~! ¡qué lata!; **to** ~ **doing** tomarse la molestia de hacer.

bottle ['bɔtl] n botella; (small) frasco; (baby's) biberón m // vt embotellar; **to** ~ **up** vt suprimir; ~**neck** n embotellamiento; ~**opener** n abrebotellas m inv.

bottom ['bɔtəm] n (of box, sea) fondo; (buttocks) trasero, culo; (of page) pie m; (of list) final m // a (low-est) más bajo; (last) último; ~**less** a sin fondo, insondable.

bough [bau] n rama.

bought [bɔ:t] pt, pp of **buy**.

boulder ['bəuldə*] n canto rodado.

bounce [bauns] vi (ball) (re)botar; (cheque) ser rechazado // vt hacer (re)botar // n (rebound) (re)bote m; ~**r** n (col) matón/ona m.

bound [baund] pt, pp of **bind** // n (leap) salto; (gen pl: limit) límite m // vi (leap) saltar // a: ~ **by** rodeado de; **to be** ~ **to do sth** (obliged) tener el deber de hacer algo; **he's** ~ **to come** es seguro que vendrá; **out of** ~s prohibido el paso; ~ **for** con destino a.

boundary ['baundrɪ] n límite m.

boundless ['baundlɪs] a ilimitado.

bouquet ['buker] n (of flowers) ramo; (of wine) aroma m.

bourgeois ['buʒwɑ:] a, n burgués/esa m/f.

bout [baut] n (of malaria etc) ataque m; (BOXING etc) combate m, encuentro.

bow [bəu] n (knot) lazo; (weapon, MUS) arco // n [bau] (of the head) reverencia; (NAUT: also: ~s) proa // vi [bau] inclinarse, hacer una reverencia; (yield): **to ~ to** or **before** ceder ante, someterse a.

bowels [bauəlz] npl intestinos mpl, vientre m.

bowl [bəul] n tazón m, cuenco; (for washing) palangana, jofaina; (ball) bola // vi (CRICKET) arrojar la pelota; **~s** n juego de las bochas, bolos mpl.

bow-legged ['bəu'legid] a estevado.

bowler ['bəulə*] n (CRICKET) lanzador m (de la pelota); (Brit: also: ~ **hat**) hongo, bombín m.

bowling ['bəuliŋ] n (game) bochas fpl, bolos mpl; **~ alley** n bolera; **~ green** n pista para bochas.

bow tie ['bəu-] n corbata de lazo, pajarita.

box [bɔks] n (also: **cardboard ~**) caja, cajón m; (for jewels) estuche m; (for money) cofre m; (THEATRE) palco // vt encajonar // vi (SPORT) boxear; **~er** n (person) boxeador m; (dog) boxer m; **~ing** n (SPORT) boxeo m; **B~ing Day** n (Brit) día de San Esteban, 26 de diciembre; **~ing gloves** npl guantes mpl de boxeo; **~ing ring** n ring m, cuadrilátero; **~ office** n taquilla, boletería (LAm); **~room** n trastero.

boy [bɔi] n (young) niño; (older) muchacho.

boycott ['bɔikɔt] n boicot m // vt boicotear.

boyfriend ['bɔifrend] n novio.

boyish ['bɔiʃ] a muchachil.

B.R. abbr = **British Rail.**

bra [brɑ:] n sostén m, sujetador m.

brace [breis] n refuerzo, abrazadera; (Brit: also: ~s: on teeth) corrector m; (tool) berbiquí m // vt abrazar, reforzar; **~s** npl (Brit) tirantes mpl; **to ~ o.s. (for)** (fig) prepararse (para).

bracelet ['breislit] n pulsera, brazale-

te m.

bracing ['breisiŋ] a vigorizante, tónico.

bracken ['brækən] n helecho.

bracket ['brækit] n (TECH) soporte m, puntal m; (group) clase f, categoría; (also: **brace ~**) soporte m, abrazadera; (also: **round ~**) paréntesis m inv; (gen: **square ~**) corchete m // vt (group) agrupar.

brag [bræg] vi jactarse.

braid [breid] n (trimming) galón m; (of hair) trenza.

brain [brein] n cerebro; **~s** npl sesos mpl; **she's got ~s** es muy lista; **~child** n parto del ingenio; **~wash** vt lavar el cerebro; **~wave** n idea luminosa; **~y** a muy inteligente.

braise [breiz] vt cocer a fuego lento.

brake [breik] n (on vehicle) freno // vt, vi frenar; **~ fluid** n líquido de frenos; **~ light** n luz f de frenado.

bramble ['bræmbl] n zarza.

bran [bræn] n salvado.

branch [brɑ:ntʃ] n rama; (fig) ramo; (COMM) sucursal f // vi (also: ~ **out**) ramificarse; (: fig) extenderse.

brand [brænd] n marca; (iron) hierro de marcar // vt (cattle) marcar con hierro candente.

brandish ['brændiʃ] vt blandir.

brand-new ['brænd'nju:] a flamante, completamente nuevo.

brandy ['brændi] n coñac m, brandy m.

brash [bræʃ] a (rough) tosco; (cheeky) descarado.

brass [brɑ:s] n latón m; **the ~** (MUS) los cobres; **~ band** n banda de metal.

brassière ['bræsiə*] n sostén m, sujetador m.

brat [bræt] n (pej) mocoso/a.

bravado [brə'vɑ:dəu] n fanfarronería.

brave [breiv] a valiente, valeroso // n guerrero indio // vt (challenge) desafiar; (resist) aguantar; **~ry** n valor m, valentía.

brawl [brɔ:l] n pendencia, reyerta //

vi pelearse.

brawn [brɔːn] *n* fuerza muscular; (*meat*) carne *f* en gelatina.

bray [breɪ] *n* rebuzno // *vi* rebuznar.

brazen ['breɪzn] *a* descarado, cínico // *vt*: to ~ **it** out echarle cara.

brazier ['breɪzɪə*] *n* brasero.

Brazil [brə'zɪl] *n* (el) Brasil; ~**ian** *a*, *n* brasileño/a *m/f*.

breach [briːtʃ] *vt* abrir brecha en // *n* (*gap*) brecha; (*breaking*): ~ **of confidence** abuso de confianza; ~ **of contract** incumplimiento *f* de contrato; ~ **of the peace** perturbación *f* del orden público.

bread [brɛd] *n* pan *m*; ~ **and butter** *n* pan con mantequilla; (*fig*) pan (de cada día) // *a* común y corriente; ~**bin**, (US) ~**box** *n* panera; ~**crumbs** *npl* migajas *fpl*; (*CULIN*) pan molido; ~**line** *n*: on the ~**line** en la miseria.

breadth [brɛtθ] *n* anchura; (*fig*) amplitud *f*.

breadwinner ['brɛdwɪnə*] *n* sostén *m* de la familia.

break [breɪk] *vb* (*pt* **broke**, *pp* **broken**) *vt* (*gen*) romper; (*promise*) faltar a; (*fall*) amortiguar; (*journey*) interrumpir; (*law*) violar, infringir; (*record*) batir; (*news*) comunicar // *vi* romperse, quebrarse; (*storm*) estallar; (*weather*) cambiar // *n* (*gap*) abertura; (*crack*) grieta; (*fracture*) fractura; (*in relations*) ruptura; (*rest*) descanso; (*time*) intervalo; (: *at school*) (período de) recreo; (*chance*) oportunidad *f*; to ~ **down** *vt* (*figures, data*) analizar, descomponer; (*undermine*) acabar con // *vi* estropearse; (*MED*) sufrir un colapso; (*AUT*) averiarse; (*person*) romper a llorar; to ~ **even** *vi* cubrir los gastos; to ~ **free** *or* **loose** *vi* escaparse; to ~ **in** *vt* (*horse etc*) domar // *vi* (*burglar*) forzar una entrada; to ~ **into** *vt fus* (*house*) forzar; to ~ **off** *vi* (*speaker*) pararse, detenerse; (*branch*) partir; to ~ **open** *vt* (*door etc*) abrir por la fuerza, forzar;

to ~ **out** *vi* estallar; to ~ **out in spots** salir a uno granos; to ~ **up** *vi* (*partnership*) disolverse; (*friends*) romper // *vi* (*rocks etc*) partir; (*crowd*) disolver; ~**age** *n* rotura; ~**down** *n* (AUT) avería; (*in communications*) interrupción *f*; (MED: *also*: **nervous** ~**down**) colapso, crisis *f* nerviosa; ~**down van** *n* (*Brit*) (camión *m*) grúa; ~**er** *n* rompiente *m*.

breakfast ['brɛkfəst] *n* desayuno.

break: ~**-in** *n* robo con allanamiento de morada; ~**ing and entering** *n* (LAW) violación *f* de domicilio, allanamiento de morada; ~**through** *n* (*fig*) avance *m*; ~**water** *n* rompeolas *m inv*.

breast [brɛst] *n* (*of woman*) pecho, seno; (*chest*) pecho; (*of bird*) pechuga; to ~**-feed** *vt*, *vi* (*irg*: *like* **feed**) amamantar, criar a los pechos; ~**stroke** *n* braza de pecho.

breath [brɛθ] *n* aliento, respiración *f*; out of ~ sin aliento, sofocado.

Breathalyser ['brɛθəlaɪzə*] *n* ® (*Brit*) alcoholímetro *m*; ~ **test** *n* prueba de alcoholemia.

breathe [briːð] *vt*, *vi* respirar; (*noisily*) resollar; to ~ **in** *vt*, *vi* aspirar; to ~ **out** *vt*, *vi* espirar; ~**r** *n* respiro; **breathing** *n* respiración *f*.

breath: ~**less** *a* sin aliento, jadeante; ~**taking** *a* imponente, pasmoso.

breed [briːd] *vb* (*pt*, *pp* **bred** [brɛd]) *vt* criar // *vi* reproducirse, procrear // *n* raza, casta; ~**er** *n* (*person*) criador(a) *m/f*; ~**ing** *n* (*of person*) educación *f*.

breeze [briːz] *n* brisa.

breezy ['briːzɪ] *a* de mucho viento, ventoso; (*person*) despreocupado.

brevity ['brɛvɪtɪ] *n* brevedad *f*.

brew [bruː] *vt* (*tea*) hacer; (*beer*) elaborar; (*plot*) tramar // *vi* hacerse; elaborarse; tramarse; (*storm*) amenazar; ~**er** *n* cervecero; ~**ery** *n* fábrica de cerveza, cervecería.

bribe [braɪb] *n* soborno // *vt* sobornar, cohechar; ~**ry** *n* soborno, cohecho.

bric-a-brac ['brɪkəbræk] n inv baratijas fpl.

brick [brɪk] n ladrillo; ~**layer** n albañil m; ~**works** n ladrillar m.

bridal ['braɪdl] a nupcial.

bride [braɪd] n novia; ~**groom** n novio; ~**smaid** n dama de honor.

bridge [brɪdʒ] n puente m; (NAUT) puente m de mando; (of nose) caballete m; (CARDS) bridge m // vt (river) tender un puente sobre.

bridle ['braɪdl] n brida, freno // vt poner la brida a; (fig) reprimir, refrenar; ~ **path** n camino de herradura.

brief [briːf] n (LAW) escrito // vt (inform) informar; (instruct) dar instrucciones a; ~**s** npl (for men) calzoncillos mpl; (for women) bragas fpl; ~**case** n cartera, portafolio (LAm); ~**ing** n (PRESS) informe m; ~**ly** ad (smile, glance) fugazmente; (explain, say) en pocas palabras.

brigadier [brɪgə'dɪə'] n general m de brigada.

bright [braɪt] a claro; (room) luminoso; (day) de sol; (person: clever) listo, inteligente; (: lively) alegre; (colour) vivo; ~**en** (also: ~en up) vt (room) hacer más alegre // vi (weather) despejarse; (person) animarse, alegrarse.

brilliance ['brɪljəns] n brillo, brillantez f.

brilliant ['brɪljənt] a brillante.

brim [brɪm] n borde m; (of hat) ala f.

brine [braɪn] n (CULIN) salmuera.

bring [brɪŋ], pt, pp **brought** vt (thing) traer; (person) conducir; **to ~ about** vt ocasionar, producir; **to ~ back** vt volver a traer; (return) devolver; **to ~ down** vt bajar; (price) rebajar; **to ~ forward** vt adelantar; **to ~ off** vt (task, plan) lograr, conseguir; **to ~ out** vt (object) sacar; **to ~ round** vt (unconscious person) hacer volver en sí; (convince) convencer; **to ~ up** vt (person) educar, criar; (carry up) subir; (question) sacar a colación;

(food: vomit) devolver, vomitar.

brink [brɪŋk] n borde m.

brisk [brɪsk] a enérgico, vigoroso; (speedy) rápido; (trade) activo.

brisket ['brɪskɪt] n carne f de vaca para asar.

bristle ['brɪsl] n cerda // vi erizarse.

Britain ['brɪtən] n (also: Great ~) Gran Bretaña.

British ['brɪtɪʃ] a británico; the ~ npl los británicos; the ~ **isles** npl las Islas Británicas; ~ **Rail (B.R.)** n ≈ RENFE f (Sp).

Briton ['brɪtən] n británico/a.

brittle ['brɪtl] a quebradizo, frágil.

broach [brəʊtʃ] vt (subject) abordar.

broad [brɔːd] a ancho, amplio; (accent) cerrado; **in ~ daylight** en pleno día; ~**cast** n emisión f // vb (pt, pp ~**cast**) vt (RADIO) emitir; (TV) transmitir // vi emitir; transmitir; ~**casting** n radiodifusión f, difusión f; ~**en** vt ensanchar // vi ensancharse; ~**ly** ad en general; ~**-minded** a tolerante, liberal.

broccoli ['brɔkəlɪ] n brécol m.

brochure ['brəʊʃjuə'] n folleto.

broil [brɔɪl] vt (US) asar a la parrilla.

broke [brəʊk] pt of break // a (col) pelado, sin blanca.

broken ['brəʊkən] pp of break // a: ~ **leg** pierna rota; **in ~ English** en un inglés imperfecto; ~**-hearted** a con el corazón partido.

broker ['brəʊkə'] n agente m/f, bolsista m/f.

brolly ['brɔlɪ] n (Brit col) paraguas m inv.

bronchitis [brɔŋ'kaɪtɪs] n bronquitis f.

bronze [brɔnz] n bronce m.

brooch [brəʊtʃ] n prendedor m.

brood [bruːd] n camada, cría; (children) progenie f // vi (hen) empollar; **to ~ over sth** dejarse obsesionar por algo.

brook [brʊk] n arroyo.

broom [brʊm] n escoba; (BOT) retama; ~**stick** n palo de escoba.

Bros. abbr (= Brothers) Hnos.

broth [brɔθ] n caldo.

brothel ['brɔθl] n burdel m.

brother ['brʌðə*] n hermano; **~-in-law** n cuñado.

brought [brɔːt] pt, pp of **bring**.

brow [brau] n (forehead) frente m; (of hill) cumbre f.

brown [braun] a moreno; (hair) castaño; (tanned) bronceado // n (colour) color m moreno o pardo // vt (tan) broncear; (CULIN) dorar; **~ bread** n pan moreno.

brownie ['brauni] n niña exploradora.

brown paper n papel m de estraza.

brown sugar n azúcar m terciado.

browse [brauz] vi (among books) hojear libros.

bruise [bruːz] n cardenal m, moretón m (LAm) // vt magullar.

brunch [brʌnʃ] n desayuno-almuerzo.

brunette [bruː'net] n morena.

brunt [brʌnt] n: **to bear the ~ of** llevar el peso de.

brush [brʌʃ] n cepillo; (large) escoba; (for painting, shaving etc) brocha; (artist's) pincel m; (BOT) maleza; (with police etc) roce m // vt cepillar; (gen: **~ past**, **~ against**) rozar al pasar; **to ~ aside** vt rechazar, no hacer caso a; **to ~ up** vt (knowledge) repasar, refrescar; **~wood** n (bushes) maleza; (sticks) leña.

brusque [bruːsk] a brusco, áspero.

Brussels ['brʌslz] n Bruselas; **~ sprout** n col de Bruselas.

brutal ['bruːtl] a brutal.

brute [bruːt] n bruto; (person) bestia // a: **by ~ force** a fuerza bruta.

B.Sc. abbr = **Bachelor of Science.**

bubble ['bʌbl] n burbuja; (in paint) ampolla // vi burbujear, borbotar; **~ gum** n chicle m de globo.

buck [bʌk] n macho; (US col) dólar m // vi corcovear; **to pass the ~** (to sb) echar (a uno) el muerto; **to ~ up** vi (cheer up) animarse, cobrar

ánimo.

bucket ['bʌkɪt] n cubo, balde m.

buckle ['bʌkl] n hebilla // vt abrochar con hebilla // vi combarse.

bud [bʌd] n brote m, yema; (of flower) capullo // vi brotar, echar brotes.

Buddhism ['budɪzm] n Budismo.

budding ['bʌdɪŋ] a en ciernes, en embrión.

buddy ['bʌdɪ] n (US) compañero, compinche m.

budge [bʌdʒ] vt mover; (fig) hacer ceder // vi moverse.

budgerigar ['bʌdʒərɪgaː*] n periquito.

budget ['bʌdʒɪt] n presupuesto // vi: **to ~ for sth** presupuestar algo.

budgie ['bʌdʒɪ] n = **budgerigar.**

buff [bʌf] a (colour) color de ante // n (enthusiast) entusiasta m/f.

buffalo ['bʌfələu], pl **~** or **~es** n (Brit) búfalo; (US: bison) bisonte m.

buffer ['bʌfə*] n amortiguador m; (COMPUT) memoria intermedia.

buffet ['bufeɪ] n (Brit: bar) bar m, cafetería; (food) buffet m // vt ['bʌfɪt] (strike) abofetear; (wind etc) golpear; **~ car** n (Brit RAIL) coche-comedor m.

bug [bʌg] n (insect) chinche m; (: gen) bicho, sabandija; (germ) microbio, bacilo; (spy device) micrófono oculto // vt (fam) fastidiar; (room) poner micrófono oculto en.

bugle ['bjuːgl] n corneta, clarín m.

build [bɪld] n (of person) talle m, tipo // vt (pt, pp **built**) construir, edificar; **to ~ up** vt (MED) fortalecer; (stocks) acumular; **~er** n constructor/a m/f; (contractor) contratista m/f; **~ing** n (act of) construcción f; (habitation, offices) edificio; **~ing society** n (Brit) sociedad f inmobiliaria, cooperativa de construcciones.

built [bɪlt] pt, pp of **build** // a: **~-in** (cupboard) empotrado; (device) interior, incorporado; **~-up** (area) urbanizado.

bulb [bʌlb] n (BOT) bulbo; (ELEC)

bombilla, foco (LAm) n.

Bulgaria [bʌl'geərɪə] n Bulgaria; ~n a, n búlgaro/a m/f.

bulge [bʌldʒ] n bombeo, pandeo // vi bombearse, pandearse; (pocket etc) hacer bulto.

bulk [bʌlk] n (mass) bulto, volumen m; (major part) grueso; **in** ~ (COMM) a granel; **the** ~ **of** la mayor parte de; ~**head** n mamparo; ~**y** a voluminoso, abultado.

bull [bul] n toro; ~**dog** n dogo.

bulldozer ['buldəuzə*] n aplanadora, motoniveladora.

bullet ['bulɪt] n bala.

bulletin ['bulɪtɪn] n anuncio, parte m; ~ **board** n (US) tablón m de anuncios.

bullet: ~**proof** a a prueba de balas; ~ **wound** n balazo.

bullfight ['bulfaɪt] n corrida de toros; ~**er** n torero; ~**ing** n los toros mpl, el toreo; (art of ~**ing**) tauromaquia.

bullion ['buljən] n oro or plata en barras.

bullock ['bulək] n novillo.

bullring ['bulrɪŋ] n plaza de toros.

bull's-eye ['bulzaɪ] n centro del blanco.

bully ['bulɪ] n valentón m, matón m // vt intimidar, tiranizar.

bum [bʌm] n (Brit: col: backside) culo; (tramp) vagabundo.

bumblebee ['bʌmblbiː] n abejorro.

bump [bʌmp] n (blow) tope m, choque m; (jolt) sacudida; (on road etc) bache m; (on head) chichón m // vt (strike) chocar contra, topetar // vi dar sacudidas; **to** ~ **into** vt fus chocar contra, tropezar con; (person) topar con; ~**er** n (Brit) parachoques m inv // a: ~**er crop/harvest** cosecha abundante; ~**er cars** npl coches mpl de choque.

bumptious ['bʌmpʃəs] a engreído, presuntuoso.

bumpy ['bʌmpɪ] a (road) lleno de baches; (journey) zarandeado.

bun [bʌn] n (Brit: cake) pastel m;

(US: bread) bollo; (of hair) moño.

bunch [bʌntʃ] n (of flowers) ramo; (of keys) manojo; (of bananas) piña; (of people) grupo; (pej) pandilla.

bundle ['bʌndl] n (gen) bulto, fardo; (of sticks) haz m; (of papers) legajo // vt (also: ~ **up**) atar, envolver; **to** ~ **sth/sb into** meter algo/a alguien precipitadamente en.

bungalow ['bʌŋgələu] n bungalow m, chalé m.

bungle ['bʌŋgl] vt chapucear.

bunion ['bʌnjən] n juanete m.

bunk [bʌŋk] n litera; ~ **beds** npl literas fpl.

bunker ['bʌŋkə*] n (coal store) carbonera; (MIL) refugio; (GOLF) bunker m.

bunny ['bʌnɪ] n (also: ~ **rabbit**) conejito.

bunting ['bʌntɪŋ] n empavesada, banderas fpl.

buoy [bɔɪ] n boya; **to** ~ **up** vt mantener a flote; (fig) animar; ~**ancy** n (of ship) capacidad f para flotar; ~**ant** a (carefree) boyante, optimista.

burden ['bəːdn] n carga // vt cargar.

bureau [bjuə'rəu], pl ~**x** [-z] n (Brit: writing desk) escritorio, buró m; (US: chest of drawers) cómoda; (office) oficina, agencia.

bureaucracy [bjuə'rɔkrəsɪ] n burocracia; **bureaucrat** ['bjuərəkræt] n burócrata m/f.

burglar ['bəːglə*] n ladrón/ona m/f; ~ **alarm** n alarma de ladrones; ~**y** n robo con allanamiento, robo de una casa.

burial ['berɪəl] n entierro.

burly ['bəːlɪ] a fornido, membrudo.

Burma ['bəːmə] n Birmania.

burn [bəːn] vb (pt, pp **burned** or **burnt**) vt quemar; (house) incendiar // vi quemarse, arder; incendiarse; (sting) escocer // n quemadura; **to** ~ **down** vt incendiar; ~**er** n (gas) quemador m; ~**ing** a ardiente.

burrow ['bʌrəu] n madriguera // vt hacer una madriguera.

bursar ['bɜːsəʳ] n tesorero; (Brit: student) becario/a; ~ **y** n (Brit) beca.

burst [bɜːst] (pt, pp **burst**) vt (balloon, pipe) reventar; (banks etc) romper // vi reventarse; romperse; (tyre) pincharse; (bomb) estallar // n (explosion) estallido; (also: ~ **pipe**) reventón m; a ~ **of energy** una explosión f de energía; **to** ~ **into flames** estallar en llamas; **to** ~ **out laughing** soltar la carcajada; **to** ~ **into tears** deshacerse en lágrimas; **to be** ~**ing with** reventar por or de; **to** ~ **into** vt fus (room etc) irrumpir en; **to** ~ **open** vi abrirse de golpe.

bury ['berɪ] n enterrar; (body) enterrar, sepultar.

bus [bʌs] n autobús m.

bush [buʃ] n arbusto; (scrub land) monte m; **to beat about the** ~ andar(se) con rodeos; ~ **y** a (thick) espeso, poblado.

busily ['bɪzɪlɪ] ad afanosamente.

business ['bɪznɪs] n (matter) asunto; (trading) comercio, negocios mpl; (firm) empresa, casa; (occupation) oficio; (affair) asunto; **to be away on** ~ estar en viaje de negocios; **it's my** ~ **to...** me toca or corresponde...; **it's none of my** ~ yo no tengo nada que ver; **he means** ~ habla en serio; ~**like** a (company) eficiente; (person) eficiente; ~**man** n hombre m de negocios; ~ **trip** n viaje m de negocios; ~**woman** n mujer f de negocios.

busker ['bʌskəʳ] n (Brit) músico/a ambulante.

bus-stop ['bʌsstɔp] n parada de autobús.

bust [bʌst] n (ANAT) pecho // a (col: broken) roto, estropeado; **to go** ~ quebrarse.

bustle ['bʌsl] n bullicio, movimiento // vi menearse, apresurarse; **bustling** a (town) animado, bullicioso.

busy ['bɪzɪ] a ocupado, atareado; (shop, street) concurrido, animado // vr: **to** ~ **o.s. with** ocuparse en;

~**body** n entrometido/a; ~ **signal** n (US TEL) señal f de comunicando.

but [bʌt] ♦ conj **1** pero; **he's not very bright,** ~ **he's hard-working** no es muy inteligente, pero es trabajador

2 (in direct contradiction) sino; **he's not English** ~ **French** no es inglés sino francés; **he didn't sing** ~ **he shouted** no cantó sino que gritó

3 (showing disagreement, surprise etc): ~ **that's far too expensive!** ¡pero eso es carísimo!; ~ **it does work!** ¡(pero) sí que funciona!

♦ prep (apart from, except) menos, salvo; **we've had nothing** ~ **trouble** no hemos tenido más que problemas; **no-one** ~ **him can do it** nadie más que él puede hacerlo; **who** ~ **a lunatic would do such a thing?** ¿sólo un loco haría una cosa así!; ~ **for you/your help** si no fuera por ti/ tu ayuda; **anything** ~ **that** cualquier cosa menos eso

♦ ad (just, only): **she's** ~ **a child** no es más que una niña; **had I** ~ **known** si lo hubiera sabido; **I can try at least lo puedo intentar; it's all** ~ **finished** está casi acabado.

butcher ['butʃəʳ] n carnicero // vt hacer una carnicería con; (cattle etc for meat) matar; ~**'s (shop)** n carnicería.

butler ['bʌtləʳ] n mayordomo.

butt [bʌt] n (cask) tonel m; (for rain) tina; (thick end) cabo, extremo; (of gun) culata; (of cigarette) colilla; (Brit fig: target) blanco // vt dar cabezadas contra, topetar; **to** ~ **in** vi (interrupt) interrumpir.

butter ['bʌtəʳ] n mantequilla // vt untar con mantequilla; ~**cup** n ranúnculo.

butterfly ['bʌtəflaɪ] n mariposa; (SWIMMING: also: ~ **stroke**) braza de mariposa.

buttocks ['bʌtəks] npl nalgas fpl.

button ['bʌtn] n botón m // vt (also: ~ **up**) abotonar, abrochar // vi abrocharse.

buttress ['bʌtrıs] n contrafuerte m; (fig) apoyo, sostén m.

buxom ['bʌksəm] a (woman) frescachona.

buy [baı] vt (pt, pp bought) comprar // n compra; **to ~ sb sth/sth from sb** comprarle algo a alguien; **to ~ sb a drink** invitar a alguien a tomar algo; **~er** n comprador(a) m/f.

buzz [bʌz] n zumbido; (col: phone call) llamada (por teléfono) // vi zumbar.

buzzer ['bʌzə*] n timbre m.

buzz word n palabra que está de moda.

─────────────
KEYWORD
─────────────

by [baı] ♦ prep 1 (referring to cause, agent) por; de; **killed ~ lightning** muerto por un relámpago; **a painting ~ Picasso** un cuadro de Picasso 2 (referring to method, manner, means): ~ **bus/car/train** en autobús/coche/tren; **to pay ~ cheque** pagar con un cheque; ~ **moonlight/candlelight** a la luz de la luna/una vela; ~ **saving hard, he ...** ahorrando, ... 3 (via, through) por; **we came ~ Dover** vinimos por Dover 4 (close to, past): **the house ~ the river** la casa junto al río; **she rushed ~ me** pasó a mi lado como una exhalación; **I go ~ the post office every day** paso por delante de Correos todos los días 5 (time: not later than) para; (: during): ~ **daylight** de día; ~ **4 o'clock** para las cuatro; ~ **this time tomorrow** para mañana a esta hora; ~ **the time I got here it was too late** cuando llegué ya era demasiado tarde 6 (amount): ~ **the kilo/metre** por kilo/metro; **paid ~ the hour** pagado/a por hora

7 (MATH, measure): **to divide/multiply ~ 3** dividir/multiplicar por 3; **a room 3 metres ~ 4** una habitación de 3 metros por 4; **it's broader ~ a metre** es un metro más ancho 8 (according to) según, de acuerdo con; **it's 3 o'clock ~ my watch** según mi reloj, son las tres; **it's all right ~ me** por mí, está bien 9: (all) ~ **oneself** etc todo solo/a; **he did it (all) ~ himself** lo hizo él solo; **he was standing (all) ~ himself in a corner** estaba de pie solo en un rincón 10: (all) ~ **the way** a propósito, por cierto; **this wasn't my idea ~ the way** pues, no fue idea mía

♦ ad 1 see go, pass etc.

2: ~ **and ~** finalmente; **they'll come back ~ and ~** acabarán volviendo; ~ **and large** en líneas generales, en general.

bye(-bye) ['baı('baı)] excl adiós, hasta luego.

by(e)-law ['baılɔ:] n ordenanza municipal.

by-election ['baıılɛkʃən] n (Brit) elección f parcial.

bygone ['baıgɒn] a pasado, del pasado // n: **let ~s be ~s** lo pasado, pasado está.

bypass ['baıpɑ:s] n carretera de circunvalación; (MED) (operación f de) by-pass m // vt evitar.

by-product ['baıprɒdʌkt] n subproducto, derivado.

bystander ['baıstændə*] n espectador(a) m/f.

byte [baıt] n (COMPUT) byte m, octeto.

byword ['baıwə:d] n: **to be a ~ for** ser conocidísimo por.

by-your-leave ['baıjɔ:'li:v] n: **without so much as a ~** sin decir nada, sin dar ningún tipo de explicación.

C

C [si:] n (MUS) do m.

C. abbr = **centigrade**.

C.A. abbr = **chartered accountant**.

cab [kæb] n taxi m; (of truck) cabina.

cabbage ['kæbɪdʒ] n col f, berza.

cabin ['kæbɪn] n cabaña; (on ship) camarote m.

cabinet ['kæbɪnɪt] n (POL) consejo de ministros; (furniture) armario; (also: **display** ~) vitrina; **~-maker** n ebanista m.

cable ['keɪbl] n cable m // vt cablegrafiar; **~-car** n teleférico; ~ **television** n televisión f por cable.

cache [kæʃ] n (of weapons, drugs etc) alijo.

cackle ['kækl] vi cacarear.

cactus ['kæktəs], pl **cacti** [-taɪ] n cacto.

cadet [kə'dɛt] n (MIL) cadete m.

cadge [kædʒ] vt gorronear.

Caesarean [si:'zɛərɪən] a: ~ (**section**) cesárea.

café ['kæfeɪ] n café m.

cafeteria [kæfɪ'tɪərɪə] n café m.

caffein(e) ['kæfi:n] n cafeína.

cage [keɪdʒ] n jaula // vt enjaular.

cagey ['keɪdʒɪ] a (col) cauteloso, reservado.

cagoule [kə'gu:l] n chubasquero.

Cairo ['kaɪərəu] n el Cairo.

cajole [kə'dʒəul] vt engatusar.

cake [keɪk] n pastel m; (of soap) pastilla; **~d** a: **~d** with cubierto de.

calculate ['kælkjuleɪt] vt calcular; **calculating** a (scheming) calculador(a); **calculation** [-'leɪʃən] n cálculo, cómputo; **calculator** n calculadora.

calendar ['kæləndə*] n calendario; ~ **month/year** n mes m/año civil.

calf [kɑ:f], pl **calves** n (of cow) ternero, becerro; (of other animals) cría; (also: **~skin**) piel f de becerro; (ANAT) pantorrilla.

calibre, (US) **caliber** ['kælɪbə*] n calibre m.

call [kɔ:l] vt (gen) llamar // vi (shout) llamar; (TEL) llamar (por teléfono), telefonear (esp LAm); (visit: also: ~ **in**, ~ **round**) hacer una visita // n (shout, TEL) llamada; (of bird) canto; (appeal) llamamiento; **to be ~ed** (person, object) llamarse; **on** ~ (nurse, doctor etc) de guardia; **to** ~ **back** vi (return) volver; (TEL) volver a llamar; **to** ~ **for** vt fus (demand) pedir, exigir; (fetch) venir por, pasar por (LAm); **to** ~ **off** vt suspender; (cancel) cancelar; **to** ~ **on** vt fus (visit) visitar; (turn to) acudir a; **to** ~ **out** vi gritar, dar voces; **to** ~ **up** vt (MIL) llamar al servicio militar; **~box** n (Brit) cabina telefónica; ~ **girl** n visita f; (TEL) usuario/a; ~ **girl** n prostituta; **~-in** n (US) (programa m) coloquio (por teléfono); **~ing** n vocación f, profesión f; **~ing card** n (US) tarjeta de visita or comercial.

callous ['kæləs] a insensible, cruel.

calm [kɑ:m] a tranquilo; (sea) liso, en calma // n calma, tranquilidad f // vt calmar, tranquilizar; **to** ~ **down** vi calmarse, tranquilizarse // vt calmar, tranquilizar.

Calor gas ['kælə*-] n ® butano.

calorie ['kælərɪ] n caloría.

calve [kɑ:v] vi parir.

calves [kɑ:vz] pl of **calf**.

camber ['kæmbə*] n (of road) combadura, comba.

Cambodia [kæm'bəudʒə] n Camboya.

came [keɪm] pt of **come**.

camel ['kæməl] n camello.

cameo ['kæmɪəu] n camafeo.

camera ['kæmərə] n máquina fotográfica; (CINEMA, TV) cámara; **in** ~ en secreto; **~man** n cámara m.

camouflage ['kæməflɑ:ʒ] n camuflaje m // vt camuflar.

camp [kæmp] n campo, campamento // vi acampar // a afectado, afeminado.

campaign [kæm'peɪn] n (MIL, POL etc) campaña // vi hacer campaña.

camp: **~bed** n (Brit) cama de campaña; **~er** n (person) campista m/f; (vehicle) caravana; **~ing** n camping m; **to go ~ing** hacer camping; **~site** n camping m.

campus ['kæmpəs] n ciudad f universitaria.

KEYWORD

can [kæn] ◆ n, vt see next headword ◆ auxiliary vb (negative cannot, can't; conditional and pt could) 1 (be able to) poder; **you ~ do it if you try** puedes hacerlo si lo intentas; **I ~'t see you** no te veo
2 (know how to) saber; **I ~ swim/play tennis/drive** sé nadar/jugar al tenis/conducir; **~ you speak French?** ¿hablas o sabes hablar francés?
3 (may) poder; **~ I use your phone?** ¿me dejas o puedo usar tu teléfono?
4 (expressing disbelief, puzzlement etc): **it ~'t be true!** no puede ser (verdad)!; **what CAN he want?** ¿qué querrá?
5 (expressing possibility, suggestion etc): **he could be in the library** podría estar en la biblioteca; **she could have been delayed** pudo haberse retrasado.

can [kæn] auxiliary vb see previous headword // n (of oil, water) bidón m; (tin) lata, bote m // vt enlatar; (preserve) conservar en lata.

Canada [kænədə] n el Canadá; **Canadian** [kə'neɪdɪən] a, n canadiense m/f.

canal [kə'næl] n canal m.

canary [kə'nɛərɪ] n canario; **C~ Islands** npl las (Islas) Canarias.

cancel ['kænsəl] vt cancelar; (train) suprimir; (appointment) anular; (cross out) tachar, borrar; **~lation** [-'leɪʃən] n cancelación f; supresión f.

cancer ['kænsə*] n cáncer m; **C~**

(ASTRO) Cáncer m.

candid ['kændɪd] a franco, abierto.

candidate ['kændɪdeɪt] n candidato/a.

candle ['kændl] n vela; (in church) cirio; **by ~ light** a la luz de una vela; **~stick** n (also: **~ holder**) (single) candelero; (low) palmatoria; (bigger, ornate) candelabro.

candour, (US) candor ['kændə*] n franqueza.

candy ['kændɪ] n azúcar m cande; (US) caramelo; **~-floss** n (Brit) algodón m (azucarado).

cane [keɪn] n (BOT) caña; (stick) vara, palmeta // vt (Brit SCOL) castigar (con palmeta).

canister ['kænɪstə*] n bote m, lata.

cannabis ['kænəbɪs] n marijuana.

canned [kænd] a en lata, de lata.

cannibal ['kænɪbəl] n caníbal m/f.

cannon ['kænən] pl ~ or **~s** n cañón m.

cannot ['kænɔt] = **can not**.

canny ['kænɪ] a astuto.

canoe [kə'nuː] n canoa; (SPORT) piragua.

canon ['kænən] n (clergyman) canónigo; (standard) canon m.

can opener ['kænəupnə*] n abrelatas m inv.

canopy ['kænəpɪ] n dosel m; toldo.

can't [kænt] = **can not**.

cantankerous [kæn'tæŋkərəs] a arisco, malhumorado.

canteen [kæn'tiːn] n (eating place) cantina; (Brit: of cutlery) juego m.

canter ['kæntə*] n medio galope // vi ir a medio galope.

canvas ['kænvəs] n (material) lona; (painting) lienzo; (NAUT) velas fpl.

canvass ['kænvəs] vt (POL) solicitar votos de; (COMM) sondear.

canyon ['kænjən] n cañón m.

cap [kæp] n (hat) gorra; (of pen) capuchón m; (of bottle) tapa, cápsula // vt (outdo) superar; (bottle etc) tapar; (tooth) poner una corona a.

capability [keɪpə'bɪlɪtɪ] n capacidad f.

capable ['keɪpəbl] a capaz.

capacity [kə'pæsɪtɪ] n capacidad f; (position) calidad f.

cape [keɪp] n capa; (GEO) cabo.

capital ['kæpɪtl] n (also: ~ city) capital f; (money) capital m; (also: ~ letter) mayúscula; ~ **gains tax** n impuesto sobre las ganancias de capital; ~**ism** n capitalismo; ~**ist** a, n capitalista m/f; ~**ize** on vt fus aprovechar; ~ **punishment** n pena de muerte.

capitulate [kə'pɪtjuleɪt] vi capitular, rendirse.

Capricorn ['kæprɪkɔːn] n Capricornio.

capsize [kæp'saɪz] vt volcar, hacer zozobrar // vi volcarse, zozobrar.

capsule ['kæpsjuːl] n cápsula.

captain ['kæptɪn] n capitán m.

caption ['kæpʃən] n (heading) título; (to picture) leyenda.

captive ['kæptɪv] a, n cautivo/a m/f; **captivity** [-'tɪvɪtɪ] n cautiverio.

capture ['kæptʃəʳ] vt prender, aprehender; (place) tomar; (attention) captar, llamar // n apresamiento; toma; (data ~) formulación f de datos.

car [kɑːʳ] n coche m, carro (LAm), automóvil m; (US RAIL) vagón m.

carafe [kə'ræf] n garrafa.

caramel ['kærəməl] n caramelo.

carat ['kærət] n quilate m.

caravan ['kærəvæn] n (Brit) caravana, ruló f; (of camels) caravana; ~ **site** n (Brit) camping m para caravanas.

carbohydrates [kɑːbəʊ'haɪdreɪts] npl hidratos mpl de carbono; (food) fécula sg.

carbon ['kɑːbən] n carbono; ~ **copy** n copia al carbón; ~ **paper** n papel m carbón.

carburettor, (US) **carburetor** [kɑːbju'retəʳ] n carburador m.

card [kɑːd] n (playing ~) carta, naipe m; (visiting ~, post~ etc) tarjeta; ~**board** n cartón m, cartulina; ~ **game** n juego de naipes.

cardiac ['kɑːdɪæk] a cardíaco.

cardigan ['kɑːdɪgən] n rebeca.

cardinal ['kɑːdɪnl] a cardinal // n cardenal m.

card index n fichero.

care [kɛəʳ] n cuidado; (worry) inquietud f; (charge) cargo, custodia // vi: to ~ **about** preocuparse por; ~ **of** en casa de, al cuidado de; **in sb's** ~ a cargo de uno; **to take** ~ to cuidarse de, tener cuidado de; **to take** ~ **of** cuidar; **I don't** ~ no me importa; **I couldn't** ~ **less** eso me trae sin cuidado; **to** ~ **for** vt fus cuidar a; (like) querer.

career [kə'rɪəʳ] n carrera // vi (also: ~ **along**) correr a toda velocidad.

carefree ['kɛəfriː] a despreocupado.

careful ['kɛəful] a cuidadoso; (cautious) cauteloso; **(be)** ~! ¡tenga cuidado!; ~**ly** ad con cuidado, cuidadosamente.

careless ['kɛəlɪs] a descuidado; (heedless) poco atento; ~**ness** n descuido, falta de atención.

caress [kə'rɛs] n caricia // vt acariciar.

caretaker ['kɛəteɪkəʳ] n portero, conserje m/f.

car-ferry ['kɑːferɪ] n transbordador m para coches.

cargo ['kɑːgəʊ], pl ~**es** n cargamento, carga.

car hire n alquiler m de automóviles.

Caribbean [kærɪ'biːən] n: **the** ~ **(Sea)** el (Mar) Caribe.

caring ['kɛərɪŋ] a humanitario.

carnal ['kɑːnl] a carnal.

carnation [kɑː'neɪʃən] n clavel m.

carnival ['kɑːnɪvl] n carnaval m; (US) parque m de atracciones.

carnivorous [kɑː'nɪvrəs] a carnívoro.

carol ['kærəl] n: (Christmas) ~ villancico.

carp [kɑːp] n (fish) carpa; **to** ~ **at** or **about** vt fus quejarse de.

car park n (Brit) aparcamiento, parking m.

carpenter ['kɑːpɪntəʳ] n carpintero/a.

carpentry [ˈkɑːpɪntrɪ] n carpintería.

carpet [ˈkɑːpɪt] n alfombra // vt alfombrar; **~ slippers** npl zapatillas fpl; **~ sweeper** n escoba mecánica.

carriage [ˈkærɪdʒ] n coche m; (Brit RAIL) vagón m; (for goods) transporte m; (: cost) porte n, flete m; (of typewriter) carro; (bearing) porte m; **~ return** n (on typewriter etc) retorno del carro; **~way** n (Brit: part of road) calzada.

carrier [ˈkærɪə*] n trajinista m/f; (company) empresa de transportes; **~ bag** n (Brit) bolsa de papel or plástico.

carrot [ˈkærət] n zanahoria.

carry [ˈkærɪ] vt (subj: person) llevar; (transport) transportar; (a motion, bill) aprobar; (involve: responsibilities etc) entrañar, implicar // vi (sound) oírse; **to get carried away** (fig) entusiasmarse; **to ~ on** vi (continue) seguir (adelante), continuar; (fam: complain) quejarse, protestar // vt proseguir, continuar; **to ~ out** vt (orders) cumplir; (investigation) llevar a cabo, realizar.

cot n (Brit) cuna portátil; **~on** n (col: fuss) lío.

cart [kɑːt] n carro, carreta // vt llevar (en carro).

carton [ˈkɑːtən] n (box) caja de cartón; (of yogurt) pote m n.

cartoon [kɑːˈtuːn] n (PRESS) caricatura; (comic strip) tira cómica; (film) dibujos mpl animados; **~ist** n dibujante m/f de historietas.

cartridge [ˈkɑːtrɪdʒ] n cartucho.

carve [kɑːv] vt (meat) trinchar; (wood, stone) cincelar, esculpir; (on tree) grabar; **to ~ up** vi dividir, repartir; **carving** n (in wood etc) escultura, (obra de) talla; **carving knife** n trinchante m.

car wash n lavado de coches.

case [keɪs] n (container) caja; (MED) caso; (for jewels etc) estuche m; (LAW) causa, proceso; (Brit: also: suit~) maleta; **in ~ of** en caso de; **in any ~** en todo caso; **just in**

~ por si acaso; **to make a good ~** tener buenos argumentos.

cash [kæʃ] n dinero en efectivo, dinero contante // vt cobrar, hacer efectivo; **to pay (in) ~** pagar al contado; **~ on delivery** cóbrese al entregar; **~book** n libro de caja; **~ card** n tarjeta f dinero; **~desk** n (Brit) caja; **~ dispenser** n cajero automático.

cashew [kæˈʃuː] n (also: ~ nut) anacardo.

cashier [kæˈʃɪə*] n cajero/a.

cashmere [ˈkæʃmɪə*] n casimir m, cachemira.

cash register n caja.

casing [ˈkeɪsɪŋ] n revestimiento.

casino [kəˈsiːnəu] n casino.

cask [kɑːsk] n tonel m, barril m.

casket [ˈkɑːskɪt] n cofre m, estuche m; (US: coffin) ataúd m.

casserole [ˈkæsərəul] n (food, pot) cazuela.

cassette [kæˈsɛt] n cassette m; **~ player/recorder** n tocacassettes m inv.

cast [kɑːst] vb (pt, pp cast) vt (throw) echar, arrojar, lanzar; (skin) mudar, perder; (metal) fundir // (THEATRE): **to ~ sb as Othello** dar a alguien el papel de Otelo // vi (FISHING) lanzar // n (THEATRE) reparto; (mould) forma, molde m; (also: plaster ~) vaciado; **to ~ one's vote** votar; **to ~ off** vi (NAUT) desamarrar.

castanets [kæstəˈnɛts] npl castañuelas fpl.

castaway [ˈkɑːstəweɪ] n náufrago/a.

caste [kɑːst] n casta.

caster sugar [ˈkɑːstə*-] n (Brit) azúcar m extrafino.

Castile [kæsˈtiːl] n Castilla.

casting vote [ˈkɑːstɪŋ-] n (Brit) voto decisivo.

cast iron n hierro fundido.

castle [ˈkɑːsl] n castillo; (CHESS) torre f.

castor [ˈkɑːstə*] n (wheel) ruedecilla; **~ oil** n aceite m de ricino.

castrate [kæs'treɪt] vt castrar.

casual ['kæʒjul] a (by chance) fortuito; (irregular: work etc) eventual, temporero; (unconcerned) despreocupado; (informal: clothes) de sport; **~ly** ad de manera despreocupada.

casualty ['kæʒjultɪ] n víctima, herido; (dead) muerto; (MIL) baja.

cat [kæt] n gato.

Catalan ['kætəlæn] a, n catalán/ana m/f.

catalogue, (US) **catalog** ['kætəlɒg] n catálogo // vt catalogar.

Catalonia [kætə'ləunɪə] n Cataluña.

catalyst ['kætəlɪst] n catalizador m.

catapult ['kætəpʌlt] n tirador m.

catarrh [kə'tɑː*] n catarro.

catastrophe [kə'tæstrəfɪ] n catástrofe f.

catch [kætʃ] vb (pt, pp **caught**) vt coger (Sp), agarrar (LAm); (arrest) detener; (grasp) asir; (breath) suspender; (person: by surprise) sorprender; (attract: attention) ganar; (MED) contagiarse de, coger; (also: **~ up**) alcanzar // vi (fire) encenderse; (in branches etc) enredarse // n (fish etc) pesca; (act of catching) cogida; (trick) trampa; (of lock) pestillo, cerradura; **to ~ fire** encenderse; **to ~ sight of** divisar; **to ~ on** vi (understand) caer en la cuenta; (grow popular) hacerse popular; **to ~ up** vi (fig) ponerse al día.

catching ['kætʃɪŋ] a (MED) contagioso.

catchment area ['kætʃmənt-] n (Brit) zona de captación.

catchphrase ['kætʃfreɪz] n lema m, eslogan m.

catchy ['kætʃɪ] a (tune) pegadizo.

categorize ['kætɪgəraɪz] vt clasificar.

category ['kætɪgərɪ] n categoría, clase f.

cater ['keɪtə*] vi: **to ~ for** (Brit) abastecer a; (needs) atender a; (consumers) proveer a; **~er** n abastecedor(a) m/f, proveedor(a) m/f; **~ing** n (trade) (ramo de la) alimentación f.

caterpillar ['kætəpɪlə*] n oruga, gusano; **~ track** n rodado de oruga.

cathedral [kə'θɪdrəl] n catedral f.

catholic [kə'θɒlɪk] a católico; **C~** a, n (REL) católico/a m/f.

cat's-eye ['kætsaɪ] n (Brit AUT) catafoto.

cattle ['kætl] npl ganado sg.

catty ['kætɪ] a malicioso, rencoroso.

caucus ['kɔːkəs] n (POL: local committee) comité m local; (: US: to elect candidates) comité m electoral.

caught [kɔːt] pt, pp of **catch**.

cauliflower ['kɔlɪflauə*] n coliflor f.

cause [kɔːz] n causa, motivo, razón f // vt causar; (provoke) provocar.

caustic ['kɔːstɪk] a cáustico; (fig) mordaz.

caution ['kɔːʃən] n cautela, prudencia; (warning) advertencia, amonestación f // vt amonestar.

cautious ['kɔːʃəs] a cauteloso, prudente, precavido; **~ly** ad con cautela.

cavalier [kævə'lɪə*] a arrogante, desdeñoso.

cavalry ['kævəlrɪ] n caballería.

cave [keɪv] n cueva, caverna; **to ~ in** vi (roof etc) derrumbarse, hundirse; **~man/woman** n cavernícola m/f, troglodita m/f.

cavern ['kævən] n caverna.

caviar(e) ['kævɪɑː*] n caviar m.

cavity ['kævɪtɪ] n hueco, cavidad f.

cavort [kə'vɔːt] vi dar cabrioladas.

CB n abbr (= Citizen's Band (Radio)) banda ciudadana.

CBI n abbr (= Confederation of British Industry) ≈ C.E.O.E. f (Sp).

cc abbr = cubic centimetres; = carbon copy.

cease [siːs] vt cesar; **~fire** n alto el fuego; **~less** a incesante; **~lessly** ad sin cesar.

cedar ['siːdə*] n cedro.

ceiling ['siːlɪŋ] n techo; (fig) límite m.

celebrate ['sɛlɪbreɪt] vt celebrar; (have a party) festejar // vi divertirse; **~d** a célebre; **celebration**

[-'breɪʃən] n fiesta, celebración f.
celery ['sɛlərɪ] n apio.
celibacy ['sɛlɪbəsɪ] n celibato.
celibate ['sɛlɪbɪt] n celibato.
cell [sɛl] n celda; (BIOL) célula; (ELEC) elemento.
cellar ['sɛlə*] n sótano; (for wine) bodega.
'cello ['tʃɛləu] n violoncelo.
cellophane ['sɛləfeɪn] n celofán m.
Celt [kɛlt, sɛlt] a, n celta m/f; ~**ic** a celta.
cement [sə'mɛnt] n cemento // vt cementar; (fig) cimentar, fortalecer; ~ **mixer** n hormigonera.
cemetery ['sɛmɪtrɪ] n cementerio.
censor ['sɛnsə*] n censor m // vt (cut) censurar; ~**ship** n censura.
censure ['sɛnʃə*] vt censurar.
census ['sɛnsəs] n censo.
cent [sɛnt] n (US: coin) centavo, céntimo; see also **per**.
centenary [sɛn'tiːnərɪ] n centenario.
center ['sɛntə*] n (US) = **centre**.
centi... [sɛntɪ] pref: ~**grade** a centígrado; ~**litre**, (US) ~**liter** n centilitro; ~**metre**, (US) ~**meter** n centímetro.
centipede ['sɛntɪpiːd] n ciempiés m inv.
central ['sɛntrəl] a central; (of house etc) céntrico; C~ **America** n Centroamérica; ~ **heating** n calefacción f central; ~**ize** vt centralizar.
centre ['sɛntə*] n centro // vt centrar; ~**forward** n (SPORT) delantero centro; ~**half** n (SPORT) medio centro.
century ['sɛntjurɪ] n siglo; **20th** ~ siglo veinte.
ceramic [sɪ'ræmɪk] a cerámico; ~**s** n cerámica.
cereal ['siːrɪəl] n cereal m.
cerebral ['sɛrɪbrəl] a cerebral; intelectual.
ceremony ['sɛrɪmənɪ] n ceremonia; **to stand on** ~ hacer ceremonias, estar de cumplido.
certain ['sɜːtən] a (sure) (correct) cierto; (person) seguro; (a particular) cierto; **for** ~ a ciencia cierta;

~**ly** ad desde luego, por supuesto; ~**ty** n certeza, certidumbre f, seguridad f.
certificate [sə'tɪfɪkɪt] n certificado.
certified ['sɜːtɪfaɪd] a: ~ **mail** n (US) correo certificado; ~ **public accountant (C.P.A)** n (US) contable m/f diplomado/a.
certify ['sɜːtɪfaɪ] vt certificar.
cervical ['sɜːvɪkl] a (of cervix: smear, cancer) cervical.
cervix ['sɜːvɪks] n cerviz f.
cessation [sə'seɪʃən] n cese m, suspensión f.
cesspit ['sɛspɪt] n pozo negro.
cf. abbr (= compare) cfr.
ch. abbr (= chapter) cap.
chafe [tʃeɪf] vt (rub) rozar; (irritate) irritar.
chaffinch ['tʃæfɪntʃ] n pinzón m (vulgar).
chagrin ['ʃægrɪn] n (annoyance) disgusto; (disappointment) desazón f.
chain [tʃeɪn] n cadena // vt (also: ~ up) encadenar; **to** ~**-smoke** vi fumar un cigarrillo tras otro; ~ **reaction** n reacción f en cadena; ~ **store** n tienda de una cadena, ≈ gran almacén.
chair [tʃeə*] n silla; (armchair) sillón m; (of university) cátedra f // vt (meeting) presidir; ~**lift** n telesilla; ~**man** n presidente m.
chalet ['ʃæleɪ] n chalet m.
chalk [tʃɔːk] n (GEO) creta; (for writing) tiza, gis m (LAm).
challenge ['tʃælɪndʒ] n desafío, reto // vt desafiar, retar; (statement, right) poner en duda; **to** ~ **sb to do sth** retar a uno a que haga algo; ~**challenging** a desafiante; (tone) de desafío.
chamber ['tʃeɪmbə*] n cámara, sala; ~ **of commerce** cámara de comercio; ~**maid** n camarera; ~ **music** n música de cámara.
champagne [ʃæm'peɪn] n champaña m, champán m.
champion ['tʃæmpɪən] n campeón/ona m/f; ~**ship** n campeonato.

chance [tʃɑːns] n (coincidence) casualidad f; (luck) suerte f; (fate) azar m; (opportunity) ocasión f, oportunidad f; (likelihood) posibilidad f; (risk) riesgo m // vt arriesgar, probar // a fortuito, casual; **to ~ it** arriesgarse, intentarlo; **to take a ~** arriesgarse; **by ~** por casualidad.

chancellor [tʃɑːnsələ*] n canciller m; **C~ of the Exchequer** n (Brit) Ministro de Hacienda.

chandelier [ʃændə'lɪə*] n araña (de luces).

change [tʃeɪndʒ] vt cambiar; (replace) reemplazar; (gear) cambiar de; (clothes, house) mudarse de; (exchange) trocar; (transform) transformar // vi cambiar(se); (trains) hacer transbordo; (be transformed): **to ~ into** transformarse en // n cambio; (alteration) modificación f, transformación f; (coins) suelto, sencillo; (money returned) vuelta; **to ~ one's mind** cambiar de opinión o idea; **for a ~** para variar; **~able** a (weather) cambiable; **~ machine** n máquina de cambio; **~over** n (to new system) cambio.

changing [tʃeɪndʒɪŋ] a cambiante; **~ room** n (Brit) vestuario.

channel [tʃænl] n (TV) canal m; (of river) cauce m; (of sea) estrecho; (groove, fig: medium) conducto, medio // vt (river etc) encauzar; **the (English) C~** el Canal (de la Mancha); **the C~ Islands** las Islas Normandas.

chant [tʃɑːnt] n canto // vt cantar.

chaos [keɪɒs] n caos m.

chap [tʃæp] n (Brit col: man) tío, tipo.

chapel [tʃæpl] n capilla.

chaperone [ʃæpərəʊn] n carabina.

chaplain [tʃæplɪn] n capellán m.

chapped [tʃæpt] a agrietado.

chapter [tʃæptə*] n capítulo.

char [tʃɑː*] vt (burn) carbonizar, chamuscar // n (Brit) = **charlady**.

character [kærɪktə*] n carácter m, naturaleza, índole f; (in novel, film)

personaje m; (role) papel m; **~istic** [-rɪstɪk] a característico n característica; **~ize** vt caracterizar.

charcoal [tʃɑːkəʊl] n carbón m vegetal; (ART) carboncillo.

charge [tʃɑːdʒ] n carga; (LAW) cargo, acusación f; (cost) precio, coste m; (responsibility) cargo; (task) encargo // vt (LAW) acusar (with de); (gun, battery, MIL: enemy) cargar; (price) pedir; (customer) cobrar; (sb with task) encargar // vi precipitarse; (make pay) cobrar; **~s** npl: **bank ~s** comisiones fpl bancarias; **free of ~** gratis; **to reverse the ~s** (Brit TEL) revertir el cobro; **to take ~ of** hacerse cargo de, encargarse de; **to be in ~ of** estar encargado de; **how much do you ~?** ¿cuánto cobra usted?; **to ~ an expense (up) to sb's account** cargar algo a cuenta de alguien; **~ card** n tarjeta de cuenta.

charitable [tʃærɪtəbl] a caritativo.

charity [tʃærɪtɪ] n (gen) caridad f; (organization) sociedad f benéfica.

charlady [tʃɑːleɪdɪ] n (Brit) mujer f de la limpieza.

charlatan [ʃɑːlətən] n farsante m/f.

charm [tʃɑːm] n encanto, atractivo // vt encantar; **~ing** a encantador(a).

chart [tʃɑːt] n (table) cuadro; (graph) gráfica; (map) carta de navegación // vt (course) trazar.

charter [tʃɑːtə*] vt (plane) alquilar; (ship) fletar // n (document) carta; **~ed accountant** n (Brit) contable m/f diplomado/a; **~ flight** n vuelo chárter.

charwoman [tʃɑːwʊmən] n = **charlady**.

chase [tʃeɪs] vt (pursue) perseguir; (hunt) cazar // n persecución f; caza; **to ~ after** correr tras.

chasm [kæzəm] n abismo.

chassis [ʃæsɪ] n chasis m.

chat [tʃæt] vi (also: **have a ~**) charlar // n charla; **~ show** n (Brit) (programa m) magazine m.

chatter [tʃætə*] vi (person) charlar; (teeth) castañetear // n (of birds) parloteo; (*of people*) charla, cháchara; **~box** *n* parlanchín/ina *m/f*.

chatty ['tʃætɪ] *a* (*style*) familiar; (*person*) hablador(a).

chauffeur ['ʃəʊfə*] *n* chófer *m*.

chauvinist ['ʃəʊvɪnɪst] *n* (*male* ~) machista *m*; (*nationalist*) chovinista *m/f*.

cheap [tʃiːp] *a* barato; (*joke*) de mal gusto; (*poor quality*) de mala calidad // *ad* barato; **~en** *vt* rebajar el precio, abaratar; **~er** *a* más barato; **~ly** *ad* barato, a bajo precio.

cheat [tʃiːt] *vi* hacer trampa // *vt* estafar, timar // *n* trampa; estafa; (*person*) tramposo/a.

check [tʃɛk] *vt* (*examine*) controlar; (*facts*) comprobar; (*count*) contar; (*halt*) parar, detener; (*restrain*) refrenar, restringir // *n* (*inspection*) control *m*, inspección *f*; (*curb*) freno; (*bill*) nota, cuenta; (*US*) = **cheque**; (*pattern: gen pl*) cuadro // *a* (*also* **~ed**: *pattern, cloth*) a cuadros; **to ~ in** *vi* (*in hotel, airport*) registrarse // *vt* (*luggage*) facturar; **to ~ out** *vi* (*of hotel*) desocupar su cuarto; **to ~ up** *vi*: **to ~ up on sth** comprobar algo; **to ~ up on sb** investigar a alguien; **~ered** *a* (*US*) = **chequered**; **~ers** *n* (*US*) juego de damas; **~-in (desk)** *n* mesa de facturación; **~ing account** *n* (*US*) cuenta corriente; **~mate** *n* jaque *m* mate; **~out** *n* caja; **~point** *n* (*punto de*) control *m*; **~room** *n* (*US*) consigna; **~up** *n* (*MED*) reconocimiento general; (*of machine*) repaso.

cheek [tʃiːk] *n* mejilla; (*impudence*) descaro; **~bone** *n* pómulo; **~y** *a* fresco, descarado.

cheep [tʃiːp] *vi* piar.

cheer [tʃɪə*] *vt* vitorear, aplaudir; (*gladden*) alegrar, animar // *vi* aplaudir, dar vivas // *n* viva *m*; **~s** *npl* aplausos *mpl*; **~s!** ¡salud!; ¡brindo!; **to ~ up** *vi* animarse // *vt* alegrar, animar; **~ful** *a* alegre.

cheerio [tʃɪərɪ'əʊ] *excl* (*Brit*) ¡hasta luego!

cheese [tʃiːz] *n* queso; **~board** *n* plato de quesos.

cheetah ['tʃiːtə] *n* leopardo cazador.

chef [ʃef] *n* jefe/a *m/f* de cocina.

chemical ['kɛmɪkəl] *a* químico // *n* producto químico.

chemist ['kɛmɪst] *n* (*Brit: pharmacist*) farmacéutico/a; (*scientist*) químico/a; **~ry** *n* química; **~'s (shop)** *n* (*Brit*) farmacia.

cheque [tʃɛk] *n* (*Brit*) cheque *m*; **~book** *n* libro de cheques, chequera (*LAm*); **~ card** *n* tarjeta de cheque.

chequered ['tʃɛkəd] *a* (*fig*) accidentado.

cherish ['tʃɛrɪʃ] *vt* (*love*) querer, apreciar; (*protect*) cuidar; (*hope etc*) abrigar.

cherry ['tʃɛrɪ] *n* cereza.

chess [tʃɛs] *n* ajedrez *m*; **~board** *n* tablero (de ajedrez); **~man** *n* pieza, trebejo.

chest [tʃɛst] *n* (*ANAT*) pecho; (*box*) cofre *m*, cajón *m*; **~ of drawers** *n* cómoda.

chestnut ['tʃɛsnʌt] *n* castaña; **~ (tree)** *n* castaño.

chew [tʃuː] *vt* mascar, masticar; **~ing gum** *n* chicle *m*.

chic [ʃiːk] *a* elegante.

chick [tʃɪk] *n* pollito, polluelo; (*US col*) chica.

chicken ['tʃɪkɪn] *n* gallina; pollo; (*food*) pollo; **to ~ out** *vi* (*col*) rajarse; **~pox** *n* varicela.

chicory ['tʃɪkərɪ] *n* (*for coffee*) achicoria; (*salad*) escarola.

chief [tʃiːf] *n* jefe/a *m/f* // *a* principal; **~ executive** *n* director(a) *m/f* general; **~ly** *ad* principalmente.

chiffon ['ʃɪfɔn] *n* gasa.

chilblain ['tʃɪlbleɪn] *n* sabañón *m*.

child [tʃaɪld], *pl* **~ren** ['tʃɪldrən] *n* niño/a; (*offspring*) hijo/a; **~birth** *n* parto; **~hood** *n* niñez *f*, infancia; **~ish** *a* pueril, aniñado; **~like** *a* de niño; **~ minder** *n* (*Brit*) niñera.

Chile ['tʃɪlɪ] *n* Chile *m*; **~an** *a, n* chileno/a *m/f*.

chill [tʃɪl] *n* frío; (*MED*) resfriado // *a*

frío // vt enfriar; (CULIN) congelar.

chilli ['tʃɪlɪ] n (Brit) chile m, ají m (LAm).

chilly ['tʃɪlɪ] a frío.

chime [tʃaɪm] n repique m, campanada // vi repicar, sonar.

chimney ['tʃɪmnɪ] n chimenea; ~ **sweep** n deshollinador m.

chimpanzee [tʃɪmpæn'ziː] n chimpancé m.

chin [tʃɪn] n mentón m, barbilla.

china ['tʃaɪnə] n porcelana; (crockery) loza.

China ['tʃaɪnə] n China; **Chinese** [tʃaɪ'niːz] a chino // n, pl inv chino/a; (LING) chino.

chink [tʃɪŋk] n (opening) grieta, hendedura; (noise) tintineo.

chip [tʃɪp] n (gen pl: CULIN: Brit) patata or papa (LAm) frita; (: US: also: **potato** ~) patata or papa frita; (of wood) astilla; (of glass, stone) lasca; (at poker) ficha; (COMPUT) chip m // vt (cup, plate) desconchar; **to ~ in** vi interrumpir; (contribute) compartir los gastos.

chiropodist [kɪ'rɔpədɪst] n (Brit) pedicuro/a.

chirp [tʃəːp] vi gorjear, piar.

chisel ['tʃɪzl] n (for wood) formón m; (for stone) cincel m.

chit [tʃɪt] n nota.

chitchat ['tʃɪtʃæt] n chismes mpl, habladurías fpl.

chivalry ['ʃɪvəlrɪ] n caballerosidad f.

chives [tʃaɪvz] npl cebollinos mpl.

chlorine ['klɔːriːn] n cloro.

chock [tʃɔk]: **~-a-block**, **~-full** a atestado.

chocolate ['tʃɔklɪt] n chocolate m.

choice [tʃɔɪs] n elección f // a escogido.

choir ['kwaɪə*] n coro; **~boy** n corista m.

choke [tʃəuk] vi sofocarse; (on food) atragantarse // vt ahogar, sofocar; (block) obstruir // n (AUT) estárter m.

choose [tʃuːz], pt **chose**, pp **chosen** vt escoger, elegir; (team) selec-

cionar.

choosy ['tʃuːzɪ] a remilgado.

chop [tʃɔp] vt (wood) cortar, tajar; (CULIN: also: ~ **up**) picar // n golpe m cortante; (CULIN) chuleta; **~s** npl (jaws) boca sg, labios mpl.

chopper ['tʃɔpə*] n (helicopter) helicóptero.

choppy ['tʃɔpɪ] a (sea) picado, agitado.

chopsticks ['tʃɔpstɪks] npl palillos mpl.

chord [kɔːd] n (MUS) acorde m.

chore [tʃɔː*] n faena, tarea; (routine task) trabajo rutinario.

chortle ['tʃɔːtl] vi reír entre dientes.

chorus ['kɔːrəs] n coro; (repeated part of song) estribillo.

chose [tʃəuz] pt of **choose**.

chosen ['tʃəuzn] pp of **choose**.

Christ [kraɪst] n Cristo.

christen ['krɪsn] vt bautizar.

Christian ['krɪstɪən] a, n cristiano/a m/f; **~ity** [-'ænɪtɪ] n cristianismo; **~ name** n nombre m de pila.

Christmas ['krɪsməs] n Navidad f; **Merry ~!** ¡Felices Pascuas!; **~ card** n crismas m inv, tarjeta de Navidad; **~ Day** n día m de Navidad; **~ Eve** n Nochebuena; **~ tree** n árbol m de Navidad.

chrome [krəum] n = **chromium plating**.

chromium ['krəumɪəm] n cromo; **~ plating** n cromado.

chronic ['krɔnɪk] a crónico.

chronicle ['krɔnɪkl] n crónica.

chronological [krɔnə'lɔdʒɪkəl] a cronológico.

chrysanthemum [krɪ'sænθəməm] n crisantemo.

chubby ['tʃʌbɪ] a rechoncho.

chuck [tʃʌk] vt lanzar, arrojar; **to ~ out** vt echar (fuera), tirar; **to ~ (up)** (Brit) abandonar.

chuckle ['tʃʌkl] vi reírse entre dientes.

chug [tʃʌg] vi resoplar.

chum [tʃʌm] n compañero/a.

chunk [tʃʌŋk] n pedazo, trozo.

church [tʃɔ:tʃ] n iglesia; **~yard** n campo santo.

churlish [ˈtʃɔ:lɪʃ] a grosero.

churn [tʃɔ:n] n (for butter) mantequera; (for milk) lechera; **to ~ out** vt producir en serie.

chute [ʃu:t] n (also: **rubbish ~**) vertedero; (Brit: children's slide) tobogán m.

chutney [ˈtʃʌtnɪ] n salsa picante.

CIA n abbr (US: = Central Intelligence Agency) CIA f.

CID n abbr (Brit: = Criminal Investigation Department) ≈ B.I.C. f (Sp).

cider [ˈsaɪdə*] n sidra.

cigar [sɪˈgɑ:*] n puro.

cigarette [sɪgəˈret] n cigarrillo, cigarro (LAm); pitillo; **~ case** n pitillera; **~ end** n colilla; **~ holder** n boquilla.

Cinderella [sɪndəˈrelə] n Cenicienta.

cine [ˈsɪnɪ]: **~-camera** n (Brit) cámara cinematográfica; **~-film** n (Brit) película de cine.

cinema [ˈsɪnəmə] n cine m.

cinnamon [ˈsɪnəmən] n canela.

cipher [ˈsaɪfə*] n cifra.

circle [ˈsɔ:kl] n círculo; (in theatre) anfiteatro // vi dar vueltas // vt (surround) rodear, cercar; (move round) dar la vuelta a.

circuit [ˈsɔ:kɪt] n circuito; (track) pista; (lap) vuelta; **~ous** [sɔ:ˈkju:təs] a indirecto.

circular [ˈsɔ:kjulə*] a circular // n circular f.

circulate [ˈsɔ:kjuleɪt] vi circular // vt poner en circulación; **circulation** [-ˈleɪʃən] n circulación f; (of newspaper) tirada.

circumcise [ˈsɔ:kəmsaɪz] vt circuncidar.

circumstances [ˈsɔ:kəmstənsɪz] npl circunstancias fpl; (financial condition) situación f económica.

circumvent [sɔ:kəmˈvent] vt burlar.

circus [ˈsɔ:kəs] n circo.

cistern [ˈsɪstən] n tanque m, depósito; (in toilet) cisterna.

citizen [ˈsɪtɪzn] n (POL) ciudadano/a;

(of city) vecino/a, habitante m/f; **~ship** n ciudadanía.

citrus fruits [ˈsɪtrəs-] npl agrios m.

city [ˈsɪtɪ] n ciudad f; **the C~** centro financiero de Londres.

civic [ˈsɪvɪk] a cívico, municipal; **~ centre** n (Brit) centro público.

civil [ˈsɪvɪl] a civil; (polite) atento, cortés; (well-bred) educado; **~ defence** n protección f civil; **~ engineer** n ingeniero civil; **~ian** [sɪˈvɪlɪən] a civil (no military) // n civil m/f, paisano/a; **~ian clothing** n ropa de paisano.

civilization [sɪvɪlaɪˈzeɪʃən] n civilización f.

civilized [ˈsɪvɪlaɪzd] a civilizado.

civil: **~ law** n derecho civil; **~ servant** n funcionario/a del Estado; **C~ Service** n administración f pública; **~ war** n guerra civil.

clad [klæd] a: **~ (in)** vestido (de).

claim [kleɪm] vt exigir, reclamar; (rights etc) reivindicar; (assert) pretender // vi (for insurance) reclamar // n reclamación f; (LAW) demanda; (pretension) pretensión f; **~ant** n (ADMIN, LAW) demandante m/f.

clairvoyant [kleəˈvɔɪənt] n clarividente m/f.

clam [klæm] n almeja.

clamber [ˈklæmbə*] vi trepar.

clammy [ˈklæmɪ] a (cold) frío y húmedo; (sticky) pegajoso.

clamour [ˈklæmə*] vi: **to ~ for** clamar por, pedir a voces.

clamp [klæmp] n abrazadera, grapa // vt afianzar (con abrazadera); **to ~ down on** vt fus (subj: government, police) reforzar la lucha contra.

clan [klæn] n clan m.

clang [klæŋ] n estruendo // vi sonar, hacer estruendo.

clap [klæp] vi aplaudir; **~ping** n aplausos mpl.

claret [ˈklærət] n clarete m.

clarify [ˈklærɪfaɪ] vt aclarar.

clarinet [klærɪˈnet] n clarinete m.

clarity [ˈklærɪtɪ] n claridad f.

clash [klæʃ] n estruendo; (fig) choque m // vi (battle) chocar; (disagree) estar en desacuerdo.

clasp [klɑːsp] n broche m; (on jewels) cierre m // vt abrochar; (hand) apretar; (embrace) abrazar.

class [klɑːs] n (gen) clase f // a clasista, de clase // vt clasificar.

classic ['klæsɪk] a, n clásico; ~al a clásico.

classified ['klæsɪfaɪd] a (information) reservado; ~ **advertisement** n anuncio por palabras.

classify ['klæsɪfaɪ] vt clasificar.

classmate n compañero/a de clase.

classroom ['klɑːsrum] n aula.

clatter ['klætə*] n ruido, estruendo; (of hooves) trápala // vi hacer ruido or estruendo.

clause [klɔːz] n cláusula; (LING) oración f.

claw [klɔː] n (of cat) uña; (of bird of prey) garra; (of lobster) pinza; (TECH) garfio; **to** ~ **at** vt fus arañar; (tear) desgarrar.

clay [kleɪ] n arcilla.

clean [kliːn] a limpio; (clear) neto, bien definido // vt limpiar; **to** ~ **out** vt limpiar; **to** ~ **up** vt limpiar, asear; ~**er** n (person) asistenta; ~**ing** n limpieza; ~**liness** ['klɛnlɪnɪs] n limpieza.

cleanse [klɛnz] vt limpiar; ~ n detergente m; (for face) crema limpiadora; **cleansing department** n (Brit) departamento de limpieza.

clear [klɪə*] a claro; (road, way) libre // a (space) despejar, limpiar; (LAW: suspect) absolver; (obstacle) salvar, saltar por encima de; (debt) liquidar; (cheque) pasar por un banco // vi (fog etc) despejarse // ad: ~ **of** a distancia de; **to** ~ **the table** recoger or levantar la mesa; **to** ~ **up** vt limpiar; (mystery) resolver, aclarar; ~**ance** n (removal) despeje m; (permission) acreditación f; ~-**cut** a bien definido, nítido, claro; ~**ing** n (in wood) claro; ~**ing bank** n (Brit) cámara de compensación; ~**ly** ad

claramente; ~**way** n (Brit) carretera donde no se puede aparcar.

cleaver ['kliːvə] n cuchilla (de carnicero).

clef [klɛf] n (MUS) clave f.

cleft [klɛft] n (in rock) grieta, hendedura.

clench [klɛntʃ] vt apretar, cerrar.

clergy ['klɜːdʒɪ] n clero; ~**man** n clérigo.

clerical ['klɛrɪkəl] a de oficina; (REL) clerical.

clerk [klɑːk, (US) klɜːrk] n oficinista m/f; (US) dependiente/a m/f, vendedor(a) m/f.

clever ['klɛvə*] a (mentally) inteligente, listo; (skilful) hábil; (device, arrangement) ingenioso.

click [klɪk] vt (tongue) chasquear; (heels) taconear.

client ['klaɪənt] n cliente m/f.

cliff [klɪf] n acantilado.

climate ['klaɪmɪt] n clima m.

climax ['klaɪmæks] n colmo, punto culminante; (sexual) clímax m.

climb [klaɪm] vi subir, trepar // (stairs) subir; (tree) trepar a; (mountain) escalar // n subida; **to** ~ **down** vi volverse atrás; ~**er** n alpinista m/f, andinista m/f (LAm); ~**ing** n alpinismo, andinismo (LAm).

clinch [klɪntʃ] vt (deal) cerrar; (argument) remachar.

cling [klɪŋ], pt, pp **clung** [klʌŋ] vi: **to** ~ **to** agrarrarse a; (clothes) pegarse a.

clinic ['klɪnɪk] n clínica.

clink [klɪŋk] vi tintinar.

clip [klɪp] n (for hair) horquilla; (also: **paper** ~) sujetapapeles m inv, clip m; (clamp) grapa // vt (cut) cortar; (hedge) podar; (also: ~ **together**) unir; ~**pers** npl (for gardening) tijeras fpl; (for hair) maquinilla sg; (for nails) cortauñas m inv; ~**ping** n (newspaper) recorte m.

clique [kliːk] n camarilla.

cloak [kləuk] n capa, manto // vt (fig) encubrir, disimular; ~**room** n guardarropa; (Brit: WC) lavabo, aseos *mpl*, baño (*LAm*).

clock [klɔk] *n* reloj *m*; (*in taxi*) taxímetro; **to ~ in** or **on** *vi* fichar, picar; **to ~ off** or **out** *vi* fichar or picar la salida; **~wise** *ad* en el sentido de las agujas del reloj; **~work** *n* aparato de relojería // *a* (*toy*) de cuerda.

clog [klɔg] *n* zueco, chanclo // *vt* atascar // *vi* atascarse.

cloister ['klɔɪstə*] *n* claustro.

close *a*, *ad and derivatives* [kləus] *a* cercano, próximo; (*near*): ~ (**to**) cerca (de); (*print, weave*) tupido, compacto; (*friend*) íntimo; (*connection*) estrecho; (*examination*) detallado, minucioso; (*weather*) bochornoso; (*atmosphere*) sofocante; (*room*) mal ventilado; **to have a ~ shave** (*fig*) escaparse por un pelo // *ad* cerca; ~ **by**, ~ **at hand** *a*, *ad* muy cerca; ~ **to** *prep* cerca de // *vb and derivatives* [kləuz] *vt* (*shut*) cerrar; (*end*) concluir, terminar // *vi* (*shop etc*) cerrarse; (*end*) concluirse, terminarse // *n* (*end*) fin *m*, final *m*, conclusión *f*; **to ~ down** *vi* cerrarse definitivamente; ~**d** *a* (*shop etc*) cerrado; ~**d shop** *n* taller *m* gremial; ~**knit** *a* (*fig*) muy unido; ~**ly** *ad* (*study*) con detalle; (*listen*) con atención; (*watch*) de cerca.

closet ['klɔzɪt] *n* (*cupboard*) armario.

close-up ['kləusʌp] *n* primer plano.

closure ['kləuʒə*] *n* cierre *m*.

clot [klɔt] *n* (*gen*: *blood*) ~ embolia; (*fam*: *idiot*) imbécil *m/f* // *vi* (*blood*) coagularse.

cloth [klɔθ] *n* (*material*) tela, paño; (*rag*) trapo.

clothe [kləuð] *vt* vestir; (*fig*) revestir; ~**s** *npl* ropa *sg*; ~**s brush** *n* cepillo (para la ropa); ~**s line** *n* cuerda (para tender la ropa); ~**s peg**, (*US*) ~**s pin** *n* pinza.

clothing ['kləuðɪŋ] *n* = **clothes**.

cloud [klaud] *n* nube *f*; (*storm* ~) nubarrón *m*; ~**y** *a* nublado, nubloso; (*liquid*) turbio.

clout [klaut] *vt* dar un tortazo.

clove [kləuv] *n* clavo; ~ **of garlic** diente *m* de ajo.

clover ['kləuvə*] *n* trébol *m*.

clown [klaun] *n* payaso // *vi* (*also*: ~ **about**, ~ **around**) hacer el payaso.

cloying [klɔɪɪŋ] *a* (*taste*) empalagoso.

club [klʌb] *n* (*society*) club *m*; (*weapon*) porra, cachiporra; (*also*: **golf** ~) palo // *vt* aporrear // *vi*: **to ~ together** (*join forces*) unir fuerzas; ~**s** *npl* (*CARDS*) tréboles *mpl*; ~ **car** (*US RAIL*) coche *m* salón; ~**house** *n* local social, *sobre todo en clubs deportivos*.

cluck [klʌk] *vi* cloquear.

clue [klu:] *n* pista; (*in crosswords*) indicación *f*; **I haven't a ~** no tengo ni idea.

clump [klʌmp] *n* (*of trees*) grupo.

clumsy ['klʌmzɪ] *a* (*person*) torpe, desmañado; (*tool*) difícil de manejar.

clung [klʌŋ] *pt*, *pp of* **cling**.

cluster ['klʌstə*] *n* grupo; (*BOT*) racimo // *vi* agruparse, apiñarse.

clutch [klʌtʃ] *n* (*AUT*) embrague *m*; (*pedal*) pedal *m* de embrague; **to fall into sb's ~es** caer en las garras de alguien // *vt* asir; agarrar.

clutter ['klʌtə*] *vt* atestar.

cm *abbr* (= *centimetre*) cm.

CND *n abbr* (= *Campaign for Nuclear Disarmament*) plataforma pro desarme nuclear.

Co. *abbr* = **county**; = **company**.

c/o *abbr* (= *care of*) c/a, a/c.

coach [kəutʃ] *n* (*bus*) autocar *m* (*Sp*), autobús *m*; (*horse-drawn*) coche *m*; (*of train*) vagón *m*, coche *m*; (*SPORT*) entrenador(a) *m/f*, instructor(a) *m/f* // *vt* (*SPORT*) entrenar; (*student*) preparar, enseñar; ~ **trip** *n* excursión *f* en autocar.

coal [kəul] *n* carbón *m*; ~ **face** *n* frente *m* de carbón; ~**field** *n* yacimiento de carbón.

coalition [kəuə'lɪʃən] *n* coalición *f*.

coal man, **coal merchant** *n* carbonero.

coalmine ['kəulmaɪn] *n* mina de carbón.

coarse [kɔːs] a basto, burdo; (*vulgar*) grosero, ordinario.

coast [kəust] n costa, litoral m // vi (AUT) ir en punto muerto; **~al** a costero, costanero; **~guard** n guardacostas m inv; **~line** n litoral m.

coat [kəut] n (*jacket*) chaqueta; (*overcoat*) abrigo; (*of animal*) pelo, lana; (*of paint*) mano f, capa // vt cubrir, revestir; **~ of arms** n escudo de armas; **~ hanger** n percha, gancho (LAm); **~ing** n capa, baño.

coax [kəuks] vt engatusar.

cob [kɔb] n see **corn**.

cobbler ['kɔblə*] n zapatero (remendón).

cobbles ['kɔblz], **cobblestones** ['kɔblstəunz] npl adoquines mpl.

cobweb ['kɔbweb] n telaraña.

cocaine [kə'keɪn] n cocaína.

cock [kɔk] n (*rooster*) gallo; (*male bird*) macho // vt (*gun*) amartillar; **~erel** n gallito; **~eyed** a (*fig: crooked*) torcido; (: *idea*) disparatado.

cockle ['kɔkl] n berberecho.

cockney ['kɔkni] n habitante m/f de ciertos barrios de Londres.

cockpit ['kɔkpit] n (*in aircraft*) cabina.

cockroach ['kɔkrəutʃ] n cucaracha.

cocktail ['kɔkteil] n coctel m, cóctel m; **~ cabinet** n mueble-bar m; **~ party** n coctel m, cóctel m.

cocoa ['kəukəu] n cacao; (*drink*) chocolate m.

coconut ['kəukənʌt] n coco.

cod [kɔd] n bacalao.

C.O.D. abbr (= cash on delivery) C.A.E.

code [kəud] n código; (*cipher*) clave f.

cod-liver oil ['kɔdlɪvə*-] n aceite m de hígado de bacalao.

coercion [kəu'əːʃən] n coacción f.

coffee ['kɔfi] n café m; **~ bar** n (Brit) cafetería; **~ break** n descanso (para tomar café); **~pot** n cafetera; **~ table** n mesita (para servir el café).

coffin ['kɔfin] n ataúd m.

cog [kɔg] n diente m.

cogent ['kəudʒənt] a convincente.

cognac ['kɔnjæk] n coñac m.

coil [kɔil] n rollo; (*rope*) adujada; (ELEC) bobina, carrete m; (*contraceptive*) espiral // vt enrollar.

coin [kɔin] n moneda // vt (*word*) inventar, idear; **~age** n moneda; **~box** n (Brit) cabina telefónica.

coincide [kəuin'said] vi coincidir; (*agree*) estar de acuerdo; **~nce** [kəu'insidəns] n casualidad f.

coke [kəuk] n (*coal*) coque m.

Coke ® [kəuk] n Coca Cola ®.

colander ['kɔləndə*] n colador m, escurridor m.

cold [kəuld] a frío // n frío; (MED) resfriado; **it's ~** hace frío; **to be ~** tener frío; **to catch ~** resfriarse, acatarrarse; **in ~ blood** a sangre fría; **~ sore** n herpes m labial.

coleslaw ['kəulslɔː] n especie de ensalada de col.

colic ['kɔlik] n cólico.

collapse [kə'læps] vi (gen) hundirse, derrumbarse; (MED) sufrir un colapso // n (gen) hundimiento; (MED) colapso; **collapsible** a plegable.

collar ['kɔlə*] n (*of coat, shirt*) cuello; **~bone** n clavícula.

collateral [kɔ'lætərəl] n garantía colateral.

colleague ['kɔliːg] n colega m/f.

collect [kə'lekt] vt reunir; (as a hobby) coleccionar; (Brit: call and pick up) recoger; (wages) cobrar; (debts) recaudar; (donations, subscriptions) colectar // vi reunirse; coleccionar; **to call ~** (US TEL) llamar a cobro revertido; **~ion** [kə'lekʃən] n colección f; (of post) recogida.

collector [kə'lektə*] n coleccionista m/f; (of taxes etc) recaudador(a) m/f.

college ['kɔlidʒ] n colegio.

collide [kə'laid] vi chocar.

collie ['kɔli] n perro pastor.

colliery ['kɔlıərı] n (Brit) mina de carbón.

collision [kə'lıʒən] n choque m.

colloquial [kə'ləukwıəl] a familiar, coloquial.

collusion [kə'luːʒən] n confabulación f, connivencia.

cologne [kə'ləun] n = **eau de cologne**.

Colombia [kə'lɔmbıə] n Colombia; **Colombian** a, n colombiano/a.

colon ['kəulən] n (sign) dos puntos; (MED) colón m.

colonel ['kɔːnl] n coronel m.

colonial [kə'ləunıəl] a colonial.

colony ['kɔlənı] n colonia.

colour, (US) **color** ['kʌlə*] n color m // vt color(e)ar; (with crayons) colorear (a pastel); (dye) teñir // vi (blush) sonrojarse; ~s npl (of party, club) colores mpl; ~ **bar** n segregación f racial; ~**blind** a daltónico; ~**ed** a de color; (photo) en color; ~**film** n película en color; ~**ful** a lleno de color; (person) excéntrico; ~**ing** n colorido; ~**less** a incoloro, sin color; ~ **scheme** n combinación f de colores; ~ **television** n televisión f en color.

colt [kəult] n potro.

column ['kɔləm] n columna; ~**ist** ['kɔləmnıst] n columnista m/f.

coma ['kəumə] n coma m.

comb [kəum] n peine m; (ornamental) peineta // vt (hair) peinar; (area) registrar a fondo.

combat ['kɔmbæt] n combate m // vt combatir.

combination [kɔmbı'neıʃən] n (gen) combinación f.

combine [kəm'baın] vt combinar; (qualities) reunir // vi combinarse // n ['kɔmbaın] (ECON) cartel m; ~ (**harvester**) n cosechadora.

come [kʌm], pt **came**, pp **come** vi venir; to ~ **undone** desatarse; to ~ **loose** aflojarse; to ~ **about** vi suceder, ocurrir; to ~ **across** vt fus (person) topar con; (thing) dar con; to ~ **away** vi marcharse; desprenderse; to ~ **back** vi volver; to ~ **by** vt fus (acquire) conseguir; to ~ **down** vi bajar; (buildings) ser derribado; derrumbarse; to ~ **forward** vi presentarse; to ~ **from** vt fus ser de; to ~ **in** vi entrar; (train) llegar; (fashion) ponerse de moda; to ~ **in for** vt fus (criticism etc) merecer; to ~ **into** vt fus (money) heredar; to ~ **off** vi (button) soltarse, desprenderse; (succeed) salir bien; to ~ **on** vi (pupil, work, project) desarrollarse; (lights) encenderse; ~ **on!** ¡vamos!; to ~ **out** vi salir; (book) aparecer; (be revealed) salir a luz; (strike) declararse en huelga; to ~ **out for/against** declararse por/contra; to ~ **round** vi (after faint, operation) volver en sí; to ~ **to** vi volver en sí; (total) sumar; to ~ **up** vi subir; (sun) salir; (problem) surgir; to ~ **up against** vt fus (resistance, difficulties) tropezar con; to ~ **up with** vt fus (idea) sugerir, proponer; to ~ **upon** vt fus dar o topar con; ~**back** n: **to make a** ~**back** (THEATRE) volver a las tablas.

comedian [kə'miːdıən] n cómico; **comedienne** [-'cn] n cómica.

comedown ['kʌmdaun] n revés m, bajón m.

comedy ['kɔmıdı] n comedia.

comet ['kɔmıt] n cometa m.

comeuppance [kʌm'ʌpəns] n: **to get one's** ~ llevar su merecido.

comfort ['kʌmfət] n comodidad f, confort m; (well-being) bienestar m; (solace) consuelo; (relief) alivio // vt consolar; ~**able** a cómodo; (fig) ad (sit) cómodamente; (live) holgadamente; ~**er** n (US: pacifier) chupete m; (: bed cover) colcha; ~ **station** n (US) servicios mpl.

comic ['kɔmık] a (also: ~**al**) cómico // n (for children) tebeo; (for adults) comic m; ~ **strip** n tira cómica.

coming ['kʌmıŋ] n venida, llegada // a que viene; ~(**s**) **and going(s)** n(pl) ir y venir m, ajetreo.

comma ['kɔmə] *n* coma.

command [kə'mɑːnd] *n* orden *f*, mandato; (*MIL: authority*) mando; (*mastery*) dominio // *vt* (*troops*) mandar; (*give orders to*) mandar, ordenar; (*be able to get*) disponer de; (*deserve*) merecer; **~eer** [kɔmən'dɪə*] *vt* requisar; **~er** *n* (*MIL*) comandante *m/f*, jefe/a *m/f*; **~ment** *n* (*REL*) mandamiento.

commando [kə'mɑːndəu] *n* comando.

commemorate [kə'meməreɪt] *vt* conmemorar.

commence [kə'mens] *vt*, *vi* comenzar, empezar.

commend [kə'mend] *vt* (*praise*) elogiar, alabar; (*recommend*) recomendar; (*entrust*) encomendar.

commensurate [kə'menʃərɪt] *a*: **~ with** en proporción a, que corresponde a.

comment ['kɔment] *n* comentario // *vi*: **to ~ on** hacer comentarios sobre; **~ary** ['kɔməntəri] *n* comentario; **~ator** ['kɔmənteɪtə*] *n* comentarista *m/f*.

commerce ['kɔmə:s] *n* comercio.

commercial [kə'mə:ʃəl] *a* comercial // *n* (*TV: also:* **~ break**) anuncio.

commiserate [kə'mɪzəreɪt] *vi*: **to ~ with** compadecerse de, condolerse de.

commission [kə'mɪʃən] *n* (*committee, fee*) comisión *f*; (*act*) perpetración *f* // *vt* (*MIL*) nombrar; (*work of art*) encargar; **out of ~** fuera de servicio; **~aire** [kəmɪʃə'neə*] *n* (*Brit*) portero; **~er** *n* comisario; (*POLICE*) comisario *m* de policía.

commit [kə'mɪt] *vt* (*act*) cometer; (*to sb's care*) entregar; **to ~ o.s. (to do)** comprometerse (a hacer); **to ~ suicide** suicidarse; **~ment** *n* compromiso.

committee [kə'mɪtɪ] *n* comité *m*.

commodity [kə'mɔdɪtɪ] *n* mercancía.

common ['kɔmən] *a* (*gen*) común; (*pej*) ordinario // *n* campo común;

the **C~s** *npl* (*Brit*) (la Cámara de) los Comunes *mpl*; **in ~** en común; **~er** *n* plebeyo; **~ law** *n* ley *f* consuetudinaria; **~ly** *ad* comúnmente; **C~ Market** *n* Mercado Común; **~place** *a* de lo más común; **~room** *n* sala común; **~ sense** *n* sentido común; **the C~wealth** *n* la Mancomunidad (Británica).

commotion [kə'məuʃən] *n* tumulto, confusión *f*.

commune ['kɔmjuːn] *n* (*group*) comuna *f* // *vi* [kə'mjuːn]: **to ~ with** comulgar o conversar con.

communicate [kə'mjuːnɪkeɪt] *vt*, *vi*: **to ~ (with)** comunicarse (con).

communication [kəmjuːnɪ'keɪʃən] *n* comunicación *f*; **~ cord** *n* (*Brit*) timbre *m* de alarma.

communion [kə'mjuːnɪən] *n* (*also:* **Holy C~**) comunión *f*.

communiqué [kə'mjuːnɪkeɪ] *n* comunicado, parte *m*.

communism ['kɔmjunɪzəm] *n* comunismo; **communist** *a*, *n* comunista *m/f*.

community [kə'mjuːnɪtɪ] *n* comunidad *f*; (*large group*) colectividad *f*; (*local*) vecindario; **~ centre** *n* centro social; **~ chest** *n* (*US*) arca comunitaria, fondo común.

commutation ticket [kɔmju-'teɪʃən-] *n* (*US*) billete *m* de abono.

commute [kə'mjuːt] *vi* viajar a diario de la casa al trabajo // *vt* conmutar; **~r** *n* persona (que ... *see vi*).

compact [kəm'pækt] *a* compacto // *n* ['kɔmpækt] (*pact*) pacto; (*also:* **powder ~**) polvera; **~ disc** *n* compact disc *m*.

companion [kəm'pænɪən] *n* compañero/a; **~ship** *n* compañerismo.

company ['kʌmpəni] *n* (*gen*) compañía; (*COMM*) sociedad *f*, compañía; **to keep sb ~** acompañar a uno; **~ secretary** *n* (*Brit*) secretario/a de compañía.

comparative [kəm'pærətɪv] *a* relativo; ~**ly** ad (*relatively*) relativamente.

compare [kəm'peə*] vt comparar; (*set side by side*) cotejar // vi: **to ~ (with)** compararse (con); **comparison** [-'pærɪsn] n comparación f; cotejo.

compartment [kəm'pɑːtmənt] n (*also: RAIL*) departamento.

compass ['kʌmpəs] n brújula; ~**es** npl compás msg.

compassion [kəm'pæʃən] n compasión f; ~**ate** a compasivo.

compatible [kəm'pætɪbl] a compatible.

compel [kəm'pel] vt obligar; ~**ling** a (*fig: argument*) convincente.

compensate ['kɒmpənseɪt] vt compensar // vi: **to ~ for** compensar; **compensation** [-'seɪʃən] n (*for loss*) indemnización f.

compère ['kɒmpeə*] n presentador m.

compete [kəm'piːt] vi (*take part*) tomar parte, concurrir; (*vie with*) competir, hacer competencia.

competence ['kɒmpɪtəns] n capacidad f, aptitud f.

competent ['kɒmpɪtənt] a competente, capaz.

competition [kɒmpɪ'tɪʃən] n (*contest*) concurso; (*ECON, rivalry*) competencia.

competitive [kəm'petɪtɪv] a (*ECON, SPORT*) competitivo; (*spirit*) competidor(a), de competencia.

competitor [kəm'petɪtə*] n (*rival*) competidor(a) m/f; (*participant*) concursante m/f.

compile [kəm'paɪl] vt recopilar.

complacency [kəm'pleɪsnsɪ] n autosatisfacción f.

complacent [kəm'pleɪsənt] a autocomplaciente.

complain [kəm'pleɪn] vi (*gen*) quejarse; (*COMM*) reclamar; ~**t** n (*gen*) queja; reclamación f; (*LAW*) demanda; (*MED*) enfermedad f.

complement n ['kɒmplɪmənt] n complemento; (*especially of ship's crew*) dotación f // [-ment] vt (*enhance*)

complementar; ~**ary** [kɒmplɪ'mentərɪ] a complementario.

complete [kəm'pliːt] a (*full*) completo; (*finished*) acabado // vt (*fulfil*) completar; (*finish*) acabar; (*a form*) llenar; ~**ly** ad completamente; **completion** [-'pliːʃən] n terminación f.

complex ['kɒmpleks] a, n complejo.

complexion [kəm'plekʃən] n (*of face*) tez f, cutis m; (*fig*) aspecto.

compliance [kəm'plaɪəns] n (*submission*) sumisión f; (*agreement*) conformidad f; **in ~ with** de acuerdo con.

complicate ['kɒmplɪkeɪt] vt complicar; ~**d** a complicado; **complication** [-'keɪʃən] n complicación f.

complicity [kəm'plɪsɪtɪ] n complicidad f.

compliment n ['kɒmplɪmənt] (*formal*) cumplido; (*flirtation*) piropo // vt felicitar; ~**s** npl saludos mpl; **to pay sb a ~** (*formal*) hacer cumplidos a alguien; (*flirt*) decir piropos a alguien; ~**ary** [-'mentərɪ] a lisonjero; (*free*) de favor.

comply [kəm'plaɪ] vi: **to ~ with** cumplir con.

component [kəm'pəunənt] a componente // n (*TECH*) pieza.

compose [kəm'pəuz] vt componer; **to ~ o.s.** tranquilizarse; ~**d** a sosegado; ~**r** n (*MUS*) compositor(a) m/f.

composite ['kɒmpəzɪt] a compuesto.

composition [kɒmpə'zɪʃən] n composición f.

compost ['kɒmpɒst] n abono.

composure [kəm'pəuʒə*] n serenidad f, calma.

compound ['kɒmpaund] n (*CHEM*) compuesto; (*LING*) palabra compuesta; (*enclosure*) recinto // a (*gen*) compuesto; (*fracture*) complicado.

comprehend [kɒmprɪ'hend] vt comprender; **comprehension** [-'henʃən] n comprensión f.

comprehensive [kɒmprɪ'hensɪv] a (*broad*) extenso; (*general*) de conjunto; (*INSURANCE*) contra todo riesgo; ~ **(school)** n centro estatal de enseñanza secundaria; ≈ Instituto Nacional de Bachillerato (*Sp*).

compress [kəm'pres] vt comprimir // n ['kɔmpres] (*MED*) compresa.

comprise [kəm'praɪz] vt (also: be ~d of) comprender, constar de.

compromise ['kɔmprəmaɪz] n (*agreement*) arreglo // vt comprometer // vi transigir.

compulsion [kəm'pʌlʃən] n obligación f.

compulsive [kəm'pʌlsɪv] a compulsivo.

compulsory [kəm'pʌlsərɪ] a obligatorio.

computer [kəm'pju:tə*] n ordenador m, computador m, computadora f; ~**ize** vt (*data*) computerizar; (*system*) informatizar; ~ **programmer** n programador(a) m/f; ~ **programming** n programación f; ~ **science** n informática f.

computing [kəm'pju:tɪŋ] n (*activity*) informática f.

comrade ['kɔmrɪd] n compañero/a; ~**ship** n camaradería, compañerismo.

con [kɔn] vt estafar // n estafa.

conceal [kən'si:l] vt ocultar; (*thoughts etc*) disimular.

conceit [kən'si:t] n presunción f; ~**ed** a presumido.

conceivable [kən'si:vəbl] a concebible.

conceive [kən'si:v] vt, vi concebir.

concentrate ['kɔnsəntreɪt] vi concentrarse // vt concentrar.

concentration [kɔnsən'treɪʃən] n concentración f; ~ **camp** n campo de concentración.

concept ['kɔnsept] n concepto.

conception [kən'sepʃən] n (*idea*) concepto, idea; (*BIOL*) concepción f.

concern [kən'sə:n] n (*matter*) asunto; (*COMM*) empresa; (*anxiety*) preocupación f // vt tener que ver con; **to be ~ed (about)** interesarse (por), preocuparse (por); ~**ing** prep

sobre, acerca de.

concert ['kɔnsət] n concierto; ~**ed** [kən'sə:tɪd] a (*efforts etc*) concertado; ~ **hall** n sala de conciertos.

concertina [kɔnsə'ti:nə] n concertina.

concerto [kən'tʃə:təu] n concierto.

concession [kən'seʃən] n concesión f; **tax** ~ privilegio fiscal.

concise [kən'saɪs] a conciso.

conclude [kən'klu:d] vt (*finish*) concluir; (*treaty etc*) firmar; (*agreement*) llegar a; (*decide*) llegar a la conclusión de; **conclusion** [-'klu:ʒən] n conclusión f; **conclusive** [-'klu:sɪv] a decisivo, concluyente.

concoct [kən'kɔkt] vt (*gen*) confeccionar; (*plot*) tramar; ~**ion** [-'kɔkʃən] n confección f.

concourse ['kɔŋkɔ:s] n (*hall*) vestíbulo.

concrete ['kɔŋkri:t] n hormigón m // a concreto.

concur [kən'kə:*] vi estar de acuerdo, asentir.

concurrently [kən'kʌrntlɪ] ad al mismo tiempo.

concussion [kən'kʌʃən] n conmoción f cerebral.

condemn [kən'dem] vt condenar; ~**ation** [kɔndem'neɪʃən] n (*gen*) condena; (*blame*) censura.

condense [kən'dens] vi condensarse // vt condensar, abreviar; ~**d milk** n leche f condensada.

condescending [kɔndɪ'sendɪŋ] a condescendiente.

condition [kən'dɪʃən] n condición f // vt condicionar; **on ~ that** a condición (de) que; ~**al** a condicional; ~**er** n (*for hair*) acondicionador m.

condolences [kən'dəulənsɪz] npl pésame msg.

condom ['kɔndəm] n condón m.

condominium [kɔndə'mɪnɪəm] n (*US*) condominio.

condone [kən'dəun] vt condonar.

conducive [kən'dju:sɪv] a: ~ **to** conducente a.

conduct ['kɒndʌkt] n conducta, comportamiento // vt [kən'dʌkt] (lead) conducir; (manage) llevar, dirigir; (MUS) dirigir // vi (MUS) llevar la batuta; **to ~ o.s.** comportarse; **~ed tour** n (Brit) visita acompañada; **~or** n (of orchestra) director m; (US: on train) revisor(a) m/f; (on bus) cobrador m; (ELEC) conductor m; **~ress** n (on bus) cobradora.

cone [kəun] n cono; (pine ~) piña; (for ice-cream) barquillo.

confectioner [kən'fɛkʃənə*] n (of cakes) pastelero; (of sweets) confitero/a; **~'s (shop)** n pastelería, confitería; **~y** n pasteles mpl; dulces mpl.

confer [kən'fə:*] vt: **to ~ sth on** otorgar algo a // vi conferenciar.

conference ['kɒnfərns] n (meeting) reunión f; (convention) congreso f.

confess [kən'fɛs] vt confesar // vi confesarse; **~ion** [-'fɛʃən] n confesión f; **~ional** [-'fɛʃənl] n confesionario.

confetti [kən'fɛtɪ] n confeti m.

confide [kən'faɪd] vi: **to ~ in** confiar en.

confidence ['kɒnfɪdns] n (gen, also: self ~) confianza; (secret) confidencia; **in ~** (speak, write) en confianza; **~ trick** n timo; **confident** a seguro de sí mismo; **confidential** [kɒnfɪ'dɛnʃl] a confidencial; (secretary) de confianza.

confine [kən'faɪn] vt (limit) limitar; (shut up) encerrar; **~s** ['kɒnfaɪnz] npl confines mpl; **~d** (space) reducido; **~ment** n (prison) prisión f; (MED) parto.

confirm [kən'fɜ:m] vt confirmar; **~ation** [kɒnfə'meɪʃən] n confirmación f; **~ed** a empedernido.

confiscate ['kɒnfɪskeɪt] vt confiscar.

conflict ['kɒnflɪkt] n conflicto // vi [kən'flɪkt] (opinions) chocar; **~ing** a contradictorio.

conform [kən'fɔ:m] vi conformarse; **to ~** ajustarse a.

confound [kən'faund] vt confundir.

confront [kən'frʌnt] vt (problems) hacer frente a; (enemy, danger) enfrentarse con; **~ation** [kɒnfrʌn'teɪʃən] n enfrentamiento.

confuse [kən'fju:z] vt (perplex) aturdir, desconcertar; (mix up) confundir; **~d** a confuso; (person) perplejo; **confusing** a confuso; **confusion** [-'fju:ʒən] n confusión f.

congeal [kən'dʒi:l] vi (blood) coagularse.

congenial [kən'dʒi:nɪəl] a agradable.

congenital [kən'dʒɛnɪtl] a congénito.

congested [kən'dʒɛstɪd] a (gen) atestado.

congestion [kən'dʒɛstʃən] n congestión f.

conglomerate [kən'glɒmərət] n (COMM, GEO) conglomerado.

conglomeration [kənglɒmə'reɪʃən] n conglomeración f.

congratulate [kən'grætjuleɪt] vt: **to ~ sb (on)** felicitar a uno (por); **congratulations** [-'leɪʃənz] npl felicidades fpl.

congregate ['kɒngrɪgeɪt] vi congregarse; **congregation** [-'geɪʃən] n (in church) fieles mpl.

congress ['kɒngrɛs] n congreso; **~man** n (US) miembro del Congreso.

conifer ['kɒnɪfə*] n conífera.

conjecture [kən'dʒɛktʃə*] n conjetura.

conjugal ['kɒndʒugl] a conyugal.

conjugate ['kɒndʒugeɪt] vt conjugar.

conjunction [kən'dʒʌŋkʃən] n conjunción f.

conjunctivitis [kəndʒʌŋktɪ'vaɪtɪs] n conjuntivitis f.

conjure ['kʌndʒə*] vi hacer juegos de manos; **to ~ up** vt (ghost, spirit) hacer aparecer; (memories) evocar; **~r** n ilusionista m/f.

conk out [kɒŋk-] vi (col) descomponerse.

con man ['kɒn-] n timador m.

connect [kə'nɛkt] vt (join) juntar, unir; (ELEC) conectar; (fig) relacionar, asociar // vi: **to ~ with** (train) enlazar con; **to be ~ed with** (*associated*) estar relacionado con; (*related*) estar emparentado con; **~ion** [-ʃən] *n* juntura, unión *f*; (*ELEC*) conexión *f*; (*RAIL*) enlace *m*; (*TEL*) comunicación *f*; (*fig*) relación *f*.

connive [kə'naiv] *vi*: **to ~ at** hacer la vista gorda a.

connoisseur [kɔni'sə*] *n* experto/a, entendido/a.

conquer ['kɔŋkə*] *vt* (*territory*) conquistar; (*enemy, feelings*) vencer; **~or** *n* conquistador *m*.

conquest ['kɔŋkwɛst] *n* conquista.

cons [kɔnz] *npl ver* **convenience, pro**.

conscience ['kɔnʃəns] *n* conciencia.

conscientious [kɔnʃi'ɛnʃəs] *a* concienzudo; (*objection*) de conciencia.

conscious ['kɔnʃəs] *a* consciente; **~ness** *n* conciencia; (*MED*) conocimiento.

conscript ['kɔnskript] *n* recluta *m*; **~ion** [kən'skripʃən] *n* servicio militar (obligatorio).

consecrate ['kɔnsikreit] *vt* consagrar.

consensus [kən'sɛnsəs] *n* consenso.

consent [kən'sɛnt] *n* consentimiento // *vi*: **to ~ (to)** consentir en.

consequence ['kɔnsikwəns] *n* consecuencia.

consequently ['kɔnsikwəntli] *ad* por consiguiente.

conservation [kɔnsə'veiʃən] *n* conservación *f*.

conservative [kən'sə:vətiv] *a* conservador(a); (*cautious*) cauteloso; **C~** *a*, *n* (*Brit POL*) conservador(a) *m/f*.

conservatory [kən'sə:vətri] *n* (*greenhouse*) invernadero.

conserve [kən'sə:v] *vt* conservar // *n* conserva.

consider [kən'sidə*] *vt* considerar; (*take into account*) tomar en cuenta; (*study*) estudiar, examinar; **to ~ doing sth** pensar en (la posibilidad de) hacer algo; **~able** *a* considerable; **~ably** *ad* notablemente.

considerate [kən'sidərit] *a* considerado; **consideration** [-'reiʃən] *n* consideración *f*; (*reward*) retribución *f*.

considering [kən'sidəriŋ] *prep* teniendo en cuenta.

consign [kən'sain] *vt* consignar; **~ment** *n* envío.

consist [kən'sist] *vi*: **to ~ of** consistir en.

consistency [kən'sistənsi] *n* (*of person, argument etc*) consecuencia; (*thickness*) consistencia.

consistent [kən'sistənt] *a* (*person, argument*) consecuente; (*results*) constante.

consolation [kɔnsə'leiʃən] *n* consuelo.

console [kən'səul] *vt* consolar // *n* ['kɔnsəul] consola.

consonant ['kɔnsənənt] *n* consonante *f*.

consortium [kən'sɔ:tiəm] *n* consorcio.

conspicuous [kən'spikjuəs] *a* (*visible*) visible; (*garish etc*) llamativo; (*outstanding*) notable.

conspiracy [kən'spirəsi] *n* conjura, complot *m*.

conspire [kən'spaiə*] *vi* conspirar.

constable ['kʌnstəbl] *n* (*Brit*) policía *m/f*; **chief ~** jefe *m* de policía.

constabulary [kən'stæbjuləri] *n* ≈ policía.

constant ['kɔnstənt] *a* (*gen*) constante; (*loyal*) leal, fiel; **~ly** *ad* constantemente.

consternation [kɔnstə'neiʃən] *n* consternación *f*.

constipated ['kɔnstipeitəd] *a* estreñido.

constipation [kɔnsti'peiʃən] *n* estreñimiento.

constituency [kən'stitjuənsi] *n* (*POL*) distrito electoral; **constituent** [-ənt] *n* (*POL*) elector(a) *m/f*; (*part*) componente *m*.

constitute ['kɔnstitjuːt] *vt* constituir.

constitution [kɔnsti'tjuːʃən] *n* constitución *f*; **~al** *a* constitucional.

constrain [kən'streın] vt obligar; **~ed** a: **to feel ~ed to ...** sentirse en la necesidad de ... .

constraint [kən'streınt] n (force) fuerza; (limit) restricción f; (restraint) reserva.

construct [kən'strʌkt] vt construir; **~ion** [-ʃən] n construcción f; **~ive** a constructivo.

construe [kən'struː] vt interpretar.

consul [‘kɔnsl] n cónsul m/f; **~ate** [‘kɔnsjulıt] n consulado f.

consult [kən'sʌlt] vt, vi consultar; **~ant** n (Brit MED) especialista m/f; (other specialist) asesor(a) m/f; **~ation** [kɔnsəl'teıʃən] n consulta; **~ing room** n (Brit) consultorio.

consume [kən'sjuːm] vt (eat) comerse; (drink) beberse; (fire etc, COMM) consumir; **~r** n consumidor/a m/f; **~r goods** npl bienes mpl de consumo; **~rism** n consumismo; **~r society** n sociedad f de consumo.

consummate [‘kɔnsʌmeıt] vt consumar.

consumption [kən'sʌmpʃən] n consumo; (MED) tisis f.

cont. abbr = (continued) sigue.

contact [‘kɔntækt] n contacto; (person) enchufe m // vt ponerse en contacto con; **~ lenses** npl lentes fpl de contacto.

contagious [kən'teıdʒəs] a contagioso.

contain [kən'teın] vt contener; **to ~ o.s.** contenerse; **~er** n recipiente m; (for shipping etc) contenedor m.

contaminate [kən'tæmıneıt] vt contaminar; **contamination** [-'neıʃən] n contaminación f.

cont'd abbr = (continued) sigue.

contemplate [‘kɔntempleıt] vt (gen) contemplar; (reflect upon) considerar; (intend) pensar.

contemporary [kən'tempərərı] a, n contemporáneo/a m/f.

contempt [kən'tempt] n desprecio; **~ of court** (LAW) desacato (a los tribunales); **~ible** a despreciable;

~uous a desdeñoso.

contend [kən'tend] vt (argue) afirmar // vi (struggle) luchar; **~er** n (SPORT) contendiente m/f.

content [kən'tent] a (happy) contento; (satisfied) satisfecho // vt contentar; satisfacer // n [‘kɔntent] contenido; (table of) **~s** índice m de materias; **~ed** a contento; satisfecho.

contention [kən'tenʃən] n discusión f; (belief) argumento.

contentment [kən'tentmənt] n contento.

contest [‘kɔntest] n contienda; (competition) concurso // vt [kən'test] (dispute) impugnar; (POL) presentarse como candidato/a en; **~ant** [kən'testənt] n concursante m/f; (in fight) contendiente m/f.

continent [‘kɔntınənt] n continente m; the C~ (Brit) el continente europeo; **~al** [-'nentl] a continental; **~al quilt** n (Brit) edredón m.

contingency [kən'tındʒənsı] n contingencia.

contingent [kən'tındʒənt] (group) grupo.

continual [kən'tınjuəl] a continuo; **~ly** ad constantemente.

continuation [kəntınju'eıʃən] n prolongación f; (after interruption) reanudación f.

continue [kən'tınjuː] vi, vt seguir, continuar.

continuous [kən'tınjuəs] a continuo; **~ stationery** n papel m continuo.

contort [kən'tɔːt] vt retorcer; **~ion** [-'tɔːʃən] n (movement) contorsión f.

contour [‘kɔntuə*] n contorno; (also: **~ line**) curva de nivel.

contraband [‘kɔntrəbænd] n contrabando.

contraception [kɔntrə'sepʃən] n contracepción f.

contraceptive [kɔntrə'septıv] a, n anticonceptivo.

contract [‘kɔntrækt] n contrato // (vb: [kən'trækt]) vi (COMM): **to do sth** comprometerse por contrato a hacer algo; (become smaller) contraerse, encogerse // vt contraer; **~ion** [kən'trækʃən] n contracción f; **~or** n contratista m/f.

contradict [kɔntrə'dikt] vt (declare to be wrong) desmentir; (be contrary to) contradecir; **~ion** [-ʃən] n contradicción f; **~ory** a (statements) contradictorio.

contraption [kən'træpʃən] n (pej) artilugio m.

contrary ['kɔntrəri] a (opposite, different) contrario; [kən'trɛəri] (perverse) terco // n: **on the ~** al contrario; **unless you hear to the ~** a no ser que le digan lo contrario.

contrast ['kɔntraːst] n contraste m // vt [kən'traːst] comparar; **~ing** a (opinion) opuesto; (colour) que hace contraste.

contravene [kɔntrə'viːn] vt infringir.

contribute [kən'tribjuːt] vi contribuir // vt: **to ~ to** (gen) contribuir a; (newspaper) escribir para; **contribution** [kɔntri'bjuːʃən] n (money) contribución f; (to debate) intervención f; (to journal) colaboración f; **contributor** n (to newspaper) colaborador(a) m/f.

contrive [kən'traiv] vt (invent) idear // vi: **to ~ to do** lograr hacer.

control [kən'trəul] vt controlar; (traffic etc) dirigir; (machinery) manejar; (temper) dominar // n (command) control m; (of car) conducción f; (check) freno; **~s** npl mando sg; **everything is under ~** todo está bajo control; **to be in ~ of** tener el mando de; **the car went out of ~** se perdió el control del coche; **~ panel** n tablero de instrumentos; **~ room** n sala de mando; **~ tower** n (AVIAT) torre f de control.

controversial [kɔntrə'vəːʃl] a polémico.

controversy ['kɔntrəvəːsi] n polémica.

conurbation [kɔnəː'beiʃən] n urbanización f.

convalesce [kɔnvə'les] vi convalecer; **convalescence** n convalecen-

cia; **convalescent** a, n convaleciente m/f.

convene [kən'viːn] vt convocar // vi reunirse.

convenience [kən'viːniəns] n (comfort) comodidad f; (advantage) ventaja; **at your ~** cuando le sea conveniente; **all modern ~s**, (Brit) all mod cons todo confort.

convenient [kən'viːniənt] a (useful) útil; (place, time) conveniente.

convent ['kɔnvənt] n convento.

convention [kən'venʃən] n convención f; (meeting) asamblea; **~al** a convencional.

conversant [kən'vəːsnt] a: **to be ~ with** estar al tanto de.

conversation [kɔnvə'seiʃən] n conversación f; **~al** a (familiar) familiar; (talkative) locuaz.

converse ['kɔnvəːs] n inversa // vi [kən'vəːs] conversar; **~ly** [-'vəːsli] ad a la inversa.

conversion [kən'vəːʃən] n conversión f.

convert [kən'vəːt] vt (REL, COMM) convertir; (alter) transformar // n ['kɔnvəːt] converso/a; **~ible** a convertible // n descapotable m.

convex ['kɔn'veks] a convexo.

convey [kən'vei] vt llevar; (thanks) comunicar; (idea) expresar; **~or belt** n cinta transportadora.

convict [kən'vikt] vt (gen) condenar; (find guilty) declarar culpable a // n ['kɔnvikt] presidiario/a; **~ion** [-ʃən] n (LAW) condena; (belief) creencia, convicción f.

convince [kən'vins] vt convencer; **~d a: ~d of/that** convencido de/de que; **convincing** a convincente.

convoluted ['kɔnvəluːtid] a (argument etc) enrevesado.

convoy ['kɔnvɔi] n convoy m.

convulse [kən'vʌls] vt convulsionar; **to be ~d with laughter** dislocarse de risa; **convulsion** [-'vʌlʃən] n convulsión f.

coo [kuː] vi arrullar.

cook [kuk] vt cocinar; (stew etc) guisar; (*meal*) preparar // *vi* cocer; (*person*) cocinar // *n* cocinero/a; ~ **book** *n* libro de cocina; ~**er** *n* cocina; ~**ery** *n* (*dishes*) cocina; (*art*) arte *m* culinario; ~**ery book** *n* (*Brit*) = ~ **book**; ~**ie** *n* (*US*) galleta; ~**ing** *n* cocina.

cool [ku:l] *a* fresco; (*not hot*) tibio; (*not afraid*) tranquilo; (*unfriendly*) frío // *vt* enfriar // *vi* enfriarse; ~**ness** *n* frescura; tranquilidad *f*; (*hostility*) frialdad *f*; (*indifference*) falta de entusiasmo.

coop [ku:p] *n* gallinero *m*, // *vt*: to ~ **up** (*fig*) encerrar.

cooperate [kəu'ɔpəreɪt] *vi* cooperar, colaborar; **cooperation** [-'reɪʃən] *n* cooperación *f*, colaboración *f*; **cooperative** [-rətɪv] *a* cooperativo // *n* cooperativa.

coordinate [kəu'ɔ:dɪneɪt] *vt* coordinar // *n* [kəu'ɔ:dɪnət] (*MATH*) coordenada; ~**s** *npl* (*clothes*) coordinados *mpl*; **coordination** [-'neɪʃən] *n* coordinación *f*.

co-ownership [kəu'əunəʃɪp] *n* copropiedad *f*.

cop [kɔp] *n* (*col*) poli *m*, tira *m* (*LAm*).

cope [kəup] *vi*: to ~ **with** poder con; (*problem*) hacer frente a.

copious ['kəupɪəs] *a* copioso, abundante.

copper ['kɔpə*] *n* (*metal*) cobre *m*; (*col: policeman*) poli *m*; ~**s** *npl* perras *fpl*, centavos *mpl* (*LAm*).

coppice ['kɔpɪs], **copse** [kɔps] *n* bosquecillo.

copulate ['kɔpjuleɪt] *vi* copularse.

copy ['kɔpɪ] *n* copia; (*of book etc*) ejemplar *m*; (*of writing*) original *m* // *vt* copiar; ~**right** *n* derechos *mpl* de autor.

coral ['kɔrəl] *n* coral *m*; ~ **reef** *n* arrecife *m* (de coral).

cord [kɔ:d] *n* cuerda; (*ELEC*) cable *m*; (*fabric*) pana.

cordial ['kɔ:dɪəl] *a* afectuoso // *n* cordial *m*.

cordon ['kɔ:dn] *n* cordón *m*; to ~

off *vt* acordonar.

corduroy ['kɔ:dərɔɪ] *n* pana.

core [kɔ:*] *n* (*gen*) centro, núcleo; (*of fruit*) corazón *m* // *vt* quitar el corazón de.

coriander [kɔrɪ'ændə*] *n* culantro.

cork [kɔ:k] *n* corcho; (*tree*) alcornoque *m*; ~**screw** *n* sacacorchos *m inv*.

corn [kɔ:n] *n* (*Brit: wheat*) trigo; (*US: maize*) maíz *m*; (*on foot*) callo; ~ **on the cob** (*CULIN*) maíz en la mazorca, choclo (*LAm*).

cornea ['kɔ:nɪə] *n* córnea.

corned beef ['kɔ:nd-] *n* carne *f* acecinada.

corner ['kɔ:nə*] *n* ángulo; (*outside*) esquina; (*inside*) rincón *m*; (*in road*) curva; (*FOOTBALL*) córner *m* // *vt* (*trap*) arrinconar; (*COMM*) acaparar // *vi* (*in car*) tomar las curvas; ~**stone** *n* piedra angular.

cornet ['kɔ:nɪt] *n* (*MUS*) corneta; (*Brit: of ice-cream*) barquillo.

cornflakes ['kɔ:nfleɪks] *npl* copos *mpl* de maíz, cornflakes *mpl*.

cornflour ['kɔ:nflauə*] *n* (*Brit*) harina de maíz.

cornstarch ['kɔ:nstɑ:tʃ] *n* (*US*) = **cornflour**

Cornwall ['kɔ:nwəl] *n* Cornualles *m*.

corny ['kɔ:nɪ] *a* (*col*) gastado.

corollary [kə'rɔləri] *n* corolario.

coronary ['kɔrənərɪ] *n*: ~ (**thrombosis**) infarto.

coronation [kɔrə'neɪʃən] *n* coronación *f*.

coroner ['kɔrənə*] *n* juez *m* (de instrucción).

coronet ['kɔrənɪt] *n* corona.

corporal ['kɔ:pərl] *n* cabo // *a*: ~ **punishment** castigo corporal.

corporate ['kɔ:pərɪt] *a* corporativo.

corporation [kɔ:pə'reɪʃən] *n* (*of town*) ayuntamiento; (*COMM*) corporación *f*.

corps [kɔ:*], *pl* **corps** [kɔ:z] *n* cuerpo.

corpse [kɔ:ps] *n* cadáver *m*.

corpuscle ['kɔ:pʌsl] *n* corpúsculo.

corral [kə'rɑːl] n corral m.

correct [kə'rekt] a (accurate) justo, exacto; (proper) correcto // vt corregir; (exam) calificar; ~**ion** [-ʃən] n rectificación f; (erasure) tachadura.

correlation [kɔrɪ'leɪʃən] n correlación f.

correspond [kɔrɪs'pɔnd] vi (write) escribirse; (be equal to) corresponder; ~**ence** n correspondencia; ~**ence course** n curso por correspondencia; ~**ent** n corresponsal m/f.

corridor ['kɔrɪdɔ:'] n pasillo.

corroborate [kə'rɔbəreit] vt corroborar.

corrode [kə'rəud] vt corroer // vi corroerse; **corrosion** [-'rəuʒən] n corrosión f.

corrugated ['kɔrəgeitid] a ondulado; ~ **iron** n chapa ondulada.

corrupt [kə'rʌpt] a corrompido; (person) corrupto // vt corromper; (bribe) sobornar; ~**ion** [-ʃən] n corrupción f.

corset ['kɔ:sit] n faja.

Corsica ['kɔ:sikə] n Córcega.

cortège [kɔ:'teiʒ] n cortejo, desfile m.

cosh [kɔʃ] n (Brit) cachiporra.

cosmetic [kɔz'metik] n cosmético.

cosmic ['kɔzmik] a cósmico.

cosmonaut ['kɔzmənɔ:t] n cosmonauta m/f.

cosmopolitan [kɔzmə'pɔlitn] a cosmopolita.

cosset ['kɔsit] vt mimar.

cost [kɔst] n (gen) coste m, costo; (price) precio; ~**s** npl costas fpl // vb (pt, pp **cost**) vi costar, valer // vt preparar el presupuesto de; **how much does it ~?** ¿cuánto cuesta?; **at all ~s** cueste lo que cueste.

co-star ['kəustɑ:'] n colega m/f de reparto.

Costa Rican ['kɔstə'ri:kən] a, n costarriqueño/a m/f.

cost-effective [kɔsti'fektiv] a rentable.

costly ['kɔstli] a (expensive) costoso.

cost-of-living [kɔstəv'liviŋ] a: ~ **al-**

lowance plus m de carestía de vida; ~ **index** n índice m del costo de vida.

cost price n (Brit) precio de coste.

costume ['kɔstju:m] n traje m; (Brit: also: **swimming** ~) traje de baño; ~ **jewellery** n bisutería.

cosy, (US) **cozy** ['kəuzi] a cómodo; (atmosphere) acogedor(a).

cot [kɔt] n (Brit: child's) cuna.

cottage ['kɔtidʒ] n casita de campo; (rustic) barraca; ~ **cheese** n requesón m; ~ **industry** n industria casera; ~ **pie** n pastel m de carne cubierta de puré de patatas.

cotton ['kɔtn] n algodón m; (thread) hilo; **to** ~ **on to** vt fus (col) caer en la cuenta de; ~ **candy** n (US) algodón m (azucarado); ~ **wool** n (Brit) algodón m (hidrófilo).

couch [kautʃ] n sofá m.

couchette [ku:'ʃet] n litera.

cough [kɔf] vi toser // n tos f; ~ **drop** n pastilla para la tos.

could [kud] pt of **can**; ~**n't** = **could not**.

council ['kaunsl] n consejo; **city** o **town** ~ consejo municipal; ~ **estate** n (Brit) urbanización f de viviendas municipales de alquiler; ~ **house** n (Brit) vivienda municipal de alquiler; ~**lor** n concejal/a m/f.

counsel ['kaunsl] n (advice) consejo; (lawyer) abogado/a // vt aconsejar; ~**lor** n consejero/a; ~**or** n (US) abogado/a.

count [kaunt] vt (gen) contar; (include) incluir // vi contar // n cuenta; (of votes) escrutinio; (nobleman) conde m; (sum) total m, suma; **to** ~ **on** vt fus contar con; **that doesn't** ~! ¡eso no vale!; ~**down** n cuenta atrás.

countenance ['kauntinəns] n semblante m, rostro // vt (tolerate) aprobar, tolerar.

counter ['kauntə'] n (in shop) mostrador m; (in games) ficha // vt contrarrestar.

counterfeit ['kauntəfit] n falsificación f, simulación f // vt falsificar // a falso, falsificado.

counterfoil ['kauntəfɔıl] n (Brit) talón m.

countermand ['kauntəmɑ:nd] vt revocar, cancelar.

counterpart ['kauntəpa:t] n (of person) homólogo/a.

counter-productive [kauntəprə'dʌktıv] a contraproducente.

countersign ['kauntəsaın] vt refrendar.

countess ['kauntıs] n condesa.

countless ['kauntlıs] a innumerable.

country ['kʌntrı] n país m; (native land) patria; (as opposed to town) campo; (region) región f, tierra; ~ **dancing** (Brit) baile m regional; ~ **house** n casa de campo; ~**man** n (national) compatriota m; (rural) campesino, paisano; ~**side** n campo.

county ['kauntı] n condado.

coup [ku:], pl ~**s** [-z] n (also: ~ **d'état**) golpe m (de estado).

coupé ['ku:peı] n cupé m.

couple ['kʌpl] n (of things) par m; (of people) pareja; (married ~) matrimonio // vt (ideas, names) unir, juntar; (machinery) acoplar; **a** ~ **of** un par de.

coupling ['kʌplıŋ] n (RAIL) enganche m.

coupon ['ku:pɔn] n cupón m; (pools ~) boleto de quiniela.

courage ['kʌrıdʒ] n valor m, valentía; ~**ous** [kə'reıdʒəs] a valiente.

courgette [kuə'ʒɛt] n (Brit) calabacín m, calabacita.

courier ['kurıə*] n mensajero/a; (diplomatic) correo; (for tourists) guía m/f (de turismo).

course [kɔ:s] n (direction) dirección f; (of river, SCOL) curso; (of ship) rumbo; (fig) proceder m; (GOLF) campo; (part of meal) plato; **of** ~ ad desde luego, naturalmente; **of** ~! ¡claro!

court [kɔ:t] n (royal) corte f; (LAW) tribunal m, juzgado; (TENNIS) pista, cancha // vt (woman) cortejar;

(danger etc) buscar; **to take to** ~ demandar.

courteous ['kə:tıəs] a cortés.

courtesan [kɔ:tı'zæn] n cortesana.

courtesy ['kə:tısı] n cortesía; **by** ~ **of** por cortesía de.

court-house ['kɔ:thaus] n (US) palacio de justicia.

courtier ['kɔ:tıə*] n cortesano.

court-martial ['kɔ:t'mɑ:ʃəl], pl **courts-martial** n consejo de guerra // vt someter a consejo de guerra.

courtroom ['kɔ:trum] n sala de justicia.

courtyard ['kɔ:tjɑ:d] n patio.

cousin ['kʌzn] n primo/a; **first** ~ primo/a carnal.

cove [kəuv] n cala, ensenada.

covenant ['kʌvənənt] n convenio.

cover ['kʌvə*] vt cubrir; (with lid) tapar; (chairs etc) revestir; (distance) recorrer; (include) abarcar; (protect) abrigar; (journalist) investigar; (issues) tratar // n cubierta; (lid) tapa; (for chair etc) funda; (for bed) cobertor m; (envelope) sobre m; (for book) forro; (of magazine) portada; (shelter) abrigo; (insurance) cobertura; **to take** ~ (shelter) protegerse, resguardarse; **under** ~ (indoors) bajo techo; **under** ~ **of darkness** al amparo de la oscuridad; **under separate** ~ (COMM) por separado; **to** ~ **up for sb** encubrir a uno; ~**age** n alcance m; ~**alls** npl (US) mono sg; ~ **charge** n precio del cubierto; ~**ing** n cubierta, envoltura; ~**ing letter**, (US) ~ **letter** n carta de explicación; ~ **note** n (INSURANCE) póliza provisional.

covert ['kʌvət] a secreto, encubierto.

cover-up ['kʌvərʌp] n encubrimiento.

covet ['kʌvıt] vt codiciar.

cow [kau] n vaca // vt intimidar.

coward ['kauəd] n cobarde m/f; ~**ice** [-ıs] n cobardía; ~**ly** a cobarde.

cowboy ['kauboı] n vaquero.

cower ['kauǝ*] vi encogerse (de miedo).

coxswain ['kɔksn] n (abbr: **cox**) timonel m/f.

coy [kɔɪ] a tímido.

cozy ['kǝuzɪ] a (US) = **cosy**.

CPA n abbr (US) = **certified public accountant**.

crab [kræb] n cangrejo; ~ **apple** n manzana silvestre.

crack [kræk] n grieta; (noise) crujido; (: of whip) chasquido; (joke) chiste m; **to have a ~ at** intentar // vt agrietar, romper; (nut) cascar; (safe) forzar; (whip etc) chasquear; (knuckles) crujir; (joke) contar // (athlete) de primera clase; **to ~ down on** vt fus reprimir fuertemente; **to ~ up** vi (MED) sufrir una crisis nerviosa; **~er** n (biscuit) crácker m; (Christmas cracker) petardo sorpresa.

crackle ['krækl] vi crepitar.

cradle ['kreɪdl] n cuna.

craft [krɑːft] n (skill) arte m; (trade) oficio; (cunning) astucia; (boat) barco.

craftsman ['krɑːftsmǝn] n artesano; **~ship** n artesanía.

crafty ['krɑːftɪ] a astuto.

crag [kræg] n peñasco.

cram [kræm] vt (fill): **to ~ sth with** llenar algo (a reventar) de; (put): **to ~ sth into** meter algo a la fuerza en // (for exams) empollar; **~med** a atestado.

cramp [kræmp] n (MED) calambre m; (TECH) grapa // vt (limit) poner trabas a; **~ed** a apretado, estrecho.

crampon ['kræmpǝn] n crampón m.

cranberry ['krænbǝrɪ] n arándano agrio.

crane [kreɪn] n (TECH) grúa; (bird) grulla.

crank [kræŋk] n manivela; (person) chiflado; **~shaft** n cigüeñal m.

cranny ['krænɪ] n see **nook**.

crash [kræʃ] n (noise) estrépito; (of cars etc) choque m; (of plane) accidente m de aviación; (COMM) quie-

bra // vt (plane) estrellar // vi (plane) estrellarse; (two cars) chocar; (fall noisily) caer con estrépito; ~ **course** n curso acelerado; ~ **helmet** n casco (protector); ~ **landing** n aterrizaje m forzado.

crass [kræs] a grosero, maleducado.

crate [kreɪt] n cajón m de embalaje.

crater ['kreɪtǝ*] n cráter m.

cravat(e) [krǝ'væt] n pañuelo.

crave [kreɪv] vt, vi: **to ~ (for)** ansiar, anhelar; **craving** n (of pregnant woman) antojo.

crawl [krɔːl] vi (drag o.s.) arrastrarse; (child) andar a gatas, gatear; (vehicle) avanzar (lentamente) // n (SWIMMING) crol m.

crayfish ['kreɪfɪʃ] n, pl inv (freshwater) cangrejo de río; (saltwater) cigala.

crayon ['kreɪǝn] n lápiz m de color.

craze [kreɪz] n manía; (fashion) moda.

crazy ['kreɪzɪ] a (person) loco; (idea) disparatado; ~ **paving** n pavimento de baldosas irregulares.

creak [kriːk] vi crujir; (hinge etc) chirriar, rechinar.

cream [kriːm] n (of milk) nata, crema; (lotion) crema; (fig) flor f y nata // a (colour) color crema; ~ **cake** n pastel m de nata; ~ **cheese** n queso crema; ~**y** a cremoso.

crease [kriːs] n (fold) pliegue m; (in trousers) raya; (wrinkle) arruga // vt (fold) doblar, plegar; (wrinkle) arrugar // vi (wrinkle up) arrugarse.

create [kriː'eɪt] vt crear; **creation** [-ʃǝn] n creación f; **creative** a creador(a); **creator** n creador(a) m/f.

creature ['kriːtʃǝ*] n (animal) animal m, bicho; (living thing) criatura.

crèche, creche [krɛʃ] n (Brit) guardería (infantil).

credence ['kriːdǝns] n: **to lend** or **give ~ to** creer en, dar crédito a.

credentials [krɪ'dɛnʃlz] npl credenciales fpl.

credible ['krɛdɪbl] a creíble.

credit ['krɛdɪt] n (gen) crédito;

(merit) honor *m*, mérito // *vt (COMM)* abonar; *(believe)* creer, prestar fe a // *a* crediticio; ~s *npl (CINEMA)* fichas *fpl* técnicas; **to be in** ~ *(person)* tener saldo a favor; **to** ~ **sb with** *(fig)* reconocer a uno el mérito de; ~ **card** *n* tarjeta de crédito; ~**or** *n* acreedor(a) *m/f*.

creed [kriːd] *n* credo.

creek [kriːk] *n* cala, ensenada; *(US)* riachuelo.

creep [kriːp], *pt, pp* **crept** *vi (animal)* deslizarse; *(gen)* arrastrarse; *(plant)* trepar; ~**er** *n* enredadera; ~**y** *a (frightening)* horripilante.

cremate [krɪˈmeɪt] *vt* incinerar.

crematorium [kreməˈtɔːrɪəm], *pl* -**ria** [-rɪə] *n* crematorio.

crêpe [kreɪp] *n (fabric)* crespón *m*; *(also:* ~ **rubber)** crepé *m*; ~ **bandage** *n (Brit)* venda de crepé.

crept [krept] *pt, pp* **of creep**.

crescent [ˈkresnt] *n* media luna; *(street)* calle *f* (en forma de semicírculo).

cress [kres] *n* berro.

crest [krest] *n (of bird)* cresta; *(of hill)* cima, cumbre *f*; *(of helmet)* cimera; *(of coat of arms)* blasón *m*; ~**fallen** *a* alicaído.

crevasse [krɪˈvæs] *n* grieta.

crevice [ˈkrevɪs] *n* grieta, hendedura.

crew [kruː] *n (of ship etc)* tripulación *f*; *(gang)* banda; *(MIL)* dotación *f*; ~**-cut** *n* corte *m* al rape; ~**-neck** *n* cuello plano.

crib [krɪb] *n* pesebre *m* // *vt (col)* plagiar.

crick [krɪk] *n (in neck)* torticolis *m*.

cricket [ˈkrɪkɪt] *n (insect)* grillo; *(game)* críquet *m*.

crime [kraɪm] *n* crimen *m*; *(less serious)* delito; **criminal** [ˈkrɪmɪnl] *n* criminal *m/f*, delincuente *m/f* // *a* criminal; *(law)* penal.

crimson [ˈkrɪmzn] *a* carmesí.

cringe [krɪndʒ] *vi* agacharse, encogerse.

crinkle [ˈkrɪŋkl] *vt* arrugar.

cripple [ˈkrɪpl] *n* lisiado/a, cojo/a // *vt*

lisiar, mutilar.

crisis [ˈkraɪsɪs], *pl* -**ses** [-siːz] *n* crisis *f inv*.

crisp [krɪsp] *a* fresco; *(cooked)* tostado; *(manner)* seco; ~s *npl (Brit)* patatas *fpl* or papas *fpl* fritas.

criss-cross [ˈkrɪskrɔs] *a* entrelazado.

criterion [kraɪˈtɪərɪən], *pl* -**ria** [-rɪə] *n* criterio.

critic [ˈkrɪtɪk] *n (paper)* crítico/a; ~**al** *a (gen)* crítico; *(illness)* grave; ~**ally** *ad (speak etc)* en tono crítico; *(ill)* gravemente; ~**ism** [ˈkrɪtɪsɪzm] *n* crítica; ~**ize** [ˈkrɪtɪsaɪz] *vt* criticar.

croak [krəuk] *n (of frog)* croar; *(raven)* graznar.

crochet [ˈkrəuʃeɪ] *n* ganchillo.

crockery [ˈkrɔkərɪ] *n* loza, vajilla.

crocodile [ˈkrɔkədaɪl] *n* cocodrilo.

crocus [ˈkrəukəs] *n* azafrán *m*.

croft [krɔft] *n (Brit)* granja pequeña.

crony [ˈkrəunɪ] *n* compinche *m*.

crook [kruk] *n (fam)* ladrón/ona *m/f*; *(of shepherd)* cayado; *(of arm)* pliegue *m*; ~**ed** [ˈkrukɪd] *a* torcido; *(path)* tortuoso; *(fam)* sucio.

crop [krɔp] *n (produce)* cultivo; *(amount produced)* cosecha; *(riding* ~) látigo de montar // *vt* cortar, recortar; **to** ~ **up** *vi* surgir, presentarse.

croquette [krəˈket] *n* croqueta.

cross [krɔs] *n* cruz *f* // *vt (street etc)* cruzar, atravesar // *a* de mal humor, enojado; **to** ~ **o.s.** santiguarse; **to** ~ **out** *vt* tachar; **to** ~ **over** *vi* cruzar; ~**bar** *n* travesaño; ~**country (race)** *n* carrera a campo traviesa, cross *m*; **to** ~**examine** *vt* interrogar; ~**eyed** *a* bizco; ~**fire** *n* fuego cruzado; ~**ing** *n (road)* cruce *m*; *(rail)* paso a nivel; *(sea passage)* travesía; *(also:* **pedestrian** ~**ing)** paso para peatones; ~**ing guard** *n (US)* persona encargada de ayudar a los niños a cruzar la calle; ~**purposes** *npl*: **to be at** ~ **purposes** malentenderse uno a otro; ~**reference** *n* contrarreferencia; ~**roads** *n* cruce *m*, encrucijada; ~

section n corte m transversal; (of population) muestra (representativa); **~walk** n (US) paso de peatones; **~wind** n viento de costado; **~word** n crucigrama m.

crotch [krɔtʃ] n (of garment) entrepierna.

crotchet ['krɔtʃit] n (Brit MUS) negra.

crotchety ['krɔtʃiti] a (person) arisco.

crouch [krautʃ] vi agacharse, acurrucarse.

crow [krəu] n (bird) cuervo; (of cock) canto, cacareo // vi (cock) cantar; (fig) jactarse.

crowbar ['krəubɑ:*] n palanca.

crowd [kraud] n muchedumbre f; (SPORT) público; (common herd) vulgo // vt (gather) amontonar; (fill) llenar // vi (gather) reunirse; (pile up) amontonarse; **~ed** a (full) atestado; (well-attended) concurrido.

crown [kraun] n corona; (of head) coronilla; (of hat) copa; (of hill) cumbre f // vt coronar; **~ jewels** npl joyas fpl reales; **~ prince** n príncipe m heredero.

crow's feet npl patas fpl de gallo.

crucial ['kru:ʃl] a decisivo.

crucifix ['kru:sifiks] n crucifijo; **~ion** [-'fikʃən] n crucifixión f.

crucify ['kru:sifai] vt crucificar.

crude [kru:d] a (materials) bruto; (fig: basic) tosco; (: vulgar) ordinario; **~ (oil)** n petróleo crudo.

cruel ['kruəl] a cruel; **~ty** n crueldad f.

cruet ['kru:it] n angarillas fpl.

cruise [kru:z] n crucero // vi (ship) hacer un crucero; (car) mantener la velocidad; **~r** n crucero.

crumb [krʌm] n miga, migaja.

crumble ['krʌmbl] vt desmenuzar // vi (gen) desmenuzarse; (building) desmoronarse; **crumbly** a desmenuzable.

crumpet ['krʌmpit] n ≈ bollo para tostar.

crumple ['krʌmpl] vt (paper) estru-

jar; (material) arrugar.

crunch [krʌntʃ] vt (with teeth) ronzar; (underfoot) hacer crujir // n (fig) crisis f; **~y** a crujiente.

crusade [kru:'seid] n cruzada.

crush [krʌʃ] n (crowd) aglomeración f // vt (gen) aplastar; (paper) estrujar; (cloth) arrugar; (fruit) exprimir.

crust [krʌst] n corteza.

crutch [krʌtʃ] n muleta.

crux [krʌks] n lo esencial.

cry [krai] vi llorar; (shout: also: ~ out) gritar // n grito; **to ~ off** vi echarse atrás.

cryptic ['kriptik] a enigmático, secreto.

crystal ['kristl] n cristal m; **~-clear** a claro como el agua; **~lize** vt cristalizar // vi cristalizarse.

cub [kʌb] n cachorro; (also: ~ scout) niño explorador.

Cuba ['kju:bə] n Cuba; **~n** a, n cubano/a m/f.

cubbyhole ['kʌbihəul] n chiribitil m.

cube [kju:b] n cubo; (of sugar) terrón m // vt (MATH) cubicar; **~ root** n raíz f cúbica; **cubic** a cúbico.

cubicle ['kju:bikl] n (at pool) caseta; (for bed) cubículo.

cuckoo ['kuku:] n cuco; **~ clock** n cucú m.

cucumber ['kju:kʌmbə*] n pepino.

cuddle ['kʌdl] vt abrazar // vi abrazarse.

cue [kju:] n (snooker ~) taco; (THEATRE etc) entrada.

cuff [kʌf] n (Brit: of shirt, coat etc) puño; (US: of trousers) vuelta; (blow) bofetada; **off the ~** ad improvisado; **~links** npl gemelos mpl.

cuisine [kwi:'zi:n] n cocina.

cul-de-sac ['kʌldəsæk] n callejón m sin salida.

cull [kʌl] vt (select) entresacar.

culminate ['kʌlmineit] vi: **to ~ in** terminar en; **culmination** [-'neiʃən] n culminación f, colmo.

culottes [ku:'lɔts] npl falda fsg pantalón.

culprit ['kʌlprɪt] n culpable m/f, delincuente m/f.

cult [kʌlt] n culto.

cultivate ['kʌltɪveɪt] vt (also fig) cultivar; **~d** a culto; **cultivation** [-'veɪʃən] n cultivo; (fig) cultura.

cultural [kʌltʃərəl] a cultural.

culture ['kʌltʃə*] n (also fig) cultura; **~d** a culto.

cumbersome ['kʌmbəsəm] a de mucho bulto, voluminoso.

cunning ['kʌnɪŋ] n astucia // a astuto.

cup [kʌp] n taza; (prize, event) copa.

cupboard ['kʌbəd] n armario; (kitchen) alacena.

cup-tie ['kʌptaɪ] n (Brit) partido de copa.

curate ['kjuərɪt] n cura m.

curator [kjuə'reɪtə*] n conservador(a) m/f.

curb [kə:b] vt refrenar // n freno; (US) bordillo.

curdle ['kə:dl] vi cuajarse.

cure [kjuə*] vt curar // n cura, curación f.

curfew ['kə:fju:] n toque m de queda.

curio ['kjuərɪəu] n curiosidad f.

curiosity [kjuərɪ'ɒsɪtɪ] n curiosidad f.

curious ['kjuərɪəs] a curioso.

curl [kə:l] n rizo // vt (hair) rizar; (paper) arrollar; (lip) fruncir // vi rizarse; arrollarse; **to ~ up** arrollarse; (person) hacerse un ovillo; **~er** n bigudí m; **~y** a rizado.

currant ['kʌrnt] n pasa.

currency ['kʌrnsɪ] n moneda; **to gain ~** (fig) difundirse.

current ['kʌrnt] n corriente f // a corriente, actual; **~ account** n (Brit) cuenta corriente; **~ affairs** npl actualidades fpl; **~ly** ad actualmente.

curriculum [kə'rɪkjuləm], pl **~s** or **curricula** [-lə] n plan m de estudios; **~ vitae (CV)** n curriculum m.

curry ['kʌrɪ] n curry m // vt: **to ~ favour with** buscar favores con; **~ powder** n curry m en polvo.

curse [kə:s] vi echar pestes // vt maldecir // n maldición f; (swearword) palabrota.

cursor ['kə:sə*] n (COMPUT) cursor m.

cursory ['kə:sərɪ] a rápido, superficial.

curt [kə:t] a corto, seco.

curtail [kə:'teɪl] vt (cut short) acortar; (restrict) restringir.

curtain ['kə:tn] n cortina; (THEATRE) telón m.

curts(e)y ['kə:tsɪ] n reverencia // vi hacer una reverencia.

curve [kə:v] n curva // vi encorvarse, torcerse; (road) hacer curva.

cushion ['kuʃən] n cojín m; (SNOOKER) banda // vt (shock) amortiguar.

custard ['kʌstəd] n (for pouring) natillas fpl.

custodian [kʌs'təudɪən] n custodio m/f.

custody ['kʌstədɪ] n custodia; **to take into ~** detener.

custom ['kʌstəm] n costumbre f; (COMM) clientela; **~ary** a acostumbrado.

customer ['kʌstəmə*] n cliente m/f.

customized ['kʌstəmaɪzd] a (car etc) hecho a encargo.

custom-made ['kʌstəm'meɪd] a hecho a la medida.

customs ['kʌstəmz] npl aduana sg; **~ duty** n derechos mpl de aduana; **~ officer** n aduanero/a.

cut [kʌt] vb (pt, pp cut) vt cortar; (price) rebajar; (record) grabar; (reduce) reducir // n corte m; (in skin) cortadura; (with sword) tajo; (of knife) cuchillada; (in salary etc) rebaja; (slice of meat) tajada; **to ~ a tooth** echar un diente; **to ~ down** vt (tree) derribar; (reduce) reducir; **to ~ off** vt cortar; (fig) aislar; (troops) cercar; **to ~ out** vt (shape) recortar; (delete) suprimir; **to ~ up** vt cortar (en pedazos); **~back** n reducción f.

cute [kju:t] a lindo; (shrewd) listo.

cuticle ['kju:tɪkl] n cutícula.

cutlery ['kʌtlərɪ] *n* cubiertos *mpl*.

cutlet ['kʌtlɪt] *n* chuleta.

cut: ~**out** *n* (*cardboard* ~) recortable *m*; ~**price**, (*US*) ~**rate** *a* a precio reducido; ~**throat** *n* asesino/a // *a* feroz.

cutting ['kʌtɪŋ] *a* (*gen*) cortante; (*remark*) mordaz // *n* (*Brit: from newspaper*) recorte *m*; (: RAIL) desmonte *m*.

CV *n abbr* = **curriculum vitae.**

cwt *abbr* = **hundredweight(s).**

cyanide ['saɪənaɪd] *n* cianuro.

cycle ['saɪkl] *n* ciclo; (*bicycle*) bicicleta // *vi* ir en bicicleta; **cycling** *n* ciclismo; **cyclist** *n* ciclista *m/f*.

cyclone ['saɪkləun] *n* ciclón *m*.

cygnet ['sɪgnɪt] *n* pollo de cisne.

cylinder ['sɪlɪndə*] *n* cilindro; ~**head gasket** *n* junta de culata.

cymbals ['sɪmblz] *npl* platillos *mpl*.

cynic ['sɪnɪk] *n* cínico/a; ~**al** *a* cínico; ~**ism** ['sɪnɪsɪzəm] *n* cinismo.

cypress ['saɪprɪs] *n* ciprés *m*.

Cypriot ['sɪprɪət] *a, n* chipriota *m/f*.

Cyprus ['saɪprəs] *n* Chipre *f*.

cyst [sɪst] *n* quiste *m*; ~**itis** *n* cistitis *f*.

czar [zɑ:*] *n* zar *m*.

Czech [tʃek] *a, n* checo/a *m/f*.

Czechoslovakia [tʃekəslə'vækɪə] *n* Checoslovaquia; ~**n** *a, n* checo/a *m/f*.

D

D [di:] *n* (MUS) re *m*.

dab [dæb] *vt* (*eyes, wound*) tocar (ligeramente); (*paint, cream*) mojar ligeramente // *n* (*light stroke*) toque *m*; (*small amount*) pizca *f*.

dabble ['dæbl] *vi*: **to ~ in** ser algo aficionado a.

Dacron ['deɪkrɔn] *n* ® (US) terylene *m*.

dad [dæd], **daddy** ['dædɪ] *n* papá *m*; **daddy-long-legs** *n* típula.

daffodil ['dæfədɪl] *n* narciso.

daft [dɑ:ft] *a* chiflado.

dagger ['dægə*] *n* puñal *m*, daga.

daily ['deɪlɪ] *a* diario, cotidiano // *n* (*paper*) diario; (*domestic help*) asistenta // *ad* todos los días, cada día.

dainty ['deɪntɪ] *a* delicado; (*tasteful*) elegante; primoroso.

dairy ['dɛərɪ] *n* (*shop*) lechería; (*on farm*) vaquería // *a* (*cow etc*) lechero; ~ **farm** *n* granja; ~ **produce** *n* productos *mpl* lácteos.

dais ['deɪs] *n* estrado.

daisy ['deɪzɪ] *n* margarita; ~ **wheel** *n* margarita.

dale [deɪl] *n* valle *m*.

dam [dæm] *n* presa // *vt* represar.

damage ['dæmɪdʒ] *n* daño; (*fig*) perjuicio; (*to machine*) avería // *vt* dañar; perjudicar; averiar; ~**s** *npl* (LAW) daños *mpl* y perjuicios.

damn [dæm] *vt* condenar; (*curse*) maldecir // *n* (*col*): **I don't give a** ~ me importa un pito // *a* (*col: also:* ~**ed**) maldito; ~ (**it**)! ¡maldito sea!; ~**ing** *a* (*evidence*) irrecusable.

damp [dæmp] *a* húmedo, mojado // *n* humedad // *vt* (*also:* ~**en**) (*cloth, rag*) mojar; (*fig*) desalentar; ~**ness** *n* humedad *f*.

damson ['dæmzən] *n* ciruela damascena.

dance [dɑ:ns] *n* baile *m* // *vi* bailar; ~ **hall** *n* salón *m* de baile; ~**r** *n* bailador(a) *m/f*; (*professional*) bailarín/ina *m/f*; **dancing** *n* baile *m*.

dandelion ['dændɪlaɪən] *n* diente *m* de león.

dandruff ['dændrəf] *n* caspa.

Dane [deɪn] *n* danés/esa *m/f*.

danger ['deɪndʒə*] *n* peligro; (*risk*) riesgo; ~! (*on sign*) ¡peligro de muerte!; **to be in** ~ **of** correr riesgo de; ~**ous** *a* peligroso; ~**ously** *ad* peligrosamente.

dangle ['dæŋgl] *vt* colgar // *vi* pender, estar colgado.

Danish ['deɪnɪʃ] *a* danés/esa // *n* (LING) danés *m*.

dapper ['dæpə*] *a* pulcro, apuesto.

dare [dɛə*] *vt*: **to ~ sb to do** desafiar a uno a hacer // *vi*: **to ~ (to)**

do sth atreverse a hacer algo; **I ~ say** (*I suppose*) puede ser, a lo mejor; **~devil** n temerario/a, atrevido/a; **daring** a atrevido, osado // n atrevimiento, osadía.

dark [dɑːk] a oscuro; (*hair, complexion*) moreno; (*fig: cheerless*) triste, sombrío // n oscuridad f; (*night*) tinieblas fpl; **in the ~ about** (*fig*) en ignorancia de; **after ~** después del anochecer; **~en** vt oscurecer; (*colour*) hacer más oscuro // vi oscurecerse; (*cloud over*) anublarse; **~ glasses** npl gafas fpl negras; **~ness** n (*in room*) oscuridad f; (*night*) tinieblas fpl; **~room** n cuarto oscuro.

darling ['dɑːlɪŋ] a, n querido/a m/f.

darn [dɑːn] vt zurcir.

dart [dɑːt] n dardo; (*in sewing*) sisa // vi precipitarse; **to ~ away/along** vi salir/marchar disparado; **~board** n diana; **~s** n dardos mpl.

dash [dæʃ] n (*small quantity: of liquid*) gota, chorrito; (*: of solid*) pizca; (*sign*) guión m; (*: long*) raya // vt (*break*) romper, estrellar; (*hopes*) defraudar // vi precipitarse, ir de prisa; **to ~ away** or **off** vi marcharse apresuradamente.

dashboard ['dæʃbɔːd] n (*AUT*) tablero de instrumentos.

dashing ['dæʃɪŋ] a gallardo.

data ['deɪtə] npl datos mpl; **~base** n base f de datos; **~ processing** n proceso de datos.

date [deɪt] n (*day*) fecha; (*with friend*) cita; (*fruit*) dátil m // vt fechar; **~ of birth** fecha de nacimiento; **to ~ ad** hasta la fecha; **out of ~** pasado de moda; **up to ~** moderno; **~d** a anticuado.

daub [dɔːb] vt embadurnar.

daughter ['dɔːtə*] n hija; **~-in-law** n nuera, hija política.

daunting ['dɔːntɪŋ] a desalentador(a).

dawdle ['dɔːdl] vi (*waste time*) perder el tiempo; (*go slowly*) andar muy despacio.

dawn [dɔːn] n alba, amanecer m // vi (*day*) amanecer; (*fig*): **it ~ed on him that...** cayó en la cuenta de que...

day [deɪ] n día m; (*working ~*) jornada; **the ~ before** el día anterior; **the ~ after tomorrow** pasado mañana; **the ~ before yesterday** anteayer; **the ~ after, the following ~** el día siguiente; **by ~** de día; **~break** n amanecer m; **~dream** vi soñar despierto; **~light** n luz f (del día); **~light saving time** n (*US*) hora de verano; **~ return** n (*Brit*) billete m de ida y vuelta (en un día); **~time** n día m; **~-to-~** a cotidiano.

daze [deɪz] vt (*stun*) aturdir // n: **in a ~** aturdido.

dazzle ['dæzl] vt deslumbrar; **dazzling** a deslumbrante.

DC abbr = **direct current**) corriente f continua.

deacon ['diːkən] n diácono.

dead [ded] a muerto; (*limb*) dormido; (*telephone*) cortado; (*battery*) agotado // ad totalmente; **to shoot sb ~** matar a uno a tiros; **~ tired** muerto (de cansancio); **to stop ~** parar en seco; **the ~** npl los muertos; **to be a ~ loss** (*col: person*) ser un inútil; (*: thing*) ser una birria; **~en** vt (*blow, sound*) amortiguar; (*make numb*) calmar, aliviar; **~ end** n callejón m sin salida; **~ heat** n (*SPORT*) empate m; **~line** n fecha or hora tope; **~lock** n punto muerto; **~ly** a mortal, fatal; **~pan** a sin expresión.

deaf [def] a sordo; **~en** vt ensordecer; **~-mute** n sordomudo/a; **~ness** n sordera.

deal [diːl] n (*agreement*) pacto, convenio; (*business*) negocio, transacción f; (*CARDS*) reparto // vt (*pt, pp dealt* [dɛlt]) (*gen*) dar; **a great ~ (of)** bastante, mucho; **to ~ in** vt fus tratar en, comerciar en; **to ~ with** vt fus (*people*) tratar con; (*problem*) ocuparse de; (*subject*) tra-

tar de; **~er** n comerciante m/f;
(CARDS) mano f; **~ings** npl
(COMM) transacciones fpl; (rela-
tions) relaciones fpl.

dean [di:n] n (REL) deán m; (SCOL)
decano/a.

dear [dɪə*] a querido; (expensive)
caro // n: my **~** mi querido/a; **~**
me! ¡Dios mío!; D**~** Sir/Madam
(in letter) Muy Señor Mío, Estimado
Señor/Estimada Señora; D**~** Mr/Mrs
X Estimado/a Señor(a) X; **~ly** ad
(love) mucho; (pay) caro.

death [dɛθ] n muerte f; **~ certificate** n partida de defunción; **~ duties** npl (Brit) derechos mpl de sucesión; **~ly** a mortal; (silence) profundo; **~ penalty** n pena de muerte; **~
rate** n mortalidad f.

debacle [deɪˈbɑːkl] n desastre m.

debar [dɪˈbɑː*] vt: to **~** sb from
doing prohibir a uno hacer.

debase [dɪˈbeɪs] vt degradar.

debatable [dɪˈbeɪtəbl] a discutible.

debate [dɪˈbeɪt] n debate m // vt discutir.

debauchery [dɪˈbɔːtʃərɪ] n libertina-
je m.

debilitating [dɪˈbɪlɪteɪtɪŋ] a (illness
etc) debilitante.

debit [ˈdɛbɪt] n debe m // vt: to **~** a
sum to sb or to sb's account car-
gar una suma en cuenta a alguien.

debris [ˈdɛbriː] n escombros mpl.

debt [dɛt] n deuda; to be in **~** tener
deudas; **~or** n deudor/a m/f.

debunk [diːˈbʌŋk] vt desprestigiar,
desacreditar.

début [ˈdeɪbjuː] n presentación f.

decade [ˈdɛkeɪd] n decenio.

decadence [ˈdɛkədəns] n decadencia.

decaffeinated [dɪˈkæfɪneɪtɪd] a descafeinado.

decanter [dɪˈkæntə*] n garrafa.

decay [dɪˈkeɪ] n (fig) decadencia; (of
building) desmoronamiento; (rotting)
pudrición f; (of tooth) caries f inv //
vi (rot) pudrirse; (fig) decaer.

deceased [dɪˈsiːst] a difunto.

deceit [dɪˈsiːt] n engaño; **~ful** a engañoso.

deceive [dɪˈsiːv] vt engañar.

December [dɪˈsɛmbə*] n diciembre
m.

decent [ˈdiːsənt] a (proper) decente;
(person) amable, bueno.

deception [dɪˈsɛpʃən] n engaño.

deceptive [dɪˈsɛptɪv] a engañoso.

decibel [ˈdɛsɪbɛl] n decibel(io) m.

decide [dɪˈsaɪd] vt (person) decidir;
(question, argument) resolver // vi:
to **~** to do/that decidir hacer/que; to
~ on sth decidir por algo; **~d** a (resolute) decidido; (clear, definite) indudable; **~dly** [-dɪdlɪ] ad decidida-
mente.

deciduous [dɪˈsɪdjuəs] a de hoja ca-
duca.

decimal [ˈdɛsɪməl] a decimal // n decimal f; **~ point** n coma decimal.

decimate [ˈdɛsɪmeɪt] vt diezmar.

decipher [dɪˈsaɪfə*] vt descifrar.

decision [dɪˈsɪʒən] n decisión f.

deck [dɛk] n (NAUT) cubierta; (of
bus) piso; (of cards) baraja; **~chair**
n tumbona.

declaration [dɛkləˈreɪʃən] n declaración f.

declare [dɪˈklɛə*] vt (gen) declarar.

decline [dɪˈklaɪn] n decaimiento, (of
cadency); (lessening) disminución f //
vt rehusar // vi declinar.

declutch [ˈdiːˈklʌtʃ] vi desembragar.

decode [diːˈkəud] vt descifrar.

decompose [diːkəmˈpəuz] vi descomponerse.

décor [ˈdeɪkɔː*] n decoración f;
(THEATRE) decorado.

decorate [ˈdɛkəreɪt] vt (adorn): to
~ (with) adornar (de), decorar
(de); (paint) pintar; (paper) empapelar; **decoration** [-ˈreɪʃən] n adorno; (act) decoración f; (medal) condecoración f; **decorative** [ˈdɛkərətɪv]
a decorativo; **decorator** n (work-
man) pintor m decorador.

decorum [dɪˈkɔːrəm] n decoro.

decoy [ˈdiːkɔɪ] n señuelo.

decrease [ˈdiːkriːs] n disminución f //

(*vb*: [diːˈkriːs]) *vt* disminuir, reducir // *vi* reducirse.

decree [diˈkriː] *n* decreto; ~ **nisi** *n* sentencia provisional de divorcio.

dedicate [ˈdedɪkeɪt] *vt* dedicar; **dedication** [-ˈkeɪʃən] *n* (*devotion*) dedicación *f*; (*in book*) dedicatoria.

deduce [dɪˈdjuːs] *vt* deducir.

deduct [dɪˈdʌkt] *vt* restar; (*from wage etc*) descontar; ~**ion** [dɪˈdʌkʃən] *n* (*amount deducted*) descuento; (*conclusion*) deducción *f*, conclusión *f*.

deed [diːd] *n* hecho, acto; (*feat*) hazaña; (*LAW*) escritura.

deem [diːm] *vt* juzgar.

deep [diːp] *a* profundo; (*voice*) bajo; (*breath*) profundo, a pleno pulmón // *ad*: the spectators stood 20 ~ los espectadores se formaron de 20 en fondo; to be 4 metres ~ tener 4 metros de profundo; ~**en** *vt* ahondar, profundizar // *vi* (*darkness*) intensificarse; ~-**freeze** *n* congeladora; ~-**fry** *vt* freír en aceite abundante; ~**ly** *ad* (*breathe*) a pleno pulmón; (*interested, moved, grateful*) profundamente, hondamente; ~-**sea diving** *n* buceo de altura; ~-**seated** *a* (*beliefs*) (profundamente) arraigado.

deer [dɪə*] *n*, *pl inv* ciervo.

deface [dɪˈfeɪs] *vt* desfigurar, mutilar.

defamation [defəˈmeɪʃən] *n* difamación *f*.

default [dɪˈfɔːlt] *vi* faltar al pago; (*SPORT*) dejar de presentarse // *n* (*COMPUT*) defecto; **by** ~ (*LAW*) en rebeldía; (*SPORT*) por incomparecencia; ~**er** *n* (*in debt*) moroso/a.

defeat [dɪˈfiːt] *n* derrota // *vt* derrotar, vencer; (*fig*) frustrar; ~**ist** *a*, *n* derrotista *m/f*.

defect *n* [ˈdiːfekt] *n* defecto // *vi* [dɪˈfekt]: to ~ to the enemy pasarse al enemigo; ~**ive** [dɪˈfektɪv] *a* (*gen*) defectuoso; (*person*) anormal.

defence [dɪˈfens] *n* defensa; ~**less** *a* indefenso.

defend [dɪˈfend] *vt* defender; ~**ant**

n acusado/a; (*in civil case*) demandado/a; ~**er** *n* defensor(a) *m/f*.

defense [dɪˈfens] *n* (*US*) = **defence**.

defensive [dɪˈfensɪv] *a* defensivo; **on the** ~ a la defensiva.

defer [dɪˈfəː*] *vt* (*postpone*) aplazar; to ~ to diferir a; ~**ence** [ˈdefərəns] *n* deferencia, respeto.

defiance [dɪˈfaɪəns] *n* desafío; **in** ~ **of** en contra de.

defiant [dɪˈfaɪənt] *a* (*insolent*) insolente; (*challenging*) retador(a).

deficiency [dɪˈfɪʃənsɪ] *n* (*lack*) falta; (*defect*) defecto.

deficient [dɪˈfɪʃənt] *a* (*lacking*) insuficiente; (*incomplete*) incompleto; (*defective*) defectuoso; (*mentally*) anormal; ~ **in** deficiente en.

deficit [ˈdefɪsɪt] *n* déficit *m*.

defile [dɪˈfaɪl] *vt* manchar; (*violate*) violar.

define [dɪˈfaɪn] *vt* definir.

definite [ˈdefɪnɪt] *a* (*fixed*) determinado; (*clear, obvious*) claro; **he was** ~ **about it** no dejó lugar a dudas (sobre ello); ~**ly** *ad* he's ~**ly mad** no cabe duda de que está loco.

definition [defɪˈnɪʃən] *n* definición *f*.

deflate [diːˈfleɪt] *vt* (*gen*) desinflar; (*person*) quitar los humos a.

deflect [dɪˈflekt] *vt* desviar.

defraud [dɪˈfrɔːd] *vt* estafar; to ~ **sb of sth** estafar algo a uno.

defray [dɪˈfreɪ] *vt*: to ~ **sb's expenses** reembolsar(le) a uno los gastos.

defrost [diːˈfrɔst] *vt* (*food*) deshelar; (*fridge*) descongelar; ~**er** *n* (*US*: *demister*) eliminador *m* de vaho.

deft [deft] *a* diestro, hábil.

defunct [dɪˈfʌŋkt] *a* difunto.

defuse [diːˈfjuːz] *vt* desarmar; (*situation*) calmar.

defy [dɪˈfaɪ] *vt* (*resist*) oponerse a; (*challenge*) desafiar; (*order*) contravenir.

degenerate [dɪˈdʒenəreɪt] *vi* degenerar // *a* [dɪˈdʒenərɪt] degenerado.

degree [dɪˈgriː] *n* grado; (*SCOL*) título; **to have a** ~ **in maths** tener una licenciatura en matemáticas; **by ~s** (*gradually*) poco a poco, por etapas; **to some ~** hasta cierto punto.

dehydrated [diːhaɪˈdreɪtɪd] *a* deshidratado; (*milk*) en polvo.

de-ice [diːˈaɪs] *vt* (*windscreen*) deshelar.

deign [deɪn] *vi*: **to ~ to do** dignarse hacer.

deity [ˈdiːɪtɪ] *n* deidad *f*, divinidad *f*.

dejected [dɪˈdʒɛktɪd] *a* abatido, desanimado.

delay [dɪˈleɪ] *vt* demorar, aplazar; (*person*) entretener; (*train*) retrasar // *vi* tardar // *n* demora, retraso; **without ~** en seguida, sin tardar.

delectable [dɪˈlɛktəbl] *a* (*person*) encantador(a); (*food*) delicioso.

delegate [ˈdɛlɪgɪt] *n* delegado/a // *vt* [ˈdɛlɪgeɪt] delegar.

delete [dɪˈliːt] *vt* suprimir, tachar.

deliberate [dɪˈlɪbərɪt] *a* (*intentional*) intencionado, (*slow*) pausado, lento // *vi* [dɪˈlɪbəreɪt] deliberar; **~ly** *ad* (*on purpose*) a propósito; (*slowly*) pausadamente.

delicacy [ˈdɛlɪkəsɪ] *n* delicadeza; (*choice food*) golosina.

delicate [ˈdɛlɪkɪt] *a* (*gen*) delicado; (*fragile*) frágil.

delicatessen [dɛlɪkəˈtɛsn] *n* ultramarinos *mpl* finos.

delicious [dɪˈlɪʃəs] *a* delicioso, rico.

delight [dɪˈlaɪt] *n* (*feeling*) placer *m*, deleite *m*; (*object*) encanto, delicia // *vt* encantar, deleitar; **to take ~ in** deleitarse en; **~ed** *a*: **~ed (at or with/to do)** encantado (con/de hacer); **~ful** *a* encantador(a), delicioso.

delinquent [dɪˈlɪŋkwənt] *a, n* delincuente *m/f*.

delirious [dɪˈlɪrɪəs] *a*: **to be ~** delirar, desvariar.

deliver [dɪˈlɪvə*] *vt* (*distribute*) repartir; (*hand over*) entregar; (*message*) comunicar; (*speech*) pronunciar; (*blow*) lanzar, dar; (*MED*) asistir al parto de; **~y** *n* reparto; entrega; (*of speaker*) modo de expresar-

se; (*MED*) parto, alumbramiento; **to take ~y of** recibir.

delude [dɪˈluːd] *vt* engañar.

deluge [ˈdɛljuːdʒ] *n* diluvio // *vt* inundar.

delusion [dɪˈluːʒən] *n* ilusión *f*, engaño.

de luxe [dəˈlʌks] *a* de lujo.

delve [dɛlv] *vi*: **to ~ into** hurgar en.

demand [dɪˈmɑːnd] *vt* (*gen*) exigir; (*rights*) reclamar // *n* (*gen*) exigencia; (*claim*) reclamación *f*; (*ECON*) demanda; **to be in ~** ser muy solicitado; **on ~** a solicitud; **~ing** *a* (*boss*) exigente; (*work*) absorbente.

demean [dɪˈmiːn] *vt*: **to ~ o.s.** rebajarse.

demeanour, (US) demeanor [dɪˈmiːnə*] *n* porte *m*, conducta.

demented [dɪˈmɛntɪd] *a* demente.

demise [dɪˈmaɪz] *n* (*death*) fallecimiento.

demister [dɪˈmɪstə*] *n* (*AUT*) eliminador *m* de vaho.

demo [ˈdɛməu] *n abbr* (col: = *demonstration*) manifestación *f*.

democracy [dɪˈmɔkrəsɪ] *n* democracia; **democrat** [ˈdɛməkræt] *n* demócrata *m/f*; **democratic** [dɛməˈkrætɪk] *a* democrático.

demolish [dɪˈmɔlɪʃ] *vt* derribar, demoler; **demolition** [dɛməˈlɪʃən] *n* derribo, demolición *f*.

demon [ˈdiːmən] *n* (*evil spirit*) demonio.

demonstrate [ˈdɛmənstreɪt] *vt* demostrar // *vi* manifestarse; **demonstration** [-ˈstreɪʃən] *n* (*POL*) manifestación *f*; (*proof*) prueba, demostración *f*; **demonstrator** *n* (*POL*) manifestante *m/f*.

demoralize [dɪˈmɔrəlaɪz] *vt* desmoralizar.

demote [dɪˈməut] *vt* degradar.

demure [dɪˈmjuə*] *a* recatado.

den [dɛn] *n* (*of animal*) guarida; (*study*) estudio.

denatured alcohol [diːˈneɪtʃəd-] *n* (*US*) alcohol *m* desnaturalizado.

denial [dɪˈnaɪəl] *n* (*refusal*) negativa;

(of report etc) negación f.

denim ['denɪm] n tela vaquera; ~s npl vaqueros mpl.

Denmark ['dɛnmɑːk] n Dinamarca.

denomination [dɪnɒmɪ'neɪʃən] n valor m; (REL) confesión f.

denote [dɪ'nəut] vt indicar, significar.

denounce [dɪ'nauns] vt denunciar.

dense [dɛns] a (thick) espeso; (: foliage etc) tupido; (stupid) torpe; ~ly ad: ~ly populated con una alta densidad de población.

density ['dɛnsɪtɪ] n densidad f; **double-~ disk** n (COMPUT) disco de doble densidad.

dent [dɛnt] n abolladura // vt (also: make a ~ in) abollar.

dental ['dɛntl] a dental; ~ **surgeon** n odontólogo/a.

dentist ['dɛntɪst] n dentista m/f; ~ry n odontología.

dentures ['dɛntʃəz] npl dentadura sg (postiza).

denunciation [dɪnʌnsɪ'eɪʃən] n denuncia, denunciación f.

deny [dɪ'naɪ] vt negar; (charge) rechazar; (report) desmentir.

deodorant [diː'əudərənt] n desodorante m.

depart [dɪ'pɑːt] vi irse, marcharse; (train) salir; ~ **from** (fig: differ from) apartarse de.

department [dɪ'pɑːtmənt] n (COMM) sección f; (SCOL) departamento; (POL) ministerio; ~ **store** n gran almacén m.

departure [dɪ'pɑːtʃə*] n partida, ida; (of train) salida; a **new** ~ un nuevo rumbo; ~ **lounge** n (at airport) sala de embarque.

depend [dɪ'pɛnd] vi: to ~ on depender de; (rely on) contar con; **it** ~s depende, según; ~**ing on the result** según el resultado; ~**able** a (person) formal, serio; ~**ant** n dependiente m/f; ~**ence** n dependencia; ~**ent** a: to be ~**ent on** depender de // n = ~**ant**.

depict [dɪ'pɪkt] vt (in picture) pintar; (describe) representar.

depleted [dɪ'pliːtɪd] a reducido.

deplorable [dɪ'plɔːrəbl] a deplorable.

deplore [dɪ'plɔː*] vt deplorar.

deploy [dɪ'plɔɪ] vt desplegar.

depopulation [diːpɒpju'leɪʃən] n despoblación f.

deport [dɪ'pɔːt] vt deportar.

deportment [dɪ'pɔːtmənt] n comportamiento.

depose [dɪ'pəuz] vt deponer.

deposit [dɪ'pɒzɪt] n depósito; (CHEM) sedimento; (of ore, oil) yacimiento // vt (gen) depositar; ~ **account** n (Brit) cuenta de ahorros; ~**or** n depositante m/f.

depot ['dɛpəu] n (storehouse) depósito; (for vehicles) parque m.

depreciate [dɪ'priːʃɪeɪt] vi depreciarse, perder valor; **depreciation** [-'eɪʃən] n depreciación f.

depress [dɪ'prɛs] vt deprimir; (press down) apretar; ~**ed** a deprimido; ~**ing** a deprimente; ~**ion** [dɪ'prɛʃən] n depresión f.

deprivation [dɛprɪ'veɪʃən] n privación f; (loss) pérdida.

deprive [dɪ'praɪv] vt: to ~ **sb of** privar a uno de; ~**d** a necesitado.

depth [dɛpθ] n profundidad f; **in the** ~**s of** en lo más hondo de.

deputation [dɛpju'teɪʃən] n delegación f.

deputize ['dɛpjutaɪz] vi: to ~ **for sb** suplir a uno.

deputy ['dɛpjutɪ] a: ~ **head** subdirector(a) m/f // n sustituto/a, suplente m/f; (POL) diputado/a; (agent) representante m/f.

derail [dɪ'reɪl] vt: to be ~**ed** descarrilarse; ~**ment** n descarrilamiento.

deranged [dɪ'reɪndʒd] a trastornado.

derby ['dɜːbɪ] n (US) hongo.

derelict ['dɛrɪlɪkt] a abandonado.

deride [dɪ'raɪd] vt ridiculizar, mofarse de.

derisive [dɪ'raɪsɪv] a burlón/ona.

derisory [dɪ'raɪzərɪ] a (sum) irrisorio.

derivative [dɪ'rɪvətɪv] n derivado // a (work) poco original.

derive [dɪ'raɪv] vt derivar // vi: to ~ from derivarse de.

derogatory [dɪ'rɔgətərɪ] a despectivo.

derrick ['derɪk] n torre f de perforación.

derv [dɔːv] n (Brit) gasoil m.

descend [dɪ'send] vt, vi descender, bajar; to ~ from descender de; ~ant n descendiente m/f.

descent [dɪ'sent] n descenso; (origin) descendencia.

describe [dɪs'kraɪb] vt describir; **description** [-'krɪpʃən] n descripción f; (sort) clase f, género.

desecrate ['desɪkreɪt] vt profanar.

desert ['dezət] n (sketch) desierto // a [dɪ'zɔːt]) vt abandonar, desamparar // vi (MIL) desertar; ~s [dɪ'zɔːts] npl: to get one's just ~s llevar su merecido; ~er n desertor/a m/f; ~ion [dɪ'zɔːʃən] n deserción f; ~ island n isla desierta.

deserve [dɪ'zɔːv] vt merecer, ser digno de; **deserving** a (person) digno; (action, cause) meritorio.

design [dɪ'zaɪn] n (sketch) bosquejo; (layout, shape) diseño; (pattern) dibujo // vt (plan) diseñar; to have ~s on sb tener la(s) mira(s) puesta(s) en uno.

designate ['dezɪgneɪt] vt (appoint) nombrar; (destine) designar // a ['dezɪgnɪt] designado.

designer [dɪ'zaɪnə*] n diseñador(a) m/f; (fashion ~) modisto/a.

desirable [dɪ'zaɪərəbl] a (proper) deseable; (attractive) atractivo.

desire [dɪ'zaɪə*] n deseo // vt desear.

desk [desk] n (in office) escritorio; (for pupil) pupitre m; (in hotel, at airport) recepción f; (Brit: in shop, restaurant) caja.

desolate ['desəlɪt] a (place) desierto; (person) afligido; **desolation** [-'leɪʃən] n (of place) desolación f; (of person) aflicción f.

despair [dɪs'peə*] n desesperación f

// vi: to ~ of desesperarse de.

despatch [dɪs'pætʃ] n, vt = dispatch.

desperate ['despərɪt] a desesperado; (fugitive) peligroso; ~**ly** ad desesperadamente; (very) terriblemente, gravemente.

desperation [despə'reɪʃən] n desesperación f; **in** ~ desesperado.

despicable [dɪs'pɪkəbl] a vil, despreciable.

despise [dɪs'paɪz] vt despreciar.

despite [dɪs'paɪt] prep a pesar de, pese a.

despondent [dɪs'pɔndənt] a deprimido, abatido.

dessert [dɪ'zɔːt] n postre m; ~**spoon** n cuchara (de postre).

destination [destɪ'neɪʃən] n destino.

destine ['destɪn] vt destinar.

destiny ['destɪnɪ] n destino.

destitute ['destɪtjuːt] a desamparado, indigente.

destroy [dɪs'trɔɪ] vt destruir; (finish) acabar con; ~**er** n (NAUT) destructor m.

destruction [dɪs'trʌkʃən] n destrucción f; (fig) ruina.

destructive [dɪs'trʌktɪv] a destructivo, destructor(a).

detach [dɪ'tætʃ] vt separar; (unstick) despegar; ~**able** a separable; (TECH) desmontable; ~**ed** a (attitude) objetivo, imparcial; (~**ed** house n ~ chalé m, chalet m; ~**ment** n separación f; (MIL) destacamento; (fig) objetividad f, imparcialidad f.

detail ['diːteɪl] n detalle m // vt detallar; (MIL) destacar; **in** ~ detalladamente; ~**ed** a detallado.

detain [dɪ'teɪn] vt retener; (in captivity) detener.

detect [dɪ'tekt] vt (gen) descubrir; (MED, POLICE) identificar; (MIL, RADAR, TECH) detectar; ~**ion** [dɪ'tekʃən] n descubrimiento; identificación f; ~**ive** n detective m/f; ~**ive story** n novela policíaca; ~**or** n detector m.

détente [deɪ'tɑːnt] *n* distensión *f.*

detention [dɪ'tenʃən] *n* detención *f,* arresto.

deter [dɪ'tɜː*] *vt* (*dissuade*) disuadir; (*prevent*) impedir; **to ~ sb from doing sth** disuadir a uno de que haga algo.

detergent [dɪ'tɜːdʒənt] *n* detergente *m.*

deteriorate [dɪ'tɪərɪəreɪt] *vi* deteriorarse; **deterioration** [-'reɪʃən] *n* deterioro.

determination [dɪtɜːmɪ'neɪʃən] *n* resolución *f.*

determine [dɪ'tɜːmɪn] *vt* determinar; **~d** *a*: **~d to do** resuelto a hacer.

deterrent [dɪ'terənt] *n* fuerza de disuasión.

detest [dɪ'test] *vt* aborrecer.

detonate ['detəneɪt] *vi* estallar // *vt* hacer detonar.

detour ['diːtuə*] *n* (*gen, US AUT: diversion*) desviación *f* // *vt* (*US AUT*) desviar.

detract [dɪ'trækt] *vt*: **to ~ from** quitar mérito a, desvirtuar.

detriment ['detrɪmənt] *n*: **to the ~ of** en perjuicio de; **~al** [detrɪ'mentl] *a*: **~ (to)** perjudicial (a).

devaluation [dɪvælju'eɪʃən] *n* devaluación *f.*

devastating ['devəsteɪtɪŋ] *a* devastador(a); (*fig*) arrollador(a).

develop [dɪ'veləp] *vt* desarrollar; (*PHOT*) revelar; (*disease*) coger; (*habit*) adquirir // *vi* desarrollarse; (*advance*) progresar; **~ing country** país *m* en (vías de) desarrollo; **~ment** *n* (*advance*) progreso; (*of affair, case*) desenvolvimiento; (*of land*) urbanización *f.*

deviate ['diːvɪeɪt] *vi*: **to ~ (from)** desviarse (de); **deviation** [-'eɪʃən] *n* desviación *f.*

device [dɪ'vaɪs] *n* (*scheme*) estratagema, recurso; (*apparatus*) aparato, mecanismo.

devil ['devl] *n* diablo, demonio; **~ish** *a* diabólico.

devious ['diːvɪəs] *a* intricado, enrevesado; (*person*) taimado.

devise [dɪ'vaɪz] *vt* idear, inventar.

devoid [dɪ'vɔɪd] *a*: **~ of** desprovisto de.

devolution [diːvə'luːʃən] *n* (*POL*) descentralización *f.*

devote [dɪ'vəut] *vt*: **to ~ sth to** dedicar algo a; **~d** *a* (*loyal*) leal, fiel; **the book is ~d to politics** el libro trata de la política; **~e** [devəu'tiː] *n* devoto/a.

devotion [dɪ'vəuʃən] *n* dedicación *f;* (*REL*) devoción *f.*

devour [dɪ'vauə*] *vt* devorar.

devout [dɪ'vaut] *a* devoto.

dew [djuː] *n* rocío.

dexterity [deks'terɪtɪ] *n* destreza.

diabetes [daɪə'biːtiːz] *n* diabetes *f;* **diabetic** [-'betɪk] *a, n* diabético/a *m/f.*

diabolical [daɪə'bɒlɪkəl] *a* (col: *weather, behaviour*) pésimo.

diagnose [daɪəg'nəuz] *vt* diagnosticar; **diagnosis** [-'nəusɪs], *pl* **-ses** [-'nəusiːz] *n* diagnóstico.

diagonal [daɪ'ægənl] *a, n* diagonal *f.*

diagram ['daɪəgræm] *n* diagrama *m,* esquema *m.*

dial ['daɪəl] *n* esfera, cuadrante *m,* cara (*Lam*); (*of phone*) disco // *vt* (*number*) marcar; **~ code** *n* (*US*) prefijo; **~ tone** *n* (*US*) señal *f* or tono de marcar.

dialect ['daɪəlekt] *n* dialecto.

dialling ['daɪəlɪŋ]: **~ code** *n* (*Brit*) prefijo; **~ tone** *n* (*Brit*) señal *f* or tono de marcar.

dialogue ['daɪəlɒg] *n* diálogo.

diameter [daɪ'æmɪtə*] *n* diámetro.

diamond ['daɪəmənd] *n* diamante *m;* **~s** *npl* (*CARDS*) diamantes *mpl.*

diaper ['daɪəpə*] *n* (*US*) pañal *m.*

diaphragm ['daɪəfræm] *n* diafragma *m.*

diarrhoea, (*US*) **diarrhea** [daɪə'riːə] *n* diarrea.

diary ['daɪərɪ] *n* (*daily account*) diario; (*book*) agenda.

dice [daɪs] *n, pl inv* dados *mpl* // *vt*

(CULIN) cortar en cuadritos.

dichotomy [dɪ'kɒtəmɪ] n dicotomía.

Dictaphone ['dɪktəfəun] n ® dictáfono ®.

dictate [dɪk'teɪt] vt dictar; **~s** ['dɪkteɪts] npl dictados mpl; **dictation** [-'teɪʃən] n dictado.

dictator [dɪk'teɪtə*] n dictador m; **~ship** n dictadura f.

dictionary ['dɪkʃənrɪ] n diccionario.

did [dɪd] pt of do.

didn't ['dɪdənt] = did not.

die [daɪ] vi morir; **to be dying for** sth/to do sth morirse por algo/de ganas de hacer algo; **to ~ away** vi (sound, light) perderse; **to ~ down** vi (gen) apagarse; (wind) amainar; **to ~ out** vi desaparecer, extinguirse.

diehard ['daɪhɑːd] n reaccionario/a.

diesel ['diːzəl]: **~ engine** n motor m Diesel; **~ (oil)** n gasoil m.

diet ['daɪət] n dieta; (restricted food) régimen m // vi (also: **be on a ~**) estar a dieta, hacer régimen.

differ ['dɪfə*] vi (be different) ser distinto, diferenciarse; (disagree) discrepar; **~ence** n diferencia; (quarrel) desacuerdo; **~ent** a diferente, distinto; **~entiate** [-'rɛnʃɪeɪt] vt distinguir // vi diferenciarse; **to ~entiate between** distinguir entre; **~ently** ad de otro modo, en forma distinta.

difficult ['dɪfɪkəlt] a difícil; **~y** n dificultad f.

diffident ['dɪfɪdənt] a tímido.

diffuse [dɪ'fjuːs] a difuso // vt [dɪ'fjuːz] difundir.

dig [dɪg] vt (pt, pp dug) (hole) cavar; (ground) remover // n (prod) empujón m; (archaeological) excavación f; (remark) indirecta; **to ~ one's nails into** clavar las uñas en; **to ~ in** vi atrincherarse; **to ~ into** vt fus (savings) consumir; **to ~ out** vt (hole) excavar; (fig) sacar; **to ~ up** vt desenterrar; (plant) desarraigar.

digest [daɪ'dʒɛst] vt (food) digerir;

(facts) asimilar // n ['daɪdʒɛst] resumen m; **~ion** [dɪ'dʒɛstʃən] n digestión f.

digit ['dɪdʒɪt] n (number) dígito; (finger) dedo; **~al** a digital.

dignified ['dɪgnɪfaɪd] a grave, solemne; (action) decoroso.

dignity ['dɪgnɪtɪ] n dignidad f.

digress [daɪ'grɛs] vi: **to ~ from** apartarse de.

digs [dɪgz] npl (Brit: col) pensión fsg, alojamiento sg.

dike [daɪk] n = dyke.

dilapidated [dɪ'læpɪdeɪtɪd] a desmoronado, ruinoso.

dilemma [daɪ'lɛmə] n dilema m.

diligent ['dɪlɪdʒənt] a diligente.

dilute [daɪ'luːt] vt diluir.

dim [dɪm] a (light) débil; (sight) turbio; (outline) indistinto; (stupid) lerdo; (room) oscuro // vt (light) bajar.

dime [daɪm] n (US) moneda de diez centavos.

dimension [dɪ'mɛnʃən] n dimensión f.

diminish [dɪ'mɪnɪʃ] vt, vi disminuir.

diminutive [dɪ'mɪnjutɪv] a diminuto // n (LING) diminutivo.

dimly ['dɪmlɪ] ad débilmente, (not clearly) indistintamente.

dimmer ['dɪmə*] n (US AUT) interruptor m.

dimple ['dɪmpl] n hoyuelo.

din [dɪn] n estruendo, estrépito.

dine [daɪn] vi cenar; **~r** n (person) comensal m/f; (Brit RAIL) = **dining car**; (US) restaurante m económico.

dinghy ['dɪŋgɪ] n bote m; (also: rubber **~**) lancha (neumática).

dingy ['dɪndʒɪ] a (room) sombrío; (dirty) sucio; (dull) deslucido.

dining ['daɪnɪŋ]: **~ car** n (Brit RAIL) coche-comedor m; **~ room** n comedor m.

dinner ['dɪnə*] n (evening meal) cena; (lunch) comida; (public) cena, banquete m; **~'s ready!** ¡la cena está servida!; **~ jacket** n smoking m; **~ party** n cena; **~ time** n hora de cenar or comer.

dinosaur ['daɪnəsɔ:ʳ] n dinosaurio.

dint [dɪnt] n: **by ~ of** a fuerza de.

diocese ['daɪəsɪs] n diócesis f inv.

dip [dɪp] n (slope) pendiente m; (in sea) baño // vt (in water) mojar; (ladle etc) meter; (Brit AUT): **to ~ one's lights** poner luces de cruce // vi inclinarse hacia abajo.

diphthong ['dɪfθɔŋ] n diptongo.

diploma [dɪ'pləʊmə] n diploma m.

diplomacy [dɪ'pləʊməsɪ] n diplomacia.

diplomat ['dɪpləmæt] n diplomático/a; **~ic** [dɪplə'mætɪk] a diplomático.

dipstick ['dɪpstɪk] n (AUT) varilla de nivel (del aceite).

dipswitch ['dɪpswɪtʃ] n (Brit AUT) interruptor m.

dire [daɪəʳ] a calamitoso.

direct [daɪ'rɛkt] a (gen) directo // vt dirigir; **can you ~ me to...?** ¿puede indicarme dónde está...?

direction [dɪ'rɛkʃən] n dirección f; **sense of ~** sentido de la dirección; **~s** npl (advice) órdenes fpl, instrucciones fpl; **~s for use** modo de empleo.

directly [dɪ'rɛktlɪ] ad (in straight line) directamente; (at once) en seguida.

director [dɪ'rɛktəʳ] n director(a) m/f.

directory [dɪ'rɛktərɪ] n (TEL) guía (telefónica).

dirt [də:t] n suciedad f; **~-cheap** a baratísimo; **~y** a sucio; (joke) verde, colorado (LAm) // vt ensuciar; (stain) manchar; **~y trick** n juego sucio.

disability [dɪsə'bɪlɪtɪ] n incapacidad f.

disabled [dɪs'eɪbld] a minusválido.

disadvantage [dɪsəd'vɑ:ntɪdʒ] n desventaja, inconveniente m.

disaffection [dɪsə'fɛkʃən] n desafecto.

disagree [dɪsə'gri:] vi (differ) discrepar; **to ~ (with)** no estar de acuerdo (con); **~able** a desagradable; **~ment** n (gen) desacuerdo; (quar-

rel) riña.

disallow ['dɪsə'laʊ] vt (goal) anular; (claim) rechazar.

disappear [dɪsə'pɪəʳ] vi desaparecer; **~ance** n desaparición f.

disappoint [dɪsə'pɔɪnt] vt decepcionar; (hopes) defraudar; **~ed** a decepcionado; **~ing** a decepcionante; **~ment** n decepción f.

disapproval [dɪsə'pru:vəl] n desaprobación f.

disapprove [dɪsə'pru:v] vi: **to ~ of** desaprobar.

disarm [dɪs'ɑ:m] vt desarmar; **~ament** n desarme m.

disarray [dɪsə'reɪ] n: **in ~** (army, organization) desorganizado; (hair, clothes) desarreglado.

disaster [dɪ'zɑ:stəʳ] n desastre m.

disband [dɪs'bænd] vt disolver // vi desbandarse.

disbelief [dɪsbə'li:f] n incredulidad f.

disc [dɪsk] n disco; (COMPUT) = **disk**.

discard [dɪs'kɑ:d] vt (old things) tirar; (fig) descartar.

discern [dɪ'sə:n] vt percibir, discernir; (understand) comprender; **~ing** a perspicaz.

discharge [dɪs'tʃɑ:dʒ] vt (task, duty) cumplir; (ship etc) descargar; (patient) dar de alta; (employee) despedir; (soldier) licenciar; (defendant) poner en libertad // n ['dɪstʃɑ:dʒ] (ELEC) descarga; (dismissal) despedida; (of duty) desempeño; (of debt) pago, descargo.

disciple [dɪ'saɪpl] n discípulo.

discipline ['dɪsɪplɪn] n disciplina // vt disciplinar.

disc jockey n pinchadiscos m/f inv.

disclaim [dɪs'kleɪm] vt negar.

disclose [dɪs'kləʊz] vt revelar; **disclosure** [-'kləʊʒəʳ] n revelación f.

disco ['dɪskəʊ] n abbr = **discothèque**.

discoloured, (US) **discolored** [dɪs'kʌləd] a descolorado.

discomfort [dɪs'kʌmfət] n incomodidad f; (unease) inquietud f; (physi-

cal) malestar *m*.

disconcert [dɪskən'səːt] *vt* desconcertar.

disconnect [dɪskə'nekt] *vt (gen)* separar; *(ELEC etc)* desconectar; *(supply)* cortar (el suministro) a.

discontent [dɪskən'tent] *n* descontento; **~ed** *a* descontento.

discontinue [dɪskən'tɪnjuː] *vt* interrumpir; *(payments)* suspender.

discord ['dɪskɔːd] *n* discordia; *(MUS)* disonancia; **~ant** [dɪs'kɔːdənt] *a* disonante.

discothèque ['dɪskəutek] *n* discoteca.

discount ['dɪskaunt] *n* descuento // *vt* [dɪs'kaunt] descontar.

discourage [dɪs'kʌrɪdʒ] *vt* desalentar; *(oppose)* oponerse a; **discouraging** *a* desalentador(a).

discover [dɪs'kʌvə*] *vt* descubrir; **~y** *n* descubrimiento.

discredit [dɪs'kredɪt] *vt* desacreditar.

discreet [dɪ'skriːt] *a (tactful)* discreto; *(careful)* circunspecto, prudente.

discrepancy [dɪ'skrepənsɪ] *n* diferencia.

discretion [dɪ'skreʃən] *n (tact)* discreción *f*; *(care)* prudencia, circunspección *f*.

discriminate [dɪ'skrɪmɪneɪt] *vi*: to ~ **between** distinguir entre; to ~ **against** discriminar contra; **discriminating** *a* entendido; **discrimination** [-'neɪʃən] *n (discernment)* perspicacia; *(bias)* discriminación *f*.

discuss [dɪs'kʌs] *vt (gen)* discutir; *(a theme)* tratar; **~ion** [dɪs'kʌʃən] *n* discusión *f*.

disdain [dɪs'deɪn] *n* desdén *m* // *vt* desdeñar.

disease [dɪ'ziːz] *n* enfermedad *f*.

disembark [dɪsɪm'bɑːk] *vt, vi* desembarcar.

disenchanted [dɪsɪn'tʃɑːntɪd] *a*: ~ **(with)** desilusionado (con).

disengage [dɪsɪn'geɪdʒ] *vt* soltar; to ~ **the clutch** *(AUT)* desembragar.

disentangle [dɪsɪn'tæŋgl] *vt* desenredar.

disfigure [dɪs'fɪgə*] *vt* desfigurar.

disgrace [dɪs'greɪs] *n* ignominia; *(shame)* vergüenza, escándalo // *vt* deshonrar; **~ful** *a* vergonzoso; *(behaviour)* escandaloso.

disgruntled [dɪs'grʌntld] *a* disgustado, descontento.

disguise [dɪs'gaɪz] *n* disfraz *m* // *vt* disfrazar; **in ~** disfrazado.

disgust [dɪs'gʌst] *n* repugnancia // *vt* repugnar, dar asco a; **~ing** *a* repugnante, asqueroso.

dish [dɪʃ] *n (gen)* plato; to **do** or **wash the ~es** fregar los platos; to ~ **up** *vt* servir; to ~ **out** *vt* repartir; **~cloth** *n* paño de cocina, bayeta.

dishearten [dɪs'hɑːtn] *vt* desalentar.

dishevelled [dɪ'ʃevəld] *a (hair)* despeinado; *(clothes, appearance)* desarreglado.

dishonest [dɪs'ɔnɪst] *a (person)* poco honrado, tramposo; *(means)* fraudulento; **~y** *n* falta de honradez.

dishonour, *(US)* **dishonor** [dɪs'ɔnə*] *n* deshonra; **~able** *a* deshonroso.

dishtowel ['dɪʃtauəl] *n (US)* trapo de fregar.

dishwasher ['dɪʃwɔʃə*] *n* lavaplatos *m inv*; *(person)* friegaplatos *m/f inv*.

disillusion [dɪsɪ'luːʒən] *vt* desilusionar.

disincentive [dɪsɪn'sentɪv] *n* desincentivo.

disinfect [dɪsɪn'fekt] *vt* desinfectar; **~ant** *n* desinfectante *m*.

disintegrate [dɪs'ɪntɪgreɪt] *vi* disgregarse, desintegrarse.

disinterested [dɪs'ɪntrəstɪd] *a* desinteresado.

disjointed [dɪs'dʒɔɪntɪd] *a* inconexo.

disk [dɪsk] *n (esp US)* = **disc**; *(COMPUT)* disco, disquete *m*; **single-/double-sided ~** disco de una cara/dos caras; ~ **drive** *n* disc drive *m*; **~ette** *n (US)* = **disk**.

dislike [dɪs'laɪk] *n* antipatía, aversión *f* // *vt* tener antipatía a.

dislocate ['dɪsləkeɪt] *vt* dislocar.

dislodge [dɪs'lɔdʒ] vt sacar; (enemy) desalojar.

disloyal [dɪs'lɔɪəl] a desleal.

dismal ['dɪzml] a (gloomy) deprimente, triste.

dismantle [dɪs'mæntl] vt desmontar, desarmar.

dismay [dɪs'meɪ] n consternación f.

dismiss [dɪs'mɪs] vt (worker) despedir; (official) destituir; (idea, LAW) rechazar; (possibility) descartar // vi (MIL) romper filas; ~**al** n despedida; destitución f.

dismount [dɪs'maunt] vi apearse.

disobedience [dɪsə'biːdɪəns] n desobediencia.

disobedient [dɪsə'biːdɪənt] a desobediente.

disobey [dɪsə'beɪ] vt desobedecer.

disorder [dɪs'ɔːdə*] n desorden m; (rioting) disturbio; (MED) trastorno; (disease) enfermedad f; ~**ly** a (untidy) desordenado; (meeting) alborotado; (conduct) escandaloso.

disorientated [dɪs'ɔːrɪəntatɪd] a desorientado.

disown [dɪs'əun] vt desconocer.

disparaging [dɪs'pærɪdʒɪŋ] a despreciativo.

disparity [dɪs'pærɪtɪ] n disparidad f.

dispassionate [dɪs'pæʃənɪt] a (unbiased) imparcial; (unemotional) desapasionado.

dispatch [dɪs'pætʃ] vt enviar // n (sending) envío; (PRESS) informe m; (MIL) parte m.

dispel [dɪs'pel] vt disipar, dispersar.

dispensary [dɪs'pensərɪ] n dispensario, farmacia.

dispense [dɪs'pens] vt dispensar, repartir; **to ~ with** vt fus prescindir de; ~**r** n (container) distribuidor m automático; **dispensing chemist** n (Brit) farmacia.

dispersal [dɪs'pɜːsl] n dispersión f.

disperse [dɪs'pɜːs] vt dispersar // vi dispersarse.

dispirited [dɪ'spɪrɪtɪd] a desanimado, desalentado.

displace [dɪs'pleɪs] vt (person) des-

plazar; (replace) reemplazar; ~**d person** n (POL) desplazado/a.

display [dɪs'pleɪ] n (exhibition) exposición f; (COMPUT) visualización f; (MIL) exhibición f; (of feeling) manifestación f; (pej) aparato, pompa f // vt exponer; manifestar; (ostentatiously) lucir.

displease [dɪs'pliːz] vt (offend) ofender; (annoy) fastidiar; ~**d** a: ~**d with** disgustado con; **displeasure** [-'pleʒə*] n disgusto.

disposable [dɪs'pəuzəbl] a (not reusable) desechable; (income) disponible; ~ **nappy** n pañal m desechable.

disposal [dɪs'pəuzl] n (sale) venta; (of house) traspaso; (arrangement) colocación f; (of rubbish) destrucción f; **at one's ~** a su disposición.

dispose [dɪs'pəuz] vt disponer; **to ~ of** vt (time, money) disponer de; (unwanted goods) deshacerse de; (throw away) tirar; ~**d** a: ~**d to do** dispuesto a hacer; **disposition** [-'zɪʃən] n disposición f.

disproportionate [dɪsprə'pɔːʃənɪt] a desproporcionado.

disprove [dɪs'pruːv] vt refutar.

dispute [dɪs'pjuːt] n disputa; (verbal) discusión f; (also: **industrial ~**) conflicto (laboral) // vt (argue) disputar; (question) cuestionar.

disqualify [dɪs'kwɔlɪfaɪ] vt (SPORT) desclasificar; **to ~ sb for sth/from doing sth** incapacitar a alguien para algo/hacer algo.

disquiet [dɪs'kwaɪət] n preocupación f, inquietud f.

disregard [dɪsrɪ'gɑːd] vt desatender; (ignore) no hacer caso de.

disrepair [dɪsrɪ'peə*] n: **to fall into ~** desmoronarse.

disreputable [dɪs'repjutəbl] a (person) de mala fama; (behaviour) vergonzoso.

disrespectful [dɪsrɪ'spektful] a irrespetuoso.

disrupt [dɪs'rʌpt] vt (plans) desbaratar, trastornar; (conversation) interrumpir; ~ion [-'rʌpʃən] n trastorno; desbaratamiento; interrupción f.

dissatisfaction [dɪssætɪs'fækʃən] n disgusto, descontento.

dissect [dɪ'sɛkt] vt disecar.

disseminate [dɪ'sɛmɪneɪt] vt divulgar, difundir.

dissent [dɪ'sɛnt] n disensión f.

dissertation [dɪsə'teɪʃən] n tesina.

disservice [dɪs'sɜːvɪs] n: to do sb a ~ perjudicar a alguien.

dissident ['dɪsɪdnt] a, n disidente m/f.

dissimilar [dɪ'sɪmɪlə*] a distinto.

dissipate ['dɪsɪpeɪt] vt disipar; (waste) desperdiciar.

dissociate [dɪ'səʊʃɪeɪt] vt disociar.

dissolute ['dɪsəluːt] a disoluto.

dissolution [dɪsə'luːʃən] n (of organization, marriage, POL) disolución f.

dissolve [dɪ'zɒlv] vt disolver // vi disolverse.

dissuade [dɪ'sweɪd] vt: to ~ sb (from) disuadir a uno (de).

distance ['dɪstns] n distancia; in the ~ a lo lejos.

distant ['dɪstnt] a lejano; (manner) reservado, frío.

distaste [dɪs'teɪst] n repugnancia; ~ful a repugnante, desagradable.

distended [dɪ'stɛndɪd] a (stomach) hinchado.

distil [dɪs'tɪl] vt destilar; ~lery n destilería.

distinct [dɪs'tɪŋkt] a (different) distinto; (clear) claro; (unmistakeable) inequívoco; as ~ from a diferencia de; ~ion [dɪs'tɪŋkʃən] n distinción f; (in exam) sobresaliente m; ~ive a distintivo.

distinguish [dɪs'tɪŋgwɪʃ] vt distinguir; ~ed a (eminent) distinguido; ~ing a (feature) distintivo.

distort [dɪs'tɔːt] vt torcer, retorcer; ~ion [dɪs'tɔːʃən] n deformación f; (of sound) distorsión f.

distract [dɪs'trækt] vt distraer; ~ed a distraído; ~ion [dɪs'trækʃən] n distracción f; (confusion) aturdimiento.

distraught [dɪs'trɔːt] a turbado, enloquecido.

distress [dɪs'trɛs] n (anguish) angustia; (pain) dolor m // a afligir; (pain) doler; ~ing a angustioso; doloroso; ~ signal n señal f de socorro.

distribute [dɪs'trɪbjuːt] vt (gen) distribuir; (share out) repartir; **distribution** [-'bjuːʃən] n distribución f; **distributor** n (AUT) distribuidor m; (COMM) distribuidora.

district ['dɪstrɪkt] n (of country) zona, región f; (of town) barrio; (ADMIN) distrito; ~ **attorney** n (US) fiscal m/f; ~ **nurse** n (Brit) enfermera que atiende a pacientes a domicilio.

distrust [dɪs'trʌst] n desconfianza // vt desconfiar de.

disturb [dɪs'tɜːb] vt (person: bother, interrupt) molestar; (meeting) interrumpir; ~**ance** n (political etc) disturbio; (violence) alboroto; ~**ed** a (worried, upset) preocupado, angustiado; **emotionally** ~**ed** trastornado; ~**ing** a inquietante, perturbador(a).

disuse [dɪs'juːs] n: to fall into ~ caer en desuso.

disused [dɪs'juːzd] a abandonado.

ditch [dɪtʃ] n zanja; (irrigation ~) acequia // vt (col) deshacerse de.

dither ['dɪðə*] vi vacilar.

ditto ['dɪtəʊ] ad ídem, lo mismo.

dive [daɪv] n (from board) salto; (underwater) buceo; (of submarine) sumersión f; (AVIAT) picada // vi saltar; bucear; sumergirse; picar; ~ **r** n (SPORT) saltador(a) m/f; (underwater) buzo.

diverge [daɪ'vɜːdʒ] vi divergir.

diverse [daɪ'vɜːs] a diversos/as, varios/as.

diversion [daɪ'vɜːʃən] n (Brit AUT) desviación f; (distraction, MIL) diversión f.

divert [daɪ'vɜːt] vt (turn aside) desviar.

divide [dɪ'vaɪd] vt dividir; (separate) separar // vi dividirse; (road) bifurcarse; **~d highway** n (US) carretera de doble calzada.

dividend ['dɪvɪdend] n dividendo; (fig) beneficio.

divine [dɪ'vaɪn] a divino.

diving ['daɪvɪŋ] n (SPORT) salto; (underwater) buceo; **~ board** n trampolín m.

divinity [dɪ'vɪnɪtɪ] n divinidad f; (SCOL) teología.

division [dɪ'vɪʒən] n división f; (sharing out) repartimiento.

divorce [dɪ'vɔːs] n divorcio // vt divorciarse de; **~d** a divorciado; **~e** ['-'siː] n divorciado/a.

divulge [daɪ'vʌldʒ] vt divulgar, revelar.

D.I.Y. a, n abbr (Brit) = **do-it-yourself.**

dizziness ['dɪzɪnɪs] n vértigo.

dizzy ['dɪzɪ] a (person) mareado; (height) vertiginoso; **to feel ~** marearse.

DJ n abbr = **disc jockey.**

KEYWORD

do [duː] ♦ n (col: party etc): we're having a little **~** on Saturday damos una fiestecita el sábado; it was rather a grand **~** fue un acontecimiento a lo grande

♦ auxiliary vb (pt did, pp done) 1 (in negative constructions) not translated: I don't understand no entiendo

2 (to form questions) not translated: didn't you know? ¿no lo sabías?; what ~ you think? ¿qué opinas?

3 (for emphasis, in polite expressions): people ~ make mistakes sometimes sí que se cometen errores a veces; she does seem rather late a mí también me parece que se ha retrasado; ~ sit down/help yourself siéntate/sírvete por favor; ~ take care! te pido

4 (used to avoid repeating vb): she sings better than I ~ canta mejor que yo; ~ you agree? — yes, I ~/ no, I don't ¿estás de acuerdo? — sí

(lo estoy)/no (lo estoy); she lives in Glasgow — so ~ I vive en Glasgow — yo también; he didn't like it and neither did we no le gustó y a nosotros tampoco; who made this mess? — I did ¿quién hizo esta chapuza? — yo; he asked me to help him and I did me pidió qué le ayudara y lo hice

5 (in question tags): you like him, don't you? te gusta, ¿verdad? or ¿no?; I don't know him, ~ I? creo que no le conozco

♦ vt 1 (gen, carry out, perform etc): what are you ~ing tonight? ¿qué haces esta noche?; what can I ~ for you? ¿en qué puedo servirle?; to ~ the washing-up/cooking fregar los platos/cocinar; to ~ one's teeth/hair/nails lavarse los dientes/arreglarse el pelo/arreglarse las uñas

2 (AUT etc): the car was ~ing 100 el coche iba a 100; we've done 200 km already ya hemos hecho 200 km; he can ~ 100 in that car puede dar los 100 en ese coche

♦ vi 1 (act, behave) hacer; ~ as I ~ haz como yo

2 (get on, fare): he's ~ing well/badly at school va bien/mal en la escuela; the firm is ~ing well la empresa anda or va bien; how ~ you ~? mucho gusto; (less formal) ¿qué tal?

3 (suit): will it ~? ¿sirve?, ¿está or va bien?

4 (be sufficient): bastar; will £10 ~? ¿será bastante con £10?; that'll ~ así está bien; that'll ~! (in annoyance) ¡ya está bien!, ¡basta ya!; to make ~ (with) arreglárselas (con)

to ~ away with vt fus (kill, disease) eliminar; (abolish: law etc) abolir; (withdraw) retirar

to ~ up vt (laces) atar; (zip, dress, shirt) abrochar; (renovate: room, house) renovar

to ~ with vt fus (need): I could ~ with a drink/some help no me ven-

dría mal un trago/un poco de ayuda; (*be connected*): tener que ver con; **what has it got to ~ with you?** ¿qué tiene que ver contigo?
to do without *vi* pasar sin; **if you're late for tea then you'll go without** si llegas tarde para la merienda pasarás sin él ♦ *vt fus* pasar sin; **I can ~ without a car** puedo pasar sin coche.

dock [dɔk] *n* (NAUT) muelle *m*; (LAW) banquillo (de los acusados); **~s** *npl* muelles *mpl*, puerto *sg* // *vi* (*enter ~*) atracar en el muelle; **~er** *n* trabajador *m* portuario, estibador *m*; **~yard** *n* astillero.

doctor ['dɔktə*] *n* médico/a; (Ph.D. etc) doctor(a) *m/f* // *vt* (*fig*) arreglar, falsificar; (*drink etc*) adulterar; **D~ of Philosophy (Ph.D.)** *n* Doctor en Filosofía y Letras.

doctrine ['dɔktrın] *n* doctrina.

document ['dɔkjumənt] *n* documento; **~ary** [-'mɛntərı] *a* documental // *n* documental *m*.

dodge [dɔdʒ] *n* (*of body*) regate *m*; (*fig*) truco *m* // *vt* (*gen*) evadir; (*blow*) esquivar.

dodgems ['dɔdʒəmz] *npl* (Brit) coches *mpl* de choque.

doe [dəu] *n* (*deer*) cierva, gama; (*rabbit*) coneja.

does [dʌz] *vb* see **do**; **~n't** = = **not**.

dog [dɔg] *n* perro // *vt* seguir los pasos de; **~ collar** *n* collar *m* de perro; (*fig*) cuello de cura; **~-eared** *a* sobado.

dogged ['dɔgıd] *a* tenaz, obstinado.

dogsbody ['dɔgzbɔdı] *n* (Brit) burro de carga.

doings ['duıŋz] *npl* (*events*) sucesos *mpl*; (*acts*) hechos *mpl*.

do-it-yourself [du:ıtjɔ:'sɛlf] *n* bricolaje *m*.

doldrums ['dɔldrəmz] *npl*: **to be in the ~** (*person*) estar abatido; (*business*) estar encalmado.

dole [dəul] *n* (Brit: *payment*) subsi-

dio de paro; **on the ~** parado; **to ~ out** *vt* repartir.

doleful ['dəulful] *a* triste, lúgubre.

doll [dɔl] *n* muñeca; **to ~ o.s. up** ataviarse.

dollar ['dɔlə*] *n* dólar *m*.

dolphin ['dɔlfın] *n* delfín *m*.

domain [də'meın] *n* (*fig*) campo, competencia; (*land*) dominios *mpl*.

dome [dəum] *n* (ARCH) cúpula; (*shape*) bóveda.

domestic [də'mɛstık] *a* (*animal*, *duty*) doméstico; (*flight, policy*) nacional; **~ated** *a* domesticado; (*home-loving*) casero, hogareño.

dominant ['dɔmınənt] *a* dominante.

dominate ['dɔmıneıt] *vt* dominar.

domineering [dɔmı'nıərıŋ] *a* dominante.

dominion [də'mınıən] *n* dominio.

domino ['dɔmınəu], *pl* **~es** *n* ficha de dominó; **~es** *n* (*game*) dominó.

don [dɔn] *n* (Brit) profesor(a) *m/f* universitario/a.

donate [də'neıt] *vt* donar; **donation** [də'neıʃən] *n* donativo.

done [dʌn] *pp* of **do**.

donkey ['dɔŋkı] *n* burro.

donor ['dəunə*] *n* donante *m/f*.

don't [dəunt] = **do not**.

doodle ['du:dl] *vi* hacer dibujitos or garabatos.

doom [du:m] *n* (*fate*) suerte *f*; (*death*) muerte *f* // *vt*: **to be ~ed to failure** ser condenado al fracaso; **~sday** *n* día *m* del juicio final.

door [dɔ:*] *n* puerta; (*entry*) entrada; **~bell** *n* timbre *m*; **~ handle** *n* tirador *m*; (*of car*) manija; **~man** *n* (*in hotel*) portero; **~mat** *n* felpudo, estera; **~step** *n* peldaño; **~way** *n* entrada, puerta.

dope [dəup] *n* (col: *person*) imbécil *m/f* // *vt* (*horse etc*) drogar.

dopey ['dəupı] *a* atontado.

dormant ['dɔ:mənt] *a* inactivo; (*latent*) latente.

dormitory ['dɔ:mıtrı] *n* (Brit) dormitorio; (US) colegio mayor.

dormouse ['dɔ:maus], *pl* **-mice**

[-maɪs] n lirón m.

DOS n abbr (= disk operating system) DOS m.

dosage ['dəʊsɪdʒ] n dosis f inv.

dose [dəʊs] n dosis f inv.

doss house ['dɒs-] n (Brit) pensión f de mala muerte.

dossier ['dɒsɪeɪ] n expediente m.

dot [dɒt] n punto; ~ted with salpicado de; **on the** ~ en punto.

dote [dəʊt]: **to** ~ **on** vt fus adorar, idolatrar.

dot matrix printer n impresora matricial (or de matriz) de puntos.

double ['dʌbl] a doble // ad (twice): **to cost** ~ costar el doble // n (gen) doble m // vt doblar; (efforts) redoblar // vi doblarse; **on the** ~, (Brit) **at the** ~ corriendo; ~s n (TENNIS) juego de dobles; ~ **bass** n contrabajo; ~ **bed** n cama matrimonial; ~ **bend** n (Brit) doble curva; ~**breasted** a cruzado; ~**cross** vt (trick) engañar; (betray) traicionar; ~**decker** n autobús m de dos pisos; ~ **glazing** n (Brit) doble acristalamiento; ~ **room** n cuarto para dos; **doubly** ad doblemente.

doubt [daʊt] n duda // vt dudar; (suspect) dudar de; **to** ~ **that** dudar que; **there is no** ~ **that** no cabe duda de que; ~**ful** a (person): **to be** ~**ful about sth** tener dudas sobre algo; ~**less** ad sin duda.

dough [dəʊ] n masa, pasta; ~**nut** n buñuelo.

douse [daʊs] vt (drench) mojar; (extinguish) apagar.

dove [dʌv] n paloma.

dovetail ['dʌvteɪl] vi (fig) encajar.

dowdy ['daʊdɪ] a (person) mal vestido; (clothes) pasado de moda.

down [daʊn] n (fluff) pelusa; (feathers) plumón m, flojel m // ad (~wards) abajo, hacia abajo; (on the ground) por tierra // prep abajo // vt (col: drink) beberse; ~ **with X!** ¡abajo X!; ~ **under** (Australia etc) Australia, Nueva Zelanda; ~**-and-out** n vagabundo/a; ~**at-**

heel a venido a menos; (appearance) desaliñado; ~**cast** a abatido; ~**fall** n caída, ruina; ~**hearted** a desanimado; ~**hill** ad: **to go** ~**hill** ir cuesta abajo; ~ **payment** n entrada, pago al contado; ~**pour** n aguacero; ~**right** a (nonsense, lie) manifiesto; (refusal) terminante; ~**stairs** ad (below) en la casa de abajo; (~wards) escaleras abajo; ~**stream** ad aguas or río abajo; ~**to-earth** a práctico; ~**town** ad en el centro de la ciudad; ~**ward** a, ad [-wəd], ~**wards** [-wədz] ad hacia abajo.

dowry ['daʊrɪ] n dote f.

doz. abbr = **dozen.**

doze [dəʊz] vi dormitar; **to** ~ **off** vi quedarse medio dormido.

dozen ['dʌzn] n docena; **a** ~ **books** una docena de libros; ~**s of** cantidad de.

Dr. abbr = **doctor; drive.**

drab [dræb] a gris, monótono.

draft [drɑːft] n (first copy) borrador m; (COMM) giro; (US: call-up) quinta // vt (write roughly) hacer un borrador de; see also **draught.**

draftsman ['drɑːftsmən] n (US) = **draughtsman.**

drag [dræg] vt arrastrar; (river) dragar, rastrear // vi arrastrarse por el suelo // n (col) lata; (women's clothing): **in** ~ vestido de travesti; **to** ~ **on** vi ser interminable.

dragon ['drægən] n dragón m.

dragonfly ['drægənflaɪ] n libélula.

drain [dreɪn] n desaguadero; (in street) sumidero // vt (land, marshes) desaguar; (MED) drenar; (reservoir) desecar; (fig) agotar // vi escurrirse; **to be a** ~ **on** agotar; ~**age** n (act) desagüe m; (MED, AGR) drenaje m; (sewage) alcantarillado; ~**ing board**, (US) ~**board** n escurridera, escurridor m; ~**pipe** n tubo de desagüe.

dram [dræm] n (drink) traguito, copita.

drama ['drɑːmə] n (art) teatro;

(*play*) drama *m*; ~**tic** [dra'mætik] *a* dramático; ~**tist** ['dræmətist] *n* dramaturgo/a; ~**tize** ['dræmətaiz] *vt* (*events*) dramatizar; (*adapt: for TV, cinema*) adaptar a la televisión al cine.

drank [dræŋk] *pt of* **drink**.

drape [dreip] *vt* cubrir; ~**s** *npl* (*US*) cortinas *fpl*; ~**r** *n* (*Brit*) pañero/a.

drastic ['dræstik] *a* (*measure, reduction*) severo; (*change*) radical.

draught, (*US*) **draft** [drɑ:ft] *n* (*of air*) corriente *f* de aire; (*drink*) trago; (*NAUT*) calado; ~**s** *n* (*Brit*) juego de damas; **on** ~ (*beer*) de barril; ~**board** (*Brit*) *n* tablero de damas.

draughtsman ['drɑ:ftsmən] *n* delineante *m*.

draw [drɔ:] *vb* (*pt* **drew**, *pp* **drawn**) *vt* (*pull*) tirar; (*take out*) sacar; (*attract*) atraer; (*picture*) dibujar; (*money*) retirar // *vi* (*SPORT*) empatar // *n* (*SPORT*) empate *m*; (*lottery*) sorteo; (*attraction*) atracción *f*; **to** ~ **near** *vi* acercarse; **to** ~ **out** *vi* (*lengthen*) alargarse; **to** ~ **up** *vi* (*stop*) pararse // *vt* (*document*) redactar; ~**back** *n* inconveniente *m*, desventaja; ~**bridge** *n* puente *m* levadizo.

drawer [drɔ:*] *n* cajón *m*; (*of cheque*) librador(a) *m/f*.

drawing ['drɔ:iŋ] *n* dibujo; ~ **board** *n* tablero de (dibujante); ~ **pin** *n* (*Brit*) chinche *m*; ~ **room** *n* salón *m*.

drawl [drɔ:l] *n* habla lenta y cansina.

drawn [drɔ:n] *pp of* **draw**.

dread [drɛd] *n* pavor *m*, terror *m* // *vt* temer, tener miedo *or* pavor a; ~**ful** *a* espantoso.

dream [dri:m] *n* sueño // *vt, vi* (*pt, pp* **dreamed** *or* **dreamt** [drɛmt]) soñar; ~**er** *n* soñador(a) *m/f*; ~**y** *a* (*distracted*) soñador/a, distraído.

dreary ['drɪərɪ] *a* monótono.

dredge [drɛdʒ] *vt* dragar.

dregs [drɛgz] *npl* heces *fpl*.

drench [drɛntʃ] *vt* empapar.

dress [drɛs] *n* vestido; (*clothing*)

ropa // *vt* vestir; (*wound*) vendar; (*CULIN*) aliñar // *vi* vestirse; **to** ~ **up** *vi* vestirse de etiqueta; (*in fancy dress*) disfrazarse; ~ **circle** *n* (*Brit*) principal *m*; ~**er** *n* (*furniture*) aparador *m*; (*: US*) cómoda con espejo (*THEAT*) camarero/a; ~**ing** *n* (*MED*) vendaje *m*; (*CULIN*) aliño; ~**ing gown** *n* (*Brit*) bata; ~**ing room** *n* (*THEATRE*) camarín *m*; (*SPORT*) vestidor *m*; ~**ing table** *n* tocador *m*; ~**maker** *n* modista, costurera; ~ **rehearsal** *n* ensayo general; ~ **shirt** *n* camisa de frac; ~**y** *a* (*col*) elegante.

drew [dru:] *pt of* **draw**.

dribble ['drɪbl] *vi* gotear, caer gota a gota; (*baby*) babear // *vt* (*ball*) regatear.

dried [draid] *a* (*gen*) seco; (*fruit*) paso; (*milk*) en polvo.

drier ['draiə*] *n* = **dryer**.

drift [drift] *n* (*of current etc*) velocidad *f*; (*of sand*) montón *m*; (*of snow*) ventisquero; (*meaning*) significado // *vi* (*boat*) ir a la deriva; (*sand, snow*) amontonarse; ~**wood** *n* madera de deriva.

drill [drɪl] *n* taladro; (*bit*) broca; (*of dentist*) fresa; (*for mining etc*) perforadora, barrena; (*MIL*) instrucción *f* // *vt* perforar, taladrar // *vi* (*for oil*) perforar.

drink [drɪŋk] *n* bebida // *vt, vi* (*pt* **drank**, *pp* **drunk**) beber; **to have a** ~ tomar algo; tomar una copa *or* un trago; **a** ~ **of water** un trago de agua; ~**er** *n* bebedor/a *m/f*; ~**ing water** *n* agua potable.

drip [drip] *n* (*act*) goteo; (*one* ~) gota; (*MED*) gota a gota *m* // *vi* gotear, caer gota a gota; (*washing*) ~**dry** *a* (*shirt*) de lava y pon; ~**ping** *n* (*animal fat*) pringue *m*.

drive [draiv] *n* paseo (en coche); (*journey*) viaje *m* (en coche); (*also:* ~**way**) entrada; (*energy*) energía, vigor *m*; (*PSYCH*) impulso; (*SPORT*) ataque *m*; (*COMPUT: also:* **disk** ~) drive *m* // *vb* (*pt* **drove**, *pp* **driven**) vt (*car*) conducir, manejar (*LAm*); (*nail*) clavar; (*push*) empujar; (*TECH: motor*) impulsar // vi (*AUT: at controls*) conducir; (: *travel*) pasearse en coche; **left-/right-hand** ~ conducción f a la izquierda/derecha; **to** ~ **sb mad** volverle loco a uno.

drivel ['drɪvl] n (*col*) tonterías fpl.

driven ['drɪvn] pp of **drive**.

driver ['draɪvə*] n conductor m/f, chofer m (*LAm*); (*of taxi, bus*) chofer; ~**'s license** n (*US*) carnet m de conducir.

driveway ['draɪvweɪ] n entrada.

driving ['draɪvɪŋ] n el conducir, el manejar (*LAm*); ~ **instructor** n instructor(a) m/f de conducción o manejo (*LAm*); ~ **lesson** n clase f de conducción o manejo (*LAm*); ~ **licence** n (*Brit*) permiso de conducir; ~ **mirror** n retrovisor m; ~ **school** n autoescuela f; ~ **test** n examen m de conducción o manejo (*LAm*).

drizzle ['drɪzl] n llovizna // vi lloviznar.

droll [drəʊl] a gracioso.

drone [drəʊn] n (*noise*) zumbido.

drool [druːl] vi babear; **to** ~ **over** sth extasiarse ante algo.

droop [druːp] vi (*fig*) decaer, desanimarse.

drop [drɔp] n (*of water*) gota; (*lessening*) baja // vt (*allow to fall*) dejar caer; (*voice, eyes, price*) bajar; (*set down from car*) dejar; (*price, temperature*) bajar; (*wind*) amainar; ~**s** npl (*MED*) gotas fpl; **to** ~ **off** vi (*sleep*) dormirse // vt (*passenger*) bajar; **to** ~ **out** vi (*withdraw*) retirarse; ~**out** n marginado/a; ~**per** n cuentagotas m inv; ~**pings** npl excremento sg.

drought [draut] n sequía.

drove [drəʊv] pt of **drive**.

drown [draun] vt ahogar // vi ahogarse.

drowsy ['drauzɪ] a soñoliento; **to be** ~ tener sueño.

drudgery ['drʌdʒərɪ] n trabajo mo-

nótono.

drug [drʌg] n medicamento; (*narcotic*) droga // vt drogar; ~ **addict** n drogadicto/a; ~**gist** n (*US*) farmacéutico; ~**store** n (*US*) farmacia.

drum [drʌm] n tambor m; (*large*) bombo; (*for oil, petrol*) bidón m; ~**s** npl batería sg // vt tocar el tambor; (*with fingers*) tamborilear; ~**mer** n tambor m.

drunk [drʌŋk] pp of **drink** // a borracho // n (*also*: ~**ard**) borracho/a; ~**en** a borracho.

dry [draɪ] a seco; (*day*) sin lluvia; (*climate*) árido, seco // vt secar; (*tears*) enjugarse // vi secarse; **to** ~ **up** vi agotarse; (*in speech*) atascarse; ~**-cleaner's** n tintorería; ~**cleaning** n lavado en seco; ~**er** n (*for hair*) secador m; (*for clothes*) secadora; ~ **goods store** n (*US*) mercería; ~**ness** n sequedad f; ~**rot** n putrefacción f fungoide.

dual ['djuəl] a doble; ~ **carriageway** n (*Brit*) carretera de doble calzada; ~**-control** n de doble mando; ~ **nationality** n doble nacionalidad f; ~**-purpose** a de doble uso.

dubbed [dʌbd] a (*CINEMA*) doblado.

dubious ['djuːbɪəs] a indeciso; (*reputation, company*) sospechoso.

duchess ['dʌtʃɪs] n duquesa.

duck [dʌk] n pato // vi agacharse; ~**ling** n patito.

duct [dʌkt] n conducto, canal m.

dud [dʌd] n (*shell*) obús m que no estalla; (*object, tool*): **it's a** ~ es una filfa // a: ~ **cheque** (*Brit*) cheque m sin fondos.

due [djuː] a (*proper*) debido; (*fitting*) conveniente, oportuno // ad: ~ **north** derecho al norte; ~**s** npl (*for club, union*) cuota sg; (*in harbour*) derechos mpl; **in** ~ **course** a su debido tiempo; ~ **to** debido a; **to be** ~ **to do** deberse a; **the train is** ~ **to arrive at 8.00** el tren debe llegar a las ocho.

duet [djuː'et] n dúo.

duffel ['dʌfl] a: ~ **bag** n bolsa de

lona; ~ **coat** n comando, abrigo de tres cuartos.

dug [dʌg] pt, pp of **dig**.

duke [djuːk] n duque m.

dull [dʌl] a (light) apagado; (stupid) torpe; (boring) pesado; (sound, pain) sordo; (weather, day) gris // vt (pain, grief) aliviar; (mind, senses) entorpecer.

duly ['djuːlɪ] ad debidamente; (on time) a su debido tiempo.

dumb [dʌm] a mudo; (stupid) estúpido; ~**founded** [dʌm'faundɪd] a pasmado.

dummy ['dʌmɪ] n (tailor's model) maniquí m; (Brit: for baby) chupete m // a falso, postizo.

dump [dʌmp] n (heap) montón m de basura; (place) basurero, vaciadero; (col) casucha; (MIL) depósito // vt (put down) dejar; (get rid of) deshacerse de; ~**ing** n (ECON) dumping m; (of rubbish) 'no ~**ing**' 'prohibido verter basura'.

dumpling ['dʌmplɪŋ] n bola de masa hervida.

dumpy ['dʌmpɪ] a regordete/a.

dunce [dʌns] n zopenco.

dung [dʌŋ] n estiércol m.

dungarees [dʌŋgə'riːz] npl mono sg.

dungeon ['dʌndʒən] n calabozo.

duo ['djuːəu] n (gen, MUS) dúo.

dupe [djuːp] n (victim) víctima // vt engañar.

duplex ['djuːplɛks] n dúplex m.

duplicate n ['djuːplɪkət] n duplicado // vt ['djuːplɪkeɪt] duplicar; (on machine) multicopiar; **in ~** por duplicado.

durable ['djuərəbl] a duradero.

duration [djuə'reɪʃən] n duración f.

duress [djuə'rɛs] n: **under ~** por compulsión.

during ['djuərɪŋ] prep durante.

dusk [dʌsk] n crepúsculo, anochecer m.

dust [dʌst] n polvo // vt (furniture) desempolvorar; (cake etc): **to ~ with** espolvorear de; ~**bin** n (Brit) cubo de la basura, balde m (LAm);

~**er** n paño, trapo; (feather ~er) plumero; ~ **jacket** n sobrecubierta; ~**man** n (Brit) basurero; ~**y** a polvoriento.

Dutch [dʌtʃ] a holandés/esa // n (LING) holandés m; **the ~** npl los holandeses; **to go ~** pagar cada uno lo suyo; ~**man/woman** n holandés/esa m/f.

dutiful ['djuːtɪful] a obediente, sumiso.

duty ['djuːtɪ] n deber m; (tax) derechos mpl de aduana; **on ~** de servicio; (at night etc) de guardia; **off ~** libre (de servicio); ~**-free** a libre de derechos de aduana.

duvet ['duːveɪ] n (Brit) edredón m.

dwarf [dwɔːf], pl **dwarves** [dwɔːvz] n enano/a // vt empequeñecer.

dwell [dwɛl], pt, pp **dwelt** [dwɛlt] vi morar; **to ~ on** vt fus explayarse en; ~**ing** n vivienda.

dwindle ['dwɪndl] vi menguar, disminuir.

dye [daɪ] n tinte m // vt teñir.

dying ['daɪɪŋ] a moribundo, agonizante; (moments) final; (words) último.

dyke [daɪk] n (Brit) dique m.

dynamic [daɪ'næmɪk] a dinámico.

dynamite ['daɪnəmaɪt] n dinamita.

dynamo ['daɪnəməu] n dínamo f.

dynasty ['dɪnəstɪ] n dinastía.

E

E [iː] n (MUS) mi m.

each [iːtʃ] a cada inv // pron cada uno; ~ **other** el uno al otro; **they hate ~ other** se odian (entre ellos o mutuamente); **they have 2 books ~** tienen 2 libros por persona.

eager ['iːgə*] a (gen) impaciente; (hopeful) ilusionado; (keen) entusiasmado; **to be ~ to do sth** tener muchas ganas de hacer algo, impacientarse por hacer algo; **to be ~ for** (news) esperar ansiosamente.

eagle ['iːgl] n águila f.

ear [ɪə*] n oreja; (sense of hearing) oído; (of corn) espiga; **~ache** n dolor m de oídos; **~drum** n tímpano.

earl [ə:l] n conde m.

early ['ə:lɪ] ad (gen) temprano; (before time) con tiempo, con anticipación // a (gen) temprano; (reply) pronto; **to have an ~ night** acostarse temprano; **in the ~ or ~ in the spring/19th century** a principios de primavera/del siglo diecinueve; **~ retirement** n jubilación f anticipada.

earmark ['ɪəmɑ:k] vt: **to ~ (for)** reservar (para), destinar (a).

earn [ə:n] vt (gen) ganar; (salary) percibir; (interest) devengar; (praise) merecerse.

earnest ['ə:nɪst] a serio, formal; **in ~** ad en serio.

earnings ['ə:nɪŋz] npl (personal) sueldo sg, ingresos mpl; (company) ganancias fpl.

ear: **~phones** npl auriculares mpl; **~ring** n pendiente m, arete m; **~shot** n: **within ~shot** al alcance del oído.

earth [ə:θ] n (gen) tierra; (Brit: ELEC) cable m de toma de tierra // vt (Brit: ELEC) conectar a tierra; **~enware** n loza (de barro); **~quake** n terremoto; **~y** a (fig: uncomplicated) sencillo; (: sensual) sensual.

earwig ['ɪəwɪg] n tijereta.

ease [i:z] n facilidad f; (comfort) comodidad f // vt (task) facilitar; (pain) aliviar; (loosen) soltar; (help pass): **to ~ sth in/out** meter/sacar algo con cuidado; **at ~!** (MIL) ¡descansen!; **to ~ off or up** vi (work, business) aflojar; (person) relajarse.

easel ['i:zl] n caballete m.

easily ['i:zɪlɪ] ad fácilmente; **it is ~ the best** es con mucho el/la mejor.

east [i:st] n este m, oriente m // a del este, oriental // ad al este, hacia el este; **the E~** el Oriente.

Easter ['i:stə*] n Pascua (de Resurrección); **~ egg** n huevo de Pascua.

easterly ['i:stəlɪ] a (to the east) al este; (from the east) del este.

eastern ['i:stən] a del este, oriental.

East Germany n Alemania Oriental.

eastward(s) ['i:stwəd(z)] ad hacia el este.

easy ['i:zɪ] a fácil; (problem) sencillo; (comfortable) holgado, cómodo; (relaxed) natural, llano // ad: **to take it or things ~** (not worry) tomarlo con calma; (go slowly) ir despacio; (rest) descansar; **~ chair** n sillón m; **~-going** a acomodadizo.

eat [i:t], pt **ate**, pp **eaten** ['i:tn] vt comer; **to ~ into**, **to ~ away** at vt fus corroer; (wear away) desgastar.

eau de Cologne [əudəkə'ləun] n (agua de) Colonia.

eaves [i:vz] npl alero sg.

eavesdrop ['i:vzdrop] vi: **to ~ (on a conversation)** escuchar (una conversación) a escondidas.

ebb [eb] n reflujo // vi bajar; (fig: also: **~ away**) decaer; **~ tide** n marea menguante.

ebony ['ebənɪ] n ébano.

eccentric [ɪk'sentrɪk] a, n excéntrico/a.

echo ['ekəu], pl **~es** n eco m // vt (sound) repetir // vi resonar, hacer eco.

eclipse [ɪ'klɪps] n eclipse m.

ecology [ɪ'kɔlədʒɪ] n ecología.

economic [i:kə'nɔmɪk] a económico; (business etc) rentable; **~al** a económico; **~s** n economía.

economize [ɪ'kɔnəmaɪz] vi economizar, ahorrar.

economy [ɪ'kɔnəmɪ] n economía.

ecstasy ['ekstəsɪ] n éxtasis m inv; **ecstatic** [-'tætɪk] a extático.

Ecuador ['ekwədɔ:r] n Ecuador m; **E~ian** a, n ecuatoriano/a m/f.

eczema ['eksɪmə] n eczema m.

edge [edʒ] n (of knife etc) filo; (of object) borde m; (of lake etc) orilla // vt (SEWING) ribetear; **on ~** (fig)

edgy; to ~ **away from** alejarse poco a poco de; ~**ways** *ad*: **he couldn't get a word in** ~**ways** no pudo meter ni baza; **edging** *n* (*SEWING*) ribete *m*; (*of path*) borde *m*.

edgy ['edʒɪ] *a* nervioso, inquieto.

edible ['edɪbl] *a* comestible.

edict ['iːdɪkt] *n* edicto.

edifice ['edɪfɪs] *n* edificio.

Edinburgh ['edɪnbərə] *n* Edimburgo.

edit ['edɪt] *vt* (*be editor of*) dirigir; (*rewrite*) redactar; (*cut*) cortar; ~**ion** [ɪ'dɪʃən] *n* (*gen*) edición *f*; (*number printed*) tirada; ~**or** *n* (*of newspaper*) director(a) *m/f*; (*of book*) redactor(a) *m/f*; ~**orial** [-'tɔːrɪəl] *a* editorial // *n* editorial *m*.

educate ['edjukeɪt] *vt* (*gen*) educar; (*instruct*) instruir.

education [edju'keɪʃən] *n* educación *f*; (*schooling*) enseñanza; (*SCOL*) pedagogía; (*teaching*) docente. ~**al** *a* (*scol etc*) educacional; (*teaching*) docente.

EEC *n abbr* (= *European Economic Community*) CEE *f*.

eel [iːl] *n* anguila.

eerie ['ɪərɪ] *a* (*sound, experience*) espeluznante.

effect [ɪ'fekt] *n* efecto // *vt* efectuar, llevar a cabo; ~**s** *npl* efectos *mpl*; **to take** ~ (*law*) entrar en vigor or vigencia; (*drug*) surtir efecto; **in** ~ en realidad; ~**ive** *a* (*gen*) eficaz; (*real*) efectivo; **to become** ~**ive** (*law*) entrar en vigor; ~**ively** *ad* eficazmente; efectivamente; ~**iveness** *n* eficacia.

effeminate [ɪ'femɪnɪt] *a* afeminado.

efficiency [ɪ'fɪʃənsɪ] *n* (*gen*) eficiencia; (*of machine*) rendimiento.

efficient [ɪ'fɪʃənt] *a* eficaz; (*person*) eficiente.

effigy ['efɪdʒɪ] *n* efigie *f*.

effort ['efət] *n* esfuerzo; ~**less** *a* sin ningún esfuerzo.

effrontery [ɪ'frʌntərɪ] *n* descaro.

effusive [ɪ'fjuːsɪv] *a* efusivo.

e.g. *ad abbr* (= *exempli gratia*) p. ej.

egg [eg] *n* huevo; **hard-boiled/soft-**

boiled/poached ~ huevo duro/pasado por agua/escalfado; **scrambled** ~**s** huevos revueltos; **to** ~ **on** *vt* incitar; ~**cup** *n* huevera; ~**plant** *n* (*esp US*) berenjena; ~**shell** *n* cáscara de huevo.

ego ['iːgəu] *n* ego; ~**tism** *n* egoísmo; ~**tist** *n* egoísta *m/f*.

Egypt ['iːdʒɪpt] *n* Egipto; ~**ian** [ɪ'dʒɪpʃən] *a*, *n* egipcio/a *m/f*.

eiderdown ['aɪdədaun] *n* edredón *m*.

eight [eɪt] *num* ocho; ~**een** *num* diez y ocho, dieciocho; ~**h** *a*, *n* octavo; ~**y** *num* ochenta.

Eire ['ɛərə] *n* Eire *m*.

either ['aɪðə*] *a* a cualquier de los dos; (*both, each*) cada; **on** ~ **side** en ambos lados // *pron*: ~ (*of them*) cualquiera de los dos; **I don't like** ~ no me gusta ninguno de los dos // *ad* tampoco; **no, I don't** ~ no, yo tampoco // *conj*: ~ **yes or no** o sí o no.

eject [ɪ'dʒekt] *vt* echar; (*tenant*) desahuciar; ~**or seat** *n* asiento proyectable.

eke [iːk]: **to** ~ **out** *vt* (*money*) hacer que alcance; (*add to*) suplir las deficiencias de.

elaborate [ɪ'læbərɪt] *a* (*design*) elaborado; (*pattern*) intrincado // [ɪ'læbəreɪt] *vt* elaborar // *vi* explicarse con muchos detalles.

elapse [ɪ'læps] *vi* transcurrir.

elastic [ɪ'læstɪk] *a*, *n* elástico; ~ **band** *n* (*Brit*) gomita.

elated [ɪ'leɪtɪd] *a*: **to be** ~ regocijarse; **elation** [ɪ'leɪʃən] *n* regocijo.

elbow [elbəu] *n* codo.

elder ['eldə*] *a* mayor // *n* (*tree*) saúco; (*person*) mayor; (*of tribe*) anciano; ~**ly** *a* de edad, mayor // *npl*: **the** ~**ly** los mayores.

eldest ['eldɪst] *a*, *n* el/la mayor.

elect [ɪ'lekt] *vt* elegir; **to** ~ **to do** optar por hacer // *a*: **the president** ~ el presidente electo; ~**ion** [ɪ'lekʃən] *n* elección *f*; ~**ioneering** [ɪlekʃə'nɪərɪŋ] *n* campaña electoral; ~**or** *n* elector(a) *m/f*; ~**oral** *a* electoral; ~**orate** *n* electorado.

electric [ɪˈlɛktrɪk] a eléctrico; **~al** a eléctrico; **~ blanket** n manta eléctrica; **~ cooker** n cocina eléctrica; **~ fire** n estufa eléctrica.

electrician [ɪlɛkˈtrɪʃən] n electricista m/f.

electricity [ɪlɛkˈtrɪsɪtɪ] n electricidad f.

electrify [ɪˈlɛktrɪfaɪ] vt (RAIL) electrificar; (fig: audience) electrizar.

electron [ɪˈlɛktrɔn] n electrón m.

electronic [ɪlɛkˈtrɔnɪk] a electrónico; **~s** n electrónica.

elegant [ˈɛlɪgənt] a elegante.

element [ˈɛlɪmənt] n (gen) elemento; (of heater, kettle etc) resistencia; **~ary** [-ˈmɛntərɪ] a elemental; (primitive) rudimentario; (school, education) primario.

elephant [ˈɛlɪfənt] n elefante m.

elevate [ˈɛlɪveɪt] vt (gen) elevar; (in rank) ascender.

elevation [ɛlɪˈveɪʃən] n elevación f; (height) altura.

elevator [ˈɛlɪveɪtə*] n (US) ascensor m.

eleven [ɪˈlɛvn] num once; **~ses** npl (Brit) café de las once; **~th** a undécimo.

elicit [ɪˈlɪsɪt] vt: to ~ (from) sacar (de).

eligible [ˈɛlɪdʒəbl] a elegible; to be ~ for sth llenar los requisitos para algo.

eliminate [ɪˈlɪmɪneɪt] vt eliminar; (strike out) suprimir; (suspect) descartar.

elm [ɛlm] n olmo.

elongated [ˈiːlɔŋgeɪtɪd] a alargado, estirado.

elope [ɪˈləup] vi fugarse (para casarse); **~ment** n fuga.

eloquent [ˈɛləkwənt] a elocuente.

else [ɛls] ad: something ~ otra cosa; somewhere ~ en otra parte; everywhere ~ en todas partes menos aquí; where ~? ¿dónde más?, ¿en qué otra parte?; there was little ~ to do apenas quedaba otra cosa que hacer; nobody ~ spoke no

habló nadie más; **~where** ad (be) en otra parte; (go) a otra parte.

elucidate [ɪˈluːsɪdeɪt] vt aclarar.

elude [ɪˈluːd] vt eludir; (blow, pursuer) esquivar.

elusive [ɪˈluːsɪv] a esquivo; (answer) difícil de encontrar.

emaciated [ɪˈmeɪsɪeɪtɪd] a demacrado.

emanate [ˈɛmǝneɪt] vi: to ~ from (idea) surgir de; (light, smell) proceder de.

emancipate [ɪˈmænsɪpeɪt] vt emancipar.

embankment [ɪmˈbæŋkmǝnt] n terraplén m; (riverside) dique m.

embargo [ɪmˈbɑːgǝu], pl **~es** n prohibición f.

embark [ɪmˈbɑːk] vi embarcarse // vt embarcar; to ~ on (fig) emprender, lanzarse a; (venture) embarcarse en; **~ation** [ɛmbɑːˈkeɪʃǝn] n (people) embarco; (goods) embarque m.

embarrass [ɪmˈbærǝs] vt avergonzar; (financially etc) poner en un aprieto; **~ed** a azorado; **~ing** a (situation) violento; (question) embarazoso; **~ment** n desconcierto, azoramiento; (financial) apuros mpl.

embassy [ˈɛmbǝsɪ] n embajada.

embed [ɪmˈbɛd] vt (jewel) empotrar; (teeth etc) clavar.

embellish [ɪmˈbɛlɪʃ] vt embellecer; (fig) adornar.

embers [ˈɛmbǝz] npl rescoldo sg, ascua sg.

embezzle [ɪmˈbɛzl] vt desfalcar, malversar.

embitter [ɪmˈbɪtǝ*] vt (person) amargar; (relationship) envenenar; **~ed** a resentido, amargado.

embody [ɪmˈbɔdɪ] vt (spirit) encarnar; (ideas) expresar.

embossed [ɪmˈbɔst] a realzado.

embrace [ɪmˈbreɪs] vt abrazar, dar un abrazo a; (include) abarcar; (adopt: idea) adherirse a // vi abrazarse // n abrazo.

embroider [ɪmˈbrɔɪdǝ*] vt bordar; (fig: story) adornar, embellecer; **~y**

n bordado.

embryo ['embriəʊ] *n* (*also fig*) embrión *m*.

emerald ['emərəld] *n* esmeralda.

emerge [ı'mɜːdʒ] *vi* (*gen*) salir; (*arise*) surgir; **~nce** *n* salida; surgimiento.

emergency [ı'mɜːdʒənsı] *n* (*event*) emergencia; (*crisis*) crisis *f inv*; **in an ~** en caso de urgencia; **state of ~** estado de emergencia; **~ cord** *n* (*US*) timbre *m* de alarma; **~ exit** *n* salida de emergencia; **~ landing** *n* aterrizaje *m* forzoso; **~ meeting** *n* reunión *f* extraordinaria; **the ~ services** *npl* (*fire, police, ambulance*) los servicios *mpl* de urgencia *or* emergencia.

emery board ['eməri-] *n* lima de uñas.

emigrant ['emıgrənt] *n* emigrante *m/f*.

emigrate ['emıgreıt] *vi* emigrar.

emit [ı'mıt] *vt* emitir; (*smoke*) arrojar; (*smell*) despedir; (*sound*) producir.

emotion [ı'məʊʃən] *n* emoción *f*; **~al** *a* (*person*) sentimental; (*scene*) conmovedor(a), emocionante; **~ally** *ad* con emoción.

emotive [ı'məʊtıv] *a* emotivo.

emperor ['empərə*] *n* emperador *m*.

emphasis ['emfəsıs], *pl* **-ses** [-sız] *n* énfasis *m inv*.

emphasize ['emfəsaız] *vt* (*word, point*) subrayar, recalcar; (*feature*) hacer resaltar.

emphatic [em'fætık] *a* (*reply*) categórico; (*person*) insistente; **~ally** *ad* con énfasis.

empire ['empaıə*] *n* imperio.

employ [ım'plɔı] *vt* emplear; **~ee** [-'iː] *n* empleado/a; **~er** *n* patrón/ona *m/f*; empresario; **~ment** *n* (*gen*) empleo; (*work*) trabajo; **~ment agency** *n* agencia de ocupaciones.

empower [ım'paʊə*] *vt*: **to ~ sb to do sth** autorizar a uno para hacer algo.

empress ['emprıs] *n* emperatriz *f*.

emptiness ['emptınıs] *n* (*gen*) vacío; (*of life etc*) vaciedad *f*.

empty ['emptı] *a* vacío; (*place*) desierto; (*house*) desocupado; (*threat*) vano // *n* (*bottle*) envase *m* // *vt* vaciar; (*place*) dejar vacío // *vi* vaciarse; (*house*) quedar desocupado; (*place*) quedar desierto; **~-handed** *a* con las manos vacías.

emulate ['emjʊleıt] *vt* emular.

emulsion [ı'mʌlʃən] *n* emulsión *f*.

enable [ı'neıbl] *vt*: **to ~ sb to do sth** (*allow*) permitir a uno hacer algo; (*prepare*) capacitar a uno para hacer algo.

enact [ın'ækt] *vt* (*law*) promulgar; (*play*) representar; (*role*) hacer.

enamel [ı'næməl] *n* esmalte *m*.

enamoured [ı'næməd] *a*: **to be ~ of** (*person*) estar enamorado de; (*activity etc*) tener gran afición a; (*idea*) aferrarse a.

encased [ın'keıst] *a*: **~ in** (*covered*) revestido de.

enchant [ın'tʃɑːnt] *vt* encantar; **~ing** *a* encantador(a).

encircle [ın'sɜːkl] *vt* rodear.

encl. *abbr* (= *enclosed*) adj.

enclose [ın'kləʊz] *vt* (*land*) cercar; (*with letter etc*) adjuntar; (*in receptacle*): **to ~ (with)** encerrar (con); **please find ~d** *te* lo mandamos adjunto.

enclosure [ın'kləʊʒə*] *n* cercado, recinto; (*COMM*) adjunto.

encompass [ın'kʌmpəs] *vt* abarcar.

encore [ɔŋ'kɔː*] *excl* ¡otra!, ¡bis! // *n* bis *m*.

encounter [ın'kaʊntə*] *n* encuentro // *vt* encontrar, encontrarse con; (*difficulty*) tropezar con.

encourage [ın'kʌrıdʒ] *vt* alentar, animar; (*growth*) estimular; **~ment** *n* estímulo; (*of industry*) fomento.

encroach [ın'krəʊtʃ] *vi*: **to ~ (up)on** (*gen*) invadir; (*time*) adueñarse de.

encrusted [ın'krʌstəd] *a*: **~ with** incrustado de.

encumber [ın'kʌmbə*] *vt*: **to be**

~ed with (*carry*) estar cargado de; (*debts*) estar gravado de.

encyclop(a)edia [ɛnsaɪkləʊ'piːdɪə] *n* enciclopedia.

end [ɛnd] *n* (*gen, also aim*) fin *m*; (*of table*) extremo; (*of street*) final *m*; (*SPORT*) lado // *vi* terminar, acabar; (*also*: **bring to an ~, put an ~ to**) acabar con // *vi* terminar, acabar; **in the ~** al fin; **~** (*object*) de punta, de cabeza; **to stand on ~** (*hair*) erizarse; **for hours on ~** hora tras hora; **to ~ up** *vi*: **to ~ up in** terminar en; (*place*) ir a parar en.

endanger [ɪn'deɪndʒə*] *vt* poner en peligro.

endearing [ɪn'dɪərɪŋ] *a* simpático, atractivo.

endeavour, (*US*) **endeavor** [ɪn'devə*] *n* esfuerzo; (*attempt*) tentativa // *vi*: **to ~ to do** esforzarse por hacer; (*try*) procurar hacer.

ending ['ɛndɪŋ] *n* fin *m*, conclusión *f*; (*of book*) desenlace *m*; (*LING*) terminación *f*.

endive ['ɛndaɪv] *n* endibia, escarola.

endless ['ɛndlɪs] *a* interminable, inacabable.

endorse [ɪn'dɔːs] *vt* (*cheque*) endosar; (*approve*) aprobar; **~ment** *n* (*on driving licence*) nota de inhabilitación.

endow [ɪn'dau] *vt* (*provide with money*) dotar (*with de*); (*found*) fundar; **to be ~ed with** (*fig*) estar dotado de.

endurance [ɪn'djuərəns] *n* resistencia.

endure [ɪn'djuə*] *vt* (*bear*) aguantar, soportar; (*resist*) resistir // *vi* (*last*) durar; (*resist*) resistir.

enemy ['ɛnəmɪ] *a, n* enemigo/a *m/f*.

energetic [ɛnə'dʒɛtɪk] *a* enérgico.

energy ['ɛnədʒɪ] *n* energía.

enforce [ɪn'fɔːs] *vt* (*LAW*) hacer cumplir; **~d** *a* forzoso, forzado.

engage [ɪn'geɪdʒ] *vt* (*attention*) llamar; (*in conversation*) abordar; (*worker*) contratar; (*clutch*) embragar // *vi* (*TECH*) engranar; **to ~ in**

dedicarse a, ocuparse en; **~d** *a* (*Brit: busy, in use*) ocupado; (*betrothed*) prometido; **to get ~d** prometerse; **he is ~d in research** se dedica a la investigación; **~d tone** *n* (*Brit TEL*) señal *f* de comunicando; **~ment** *n* (*appointment*) compromiso, cita; (*battle*) combate *m*; (*to marry*) compromiso; (*period*) noviazgo; **~ment ring** *n* alianza, anillo de prometida.

engaging [ɪn'geɪdʒɪŋ] *a* atractivo, simpático.

engender [ɪn'dʒɛndə*] *vt* engendrar.

engine ['ɛndʒɪn] *n* (*AUT*) motor *m*; (*RAIL*) locomotora; **~ driver** *n* maquinista *m/f*.

engineer [ɛndʒɪ'nɪə*] *n* ingeniero; (*US RAIL*) maquinista *m/f*; **~ing** *n* ingeniería.

England ['ɪŋglənd] *n* Inglaterra.

English ['ɪŋglɪʃ] *a* inglés/esa // (*LING*) inglés *m*; **the ~ npl** los ingleses *mpl*; **the ~ Channel** *n* (el Canal de) la Mancha; **~man/woman** *n* inglés/esa *m/f*.

engraving [ɪn'greɪvɪŋ] *n* grabado.

engrossed [ɪn'grəust] *a*: **~ in** absorto en.

engulf [ɪn'gʌlf] *vt* sumergir, hundir.

enhance [ɪn'hɑːns] *vt* (*gen*) aumentar; (*beauty*) realzar.

enjoy [ɪn'dʒɔɪ] *vt* (*health, fortune*) disfrutar de, gozar de; (*food*) comer con gusto; **I enjoy dancing** me gusta bailar; **to ~ o.s.** divertirse; **~able** *a* (*pleasant*) agradable; (*amusing*) divertido; **~ment** *n* (*use*) disfrute *m*; (*joy*) placer *m*.

enlarge [ɪn'lɑːdʒ] *vt* aumentar; (*broaden*) extender; (*PHOT*) ampliar // *vi*: **to ~ on** (*subject*) tratar con más detalles.

enlighten [ɪn'laɪtn] *vt* (*inform*) informar; **~ed** *a* iluminado; (*tolerant*) comprensivo; **the E~ment** *n* (*HISTORY*) ≈ la Ilustración, el Siglo de las Luces.

enlist [ɪn'lɪst] *vt* alistar; (*support*) conseguir // *vi* alistarse.

enmity ['ɛnmɪtɪ] n enemistad f.

enormous [ɪ'nɔːməs] a enorme.

enough [ɪ'nʌf] a: ~ time/books bastante tiempo/bastantes libros // n: have you got ~? ¿tiene usted bastante? // ad: big ~ bastante grande; he has not worked ~ no ha trabajado bastante; ~! ¡basta ya!; that's ~, thanks con eso basta, gracias; I've had ~ of him estoy harto de él; ...which, funnily ~ ... ...lo que, por extraño que parezca... .

enquire [ɪn'kwaɪə*] vt, vi = **inquire**.

enrage [ɪn'reɪdʒ] vt enfurecer.

enrich [ɪn'rɪtʃ] vt enriquecer.

enrol [ɪn'rəul] vt (members) inscribir; (SCOL) matricular // vi inscribirse; matricularse; ~ment n inscripción f; matriculación f.

en route [ɔn'ruːt] ad durante el viaje.

ensign ['ɛnsaɪn] n (flag) bandera, (NAUT) alférez m.

enslave [ɪn'sleɪv] vt esclavizar.

ensue [ɪn'sjuː] vi seguirse; (result) resultar.

ensure [ɪn'ʃuə*] vt asegurar.

entail [ɪn'teɪl] vt suponer.

entangle [ɪn'tæŋgl] vt enredar, enmarañar.

enter ['ɛntə*] vt (room) entrar en; (club) hacerse socio de; (army) alistarse en; (sb for a competition) inscribir; (write down) anotar, apuntar; (COMPUT) meter // vi entrar; **to ~ for** vt fus presentarse para; **to ~ into** vt fus (relations) establecer; (plans) formar parte de; (debate) tomar parte en; (agreement) llegar a, firmar; **to ~ (up)on** vt fus (career) emprender.

enterprise ['ɛntəpraɪz] n empresa; (spirit) iniciativa; **free ~** la libre empresa; **private ~** la iniciativa privada; **enterprising** a emprendedor(a).

entertain [ɛntə'teɪn] vt (amuse) divertir; (receive: guest) recibir (en casa); (idea) abrigar; **~er** n artista m/f; **~ing** a divertido, entretenido;

~ment n (amusement) diversión f; (show) espectáculo; (party) fiesta.

enthralled [ɪn'θrɔːld] a encantado.

enthusiasm [ɪn'θuːziæzəm] n entusiasmo.

enthusiast [ɪn'θuːziæst] n entusiasta m/f; **~ic** [-'æstɪk] a entusiasta; **to be ~ic about** entusiasmarse por.

entice [ɪn'taɪs] vt tentar; (seduce) seducir.

entire [ɪn'taɪə*] a entero; **~ly** ad totalmente; **~ty** [ɪn'taɪərətɪ] n: **in its ~ty** en su totalidad.

entitle [ɪn'taɪtl] vt: **to ~ sb to sth** dar a uno derecho a algo; **~d a** (book) que se titula; **to be ~d to** do tener derecho a hacer.

entourage [ɔntu'rɑːʒ] n séquito.

entrails ['ɛntreɪlz] npl entrañas fpl; (US) asadura sg, menudos mpl.

entrance ['ɛntrəns] n entrada // [ɪn'trɑːns] encantar, hechizar; **to gain ~ to** (university etc) ingresar en; **~ examination** n examen m de ingreso; **~ fee** n cuota; **~ ramp** n (US AUT) rampa de acceso.

entrant ['ɛntrənt] n (race, competition) participante m/f; (examination) candidato/a.

entreat [ɛn'triːt] vt rogar, suplicar.

entrenched [ɛn'trentʃd] a: **~ interests** intereses mpl creados.

entrepreneur [ɔntrəprə'nəː] n empresario.

entrust [ɪn'trʌst] vt: **to ~ sth to sb** confiar algo a uno.

entry ['ɛntrɪ] n entrada; (permission to enter) acceso; (in register) apunte m; (in account) partida; **no ~** prohibido el paso; (AUT) dirección prohibida; **~ phone** n portero automático.

enunciate [ɪ'nʌnsɪeɪt] vt pronunciar; (principle etc) enunciar.

envelop [ɪn'vɛləp] vt envolver.

envelope ['ɛnvələup] n sobre m.

envious ['ɛnvɪəs] a envidioso; (look) de envidia.

environment [ɪn'vaɪrənmənt] n medio ambiente; **~al** [-'mɛntl] a ambiental.

envisage [ɪnˈvɪzɪdʒ] vt (foresee) prever; (imagine) concebir.

envoy [ˈenvɔɪ] n enviado.

envy [ˈenvɪ] n envidia // vt tener envidia a; to ~ sb sth envidiar algo a uno.

epic [ˈepɪk] n épica // a épico.

epidemic [epɪˈdemɪk] n epidemia.

epilepsy [ˈepɪlepsɪ] n epilepsia.

episode [ˈepɪsəud] n episodio.

epistle [ɪˈpɪsl] n epístola.

epitome [ɪˈpɪtəmɪ] n epítome m; **epitomize** vt epitomar, resumir.

equable [ˈekwəbl] a (climate) templado; (character) tranquilo, afable.

equal [ˈiːkwl] a (gen) igual; (treatment) equitativo // n igual m/f // vt ser igual a; (fig) igualar; to be ~ to (task) estar a la altura de; ~ity [iːˈkwɔlɪtɪ] n igualdad f; ~ize vt, vi igualar; (SPORT) empatar; ~izer n igualada; ~ly ad igualmente; (share etc) a partes iguales.

equanimity [ekwəˈnɪmɪtɪ] n ecuanimidad f.

equate [ɪˈkweɪt] vt: to ~ sth with equiparar algo con; **equation** [ɪˈkweɪʒən] n (MATH) ecuación f.

equator [ɪˈkweɪtə*] n ecuador m; ~ial [ekwəˈtɔːrɪəl] a ecuatorial.

equilibrium [iːkwɪˈlɪbrɪəm] n equilibrio.

equip [ɪˈkwɪp] vt (gen) equipar; (person) proveer; to be well ~ped estar bien equipado; ~ment n equipo; (tools) avíos mpl.

equitable [ˈekwɪtəbl] a equitativo.

equities [ˈekwɪtɪz] npl (Brit COMM) derechos mpl sobre or en el activo.

equivalent [ɪˈkwɪvələnt] a: ~ (to) equivalente (a) // n equivalente m.

equivocal [ɪˈkwɪvəkl] a equívoco.

era [ˈɪərə] n época.

eradicate [ɪˈrædɪkeɪt] vt erradicar, extirpar.

erase [ɪˈreɪz] vt borrar; ~r n goma de borrar.

erect [ɪˈrekt] a erguido // vt erigir, levantar; (assemble) montar.

erection [ɪˈrekʃən] n construcción f; (assembly) montaje m; (structure) edificio; (MED) erección f.

ermine [ˈəːmɪn] n armiño.

erode [ɪˈrəud] vt (GEO) erosionar; (metal) corroer, desgastar.

erotic [ɪˈrɔtɪk] a erótico.

err [əː*] vi equivocarse; (REL) pecar.

errand [ˈernd] n recado, mandado (LAm); ~ boy n recadero.

erratic [ɪˈrætɪk] a variable; (results etc) desigual, poco uniforme.

erroneous [ɪˈrəunɪəs] a erróneo.

error [ˈerə*] n error m, equivocación f.

erupt [ɪˈrʌpt] vi entrar en erupción; (MED) hacer erupción; (fig) estallar; ~ion [ɪˈrʌpʃən] n erupción f.

escalate [ˈeskəleɪt] vi extenderse, intensificarse.

escalation [eskəˈleɪʃən] n escalamiento, intensificación f.

escalator [ˈeskəleɪtə*] n escalera móvil.

escapade [eskəˈpeɪd] n travesura.

escape [ɪˈskeɪp] n (gen) fuga; (from duties) evasión f // vi (gen) escaparse; (flee) huir, evadirse; (leak) fugarse // vt evitar, eludir; (consequences) escapar a; to ~ from (place) escaparse de; (person) escaparse a; **escapism** n escapismo.

escort [ˈeskɔːt] n acompañante m/f; (MIL) escolta; (NAUT) convoy m // vt [ɪˈskɔːt] acompañar; (MIL, NAUT) escoltar.

Eskimo [ˈeskɪməu] n esquimal m/f.

especially [ɪˈspeʃlɪ] ad (gen) especialmente; (above all) sobre todo; (particularly) en particular.

espionage [ˈespɪənɑːʒ] n espionaje m.

esplanade [espləˈneɪd] n (by sea) paseo marítimo.

espouse [ɪˈspauz] vt adherirse a.

Esquire [ɪˈskwaɪə*] n (abbr Esq.): J. Brown, ~ Sr. D. J. Brown.

essay [ˈeseɪ] n (SCOL) ensayo.

essence [ˈesns] n esencia.

essential [ɪ'sɛnʃl] a (*necessary*) imprescindible; (*basic*) esencial; **~s** npl lo esencial sg; **~ly** ad esencialmente.

establish [ɪ'stæblɪʃ] vt establecer; (*identity*) verificar; (*prove*) demostrar; (*relations*) entablar; **~ment** n establecimiento; **the E~ment** la clase dirigente.

estate [ɪ'steɪt] n (*land*) finca, hacienda; (*property*) propiedad f; (*inheritance*) herencia; (POL) estado; ~ **agent** n (*Brit*) agente m/f inmobiliario/a; ~ **car** n (*Brit*) furgoneta.

esteem [ɪ'stiːm] n: **to hold sb in high** ~ estimar en mucho a alg // vt estimar.

esthetic [ɪs'θɛtɪk] a (US) = **aesthetic**.

estimate ['ɛstɪmət] n estimación f, apreciación f; (*assessment*) tasa, cálculo; (COMM) presupuesto // vt [-meɪt] estimar, tasar, calcular; **estimation** [-'meɪʃən] n opinión f, juicio; (*esteem*) aprecio.

estranged [ɪ'streɪndʒd] a separado.

estuary ['ɛstjuərɪ] n estuario, ría.

etc abbr (= *et cetera*) etc.

etching ['ɛtʃɪŋ] n aguafuerte m o f.

eternal [ɪ'təːnl] a eterno.

eternity [ɪ'təːnɪtɪ] n eternidad f.

ethical ['ɛθɪkl] a ético; (*honest*) honrado.

ethics ['ɛθɪks] n ética // npl moralidad fsg.

Ethiopia [iːθɪ'əupɪə] n Etiopía.

ethnic ['ɛθnɪk] a étnico.

ethos ['iːθɔs] n genio, carácter m.

etiquette ['ɛtɪkɛt] n etiqueta.

Eurocheque [juːərəʊtʃɛk] n Eurocheque m.

Europe ['juərəp] n Europa; **~an** [-'piːən] a, n europeo/a m/f.

evacuate [ɪ'vækjueɪt] vt desocupar; **evacuation** [-'eɪʃən] n evacuación f.

evade [ɪ'veɪd] vt evadir, eludir.

evaluate [ɪ'væljueɪt] vt evaluar; (*value*) tasar; (*evidence*) interpretar.

evangelist [ɪ'vændʒəlɪst] n (*biblical*)

evangelista m; (*preacher*) evangelizador(a) m/f.

evaporate [ɪ'væpəreɪt] vi evaporarse; (*fig*) desvanecerse // vt evaporar; **~d milk** n leche f evaporada.

evasion [ɪ'veɪʒən] n evasiva, evasión f.

eve [iːv] n: **on the** ~ **of** en vísperas de.

even ['iːvn] a (*level*) llano; (*smooth*) liso; (*speed, temperature*) uniforme; (*number*) par; (SPORT) igual(es) // ad hasta, incluso; ~ **if,** ~ **though** aunque + subjun; ~ **more** aun más; ~ **so** aun así; **not** ~ ni siquiera; ~ **he was there** hasta él estuvo allí; ~ **on Sundays** incluso los domingos; **to get** ~ **with sb** ajustar cuentas con uno; **to** ~ **out** vi nivelarse.

evening ['iːvnɪŋ] n tarde f; (*dusk*) atardecer m; (*night*) noche f; **in the** ~ por la tarde; ~ **class** n clase f nocturna; ~ **dress** n (*man's*) traje m de etiqueta; (*woman's*) traje m de noche.

event [ɪ'vɛnt] n suceso, acontecimiento; (SPORT) prueba; **in the** ~ **of** en caso de; ~**ful** a accidentado; (*game etc*) lleno de emoción.

eventual [ɪ'vɛntʃuəl] a final; ~**ity** [-'ælɪtɪ] n eventualidad f; ~**ly** ad (*finally*) finalmente.

ever ['ɛvə] ad nunca, jamás; (*at all times*) siempre; **the best** ~ lo nunca visto; **have you** ~ **seen it?** ¿lo ha visto usted alguna vez?; **better than** ~ mejor que nunca; ~ **since** ad desde entonces // conj después de que; ~**green** n árbol m de hoja perenne; ~**lasting** a eterno, perpetuo.

───────────────

KEYWORD

───────────────

every ['ɛvrɪ] a **1** (*each*) cada; ~ **one of them** (*persons*) todos ellos/as; (*objects*) cada uno de ellos/as; ~ **shop in the town was closed** todas las tiendas de la ciudad estaban cerradas

2 (*all possible*) todo/a; **I gave you** ~ **assistance** te di toda la ayuda posible; **I have ~ confidence in him** tiene toda mi confianza; **we wish you ~ success** te deseamos toda suerte de éxitos

3 (*showing recurrence*) todo/a; **~ day/week** todos los días/todas las semanas; **~ other car had been broken into** habían entrado en uno de cada dos coches; **she visits me ~ other/third day** me visita cada dos/ tres días; **~ now and then** de vez en cuando.

everybody ['εvrɪbɔdɪ] *pron* = **everyone.**

everyone ['εvrɪwʌn] *pron* todos, todo el mundo; **~ knows that** todo el mundo lo sabe; **~ has his own view** cada uno piensa de una manera.

everything ['εvrɪθɪŋ] *pron* todo; **~'s ready** está todo listo; **~ you say is true** todo lo que dices es cierto; **this shop sells ~** esta tienda vende de todo.

everywhere ['εvrɪwεə*] *ad*: **I've been looking for you ~** te he estado buscando por todas partes; **~ you go you meet...** en todas partes encuentras....

evict [ɪ'vɪkt] *vt* desahuciar; **~ion** [ɪ'vɪkʃən] *n* desahucio.

evidence ['εvɪdəns] *n* (*proof*) prueba; (*of witness*) testimonio; (*facts*) datos *mpl*, hechos *mpl*; **to give ~** prestar declaración, dar testimonio.

evident ['εvɪdənt] *a* evidente, manifiesto; **~ly** *ad*: **it is ~ly difficult** por lo visto es difícil.

evil ['iːvl] *a* malo; (*influence*) funesto; (*smell*) horrible // *n* mal *m*, maldad *f*.

evocative [ɪ'vɔkətɪv] *a* sugestivo, evocador(a).

evoke [ɪ'vəuk] *vt* evocar.

evolution [iːvə'luːʃən] *n* evolución *f*, desarrollo.

evolve [ɪ'vɔlv] *vt* desarrollar // *vi* evolucionar, desarrollarse.

ewe [juː] *n* oveja.

ex- [εks] *pref* ex.

exacerbate [εk'sæsəbeɪt] *vt* (*pain, disease*) exacerbar; (*fig*) empeorar.

exact [ɪg'zækt] *a* exacto // *vt*: **to ~ sth (from)** exigir algo (de); **~ing** *a* exigente; (*conditions*) arduo; **~ly** *ad* exactamente.

exaggerate [ɪg'zædʒəreɪt] *vt, vi* exagerar; **exaggeration** [-'reɪʃən] *n* exageración *f*.

exalted [ɪg'zɔːltɪd] *a* (*position*) exaltado; (*elated*) excitado.

exam [ɪg'zæm] *n abbr* (*SCOL*) = **examination.**

examination [ɪgzæmɪ'neɪʃən] *n* (*gen*) examen *m*; (*LAW*) interrogación *f*; (*inquiry*) investigación *f*.

examine [ɪg'zæmɪn] *vt* (*gen*) examinar; (*inspect*) inspeccionar, escudriñar; (*SCOL, LAW: person*) interrogar; (*at customs: luggage*) registrar; **~r** *n* inspector(a) *m/f*.

example [ɪg'zɑːmpl] *n* ejemplo; **for ~** por ejemplo.

exasperate [ɪg'zɑːspəreɪt] *vt* exasperar, irritar; **exasperation** [-ʃən] *n* exasperación *f*, irritación *f*.

excavate ['εkskəveɪt] *vt* excavar.

exceed [ɪk'siːd] *vt* exceder; (*number*) pasar de; (*speed limit*) sobrepasar; (*limits*) rebasar; (*powers*) excederse en; (*hopes*) superar; **~ingly** *ad* sumamente, sobremanera.

excel [ɪk'sεl] *vi* sobresalir.

excellent ['εksələnt] *a* excelente.

except [ɪk'sεpt] *prep* (*also*: **~ for, ~ing**) excepto, salvo // *vt* exceptuar, excluir; **~ if/when** excepto si/ cuando; **~ that** salvo que; **~ion** [ɪk'sεpʃən] *n* excepción *f*; **to take ~ion to** ofenderse por; **~ional** [ɪk'sεpʃənl] *a* excepcional.

excerpt ['εksɜːpt] *n* extracto.

excess [ɪk'sεs] *n* exceso; **~ baggage** *n* exceso de equipaje; **~ fare** *n* suplemento; **~ive** *a* excesivo.

exchange [ɪks'tʃeɪndʒ] *n* cambio; (*of goods*) canje *m*; (*of ideas*) intercambio; (*also*: **telephone ~**) central *f* (telefónica) // *vt*: **to ~ (for)** cam-

biar (por); ~ **rate** n tipo de cambio.
exchequer [ɪks'tʃekə*] n: **the** ~
(Brit) la Hacienda del Fisco.
excise ['eksaɪz] n impuestos mpl sobre el comercio exterior.
excite [ɪk'saɪt] vt (stimulate) estimular; (anger) provocar; (move) entusiasmar; ~**d** a: **to get** ~**d** emocio-
narse; ~**ment** n emoción f; **exciting** a emocionante.
exclaim [ɪk'skleɪm] vi exclamar; **exclamation** [eksklə'meɪʃən] n exclamación f; **exclamation mark** n
punto de admiración.
exclude [ɪk'skluːd] vt excluir; (except) exceptuar.
exclusive [ɪk'skluːsɪv] a exclusivo;
(club, district) selecto; ~ **of tax** ex-
cluyendo impuestos; ~**ly** ad únicamente.
excommunicate [ekskə'mjuːnɪkeɪt]
vt excomulgar.
excruciating [ɪk'skruːʃɪeɪtɪŋ] a
(pain) agudísimo, atroz.
excursion [ɪk'skəːʃən] n excursión f.
excusable [ɪk'skjuːzəbl] a perdona-
ble.
excuse [ɪk'skjuːs] n disculpa, excusa;
(evasion) pretexto // vt [ɪk'skjuːz] disculpar, perdonar; **to** ~ **sb from
doing sth** dispensar a uno de hacer
algo; ~ **me!** ¡perdón!; **if you will**
~ **me** con su permiso.
ex-directory ['eksdɪ'rektərɪ] a (Brit)
que no consta en la guía.
execute ['eksɪkjuːt] vt (plan) realizar; (order) cumplir; (person) ajusti-
ciar, ejecutar; **execution** [-'kjuːʃən]
n realización f; cumplimiento; ejecución f; **executioner** [-'kjuːʃənə*] n
verdugo.
executive [ɪg'zekjutɪv] n (COMM)
ejecutivo; (POL) poder m ejecutivo //
a ejecutivo.
executor [ɪg'zekjutə*] n albacea m,
testamentario.
exemplify [ɪg'zemplɪfaɪ] vt ejemplifi-
car.
exempt [ɪg'zempt] a: ~ **from** exento de // vt: **to** ~ **sb from** eximir a

uno de; ~**ion** [-ʃən] n exención f;
(immunity) inmunidad f.
exercise ['eksəsaɪz] n ejercicio // vt
ejercer; (right) valerse de; (dog) llevar de paseo // vi hacer ejercicio(s);
~ **book** n cuaderno.
exert [ɪg'zəːt] vt ejercer; **to** ~ **o.s.**
esforzarse; ~**ion** [-ʃən] n esfuerzo.
exhale [eks'heɪl] vt despedir // vi exhalar.
exhaust [ɪg'zɔːst] n (pipe) escape m;
(fumes) gases mpl de escape // vt
agotar; ~**ed** a agotado; ~**ion**
[ɪg'zɔːstʃən] n agotamiento; **nervous**
~**ion** postración f nerviosa; ~**ive** a
exhaustivo.
exhibit [ɪg'zɪbɪt] n (ART) obra ex-
puesta; (LAW) objeto expuesto // vt
(show: emotions) manifestar; (: courage, skill) demostrar; (paintings)
exponer; ~**ion** [eksɪ'bɪʃən] n exposición f.
exhilarating [ɪg'zɪləreɪtɪŋ] a estimulante, tónico.
exile ['eksaɪl] n exilio; (person)
exiliado/a // vt desterrar, exiliar.
exist [ɪg'zɪst] vi existir; ~**ence** n
existencia; ~**ing** a existente, actual.
exit ['eksɪt] n salida // vi (THEATRE)
hacer mutis; (COMPUT) salir (al sistema); ~ **ramp** n (US AUT) vía de
acceso.
exodus ['eksədəs] n éxodo.
exonerate [ɪg'zɔnəreɪt] vt: **to** ~
from exculpar de.
exotic [ɪg'zɔtɪk] a exótico.
expand [ɪk'spænd] vt ampliar; (number) aumentar // vi (trade etc) ex-
pandirse; (gas, metal) dilatarse.
expanse [ɪk'spæns] n extensión f.
expansion [ɪk'spænʃən] n ampliación f; aumento; (of trade) expansión
f.
expect [ɪk'spekt] vt (gen) esperar;
(count on) contar con; (suppose) suponer // vi: **to be** ~**ing** estar encinta; ~**ancy** n (anticipation) esperanza; **life** ~**ancy** esperanza de vida;
~**ant mother** n mujer f encinta;
~**ation** [ekspek'teɪʃən] n esperanza,

expectativa.

expedience [ɪk'spiːdɪəns], **expediency** [ɪk'spiːdɪənsɪ] n conveniencia.

expedient [ɪk'spiːdɪənt] a conveniente, oportuno // n recurso, expediente m.

expedition [ɛkspə'dɪʃən] n expedición f.

expel [ɪk'spɛl] vt arrojar; (SCOL) expulsar.

expend [ɪk'spɛnd] vt gastar; (use up) consumir; **~able** a prescindible; **~iture** n gastos mpl, desembolso.

expense [ɪk'spɛns] n gasto, gastos mpl; (high cost) costa; **~s** npl (COMM) gastos mpl; **at the ~ of** a costa de; **~ account** n cuenta de gastos.

expensive [ɪk'spɛnsɪv] a caro, costoso.

experience [ɪk'spɪərɪəns] n experiencia // vt experimentar; (suffer) sufrir; **~d** a experimentado.

experiment [ɪk'spɛrɪmənt] n experimento // vi hacer experimentos; **~al** [-'mɛntl] a experimental.

expert ['ɛkspəːt] a experto, perito // n experto/a, perito/a; (specialist) especialista m/f; **~ise** [-'tiːz] n pericia.

expire [ɪk'spaɪə*] vi (gen) caducar, vencerse; **expiry** n vencimiento.

explain [ɪk'spleɪn] vt explicar; (mystery) aclarar; **explanation** [ɛksplə'neɪʃən] n explicación f; aclaración f; **explanatory** [ɪk'splænətrɪ] a explicativo; aclaratorio.

explicit [ɪk'splɪsɪt] a explícito.

explode [ɪk'spləʊd] vi estallar, explotar; (with anger) reventar // vt volar, explotar.

exploit ['ɛksplɔɪt] n hazaña // vt [ɪk'splɔɪt] explotar; **~ation** [-'teɪʃən] n explotación f.

exploratory [ɛk'splɔrətrɪ] a (fig: talks) exploratorio, preliminar.

explore [ɪk'splɔː*] vt explorar; (fig) examinar, sondear; **~r** n explorador/a m/f.

explosion [ɪk'spləʊʒən] n explosión f.

explosive [ɪks'pləʊsɪv] a, n explosivo.

exponent [ɪk'spəʊnənt] n partidario/a, intérprete m/f.

export [ɪk'spɔːt] vt exportar // n ['ɛkspɔːt] exportación f // cpd de exportación; **~er** n exportador m.

expose [ɪk'spəʊz] vt exponer; (unmask) desenmascarar; **~d** a expuesto.

exposure [ɪk'spəʊʒə*] n exposición f; (PHOT: speed) velocidad f de obturación (: shot) fotografía; **to die from ~** (MED) morir de frío; **~ meter** n fotómetro.

expound [ɪk'spaʊnd] vt exponer.

express [ɪk'sprɛs] a (definite) expreso, explícito; (Brit: letter etc) urgente // n (train) rápido // ad (send) por correo extraordinario // vt expresar; **~ion** [ɪk'sprɛʃən] n expresión f; **~ly** ad expresamente; **~way** n (US: urban motorway) autopista.

exquisite [ɛk'skwɪzɪt] a exquisito.

extend [ɪk'stɛnd] vt (visit, street) prolongar; (building) ensanchar; (thanks, friendship etc) extender // vi (land) extenderse.

extension [ɪk'stɛnʃən] n extensión f; (building) ampliación f; (TEL: line) línea derivada; (: telephone) extensión f; (of deadline) prórroga.

extensive [ɪk'stɛnsɪv] a (gen) extenso; (damage) importante; (knowledge) amplio; **~ly** ad: **he's travelled ~ly** ha viajado por muchos países.

extent [ɪk'stɛnt] n (breadth) extensión f; (scope) alcance m; **to some ~** hasta cierto punto; **to the ~ of...** hasta el punto de...; **to such an ~ that...** hasta tal punto que...; **to what ~?** ¿hasta qué punto?

extenuating [ɪk'stɛnjueɪtɪŋ] a: **~ circumstances** circunstancias fpl atenuantes.

exterior [ɛk'stɪərɪə*] a exterior, externo // n exterior m.

exterminate [ɪk'stəːmɪneɪt] vt exterminar; **extermination** [-'neɪʃən] n exterminación f.

external [ɛkˈstɜːnl] a externo, exterior; **~ly** ad por fuera.

extinct [ɪkˈstɪŋkt] a (volcano) extinguido; (race) extinto.

extinguish [ɪkˈstɪŋgwɪʃ] vt extinguir, apagar; **~er** n extintor m.

extort [ɪkˈstɔːt] vt: to ~ sth from sb sacar algo de uno a la fuerza; **~ion** [ɪkˈstɔːʃən] n exacción f; **~ionate** [ɪkˈstɔːʃnət] a excesivo, exorbitante.

extra [ˈɛkstrə] a adicional // ad (in addition) de más // n (addition) extra m, suplemento; (THEATRE) extra m/f, comparsa m/f; (newspaper) edición f extraordinaria.

extra... [ˈɛkstrə] pref extra... .

extract [ɪkˈstrækt] vt sacar; (tooth) extraer; (confession) arrancar, obtener // n [ˈɛkstrækt] extracto.

extracurricular [ɛkstrəkəˈrɪkjulə*] a extraescolar, extra-académico.

extradite [ˈɛkstrədaɪt] vt extraditar.

extramarital [ɛkstrəˈmærɪtl] a extra-matrimonial.

extramural [ɛkstrəˈmjuərl] a extraescolar.

extraordinary [ɪkˈstrɔːdnrɪ] a extraordinario; (: building) dar a; ~ down raro.

extravagance [ɪkˈstrævəgəns] n prodigalidad f; derroche m; (thing bought) extravagancia.

extravagant [ɪkˈstrævəgənt] a (lavish) pródigo; (wasteful) derrochador(a); (price) exorbitante.

extreme [ɪkˈstriːm] a extremo; (poverty etc) extremado; (case) excepcional // n extremo, extremidad f; **~ly** ad sumamente, extremadamente; **extremist** a, n extremista m/f.

extremity [ɪkˈstrɛmətɪ] n extremidad f, punta; (need) apuro, necesidad f.

extricate [ˈɛkstrɪkeɪt] vt: to ~ o.s. from librarse de.

extrovert [ˈɛkstrəvɜːt] a, n extrovertido/a.

exuberant [ɪgˈzjuːbərnt] a (person) eufórico; (style) exuberante.

exude [ɪgˈzjuːd] vt rezumar, sudar.

exult [ɪgˈzʌlt] vi regocijarse.

eye [aɪ] n ojo // vt mirar de soslayo, ojear; to keep an ~ on vigilar; **~ball** n globo del ojo; **~bath** n ojera; **~brow** n ceja; **~brow pencil** n lápiz m de cejas; **~drops** npl gotas fpl para los ojos; **~lash** n pestaña; **~lid** n párpado; **~liner** n lápiz m de ojos; **~opener** n revelación f, gran sorpresa; **~shadow** n sombreador m de ojos; **~sight** n vista; **~sore** n monstruosidad f; **~witness** n testigo m/f presencial.

F

F [ɛf] n (MUS) fa m.

F. abbr = **Fahrenheit**.

fable [ˈfeɪbl] n fábula.

fabric [ˈfæbrɪk] n tejido, tela.

fabrication [fæbrɪˈkeɪʃən] n invención f.

fabulous [ˈfæbjuləs] a fabuloso.

façade [fəˈsɑːd] n fachada.

face [feɪs] n (ANAT) cara, rostro; (of clock) esfera, cara (LAm); (side, surface) superficie f // vt (subj: person) encararse con; (: building) dar a; ~ down (person, card) boca abajo; to lose ~ desprestigiarse; to make or pull a ~ hacer muecas; in the ~ of (difficulties etc) ante; on the ~ of it a primera vista; ~ to cara a cara; to ~ up to vt fus hacer frente a, arrostrar; ~ cloth n (Brit) manopla; ~ cream n crema (de belleza); ~ lift n estirado facial; ~ powder n polvos mpl; **~-saving** a para salvar las apariencias.

facetious [fəˈsiːʃəs] a chistoso.

face value n (of stamp) valor m nominal; to take sth at ~ (fig) tomar algo en sentido literal.

facile [ˈfæsaɪl] a superficial.

facilities [fəˈsɪlɪtɪz] npl facilidades fpl; credit ~ facilidades de crédito.

facing [ˈfeɪsɪŋ] prep frente a // a de enfrente.

facsimile [fækˈsɪmɪlɪ] n (document) facsímil(e) m; (machine) telefax m.

fact [fækt] n hecho; **in ~** en realidad.

factor ['fæktə*] n factor m.

factory ['fæktərɪ] n fábrica.

factual ['fæktjuəl] a basado en los hechos.

faculty ['fækltɪ] n facultad f; (US: teaching staff) personal m docente.

fad [fæd] n novedad f, moda.

fade [feɪd] vi desteñirse; (sound, hope) desvanecerse; (light) apagarse; (flower) marchitarse.

fag [fæg] n (Brit: col: cigarette) pitillo (Sp), cigarro; (US: pej: homosexual) maricón m.

fail [feɪl] vt (candidate) suspender; (exam) no aprobar (Sp), reprobar (LAm); (subj: memory etc) fallar a // vi suspender; (be unsuccessful) fracasar; (strength, engine) fallar; **to ~ to do sth** (neglect) dejar de hacer algo; (be unable) no poder hacer algo; **without ~** sin falta; **~ing** n falta, defecto // prep a falta de; **~ure** ['feɪljə*] n fracaso; (person) fracasado/a; (mechanical etc) fallo.

faint [feɪnt] a débil; (recollection) vago; (mark) apenas visible // n desmayo // vi desmayarse; **to feel ~** estar mareado, marearse.

fair [feə*] a justo; (hair, person) rubio; (weather) bueno; (good enough) regular; (sizeable) considerable // ad (play) limpio // n feria; (Brit: funfair) parque m de atracciones; **~ly** ad (justly) con justicia; (equally) equitativamente; (quite) bastante; **~ness** n justicia; (impartiality) imparcialidad f; **~ play** n juego limpio.

fairy ['feərɪ] n hada; **~ tale** n cuento de hadas.

faith [feɪθ] n fe f; (trust) confianza; (sect) religión f; **~ful** a fiel; **~fully** ad fielmente; **yours ~fully** (Brit: in letters) le saluda atentamente.

fake [feɪk] n (painting etc) falsificación f; (person) impostor(a) m/f // a falso // vt fingir; (painting etc) falsificar.

falcon ['fɔːlkən] n halcón m.

fall [fɔːl] n caída; (US) otoño // vi (pt **fell**, pp **fallen** ['fɔːlən]) caer(se); (price) bajar; **~s** npl (waterfall) cascada f, salto sg de agua; **to ~ flat** vi (on one's face) caerse (boca abajo); (joke, story) no hacer gracia; **to ~ back** vi retroceder; **to ~ back on** vt fus (remedy etc) recurrir a; **to ~ behind** vi quedarse atrás; **to ~ down** vi (person) caerse; (building, hopes) derrumbarse; **to ~ for** vt fus (trick) dejarse engañar por; (person) enamorarse de; **to ~ in** vi (roof) hundirse; (MIL) alinearse; **to ~ off** vi caerse; (diminish) disminuir; **to ~ out** vi (friends etc) reñir; (MIL) romper filas; **to ~ through** vi (plan, project) fracasar.

fallacy ['fæləsɪ] n error m.

fallen ['fɔːlən] pp of **fall**.

fallout ['fɔːlaut] n lluvia radioactiva; **~ shelter** n refugio antiatómico.

fallow ['fæləu] a en barbecho.

false [fɔːls] a (gen) falso; (hair, teeth etc) postizo; (disloyal) desleal, traidor(a); **under ~ pretences** con engaños; **~ alarm** n falsa alarma; **~ teeth** npl (Brit) dentadura sg postiza.

falter ['fɔːltə*] vi vacilar.

fame [feɪm] n fama.

familiar [fə'mɪlɪə*] a familiar; (well-known) conocido; (tone) de confianza; **to be ~ with** (subject) estar enterado de; **~ity** [fəmɪlɪ'ærɪtɪ] n familiaridad f.

family ['fæmɪlɪ] n familia; **~ business** n negocio familiar; **~ doctor** n médico/a de cabecera.

famine ['fæmɪn] n hambruna.

famished ['fæmɪʃt] a hambriento.

famous ['feɪməs] a famoso, célebre; **~ly** ad (get on) estupendamente.

fan [fæn] n abanico; (ELEC) ventilador m; (person) aficionado/a // vt abanicar; (fire, quarrel) atizar; **to ~ out** vi desparramarse.

fanatic [fə'nætɪk] n fanático/a.

fan belt n correa de ventilador.

fanciful ['fænsiful] a (gen) fantástico; (imaginary) fantasioso.

fancy ['fænsi] n (whim) capricho, antojo; (imagination) imaginación f // a (luxury) de lujo; (price) exorbitado // vt (feel like, want) tener ganas de; (imagine) imaginarse; **to take a ~** to sb tomar cariño a uno; **he fancies her** le gusta (ella) mucho; **~dress** n disfraz m; **~-dress ball** n baile m de disfraces.

fanfare ['fænfɛə'] n fanfarria (de trompeta).

fang [fæŋ] n colmillo.

fantastic [fæn'tæstik] a fantástico.

fantasy ['fæntəzi] n fantasía.

far [fɑ:'] a (distant) lejano // ad lejos; **~ away**, **~ off** (a lo lejos); **~ better** mucho mejor; **~ from** lejos de; **by ~** con mucho; **go as ~ as the farm** vaya hasta la granja; **as ~ as I know** que yo sepa; **how ~?** ¿hasta dónde?; ¿hasta qué punto?; **~away** a remoto.

farce [fɑ:s] n farsa; **farcical** a absurdo.

fare [fɛə'] n (on trains, buses) precio (del billete); (in taxi: cost) tarifa; (: passenger) pasajero/a; (food) comida; **half/full ~** medio pasaje/pasaje m completo.

Far East n: **the ~** el Extremo Oriente.

farewell [fɛə'wɛl] excl, n adiós m.

farm [fɑ:m] n granja, finca (LAm), estancia (LAm) // vt cultivar; **~er** n granjero, estanciero (LAm); **~hand** n peón m, **~house** n granja, casa de hacienda (LAm); **~ing** n (gen) agricultura; (tilling) cultivo; **~land** n tierra de cultivo; **~ worker** n = **~hand**; **~yard** n corral m.

far-reaching [fɑ:'ri:tʃiŋ] a (reform, effect) de gran alcance.

fart [fɑ:t] (col!) n pedo(!) // vi tirarse un pedo(!)

farther ['fɑ:ðə'] ad más lejos, más allá// a más lejano.

farthest ['fɑ:ðist] superlative of **far**.

fascinate ['fæsineit] vt fascinar; **fas-**cinating a fascinante; **fascination** [-'neiʃən] n fascinación f.

fascism ['fæʃizəm] n fascismo.

fashion ['fæʃən] n moda; (manner) manera // vt formar; **in ~** a la moda; **out of ~** pasado de moda; **~able** a de moda; **~ show** n desfile m de modelos.

fast [fɑ:st] a rápido; (dye, colour) sólido; (clock): **to be ~** estar adelantado // ad rápidamente, de prisa; (stuck, held) firmemente // n ayuno // vi ayunar; **~ asleep** profundamente dormido.

fasten ['fɑ:sn] vt asegurar, sujetar; (coat, belt) abrochar // vi cerrarse; **~er**, **~ing** n cierre m; (of door etc) cerrojo.

fast food n comida rápida, platos mpl preparados.

fastidious [fæs'tidiəs] a (fussy) delicado; (demanding) exigente.

fat [fæt] a gordo; (meat) con mucha grasa; (greasy) grasiento // n grasa; (on person) carnes fpl; (lard) manteca.

fatal ['feitl] a (mistake) fatal; (injury) mortal; (consequence) funesto; **~ism** n fatalismo; **~ity** [fə'tæliti] n (road death etc) víctima f; **~ly** ad: **~ly injured** herido a muerte.

fate [feit] n destino; **~ful** a fatídico.

father ['fɑ:ðə'] n padre m; **~-in-law** n suegro; **~ly** a paternal.

fathom ['fæðəm] n braza // vt (mystery) desentrañar; (understand) lograr comprender.

fatigue [fə'ti:g] n fatiga, cansancio.

fatten ['fætn] vt, vi engordar.

fatty ['fæti] a (food) graso // n (fam) gordito/a, gordinflón/ona m/f.

fatuous ['fætjuəs] a fatuo, necio.

faucet ['fɔ:sit] n (US) grifo, llave f (LAm).

fault [fɔ:lt] n (blame) culpa; (defect: in character) defecto; (in manufacture) desperfecto; (GEO) falla // vt criticar; **it's my ~** es culpa mía; **to find ~ with** criticar, poner peros a; **at ~** culpable; **~less** a (action) intachable; (person) sin defectos; ~**y** a defectuoso.

fauna ['fɔːnə] n fauna.

faux pas ['fəʊ'pɑː] n plancha.

favour, (US) **favor** ['feɪvə*] n favor m; (approval) aprobación f // vt (proposition) estar a favor de, aprobar; (person ete) favorecer; (assist) ser propicio a; **to ask a** ~ **of** pedir un favor a; **to do sb a** ~ hacer un favor a uno; **to find** ~ **with** caer en gracia de; **in** ~ **of** a favor de; ~**able** a favorable; ~**ite** [-rɪt] a, n favorito, preferido; ~**itism** n favoritismo.

fawn [fɔːn] n cervato // a (also: ~ **coloured**) color de cervato, leonado // vi: **to** ~ **(up)on** adular.

fax [fæks] n (document) facsímil(e) m; (machine) telefax m // vt mandar por telefax.

FBI n abbr (US: = Federal Bureau of Investigation) ≈ BIC f (Sp).

fear [fɪə*] n miedo, temor m // vt temer; **for** ~ **of** por temor a; ~**ful** a temeroso, miedoso; (awful) terrible.

feasible ['fiːzəbl] a factible.

feast [fiːst] n banquete m; (REL: also: ~ **day**) fiesta // vi banquetear.

feat [fiːt] n hazaña.

feather ['feðə*] n pluma.

feature ['fiːtʃə*] n (gen) característica; (ANAT) rasgo; (article) artículo de fondo // vt (subj: film) presentar // vi figurar; ~**s** npl (of face) facciones fpl; ~ **film** n largometraje m.

February ['februərɪ] n febrero.

fed [fed] pt, pp de **feed**.

federal ['fedərəl] a federal.

fed-up [fed'ʌp] a: **to be** ~ **(with)** estar harto (de).

fee [fiː] n (professional) derechos mpl; honorarios mpl; (of school) matrícula; (of club) cuota.

feeble ['fiːbl] a débil.

feed [fiːd] n (gen, of baby) comida; (of animal) pienso; (on printer) dispositivo de alimentación // vt (pt, pp **fed**) (gen) alimentar; (Brit: baby: breastfeed) dar el pecho a; (animal)

dar de comer a; (data, information): **to** ~ **into** meter en; **to** ~ **on** vt fus alimentarse de; ~**back** n reacción f, feedback m; ~**ing bottle** n (Brit) biberón m.

feel [fiːl] n (sensation) sensación f; (sense of touch) tacto // vt (pt, pp **felt**) tocar; (cold, pain etc) sentir; (think, believe) creer; **to** ~ **hungry/cold** tener hambre/frío; **to** ~ **lonely/better** sentirse solo/mejor; **I don't** ~ **well** no me siento bien; **it** ~**s soft** es suave al tacto; **to** ~ **like** (want) tener ganas de; **to** ~ **about** or **around** vi tantear; ~**er** n (of insect) antena; **to put out** ~**ers** (fig) sondear; ~**ing** n (physical) sensación f; (foreboding) presentimiento; (emotion) sentimiento.

feet [fiːt] npl of **foot**.

feign [feɪn] vt fingir.

fell [fel] pt of **fall** // vt (tree) talar.

fellow ['feləʊ] n tipo, tío (Sp); (of learned society) socio/a // cpd: ~ **students** compañeros/as m/pl de curso, condiscípulos/as m/fpl; ~ **citizen** n conciudadano/a; ~ **countryman** n compatriota m; ~ **men** npl semejantes mpl; ~**ship** n compañerismo; (grant) beca; ~ **student** n compañero/a de curso.

felony ['felənɪ] n crimen m.

felt [felt] pt, pp of **feel** // n fieltro; ~**-tip pen** n rotulador m.

female ['fiːmeɪl] n (ZOOL) hembra // a femenino.

feminine ['femɪnɪn] a femenino.

feminist ['femɪnɪst] n feminista.

fence [fens] n valla, cerca // vt (also: ~ **in**) cercar // vi (SPORT) hacer esgrima; **fencing** n esgrima.

fend [fend] vi: **to** ~ **for o.s.** valerse por sí mismo; **to** ~ **off** vt (attack) rechazar.

fender ['fendə*] n guardafuego; (US: AUT) parachoques m inv; (: RAIL) trompa.

ferment [fə'ment] vi fermentar // n ['fɜːment] (fig) agitación f.

fern [fɜːn] n helecho.

ferocious [fə'rəʊʃəs] a feroz; **fero-city** ['rɒsɪtɪ] n ferocidad f.

ferret ['ferɪt] n hurón m // vt: to ~ **out** desentrañar.

ferry ['ferɪ] n (small) barca (de pasaje), balsa; (large: also: ~ **boat**) transbordador m (Sp), embarcadero (LAm) // vt transportar.

fertile ['fɜːtaɪl] a fértil; (BIOL) fecundo; **fertility** [fə'tɪlɪtɪ] n fertilidad f; fecundidad f; **fertilize** ['fɜːtɪlaɪz] vt (BIOL) fecundar; (AGR) abonar; **fertilizer** n abono.

fervent ['fɜːvənt] a (admirer) entusiasta; (hope) ferviente.

fervour ['fɜːvə*] n fervor m, ardor m.

fester ['festə*] vi ulcerarse.

festival ['festɪvəl] n (REL) fiesta; (ART, MUS) festival m.

festive ['festɪv] a festivo; the ~ **season** (Brit: Christmas) las Navidades.

festivities [fes'tɪvɪtɪz] npl fiestas fpl.

festoon [fes'tuːn] vt: to ~ **with** engalanar de.

fetch [fetʃ] vt ir a buscar; (sell for) venderse por.

fetching ['fetʃɪŋ] a atractivo.

fête [feɪt] n fiesta.

fetus ['fiːtəs] n (US) = **foetus**.

feud [fjuːd] n (hostility) enemistad f; (quarrel) disputa.

feudal ['fjuːdl] a feudal.

fever ['fiːvə*] n fiebre f; ~**ish** a febril.

few [fjuː] a (not many) pocos; (some) algunos, unos; a ~ a unos pocos // pron algunos; ~**er** a menos; ~**est** a los/las menos.

fiancé [fɪ'ɑːŋseɪ] n novio, prometido; ~**e** n novia, prometida.

fib [fɪb] n mentirilla // vi decir mentirillas.

fibre, (US) **fiber** ['faɪbə*] n fibra; ~**-glass** n fibra de vidrio.

fickle ['fɪkl] a inconstante.

fiction ['fɪkʃən] n (gen) ficción f; ~**al** a novelesco; **fictitious** [fɪk'tɪʃəs] a ficticio.

fiddle ['fɪdl] n (MUS) violín m;

(cheating) trampa // vt (Brit: accounts) falsificar; **to** ~ **with** vt fus jugar con.

fidelity [fɪ'delɪtɪ] n fidelidad f.

fidget ['fɪdʒɪt] vi inquietarse.

field [fiːld] n campo; (fig) campo, esfera; (SPORT) campo, cancha (LAm); (competitors) competidores mpl; ~ **marshal** n mariscal m; ~**work** n trabajo de campo.

fiend [fiːnd] n demonio; ~**ish** a diabólico.

fierce [fɪəs] a feroz; (wind, attack) violento; (heat) intenso; (fighting, enemy) encarnizado.

fiery ['faɪərɪ] a (burning) ardiente; (temperament) apasionado.

fifteen [fɪf'tiːn] num quince.

fifth [fɪfθ] a, n quinto.

fifty ['fɪftɪ] num cincuenta; ~-~ a: a ~-~ **chance** el cincuenta por ciento de posibilidades // ad a medias, mitad por mitad.

fig [fɪg] n higo.

fight [faɪt] n (gen) pelea; (MIL) combate m; (struggle) lucha // (vb: pt, pp **fought**) vt luchar contra; (cancer, alcoholism) combatir // vi pelear, luchar; ~**er** n combatiente m/f; (fig) luchador(a) m/f; (plane) caza m; ~**ing** n combate m.

figment ['fɪgmənt] n: **a** ~ **of the imagination** una quimera.

figurative ['fɪgjʊrətɪv] a (meaning) figurado.

figure ['fɪgə*] n (DRAWING, GEOM) figura, dibujo; (number, cipher) cifra; (body, outline) talle m, tipo // vt (esp US) imaginar // vi (appear) figurar; (US: make sense) ser lógico; **to** ~ **out** vt (understand) comprender; ~**head** n (fig) testaferro; (of speech) n figura retórica.

filch [fɪltʃ] vt (col: steal) hurtar, robar.

file [faɪl] n (tool) lima; (dossier) expediente m; (folder) carpeta; (COMPUT) fichero; (row) fila // vt limar; (papers) clasificar; (LAW: claim) presentar; (store) archivar; **to** ~

in/out vi entrar/salir en fila; **to ~ past** vt fus desfilar ante; **filing** n: **to do the filing** llevar los archivos; **filing cabinet** n fichero, archivo.

fill [fɪl] vt llenar // n: **to eat one's ~** llenarse; **to ~ in** vt rellenar; **to ~ up** vt llenar (hasta el borde) // vi (AUT) poner gasolina.

fillet ['fɪlɪt] n filete m; **~ steak** n filete m de ternera.

filling ['fɪlɪŋ] n (CULIN) relleno; (for tooth) empaste m; **~ station** n estación f de servicio.

film [fɪlm] n película // vt (scene) filmar // vi rodar (una película); **~ star** n astro, estrella de cine; **~strip** n tira de película.

filter ['fɪltə*] n filtro // vt filtrar; **~ lane** n (Brit) carril m de selección; **~-tipped** a con filtro.

filth [fɪlθ] n suciedad f; **~y** a sucio; (language) obsceno.

fin [fɪn] n (gen) aleta.

final ['faɪnl] a (last) final, último; (definitive) definitivo, terminante // n (Brit: SPORT) final f; **~s** npl (SCOL) examen m de fin de curso; (US: SPORT) final f.

finale [fɪ'nɑːlɪ] n final m.

final: ~ist n (SPORT) finalista m/f; **~ize** vt concluir, completar; **~ly** ad (lastly) por último, finalmente; (eventually) por fin.

finance [faɪ'næns] n (money) fondos mpl; **~s** npl finanzas fpl // vt financiar; **financial** [-'nænʃəl] a financiero; **financier** n financiero/a.

find [faɪnd] vt (pt, pp found) (gen) encontrar, hallar; (come upon) descubrir // n hallazgo; descubrimiento; **to ~ sb guilty** (LAW) declarar culpable a uno; **to ~ out** vt averiguar; (truth, secret) descubrir; **to ~ out about** enterarse de; **~ings** npl (LAW) veredicto sg, fallo sg; (of report) recomendaciones fpl.

fine [faɪn] a (delicate) fino; (beautiful) hermoso // ad (well) bien // n (LAW) multa // vt (LAW) multar; **the weather is ~** hace buen tiempo;

~ arts npl bellas artes fpl.

finery ['faɪnərɪ] n adornos mpl.

finesse [fɪ'nɛs] n sutileza.

finger ['fɪŋgə*] n dedo // vt (touch) manosear; (MUS) puntear; **little/ index ~** (dedo) meñique m/índice m; **~nail** n uña; **~print** n huella dactilar; **~tip** n yema del dedo.

finicky ['fɪnɪkɪ] a (fussy) delicado.

finish ['fɪnɪʃ] n (end) fin m; (SPORT) meta; (polish etc) acabado // vt, vi terminar; **to ~ doing sth** acabar de hacer algo; **to ~ third** llegar el tercero; **to ~ off** vt acabar, terminar; (kill) acabar con; **to ~ up** vt acabar, terminar // vi ir a parar, terminar; **~ing line** n línea de llegada or meta; **~ing school** n academia para señoritas.

finite ['faɪnaɪt] a finito; (verb) conjugado.

Finland ['fɪnlənd] n Finlandia.

Finn [fɪn] n finlandés/esa m/f; **~ish** a finlandés/esa // n (LING) finlandés m.

fir [fə:*] n abeto.

fire ['faɪə*] n (gen) fuego; (accidental) incendio // vt (gun) disparar; (set fire to) incendiar; (excite) exaltar; (interest) despertar; (dismiss) despedir // vi encenderse; **on ~** ardiendo, en llamas; **~ alarm** n alarma de incendios; **~ arm** n arma de fuego; **~ brigade**, (US) **~ department** n (cuerpo de) bomberos mpl; **~ engine** n coche m de bomberos; **~ escape** n escalera de incendios; **~ extinguisher** n extintor m (de fuego); **~man** n bombero; **~place** n chimenea; **~side** n: **by the ~** al lado de la chimenea; **~ station** n parque m de bomberos; **~wood** n leña; **~works** npl fuegos mpl artificiales.

firing ['faɪərɪŋ] n (MIL) disparos mpl, tiroteo; **~ squad** n pelotón m de ejecución.

firm [fə:m] a firme // n firma, empresa; **~ly** ad firmemente; **~ness** n firmeza.

first [fə:st] a primero // ad (before

others) primero/a; (*when listing reasons etc*) en primer lugar, primeramente // n (*person: in race*) primero/a; (*AUT*) primera; at ~ al principio; ~ of all ante todo; ~ aid n primera ayuda, primeros auxilios mpl; ~aid kit n botiquín m; ~class a de primera clase; ~hand a de primera mano; F~ Lady n (*esp US*) primera dama; ~ly ad en primer lugar; ~name n nombre m de pila; ~rate a de primera clase.

fish [fɪʃ] n, pl inv pez m; (*food*) pescado // vt, vi pescar; to go ~ing ir de pesca; ~erman n pescador m; ~farm n criadero de peces; ~fingers npl (*Brit*) croquetas fpl de pescado; ~ing boat n barca de pesca; ~ing line n sedal m; ~ing rod n caña (de pescar); ~ing tackle n aparejo (de pescar); ~ market n mercado de pescado; ~monger n (*Brit*) pescadero; ~monger's (shop) n (*Brit*) pescadería; ~seller n (*US*) = fishmonger; ~y a (*fig*) sospechoso; ~store n (*US*) = fishmonger's.

fist [fɪst] n puño.

fit [fɪt] a (*MED, SPORT*) en (buena) forma; (*proper*) adecuado, apropiado // vt (*subj: clothes*) sentar bien a; (*try on: clothes*) probar; (*facts*) cuadrar or corresponder con; (*accommodate*) ajustar, adaptar // vi (*clothes*) entallar; (*in space, gap*) caber; (*facts*) coincidir // n (*MED*) ataque m; ~ to apto para; ~ for apropiado para; a ~ of anger/pride un arranque de cólera/orgullo; this dress is a good ~ este vestido me sienta bien; by ~s and starts a rachas; to ~ in vi (*gen*) encajarse; (*fig: person*) llevarse bien (con todos); to ~ out (*Brit: also: ~ up*) vt equipar; ~ful a espasmódico, intermitente; ~ment n módulo adosable; ~ness n (*MED*) salud f; (*of remark*) conveniencia; ~ted carpet n moqueta, ~ted kitchen n cocina amueblada;

~ter n ajustador m; ~ting a apropiado // n (*of dress*) prueba; ~ting room n probador m; ~tings npl instalaciones fpl.

five [faɪv] num cinco; ~r n (*col: Brit*) billete m de cinco libras; (: *US*) billete m de cinco dólares.

fix [fɪks] vt (*secure*) fijar, asegurar; (*mend*) arreglar // n: to be in a ~ estar en un aprieto; to ~ up vt (*meeting*) arreglar; to ~ sb up with sth proveer a uno de algo; ~ation [fɪkˈseɪʃən] n obsesión f; ~ed [fɪkst] a (*prices etc*) fijo; ~ture [ˈfɪkstʃəʳ] n (*SPORT*) encuentro; ~tures npl instalaciones fpl fijas.

fizz [fɪz] vi hacer efervescencia.

fizzle out [ˈfɪzl] vi apagarse.

fizzy [ˈfɪzɪ] a (*drink*) gaseoso.

flabbergasted [ˈflæbəgɑːstd] a pasmado.

flabby [ˈflæbɪ] a flojo (de carnes); (*skin*) fofo.

flag [flæg] n bandera; (*stone*) losa // vi decaer; to ~ sb down hacer señas a uno para que se pare; ~pole n asta de bandera; ~ stop n (*US*) parada a petición.

flair [fleə*] n aptitud f especial.

flak [flæk] n (*MIL*) fuego antiaéreo; (*col: criticism*) lluvia de críticas.

flake [fleɪk] n (*of rust, paint*) escama; (*of snow, soap powder*) copo // vi (*also: ~ off*) (*paint*) desconcharse; (*skin*) descamarse.

flamboyant [flæmˈbɔɪənt] a (*dress*) vistoso; (*person*) extravagante.

flame [fleɪm] n llama.

flamingo [fləˈmɪŋɡəu] n flamenco.

flammable [ˈflæməbl] a inflamable.

flan [flæn] n (*Brit*) tarta.

flank [flæŋk] n flanco; (*of person*) costado // vt flanquear.

flannel [ˈflænl] n (*Brit: also: face ~*) manopla; (*fabric*) franela; ~s npl pantalones mpl de franela.

flap [flæp] n (*of pocket*) solapa; (*envelope*) solapa; (*of table*) hoja (plegadiza); (*wing movement*) aleteo // vt (*wings*) aletear // vi (*sail, flag*) ondear.

flare |fleə*| n llamarada; (*MIL*) bengala; (*in skirt etc*) vuelo; **to ~ up** vi encenderse; (: *person*) encolerizarse; (: *revolt*) estallar.

flash |flæʃ| n relámpago; (*also*: **news ~**) noticias *fpl* de última hora; (*PHOT*) flash *m* // *vt* (*light, headlights*) encender y apagar; (*torch*) encender // *vi* brillar; **in a ~** un instante; **he ~ed by** *or* **past** pasó como un rayo; **~bulb** n bombilla fusible; **~ cube** n cubo de flash; **~light** n linterna.

flashy |ˈflæʃɪ| a (*pej*) ostentoso.

flask |flɑːsk| n frasco; (*also*: **vacuum ~**) termo(s) *m*.

flat |flæt| a llano; (*smooth*) liso; (*tyre*) desinflado; (*beer*) muerto; (*MUS*) desafinado // *n* (*Brit*: *apartment*) piso (*Sp*), departamento (*LAm*), apartamento (*AUT*) pinchazo; (*MUS*) bemol *m*; **to work ~ out** trabajar a toda mecha; **~ly** *ad* terminantemente, de plano; **~ten** *vt* (*also*: **~ten out**) allanar; (*smooth out*) alisar.

flatter |ˈflætə*| *vt* adular, halagar; **~ing** a halagüeño; **~y** n adulación *f*.

flaunt |flɔːnt| *vt* ostentar, lucir.

flavour, (*US*) **flavor** |ˈfleɪvə*| n sabor *m*, gusto // *vt* sazonar, condimentar; **~ed** a: **strawberry ~ed** con sabor a fresa; **~ing** n (*in product*) aromatizante *m*.

flaw |flɔː| n defecto.

flax |flæks| n lino; **~en** a rubio.

flea |fliː| n pulga.

fleck |flɛk| n (*mark*) mota; (*pattern*) punto.

flee |fliː|, *pt, pp* **fled** |flɛd| *vt* huir de, abandonar // *vi* huir, fugarse.

fleece |fliːs| n vellón *m*; (*wool*) lana // *vt* (*col*) pelar.

fleet |fliːt| n flota; (*of lorries etc*) escuadra.

fleeting |ˈfliːtɪŋ| a fugaz.

Flemish |ˈflɛmɪʃ| a flamenco.

flesh |flɛʃ| n carne *f*; (*of fruit*) pul-

pa; **of ~ and blood** de carne y hueso; **~ wound** n herida superficial.

flew |fluː| *pt of* **fly**.

flex |flɛks| n cordón *m* // *vt* (*muscles*) tensar; **~ibility** |-ɪˈbɪlɪtɪ| n flexibilidad *f*; **~ible** a flexible.

flick |flɪk| n golpecito; (*with finger*) capirotazo // *vt* dar un golpecito a; **to ~ through** *vt fus* hojear.

flicker |ˈflɪkə*| *vi* (*light*) parpadear; (*flame*) vacilar // n parpadeo.

flier |ˈflaɪə*| n aviador(a) *m/f*.

flight |flaɪt| n vuelo; (*escape*) huida, fuga; (*also*: **~ of steps**) tramo (de escaleras); **to take ~** huir, darse a la fuga; **to put to ~** ahuyentar; **~ attendant** n (*US*) (*male*) camarero, (*female*) azafata; **~ deck** n (*AVIAT*) cabina de mandos.

flimsy |ˈflɪmzɪ| a (*thin*) muy ligero; (*excuse*) flojo.

flinch |flɪntʃ| *vi* encogerse.

fling |flɪŋ|, *pt, pp* **flung** *vt* arrojar.

flint |flɪnt| n pedernal *m*; (*in lighter*) piedra.

flip |flɪp| *vt* dar la vuelta a; (*coin*) echar a cara o cruz.

flippant |ˈflɪpənt| a poco serio.

flipper |ˈflɪpə*| n aleta.

flirt |flɜːt| *vi* coquetear, flirtear // n coqueta *f*; **~ation** |-ˈteɪʃən| n coqueteo, flirteo.

flit |flɪt| *vi* revolotear.

float |fləʊt| n flotador *m*; (*in procession*) carroza; (*money*) reserva // *vi* flotar; (*swimmer*) hacer la plancha // *vt* (*gen*) hacer flotar; (*company*) lanzar.

flock |flɒk| n (*of sheep*) rebaño, (*of birds*) bandada; (*of people*) multitud *f*.

flog |flɒg| *vt* azotar; (*col*) vender.

flood |flʌd| n inundación *f*; (*of words, tears etc*) torrente *m* // *vt* inundar; **~ing** n inundación *f*; **~light** n foco.

floor |flɔː*| n suelo; (*storey*) piso; (*of sea*) fondo; (*dance ~*) pista // (*fig*) dejar sin respuesta; **ground ~**, (*US*) **first ~** planta baja; **first ~**, (*US*) second ~ primer piso; ~**board** n tabla; ~ **lamp** n (US) lámpara de pie; ~ **show** n cabaret m.

flop [flɔp] n fracaso.

floppy ['flɔpi] a flojo // n (COMPUT: also = **disk**) floppy m.

flora ['flɔːrə] n flora.

florist ['flɔrist] n florista m/f; ~'**s** (**shop**) n florería.

flounce [flauns] n volante m; **to ~ out** vi salir enfadado.

flounder ['flaundə*] vi tropezar // n (ZOOL) platija.

flour ['flauə*] n harina.

flourish ['flʌriʃ] vi florecer // n ademán m, movimiento (ostentoso); ~**ing** a floreciente.

flout [flaut] vt burlarse de.

flow [fləu] n (movement) flujo; (direction) curso; (tide) corriente f // vi (river, traffic, blood) fluir; ~ **chart** n organigrama m.

flower ['flauə*] n flor f // vi florecer; ~ **bed** n macizo; ~**pot** n tiesto; ~**y** a florido.

flown [fləun] pp of **fly**.

flu [fluː] n gripe f.

fluctuate ['flʌktjueit] vi fluctuar.

fluent ['fluːənt] a (speech) elocuente; he speaks ~ French, he's ~ in French domina el francés; ~**ly** ad con fluidez.

fluff [flʌf] n pelusa; ; ~**y** a velloso.

fluid ['fluːid] a, n fluido, líquido.

fluke [fluːk] n (col) chiripa.

flung [flʌŋ] pt, pp of **fling**.

fluoride ['fluəraid] n fluoruro.

flurry ['flʌri] n (of snow) temporal m; (haste) agitación f; ~ **of activity** frenesí m de actividad.

flush [flʌʃ] n (on face) rubor m; (fig: of youth, beauty) resplandor m // vt limpiar con agua // vi ruborizarse // a: ~ **with** a ras de; **to ~ the toilet** hacer funcionar el WC; **to ~ out** vt (game, birds) levantar; (fig) desalojar; ~**ed** a ruborizado.

flustered ['flʌstəd] a aturdido.

flute [fluːt] n flauta.

flutter ['flʌtə*] n (of wings) revolo-

teo, aleteo // vi revolotear.

flux [flʌks] n: **to be in a state of ~** estar continuamente cambiando.

fly [flai] n (insect) mosca; (on trousers: also = **flies**) bragueta // vb (pt **flew**, pp **flown**) vt (plane) pilot(e)ar; (cargo) transportar (en avión); (distances) recorrer (en avión) // vi volar; (passengers) ir en avión; (escape) evadirse; (flag) ondear; **to ~ away** or **off** vi (bird, insect) emprender el vuelo; ~**ing** n (activity) (el) volar // a: ~**ing visit** visita relámpago; **with ~ing colours** con lucimiento; ~**ing saucer** n platillo volante; ~**ing start** n: **to get off to a ~ing start** empezar con buen pie; ~**over** n (Brit: bridge) paso a desnivel or superior; ~**past** n desfile m aéreo; ~**sheet** n (for tent) doble techo.

foal [fəul] n potro.

foam [fəum] n espuma // vi echar espuma; ~ **rubber** n espuma de caucho.

fob [fɔb] vt: **to ~ sb off with sth** despachar a uno con algo.

focus ['fəukəs] pl ~**es** n foco // vt (field glasses etc) enfocar // vt: **to ~ on** enfocar a; (issue etc) centrarse en; **in/out of ~** enfocado/ desenfocado.

fodder ['fɔdə*] n pienso.

foe [fəu] n enemigo.

foetus ['fiːtəs] n feto.

fog [fɔg] n niebla; ~**gy** a: **it's ~gy** hay niebla, está brumoso; ~ **lamp**, (US) ~ **light** n (AUT) faro de niebla.

foil [fɔil] vt frustrar // n hoja; (kitchen ~) papel m de aluminio; (FENCING) florete m.

fold [fəuld] n (bend, crease) pliegue m; (AGR) redil m // vt doblar; **to ~ up** vi plegarse, doblarse; (business) quebrar // vt (map etc) plegar; ~**er** n (for papers) carpeta; (brochure) folleto; ~**ing** a (chair, bed) plegable.

foliage ['fəulidʒ] n follaje m.

folk [fəuk] npl gente f // a popular, folklórico; **~s** npl familia, parientes mpl; **~lore** ['fəuklɔ:*] n folklore m; **~ song** n canción f popular or folklórica.

follow ['fɔləu] vt seguir // vi seguir; (result) resultar; he **~ed** suit hizo lo mismo; **to ~ up** vt (letter, offer) responder a; (case) investigar; **~er** n seguidor(a) m/f; (POL) partidario/ a; **~ing** a siguiente // n afición f, partidarios mpl.

folly ['fɔlı] n locura.

fond [fɔnd] a (loving) cariñoso; **to be ~ of** tener cariño a.

fondle ['fɔndl] vt acariciar.

fondness ['fɔndnıs] n (for things) gusto; (for people) cariño m.

font [fɔnt] n pila bautismal.

food [fu:d] n comida; **~ mixer** n batidora; **~ poisoning** n botulismo; **~ processor** n robot m de cocina; **~stuffs** npl comestibles mpl.

fool [fu:l] n tonto/a; (CULIN) puré m de frutas con nata // vt engañar // vi (gen: **~ around**) bromear; (waste time) perder el tiempo; **~hardy** a temerario; **~ish** a tonto; (careless) imprudente; **~proof** a (plan etc) infalible.

foot [fut], pl **feet** n pie m; (measure) pie m (= 304 mm); (of animal) pata // vt (bill) pagar; **on ~** a pie; **~age** n (CINEMA) imagenes fpl; **~ball** n balón m; (game: Brit) fútbol m; (: US) fútbol m americano; **~ball player** n (Brit: also: **~er**) n futbolista m; (US) jugador m de fútbol americano; **~brake** n freno de pie; **~bridge** n puente m para peatones; **~hills** npl estribaciones fpl; **~hold** n pie m firme; **~ing** n (fig) posición f; **to lose one's ~ing** perder el pie; **on an equal ~ing** en pie de igualdad; **~lights** npl candilejas fpl; **~man** n lacayo; **~note** n nota de pie; **~path** n sendero; **~print** n huella, pisada; **~sore** a con los pies doloridos; **~step** n paso; **~wear** n calzado.

for [fɔ:] ◆ prep **1** (indicating destination, intention) para; **the train ~ London** el tren con destino a or de Londres; **he left ~ Rome** marchó para Roma; **he went ~ the paper** fue por el periódico; **is this ~ me?** ¿es esto para mí?; **it's time ~ lunch** es la hora de comer

2 (indicating purpose) para; **what('s it) ~?** ¿para qué (es)?; **to pray ~ peace** rezar por la paz

3 (on behalf of, representing): **the MP ~ Hove** el diputado por Hove; **he works ~ the government/a local firm** trabaja para el gobierno/en una empresa local; **I'll ask him ~ you** se lo pediré por ti; **G ~ George** G de George

4 (because of) por esta razón; **~ fear of being criticized** por temor a ser criticado

5 (with regard to) para; **it's cold ~ July** hace frío para julio; **he has a gift ~ languages** tiene don de lenguas

6 (in exchange for) por; **I sold it ~ £5** lo vendí por £5; **to pay 50 pence ~ a ticket** pagar 50p por un billete

7 (in favour of): **are you ~ or against us?** ¿estás con nosotros o contra nosotros?; **I'm all ~ it** estoy totalmente a favor; **vote ~ X** vote (a) X

8 (referring to distance): **there are roadworks ~ 5 km** hay obras en 5 km; **we walked ~ miles** caminamos kilómetros y kilómetros

9 (referring to time): **he was away ~ 2 years** estuvo fuera (durante) dos años; **it hasn't rained ~ 3 weeks** no ha llovido durante en 3 semanas; **I have known her ~ years** la conozco desde hace años; **can you do it ~ tomorrow?** ¿lo podrás hacer para mañana?

10 (with infinitive clauses): **~ this ~ me to decide** la decisión no es cosa mía; **it would be best ~ you**

to leave sería mejor que te fueras; there is still time ~ **you to do it** todavía te queda tiempo para hacerlo; ~ **this to be possible...** para que esto sea posible...

11 (*in spite of*) a pesar de; ~ **all his complaints** a pesar de tus quejas ◆ *conj* (*since, as: rather formal*) puesto que.

forage ['fɔrɪdʒ] *n* forraje *m*.

foray ['fɔreɪ] *n* incursión *f*.

forbid [fə'bɪd], *pt* **forbad(e)** [fə'bæd], *pp* **forbidden** [fə'bɪdn] *vt* prohibir; **to ~ sb to do sth** prohibir a uno hacer algo; **~ding** *a* (*landscape*) inhóspito; (*severe*) severo.

force [fɔ:s] *n* fuerza // *vt* forzar; **to ~ o.s.** to do hacer un esfuerzo por hacer; **the F~s** *npl* (*Brit*) las Fuerzas Armadas; **in ~** en vigor; **~d** [fɔ:st] *a* forzado; **to ~feed** (*animal, prisoner*) alimentar a la fuerza; **~ful** *a* enérgico.

forcibly ['fɔ:səblɪ] *ad* a la fuerza.

ford [fɔ:d] *n* vado *m* // *vt* vadear.

fore [fɔ:*] *n*: **to the ~** en evidencia.

forearm ['fɔ:rɑ:m] *n* antebrazo.

foreboding [fɔ:'bəudɪŋ] *n* presentimiento.

forecast ['fɔ:kɑ:st] *n* pronóstico *m* (*irg: like* cast) pronosticar.

forecourt ['fɔ:kɔ:t] *n* (*of garage*) patio.

forefathers ['fɔ:fɑ:ðəz] *npl* antepasados *mpl*.

forefinger ['fɔ:fɪŋgə*] *n* (dedo) índice *m*.

forefront ['fɔ:frʌnt] *n*: **in the ~ of** en la vanguardia de.

forego *vt* = **forgo**.

foregone ['fɔ:gɒn] *a*: **it's a ~ conclusion** es una conclusión evidente.

foreground ['fɔ:graund] *n* primer plano.

forehead ['fɔrɪd] *n* frente *f*.

foreign ['fɔrɪn] *a* extranjero; (*trade*) exterior; **~er** *n* extranjero/a; ~ **exchange** *n* divisas *fpl*; **F~ Office** *n* (*Brit*) Ministerio de Asuntos Exterio-

res; **F~ Secretary** *n* (*Brit*) Ministro de Asuntos Exteriores.

foreleg ['fɔ:leg] *n* pata delantera.

foreman ['fɔ:mən] *n* capataz *m*; (*in construction*) maestro de obras.

foremost ['fɔ:məust] *a* principal // *ad*: **first and ~** ante todo.

forensic [fə'rensɪk] *a* forense.

forerunner ['fɔ:rʌnə*] *n* precursor(a) *m/f*.

foresee [fɔ:'si:], *pt* **foresaw** [fɔ:'sɔ:, -'sɒ:, -si:n] *vt* prever; **~able** *a* previsible.

foreshadow [fɔ:'fædəu] *vt* prefigurar, anunciar.

foresight ['fɔ:saɪt] *n* previsión *f*.

forest ['fɔrɪst] *n* bosque *m*.

forestall [fɔ:'stɔ:l] *vt* prevenir.

forestry ['fɔrɪstrɪ] *n* silvicultura.

foretaste ['fɔ:teɪst] *n* muestra.

foretell [fɔ:'tel], *pt*, *pp* **foretold** [fɔ:'təuld] *vt* predecir, pronosticar.

forever [fə'revə*] *ad* para siempre.

foreword ['fɔ:wɜ:d] *n* prefacio.

forfeit ['fɔ:fɪt] *n* (*in game*) prenda // *vt* perder (derecho a).

forgave [fə'geɪv] *pt* de **forgive**.

forge [fɔ:dʒ] *n* fragua; (*smithy*) herrería // *vt* (*signature, Brit: money*) falsificar; (*metal*) forjar; **to ~ ahead** *vi* avanzar constantemente; **~r** *n* falsificador(a) *m/f*; **~ry** *n* falsificación *f*.

forget [fə'get], *pt* **forgot**, *pp* **forgotten** *vt* olvidar // *vi* olvidarse; **~ful** *a* olvidadizo; **~-me-not** *n* nomeolvides *f inv*.

forgive [fə'gɪv], *pt* **forgave**, *pp* **forgiven** *vt* perdonar; **to ~ sb for sth** perdonar algo a uno; **~ness** *n* perdón *m*.

forgo [fɔ:'gəu], *pt* **forwent**, *pp* **forgone** *vt* (*give up*) renunciar a; (*go without*) privarse de.

forgot [fə'gɒt] *pt* de **forget**.

forgotten [fə'gɒtn] *pp* de **forget**.

fork [fɔ:k] *n* (*for eating*) tenedor *m*; (*for gardening*) horca; (*of roads*) bifurcación *f* // *vi* (*road*) bifurcarse; **to ~ out** *vt* (*col: pay*) desembolsar;

~-**lift truck** n máquina elevadora.

forlorn [fə'lɔ:n] (person) triste, melancólico; (place) abandonado; (attempt, hope) desesperado.

form [fɔ:m] n forma; (Brit SCOL) clase f; (document) formulario // vt formar; **in top** ~ en plena forma.

formal ['fɔ:məl] a (offer, receipt) por escrito; (person etc) correcto; (occasion, dinner) ceremonioso; (dress) de etiqueta; ~**ity** [-'mælɪtɪ] n ceremonia; ~**ly** ad oficialmente.

format ['fɔ:mæt] n formato // vt (COMPUT) formatear.

formation [fɔ:'meɪʃən] n formación f.

formative ['fɔ:mətɪv] a (years) formativo.

former ['fɔ:mə*] a anterior; (earlier) antiguo; (ex) ex; **the** ~ ... **the latter** ... aquél ... éste ...; ~**ly** ad antiguamente.

formula ['fɔ:mjulə] n fórmula.

forsake, pt **forsook**, pp **forsaken** [fə'seɪk, -'suk, -'seɪkən] vt (gen) abandonar; (plan) renunciar a.

fort [fɔ:t] n fuerte m.

forte ['fɔ:tɪ] n fuerte m.

forth [fɔ:θ] ad: **back and** ~ de acá para allá; **and so** ~ y así sucesivamente; ~**coming** a próximo, venidero; (character) comunicativo; ~**right** a franco; ~**with** ad en el acto.

fortify ['fɔ:tɪfaɪ] vt fortalecer.

fortitude ['fɔ:tɪtju:d] n fortaleza.

fortnight ['fɔ:tnaɪt] n (Brit) quincena; ~**ly** ad/a quincenal, quincenalmente.

fortress ['fɔ:trɪs] n fortaleza.

fortunate ['fɔ:tʃənɪt] a: **it is** ~ **that...** (es una) suerte que...; ~**ly** ad afortunadamente.

fortune ['fɔ:tʃən] n suerte f; (wealth) fortuna; ~-**teller** n adivino/a.

forty ['fɔ:tɪ] num cuarenta.

forum ['fɔ:rəm] n foro.

forward ['fɔ:wəd] a (movement, position) avanzado; (front) delantero;

(not shy) atrevido // n (SPORT) delantero // vt (letter) remitir; (career) promocionar; **to move** ~ avanzar; ~**(s)** ad (hacia) adelante.

forwent [fɔ:'went] pt of **forgo**.

fossil ['fɔsl] n fósil m.

foster ['fɔstə*] vt fomentar; ~ **child** n hijo/a adoptivo/a; ~ **mother** n madre f adoptiva.

fought [fɔ:t] pt, pp of **fight**.

foul [faul] a (gen) sucio, puerco; (weather, smell etc) asqueroso // n (FOOTBALL) falta f vt (dirty) ensuciar; (block) atascar; (football player) cometer una falta contra; ~ **play** n (SPORT) mala jugada; (LAW) muerte f violenta.

found [faund] pt, pp of **find** // vt (establish) fundar; ~**ation** [-'deɪʃən] n (act) fundación f; (basis) base f; (also: ~**ation cream**) crema base; ~**ations** npl (of building) cimientos mpl.

founder ['faundə*] n fundador(a) m/f // vi hundirse.

foundry ['faundrɪ] n fundición f.

fountain ['fauntɪn] n fuente f; ~ **pen** n (pluma) estilográfica, plumafuente f (LAm).

four [fɔ:*] num cuatro; **on all** ~s a gatas; ~-**poster** (**bed**) n cama de dosel; ~**some** ['fɔ:səm] n grupo de cuatro personas; ~**teen** num catorce; ~**th** a cuarto.

fowl [faul] n ave f (de corral).

fox [fɔks] n zorro // vt confundir.

foyer ['fɔɪeɪ] n vestíbulo.

fracas ['fræka:] n gresca, riña.

fraction ['frækʃən] n fracción f.

fracture ['fræktʃə*] n fractura.

fragile ['frædʒaɪl] a frágil.

fragment ['frægmənt] n fragmento.

fragrance ['freɪgrəns] n (of flowers) fragancia; (perfume) perfume m.

fragrant ['freɪgrənt] a fragante, oloroso.

frail [freɪl] a frágil; (person) débil.

frame [freɪm] n (TECH) armazón m; (of picture, door, house) marco; (of spectacles: also: ~**s**) montura // vt

encuadrar; (*reply*) formular; (*fam*) incriminar; ~ **of mind** *n* estado de ánimo; ~**work** *n* marco.

France [frɑːns] *n* Francia.

franchise ['fræntʃaɪz] *n* (*POL*) derecho de votar, sufragio; (*COMM*) licencia, concesión *f*.

frank [fræŋk] *a* franco *// vt* (*Brit: letter*) franquear; ~**ly** *ad* francamente; ~**ness** *n* franqueza.

frantic ['fræntɪk] *a* frenético.

fraternal [frə'təːnl] *a* fraterno.

fraternity [frə'təːnɪtɪ] *n* (*club*) fraternidad *f*; (*US*) club *m* de estudiantes; (*guild*) cofradía.

fraud [frɔːd] *n* fraude *m*; (*person*) impostor(a) *m/f*.

fraught [frɔːt] *a*: ~ **with** cargado de.

fray [freɪ] *n* combate *m*, lucha *// vi* deshilacharse; **tempers were** ~**ed** el ambiente se ponía tenso.

freak [friːk] *n* (*person*) fenómeno; (*event*) suceso anormal.

freckle ['frekl] *n* peca.

free [friː] *a* (*person: at liberty*) libre; (*not fixed*) suelto; (*gratis*) gratuito; (*unoccupied*) desocupado; (*liberal*) generoso *// vt* (*prisoner etc*) poner en libertad; (*jammed object*) soltar; ~ (*of charge*), **for** ~ *ad* gratis; ~**dom** ['friːdəm] *n* libertad *f*; ~**for-all** *n* riña general; ~ **gift** *n* prima; ~**hold** *n* propiedad *f* vitalicia; ~ **kick** *n* tiro libre; ~**lance** *a*, *ad* por cuenta propia; ~**ly** *ad* libremente; generosamente; ~**mason** *n* francmasón *m*; ~**post** *n* porte *m* pagado; ~**range** *a* (*hen, eggs*) de granja; ~ **trade** *n* libre comercio; ~**way** *n* (*US*) autopista; ~**wheel** *vi* ir en punto muerto; ~ **will** *n* libre albedrío *m*; **of one's own** ~ **will** por su propia voluntad.

freeze [friːz] *vb* (*pt* **froze**, *pp* **frozen**) *vi* helarse, congelarse *// vt* helar; (*prices, food, salaries*) congelar *// n* helada; congelación *f*; ~**-dried** *a* liofilizado; ~**r** *n* congelador *m* (*Sp*), congeladora (*LAm*).

freezing ['friːzɪŋ] *a* helado; ~ **point** *n* punto de congelación; **3 degrees below** ~ tres grados bajo cero.

freight [freɪt] *n* (*goods*) carga; (*money charged*) flete *m*; ~ **train** *n* (*US*) tren *m* de mercancías.

French [frentʃ] *a* francés/esa *// n* (*LING*) francés *m*; **the** ~ *npl* los franceses; ~ **bean** *n* judía verde; ~ **fried (potatoes)**, (*US*) ~ **fries** *npl* patatas *fpl* or papas *fpl* (*LAm*) fritas; ~**man/woman** *n* francés/esa *m/f*; ~ **window** *n* puertaventana.

frenzy ['frenzɪ] *n* frenesí *m*.

frequent ['friːkwənt] *a* frecuente *// vt* [frɪ'kwent] frecuentar; ~**ly** [-əntlɪ] *ad* frecuentemente, a menudo.

fresh [freʃ] *a* (*gen*) fresco; (*new*) nuevo; (*water*) dulce; (*wind, air*) soplar más recio; **to** ~**en up** *vi* (*person*) refrescarse; ~**er** *n* (*Brit SCOL: col*) estudiante *m/f* de primer año; ~**ly** *ad* (*newly*) nuevamente; (*recently*) recientemente; ~**man** *n* (*US*) = ~**er**; ~**ness** *n* frescura; ~**water** *a* (*fish*) de agua dulce.

fret [fret] *vi* inquietarse.

friar ['fraɪə*] *n* fraile *m*; (*before name*) fray *m*.

friction ['frɪkʃən] *n* fricción *f*.

Friday ['fraɪdɪ] *n* viernes *m* *inv*.

fridge [frɪdʒ] *n* (*Brit*) nevera, frigo, refrigerada (*LAm*).

friend [frend] *n* amigo/a; ~**liness** *n* simpatía; ~**ly** *a* simpático; ~**ship** *n* amistad *f*.

frieze [friːz] *n* friso.

frigate ['frɪgɪt] *n* fragata.

fright [fraɪt] *n* susto; **to take** ~ asustarse; ~**en** *vt* asustar; ~**ened** *a* asustado; ~**ening** *a* espantoso; ~**ful** *a* espantoso, horrible; ~**fully** *ad* terriblemente.

frigid ['frɪdʒɪd] *a* (*MED*) frígido, frío.

frill [frɪl] *n* volante *m*.

fringe [frɪndʒ] *n* (*Brit: of hair*) flequillo; (*edge: of forest etc*) borde *m*, margen *m*; ~ **benefits** *npl* ventajas *fpl* supletorias.

frisk [frɪsk] *vt* cachear, registrar.

frisky ['frɪskɪ] *a* juguetón/ona.

fritter ['frɪtə*] *n* buñuelo; **to ~ away** *vt* desperdiciar.

frivolous ['frɪvələs] *a* frívolo.

frizzy ['frɪzɪ] *a* rizado.

fro [frəu] *see* to.

frock [frɒk] *n* vestido.

frog [frɒg] *n* rana; **~man** *n* hombrerana *m*.

frolic ['frɒlɪk] *vi* juguetear.

KEYWORD

from [frɒm] *prep* **1** (*indicating starting place*) de, desde; **where do you come ~?** ¿de dónde eres?; **~ London to Glasgow** de Londres a Glasgow; **to escape ~ sth/sb** escaparse de algo/alguien

2 (*indicating origin etc*) de; **a letter/telephone call ~ my sister** una carta/llamada de mi hermana; **tell him ~ me that...** dígale de mi parte que...

3 (*indicating time*): **~ one o'clock to or until or till two de(sde)** la una a o hasta las 2; **~ January (on)** desde enero

4 (*indicating distance*) de; **the hotel is 1 km from the beach** el hotel está a 1 km de la playa

5 (*indicating price, number etc*) de; **prices range ~ £10 to £50** los precios van desde £10 a o hasta £50; **the interest rate was increased 9% to 10%** el tipo de interés fue incrementado de un 9% a un 10%

6 (*indicating difference*) de; **he can't tell red ~ green** no sabe distinguir el rojo del verde; **to be different ~ sb/sth** ser diferente a algo/alguien

7 (*because of, on the basis of*): **~ what he says** por lo que dice; **weak ~ hunger** debilitado/a por el hambre.

front [frʌnt] *n* (*foremost part*) parte *f* delantera; (*of house*) fachada; (*promenade: also*: **sea ~**) paseo marítimo; (*MIL, POL, METEOROLOGY*)

frente *m*; (*fig*: *appearances*) apariencias *fpl* // *a* (*wheel, leg*) delantero; (*row, line*) primero; **in ~ (of)** delante (de); **~ door** *n* puerta principal; **~ier** ['frʌntɪə*] *n* frontera; **~ page** *n* primera plana; **~ room** *n* (*Brit*) salón *m*, sala; **~-wheel drive** *n* tracción *f* delantera.

frost [frɒst] *n* (*gen*) helada; (*also*: **hoar~**) escarcha // *vt* (*US CULIN*) escarchar; **~bite** *n* congelación *f*; **~ed** *a* (*glass*) deslustrado; **~y** *a* (*surface*) cubierto de escarcha; (*welcome etc*) glacial.

froth [frɒθ] *n* espuma.

frown [fraun] *vi* fruncir el ceño.

froze [frəuz] *pt of* freeze.

frozen ['frəuzn] *pp of* freeze // *a* (*food*) congelado.

fruit [fruːt] *n, pl inv* fruta; **~erer** *n* frutero/a; **~erer's (shop)** *n* frutería; **~ful** *a* provechoso; **~ion** [fruː'ɪʃən] *n*: **to come to ~ion** realizarse; **~ juice** *n* zumo or jugo (*LAm*) de fruta; **~ machine** *n* (*Brit*) máquina *f* tragaperras; **~ salad** *n* macedonia *or* ensalada (*LAm*) de frutas.

frustrate [frʌs'treɪt] *vt* frustrar; **~d** *a* frustrado/a.

fry [fraɪ], *pt, pp* **fried** *vt* freír; **small ~** *n* gente *f* menuda; **~ing pan** *n* sartén *f*.

ft. *abbr* = **foot, feet**.

fuddy-duddy ['fʌdɪdʌdɪ] *n* carroza *m/f*.

fudge [fʌdʒ] *n* (*CULIN*) caramelo blando.

fuel [fjuəl] *n* (*for heating*) combustible *m*; (*coal*) carbón *m*; (*wood*) leña; (*for engine*) carburante *m*; **~ oil** *n* fuel oil *m*; **~ tank** *n* depósito (de combustible).

fugitive ['fjuːdʒɪtɪv] *n* fugitivo/a.

fulfil [ful'fɪl] *vt* (*function*) cumplir con; (*condition*) satisfacer; (*wish, desire*) realizar; **~ment** *n* satisfacción *f*; realización *f*.

full [ful] *a* lleno; (*fig*) pleno; (*complete*) completo; (*information*) deta-

llado // ad: ~ **well** perfectamente;
I'm ~ (up) no puedo más; ~ employment pleno empleo; **a ~ two
hours** dos horas completas; **at ~
speed** a máxima velocidad; **in ~**
(reproduce, quote) íntegramente; ~
moon n luna llena; ~**-scale** a (attack, war) en gran escala; (model)
de tamaño natural; ~ **stop** n punto;
~**-time** a (work) de tiempo completo // ad: **to work** ~**-time** trabajar a
tiempo completo; ~**y** ad completamente; ~**y-fledged** a (teacher, barrister) diplomado.

fulsome ['fulsəm] a (pej: praise,
gratitude) excesivo, exagerado.

fumble ['fʌmbl] vi: **to ~ for sth**
buscar algo con las manos; **to ~
with sth** manejar algo torpemente.

fume [fju:m] vi humear, echar humo;
~**s** npl humo sg, gases mpl.

fun [fʌn] n (amusement) diversión f;
(joy) alegría; **to have ~** divertirse;
for ~ en broma; **to make ~ of** vt
fus burlarse de.

function ['fʌŋkʃən] n función f // vi
funcionar; ~**al** a funcional.

fund [fʌnd] n fondo; (reserve) reserva; ~**s** npl fondos mpl.

fundamental [fʌndə'mentl] a fundamental.

funeral ['fju:nərəl] n (burial) entierro; (ceremony) funerales mpl; ~
parlour n (Brit) funeraria; ~ **service** n misa de difuntos.

funfair ['fʌnfεə*] n (Brit) parque m
de atracciones.

fungus ['fʌŋgəs], pl **-gi** [-gaɪ] n hongo.

funnel ['fʌnl] n embudo; (of ship)
chimenea.

funny ['fʌnɪ] a gracioso, divertido;
(strange) curioso, raro.

fur [fɜ:*] n piel f; (Brit: on tongue
etc) sarro; ~ **coat** n abrigo de pie-
les.

furious ['fjuərɪəs] a furioso; (effort)
violento.

furlong ['fɜ:lɔŋ] n octava parte de
una milla, = 201.17 m.

furlough ['fɜ:ləu] n (MIL, US) permiso.

furnace ['fɜ:nɪs] n horno.

furnish ['fɜ:nɪʃ] vt amueblar;
(supply) suministrar; (information)
facilitar; ~**ings** npl muebles mpl.

furniture ['fɜ:nɪtʃə*] n muebles mpl;
piece of ~ mueble m.

furrow ['fʌrəu] n surco.

furry ['fɜ:rɪ] a peludo.

further ['fɜ:ðə*] a (new) nuevo, adicional; (place) más lejano // ad más
lejos; (more) más; (moreover) además // vt promover, adelantar; ~
education n educación f superior;
~**more** [fɜ:ðə'mɔ:*] ad además.

furthest ['fɜ:ðɪst] superlative of **far**.

fury ['fjuərɪ] n furia.

fuse, (US) **fuze** [fju:z] n fusible m;
(for bomb etc) mecha // vt (metal)
fundir; (fig) fusionar // vi fundirse;
fusionarse; (Brit ELEC): **to ~ the
lights** fundir los plomos; ~ **box** n
caja de fusibles.

fuss [fʌs] n (noise) bulla; (dispute)
lío; (complaining) protesta; **to make
a ~** armar un lío or jaleo; ~**y** a
(person) exigente.

futile ['fju:taɪl] a vano; **futility**
[-'tɪlɪtɪ] n inutilidad f.

future ['fju:tʃə*] a (gen) futuro;
(coming) venidero // n futuro; porvenir; **in ~** de ahora en adelante.

fuze [fju:z] (US) = **fuse**.

fuzzy ['fʌzɪ] a (PHOT) borroso;
(hair) muy rizado.

G

G [dʒi:] n (MUS) sol m.

g. abbr = **gram(s)**.

gabble ['gæbl] vi hablar atropellada-
mente; (gossip) cotorrear.

gable ['geɪbl] n aguilón m.

gadget ['gædʒɪt] n aparato.

Gaelic ['geɪlɪk] a, n (LING) gaélico.

gaffe [gæf] n plancha.

gag [gæg] n (on mouth) mordaza;
(joke) chiste m // vt amordazar;

gaiety ['geɪɪtɪ] n alegría.

gaily ['geɪlɪ] ad alegremente.

gain [geɪn] n ganancia // vt ganar // vi (watch) adelantarse; **to ~ by sth** sacar provecho de algo; **to ~ on sb** ganar terreno a uno; **to ~ 3 lbs** (in weight) engordar 3 libras.

gait [geɪt] n (modo de) andar m.

gal. abbr. = **gallon.**

gala ['gɑːlə] n fiesta.

gale [geɪl] n (wind) vendaval m.

gallant ['gælənt] a valiente; (towards ladies) atento.

gall bladder ['gɔːl-] n vesícula biliar.

gallery ['gælərɪ] n galería; (also: art ~) pinacoteca.

galley ['gælɪ] n (ship's kitchen) cocina; (ship) galera.

gallon ['gælən] n galón m (= 8 pints; Brit = 4,546 litros, US = 3,785 litros).

gallop ['gæləp] n galope m // vi galopar.

gallows ['gæləuz] n horca.

gallstone ['gɔːlstəun] n cálculo biliario.

galore [gə'lɔː*] ad en cantidad, en abundancia.

galvanize ['gælvənaɪz] vt (metal) galvanizar; (fig): **to ~ sb into action** animar a uno para que haga algo.

gambit ['gæmbɪt] n (fig): **opening ~** estrategia inicial.

gamble ['gæmbl] n (risk) riesgo; (bet) apuesta // vt: **to ~ on** apostar a; (fig) confiar en algo // vi jugar; (COMM) especular; **~r** n jugador(a) m/f; **gambling** n juego.

game [geɪm] n juego; (match) partido; (of cards) partida; (HUNTING) caza // a valiente; (ready): **to be ~ for anything** atreverse a todo; **big ~** caza mayor; **~keeper** n guardabosques m inv.

gammon ['gæmən] n tocino or jamón m ahumado.

gamut ['gæmət] n gama.

gang [gæŋ] n pandilla; (of workmen) brigada // vi: **to ~ up on sb** conspi-

rar contra uno.

gangster ['gæŋstə*] n gángster m.

gangway ['gæŋweɪ] n (Brit: in theatre, bus etc) pasillo; (on ship) pasarela.

gaol [dʒeɪl] n, vt (Brit) = **jail.**

gap [gæp] n vacío, hueco (LAm); (in trees, traffic) claro; (in time) intervalo.

gape [geɪp] vi mirar boquiabierto; **gaping** a (hole) muy abierto.

garage ['gærɑːʒ] n garaje m.

garbage ['gɑːbɪdʒ] n (US) basura; **~ can** n cubo or bote m (LAm) de la basura; **~ man** n basurero.

garbled ['gɑːbld] a (distorted) falsificado, amañado.

garden ['gɑːdn] n jardín m; **~er** n jardinero/a; **~ing** n jardinería.

gargle ['gɑːgl] vi hacer gárgaras, gargarear (LAm).

gargoyle ['gɑːgɔɪl] n gárgola.

garish ['gɛərɪʃ] a chillón/ona.

garland ['gɑːlənd] n guirnalda.

garlic ['gɑːlɪk] n ajo.

garment ['gɑːmənt] n prenda (de vestir).

garnish ['gɑːnɪʃ] vt adornar; (CULIN) aderezar.

garrison ['gærɪsn] n guarnición f.

garrulous ['gærjuləs] a charlatán/ana.

garter ['gɑːtə*] n (US) liga.

gas [gæs] n gas m; (US: gasoline) gasolina // vt asfixiar con gas; **~ cooker** n (Brit) cocina de gas; **~ cylinder** n bombona de gas; **~ fire** n estufa de gas; **~ pedal** n (esp US) acelerador m.

gash [gæʃ] n raja; (on face) cuchillada // vt rajar; (with knife) acuchillar.

gasket ['gæskɪt] n (AUT) junta de culata.

gas mask n careta antigás.

gas meter n contador m de gas.

gasoline ['gæsəliːn] n (US) gasolina.

gasp [gɑːsp] n grito sofocado // vi (pant) jadear; **to ~ out** vt (say) decir con voz entrecortada.

gas ring n hornillo de gas.

gas station n (US) gasolinera.

gassy ['gæsɪ] a gaseoso.

gas tap n llave f del gas.

gastric ['gæstrɪk] a gástrico.

gate [geɪt] n puerta; (RAIL) barrera; **~crash** vt (Brit) colarse en; **~way** n puerta.

gather ['gæðə*] vt (flowers, fruit) coger (Sp), recoger; (assemble) reunir; (pick up) recoger; (SEWING) fruncir; (understand) entender // (assemble) reunirse; **to ~ speed** ganar velocidad; **~ing** n reunión f, asamblea.

gauche [gəʊʃ] a torpe.

gaudy ['gɔːdɪ] a chillón/ona.

gauge [geɪdʒ] n calibre m; (RAIL) entrevía; (instrument) indicador m // vt medir.

gaunt [gɔːnt] a descarnado.

gauntlet ['gɔːntlɪt] n (fig): **to run the ~ of** exponerse a; **to throw down the ~** arrojar el guante.

gauze [gɔːz] n gasa.

gave [geɪv] pt of **give**.

gay [geɪ] a (person) alegre; (colour) vivo; (homosexual) gay.

gaze [geɪz] n mirada fija // vi: **to ~ at** sth mirar algo fijamente.

gazelle [gə'zɛl] n gacela.

gazetteer [gæzə'tɪə*] n diccionario geográfico.

gazumping [gə'zʌmpɪŋ] n (Brit) la subida del precio de una casa una vez que ya ha sido apalabrado.

GB abbr = **Great Britain**.

GCE n abbr (Brit) = **General Certificate of Education**.

GCSE n abbr (Brit) = **General Certificate of Secondary Education**) = Bachillerato Elemental y Superior.

gear [gɪə*] n equipo, herramientas fpl; (TECH) engranaje m; (AUT) velocidad f, marcha // vt (fig: adapt): **to ~ sth to** adaptar o ajustar algo a; **top** or (US) **high/low** = en marcha; **in ~** en marcha; **~ box** n caja de cambios; **~ lever**, (US) **~ shift** n palanca de cambio; **~ wheel** n rueda dentada.

geese [giːs] pl of **goose**.

gel [dʒɛl] n gel m.

gelignite ['dʒɛlɪgnaɪt] n gelignita.

gem [dʒɛm] n joya.

Gemini ['dʒɛmɪnaɪ] n Géminis m, Gemelos mpl.

gender ['dʒɛndə*] n género.

gene [dʒiːn] n gen(e) m.

general ['dʒɛnərl] n general m // a: **in ~** en general; **~ delivery** n (US) lista de correos; **~ election** n elecciones fpl generales; **~ization** [-aɪ'zeɪʃən] n generalización f; **~ize** vi generalizar; **~ly** ad generalmente, en general; **~ practitioner (G.P.)** n médico general.

generate ['dʒɛnəreɪt] vt (ELEC) generar; (fig) producir.

generation [dʒɛnə'reɪʃən] n generación f.

generator ['dʒɛnəreɪtə*] n generador m.

generosity [dʒɛnə'rɔsɪtɪ] n generosidad f.

generous ['dʒɛnərəs] a generoso; (copious) abundante.

genetics [dʒɪ'nɛtɪks] n genética.

Geneva [dʒɪ'niːvə] n Ginebra.

genial ['dʒiːnɪəl] a afable, simpático.

genitals ['dʒɛnɪtlz] npl (órganos mpl) genitales mpl.

genius ['dʒiːnɪəs] n genio.

gent [dʒɛnt] n abbr = **gentleman**.

genteel [dʒɛn'tiːl] a fino, elegante.

gentle ['dʒɛntl] a (sweet) amable, dulce; (touch etc) ligero, suave.

gentleman ['dʒɛntlmən] n señor m; (well-bred man) caballero.

gentleness ['dʒɛntlnɪs] n dulzura; (of touch) suavidad f.

gently ['dʒɛntlɪ] ad suavemente.

gentry ['dʒɛntrɪ] n alta burguesía.

gents [dʒɛnts] n aseos mpl (de caballeros).

genuine ['dʒɛnjuɪn] a auténtico; (person) sincero.

geography [dʒɪ'ɔgrəfɪ] n geografía.

geology [dʒɪ'ɔlədʒɪ] n geología.

geometric(al) [dʒɪə'mɛtrɪk(l)] a geométrico.

geometry [dʒɪˈɒmətrɪ] n geometría.

geranium [dʒɪˈreɪnɪəm] n geranio.

geriatric [dʒerɪˈætrɪk] a, n geriátrico/a m/f.

germ [dʒɜːm] n (microbe) microbio, bacteria; (seed, fig) germen m.

German [ˈdʒɜːmən] a alemán/ana // n alemán/ana m/f; (LING) alemán m; ~ **measles** n rubéola; ~ **Shepherd Dog** n pastor m alemán.

Germany [ˈdʒɜːmənɪ] n Alemania.

gesture [ˈdʒestjə*] n gesto.

get [get], pt, pp **got**, pp **gotten** (US) vi **1** (become, be) ponerse, volverse; **to** ~ **old/tired** envejecerse/cansarse; **to** ~ **drunk** emborracharse; **to** ~ **dirty** ensuciarse; **to** ~ **married** casarse; **when do I** ~ **paid?** ¿cuándo me pagan or se me paga?; **it's** ~**ting late** se está haciendo tarde

2 (go): **to** ~ **to/from** llegar a/de; **to** ~ **home** llegar a casa

3 (begin) empezar a; **to** ~ **to know sb** (llegar a) conocer a uno; **I'm** ~**ting to like him** me está empezando a gustar; **let's** ~ **going** or **started** (vamos a empezar)!

4 (modal auxiliary vb): **you've got to do it** tienes que hacerlo

◆ vt **1**: **to** ~ **sth done** (finish) terminar algo; (have done) mandar hacer algo; **to** ~ **one's hair cut** cortarse el pelo; **to** ~ **the car going** or **to go** arrancar el coche; **to** ~ **sb to do sth** conseguir or hacer que alguien haga algo; **to** ~ **sth/sb ready** preparar algo/a alguien

2 (obtain: money, permission, results) conseguir; (find: job, flat) encontrar; (fetch: person, doctor) buscar; (object) ir a buscar, traer; **to** ~ **sth for sb** conseguir algo para alguien; ~ **me Mr Jones, please** (TEL) póngame or comuníqueme (LAm) con el Sr. Jones, por favor; **can I** ~ **you a drink?** ¿te pido algo?

3 (receive: present, letter) recibir;

(acquire: reputation) alcanzar; (: prize) ganar; **what did you** ~ **for your birthday?** ¿qué te regalaron por tu cumpleaños?; **how much did you** ~ **for the painting?** ¿cuánto sacaste por el cuadro?

4 (catch) coger (Sp), agarrar (LAm); (hit: target etc) dar en; **to** ~ **sb by the arm/throat** coger (Sp) or agarrar (LAm) a uno del brazo/cuello; ~ **him!** ¡cógelo! (Sp), ¡atrápalo! (LAm); **the bullet got him in the leg** la bala le dio en la pierna

5 (take, move) llevar; **to** ~ **sth to sb** llevar algo a alguien; **do you think we'll** ~ **it through the door?** ¿crees que lo podremos meter por la puerta?

6 (catch, take: plane, bus etc) coger (Sp), tomar (LAm); **where do I** ~ **the train for Birmingham?** ¿dónde se se coge (Sp) or se toma (LAm) el tren para Birmingham?

7 (understand) entender; (hear) oír; **I've got it!** ¡ya lo tengo!; ¡eureka!; **I don't** ~ **your meaning** no te entiendo; **I'm sorry, I didn't** ~ **your name** lo siento, no cogí su nombre

8 (have, possess): **to have got** tener.

get about vi salir mucho; (news) divulgarse

get along vi (agree) llevarse bien; (depart) marcharse; (manage) = **get by**

get at vt fus (attack) atacar; (reach) alcanzar

get away vi marcharse; (escape) escaparse

get away with vt fus hacer impunemente

get back vi (return) volver // vt recobrar

get by vi (pass) lograr pasar; (manage) arreglárselas

get down vi bajarse // vt fus bajar // vt (object) bajar; (depress) deprimir

get down to vt fus (work) ponerse a

get in vi entrar; (train) llegar; (arrive home) volver a casa, regresar

get into vt fus entrar en; (vehicle) subir a; **to ~ into a rage** enfadarse

get off vi (from train etc) bajar; (depart: person, car) marcharse // vt (remove) quitar // vt fus (train, bus) bajar de

get on vi (at exam etc): **how are you ~ting on?** ¿cómo te va?; (agree): **to ~ on (with)** llevarse bien (con) // vt fus subir a

get out vi salir; (of vehicle) bajar // vt sacar

get out of vt fus salir de; (duty etc) escaparse de

get over vt fus (illness) recobrarse de

get round vt fus rodear; (fig: person) engatusar a

get through vi (TEL) lograr) comunicarse

get through to vt fus (TEL) comunicar con

get together vi reunirse // vt reunir, juntar

get up vi (rise) levantarse // vt fus subir

get up to vt fus (reach) llegar a; (prank) hacer.

geyser ['giːzə*] n (water heater) calentador m de agua; (GEO) géiser m.

Ghana ['gɑːnə] n Ghana.

ghastly ['gɑːstlɪ] a horrible.

gherkin ['gəːkɪn] n pepinillo.

ghost [gəust] n fantasma m.

giant ['dʒaɪənt] n gigante m/f // a gigantesco, gigante.

gibberish ['dʒɪbərɪʃ] n galimatías m.

gibe [dʒaɪb] n mofa.

giblets ['dʒɪblɪts] npl menudillos mpl.

Gibraltar [dʒɪ'brɔːltə*] n Gibraltar m.

giddiness ['gɪdɪnɪs] n vértigo.

giddy ['gɪdɪ] a (height, speed) vertiginoso; **to be ~** estar mareado/a.

gift [gɪft] n regalo; (offering) obse-

quio; (ability) talento; **~ed** a dotado; **~ token** or **voucher** n vale m canjeable por un regalo.

gigantic [dʒaɪ'gæntɪk] a gigantesco.

giggle ['gɪgl] vi reírse tontamente // n risilla.

gill [dʒɪl] n (measure) = 0.25 pints (Brit = 0.148 l, US = 0.118l).

gills [gɪlz] npl (of fish) branquias fpl, agallas fpl.

gilt [gɪlt] a, n dorado; **~-edged** a (COMM) de máxima garantía.

gimmick ['gɪmɪk] n truco.

gin [dʒɪn] n (liquor) ginebra.

ginger ['dʒɪndʒə*] n jengibre m; **~ ale**, **~ beer** n (Brit) gaseosa de jengibre; **~bread** n pan m de jengibre; **~-haired** a pelirrojo.

gingerly ['dʒɪndʒəlɪ] ad con cautela.

gipsy ['dʒɪpsɪ] n gitano/a.

giraffe [dʒɪ'rɑːf] n jirafa.

girder ['gəːdə*] n viga.

girdle ['gəːdl] n (corset) faja.

girl [gəːl] n (small) niña; (young woman) chica, joven f, muchacha; **an English ~** una (chica) inglesa; **~friend** n (of girl) amiga; (of boy) novia; **~ish** a de niña.

giro ['dʒaɪrəu] n (Brit: bank ~) giro bancario; (post office ~) giro postal; (state benefit) cheque quincenal del subsidio de desempleo.

girth [gəːθ] n circunferencia; (of saddle) cincha.

gist [dʒɪst] n lo esencial.

give [gɪv], pt **gave**, pp **given** vt dar; (deliver) entregar; (as gift) regalar // vi (break) romperse; (stretch: fabric) dar de sí; **to ~ sb sth**, **~ sth to sb** dar algo a uno; **to ~ away** vt (give free) regalar; (betray) traicionar; (disclose) revelar; **to ~ back** vt devolver; **to ~ in** vi ceder // vt entregar; **to ~ off** vt desprender; **to ~ out** vt distribuir; **to ~ up** vi rendirse, darse por vencido // vt renunciar a; **to ~ up smoking** dejar de fumar; **to ~ o.s. up** entregarse; **to ~ way** vi ceder; (Brit AUT) ceder el paso.

glacier ['glæsɪə*] n glaciar m.

glad [glæd] a contento.

gladly ['glædlɪ] ad con mucho gusto.

glamorous ['glæmərəs] a encantador(a), atractivo.

glamour ['glæmə*] n encanto, atractivo.

glance [glɑːns] n ojeada, mirada // vi: **to ~** at echar una ojeada a; **to ~ off** (bullet) rebotar; **glancing** a (blow) oblicuo.

gland [glænd] n glándula.

glare [glɛə*] n deslumbramiento, brillo // vi deslumbrar; **to ~ at** mirar ferozmente; **glaring** a (mistake) manifiesto.

glass [glɑːs] n vidrio, cristal m; (for drinking) vaso; (: with stem) copa; (also: looking ~) espejo; ~es npl gafas fpl; **~house** n invernadero; **~ware** n cristalería; **~y** a (eyes) vidrioso.

glaze [gleɪz] vt (window) poner cristales a; (pottery) barnizar // n barniz m.

glazier ['gleɪzɪə*] n vidriero/a.

gleam [gliːm] n destello // vi brillar; **~ing** a reluciente.

glean [gliːn] vt (information) recoger.

glee [gliː] n alegría, regocijo.

glen [glɛn] n cañada.

glib [glɪb] a de mucha labia.

glide [glaɪd] vi deslizarse; (AVIAT, birds) planear; **~r** n (AVIAT) planeador m; **gliding** n (AVIAT) vuelo sin motor.

glimmer ['glɪmə*] n luz f tenue.

glimpse [glɪmps] n vislumbre m // vt vislumbrar, entrever.

glint [glɪnt] vi centellear.

glisten ['glɪsn] vi relucir, brillar.

glitter ['glɪtə*] vi relucir, brillar // n brillo.

gloat [gləʊt] vi: **to ~ over** (money) recrearse en; (sb's misfortune) saborear.

global ['gləʊbl] a mundial.

globe [gləʊb] n globo, esfera.

gloom [gluːm] n tinieblas fpl, oscuri-

dad f; (sadness) tristeza, melancolía; **~y** a (dark) oscuro; (sad) triste; (pessimistic) pesimista.

glorious ['glɔːrɪəs] a glorioso.

glory ['glɔːrɪ] n gloria.

gloss [glɒs] n (shine) brillo; (paint) pintura de aceite; **to ~ over** vt fus encubrir.

glossary ['glɒsərɪ] n glosario.

glossy ['glɒsɪ] a lustroso.

glove [glʌv] n guante m; **~ compartment** n (AUT) guantera.

glow [gləʊ] vi (shine) brillar // n brillo.

glower ['glaʊə*] vi: **to ~ at** mirar con ceño.

glue [gluː] n goma (de pegar), cemento (LAm) // vt pegar.

glum [glʌm] a (mood) abatido; (person, tone) melancólico.

glut [glʌt] n superabundancia.

glutton ['glʌtn] n glotón/ona m/f; a **~ for punishment** masoquista m/f.

gnarled [nɑːld] a nudoso.

gnat [næt] n mosquito.

gnaw [nɔː] vt roer.

gnome [nəʊm] n gnomo.

go [gəʊ] vb (pt **went**, pp **gone**) vi ir; (travel) viajar; (depart) irse, marcharse; (work) funcionar, marchar; (be sold) venderse; (time) pasar; (fit, suit): **to ~ with** hacer juego con; (become) ponerse; (break etc) estropearse, romperse // n (pl: ~es): **to have a ~ (at)** probar suerte (con); **to be on the ~** no parar; **whose ~ is it?** ¿a quién le toca?; **he's going to do it** va a hacerlo; **to ~ for a walk** ir de paseo; **to ~ dancing** ir a bailar; **how did it ~?** ¿qué tal salió or resultó?, ¿cómo ha ido?; **to ~ round the back** pasar por detrás; **to ~ about** vi (rumour) propagarse // vt fus: **how do I ~ about this?** ¿cómo me las arreglo para hacer esto?; **to ~ ahead** vi seguir adelante; **to ~ along** vi ir // vt fus bordear; **to ~ along with** (agree) estar de acuerdo con; **to ~ away** vi irse, marcharse; **to ~**

back *vi* volver; **to ~ back on** *vt fus* (*promise*) faltar a; **to ~ by** *vi* (*years, time*) pasar // *vt fus* guiarse por; **to ~ down** *vi* bajar; por; hundirse; (*sun*) ponerse // *vt fus* bajar por; **to ~ for** *vt fus* (*fetch*) ir por; (*like*) gustar; (*attack*) atacar; **to ~ in** *vi* entrar; **to ~ in for** *vt fus* (*competition*) presentarse a; **to ~ into** *vt fus* entrar en; (*investigate*) investigar; (*embark on*) dedicarse a; **to ~ off** *vi* irse, marcharse; (*food*) pasarse; (*explode*) estallar; (*event*) realizarse; **I'm going off her/the idea** ya no me gusta tanto ella/la idea // *vt fus* dejar de gustar; **to ~ on** *vi* (*continue*) seguir, continuar; (*happen*) pasar, ocurrir; **to ~ on doing sth** seguir haciendo algo; **to ~ out** *vi* salir; (*fire, light*) apagarse; **to ~ over** *vi* (*ship*) zozobrar // *vt fus* (*check*) revisar; **to ~ through** *vt fus* (*town etc*) atravesar; **to ~ up** *vi* subir; **to ~ without** *vt fus* pasarse sin.

goad [gəud] *vt* aguijonear.

go-ahead ['gəuəhɛd] *a* emprendedor(a) // *n* luz *f* verde.

goal [gəul] *n* meta; (*score*) gol *m*; **~keeper** *n* portero; **~-post** *n* poste *m* (de la portería).

goat [gəut] *n* cabra *f*.

gobble ['gɔbl] *vt* (*also:* **~ down, ~ up**) engullir.

go-between ['gəubɪtwiːn] *n* medianero/a, intermediario/a.

goblet ['gɔblɪt] *n* copa.

god [gɔd] *n* dios *m*; **G~** *n* Dios *m*; **~child** *n* ahijado/a; **~daughter** *n* ahijada; **~dess** *n* diosa; **~father** *n* padrino; **~forsaken** *a* dejado de la mano de Dios; **~mother** *n* madrina; **~send** *n* don *m* del cielo; *n* ahijado.

goggles ['gɔglz] *npl* (*AUT*) anteojos *mpl*; (*of skindiver*) gafas *fpl* submarinas.

going ['gəuɪŋ] *n* (*conditions*) estado del terreno // *a*: **the ~ rate** la tarifa corriente *or* en vigor.

gold [gəuld] *n* oro // *a* de oro; **~en** *a* (*made of ~*) de oro; (*~ in colour*) dorado; **~fish** *n* pez *m* de colores; **~-plated** *a* chapado en oro; **~smith** *n* orfebre *m/f*.

golf [gɔlf] *n* golf *m*; **~ ball** *n* (*for game*) pelota de golf; (*on typewriter*) esfera; **~ club** *n* club *m* de golf; (*stick*) palo de golf; **~ course** *n* campo de golf; **~er** *n* golfista *m/f*.

good [gud] *a* bueno; (*kind*) bueno, amable; (*well-behaved*) educado // *n* bien *m*, provecho; **~s** *npl* bienes *mpl*; (*COMM*) mercancías *fpl*; ~! ¡qué bien!; **to be ~ at** tener aptitud para; **to be ~ for** servir para; **it's ~ for you** te hace bien; **would you be ~ enough to...?** ¿podría hacerme el favor de...?; ¿sería tan amable de...?; **a ~ deal (of)** mucho; **a ~ many** muchos; **to make ~** reparar; **it's no ~ complaining** no vale la pena de quejarse; **for ~** para siempre, definitivamente; **~ morning/afternoon** ¡buenos días/ buenas tardes!; **~ evening!** ¡buenas noches!; **~ night!** ¡buenas noches!; **~-bye!** ¡adiós!; **to say ~-bye** despedirse; **G~ Friday** *n* Viernes *m* Santo; **~-looking** *a* guapo; **~-natured** *a* amable, simpático; **~ness** *n* (*of person*) bondad *f*; **for ~ness sake!** ¡por Dios!; **~ness gracious!** ¡Dios mío!; **~s train** *n* (*Brit*) tren *m* de mercancías; **~will** *n* buena voluntad *f*.

goose [guːs], *pl* **geese** *n* ganso, oca.

gooseberry ['guzbəri] *n* grosella espinosa.

gooseflesh ['guːsflɛʃ] *n*, **goose pimples** *npl* carne *f* de gallina.

gore [gɔː*] *vt* cornear // *n* sangre *f*.

gorge [gɔːdʒ] *n* barranco // *vr*: **to ~ o.s. (on)** atracarse (de).

gorgeous ['gɔːdʒəs] *a* magnífico, maravilloso.

gorilla [gəˈrɪlə] *n* gorila *m*.

gorse [gɔːs] *n* aulaga.

gory ['gɔːrɪ] *a* sangriento.

go-slow ['gəuˈsləu] *n* (*Brit*) huelga

de manos caídas.

gospel ['gɔspl] n evangelio.

gossip ['gɔsɪp] n (scandal) chismorreo, chismes mpl; (chat) charla; (scandalmonger) chismoso/a; (talker) hablador(a) m/f // vi chismear.

got [gɔt] pt, pp of **get**; ~**ten** (US) pp of **get**.

gout [gaut] n gota.

govern ['gʌvən] vt gobernar.

governess ['gʌvənɪs] n institutriz f.

government ['gʌvnmənt] n gobierno; ~**al** [-'mɛntl] a gubernamental.

governor ['gʌvənə*] n gobernador(a) m/f; (of jail) director(a) m/f.

gown [gaun] n traje m; (of teacher; Brit: of judge) toga.

G.P. n abbr = **general practitioner.**

grab [græb] vt coger (Sp) or agarrar (LAm), arrebatar.

grace [greɪs] n gracia // n **5 days' ~** un plazo de 5 días; **to say ~** bendecir la mesa; **to fall from ~** caer en desgracia; **~ful** a elegante, gracioso; **gracious** ['greɪʃəs] a amable.

grade [greɪd] n (quality) clase f, calidad f; (in hierarchy) grado; (US SCOL) curso // vt clasificar; ~ **crossing** n (US) paso a nivel; ~ **school** n (US) escuela primaria.

gradient ['greɪdɪənt] n pendiente f.

gradual ['grædjuəl] a paulatino; ~**ly** ad paulatinamente.

graduate ['grædjuɪt] n graduado/a, licenciado/a // vi ['grædjueɪt] graduarse, licenciarse; **graduation** [-'eɪʃən] n graduación f.

graffiti [grə'fiːtɪ] n pintadas fpl.

graft [grɑːft] n (AGR, MED) injerto; (bribery) corrupción f // vt injertar; **hard ~** (col) trabajo duro.

grain [greɪn] n (single particle) grano; (corn) granos mpl, cereales mpl.

gram [græm] n (US) gramo.

grammar ['græmə*] n gramática; ~ **school** n (Brit) ≈ instituto de segunda enseñanza, liceo (Sp).

grammatical [grə'mætɪkl] a gramatical.

gramme [græm] n = **gram.**

gramophone ['græməfəun] n (Brit) tocadiscos m inv.

granary ['grænərɪ] n granero, troj f.

grand [grænd] a magnífico, imponente; ~**children** npl nietos mpl; ~**dad** n yayo, abuelito; ~**daughter** n nieta; ~**eur** ['grændjə*] n magnificencia, lo grandioso; ~**father** n abuelo; ~**ma** n yaya, abuelita; ~**mother** n abuela; ~**pa** n = ~**dad**; ~**parents** npl abuelos mpl; ~ **piano** n piano de cola; ~**son** n nieto; ~**stand** n (SPORT) tribuna.

granite ['grænɪt] n granito.

granny ['grænɪ] n abuelita, yaya.

grant [grɑːnt] vt (concede) conceder; (admit) reconocer // n (SCOL) beca; **to take sth for ~ed** dar algo por sentado.

granulated ['grænjuleɪtɪd] n: ~ **sugar** (Brit) azúcar m blanquilla refinado.

granule ['grænjuːl] n gránulo.

grape [greɪp] n uva.

grapefruit ['greɪpfruːt] n pomelo, toronja (LAm).

graph [grɑːf] n gráfica; ~**ic** a gráfico; ~**ics** n artes fpl gráficas // npl (COMPUT) gráficos mpl.

grapple ['græpl] vi: **to ~ with** a problem enfrentar un problema.

grasp [grɑːsp] vt agarrar, asir; (understand) comprender // n (grip) asimiento; (reach) alcance m; (understanding) comprensión f; ~**ing** a avaro.

grass [grɑːs] n hierba; (lawn) césped m; ~**hopper** n saltamontes m inv; ~**land** n pradera, pampa (LAm); ~**roots** a popular; ~ **snake** n culebra.

grate [greɪt] n parrilla de chimenea // vi chirriar // vt (CULIN) rallar.

grateful ['greɪtful] a agradecido.

grater ['greɪtə*] n rallador m.

gratify ['grætɪfaɪ] vt complacer; (whim) satisfacer; ~**ing** a grato.

grating ['greɪtɪŋ] n (iron bars) rejilla // a (noise) áspero.

gratitude ['grætɪtjuːd] n agradecimiento.

gratuity [grə'tjuːɪtɪ] n gratificación f.

grave [greɪv] n tumba // a serio, grave.

gravel ['grævl] n grava.

gravestone ['greɪvstəun] n lápida.

graveyard ['greɪvjɑːd] n cementerio.

gravity ['grævɪtɪ] n gravedad f.

gravy ['greɪvɪ] n salsa de carne.

gray [greɪ] a = **grey**.

graze [greɪz] vi pacer // vt (touch lightly) rozar; (scrape) raspar // n (MED) abrasión f.

grease [griːs] n (fat) grasa; (lubricant) lubricante m // vt engrasar; **~proof** a a prueba de grasa; **~proof paper** n (Brit) papel m apergaminado; **greasy** a grasiento.

great [greɪt] a grande; (col) magnífico, estupendo; **G~ Britain** n Gran Bretaña; **~-grandfather/ -grandmother** n bisabuelo/a; **~ly** ad muy; (with verb) mucho; **~ness** n grandeza.

Greece [griːs] n Grecia.

greed [griːd] n (also: **~iness**) codicia, avaricia; (for food) gula; **~y** a avaro; (for food) glotón/ona.

Greek [griːk] a griego // n griego/a; (LING) griego.

green [griːn] a verde; (inexperienced) novato // n verde m; (stretch of grass) césped m; **~s** npl verduras fpl; **~ belt** n zona verde; **~ card** n (AUT) carta verde; **~ery** n verdura; **~gage** n claudia; **~grocer** n (Brit) verdulero/a; **~house** n invernadero; **~ish** a verdoso.

Greenland ['griːnlənd] n Groenlandia.

greet [griːt] vt saludar; (welcome) dar la bienvenida a; **~ing** n (gen) saludo; (welcome) bienvenida; **~ing(s) card** n tarjeta de felicitaciones.

grenade [grə'neɪd] n granada.

grew [gruː] pt of **grow**.

grey [greɪ] a gris; **~-haired** a canoso; **~hound** n galgo.

grid [grɪd] n reja; (ELEC) red f.

grief [griːf] n dolor m, pena.

grievance ['griːvəns] n motivo de queja, agravio.

grieve [griːv] vi afligirse, acongojarse // vt dar pena a; **to ~ for** llorar por.

grievous ['griːvəs] a : **~ bodily harm** (LAW) daños mpl corporales graves.

grill [grɪl] n (on cooker) parrilla // vt (Brit) asar a la parrilla; (question) interrogar.

grille [grɪl] n reja.

grim [grɪm] a (place) sombrío; (person) ceñudo.

grimace [grɪ'meɪs] n mueca // vi hacer muecas.

grimy ['graɪmɪ] a mugriento.

grin [grɪn] n sonrisa abierta // vi sonreír abiertamente.

grind [graɪnd] vt (pt, pp **ground**) (coffee, pepper etc) moler; (US: meat) picar; (make sharp) afilar // n: **the daily ~** la rutina diaria; **to ~ one's teeth** hacer rechinar los dientes.

grip [grɪp] n (hold) asimiento; (of hands) apretón m; (handle) asidero; (holdall) maletín m // vt agarrar; **to get to ~s with** enfrentarse con; **~ping** a absorbente.

grisly ['grɪzlɪ] a horripilante, horrible.

gristle ['grɪsl] n cartílago.

grit [grɪt] n gravilla; (courage) valor m // vt (road) poner gravilla en; **to ~ one's teeth** apretar los dientes.

groan [grəun] n gemido; quejido // vi gemir; quejarse.

grocer ['grəusə*] n tendero (de ultramarinos); **~ies** npl comestibles mpl; **~'s (shop)** n tienda de ultramarinos or de abarrotes (LAm).

groggy ['grɒgɪ] a atontado.

groin [grɔɪn] n ingle f.

groom [gruːm] n mozo/a de cuadra; (also: **bride~**) novio // vt (horse) almohazar.

groove [gruːv] n ranura, surco.

grope [grəup] vi ir a tientas; **to ~ for** vt fus buscar a tientas.

gross [grəus] a grueso, (COMM) bruto; ~ly ad (greatly) enormemente.

grotesque [grə'tɛsk] a grotesco.

grotto ['grɔtəu] n gruta.

ground [graund] n (gen) suelo; tierra; (SPORT) campo, terreno; (reason: gen pl) causa, razón f; (US: also: ~ wire) tierra // vt (plane) mantener en tierra; (US ELEC) conectar con tierra // vi (ship) varar, encallar; ~s npl (of coffee etc) poso sg; (gardens etc) jardines mpl, parque m; on the ~ en el suelo; to gain/lose ~ ganar/perder terreno; to ~ cloth n (US) = ~sheet; ~ing n (in education) conocimientos mpl básicos; ~less a infundado; ~sheet n (Brit) tela impermeable; ~ staff n personal m de tierra; ~work n preparación f.

group [gru:p] n grupo; (musical) conjunto // (vb: also: ~ together) vt agrupar // vi agruparse.

grouse [graus] n, pl inv (bird) urogallo // vi (complain) quejarse.

grove [grəuv] n arboleda.

grovel ['grɔvl] vi arrastrarse.

grow [grəu], pt grew, pp grown vi crecer; (increase) aumentarse; (expand) desarrollarse; (become) volverse; to ~ rich/weak enriquecerse/debilitarse // vt cultivar; (hair, beard) dejar crecer; to ~ up vi crecer, hacerse hombre/mujer; ~er n cultivador(a) m/f, productor(a) m/f; ~ing a creciente.

growl [graul] vi gruñir.

grown [grəun] pp of grow; ~-up n adulto, mayor m/f.

growth [grəuθ] n crecimiento, desarrollo; (what has grown) brote m; (MED) tumor m.

grub [grʌb] n gusano; (col: food) comida.

grubby ['grʌbi] a sucio, mugriento.

grudge [grʌdʒ] n rencor // vt: to ~ sb sth dar algo a uno de mala gana; to bear sb a ~ guardar rencor a uno; he ~s (giving) the money da el dinero de mala gana

gruelling ['gruəlɪŋ] a penoso, duro.

gruesome ['gru:səm] a horrible.

gruff [grʌf] a (voice) ronco; (manner) brusco.

grumble ['grʌmbl] vi refunfuñar, quejarse.

grumpy ['grʌmpi] a gruñón/ona.

grunt [grʌnt] vi gruñir // n gruñido.

G-string ['dʒi:strɪŋ] n taparrabo.

guarantee [gærən'ti:] n garantía // vt garantizar.

guard [ga:d] n guardia; (one man) guardia m; (Brit RAIL) jefe m de tren // vt guardar; ~ed a (fig) cauteloso; ~ian n guardián/ana m/f; (of minor) tutor(a) m/f; ~'s van n (Brit RAIL) furgón m.

Guatemala [gwætɪ'mɑːlə] n Guatemala; ~n a, n guatemalteco/a m/f.

guerrilla [gə'rɪlə] n guerrillero/a; ~ warfare n guerra de guerrillas.

guess [gɛs] vi adivinar // vt adivinar; (US) suponer // n suposición f, conjetura; to take or have a ~ tratar de adivinar; ~work n conjeturas fpl.

guest [gɛst] n invitado/a; (in hotel) huésped/a m/f; ~-house n casa de huéspedes, pensión f; ~ room n cuarto de huéspedes.

guffaw [gʌ'fɔː] n reírse a carcajadas.

guidance ['gaɪdəns] n (gen) dirección f; (advice) consejos mpl.

guide [gaɪd] n (person) guía m/f; (book, fig) guía f // vt guiar; (girl) ~ n exploradora; ~book n guía; ~ dog n perro m guía; ~lines npl (fig) directiva sg.

guild [gɪld] n gremio; ~hall n (Brit) ayuntamiento.

guile [gaɪl] n astucia.

guillotine ['gɪlətiːn] n guillotina.

guilt [gɪlt] n culpabilidad f; ~y a culpable.

guinea pig n cobayo.

guise [gaɪz] n: in or under the ~ of bajo apariencia de.

guitar [gɪ'tɑː*] n guitarra.

gulf [gʌlf] n golfo; (abyss) abis-

mo.
gull [gʌl] *n* gaviota.
gullet [ˈgʌlɪt] *n* esófago.
gullible [ˈgʌlɪbl] *a* crédulo.
gully [ˈgʌlɪ] *n* barranco.
gulp [gʌlp] *vi* tragar saliva // *vt* (*also:* ~ **down**) tragarse.
gum [gʌm] *n* (*ANAT*) encía; (*glue*) goma, cemento (*LAm*); (*sweet*) caramelo de goma; (*also:* **chewing-~**) chicle *m* // *vt* pegar con goma; **~boots** *npl* (*Brit*) botas *fpl* de goma.
gun [gʌn] *n* (*small*) pistola, revólver *m*; (*shotgun*) escopeta; (*rifle*) fusil *m*; (*cannon*) cañón *m*; **~boat** *n* cañonero; **~fire** *n* disparos *mpl*; **~man** *n* pistolero; **~ner** *n* artillero; **~point** *n*: **at ~point** a mano armada; **~powder** *n* pólvora; **~shot** *n* escopetazo; **~smith** *n* armero.
gurgle [ˈgɔːgl] *vi* gorgotear.
guru [ˈguːruː] *n* gurú *m*.
gush [gʌʃ] *vi* chorrear; (*fig*) deshacerse en efusiones.
gusset [ˈgʌsɪt] *n* escudete *m*.
gust [gʌst] *n* (*of wind*) ráfaga.
gusto [ˈgʌstəu] *n* entusiasmo.
gut [gʌt] *n* intestino; (*MUS etc*) cuerda de tripa; **~s** *npl* (*courage*) valor *m*.
gutter [ˈgʌtə*] *n* (*of roof*) canalón *m*; (*in street*) arroyo.
guy [gaɪ] *n* (*also:* **~rope**) cuerda; (*col: man*) tío (*Sp*), tipo.
guzzle [ˈgʌzl] *vi* tragar // *vt* engullir.
gym [dʒɪm] *n* (*also:* **gymnasium**) gimnasio; (*also:* **gymnastics**) gimnasia; **~nast** *n* gimnasta *m/f*; **~ shoes** *npl* zapatillas *fpl* deportivas; **~ slip** *n* (*Brit*) túnica de colegiala.
gynaecologist, (*US*) **gynecologist** [gaɪnɪˈkɔlədʒɪst] *n* ginecólogo/a.
gypsy [ˈdʒɪpsɪ] *n* = **gipsy**.
gyrate [dʒaɪˈreɪt] *vi* girar.

H

haberdashery [ˈhæbəˈdæʃərɪ] *n* (*Brit*) mercería; (*US: men's clothing*) prendas *fpl* de caballero.
habit [ˈhæbɪt] *n* hábito, costumbre *f*.
habitat [ˈhæbɪtæt] *n* habitat *m*.
habitual [həˈbɪtjuəl] *a* acostumbrado, habitual; (*drinker, liar*) empedernido; **~ly** *ad* por costumbre.
hack [hæk] *vt* (*cut*) cortar; (*slice*) tajar // *n* corte *m*; (*axe blow*) hachazo; (*pej: writer*) escritor(a) *m/f* a sueldo.
hackneyed [ˈhæknɪd] *a* trillado, gastado.
had [hæd] *pt, pp* of **have**.
haddock [ˈhædək] *pl ~ or ~s n* especie de merluza.
hadn't [ˈhædnt] = **had not**.
haemorrhage, (*US*) **hemorrhage** [ˈhemərɪdʒ] *n* hemorragia.
haemorrhoids, (*US*) **hemorrhoids** [ˈhemərɔɪdz] *npl* hemorroides *fpl*.
haggard [ˈhægəd] *a* ojeroso.
haggle [ˈhægl] *vi* (*argue*) discutir; (*bargain*) regatear.
Hague [heɪg] *n*: **The ~** La Haya.
hail [heɪl] *n* (*weather*) granizo // *vt* saludar; (*call*) llamar a // *vi* granizar; **~stone** *n* (piedra de) granizo.
hair [heə*] *n* (*gen*) pelo, cabellos *mpl*; (*one ~*) pelo, cabello; (*head of ~*) pelo, cabellera; (*on legs etc*) vello; **to do one's ~** arreglarse el pelo; **grey ~** canas *fpl*; **~brush** *n* cepillo (para el pelo); **~cut** *n* corte *m* (de pelo); **~do** *n* peinado; **~dresser** *n* peluquero/a; **~dresser's** *n* peluquería; **~-dryer** *n* secador *m* de pelo; **~grip,** **~pin** *n* horquilla; **~net** *n* redecilla; **~piece** *n* postizo; **~pin bend,** (*US*) **~pin curve** *n* curva de horquilla; **~raising** *a* espeluznante; **~ remover** *n* depilatorio; **~ spray** *n* laca; **~style** *n* peinado; **~y** *a* peludo; velludo.

hake [heɪk] n merluza.

half [hɑ:f], pl **halves** n mitad f // a medio // al medio, a medias; ~**an-hour** media hora; **two and a** ~ dos y media; ~ **a dozen** media docena; ~ **a pound** media libra; **to cut sth in** ~ cortar algo por la mitad; ~ **asleep** medio dormido; ~**back** n (SPORT) medio; ~**breed**, ~**caste** n mestizo/a; ~**hearted** a indiferente, poco entusiasta; ~**hour** n media hora; ~**mast** n: **at** ~**mast** (flag) a media asta; ~**price** a a mitad de precio; ~ **term** n (Brit SCOL) vacaciones de mediados del trimestre; ~**time** n descanso; ~**way** ad a medio camino.

halibut ['hælɪbət] n, pl inv halibut m.

hall [hɔ:l] n (for concerts) sala; (entrance way) entrada, vestíbulo; ~ **of residence** n (Brit) colegio mayor.

hallmark ['hɔ:lmɑ:k] n (mark) contraste m; (fig) sello.

hallo [hə'ləu] excl = **hello**.

Hallowe'en [hæləu'i:n] n víspera de Todos los Santos.

hallucination [həlu:sɪ'neɪʃən] n alucinación f.

hallway ['hɔ:lweɪ] n vestíbulo.

halo ['heɪləu] n (of saint) aureola.

halt [hɔ:lt] n (stop) alto, parada; (RAIL) apeadero // vt parar // vi pararse; (process) interrumpirse.

halve [hɑ:v] vt partir por la mitad.

halves [hɑ:vz] pl of **half**.

ham [hæm] n jamón m (cocido).

hamburger ['hæmbə:gə*] n hamburguesa.

hamlet ['hæmlɪt] n aldea.

hammer ['hæmə*] n martillo // vt (nail) clavar.

hammock ['hæmək] n hamaca.

hamper ['hæmpə*] vt estorbar // n cesto.

hand [hænd] n mano f; (of clock) aguja; (writing) letra; (worker) obrero // vt dar, pasar; **to give sb a** ~ echar una mano a uno, ayudar a uno; **at** ~ a la mano; **in** ~ entre manos; **on** ~ (person, services) a

mano, al alcance; **to** ~ (information etc) a mano; **on the one** ~ ..., **on the other** ~ ... por una parte ... por otra (parte) ...; **to** ~ **in** vt entregar; **to** ~ **out** vt distribuir; **to** ~ **over** vt (deliver) entregar; (surrender) ceder; ~**bag** n bolso, cartera (LAm); ~**book** n manual m; ~**brake** n freno de mano; ~**cuffs** npl esposas fpl; ~**ful** n puñado.

handicap ['hændɪkæp] n desventaja, (SPORT) handicap m // vt estorbar; **handicapped** a: **to be mentally/physically** ~**ped** ser deficiente m/f (mental)/minusválido/a (físico/a).

handicraft ['hændɪkrɑ:ft] n artesanía.

handiwork ['hændɪwə:k] n manualidad(es) f(pl); (fig) obra.

handkerchief ['hæŋkətʃɪf] n pañuelo.

handle ['hændl] n (of door etc) manija; (of cup etc) asa; (of knife etc) mango; (for winding) manivela // vt (touch) tocar; (deal with) encargarse de; (treat: people) manejar; '~ **with care**' (manéjese) con cuidado); **to fly off the** ~ perder los estribos; ~**bar(s)** n(pl) manillar msg.

hand: ~**luggage** n equipaje m de mano; ~**made** ['hændmeɪd] a hecho a mano; ~**out** ['hændaut] n (leaflet) folleto; ~**rail** ['hændreɪl] n pasamanos m inv; ~**shake** ['hændʃeɪk] n apretón m de manos.

handsome ['hænsəm] a guapo.

handwriting ['hændraɪtɪŋ] n letra.

handy ['hændɪ] a (close at hand) a la mano; (tool etc) práctico; (skilful) hábil, diestro; ~**man** n manitas m inv.

hang [hæŋ], pt, pp **hung** vt colgar; (head) bajar; (criminal: pt, pp **hanged**) ahorcar // vi colgar; **to get the** ~ **of sth** (col) lograr dominar algo; **to** ~ **about** vi haraganear; **to** ~ **on** vi (wait) esperar; **to** ~ **up** vi (TEL) colgar.

hanger ['hæŋə*] n percha.

hang-gliding ['hæŋglaɪdɪŋ] n vuelo

libre.

hangover ['hæŋəuvə*] n (after drinking) resaca.

hang-up ['hæŋʌp] n complejo.

hanker ['hæŋkə*] vi: to ~ after añorar.

hankie, hanky ['hæŋkɪ] n abbr = **handkerchief.**

haphazard [hæp'hæzəd] a fortuito.

happen ['hæpən] vi suceder, ocurrir; (take place) tener lugar, realizarse; as it ~s da la casualidad de que; ~ing n suceso, acontecimiento.

happily ['hæpɪlɪ] ad (luckily) afortunadamente; (cheerfully) alegremente.

happiness ['hæpɪnɪs] n (contentment) felicidad f; (joy) alegría.

happy ['hæpɪ] a feliz; (cheerful) alegre; to be ~ (with) estar contento (con); ~ **birthday!** ¡feliz cumpleaños!; ~**-go-lucky** a despreocupado.

harangue [hə'ræŋ] vt arengar.

harass ['hærəs] vt acosar, hostigar; ~**ment** n persecución f.

harbour, (US) harbor ['hɑ:bə*] n puerto // vt dar abrigo a.

hard [hɑ:d] a duro; (difficult) difícil; (work) arduo; (person) severo // ad (work) mucho, duro; (think) profundamente; to look ~ at sb/sth clavar los ojos en uno/algo; to try ~ esforzarse; no ~ feelings! ¡sin rencor(es)!; to be ~ of hearing ser duro de oído; to be ~ done by ser tratado injustamente; ~ **cash** n dinero contante; ~ **disk** n (COMPUT) disco duro or rígido; ~**en** vt endurecer; (fig) curtir // vi endurecerse; ~**-headed** a poco sentimental, realista; ~ **labour** n trabajos mpl forzados.

hardly ['hɑ:dlɪ] ad (scarcely) apenas; that can ~ be true eso difícilmente puede ser cierto; ~ ever casi nunca.

hardship ['hɑ:dʃɪp] n (troubles) penas fpl; (financial) apuro.

hard-up [hɑ:d'ʌp] a (col) sin un duro

(Sp), sin plata (LAm).

hardware ['hɑ:dwɛə*] n ferretería; (COMPUT) hardware m; ~ **shop** n ferretería.

hard-wearing [hɑ:d'wɛərɪŋ] a resistente, duradero.

hard-working [hɑ:d'wɜ:kɪŋ] a trabajador(a).

hardy ['hɑ:dɪ] a fuerte; (plant) resistente.

hare [hɛə*] n liebre f; ~**-brained** a casquivano.

haricot (bean) ['hærɪkəu-] n alubia.

harm [hɑ:m] n daño, mal m // vt (person) hacer daño a; (health, interests) perjudicar; (thing) dañar; **out of** ~'**s way** a salvo; ~**ful** a (gen) dañino; (to reputation) perjudicial; ~**less** a (person) inofensivo; (drugs) inocuo.

harmonize ['hɑ:mənaɪz] vt, vi armonizar.

harmony ['hɑ:mənɪ] n armonía.

harness ['hɑ:nɪs] n arreos mpl // vt (horse) enjaezar; (resources) aprovechar.

harp [hɑ:p] n arpa // vi: to ~ on (about) machacar (con).

harpoon [hɑ:'pu:n] n arpón m.

harrowing ['hærəuɪŋ] a angustioso.

harsh [hɑ:ʃ] a (cruel) duro, cruel; (severe) severo; (words) hosco; (colour) chillón/ona; (contrast) violento.

harvest ['hɑ:vɪst] n cosecha; (of grapes) vendimia // vt, vi cosechar; ~**er** n (machine) cosechadora.

has [hæz] vb see **have.**

hash [hæʃ] n (CULIN) picadillo; (fig: mess) lío.

hashish ['hæʃɪʃ] n hachís m, hachich m.

hasn't ['hæznt] = **has not.**

hassle ['hæsl] n pelea.

haste [heɪst] n prisa; ~**n** ['heɪsn] vt acelerar // vi darse prisa; **hastily** ad de prisa; **hasty** a apresurado.

hat [hæt] n sombrero.

hatch [hætʃ] n (NAUT: also: ~**way**) escotilla // vi salir del cascarón // vt incubar; (plot) tramar.

hatchback ['hætʃbæk] n (AUT) tres or cinco puertas m.

hatchet ['hætʃɪt] n hacha.

hate [heɪt] vt odiar, aborrecer // n odio; **~ful** a odioso; **hatred** ['heɪtrɪd] a odio.

hat trick n: to score a ~ (Brit: SPORT) marcar tres goles or tantos.

haughty ['hɔːtɪ] a altanero, arrogante.

haul [hɔːl] vt tirar; (by lorry) transportar // n (of fish) redada; (of stolen goods etc) botín m; **~age** n (Brit) transporte m; (costs) gastos mpl de transporte; **~ier**, (US) **~er** n transportista m/f.

haunch [hɔːntʃ] n anca; (of meat) pierna.

haunt [hɔːnt] vt (subj: ghost) aparecer en; (frequent) frecuentar; (obsess) obsesionar // n guarida.

KEYWORD

have [hæv], pt, pp **had** ♦ auxiliary vb 1 (gen) haber; **to ~ arrived/eaten** haber llegado/comido; **having finished or when he had finished, he left** cuando terminó, se fue
2 (in tag questions): **you've done it, ~n't you?** lo has hecho, ¿verdad? or ¿no?
3 (in short answers and questions): **I ~n't** no; **so I ~** pues, es verdad; **we ~n't paid — yes we ~!** no hemos pagado — sí que hemos pagado!; **I've been there before, ~ you?** he estado allí antes, ¿y tú?
♦ modal auxiliary vb (be obliged): **to ~ (got) to do sth** tener que hacer algo; **you ~n't to tell her** no hay que or no debes decírselo
♦ vt 1 (possess): **he has (got) blue eyes/dark hair** tiene los ojos azules/el pelo negro
2 (referring to meals etc): **to ~ breakfast/lunch/dinner** desayunar/comer/cenar; **to ~ a drink/a cigarette** tomar algo/fumar un cigarrillo
3 (receive) recibir; (obtain) obtener; **may I ~ your address?** ¿puedes

darme tu dirección?; **you can ~ it for £5** te lo puedes quedar por £5; **I must ~ it by tomorrow** lo necesito para mañana; **to ~ a baby** tener un niño or bebé
4 (maintain, allow): **I won't ~ it/this nonsense!** ¡no lo permitiré!/¡no permitiré estas tonterías!; **we can't ~ that** no podemos permitir eso
5: **to ~ sth done** hacer or mandar hacer algo; **to ~ one's hair cut** cortarse el pelo; **to ~ sb do sth** hacer que alguien haga algo
6 (experience, suffer): **to ~ a cold/flu** tener un resfriado/gripe; **she had her bag stolen/her arm broken** le robaron el bolso/se rompió un brazo; **to ~ an operation** operarse
7 (+ noun): **to ~ a swim/walk/bath/rest** nadar/dar un paseo/darse un baño/descansar; **let's ~ a look** vamos a ver; **to ~ a meeting/party** celebrar una reunión/una fiesta; **let me ~ a try** déjame intentarlo;
to ~ out vt: **to ~ it out with sb** (settle a problem etc) dejar las cosas en claro con alguien.

---

haven ['heɪvn] n puerto; (fig) refugio.

haven't ['hævnt] = **have not**.

haversack ['hævəsæk] n mochila.

havoc ['hævək] n estragos mpl.

hawk ['hɔːk] n halcón m.

hay [heɪ] n heno; **~ fever** n fiebre f del heno; **~stack** n almiar m.

haywire ['heɪwaɪə'] a (col): **to go ~** (person) volverse loco; (plan) embrollarse.

hazard ['hæzəd] n riesgo; (danger) peligro // vt aventurar; **~ous** a peligroso; **~ warning lights** npl (AUT) señales fpl de emergencia.

haze [heɪz] n neblina.

hazelnut ['heɪzlnʌt] n avellana.

hazy ['heɪzɪ] a brumoso; (idea) vago.

he [hiː] pron él; **~ who...** él que..., quien...

head [hɛd] n cabeza; (leader) jefe/a m/f // vt (list) encabezar; (group) capitanear; ~s **(or tails)** cara (o cruz); ~ **first** de cabeza; ~ **over heels** patas arriba; to ~ **the ball** cabecear (la pelota); to ~ **for** vt fus dirigirse a; ~**ache** n dolor m de cabeza; ~**dress** n tocado; ~**ing** n título; ~**lamp** n (Brit) = ~**light**; ~**land** n promontorio; ~**light** n faro; ~**line** n titular m; ~**long** ad (fall) de cabeza; (rush) precipitadamente; ~**master/mistress** n director(a) m/f (de escuela); ~ **office** n oficina central, central f; ~**on** a (collision) de frente; ~**phones** npl auriculares mpl; ~**quarters (HQ)** npl sede f central; (MIL) cuartel m general; ~**rest** n reposa-cabezas m inv; ~**room** n (in car) altura interior; (under bridge) (límite m de) altura; ~**scarf** n pañuelo; ~**strong** a testarudo; ~ **waiter** n maître m; ~**way** n: to make ~ (fig) hacer progresos; ~**wind** n viento contrario; ~**y** a (experience, period) apasionante; (wine) cabezón.

heal [hi:l] n salud f; ~ **food** n alimentos mpl orgánicos; **the H~ Service** n (Brit) servicio de salud pública; = Insalud m (Sp); ~**y** a (gen) sano.

heap [hi:p] n montón m // vt amontonar.

hear [hɪə*], pt, pp **heard** [hɜːd] vt oír; (perceive) sentir; (listen to) escuchar; (lecture) asistir a // vi oír; to ~ **about** oír hablar de; to ~ **from sb** tener noticias de uno; ~**ing** n (sense) oído; (LAW) vista; ~**ing aid** n audífono; ~**say** n rumores mpl, habillas fpl.

hearse [hɜːs] n coche m fúnebre.

heart [hɑːt] n corazón m; ~s npl (CARDS) corazones m; **at** ~ en el fondo; **by** ~ (learn, know) de memoria; ~ **attack** n infarto (de miocardio); ~**beat** n latido (del corazón); ~**breaking** a desgarrador(a); ~**broken** a: she was ~**broken about it** esto le partió el corazón;

~**burn** n acedía; ~ **failure** n fallo cardíaco; ~**felt** a (cordial) cordial; (deeply felt) más sentido.

hearth [hɑːθ] n (gen) hogar m; (fireplace) chimenea.

heartily ['hɑːtɪlɪ] ad sinceramente, cordialmente; (laugh) a carcajadas; (eat) con buen apetito.

heartless ['hɑːtlɪs] a cruel.

hearty ['hɑːtɪ] a cordial.

heat [hi:t] n (gen) calor m; (SPORT: also: qualifying ~) prueba eliminatoria // vt calentar; to ~ **up** vi (gen) calentarse; ~**ed** a caliente; (fig) acalorado; ~**er** n calentador m.

heath [hi:θ] n (Brit) brezal m.

heathen ['hi:ðən] a, n pagano/a m/f.

heather ['hɛðə*] n brezo.

heating ['hi:tɪŋ] n calefacción f.

heatstroke ['hi:tstrəuk] n insolación f.

heatwave ['hi:tweɪv] n ola de calor.

heave [hi:v] vt (pull) tirar; (push) empujar con esfuerzo; (lift) levantar (con esfuerzo) // vi (water) subir y bajar // n tirón m; empujón m.

heaven ['hɛvn] n cielo; ~**ly** a celestial.

heavily ['hɛvɪlɪ] ad pesadamente; (drink, smoke) con exceso; (sleep, sigh) profundamente.

heavy ['hɛvɪ] a pesado; (work) duro; (sea, rain, meal) fuerte; (drinker, smoker) gran; ~ **goods vehicle (HGV)** n vehículo pesado; ~**weight** n (SPORT) peso pesado.

Hebrew ['hi:bru:] a, n (LING) hebreo.

Hebrides ['hɛbrɪdiːz] npl: **the** ~ las Hébridas.

heckle ['hɛkl] vt interrumpir.

hectic ['hɛktɪk] a agitado.

he'd [hi:d] = he would, he had.

hedge [hɛdʒ] n seto // vt cercar (con un seto) // vi contestar con evasivas; to ~ **one's bets** (fig) cubrirse.

hedgehog ['hɛdʒhɔg] n erizo.

heed [hi:d] vt: also: **take ~ of** (pay attention) hacer caso de; (bear in mind) tener en cuenta; ~**less** a desatento.

heel [hi:l] *n* talón *m* // *vt* (*shoe*) poner tacón a.

hefty ['heftɪ] *a* (*person*) fornido; (*piece*) grande; (*price*) gordo.

heifer ['hefə*] *n* novilla, ternera.

height [haɪt] *n* (*of person*) talle *m*; (*of building*) altura; (*high ground*) cerro; (*altitude*) altitud *f*; **~en** *vt* elevar; (*fig*) aumentar.

heir [ɛə*] *n* heredero; **~ess** *n* heredera; **~loom** *n* reliquia de familia.

held [held] *pt, pp* of **hold**.

helicopter ['helɪkɒptə*] *n* helicóptero.

helium ['hi:lɪəm] *n* helio.

hell [hel] *n* infierno; **~!** (*col*) ¡demonios!

he'll [hi:l] = **he will, he shall.**

hellish ['helɪʃ] *a* infernal.

hello [hə'ləu] *excl* ¡hola!; (*surprise*) ¡caramba!

helm [helm] *n* (*NAUT*) timón *m*.

helmet ['helmɪt] *n* casco.

help [help] *n* ayuda; (*charwoman*) criada, asistenta // *vt* ayudar; **~!** ¡socorro!; **~** **yourself** sírvete; **he can't ~** it no es culpa suya; **~er** *n* ayudante *m/f*; **~ful** *a* útil; (*person*) servicial; **~ing** *n* ración *f*; **~less** *a* (*incapable*) incapaz; (*defenceless*) indefenso.

hem [hem] *n* dobladillo // *vt* poner or coser el dobladillo; **to ~ in** *vt* cercar.

he-man ['hi:mæn] *n* macho.

hemorrhage ['hemərɪdʒ] *n* (*US*) = **haemorrhage.**

hemorrhoids ['hemərɔɪdʒ] *npl* (*US*) = **haemorrhoids.**

hen [hen] *n* gallina.

hence [hens] *ad* (*therefore*) por lo tanto; **2 years ~** de aquí a 2 años; **~forth** *ad* de hoy en adelante.

henchman ['hentʃmən] *n* (*pej*) secuaz *m*.

henpecked ['henpekt] *a*: **to be ~** ser un calzonazos.

hepatitis [hepə'taɪtɪs] *n* hepatitis *f*.

her [hə:*] *pron* (*direct*) la; (*indirect*) le; (*stressed, after prep*) ella // *a* su; *see also* **me, my.**

herald ['herəld] *n* heraldo // *vt* anunciar.

herb [hə:b] *n* hierba.

herd [hə:d] *n* rebaño.

here [hɪə*] *ad* aquí, ~! (*present*) ¡presente!; (*offering sth*) ¡toma!; **~ is/are** aquí está/están; **~ she is** aquí está; **~after** *ad* en el futuro // *n*: **the ~after** el más allá; **~by** *ad* (*in letter*) por la presente.

heredity [hɪ'redɪtɪ] *n* herencia.

heresy ['herəsɪ] *n* herejía.

heretic ['heretɪk] *n* hereje *m/f*.

heritage ['herɪtɪdʒ] *n* (*gen*) herencia; (*fig*) patrimonio.

hermetically [hə:'metɪklɪ] *ad*: **~ sealed** cerrado herméticamente.

hermit ['hə:mɪt] *n* ermitaño/a.

hernia ['hə:nɪə] *n* hernia.

hero ['hɪərəu], *pl* **~es** *n* héroe *m*; (*in book, film*) protagonista *m*; **~ic** [hɪ'rəuɪk] *a* heroico.

heroin ['herəuɪn] *n* heroína.

heroine ['herəuɪn] *n* heroína; (*in book, film*) protagonista.

heron ['herən] *n* garza.

herring ['herɪŋ] *n* arenque *m*.

hers [hə:z] *pron* (el) suyo/(la) suya etc; *see also* **mine.**

herself [hə:'self] *pron* (*reflexive*) se; (*emphatic*) ella misma; (*after prep*) sí (misma); *see also* **oneself.**

he's [hi:z] = **he is; he has.**

hesitant ['hezɪtənt] *a* vacilante.

hesitate ['hezɪteɪt] *vi* vacilar; **hesitation** ['-teɪʃən] *n* indecisión *f*.

heterosexual [hetərəu'seksjuəl] *a, n* heterosexual *m/f*.

heyday ['heɪdeɪ] *n*: **the ~ of** el apogeo de.

HGV *n* abbr = **heavy goods vehicle.**

hi [haɪ] *excl* ¡hola!

hiatus [haɪ'eɪtəs] *n* laguna; (*LING*) hiato.

hibernate ['haɪbəneɪt] *vi* invernar.

hiccough, hiccup ['hɪkʌp] *vi* hipar; **~s** *npl* hipo *sg*.

hide [haɪd] n (*skin*) piel f // vb (*pt* **hid**, *pp* **hidden**) vt esconder, ocultar // vi: **to ~ (from sb)** esconderse or ocultarse (de uno); **~-and-seek** n escondite m; **~away** n escondite m.

hideous ['hɪdɪəs] a horrible.

hiding ['haɪdɪŋ] n (*beating*) paliza; **to be in ~** (*concealed*) estar escondido; **~ place** n escondrijo.

hierarchy ['haɪərɑːkɪ] n jerarquía.

hi-fi ['haɪfaɪ] n estéreo, hifi m // a de alta fidelidad.

high [haɪ] a alto; (*speed, number*) grande; (*price*) elevado; (*wind*) fuerte; (*voice*) agudo // ad alto, a gran altura; **it is 20 m ~** tiene 20 m de altura; **~ in the air** en las alturas; **~brow** n (*US*) cómoda alta; **~brow** a, n intelectual m/f; **~chair** n silla alta; **~er education** n educación f or enseñanza superior; **~-handed** a despótico; **~jack** = **hijack**; **~ jump** n (*SPORT*) salto de altura; **the H~lands** npl las tierras altas de Escocia; **~light** n (*fig: of event*) punto culminante // vt subrayar; **~ly** ad sumamente; **~ly strung** a hipertenso; **~ness** n altura; **Her** or **His H~ness** Su Alteza; **~pitched** a agudo; **~rise block** n torre f de pisos; **~ school** n centro de enseñanza secundaria; = Instituto Nacional de Bachillerato (*Sp*); **~ season** n (*Brit*) temporada alta; **~ street** n (*Brit*) calle f mayor; **~way** n carretera; **H~way Code** n (*Brit*) código de la circulación.

hijack ['haɪdʒæk] vt secuestrar; **~er** n secuestrador(a) m/f.

hike [haɪk] vi (*go walking*) ir de excursión (de pie) // n caminata; **~r** n excursionista m/f.

hilarious [hɪ'lɛərɪəs] a divertidísimo.

hill [hɪl] n colina; (*high*) montaña; (*slope*) cuesta; **~side** n ladera; **~y** a montañoso; (*uneven*) accidentado.

hilt [hɪlt] n (*of sword*) empuñadura; **to the ~** (*fig: support*) incondicionalmente.

him [hɪm] pron (*direct*) le, lo; (*indi-*

rect) le; (*stressed, after prep*) él; *see also* **me**; **~self** pron (*reflexive*) se; (*emphatic*) él mismo; (*after prep*) sí (mismo); *see also* **oneself**.

hind [haɪnd] a posterior // n cierva.

hinder ['hɪndə*] vt estorbar, impedir; **hindrance** ['hɪndrəns] n estorbo, obstáculo.

hindsight ['haɪndsaɪt] n: **with ~** en retrospectiva.

Hindu ['hɪnduː] n hindú m/f.

hinge [hɪndʒ] n bisagra, gozne m // vi (*fig*): **to ~ on** depender de.

hint [hɪnt] n indirecta; (*advice*) consejo // vt: **to ~** that insinuar que // vi: **to ~ at** hacer alusión a.

hip [hɪp] n cadera.

hippopotamus [hɪpə'pɔtəməs], pl **~es** or **-mi** [-maɪ] n hipopótamo.

hire ['haɪə*] vt (*Brit: car, equipment*) alquilar; (*worker*) contratar // n alquiler m; **for ~** se alquila; (*taxi*) libre; **~ purchase (H.P.)** n (*Brit*) compra a plazos.

his [hɪz] pron (el) suyo/(la) suya *etc* // a su; *see also* **my, mine**.

Hispanic [hɪs'pænɪk] a hispánico.

hiss [hɪs] vi silbar.

historian [hɪ'stɔːrɪən] n historiador(a) m/f.

historic(al) [hɪ'stɔrɪk(l)] a histórico.

history ['hɪstərɪ] n historia.

hit [hɪt] vt (*pt, pp* **hit**) (*strike*) golpear, pegar; (*reach: target*) alcanzar; (*collide with: car*) chocar contra; (*fig: affect*) afectar // n golpe m; (*success*) éxito; **to ~ it off with sb** llevarse bien con uno; **~-and-run driver** n conductor(a) que atropella y huye.

hitch [hɪtʃ] vt (*fasten*) atar, amarrar; (*also: ~ up*) remangar // n (*difficulty*) dificultad f; **to ~ a lift** hacer autostop.

hitch-hike ['hɪtʃhaɪk] vi hacer autostop; **~r** n autostopista m/f.

hi-tech [haɪ'tɛk] a de alta tecnología.

hitherto ['hɪðə'tuː] ad hasta ahora.

hive [haɪv] n colmena; **to ~ off** vt transferir; (*privatize*) privatizar.

HMS abbr = His (Her) Majesty's Ship.

hoard [hɔːd] n (treasure) tesoro; (stockpile) provisión f // vt acumular; ~**ing** n (for posters) cartelera.

hoarfrost ['hɔːfrɒst] n escarcha.

hoarse [hɔːs] a ronco.

hoax [həuks] n trampa.

hob [hɒb] n quemador m.

hobble ['hɒbl] vi cojear.

hobby ['hɒbɪ] n pasatiempo, afición f; ~**horse** n (fig) caballo de batalla.

hobo ['həubəu] n (US) vagabundo.

hockey ['hɒkɪ] n hockey m.

hoe [həu] n azadón m // vt azadonar.

hog [hɒg] n cerdo, puerco // vt (fig) acaparar; **to go the whole** ~ poner toda la carne en el asador.

hoist [hɔɪst] n (crane) grúa // vt levantar, alzar.

hold [həuld] vt (pt, pp **held**) tener; (contain) contener; (keep back) retener; (believe) sostener; (take ~ of) coger (Sp), agarrar (LAm); (take weight) soportar; (meeting) celebrar // vi (withstand pressure) resistir; (be valid) valer; (stick) pegarse // n (grasp) asimiento; (fig) dominio; (WRESTLING) presa; (NAUT) bodega; ~ **the line!** (TEL) ¡no cuelgue!; **to** ~ **one's own** (fig) defenderse; **to catch or get** (a) ~ **of** agarrarse or asirse de; **to** ~ **back** vt retener; (secret) ocultar; **to** ~ **down** vt (person) sujetar; (job) mantener; **to** ~ **off** vt (enemy) rechazar; **to** ~ **on** vi agarrarse bien; (wait) esperar; **to** ~ **on to** vt fus agarrarse a; (keep) guardar; **to** ~ **out** vt ofrecer // vi (resist) resistir; **to** ~ **up** vt (raise) levantar; (support) apoyar; (delay) retrasar; (rob) asaltar; ~**all** n (Brit) bolsa; ~**er** n (of ticket, record) poseedor(a) m/f; (of office, title etc) titular m/f; ~**ing** n (share) interés m; ~**up** n (robbery) atraco; (delay) retraso; (Brit: in traffic) embotellamiento.

hole [həul] n agujero // vt agujerear.

holiday ['hɒlədɪ] n vacaciones fpl; (day off) día m de fiesta, día m feriado; **on** ~ de vacaciones; ~ **camp** n colonia veraniega; ~**maker** n (Brit) turista m/f; ~ **resort** n centro turístico.

holiness ['həulɪnɪs] n santidad f.

Holland ['hɒlənd] n Holanda.

hollow ['hɒləu] a hueco; (fig) vacío; (eyes) hundido; (sound) sordo // n (gen) hueco; (in ground) hoyo // vt: **to** ~ **out** ahuecar.

holly ['hɒlɪ] n acebo.

holocaust ['hɒləkɔːst] n holocausto.

holster ['həulstə*] n pistolera.

holy ['həulɪ] a (gen) santo, sagrado; (water) bendito; **H~ Ghost or Spirit** n Espíritu m Santo.

homage ['hɒmɪdʒ] n homenaje m.

home [həum] n casa; (country) patria; (institution) asilo // a (domestic) casero, de casa; (ECON, POL) nacional // ad (direction) a casa; **at** ~ en casa; **to go/come** ~ ir/volver a casa; **make yourself at** ~ ¡estás en tu casa!; ~ **address** n domicilio; ~ **computer** n ordenador m doméstico; ~**land** n tierra natal; ~**less** a sin hogar, sin casa; ~**ly** a (domestic) casero; (simple) sencillo; ~**made** a hecho en casa; **H~ Office** n (Brit) Ministerio del Interior; ~ **rule** n autonomía; **H~ Secretary** n (Brit) Ministro del Interior; ~**sick** a: **to be** ~**sick** tener morriña, sentir nostalgia; ~ **town** n ciudad f natal; ~**ward** ['həumwəd] a (journey) hacia casa; ~**work** n deberes mpl.

homogeneous [hɒmə'dʒiːnɪəs] a homogéneo.

homicide ['hɒmɪsaɪd] n (US) homicidio.

homosexual [hɒməu'sɛksjuəl] a, n homosexual m/f.

Honduran [hɒn'djuərən] a, n hondureño/a m/f.

Honduras [hɒn'djuərəs] n Honduras f.

honest ['ɒnɪst] a honrado; (sincere) franco, sincero; ~**ly** ad honradamente; francamente; **~y** n honradez f.

honey ['hʌni] n miel f; **~comb** n panal m; **~moon** n luna de miel; **~ suckle** n madreselva.

honk [hɒŋk] vi (AUT) tocar la bocina.

honorary ['ɒnərəri] a (member, president) de honor; **~ degree** doctorado honoris causa.

honour, (US) **honor** ['ɒnə] vt honrar // n honor m, honra; **~able** a honorable; **~s degree** (SCOL) título de licenciado de categoría superior.

hood [hud] n capucha; (Brit AUT) capota; (US: AUT) capó m.

hoodlum ['huːdləm] n matón m.

hoodwink ['hudwɪŋk] vt (Brit) timar.

hoof [huːf], pl **hooves** n pezuña.

hook [huk] n gancho; (on dress) corchete m, broche m; (for fishing) anzuelo // vt enganchar.

hooligan ['huːlɪɡən] n gamberro.

hoop [huːp] n aro.

hoot [huːt] vi (Brit AUT) tocar la bocina; (siren) sonar la sirena // n bocinazo, toque m de sirena; to ~ **with laughter** morirse de risa; **~er** n (Brit AUT) bocina; (NAUT) sirena.

hoover ® ['huːvə] n (Brit) aspiradora // vt pasar la aspiradora por.

hooves [huːvz] pl of **hoof**.

hop [hɒp] vi saltar, brincar; (on one foot) saltar con un pie.

hope [həup] vt, vi esperar // n esperanza; I ~ **so/not** espero que sí/no; **~ful** a (person) optimista; (situation) prometedor/a; **~fully** ad con optimismo, con esperanza; **~less** a desesperado.

hops [hɒps] npl lúpulo sg.

horizon [hə'raɪzn] n horizonte m; **~tal** [hɒrɪ'zɒntl] a horizontal.

hormone ['hɔːməun] n hormona.

horn [hɔːn] n cuerno; (MUS: also: French ~) trompa; (AUT) bocina, claxon m (LAm).

hornet ['hɔːnɪt] n avispón m.

horny ['hɔːnɪ] a (material) córneo; (hands) calloso; (col) cachondo.

horoscope ['hɒrəskəup] n horóscopo.

horrendous [hə'rɛndəs] a horrendo.

horrible ['hɒrɪbl] a horrible.

horrid ['hɒrɪd] a horrible, horroroso.

horrify ['hɒrɪfaɪ] vt horrorizar.

horror ['hɒrə] n horror m; ~ **film** n película de horror.

hors d'œuvre [ɔː'dəːvrə] n entremeses mpl.

horse [hɔːs] n caballo; **on ~back** a caballo; **~ chestnut** n (tree) castaño de Indias; **~man/woman** n jinete/a m(f); **~power (h.p.)** n caballo (de fuerza); **~-racing** n carreras fpl de caballos; **~radish** n rábano picante; **~shoe** n herradura.

hose [həuz] n (also: **~pipe**) manga.

hosiery ['həuzɪərɪ] n calcetería.

hospitable [hɒs'pɪtəbl] a hospitalario.

hospital ['hɒspɪtl] n hospital m.

hospitality [hɒspɪ'tælɪtɪ] n hospitalidad f.

host [həust] n anfitrión m; (of inn etc) mesonero (REL) hostia; (large number): **a ~ of** multitud de.

hostage ['hɒstɪdʒ] n rehén m.

hostel ['hɒstl] n hostal m; (youth) ~ n albergue m juvenil.

hostess ['həustɪs] n anfitriona.

hostile ['hɒstaɪl] a hostil; **hostility** [-'stɪlɪtɪ] n hostilidad f.

hot [hɒt] a caliente; (weather) caluroso, de calor; (as opposed to only warm) muy caliente; (spicy) picante; (fig) ardiente, acalorado; to be ~ (person) tener calor; (object) estar caliente; (weather) hacer calor; **~bed** n (fig) semillero; ~ **dog** n perro caliente.

hotel [həu'tɛl] n hotel m; **~ier** n hotelero.

hot: **~headed** a exaltado; **~house** n invernadero; **~ line** n (POL) teléfono rojo; **~ly** ad con pasión, apasionadamente; **~plate** n (on cooker) hornillo; **~-water bottle** n bolsa de agua caliente.

hound [haund] vt acosar // n perro de caza.

hour ['auə*] n hora; **~ly** a (de) cada hora // ad cada hora.

house (haus, pl: 'hauziz) n (also: firm) casa; (POL) cámara; (THEATRE) sala // vt [hauz] (person) alojar; **on the ~** (fig) la casa invita; **~arrest** n arresto domiciliario; **~boat** n casa flotante; **~breaking** n allanamiento de morada; **~hold** n familia; **~keeper** n ama de llaves; **~keeping** n (work) trabajos mpl domésticos; **~keeping (money)** n dinero para gastos domésticos; **~warming party** n fiesta de estreno de una casa; **~wife** n ama de casa; **~work** n faenas fpl (de la casa).

housing ['hauziŋ] n (act) alojamiento; (houses) viviendas fpl; **~ development**, (Brit) **~ estate** n urbanización f.

hovel ['hɔvl] n casucha.

hover ['hɔvə*] vi flotar (en el aire); **~craft** n aerodeslizador m.

how [hau] ad (in what way) cómo; **~ are you?** ¿cómo estás?; **~ much milk/many people?** ¿cuánta leche/gente?; **~ much does it cost?** ¿cuánto cuesta?; **~ long have you been here?** ¿cuánto hace que estás aquí?; **~ old are you?** ¿cuántos años tienes?; **~ tall is he?** ¿cuánto es de alto?; **~ is school?** ¿cómo (te) va (en) la escuela?; **~ was the film?** ¿qué tal la película?; **~ lovely/awful!** ¡qué bonito/horror!

howl [haul] n aullido // vi aullar.

H.P. n abbr = **hire purchase.**

h.p. abbr = **horse power.**

HQ n abbr = **headquarters.**

hub [hʌb] n (of wheel) centro.

hubbub ['hʌbʌb] n barahúnda, barullo.

hubcap ['hʌbkæp] n tapacubos m inv.

huddle ['hʌdl] vi: **to ~ together** amontonarse.

hue [hju:] n color m, matiz m; **~ and cry** n alarma.

huff [hʌf] n: **in a ~** enojado.

hug [hʌg] vt abrazar // n abrazo.

huge [hju:dʒ] a enorme.

hulk [hʌlk] n (ship) barco viejo; (person, building etc) mole f.

hull [hʌl] n (of ship) casco.

hullo [hə'ləu] excl = **hello.**

hum [hʌm] vt tararear, canturrear // vi tararear, canturrear; (insect) zumbar.

human ['hju:mən] a, n humano m/f.

humane [hju:'meɪn] a humano, humanitario.

humanitarian [hju:mæni'tɛərɪən] a humanitario.

humanity [hju:'mænɪtɪ] n humanidad f.

humble ['hʌmbl] a humilde // vt humillar.

humbug ['hʌmbʌg] n tonterías fpl; (Brit: sweet) caramelo de menta.

humdrum ['hʌmdrʌm] a (boring) monótono, aburrido; (routine) rutinario.

humid ['hju:mɪd] a húmedo; **~ity** [-'mɪdɪtɪ] n humedad f.

humiliate [hju:'mɪlɪeɪt] vt humillar; **humiliation** [-'eɪʃən] n humillación f.

humility [hju:'mɪlɪtɪ] n humildad f.

humorous ['hju:mərəs] a gracioso, divertido.

humour, (US) **humor** ['hju:mə*] n humorismo, sentido del humor; (mood) humor m // vt (person) complacer.

hump [hʌmp] n (in ground) montículo; (camel's) giba.

hunch [hʌntʃ] n (premonition) presentimiento; **~back** n joroba m/f; **~ed** a jorobado.

hundred ['hʌndrəd] num ciento; (before n) cien; **~s of** centenares de; **~weight** n (Brit) = 50.8 kg; 112 lb; (US) = 45.3 kg; 100 lb.

hung [hʌŋ] pt, pp of **hang.**

Hungarian [hʌŋ'gɛərɪən] a, n húngaro/a m/f.

Hungary ['hʌŋgərɪ] n Hungría.

hunger ['hʌŋgə*] n hambre f // vi: **~ for** (fig) tener hambre de, anhelar; ~ **strike** n huelga de hambre.

hungry ['hʌŋgrɪ] a hambriento; to be ~ tener hambre.

hunk [hʌŋk] n (of bread etc) trozo, pedazo.

hunt [hʌnt] vt (seek) buscar; (SPORT) cazar // vi cazar // n caza, cacería; ~**er** n cazador(a) m/f; ~**ing** n caza.

hurdle ['həːdl] n (SPORT) valla; (fig) obstáculo.

hurl [həːl] vt lanzar, arrojar.

hurrah [hu'rɑː], **hurray** [hu'reɪ] n ¡viva!, ¡vítor!

hurricane ['hʌrɪkən] n huracán m.

hurried ['hʌrɪd] a (fast) apresurado; (rushed) hecho de prisa; ~**ly** ad con prisa, apresuradamente.

hurry ['hʌrɪ] n prisa // vi (also: ~ up) vi apresurarse, darse prisa // vt (person) dar prisa a; (work) apresurar, hacer de prisa; to be in a ~ tener prisa.

hurt [həːt], pt, pp **hurt** vt hacer daño a // vi doler // a lastimado; ~**ful** a (remark etc) dañoso.

hurtle ['həːtl] vi: to ~ past pasar como un rayo.

husband ['hʌzbənd] n marido.

hush [hʌʃ] n silencio // vt hacer callar; (cover up) encubrir; ~! ¡chitón!, ¡cállate!

husk [hʌsk] n (of wheat) cáscara.

husky ['hʌskɪ] a ronco // n perro esquimal.

hustle ['hʌsl] vt (push) empujar; (hurry) dar prisa a // n bullicio, actividad f febril; ~ **and bustle** n vaivén m.

hut [hʌt] n cabaña; (shed) cobertizo.

hutch [hʌtʃ] n conejera.

hyacinth ['haɪəsɪnθ] n jacinto.

hydrant ['haɪdrənt] n (also: fire ~) boca de incendios.

hydraulic [haɪ'drɔːlɪk] a hidráulico.

hydroelectric [haɪdrəʊ'lektrɪk] a hidroeléctrico.

hydrofoil ['haɪdrəfɔɪl] n aerodeslizador m.

hydrogen ['haɪdrədʒən] n hidrógeno.

hyena [haɪ'iːnə] n hiena.

hygiene ['haɪdʒiːn] n higiene f; **hygienic** [-'dʒiːnɪk] a higiénico.

hymn [hɪm] n himno.

hype [haɪp] n (col) bombardeo publicitario.

hypermarket ['haɪpəmɑːkɪt] n hipermercado.

hyphen ['haɪfn] n guión m.

hypnotize ['hɪpnətaɪz] vt hipnotizar.

hypochondriac [haɪpəʊ'kɒndrɪæk] n hipocondríaco/a.

hypocrisy [hɪ'pɒkrɪsɪ] n hipocresía; **hypocrite** ['hɪpəkrɪt] n hipócrita m/f; **hypocritical** [hɪpə'krɪtɪkl] a hipócrita.

hypothesis [haɪ'pɒθɪsɪs], pl **-ses** [-siːz] n hipótesis f inv.

hysteria [hɪ'stɪərɪə] n histeria; **hysterical** [-'sterɪkl] a histérico; **hysterics** [-'sterɪks] npl histeria sg, histerismo sg.

I

I [aɪ] pron yo.

ice [aɪs] n hielo // vt (cake) alcorzar // vi (also: ~ **over**, ~ **up**) helarse; ~**axe** n piqueta de alpinista); ~**berg** n iceberg m; ~**box** n (Brit) congelador m; (US) nevera, refrigeradora (LAm); ~ **cream** n helado; ~ **cube** n cubito de hielo; ~ **hockey** n hockey m sobre hielo.

Iceland ['aɪslənd] n Islandia.

ice: ~ **lolly** n (Brit) polo; ~ **rink** n pista de hielo; ~ **skating** n patinaje m sobre hielo.

icicle ['aɪsɪkl] n carámbano.

icing ['aɪsɪŋ] n (CULIN) alcorza; (AVIAT) formación f de hielo; ~ **sugar** n (Brit) azúcar m glas(eado).

icy ['aɪsɪ] a (road) helado; (fig) glacial.

I'd [aɪd] = **I would; I had.**

idea [aɪ'dɪə] n idea.

ideal [aɪ'dɪəl] n ideal m // a ideal; ~**ist** n idealista m/f.

identical [aɪ'dentɪkl] a idéntico.

identification [aɪdentɪfɪˈkeɪʃən] n identificación f; **means of ~** documentos mpl personales.

identify [aɪˈdentɪfaɪ] vt identificar.

identikit picture [aɪˈdentɪkɪt-] n retrato-robot m.

identity [aɪˈdentɪtɪ] n identidad f; **~ card** n carnet m de identidad.

ideology [aɪdɪˈɒlədʒɪ] n ideología.

idiom [ˈɪdɪəm] n modismo; (style of speaking) lenguaje m; **~atic** [-ˈmætɪk] a idiomático.

idiosyncrasy [ɪdɪəʊˈsɪŋkrəsɪ] n idiosincrasia.

idiot [ˈɪdɪət] n (gen) idiota m/f; (fool) tonto/a; **~ic** [-ˈɒtɪk] a idiota; tonto.

idle [ˈaɪdl] a (lazy) holgazán/ana; (unemployed) parado, desocupado; (talk) frívolo // vt (machine) marchar en vacío // vt: **to ~ away the time** malgastar el tiempo; **~ness** n holgazanería; paro, desocupación f.

idol [ˈaɪdl] n ídolo; **~ize** vt idolatrar.

idyllic [ɪˈdɪlɪk] a idílico.

i.e. abbr (= that is) esto es.

if [ɪf] conj si; **~ necessary** si fuera necesario, si hiciese falta; **~ I were you** yo en tu lugar; **~ so/not** de ser así/si no; **~ only I could!** ¡ojalá pudiera!; see also as, even.

igloo [ˈɪgluː] n iglú m.

ignite [ɪgˈnaɪt] vt (set fire to) encender // vi encenderse.

ignition [ɪgˈnɪʃən] n (AUT) encendido; **to switch on/off the ~** arrancar/apagar el motor; **~ key** n (AUT) llave f de contacto.

ignorance [ˈɪgnərəns] n ignorancia.

ignorant [ˈɪgnərənt] a ignorante; **to be ~ of** ignorar.

ignore [ɪgˈnɔː] vt (person) no hacer caso de; (fact) pasar por alto.

ill [ɪl] a enfermo, malo // n mal m // ad mal; **to take or be taken ~** caer or ponerse enfermo; **~-advised** (decision) imprudente; **he was ~-advised to go** se equivocó al ir; **~-at-ease** a incómodo.

I'll [aɪl] = **I will, I shall.**

illegal [ɪˈliːgl] a ilegal.

illegible [ɪˈledʒɪbl] a ilegible.

illegitimate [ɪlɪˈdʒɪtɪmət] a ilegítimo.

ill-fated [ɪlˈfeɪtɪd] a malogrado.

ill feeling n rencor m.

illicit [ɪˈlɪsɪt] a ilícito.

illiterate [ɪˈlɪtərət] a analfabeto.

ill-mannered [ɪlˈmænəd] a mal educado.

illness [ˈɪlnɪs] n enfermedad f.

illuminate [ɪˈluːmɪneɪt] vt (room, street) iluminar, alumbrar; (subject) aclarar; **illumination** [-ˈneɪʃən] n alumbrado; **illuminations** npl iluminaciones fpl, luces fpl.

illusion [ɪˈluːʒən] n ilusión f; **to be under the ~ that...** hacerse ilusiones de que ....

illusory [ɪˈluːsərɪ] a ilusorio.

illustrate [ˈɪləstreɪt] vt ilustrar.

illustration [ɪləˈstreɪʃən] n (example) ejemplo, ilustración f; (in book) lámina.

illustrious [ɪˈlʌstrɪəs] a ilustre.

ill will n rencor m.

I'm [aɪm] = **I am.**

image [ˈɪmɪdʒ] n imagen f; **~ry** [-ərɪ] n imágenes fpl.

imaginary [ɪˈmædʒɪnərɪ] a imaginario.

imagination [ɪˈmædʒɪˈneɪʃən] n imaginación f; (inventiveness) inventiva; (illusion) fantasía.

imaginative [ɪˈmædʒɪnətɪv] a imaginativo.

imagine [ɪˈmædʒɪn] vt imaginarse; (delude o.s.) hacerse la ilusión (de que).

imbalance [ɪmˈbæləns] n desequilibrio.

imbecile [ˈɪmbəsiːl] n imbécil m/f.

imitate [ˈɪmɪteɪt] vt imitar; **imitation** [-ˈteɪʃən] n imitación f; (copy) copia; (pej) remedo.

immaculate [ɪˈmækjʊlət] a perfectamente limpio; (REL) inmaculado.

immaterial [ɪməˈtɪərɪəl] a incorpóreo; **it is ~ whether...** no importa si... .

immature [ɪmə'tjuə*] a (person) inmaduro; (of one's youth) joven.

immediate [ɪ'miːdɪət] a inmediato; (pressing) urgente, apremiante; **~ly** ad (at once) en seguida; **~ly next to** muy junto a.

immense [ɪ'mɛns] a inmenso, enorme.

immerse [ɪ'məːs] vt (submerge) sumergir; **to be ~d in** (fig) estar absorto en.

immersion heater [ɪ'məːʃən-] n (Brit) calentador m de inmersión.

immigrant ['ɪmɪɡrənt] n inmigrante m/f.

immigrate ['ɪmɪɡreɪt] vi inmigrar; **immigration** [-'ɡreɪʃən] n inmigración f.

imminent ['ɪmɪnənt] a inminente.

immobile [ɪ'məubaɪl] a inmóvil.

immoral [ɪ'mɔrl] a inmoral.

immortal [ɪ'mɔːtl] a inmortal.

immune [ɪ'mjuːn] a: **~ (to)** inmune (contra); **immunity** n (MED, of diplomat) inmunidad f.

immunize ['ɪmjunaɪz] vt inmunizar.

imp [ɪmp] n diablillo.

impact ['ɪmpækt] n (gen) impacto.

impair [ɪm'pɛə*] vt perjudicar.

impart [ɪm'pɑːt] vt comunicar.

impartial [ɪm'pɑːʃl] a imparcial.

impassable [ɪm'pɑːsəbl] a (barrier) infranqueable; (river, road) intransitable.

impasse [æm'pɑːs] n: **to reach an ~** alcanzar un punto muerto.

impassive [ɪm'pæsɪv] a impasible.

impatience [ɪm'peɪʃəns] n impaciencia.

impatient [ɪm'peɪʃənt] a impaciente; **to get o grow ~** impacientarse.

impeccable [ɪm'pɛkəbl] a impecable.

impede [ɪm'piːd] vt estorbar.

impediment [ɪm'pedɪmənt] n obstáculo, estorbo; (also: speech **~**) defecto (del habla).

impending [ɪm'pendɪŋ] a inminente.

impenetrable [ɪm'penɪtrəbl] a (gen) impenetrable; (unfathomable) insondable.

imperative [ɪm'perətɪv] a (tone) imperioso; (necessary) imprescindible // n (LING) imperativo.

imperfect [ɪm'pəːfɪkt] a imperfecto; (goods etc) defectuoso; **~ion** [-'fekʃən] n (blemish) desperfecto; (fault) defecto.

imperial [ɪm'pɪərɪəl] a imperial; **~ism** n imperialismo.

impersonal [ɪm'pəːsənl] a impersonal.

impersonate [ɪm'pəːsəneɪt] vt hacerse pasar por.

impertinent [ɪm'pəːtɪnənt] a impertinente, insolente.

impervious [ɪm'pəːvɪəs] a impermeable; (fig): **~ to** insensible a.

impetuous [ɪm'petjuəs] a impetuoso.

impetus ['ɪmpɪtəs] n ímpetu m; (fig) impulso.

impinge [ɪm'pɪndʒ]: **to ~ on** vt fus (affect) afectar a.

implacable [ɪm'plækəbl] a implacable.

implement ['ɪmplɪmənt] n instrumento, herramienta // vt ['ɪmplɪment] hacer efectivo; (carry out) realizar.

implicate ['ɪmplɪkeɪt] vt (compromise) comprometer; (involve) enredar; **implication** [-'keɪʃən] n consecuencia.

implicit [ɪm'plɪsɪt] a (gen) implícito; (complete) absoluto.

implore [ɪm'plɔː*] vt (person) suplicar.

imply [ɪm'plaɪ] vt (involve) suponer; (hint) dar a entender que.

impolite [ɪmpə'laɪt] a mal educado.

import vt [ɪm'pɔːt] vt importar // n ['ɪmpɔːt] (COMM) importación f; (meaning) significado, sentido.

importance [ɪm'pɔːtəns] n importancia.

important [ɪm'pɔːtənt] a importante; **it's not ~** no importa, no tiene importancia.

importer [ɪm'pɔːtə*] n importador(a) m/f.

impose [ɪm'pəuz] vt imponer // vi:

~ **on sb** abusar de uno; **imposing**
a imponente, impresionante.

imposition [ɪmpə'zɪʃn] *n* (*of tax
etc*) imposición *f*; **to be an ~** (*on
person*) molestar.

impossible [ɪm'pɒsɪbl] *a* imposible;
(*person*) insoportable.

impostor [ɪm'pɒstə*] *n* impostor(a)
m/f.

impotent ['ɪmpətənt] *a* impotente.

impound [ɪm'paʊnd] *vt* embargar.

impoverished [ɪm'pɒvərɪʃt] *a* necesitado; (*land*) agotado.

impracticable [ɪm'præktɪkəbl] *a* no
factible, irrealizable.

impractical [ɪm'præktɪkl] *a* (*person*)
poco práctico.

imprecise [ɪmprɪ'saɪs] *a* impreciso.

impregnable [ɪm'pregnəbl] *a* invul-
nerable; (*castle*) inexpugnable.

impregnate ['ɪmpregneɪt] *vt* impregnar; (*BIOL*) fecundar.

impress [ɪm'pres] *vt* (*person*);
(*mark*) estampar // *vi* hacer buena
impresión; **to ~ sth on sb** hacer entender algo a uno.

impression [ɪm'preʃən] *n* impresión
f; (*footprint etc*) huella; (*print run*)
edición *f*; **to be under the ~** that
tener la impresión de que; **~able** *a*
impresionable; **~ist** *n* impresionista
m/f.

impressive [ɪm'presɪv] *a* impresionante.

imprint ['ɪmprɪnt] *n* (*PUBLISHING*)
pie *m* de imprenta; (*fig*) sello.

imprison [ɪm'prɪzn] *vt* encarcelar;
~ment *n* encarcelamiento; (*term of
~*) cárcel *f*.

improbable [ɪm'prɒbəbl] *a* improbable, inverosímil.

impromptu [ɪm'prɒmptju:] *a* improvisado // *ad* de improviso.

improper [ɪm'prɒpə*] *a* (*incorrect*)
impropio; (*unseemly*) indecoroso;
(*indecent*) indecente.

improve [ɪm'pru:v] *vt* mejorar; (*foreign language*) perfeccionar // *vi* mejorarse; (*pupils*) hacer progresos;
~ment *n* mejoramiento; perfección

f; progreso.

improvise ['ɪmprəvaɪz] *vt, vi* improvisar.

imprudent [ɪm'pru:dnt] *a* imprudente.

impudent ['ɪmpjudnt] *a* descarado,
insolente.

impulse ['ɪmpʌls] *n* impulso; **to act
on ~** obrar sin reflexión; **impulsive**
[-'pʌlsɪv] *a* irreflexivo.

impunity [ɪm'pju:nɪtɪ] *n*: **with ~** impunemente.

impure [ɪm'pjuə*] *a* (*adulterated*)
adulterado; (*morally*) impuro; **impurity** *n* (*gen*) impureza.

KEYWORD

in [ɪn] ◆ *prep* 1 (*indicating place, position, with place names*) en; **the
house/garden** en (la) casa/el jardín;
~ here/there aquí/ahí *or* allí dentro;
~ London/England en Londres/
Inglaterra

2 (*indicating time*) en; **~ spring** en
(la) primavera; **~ the afternoon** por
la tarde; **at 4 o'clock ~ the
afternoon** a las 4 de la tarde; **I did
it ~ 3 hours/days** lo hice en 3
horas/días; **I'll see you ~ 2 weeks
or ~ 2 weeks' time** te veré dentro
de 2 semanas

3 (*indicating manner etc*) en; **~ a
loud/soft voice** en voz alta/baja; **~
pencil/ink** a lápiz/bolígrafo; **the boy
~ the blue shirt** el chico de la camisa azul

4 (*indicating circumstances*): **~ the
sun/shade/rain** al sol/a la sombra/
bajo la lluvia; **a change ~ policy**
un cambio de política

5 (*indicating mood, state*): **~ tears**
en lágrimas, llorando; **~ anger/
despair** enfadado(a)/desesperado(a);
to live ~ luxury vivir lujosamente

6 (*with ratios, numbers*): **1 ~ 10
households, 1 household ~ 10** una
de cada 10 familias; **2 pence ~ the
pound** 20 peniques por libra; **they
lined up ~ twos** se alinearon de dos
en dos

7 (referring to people, works) en; entre; the disease is common ~ children la enfermedad es común entre los niños; ~ (the works of) Dickens en (las obras de) Dickens

8 (indicating profession etc): to be ~ teaching estar en la enseñanza

9 (after superlative) de; the best pupil ~ the class el/la mejor alumno/a de la clase

10 (with present participle): ~ saying this al decir esto

◆ ad: to be ~ (person: at home) estar en casa; (work) estar; (train, ship, plane) haber llegado; (in fashion) estar de moda; she'll be ~ later today llegará más tarde hoy; to ask sb ~ hacer pasar a uno; to run/limp etc ~ entrar corriendo/cojeando etc

◆ n: the ~s and outs (of proposal, situation etc) los detalles

in., ins abbr = **inch(es)**.

inability [ɪnəˈbɪlɪtɪ] n incapacidad f.

inaccessible [ɪnəkˈsesɪbl] a inaccesible.

inaccurate [ɪnˈækjurət] a inexacto, incorrecto.

inactivity [ɪnækˈtɪvɪtɪ] n inactividad f.

inadequate [ɪnˈædɪkwət] a (insufficient) insuficiente; (unsuitable) inadecuado; (person) incapaz.

inadvertently [ɪnədˈvɜːtntlɪ] ad por descuido.

inadvisable [ɪnədˈvaɪzəbl] a poco aconsejable.

inane [ɪˈneɪn] a necio, fatuo.

inanimate [ɪnˈænɪmət] a inanimado.

inappropriate [ɪnəˈprəuprɪət] a inadecuado.

inarticulate [ɪnɑːˈtɪkjulət] a (person) incapaz de expresarse; (speech) mal pronunciado.

inasmuch as [ɪnəzˈmʌtʃæz] conj puesto que, ya que.

inaudible [ɪnˈɔːdɪbl] a inaudible.

inaugural [ɪˈnɔːgjurəl] a (speech) de apertura.

inaugurate [ɪˈnɔːgjureɪt] vt inaugurar; **inauguration** [-ˈreɪʃən] n ceremonia de apertura.

in-between [ɪnbɪˈbɔːn] a (feeling) innato.

inborn [ɪnˈbɔːn] a (feeling) innato.

inbred [ɪnˈbred] a innato; (family) engendrado por endogamia.

Inc. abbr (US) = **incorporated**.

incapable [ɪnˈkeɪpəbl] a incapaz.

incapacitate [ɪnkəˈpæsɪtet] vt: to ~ sb incapacitar a uno.

incapacity [ɪnkəˈpæsɪtɪ] n (inability) incapacidad f.

incarcerate [ɪnˈkɑːsəreɪt] vt encarcelar.

incarnation [ɪnkɑːˈneɪʃən] n encarnación f.

incendiary [ɪnˈsendɪərɪ] a incendiario.

incense [ˈɪnsens] n incienso // [ɪnˈsens] (anger) indignar, encolerizar.

incentive [ɪnˈsentɪv] n incentivo, estímulo.

incessant [ɪnˈsesnt] a incesante, continuo; ~**ly** ad constantemente.

incest [ˈɪnsest] n incesto.

inch [ɪntʃ] n pulgada; to be within an ~ of estar a dos dedos de; he didn't give an ~ no dio concesión alguna; to ~ forward vi avanzar palmo a palmo.

incidence [ˈɪnsɪdns] n (of crime, disease) incidencia.

incident [ˈɪnsɪdnt] n incidente m; (in book) episodio.

incidental [ɪnsɪˈdentl] a circunstancial, accesorio; (unplanned) fortuito; ~ to relacionado con; ~ **music** ambientación f musical; ~**ly** [-ˈdentlɪ] ad (by the way) a propósito.

incinerator [ɪnˈsɪnəreɪtə*] n incinerador m.

incipient [ɪnˈsɪpɪənt] a incipiente.

incision [ɪnˈsɪʒən] n incisión f.

incisive [ɪnˈsaɪsɪv] a (mind) penetrante; (remark etc) incisivo.

incite [ɪnˈsaɪt] vt provocar.

inclination [ɪnklɪˈneɪʃən] n (ten-

dency) tendencia, inclinación f.

incline ['ɪnklaɪn] n pendiente m, cuesta // vb [ɪn'klaɪn] vt (*slope*) inclinar; (*head*) poner de lado // vi inclinarse; **to be ~d to** (*tend*) ser propenso a; (*be willing*) estar dispuesto a.

include [ɪn'klu:d] vt incluir, comprender; (*in letter*) adjuntar; **including** prep incluso, inclusive.

inclusion [ɪn'klu:ʒən] n inclusión f.

inclusive [ɪn'klu:sɪv] a inclusivo // ad inclusive; **~ of tax** incluidos los impuestos.

incognito [ɪnkɔg'ni:təu] ad de incógnito.

incoherent [ɪnkəu'hɪərənt] a incoherente.

income ['ɪnkʌm] n (*personal*) ingresos mpl; (*from property etc*) renta; (*profit*) rédito; **~ tax** n impuesto sobre la renta; **~ tax return** n declaración f de renta.

incoming ['ɪnkʌmɪŋ] a: **~ flight** vuelo entrante.

incomparable [ɪn'kɔmpərəbl] a incomparable, sin par.

incompatible [ɪnkəm'pætɪbl] a incompatible.

incompetence [ɪn'kɔmpɪtəns] n incompetencia.

incompetent [ɪn'kɔmpɪtənt] a incompetente.

incomplete [ɪnkəm'pli:t] a incompleto; (*unfinished*) sin terminar.

incomprehensible [ɪnkɔmprɪ'hensɪbl] a incomprensible.

inconceivable [ɪnkən'si:vəbl] a inconcebible.

incongruous [ɪn'kɔŋgruəs] a discordante.

inconsiderate [ɪnkən'sɪdərət] a desconsiderado; **how ~ of him!** ¡qué falta de consideración (de su parte)!

inconsistency [ɪnkən'sɪstənsɪ] n inconsecuencia.

inconsistent [ɪnkən'sɪstnt] a inconsecuente; **~ with** (que) no concuerda con.

inconspicuous [ɪnkən'spɪkjuəs] a

discreet) discreto; (*person*) que llama poca la atención.

inconvenience [ɪnkən'vi:njəns] n (*gen*) inconvenientes mpl; (*trouble*) molestia, incomodidad f // vt incomodar.

inconvenient [ɪnkən'vi:njənt] a incómodo, poco práctico; (*time, place*) inoportuno.

incorporate [ɪn'kɔ:pəreɪt] vt incorporar; (*contain*) comprender; (*add*) agregar; **~d company** (US: *abbr* Inc.) ≈ Sociedad f Anónima (S.A.).

incorrect [ɪnkə'rɛkt] a incorrecto.

incorrigible [ɪn'kɔrɪdʒəbl] a incorregible.

increase ['ɪnkri:s] n aumento // [ɪn'kri:s] aumentarse; (*grow*) crecer; (*price*) subir // vt aumentar; **increasing** [ɪn'kri:sɪŋ] a (*number*) creciente, que va en aumento; **increasingly** [ɪn'kri:sɪŋlɪ] ad de más en más, cada vez más.

incredible [ɪn'krɛdɪbl] a increíble.

incredulous [ɪn'krɛdjuləs] a incrédulo.

increment ['ɪnkrɪmənt] n aumento, incremento.

incriminate [ɪn'krɪmɪneɪt] vt incriminar.

incubator ['ɪnkjubeɪtə*] n incubadora.

incumbent [ɪn'kʌmbənt] n titular mf // a: **it is ~ on him to...** le incumbe... .

incur [ɪn'kə:*] vt (*expenditure*) incurrir; (*loss*) sufrir.

incurable [ɪn'kjuərəbl] a incurable.

indebted [ɪn'detɪd] a: **to be ~ to sb** estar agradecido a uno.

indecent [ɪn'di:snt] a indecente; **~ assault** n (*Brit*) atentado contra el pudor; **~ exposure** n exhibicionismo.

indecisive [ɪndɪ'saɪsɪv] a indeciso; (*discussion*) no resuelto, inconcluyente.

indeed [ɪn'di:d] ad efectivamente, en realidad; **yes ~!** ¡claro que sí!

indefinite [ɪnˈdefɪnɪt] a indefinido; (*uncertain*) incierto; **~ly** ad (*wait*) indefinidamente.

indelible [ɪnˈdelɪbl] a imborrable.

indemnify [ɪnˈdemnɪfaɪ] vt indemnizar, resarcir.

indemnity [ɪnˈdemnɪtɪ] n (*insurance*) indemnidad f; (*compensation*) indemnización f.

independence [ɪndɪˈpendns] n independencia.

independent [ɪndɪˈpendənt] a independiente; **to become ~** independizarse.

indestructible [ɪndɪsˈtrʌktəbl] a indestructible.

index [ˈɪndeks] n (pl: **~es**: in book) índice m; (: in library etc) catálogo; (pl: **indices** [ˈɪndɪsiːz]: ratio, sign) exponente m; **~ card** n ficha; **~ finger** n índice m; **~-linked**, (US) **~ed** a vinculado al índice del coste de la vida.

India [ˈɪndɪə] n la India; **~ n**, a, n indio/a m/f; **Red ~n** piel roja m/f; **the ~n Ocean** n el Océano Indico.

indicate [ˈɪndɪkeɪt] vt indicar; **indication** [-ˈkeɪʃən] n indicio, señal f; **indicative** [ɪnˈdɪkətɪv] a: **to be ~ of** indicar // n (LING) indicativo; **indicator** n (gen) indicador m.

indices [ˈɪndɪsiːz] pl of **index**.

indict [ɪnˈdaɪt] vt acusar; **~ment** n acusación f.

indifference [ɪnˈdɪfrəns] n indiferencia.

indifferent [ɪnˈdɪfrənt] a indiferente; (*poor*) regular.

indigenous [ɪnˈdɪdʒɪnəs] a indígena.

indigestion [ɪndɪˈdʒestʃən] n indigestión f.

indignant [ɪnˈdɪɡnənt] a: **to be ~ about sth** indignarse por algo.

indignity [ɪnˈdɪɡnɪtɪ] n indignidad f.

indigo [ˈɪndɪɡəu] a de color añil // n añil m.

indirect [ɪndɪˈrekt] a indirecto; **~ly** ad indirectamente.

indiscreet [ɪndɪsˈkriːt] a indiscreto, imprudente.

indiscriminate [ɪndɪsˈkrɪmɪnət] a indiscriminado.

indispensable [ɪndɪsˈpensəbl] a indispensable, imprescindible.

indisposed [ɪndɪsˈpəuzd] a (*unwell*) indispuesto.

indisputable [ɪndɪsˈpjuːtəbl] a incontestable.

individual [ɪndɪˈvɪdjuəl] n individuo // a (*single*); (*personal*) personal; (*for/of one only*) particular; **~ist** n individualista m/f; **~ity** [-ˈælɪtɪ] n individualidad f; **~ly** ad individualmente; particularmente.

indoctrinate [ɪnˈdɒktrɪneɪt] vt adoctrinar; **indoctrination** [-ˈneɪʃən] n adoctrinamiento.

indolent [ˈɪndələnt] a indolente, perezoso.

Indonesia [ɪndəuˈniːzɪə] n Indonesia.

indoor [ˈɪndɔːʳ] a (*swimming pool*) cubierto; (*plant*) de interior; (*sport*) bajo cubierta; **~s** [ɪnˈdɔːz] ad adentro; (*at home*) en casa.

induce [ɪnˈdjuːs] vt inducir, persuadir; (*bring about*) producir; **~ment** n (*incentive*) incentivo, aliciente m.

induction [ɪnˈdʌkʃən] n (MED: of birth) inducción f; **~ course** n (Brit) curso de inducción.

indulge [ɪnˈdʌldʒ] vt (*whim*) satisfacer; (*person*) complacer; (*child*) mimar // vi: **to ~ in** darse el gusto de; **~nce** n vicio; **~nt** a indulgente.

industrial [ɪnˈdʌstrɪəl] a industrial; **~ action** n huelga; **~ estate** n (Brit) polígono or zona (LAm) industrial; **~ist** n industrial m/f; **~ize** vt industrializar; **~ park** n (US) = **estate**.

industrious [ɪnˈdʌstrɪəs] a (*gen*) trabajador(a); (*student*) aplicado.

industry [ˈɪndəstrɪ] n industria; (*diligence*) aplicación f.

inebriated [ɪˈniːbrɪeɪtɪd] a borracho.

inedible [ɪnˈedɪbl] a incomible; (*plant etc*) no comestible.

ineffective [ɪnɪˈfektɪv], **ineffectual** [ɪnɪˈfektʃuəl] a ineficaz, inútil.

inefficiency [ɪnɪˈfɪʃənsɪ] n ineficacia.

inefficient [ɪnɪ'fɪʃənt] a ineficaz, ineficiente.

inept [ɪ'nept] a incompetente.

inequality [ɪnɪ'kwɔlɪtɪ] n desigualdad f.

inert [ɪ'nɜːt] a inerte, inactivo; (*immobile*) inmóvil; ~**ia** [ɪ'nɜːʃə] n inercia; (*laziness*) pereza.

inescapable [ɪnɪ'skeɪpəbl] a ineludible.

inevitable [ɪn'evɪtəbl] a inevitable; (*necessary*) forzoso; **inevitably** ad inevitablemente.

inexcusable [ɪnɪks'kjuːzəbl] a imperdonable.

inexhaustible [ɪnɪg'zɔːstɪbl] a inagotable.

inexpensive [ɪnɪk'spensɪv] a económico.

inexperience [ɪnɪk'spɪərɪəns] n falta de experiencia; ~**d** a inexperto.

inextricably [ɪnɪks'trɪkəblɪ] ad indisolublemente.

infallible [ɪn'fælɪbl] a infalible.

infamous ['ɪnfəməs] a infame.

infancy ['ɪnfənsɪ] n infancia.

infant ['ɪnfənt] n niño/a; ~**ile** a infantil; (*pej*) aniñado; ~ **school** n (*Brit*) escuela de párvulos.

infantry ['ɪnfəntrɪ] n infantería.

infatuated [ɪn'fætjueɪtɪd] a: ~ **with** (*in love*) loco por.

infatuation [ɪnfætju'eɪʃən] n enamoramiento.

infect [ɪn'fekt] vt (*wound*) infectar; (*person*) contagiar; (*fig: pej*) corromper; ~**ed with** (*illness*) contagiado de; ~**ion** [ɪn'fekʃən] n infección f; (*fig*) contagio; ~**ious** [ɪn'fekʃəs] a contagioso; (*also fig*) infeccioso.

infer [ɪn'fɜː*] vt deducir, inferir; ~**ence** ['ɪnfərəns] n deducción f, inferencia.

inferior [ɪn'fɪərɪə*] a, n inferior m/f; ~**ity** [-rɪ'ɔrɪtɪ] n inferioridad f; ~**ity complex** n complejo de inferioridad.

inferno [ɪn'fɜːnəu] n (*fire*) hoguera.

infertile [ɪn'fɜːtaɪl] a estéril; (*person*) infecundo; **infertility** [-'tɪlɪtɪ] n

esterilidad f; infecundidad f.

infested [ɪn'festɪd] a: ~ **with** plagado de.

in-fighting ['ɪnfaɪtɪŋ] n (*fig*) lucha(s) f(pl) interna(s).

infiltrate ['ɪnfɪltreɪt] vt (*troops etc*) infiltrar en // vi infiltrarse.

infinite ['ɪnfɪnɪt] a infinito.

infinitive [ɪn'fɪnɪtɪv] n infinitivo.

infinity [ɪn'fɪnɪtɪ] n (*also MATH*) infinito; (*an* ~) infinidad f.

infirm [ɪn'fɜːm] a enfermo, débil; ~**ary** n hospital m; ~**ity** n debilidad f; (*illness*) enfermedad f, achaque m.

inflamed [ɪn'fleɪmd] a: to become ~ inflamarse.

inflammable [ɪn'flæməbl] a (*Brit*) inflamable; (*situation etc*) explosivo.

inflammation [ɪnflə'meɪʃən] n inflamación f.

inflatable [ɪn'fleɪtəbl] a (*ball, boat*) inflable.

inflate [ɪn'fleɪt] vt (*tyre, balloon*) inflar; (*fig*) hinchar; **inflation** [ɪn'fleɪʃən] n (*ECON*) inflación f.

inflict [ɪn'flɪkt] vt: to ~ **on** infligir en; (*tax etc*) imponer a.

influence ['ɪnfluəns] n influencia // vt influir en, influenciar; **under the** ~ **of** alcohol en estado de embriaguez; **influential** [-'enʃl] a influyente.

influenza [ɪnflu'enzə] n gripe f.

influx ['ɪnflʌks] n afluencia.

inform [ɪn'fɔːm] vt: to ~ **sb of sth** informar a uno sobre or de algo; (*warn*) avisar a uno de algo; (*communicate*) comunicar algo a uno // vi: to ~ **on sb** delatar a uno.

informal [ɪn'fɔːml] a (*manner, tone*) desenfadado; (*dress, interview, occasion*) informal; ~**ity** [-'mælɪtɪ] n desenfado; falta de ceremonia.

informant [ɪn'fɔːmənt] n informante m/f.

information [ɪnfə'meɪʃən] n información f; (*news*) noticias fpl; (*knowledge*) conocimientos mpl; (*LAW*) delación f; **a piece of** ~ un dato; ~ **office** n información f.

informative [ɪn'fɔːmətɪv] a informativo.

informer [ɪnˈfɔːmə*] n delator(a) m/f; (also: police ~) soplón/ona m/f.

infra-red [ɪnfrəˈred] a infrarrojo.

infrastructure [ˈɪnfrəstrʌktʃə*] n (of system etc, ECON) infraestructura.

infringe [ɪnˈfrɪndʒ] vt infringir, violar // vi: to ~ on abusar de; **~ment** n infracción f; (of rights) usurpación f; (SPORT) falta.

infuriating [ɪnˈfjuərɪeɪtɪŋ] a: I find it ~ me saca de quicio.

infusion [ɪnˈfjuːʒən] n (tea etc) infusión f.

ingenious [ɪnˈdʒiːnjəs] a ingenioso; **ingenuity** [-dʒɪˈnjuːɪtɪ] n ingeniosidad f.

ingenuous [ɪnˈdʒɛnjuəs] a ingenuo.

ingot [ˈɪŋɡət] n lingote m, barra.

ingrained [ɪnˈgreɪnd] a arraigado.

ingratiate [ɪnˈgreɪʃɪeɪt] vt: to ~ o.s. with congraciarse con.

ingredient [ɪnˈgriːdɪənt] n ingrediente m.

inhabit [ɪnˈhæbɪt] vt vivir en; (occupy) ocupar; **~ant** n habitante m/f.

inhale [ɪnˈheɪl] vt inhalar // vi (in smoking) tragar.

inherent [ɪnˈhɪərənt] a: ~ in or to inherente a.

inherit [ɪnˈherɪt] vt heredar; **~ance** n herencia f; (fig) patrimonio.

inhibit [ɪnˈhɪbɪt] vt inhibir, impedir; to ~ sb from doing sth impedir a uno hacer algo; ~ed a cohibido; **~ion** [-ˈbɪʃən] n cohibición f.

inhospitable [ɪnhɔsˈpɪtəbl] a (person) inhospitalario; (place) inhóspito.

inhuman [ɪnˈhjuːmən] a inhumano.

iniquity [ɪˈnɪkwɪtɪ] n iniquidad f; (injustice) injusticia.

initial [ɪˈnɪʃl] a inicial; (first) primero // n inicial f // vt firmar con las iniciales; ~s npl iniciales fpl; (abbreviation) siglas fpl; **~ly** al principio.

initiate [ɪˈnɪʃɪeɪt] vt (start) iniciar; to ~ proceedings against sb (LAW) entablar proceso contra uno; **initiation** [-ˈeɪʃən] n (into secret etc)

iniciación f; (beginning) comienzo.

initiative [ɪˈnɪʃətɪv] n iniciativa.

inject [ɪnˈdʒekt] vt inyectar; **~ion** [ɪnˈdʒekʃən] n inyección f.

injunction [ɪnˈdʒʌŋkʃən] n interdicto.

injure [ˈɪndʒə*] vt herir; (hurt) lastimar; (fig: reputation etc) perjudicar; **~d** a (person, arm) herido; **injury** n herida, lesión f; (wrong) perjuicio, daño; **injury time** n (SPORT) descuento.

injustice [ɪnˈdʒʌstɪs] n injusticia.

ink [ɪŋk] n tinta.

inkling [ˈɪŋklɪŋ] n sospecha; (idea) idea.

inlaid [ˈɪnleɪd] a (wood) taraceado; (tiles) entarimado.

inland [ˈɪnlənd] a interior; (town) del interior // ad [ɪnˈlænd] tierra adentro; **I~ Revenue** n (Brit) departamento de impuestos; ≈ Hacienda (Sp).

in-laws [ˈɪnlɔːz] npl suegros mpl.

inlet [ˈɪnlet] n (GEO) ensenada, cala; (TECH) admisión f, entrada.

inmate [ˈɪnmeɪt] n (in prison) preso/a; (in asylum) internado/a.

inn [ɪn] n posada, mesón m.

innate [ɪˈneɪt] a innato.

inner [ˈɪnə*] a interior, interno; **~ city** n barrios deprimidos del centro de una ciudad; **~ tube** n (of tyre) cámara or llanta (LAm).

innings [ˈɪnɪŋz] n (CRICKET) entrada, turno.

innocence [ˈɪnəsns] n inocencia.

innocent [ˈɪnəsnt] a inocente.

innocuous [ɪˈnɔkjuəs] a inocuo.

innovation [ɪnəuˈveɪʃən] n novedad f.

innuendo [ɪnjuˈendəu] pl ~es n indirecta.

inoculation [ɪnɔkjuˈleɪʃən] n inoculación f.

inopportune [ɪnˈɔpətjuːn] a inoportuno.

inordinately [ɪˈnɔːdɪnətlɪ] ad desmesuradamente.

in-patient ['ɪnpeɪʃənt] n paciente m/f interno/a.

input ['ɪnput] n (ELEC) entrada; (COMPUT) entrada de datos.

inquest ['ɪnkwɛst] n (coroner's) encuesta judicial.

inquire [ɪn'kwaɪə*] vi preguntar // vt: to ~ whether preguntar si; to ~ about (person) preguntar por; (fact) informarse de; to ~ into vt fus investigar, indagar; **inquiry** n pregunta; (LAW) investigación f, pesquisa; (commission) comisión f investigadora; **inquiry office** n (Brit) oficina de informaciones.

inquisitive [ɪn'kwɪzɪtɪv] a (mind) inquisitivo; (person) fisgón/ona.

inroad ['ɪnrəud] n incursión f; (fig) invasión f.

insane [ɪn'seɪn] a loco; (MED) demente.

insanity [ɪn'sænɪtɪ] n demencia, locura.

insatiable [ɪn'seɪʃəbl] a insaciable.

inscribe [ɪn'skraɪb] vt inscribir; (book etc) to ~ (to sb) dedicar (a uno).

inscription [ɪn'skrɪpʃən] n (gen) inscripción f; (in book) dedicatoria.

inscrutable [ɪn'skruːtəbl] a inescrutable, insondable.

insect ['ɪnsɛkt] n insecto; ~**icide** [ɪn'sɛktɪsaɪd] n insecticida m.

insecure [ɪnsɪ'kjuə*] a inseguro.

insemination [ɪnsɛmɪ'neɪʃən] n : artificial ~ inseminación f artificial.

insensible [ɪn'sɛnsɪbl] a inconsciente; (unconscious) sin conocimiento.

insensitive [ɪn'sɛnsɪtɪv] a insensible.

inseparable [ɪn'sɛprəbl] a inseparable.

insert [ɪn'səːt] vt (into sth) introducir; // n ['ɪnsəːt] encarte m; ~**ion** [ɪn'səːʃən] n inserción f.

in-service [ɪn'səːvɪs] a (training, course) a cargo de la empresa.

inshore [ɪn'ʃɔː*] a : ~ fishing pesca f costera // ad (fish) a lo largo de la costa; (move) hacia la orilla.

inside ['ɪn'saɪd] n interior m; (lining) forro // a interior, interno; (information) confidencial // ad (within) (por) dentro; (with movement) hacia dentro; (fam: in prison) en la cárcel // prep dentro de; (of time): ~ 10 minutes en menos de 10 minutos; ~**s** npl (col) tripas fpl; ~ **forward** n (SPORT) interior m; ~ **lane** n (AUT: in Britain) carril m izquierdo; ~ **out** ad (turn) al revés; (know) a fondo.

insidious [ɪn'sɪdɪəs] a insidioso.

insight ['ɪnsaɪt] n perspicacia.

insignia [ɪn'sɪgnɪə] npl insignias fpl.

insignificant [ɪnsɪg'nɪfɪknt] a insignificante.

insincere [ɪnsɪn'sɪə*] a poco sincero.

insinuate [ɪn'sɪnjueɪt] vt insinuar.

insipid [ɪn'sɪpɪd] a soso, insulso.

insist [ɪn'sɪst] vi insistir; to ~ **on** doing empeñarse en hacer; to ~ **that** insistir en que; (claim) exigir que; ~**ence** n insistencia; (stubbornness) empeño; ~**ent** a insistente.

insole ['ɪnsəul] n plantilla.

insolent ['ɪnsələnt] a insolente, descarado.

insoluble [ɪn'sɔljubl] a insoluble.

insomnia [ɪn'sɔmnɪə] n insomnio.

inspect [ɪn'spɛkt] vt inspeccionar, examinar; (troops) pasar revista a; ~**ion** [ɪn'spɛkʃən] n inspección f, examen m; ~**or** n inspector(a) m/f; (Brit: on buses, trains) revisor(a) m/f.

inspiration [ɪnspə'reɪʃən] n inspiración f; **inspire** [ɪn'spaɪə*] vt inspirar.

instability [ɪnstə'bɪlɪtɪ] n inestabilidad f.

install [ɪn'stɔːl] vt instalar; ~**ation** [ɪnstə'leɪʃən] n instalación f.

instalment, (US) **installment** [ɪn'stɔːlmənt] n plazo; (of story) entrega; (of TV serial etc) capítulo; **in** ~**s** (pay, receive) a plazos; ~ **plan** n (US) compra a plazos.

instance ['ɪnstəns] n ejemplo, caso; **for** ~ por ejemplo; **in the first** ~ en primer lugar.

instant ['ɪnstənt] n instante m, momento // a inmediato; (coffee) instantáneo.

instantly ['ɪnstəntlɪ] ad en seguida.

instead [ɪn'sted] ad en cambio; ~ of en lugar de, en vez de.

instep ['ɪnstep] n empeine m.

instil [ɪn'stɪl] vt: to ~ into inculcar a.

instinct ['ɪnstɪŋkt] n instinto; ~ive [-'stɪŋktɪv] a instintivo.

institute ['ɪnstɪtjuːt] n instituto; (professional body) colegio // vt (begin) iniciar, empezar; (proceedings) entablar.

institution [ɪnstɪ'tjuːʃən] n institución f; (MED: home) asilo; (: asylum) manicomio.

instruct [ɪn'strʌkt] vt: to ~ sb in sth instruir a uno en or sobre algo; to ~ sb to do sth dar instrucciones a uno de hacer algo; ~ion [ɪn'strʌkʃən] n (teaching) instrucción f; ~ions npl órdenes fpl; ~ions (for use) modo sg de empleo; ~ive a instructivo; ~or n instructor(a) m/f.

instrument ['ɪnstrəmənt] n instrumento; ~ panel n tablero (de instrumentos); ~al [-'mentl] a (MUS) instrumental; to be ~al in ser (el) artífice de.

insubordinate [ɪnsə'bɔːdɪnət] a insubordinado.

insufferable [ɪn'sʌfrəbl] a insoportable.

insufficient [ɪnsə'fɪʃənt] a insuficiente.

insular ['ɪnsjulə] a insular; (person) estrecho de miras.

insulate ['ɪnsjuleɪt] vt aislar; **insulating tape** n cinta aislante; **insulation** [-'leɪʃən] n aislamiento.

insulin ['ɪnsjulɪn] n insulina.

insult ['ɪnsʌlt] n insulto; (offence) ofensa // vt [ɪn'sʌlt] insultar; ofender; ~ing a insultante; ofensivo.

insuperable [ɪn'sjuːprəbl] a insuperable.

insurance [ɪn'ʃuərəns] n seguro; fire/life ~ seguro contra incendios/

sobre la vida; ~ **agent** n agente m/f de seguros; ~ **policy** n póliza (de seguros).

insure [ɪn'ʃuə] vt asegurar.

intact [ɪn'tækt] a íntegro; (untouched) intacto.

intake ['ɪnteɪk] n (TECH) entrada, toma; (: pipe) tubo de admisión; (of food) ingestión f; (Brit SCOL): **an** ~ **of 200 a year** 200 matriculados al año.

integral ['ɪntɪgrəl] a (whole) íntegro; (part) integrante.

integrate ['ɪntɪgreɪt] vt integrar // vi integrarse.

integrity [ɪn'tegrɪtɪ] n honradez f, rectitud f.

intellect ['ɪntɪlekt] n intelecto; ~**ual** [-'lektjuəl] a, n intelectual m/f.

intelligence [ɪn'telɪdʒəns] n inteligencia; **I~ Service** n Servicio de Inteligencia.

intelligent [ɪn'telɪdʒənt] a inteligente.

intelligentsia [ɪntelɪ'dʒentsɪə] n intelectualidad f.

intelligible [ɪn'telɪdʒɪbl] a inteligible, comprensible.

intend [ɪn'tend] vt (gift etc): to ~ sth for destinar algo a; to ~ to do sth tener intención de or pensar hacer algo; ~ed a (effect) deseado.

intense [ɪn'tens] a (gen) intenso; ~**ly** ad intensamente; (very) sumamente.

intensify [ɪn'tensɪfaɪ] vt intensificar; (increase) aumentar.

intensity [ɪn'tensɪtɪ] n (gen) intensidad f.

intensive [ɪn'tensɪv] a intensivo; ~ **care unit** n unidad de vigilancia intensiva.

intent [ɪn'tent] n propósito // a (absorbed) absorto; (attentive) atento; **to all** ~**s and purposes** prácticamente; **to be** ~ **on doing sth** estar resuelto a hacer algo.

intention [ɪn'tenʃən] n intención f, propósito; ~**al** a deliberado; ~**ally** ad a propósito.

intently [ɪn'tɛntlɪ] *ad* atentamente, fijamente.

interact [ɪntər'ækt] *vi* influirse mutuamente; **~ion** [-'ækʃən] *n* interacción *f*, acción *f* recíproca.

intercede [ɪntə'siːd] *vi*: to ~ (with) interceder (con).

intercept [ɪntə'sɛpt] *vt* interceptar; (*stop*) detener.

interchange ['ɪntətʃeɪndʒ] *n* intercambio; (*on motorway*) intersección *f* // *vt* [ɪntə'tʃeɪndʒ] intercambiar; canjear; **~able** *a* intercambiable.

intercom ['ɪntəkɔm] *n* interfono.

intercourse ['ɪntəkɔːs] *n* (*sexual*) relaciones *fpl* sexuales; (*social*) trato.

interest ['ɪntrɪst] *n* (*also* COMM) interés *m* // *vt* interesar; **to be ~ed in** interesarse por; **~ing** *a* interesante; **~ rate** *n* tipo *or* tasa de interés.

interface ['ɪntəfeɪs] *n* (COMPUT) junción *f*.

interfere [ɪntə'fɪə*] *vi*: to ~ in (*quarrel, other people's business*) entrometerse en; to ~ with (*hinder*) estorbar; (*damage*) estropear; (*radio*) interferir con.

interference [ɪntə'fɪərəns] *n* (*gen*) intromisión *f*; (RADIO, TV) interferencia.

interim ['ɪntərɪm] *n*: in the ~ en el ínterin // *a* provisional.

interior [ɪn'tɪərɪə*] *n* interior *m* // *a* interior; **~ designer** *n* interiorista *m/f*.

interlock [ɪntə'lɔk] *vi* entrelazarse; (*wheels etc*) endentarse.

interloper ['ɪntələupə*] *n* intruso/a.

interlude ['ɪntəluːd] *n* intervalo; (*rest*) descanso; (THEATRE) intermedio.

intermediary [ɪntə'miːdɪərɪ] *n* intermediario/a.

intermediate [ɪntə'miːdɪət] *a* intermedio.

interminable [ɪn'tɜːmɪnəbl] *a* inacabable.

intermission [ɪntə'mɪʃən] *n* (THEATRE) descanso.

intermittent [ɪntə'mɪtnt] *a* intermi-

tente.

intern [ɪn'tɜːn] *vt* internar; (*enclose*) encerrar // *n* ['ɪntɜːn] (US) interno/a.

internal [ɪn'tɜːnl] *a* interno, interior; **~ly** *ad* interiormente; **'not to be taken ~ly'** 'uso externo'; I~ **Revenue Service (IRS)** *n* (US) departamento de impuestos; ≈ Hacienda (Sp).

international [ɪntə'næʃənl] *a* internacional; ~ (**game**) partido internacional; ~ (**player**) jugador(a) *m/f* internacional.

interplay ['ɪntəpleɪ] *n* interacción *f*.

interpret [ɪn'tɜːprɪt] *vt* interpretar; (*translate*) traducir; (*understand*) entender // *vi* hacer de intérprete; **~ation** [-'teɪʃən] *n* interpretación *f*; traducción *f*; entendimiento; **~er** *n* intérprete *m/f*.

interrelated [ɪntərɪ'leɪtɪd] *a* interrelacionado.

interrogate [ɪn'tɛrəuɡeɪt] *vt* interrogar; **interrogation** [-'ɡeɪʃən] *n* interrogatorio; **interrogative** [ɪntə'rɔɡətɪv] *a* interrogativo.

interrupt [ɪntə'rʌpt] *vt*, *vi* interrumpir; **~ion** [-'rʌpʃən] *n* interrupción *f*.

intersect [ɪntə'sɛkt] *vt* cruzar // *vi* (*roads*) cruzarse; **~ion** [-'sɛkʃən] *n* intersección *f*; (*of roads*) cruce *m*.

intersperse [ɪntə'spɜːs] *vt*: to ~ with salpicar de.

intertwine [ɪntə'twaɪn] *vt* entrelazar // *vi* entrelazarse.

interval ['ɪntəvl] *n* intervalo; (*Brit*: THEATRE, SPORT) descanso; **at ~s** a ratos, de vez en cuando.

intervene [ɪntə'viːn] *vi* intervenir; (*take part*) participar; (*occur*) sobrevenir; **intervention** [-'vɛnʃən] *n* intervención *f*.

interview ['ɪntəvjuː] *n* (RADIO, TV etc) entrevista // *vt* entrevistarse con; **~er** *n* entrevistador(a) *m/f*.

intestine [ɪn'tɛstɪn] *n*: **large/small** ~ intestino grueso/delgado.

intimacy ['ɪntɪməsɪ] *n* intimidad *f*; (*relations*) relaciones *fpl* íntimas.

intimate ['ɪntɪmət] *a* íntimo;

(friendship) estrecho; *(knowledge)* profundo // *vt* ['ɪntɪmeɪt] *(announce)* dar a entender.

intimidate [ɪn'tɪmɪdeɪt] *vt* intimidar, amedrentar.

into ['ɪntu:] *prep (gen)* en; *(towards)* a; *(inside)* hacia el interior de; ~ 3 pieces/French en 3 pedazos/al francés.

intolerable [ɪn'tɔlərəbl] *a* intolerable, insoportable.

intolerance [ɪn'tɔlərəns] *n* intolerancia.

intolerant [ɪn'tɔlərənt] *a*: ~ of intolerante con *or* para.

intonation [ɪntəu'neɪʃən] *n* entonación *f*.

intoxicate [ɪn'tɔksɪkeɪt] *vt* embriagar; ~d *a* embriagado; **intoxication** [-'keɪʃən] *n* embriaguez *f*.

intractable [ɪn'træktəbl] *a (person)* intratable; *(problem)* espinoso.

intransitive [ɪn'trænsɪtɪv] *a* intransitivo.

intravenous [ɪntrə'vi:nəs] *a* intravenoso.

in-tray ['ɪntreɪ] *n* bandeja de entrada.

intricate ['ɪntrɪkət] *a* intrincado; *(plot, problem)* complejo.

intrigue [ɪn'tri:g] *n* intriga // *vt* fascinar // *vi* andar en intrigas; **intriguing** *a* fascinante.

intrinsic [ɪn'trɪnsɪk] *a* intrínseco.

introduce [ɪntrə'dju:s] *vt* introducir, meter; **to** ~ **sb (to sb)** presentar uno (a otro); **to** ~ **sb to** *(pastime, technique)* introducir a uno a; **introduction** [-'dʌkʃən] *n* introducción *f*; *(of person)* presentación *f*; **introductory** [-'dʌktərɪ] *a* introductorio.

introvert ['ɪntrəvɜ:t] *a*, *n* introvertido/a *m/f*.

intrude [ɪn'tru:d] *vi (person)* entrometerse; **to** ~ **on** *or* **into** estorbar; ~ **r** *n* intruso/a; **intrusion** [-ʒən] *n* invasión *f*.

intuition [ɪntju:'ɪʃən] *n* intuición *f*.

inundate ['ɪnʌndeɪt] *vt*: **to** ~ **with** inundar de.

invade [ɪn'veɪd] *vt* invadir; ~ **r** *n* in-

vasor(a) *m/f*.

invalid ['ɪnvəlɪd] *n* minusválido/a *f* // [ɪn'vælɪd] *(not valid)* inválido, nulo.

invaluable [ɪn'væljuəbl] *a* inestimable.

invariably [ɪn'veərɪəblɪ] *ad* sin excepción.

invasion [ɪn'veɪʒən] *n* invasión *f*.

invent [ɪn'vent] *vt* inventar; ~**ion** [ɪn'venʃən] *n* invento; *(inventiveness)* inventiva; *(lie)* ficción *f*, mentira; ~**ive** *a* inventivo; ~**iveness** *n* ingenio, inventiva; ~**or** *n* inventor(a) *m/f*.

inventory ['ɪnvəntrɪ] *n* inventario.

invert [ɪn'vɜ:t] *vt* invertir; ~**ed commas** *npl (Brit)* comillas *fpl*.

invertebrate [ɪn'vɜ:tɪbrət] *n* invertebrado.

invest [ɪn'vest] *vt*, *vi* invertir.

investigate [ɪn'vestɪgeɪt] *vt* investigar; *(study)* estudiar, examinar; **investigation** [-'geɪʃən] *n* investigación *f*, pesquisa; examen *m*; **investigator** *n* investigador(a) *m/f*.

investment [ɪn'vestmənt] *n* inversión *f*.

investor [ɪn'vestə*] *n* inversionista *m/f*.

inveterate [ɪn'vetərət] *a* empedernido.

invidious [ɪn'vɪdɪəs] *a* odioso.

invigilate [ɪn'vɪdʒɪleɪt] *vt*, *vi (in exam)* vigilar.

invigorating [ɪn'vɪgəreɪtɪŋ] *a* vigorizante.

invincible [ɪn'vɪnsɪbl] *a* invencible.

invisible [ɪn'vɪzɪbl] *a* invisible; ~ **ink** *n* tinta simpática.

invitation [ɪnvɪ'teɪʃən] *n* invitación *f*.

invite [ɪn'vaɪt] *vt* invitar; *(opinions etc)* solicitar, pedir; *(trouble)* buscarse; **inviting** *a* atractivo; *(look)* provocativo; *(food)* apetitoso.

invoice ['ɪnvɔɪs] *n* factura // *vt* facturar.

invoke [ɪn'vəuk] *vt* invocar; *(aid)* pedir; *(law)* recurrir a.

involuntary [ɪn'vɔləntrɪ] *a* involuntario.

involve [ɪn'vɔlv] vt (entail) suponer, implicar; **to ~ sb (in)** comprometer a uno (con); **~d** a complicado; **~ment** n (gen) enredo; (obligation) compromiso; (difficulty) apuro.

inward ['ɪnwəd] a (movement) interior, interno; (thought, feeling) íntimo; **~(s)** ad hacia dentro.

I/O abbr (COMPUT = input/output) entrada/salida.

iodine ['aɪəʊdiːn] n yodo.

iota [aɪ'əʊtə] n (fig) jota, ápice m.

IOU n abbr (= I owe you) pagaré m.

IQ n abbr (= intelligence quotient) cociente m intelectual.

IRA n abbr (= Irish Republican Army) IRA m.

Iran [ɪ'rɑːn] n Irán m; **~ian** [ɪ'reɪnɪən] a, n iraní m/f.

Iraq [ɪ'rɑːk] n Irak; **~i** a, n iraquí m/f.

irascible [ɪ'ræsɪbl] a irascible.

irate [aɪ'reɪt] a enojado, airado.

Ireland ['aɪələnd] n Irlanda.

iris ['aɪrɪs], pl **~es** n (ANAT) iris m; (BOT) lirio.

Irish ['aɪrɪʃ] a irlandés/esa // npl: **the ~** los irlandeses; **~man/woman** n irlandés m/irlandesa m/f; **the ~ Sea** n el Mar de Irlanda.

irk [əːk] vt fastidiar; **~some** a fastidioso.

iron ['aɪən] n hierro; (for clothes) plancha // a de hierro // vt (clothes) planchar; **to ~ out** vt (crease) quitar; (fig) allanar; **the I~ Curtain** n el Telón de Acero.

ironic(al) [aɪ'rɔnɪk(l)] a irónico.

ironing ['aɪənɪŋ] n (act) planchado; (clothes: ironed) ropa planchada; (: to be ironed) ropa por planchar; **~ board** n tabla de planchar.

ironmonger ['aɪənmʌŋgə*] n (Brit) ferretero/a; **~'s (shop)** n ferretería, quincallería.

iron ore n mineral m de hierro.

irony ['aɪrənɪ] n ironía.

irrational [ɪ'ræʃənl] a irracional.

irreconcilable [ɪrekən'saɪləbl] a (idea) incompatible; (enemies) irre-

conciliable.

irregular [ɪ'regjulə*] a irregular; (surface) desigual.

irrelevant [ɪ'reləvənt] a fuera de lugar, inoportuno.

irreplaceable [ɪrɪ'pleɪsəbl] a irremplazable.

irrepressible [ɪrɪ'presəbl] a incontenible.

irresistible [ɪrɪ'zɪstɪbl] a irresistible.

irresolute [ɪ'rezəluːt] a indeciso.

irrespective [ɪrɪ'spektɪv]: **~ of** prep sin tener en cuenta, no importa.

irresponsible [ɪrɪ'spɔnsɪbl] a (act) irresponsable; (person) poco serio.

irrigate ['ɪrɪgeɪt] vt regar; **irrigation** [-'geɪʃən] n riego.

irritable ['ɪrɪtəbl] a (person: temperament) de (mal) carácter; (: mood) de mal humor.

irritate ['ɪrɪteɪt] vt fastidiar; (MED) picar; **irritating** a fastidioso; **irritation** [-'teɪʃən] n fastidio; picazón f, picor m.

IRS n abbr (US) = **Internal Revenue Service**.

is [ɪz] vb see **be**.

Islam ['ɪzlɑːm] n Islam m.

island ['aɪlənd] n isla; (also: **traffic ~**) isleta; **~er** n isleño/a.

isle [aɪl] n isla.

isn't ['ɪznt] = **is not**.

isolate ['aɪsəleɪt] vt aislar; **~d** a aislado; **isolation** [-'leɪʃən] n aislamiento.

Israel ['ɪzreɪl] n Israel m; **~i** [ɪz'reɪlɪ] a, n israelí m/f.

issue ['ɪsjuː] n cuestión f, asunto; (outcome) resultado; (of banknotes etc) emisión f; (of newspaper etc) número; (offspring) sucesión f, descendencia // vt (rations, equipment) distribuir, repartir; (orders) dar; (certificate, passport) expedir; (decree) promulgar; (magazine) publicar; (cheques) extender; (banknotes, stamps) emitir; **at ~** en cuestión; **to take ~ with sb (over)** estar en desacuerdo con uno (sobre).

isthmus ['ɪsməs] n istmo.

---

it [ɪt] *pron* 1 *(specific: subject: not generally translated)* él/ella; *(: direct object)* lo, la; *(: indirect object)* le; *(after prep)* ello; ~'s *(abstract concept)* ello; ~'s on the table está en la mesa; I can't find ~ no lo *(or* la) encuentro; give ~ to me dámelo *(or* dámela); I spoke to him about ~ le hablé del asunto; what did you learn from ~? ¿qué aprendiste de él *(or* ella)?; did you go to ~? *(party, concert etc)* ¿fuiste? 2 *(impersonal)*: ~'s raining llueve, está lloviendo; ~'s 6 o'clock/the 10th of August son las 6/es el 10 de agosto; how far is ~? — ~'s 10 miles/2 hours on the train ¿a qué distancia está? — a 10 millas/2 horas en tren; who is ~? — ~'s me ¿quién es? — soy yo.

Italian [ɪ'tæljən] *a* italiano // *n* italiano/a; *(LING)* italiano.
italic [ɪ'tælɪk] *a* cursivo // ~s *npl* cursiva *sg*.
Italy ['ɪtəlɪ] *n* Italia.
itch [ɪtʃ] *n* picazón *f*; *(fig)* prurito // *vi (person)* sentir *or* tener comezón; *(part of body)* picar; **to be ~ing to** do sth rabiar por hacer algo; **~y** *a*: **to be ~y** = **to ~**.
it'd ['ɪtd] = **it would, it had.**
item ['aɪtəm] *n* artículo; *(on agenda)* asunto (a tratar); *(in programme)* número; *(also:* **news ~)** noticia; **~ize** *vt* detallar.
itinerant [ɪ'tɪnərənt] *a* ambulante.
itinerary [aɪ'tɪnərərɪ] *n* itinerario.
it'll ['ɪtl] = **it will, it shall.**
its [ɪts] *a* su.
it's [ɪts] = **it is, it has.**
itself [ɪt'sɛlf] *pron (reflexive)* sí mismo/a; *(emphatic)* él mismo/ella misma.
ITV *n abbr (Brit:* = *Independent Television)* cadena de TV comercial independiente del Estado.
I.U.D. *n abbr* (= *intra-uterine device*)

DIU *m.*
I've [aɪv] = **I have.**
ivory ['aɪvərɪ] *n* marfil *m.*
ivy ['aɪvɪ] *n* hiedra.

J

jab [dʒæb] *vt*: **to ~ sth into sth** clavar algo en algo // *n (MED: col)* pinchazo.
jabber ['dʒæbə*] *vt, vi* farfullar.
jack [dʒæk] *n (AUT)* gato; *(BOWLS)* boliche *m*; *(CARDS)* sota; **to ~ up** *vt (AUT)* levantar con el gato.
jackal ['dʒækɔːl] *n (ZOOL)* chacal *m.*
jackdaw ['dʒækdɔː] *n* grajo.
jacket ['dʒækɪt] *n* chaqueta, americana, saco *(LAm)*; *(of boiler etc)* camisa; *(of book)* sobrecubierta.
jack-knife ['dʒæknaɪf] *vi* colear.
jack plug *n (ELEC)* enchufe *m* de clavija.
jackpot ['dʒækpɔt] *n* premio gordo.
jaded ['dʒeɪdɪd] *a (tired)* cansado; *(fed-up)* hastiado.
jagged ['dʒægɪd] *a* dentado.
jail [dʒeɪl] *n* cárcel *f* // *vt* encarcelar; **~break** *n* fuga *or* evasión *f* (de la cárcel); **~er** *n* carcelero/a.
jam [dʒæm] *n* mermelada, jalea; *(also:* **traffic ~)** embotellamiento; *(difficulty)* apuro // *vt (passage etc)* obstruir; *(mechanism, drawer etc)* atascar; *(RADIO)* interferir // *vi* atascarse, trabarse; **to ~ sth into** sth meter algo a la fuerza en algo.
Jamaica [dʒə'meɪkə] *n* Jamaica.
jangle ['dʒæŋgl] *vi* sonar (de manera) discordante.
janitor ['dʒænɪtə*] *n (caretaker)* portero, conserje *m.*
January ['dʒænjuərɪ] *n* enero.
Japan [dʒə'pæn] *n* (el) Japón; **~ese** [dʒæpə'niːz] *a* japonés/esa // *n, pl inv* japonés/esa *m/f*; *(LING)* japonés *m.*
jar [dʒɑː*] *n (glass: large)* jarra; *(: small)* tarro // *vi (sound)* chirriar; *(colours)* desentonar.
jargon ['dʒɑːgən] *n* jerga.

jasmin(e) ['dʒæzmɪn] *n* jazmín *m*.

jaundice ['dʒɔːndɪs] *n* ictericia; ~*d a* (*fig: embittered*) amargado; (: *disillusioned*) desilusionado.

jaunt [dʒɔːnt] *n* excursión *f*; ~**y** *a* alegre.

javelin ['dʒævlɪn] *n* jabalina.

jaw [dʒɔː] *n* mandíbula.

jay [dʒeɪ] *n* (ZOOL) arrendajo.

jaywalker ['dʒeɪwɔːkə*] *n* peatón/ona *m/f* imprudente.

jazz [dʒæz] *n* jazz *m*; **to ~ up** *a* (*liven up*) animar, avivar.

jealous ['dʒeləs] *a* celoso; (*envious*) envidioso; **to be ~** tener celos; tener envidia; ~**y** *n* celos *mpl*; envidia.

jeans [dʒiːnz] *npl* (*pantalones mpl*) vaqueros *mpl* or tejanos *mpl*.

jeep [dʒiːp] *n* jeep *m*.

jeer [dʒɪə*] *vi*: **to ~ (at)** (*boo*) abuchear; (*mock*) mofarse (de).

jelly ['dʒelɪ] *n* jalea, gelatina; ~**fish** *n* medusa.

jeopardize ['dʒepədaɪz] *vt* arriesgar, poner en peligro.

jeopardy ['dʒepədɪ] *n*: **to be in ~** estar en peligro.

jerk [dʒɜːk] *n* (*jolt*) sacudida; (*wrench*) tirón *m* // *vt* dar una sacudida a; tirar bruscamente de // (*vehicle*) traquetear.

jerkin ['dʒɜːkɪn] *n* chaleco.

jerky ['dʒɜːkɪ] *a* espasmódico.

jersey ['dʒɜːzɪ] *n* jersey *m*.

jest [dʒest] *n* broma.

Jesus ['dʒiːzəs] *n* Jesús *m*.

jet [dʒet] *n* (*of gas, liquid*) chorro; (AVIAT) avión *m* a reacción; ~-**black** *a* negro como el azabache; ~-**engine** *n* motor *m* a reacción; ~-**lag** *n* desorientación *f* después de un largo vuelo.

jettison ['dʒetɪsn] *vt* desechar.

jetty ['dʒetɪ] *n* muelle *m*, embarcadero.

Jew [dʒuː] *n* judío.

jewel ['dʒuːəl] *n* joya; (*in watch*) rubí *m*; ~**ler**, (US) ~**er** *n* joyero/a; ~**ler's** (*shop*), (US) ~**ry store** *n* joyería; (US) ~**ery**, ~**lery** *n* joyas *fpl*, alhajas *fpl*.

Jewess ['dʒuːɪs] *n* judía.

Jewish ['dʒuːɪʃ] *a* judío.

jibe [dʒaɪb] *n* mofa.

jiffy ['dʒɪfɪ] *n* (col): **in a ~** en un santiamén.

jig [dʒɪg] *n* jiga.

jigsaw ['dʒɪgsɔː] *n* (*also*: ~ **puzzle**) rompecabezas *m inv*.

jilt [dʒɪlt] *vt* dejar plantado a.

jingle ['dʒɪŋgl] *n* (*advert*) musiquilla // *vi* tintinear.

jinx [dʒɪŋks] *n*: **there's a ~ on it** está gafado.

jitters ['dʒɪtəz] *npl* (col): **to get the ~** ponerse nervioso.

job [dʒɒb] *n* trabajo; (*task*) tarea; (*duty*) deber *m*; (*post*) empleo; **it's a good ~ that...** menos mal que...; **just the ~!** ¡estupendo!; ~ **centre** *n* (Brit) oficina estatal de colocaciones; ~**less** *a* sin trabajo.

jockey ['dʒɒkɪ] *n* jockey *m/f* // *vi*: **to ~ for position** maniobrar para conseguir una posición.

jocular ['dʒɒkjulə*] *a* (*humorous*) gracioso; (*merry*) alegre.

jog [dʒɒg] *vt* empujar (ligeramente) // *vi* (*run*) hacer footing; **to ~ along** ir tirando; **to ~ sb's memory** refrescar la memoria a uno; ~**ging** *n* footing *m*.

join [dʒɔɪn] *vt* (*things*) juntar, unir; (*become member of: club*) hacerse socio de; (POL: *party*) afiliarse a; (*meet: people*) reunirse con // *vi* (*roads*) empalmar; (*rivers*) confluir // *n* juntura; **to ~ in** tomar parte, participar // *vt fus* tomar parte en o participar en // **to ~ up** *vi* unirse; (MIL) alistarse.

joiner ['dʒɔɪnə*] *n* carpintero; ~**y** *n* carpintería.

joint [dʒɔɪnt] *n* (TECH) junta, unión *f*; (ANAT) articulación *f*; (Brit CULIN) pieza de carne (para asar); (col: *place*) garito *a* (*common*) común; (*combined*) mixto; ~ **account** (*with bank etc*) cuenta común; ~**ly** *ad* común; conjuntamente.

joist [dʒɔɪst] n viga.

joke [dʒəuk] n chiste m; (also: **practical** ~) broma // vi bromear; **to play a ~ on** gastar una broma a; **~r** n chistoso/a, bromista m/f; (CARDS) comodín m.

jolly ['dʒɔlɪ] a (merry) alegre; (enjoyable) divertido // ad (col) muy, terriblemente.

jolt [dʒəult] n (shake) sacudida; (blow) golpe m; (shock) susto // vt sacudir; asustar.

Jordan ['dʒɔːdən] n Jordania.

jostle ['dʒɔsl] vt dar empellones a, codear.

jot [dʒɔt] n: **not one** ~ ni jota, ni pizca; **to** ~ **down** vt apuntar; **~ter** n (Brit) bloc m.

journal ['dʒɜːnl] n (paper) periódico; (magazine) revista; (diary) diario; **~ism** n periodismo; **~ist** n periodista m/f, reportero/a.

journey ['dʒɜːnɪ] n viaje m; (distance covered) trayecto // vi viajar.

jovial ['dʒəuvɪəl] a risueño.

joy [dʒɔɪ] n alegría; **~ful, ~ous** a alegre; ~ **ride** n (illegal) paseo en coche robado; ~ **stick** n (AVIAT) palanca de mando; (COMPUT) palanca de control.

J.P. n abbr = **Justice of the Peace.**

Jr abbr = **junior.**

jubilant ['dʒuːbɪlənt] a jubiloso.

jubilee ['dʒuːbɪliː] n aniversario.

judge [dʒʌdʒ] n juez m/f // vt juzgar; (estimate) considerar; **judg(e)ment** n juicio; (punishment) sentencia, fallo.

judiciary [dʒuː'dɪʃɪərɪ] n poder m judicial.

judicious [dʒuː'dɪʃəs] a juicioso.

judo ['dʒuːdəu] n judo.

jug [dʒʌg] n jarro.

juggernaut ['dʒʌgənɔːt] n (Brit: huge truck) camionazo.

juggle ['dʒʌgl] vi hacer juegos malabares; **~r** n malabarista m/f.

Jugoslav ['juːgəuslɑːv] etc = **Yugo-**

slav etc.

juice [dʒuːs] n zumo, jugo (esp LAm); **juicy** a jugoso.

jukebox ['dʒuːkbɔks] n tocadiscos m inv tragaperras.

July [dʒuː'laɪ] n julio.

jumble ['dʒʌmbl] n revoltijo // vt (also: ~ **up**: mix up) revolver; (: disarrange) mezclar; ~ **sale** n (Brit) venta de objetos usados con fines benéficos.

jumbo (jet) ['dʒʌmbəu–] n jumbo.

jump [dʒʌmp] vi saltar, dar saltos; (start) asustarse, sobresaltarse; (increase) aumentar // vt saltar // n salto; aumento; **to** ~ **the queue** (Brit) colarse.

jumper ['dʒʌmpə*] n (Brit: pullover) suéter m, jersey m; (US: dress) mandil m; ~ **cables** npl (US) = **jump leads.**

jump leads npl (Brit) cables mpl puente de batería.

jumpy ['dʒʌmpɪ] a nervioso.

Jun. abbr = **junior.**

junction ['dʒʌŋkʃən] n (Brit: of roads) cruce m; (RAIL) empalme m.

juncture ['dʒʌŋktʃə*] n: **at this** ~ en este momento, en esta coyuntura.

June [dʒuːn] n junio.

jungle ['dʒʌŋgl] n selva, jungla.

junior ['dʒuːnɪə*] a (in age) menor, más joven; (competition) juvenil; (position) subalterno // n menor m/f, joven m/f; **he's ~ to me** es menor que yo; ~ **school** n (Brit) escuela primaria.

junk [dʒʌŋk] n (cheap goods) baratijas fpl; (lumber) trastos mpl viejos; (rubbish) basura; ~ **food** n alimentos preparados y envasados de escaso valor nutritivo; ~ **shop** n tienda de objetos usados.

Junr abbr = **junior.**

jurisdiction [dʒuərɪs'dɪkʃən] n jurisdicción f.

juror ['dʒuərə*] n jurado.

jury ['dʒuərɪ] n jurado.

just [dʒʌst] a justo // ad (exactly) exactamente; (only) sólo, solamente;

he's ~ done it/left acaba de hacerlo/irse; ~ **right** perfecto; ~ **two o'clock** las dos en punto; **she's ~ as clever as you** (ella) es tan lista como tú; ~ **as well that...** menos mal que...; ~ **as he was leaving** en el momento en que se marchaba; ~ **before/enough** justo antes/lo suficiente; ~ **here** aquí mismo; he ~ **missed** ha fallado por poco; ~ **listen to this** escucha esto un poco.

justice ['dʒʌstɪs] n justicia; **J~ of the Peace (J.P.)** n juez m de paz.

justifiable [dʒʌstɪ'faɪəbl] a justificable.

justify ['dʒʌstɪfaɪ] vt justificar; (text) alinear.

justly ['dʒʌstlɪ] ad (gen) justamente; (with reason) con razón.

jut [dʒʌt] vi (also: ~ **out**) sobresalir.

juvenile ['dʒuːvənaɪl] a juvenil; (court) de menores // n joven m/f, menor m de edad.

juxtapose ['dʒʌkstəpəʊz] vt yuxtaponer.

K

K abbr (= one thousand) mil; (= kilobyte) kilobyte m, kilocteto.

kaleidoscope [kə'laɪdəskəʊp] n calidoscopio.

Kampuchea [kæmpu'tʃɪə] n Kampuchea.

kangaroo [kæŋɡə'ruː] n canguro.

karate [kə'rɑːtɪ] n karate m.

kebab [kə'bæb] n pincho moruno.

keel [kiːl] n quilla; **on an even ~** (fig) en equilibrio.

keen [kiːn] a (interest, desire) grande, vivo; (eye, intelligence) agudo; (competition) intenso; (edge) afilado; (Brit: eager) entusiasta; **to be ~ to do or on doing sth** tener muchas ganas de hacer algo; **to be ~ on sth/ sb** interesarse por algo/uno.

keep [kiːp] vb (pt, pp kept) vt (retain, preserve) guardar; (hold back)

quedarse con; (shop) ser propietario de; (feed: family etc) mantener; (promise) cumplir; (chickens, bees etc) criar // vi (food) conservarse; (remain) seguir, continuar // n (of castle) torreón m; (food etc) comida, subsistencia; (col): **for ~s** para siempre; **to ~ doing sth** seguir haciendo algo; **to ~ sb from doing sth** impedir a uno hacer algo; **to ~ sth from happening** impedir que algo ocurra; **to ~ sb happy** tener a uno contento; **to ~ a place tidy** mantener un lugar limpio; **to ~ sth to o.s.** guardar algo para uno mismo; **to ~ sth (back) from sb** ocultar algo a uno; **to ~ time** (clock) mantener la hora exacta; **to ~ on** vi seguir, continuar; **to ~ out** (stay out) permanecer fuera; '**~ out**' prohibida la entrada; **to ~ up** vt mantener, conservar // vi no retrasarse; **to ~ up with** (pace) ir al paso de; (level) mantenerse a la altura de; **~er** n guardián/ana m/f; **~-fit** n gimnasia (para mantenerse en forma); **~ing** n (care) cuidado; **in ~ing with** de acuerdo con; **~sake** n recuerdo.

keg [kɛɡ] n barrilete m, barril m.

kennel ['kɛnl] n perrera; **~s** npl perreras fpl.

Kenya ['kɛnjə] n Kenia; **~n** a, n keniano/a m/f.

kept [kɛpt] pt, pp of **keep**.

kerb [kəːb] n (Brit) bordillo.

kernel ['kəːnl] n (nut) fruta; (fig) meollo.

kerosene ['kɛrəsiːn] n keroseno.

ketchup ['kɛtʃəp] n salsa de tomate, catsup m.

kettle ['kɛtl] n hervidor m, olla; **~drum** n (MUS) timbal m.

key [kiː] n (gen) llave f; (MUS) tono; (of piano, typewriter) tecla // vt (also: ~ **in**) teclear; **~board** n teclado; **~ed up** a (person) nervioso; **~hole** n ojo (de la cerradura); **~note** n (MUS) tónica; **~ring** n llavero.

khaki ['kɑːkɪ] n caqui.

kick [kɪk] vt (person) dar una patada a; (ball) dar un puntapié a // vi (horse) dar coces // n patada; puntapié m; (of rifle) culetazo; (thrill): **he does it for ~s** lo hace por pura diversión; **to ~ off** vi (SPORT) hacer el saque inicial.

kid [kɪd] n (col: child) chiquillo/a; (animal) cabrito; (leather) cabritilla // vi (col) bromear.

kidnap ['kɪdnæp] vt secuestrar; **~per** n secuestrador/a m/f; **~ping** n secuestro.

kidney ['kɪdnɪ] n riñón m.

kill [kɪl] vt matar; (murder) asesinar; (fig: story) suprimir; (: rumour) acabar con; **to be ~ed (by a bullet)** ser muerto (por una bala) // n matanza; **~er** n asesino/a; **~ing** n (one) asesinato; (several) matanza; **~joy** n (Brit) aguafiestas m/f inv.

kiln [kɪln] n horno.

kilo ['kiːləʊ] n kilo; **~byte** n (COMPUT) kilobyte m, kiloocteto; **~gram(me)** ['kɪləʊɡræm] n kilo, kilogramo; **~metre**, (US) **~meter** ['kɪləmiːtə*] n kilómetro; **~watt** ['kɪləʊwɔt] n kilovatio.

kilt [kɪlt] n falda escocesa.

kin [kɪn] n parientes mpl.

kind [kaɪnd] a (treatment) bueno, cariñoso; (person, act, word) amable, atento // n clase f, especie f; (species) género; **in ~** (COMM) en especie; **a ~ of** una especie de; **to be two of a ~** ser tal para cual.

kindergarten ['kɪndəɡɑːtn] n jardín m de infantes.

kind-hearted ['kaɪnd'hɑːtɪd] a bondadoso, de buen corazón.

kindle ['kɪndl] vt encender.

kindly ['kaɪndlɪ] a bondadoso; (gentle) cariñoso // ad bondadosamente, amablemente; **will you ~...** sea usted tan amable de... .

kindness ['kaɪndnɪs] n bondad f, amabilidad f.

kindred ['kɪndrɪd] a: **~ spirits** almas fpl gemelas.

kinetic [kɪ'netɪk] a cinético.

king [kɪŋ] n rey m; **~dom** n reino; **~fisher** n martín m pescador; **~-size** a de tamaño gigante.

kinky ['kɪŋkɪ] a (pej) perverso.

kiosk ['kiːɔsk] n quiosco; (Brit TEL) cabina.

kipper ['kɪpə*] n arenque m ahumado.

kiss [kɪs] n beso // vt besar; **to ~ (each other)** besarse.

kit [kɪt] n avíos mpl; (equipment) equipo; (set of tools etc) (caja de herramientas fpl; (assembly ~) juego de armar.

kitchen ['kɪtʃɪn] n cocina; **~ sink** n fregadero.

kite [kaɪt] n (toy) cometa.

kith [kɪθ] n: **~ and kin** parientes mpl y allegados.

kitten ['kɪtn] n gatito/a.

kitty ['kɪtɪ] n (pool of money) fondo común; (CARDS) puesta.

km abbr (= kilometre) km.

knack [næk] n: **to have the ~ of doing sth** tener el don de hacer algo.

knapsack ['næpsæk] n mochila.

knead [niːd] vt amasar.

knee [niː] n rodilla; **~cap** n rótula.

kneel [niːl], pt, pp **knelt** vi (also: ~ down) arrodillarse.

knell [nel] n toque m de difuntos.

knelt [nelt] pt, pp of **kneel**.

knew [njuː] pt of **know**.

knickers ['nɪkəz] npl (Brit) bragas fpl.

knife [naɪf], pl **knives** n cuchillo // vt acuchillar.

knight [naɪt] n caballero; (CHESS) caballo; **~hood** n (title) título de caballero; **to get a ~hood** recibir el título de Sir.

knit [nɪt] vt tejer, tricotar; (brows) fruncir // vi tejer, tricotar; (bones) soldarse; **to ~ together** vt (fig) unir, juntar; **~ting** n labor f de punto; **~ting machine** n máquina de tricotar; **~ting needle**, (US) **~ pin** n aguja de tejer; **~wear** n prendas fpl de punto.

knives [naɪvz] pl of **knife**.

knob [nɔb] n (of door) tirador m; (of stick) puño; **a ~ of butter** (Brit) un pedazo de mantequilla.

knock [nɔk] vt (strike) golpear; (bump into) chocar contra; (fig: col) criticar // vi (at door etc): **to ~ at/ on** llamar a // n golpe m; (on door) llamada; **to ~ down** vt (pedestrian) atropellar; **to ~ off** vi (col: finish) salir del trabajo // vt (col: steal) birlar; **to ~ out** vt dejar sin sentido; (BOXING) poner fuera de combate, dejar K.O.; **to ~ over** vt (object) tirar; (person) atropellar; **~er** n (on door) aldaba; **~-kneed** a patizambo; **~out** n (BOXING) K.O. m, knockout m.

knot [nɔt] n (gen) nudo // vt anudar; **~ty** a (fig) complicado.

know [nəu], pt **knew**, pp **known** vt (gen) saber; (person, author, place) conocer; **to ~ how to** do sth saber como hacer; **to ~ how to swim** saber nadar; **to ~ about** or of sb/sth saber de uno/algo; **~all** n sabelotodo m/f; **~-how** n conocimientos mpl; **~ing** a (look) de complicidad; **~ingly** ad (purposely) adrede; (smile, look) con complicidad.

knowledge ['nɔlɪdʒ] n (gen) conocimiento; (learning) saber m, conocimientos mpl; **~able** a: **~able about** enterado de.

known [nəun] pp of **know**.

knuckle ['nʌkl] n nudillo n.

K.O. n abbr = **knockout**.

Koran [kɔ'rɑːn] n Corán m.

Korea [kɔ'rɪə] n Corea.

kosher ['kəuʃə*] a autorizado por la ley judía.

L

l. abbr = **litre**.

lab [læb] n abbr = **laboratory**.

label ['leɪbl] n etiqueta; (brand: of record) sello (discográfico) // vt poner etiqueta a.

laboratory [lə'bɔrətəri] n laborato-

rio.

laborious [lə'bɔːrɪəs] a penoso.

labour, (US) **labor** ['leɪbə*] n (task) trabajo; (~ force) mano de obra; (MED) parto // vi: **to ~ (at)** trabajar (en) // vt insistir en; **in ~** (MED) de parto; **L~, the L~ party** (Brit) el partido laborista, los laboristas mpl; **~ed** a (breathing) fatigoso; (style) pesado; **~er** n peón m; (on farm) peón m; (day ~er) jornalero.

labyrinth ['læbɪrɪnθ] n laberinto.

lace [leɪs] n encaje m; (of shoe etc) cordón m // vt (shoes: also: ~ up) atarse (los zapatos).

lack [læk] n (absence) falta; (scarcity) escasez f // vt faltarle a uno, carecer de; **through** or **for ~ of** por falta de; **to be ~ing** faltar, no haber.

lackadaisical [lækə'deɪzɪkl] a (careless) descuidado; (indifferent) indiferente.

lacquer ['lækə*] n laca.

lad [læd*] n muchacho, chico; (in stable etc) mozo.

ladder ['lædə*] n escalera (de mano); (Brit: in tights) carrera // vt (Brit: tights) hacer una carrera en.

laden ['leɪdn] a: **~ (with)** cargado (de).

ladle ['leɪdl] n cucharón m.

lady ['leɪdɪ] n señora; (distinguished, noble) dama; **young ~** señorita; **the ladies' (room)** los servicios de señoras; **~bird, ~bug** (US) n mariquita; **~-in-waiting** n dama de honor; **~like** a fino; **L~ship** n: **your L~ship** su Señoría.

lag [læg] vi (also: **~ behind**) retrasarse, quedarse atrás // vt (pipes) revestir.

lager ['lɑːgə*] n cerveza (rubia).

lagoon [lə'guːn] n laguna.

laid [leɪd] pt, pp of **lay**; **~ back** a (col) relajado.

lain [leɪn] pp of **lie**.

lair [lɛə*] n guarida.

laity ['leɪtɪ] n laicado.

lake [leɪk] n lago.

lamb [læm] *n* cordero; (*meat*) carne *f* de cordero; ~ **chop** *n* chuleta de cordero; ~**swool** *n* lana de cordero.

lame [leɪm] *a* cojo; (*excuse*) poco convincente.

lament [lə'mɛnt] *vi* lamentarse de.

laminated [læmineɪtɪd] *a* laminado.

lamp [læmp] *n* lámpara.

lampoon [læm'puːn] *vt* satirizar.

lamp: ~**post** *n* (*Brit*) (poste *m* de farol *m*); ~**shade** *n* pantalla.

lance [lɑːns] *n* lanza // *vt* (*MED*) abrir con lanceta; ~ **corporal** *n* (*Brit*) soldado de primera clase.

land [lænd] *n* tierra; (*country*) país *m*; (*piece of* ~) terreno; (*estate*) tierras *fpl*, finca; (*AGR*) campo // *vi* (*from ship*) desembarcar; (*AVIAT*) aterrizar; (*fig: fall*) caer, terminar // *vt* (*obtain*) conseguir; (*passengers, goods*) desembarcar; **to** ~ **up** in/at ir a parar a/en; ~**ing** *n* desembarco; aterrizaje *m*; (*of staircase*) rellano; ~**ing stage** *n* (*Brit*) desembarcadero; ~**ing strip** *n* pista de aterrizaje; ~**lady** *n* (*of boarding house*) patrona; (*owner*) dueña; ~**lord** *n* propietario; (*of pub etc*) patrón *m*; ~**mark** *n* lugar *m* conocido; **to be a** ~**mark** (*fig*) hacer época; ~**owner** *n* terrateniente *m/f*.

landscape [lænskeɪp] *n* paisaje *m*.

landslide [lændslaɪd] *n* (*GEO*) corrimiento de tierras; (*fig: POL*) victoria arrolladora.

lane [leɪn] *n* (*in country*) camino; (*in town*) callejón *m*; (*AUT*) carril *m*; (*in race*) calle *f*; (*for air or sea traffic*) ruta.

language [læŋgwɪdʒ] *n* lenguaje *m*; (*national tongue*) idioma *m*, lengua; **bad** ~ palabrotas *fpl*; ~ **laboratory** *n* laboratorio de idiomas.

languid [læŋgwɪd] *a* lánguido.

languish [læŋgwɪʃ] *vi* languidecer.

lank [læŋk] *a* (*hair*) lacio.

lanky [læŋkɪ] *a* larguirucho.

lantern [læntn] *n* linterna, farol *m*.

lap [læp] *n* (*of track*) vuelta; (*of body*): **to sit on sb's** ~ sentarse en

las rodillas de uno // *vt* (*also:* ~ **up**) lamer // *vi* (*waves*) chapotear.

lapel [lə'pɛl] *n* solapa.

Lapland [læplænd] *n* Laponia.

lapse [læps] *n* error *m*, fallo; (*moral*) desliz *m* // *vi* (*expire*) caducar; (*morally*) cometer un desliz; (*time*) pasar, transcurrir; **to** ~ **into bad habits** caer en malos hábitos; ~ **of time** lapso, período.

larceny [lɑːsənɪ] *n* latrocinio *m*.

lard [lɑːd] *n* manteca (de cerdo).

larder [lɑːdə*] *n* despensa.

large [lɑːdʒ] *a* grande; **at** ~ (*free*) en libertad; (*generally*) en general; ~**ly** *ad* en gran parte; ~**-scale** *a* (*map*) en gran escala; (*fig*) importante.

largesse [lɑːˈʒɛs] *n* generosidad *f*.

lark [lɑːk] *n* (*bird*) alondra; (*joke*) broma; **to** ~ **about** *vi* bromear, hacer el tonto.

laryngitis [lærɪnˈdʒaɪtɪs] *n* laringitis *f*.

larynx [lærɪŋks] *n* laringe *f*.

laser [leɪzə*] *n* láser *m*; ~ **printer** *n* impresora (*f*) por láser.

lash [læʃ] *n* latigazo; (*punishment*) azote *m*; (*also: eyelash*) pestaña // *vt* azotar; (*tie*) atar; **to** ~ **out** (*col: spend*) gastar a la loca; **to** ~ **out at or against sb** lanzar invectivas contra uno.

lass [læs] *n* chica.

lasso [læ'suː] *n* lazo.

last [lɑːst] *a* (*gen*) último; (*final*) último, final // *ad* por último // *vi* (*endure*) durar; (*continue*) continuar, seguir; ~ **night** anoche; ~ **week** la semana pasada; **at** ~ por fin; ~ **but one** penúltimo; ~**-ditch** *a* (*attempt*) último, desesperado; ~**ing** *a* duradero; ~**ly** *ad* por último, finalmente; ~**-minute** *a* de última hora.

latch [lætʃ] *n* picaporte *m*, pestillo.

late [leɪt] *a* (*not on time*) tarde, atrasado; (*towards end of period, life*) tardío; (*hour*) avanzado; (*dead*) fallecido // *ad* tarde; (*behind time, schedule*) con retraso; **of** ~ últimamente; **in ~ May** hacia fines de mayo; **the ~ Mr X** el difunto Sr X; **~comer** n recién llegado/a; **~ly** ad últimamente.

later ['leɪtə*] a (date etc) posterior; (version etc) más reciente // ad más tarde, después.

lateral ['lætərl] a lateral.

latest ['leɪtɪst] a último; **at the ~** a más tardar.

lathe [leɪð] n torno.

lather ['lɑːðə*] n espuma (de jabón) // vt enjabonar.

Latin ['lætɪn] n latín m // a latino; **~ America** n América latina; **~ American** a latinoamericano.

latitude ['lætɪtjuːd] n latitud f.

latrine [lə'triːn] n letrina.

latter ['lætə*] a último; (of two) segundo // n: **the ~** el último, éste; **~ly** ad últimamente.

lattice ['lætɪs] n enrejado.

laudable ['lɔːdəbl] a loable.

laugh [lɑːf] n risa; (loud) carcajada // vi reír(se); **to ~ at** vt fus reírse de; **to ~ off** vt tomar algo a risa; **~able** a ridículo; **~ing stock** n: **the ~ing stock of** el hazmerreír de; **~ter** n risa.

launch [lɔːntʃ] n (boat) lancha; see also **~ing** // vt (ship, rocket, plan) lanzar; **~ing** n (of rocket etc) lanzamiento; (inauguration) estreno; **~(ing) pad** n plataforma de lanzamiento.

launder ['lɔːndə*] vt lavar.

launderette [lɔːn'drɛt], (US) **laundromat** ['lɔːdrəmæt] n lavandería (automática).

laundry ['lɔːndrɪ] n lavandería; (clothes) ropa sucia; **to do the ~** hacer la colada.

laureate ['lɔːrɪət] a see **poet**.

lavatory ['lævətərɪ] n wáter m; lavatories npl servicios mpl, aseos mpl, sanitarios mpl (LAm).

lavender ['lævəndə*] n lavanda.

lavish ['lævɪʃ] a abundante; (giving freely): **~ with** pródigo en // vt: **to ~ sth on sb** colmar a uno de algo.

law [lɔː] n ley f; (study) derecho; (of game) regla; **~-abiding** a respetuoso de la ley; **~ and order** n orden m público; **~ court** n tribunal m (de justicia); **~ful** a legítimo, lícito; **~fully** ad legalmente.

lawn [lɔːn] n césped m; **~mower** n cortacésped m; **~ tennis** n tenis m sobre hierba.

law school n facultad f de derecho.

lawsuit ['lɔːsuːt] n pleito.

lawyer ['lɔːjə*] n abogado/a; (for sales, wills etc) notario/a.

lax [læks] a (discipline) relajado; (person) negligente al hacer.

laxative ['læksətɪv] n laxante m.

laxity ['læksɪtɪ] n flojedad f; (moral) relajamiento; (negligence) negligencia.

lay [leɪ] pt of **lie** // a laico; (not expert) lego // vt (pt, pp **laid**) (place) colocar; (eggs, table) poner; (trap) tender; **to ~ aside** or **by** vt dejar a un lado; **to ~ down** vt (pen etc) dejar; (arms) rendir; (policy) asentar; **to ~ down the law** imponer las normas; **to ~ off** vt (workers) despedir; **to ~ on** vt (water, gas) instalar; (meal, facilities) proveer; **to ~ out** vt (plan) trazar; (display) disponer; (spend) gastar; **to ~ up** vt (store) guardar; (ship) desarmar; (subj: illness) obligar a guardar cama; **~about** n vago/a; **~-by** n (Brit AUT) área de aparcamiento.

layer ['leɪə*] n capa.

layette [leɪ'ɛt] n ajuar m (de niño).

layman ['leɪmən] n lego.

layout ['leɪaʊt] n (design) plan m, trazado; (disposition) disposición f; (PRESS) composición f.

laze [leɪz] vi holgazanear.

laziness ['leɪzɪnɪs] n pereza.

lazy ['leɪzɪ] a perezoso, vago.

lb. abbr = **pound** (weight).

lead [liːd] n (front position) delantera; (distance, time ahead) ventaja; (clue) pista; (ELEC) cable m; (for dog) correa; (THEATRE) papel m principal; [lɛd] (metal) plomo; (in pencil) mina // (vb: pt, pp led) vt conducir; (life) llevar; (be leader of) dirigir; (SPORT) ir en cabeza de // vi ir primero; **to be in the ~** (SPORT) llevar la delantera; (fig) ir a la cabeza; **to ~ astray** llevar por mal camino; **to ~ away** vt llevar; **to ~ back** vt (person, route) llevar de vuelta; **to ~ on** vt (tease) engañar; **to ~ on** vt (induce) incitar a; **to ~ to** vt fus producir, provocar; **to ~ up to** vt fus conducir a.

leaden ['lɛdn] a (sky, sea) plomizo; (heavy: footsteps) pesado.

leader ['liːdə*] n jefe/a m/f, líder m; (of union etc) dirigente m/f; (guide) guía m/f; (of newspaper) artículo de fondo; **~ship** n dirección f.

leading ['liːdɪŋ] a (main) principal; (outstanding) destacado; (first) primero; (front) delantero; **~ lady** n (THEATRE) primera actriz f; **~ light** n (person) figura principal.

leaf [liːf], pl **leaves** n hoja // vi: **to ~ through** hojear; **to turn over a new ~** reformarse.

leaflet ['liːflɪt] n folleto.

league [liːg] n sociedad f; (FOOTBALL) liga; **to be in ~ with** estar de manga con.

leak [liːk] n (of liquid, gas) escape m, fuga; (in pipe) agujero; (in roof) gotera; (in security) filtración f // vi (shoes, ship) hacer agua; (pipe) tener (un) escape; (roof) gotear; (also: **~ out**: liquid, gas) escaparse, fugarse; (fig: news) divulgarse // vt (fig: information) filtrarse.

lean [liːn] a (thin) flaco; (meat) magro // (vb: pt, pp **leaned** or **leant** [lɛnt]) vt: **to ~ sth on sth** apoyar algo en algo // vi (slope) inclinarse; (rest): **to ~ against** apoyarse contra; **to ~ on** apoyarse en; (fig: rely on) contar con (el apoyo de); **to ~ back/forward** vi inclinarse hacia atrás/adelante; **to ~ out** vi asomarse; **to ~ over** vi inclinarse; **~ing** n: **~ing (towards)** inclinación f (ha-

cia); **~-to** n cobertizo.

leap [liːp] n salto // vi (pt, pp **leaped** or **leapt** [lɛpt]) saltar; **~frog** n pídola; **~ year** n año bisiesto.

learn [ləːn], pt, pp **learned** or **learnt** vt (gen) aprender; (come to know of) enterarse de // vi aprender; **to ~ how to do sth** aprender a hacer algo; **~ed** ['ləːnɪd] a erudito; **~er** n principiante m/f; (Brit: also: **~er driver**) aprendiz(a) m/f; **~ing** n el saber m, conocimientos mpl.

lease [liːs] n arriendo // vt arrendar.

leash [liːʃ] n correa.

least [liːst] a (slightest) menor, más pequeño; (smallest amount of) mínimo // ad menos // n: **the ~** lo menos; **the ~ expensive car** el coche menos costoso; **at ~** por lo menos, al menos; **not in the ~** en absoluto.

leather ['lɛðə*] n cuero.

leave [liːv], pt, pp **left** vt dejar; (go away from) abandonar // vi irse; (train) salir // n permiso; **to be left** quedar, sobrar; **there's some milk left over** sobra o queda algo de leche; **on ~** de permiso; **to ~ behind** vt (on purpose) dejar (atrás); (accidentally) olvidar; **to take one's ~ of** despedirse de; **to ~ out** vt omitir; **~ of absence** n permiso de ausentarse.

leaves [liːvz] pl of **leaf**.

Lebanon ['lɛbənən] n: **the ~** el Líbano.

lecherous ['lɛtʃərəs] a lascivo.

lecture ['lɛktʃə*] n conferencia; (SCOL) clase f // vi dar una clase // vt (scold) sermonear; **to give a ~ on** dar una conferencia sobre; **~r** n conferenciante m/f; (Brit: at university) profesor(a) m/f.

led [lɛd] pt, pp of **lead**.

ledge [lɛdʒ] n (of window, on wall) repisa, reborde m; (of mountain) saliente m.

ledger ['lɛdʒə*] n libro mayor.

lee [liː] n sotavento.

leech [liːtʃ] n sanguijuela.

leek [liːk] n puerro.

leer [lɪə*] vi: to ~ at sb mirar de manera lasciva a uno.

leeway ['liːweɪ] n (fig): to have some ~ tener cierta libertad de acción.

left [left] pt, pp of **leave** // a izquierdo // n izquierda // ad a la izquierda; **on** or **to the** ~ a la izquierda; **the L~** (POL) la izquierda; **~-handed** a zurdo; **the ~-hand side** n la izquierda; **~-luggage (office)** n (Brit) consigna; **~-overs** npl sobras fpl; **~-wing** a (POL) de izquierda, izquierdista.

leg [leg] n pierna; (of animal) pata; (of chair) pie m; (CULIN: of meat) pierna; (of journey) etapa; **lst/2nd** ~ (SPORT) partido de ida/de vuelta.

legacy ['legəsɪ] n herencia.

legal ['liːgl] a (permitted by law) lícito; (of law) legal; (inquiry etc) jurídico; ~ **holiday** n (US) fiesta oficial; **~ize** vt legalizar; **~ly** ad legalmente; ~ **tender** n moneda de curso legal.

legend ['ledʒənd] n leyenda.

legislation [ledʒɪs'leɪʃən] n legislación f.

legislature ['ledʒɪslətʃə*] n cuerpo legislativo.

legitimate [lɪ'dʒɪtɪmət] a legítimo.

leg-room ['legruːm] n espacio para las piernas.

leisure ['leʒə*] n ocio, tiempo libre; **at** ~ con tranquilidad; ~ **centre** n centro de recreo; **~ly** a sin prisa, lento.

lemon ['lemən] n limón m; **~ade** [-'neɪd] n (fruit juice) limonada; (fizzy) gaseosa; ~ **tea** n té m con limón.

lend [lend], pt, pp **lent** vt: to ~ sth to sb prestar algo a alguien; **~ing library** n biblioteca de préstamo.

length [leŋθ] n (size) largo, longitud f; (section: of road, pipe) tramo; (: rope etc) largo; **at** ~ (at last) por fin; (lengthily) largamente; **~en** vt alargar // vi alargarse; **~ways** ad a lo largo; **~y** a largo,

extenso; (meeting) prolongado.

lenient ['liːnɪənt] a indulgente.

lens [lenz] n (of spectacles) lente f; (of camera) objetivo.

lent [lent] pt, pp of **lend**.

Lent [lent] n Cuaresma.

lentil ['lentl] n lenteja.

Leo ['liːəu] n Leo.

leotard ['liːətɑːd] n leotardo.

leper ['lepə*] n leproso/a.

leprosy ['leprəsɪ] n lepra.

lesbian ['lezbɪən] n lesbiana.

less [les] a (in size, degree etc) menor; (in quantity) menos // pron, ad menos; ~ **than half** menos de la mitad; ~ **than ever** menos que nunca; ~ **and** ~ cada vez menos; **the ~ he works...** cuanto menos trabaja...

lessen ['lesn] vi disminuir, reducirse // vt disminuir, reducir.

lesser ['lesə*] a menor; **to a** ~ **extent** en menor grado.

lesson ['lesn] n clase f; **a maths** ~ una clase de matemáticas.

lest [lest] conj: ~ **it happen** para que no pase.

let [let], pt, pp **let** vt (allow) dejar, permitir; (Brit: lease) alquilar; **to** ~ **sb do sth** dejar que uno haga algo; **to** ~ **sb know sth** comunicar algo a uno; **~'s go** ¡vamos!; **to** ~ **him come** que venga; **'to** ~' 'se alquila'; **to** ~ **down** vt (lower) bajar; (dress) alargar; (tyre) desinflar; (hair) soltar; (disappoint) defraudar; **to** ~ **go** vi soltar; (fig) dejarse ir // vt soltar; **to** ~ **in** vt dejar entrar; (visitor etc) hacer pasar; **to** ~ **off** vt dejar escapar; (firework etc) disparar; (bomb) accionar; **to** ~ **on** vi (col) divulgar; **to** ~ **out** vt dejar salir; (dress) ensanchar; **to** ~ **up** vi amainar, disminuir.

lethal ['liːθl] a (weapon) mortífero; (poison, wound) mortal.

lethargy ['leθədʒɪ] n letargo.

letter ['letə*] n (of alphabet) letra; (correspondence) carta; ~ **bomb** n carta-bomba; **~box** n (Brit) buzón m; ~ **of credit** n carta de crédito;

~ing n letras fpl.

lettuce ['letɪs] n lechuga.

leukaemia, (US) **leukemia** [luːˈkiːmɪə] n leucemia.

level ['levl] a (flat) llano; (flattened) nivelado; (uniform) igual // ad a nivel // n nivel m // vt nivelar; allanar; **to be ~ with** estar a nivel de; **'A' ~s** npl (Brit) ≈ Bachillerato Superior, B.U.P.; **'O' ~s** npl (Brit) ≈ bachillerato elemental, octavo de básica; **on the ~** (fig: honest) en serio; **to ~ off** or **out** vi (prices etc) estabilizarse; **~ crossing** n (Brit) paso a nivel; **~-headed** a sensato.

lever ['liːvə*] n palanca // vt: **to ~ up** levantar con palanca; **~age** n (fig: influence) influencia.

levy ['levɪ] n impuesto // vt exigir, recaudar.

lewd [luːd] a lascivo; (joke) obsceno, colorado (LAm).

liability [laɪəˈbɪlɪtɪ] n responsabilidad f; (handicap) desventaja; **liabilities** npl obligaciones fpl; (COMM) pasivo sg.

liable ['laɪəbl] a (subject): **~ to** sujeto a; (responsible): **~ for** responsable de; (likely): **~ to do** propenso a hacer.

liaise [lɪˈeɪz] vi: **to ~ with** enlazar con.

liaison [lɪˈeɪzɒn] n (coordination) enlace m; (affair) relación f.

liar ['laɪə*] n mentiroso/a.

libel ['laɪbl] n calumnia // vt calumniar.

liberal ['lɪbərl] a (gen) liberal; (generous): **~ with** generoso con.

liberty ['lɪbətɪ] n libertad f; **to be at ~ to do** estar libre para hacer.

Libra ['liːbrə] n Libra.

librarian [laɪˈbreərɪən] n bibliotecario/a.

library ['laɪbrərɪ] n biblioteca.

libretto [lɪˈbretəʊ] n libreto.

Libya ['lɪbɪə] n Libia; **~n** a, n libio/a m/f.

lice [laɪs] pl of **louse**.

licence, (US) **license** ['laɪsns] n li-

cencia; (permit) permiso; (also: **driving ~**, (US) **driver's ~**) carnet m de conducir (Sp), permiso (LAm); (excessive freedom) libertad f; **~ number** n matrícula; **~ plate** n placa (de matrícula).

license ['laɪsns] n (US) = **licence** // vt autorizar, dar permiso a; **~d** a (for alcohol) autorizado para vender bebidas alcohólicas.

licentious [laɪˈsenʃəs] a licencioso.

lichen ['laɪkən] n liquen m.

lick [lɪk] vt lamer // n lamedura; **a ~ of paint** una mano de pintura.

licorice ['lɪkərɪs] n = **liquorice**.

lid [lɪd] n (of box, case) tapa; (of pan) cobertera.

lido ['laɪdəʊ] n (Brit) piscina.

lie [laɪ] n mentira // vi mentir; (pt lay, pp lain) (rest) estar echado, estar acostado; (of object: be situated) estar, encontrarse; **to ~ low** (fig) mantenerse a escondidas; **~ about** vi (things) estar tirado; (Brit) (people) estar tumbado; **to have a ~-down** (Brit) echarse (una siesta); **to have a ~-in** (Brit) quedarse en la cama.

lieu [luː]: **in ~ of** prep en lugar de.

lieutenant [lefˈtenənt, (US) luːˈtenənt] n (MIL) teniente m.

life [laɪf], pl **lives** n vida; (way of ~) modo de vivir; (of licence etc) vigencia; **~ assurance** n (Brit) seguro de vida; **~belt** n (Brit) cinturón m salvavidas; **~boat** n lancha de socorro; **~guard** n vigilante m/f; **~ insurance** n = **~ assurance**; **~ jacket** n chaleco salvavidas; **~less** a sin vida; (dull) soso; **~like** a natural; **~line** n (fig) cordón m umbilical; **~long** a de toda la vida; **~ preserver** n (US) = **~belt**; **~ saver** n socorrista m/f; **~ sentence** n condena perpetua; **~sized** a de tamaño natural; **~ span** n vida; **lifestyle** n estilo de vida; **~ support system** n (MED) sistema m de respiración asistida; **~time** n: in his **~time** durante su vida; **once in**

a ~**time** una vez en la vida.

lift [lɪft] vt levantar; (copy) plagiar // vi (fog) disiparse // n (Brit: elevator) ascensor m; **to give sb a** ~ (Brit) llevar a uno en el coche; ~**-off** n despegue m.

light [laɪt] n luz f; (flame) lumbre f; (lamp) luz f, lámpara; (daylight) luz f del día; (headlight) faro; (rear ~) luz f trasera; (for cigarette etc): **have you got a** ~? ¿tienes fuego? // vt (pt, pp **lighted** or **lit**) (candle, cigarette, fire) encender (Sp), prender (LAm); (room) alumbrar // a (colour) claro; (not heavy, also fig) ligero; (room) alumbrado; **to come to** ~ salir a luz; **to** ~ **up** vi (smoke) encender un cigarrillo; (face) iluminarse // vt (illuminate) iluminar, alumbrar; ~ **bulb** n bombilla, foco (LAm); ~**en** vi (grow ~) clarear // vt (give light to) iluminar; (make lighter) aclarar; (make less heavy) aligerar; ~**er** n (also: cigarette ~) encendedor m, mechero; ~**headed** a (dizzy) mareado; (excited) exaltado; (by nature) casquivano; ~**hearted** a alegre; ~**house** n faro; ~**ing** n (act) iluminación f; (system) alumbrado; ~**ly** ad ligeramente; (not seriously) con poca seriedad; **to get off** ~**ly** ser castigado con poca severidad; ~**ness** n claridad f; (in weight) ligereza.

lightning ['laɪtnɪŋ] n relámpago, rayo; ~ **conductor**, (US) ~ **rod** n pararrayos m inv.

light: ~**pen** n lápiz m óptico; ~**weight** a (suit) ligero // n (BOXING) peso ligero; ~**year** n año luz.

like [laɪk] vt gustarle a uno // prep como // a parecido, semejante // n: **the** ~ semejante m/f; **his** ~**s and dislikes** sus gustos y aversiones; **I would** ~, **I'd** ~ me gustaría; (for purchase) quisiera; **would you** ~ **a coffee?** ¿te apetece un café? **I** ~ **swimming** me gusta nadar; **she** ~**s apples** le gustan las manzanas; **to be** or **look** ~ sb/sth parecerse a

alguien/algo; **that's just** ~ **him** es muy de él, es característico de él; **do it** ~ **this** hazlo así; **it is nothing** ~... no tiene parecido alguno con...; ~**able** a simpático, agradable.

likelihood ['laɪklɪhud] n probabilidad f.

likely ['laɪklɪ] a probable; **he's** ~ **to leave** es probable que se vaya; **not** ~! ¡ni hablar!

likeness ['laɪknɪs] n semejanza, parecido.

likewise ['laɪkwaɪz] ad igualmente.

liking ['laɪkɪŋ] n: ~ (**for**) (person) cariño (a); (thing) afición (a).

lilac ['laɪlək] n lila // a (colour) de color lila.

lily ['lɪlɪ] n lirio, azucena; ~ **of the valley** n lirio de los valles.

limb [lɪm] n miembro.

limber ['lɪmbə']: **to** ~ **up** vi (fig) entrenarse; (SPORT) desentumecerse.

limbo ['lɪmbəu] n: **to be in** ~ (fig) quedar a la expectativa.

lime [laɪm] n (tree) limero; (fruit) lima; (GEO) cal f.

limelight ['laɪmlaɪt] n: **to be in the** ~ (fig) ser el centro de atención.

limerick ['lɪmərɪk] n quintilla humorística.

limestone ['laɪmstəun] n piedra caliza.

limit ['lɪmɪt] n límite m // vt limitar; ~**ed** a limitado; **to be** ~**ed to** limitarse a; ~**ed (liability) company (Ltd)** n (Brit) sociedad f anónima.

limousine ['lɪməzi:n] n limusina.

limp [lɪmp] n: **to have a** ~ tener cojera // vi cojear // a flojo.

limpet ['lɪmpɪt] n lapa.

line [laɪn] n (gen) línea; (straight ~) raya; (rope) cuerda; (for fishing) sedal m; (wire) hilo; (row, series) fila, hilera; (of writing) renglón m; (on face) arruga; (speciality) rama // vt (SEWING) forrar (with de); **to** ~ **the streets** ocupar las aceras; **in** ~ **with** de acuerdo con; **to** ~ **up** vi hacer cola // vt alinear, poner en fila.

linear ['lɪnɪə'] a lineal.

lined [laɪnd] a (face) arrugado; (paper) rayado.

linen ['lɪnɪn] n ropa blanca; (cloth) lino.

liner ['laɪnə*] n vapor m de línea, transatlántico.

linesman ['laɪnzmən] n (SPORT) juez m de línea.

line-up ['laɪnʌp] n alineación f.

linger ['lɪŋgə*] vi retrasarse, tardar en marcharse; (smell, tradition) persistir.

lingerie ['lænʒəriː] n ropa interior (de mujer).

lingo ['lɪŋgəʊ], pl ~es n (pej) jerga.

linguist ['lɪŋgwɪst] n lingüista m/f; ~ic a lingüístico; ~ics n lingüística.

lining ['laɪnɪŋ] n forro.

link [lɪŋk] n (of a chain) eslabón m; (connection) conexión f; (bond) vínculo, lazo // vt vincular, unir; ~s npl (GOLF) campo sg de golf; **to** ~ **up** vt acoplar // vi unirse; **~-up** n (gen) unión f; (in space) acoplamiento.

lino ['laɪnəʊ], **linoleum** [lɪ'nəʊlɪəm] n linóleo.

lion ['laɪən] n león m; ~ess n leona.

lip [lɪp] n labio; (of jug) pico; (of cup etc) borde m; (: fam) descaro; ~**read** vi leer los labios; ~**salve** n crema protectora para labios; ~**service** n: **to pay** ~ **service to sth** prometer algo de palabra; ~**stick** n lápiz m de labios, carmín m.

liqueur [lɪ'kjʊə*] n licor m.

liquid ['lɪkwɪd] a, n líquido.

liquidize ['lɪkwɪdaɪz] vt (CULIN) licuar.

liquidizer ['lɪkwɪdaɪzə*] n licuadora.

liquor ['lɪkə*] n licor m, bebidas fpl alcohólicas.

liquorice ['lɪkərɪs] n regaliz m.

liquor store n (US) bodega, tienda de vinos y bebidas alcohólicas.

Lisbon ['lɪzbən] n Lisboa.

lisp [lɪsp] n ceceo.

list [lɪst] n lista; (of ship) inclinación f // vt (write down) hacer una lista de; (enumerate) catalogar // vi (ship) inclinarse.

listen ['lɪsn] vi escuchar, oír; (pay attention) atender; ~**er** n oyente m/f.

listless ['lɪstlɪs] a apático, indiferente.

lit [lɪt] pt, pp of **light**.

litany ['lɪtənɪ] n letanía.

liter ['liːtə*] n (US) = **litre**.

literacy ['lɪtərəsɪ] n capacidad f de leer y escribir.

literal ['lɪtərl] a literal.

literary ['lɪtərərɪ] a literario.

literate ['lɪtərət] a que sabe leer y escribir; (fig) culto.

literature ['lɪtrɪtʃə*] n literatura; (brochures etc) folletos mpl.

lithe [laɪð] a ágil.

litigation [lɪtɪ'geɪʃən] n litigio.

litre, (US) **liter** ['liːtə*] n litro.

litter ['lɪtə*] n (rubbish) basura; (paper) papel m tirado; (young animals) camada, cría; ~ **bin** n (Brit) papelera; ~**ed** a: ~**ed with** (scattered) esparcido con; (covered with) lleno de.

little ['lɪtl] a (small) pequeño; (not much) poco; (often translated by suffix: eg = **house** casita) // ad poco; **a** ~ **un poco (de)**; ~ **by** ~ poco a poco.

live [lɪv] vi vivir // vt (a life) llevar; (experience) vivir // a [laɪv] (animal) vivo; (wire) conectado; (broadcast) en directo; (shell) cargado; **to** ~ **down** vt hacer olvidar; **to** ~ **on** vt fus (food) vivirse de, alimentarse de; **to** ~ **together** vi vivir juntos; **to** ~ **up to** vt fus (fulfil) cumplir con; (justify) justificar.

livelihood ['laɪvlɪhʊd] n sustento.

lively ['laɪvlɪ] a (gen) vivo; (talk) animado; (pace) rápido; (party, tune) alegre.

liven up ['laɪvn-] vt animar.

liver ['lɪvə*] n hígado.

livery ['lɪvərɪ] n librea.

lives [laɪvz] pl of **life**.

livestock ['laɪvstɒk] n ganado.

livid ['lɪvɪd] a lívido; (furious) furioso.

living ['lɪvɪŋ] a (alive) vivo // n: to earn or make a ~ ganarse la vida; ~ **conditions** npl condiciones fpl de vida; ~ **room** n sala (de estar); ~ **wage** n sueldo suficiente para vivir.

lizard ['lɪzəd] n lagartija.

load [ləʊd] n (gen) carga; (weight) peso // vt (COMPUT) cargar; (also: ~ up): to ~ (with) cargar (con or de); a ~ of, ~s of (fig) (gran) cantidad de, montones de; ~ed a (dice) cargado; (question) intencionado; (col: rich) forrado de dinero; ~ing **bay** n área de carga y descarga.

loaf [ləʊf], pl **loaves** n (barra de) pan m // vi (also: ~ about, ~ around) holgazanear.

loan [ləʊn] n préstamo; (COMM) empréstito // vt prestar; **on** ~ prestado.

loath [ləʊθ] a: to be ~ to do sth estar poco dispuesto a hacer algo.

loathe [ləʊð] vt aborrecer; (person) odiar; **loathing** n aversión f; odio.

loaves [ləʊvz] pl of **loaf**.

lobby ['lɒbɪ] n vestíbulo, sala de espera; (POL: pressure group) grupo de presión // vt presionar.

lobe [ləʊb] n lóbulo.

lobster ['lɒbstə*] n langosta.

local ['ləʊkl] a local // n (pub) bar m; the ~s npl los vecinos, los del lugar; ~ **anaesthetic** n (MED) anestesia local; ~ **authority** n municipio, ayuntamiento (Sp); ~ **call** n (TEL) llamada local; ~ **government** n gobierno municipal; ~**ity** [-'kælɪtɪ] n localidad f; ~**ly** [-kəlɪ] ad en la vecindad.

locate [ləʊ'keɪt] vt (find) localizar; (situate) colocar.

location [ləʊ'keɪʃən] n situación f; **on** ~ (CINEMA) en exteriores.

loch [lɒx] n lago.

lock [lɒk] n (of door, box) cerradura; (of canal) esclusa; (of hair) mechón m // vt (with key) cerrar con llave; (immobilize) inmovilizar // vi (door etc) cerrarse con llave; (wheels) trabarse.

locker ['lɒkə*] n casillero; ~**room** n (US SPORT) vestuario.

locket ['lɒkɪt] n medallón m.

lockout ['lɒkaʊt] n paro patronal, lockout m.

locksmith ['lɒksmɪθ] n cerrajero/a.

lock-up ['lɒkʌp] n (garage) cochera.

locomotive [ləʊkə'məʊtɪv] n locomotora.

locum ['ləʊkəm] n (MED) (médico/a) interino/a.

locust ['ləʊkəst] n langosta.

lodge [lɒdʒ] n casa del guarda; (porter's) portería; (FREEMASONRY) logia // vi (person): to ~ (with) alojarse (en casa de) // vt (complaint) presentar; ~**r** n huésped/a m/f.

lodgings ['lɒdʒɪŋz] npl alojamiento sg; (house) casa sg de huéspedes.

loft [lɒft] n desván m.

lofty ['lɒftɪ] a (tall) alto; (haughty) orgulloso.

log [lɒg] n (of wood) leño, tronco; (book) = **logbook**.

logbook ['lɒgbʊk] n (NAUT) diario de a bordo; (AVIAT) libro de vuelo; (of car) documentación f (del coche).

loggerheads ['lɒgəhedz] npl: **at** ~ (with) de punta (con).

logic ['lɒdʒɪk] n lógica; ~**al** a lógico.

logo ['ləʊgəʊ] n logotipo.

loin [lɔɪn] n (CULIN) lomo, solomillo; ~s npl lomos mpl.

loiter ['lɔɪtə*] vi vagar; (pej) merodear.

loll [lɒl] vi (also: ~ about) repantigarse.

lollipop ['lɒlɪpɒp] n piruli m; (iced) polo; ~ **man/lady** n (Brit) persona encargada de ayudar a los niños a cruzar la calle.

London ['lʌndən] n Londres; ~**er** n londinense m/f.

lone [ləʊn] a solitario.

loneliness ['ləʊnlɪnɪs] n soledad f, aislamiento.

lonely ['ləʊnlɪ] a solitario, solo.

long [lɒŋ] a largo // ad mucho tiempo, largamente // vi: to ~ **for sth** anhelar algo; **in the** ~ **run** a la larga; **so** or **as** ~ **as** mientras, con tal que; **don't be** ~! ¡no tardes!, ¡vuelve pronto!; **how ~ is the street?** ¿cuánto tiene la calle de largo?; **how ~ is the lesson?** ¿cuánto dura la clase?; **6 metres ~** que mide 6 metros, de 6 metros de largo; **6 months ~** que dura 6 meses, de 6 meses de duración; **all night ~** toda la noche; **he no ~er comes** ya no viene; **~ before** mucho antes; **before ~** (+ *future*) dentro de poco; (+ *past*) poco tiempo después; **at ~ last** al fin, por fin; **~distance** *a* (*race*) de larga distancia; (*call*) interurbano; **~haired** *a* de pelo largo; **~hand** *n* escritura sin abreviaturas; **~ing** *n* anhelo, ansia; (*nostalgia*) nostalgia // *a* anhelante.

longitude ['lɒŋgɪtjuːd] *n* longitud *f*.

long: ~ jump *n* salto de longitud; **~lost** *a* desaparecido hace mucho tiempo; **~playing record (L.P.)** *n* elepé *m*, disco de larga duración; **~-range** *a* de gran alcance; **~-sighted** *a* (*Brit*) présbita; **~-standing** *a* de mucho tiempo; **~-suffering** *a* sufrido; **~-term** *a* a largo plazo; **~ wave** *n* onda larga; **~-winded** *a* prolijo.

loo [luː] *n* (*Brit*: *col*) wáter *m*.

look [luk] *vi* mirar; (*seem*) parecer; (*building etc*): **to ~ south/on to** the sea dar al sur/al mar // *n* mirada; (*glance*) vistazo; (*appearance*) aire *m*, aspecto; **~s** *npl* físico *sg*, apariencia *sg*; **to ~ after** *vt fus* cuidar; **to ~ at** *vt fus* mirar; (*consider*) considerar; **to ~ back** *vi* mirar hacia atrás; **to ~ down on** *vt fus* (*fig*) despreciar, mirar con desprecio; **to ~ for** *vt fus* buscar; **to ~ forward to** *vt fus* esperar con ilusión; (*in letters*): **we ~ forward to hearing from you** quedamos a la espera de sus gratas noticias; **to ~ into** *vt* investigar; **to ~ on** *vi* mirar (como espectador); **to ~ out** *vi* (*beware*) tener cuidado (de); **to ~ out for** *vt fus* (*seek*) buscar; (*await*) esperar; **to ~ round** *vi* volver la cabeza; **to ~ up** *vt fus* ocu-

parse de; (*rely on*) contar con; **to ~ up** *vi* mirar hacia arriba; (*improve*) mejorar // *vt* (*word*) buscar; (*friend*) visitar; **to ~ up to** *vt fus* admirar; **~-out** *n* (*tower etc*) puesto de observación; (*person*) vigía *m/f*; **to be on the ~-out for sth** estar al acecho de algo.

loom [luːm] *n* telar *m* // *vi* (*threaten*) amenazar.

loony ['luːnɪ] *n* (*col*) loco/a.

loop [luːp] *n* lazo; (*bend*) vuelta, recodo; **~hole** *n* escapatoria.

loose [luːs] *a* (*gen*) suelto; (*not tight*) flojo; (*wobbly etc*) movedizo; (*clothes*) ancho; (*morals*, *discipline*) relajado; **to be at a ~ end** *or* (*US*) **at ~ ends** no saber qué hacer; **~ change** *n* cambio; **~ chippings** *npl* (*on road*) gravilla *sg* suelta; **~ly** *ad* libremente, aproximadamente; **~n** *vt* (*free*) soltar; (*untie*) desatar; (*slacken*) aflojar.

loot [luːt] *n* botín *m* // *vt* saquear.

lop [lɒp]: **to ~ off** *vt* cortar; (*branches*) podar.

lop-sided ['lɒp'saɪdɪd] *a* desequilibrado.

lord [lɔːd] *n* señor *m*; **L~ Smith** Lord Smith; **the (House of) L~s** (*Brit*) la Cámara de los Lores; **~ship** *n*: **your L~ship** su Señoría.

lore [lɔː*] *n* tradiciones *fpl*.

lorry ['lɔrɪ] *n* (*Brit*) camión *m*; **~ driver** *n* camionero/a.

lose [luːz], *pt*, *pp* **lost** *vt* perder // *vi* perder, ser vencido; **to ~** (*time*) (*clock*) atrasarse; **~r** *n* perdedor/a *m/f*.

loss [lɒs] *n* pérdida; **heavy ~es** (*MIL*) grandes pérdidas; **to be at a ~** no saber qué hacer; **to make a ~** sufrir pérdidas.

lost [lɒst] *pt*, *pp* of **lose** // *a* perdido; **~ property**, (*US*) **~ and found** *n* objetos *mpl* perdidos.

lot [lɒt] *n* (*at auctions*) lote *m*; (*destiny*) suerte *f*; **the ~** el todo, todos; **a ~** mucho, bastante; **a ~ of**, **~s of**

mucho(s) (pl); I read a ~ leo bastante; to draw ~s (for sth) echar suertes (para decidir algo).

lotion ['ləʊʃən] n loción f.

lottery ['lɒtərɪ] n lotería.

loud [laʊd] a (voice, sound) fuerte; (laugh, shout) estrepitoso; (gaudy) chillón/ona // ad (speak etc) en alta voz; ~**hailer** n (Brit) megáfono; ~**ly** ad (noisily) fuerte; (aloud) en alta voz; ~**speaker** n altavoz m.

lounge [laʊndʒ] n salón m, sala (de estar) // n reposar, holgazanear; ~ **suit** n (Brit) traje m de calle.

louse [laʊs], pl **lice** n piojo.

lousy ['laʊzɪ] a (fig) vil, asqueroso.

lout [laʊt] n gamberro/a.

louvre, (US) **louver** ['luːvəˈ] a (door) de rejilla; (window) de libro.

lovable ['lʌvəbl] a amable, simpático.

love [lʌv] n amor m // vt amar, querer; to ~ to do encantarle a uno hacer; to be in ~ with estar enamorado de; to make ~ hacer el amor; for the ~ of por amor de; '15 ~' (TENNIS) 15 a cero; I ~ paella me encanta la paella; ~ **affair** n aventura sentimental; ~ **letter** n carta de amor; ~ **life** n vida sentimental.

lovely ['lʌvlɪ] a (delightful) precioso, encantador(a); (beautiful) hermoso.

lover ['lʌvəˈ] n amante m/f; (amateur): a ~ of un aficionado/a or un amante de.

loving ['lʌvɪŋ] a amoroso, cariñoso.

low [ləʊ] a, ad bajo // n (METEOROLOGY) área de baja presión // a (cow) mugir; to feel ~ sentirse deprimido; to turn (down) ~ bajar; ~**cut** a (dress) escotado.

lower ['ləʊəˈ] vt bajar; (reduce) reducir // vr: to ~ o.s. to (fig) rebajarse a.

low: ~**fat** a (milk, yoghurt) desnatado; (diet) bajo en calorías; ~**lands** npl (GEO) tierras fpl bajas; ~**ly** a humilde; ~**lying** a bajo.

loyal ['lɔɪəl] a leal; ~**ty** n lealtad f.

lozenge ['lɒzɪndʒ] n (MED) pastilla.

L.P. n abbr = **long-playing record**.

L-plates ['elpleɪts] npl (Brit) placas de aprendiz de conductor.

Ltd abbr (= limited company) S.A.

lubricant ['luːbrɪkənt] n lubricante m.

lubricate ['luːbrɪkeɪt] vt lubricar, engrasar.

lucid ['luːsɪd] a lúcido.

luck [lʌk] n suerte f; bad ~ mala suerte; good ~! ¡que tengas suerte!, ¡suerte!; ~**ily** ad afortunadamente; ~**y** a afortunado.

ludicrous ['luːdɪkrəs] a absurdo.

lug [lʌg] vt (drag) arrastrar.

luggage ['lʌgɪdʒ] n equipaje m; ~ **rack** n (in train) rejilla, redecilla; (on car) baca, portaequipajes m inv.

lukewarm ['luːkwɔːm] a tibio, templado.

lull [lʌl] n tregua // vt (child) acunar; (person, fear) calmar.

lullaby ['lʌləbaɪ] n nana.

lumbago [lʌm'beɪgəʊ] n lumbago.

lumber ['lʌmbəˈ] n (junk) trastos mpl viejos; (wood) maderas mpl; ~**jack** n leñador.

luminous ['luːmɪnəs] a luminoso.

lump [lʌmp] n terrón m; (fragment) trozo; (in sauce) grumo; (in throat) nudo; (swelling) bulto // vt (also: ~ **together**) juntar; ~ **sum** n suma global.

lunacy ['luːnəsɪ] n locura.

lunar ['luːnəˈ] a lunar.

lunatic ['luːnətɪk] a, n loco/a; ~ **asylum** n manicomio.

lunch [lʌntʃ] n almuerzo, comida // vi almorzar.

luncheon ['lʌntʃən] n almuerzo; ~ **meat** n tipo de fiambre; ~ **voucher** n vale m de comida.

lung [lʌŋ] n pulmón m.

lunge [lʌndʒ] vi (also: ~ **forward**) abalanzarse; to ~ **at** arremeter contra.

lurch [lɜːtʃ] vi dar sacudidas // n sacudida; to leave sb in the ~ dejar a uno plantado.

lure [luəˈ] n (bait) cebo; (decoy) sefíuelo // vt convencer con engaños.

lurid ['luərɪd] a (colour) chillón/ona; (account) sensacional; (detail) horripilante.

lurk [lə:k] vi (hide) esconderse; (wait) estar al acecho.

luscious ['lʌʃəs] a delicioso.

lush [lʌʃ] a exuberante.

lust [lʌst] n lujuria; (greed) codicia; **to ~ after** vt fus codiciar.

lustre, (US) **luster** ['lʌstə*] n lustre m, brillo.

lusty ['lʌstɪ] a robusto, fuerte.

Luxembourg ['lʌksəmbə:g] n Luxemburgo.

luxuriant [lʌg'zjuərɪənt] a exuberante.

luxurious [lʌg'zjuərɪəs] a lujoso.

luxury ['lʌkʃərɪ] n lujo // cpd de lujo.

lying ['laɪɪŋ] n mentiras fpl.

lyric ['lɪrɪk] a lírico // ~s npl (of song) letra sg; ~**al** a lírico.

M

m. abbr = metre; mile; million.

M.A. abbr = Master of Arts.

mac [mæk] n (Brit) impermeable m.

macaroni [mækə'rəʊnɪ] n macarrones mpl.

mace [meɪs] n (weapon, ceremonial) maza; (spice) macis f.

machine [mə'ʃi:n] n máquina // vt (dress etc) coser a máquina; ~ **gun** n ametralladora; ~ **language** n (COMPUT) lenguaje m máquina; ~**ry** n maquinaria; (fig) mecanismo.

mackerel ['mækrl] n, pl inv caballa.

mackintosh ['mækɪntɒʃ] n (Brit) impermeable m.

mad [mæd] a loco; (idea) disparatado; (angry) furioso.

madam ['mædəm] n señora.

madden ['mædn] vt volver loco.

made [meɪd] pt, pp of **make**.

Madeira [mə'dɪərə] n (GEO) Madera; (wine) vino de Madera.

made-to-measure ['meɪdtəmeʒə*] a (Brit) hecho a la medida.

madly ['mædlɪ] ad locamente.

madman ['mædmən] n loco.

madness ['mædnɪs] n locura.

Madrid [mə'drɪd] n Madrid.

Mafia ['mæfɪə] n Mafia.

magazine [mægə'zi:n] n revista; (MIL: store) almacén m; (of firearm) recámara.

maggot ['mægət] n gusano.

magic ['mædʒɪk] n magia // a mágico; ~**al** a mágico; ~**ian** [mə'dʒɪʃən] n mago/a; (conjurer) prestidigitador(a) m/f.

magistrate ['mædʒɪstreɪt] n juez m/f (municipal).

magnet ['mægnɪt] n imán m; ~**ic** [-'nɛtɪk] a magnético.

magnificent [mæg'nɪfɪsnt] a magnífico.

magnify ['mægnɪfaɪ] vt aumentar; (fig) exagerar; ~**ing glass** n lupa.

magnitude ['mægnɪtju:d] n magnitud f.

magpie ['mægpaɪ] n urraca.

mahogany [mə'hɒgənɪ] n caoba // cpd de caoba.

maid [meɪd] n criada; **old ~** (pej) solterona.

maiden ['meɪdn] n doncella // a (aunt etc) solterona; (speech, voyage) inaugural; ~ **name** n nombre m de soltera.

mail [meɪl] n correo; (letters) cartas fpl // vt (post) enviar al correo; (send) mandar por correo; ~**box** n (US) buzón m; ~**ing list** n lista de direcciones; ~**order** n pedido postal; (business) venta por correo.

maim [meɪm] vt mutilar, lisiar.

main [meɪn] a principal, mayor // n (pipe) cañería maestra; (US) red f eléctrica; **the ~s** (Brit ELEC) la red eléctrica; **in the ~** en general; ~**frame** n (COMPUT) ordenador m central; ~**land** n continente m; ~**ly** ad principalmente; ~ **road** n carretera; ~**stay** n (fig) pilar m; ~**stream** n corriente f principal; ~ **street** n calle f mayor.

maintain [meɪn'teɪn] vt mantener;

(*affirm*) sostener; **maintenance** ['meɪntənəns] *n* mantenimiento; (*alimony*) pensión *f* alimenticia.

maize [meɪz] *n* (*Brit*) maíz *m*, choclo (*LAm*).

majestic [mə'dʒestɪk] *a* majestuoso.

majesty ['mædʒɪstɪ] *n* majestad *f*.

major ['meɪdʒə*] *n* (*MIL*) comandante *m* // *a* principal; (*MUS*) mayor.

Majorca [mə'jɔːkə] *n* Mallorca.

majority [mə'dʒɔrɪtɪ] *n* mayoría.

make [meɪk] *vt* (*pt, pp* **made**) hacer; (*manufacture*) hacer, fabricar; (*cause to be*): **to ~ sb sad** hacer or poner triste a alguien; (*force*): **to ~ sb do sth** obligar a alguien a hacer algo; (*equal*): **2 and 2 ~ 4** 2 y 2 son 4 // *n* marca; **to ~ a fool of sb** poner a alguien en ridículo; **to ~ a profit/loss** obtener ganancias/sufrir pérdidas; **to ~ it** (*arrive*) llegar; (*achieve sth*) tener éxito; **what time do you ~ it?** ¿qué hora tienes?; **to ~ do with** contentarse con; **to ~ for** *vt fus* (*place*) dirigirse a; **to ~ out** *vt* (*decipher*) descifrar; (*understand*) entender; (*see*) distinguir; (*write*: *cheque*) extender; **to ~ up** *vt* (*invent*) inventar; (*parcel*) hacer // *vi* reconciliarse; (*with cosmetics*) maquillarse; **to ~ up for** *vt fus* compensar; **~believe** *n* ficción *f*, invención *f*; **~r** *n* fabricante *m/f*; **~shift** *a* improvisado; **~up** *n* maquillaje *m*; **~up remover** *n* desmaquillador *m*.

making ['meɪkɪŋ] *n* (*fig*): **in the ~** en vías de formación; **to have the ~s of** (*person*) tener madera de.

malaise [mæ'leɪz] *n* malestar *m*.

malaria [mə'leərɪə] *n* malaria.

Malaya [mə'leɪə] *n* Malaya, Malaca.

Malaysia [mə'leɪzɪə] *n* Malasia.

male [meɪl] *n* (*BIOL, ELEC*) macho // *a* (*sex, attitude*) masculino; (*child etc*) varón.

malevolent [mə'levələnt] *a* malévolo.

malfunction [mæl'fʌŋkʃən] *n* mal funcionamiento.

malice ['mælɪs] *n* (*ill will*) malicia; (*rancour*) rencor *m*; **malicious** [mə'lɪʃəs] *a* malicioso; rencoroso.

malign [mə'laɪn] *vt* difamar, calumniar // *a* maligno.

malignant [mə'lɪgnənt] *a* (*MED*) maligno.

mall [mɔːl] *n* (*US*: *also*: **shopping ~**) centro comercial.

malleable ['mælɪəbl] *a* maleable.

mallet ['mælɪt] *n* mazo.

malnutrition [mælnjuː'trɪʃən] *n* desnutrición *f*.

malpractice [mæl'præktɪs] *n* negligencia profesional.

malt [mɔːlt] *n* malta.

Malta ['mɔːltə] *n* Malta.

maltreat [mæl'triːt] *vt* maltratar.

mammal ['mæml] *n* mamífero.

mammoth ['mæməθ] *n* mamut *m* // *a* gigantesco.

man [mæn], *pl* **men** *n* hombre *m*; (*CHESS*) pieza *f* // *vt* (*NAUT*) tripular; (*MIL*) guarnecer; **an old ~** un viejo; **~ and wife** marido y mujer.

manage ['mænɪdʒ] *vi* arreglárselas, ir tirando // *vt* (*be in charge of*) dirigir; (*person etc*) manejar; **~able** *a* manejable; **~ment** *n* dirección *f*, administración *f*; **~r** *n* director *m*; (*SPORT*) entrenador *m*; **~ress** *n* directora; (*SPORT*) entrenadora; **~rial** [-ə'dʒɪərɪəl] *a* directivo; **managing director** *n* director(a) *m/f* general.

mandarin ['mændərɪn] *n* (*also*: **~ orange**) mandarina.

mandate ['mændeɪt] *n* mandato.

mandatory ['mændətərɪ] *a* obligatorio.

mane [meɪn] *n* (*of horse*) crin *f*; (*of lion*) melena.

maneuver [mə'nuːvə*] (*US*) = **manoeuvre**.

manfully ['mænfəlɪ] *ad* valientemente.

mangle ['mæŋgl] *vt* mutilar, destrozar // *n* rodillo.

mango ['mæŋgəu], *pl* **~es** *n* mango.

mangy ['meɪndʒɪ] *a* roñoso; (*MED*) sarnoso.

manhandle ['mænhændl] vt maltratar.

manhood ['mænhud] n edad f viril; virilidad f.

man-hour ['mæn'auə*] n hora-hombre f.

mania ['meɪnɪə] n manía; **~c** ['meɪnɪæk] n maníaco/a; (fig) maníático.

manic ['mænɪk] a (behaviour, activity) frenético; **~-depressive** n maníaco/a depresivo/a.

manicure ['mænɪkjuə*] n manicura; **~ set** n estuche m de manicura.

manifest ['mænɪfest] vt manifestar, mostrar // a manifiesto.

manifesto [mænɪ'festəu] n manifiesto.

manipulate [mə'nɪpjuleɪt] vt manipular.

mankind [mæn'kaɪnd] n humanidad f, género humano.

manly ['mænlɪ] a varonil.

man-made ['mæn'meɪd] a artificial.

manner ['mænə*] n manera, modo; (behaviour) conducta, manera de ser; (type) clase f; **~s** npl modales mpl, educación fsg; **bad ~s** mala educación; **~ism** n peculiaridad f de lenguaje (or de comportamiento).

manoeuvre, (US) **maneuver** [mə'nuːvə*] vt, vi maniobrar // n maniobra.

manor ['mænə*] n (also: **~ house**) casa solariega.

manpower ['mænpauə*] n mano f de obra.

mansion ['mænʃən] n palacio, casa grande.

manslaughter ['mænslɔːtə*] n homicidio no premeditado.

mantelpiece ['mæntlpiːs] n repisa, chimenea.

manual ['mænjuəl] a manual // n manual m.

manufacture [mænju'fæktʃə*] vt fabricar // n fabricación f; **~r** n fabricante m/f.

manure [mə'njuə*] n estiércol m, abono.

manuscript ['mænjuskrɪpt] n manuscrito.

many ['menɪ] a muchos/as // pron muchos/as; **a great ~** muchísimos, buen número de; **~ a time** muchas veces.

map [mæp] n mapa m // vt trazar el mapa de; **to ~ out** vt proyectar.

maple ['meɪpl] n arce m, maple m (LAm).

mar [maː*] vt estropear.

marathon ['mærəθən] n maratón m.

marauder [mə'rɔːdə*] n merodeador(a) m/f, intruso/a.

marble ['maːbl] n mármol m; (toy) canica.

March [maːtʃ] n marzo.

march [maːtʃ] vi (MIL) marchar; (fig) caminar con resolución // n marcha; (demonstration) manifestación f; **~-past** n desfile m.

mare [meə*] n yegua.

margarine [maːdʒə'riːn] n margarina.

margin ['maːdʒɪn] n margen m; **~al** a marginal; **~al seat** n (POL) escaño electoral difícil de asegurar.

marigold ['mærɪgəuld] n caléndula.

marijuana [mærɪ'waːnə] n marijuana.

marinate ['mærɪneɪt] vt adobar.

marine [mə'riːn] a marino // n soldado de marina.

marital ['mærɪtl] a matrimonial; **~ status** estado civil.

maritime ['mærɪtaɪm] a marítimo.

marjoram ['maːdʒərəm] n mejorana.

mark [maːk] n marca, señal f; (imprint) huella; (stain) mancha; (Brit SCOL) nota; (currency) marco // vt marcar; manchar; (Brit SCOL) calificar, corregir; **to ~ time** marcar el paso; **to ~ out** vt trazar; **~ed** a marcado, acusado; **~er** n (sign) marcador m; (bookmark) registro.

market ['maːkɪt] n mercado // vt (COMM) comercializar; **~ garden** n (Brit) huerto; **~ing** n márketing m, mercadotecnia; **~place** n mercado; **~ research** n (COMM) análisis m *inv* de mercados; ~ **value** *n* valor *m* en el mercado.

marksman ['mɑːksmən] *n* tirador *m*.

marmalade ['mɑːməleid] *n* mermelada de naranja.

maroon [mə'ruːn] *vt* (*fig*): to be ~**ed** (**in** *or* **at**) quedar bloqueado (en) // a marrón.

marquee [mɑː'kiː] *n* entoldado.

marriage ['mærɪdʒ] *n* (*state*) matrimonio; (*wedding*) boda; (*act*) casamiento; ~ **bureau** *n* agencia matrimonial; ~ **certificate** *n* partida de casamiento.

married ['mærid] *a* casado; (*life, love*) conyugal.

marrow ['mærəu] *n* médula; (*vegetable*) calabacín *m*.

marry ['mærɪ] *vt* casarse con; (*subj: father, priest etc*) casar // *vi* (*also: get married*) casarse.

Mars [mɑːz] *n* Marte *m*.

marsh [mɑːʃ] *n* pantano; (*salt ~*) marisma.

marshal ['mɑːʃl] *n* (*MIL*) mariscal *m*; (*at sports meeting etc*) oficial *m*; (*US: of police, fire department*) jefe/a // *vt* (*facts*) ordenar; (*soldiers*) formar.

marshy ['mɑːʃɪ] *a* pantanoso.

martial ['mɑːʃl] *a* marcial; ~ **law** *n* ley *f* marcial.

martyr ['mɑːtə*] *n* mártir *m/f* // *vt* martirizar; ~**dom** *n* martirio.

marvel ['mɑːvl] *n* maravilla, prodigio // *vi*: to ~ (**at**) maravillarse (de); ~**lous**, (*US*) ~**ous** *a* maravilloso.

Marxist ['mɑːksist] *n, a* marxista *m/f*.

marzipan ['mɑːzɪpæn] *n* mazapán *m*.

mascara [mæs'kɑːrə] *n* rimel *m*.

masculine ['mæskjulɪn] *a* masculino.

mash [mæʃ] *n* (*mix*) mezcla; (*pulp*) amasijo; ~**ed potatoes** *npl* puré *m* de patatas o papas (*LAm*).

mask [mɑːsk] *n* máscara // *vt* enmascarar.

masochist ['mæsəkist] *n* masoquista *m/f*.

mason ['meɪsn] *n* (*also: stone~*) al-

bañil *m*; (*also: free~*) masón *m*; ~**ic** [mə'sɔnik] *a* masónico; ~**ry** *n* masonería; (*in building*) mampostería.

masquerade [mæskə'reid] *n* baile *m* de máscaras; (*fig*) mascarada // *vi*: to ~ **as** disfrazarse de, hacerse pasar por.

mass [mæs] *n* (*people*) muchedumbre *f*; (*PHYSICS*) masa; (*REL*) misa; (*great quantity*) montón *m* // *vi* reunirse; (*MIL*) concentrarse; **the ~es** las masas.

massacre ['mæsəkə*] *n* masacre *f*.

massage ['mæsɑːʒ] *n* masaje *m* // *vt* dar masaje.

masseur [mæ'səː*] *n* masajista *m*; **masseuse** [-'səːz] *n* masajista *f*.

massive ['mæsɪv] *a* enorme; (*support, intervention*) masivo.

mass media *npl* medios *mpl* de comunicación masiva.

mass-production ['mæsprə'dʌkʃən] *n* fabricación *f* en serie.

mast [mɑːst] *n* (*NAUT*) mástil *m*; (*RADIO etc*) torre *f*.

master ['mɑːstə*] *n* maestro; (*in secondary school*) profesor *m*; (*title for boys*): **M~ X** Señorito *m* X // *vt* dominar; (*learn*) aprender a fondo; **M~ of Arts/Science (M.A./M.Sc.)** *n* licenciatura superior en Letras/Ciencias; ~ **key** *n* llave *f* maestra; ~**ly** *a* magistral; ~**mind** *n* inteligencia superior // *vt* dirigir, planear; ~**piece** *n* obra maestra; ~**y** *n* maestría.

mat [mæt] *n* estera; (*also: door~*) felpudo // *a* = **matt**.

match [mætʃ] *n* cerilla, fósforo; (*game*) partido; (*fig*) igual *m/f* // *vt* emparejar; (*go well with*) hacer juego con; (*equal*) igualar // *vi* hacer juego; **to be a good ~** hacer buena pareja; ~**box** *n* caja de cerillas; ~**ing** *a* que hace juego.

mate [meit] *n* (*work~*) colega *m/f*; (*col: friend*) amigo/a; (*animal*) macho *m*/hembra *f*; (*in merchant navy*) segundo a bordo // *vi* acoplarse.

parearse // vt acoplar, parear.

material [mə'tɪərɪəl] n (substance) materia; (equipment) material m; (cloth) tela, tejido // a material; (important) esencial; ~s npl materiales mpl.

maternal [mə'təːnl] a maternal.

maternity [mə'təːnɪtɪ] n maternidad f; ~ **dress** n vestido premamá; ~ **hospital** n hospital m de maternidad.

math [mæθ] n (US) = maths.

mathematical [mæθə'mætɪkl] a matemático.

mathematician [mæθəmə'tɪʃən] n matemático/a.

mathematics [mæθə'mætɪks], **maths** [mæθs], (US) **math** [mæθ] n matemáticas fpl.

matinée ['mætɪneɪ] n función f de la tarde.

mating ['meɪtɪŋ] n apareamiento; ~ **call** n llamada del macho.

matrices ['meɪtrɪsiːz] pl of matrix.

matrimonial [mætrɪ'məʊnɪəl] a matrimonial.

matrimony ['mætrɪmənɪ] n matrimonio.

matrix ['meɪtrɪks], pl **matrices** n matriz f.

matron ['meɪtrən] n (in hospital) enfermera f jefe; (in school) ama de llaves; ~**ly** a de matrona; (fig: figure) corpulento.

mat(t) [mæt] a mate.

matted ['mætɪd] a enmarañado.

matter ['mætə*] n cuestión f, asunto; (PHYSICS) sustancia, materia; (content) contenido; (MED: pus) pus m // vi importar; **it doesn't** ~ no importa; **what's the** ~? ¿qué pasa?; **no** ~ what pase lo que pase; **as a** ~ **of course** por rutina; **as a** ~ **of fact** de hecho; ~-**of-fact** a prosaico, práctico.

mattress ['mætrɪs] n colchón m.

mature [mə'tjuə*] a maduro // vi madurar; **maturity** n madurez f.

maul [mɔːl] vt magullar.

mauve [məʊv] a de color malva or

guinda (LAm).

maxim ['mæksɪm] n máxima.

maximum ['mæksɪməm] a máximo // n (pl **maxima** ['mæksɪmə]) máximo.

May [meɪ] n mayo.

may [meɪ] vi (conditional: **might**) (indicating possibility): **he** ~ **come** puede que venga; (be allowed to): ~ **I smoke?** ¿puedo fumar?; (wishes): ~ **God bless you!** ¡que Dios le bendiga!

maybe ['meɪbɪ] ad quizá(s).

May Day n el primero de Mayo.

mayday ['meɪdeɪ] n S.O.S. m.

mayhem ['meɪhem] n caos m total.

mayonnaise [meɪə'neɪz] n mayonesa.

mayor [mɛə*] n alcalde m; ~**ess** n alcaldesa.

maze [meɪz] n laberinto.

M.D. abbr = Doctor of Medicine.

me [miː] pron (direct) me; (stressed, after pronoun) mí; **can you hear** ~? ¿me oyes?; **he heard ME!** me oyó a mí; **it's** ~ soy yo; **give them to** ~ dámelos (or dámelas); **with/without** ~ conmigo/sin mí.

meadow ['medəʊ] n prado, pradera.

meagre, (US) **meager** ['miːgə*] a escaso, pobre.

meal [miːl] n comida; (flour) harina; ~**time** n hora de comer.

mean [miːn] a (with money) tacaño; (unkind) mezquino, malo; (average) medio // vt (pt, pp **meant**) (signify) querer decir, significar; (intend): **to** ~ **to do sth** pensar or pretender hacer algo // n medio, término medio; ~s npl medio sg, manera sg; (resource) recursos mpl, medios mpl; **by** ~s **of** mediante, por medio de; **by all** ~s! ¡naturalmente!, ¡claro que sí!; **do you** ~ **it?** ¿lo dices en serio?; **what do you** ~? ¿qué quieres decir?; **to be meant for sb/sth** ser para uno/algo.

meander [mɪ'ændə*] vi (river) serpentear; (person) vagar.

meaning ['miːnɪŋ] n significado, sentido; ~**ful** a significativo; ~**less** a sin sentido.

meanness ['mi:nnɪs] n (with money) tacañería; (unkindness) maldad f, mezquindad f.

meant [mɛnt] pt, pp of **mean**.

meantime ['mi:ntaɪm], **meanwhile** ['mi:nwaɪl] ad (also: **in the ~**) mientras tanto.

measles ['mi:zlz] n sarampión m.

measly ['mi:zlɪ] a (col) miserable.

measure ['mɛʒə*] vt medir; (for clothes etc) tomar las medidas a // vi medir // n medida; (ruler) regla; **~ments** npl medidas fpl.

meat [mi:t] n carne f; **cold ~** fiambre m; **~ball** n albóndiga; **~ pie** n pastel m de carne; **~y** a carnoso; (fig) sustancioso.

Mecca ['mɛkə] n La Meca.

mechanic [mɪ'kænɪk] n mecánico/a; **~s** n mecánica // npl mecanismo sg; **~al** a mecánico.

mechanism ['mɛkənɪzəm] n mecanismo.

medal ['mɛdl] n medalla; **~lion** [mɪ'dælɪən] n medallón m; **~list**, (US) **~ist** n (SPORT) medallero/a.

meddle ['mɛdl] vi: **to ~ in** entrometerse en; **to ~ with sth** manosear algo.

media ['mi:dɪə] npl medios mpl de comunicación.

mediaeval [mɛdɪ'i:vl] a = **medieval**.

median ['mi:dɪən] n (US: also: **~ strip**) mediana.

mediate ['mi:dɪeɪt] vi mediar; **mediator** n intermediario/a, mediador(a) m/f.

Medicaid ['mɛdɪkeɪd] n (US) programa de ayuda médica.

medical ['mɛdɪkl] a médico // n reconocimiento médico.

Medicare ['mɛdɪkɛə*] n (US) seguro médico del Estado.

medicated ['mɛdɪkeɪtɪd] a medicinal.

medicine ['mɛdsɪn] n medicina; (drug) medicamento.

medieval [mɛdɪ'i:vl] a medieval.

mediocre [mi:dɪ'əukə*] a mediocre.

meditate ['mɛdɪteɪt] vi meditar.

Mediterranean [mɛdɪtə'reɪnɪən] a mediterráneo // n: **the ~ (Sea)** el (Mar) Mediterráneo.

medium ['mi:dɪəm] a mediano, regular // n (pl **media**: means) medio; (pl **mediums**: person) médium m/f; **happy ~** justo medio; **~ wave** n onda media.

medley ['mɛdlɪ] n mezcla; (MUS) popurrí m.

meek [mi:k] a manso, sumiso.

meet [mi:t], pt, pp met vt encontrar; (accidentally) encontrarse con, tropezar con; (by arrangement) reunirse con; (for the first time) conocer; (go and fetch) ir a buscar; (opponent) enfrentarse con; (obligations) cumplir // vi encontrarse; (in session) reunirse; (join: objects) unirse; (get to know) conocerse; **to ~ with** vt fus reunirse con; (difficulty) tropezar con; **~ing** n encuentro; (arranged) cita, compromiso (LAm); (session, business ~) reunión f; (POL) mitin m.

megabyte ['mɛgə'baɪt] n (COMPUT) megabyte m, megaocteto.

megaphone ['mɛgəfəun] n megáfono.

melancholy ['mɛlənkəlɪ] n melancolía // a melancólico.

mellow ['mɛləu] a (wine) añejo; (sound, colour) suave; (fruit) maduro // vi (person) ablandar.

melody ['mɛlədɪ] n melodía.

melon ['mɛlən] n melón m.

melt [mɛlt] vi (metal) fundirse; (snow) derretirse; (fig) ablandarse // vt (also: **~ down**) fundir; **to ~ away** vi desvanecerse; **~down** n (in nuclear reactor) fusión f de un reactor (nuclear); **~ing point** n punto de fusión; **~ing pot** n (fig) crisol m.

member ['mɛmbə*] n (gen) miembro; (of club) socio/a; **M~ of Parliament (MP)** (Brit) diputado/a; **M~ of the European Parliament**

(MEP) (*Brit*) eurodiputado/a; **~ship** *n* (*members*) número de miembros; **to seek ~ship** of pedir el ingreso a; **~ship card** carnet *m* de socio.

memento [mə'mɛntəu] *n* recuerdo.

memo ['mɛmɒu] *n* apunte *m*, nota.

memoirs ['mɛmwɑːz] *npl* memorias *fpl*.

memorandum [mɛmə'rændəm], *pl* **-da** [-də] *n* apunte *m*, nota; (*POL*) memorándum *m*.

memorial [mɪ'mɔːrɪəl] *n* monumento conmemorativo // *a* conmemorativo.

memorize ['mɛmərɑɪz] *vt* aprender de memoria.

memory ['mɛmərɪ] *n* memoria; (*recollection*) recuerdo *m*.

men [mɛn] *pl* of **man**.

menace ['mɛnəs] *n* amenaza // *vt* amenazar; **menacing** *a* amenazador(a).

menagerie [mɪ'nædʒərɪ] *n* casa de fieras.

mend [mɛnd] *vt* reparar, arreglar; (*darn*) zurcir // *vi* reponerse // *n* (*gen*) remiendo; (*darn*) zurcido; **to be on the ~** ir mejorando; **~ing** *n* reparación *f*; (*clothes*) ropa por remendar.

menial ['miːnɪəl] *a* doméstico; (*pej*) bajo.

meningitis [mɛnɪn'dʒaɪtɪs] *n* meningitis *f*.

menopause ['mɛnəupɔːz] *n* menopausia.

menstruation [mɛnstru'eɪʃən] *n* menstruación *f*.

mental ['mɛntl] *a* mental; **~ity** [-'tælɪtɪ] *n* mentalidad *f*.

mention ['mɛnʃən] *n* mención *f* // *vt* mencionar; (*speak of*) hablar de; **don't ~ it!** ¡de nada!

mentor ['mɛntɔː*] *n* mentor *m*.

menu ['mɛnjuː] *n* (*set ~*) menú *m*; (*printed*) carta; (*COMPUT*) menú *m*.

MEP *n* abbr = **Member of the European Parliament**.

mercenary ['mɜːsɪnərɪ] *a*, *n* mercenario.

merchandise ['mɜːtʃəndaɪz] *n* mercancías *fpl*.

merchant ['mɜːtʃənt] *n* comerciante *m/f*; **~ bank** *n* (*Brit*) banco comercial; **~ navy**, (*US*) **~ marine** *n* marina mercante.

merciful ['mɜːsɪful] *a* compasivo.

merciless ['mɜːsɪlɪs] *a* despiadado.

mercury ['mɜːkjurɪ] *n* mercurio.

mercy ['mɜːsɪ] *n* compasión *f*; (*REL*) misericordia; **at the ~ of** a la merced de.

mere [mɪə*] *a* simple, mero; **~ly** *ad* simplemente, sólo.

merge [mɜːdʒ] *vt* (*join*) unir; (*mix*) mezclar; (*fuse*) fundir // *vi* unirse; (*COMM*) fusionarse; **~r** *n* (*COMM*) fusión *f*.

meringue [mə'ræŋ] *n* merengue *m*.

merit ['mɛrɪt] *n* mérito // *vt* merecer.

mermaid ['mɜːmeɪd] *n* sirena.

merry ['mɛrɪ] *a* alegre; **M~ Christmas!** ¡Felices Pascuas!; **~-go-round** *n* tiovivo.

mesh [mɛʃ] *n* malla; (*TECH*) engranaje *m* // *vi* (*gears*) engranar.

mesmerize ['mɛzmərɑɪz] *vt* hipnotizar.

mess [mɛs] *n* (*of objects*) confusión *f*; (*objects*) revoltijo; (*tangle*) lío; (*MIL*) comedor *m*; **to ~ about** *or* **around** *vi* (*col*) perder el tiempo; (*pass the time*) entretenerse; **to ~ about** *or* **around with** *vt fus* (*col*: *play with*) divertirse con; (: *handle*) manosear; **to ~ up** *vt* (*disarrange*) desordenar; (*spoil*) estropear; (*dirty*) ensuciar.

message ['mɛsɪdʒ] *n* recado, mensaje *m*.

messenger ['mɛsɪndʒə*] *n* mensajero/a.

Messrs *abbr* (*on letters*: = *Messieurs*) Sres.

messy ['mɛsɪ] *a* (*dirty*) sucio; (*untidy*) desordenado.

met [mɛt] *pt*, *pp* of **meet**.

metabolism [mɛ'tæbəlɪzəm] *n* metabolismo.

metal ['mɛtl] *n* metal *m*; **~lic** [-'tælɪk] *a* metálico; **~lurgy**

[-'tælədʒɪ] n metalurgia.

metaphor ['mɛtəfə*] n metáfora.

mete [miːt]: to ~ out vt fus (punishment) imponer.

meteor ['miːtɪə*] n meteoro; ~ite [-aɪt] n meteorito.

meteorology [miːtɪə'rɔlədʒɪ] n meteorología.

meter ['miːtə*] n (instrument) contador m; (US: unit) = metre // vt (US POST) franquear.

method ['mɛθəd] n método; ~ical [mɪ'θɔdɪkl] a metódico.

Methodist ['mɛθədɪst] a, n metodista m/f.

meths [mɛθs], **methylated spirit** ['mɛθɪleɪtɪd-] n (Brit) alcohol m metilado or desnaturalizado.

metre, (US) **meter** ['miːtə*] n metro.

metric ['mɛtrɪk] a métrico.

metropolis [mɪ'trɔpəlɪs] n metrópoli f.

metropolitan [mɛtrə'pɔlɪtən] a metropolitano; the M~ Police n (Brit) la policía londinense.

mettle ['mɛtl] n valor m, ánimo.

mew [mjuː] vi (cat) maullar.

mews [mjuːz] n: ~ cottage (Brit) casa acondicionada en antiguos establos o cocheras.

Mexican ['mɛksɪkən] a, n mejicano/a m/f, mexicano/a m/f (LAm).

Mexico ['mɛksɪkəu] n Méjico, México (LAm); ~ City n Ciudad f de Méjico or México (LAm).

mezzanine ['mɛtsəniːn] n entresuelo.

miaow [miːˈau] vi maullar.

mice [maɪs] pl of **mouse**.

micro... [maɪkrəu] pref micro...

micro: ~**chip** n microplaqueta; ~ **(computer)** n microordenador m; ~**cosm** n microcosmo; ~**phone** n micrófono; ~**processor** n microprocesador m; ~**scope** n microscopio; ~**wave** n (also: ~**wave oven**) horno microondas.

mid [mɪd] a: in ~ May a mediados de mayo; in ~ afternoon a media

tarde; in ~ air en el aire; ~**day** n mediodía m.

middle ['mɪdl] n medio, centro; (waist) cintura f // a de en medio; in the ~ of the night en plena noche; ~-**aged** a de mediana edad; the M~ Ages npl la Edad Media; ~-**class** a de clase media; the ~ **class(es)** n(pl) la clase media; M~ **East** n Oriente m Medio; ~**man** n intermediario; ~ **name** n segundo nombre; ~**weight** n (BOXING) peso medio.

middling ['mɪdlɪŋ] a mediano.

midge [mɪdʒ] n mosca.

midget ['mɪdʒɪt] n enano/a.

Midlands ['mɪdləndz] npl la región central de Inglaterra.

midnight ['mɪdnaɪt] n medianoche f.

midriff ['mɪdrɪf] n diafragma m.

midst [mɪdst] n: in the ~ of en medio de.

midsummer [mɪd'sʌmə*] n: in ~ en pleno verano.

midway [mɪd'weɪ] a, ad: ~ (between) a medio camino (entre).

midweek [mɪd'wiːk] ad entre semana.

midwife ['mɪdwaɪf], pl -**wives** [-waɪvz] n comadrona, partera; ~**ry** [-wɪfərɪ] n partería.

midwinter [mɪd'wɪntə*] n: in ~ en pleno invierno.

might [maɪt] vb see **may**: he ~ be there podría estar allí, puede que esté allí; I ~ as well go lo más vale que vaya; you ~ like to try podría intentar // n fuerza, poder m; ~**y** a fuerte, poderoso.

migraine ['miːgreɪn] n jaqueca.

migrant ['maɪgrənt] n a (bird) migratorio; (worker) emigrante.

migrate [maɪ'greɪt] vi emigrar.

mike [maɪk] n abbr (= microphone) micro.

mild [maɪld] n (person) apacible; (climate) templado; (slight) ligero; (taste) suave; (illness) leve.

mildew ['mɪldjuː] n moho.

mildly ['maɪldlɪ] ad ligeramente; suavemente; **to put it** ~ para no decir más.

mile [maɪl] n milla; **~age** n número de millas, ≈ kilometraje m; **~stone** n mojón m.

milieu [ˈmiːljəː] n (medio) ambiente m.

militant [ˈmɪlɪtnt] a, n militante m/f.

military [ˈmɪlɪtərɪ] n militar.

militia [mɪˈlɪʃə] n milicia.

milk [mɪlk] n leche f // vt (cow) ordeñar; (fig) chupar; ~ **chocolate** n chocolate m con leche; **~man** n lechero; ~ **shake** n batido, malteada (LAm); **~y** a lechoso; **M~y Way** n Vía Láctea.

mill [mɪl] n (windmill etc) molino; (coffee ~) molinillo; (factory) fábrica; (spinning ~) hilandería // vt moler // vi (also: ~ **about**) arremolinarse.

millennium [mɪˈleniəm], pl **~s** or **-ia** [-nɪə] n milenio, milenario.

miller [ˈmɪlə*] n molinero.

millet [ˈmɪlɪt] n mijo.

milli... [ˈmɪlɪ] pref: **~gram(me)** n miligramo; **~litre**, n, (US) **~liter** n mililitro; **~metre**, (US) **~meter** n milímetro.

milliner [ˈmɪlɪnə*] n sombrerero/a; **~y** n sombrerería.

million [ˈmɪljən] n millón m; **a** ~ **times** un millón de veces; **~aire** n millonario/a.

millstone [ˈmɪlstəun] n piedra de molino.

milometer [maɪˈlɔmɪtə*] n (Brit) ≈ cuentakilómetros m inv.

mime [maɪm] n mímica, (actor) mimo/a // vt remedar // vi actuar de mimo.

mimic [ˈmɪmɪk] n imitador(a) m/f // a mímico // vt remedar, imitar; **~ry** n imitación f.

min. abbr = **minute(s); minimum.**

minaret [mɪnəˈret] n alminar m.

mince [mɪns] vt picar // vi (in walking) andar con pasos menudos // n (Brit CULIN) carne f picada, picadillo; **~meat** n conserva de fruta pi-

cada; ~ **pie** n empanadilla rellena de fruta picada; **~r** n picadora de carne.

mind [maɪnd] n (gen) mente f; (contrasted with matter) espíritu // vt (attend to, look after) ocuparse de, cuidar; (be careful of) tener cuidado con; (object to): **I don't** ~ **the noise** no me molesta el ruido; **it is on my** ~ me preocupa; **to my** ~ en mi opinión; **to be out of one's** ~ estar fuera de juicio; **to bear sth in** ~ tomar or tener algo en cuenta; **to make up one's** ~ decidirse; **I don't** ~ me es igual; ~ **you,** ... te advierto que ...; **never** ~! ¡es igual!, ¡no importa!; (don't worry) ¡no te preocupes!; '~ **the step**' 'cuidado con el escalón'; **~er** n guardaespaldas m inv; **~ful** a: **~ful of** consciente de; **~less** a (crime) sin motivo; (work) de autómata.

mine [maɪn] pron el mío/la mía etc; **a friend of** ~ un/a amigo/a mío/ mía // a: **this book is** ~ este libro es mío // n mina // vt (coal) extraer; (ship, beach) minar; **~field** n campo de minas; **~r** n minero/a.

mineral [ˈmɪnərəl] a mineral // n mineral m; **~s** npl (Brit: soft drinks) aguas fpl minerales, gaseosa sg; ~ **water** n agua mineral.

minesweeper [ˈmaɪnswiːpə*] n dragaminas m inv.

mingle [ˈmɪŋɡl] vi: **to** ~ **with** mezclarse con.

miniature [ˈmɪnətʃə*] a (en) miniatura // n miniatura.

minibus [ˈmɪnɪbʌs] n microbús m.

minim [ˈmɪnɪm] n (Brit MUS) blanca.

minimal [ˈmɪnɪml] a mínimo.

minimum [ˈmɪnɪməm] n, pl **minima** [ˈmɪnɪmə] mínimo // a mínimo.

mining [ˈmaɪnɪŋ] n explotación minera // a minero.

miniskirt [ˈmɪnɪskəːt] n minifalda.

minister [ˈmɪnɪstə*] n (Brit POL) ministro/a (Sp), secretario/a (LAm); (REL) pastor m // vi: **to** ~ **to** atender a; **~ial** [-ˈtɪərɪəl] a (Brit POL) ministerial.

ministry ['mɪnɪstrɪ] *n* (*Brit POL*) ministerio (*Sp*); secretaría (*LAm*); (*REL*) sacerdocio.

mink [mɪŋk] *n* visón *m*.

minnow ['mɪnəu] *n* pececillo (*de agua dulce*).

minor ['maɪnə*] *a* (*unimportant*) secundario; (*MUS*) menor // *n* (*LAW*) menor *m/f* de edad.

Minorca [mɪ'nɔ:kə] *n* Menorca.

minority [maɪ'nɔrɪtɪ] *n* minoría.

mint [mɪnt] *n* (*plant*) menta, hierbabuena; (*sweet*) caramelo de menta // *vt* (*coins*) acuñar; the (*Royal*) M~, (*US*) the (*US*) M~ la Casa de la Moneda; **in ~ condition** en perfecto estado.

minus ['maɪnəs] *n* (*also*: ~ **sign**) signo de menos // *prep* menos.

minute ['mɪnɪt] *n* minuto; (*fig*) momento; ~**s** *npl* actas *fpl* // *a* [maɪ'nju:t] diminuto; (*search*) minucioso; **at the last** ~ a última hora.

miracle ['mɪrəkl] *n* milagro; **miraculous** [mɪ'rækjuləs] *a* milagroso.

mirage ['mɪrɑ:ʒ] *n* espejismo.

mire [maɪə*] *n* fango, lodo.

mirror ['mɪrə*] *n* espejo; (*in car*) retrovisor *m* // *vt* reflejar.

mirth [mɜ:θ] *n* alegría.

misadventure [mɪsəd'ventʃə*] *n* desgracia; **death by ~** muerte *f* accidental.

misanthropist [mɪ'zænθrəpɪst] *n* misántropo/a.

misapprehension ['mɪsæprɪ'henʃən] *n* equivocación *f*.

misbehave [mɪsbɪ'heɪv] *vi* portarse mal.

miscalculate [mɪs'kælkjuleɪt] *vt* calcular mal.

miscarriage ['mɪskærɪdʒ] *n* (*MED*) aborto; ~ **of justice** error *m* judicial.

miscellaneous [mɪsɪ'leɪnɪəs] *a* varios/as, diversos/as.

mischief ['mɪstʃɪf] *n* (*naughtiness*) travesura; (*harm*) mal *m*, daño; (*maliciousness*) malicia; **mischie-**

vous [-ʃɪvəs] *a* travieso; dañoso; (*playful*) malicioso.

misconception ['mɪskən'sepʃən] *n* concepto erróneo; equivocación *f*.

misconduct [mɪs'kɔndʌkt] *n* mala conducta; **professional** ~ falta profesional.

miscount [mɪs'kaunt] *vt, vi* contar mal.

misconstrue [mɪskən'stru:] *vt* interpretar mal.

misdeed [mɪs'di:d] *n* delito.

misdemeanour, (*US*) **misdemeanor** [mɪsdɪ'mi:nə*] *n* delito, ofensa.

miser ['maɪzə*] *n* avaro/a.

miserable ['mɪzərəbl] *a* (*unhappy*) triste, desgraciado; (*wretched*) miserable.

miserly ['maɪzəlɪ] *a* avariento, tacaño.

misery ['mɪzərɪ] *n* (*unhappiness*) tristeza; (*wretchedness*) miseria, desdicha.

misfire [mɪs'faɪə*] *vi* fallar.

misfit ['mɪsfɪt] *n* (*person*) inadaptado/a.

misfortune [mɪs'fɔ:tʃən] *n* desgracia.

misgiving(s) [mɪs'gɪvɪŋ(z)] *n(pl)* (*mistrust*) recelo; (*apprehension*) presentimiento.

misguided [mɪs'gaɪdɪd] *a* equivocado.

mishandle [mɪs'hændl] *vt* (*treat roughly*) maltratar; (*mismanage*) manejar mal.

mishap ['mɪshæp] *n* desgracia, contratiempo.

misinform [mɪsɪn'fɔ:m] *vt* informar mal.

misinterpret [mɪsɪn'tə:prɪt] *vt* interpretar mal.

misjudge [mɪs'dʒʌdʒ] *vt* juzgar mal.

mislay [mɪs'leɪ] (*irg*: *like* **lay**) *vt* extraviar, perder.

mislead [mɪs'li:d] (*irg*: *like* **lead**) *vt* llevar a conclusiones erróneas; ~**ing** *a* engañoso.

mismanage [mɪs'mænɪdʒ] *vt* administrar mal.

misnomer [mɪs'nəumə*] n término inapropiado o equivocado.

misogynist [mɪ'sɔdʒɪnɪst] n misógino.

misplace [mɪs'pleɪs] vt (lose) extraviar.

misprint ['mɪsprɪnt] n errata, error m de imprenta.

Miss [mɪs] n Señorita.

miss [mɪs] vt (train etc) perder; (fail to hit: target) no dar en; (regret the absence of): **I ~ him** (yo) le echo de menos or a faltar // vi fallar // n (shot) tiro fallido or perdido; **to ~ out** (Brit) omitir.

misshapen [mɪs'ʃeɪpən] a deforme.

missile ['mɪsaɪl] n (AVIAT) misil m; (object thrown) proyectil m.

missing ['mɪsɪŋ] a (pupil) ausente; (thing) perdido; (MIL) desaparecido; **to be ~** faltar.

mission ['mɪʃən] n misión f; **~ary** n misionero/a.

misspent ['mɪs'spɛnt] a: **his ~ youth** su juventud disipada.

mist [mɪst] n (light) neblina; (heavy) niebla; (at sea) bruma // vi (also: ~ over, ~ up: weather) nublarse; (: Brit: windows) empañarse.

mistake [mɪs'teɪk] n error m // vt (irg: like **take**) entender mal; **by ~** por equivocación; **to make a ~** equivocarse; **to ~ A for B** confundir A con B; **~n** a (idea etc) equivocado; **to be ~n** equivocarse, engañarse.

mister ['mɪstə*] n (col) señor m; see **Mr**.

mistletoe ['mɪsltəu] n muérdago.

mistook [mɪs'tuk] pt of **mistake**.

mistress ['mɪstrɪs] n (lover) amante f; (of house) señora (de la casa); (Brit: in primary school) maestra; (in secondary school) profesora, see **Mrs**.

mistrust [mɪs'trʌst] vt desconfiar de.

misty ['mɪstɪ] a nebuloso, brumoso; (day) de niebla; (glasses) empañado.

misunderstand [misʌndə'stænd] (irg: like **understand**) vt, vi enten-

der mal; **~ing** n malentendido.

misuse [mɪs'juːs] n mal uso; (of power) abuso // vt [mɪs'juːz] abusar de; (funds) malversar.

mitre, (US) **miter** ['maɪtə*] n mitra.

mitt(en) ['mɪt(n)] n manopla.

mix [mɪks] vt (gen) mezclar; (combine) unir // vi mezclarse; (people) llevarse bien // n mezcla; **to ~ up** vt mezclar; (confuse) confundir; **~ed** a (assorted) variado, surtido; (school etc) mixto; **~ed-up** a (confused) confuso, revuelto; **~er** n (for food) licuadora; (person): **he's a good ~er** tiene don de gentes; **~ture** n mezcla; **~-up** n confusión f.

mm abbr (= millimetre) mm.

moan [məun] n gemido // vi gemir; (col: complain): **to ~ (about)** quejarse (de).

moat [məut] n foso.

mob [mɔb] n multitud f; (pej): **the ~** el populacho // vt acosar.

mobile ['məubaɪl] a móvil // n móvil m; **~ home** n caravana.

mock [mɔk] vt (make ridiculous) ridiculizar; (laugh at) burlarse de // a fingido; **~ery** n burla.

mod [mɔd] a see **convenience**.

mode [məud] n modo.

model ['mɔdl] n (gen) modelo; (ARCH) maqueta; (person: for fashion, ART) modelo m/f // a modelo // vt modelar // vi ser modelo; **~ railway** ferrocarril m de juguete; **to ~ clothes** pasar modelos, ser modelo.

modem ['məudəm] n módem m.

moderate ['mɔdərət] a, n moderado/a // vb ['mɔdəreɪt] vi moderarse, calmarse // vt moderar.

modern ['mɔdən] a moderno; **~ize** vt modernizar.

modest ['mɔdɪst] a modesto; **~y** n modestia.

modicum ['mɔdɪkəm] n: **a ~ of** un mínimo de.

modify ['mɔdɪfaɪ] vt modificar.

module ['mɔdjuːl] n (unit, component, SPACE) módulo.

mogul ['məʊgəl] n (fig) magnate m.

mohair ['məʊheə*] n mohair m.

moist [mɔist] a húmedo; ~**en** ['mɔisn] vt humedecer; ~**ure** ['mɔistʃə*] n humedad f; ~**urizer** ['mɔistʃəraizə*] n crema hidratante.

molar ['məʊlə*] n muela.

molasses [məʊ'læsiz] n melaza.

mold [məʊld] n, vt (US) = **mould**.

mole [məʊl] n (animal) topo; (spot) lunar m.

molecule ['mɔlikju:l] n molécula.

molest [məʊ'lest] vt importunar.

mollycoddle ['mɔlikɔdl] vt mimar.

molt [məʊlt] vi (US) = **moult**.

molten ['məʊltən] a fundido; (lava) líquido.

mom [mɔm] n (US) = **mum**.

moment ['məʊmənt] n momento; at the ~ de momento, por ahora; ~**ary** a momentáneo; ~**ous** [-'mentəs] a trascendental, importante.

momentum [məʊ'mentəm] n momento; (fig) ímpetu m; **to gather** ~ cobrar velocidad.

mommy ['mɔmi] n (US) = **mummy**.

Monaco ['mɔnəkəʊ] n Mónaco.

monarch ['mɔnək] n monarca m/f; ~**y** n monarquía.

monastery ['mɔnəstəri] n monasterio.

Monday ['mʌndi] n lunes m inv.

monetary ['mʌnitəri] a monetario.

money ['mʌni] n dinero; **to make** ~ ganar dinero; ~**lender** n prestamista m/f; ~ **order** n giro; ~**-spinner** n (col): **to be a** ~**-spinner** dar mucho dinero.

mongol ['mɔngəl] a, n (MED) mongólico.

mongrel ['mʌngrəl] n (dog) perro mestizo.

monitor ['mɔnitə*] n (SCOL) monitor m; (also: **television** ~) receptor m de control; (of computer) monitor m // vt controlar.

monk [mʌŋk] n monje m.

monkey ['mʌŋki] n mono; ~ **nut** n (Brit) cacahuete m, maní (LAm); ~

wrench n llave f inglesa.

mono... ['mɔnəʊ] pref: ~**chrome** a monocromo.

monocle ['mɔnəkl] n monóculo.

monologue ['mɔnəlɔg] n monólogo.

monopoly [mə'nɔpəli] n monopolio.

monotone ['mɔnətəʊn] n voz f (or tono) monocorde.

monotonous [mə'nɔtənəs] a monótono.

monotony [mə'nɔtəni] n monotonía.

monsoon [mɔn'su:n] n monzón m.

monster ['mɔnstə*] n monstruo.

monstrosity [mɔns'trɔsiti] n monstruosidad f.

monstrous ['mɔnstrəs] a (huge) enorme; (atrocious) monstruoso.

montage ['mɔntɑ:ʒ] n montaje m.

month [mʌnθ] n mes m; ~**ly** a mensual // ad mensualmente // n (magazine) revista mensual.

monument ['mɔnjumənt] n monumento; ~**al** [-'mentl] a monumental.

moo [mu:] vi mugir.

mood [mu:d] n humor m; **to be in a good/bad** ~ estar de buen/mal humor; ~**y** a (changeable) de humor variable; (sullen) malhumorado.

moon [mu:n] n luna; ~**light** n luz f de la luna; ~**lighting** n pluriempleo; ~**lit** a: a ~**lit night** una noche de luna.

Moor [muə*] n moro/a.

moor [muə*] n páramo // vt (ship) amarrar // vi echar las amarras.

Moorish ['muəriʃ] a moro; (architecture) árabe, morisco.

moorland ['muələnd] n páramo, brezal m.

moose [mu:s] n, pl inv alce m.

mop [mɔp] n fregona; (of hair) greña, melena // vt fregar; **to** ~ **up** vt limpiar.

mope [məʊp] vi estar or andar deprimido.

moped ['məʊped] n ciclomotor m.

moral ['mɔrl] a moral // n moraleja; ~**s** npl moralidad f, moral f.

morale [mɔ'rɑ:l] n moral f.

morality [mə'ræliti] n moralidad f.

morass [mə'ræs] n pantano.

morbid ['mɔːbɪd] a (interest) morboso; (MED) mórbido.

KEYWORD

more [mɔː*] ♦ a 1 (greater in number etc) más (greater in number etc) más; ~ **people/work than** before más gente/trabajo que antes 2 (additional) más; **do you want (some) ~ tea?** ¿quieres más té?; **is there any ~ wine?** ¿queda vino?; **it'll take a few ~ weeks** tardará unas semanas más; **it's 2 kms ~ to the house** faltan 2 kms para la casa; **~ time/letters than we expected** más tiempo del que/ más cartas de las que esperábamos ♦ pron (greater amount, additional amount) más; ~ **than 10 más de 10**; **it cost ~ than the other one/than we expected** costó más que el otro/ más de lo que esperábamos; **is there any ~?** ¿hay más?; **many/much ~** mucho(a)/muchos(as) más ♦ ad más; ~ **dangerous/easily (than)** más peligroso/fácilmente (que); ~ **and ~** expensive cada vez más caro; ~ **or less** más o menos; ~ **than ever** más que nunca.

---

moreover [mɔː'rəʊvə*] ad además, por otra parte.

morgue [mɔːg] n depósito de cadáveres.

Mormon ['mɔːmən] n mormón/ona m/f.

morning ['mɔːnɪŋ] n (gen) mañana; (early ~) madrugada; **in the ~** por la mañana; **7 o'clock in the ~** las 7 de la mañana.

Moroccan [mə'rɒkən] a, n marroquí m/f.

Morocco [mə'rɒkəʊ] n Marruecos m.

moron ['mɔːrɒn] n imbécil m/f.

morose [mə'rəʊs] a hosco, malhumorado.

morphine ['mɔːfiːn] n morfina.

Morse [mɔːs] n (also: ~ **code**) (código) morse.

morsel ['mɔːsl] n (of food) bocado.

---

mortal ['mɔːtl] a, n mortal m; ~**ity** [-'tælɪtɪ] n mortalidad f.

mortar ['mɔːtə*] n argamasa; (implement) mortero.

mortgage ['mɔːgɪdʒ] n hipoteca // vt hipotecar; ~ **company** n (US) banco hipotecario.

mortify ['mɔːtɪfaɪ] vt mortificar, humillar.

mortuary ['mɔːtjuərɪ] n depósito de cadáveres.

mosaic [məʊ'zeɪɪk] n mosaico.

Moscow ['mɒskəʊ] n Moscú m.

Moslem ['mɒzləm] a, n = **Muslim**.

mosque [mɒsk] n mezquita.

mosquito [mɒs'kiːtəʊ], pl ~**es** n mosquito (Sp), zancudo (LAm).

moss [mɒs] n musgo.

most [məʊst] a la mayor parte de, la mayoría de // pron la mayor parte, la mayoría // ad el más; (very) muy; **the ~** (also: + adjective) el más; ~ **of them** la mayor parte de ellos; **I saw the ~** yo vi el que más; **at the (very) ~** a lo sumo, todo lo más; **to make the ~ of** aprovechar (al máximo); **a ~ interesting book** un libro interesantísimo; ~**ly** ad en su mayor parte, principalmente.

MOT n abbr (Brit = Ministry of Transport): **the ~ (test)** inspección (anual) obligatoria de coches y camiones.

motel [məʊ'tel] n motel m.

moth [mɒθ] n mariposa nocturna; (clothes ~) polilla; ~**ball** n bola de naftalina.

mother ['mʌðə*] n madre f // a materno // vt (care for) cuidar (como una madre); ~**hood** n maternidad f; ~**in-law** n suegra; ~**ly** a maternal; ~**of-pearl** n nácar m; ~**to-be** n futura madre; ~**tongue** n lengua materna.

motif [məʊ'tiːf] n motivo, (theme) tema m.

motion ['məʊʃən] n movimiento; (gesture) ademán m, señal f; (at meeting) moción f // vt, vi: **to ~ (to) sb to do sth** hacer señas a uno para

que haga algo; **~less** a inmóvil; **~
picture** n película.
motivated ['məʊtɪveɪtɪd] a motiva-
do.
motive ['məʊtɪv] n motivo.
motley ['mɒtlɪ] a variado.
motor ['məʊtə*] n motor m; (Brit:
col: vehicle) coche m, carro (LAm),
automóvil m // a motor (f: motora,
motriz); **~bike** n moto f; **~boat** n
lancha motora; **~car** n (Brit) coche
m, carro (LAm), automóvil m;
~cycle n motocicleta; **~cycle racing** n motociclismo; **~cyclist** n
motociclista m/f; **~ing** n (Brit) automovilismo; **~ist** n conductor(a) m/f,
automovilista m/f; **~ racing** n
(Brit) carreras fpl de coches, automovilismo; **~ scooter** n moto f; **~
vehicle** n automóvil m; **~way** n
(Brit) autopista.
mottled ['mɒtld] a abigarrado, multi-
color.
motto ['mɒtəʊ], pl **~es** n lema m;
(watchword) consigna.
mould, (US) **mold** [məʊld] n molde
m; (mildew) moho // vt moldear;
(fig) formar; **~er** vi (decay) decaer;
~ing n moldura; **~y** a enmohecido.
moult, (US) **molt** [məʊlt] vi mudar
(la piel/las plumas).
mound [maʊnd] n montón m, monti-
culo.
mount [maʊnt] n monte m; (horse)
montura; (for jewel etc) engarce m;
(for picture) marco m // vt montar,
subir a // vi (also: **~ up**) subirse,
montarse.
mountain ['maʊntɪn] n montaña //
cpd de montaña; **~eer** [-'nɪə*] n alpinista m/f, andinista m/f (LAm);
~eering [-'nɪərɪŋ] n alpinismo, andinismo (LAm); **~ous** a montañoso;
~side n ladera de la montaña.
mourn [mɔːn] vt llorar, lamentar //
vi: to **~ for** llorar la muerte de, lamentarse por; **~er** n doliente m/f;
dolorido/a; **~ful** a triste, lúgubre;
~ing n luto // cpd (dress) de luto; in
~ing de luto.

mouse [maʊs], pl **mice** n ratón m;
(COMPUT) ratón m; **~trap** n ratonera.
mousse [muːs] n (CULIN) crema ba-
tida; (for hair) espuma (moldeado-
ra).
moustache [məs'tɑːʃ] n bigote m.
mousy ['maʊsɪ] a (person) tímido;
(hair) pardusco.
mouth [maʊθ], pl **~s** [-ðz] n boca;
(of river) desembocadura; **~ful** n
bocado; **~ organ** n armónica;
~piece n (of musical instrument)
boquilla; (spokesman) portavoz m/f;
~wash n enjuague m; **~watering**
a apetitoso.
movable ['muːvəbl] a movible.
move [muːv] n (movement) movimiento; (in game) jugada; (: turn to
play) turno; (change of house) mudanza // vt mover; (emotionally) conmover; (POL: resolution etc) proponer // vi (gen) moverse; (traffic) circular; (also: Brit: **~ house**) trasla-
darse, mudarse; to **~ sb** to do sth
mover a uno a hacer algo; to **get a
~ on** darse prisa; to **~ about** or
around vi moverse; (travel) viajar;
to **~ along** vi avanzar, adelantarse; to **~ away** vi alejarse; to **~
back** vi retroceder; to **~ forward**
vi avanzar // vt adelantar; to **~ in**
vi (a house) instalarse; to **~ on** vi
ponerse en camino; to **~ out** vi
(of house) mudarse; to **~ over** vi
apartarse; to **~ up** vi subir; (employee) ser ascendido.
movement ['muːvmənt] n movimiento; (TECH) mecanismo.
movie ['muːvɪ] n película; to go to
the **~s** ir al cine; **~ camera** n cámara cinematográfica.
moving ['muːvɪŋ] a (emotional) con-
movedor(a); (that moves) móvil.
mow [maʊ], pt **mowed**, pp **mowed**
or **mown** vt (grass) cortar; (corn:
also: **~ down**) segar; (shoot) acribillar; **~er** n (also: **lawnmower**) cor-
tacéspedes m inv.
MP n abbr = Member of Parlia-

ment.

m.p.h. *abbr* = miles per hour (60 m.p.h. = 96 k.p.h.).

Mr, Mr. ['mɪstə*] *n*: ~ Smith (el) Sr. Smith.

Mrs, Mrs. ['mɪsɪz] *n*: ~ Smith (la) Sra. Smith.

Ms, Ms. [mɪz] *n* (= Miss or Mrs): ~ Smith (la) Sr(ta). Smith.

M.Sc. *abbr* = **Master of Science.**

much [mʌtʃ] *a* mucho // *ad, n or pron* mucho; (before pp) muy; **how ~ is it?** ¿cuánto es?, ¿cuánto cuesta?; **too ~** demasiado; **it's not ~** no es mucho; **as ~ as** tanto como; **however ~ he tries** por mucho que se esfuerce.

muck [mʌk] *n* (dirt) suciedad *f*; (fig) porquería; **to ~ about** or **around** *vi* (col) perder el tiempo; (enjoy o.s.) entretenerse; **to ~ up** *vt* (col: ruin) arruinar, estropear; **~y** *a* (dirty) sucio.

mucus ['mjuːkəs] *n* moco.

mud [mʌd] *n* barro, lodo.

muddle ['mʌdl] *n* desorden *m*, confusión *f*; (mix-up) embrollo, lío // *vt* (also: ~ up) embrollar, confundir; **to ~ through** *vi* salir del paso.

muddy ['mʌdɪ] *a* fangoso, cubierto de lodo.

mud: ~**guard** *n* guardabarros *m inv*; ~**slinging** *n* injurias *fpl*, difamación *f*.

muff [mʌf] *n* manguito // *vt* (chance) desperdiciar; (lines) estropear.

muffin ['mʌfin] *n* mollete *m*.

muffle ['mʌfl] *vt* (sound) amortiguar; (against cold) embozar; ~**r** *n* (US AUT) silenciador *m*.

mug [mʌg] *n* (cup) taza grande (sin platillo); (for beer) jarra; (col: face) jeta; (: fool) bobo // *vt* (assault) asaltar; ~**ging** *n* asalto.

muggy ['mʌgɪ] *a* bochornoso.

mule [mjuːl] *n* mula.

mull [mʌl]: **to ~ over** *vt* meditar sobre.

mulled [mʌld] *a*: ~ **wine** vino caliente.

multifarious [mʌltɪ'fɛərɪəs] *a* múltiple.

multi-level [mʌltɪ'lɛvl] *a* (US) = **multistorey.**

multiple ['mʌltɪpl] *a, n* múltiplo; ~ **sclerosis** *n* esclerosis *f* múltiple; ~ **store** *n* (Brit) (cadena de) grandes almacenes.

multiplication [mʌltɪplɪ'keɪʃən] *n* multiplicación *f*.

multiply ['mʌltɪplaɪ] *vt* multiplicar // *vi* multiplicarse.

multistorey [mʌltɪ'stɔːrɪ] *a* (Brit: building, car park) de muchos pisos.

multitude ['mʌltɪtjuːd] *n* multitud *f*.

mum [mʌm] *n* (Brit) mamá // *a*: **to keep ~** mantener la boca cerrada.

mumble ['mʌmbl] *vt, vi* hablar entre dientes, refunfuñar.

mummy ['mʌmɪ] *n* (Brit: mother) mamá; (embalmed) momia.

mumps [mʌmps] *n* paperas *fpl*.

munch [mʌntʃ] *vt, vi* mascar.

mundane [mʌn'deɪn] *a* trivial.

municipal [mjuː'nɪsɪpl] *a* municipal; ~**ity** [-'pælɪtɪ] *n* municipio.

mural ['mjuərl] *n* (pintura) mural *m*.

murder ['məːdə*] *n* asesinato; (in law) homicidio // *vt* asesinar; matar; ~**er/~ess** *n* asesino/a; ~**ous** *a* homicida.

murky ['məːkɪ] *a* (water, past) turbio; (room) sombrío.

murmur ['məːmə*] *n* murmullo // *vt, vi* murmurar.

muscle ['mʌsl] *n* músculo; **to ~ in** *vi* entrometerse; **muscular** ['mʌskjulə*] *a* muscular; (person) musculoso.

muse [mjuːz] *vi* meditar // *n* musa.

museum [mjuː'zɪəm] *n* museo.

mushroom ['mʌʃrum] *n* (gen) seta, hongo; (small) champiñón *m* // *vi* (fig) crecer de la noche a la mañana.

music ['mjuːzɪk] *n* música; ~**al** *a* melodioso; (person) musical // *n* (show) comedia musical; ~**al instrument** *n* instrumento musical; ~

hall *n* teatro de variedades; ~**ian**
[-'zɪʃən] *n* músico/a.
Muslim ['mʌzlɪm] *a, n* musulmán/
ana *m/f*.
muslin ['mʌzlɪn] *n* muselina.
mussel ['mʌsl] *n* mejillón *m*.
must [mʌst] *auxiliary vb* (obligation): I ~ do it debo hacerlo, tengo
que hacerlo; (probability): **he ~ be
there by now** ya debe (de) estar allí
// *n*: **it's a ~** es imprescindible.
mustard ['mʌstəd] *n* mostaza.
muster ['mʌstə*] *vt* juntar, reunir.
mustn't ['mʌsnt] = **must not.**
musty ['mʌstɪ] *a* mohoso, que huele a
humedad.
mute [mjuːt] *a, n* mudo/a.
muted ['mjuːtɪd] *a* callado.
mutiny ['mjuːtɪnɪ] *n* motín *m* // *vi*
amotinarse.
mutter ['mʌtə*] *vt, vi* murmurar.
mutton ['mʌtn] *n* carne *f* de cordero.
mutual ['mjuːtʃuəl] *a* mutuo;
(friend) común; ~**ly** *ad* mutuamente.
muzzle ['mʌzl] *n* hocico; (protective
device) bozal *m*; (of gun) boca // *vt*
amordazar; (dog) poner un bozal a.
my [maɪ] *a* mi/is; ~ **house/brother/
sisters** mi casa/mi hermano/mis her-
manas; **I've washed** ~ **hair/cut** ~
finger me he lavado el pelo/cortado
un dedo; **is this** ~ **pen or yours?**
¿es este bolígrafo mío o tuyo?
myriad ['mɪrɪəd] *n* (of people, things)
miríada.
myself [maɪ'self] *pron* (reflexive)
me; (emphatic) yo mismo; (after
prep) mí (mismo); see also **oneself**.
mysterious [mɪs'tɪərɪəs] *a* misterioso.
mystery ['mɪstərɪ] *n* misterio.
mystify ['mɪstɪfaɪ] *vt* (perplex) dejar
perplejo; (disconcert) desconcertar.
mystique [mɪs'tiːk] *n* misterio (profesional etc).
myth [mɪθ] *n* mito; ~**ical** *a* mítico.

N

n/a *abbr* (= not applicable) ≈ no in-
teresa.
nab [næb] *vt* (col: grab) coger (Sp),
agarrar (LAm); (: catch out) pillar.
nag [næg] *n* (pej: horse) rocín *m* // *vt*
(scold) regañar; (annoy) fastidiar;
~**ging** *a* (doubt) persistente; (pain)
continuo // *n* quejas *fpl*.
nail [neɪl] *n* (human) uña; (metal)
clavo // *vt* clavar; (fig: catch) coger
(Sp), pillar; **to** ~ **sb down to** hacer
sth comprometer a uno a que haga
algo; ~**brush** *n* cepillo para las
uñas; ~**file** *n* lima para las uñas; ~
polish *n* esmalte *m* or laca para las
uñas; ~ **polish remover** *n* quitaesmalte *m*; ~ **scissors** *npl* tijeras *fpl*
para las uñas; ~ **varnish** *n* (Brit) =
~ **polish.**
naïve [naɪ'iːv] *a* ingenuo.
naked ['neɪkɪd] *a* (nude) desnudo;
(flame) expuesto al aire.
name [neɪm] *n* (gen) nombre *m*;
(surname) apellido; (reputation)
fama, renombre *m* // *vt* (child) poner
nombre a; (appoint) nombrar; **by** ~
de nombre; **in the** ~ **of** en nombre
de; **what's your** ~? ¿cómo se llama?; **to give one's** ~ **and address**
dar sus señas; ~**less** *a* anónimo, sin
nombre; ~**ly** *ad* a saber; ~**sake** *n*
tocayo/a.
nanny ['nænɪ] *n* niñera.
nap [næp] *n* (sleep) sueñecito, siesta;
to be caught ~**ping** estar desprevenido.
napalm ['neɪpɑːm] *n* napalm *m*.
nape [neɪp] *n*: ~ **of the neck** nuca,
cogote *m*.
napkin ['næpkɪn] *n* (also: **table** ~)
servilleta.
nappy ['næpɪ] *n* (Brit) pañal *m*; ~
liner *n* gasa; ~ **rash** *n* prurito.
narcissus [nɑː'sɪsəs], *pl* -**si** [-saɪ] *n*
narciso.
narcotic [nɑː'kɔtɪk] *a, n* narcótico.

narrative ['nærətɪv] n narrativa // a narrativo.

narrow ['nærəʊ] a estrecho, angosto // vi estrecharse, angostarse; (diminish) reducirse; **to have a ~ escape** escaparse por los pelos; **to ~ sth down** reducir algo; **~ly** ad (miss) por poco; **~-minded** a de miras estrechas.

nasty ['nɑːstɪ] a (remark) feo; (person) antipático; (revolting: taste, smell) asqueroso; (wound, disease etc) peligroso, grave.

nation ['neɪʃən] n nación f.

national ['næʃənl] a, n nacional m/f; **~ dress** n vestido nacional; **N~ Health Service (NHS)** n (Brit) servicio nacional de salud pública; ≈ Insalud m (Sp); **N~ Insurance** n (Brit) seguro nacional social; **~ism** n nacionalismo; **~ist** a, n nacionalista m/f; **~ity** [-'nælɪtɪ] n nacionalidad f; (ship) nacionalizar; **~ly** ad (nationwide) en escala nacional; (as a nation) nacionalmente, como nación.

nationwide ['neɪʃənwaɪd] a en escala o a nivel nacional.

native ['neɪtɪv] n (local inhabitant) natural m/f, nacional m/f; (in colonies) indígena m/f, nativo/a // a (indigenous) indígena; (country) natal; (innate) innato; a ~ of Russia un(a) natural m/f de Rusia; **~ language** n lengua materna; **a ~ speaker of French** un hablante nativo de francés.

Nativity [nə'tɪvɪtɪ] n: **the ~** Navidad f.

NATO ['neɪtəʊ] n abbr (= North Atlantic Treaty Organization) OTAN f.

natural ['nætʃrəl] a natural; **~ gas** n gas m natural; **~ize** vt: **to become ~ized** (person) naturalizarse; (plant) aclimatarse; **~ly** ad (speak etc) naturalmente; (of course) desde luego, por supuesto; (instinctively) por instinto, por naturaleza.

nature ['neɪtʃə*] n naturaleza; (group, sort) género, clase f; (character) carácter m, genio; **by ~** por

or de naturaleza.

naught [nɔːt] n = **nought**.

naughty ['nɔːtɪ] a (child) travieso; (story, film) verde, escabroso, colorado (LAm).

nausea ['nɔːsɪə] n náusea; **~te** [-sɪeɪt] vt dar náuseas a; (fig) dar asco a.

nautical ['nɔːtɪkl] a náutico, marítimo; (mile) marino.

naval ['neɪvl] a naval, de marina; **~ officer** n oficial m/f de marina.

nave [neɪv] n nave f.

navel ['neɪvl] n ombligo.

navigate ['nævɪgeɪt] vt gobernar // vi navegar; **navigation** [-'geɪʃən] n (action) navegación f; (science) náutica; **navigator** n navegador(a) m/f, navegante m/f.

navvy ['nævɪ] n (Brit) peón m caminero.

navy ['neɪvɪ] n marina de guerra; (ships) armada, flota; **~-(blue)** a azul marino.

Nazi ['nɑːtsɪ] n nazi m/f.

NB abbr (= nota bene) nótese.

near [nɪə*] a (place, relation) cercano; (time) próximo // ad cerca // prep (also: **~ to**: space) cerca de, junto a; (: time) cerca de // vt acercarse a, aproximarse a; **~by** [nɪə'baɪ] a cercano, próximo // ad cerca; **~ly** ad casi, por poco; **I ~ly fell** por poco me caigo; **~ miss** n tiro cercano; **~side** n (AUT) lado derecho; **~sighted** a miope, corto de vista.

neat [niːt] a (place) ordenado, bien cuidado; (person) pulcro; (plan) ingenioso; (spirits) solo; **~ly** ad (tidily) con esmero; (skilfully) ingeniosamente.

nebulous ['nebjʊləs] a (fig) vago, confuso.

necessarily ['nesɪsrɪlɪ] ad necesariamente.

necessary ['nesɪsrɪ] a necesario, preciso; **he did all that was ~** hizo todo lo necesario.

necessity [nɪ'sesɪtɪ] n necesidad f; **necessities** npl artículos mpl de primera necesidad.

neck [nek] *n* (ANAT) cuello; (*of animal*) pescuezo // *vi* besuquearse; ~ **and** ~ parejos.

necklace ['neklɪs] *n* collar *m*.

neckline ['neklaɪn] *n* escote *m*.

necktie ['nektaɪ] *n* (US) corbata.

née [neɪ] *a*: ~ Scott de soltera Scott.

need [niːd] *n* (*lack*) escasez *f*, falta; (*necessity*) necesidad *f* // *vt* (*require*) necesitar; **I** ~ **to do it** tengo que or debo hacerlo; **you don't** ~ **to go** no hace falta que vayas.

needle ['niːdl] *n* aguja // *vt* (*fig: col*) picar, fastidiar.

needless ['niːdlɪs] *a* innecesario, inútil; ~ **to say** huelga decir que.

needlework ['niːdlwɜːk] *n* (*activity*) costura, labor *f* de aguja.

needn't ['niːdnt] = **need not.**

needy ['niːdɪ] *a* necesitado.

negative ['negətɪv] *n* (PHOT) negativo; (LING) negación *f* // *a* negativo.

neglect [nɪ'glekt] *vt* (*one's duty*) faltar a, no cumplir con; (*child*) descuidar, desatender // *n* (*state*) abandono; (*personal*) dejadez *f*; (*of duty*) incumplimiento.

negligee ['neglɪʒeɪ] *n* (*nightdress*) salto de cama.

negligence ['neglɪdʒəns] *n* negligencia, descuido.

negligible ['neglɪdʒɪbl] *a* insignificante, despreciable.

negotiate [nɪ'gəʊʃɪeɪt] *vt* (*treaty, loan*) negociar; (*obstacle*) franquear // *vi*: **to** ~ (**with**) negociar (con); **negotiation** [-'eɪʃən] *n* negociación *f*, gestión *f*.

Negress ['niːgrɪs] *n* negra.

Negro ['niːgrəʊ] *a*, *n* negro.

neigh [neɪ] *n* relincho // *vi* relinchar.

neighbour, (US) **neighbor** ['neɪbə*] *n* vecino/a; ~**hood** *n* (*place*) vecindad *f*, barrio; (*people*) vecindario; ~**ing** *a* vecino.

neither ['naɪðə*] *a* ni // *conj*: **I didn't move and** ~ **did John** no me he movido, ni Juan tampoco // *pron* ninguno; ~ **is true** ninguno/a de los/

las dos es cierto/a // *ad*: ~ **good nor bad** ni bueno ni malo.

neon ['niːɔn] *n* neón *m*; ~ **light** *n* lámpara de neón.

nephew ['nevjuː] *n* sobrino.

nerve [nɜːv] *n* (ANAT) nervio; (*courage*) valor *m*; (*impudence*) descaro, frescura; **a fit of** ~**s** un ataque de nervios; ~-**racking** *a* desquiciante.

nervous ['nɜːvəs] *a* (*anxious*, ANAT) nervioso; (*timid*) tímido, miedoso; ~ **breakdown** *n* crisis *f* nerviosa.

nest [nest] *n* (*of bird*) nido // *vi* anidar; ~ **egg** *n* (*fig*) ahorros *mpl*.

nestle ['nesl] *vi*: **to** ~ **down** acurrucarse.

net [net] *n* (*gen*) red *f*; (COMM) neto, líquido // *vt* coger (*Sp*) or agarrar (*LAm*) con red; (SPORT) marcar; ~**ball** *n* básquet *m*; ~ **curtain** *n* visillo.

Netherlands ['neðələndz] *npl*: **the** ~ **los** Países Bajos.

nett [net] *a* = **net.**

netting ['netɪŋ] *n* red *f*, redes *fpl*.

nettle ['netl] *n* ortiga.

network ['netwɜːk] *n* red *f*.

neurosis [njuə'rəʊsɪs], *pl* **-ses** [-siːz] *n* neurosis *f inv*; **neurotic** [-'rɔtɪk] *a*, *n* neurótico/a *m/f*.

neuter ['njuːtə*] *a* (LING) neutro // *vt* castrar, capar.

neutral ['njuːtrəl] *a* (*person*) neutral; (*colour etc*, ELEC) neutro // *n* (AUT) punto muerto; ~**ity** [-'trælɪtɪ] *n* neutralidad *f*; ~**ize** *vt* neutralizar.

neutron ['njuːtrɔn] *n* neutrón *m*; ~ **bomb** *n* bomba de neutrones.

never ['nevə*] *ad* nunca, jamás; **I** ~ **went no fui nunca;** ~ **in my life** jamás en la vida; *see also* **mind**; ~-**ending** *a* interminable, sin fin; ~**theless** [nevəðə'les] *ad* sin embargo, no obstante.

new [njuː] *a* nuevo; (*recent*) reciente; ~-**born** *a* recién nacido; ~-**comer** ['njuːkʌmə*] *n* recién venido/a or llegado/a; ~-**fangled** *a* (*pej*) modernísimo; ~-**found** *a* (*friend*) nuevo; (*enthusiasm*) recién adquirido;

~ly *ad* nuevamente, recién; **~ly-weds** *npl* recién casados *mpl*; **~ moon** *n* luna nueva.

news [nju:z] *n* noticias *fpl*; **a piece of ~** una noticia; **the ~** (*RADIO, TV*) las noticias *fpl*, telediario; **~ agency** *n* agencia de noticias; **~agent** *n* (*Brit*) vendedor(a) *m/f* de periódicos; **~caster** *n* presentador(a) *m/f*, locutor(a) *m/f*; **~ dealer** *n* (*US*) = **~agent**; **~ flash** *n* noticia de última hora; **~letter** *n* hoja informativa, boletín *m*; **~paper** *n* periódico, diario; **~print** *n* papel *m* de periódico; **~reader** *n* = **~caster**; **~reel** *n* noticiario; **~ stand** *n* quiosco o puesto de periódicos.

newt [nju:t] *n* tritón *m*.

New Year *n* Año Nuevo; **~'s Day** *n* Día *m* de Año Nuevo; **~'s Eve** *n* Nochevieja.

New York [nju:'jɔ:k] *n* Nueva York.

New Zealand [nju:'zi:lənd] *n* Nueva Zelanda; **~er** *n* neozelandés/esa *m/f*.

next [nɛkst] *a* (*house, room*) vecino; (*bus stop, meeting*) próximo; (*page*) siguiente // *ad* después; **the ~ day** el día siguiente; **~ time** la próxima vez; **~ year** el año próximo or que viene; **~ door** *ad* en la casa de al lado // *a* vecino, de al lado; **~-of-kin** *n* pariente *m* más cercano; **~ to** *prep* junto a, al lado de; **~ to nothing** casi nada.

NHS *n abbr* = **National Health Service**.

nib [nɪb] *n* plumilla.

nibble ['nɪbl] *vt* mordisquear, mordiscar.

Nicaragua [nɪkə'rægjuə] *n* Nicaragua; **~n** *a*, *n* nicaragüense *m/f*.

nice [naɪs] *a* (*likeable*) simpático; (*kind*) amable; (*pleasant*) agradable; (*attractive*) bonito, mono, lindo (*LAm*); (*distinction*) fino; **~-looking** *a* guapo; **~ly** *ad* amablemente; bien.

niche [ni:ʃ] *n* nicho.

nick [nɪk] *n* (*wound*) rasguño; (*cut, indentation*) mella, muesca // *vt* (*col*)

birlar, robar; **in the ~ of time** justo a tiempo.

nickel ['nɪkl] *n* níquel *m*; (*US*) moneda de 5 centavos.

nickname ['nɪkneɪm] *n* apodo, mote *m* // *vt* apodar.

nicotine ['nɪkəti:n] *n* nicotina.

niece [ni:s] *n* sobrina.

Nigeria [naɪ'dʒɪərɪə] *n* Nigeria; **~n** *a*, *n* nigeriano/a *m/f*.

nigger ['nɪgə*] *n* (*col!: highly offensive*) negro/a.

niggling ['nɪglɪŋ] *a* (*trifling*) nimio, insignificante; (*annoying*) molesto.

night [naɪt] *n* (*gen*) noche *f*; (*evening*) tarde *f*; **last ~** anoche; **the ~ before last** antenoche; **at ~, by ~** de noche, por la noche; **~cap** *n* (*drink*) bebida que se toma antes de acostarse; **~ club** *n* cabaret *m*; **~dress** *n* (*Brit*) camisón *m*; **~fall** *n* anochecer *m*; **~gown**, (*US*) **~ie** ['naɪtɪ] *n* (*Brit*) = **~dress**.

nightingale ['naɪtɪŋgeɪl] *n* ruiseñor *m*.

nightly ['naɪtlɪ] *a* de todas las noches // *ad* todas las noches, cada noche.

nightmare ['naɪtmɛə*] *n* pesadilla.

night: **~ porter** *n* guardián *m* nocturno; **~ school** *n* clase(s) *f(pl)* nocturna(s); **~ shift** *n* turno nocturno or de noche; **~-time** *n* noche *f*.

nil [nɪl] *n* (*Brit SPORT*) cero, nada.

Nile [naɪl] *n*: **the ~** el Nilo.

nimble ['nɪmbl] *a* (*agile*) ágil, ligero; (*skilful*) diestro.

nine [naɪn] *num* nueve; **~teen** *num* diecinueve, diez y nueve; **~ty** *num* noventa.

ninth [naɪnθ] *a* noveno.

nip [nɪp] *vt* (*pinch*) pellizcar; (*bite*) morder.

nipple ['nɪpl] *n* (*ANAT*) pezón *m*; (*of bottle*) tetilla.

nitrogen ['naɪtrədʒən] *n* nitrógeno.

KEYWORD

no [nəu] ◆ *ad* (*opposite of 'yes'*) no; **are you coming? — ~** (**I'm not**) ¿vienes? — no; **would you like**

some more? — ~ thank you ¿quieres más? no gracias
♦ a (not any): I have ~ money/time/books no tengo dinero/tiempo/libros; ~ other man would have done it ningún otro lo hubiera hecho; '~ entry' 'prohibido el paso'; '~ smoking' 'prohibido fumar'
♦ n (pl ~es) no m.

nobility [nəʊ'bɪlɪtɪ] n nobleza.

noble ['nəʊbl] a noble.

nobody ['nəʊbədɪ] pron nadie.

nod [nɒd] vi saludar con la cabeza; (in agreement) decir que sí con la cabeza // vt: to ~ one's head inclinar la cabeza // n inclinación f de cabeza; to ~ off vi cabecear.

noise [nɔɪz] n ruido; (din) escándalo, estrépito; **noisy** a (gen) ruidoso; (child) escandaloso.

nominal ['nɒmɪnl] a nominal.

nominate ['nɒmɪneɪt] vt (propose) proponer; (appoint) nombrar; **nomination** [-'neɪʃən] n propuesta; nombramiento.

nominee [nɒmɪ'niː] n candidato/a.

non... [nɒn] pref no, des..., in...; ~-alcoholic a no alcohólico; ~-aligned a no alineado.

nonchalant ['nɒnʃələnt] a indiferente.

non-committal ['nɒnkə'mɪtl] a (reserved) reservado; (uncommitted) evasivo.

nonconformist [nɒnkən'fɔːmɪst] a (attitude) heterodoxo; (person) inconformista m/f.

nondescript ['nɒndɪskrɪpt] a soso.

none [nʌn] pron ninguno/a // de ninguna manera; ~ of you ninguno de vosotros; I've ~ left no me queda ninguno/a; he's ~ the worse for it no está peor por ello.

nonentity [nɒ'nentɪtɪ] n cero a la izquierda, nulidad f.

nonetheless [nʌnðə'les] ad sin embargo, no obstante.

non-existent [nɒnɪg'zɪstənt] a inexistente.

non-fiction [nɒn'fɪkʃən] n literatura no novelesca.

nonplussed [nɒn'plʌst] a perplejo.

nonsense ['nɒnsəns] n tonterías fpl, disparates fpl; ~! ¡qué tonterías!

non: ~-**smoker** n no fumador(a) m/f; ~-**stick** a (pan, surface) antiadherente; ~-**stop** a continuo; (RAIL) directo // ad sin parar.

noodles ['nuːdlz] npl tallarines mpl.

nook [nuk] n rincón m; ~s and crannies escondrijos mpl.

noon [nuːn] n mediodía m.

no-one ['nəʊwʌn] pron = **nobody**.

noose [nuːs] n lazo corredizo.

nor [nɔː*] conj = **neither** // ad see **neither**.

norm [nɔːm] n norma.

normal ['nɔːml] a normal; ~**ly** ad normalmente.

north [nɔːθ] n norte m // a del norte, norteño // ad hacia el norte; N~ **America** n América del Norte; ~-**east** n nor(d)este m; ~**erly** ['nɔːðəlɪ] a (point, direction) norteño; ~**ern** ['nɔːðən] a norteño, del norte; **N~ern Ireland** n Irlanda del Norte; **N~ Pole** n Polo Norte; **N~ Sea** n Mar m del Norte; ~**ward(s)** ['nɔːθwəd(z)] ad hacia el norte; ~-**west** n nor(d)oeste m.

Norway ['nɔːweɪ] n Noruega; **Norwegian** [-'wiːdʒən] a, n noruego/a m/f.

nose [nəʊz] n (ANAT) nariz f; (ZOOL) hocico; (sense of smell) olfato // vi: to ~ **about** curiosear; ~**bleed** n hemorragia nasal; ~-**dive** n picado vertical; ~**y** a curioso, fisgón/ona.

nostalgia [nɒs'tældʒɪə] n nostalgia.

nostril ['nɒstrɪl] n ventana de la nariz.

nosy ['nəʊzɪ] a = **nosey**.

not [nɒt] ad no; ~ **that**... no es que...; it's too late, isn't it? es demasiado tarde, ¿verdad or no?; ~ **yet/now** todavía/ahora no; why ~? ¿por qué no?; see also **all**, **only**.

notably ['nəʊtəblɪ] ad especialmente.

notary ['nəʊtərɪ] n notario/a.

notch [nɒtʃ] n muesca, corte m.

note [nəʊt] n (MUS, record, letter) nota; (banknote) billete m; (tone) tono // vt (observe) notar, observar; ~**book** n libreta, cuaderno; ~**d** ['nəʊtɪd] a célebre, conocido; ~**pad** n bloc m; ~**paper** n papel m para cartas.

nothing ['nʌθɪŋ] n nada; (zero) cero; he does ~ no hace nada; ~ new nada nuevo; for ~ (free) gratis, sin pago; (in vain) en balde.

notice ['nəʊtɪs] n (announcement) anuncio; (dismissal) despido; (resignation) dimisión f // vt (observe) notar, observar; to take ~ of tomar nota de, prestar atención a; at short ~ con poca anticipación; until further ~ hasta nuevo aviso; to hand in one's ~ dimitir; ~**able** a evidente, obvio; ~ **board** n (Brit) tablón m de anuncios.

notify ['nəʊtɪfaɪ] vt: to ~ sb (of sth) comunicar (algo) a uno.

notion ['nəʊʃən] n noción f, concepto; (opinion) opinión f; ~s pl (US) mercería.

notorious [nəʊ'tɔːrɪəs] a notorio.

notwithstanding [nɒtwɪθ'stændɪŋ] ad no obstante, sin embargo; ~ **this** a pesar de esto.

nougat ['nuːgɑː] n turrón m.

nought [nɔːt] n cero.

noun [naʊn] n nombre m, sustantivo.

nourish ['nʌrɪʃ] vt nutrir; ~**ing** a nutritivo; ~**ment** n alimento, sustento.

novel ['nɒvl] n novela // a (new) nuevo, original; (unexpected) insólito; ~**ist** n novelista m/f; ~**ty** n novedad f.

November [nəʊ'vɛmbə*] n noviembre m.

novice ['nɒvɪs] n principiante m/f, novato/a; (REL) novicio/a.

now [naʊ] ad (at the present time) ahora; (these days) actualmente, hoy día // conj: ~ (that) ya que, ahora que; right ~ ahora mismo; by ~ ya; just ~: I'll do it just ~ ahora mismo lo hago; ~ and then, ~ and again de vez en cuando; from ~ on de ahora en adelante; ~**adays** ['naʊədeɪz] ad hoy (en) día, actualmente.

nowhere ['nəʊwɛə*] ad (direction) a ninguna parte; (location) en ninguna parte.

nozzle ['nɒzl] n boquilla.

nuance ['njuːɑːns] n matiz m.

nuclear ['njuːklɪə*] a nuclear.

nucleus ['njuːklɪəs], pl -**lei** [-lɪaɪ] n núcleo.

nude [njuːd] a, n desnudo/a m/f; in the ~ desnudo.

nudge [nʌdʒ] vt dar un codazo a.

nudist ['njuːdɪst] n nudista m/f.

nudity ['njuːdɪtɪ] n desnudez f.

nuisance ['njuːsns] n molestia, fastidio; (person) pesado, latoso; what a ~! ¡qué lata!

nuke ['njuːk] (col) n bomba atómica // vt atacar con arma nuclear.

null [nʌl] a: ~ and void nulo y sin efecto.

numb [nʌm] a entumecido; (fig) insensible // vt entumecer, entorpecer.

number ['nʌmbə*] n (gen) número; (numeral) número, cifra // vt (pages etc) numerar, poner número a; (amount to) sumar, ascender a; to be ~**ed** among figurar entre; a ~ of varios, algunos; they were ten in ~ eran diez; ~ **plate** n (Brit) matrícula, placa.

numeral ['njuːmərəl] n número, cifra.

numerate ['njuːmərɪt] a competente en la aritmética.

numerical [njuː'mɛrɪkl] a numérico.

numerous ['njuːmərəs] a numeroso, muchos.

nun [nʌn] n monja, religiosa.

nurse [nɜːs] n enfermero/a (nanny) niñera // vt (patient) cuidar, atender; (baby: Brit) mecer; (: US) criar, amamantar.

nursery ['nɜːsərɪ] n (institution)

guardería infantil; (room) cuarto de los niños; (for plants) criadero, semillero; ~ **rhyme** n canción f infantil; ~ **school** n parvulario, escuela de párvulos; ~ **slope** n (Brit SKI) cuesta para principiantes.

nursing ['nɜ:sɪŋ] n (profession) profesión f de enfermera; (care) asistencia, cuidado; ~ **home** n clínica de reposo.

nurture ['nɜ:tʃə*] vt (child, plant) alimentar, nutrir.

nut [nʌt] n (TECH) tuerca; (BOT) nuez f; ~**crackers** npl cascanueces m inv; ~**s** a (col) loco.

nutmeg ['nʌtmeg] n nuez f moscada.

nutritious [nju:'trɪʃəs] a nutritivo, rico.

nutshell ['nʌtʃel] n cáscara de nuez; **in a** ~ en resumidas cuentas.

nylon ['naɪlən] n nilón m // a de nilón.

O

oak [əuk] n roble m // a de roble.

O.A.P. abbr = **old-age pensioner**.

oar [ɔ:*] n remo.

oasis [əu'eɪsɪs], pl **-ses** [-siːz] n oasis m inv.

oath [əuθ] n juramento; (swear word) palabrota; **on** (Brit) or **under** ~ bajo juramento.

oatmeal ['əutmiːl] n harina de avena.

oats [əuts] n avena.

obedience [ə'biːdɪəns] n obediencia, cumplimiento; (ritual) práctica.

obedient [ə'biːdɪənt] a obediente.

obey [ə'beɪ] vt obedecer; (instructions, regulations) cumplir.

obituary [ə'bɪtjuərɪ] n necrología.

object ['ɔbdʒɪkt] n (gen) objeto; (purpose) objeto, propósito; (LING) complemento // vi [əb'dʒɛkt]: **to** ~ **to** (attitude) protestar contra; (proposal) oponerse a; **expense is no** ~ no importa cuánto cuesta; **I** ~! ¡yo protesto!; **to** ~ **that** objetar que; ~**ion** [əb'dʒɛkʃən] n protesta; **I**

have no ~**ion to...** no tengo inconveniente en que...; ~**ionable** [əb'dʒɛkʃənəbl] a (gen) desagradable; (conduct) censurable; ~**ive** a, n objetivo.

obligation [ɔblɪ'geɪʃən] n obligación f; (debt) deber m; **without** ~ sin compromiso.

oblige [ə'blaɪdʒ] vt (do a favour for) complacer, hacer un favor a; **to** ~ **sb to do sth** forzar or obligar a uno a hacer algo; **to be** ~**d to sb for sth** estarle agradecido a uno por algo; **obliging** a servicial, atento.

oblique [ə'bliːk] a oblicuo; (allusion) indirecto.

obliterate [ə'blɪtəreɪt] vt borrar.

oblivion [ə'blɪvɪən] n olvido; **oblivious** [-ɪəs] a: **oblivious of** inconsciente de.

oblong ['ɔblɔŋ] a rectangular // n rectángulo.

obnoxious [əb'nɔkʃəs] a odioso, detestable; (smell) nauseabundo.

oboe ['əubəu] n oboe m.

obscene [əb'siːn] a obsceno.

obscure [əb'skjuə*] a oscuro // vt oscurecer; (hide: sun) esconder.

observance [əb'zɜːvns] n observancia, cumplimiento; (ritual) práctica.

observant [əb'zɜːvnt] a observador(a).

observation [ɔbzə'veɪʃən] n observación f; (by police etc) vigilancia; (MED) examen m.

observatory [əb'zɜːvətrɪ] n observatorio.

observe [əb'zɜːv] vt (gen) observar; (rule) cumplir; ~**r** n observador(a) m/f.

obsess [əb'sɛs] vt obsesionar; ~**ive** a obsesivo; obsesionante.

obsolescence [ɔbsə'lɛsns] n obsolescencia.

obsolete ['ɔbsəliːt] a: **to be** ~ estar en desuso.

obstacle ['ɔbstəkl] n obstáculo; (nuisance) estorbo; ~ **race** n carrera de obstáculos.

obstinate ['ɔbstɪnɪt] a terco, porfiado; (determined) tenaz.

obstruct [əb'strʌkt] vt (block) obstruir; (hinder) estorbar, obstaculizar; ~**ion** [əb'strʌkʃən] n obstrucción f; estorbo, obstáculo.

obtain [əb'teɪn] vt (get) obtener; (achieve) conseguir; ~**able** a asequible.

obtrusive [əb'truːsɪv] a (person) importuno, entrometido; (building etc) demasiado visible.

obvious ['ɔbvɪəs] a (clear) obvio, evidente; (unsubtle) poco sutil; ~**ly** ad evidentemente, naturalmente.

occasion [ə'keɪʒən] n oportunidad f, ocasión f; (event) acontecimiento // vt ocasionar, causar; ~**al** a poco frecuente, ocasional; ~**ally** ad de vez en cuando.

occupant ['ɔkjupənt] n (of house) inquilino/a; (of car) ocupante m/f.

occupation [ɔkju'peɪʃən] n (of house) tenencia; (job) trabajo; (: calling) oficio, ~**al hazard** n riesgo profesional.

occupier ['ɔkjupaɪə*] n inquilino/a.

occupy ['ɔkjupaɪ] vt (seat, post, time) ocupar; (house) habitar; to o.s. with or by doing (as job) dedicarse a hacer; (to pass time) pasar el tiempo haciendo.

occur [ə'kə:*] vi pasar, suceder; to ~ to sb ocurrírsele a uno; ~**rence** [ə'kʌrəns] n acontecimiento.

ocean ['əuʃən] n océano; ~**-going** a de alta mar.

ochre, (US) **ocher** ['əukə*] n ocre m.

OCR n abbr = optical character recognition/reader.

o'clock [ə'klɔk] ad: it is 5 ~ son las 5.

octave ['ɔktɪv] n octava.

October [ɔk'təubə*] n octubre m.

octopus ['ɔktəpəs] n pulpo.

odd [ɔd] a (strange) extraño, raro; (number) impar; (left over) sobrante, suelto; 60~ 60 y pico; at times de vez en cuando; to be the ~ one out estar de más; ~**s** and

ends npl minucias fpl; ~**ity** n rareza; (person) excéntrico; ~**job bricolaje** m; ~**ly** ad curiosamente, extrañamente; ~**ments** npl (Brit COMM) retales mpl; ~**s** npl (in betting) puntos mpl de ventaja; it makes no ~**s** da lo mismo; at ~**s** reñidos/as.

odometer [ɔ'dɔmɪtə*] n (US) cuentakilómetros m inv.

odour, (US) **odor** ['əudə*] n olor m; (perfume) perfume m.

KEYWORD

of prep 1 (gen) de; **a friend ~ ours** un amigo nuestro; **a boy ~ 10** un chico de 10 años; **that was kind ~ you** muy amable por or de tu parte 2 (expressing quantity, amount, dates etc) de; **a kilo ~ flour** un kilo de harina; **there were 3 ~ them** había tres; **3 ~ us went** tres de nosotros fuimos; **the 5th ~ July** el 5 de julio 3 (from, out of) de; **made ~ wood** (hecho) de madera.

off [ɔf] a, ad (engine) desconectado; (light) apagado; (tap) cerrado; (Brit: food: bad) pasado, malo; (: milk) cortado; (cancelled) cancelado // prep de; **to be ~** (to leave) irse, marcharse; **to be ~ sick** estar enfermo or de baja; **a day ~** un día libre or sin trabajar; **to have an ~ day** tener un día malo; **he had his coat ~** se había quitado el abrigo; **10% ~** (COMM) (con el) 10% de descuento; **5 km ~** (the road) a 5 km (de la carretera); **the coast ~** the coast frente a la costa; **I'm ~ meat** (no longer eat/like it) paso de la carne; **on the ~ chance** por si acaso; ~ **and on** en ocasiones.

offal ['ɔfl] n (Brit CULIN) menudencias fpl.

off-colour ['ɔf'kʌlə*] a (Brit: ill) indispuesto.

offence, (US) **offense** [ə'fɛns] n (crime) delito; (insult) ofensa; **to take ~ at** ofenderse por.

offend [ə'fɛnd] vt (person) ofender; **~er** n delincuente m/f; (against regulations) infractor(a) m/f.

offensive [ə'fɛnsɪv] a ofensivo; (smell etc) repugnante // n (MIL) ofensiva.

offer ['ɔfə*] n (gen) oferta, ofrecimiento; (proposal) propuesta // vt ofrecer; (opportunity) facilitar; **on ~'** (COMM) 'en oferta'; **~ing** n ofrenda.

offhand [ɔf'hænd] a informal // ad de improviso.

office ['ɔfɪs] n (place) oficina; (room) despacho; (position) carga, oficio; **doctor's ~** (US) consultorio; **to take ~** entrar en funciones; **~ automation** n ofimática, buromática; **~ block**, (US) **~ building** n bloque m de oficinas; **~ hours** npl horas fpl de oficina; (US MED) horas fpl de consulta.

officer ['ɔfɪsə*] n (MIL etc) oficial m/f; (of organization) director(a) m/f; (also: **police officer**) agente m/f de policía.

office worker n oficinista m/f.

official [ə'fɪʃl] a (authorized) oficial, autorizado // n funcionario, oficial m; **~dom** n burocracia.

offing ['ɔfɪŋ] n: **in the ~** (fig) en perspectiva.

off: ~licence n (Brit: shop) bodega, tienda de vinos y bebidas alcohólicas; **~line** a, ad (COMPUT) fuera de línea; **~peak** a (holiday) de temporada baja; (electricity) de banda económica; **~putting** a (Brit) asqueroso; desalentador(a); **~season** a, ad fuera de temporada.

offset ['ɔfsɛt] (irg: like set) vt (counteract) contrarrestar, compensar.

offshoot ['ɔfʃuːt] n (fig) ramificación f.

offshore [ɔf'ʃɔː*] a (breeze, island) costera; (fishing) de bajura.

offside ['ɔf'saɪd] a (SPORT) fuera de juego; (AUT) del lado izquierdo.

offspring ['ɔfsprɪŋ] n descendencia.

off: ~stage ad entre bastidores; **~-the-peg**, (US) **~-the-rack** ad confeccionado; **~-white** a blanco grisáceo.

often ['ɔfn] ad a menudo, con frecuencia; **how ~ do you go?** ¿cada cuánto vas?

ogle ['əʊgl] vt comerse con los ojos a.

oh [əʊ] excl ¡ah!

oil [ɔɪl] n aceite m; (petroleum) petróleo // vt (machine) engrasar; **~can** n lata de aceite; **~field** n campo petrolífero; **~ filter** n (AUT) filtro de aceite; **~-fired** a que quema aceite combustible; **~ painting** n pintura al óleo; **~ rig** n torre f de perforación; **~skins** npl impermeables mpl de hule, chubasquero sg; **~ tanker** n petrolero; **~ well** n pozo (de petróleo); **~y** a aceitoso; (food) grasiento.

ointment ['ɔɪntmənt] n ungüento.

O.K., okay ['əʊ'keɪ] excl O.K., ¡está bien!, ¡vale! // a bien // vt dar el visto bueno a.

old [əʊld] a viejo; (former) antiguo; **how ~ are you?** ¿cuántos años tienes?, ¿qué edad tienes?; **he's 10 years ~** tiene 10 años; **~er brother** hermano mayor; **~ age** n vejez f; **~age pensioner (O.A.P.)** n (Brit) jubilado/a; **~-fashioned** a anticuado, pasado de moda.

olive ['ɔlɪv] n (fruit) aceituna; (tree) olivo // a (also: **~-green**) verde oliva; **~ oil** n aceite m de oliva.

Olympic [əʊ'lɪmpɪk] a olímpico; **the ~ Games, the ~s** npl las Olimpiadas fpl.

omelet(te) ['ɔmlɪt] n tortilla, tortilla de huevo (LAm).

omen ['əʊmən] n presagio.

ominous ['ɔmɪnəs] a de mal agüero, amenazador(a).

omit [əʊ'mɪt] vt omitir.

KEYWORD

---

on [ɔn] ◆ prep 1 (indicating position) en; sobre; **~ the wall** en la pared;

it's ~ the table está sobre or en la mesa; ~ the left a la izquierda
2 (*indicating means, method, condition etc*): ~ foot a pie; ~ the train/plane (*go*) en tren/avión; (*be*) en el tren/el avión; ~ the radio/television/telephone por or en la radio/televisión/al teléfono; to be ~ drugs drogarse; to be ~ holiday/business estar de vacaciones/en viaje de negocios
3 (*referring to time*): ~ Friday el viernes; ~ Fridays los viernes; ~ June 20th el 20 de junio; a week ~ Friday del viernes en una semana; ~ arrival al llegar; ~ seeing this al ver esto
4 (*about, concerning*) sobre, acerca de; a book ~ physics un libro de or sobre física
♦ *ad* **1** (*referring to dress*): to have one's coat ~ tener or llevar el abrigo puesto; she put her gloves ~ se puso los guantes
2 (*referring to covering*): 'screw the lid ~ tightly' 'cerrar bien la tapa'
3 (*further, continuously*): to walk etc ~ seguir caminando etc
♦ *a* **1** (*functioning, in operation: machine, radio, TV, light*) encendido/a, prendido/a (*LAm*); (: *tap*) abierto/a; (: *brakes*) echado/a, puesto/a; is the meeting still ~? (*in progress; not cancelled*) ¿todavía continúa la reunión?; there's a good film ~ at the cinema ponen una buena película en el cine
2: that's not ~! (*col : not possible*) ¡eso ni hablar!, ¡eso no está bien!; (: *not acceptable*) ¡eso no se hace!

once [wʌns] *ad* una vez; (*formerly*) antiguamente // *conj* una vez que; ~ he had left/it was done una vez que se había marchado/se hizo; at ~ en seguida, inmediatamente; (*simultaneously*) a la vez; ~ a week una vez por semana; ~ more otra vez; ~

and for all de una vez por todas; ~ upon a time érase una vez.
oncoming ['ɔnkʌmɪŋ] *a* (*traffic*) que viene de frente.

one [wʌn] ♦ *num* un(o)/una; ~ hundred and fifty ciento cincuenta; ~ by ~ uno a uno
♦ *a* **1** (*sole*) único; the ~ book which el único libro que; the ~ man who el único que
2 (*same*): they came in the ~ car vinieron en un solo coche
♦ *pron* **1**: this ~ éste/ésta; that ~ ése/ésa; (*more remote*) aquél/aquella; I've already got a (red) ~ ya tengo una/o (roja/o); ~ by ~ uno por uno/a
2: ~ another os (*Sp*), se (+ *el uno al otro, unos a otros etc*); do you two ever see ~ another? ¿vosotros dos os veis alguna vez? (*Sp*), ¿se ven ustedes dos alguna vez?; the boys didn't dare look at ~ another los chicos no se atrevieron a mirarse (el uno al otro); they all kissed ~ another se besaron unos a otros
3 (*impersonal*): ~ never knows nunca se sabe; to cut ~'s finger cortarse el dedo; ~ needs to eat hay que comer.

one: ~-armed bandit *n* máquina tragaperras; ~-day excursion *n* (*US*) billete *m* de ida y vuelta en un día; ~-man *a* (*business*) individual; ~-man band *n* hombre-orquesta *m*; ~-off *n* (*Brit col: event*) acontecimiento único.
oneself [wʌn'sɛlf] *pron* (*reflexive*) se; (*after prep*) sí; (*emphatic*) mismo/a; to hurt ~ hacerse daño; to keep sth for ~ guardarse algo; to talk to ~ hablar solo.
one: ~-sided *a* (*argument*) parcial; ~-to-~ *a* (*relationship*) de dos; ~-upmanship *n* arte *m* de aventajar a los demás.
ongoing ['ɔngəʊɪŋ] *a* continuo.

onion [ˈʌnjən] *n* cebolla.

on-line [ˈɒnlaɪn] *a, ad* (COMPUT) en línea.

onlooker [ˈɒnlukəʳ] *n* espectador(a) *m/f*.

only [ˈəʊnlɪ] *ad* solamente, sólo // *a* único, solo // *conj* solamente que, pero; **an ~ child** un hijo único; **not ~ ...but also...** no sólo ... sino también...

onset [ˈɒnsɛt] *n* comienzo.

onshore [ˈɒnʃɔːʳ] *a* (wind) que sopla del mar hacia la tierra.

onslaught [ˈɒnslɔːt] *n* ataque *m*, embestida.

onto [ˈɒntʊ] *prep* = **on to.**

onus [ˈəʊnəs] *n* responsabilidad *f*.

onward(s) [ˈɒnwəd(z)] *ad* (move) (hacia) adelante.

ooze [uːz] *vi* rezumar.

opaque [əʊˈpeɪk] *a* opaco.

OPEC [ˈəʊpɛk] *n abbr* (= Organization of Petroleum-Exporting Countries) OPEP *f*.

open [ˈəʊpn] *a* abierto; (car) descubierto; (road, view) despejado; (meeting) público; (admiration) manifiesto // *vt* abrir // *vi* (flower, eyes, door, debate) abrirse; (book etc: commence) comenzar; **in the ~** (air) al aire libre; **to ~ on to** *vt fus* (subj: room, door) dar a; **to ~ up** *vt* abrir; (blocked road) despejar // *vi* abrirse, empezar; **~ing** *n* apertura, comienzo; (opportunity) oportunidad *f*; (job) puesto vacante, vacante *f*; **~ly** *ad* abiertamente; **~-minded** *a* imparcial; **~-plan** *a*: **~-plan office** gran oficina sin particiones.

opera [ˈɒpərə] *n* ópera; **~ house** *n* teatro de la ópera.

operate [ˈɒpəreɪt] *vt* (machine) hacer funcionar; (manage) dirigir // *vi* funcionar; (drug) hacer efecto; **to ~ on sb** (MED) operar a uno.

operatic [ɒpəˈrætɪk] *a* de ópera.

operating [ˈɒpəreɪtɪŋ] *a*: **~ table/theatre** mesa/sala de operaciones.

operation [ɒpəˈreɪʃən] *n* (gen) ope-

ración *f*; (of machine) funcionamiento; **to be in ~** estar funcionando *or* en funcionamiento; **to have an ~** (MED) ser operado; **~al** *a* operacional, en buen estado.

operative [ˈɒpərətɪv] *a* (measure) en vigor.

operator [ˈɒpəreɪtəʳ] *n* (of machine) maquinista *m/f*, operario/a, *m/f*; (TEL) operador(a) *m/f*, telefonista *m/f*.

ophthalmic [ɒfˈθælmɪk] *a* oftálmico.

opinion [əˈpɪnjən] *n* (gen) opinión *f*; **in my ~** en mi opinión, a mi juicio; **~ated** *a* testarudo; **~ poll** *n* encuesta, sondeo.

opponent [əˈpəʊnənt] *n* adversario/a, contrincante *m/f*.

opportunist [ɒpəˈtjuːnɪst] *n* oportunista *m/f*.

opportunity [ɒpəˈtjuːnɪtɪ] *n* oportunidad *f*; **to take the ~ of doing** aprovechar la ocasión para hacer.

oppose [əˈpəʊz] *vt* oponerse a; **to be ~d to sth** oponerse a algo; **as ~d to** a diferencia de; **opposing** *a* (side) opuesto, contrario.

opposite [ˈɒpəzɪt] *a* opuesto, contrario; (house etc) de enfrente // *ad* en frente // *prep* en frente de, frente a // *n* lo contrario.

opposition [ɒpəˈzɪʃən] *n* oposición *f*.

oppress [əˈprɛs] *vt* oprimir.

opt [ɒpt] *vi*: **to ~ for** optar por; **to ~ to do** optar por hacer; **to ~ out of** optar por no hacer.

optical [ˈɒptɪkl] *a* óptico; **~ character recognition/reader (OCR)** *n* reconocimiento/lector *m* óptico de caracteres.

optician [ɒpˈtɪʃən] *n* óptico *m/f*.

optimist [ˈɒptɪmɪst] *n* optimista *m/f*; **~ic** [-ˈmɪstɪk] *a* optimista.

optimum [ˈɒptɪməm] *a* óptimo.

option [ˈɒpʃən] *n* opción *f*; **to keep one's ~s open** (fig) mantener las opciones abiertas; **~al** *a* facultativo, discrecional.

or [ɔːʳ] *conj* o; (before o, ho) u; (with negative): **he hasn't seen ~ heard anything** no ha visto ni oído nada; **~**

else si no.

oracle ['ɔrəkl] *n* oráculo.

oral ['ɔːrəl] *a* oral // *n* examen *m* oral.

orange ['ɒrɪndʒ] *n* (*fruit*) naranja // *a* color naranja.

orator ['ɒrətə*] *n* orador(a) *m/f*.

orbit ['ɔːbɪt] *n* órbita // *vt, vi* orbitar.

orchard ['ɔːtʃəd] *n* huerto.

orchestra ['ɔːkɪstrə] *n* orquesta; (*US: seating*) platea; **~l** [-'kestrəl] *a* de orquesta.

orchid ['ɔːkɪd] *n* orquídea.

ordain [ɔː'deɪn] *vt* (*REL*) ordenar, decretar; (*decide*) mandar.

ordeal [ɔː'diːl] *n* experiencia horrorosa.

order ['ɔːdə*] *n* orden *m*; (*command*) orden *f*; (*type, kind*) clase *f*; (*state*) estado; (*COMM*) pedido, encargo // *vt* (*also*: **put in ~**) arreglar, poner en orden; (*COMM*) encargar, pedir; (*command*) mandar, ordenar; **in ~** (*gen*) en orden; (*of document*) en regla; **in** (*working*) **~** en funcionamiento; **in ~ to do** para hacer; **in ~ that** para que; **on ~** (*COMM*) pedido; **to ~ sb to do sth** mandar a uno hacer algo; **~ form** *n* hoja de pedido; **~ly** *n* (*MIL*) ordenanza *m*; (*MED*) enfermero/a (auxiliar) // *a* ordenado.

ordinary ['ɔːdnrɪ] *a* corriente, normal; (*pej*) común y corriente; **out of the ~** fuera de lo común.

ordnance ['ɔːdnəns] *n* (*MIL: unit*) artillería.

ore [ɔː*] *n* mineral *m*.

organ ['ɔːgən] *n* órgano; **~ic** [ɔː'gænɪk] *a* orgánico.

organization [ɔːgənaɪ'zeɪʃən] *n* organización *f*.

organize ['ɔːgənaɪz] *vt* organizar; **~r** *n* organizador(a) *m/f*.

orgasm ['ɔːgæzəm] *n* orgasmo.

orgy ['ɔːdʒɪ] *n* orgía.

Orient ['ɔːrɪənt] *n* Oriente *m*; **oriental** [-'ɛntl] *a* oriental.

origin ['ɒrɪdʒɪn] *n* origen *m*; (*point of departure*) procedencia.

original [ə'rɪdʒɪnl] *a* original; (*first*) primero; (*earlier*) primitivo // *n* original *m*; **~ity** [-'nælɪtɪ] *n* originalidad *f*; **~ly** *ad* (*at first*) al principio; (*with originality*) con originalidad.

originate [ə'rɪdʒɪneɪt] *vi*: **to ~ from, to ~ in** surgir de, tener su origen en.

Orkneys ['ɔːknɪz] *npl*: **the ~** (*also*: **the Orkney Islands**) las Orcadas.

ornament ['ɔːnəmənt] *n* adorno; (*trinket*) chuchería; **~al** [-'mɛntl] *a* decorativo, de adorno.

ornate [ɔː'neɪt] *a* muy ornado, vistoso.

orphan ['ɔːfn] *n* huérfano // *vt*: **to be ~ed** quedar huérfano/a; **~age** *n* orfanato.

orthodox ['ɔːθədɒks] *a* ortodoxo; **~y** *n* ortodoxia.

orthopaedic, (*US*) **orthopedic** [ɔːθə'piːdɪk] *a* ortopédico.

oscillate ['ɒsɪleɪt] *vi* oscilar; (*person*) vacilar.

ostensibly [ɒs'tɛnsɪblɪ] *ad* aparentemente.

ostentatious [ɒstɛn'teɪʃəs] *a* ostentoso.

osteopath ['ɒstɪəpæθ] *n* osteópata *m/f*.

ostracize ['ɒstrəsaɪz] *vt* hacer el vacío a.

ostrich ['ɒstrɪtʃ] *n* avestruz *m*.

other ['ʌðə*] *a* otro // *pron*: **the ~ (one)** el/la otro/a; **~s** (**~ people**) otros; **~ than** (*apart from*) aparte de; **~wise** *ad, conj* de otra manera; (*if not*) si no.

otter ['ɒtə*] *n* nutria.

ouch [autʃ] *excl* ¡ay!

ought [ɔːt], *pt* **ought** *auxiliary vb*: **I ~ to do it** debería hacerlo; **this ~ to have been corrected** esto debiera de haberse corregido; **he ~ to win** (*probability*) debe *or* debiera ganar.

ounce [auns] *n* onza (*28.35g*).

our ['auə*] *a* nuestro; *see also* **my**; **~s** *pron* (el) nuestro/(la) nuestra *etc*; *see also* **mine**; **~selves** *pron* (*reflexive, after prep*) nosotros; (*emphatic*) nosotros mismos; *see* *also* **oneself.**

oust [aust] *vt* desalojar.

out [aut] *ad* fuera, afuera; (*not at home*) fuera (de casa); (*light, fire*) apagado; ~ **there** allí (fuera); **he's** ~ (*absent*) no está, ha salido; **to be** ~ **in one's calculations** equivocarse (en sus cálculos); **to run** ~ salir corriendo; ~ **loud** en alta voz; ~ **of** (*outside*) fuera de; (*because of*: *anger etc*) por; ~ **of petrol** sin gasolina; '~ **of order**' 'no funciona'; ~ **-and-**~ *a* (*liar, thief etc*) redomado, empedernido.

outback ['autbæk] *n* interior *m*.

outboard ['autbɔːd] *a*: ~ **motor** (motor *m*) fuera borda *m*.

outbreak ['autbreik] *n* (*of war*) comienzo, (*of disease*) epidemia, (*of violence etc*) ola.

outburst ['autbəːst] *n* explosión *f*, arranque *m*.

outcast ['autkɑːst] *n* paria *m/f*.

outcome ['autkʌm] *n* resultado.

outcrop ['autkrɔp] *n* (*of rock*) afloramiento.

outcry ['autkrai] *n* protestas *fpl*.

outdated [aut'deitid] *a* anticuado, fuera de moda.

outdo [aut'duː] (*irg*: *like* **do**) *vt* superar.

outdoor [aut'dɔː*] *a* al aire libre.

outdoors [aut'dɔːz] *ad* al aire libre.

outer ['autə*] *a* exterior, externo; ~ **space** *n* espacio exterior.

outfit ['autfit] *n* equipo; (*clothes*) traje *m*; ~**ter's** *n* (*Brit*) sastrería.

outgoing ['autgəuiŋ] *a* (*character*) extrovertido; ~**s** *npl* (*Brit*) gastos *mpl*.

outgrow [aut'grəu] (*irg*: *like* **grow**) *vt*: **he has** ~**n his clothes** su ropa le queda pequeña ya.

outhouse ['authaus] *n* dependencia.

outing ['autiŋ] *n* excursión *f*, paseo.

outlandish [aut'lændiʃ] *a* estrafalario.

outlaw ['autlɔː] *n* proscrito.

outlay ['autlei] *n* inversión *f*.

outlet ['autlet] *n* salida; (*of pipe*)

desagüe *m*; (*US ELEC*) toma de corriente; (*for emotion*) desahogo; (*also*: **retail** ~) punto de venta.

outline ['autlain] *n* (*shape*) contorno, perfil *m*; **in** ~ (*fig*) a grandes rasgos.

outlive [aut'liv] *vt* sobrevivir a.

outlook ['autluk] *n* perspectiva; (*opinion*) punto de vista.

outlying ['autlaiiŋ] *a* remoto, aislado.

outmoded [aut'məudid] *a* anticuado, pasado de moda.

outnumber [aut'nʌmbə*] *vt* exceder en número.

out-of-date [autəv'deit] *a* (*passport*) caducado; (*clothes*) pasado de moda.

out-of-the-way [autəvðə'wei] *a* (*place*) apartado.

outpatient ['autpeiʃənt] *n* paciente *m/f* externo/a.

outpost ['autpəust] *n* puesto avanzado.

output ['autput] *n* (volumen *m* de) producción *f*, rendimiento; (*COMPUT*) salida.

outrage ['autreidʒ] *n* (*scandal*) escándalo; (*atrocity*) atrocidad *f* // *vt* ultrajar; ~**ous** [-'reidʒəs] *a* monstruoso.

outright [aut'rait] *ad* (*win*) de manera absoluta; (*be killed*) en el acto; (*completely*) completamente // *a* ['autrait] completo.

outset ['autset] *n* principio.

outside [aut'said] *n* exterior *m* // *a* exterior, externo // *ad* fuera // *prep* fuera de; (*beyond*) más allá de; **at the** ~ (*fig*) a lo sumo; ~ **lane** *n* (*AUT*: *in Britain*) carril *m* de la derecha; ~**-left/right** *n* (*FOOTBALL*) extremo izquierdo/derecho; ~ **line** *n* (*TEL*) línea (exterior); ~**r** *n* (*stranger*) extraño, forastero.

outsize ['autsaiz] *a* (*clothes*) de talla grande.

outskirts ['autskəːts] *npl* alrededores *mpl*, afueras *fpl*.

outspoken [aut'spəukən] *a* muy franco.

outstanding [aut'stændɪŋ] a excepcional, destacado; (unfinished) pendiente.

outstay [aut'steɪ] vt: to ~ one's welcome quedarse más de la cuenta.

outstretched [aut'stretʃt] a (hand) extendido.

outstrip [aut'strɪp] vt (competitors, demand) dejar atrás, aventajar.

out-tray ['auttreɪ] n bandeja de salida.

outward ['autwəd] a (sign, appearances) externo; (journey) de ida; ~ly ad por fuera.

outweigh [aut'weɪ] vt pesar más que.

outwit [aut'wɪt] vt ser más listo que.

oval ['əuvl] a ovalado // n óvalo.

ovary ['əuvərɪ] n ovario.

oven ['ʌvn] n horno; ~proof a resistente al horno.

over ['əuvə*] ad encima, por encima // a (or ad) (finished) terminado; (surplus) de sobra // prep por encima de; (above) sobre; (on the other side of) al otro lado de; (more than) más de; (during) durante; ~ here (por) aquí; ~ there (por) allí or allá; all ~ (everywhere) por todas partes; ~ and ~ (again) una y otra vez; ~ and above además de; to ask sb ~ invitar a uno a casa; to bend ~ inclinarse.

overall ['əuvərɔːl] a (length) total; (study) de conjunto // ad [əuvər'ɔːl] en conjunto // n (Brit) guardapolvo; ~s npl mono sg, overol msg (LAm).

overawe [əuvər'ɔː] vt: to be ~d (by) quedar impresionado (con).

overbalance [əuvə'bæləns] vi perder el equilibrio.

overbearing [əuvə'beərɪŋ] a autoritario, imperioso.

overboard ['əuvəbɔːd] ad (NAUT) por la borda.

overbook [əuvə'buk] vt sobrereservar.

overcast ['əuvəkɑːst] a encapotado.

overcharge [əuvə'tʃɑːdʒ] vt: to ~ sb cobrar un precio excesivo a uno.

overcoat ['əuvəkəut] n abrigo, sobretodo.

overcome [əuvə'kʌm] (irg: like come) vt (gen) vencer; (difficulty) superar.

overcrowded [əuvə'kraudɪd] a atestado de gente; (city, country) superpoblado.

overdo [əuvə'duː] (irg: like do) vt exagerar; (overcook) cocer demasiado.

overdose ['əuvədəus] n sobredosis f inv.

overdraft ['əuvədrɑːft] n saldo deudor.

overdrawn [əuvə'drɔːn] a (account) en descubierto.

overdue [əuvə'djuː] a retrasado; (recognition) tardío.

overestimate [əuvər'estɪmeɪt] vt sobrestimar.

overflow [əuvə'fləu] vi desbordarse // n ['əuvəfləu] (excess) exceso; (of river) desbordamiento; (also: ~ pipe) (cañería de) desagüe m.

overgrown [əuvə'grəun] a (garden) invadido por la vegetación.

overhaul [əuvə'hɔːl] vt revisar, reparar // n ['əuvəhɔːl] revisión f.

overhead [əuvə'hed] ad por arriba or encima // a ['əuvəhed] (cable) aéreo; (railway) elevado, aéreo // n (US) = ~s; ~s npl gastos mpl generales.

overhear [əuvə'hɪə*] (irg: like hear) vt oír por casualidad.

overheat [əuvə'hiːt] vi (engine) recalentarse.

overjoyed [əuvə'dʒɔɪd] a encantado, lleno de alegría.

overkill ['əuvəkɪl] n: that would be ~ eso sería sobrepasarse.

overland [əuvə'lænd] a, ad por tierra.

overlap [əuvə'læp] vi traslaparse.

overleaf [əuvə'liːf] ad al dorso.

overload [əuvə'ləud] vt sobrecargar.

overlook [əuvə'luk] vt (have view of) dar a, tener vistas a; (miss) pasar por alto; (forgive) hacer la vista gorda a.

overnight [əuvə'naɪt] ad durante la noche; (fig) de la noche a la mañana // a de noche; **to stay** ~ pasar la noche.

overpass ['əuvəpɑːs] n (US) paso superior.

overpower [əuvə'pauə*] vt dominar; (fig) embargar; ~**ing** a (heat) agobiante; (smell) penetrante.

overrate [əuvə'reɪt] vt sobreestimar.

override [əuvə'raɪd] (irg: like ride) vt (order, objection) no hacer caso de; **overriding** a predominante.

overrule [əuvə'ruːl] vt (decision) anular; (claim) denegar.

overrun [əuvə'rʌn] (irg: like run) vt (country) invadir; (time limit) rebasar, exceder.

overseas [əuvə'siːz] ad en ultramar; (abroad) en el extranjero // a (trade) exterior; (visitor) extranjero.

overseer ['əuvəsɪə*] n (in factory) superintendente m/f; (foreman) capataz m.

overshadow [əuvə'ʃædəu] vt (fig) eclipsar.

overshoot [əuvə'ʃuːt] (irg: like shoot) vt excederse.

oversight ['əuvəsaɪt] n descuido.

oversleep [əuvə'sliːp] (irg: like sleep) vi quedarse dormido.

overspill ['əuvəspɪl] n exceso de población.

overstep [əuvə'step] vt: **to** ~ **the mark** pasarse de la raya.

overt [əu'vɜːt] a abierto.

overtake [əuvə'teɪk] (irg: like take) vt sobrepasar; (Brit AUT) adelantar.

overthrow [əuvə'θrəu] (irg: like throw) vt (government) derrocar.

overtime ['əuvətaɪm] n horas fpl extraordinarias.

overtone ['əuvətəun] n (fig) tono.

overture ['əuvətʃuə*] n (MUS) obertura; (fig) preludio.

overturn [əuvə'tɜːn] vt, vi volcar.

overweight [əuvə'weɪt] a demasiado gordo or pesado.

overwhelm [əuvə'welm] vt aplas-

tar; ~**ing** a (victory, defeat) arrollador(a); (desire) irresistible.

overwork [əuvə'wɜːk] n trabajo excesivo // vi trabajar demasiado.

overwrought [əuvə'rɔːt] a sobreexcitado.

owe [əu] vt deber; **to** ~ **sb sth, to** ~ **sth to sb** deber algo a uno; **owing to** prep debido a, por causa de.

owl [aul] n búho, lechuza.

own [əun] vt tener, poseer // a propio; **a room of my** ~ una habitación propia; **to get one's** ~ **back** tomar revancha; **on one's** ~ solo, a solas; **to** ~ **up** vi confesar; ~**er** n dueño/a; ~**ership** n posesión f.

ox [ɔks], pl ~**en** ['ɔksn] n buey m.

oxtail ['ɔksteɪl] n: ~ **soup** sopa de rabo de buey.

oxygen ['ɔksɪdʒən] n oxígeno; ~ **mask/tent** n máscara/tienda de oxígeno.

oyster ['ɔɪstə*] n ostra.

oz. abbr = **ounce(s)**.

ozone ['əuzəun] n: ~ **layer** capa de ozono or ozónica.

P

p [piː] abbr = **penny, pence**.

P.A. n abbr = **personal assistant; public address system**.

p.a. abbr = **per annum**.

pa [pɑː] n (col) papá m.

pace [peɪs] n paso; (rhythm) ritmo // vi: **to** ~ **up and down** pasearse de un lado a otro; **to keep** ~ **with** llevar el mismo paso que; (events) mantenerse a la altura de or al corriente de; ~**maker** n (MED) regulador m cardíaco, marcapasos m inv.

pacific [pə'sɪfɪk] a pacífico // n: **the P**~ **(Ocean)** el Océano m Pacífico.

pacify ['pæsɪfaɪ] vt (soothe) apaciguar; (country) pacificar.

pack [pæk] n (packet) paquete m; (of hounds) jauría; (of thieves etc) manada, bando; (of cards) baraja;

(*bundle*) fardo; (*US: of cigarettes*) paquete *m* // *vt* (*wrap*) empaquetar; (*fill*) llenar; (*in suitcase etc*) meter, poner; (*cram*) llenar, atestar; (*fig: meeting etc*) llenar de partidarios; **to ~** (*one's bags*) hacerse la maleta; **to ~ sb off** despachar a uno; **~ it in!** (*col*) ¡déjalo!

package ['pækɪdʒ] *n* paquete *m*; (*bulky*) bulto; (*also: ~ deal*) acuerdo global; **~ tour** *n* viaje *m* organizado.

packed lunch *n* almuerzo frío.

packet ['pækɪt] *n* paquete *m*.

packing ['pækɪŋ] *n* embalaje *m*; **~ case** *n* cajón *m* de embalaje.

pact [pækt] *n* pacto.

pad [pæd] *n* (*of paper*) bloc *m*; (*cushion*) cojinete *m*; (*launching ~*) plataforma *f* de lanzamiento; (*col: flat*) casa // *vt* rellenar; **~ding** *n* relleno; (*fig*) paja.

paddle ['pædl] *n* (*oar*) canalete *m*; (*US: for table tennis*) raqueta // *vt* impulsar con canalete // *vi* (*with feet*) chapotear; **~ steamer** *n* vapor *m* de ruedas; **paddling pool** *n* (*Brit*) estanque *m* de juegos.

paddock ['pædǝk] *n* corral *m*.

paddy field ['pædɪ-] *n* arrozal *m*.

padlock ['pædlɔk] *n* candado.

paediatrics [piːdɪ'ætrɪks] *n* pediatría.

pagan ['peɪgǝn] *a*, *n* pagano/a *m/f*.

page [peɪdʒ] *n* (*of book*) página; (*of newspaper*) plana; (*also: ~ boy*) paje *m* // *vt* (*in hotel etc*) llamar por altavoz *m*.

pageant ['pædʒǝnt] *n* (*procession*) desfile *m*; (*show*) espectáculo *m*; **~ry** *n* pompa.

paid [peɪd] *pt*, *pp of* **pay** // *a* (*work*) remunerado; (*official*) asalariado; **to put ~ to** (*Brit*) acabar con.

pail [peɪl] *n* cubo, balde *m*.

pain [peɪn] *n* dolor *m*; **to be in ~** sufrir; **to take ~s over/to do sth** tomarse grandes molestias con/en hacer algo; **~ed** *a* (*expression*) afligido; **~ful** *a* doloroso; (*difficult*) peno-

so; (*disagreeable*) desagradable; **~fully** *ad* (*fig: very*) terriblemente; **~killer** *n* analgésico; **~less** *a* que no causa dolor; **~staking** ['peɪnzteɪkɪŋ] *a* (*person*) concienzudo, esmerado.

paint [peɪnt] *n* pintura // *vt* pintar; **to ~ the door blue** pintar la puerta de azul; **~brush** *n* (*artist's*) pincel *m*; (*decorator's*) brocha; **~er** *n* pintor(a) *m/f*; **~ing** *n* pintura; **~work** *n* pintura.

pair [pɛǝ*] *n* (*of shoes, gloves etc*) par *m*; (*of people*) pareja; **a ~ of scissors** unas tijeras; **a ~ of trousers** unos pantalones, un pantalón.

pajamas [pɪ'dʒɑːmǝz] *npl* (*US*) pijama *msg*.

Pakistan [pɑːkɪ'stɑːn] *n* Paquistán // *~i a*, *n* paquistaní *m/f*.

pal [pæl] *n* (*col*) compinche *m*, compañero/a.

palace ['pælǝs] *n* palacio.

palatable ['pælɪtǝbl] *a* sabroso; (*acceptable*) aceptable.

palate ['pælɪt] *n* paladar *m*.

palatial [pǝ'leɪʃǝl] *a* (*surroundings, residence*) suntuoso, espléndido.

palaver [pǝ'lɑːvǝ*] *n* (*fuss*) lío.

pale [peɪl] *a* (*gen*) pálido; (*colour*) claro // *n*: **to be beyond the ~** pasarse de la raya; **to grow ~** palidecer.

Palestine ['pælɪstaɪn] *n* Palestina; **Palestinian** [-'tɪnɪǝn] *a*, *n* palestino/a *m/f*.

palette ['pælɪt] *n* paleta.

paling ['peɪlɪŋ] *n* (*stake*) estaca; (*fence*) valla.

pall [pɔːl] *n* (*of smoke*) capa (de humo) // *vi* perder el sabor.

pallet ['pælɪt] *n* (*for goods*) pallet *m*.

pallor ['pælǝ*] *n* palidez *f*.

pallid ['pælɪd] *a* pálido.

palm [pɑːm] *n* (*ANAT*) palma; (*also: ~ tree*) palmera, palma // *vt*: **to ~ sth off on sb** (*Brit col*) encajar algo a uno; **P~ Sunday** *n* Domingo de Ramos.

palpable ['pælpǝbl] *a* palpable.

palpitation [pælpɪ'teɪʃən] n palpitación f; to have ~s tener vahídos.

paltry ['pɔːltrɪ] a (quantity) irrisorio; (person) insignificante.

pamper ['pæmpə*] vt mimar.

pamphlet ['pæmflət] n folleto.

pan [pæn] n (also: sauce~) cacerola, cazuela, olla; (also: frying ~) sartén m; (of lavatory) taza f // vi (CINEMA) tomar panorámicas.

panache [pə'næʃ] n: with ~ con estilo.

Panama ['pænəmɑː] n Panamá m; the ~ Canal el Canal de Panamá.

pancake ['pænkeɪk] n crepe f.

panda ['pændə] n panda m; ~ car n (Brit) coche m Z.

pandemonium [pændɪ'məunɪəm] n: there was ~ se armó un tremendo jaleo.

pander ['pændə*] vi: to ~ to complacer a.

pane [peɪn] n cristal m.

panel ['pænl] n (of wood) panel m; (of cloth) paño; (RADIO, TV) panel m de invitados; ~ling, (US) ~ing n paneles mpl.

pang [pæŋ] n: ~s of conscience remordimiento sg; ~s of hunger dolores mpl del hambre.

panic ['pænɪk] n (terror m) pánico // vi dejarse llevar por el pánico; ~ky a (person) asustadizo; ~-stricken a preso de pánico.

pansy ['pænzɪ] n (BOT) pensamiento; (col: pej) maricón m.

pant [pænt] vi jadear.

panther ['pænθə*] n pantera.

panties ['pæntɪz] npl bragas fpl, pantis mpl.

pantihose ['pæntɪhəuz] n (US) pantimedias fpl.

pantomime ['pæntəmaɪm] n (Brit) revista musical representada en Navidad, basada en cuentos de hadas.

pantry ['pæntrɪ] n despensa.

pants [pænts] n (Brit: underwear: woman's) bragas fpl; (: man's) calzoncillos mpl; (US: trousers) pantalones mpl.

papal ['peɪpəl] a papal.

paper ['peɪpə*] n papel m; (also: news~) periódico, diario; (study, article) artículo; (exam) examen m // a de papel // vt empapelar, tapizar (LAm); (identity) ~s npl papeles mpl, documentos mpl; ~back n libro de bolsillo; ~ bag n bolsa de papel; ~ clip n clip m; ~ hankie n pañuelo de papel; ~weight n pisapapeles m inv; ~work n trabajo administrativo; (pej) papeleo.

papier-mâché ['pæpɪeɪ'mæʃeɪ] n cartón m piedra.

paprika ['pæprɪkə] n pimienta húngara or roja.

par [pɑː*] n par f; (GOLF) par m; to be on a ~ with estar a la par con.

parable ['pærəbl] n parábola.

parachute ['pærəʃuːt] n paracaídas m inv // vi lanzarse en paracaídas.

parade [pə'reɪd] n desfile m // vt (gen) recorrer, desfilar por; (show off) hacer alarde de // vi desfilar; (MIL) pasar revista.

paradise ['pærədaɪs] n paraíso.

paradox ['pærədɔks] n paradoja; ~ically [-'dɔksɪklɪ] ad paradójicamente.

paraffin ['pærəfɪn] n (Brit): ~ (oil) parafina.

paragon ['pærəgən] n modelo.

paragraph ['pærəgrɑːf] n párrafo.

Paraguay ['pærəgwaɪ] n Paraguay m.

parallel ['pærəlel] a en paralelo; (fig) semejante // n (line) paralela; (fig, GEO) paralelo.

paralysis [pə'rælɪsɪs] n parálisis f inv.

paralyze ['pærəlaɪz] vt paralizar.

paramedic [pærə'medɪk] n (US) ambulanciero/a.

paramount ['pærəmaunt] a: of ~ importance de suma importancia.

paranoid ['pærənɔɪd] a (person, feeling) paranoico.

paraphernalia [pærəfə'neɪlɪə] n (gear) avíos mpl.

parasite ['pærəsaɪt] n parásito/a.

parasol ['pærəsɒl] n sombrilla, quitasol m.

paratrooper ['pærətru:pə*] n paracaidista m/f.

parcel ['pɑ:sl] n paquete m // vt (also: ~ up) empaquetar, embalar.

parch [pɑ:tʃ] vt secar, resecar; ~**ed** a (person) muerto de sed.

parchment ['pɑ:tʃmənt] n pergamino.

pardon ['pɑ:dn] n perdón m; (LAW) indulto // vt perdonar; indultar; ~ me!, I beg your ~! ¡perdone usted!; (I beg your) ~?, (US) ~ me? ¿cómo?

parent ['pɛərənt] n: ~s npl padres mpl; ~al [pə'rɛntl] a paternal/maternal.

parenthesis [pə'rɛnθɪsɪs], pl -theses [-θɪsi:z] n paréntesis m inv.

Paris ['pærɪs] n París m.

parish ['pærɪʃ] n parroquia.

parity ['pærɪtɪ] n paridad f, igualdad f.

park [pɑ:k] n parque m // vt aparcar, estacionar // vi aparcar, estacionarse.

parking ['pɑ:kɪŋ] n aparcamiento, estacionamiento; 'no ~' 'prohibido estacionarse'; ~ **lot** n (US) parking m; ~ **meter** n parquímetro; ~ **ticket** n multa de aparcamiento.

parlance ['pɑ:ləns] n lenguaje m.

parliament ['pɑ:ləmənt] n parlamento; (Spanish) Cortes fpl; ~**ary** [-'mɛntərɪ] a parlamentario.

parlour, (US) **parlor** ['pɑ:lə*] n sala de recibo, salón m, living (LAm).

parochial [pə'rəukɪəl] a parroquial; (pej) de miras estrechas.

parody ['pærədɪ] n parodia.

parole [pə'rəul] n: on ~ libre bajo palabra.

parquet ['pɑ:keɪ] n: ~ **floor(ing)** n parquet m.

parrot ['pærət] n loro, papagayo.

parry ['pærɪ] vt parar.

parsimonious [pɑ:sɪ'məunɪəs] a tacaño.

parsley ['pɑ:slɪ] n perejil m.

parsnip ['pɑ:snɪp] n chirivía.

parson ['pɑ:sn] n cura m.

part [pɑ:t] n (gen, MUS) parte f; (bit) trozo; (of machine) pieza; (THEATRE) papel m; (of serial) entrega; (US: in hair) raya // ad = **partly** // vt separar; (break) partir // vi (people) separarse; (roads) bifurcarse; (crowd) apartarse; (break) romperse; **to take ~ in** participar or tomar parte en; **to take sth in good ~** tomar algo en buena parte; **to take sb's ~** defender a uno; **for my ~** por mi parte; **for the most ~** en su mayor parte; (people) en su mayoría; **to ~ with** vt fus ceder, entregar; (money) pagar; (get rid of) deshacerse de; ~ **exchange** n (Brit): **in ~ exchange** como parte del pago.

partial ['pɑ:ʃl] a parcial; **to be ~ to** ser aficionado a.

participant [pɑ:'tɪsɪpənt] n (in competition) concursante m/f.

participate [pɑ:'tɪsɪpeɪt] vi: **to ~ in** participar en; **participation** ['peɪʃən] n participación f.

participle ['pɑ:tɪsɪpl] n participio.

particle ['pɑ:tɪkl] n partícula; (of dust) grano; (fig) pizca.

particular [pə'tɪkjulə*] a (special) particular; (concrete) concreto; (given) determinado; (detailed) detallado, minucioso; (fussy) quisquilloso, exigente; ~s npl (information) datos mpl, detalles mpl; (details) pormenores mpl; **in ~** en particular; ~**ly** ad especialmente, en particular.

parting ['pɑ:tɪŋ] n (act of) separación f; (farewell) despedida; (Brit: in hair) raya // a de despedida.

partisan [pɑ:tɪ'zæn] a, n partidario/a.

partition [pɑ:'tɪʃən] n (POL) división f; (wall) tabique m.

partly ['pɑ:tlɪ] ad en parte.

partner ['pɑ:tnə*] n (COMM) socio/a; (SPORT, at dance) pareja; (spouse) cónyuge m/f; (friend etc) compañero/a // vt acompañar; ~**ship** n (gen) asociación f; (COMM) sociedad f.

partridge ['pɑːtrɪdʒ] n perdiz f.

part-time ['pɑːt'taɪm] a, ad a tiempo parcial.

party ['pɑːtɪ] n (POL) partido; (celebration) fiesta; (group) grupo; (LAW) parte f, interesado a (POL) de partido; (dress etc) de fiesta, de gala; ~ **line** n (TEL) línea compartida.

pass [pɑːs] vt (time, object) pasar; (place) pasar por; (exam) aprobar; (overtake, surpass) rebasar; (approve) aprobar // vi pasar; (SCOL) aprobar, ser aprobado // n (permit) permiso; (membership card) carnet m; (in mountains) puerto, desfiladero; (SPORT) pase m; (SCOL: also: ~ **mark**): **to get a ~ in** aprobar en; **to ~ sth through sth** pasar algo por algo; **to make a ~ at sb** (col) hacer proposiciones a uno; **to ~ away** vi fallecer; **to ~ by** vi pasar // vt (ignore) pasar por alto; **to ~ for** pasar por; **to ~ on** vt transmitir; **to ~ out** vi desmayarse; **to ~ up** vt (opportunity) renunciar a; ~**able** a (road) transitable; (tolerable) pasable.

passage ['pæsɪdʒ] n (also: ~**way**) pasillo; (act of passing) tránsito; (fare, in book) pasaje m; (by boat) travesía.

passbook ['pɑːsbuk] n libreta de banco.

passenger ['pæsɪndʒə*] n pasajero/a, viajero/a.

passer-by ['pɑːsə'baɪ] n transeúnte m/f.

passing ['pɑːsɪŋ] a (fleeting) pasajero; **in ~** de paso; ~ **place** n (AUT) apartadero.

passion ['pæʃən] n pasión f; ~**ate** a apasionado.

passive ['pæsɪv] a (also LING) pasivo.

Passover ['pɑːsəuvə*] n Pascua (de los judíos).

passport ['pɑːspɔːt] n pasaporte m; ~ **control** n control m de pasaporte.

password ['pɑːswɜːd] n contraseña.

past [pɑːst] prep (further than) más allá de; (later than) después de // a pasado; (president etc) antiguo // n (time) el pasado; (of person) antecedentes mpl; **he's ~ forty** tiene más de cuarenta años; **for the ~ few/3 days** durante los últimos días/últimos 3 días; **to run ~ sb** pasar a uno corriendo.

pasta ['pæstə] n pasta.

paste [peɪst] n (gen) pasta; (glue) engrudo // vt (stick) pegar; (glue) engomar.

pasteurized ['pæstəraɪzd] a pasteurizado.

pastille ['pæstɪl] n pastilla.

pastime ['pɑːstaɪm] n pasatiempo.

pastor ['pɑːstə*] n pastor m.

pastry ['peɪstrɪ] n (dough) pasta; (cake) pastel m.

pasture ['pɑːstʃə*] n (grass) pasto.

pasty ['pæstɪ] n empanada // a ['peɪstɪ] (complexion) pálido.

pat [pæt] vt dar una palmadita a; (dog etc) acariciar.

patch [pætʃ] n (of material) parche m; (mended part) remiendo; (of land) terreno // vt (clothes) remendar; (to go through) **a bad ~** (pasar por) una mala racha; **to ~ up** vt (mend temporarily) reparar; (quarrel) hacer las paces con; ~**work** n labor m de retazos; ~**y** a desigual.

pâté ['pæteɪ] n paté m.

patent ['peɪtnt] n patente f // vt patentar // a patente, evidente; ~ **leather** n charol m.

paternal [pə'tɜːnl] a paternal; (relation) paterno.

paternity [pə'tɜːnɪtɪ] n paternidad f.

path [pɑːθ] n camino, sendero; (trail, track) pista; (of missile) trayectoria.

pathetic [pə'θetɪk] a (pitiful) patético, lastimoso; (very bad) malísimo; (moving) conmovedor(a).

pathological [pæθə'lɔdʒɪkəl] a patológico.

pathology [pə'θɔlədʒɪ] n patología.

pathos ['peɪθɔs] n patetismo.

pathway ['pɑːθweɪ] n sendero, vereda.

patience ['peɪʃns] n paciencia; (Brit CARDS) solitario.

patient ['peɪʃnt] n paciente m/f // a paciente, sufrido.

patio ['pætɪəʊ] n patio.

patriotic [pætrɪ'ɒtɪk] a patriótico.

patrol [pə'trəʊl] n patrulla // vt patrullar por; ~ **car** n coche m patrulla; ~**man** n (US) policía m.

patron ['peɪtrən] n (in shop) cliente m/f; (of charity) patrocinador(a) m/f; ~ **of the arts** mecenas m; ~**ize** ['pætrənaɪz] vt (shop) ser cliente de; (look down on) condescender con.

patter ['pætə*] n golpeteo; (sales talk) labia // vi (rain) tamborilear.

pattern ['pætən] n (SEWING) patrón m; (design) dibujo.

paunch [pɔːntʃ] n panza, barriga.

pauper ['pɔːpə*] n pobre m/f.

pause [pɔːz] n pausa; (interval) intérvalo // vi hacer una pausa.

pave [peɪv] vt pavimentar; **to ~ the way for** preparar el terreno para.

pavement ['peɪvmənt] n (Brit) acera, vereda (LAm).

pavilion [pə'vɪlɪən] n pabellón m; (SPORT) caseta.

paving ['peɪvɪŋ] n pavimento, enlosado; ~ **stone** n losa.

paw [pɔː] n pata; (claw) garra.

pawn [pɔːn] n (CHESS) peón m; (fig) instrumento // vt empeñar; ~**broker** n prestamista m/f; ~**shop** n monte de piedad.

pay [peɪ] n paga; (wage etc) sueldo, salario // (vb: pt, pp **paid**) vt pagar // vi pagar; (be profitable) rendir; **to ~ attention (to)** prestar atención (a); **to ~ back** (money) reembolsar; (person) pagar; **to ~ for** vt pagar; **to ~ in** vt ingresar; **to ~ off** vt liquidar // vi (scheme, decision) dar resultado; **to ~ up** vt pagar (de mala gana); ~**able** a pagadero; ~**ee** n portador(a) m/f; ~ **envelope** n (US) =

~ **packet**; ~**ment** n pago; advance ~**ment** anticipo; monthly ~**ment** mensualidad f; ~ **packet** n (Brit) sobre m (de paga); ~-**phone** n teléfono público; ~**roll** n nómina; ~ **slip** n recibo de sueldo.

PC n abbr = **personal computer**.

p.c. abbr = **per cent**.

pea [piː] n guisante m, chícharo (LAm), arveja (LAm).

peace [piːs] n paz f; (calm) paz f, tranquilidad f; ~**able** a pacífico; ~**ful** a (gentle) pacífico; (calm) tranquilo, sosegado.

peach [piːtʃ] n melocotón m, durazno (LAm).

peacock ['piːkɔk] n pavo real.

peak [piːk] n (of mountain: top) cumbre f, cima; (: point) pico; (of cap) visera; (fig) cumbre f; ~ **hours** npl, ~ **period** n horas fpl punta.

peal [piːl] n (of bells) repique m; ~ **of laughter** carcajada.

peanut ['piːnʌt] n cacahuete m, maní m (LAm).

pear [pɛə*] n pera.

pearl [pɜːl] n perla.

peasant ['pɛznt] n campesino/a.

peat [piːt] n turba.

pebble ['pɛbl] n guijarro.

peck [pɛk] vt (also: ~ **at**) picotear; (food) comer sin ganas // n picotazo; (kiss) besito; ~**ing order** n orden m de jerarquía; ~**ish** a (Brit col): **I feel** ~**ish** tengo ganas de picar algo.

peculiar [pɪ'kjuːlɪə*] a (odd) extraño, raro; (typical) propio, característico; ~ **to** propio de; ~**ity** [pɪkjuːlɪ'ærɪtɪ] n peculiaridad f, característica.

pedal ['pɛdl] n pedal m // vi pedalear.

pedantic [pɪ'dæntɪk] a pedante.

peddler ['pɛdlə*] n vendedor(a) m/f ambulante.

pedestal ['pɛdəstl] n pedestal m.

pedestrian [pɪ'dɛstrɪən] n peatón m/ona m/f // a pedestre; ~ **crossing** n (Brit) paso de peatones.

pediatrics [piːdɪ'ætrɪks] n (US) = **paediatrics**.

pedigree ['pedɪgriː] n genealogía; (of animal) raza // cpd (animal) de raza, de casta.

pedlar ['pedlə*] n = peddler.

pee [piː] vi (col) mear.

peek [piːk] vi mirar a hurtadillas.

peel [piːl] n piel f; (of orange, lemon) cáscara; (: removed) peladuras fpl // vt pelar // vi (paint etc) desconcharse; (wallpaper) despegarse, desprenderse.

peep [piːp] n (Brit: look) mirada furtiva; (sound) pío // vi (Brit) piar; to ~ out vi asomar la cabeza; ~hole n mirilla.

peer [pɪə*] vi: to ~ at escudriñar // n (noble) par m; (equal) igual m; ~age n nobleza.

peeved [piːvd] a enojado.

peevish ['piːvɪʃ] a malhumorado.

peg [peg] n clavija; (for coat etc) gancho, colgadero; (Brit: also: clothes ~) pinza; (tent ~) estaca // vt (prices) fijar.

Peking [piː'kɪŋ] n Pekín.

pekinese [piːkɪ'niːz] n pequinés/esa m/f.

pelican ['pelɪkən] n pelícano; ~ crossing n (Brit AUT) paso de peatones señalizado.

pellet ['pelɪt] n bolita; (bullet) perdigón m.

pelmet ['pelmɪt] n galería.

pelt [pelt] vt: to ~ sb with sth arrojarle algo a uno // vi (rain) llover a cántaros // n pellejo.

pen [pen] n pluma; (for sheep) redil m.

penal ['piːnl] a penal; ~ize vt (punish- SPORT) castigar.

penalty ['penltɪ] n (gen) pena; (fine) multa; (SPORT) castigo; ~ (kick) n (FOOTBALL) penalty m.

penance ['penəns] n penitencia.

pence [pens] pl of **penny**.

pencil ['pensl] n lápiz m, lapicero (LAm); ~ case n estuche m; ~ sharpener n sacapuntas m inv.

pendant ['pendnt] n pendiente m.

pending ['pendɪŋ] prep antes de // a

pendiente; ~ the arrival of ... hasta que llegue ...

pendulum ['pendjuləm] n péndulo.

penetrate ['penɪtreɪt] vt penetrar.

penfriend ['penfrend] n (Brit) amigo/a por carta.

penguin ['peŋgwɪn] n pingüino.

penicillin [penɪ'sɪlɪn] n penicilina.

peninsula [pə'nɪnsjulə] n península.

penis ['piːnɪs] n pene m.

penitent ['penɪtnt] a arrepentido; (REL) penitente.

penitentiary [penɪ'tenʃərɪ] n (US) cárcel f, presidio.

penknife ['pennaɪf] n navaja.

pen name n seudónimo.

penniless ['penɪlɪs] a sin dinero.

penny ['penɪ], pl **pennies** ['penɪz] or (Brit) **pence** [pens] n penique m; (US) centavo.

penpal ['penpæl] n amigo/a por carta.

pension ['penʃən] n (allowance, state payment) pensión f; (old-age) jubilación f; ~er n (Brit) jubilado/a.

pensive ['pensɪv] a pensativo; (withdrawn) preocupado.

pentagon ['pentəgən] n: the P~ (US POL) el Pentágono.

Pentecost ['pentɪkɔst] n Pentecostés m.

penthouse ['penthaus] n ático de lujo.

pent-up ['pentʌp] a (feelings) reprimido.

people ['piːpl] npl gente f; (citizens) pueblo sg, ciudadanos mpl // n (nation, race) pueblo, nación f // vt poblar; several ~ came vinieron varias personas; ~ say that... dice la gente que... .

pep [pep] n (col) energía; to ~ up vt animar.

pepper ['pepə*] n (spice) pimienta; (vegetable) pimiento // vt (fig) salpicar; ~mint n menta; (sweet) pastilla de menta.

peptalk ['peptɔːk] n: to give sb a ~ darle a uno una inyección de ánimo.

per [pɜː*] prep por; ~ day/person

por día/persona; ~ **annum** ad al año; ~ **capita** a, ad per capita.
perceive [pə'siːv] vt percibir; (realize) darse cuenta de.
per cent n por ciento.
percentage [pə'sentɪdʒ] n porcentaje m.
perception [pə'sepʃən] n percepción f; (insight) perspicacia; **perceptive** ['-septɪv] a perspicaz.
perch [pɜːtʃ] n (fish) perca; (for bird) percha // vi posarse.
percolator ['pɜːkəleɪtə*] n cafetera de filtro.
perennial [pə'renɪəl] a perenne.
perfect ['pɜːfɪkt] a perfecto // n (also: ~ **tense**) perfecto // vt [pə'fekt] perfeccionar; ~**ly** ad perfectamente.
perforate ['pɜːfəreɪt] vt perforar; **perforation** ['-'reɪʃən] n perforación f.
perform [pə'fɔːm] vt (carry out) realizar, llevar a cabo; (THEATRE) representar; (piece of music) interpretar // vi (THEATRE) actuar; (TECH) funcionar; ~**ance** n (of task) realización f; (of a play) representación f; (of player etc) actuación f; (of car, engine) rendimiento; (of function) desempeño; ~**er** n (actor) actor m, actriz f; (MUS) intérprete m/f; ~**ing** a (animal) amaestrado.
perfume ['pɜːfjuːm] n perfume m.
perfunctory [pə'fʌŋktərɪ] a superficial.
perhaps [pə'hæps] ad quizá(s), tal vez.
peril ['perɪl] n peligro, riesgo.
perimeter [pə'rɪmɪtə*] n perímetro.
period ['pɪərɪəd] n período; (HISTORY) época; (SCOL) clase f; (full stop) punto; (MED) regla // a (costume, furniture) de época; ~**ic** ['-'ɔdɪk] a periódico; ~**ical** ['-'ɔdɪk] n periódico; ~**ically** ['-'ɔdɪklɪ] ad de vez en cuando, cada cierto tiempo.
peripheral [pə'rɪfərəl] a periférico // n (COMPUT) periférico, unidad f periférica.

perish ['perɪʃ] vi perecer; (decay) echarse a perder; ~**able** a perecedero.
perjury ['pɜːdʒərɪ] n (LAW) perjurio.
perk [pɜːk] n extra m; **to** ~ **up** vi (cheer up) animarse; ~**y** a alegre, despabilado.
perm [pɜːm] n permanente f.
permanent ['pɜːmənənt] a permanente.
permeate ['pɜːmɪeɪt] vi penetrar, trascender // vt penetrar, trascender a.
permissible [pə'mɪsɪbl] a permisible, lícito.
permission [pə'mɪʃən] n permiso.
permissive [pə'mɪsɪv] a permisivo.
permit ['pɜːmɪt] n permiso, licencia // vt [pə'mɪt] permitir; (accept) tolerar.
pernicious [pɜː'nɪʃəs] a nocivo; (MED) pernicioso.
perpetrate ['pɜːpɪtreɪt] vt cometer.
perpetual [pə'petjuəl] a perpetuo.
perplex [pə'pleks] vt dejar perplejo.
persecute ['pɜːsɪkjuːt] vt (pursue) perseguir; (harass) acosar.
perseverance [pɜːsɪ'vɪərəns] n perseverancia.
persevere [pɜːsɪ'vɪə*] vi persistir.
Persian ['pɜːʃən] a, n persa m/f; **the** (~) **Gulf** n el Golfo Pérsico.
persist [pə'sɪst] vi: **to** ~ (**in doing sth**) persistir (en hacer algo); ~**ence** n empeño; ~**ent** a persistente; (determined) porfiado; (continuing) constante.
person ['pɜːsn] n persona; **in** ~ en persona; ~**able** a atractivo; ~**al** a personal, individual; (visit) en persona; ~**al assistant** (**P.A.**) n ayudante m/f personal; ~**al column** n anuncios mpl personales; ~**al computer** (**PC**) n computador m personal; ~**ality** ['-'nælɪtɪ] n personalidad f; ~**ally** ad personalmente; ~**ify** ['-'sɔnɪfaɪ] vt encarnar.
personnel [pɜːsə'nel] n personal m.
perspective [pə'spektɪv] n perspectiva.

Perspex ['pɜːspeks] n ® plexiglás m.

perspiration [pɜːspɪ'reɪʃən] n transpiración f.

persuade [pə'sweɪd] vt: to ~ sb to do sth persuadir a uno para que haga algo.

pert [pɜːt] a impertinente, fresco.

pertaining [pə'teɪnɪŋ]: ~ to prep relacionado con.

pertinent ['pɜːtɪnənt] a pertinente, a propósito.

Peru [pə'ruː] n el Perú.

peruse [pə'ruːz] vt leer con detención, examinar.

Peruvian [pə'ruːvɪən] a, n peruano/a m/f.

pervade [pə'veɪd] vt impregnar, infundirse en.

perverse [pə'vɜːs] a perverso; (stubborn) terco; (wayward) travieso.

pervert ['pɜːvɜːt] n pervertido/a // vt [pə'vɜːt] pervertir.

pessimist ['pesɪmɪst] n pesimista m/f; ~**ic** ['mɪstɪk] a pesimista.

pest [pest] n (insect) insecto nocivo; (fig) lata, molestia.

pester ['pestə*] vt molestar, acosar.

pet [pet] n animal m doméstico; (favourite) favorito/a // vt acariciar // vi (col) besuquearse.

petal ['petl] n pétalo.

peter ['piːtə*]: to ~ out vi agotarse, acabarse.

petite [pə'tiːt] a chiquito.

petition [pə'tɪʃən] n petición f.

petrified ['petrɪfaɪd] a horrorizado.

petrol ['petrəl] (Brit) n gasolina; (for lighter) bencina; **two/four-star ~** gasolina normal/súper; ~ **can** n bidón m de gasolina.

petroleum [pə'trəʊlɪəm] n petróleo.

petrol: ~ **pump** n (Brit) (in car) bomba de gasolina; (in garage) surtidor m de gasolina; ~ **station** n (Brit) gasolinera; ~ **tank** n (Brit) depósito de gasolina.

petticoat ['petɪkəʊt] n enaguas fpl.

petty ['petɪ] a (mean) mezquino; (unimportant) insignificante; ~ **cash** n dinero para gastos menores; ~

officer n contramaestre m.

petulant ['petjulənt] a malhumorado.

pew [pjuː] n banco.

pewter ['pjuːtə*] n peltre m.

phantom ['fæntəm] n fantasma m.

pharmacist ['fɑːməsɪst] n farmacéutico/a.

pharmacy ['fɑːməsɪ] n farmacia.

phase [feɪz] n fase f // vt: to ~ sth in/out introducir/retirar algo por etapas.

Ph.D. abbr = Doctor of Philosophy.

pheasant ['feznt] n faisán m.

phenomenon [fə'nɒmɪnən], pl **phenomena** [-nə] n fenómeno.

phial ['faɪəl] n ampolla.

Philippines ['fɪlɪpiːnz]: the ~ las Filipinas.

philosopher [fɪ'lɒsəfə*] n filósofo/a.

philosophy [fɪ'lɒsəfɪ] n filosofía.

phlegm [flem] n flema; ~**atic** [fleg'mætɪk] a flemático.

phobia ['fəʊbjə] n fobia.

phone [fəʊn] n teléfono // vt telefonear, llamar por teléfono; **to be on the** ~ tener teléfono; (be calling) estar hablando por teléfono; **to ~ back** vt, vi volver a llamar; **to ~ up** vt, vi llamar por teléfono; ~ **book** n guía telefónica; ~ **box** o **booth** cabina telefónica; ~ **call** n llamada (telefónica); ~**-in** n (Brit RADIO, TV) programa m de participación telefónica.

phonetics [fə'netɪks] n fonética.

phoney ['fəʊnɪ] a falso // n (person) farsante m/f.

phonograph ['fəʊnəgræf] n (US) fonógrafo, tocadiscos m inv.

phosphate ['fɒsfeɪt] n fosfato.

photo ['fəʊtəʊ] n foto f.

photo... ['fəʊtəʊ] pref: ~**copier** n fotocopiadora; ~**copy** n fotocopia // vt fotocopiar; ~**graph** n fotografía // vt fotografiar; ~**grapher** [fə'tɒgrəfə*] n fotógrafo; ~**graphy** [fə'tɒgrəfɪ] n fotografía.

phrase [freɪz] n frase f // vt expresar; ~ **book** *n* libro de frases.

physical ['fɪzɪkl] *a* físico; ~ **educa-tion** *n* educación *f* física; **~ly** *ad* físicamente.

physician [fɪ'zɪʃən] *n* médico/a.

physicist ['fɪzɪsɪst] *n* físico/a.

physics ['fɪzɪks] *n* física.

physiotherapy [fɪzɪəʊ'θerəpɪ] *n* fisioterapia.

physique [fɪ'ziːk] *n* físico.

pianist ['piːənɪst] *n* pianista *m/f*.

piano [pɪ'ænəʊ] *n* piano.

piccolo ['pɪkələʊ] *n* (*MUS*) flautín *m*.

pick [pɪk] *n* (*tool: also:* ~**axe**) pico, piqueta // *vt* (*select*) elegir, escoger; (*gather*) coger (*Sp*), recoger (*LAm*); (*lock*) abrir con ganzúa; **take your** ~ escoja lo que quiera; **the** ~ **of** lo mejor de; **to** ~ **one's nose/teeth** hurgarse las narices/limpiarse los dientes; **to** ~ **pockets** ratear, ser carterista; **to** ~ **off** *vt* (*kill*) matar uno a uno; **to** ~ **on** *vt fus* (*person*) meterse con; **to** ~ **out** *vt* escoger; (*distinguish*) identificar; **to** ~ **up** *vi* (*improve: sales*) ir mejor; (: *patient*) reponerse; (: *FINANCE*) recobrarse // *vt* (*from floor*) recoger; (*buy*) comprar; (*find*) encontrar; (*learn*) aprender; **to** ~ **up speed** acelerarse; **to** ~ **o.s. up** levantarse.

picket ['pɪkɪt] *n* (*in strike*) piquete *m* // *vt* piquetear; ~ **line** *n* piquete *m*.

pickle ['pɪkl] *n* (*also:* ~**s:** *as condiment*) escabeche *m*; (*fig: mess*) apuro // *vt* encurtir; (*in vinegar*) envinagrar.

pickpocket ['pɪkpɒkɪt] *n* carterista *m/f*.

pickup ['pɪkʌp] *n* (*Brit: on record player*) pickup *m*; (*small truck*) furgoneta.

picnic ['pɪknɪk] *n* merienda // *vi* ir de merienda.

pictorial [pɪk'tɔːrɪəl] *a* pictórico; (*magazine etc*) ilustrado.

picture ['pɪktʃə*] *n* cuadro; (*painting*) pintura; (*photograph*) fotografía; (*film*) película // *vt* pintar; **the** ~**s** (*Brit*) el cine; ~ **book** *n* libro de

dibujos.

picturesque [pɪktʃə'resk] *a* pintoresco.

pie [paɪ] *n* pastel *m*; (*open*) tarta; (*small: of meat*) empanada.

piece [piːs] *n* pedazo, trozo; (*of cake*) trozo; (*item*): **a** ~ **of furniture/ advice** un mueble/un consejo // *vt*: **to** ~ **together** juntar; (*TECH*) armar; **to take to** ~**s** desmontar; ~**meal** *ad* poco a poco; ~**work** *n* trabajo a destajo.

pie chart *n* gráfico de sectores *or* tarta.

pier [pɪə*] *n* muelle *m*, embarcadero.

pierce [pɪəs] *vt* penetrar en; perforar.

piercing ['pɪəsɪŋ] *a* (*cry*) penetrante.

piety ['paɪətɪ] *n* piedad *f*.

pig [pɪg] *n* cerdo, puerco; (*fig*) cochino.

pigeon ['pɪdʒən] *n* paloma; (*as food*) pichón *m*; ~**hole** *n* casilla.

piggy bank ['pɪgɪbæŋk] *n* hucha (*en forma de cerdito*).

pigheaded ['pɪg'hedɪd] *a* terco, testarudo.

pigskin ['pɪgskɪn] *n* piel *f* de cerdo.

pigsty ['pɪgstaɪ] *n* pocilga.

pigtail ['pɪgteɪl] *n* (*girl's*) trenza; (*Chinese, TAUR*) coleta.

pike [paɪk] *n* (*spear*) pica; (*fish*) lucio.

pilchard ['pɪltʃəd] *n* sardina.

pile [paɪl] *n* (*heap*) montón *m*; (*of carpet*) pelo // (*vb: also:* ~ **up**) *vt* amontonar; (*fig*) acumular // *vi* amontonarse; **to** ~ **into** (*car*) meterse en.

piles [paɪlz] *npl* (*MED*) almorranas *fpl*, hemorroides *mpl*.

pile-up ['paɪlʌp] *n* (*AUT*) accidente *m* múltiple.

pilfering ['pɪlfərɪŋ] *n* ratería.

pilgrim ['pɪlgrɪm] *n* peregrino/a; ~**age** *n* peregrinación *f*, romería.

pill [pɪl] *n* píldora; **the** ~ la píldora.

pillage ['pɪlɪdʒ] *vt* pillar, saquear.

pillar ['pɪlə*] *n* (*gen*) pilar *m*; (*concrete*) columna; ~ **box** *n* (*Brit*) buzón m.

pillion ['pıljən] n (of motorcycle) asiento trasero.

pillow ['pıləu] n almohada; **~case** n funda.

pilot ['paılət] n piloto // a (scheme etc) piloto // vt pilotar; (fig) guiar, conducir; **~ light** n piloto.

pimp [pımp] n chulo, cafiche m (LAm).

pimple ['pımpl] n grano.

pin [pın] n alfiler m; (TECH) perno m; (: wooden) clavija // vt prender (con alfiler); sujetar con perno; **~s and needles** npl hormigueo sg; **to ~ sb down** (fig) hacer que uno concrete; **to ~ sth on sb** (fig) colgarle a uno el sambenito de algo.

pinafore ['pınəfɔ:*] n delantal m; **~ dress** n (Brit) mandil m.

pinball ['pınbɔ:l] n fliper m.

pincers ['pınsəz] npl pinzas fpl, tenazas fpl.

pinch [pıntʃ] n pellizco; (of salt etc) pizca // vt pellizcar; (col: steal) birlar // vi (shoe) apretar; **at a ~** en caso de apuro.

pincushion ['pınkuʃən] n acerico.

pine [paın] n (also: **~ tree**) pino // vi: **to ~ for** suspirar por; **to ~ away** vi morirse de pena.

pineapple ['paınæpl] n piña, ananás m.

ping [pıŋ] n (noise) sonido agudo; **~-pong** n ® pingpong m ®.

pink [pıŋk] n rosado, (color de) rosa // a (colour) rosa; (BOT) clavel m, clavellina.

pinnacle ['pınəkl] n cumbre f.

pinpoint ['pınpɔınt] vt precisar.

pint [paınt] n pinta (Brit = 0.57 l; US = 0.47 l); (Brit col: of beer) pinta de cerveza, ≈ jarra (Sp).

pioneer [paıə'nıə*] n pionero/a.

pious ['paıəs] a piadoso, devoto.

pip [pıp] n (seed) pepita; **the ~s** (Brit TEL) la señal.

pipe [paıp] n tubo, caño; (for smoking) pipa // vt conducir en cañerías; **~s** npl (gen) cañería sg; (also:

bag~s) gaita sg; **to ~ down** vi (col) callarse; **~ cleaner** n limpiapipas m inv; **~ dream** n sueño imposible; **~line** n tubería, cañería; (for oil) oleoducto; (for gas) gasoducto; **~r** n (gen) flautista m/f; (with bagpipes) gaitero/a.

piping ['paıpıŋ] ad: **to be ~ hot** estar que quema.

piquant ['pi:kənt] a picante.

pique [pi:k] n pique m, resentimiento.

pirate ['paıərət] n pirata m/f; **~ radio** n (Brit) emisora pirata.

pirouette [pıru'et] n pirueta // vi piruetear.

Pisces ['paısi:z] n Piscis m.

piss [pıs] vi (col) mear; **~ed** a (col: drunk) borracho.

pistol ['pıstl] n pistola.

piston ['pıstən] n pistón m, émbolo.

pit [pıt] n hoyo; (also: **coal ~**) mina; (in garage) foso de inspección; (also: **orchestra ~**) platea // vt: **to ~ A against B** oponer A a B; **~s** npl (AUT) box msg.

pitch [pıtʃ] n (throw) lanzamiento; (MUS) tono; (Brit SPORT) campo, terreno; (tar) brea; (in market etc) puesto // vt (throw) arrojar, lanzar // vi (fall) caer(se); (NAUT) cabecear; **to ~ a tent** montar una tienda de campaña; **~-black** a negro como boca de lobo; **~ed battle** n batalla campal.

pitcher ['pıtʃə*] n cántaro, jarro.

pitchfork ['pıtʃfɔ:k] n horca.

piteous ['pıtıəs] a lastimoso.

pitfall ['pıtfɔ:l] n riesgo.

pith [pıθ] n (of orange) médula; (fig) meollo.

pithy ['pıθı] a jugoso.

pitiful ['pıtıful] a (touching) lastimoso, conmovedor(a); (contemptible) lamentable, miserable.

pitiless ['pıtılıs] a despiadado.

pittance ['pıtns] n miseria.

pity ['pıtı] n compasión f, piedad f // vt compadecer(se de); **what a ~!** ¡qué pena!

pivot ['pivət] *n* eje *m*.

pizza ['pi:tsə] *n* pizza.

placard ['plækɑ:d] *n* (*in march etc*) pancarta.

placate [plə'keit] *vt* apaciguar.

place [pleis] *n* lugar *m*, sitio; (*rank*) rango; (*seat*) plaza, asiento; (*post*) puesto; **at/to his ~** en/a su casa // *vt* (*object*) poner, colocar; (*identify*) reconocer; (*find a post for*) dar un puesto a, colocar; **to take ~** tener lugar; **to be ~d** (*in race, exam*) colocarse; **out of ~** (*not suitable*) fuera de lugar; **in the first ~** (*first of all*) en primer lugar; **to change ~s with sb** cambiarse de sitio con alguien.

placid ['plæsid] *a* apacible.

plague [pleig] *n* plaga; (*MED*) peste *f* // *vt* (*fig*) acosar, atormentar.

plaice [pleis] *n, pl inv* platija.

plaid [plæd] *n* (*material*) tartán *m*.

plain [plein] *a* (*clear*) claro, evidente; (*simple*) sencillo; (*frank*) franco, abierto; (*not handsome*) poco atractivo; (*pure*) natural, puro // *ad* claramente // *n* llano, llanura; **in ~ clothes** (*police*) vestido de paisano; **~ly** *ad* claramente, evidentemente; (*frankly*) francamente.

plaintiff ['pleintif] *n* demandante *m/f*.

plait [plæt] *n* trenza // *vt* trenzar.

plan [plæn] *n* (*drawing*) plano; (*scheme*) plan *m*, proyecto // *vt* (*think*) pensar; (*prepare*) proyectar, planificar // *vi* hacer proyectos; **to ~ to do** pensar hacer.

plane [plein] *n* (*AVIAT*) avión *m*; (*tree*) plátano; (*tool*) cepillo; (*MATH*) plano.

planet ['plænit] *n* planeta *m*.

plank [plæŋk] *n* tabla.

planner ['plænə*] *n* planificador(a) *m/f*.

planning ['plæniŋ] *n* planificación *f*; **family ~** planificación familiar; **~ permission** *n* permiso para realizar obras.

plant [plɑ:nt] *n* planta; (*machinery*) maquinaria; (*factory*) fábrica // *vt*

plantar; (*field*) sembrar; (*bomb*) colocar.

plaque [plæk] *n* placa.

plaster ['plɑ:stə*] *n* (*for walls*) yeso; (*also*: **~ of Paris**) yeso mate; (*Brit: also*: **sticking ~**) tirita, esparadrapo, curita (*LAm*) // *vt* enyesar; (*cover*): **to ~ with** llenar or cubrir de; **~ed** *a* (*col*) borracho; **~er** *n* yesero.

plastic ['plæstik] *n* plástico // *a* plástico; **~ bag** *n* bolsa de plástico.

plasticine ['plæstisi:n] *n* (*Brit*) ® plastilina ®.

plastic surgery *n* cirujía plástica.

plate [pleit] *n* (*dish*) plato; (*metal, in book*) lámina; (*PHOT*) placa.

plateau ['plætəu], *pl* **~s** *or* **~x** [-z] *n* meseta, altiplanicie *f*.

plate glass *n* vidrio cilindrado.

platform ['plætfɔ:m] *n* (*RAIL*) andén *m*; (*stage*) plataforma; (*at meeting*) tribuna; (*POL*) programa *m* (electoral); **~ ticket** *n* (*Brit*) billete *m* de andén.

platinum ['plætinəm] *n* platino.

platitude ['plætitju:d] *n* lugar *m* común, tópico.

platoon [plə'tu:n] *n* pelotón *m*.

platter ['plætə*] *n* fuente *f*.

plausible ['plɔ:zibl] *a* verosímil; (*person*) convincente.

play [plei] *n* (*gen*) juego; (*THEATRE*) obra, comedia // *vt* (*game*) jugar; (*instrument*) tocar; (*THEATRE*) representar; (: *part*) hacer el papel de; (*fig*) desempeñar // *vi* jugar; (*THEATRE*) actuar; (*MUS*) tocar; (*frolic*) juguetear; **to ~ safe** ir a lo seguro; **to ~ down** *vt* quitar importancia a; **to ~ up** *vi* (*cause trouble to*) dar guerra; **~boy** *n* playboy *m*; **~er** *n* jugador(a) *m/f*; (*THEATRE*) actor *m*/actriz *f*; (*MUS*) músico/a; **~ful** *a* juguetón/ona; **~ground** *n* (*in school*) patio de recreo; **~group** *n* jardín *m* de niños; **~ing card** *n* naipe *m*, carta; **~ing field** *n* campo de deportes; **~mate** *n* compañero/a de juego; **~-off** *n* (*SPORT*) (partido de) desempate *m*;

~**pen** n corral m; ~**school** n = ~ **group**; ~**thing** n juguete m; ~**wright** n dramaturgo/a.

plc abbr (= public limited company) S.A.

plea [pliː] n (request) súplica, petición f; (excuse) pretexto, disculpa; (LAW) alegato, defensa.

plead [pliːd] vt (LAW): to ~ sb's case defender a uno; (give as excuse) poner como pretexto // vi (LAW) declararse; (beg): to ~ with sb suplicar or rogar a uno.

pleasant ['plɛznt] a agradable; ~**ries** npl (polite remarks) cortesías fpl.

please [pliːz] vt (give pleasure to) dar gusto a, agradar // vi (think fit): do as you ~ haz lo que quieras; ~! ¡por favor!; ~ **yourself**! ¡haz lo que quieras!, ¡como quieras!; ~**d** (happy) alegre, contento; ~**d** (**with**) satisfecho (de); ~**d to meet you** ¡encantado!, ¡tanto gusto!; **pleasing** a agradable, grato.

pleasure ['plɛʒə*] n placer m, gusto; (will) voluntad f; **'it's a** ~' el gusto es mío.

pleat [pliːt] n pliegue m.

pledge [plɛdʒ] n (object) prenda; (promise) promesa, voto // vt empeñar; prometer.

plentiful ['plɛntiful] a copioso, abundante.

plenty ['plɛnti] n abundancia; ~ **of** mucho(s)/a(s).

pliable ['plaɪəbl] a flexible.

pliers ['plaɪəz] npl alicates mpl, tenazas fpl.

plight [plaɪt] n situación f difícil.

plimsolls ['plɪmsəlz] npl (Brit) zapatos mpl de tenis.

plinth [plɪnθ] n plinto.

plod [plɔd] vi caminar con paso pesado; (fig) trabajar laboriosamente; ~**der** n trabajador(a) m/f diligente pero lento/a.

plonk [plɔŋk] (col) n (Brit: wine) vino peleón // vt: to ~ **sth down** dejar caer algo.

plot [plɔt] n (scheme) complot m, conjura; (of story, play) argumento; (of land) terreno, lote m (LAM) // vt (mark out) trazar; (conspire) tramar, urdir // vi conspirar; ~**ter** n (instrument) trazador m de gráficos.

plough, (US) **plow** [plau] n arado // vt (earth) arar; to ~ **back** vt (COMM) reinvertir; to ~ **through** vt fus (crowd) abrirse paso por la fuerza por; (book, work) roer.

ploy [plɔɪ] n truco, estratagema.

pluck [plʌk] vt (fruit) coger (Sp), recoger (LAm); (musical instrument) puntear; (bird) desplumar // n valor m, ánimo; to ~ **up courage** hacer de tripas corazón; ~**y** a valiente.

plug [plʌg] n tapón m; (ELEC) enchufe m, clavija; (AUT: also: **spark(ing)** ~) bujía // vt (hole) tapar; (col: advertise) dar publicidad a; to ~ **in** vt (ELEC) enchufar.

plum [plʌm] n (fruit) ciruela // a: ~ **job** (col) puesto (de trabajo) muy codiciado.

plumb [plʌm] a vertical // n plomo // ad (exactly) exactamente, en punto // vt sondar; (fig) sondear.

plumber ['plʌmə*] n fontanero/a, plomero/a.

plumbing ['plʌmɪŋ] n (trade) fontanería; (piping) cañería.

plume [pluːm] n pluma.

plummet ['plʌmɪt] vi: to ~ (**down**) caer a plomo.

plump [plʌmp] a rechoncho, rollizo // vt: to ~ **sth** (**down**) **on** dejar caer algo en; to ~ **for** vt fus (col: choose) optar por.

plunder ['plʌndə*] n pillaje m; (loot) botín m // vt pillar, saquear.

plunge [plʌndʒ] n zambullida // vt sumergir, hundir // vi (fall) caer; (dive) saltar; (person) arrojarse; (sink) hundirse; to **take the** ~ lanzarse; ~**r** n émbolo; (for drain) desatascador m.

pluperfect [pluː'pəːfɪkt] n pluscuamperfecto.

plural ['pluərl] *n* plural *m*.

plus [plʌs] *n* (*also*: ~ **sign**) signo más // *prep* más, y, además de; **ten/ twenty** ~ más de diez/veinte.

plush [plʌʃ] *a* de felpa.

plutonium [pluː'təuniəm] *n* plutonio.

ply [plaɪ] *vt* (*a trade*) ejercer // *n* (*ship*) ir y venir; (*for hire*) ofrecerse (para alquilar); **to ~ sb with drink** insistir en ofrecer a alguien muchas copas; **~wood** *n* madera contrachapada.

P.M. *abbr* = **Prime Minister**.

p.m. *ad abbr* (= *post meridiem*) de la tarde *o* noche.

pneumatic [njuː'mætɪk] *a* neumático; ~ **drill** *n* martillo neumático.

pneumonia [njuː'məunɪə] *n* pulmonía.

poach [pəutʃ] *vt* (*cook*) escalfar; (*steal*) cazar/pescar en vedado // *vi* cazar/pescar en vedado; **~ed** *a* (*egg*) escalfado; **~er** *n* cazador/a *m/f* furtivo/a; **~ing** *n* caza/pesca furtiva.

P.O. Box *n abbr* = **Post Office Box**.

pocket ['pɔkɪt] *n* bolsillo; (*of air, GEO, fig*) bolsa; (*BILLIARDS*) tronera // *vt* meter en el bolsillo; (*steal*) embolsar; (*BILLIARDS*) entronerar; **to be out of** ~ salir perdiendo; **~book** *n* (*US*: *wallet*) cartera; ~ **knife** *n* navaja; ~ **money** *n* asignación *f*.

pod [pɔd] *n* vaina.

podgy ['pɔdʒɪ] *a* gordinflón/ona.

pediatrist [pə'diːətrɪst] *n* (*US*) pedicuro/a.

poem ['pəuɪm] *n* poema *m*.

poet ['pəuɪt] *n* poeta *m/f*; ~**ic** [-'ɛtɪk] *a* poético; ~ **laureate** *n* poeta *m* laureado; ~**ry** *n* poesía.

poignant ['pɔɪnjənt] *a* conmovedor(a).

point [pɔɪnt] *n* punto; (*tip*) punta; (*purpose*) fin *m*, propósito; (*use*) utilidad *f*; (*significant point*) lo significativo; (*also*: **decimal** ~): **2 ~ 3 (2.3)** dos coma tres (2,3) // *vt* (*gun etc*): **to**

~ **sth at sb** apuntar algo a uno // *vi* señalar con el dedo; **~s** *npl* (*AUT*) contactos *mpl*; (*RAIL*) agujas *fpl*; **to be on the** ~ **of doing sth** estar a punto de hacer algo; **to make a** ~ **of** poner empeño en; **to get the** ~ comprender; **to come to the** ~ ir al meollo; **there's no** ~ **(in doing)** no tiene sentido (hacer); **to** ~ **out** *vt* señalar; **to** ~ **to** *vt fus* indicar con el dedo; (*fig*) indicar, señalar; ~**blank** *ad* (*also*: **at** ~**-blank range**) a quemarropa; ~**ed** *a* (*shape*) puntiagudo, afilado; (*remark*) intencionado; ~**edly** *ad* intencionadamente; ~**er** *n* (*stick*) puntero; (*needle*) aguja, indicador *m*; ~**less** *a* sin sentido; ~ **of view** *n* punto de vista.

poise [pɔɪz] *n* (*of head, body*) porte *m*; (*calmness*) aplomo, elegancia.

poison ['pɔɪzn] *n* veneno // *vt* envenenar; ~**ing** *n* envenenamiento; ~**ous** *a* venenoso; (*fumes etc*) tóxico; (*fig*) pernicioso.

poke [pəuk] *vt* (*fire*) hurgar, atizar; (*jab with finger, stick etc*) empujar; (*put*): **to** ~ **sth in(to)** introducir algo en; **to** ~ **about** *vi* fisgonear.

poker ['pəukə*] *n* atizador *m*; (*CARDS*) póker *m*; ~**-faced** *a* de cara impasible.

poky ['pəukɪ] *a* estrecho.

Poland ['pəulənd] *n* Polonia.

polar ['pəulə*] *a* polar.

Pole [pəul] *n* polaco/a.

pole [pəul] *n* palo; (*GEO*) polo; (*TEL*) poste *m*; (*flag*) ~ asta; (*tent* ~) mástil *m*; ~ **bean** *n* (*US*) judía trepadora; ~ **vault** *n* salto con pértiga.

police [pə'liːs] *n* policía // *vt* vigilar; ~ **car** *n* coche-patrulla *m*; ~**man** *n* policía *m*, guardia *m*; ~ **state** *n* estado policial; ~ **station** *n* comisaría; ~**woman** *n* mujer *f* policía.

policy ['pɔlɪsɪ] *n* política; (*also*: **insurance** ~) póliza.

polio ['pəulɪəu] *n* polio *f*.

Polish ['pəulɪʃ] *a* polaco // *n* (*LING*) polaco.

polish ['pɒlɪʃ] n (for shoes) betún m; (for floor) cera (de lustrar); (for nails) esmalte m; (shine) brillo, lustre m; (fig: refinement) educación f // vt (shoes) limpiar; (make shiny) pulir, sacar brillo a; (fig: improve) perfeccionar; **to ~ off** vt (work) terminar; (food) despachar; **~ed** a (fig: person) elegante.

polite [pə'laɪt] a cortés, atento; (formal) correcto; **~ness** n cortesía.

politic ['pɒlɪtɪk] a prudente; **~al** [pə'lɪtɪkl] a político; **~ian** [-'tɪʃən] n político/a; **~s** n política.

polka ['pɒlkə] n polca; **~ dot** n lunar m.

poll [pəul] n (votes) votación f, votos mpl; (also: opinion ~) sondeo, encuesta // vt (votes) obtener.

pollen ['pɒlən] n polen m.

polling ['pəulɪŋ] (Brit): **~ booth** n cabina de votar; **~ day** n día m de elecciones; **~ station** n centro electoral.

pollution [pə'lu:ʃən] n polución f, contaminación f del medio ambiente.

polo ['pəuləu] n (sport) polo; **~-neck** a de cuello vuelto.

polyester [pɒlɪ'estə*] n poliéster m.

polyethylene ['pɒlɪ'eθɪli:n] n (US) politeno.

Polynesia [pɒlɪ'ni:zɪə] n Polinesia.

polystyrene [pɒlɪ'staɪri:n] n poliestireno.

polytechnic [pɒlɪ'teknɪk] n ≈ escuela de formación profesional.

polythene ['pɒlɪθi:n] n (Brit) politeno.

pomegranate ['pɒmɪgrænɪt] n granada.

pomp [pɒmp] n pompa.

pompom ['pɒmpɒm], **pompon** ['pɒmpɒn] n borla.

pompous ['pɒmpəs] a pomposo.

pond [pɒnd] n (natural) charca; (artificial) estanque m.

ponder ['pɒndə*] vt meditar; **~ous** a pesado.

pong [pɒŋ] n (Brit col) hedor m.

pontoon [pɒn'tu:n] n pontón m;

(Brit: card game) veintiuna.

pony ['pəunɪ] n poney m, jaca, potro (LAm); **~tail** n cola de caballo; **~ trekking** n (Brit) excursión f a caballo.

poodle ['pu:dl] n caniche m.

pool [pu:l] n (natural) charca; (pond) estanque m; (also: swimming ~) piscina, alberca (LAm); (billiards) chapolín // vt juntar; typing ~ servicio de mecanografía; (football) **~s** npl quinielas fpl.

poor [puə*] a pobre; (bad) de mala calidad // npl: **the ~** los pobres; **~ly** a mal, enfermo.

pop [pɒp] n (sound) ruido seco; (MUS) (música) pop m; (US: col: father) papá m; (lemonade) gaseosa // vt (burst) hacer reventar // vi reventar; (cork) saltar; **to ~ in/out** vi entrar/salir un momento; **to ~ up** vi aparecer inesperadamente; **~ concert** n concierto pop; **~corn** n palomitas fpl.

pope [pəup] n papa m.

poplar ['pɒplə*] n álamo.

poppy ['pɒpɪ] n amapola.

popsicle ['pɒpsɪkl] n (US) polo.

populace ['pɒpjuləs] n pueblo, plebe f.

popular ['pɒpjulə*] a popular; **~ize** vt popularizar; (disseminate) vulgarizar.

population [pɒpju'leɪʃən] n población f.

porcelain ['pɒːslɪn] n porcelana.

porch [pɒːtʃ] n pórtico, entrada.

porcupine ['pɒːkjupaɪn] n puerco m espín.

pore [pɒː*] n poro // vi: **to ~ over** engolfarse en.

pork [pɒːk] n carne f de cerdo or chancho (LAm).

pornography [pɒː'nɒgrəfɪ] n pornografía.

porous ['pɒːrəs] a poroso.

porpoise ['pɒːpəs] n marsopa.

porridge ['pɒrɪdʒ] n gachas fpl de avena.

port [pɒːt] n (harbour) puerto;

(NAUT: left side) babor m; (wine) vino de Oporto; ~ of call puerto de escala.

portable ['pɔ:təbl] a portátil.

portent ['pɔ:tent] n presagio, augurio.

porter ['pɔ:tə*] n (for luggage) maletero; (doorkeeper) portero/a, conserje m/f.

portfolio [pɔ:t'fəuliəu] n (case, of artist) cartera, carpeta; (POL, FINANCE) cartera.

porthole ['pɔ:thəul] n portilla.

portion ['pɔ:ʃən] n porción f; (helping) ración f.

portly ['pɔ:tli] a corpulento.

portrait ['pɔ:treit] n retrato.

portray [pɔ:'trei] vt retratar; (in writing) representar.

Portugal ['pɔ:tjugl] n Portugal m.

Portuguese [pɔ:tju'gi:z] a portugués/esa // n, pl inv portugués/esa m/f; (LING) portugués m.

pose [pəuz] n postura, actitud f; (pej) afectación f, pose f // vi posar; (pretend): to ~ as hacerse pasar por // vt (question) plantear.

posh [pɔʃ] a (col) elegante, de lujo.

position [pə'ziʃən] n posición f; (job) puesto // vt colocar.

positive ['pɔzitiv] a positivo; (certain) seguro; (definite) definitivo.

posse ['pɔsi] n (US) pelotón m.

possess [pə'zɛs] vt poseer; ~ion [pə'zɛʃən] n posesión f.

possibility [pɔsi'biliti] n posibilidad f.

possible ['pɔsibl] a posible; as big as ~ lo más grande posible; **possibly** ad (perhaps) posiblemente, tal vez; I cannot possibly come no me es imposible venir.

post [pəust] n (Brit: letters, delivery) correo; (job, situation) puesto; (pole) poste m // vt (Brit: send by post) echar al correo; (MIL) apostar; (bills) fijar, pegar; (Brit: appoint): to ~ to enviar a; ~age n porte m, franqueo; ~al a postal, de correos; ~al order n giro postal; ~box n

(Brit) buzón m; ~card n tarjeta postal; ~code n (Brit) código postal.

postdate [pəust'deit] vt (cheque) poner fecha adelantada a.

poster ['pəustə*] n cartel m.

poste restante [pəust'rɛstɔ̃t] n (Brit) lista de correos.

posterior [pɔs'tiəriə*] n (col) culo, trasero.

postgraduate ['pəust'grædjuət] n posgraduado/a.

posthumous ['pɔstjuməs] a póstumo.

post: ~man n cartero; ~mark n matasellos m inv; ~master n administrador m de correos.

post-mortem [pəust'mɔ:təm] n autopsia.

post office n (building) (oficina de) correos m; (organization): the P~O~ Administración f General de Correos; P~ O~ Box (P.O. Box) n apartado postal, casilla de correos (LAm).

postpone [pəs'pəun] vt aplazar.

postscript ['pəustskript] n posdata.

posture ['pɔstʃə*] n postura, actitud f.

postwar [pəust'wɔ:*] a de la posguerra.

posy ['pəuzi] n ramillete m (de flores).

pot [pɔt] n (for cooking) olla; (for flowers) maceta; (for jam) tarro, pote m; (col: marijuana) costo // vt (plant) poner en tiesto; (conserve) conservar; to go to ~ (col: work, performance) irse al traste.

potato [pə'teitəu], pl ~es n patata, papa (LAm); ~ peeler n pelapatatas m inv.

potent ['pəutnt] a potente, poderoso; (drink) fuerte.

potential [pə'tenʃl] a potencial, posible // n potencial m; ~ly ad en potencia.

pothole ['pɔthəul] n (in road) bache m; (Brit: underground) gruta; **potholing** n (Brit): to go potholing dedicarse a la espeleología.

potion ['pəʊʃən] n poción f, pócima.

potluck [pɔt'lʌk] n: **to take ~** to-mar lo que haya.

potshot ['pɔtʃɔt] n: **to take a ~** at sth tirar a algo sin apuntar.

potted ['pɔtɪd] a (food) en conserva; (plant) en tiesto or maceta.

potter ['pɔtə*] n alfarero/a // vi: **to ~ around, ~ about** hacer trabaji-tos; **~y** n cerámica; alfarería.

potty ['pɔtɪ] a (col: mad) chiflado // n orinal m de niño.

pouch [paʊtʃ] n (ZOOL) bolsa; (for tobacco) petaca.

poultry ['pəʊltrɪ] n aves fpl de co-rral; (dead) pollos mpl.

pounce [paʊns] vi: **to ~ on** precipi-tarse sobre

pound [paʊnd] n libra (weight = 453g, 16oz; money = 100 pence); (for dogs) corral m; (for cars) depósito m // vt (beat) golpear; (crush) machacar // vi (beat) dar golpes.

pour [pɔ:*] vt echar; (tea) servir // vi correr, fluir; (rain) llover a cánta-ros; **to ~ away or off** vt vaciar, verter; **to ~ in/out** vi (people) entrar/salir en tropel // vt (drink) echar, servir; **~ing a: ~ing rain** lluvia torrencial.

pout [paʊt] vi hacer pucheros.

poverty ['pɔvətɪ] n pobreza, miseria; **~-stricken** a necesitado.

powder ['paʊdə*] n polvo; (face ~) polvos mpl; (gun ~) pólvora // vt pol-vorear; **to ~ one's face** ponerse pol-vos; **~ compact** n polvera; **~ed milk** n leche f en polvo; **~ puff** n borla; **~ room** n aseos mpl.

power ['paʊə*] n poder m; (strength) fuerza; (nation, TECH) po-tencia; (drive) empuje m; (ELEC) fuerza, energía // vt impulsar; **to be in ~** (POL) estar en el poder; **~ cut** n (Brit) apagón m; **~ed a: ~ed by** impulsado por; **~ failure** n = **~ cut**; **~ful** a poderoso; (engine) po-tente; **~less** a impotente, ineficaz; **~ point** n (Brit) enchufe m; **~ sta-**

tion n central f eléctrica.

p.p. abbr (= per procurationem): **~ J. Smith** p.p. (por poder de) J. Smith.

PR n abbr = **public relations**.

practicable ['præktɪkəbl] a (scheme) factible.

practical ['præktɪkl] a práctico; **~ity** [-'kælɪtɪ] n (of situation etc) factibili-dad f; **~ joke** n broma pesada; **~ly** ad (almost) casi.

practice ['præktɪs] n (habit) costum-bre f; (exercise) práctica, ejercicio; (training) adiestramiento; (MED) clientela // vt, vi (US) = **practise**; **in ~** (in reality) en la práctica; **out of ~** desentrenado.

practise, (US) **practice** ['præktɪs] vt (carry out) practicar; (profession) ejercer; (train at) practicar // vi ejercer; (train) practicar; **practis-ing** a (Christian etc) practicante; (lawyer) que ejerce.

practitioner [præk'tɪʃənə*] n practi-cante m/f; (MED) médico/a.

prairie ['prɛərɪ] n (in N. America) pampa.

praise [preɪz] n alabanza(s) f(pl), elogio(s) m(pl); **~worthy** a loable.

pram [præm] n (Brit) cochecito de ni-ño.

prance [prɑ:ns] vi (horse) hacer ca-briolas.

prank [præŋk] n travesura.

prawn [prɔ:n] n gamba.

pray [preɪ] vi rezar.

prayer [prɛə*] n oración f, rezo; (en-treaty) ruego, súplica; **~ book** n de-vocionario, misal m.

preach [pri:tʃ] vi predicar.

precaution [prɪ'kɔ:ʃən] n precaución f.

precede [prɪ'si:d] vt, vi preceder.

precedence ['presɪdəns] n preceden-cia; (priority) prioridad f.

precedent ['presɪdənt] n precedente m.

precinct ['pri:sɪŋkt] n recinto; **~s** npl contornos mpl; **pedestrian ~** (Brit) zona peatonal; **shopping ~**

(Brit) centro comercial.

precious ['prɛʃəs] a precioso.

precipice ['prɛsɪpɪs] n precipicio.

precipitate [prɪ'sɪpɪtɪt] a (hasty) precipitado // vt [prɪ'sɪpɪteɪt] precipitar.

precise [prɪ'saɪs] a preciso, exacto; ~**ly** ad exactamente, precisamente.

preclude [prɪ'kluːd] vt excluir.

precocious [prɪ'kəʊʃəs] a precoz.

precondition [priːkən'dɪʃən] n condición f previa.

predator ['prɛdətə*] n animal m de rapiña.

predecessor ['priːdɪsɛsə*] n antecesor(a) m/f.

predicament [prɪ'dɪkəmənt] n apuro.

predict [prɪ'dɪkt] vt pronosticar; ~**able** a previsible.

predominantly [prɪ'dɒmɪnəntlɪ] ad en su mayoría.

preen [priːn] vt: to ~ itself (bird) limpiarse (las plumas); to ~ o.s. pavonearse.

prefab ['priːfæb] n casa prefabricada.

preface ['prɛfəs] n prefacio.

prefect ['priːfɛkt] n (Brit: in school) monitor(a) m/f.

prefer [prɪ'fɜː*] vt preferir; ~**able** ['prɛfrəbl] a preferible; ~**ably** ['prɛfrəblɪ] ad de preferencia; ~**ence** ['prɛfrəns] n preferencia; (priority) prioridad f; ~**ential** [prɛfə'rɛnʃəl] a preferente.

prefix ['priːfɪks] n prefijo.

pregnancy ['prɛgnənsɪ] n embarazo.

pregnant ['prɛgnənt] a embarazada.

prehistoric ['priːhɪs'tɒrɪk] a prehistórico.

prejudice ['prɛdʒudɪs] n (bias) prejuicio; (harm) perjuicio // vt (bias) predisponer; (harm) perjudicar; ~**d** a (person) predispuesto; (view) parcial, interesado.

prelude ['prɛljuːd] n preludio.

premarital [priː'mærɪtl] a premarital.

premature ['prɛmətʃuə*] a prematuro.

premier ['prɛmɪə*] a primero, principal // n (POL) primer(a) ministro/a.

première ['prɛmɪɛə*] n estreno.

premise ['prɛmɪs] n premisa; ~s npl local msg; on the ~s en el lugar mismo.

premium ['priːmɪəm] n premio; (COMM) prima; to be at a ~ ser muy solicitado; ~ bond n (Brit) bono del estado que participa en una lotería nacional.

premonition [prɛmə'nɪʃən] n presentimiento.

preoccupied [priː'ɒkjupaɪd] a (worried) preocupado; (absorbed) ensimismado.

prep [prɛp] n (SCOL: study) deberes mpl; ~ **school** n = preparatory school.

prepaid [priː'peɪd] a porte pagado.

preparation [prɛpə'reɪʃən] n preparación f; ~s npl preparativos mpl.

preparatory [prɪ'pærətərɪ] a preparatorio, preliminar; ~ **school** n escuela preparatoria.

prepare [prɪ'pɛə*] vt preparar, disponer // vi: to ~ for prepararse or disponerse para; (make preparations) hacer preparativos para; ~**d** to a dispuesto a.

preposition [prɛpə'zɪʃən] n preposición f.

preposterous [prɪ'pɒstərəs] a absurdo, ridículo.

prerequisite [priː'rɛkwɪzɪt] n requisito.

prerogative [prɪ'rɒgətɪv] n prerrogativa.

preschool [priː'skuːl] a preescolar.

prescribe [prɪ'skraɪb] vt prescribir; (MED) recetar.

prescription [prɪ'skrɪpʃən] n (MED) receta.

presence ['prɛzns] n presencia; (attendance) asistencia; ~ of mind aplomo.

present ['prɛznt] a (in attendance) presente; (current) actual // n (gift) regalo; (actuality) actualidad f, presente m // vt [prɪ'zɛnt] (introduce) presentar; (*expound*) exponer; (*give*) presentar, dar, ofrecer; (*THEATRE*) representar; **to give sb a** ~ regalar algo a uno; **at** ~ actualmente; **~able** [prɪ'zɛntəbl] *a*: **to make o.s. ~able** arreglarse; **~ation** [-'teɪʃən] *n* presentación *f*; (*gift*) obsequio, (*of case*) exposición *f*; (*THEATRE*) representación *f*; **~-day** *a* actual; **~er** [prɪ'zɛntə*] *n* (*RADIO, TV*) locutor/a *m/f*; **~ly** *ad* (*soon*) dentro de poco.

preservation [prɛzə'veɪʃən] *n* conservación *f*.

preservative [prɪ'zəːvətɪv] *n* conservante *m*.

preserve [prɪ'zəːv] *vt* (*keep safe*) preservar, proteger; (*maintain*) mantener; (*food*) conservar; (*in salt*) salar // *n* (*for game*) coto, vedado; (*often pl: jam*) conserva, confitura.

president ['prɛzɪdənt] *n* presidente *m/f*; **~ial** [-'dɛnʃl] *a* presidencial.

press [prɛs] *n* (*tool, machine, newspapers*) prensa; (*printer's*) imprenta; (*of hand*) apretón *m* // *vt* (*push*) empujar; (*squeeze*) apretar; (*grapes*) pisar; (*clothes: iron*) planchar; (*pressure*) presionar; (*insist*): **to** ~ **sth on sb** insistir en que uno acepte algo // *vi* (*squeeze*) apretar; (*pressurize*) ejercer presión; **we are ~ed for time** tenemos poco tiempo; **to** ~ **on** *vi* avanzar; (*hurry*) apretar el paso; ~ **agency** *n* agencia de prensa; ~ **conference** *n* rueda de prensa; ~**ing** *a* apremiante; ~ **stud** *n* (*Brit*) botón *m* de presión; ~**-up** *n* (*Brit*) plancha.

pressure ['prɛʃə*] *n* presión *f*; ~ **cooker** *n* olla a presión; ~ **gauge** *n* manómetro; ~ **group** *n* grupo de presión; **pressurized** (*container*) a presión.

prestige [prɛs'tiːʒ] *n* prestigio.

presumably [prɪ'zjuːməblɪ] *ad* es de suponer que, cabe presumir que.

presume [prɪ'zjuːm] *vt* presumir, suponer; **to** ~ **to do** (*dare*) atreverse a hacer.

presumption [prɪ'zʌmpʃən] *n* supo-

sición *f*; (*pretension*) presunción *f*.

presumptuous [prɪ'zʌmptjuəs] *a* presumido.

pretence, pretense [prɪ'tɛns] *n* (*claim*) pretensión *f*; (*pretext*) pretexto; (*make-believe*) fingimiento; **on the** ~ **of** bajo pretexto de.

pretend [prɪ'tɛnd] *vt* (*feign*) fingir // *vi* (*feign*) fingir; (*claim*): **to** ~ **to sth** pretender a algo.

pretense [prɪ'tɛns] *n* (*US*) = **pretence**.

pretension [prɪ'tɛnʃən] *n* (*claim*) pretensión *f*.

pretentious [prɪ'tɛnʃəs] *a* presumido; (*ostentatious*) ostentoso, aparatoso.

pretext ['priːtɛkst] *n* pretexto.

pretty ['prɪtɪ] *a* (*gen*) bonito, lindo (*LAm*) // *ad* bastante.

prevail [prɪ'veɪl] *vi* (*gain mastery*) prevalecer; (*be current*) predominar; (*persuade*): **to** ~ **(up)on sb to do sth** persuadir a uno para que haga algo; ~**ing** *a* (*dominant*) predominante.

prevalent ['prɛvələnt] *a* (*dominant*) dominante; (*widespread*) extendido; (*fashionable*) de moda.

prevent [prɪ'vɛnt] *vt*: **to** ~ **(sb from doing sth)** impedir (a uno hacer algo); ~**ive** *a* preventivo.

preview ['priːvjuː] *n* (*of film*) preestreno.

previous ['priːvɪəs] *a* previo, anterior; ~**ly** *ad* antes.

prewar [priː'wɔː*] *a* de antes de la guerra.

prey [preɪ] *n* presa // *vi*: **to** ~ **on** vivir a costa de; (*feed on*) alimentarse de.

price [praɪs] *n* precio // *vt* (*goods*) fijar el precio a; ~**less** *a* que no tiene precio; ~ **list** *n* tarifa.

prick [prɪk] *n* pinchazo; (*sting*) picadura // *vt* pinchar; picar; **to** ~ **up one's ears** aguzar el oído.

prickle ['prɪkl] *n* (*sensation*) picor *m*; (*BOT*) espina; (*ZOOL*) púa; **prickly** *a* espinoso; (*fig: person*) enojadizo;

prickly heat n sarpullido causado por exceso de calor.

pride [praɪd] n orgullo; (pej) soberbia // vt: **to ~ o.s. on** enorgullecerse de.

priest [priːst] n sacerdote m; **~ess** n sacerdotisa; **~hood** n (practice) sacerdocio; (priests) clero.

prig [prɪg] n gazmoño/a.

prim [prɪm] a (demure) remilgado; (prudish) gazmoño.

primarily ['praɪmərɪlɪ] ad (above all) ante todo.

primary ['praɪmərɪ] a primario; (first in importance) principal; **~ school** n (Brit) escuela primaria.

primate [praɪmeɪt] n (REL) primado // ['praɪmeɪt] (ZOOL) primate m.

prime [praɪm] a primero, principal; (basic) fundamental; (excellent) selecto, de primera clase // n: **in the ~ of life** en la flor de la vida // vt (gun, pump) cebar; (fig) preparar; **P~ Minister (P.M.)** n primer/a ministro/a.

primer [praɪmə*] n (book) texto elemental; (paint) imprimación f.

primeval [praɪˈmiːvəl] a primitivo.

primitive ['prɪmɪtɪv] a primitivo; (crude) rudimentario.

primrose ['prɪmrəʊz] n primavera, prímula.

primus (stove) ['praɪməs-] n ® (Brit) hornillo de camping.

prince [prɪns] n príncipe m.

princess [prɪnˈses] n princesa.

principal ['prɪnsɪpl] a principal, mayor // n director/a m/f.

principle ['prɪnsɪpl] n principio; **in ~** en principio; **on ~** por principio.

print [prɪnt] n (impression) marca, impresión f; huella; (letters) letra de molde; (fabric) estampado; (ART) grabado; (PHOT) impresión f // vt (gen) imprimir; (on mind) grabar; (write in capitals) escribir en letras de molde; **out of ~** agotado; **~ed matter** n impresos mpl; **~er** n (person) impresor/a m/f; (machine) impresora; **~ing** n (art) imprenta.

(act) impresión f; (quantity) tirada; **~out** n (COMPUT) impresión f.

prior ['praɪə*] a anterior, previo // n prior m; **~ to doing** antes de hacer.

priority [praɪˈɒrɪtɪ] n prioridad f.

prise [praɪz] vt: **to ~ open** abrir con palanca.

prison ['prɪzn] n cárcel f, prisión f // cpd carcelario; **~er** n (in prison) preso/a; (under arrest) detenido/a; (in dock) acusado/a.

privacy ['prɪvəsɪ] n (seclusion) soledad f; (intimacy) intimidad f.

private ['praɪvɪt] a (personal) particular; (confidential) secreto, confidencial; (sitting etc) a puertas cerradas // n soldado raso; **'~'** (on envelope) 'confidencial'; (on door) 'prohibido el paso'; **in ~** en privado; **~ enterprise** n la empresa privada; **~ eye** n detective m/f privado/a; **~ly** ad en privado; (in o.s.) personalmente; **~ property** n propiedad f privada; **~ school** n colegio particular.

privet ['prɪvɪt] n alheña.

privilege ['prɪvɪlɪdʒ] n privilegio; (prerogative) prerrogativa f.

privy ['prɪvɪ] a: **to be ~ to** estar enterado de; **P~ Council** n Consejo del Estado.

prize [praɪz] n premio // a (first class) de primera clase // vt apreciar, estimar; **~giving** n distribución f de premios; **~winner** n premiado/a.

pro [prəʊ] n (SPORT) profesional m/f; **the ~s and cons** los pros y los contras.

probability [prɒbəˈbɪlɪtɪ] n probabilidad f.

probable ['prɒbəbl] a probable.

probably ['prɒbəblɪ] ad probablemente.

probation [prəˈbeɪʃən] n: **on ~** (employee) a prueba; (LAW) en libertad condicional.

probe [prəʊb] n (MED, SPACE) sonda; (enquiry) encuesta, investigación f // vt sondar; (investigate) investigar.

problem ['prɒbləm] n problema m.

procedure [prə'si:dʒə*] *n* procedimiento; (*bureaucratic*) trámites *mpl*.

proceed [prə'si:d] *vi* proceder; (*continue*): **to ~ (with)** continuar or seguir (con); **~s** ['prəusi:dz] *npl* ganancias *fpl*, ingresos *mpl*; **~ings** *npl* acto *sg*, actos *mpl*; (*LAW*) proceso *sg*; (*meeting*) función *fsg*; (*records*) actas *fpl*.

process ['prəuses] *n* proceso; (*method*) método, sistema *m* // *vt* tratar, elaborar; **in ~** en curso; **~ing** *n* tratamiento, elaboración *f*.

procession [prə'sɛʃən] *n* desfile *m*; **funeral ~** cortejo fúnebre.

proclaim [prə'kleim] *vt* proclamar; (*announce*) anunciar; **proclamation** [prɔklə'meiʃən] *n* proclamación *f*; (*written*) proclama.

procrastinate [prəu'kræstineit] *vi* demorarse.

procure [prə'kjuə*] *vt* conseguir.

prod [prɔd] *vt* empujar.

prodigal ['prɔdigl] *a* pródigo.

prodigy ['prɔdidʒi] *n* prodigio.

produce ['prɔdju:s] *n* (*AGR*) productos *mpl* agrícolas // *vt* [prə'dju:s] producir; (*yield*) rendir; (*show*) presentar, mostrar; (*THEATRE*) presentar, poner en escena; (*offspring*) dar a luz; **~ dealer** *n* (*US*) verdulero/a; **~r** *n* (*THEATRE*) director(a) *m/f*; (*AGR, CINEMA*) productor(a) *m/f*.

product ['prɔdʌkt] *n* producto; (*result*) fruto, producto.

production [prə'dʌkʃən] *n* (*act*) producción *f*; (*THEATRE*) presentación *f*; **~ line** *n* línea de producción.

productive [prə'dʌktiv] *a* productivo; **productivity** [prɔdʌk'tiviti] *n* productividad *f*.

profane [prə'fein] *a* profano.

profession [prə'fɛʃən] *n* profesión *f*; **~al** *n* profesional *m/f* // *a* profesional; (*by profession*) de profesión.

professor [prə'fɛsə*] *n* (*Brit*) catedrático/a; (*US*) profesor(a) *m/f*.

proficiency [prə'fiʃənsi] *n* capacidad, habilidad *f*.

proficient [prə'fiʃənt] *a* experto, há-

bil.

profile ['prəufail] *n* perfil *m*.

profit ['prɔfit] *n* (*COMM*) ganancia; (*fig*) provecho; **to make a ~** obtener beneficios // *vi*: **to ~ by or from** aprovechar or sacar provecho de; **~ability** [-ə'biliti] *n* rentabilidad *f*; **~able** *a* (*ECON*) rentable; (*beneficial*) provechoso; **~eering** [-'tiəriŋ] *n* (*pej*) explotación *f*.

profound [prə'faund] *a* profundo.

profusely [prə'fju:sli] *ad* profusamente; **profusion** [-'fju:ʒən] *n* profusión *f*, abundancia.

progeny ['prɔdʒini] *n* progenie *f*.

programme, (*US*) **program** ['prəugræm] *n* programa *m* // *vt* programar; **~r**, (*US*) **programer** *n* programador(a) *m/f*; **programming**, (*US*) **programing** *n* programación *f*.

progress ['prəugres] *n* progreso; (*development*) desarrollo // *vi* [prə'gres] progresar, avanzar; desarrollarse; **in ~** en curso; **~ive** [-'gresiv] *a* progresivo; (*person*) progresista.

prohibit [prə'hibit] *vt* prohibir; **to ~ sb from doing sth** prohibir a uno hacer algo.

project ['prɔdʒekt] *n* proyecto // (*vb*: [prə'dʒekt]) *vt* proyectar // *vi* (*stick out*) salir, sobresalir.

projectile [prə'dʒektail] *n* proyectil *m*.

projection [prə'dʒekʃən] *n* proyección *f*; (*overhang*) saliente *m*.

projector [prə'dʒektə*] *n* proyector *m*.

proletariat [prəuli'teəriət] *n* proletariado.

prologue ['prəulɔg] *n* prólogo.

prolong [prə'lɔŋ] *vt* prolongar, extender.

prom [prɔm] *n abbr* = **promenade**; (*US*: *ball*) baile *m* de gala.

promenade [prɔmə'nɑːd] *n* (*by sea*) paseo marítimo; **~ concert** *n* concierto (en que parte del público permanece de pie).

prominence ['prɔminəns] *n* (*fig*) importancia.

prominent ['prɒmɪnənt] *a* (*standing out*) saliente; (*important*) eminente, importante.

promiscuous [prə'mɪskjuəs] *a* (*sexually*) promiscuo.

promise ['prɒmɪs] *n* promesa *f* // *vt, vi* prometer; **promising** *a* prometedor(a).

promontory ['prɒməntrɪ] *n* promontorio.

promote [prə'məut] *vt* promover; (*new product*) hacer propaganda por; (*MIL*) ascender; **~r** *n* (*of sporting event*) promotor(a) *m/f*; **promotion** [-'məuʃən] *n* (*advertising*) promoción *f*; (*in rank*) ascenso.

prompt [prɒmpt] *a* (*punctual*) puntual; (*quick*) rápido // *ad*: **at 6 o'clock ~** a las seis en punto // *n* (*COMPUT*) aviso // *vt* (*urge*) mover, incitar; (*THEATRE*) apuntar; **to ~ sb to do sth** instar a uno a hacer algo; **~ly** *ad* puntualmente; rápidamente.

prone [prəun] *a* (*lying*) postrado; **~ to** propenso a.

prong [prɒŋ] *n* diente *m*, punta.

pronoun ['prəunaun] *n* pronombre *m*.

pronounce [prə'nauns] *vt* pronunciar // *vi*: **to ~ (up)on** pronunciarse sobre; **~d** *a* (*marked*) marcado; **~ment** *n* declaración *f*.

pronunciation [prənʌnsɪ'eɪʃən] *n* pronunciación *f*.

proof [pruːf] *n* prueba; **70° ~** graduación *f* del 70 por 100 // *a*: **~ against** a prueba de.

prop [prɒp] *n* apoyo, (*fig*) sostén *m* // *vt* (*also*: **~ up**) apoyar; (*lean*): **to ~ sth against** apoyar algo contra.

propaganda [prɒpə'gændə] *n* propaganda.

propel [prə'pel] *vt* impulsar, propulsar; **~ler** *n* hélice *f*; **~ling pencil** (*Brit*) lapicero.

propensity [prə'pensɪtɪ] *n* propensión *f*.

proper ['prɒpə*] *a* (*suited, right*)

propio; (*exact*) justo; (*apt*) apropiado, conveniente; (*timely*) oportuno; (*seemly*) correcto, decente; (*authentic*) verdadero; (*col: real*) auténtico; **~ly** *ad* (*adequately*) correctamente; (*decently*) decentemente; **~ noun** *n* nombre *m* propio.

property ['prɒpətɪ] *n* propiedad *f*; (*personal*) bienes *mpl* muebles; (*estate*) finca; **~ owner** *n* dueño/a de propiedades.

prophecy ['prɒfɪsɪ] *n* profecía.

prophesy ['prɒfɪsaɪ] *vt* profetizar; (*fig*) predecir.

prophet ['prɒfɪt] *n* profeta *m*.

proportion [prə'pɔːʃən] *n* proporción *f*; (*share*) parte *f*; **~al** *a* proporcional; **~ate** *a* proporcionado.

proposal [prə'pəuzl] *n* propuesta; (*offer of marriage*) oferta de matrimonio; (*plan*) proyecto.

propose [prə'pəuz] *vt* proponer // *vi* declararse; **to ~ to do sth** tener intención de hacer algo.

proposition [prɒpə'zɪʃən] *n* propuesta.

proprietor [prə'praɪətə*] *n* propietario/a, dueño/a.

propriety [prə'praɪətɪ] *n* decoro.

pro rata [prəu'rɑːtə] *ad* a prorrateo.

prose [prəuz] *n* prosa; (*SCOL*) traducción *f* inversa.

prosecute ['prɒsɪkjuːt] *vt* (*LAW*) procesar; **prosecution** [-'kjuːʃən] *n* proceso, causa; (*accusing side*) acusación *f*; **prosecutor** *n* acusador *m/f*; (*also*: **public prosecutor**) fiscal *m*.

prospect ['prɒspekt] *n* (*view*) vista; (*outlook*) perspectiva; (*hope*) esperanza // *vi* (*for mineral*) explorar // *vi* buscar; **~s** *npl* (*for work etc*) perspectivas *fpl*; **~ing** *n* prospección *f*; **~ive** [prə'spektɪv] *a* (*possible*) probable, eventual; (*certain*) futuro; **~or** [prə'spektə*] *n* explorador/a *m/f*.

prospectus [prə'spektəs] *n* prospecto.

prosper ['prɒspə*] *vi* prosperar; **~ity** [-'sperɪtɪ] *n* prosperidad *f*;

~**ous** a próspero.

prostitute ['prɒstɪtjuːt] n prostituta.

prostrate ['prɒstreɪt] a postrado.

protagonist [prə'tægənɪst] n protagonista m/f.

protect [prə'tekt] vt proteger; ~**ion** [-'tekʃən] n protección f; ~**ive** a protector(a).

protégé ['prəʊteʒeɪ] n protegido/a.

protein ['prəʊtiːn] n proteína.

protest ['prəʊtest] n protesta // vb: [prə'test] vi protestar // vt (affirm) afirmar, declarar.

Protestant ['prɒtɪstənt] a, n protestante m/f.

protester [prə'testə*] n manifestante m/f.

protracted [prə'træktɪd] a prolongado.

protrude [prə'truːd] vi salir, sobresalir.

proud [praud] a orgulloso; (pej) soberbio, altanero.

prove [pruːv] vt probar; (verify) comprobar; (show) demostrar // vi: to ~ correct resultar correcto; to ~ o.s. probar su valía.

proverb ['prɒvɜːb] n refrán m.

provide [prə'vaɪd] vt proporcionar, dar; to ~ sb with sth proveer a uno de algo; ~**d** (that) conj con tal de que, a condición de que; to ~ **for** vt fus (person) mantener a; (problem etc) tener en cuenta.

providing [prə'vaɪdɪŋ] conj a condición de que, con tal de que.

province ['prɒvɪns] n provincia; (fig) esfera; **provincial** [prə'vɪnʃəl] a provincial; (pej) provinciano.

provision [prə'vɪʒən] n provisión f; (supply) suministro, abastecimiento; ~**s** npl (food) comestibles mpl; ~**al** a provisional; (temporary) interino.

proviso [prə'vaɪzəʊ] n condición f, estipulación f.

provocative [prə'vɒkətɪv] a provocativo.

provoke [prə'vəʊk] vt (arouse) provocar; (anger) enojar.

prow [prau] n proa.

prowess ['prauɪs] n destreza.

prowl [praul] vi (also: ~ **about**, ~ **around**) merodear // n: on the ~ de merodeo; ~**er** n merodeador(a) m/f.

proxy ['prɒksɪ] n poder m; (person) apoderado/a; **by** ~ por poderes.

prudence ['pruːdns] n prudencia.

prudent ['pruːdənt] a prudente.

prudish ['pruːdɪʃ] a gazmoño.

prune [pruːn] n ciruela pasa // vt podar.

pry [praɪ] vi: to ~ **into** entrometerse en.

PS n abbr (= postscript) P.D.

psalm [sɑːm] n salmo.

pseudo- [sjuːdəʊ] pref seudo-; **pseudonym** n seudónimo.

psyche ['saɪkɪ] n psique f.

psychiatric [saɪkɪ'ætrɪk] a psiquiátrico.

psychiatrist [saɪ'kaɪətrɪst] n psiquiatra m/f.

psychiatry [saɪ'kaɪətrɪ] n psiquiatría.

psychic ['saɪkɪk] a (also: ~**al**) psíquico.

psychoanalysis [saɪkəʊə'nælɪsɪs] n psicoanálisis m inv; **psychoanalyst** [-'ænəlɪst] n psicoanalista m/f.

psychological [saɪkə'lɒdʒɪkl] a psicológico.

psychologist [saɪ'kɒlədʒɪst] n psicólogo/a.

psychology [saɪ'kɒlədʒɪ] n psicología.

PTO abbr (= please turn over) sigue.

pub [pʌb] n abbr (= public house) pub m, taberna.

puberty ['pjuːbətɪ] n pubertad f.

pubic ['pjuːbɪk] a púbico.

public ['pʌblɪk] a, n público; **in** ~ en público; ~ **address system (P.A.)** n megafonía.

publican ['pʌblɪkən] n tabernero/a.

publication [pʌblɪ'keɪʃən] n publicación f.

public: ~ **company** n sociedad f anónima; ~ **convenience** n (Brit) aseos mpl públicos, sanitarios mpl (LAm); ~ **holiday** n día de fiesta, (día) feriado (LAm); ~ **house**

(*Brit*) bar *m*, pub *m*.

publicity [pʌb'lɪsɪtɪ] *n* publicidad *f.*

publicize ['pʌblɪsaɪz] *vt* publicitar; (*advertise*) hacer propaganda para.

publicly ['pʌblɪklɪ] *ad* públicamente, en público.

public: ~ **opinion** *n* opinión *f* pública; ~ **relations (PR)** *n* relaciones *fpl* públicas; ~ **school** *n* (*Brit*) escuela privada; (*US*) instituto; ~ **spirited** *a* que tiene sentido del deber ciudadano; ~ **transport** *n* transporte *m* público.

publish ['pʌblɪʃ] *vt* publicar; ~**er** *n* (*person*) editor *m/f*; (*firm*) editorial *f*; ~**ing** *n* (*industry*) industria del libro.

puce [pjuːs] *a* de color pardo rojizo.

pucker ['pʌkə*] *vt* (*pleat*) arrugar; (*brow etc*) fruncir.

pudding ['pudɪŋ] *n* pudín *m*; (*Brit: sweet*) postre *m*; **black** ~ morcilla.

puddle ['pʌdl] *n* charco.

puff [pʌf] *n* soplo; (*of smoke*) bocanada; (*of breathing, engine*) resoplido // *vt*: **to** ~ **one's pipe** chupar la pipa // *vi* (*gen*) soplar; (*pant*) jadear; **to** ~ **out smoke** echar humo; ~**ed** *a* (*col: out of breath*) sin aliento.

puff pastry *n* hojaldre *m.*

puffy ['pʌfɪ] *a* hinchado.

pull [pul] *n* (*tug*): **to give sth a** ~ dar un tirón a algo; (*influence*) influencia // *vt* tirar de; (*muscle*) agarrotarse; (*haul*) tirar, arrastrar // *vi* tirar; **to** ~ **to pieces** hacer pedazos; **to** ~ **one's punches** (*fig*) no andarse con bromas; **to** ~ **o.s. together** tranquilizarse; **to** ~ **sb's leg** tomar el pelo a uno; **to** ~ **apart** *vt* (*take apart*) desmontar; **to** ~ **down** *vt* (*house*) derribar; **to** ~ **in** *vi* (*AUT: at the kerb*) parar (junto a la acera); (*RAIL*) llegar a la estación; **to** ~ **off** *vt* (*deal etc*) cerrar; **to** ~ **out** *vi* irse, marcharse; (*AUT: from kerb*) salir // *vt* sacar, arrancar; **to** ~ **over** *vi* (*AUT*) hacerse a un lado;

to ~ **through** *vi* salir adelante; (*MED*) recobrar la salud; **to** ~ **up** *vi* (*stop*) parar // *vt* (*uproot*) arrancar, desarraigar; (*stop*) parar.

pulley ['pulɪ] *n* polea.

pullover ['puləuvə*] *n* jersey *m*, suéter *m.*

pulp [pʌlp] *n* (*of fruit*) pulpa; (*for paper*) pasta.

pulpit ['pulpɪt] *n* púlpito.

pulsate [pʌl'seɪt] *vi* pulsar, latir.

pulse [pʌls] *n* (*ANAT*) pulso; (*of music, engine*) pulsación *f*; (*BOT*) legumbre *f.*

pummel ['pʌml] *vt* aporrear.

pump [pʌmp] *n* bomba; (*shoe*) zapatilla // *vt* sacar con una bomba; (*fig: col*) sonsacar; **to** ~ **up** *vt* inflar.

pumpkin ['pʌmpkɪn] *n* calabaza.

pun [pʌn] *n* juego de palabras.

punch [pʌntʃ] *n* (*blow*) golpe *m*, puñetazo; (*tool*) punzón *m*; (*for paper*) perforadora; (*for tickets*) taladro; (*drink*) ponche *m* // *vt* (*hit*): **to** ~ **sb/sth** dar un puñetazo or golpear a uno/algo; (*make a hole in*) punzar; perforar; (*tickets*) picar; **to** ~ **ina joke** rematan un chiste; ~-**up** *n* (*Brit col*) riña.

punctual ['pʌŋktjuəl] *a* puntual.

punctuation [pʌŋktju'eɪʃən] *n* puntuación *f.*

puncture ['pʌŋktʃə*] (*Brit*) *n* pinchazo // *vt* pinchar.

pundit ['pʌndɪt] *n* experto/a.

pungent ['pʌndʒənt] *a* acre.

punish ['pʌnɪʃ] *vt* castigar; ~**ment** *n* castigo.

punk [pʌŋk] *n* (*also:* ~ **rocker**) punk *m/f*; (*also:* ~ **rock**) música punk; (*US col: hoodlum*) rufián *m.*

punt [pʌnt] *n* (*boat*) batea.

punter ['pʌntə*] *n* (*Brit: gambler*) jugador/a *m/f.*

puny ['pjuːnɪ] *a* débil.

pup [pʌp] *n* cachorro.

pupil ['pjuːpl] *n* alumno/a.

puppet ['pʌpɪt] *n* títere *m.*

puppy ['pʌpɪ] *n* cachorro, perrito.

purchase ['pəːtʃɪs] *n* compra // *vt*

comprar; ~**r** *n* comprador(a) *m/f*.

pure [pjuə*] *a* puro.

purée ['pjuəreɪ] *n* puré *m*.

purely ['pjuəlɪ] *ad* puramente.

purge [pɜːdʒ] *n* (MED, POL) purga *f*; *vt* purgar.

purify ['pjuərɪfaɪ] *vt* purificar, depurar.

puritan ['pjuərɪtən] *n* puritano/a.

purity ['pjuərɪtɪ] *n* pureza.

purl [pɜːl] *n* punto del revés.

purple ['pɜːpl] *a* purpúreo; morado.

purport [pə'pɔːt] *vi*: **to ~** to be/do dar a entender que es/hace.

purpose ['pɜːpəs] *n* propósito; **on ~** a propósito, adrede; ~**ful** *a* resuelto, determinado.

purr [pɜː*] *vi* ronronear.

purse [pɜːs] *n* monedero; (US) bolsa, cartera (LAm) *vt* fruncir.

purser ['pɜːsə*] *n* (NAUT) comisario/a.

pursue [pə'sjuː] *vt* seguir; *n* perseguidor(a) *m/f*.

pursuit [pə'sjuːt] *n* (chase) caza; (occupation) actividad *f*.

purveyor [pə'veɪə*] *n* proveedor/a *m/f*.

push [puʃ] *n* empuje *m*, empujón *m*; (MIL) ataque *m*; (drive) empuje *m* *vt* empujar; (button) apretar; (promote) promover; (thrust): **to ~ sth (into)** meter algo a la fuerza (en) *vi* empujar; (fig) hacer esfuerzos; **to ~ aside** *vt* apartar con la mano; **to ~ off** *vi* (col) largarse; **to ~ on** *vi* (continue) seguir adelante; **to ~ through** *vt* (measure) despachar; **to ~ up** *vt* (total, prices) hacer subir; ~**chair** *n* (Brit) sillita de ruedas; ~**er** *n* (drug ~er) traficante *m/f* de drogas; ~**over** *n* (col): **it's a ~over** está tirado; ~**-up** *n* (US) plancha; ~**y** *a* (pej) agresivo.

puss [pus], **pussy(-cat)** ['pusɪ(kæt)] *n* minino.

put [put], *pt*, *pp* **put** *vt* (place) poner, colocar; (~ into) meter; (say) expresar; (a question) hacer; **to ~ about** *vi* (NAUT) virar *vt* (ru-

mour) diseminar; **to ~ across** *vt* (ideas etc) comunicar; **to ~ away** *vt* (store) guardar; **to ~ back** *vt* (replace) devolver a su lugar; (postpone) aplazar; **to ~ by** *vt* (money) guardar; **to ~ down** *vt* (on ground) poner en el suelo; (animal) sacrificar; (in writing) apuntar; (suppress: revolt etc) sofocar; (attribute) atribuir; **to ~ forward** *vt* (ideas) presentar, proponer; (date) adelantar; **to ~ in** *vt* (application, complaint) presentar; **to ~ off** *vt* (postpone) aplazar; (discourage) desanimar; **to ~ on** *vt* (clothes, lipstick etc) ponerse; (light etc) encender; (play etc) presentar; (weight) ganar; (brake) echar; **to ~ out** *vt* (fire, light) apagar; (one's hand) alargar; (news, rumour) hacer circular; (tongue etc) sacar; (person: inconvenience) molestar, fastidiar; **to ~ up** *vt* (raise) levantar, alzar; (hang) colgar; (build) construir; (increase) aumentar; (accommodate) alojar; **to ~ up with** *vt fus* aguantar.

putrid ['pjuːtrɪd] *a* podrido.

putt [pʌt] *vt* hacer un putt / *n* putt *m*, golpe *m* corto; ~**ing green** *n* green *m*; minigolf *m*.

putty ['pʌtɪ] *n* masilla.

puzzle ['pʌzl] *n* (riddle) acertijo; (jigsaw) rompecabezas *m inv*; (also: crossword ~) crucigrama *m*; (mystery) misterio *vt* dejar perplejo, confundir / *vi*: **to ~ about** quebrar la cabeza por; **puzzling** *a* misterioso, extraña.

pyjamas [pɪ'dʒɑːməz] *npl* (Brit) pijama *m*.

pylon ['paɪlən] *n* torre *f* de conducción eléctrica.

pyramid ['pɪrəmɪd] *n* pirámide *f*.

Pyrenees [pɪrə'niːz] *npl*: **the ~** los Pirineos.

python ['paɪθən] *n* pitón *m*.

Q

quack [kwæk] *n* (*of duck*) graznido; (*pej: doctor*) curandero/a.

quad [kwɔd] *n abbr* = **quadrangle**; **quadruplet**.

quadrangle ['kwɔdræŋgl] *n* (*Brit: courtyard: abbr:* **quad**) patio.

quadruple [kwɔ'drupl] *vt, vi* cuadruplicar.

quadruplet [kwɔ'dru:plɪt] *n* cuatrillizo/a.

quagmire ['kwægmaɪə*] *n* lodazal *m*, cenagal *m*.

quail [kweɪl] *n* (*bird*) codorniz *f* // *vi* amedrentarse.

quaint [kweɪnt] *a* extraño; (*picturesque*) pintoresco.

quake [kweɪk] *vi* temblar // *n abbr* = earthquake.

Quaker ['kweɪkə*] *n* cuáquero/a.

qualification [kwɔlɪfɪ'keɪʃən] *n* (*ability*) capacidad *f*; (*requirement*) requisito; (*diploma etc*) título.

qualified ['kwɔlɪfaɪd] *a* (*trained, fit*) capacitado; (*professionally*) titulado; (*limited*) limitado.

qualify ['kwɔlɪfaɪ] *vt* (*LING*) calificar a; (*capacitate*) capacitar; (*modify*) modificar // *vi* (*SPORT*) clasificarse; **to ~ (as)** calificarse (de), graduarse (en); **to ~ (for)** reunir los requisitos (para).

quality ['kwɔlɪtɪ] *n* calidad *f*; (*moral*) cualidad *f*.

qualm [kwɑːm] *n* escrúpulo.

quandary ['kwɔndrɪ] *n*: **to be in a ~** tener dudas.

quantity ['kwɔntɪtɪ] *n* cantidad *f*; **~ surveyor** *n* aparejador/a *m/f*.

quarantine ['kwɔrntiːn] *n* cuarentena.

quarrel ['kwɔrl] *n* riña, pelea // *vi* reñir, pelearse; **~some** *a* pendenciero.

quarry ['kwɔrɪ] *n* (*for stone*) cantera; (*animal*) presa.

quart [kwɔːt] *n* cuarto de galón =

1.136 l.

quarter ['kwɔːtə*] *n* cuarto, cuarta parte *f*; (*of year*) trimestre *m*; (*district*) barrio // *vt* dividir en cuartos; (*MIL: lodge*) alojar; **~s** *npl* (*barracks*) cuartel *m*; (*living* **~s**) alojamiento *sg*; **a ~ of an hour** un cuarto de hora; **~ final** *n* cuarto de final; **~ly** *a* trimestral // *ad* cada 3 meses, trimestralmente; **~master** *n* (*MIL*) comisario, intendente *m* militar.

quartet(te) [kwɔː'tɛt] *n* cuarteto.

quartz [kwɔːts] *n* cuarzo.

quash [kwɔʃ] *vt* (*verdict*) anular.

quasi- ['kweɪzaɪ] *pref* cuasi.

quaver ['kweɪvə*] *n* (*Brit MUS*) corchea // *vi* temblar.

quay [kiː] *n* (*also:* **~side**) muelle *m*.

queasy ['kwiːzɪ] *a*: **to feel ~** tener náuseas.

queen [kwiːn] *n* reina; (*CARDS etc*) dama; **~ mother** *n* reina madre.

queer [kwɪə*] *a* (*odd*) raro, extraño // *n* (*pej: col*) maricón *m*.

quell [kwɛl] *vt* (*feeling*) calmar; (*rebellion etc*) sofocar.

quench [kwɛntʃ] *vt* (*flames*) apagar; **to ~ one's thirst** apagar la sed.

querulous ['kwɛruləs] *a* (*person, voice*) quejumbroso.

query ['kwɪərɪ] *n* (*question*) pregunta; (*doubt*) duda // *vt* dudar de.

quest [kwɛst] *n* busca, búsqueda.

question ['kwɛstʃən] *n* pregunta; (*matter*) asunto, cuestión *f* // *vt* (*doubt*) dudar de; (*interrogate*) interrogar, hacer preguntas a; **beyond ~** fuera de toda duda; **it's out of the ~** imposible; ni hablar; **~able** *a* discutible; (*doubtful*) dudoso; **~ mark** *n* punto de interrogación; **~naire** [-'nɛə*] *n* cuestionario.

queue [kjuː] (*Brit*) *n* cola // *vi* hacer cola.

quibble ['kwɪbl] *vi* sutilizar.

quick [kwɪk] *a* rápido; (*temper*) vivo; (*mind*) listo; (*eye*) agudo // *n*: **cut to the ~** (*fig*) herido en lo vivo; **be ~!** ¡dare prisa!; **~en** *vt* apresu-

rar // vi apresurarse, darse prisa;
~**ly** ad rápidamente, de prisa;
~**sand** n arenas fpl movedizas; ~-
witted a perspicaz.

quid [kwɪd] n, pl inv (Brit col) libra.

quiet ['kwaɪət] a tranquilo; (person)
callado; (discreet) discreto // n silencio, tranquilidad f // vt, vi (US) =
~**en**; **keep** ~! ¡cállate!; ¡silencio!;
~**en** (also: ~**en down**) vi (grow
calm) calmarse; (grow silent) callarse // vt calmar, hacer callar; ~**ly** ad
tranquilamente, (silently) silenciosa-
mente; ~**ness** n (silence) silencio;
(calm) tranquilidad f.

quilt [kwɪlt] n (Brit) edredón m.

quin [kwɪn] n abbr = **quintuplet**.

quinine [kwɪ'niːn] n quinina.

quintet(te) [kwɪn'tɛt] n quinteto.

quintuplet [kwɪn'tjuːplɪt] n
quintillizo/a

quip [kwɪp] n pulla.

quirk [kwəːk] n peculiaridad f.

quit [kwɪt], pt, pp quit or quitted vt
dejar, abandonar; (premises) desocupar // vi (give up) renunciar; (go
away) irse; (resign) dimitir.

quite [kwaɪt] ad (rather) bastante;
(entirely) completamente; ~ **a few**
of them un buen número de ellos; ~
(so)! ¡así es!, ¡exactamente!

quits [kwɪts] a: ~ (with) en paz
(con); **let's call it** ~ dejémoslo en
tablas.

quiver ['kwɪvə*] vi estremecerse
// n (for arrows) carcaj m, aljaba.

quiz [kwɪz] n (game) concurso //
(: TV, RADIO) programa-concurso //
vt interrogar; ~**zical** a burlón(ona).

quota ['kwəʊtə] n cuota.

quotation [kwəʊ'teɪʃən] n cita; (estimate) presupuesto; ~ **marks** npl
comillas fpl.

quote [kwəʊt] n cita // vt (sentence)
citar; (price) cotizar // vi: **to** ~
from citar de.

quotient ['kwəʊʃənt] n cociente m.

R

rabbi ['ræbaɪ] n rabino.

rabbit ['ræbɪt] n conejo; ~ **hutch** n
conejera.

rabble ['ræbl] n (pej) chusma, populacho.

rabies ['reɪbiːz] n rabia.

RAC n abbr (Brit) = Royal Automobile Club.

race [reɪs] n carrera; (species) raza
// vt (horse) hacer correr; (person)
competir contra; (engine) acelerar //
vi (compete) competir; (run) correr;
(pulse) latir a ritmo acelerado; ~
car n (US) = **racing car**; ~ **car
driver** n (US) = **racing driver**;
~**course** n hipódromo; ~**horse** n
caballo de carreras; ~**track** n hipódromo; (for cars) autódromo.

racial ['reɪʃl] a racial; ~**ist** a, n racista m/f.

racing ['reɪsɪŋ] n carreras fpl; ~ **car**
n (Brit) coche m de carreras; ~
driver n (Brit) corredor/a m/f de
coches.

racism ['reɪsɪzəm] n racismo; **racist**
[-sɪst] a, n racista m/f.

rack [ræk] n (also: **luggage** ~) rejilla; (shelf) estante m; (also: **roof** ~)
baca, portaequipajes m inv; (clothes
~) percha // vt (cause pain to) atormentar; **to** ~ **one's brains** devanar-
se los sesos.

racket ['rækɪt] n (for tennis) raqueta;
(noise) ruido, estrépito; (swindle) estafa, timo.

racquet ['rækɪt] n raqueta.

racy ['reɪsɪ] a picante, salado.

radar ['reɪdɑː*] n radar m.

radiance ['reɪdɪəns] n brillantez f,
resplandor m.

radiant ['reɪdɪənt] a brillante, resplandeciente.

radiate ['reɪdɪeɪt] vt (heat) radiar,
irradiar // vi (lines) extenderse.

radiation [reɪdɪ'eɪʃən] n radiación f.

radiator ['reɪdɪeɪtə*] n radiador m.

radical ['rædɪkl] a radical.

radii ['reɪdɪaɪ] npl of **radius**.

radio ['reɪdɪəʊ] n radio f; **on the ~** por radio.

radio... [reɪdɪəʊ] pref: **~active** a radioactivo.

radio-controlled [reɪdɪəʊkən'trəʊld] a teledirigido.

radiography [reɪdɪ'ɒgrəfɪ] n radiografía.

radiology [reɪdɪ'ɒlədʒɪ] n radiología.

radio station n emisora.

radiotherapy ['reɪdɪəʊθerəpɪ] n radioterapia.

radish ['rædɪʃ] n rábano.

radius ['reɪdɪəs], pl **radii** [-ɪaɪ] n radio.

RAF n abbr = **Royal Air Force**.

raffle ['ræfl] n rifa, sorteo // vt rifar.

raft [rɑːft] n (craft) baba; (also: life ~) balsa salvavidas.

rafter ['rɑːftə*] n viga.

rag [ræg] n (piece of cloth) trapo; (torn cloth) harapo; (pej: newspaper) periodicucho; (for charity) actividades estudiantiles benéficas // vt (Brit) tomar el pelo a; **~s** npl harapos mpl; **~-and-bone man** n (Brit) = **~man**; **~ doll** n muñeca de trapo.

rage [reɪdʒ] n (fury) rabia, furor m // vi (person) rabiar, estar furioso; (storm) bramar; **it's all the ~ es** lo último.

ragged ['rægɪd] a (edge) desigual, mellado; (cuff) roto; (appearance) andrajoso, harapiento.

ragman ['rægmæn] n trapero.

raid [reɪd] n (MIL) incursión f; (criminal) asalto; (by police) redada // vt invadir, atacar, asaltar; **~er** n invasor/a m/f.

rail [reɪl] n (on stair) barandilla, pasamanos m inv; (on bridge, balcony) pretil m; (of ship) barandilla; (for train) riel m, carril m; **~s** npl vía sg; **by ~** por ferrocarril; **~ing(s)** n(pl) verja sg, enrejado sg; **~road** n (US) = **~way**; **~way** n (Brit) ferrocarril m, vía férrea; **~way line**

n (Brit) línea (de ferrocarril); **~wayman** n (Brit) ferroviario; **~way station** n (Brit) estación f de ferrocarril.

rain [reɪn] n lluvia // vi llover; **in the ~** bajo la lluvia; **it's ~ing** llueve, está lloviendo; **~bow** n arco iris; **~coat** n impermeable m; **~drop** n gota de lluvia; **~fall** n lluvia; **~y** a lluvioso.

raise [reɪz] n aumento // vt (lift) levantar; (build) erigir, edificar; (increase) aumentar; (doubts) suscitar; (a question) plantear; (cattle, family) criar; (crop) cultivar; (army) reclutar; (funds) reunir; (loan) obtener; to **~ one's voice** alzar la voz.

raisin ['reɪzn] n pasa de Corinto.

rake [reɪk] n (tool) rastrillo; (person) libertino // vt (garden) rastrillar; (fire) hurgar; (with machine gun) barrer.

rally ['rælɪ] n (POL etc) reunión f, mitin m; (AUT) rallye m; (TENNIS) peloteo // vt reunir // vi reunirse; (sick person, Stock Exchange) recuperarse; to **~ round** vt fus (fig) dar apoyo a.

RAM [ræm] n abbr (= random access memory) RAM f.

ram [ræm] n carnero; (TECH) pisón m // vt (crash into) dar contra, chocar con; (tread down) apisonar.

ramble ['ræmbl] n caminata, excursión f en el campo // vi (pej: also: ~on) divagar; **~r** n excursionista m/f; (BOT) trepadera; **rambling** a (speech) inconexo; (BOT) trepador(a).

ramp [ræmp] n rampa; **on/off ~** n (US AUT) vía de acceso/salida.

rampage [ræm'peɪdʒ] n: to **be on the ~** desmandarse.

rampant ['ræmpənt] a (disease etc): to **be ~** estar extendiéndose mucho.

rampart ['ræmpɑːt] n terraplén m; (wall) muralla.

ramshackle ['ræmʃækl] a destartalado.

ran [ræn] pt of **run**.

ranch [rɑːntʃ] n (US) hacienda, estancia; **~er** n ganadero.

rancid [ˈrænsɪd] a rancio.

rancour, (US) **rancor** [ˈræŋkə*] n rencor m.

random [ˈrændəm] a fortuito, sin orden; (COMPUT, MATH) aleatorio // n: **at ~** al azar.

randy [ˈrændɪ] a (Brit col) cachondo.

rang [ræŋ] pt of **ring**.

range [reɪndʒ] n (of mountains) cadena de montañas, cordillera; (of missile) alcance m; (of voice) registro; (series) serie f; (of products) surtido; (MIL: also: **shooting ~**) campo de tiro; (also: **kitchen ~**) fogón m // vt (place) colocar; (arrange) arreglar // vi: **to ~ over** (wander) recorrer; (extend) extenderse por; **to ~ from ... to...** oscilar entre ... y...

ranger [reɪndʒə*] n guardabosques m inv.

rank [ræŋk] n (row) fila; (MIL) rango; (status) categoría; (Brit: also: **taxi ~**) parada // vi: **to ~ among** figurar entre // a (stinking) fétido, rancio; **the ~ and file** (fig) la base.

rankle [ˈræŋkl] vi (insult) doler.

ransack [ˈrænsæk] vt (search) registrar; (plunder) saquear.

ransom [ˈrænsəm] n rescate m; **to hold sb to ~** (fig) hacer chantaje a uno.

rant [rænt] vi divagar, desvariar.

rap [ræp] vt golpear, dar un golpecito en.

rape [reɪp] n violación f; (BOT) colza // vt violar; **~ (seed) oil** n aceite m de colza.

rapid [ˈræpɪd] a rápido; **~s** npl (GEO) rápidos mpl; **~ity** [rəˈpɪdɪtɪ] n rapidez f; **~ly** ad rápidamente.

rapist [ˈreɪpɪst] n violador m.

rapport [ræˈpɔː*] n simpatía.

rapture [ˈræptʃə*] n éxtasis m.

rare [reə*] a raro, poco común; (CULIN: steak) poco hecho.

rarely [ˈreəlɪ] ad poca veces.

raring [ˈreərɪŋ] a: **to be ~ to go** (col) tener muchas ganas de empezar.

rarity [ˈreərɪtɪ] n rareza.

rascal [ˈrɑːskl] n pillo, pícaro.

rash [ræʃ] a imprudente, precipitado // n (MED) salpullido, erupción f (cutánea).

rasher [ˈræʃə*] n lonja.

raspberry [ˈrɑːzbərɪ] n frambuesa.

rasping [ˈrɑːspɪŋ] a: **a ~ noise** un ruido áspero.

rat [ræt] n rata.

rate [reɪt] n (ratio) razón f; (percentage) tanto por ciento; (price) precio; (: of hotel) tarifa; (of interest) tipo; (speed) velocidad f // vt (value) tasar; (estimate) estimar; **to ~ as** ser considerado como; **~s** npl (Brit) impuesto sg municipal; (fees) tarifa sg; **~able value** n (Brit) valor m imposible; **~payer** n (Brit) contribuyente m/f.

rather [ˈrɑːðə*] ad: **it's ~ expensive** es algo caro; (too much) es demasiado caro; **there's ~ a lot** hay bastante; **I would** or **I'd ~ go** preferiría ir; or mejor dicho.

ratify [ˈrætɪfaɪ] vt ratificar.

rating [ˈreɪtɪŋ] n (valuation) tasación f; (standing) posición f; (Brit NAUT: sailor) marinero.

ratio [ˈreɪʃɪəʊ] n razón f; **in the ~ of 100 to 1** a razón de 100 a 1.

ration [ˈræʃən] n ración f; **~s** npl víveres mpl // vt racionar.

rational [ˈræʃənl] a racional; (solution, reasoning) lógico, razonable; (person) cuerdo, sensato; **~e** [-ˈnɑːl] n razón f fundamental; **~ize** vt (industry) reconvertir; (behaviour) justificar.

rationing [ˈræʃnɪŋ] n racionamiento m.

rat race n lucha incesante por la supervivencia.

rattle [ˈrætl] n golpeteo; (of train etc) traqueteo; (object: of baby) sonaja, sonajero; (: of sports fan) matraca // vi sonar, golpear; traquetear; (small objects) castañetear // vt hacer sonar agitando; **~snake** n serpiente f de cascabel.

raucous [ˈrɔːkəs] a estridente, ronco.

ravage ['rævidʒ] vt hacer estragos en, destrozar; ~s npl estragos mpl.

rave [reiv] vi (in anger) encolerizarse; (with enthusiasm) entusiasmarse; (MED) delirar, desvariar.

raven ['reivən] n cuervo.

ravenous ['rævənəs] a hambriento.

ravine [rə'vi:n] n barranco.

raving ['reivin] a: ~ **lunatic** loco de atar.

ravishing ['rævifin] a encantador(a).

raw [rɔ:] a (uncooked) crudo; (not processed) bruto; (sore) vivo; (inexperienced) novato, inexperto; ~ **deal** n injusticia; ~ **material** n materia prima.

ray [rei] n rayo; ~ **of hope** (rayo de) esperanza.

rayon ['reiɔn] n rayón m.

raze [reiz] vt arrasar.

razor ['reizə*] n (open) navaja; (safety ~) máquina de afeitar; ~ **blade** n hoja de afeitar.

Rd abbr = **road**.

re [ri:] prep con referencia a.

reach [ri:tʃ] n alcance m; (BOXING) envergadura; (of river etc) extensión f entre dos recodos // vt alcanzar, llegar a; (achieve) lograr // vi extenderse; **within** ~ al alcance (de la mano); **out of** ~ fuera del alcance; **to** ~ **out for sth** alargar or tender la mano para tomar algo.

react [ri:'ækt] vi reaccionar; ~**ion** [-'ækʃən] n reacción f.

reactor [ri:'æktə*] n reactor m.

read [ri:d], pt, pp **read** [rɛd] vi leer // vt leer; (understand) entender; (study) estudiar; **to** ~ **out** vt leer en alta voz; ~**able** a (writing) legible; (book) leíble; ~**er** n lector(a) m/f; (book) libro de lecturas; (Brit: at university) profesor(a) m/f adjunto/a; ~**ership** n (of paper etc) (número de) lectores mpl.

readily ['rɛdili] ad (willingly) de buena gana; (easily) fácilmente; (quickly) en seguida.

readiness ['rɛdinis] n buena voluntad; (preparedness) preparación f;

in ~ (prepared) listo, preparado.

reading ['ri:din] n lectura; (understanding) comprensión f; (on instrument) indicación f.

readjust [ri:ə'dʒʌst] vt reajustar // vi (person): **to** ~ **to** reajustarse a.

ready ['rɛdi] a listo, preparado; (willing) dispuesto; (available) disponible // ad: ~-**cooked** listo para comer // n: **at the** ~ (MIL) listo para tirar; **to get** ~ vi prepararse // vt preparar; ~-**made** a confeccionado; ~ **money** n dinero contante; ~ **reckoner** n libro de cálculos hechos; ~-**to-wear** a confeccionado.

real [riəl] a verdadero, auténtico; **in** ~ **terms** en términos reales; ~ **estate** n bienes mpl raíces; ~**istic** [-'listik] a realista.

reality [ri:'æliti] n realidad f.

realization [riəlai'zeifən] n comprensión f; realización f.

realize ['riəlaiz] vt (understand) darse cuenta de; (a project; COMM: asset) realizar.

really ['riəli] ad realmente; ~? ¿de veras?

realm [rɛlm] n reino; (fig) esfera.

realtor ['riəltɔ:*] n (US) corredor(a) m/f de bienes raíces.

reap [ri:p] vt segar; (fig) cosechar, recoger.

reappear [ri:ə'piə*] vi reaparecer.

rear [riə*] a trasero // n parte f trasera // vt (cattle, family) criar // vi (also: ~ **up**) (animal) encabritarse; ~**guard** n retaguardia.

rearmament [ri:'ɑ:məmənt] n rearme m.

rearrange [ri:ə'reindʒ] vt ordenar or arreglar de nuevo.

rear-view ['riəvju:]: ~ **mirror** n (AUT) (espejo) retrovisor m.

reason ['ri:zn] n razón f // vi: **to** ~ **with sb** tratar de que uno entre en razón; **it stands to** ~ **that** es lógico que; ~**able** a razonable; (sensible) sensato; ~**ably** ad razonablemente; ~**ed** a (argument) razonado; ~**ing** n razonamiento, argumentos mpl.

reassurance [riːəˈʃuərəns] n consuelo.

reassure [riːəˈʃuəʳ] vt tranquilizar, alentar; **to ~ sb that** tranquilizar a uno asegurando que; **reassuring** a alentador(a).

rebate [ˈriːbeɪt] n (on product) rebaja; (on tax etc) descuento; (repayment) reembolso.

rebel [ˈrɛbl] n rebelde m/f // [rɪˈbɛl] rebelarse, sublevarse; **~lion** [rɪˈbɛljən] n rebelión f, sublevación f; **~lious** [rɪˈbɛljəs] a rebelde; (child) revoltoso.

rebound [rɪˈbaund] vi (ball) rebotar // [ˈriːbaund] rebote m.

rebuff [rɪˈbʌf] n desaire m, rechazo.

rebuild [riːˈbɪld] (irg: like **build**) vt reconstruir.

rebuke [rɪˈbjuːk] vt reprender.

rebut [rɪˈbʌt] vt rebatir.

recalcitrant [rɪˈkælsɪtrənt] a reacio.

recall [rɪˈkɔːl] vt (remember) recordar; (ambassador etc) retirar // n recuerdo.

recant [rɪˈkænt] vi retractarse.

recap [ˈriːkæp] vi, vi recapitular.

recapitulate [riːkəˈpɪtjuleɪt] vt, vi = **recap.**

rec'd abbr (= received) rbdo.

recede [rɪˈsiːd] vi retroceder; **receding** a (forehead, chin) huidizo; **receding hairline** entradas fpl.

receipt [rɪˈsiːt] n (document) recibo; (for parcel etc) acuse m de recibo; (act of receiving) recepción f; **~s** npl (COMM) ingresos mpl.

receive [rɪˈsiːv] vt recibir; (guest) acoger; (wound) sufrir; **~r** n (TEL) auricular m; (RADIO) receptor m; (of stolen goods) perista m/f; (LAW) administrador m jurídico.

recent [ˈriːsnt] a reciente; **~ly** ad recientemente; **~ly arrived** recién llegado.

receptacle [rɪˈsɛptɪkl] n receptáculo.

reception [rɪˈsɛpʃən] n (gen) recepción f; (welcome) acogida; **~ desk** n recepción f; **~ist** n recepcionista m/f.

recess [rɪˈsɛs] n (in room) hueco; (for bed) nicho; (secret place) escondrijo; (POL etc: holiday) clausura; **~ion** [-ˈsɛʃən] n recesión f.

recharge [riːˈtʃɑːdʒ] vt (battery) recargar.

recipe [ˈrɛsɪpɪ] n receta.

recipient [rɪˈsɪpɪənt] n recibidor(a) m/f; (of letter) destinatario/a.

recital [rɪˈsaɪtl] n recital m.

recite [rɪˈsaɪt] vt (poem) recitar; (complaints etc) enumerar.

reckless [ˈrɛkləs] a temerario, imprudente; (speed) peligroso; **~ly** ad imprudentemente; de modo peligroso.

reckon [ˈrɛkən] vt (count) contar; (consider) considerar; **I ~ that...** me parece que...; **to ~ on** vt fus contar con; **~ing** n (calculation) cálculo.

reclaim [rɪˈkleɪm] vt (land) recuperar; (: from sea) rescatar; (demand back) reclamar.

recline [rɪˈklaɪn] vi reclinarse; **reclining** a (seat) reclinable.

recluse [rɪˈkluːs] n recluso/a.

recognition [rɛkəɡˈnɪʃən] n reconocimiento; **transformed beyond ~** irreconocible.

recognizable [ˈrɛkəɡnaɪzəbl] a: **~ (by)** reconocible (por).

recognize [ˈrɛkəɡnaɪz] vt: **to ~ (by/as)** reconocer (por/como).

recoil [rɪˈkɔɪl] vi (person): **to ~ from doing sth** retraerse de hacer algo // n (of gun) retroceso.

recollect [rɛkəˈlɛkt] vt recordar, acordarse de; **~ion** [-ˈlɛkʃən] n recuerdo.

recommend [rɛkəˈmɛnd] vt recomendar.

recompense [ˈrɛkəmpɛns] vt recompensar // n recompensa.

reconcile [ˈrɛkənsaɪl] vt (two people) reconciliar; (two facts) compaginar; **to ~ o.s. to sth** conformarse a algo.

recondition [riːkənˈdɪʃən] vt (machine) reacondicionar.

reconnaissance [rɪˈkɒnɪsns] n (MIL) reconocimiento.

reconnoitre, (US) **reconnoiter** [rekə'nɔıtə*] vt, vi (MIL) reconocer.

reconsider [ri:kən'sıdə*] vt repensar.

reconstruct [ri:kən'strʌkt] vt reconstruir.

record ['rekɔ:d] n (MUS) disco; (of meeting etc) relación f; (register) registro, partida; (file) archivo; (also: police ~) antecedentes mpl; (written) expediente m; (SPORT) récord m // vt [rı'kɔ:d] (set down) registrar; (relate) hacer constar; (MUS: song etc) grabar; in ~ time en un tiempo récord; off the ~ a no oficial // ad confidencialmente; ~ card n (in file) ficha; ~ed delivery n (Brit POST) entrega con acuse de recibo; ~er n (MUS) flauta de pico; (TECH) contador m; ~ holder n (SPORT) actual poseedor(a) m/f del récord; ~ing n (MUS) grabación f; ~ player n tocadiscos m inv.

recount [rı'kaunt] vt contar.

re-count [rı'kaunt] n (POL: of votes) segundo escrutinio // vt [ri:'kaunt] volver a contar.

recoup [rı'ku:p] vt: to ~ one's losses recuperar las pérdidas.

recourse [rı'kɔ:s] n recurso.

recover [rı'kʌvə*] vt recuperar; (rescue) rescatar // vi (from illness, shock) recuperarse; (country) recuperar; ~y n recuperación f; rescate m; (MED): to make a ~y restablecerse.

recreation [rekrı'eıʃən] n (amusement, SCOL) recreo; ~al a de recreo.

recruit [rı'kru:t] n recluta m/f // vt reclutar; (staff) contratar (personal); ~ment n reclutamiento.

rectangle ['rektæŋgl] n rectángulo; **rectangular** [-'tæŋgjulə*] a rectangular.

rectify ['rektıfaı] vt rectificar.

rector ['rektə*] n (REL) párroco; ~y n casa del párroco.

recuperate [rı'ku:pəreıt] vi reponerse, restablecerse.

recur [rı'kə:*] vi repetirse; (pain, illness) producirse de nuevo; ~rence [rı'kʌrəns] n repetición f; ~rent [rı'kʌrənt] a repetido.

red [red] n rojo // a rojo; to be in the ~ (account) estar en números rojos; (business) tener un saldo negativo; to give sb the ~ carpet treatment recibir a uno con todos los honores; R~ Cross n Cruz f Roja; ~currant n grosella roja; ~den vt enrojecer // vi enrojecerse; ~dish a (hair) rojizo.

redeem [rı'di:m] vt (in pawn) desempeñar; (fig, also REL) rescatar; ~ing a: ~ing feature rasgo bueno or favorable.

redeploy [ri:dı'plɔı] vt (resources) reorganizar.

red: ~-haired a pelirrojo; ~-handed a: to be caught ~-handed cogerse (Sp) or pillarse (LAm) con las manos en la masa; ~head n pelirrojo/a; ~ herring n (fig) pista falsa; ~-hot a candente.

redirect [ri:daı'rekt] vt (mail) reexpedir.

red light n: to go through a ~ (AUT) pasar la luz roja; **red-light district** n barrio chino.

redo [ri:'du:] vt (irg: like do) vt rehacer.

redolent ['redələnt] a: ~ of (smell) con fragancia a; ~ of (fig) recordar.

redouble [ri:'dʌbl] vt: to ~ one's efforts intensificar sus esfuerzos.

redress [rı'dres] n reparación f // vt reparar.

Red Sea n: the ~ el mar Rojo.

redskin ['redskın] n piel roja m/f.

red tape n (fig) trámites mpl.

reduce [rı'dju:s] vt reducir; (lower) rebajar; '~ speed now' (AUT) 'reduzca la velocidad'; at a ~d price (of goods) (a precio) rebajado; re-**duction** [rı'dʌkʃən] n reducción f; (of price) rebaja; (discount) descuento.

redundancy [rı'dʌndənsı] n desempleo.

redundant [rɪ'dʌndnt] a (Brit) (worker) parado, sin trabajo; (detail, object) superfluo; **to be made ~** quedar(se) sin trabajo.

reed [riːd] n (BOT) junco, caña.

reef [riːf] n (at sea) arrecife m.

reek [riːk] vi: **to ~ (of)** apestar (a).

reel [riːl] n carrete m, bobina; (of film) rollo // vt (TECH) devanar; (also: ~ **in**) sacar // vi (sway) tambalear(se).

ref [ref] n abbr (col) = referee.

refectory [rɪ'fektəri] n comedor m.

refer [rɪ'fɜː*] vt (send) remitir; (ascribe) referir a, relacionar con // vi: **to ~ to** (allude to) referirse a, aludir a; (apply to) relacionarse con; (consult) consultar.

referee [refə'riː] n árbitro; (Brit: for job application) valedor m; **to be a ~** (for job application) proporcionar referencias // vt (match) arbitrar en.

reference ['refrəns] n (mention) referencia; (for job application: letter) carta de recomendación; **with ~ to** con referencia a; (COMM: in letter) me remito a; ~ **book** n libro de consulta; ~ **number** n número de referencia.

refill [riː'fɪl] vt rellenar // n ['riːfɪl] repuesto, recambio.

refine [rɪ'faɪn] vt (sugar, oil) refinar; ~**d** a (person, taste) fino; ~**ment** n (of person) cultura, educación f.

reflect [rɪ'flekt] vt (light, image) reflejar // vi (think) reflexionar, pensar; **it ~s badly/well on him** le perjudica/le hace honor; ~**ion** [-'flekʃən] n (act) reflexión f; (image) reflejo; (discredit) crítica; **on ~ion** pensándolo bien; ~**or** n (AUT) captafaros m inv; (telescope) reflector m.

reflex ['riːfleks] a, n reflejo; ~**ive** [rɪ'fleksɪv] a (LING) reflexivo.

reform [rɪ'fɔːm] n reforma // vt reformar; **the R~ation** [refə'meɪʃən] n la Reforma; ~**atory** n (US) reformatorio; ~**er** n reformador(a) m/f.

refrain [rɪ'freɪn] vi: **to ~ from doing** abstenerse de hacer // n estribillo.

refresh [rɪ'freʃ] vt refrescar; ~**er course** n (Brit) curso de repaso; ~**ing** a (drink) refrescante; (change etc) estimulante; ~**ments** npl (drinks) refrescos mpl.

refrigerator [rɪ'frɪdʒəreɪtə*] n nevera, refrigeradora (LAm).

refuel [riː'fjuəl] vi repostar (combustible).

refuge ['refjuːdʒ] n refugio, asilo; **to take ~ in** refugiarse en.

refugee [refju'dʒiː] n refugiado/a.

refund ['riːfʌnd] n reembolso // vt [rɪ'fʌnd] devolver, reembolsar.

refurbish [riː'fɜːbɪʃ] vt restaurar, renovar.

refusal [rɪ'fjuːzəl] n negativa; **to have first ~ on** tener la primera opción a.

refuse ['refjuːs] n basura // vb [rɪ'fjuːz] vt rechazar // vi negarse; (horse) rehusar; ~ **collection** recolección f de basuras.

regain [rɪ'geɪn] vt recobrar, recuperar.

regal ['riːgl] a regio, real.

regalia [rɪ'geɪlɪə] n insignias fpl.

regard [rɪ'gɑːd] n (esteem) respeto, consideración f // vt (consider) considerar; **to give one's ~s to** saludar de su parte a; **'with kindest ~s'** 'con muchos recuerdos'; ~**ing, as ~s, with ~ to** prep con respecto a, en cuanto a; ~**less** ad a pesar de todo; ~**less of** sin reparar en.

régime [reɪ'ʒiːm] n régimen m.

regiment ['redʒɪmənt] n regimiento // vt reglamentar; ~**al** [-'mentl] a militar.

region ['riːdʒən] n región f; **in the ~ of** (fig) alrededor de; ~**al** a regional.

register ['redʒɪstə*] n registro // vt registrar; (birth) declarar; (letter) certificar; (subj: instrument) marcar, indicar // vi (at hotel) registrarse; (sign on) inscribirse; (make impression) producir impresión; ~**ed** a (*design*) registrado; (*Brit: letter*) certificado; ~**ed trademark** *n* marca registrada.

registrar ['rɛdʒɪstra:ˁ] *n* secretario/a (del registro civil).

registration [rɛdʒɪs'treɪʃən] *n* (*act*) declaración *f*; (*AUT: also:* ~ **number**) matrícula.

registry ['rɛdʒɪstrɪ] *n* registro; ~ **office** *n* (*Brit*) registro civil; **to get married in a** ~ **office** casarse por lo civil.

regret [rɪ'grɛt] *n* sentimiento, pesar *m*; (*remorse*) remordimiento *// vt* sentir, lamentar; (*repent of*) arrepentirse de; ~**fully** *ad* con pesar; ~**table** *a* lamentable; (*loss*) sensible.

regroup [ri:'gru:p] *vt* reagrupar *// vi* reagruparse.

regular ['rɛgjulə*ˁ*] *a* regular; (*soldier*) profesional; (*col: intensive*) verdadero *// n* (*client etc*) cliente/a *m/f* habitual; ~**ity** [-'lærɪtɪ] *n* regularidad *f*; ~**ly** *ad* con regularidad.

regulate ['rɛgjuleɪt] *vt* (*gen*) controlar; **regulation** [-'leɪʃən] *n* (*rule*) regla, reglamento; (*adjustment*) regulación *f*.

rehearsal [rɪ'hə:səl] *n* ensayo.

rehearse [rɪ'hə:s] *vt* ensayar.

reign [reɪn] *n* reinado; (*fig*) predominio *// vi* reinar; (*fig*) imperar.

reimburse [ri:ɪm'bə:s] *vt* reembolsar.

rein [reɪn] *n* (*for horse*) rienda.

reindeer ['reɪndɪəˁ] *n*, *pl inv* reno.

reinforce [ri:ɪn'fɔ:s] *vt* reforzar; ~**d concrete** *n* hormigón *m* armado; ~**ment** *n* (*action*) refuerzo; ~**ments** *npl* (*MIL*) refuerzos *mpl*.

reinstate [ri:ɪn'steɪt] *vt* (*worker*) reintegrar (a su puesto).

reiterate [ri:'ɪtəreɪt] *vt* reiterar, repetir.

reject ['ri:dʒɛkt] *n* (*thing*) desecho *// vt* [rɪ'dʒɛkt] rechazar; (*suggestion*) descartar; ~**ion** [rɪ'dʒɛkʃən] *n* rechazo.

rejoice [rɪ'dʒɔɪs] *vi*: **to** ~ **at** *or* **over** regocijarse *or* alegrarse de.

rejuvenate [rɪ'dʒu:vəneɪt] *vt* rejuvenecer.

relapse [rɪ'læps] *n* (*MED*) recaída.

relate [rɪ'leɪt] *vt* (*tell*) contar, relatar; (*connect*) relacionar *// vi* relacionarse; ~**d a** a fin; (*person*) emparentado; ~**d to** (*subject*) relacionado con; **relating to** *prep* referente a.

relation [rɪ'leɪʃən] *n* (*person*) pariente/a *m/f*; (*link*) relación *f*; ~**ship** *n* relación *f*; (*personal*) relaciones *fpl*; (*also: family* ~**ship**) parentesco.

relative ['rɛlətɪv] *n* pariente/a *m/f*, familiar *m/f* // *a* relativo; ~**ly** *ad* (*comparatively*) relativamente.

relax [rɪ'læks] *vi* descansar; (*unwind*) relajarse *// vt* relajar; (*mind, person*) descansar; ~**ation** [ri:læk'seɪʃən] *n* (*rest*) descanso; (*entertainment*) diversión *f*; ~**ed** *a* relajado; (*tranquil*) tranquilo; ~**ing** *a* relajante.

relay ['ri:leɪ] *n* (*race*) carrera de relevos *// vt* (*RADIO, TV, pass on*) retransmitir.

release [rɪ'li:s] *n* (*liberation*) liberación *f*; (*discharge*) puesta en libertad *f*; (*of gas etc*) escape *m*; (*of film etc*) estreno *// vt* (*prisoner*) poner en libertad; (*film*) estrenar; (*book*) publicar; (*piece of news*) difundir; (*gas etc*) despedir, arrojar; (*free: from wreckage etc*) soltar; (*TECH: catch, spring etc*) desenganchar; (*let go*) soltar, aflojar.

relegate ['rɛləgeɪt] *vt* relegar; (*SPORT*): **to be** ~**d** to bajar a.

relent [rɪ'lɛnt] *vi* ablandarse; ~**less** *a* implacable.

relevant ['rɛləvənt] *a* (*fact*) pertinente; **relevant to** relacionado con.

reliability [rɪlaɪə'bɪlɪtɪ] *n* fiabilidad *f*; seguridad *f*; veracidad *f*.

reliable [rɪ'laɪəbl] *a* (*person, firm*) de confianza, de fiar; (*method, machine*) seguro; (*source*) fidedigno; **reliably** *ad*: **to be reliably informed that...** saber de fuente fidedigna que...

reliance [rɪ'laɪəns] *n*: ~ (**on**) dependencia (de).

relic ['rɛlɪk] n (REL) reliquia; (of the past) vestigio.

relief [rɪ'li:f] n (from pain, anxiety) alivio; (help, supplies) socorro, ayuda; (ART, GEO) relieve m.

relieve [rɪ'li:v] vt (pain, patient) aliviar; (bring help to) ayudar, socorrer; (burden) aligerar; (take over from: gen) sustituir; (: guard) relevar; to ~ sb of sth quitar algo a uno; to ~ o.s. hacer sus necesidades.

religion [rɪ'lɪdʒən] n religión f; **religious** a religioso.

relinquish [rɪ'lɪŋkwɪʃ] vt abandonar; (plan, habit) renunciar a.

relish ['rɛlɪʃ] n (CULIN) salsa; (enjoyment) entusiasmo // vt (food etc) saborear; to ~ doing gustar mucho de hacer.

relocate [ri:ləu'keɪt] vt cambiar de lugar, mudar // vi mudarse.

reluctance [rɪ'lʌktəns] n renuencia; **reluctant** a renuente; **reluctantly** ad de mala gana.

rely [rɪ'laɪ]: to ~ on vt fus confiar en, fiarse de; (be dependent on) depender de.

remain [rɪ'meɪn] vi (survive) quedar; (be left) sobrar; (continue) quedar(se), permanecer; ~der n resto; ~ing a sobrante; ~s npl restos mpl.

remand [rɪ'mɑ:nd] n: on ~ detenido (bajo custodia) // vt: to ~ in custody mantener bajo custodia; ~ home n (Brit) reformatorio.

remark [rɪ'mɑ:k] n comentario // vt comentar; ~able a notable; (outstanding) extraordinario.

remarry [rɪ'mærɪ] vi volver a casarse.

remedial [rɪ'mi:dɪəl] a: ~ education educación f de los niños atrasados.

remedy ['rɛmədɪ] n remedio // vt remediar, curar.

remember [rɪ'mɛmbə*] vt recordar, acordarse de; (bear in mind) tener presente; **remembrance** n: in remembrance of en conmemoración de.

remind [rɪ'maɪnd] vt: to ~ sb to do sth recordar a uno que haga algo; to ~ sb of sth recordar algo a uno; she ~s me of her mother me recuerda a su madre; ~er n notificación f; (memento) recuerdo.

reminisce [rɛmɪ'nɪs] vi recordar (viejas historias); ~nt a: to be ~nt of sth recordar algo.

remiss [rɪ'mɪs] a descuidado; it was ~ of him fue un descuido de su parte.

remission [rɪ'mɪʃən] n remisión f; (of sentence) disminución f de pena.

remit [rɪ'mɪt] vt (send: money) remitir, enviar; ~tance n remesa, envío.

remnant ['rɛmnənt] n resto; (of cloth) retazo; ~s npl (COMM) restos mpl de serie.

remorse [rɪ'mɔ:s] n remordimientos mpl; ~ful a arrepentido; ~less a (fig) implacable; inexorable.

remote [rɪ'məut] a (distant) lejano; (person) distante; ~ control n telecontrol m; ~ly ad remotamente; (slightly) levemente.

remould ['ri:məuld] n (Brit: tyre) neumático or llanta (LAm) recauchutado/a.

removable [rɪ'mu:vəbl] a (detachable) separable.

removal [rɪ'mu:vəl] n (taking away) el quitar; (Brit: from house) mudanza; (from office: dismissal) destitución f; (MED) extirpación f; ~ van n (Brit) camión m de mudanzas.

remove [rɪ'mu:v] vt quitar; (employee) destituir; (name: from list) tachar, borrar; (doubt) disipar; (abuse) suprimir, acabar con; (TECH) retirar, separar; (MED) extirpar; ~rs npl (Brit: company) agencia de mudanzas.

Renaissance [rɪ'neɪsɔ̃s] n: the ~ el Renacimiento.

render ['rɛndə*] vt (thanks) dar; (aid) proporcionar, prestar; (honour) dar, conceder; (assistance) dar, prestar; to ~ sth + a volver algo + a; ~ing n (MUS etc) interpretación f.

rendez-vous ['rɔndıvuː] *n* cita.

renegade ['rɛnıgeıd] *n* renegado/a.

renew [rı'njuː] *vt* renovar; *(resume)* reanudar; *(extend date)* prorrogar; ~**al** *n* renovación *f*; reanudación *f*; prórroga.

renounce [rı'nauns] *vt* renunciar a; *(right, inheritance)* renunciar.

renovate ['rɛnəveıt] *vt* renovar.

renown [rı'naun] *n* renombre *m*; ~**ed** *a* renombrado.

rent [rɛnt] *n* alquiler *m*; *(for house)* arriendo, renta // *vt* alquilar; ~**al** *n* *(for television, car)* alquiler *m*.

renunciation [rınʌnsı'eıʃən] *n* renuncia.

rep [rɛp] *n abbr* = **representative; repertory**.

repair [rı'pɛə*] *n* reparación *f*, compostura // *vt* reparar, componer; *(shoes)* remendar; **in good/bad** ~ en buen/mal estado; ~ **kit** *n* caja de herramientas.

repartee [rɛpɑː'tiː] *n* réplicas *fpl* agudas.

repatriate [riː'pætrıeıt] *vt* repatriar.

repay [riː'peı] *vt (irg: like* **pay***) vt (money)* devolver, reembolsar; *(person)* pagar; *(debt)* liquidar; *(sb's efforts)* devolver, corresponder a; ~**ment** *n* reembolso, devolución *f*; *(sum of money)* recompensa.

repeal [rı'piːl] *n* revocación *f* // *vt* revocar.

repeat [rı'piːt] *n (RADIO, TV)* reposición *f* // *vt* repetir // *vi* repetirse; ~**edly** *ad* repetidas veces.

repel [rı'pɛl] *vt (fig)* repugnar; ~**lent** *a* repugnante // *n:* **insect** ~**lent** crema/loción *f* anti-insectos.

repent [rı'pɛnt] *vi:* **to** ~ **(of)** arrepentirse (de); ~**ance** *n* arrepentimiento.

repercussion [riːpə'kʌʃən] *n (consequence)* repercusión *f*; **to have** ~**s** repercutir.

repertoire ['rɛpətwɑː*] *n* repertorio *m*.

repertory ['rɛpətərı] *n (also:* ~ **theatre)** teatro de repertorio.

repetition [rɛpı'tıʃən] *n* repetición *f*.

repetitive [rı'pɛtıtıv] *a* repetitivo.

replace [rı'pleıs] *vt (put back)* devolver a su sitio; *(take the place of)* reemplazar, sustituir; ~**ment** *n (act)* reposición *f*; *(thing)* recambio; *(person)* suplente *m/f*.

replay ['riːpleı] *n (SPORT)* desempate *m*; *(of tape, film)* repetición *f*.

replenish [rı'plɛnıʃ] *vt (tank etc)* rellenar; *(stock etc)* reponer.

replete [rı'pliːt] *a* repleto, lleno.

replica ['rɛplıkə] *n* copia, reproducción *f* (exacta).

reply [rı'plaı] *n* respuesta, contestación *f* // *vi* contestar, responder; ~ **coupon** *n* cupón-respuesta *m*.

report [rı'pɔːt] *n* informe *m*; *(PRESS etc)* reportaje *m*; *(Brit: also:* **school** ~) boletín *m* escolar; *(of gun)* estallido // *vt* informar de; *(PRESS etc)* hacer un reportaje sobre; *(notify: accident, culprit)* denunciar // *vi (make a report)* presentar un informe; *(present o.s.):* **to** ~ **(to sb)** presentarse (ante uno); ~ **card** *n (US, Scottish)* cartilla escolar; ~**edly** *ad* según se dice; ~**er** *n* periodista *m/f*.

repose [rı'pəuz] *n:* **in** ~ *(face, mouth)* en reposo.

reprehensible [rɛprı'hɛnsıbl] *a* reprensible, censurable.

represent [rɛprı'zɛnt] *vt* representar; *(COMM)* ser agente de; ~**ation** [-'teıʃən] *n* representación *f*; ~**ations** *npl (protest)* quejas *fpl*; ~**ative** *a (gen)* representante *m/f*; *(US POL)* diputado/a *m/f* // *a* representativo.

repress [rı'prɛs] *vt* reprimir; ~**ion** [-'prɛʃən] *n* represión *f*.

reprieve [rı'priːv] *n (LAW)* indulto; *(fig)* alivio.

reprimand ['rɛprımɑːnd] *n* reprimenda // *vt* reprender.

reprisal [rı'praızl] *n* represalia.

reproach [rı'prəutʃ] *n* reproche *m* // *vt:* **to** ~ **sb with sth** reprochar algo a uno; ~**ful** *a* de reproche, de acusación.

reproduce [riːprə'djuːs] *vt* reproducir // vi reproducirse; **reproduction** [-'dʌkʃən] n reproducción f.

reproof [rɪ'pruːf] n reproche m.

reprove [rɪ'pruːv] vt: to ~ sb for sth reprochar algo a uno.

reptile ['reptaɪl] n reptil m.

republic [rɪ'pʌblɪk] n república; ~**an** a, n republicano/a m/f.

repudiate [rɪ'pjuːdɪeɪt] vt (accusation) rechazar; (obligation) desconocer.

repulse [rɪ'pʌls] vt rechazar; **repulsive** a repulsivo.

reputable ['repjʊtəbl] a (make etc) de renombre.

reputation [repju'teɪʃən] n reputación f.

repute [rɪ'pjuːt] n reputación f, fama; ~**d** a supuesto; ~**dly** ad según dicen or se dice.

request [rɪ'kwest] n solicitud f; petición f // vt: to ~ sth of or from sb solicitar algo a uno; ~ **stop** n (Brit) parada discrecional.

require [rɪ'kwaɪə*] vt (need: subj: person) necesitar, tener necesidad de; (: thing, situation) exigir; (want) pedir; (demand) insistir en que; ~**ment** n requisito; (need) necesidad f.

requisite ['rekwɪzɪt] n requisito // a necesario.

requisition [rekwɪ'zɪʃən] n: ~ (**for**) solicitud f (de) // vt (MIL) requisar.

rescind [rɪ'sɪnd] vt (LAW) abrogar; (contract, order etc) anular.

rescue ['reskjuː] n rescate m // vt rescatar; to ~ **from** librar de; ~ **party** n expedición f de salvamento; ~**r** n salvador(a) m/f.

research [rɪ'sɜːtʃ] n investigaciones fpl // vt investigar; ~**er** n investigador(a) m/f.

resemblance [rɪ'zembləns] n parecido.

resemble [rɪ'zembl] vt parecerse a.

resent [rɪ'zent] vt tomar a mal; ~**ful** a resentido; ~**ment** n resentimiento.

reservation [rezə'veɪʃən] n (area of land, doubt) reserva; (booking) re-

servación f; (Brit: also: **central** ~) mediana.

reserve [rɪ'zɜːv] n reserva; (SPORT) suplente m/f // vt (seats etc) reservar; ~**s** npl (MIL) reserva sg; **in** ~ de reserva; ~**d** a reservado.

reservoir ['rezəvwɑː*] n (for irrigation, etc) embalse m; (tank etc) depósito.

reshape [riː'ʃeɪp] vt (policy) reformar, rehacer.

reshuffle [riː'ʃʌfl] n: **cabinet** ~ (POL) remodelación f del gabinete.

reside [rɪ'zaɪd] vi residir, vivir.

residence ['rezɪdəns] n residencia; (formal: home) domicilio; (length of stay) permanencia; ~ **permit** n (Brit) permiso de permanencia.

resident ['rezɪdənt] n (of area) vecino/a; (in hotel) huésped/a m/f // a (population) permanente; ~**ial** [-'denʃəl] a residencial.

residue ['rezɪdjuː] n resto, (CHEM, PHYSICS) residuo.

resign [rɪ'zaɪn] vt (gen) renunciar a // vi dimitir; to ~ **o.s. to** (endure) resignarse a; ~**ation** [rezɪg'neɪʃən] n dimisión f; (state of mind) resignación f; ~**ed** a resignado.

resilience [rɪ'zɪlɪəns] n (of material) elasticidad f; (of person) resistencia.

resilient [rɪ'zɪlɪənt] a (person) resistente.

resin ['rezɪn] n resina.

resist [rɪ'zɪst] vt resistir, oponerse a; ~**ance** n resistencia.

resolute ['rezəluːt] a resuelto.

resolution [rezə'luːʃən] n (gen) resolución f.

resolve [rɪ'zɔlv] n resolución f // vt resolver // vi resolverse; to ~ **to do** resolver hacer; ~**d** a resuelto.

resort [rɪ'zɔːt] n (town) centro turístico; (recourse) recurso // vi: to ~ **to** recurrir a; **in the last** ~ como último recurso.

resound [rɪ'zaund] vi: to ~ (**with**) resonar (con); ~**ing** a sonoro; (fig) clamoroso.

resource [rɪ'sɔːs] n recurso; ~**s** npl

recursos *mpl*; ~**ful** *a* despabilado, ingenioso.

respect [ris'pɛkt] *n* (*consideration*) respeto; ~**s** *npl* recuerdos *mpl*, saludos *mpl* // *vt* respetar; **with** ~ **to** con respecto a; **in this** ~ en cuanto a eso; ~**able** *a* respetable; (*large*) apreciable; (*passable*) tolerable; ~**ful** *a* respetuoso.

respective [ris'pɛktiv] *a* respectivo; ~**ly** *ad* respectivamente.

respite ['rɛspait] *n* respiro; (*LAW*) prórroga.

resplendent [ris'plɛndənt] *a* resplandeciente.

respond [ris'pɔnd] *vi* responder; (*react*) reaccionar; **response** [-'pɔns] *n* respuesta; reacción *f*.

responsibility [rispɔnsi'biliti] *n* responsabilidad *f*.

responsible [ris'pɔnsibl] *a* (*character*) serio, formal; (*job*) de confianza; (*liable*): ~ (**for**) responsable (de).

responsive [ris'pɔnsiv] *a* sensible.

rest [rɛst] *n* descanso, reposo; (*MUS*) pausa, silencio; (*support*) apoyo; (*remainder*) resto // *vi* descansar; (*be supported*): **to** ~ **on** descansar sobre // *vt* (*lean*): **to** ~ **sth on/against** apoyar algo en or sobre/contra; **the** ~ **of them** (*people, objects*) los demás; **it** ~**s with him** depende de él.

restaurant ['rɛstərɔŋ] *n* restorán *m*, restaurante *m*; ~ **car** *n* (*Brit RAIL*) coche-comedor *m*.

restful ['rɛstful] *a* descansado, tranquilo.

rest home *n* residencia para jubilados.

restitution [rɛsti'tju:ʃən] *n*: **to make** ~ **to sb for sth** indemnizar a uno por algo.

restive ['rɛstiv] *a* inquieto; (*horse*) rebelón(ona).

restless ['rɛstlis] *a* inquieto.

restoration [rɛstə'reiʃən] *n* restauración *f*; devolución *f*.

restore [ri'stɔ:*] *vt* (*building*) restaurar; (*sth stolen*) devolver; (*health*)

restablecer.

restrain [ris'trein] *vt* (*feeling*) contener, refrenar; (*person*): **to** ~ (**from doing**) disuadir (de hacer); ~**ed** *a* (*style*) reservado; ~**t** *n* (*restriction*) restricción *f*; (*of manner*) reserva.

restrict [ris'trikt] *vt* restringir, limitar; ~**ion** [-kʃən] *n* restricción *f*, limitación *f*; ~**ive** *a* restrictivo.

rest room *n* (*US*) aseos *mpl*.

result [ri'zʌlt] *n* resultado // *vi*: **to** ~ **in** terminar en, tener por resultado; **as a** ~ **of** a consecuencia de.

resume [ri'zju:m] *vt* (*work, journey*) reanudar // *vi* (*meeting*) continuar.

résumé ['reizju:mei] *n* resumen *m*.

resumption [ri'zʌmpʃən] *n* reanudación *f*.

resurgence [ri'sə:dʒəns] *n* resurgimiento.

resurrection [rɛzə'rɛkʃən] *n* resurrección *f*.

resuscitate [ri'sʌsiteit] *vt* (*MED*) resucitar.

retail ['ri:teil] *n* venta al por menor // *cpd* al por menor // *vt* vender al por menor; ~**er** *n* detallista *m/f* ~ **price** *n* precio de venta al público.

retain [ri'tein] *vt* (*keep*) retener, conservar; (*employ*) contratar; ~**er** *n* (*servant*) criado; (*fee*) anticipo.

retaliate [ri'tælieit] *vi*: **to** ~ (**against**) tomar represalias (contra); **retaliation** [-'eiʃən] *n* represalias *fpl*.

retarded [ri'tɑ:did] *a* retrasado.

retch [rɛtʃ] *vi* hacer uno arcadas.

retentive [ri'tɛntiv] *a* (*memory*) retentivo.

reticent ['rɛtisnt] *a* reservado.

retina ['rɛtinə] *n* retina.

retinue ['rɛtinju:] *n* séquito, comitiva.

retire [ri'taiə*] *vi* (*give up work*) jubilarse; (*withdraw*) retirarse; (*go to bed*) acostarse; ~**d** *a* (*person*) jubilado; ~**ment** *n* (*state*) retiro; (*act*) jubilación *f*; **retiring** *a* (*leaving*) saliente; (*shy*) retraído.

retort [ri'tɔ:t] *n* (*reply*) réplica // *vi*

contestar.

retrace [ri'treis] *vt*: to ~ one's steps volver sobre sus pasos, desandar lo andado.

retract [ri'trækt] *vt* (*statement*) retirar; (*claws*) retraer; (*undercarriage, aerial*) replegar // *vi* retractarse.

retrain [ri:'trein] *vt* reciclar; **~ing** *n* readaptación *f* profesional.

retread [ri:'tred] *n* neumático *m* or llanta (*LAm*) recauchutado/a.

retreat [ri'tri:t] *n* (*place*) retiro; (*MIL*) retirada // *vi* retirarse; (*flood*) bajar.

retribution [retri'bju:ʃən] *n* desquite *m*.

retrieval [ri'tri:vəl] *n* recuperación *f*; **information ~** recuperación *f* de datos.

retrieve [ri'tri:v] *vt* recobrar; (*situation, honour*) salvar; (*COMPUT*) recuperar; (*error*) reparar; **~r** *n* perro cobrador.

retrograde ['retrəgreid] *a* retrógrado.

retrospect ['retrəspekt] *n*: **in ~** retrospectivamente; **~ive** [-'spektiv] *a* restrospectivo; (*law*) retroactivo.

return [ri'tə:n] *n* (*going or coming back*) vuelta, regreso; (*of sth stolen etc*) devolución *f*; (*recompense*) recompensa; (*FINANCE: from land, shares*) ganancia, ingresos *mpl* // *cpd* (*journey*) de regreso; (*Brit: ticket*) de ida y vuelta; (*match*) de desquite // *vi* (*person etc: come or go back*) volver, regresar; (*symptoms etc*) reaparecer // *vt* devolver; (*favour, love etc*) corresponder a; (*verdict*) pronunciar; (*POL: candidate*) elegir; **~s** *npl* (*COMM*) ingresos *mpl*; **in ~** (**for**) en cambio (de); **by ~ of post** a vuelta de correo; **many happy ~s (of the day)!** ¡feliz cumpleaños!

reunion [ri:'ju:niən] *n* reunión *f*.

reunite [ri:ju:'nait] *vt* reunir; (*reconcile*) reconciliar.

rev [rev] (*AUT*) *n abbr* (= *revolution*) revolución // (*vb: also:* ~ **up**) *vt* girar // *vi* (*engine*) girarse; (*driver*) gi-

rar el motor.

revamp [ri:'væmp] *vt* (*company, organization*) reorganizar.

reveal [ri'vi:l] *vt* (*make known*) revelar; **~ing** *a* revelador(a).

reveille [ri'væli] *n* (*MIL*) diana.

revel ['revl] *vi*: to ~ **in sth/in doing sth** gozar de algo/con hacer algo.

revelry ['revlri] *n* jarana, juerga.

revenge [ri'vendʒ] *n* venganza; (*in sport*) revancha; **to take ~ on** vengarse de.

revenue ['revənju:] *n* ingresos *mpl*, rentas *fpl*.

reverberate [ri'və:bəreit] *vi* (*sound*) resonar, retumbar; **reverberation** [-'reiʃən] *n* retumbo, eco.

revere [ri'viə*] *vt* venerar; **~nce** ['revərəns] *n* reverencia.

Reverend ['revərənd] *a* (*in titles*): **the ~ John Smith** (*Anglican*) el Reverendo John Smith; (*Catholic*) el Padre John Smith; (*Protestant*) el Pastor John Smith.

reverie ['revəri] *n* ensueño.

reversal [ri'və:sl] *n* (*of order*) inversión *f*; (*of policy*) cambio; (*of decision*) revocación *f*.

reverse [ri'və:s] *n* (*opposite*) contrario; (*back: of cloth*) revés *m*; (: *of coin*) reverso, (: *of paper*) dorso; (*AUT: also:* ~ **gear**) marcha atrás // *a* (*order*) inverso; (*direction*) contrario // *vt* (*decision, AUT*) dar marcha atrás a; (*position, function*) invertir // *vi* (*Brit AUT*) dar marcha atrás; **~-charge call** *n* (*Brit*) llamada a cobro revertido; **reversing lights** *npl* (*Brit AUT*) luces *fpl* de marcha atrás.

revert [ri'və:t] *vi*: to ~ **to** volver a.

review [ri'vju:] *n* (*magazine, MIL*) revista; (*of book, film*) reseña; (*US: examination*) repaso, examen *m* // *vt* repasar, examinar; (*MIL*) pasar revista a; (*book, film*) reseñar; **~er** *n* crítico/a.

revile [ri'vail] *vt* injuriar, vilipendiar.

revise [ri'vaiz] *vt* (*manuscript*) corregir; (*opinion*) modificar; (*Brit:*

study: subject) repasar; *(look over)* revisar; **revision** [rɪ'vɪʒən] *n* corrección *f*; modificación *f*; repaso; revisión *f*.

revitalize [ri:'vaɪtəlaɪz] *vt* revivificar.

revival [rɪ'vaɪvəl] *n (recovery)* reanimación *f*; *(POL)* resurgimiento; *(of interest)* renacimiento; *(THEATRE)* reestreno; *(of faith)* despertar *m*.

revive [rɪ'vaɪv] *vt* resucitar; *(custom)* restablecer; *(hope, interest)* despertar; *(play)* reestrenar // *vi (person)* volver en sí; *(from tiredness)* reponerse; *(business)* reactivarse.

revolt [rɪ'vəʊlt] *n* rebelión *f* // *vi* rebelarse, sublevarse // *vt* dar asco a, repugnar; **~ing** *a* asqueroso, repugnante.

revolution [rɛvə'lu:ʃən] *n* revolución *f*; **~ary** *a, n* revolucionario/a *m/f*.

revolve [rɪ'vɒlv] *vi* dar vueltas, girar.

revolver [rɪ'vɒlvə*] *n* revólver *m*.

revolving [rɪ'vɒlvɪŋ] *a (chair, door etc)* giratorio.

revue [rɪ'vju:] *n (THEATRE)* revista.

revulsion [rɪ'vʌlʃən] *n* asco, repugnancia.

reward [rɪ'wɔːd] *n* premio, recompensa *f* // *vt*: to ~ (for) recompensar *or* premiar (por); **~ing** *a (fig)* valioso.

rewire [ri:'waɪə*] *vt (house)* renovar la instalación eléctrica de.

reword [ri:'wɜːd] *vt* expresar en otras palabras.

rewrite [ri:'raɪt] *(irg: like write) vt* reescribir.

rhapsody ['ræpsədɪ] *n (MUS)* rapsodia.

rhetoric ['rɛtərɪk] *n* retórica; **~al** [rɪ'tɒrɪkl] *a* retórico.

rheumatism ['ru:mətɪzəm] *n* reumatismo, reúma *m*.

Rhine [raɪn] *n*: the ~ el (río) Rin.

rhinoceros [raɪ'nɒsərəs] *n* rinoceronte *m*.

rhododendron [rəʊdə'dɛndrn] *n* rododendro.

Rhone [rəʊn] *n*: the ~ el (río) Ródano.

rhubarb ['ru:bɑːb] *n* ruibarbo.

rhyme [raɪm] *n* rima; *(verse)* poesía.

rhythm ['rɪðm] *n* ritmo.

rib [rɪb] *n (ANAT)* costilla // *vt (mock)* tomar el pelo a.

ribald ['rɪbəld] *a* escabroso.

ribbon ['rɪbən] *n* cinta; **in ~s** *(torn)* hecho trizas.

rice [raɪs] *n* arroz *m*; ~ **pudding** *n* arroz *m* con leche.

rich [rɪtʃ] *a* rico; *(soil)* fértil; *(food)* pesado; (: *sweet)* empalagoso; **the ~ npl** los ricos; **~es** *npl* riqueza *sg*; **~ly** *ad* ricamente; **~ness** *n* riqueza; fertilidad *f*.

rickets ['rɪkɪts] *n* raquitismo.

rickety ['rɪkɪtɪ] *a (old)* desvencijado; *(shaky)* tambaleante.

rickshaw ['rɪkʃɔː] *n* carro de culi.

ricochet ['rɪkəʃeɪ] *n* rebote *m* // *vi* rebotar.

rid [rɪd], *pt, pp* **rid** *vt*: to ~ **sb** *of* **sth** librar a uno de algo; **to get ~ of** deshacerse *or* desembarazarse de.

ridden ['rɪdn] *pp of* **ride**.

riddle ['rɪdl] *n (puzzle)* acertijo; *(mystery)* enigma *m*, misterio // *vt*: **to be ~d** *with* ser lleno *o* plagado de.

ride [raɪd] *n* paseo; *(distance covered)* viaje *m*, recorrido // *(vb: pt* rode, *pp* ridden) *vi (horse: as sport)* montar; *(go somewhere: on horse, bicycle)* dar un paseo, pasearse; *(journey: on bicycle, motor cycle, bus)* viajar // *vt (a horse)* montar a; *(distance)* recorrer; **to ~ a bicycle** andar en bicicleta; **to ~ at anchor** *(NAUT)* estar fondeado; **to take sb for a ~** *(fig)* engañar a uno; **~r** *n (on horse)* jinete/a *m/f*; *(on bicycle)* ciclista *m/f*; *(on motorcycle)* motociclista *m/f*.

ridge [rɪdʒ] *n (of hill)* cresta; *(of roof)* caballete *m*.

ridicule ['rɪdɪkjuːl] *n* irrisión *f*, burla // *vt* poner en ridículo, burlarse de; **ridiculous** [-'dɪkjuləs] *a* ridículo.

riding ['raɪdɪŋ] n equitación f; I like ~ me gusta montar a caballo; ~ **school** n escuela f de equitación.

rife [raɪf] a: to be ~ ser muy común; to be ~ **with** abundar en.

riffraff ['rɪfræf] n gentuza.

rifle ['raɪfl] n rifle m, fusil m // vt saquear; ~ **range** n campo de tiro; (at fair) tiro al blanco.

rift [rɪft] n (fig: between friends) desavenencia; (: in party) ruptura f.

rig [rɪg] n (also: **oil** ~: on land) torre f de perforación; (: at sea) plataforma petrolera // vt (election etc) amañar; **to** ~ **out** vt (Brit) ataviar; **to** ~ **up** vt improvisar; ~**ging** n (NAUT) aparejo.

right [raɪt] a (true, correct) correcto, exacto; (suitable) indicado, debido; (proper) apropiado; (just) justo; (morally good) bueno; (not left) derecho // n (title, claim) derecho; (not left) derecha // ad (correctly) bien, correctamente; (straight) derecho, directamente; (not left) a la derecha; (to the ~) hacia la derecha // vt enderezar // excl ¡bueno!, ¡está bien!; **to be** ~ (person) tener razón; **by** ~**s** en justicia; **on the** ~ a la derecha; **to be in the** ~ tener razón; ~ **now** ahora mismo; ~ **in the middle** exactamente en el centro; ~ **away** en seguida; ~ **angle** n ángulo recto; ~**eous** ['raɪtʃəs] a justado, honrado; (anger) justificado; ~**ful** a (heir) legítimo; ~**handed** a (person) que usa la mano derecha; ~**hand man** n brazo derecho; **the** ~**-hand side** n la derecha; ~**ly** ad correctamente, debidamente; (with reason) con razón; ~ **of way** n (on path etc) derecho de paso; (AUT) prioridad f; ~**wing** a (POL) derechista.

rigid ['rɪdʒɪd] a rígido; (person, ideas) inflexible; ~**ity** [rɪ'dʒɪdɪtɪ] n rigidez f; inflexibilidad n.

rigmarole ['rɪgmərəʊl] n galimatías m inv.

rigorous ['rɪgərəs] a riguroso.

rigour, (US) rigor ['rɪgə*] n rigor m, severidad f.

rile [raɪl] vt irritar.

rim [rɪm] n borde m; (of spectacles) aro; (of wheel) llanta.

rind [raɪnd] n (of bacon) corteza; (of lemon etc) cáscara; (of cheese) costra.

ring [rɪŋ] n (of metal) aro; (on finger) anillo; (also: **wedding** ~) alianza; (of people) corro; (of objects) círculo; (gang) banda; (for boxing) cuadrilátero; (of circus) pista; (bull ~) ruedo, plaza; (sound of bell) toque m; (telephone call) llamada // vb (pt **rang**, pp **rung**) vi (on telephone) llamar por teléfono; (large bell) repicar; (also: ~ **out**: voice, words) sonar; (ears) zumbar // vt (Brit TEL: also: ~ **up**) llamar, telefonear (esp LAm); (bell etc) hacer sonar; (doorbell) tocar; **to** ~ **back** vt, vi (TEL) devolver la llamada; **to** ~ **off** vi (Brit TEL) colgar, cortar la comunicación; ~**ing** n (of large bell) repique m; (in ears) zumbido; ~**ing tone** n (TEL) tono de llamada; ~**leader** n (of gang) cabecilla m.

ringlets ['rɪŋlɪts] npl rizos mpl, bucles mpl.

ring road n (Brit) carretera periférica or de circunvalación.

rink [rɪŋk] n (also: **ice** ~) pista de hielo.

rinse [rɪns] vt (dishes) enjuagar; (clothes) aclarar; (hair) dar reflejos a.

riot ['raɪət] n motín m, disturbio // vi amotinarse; **to run** ~ desmandarse; ~**er** n amotinado/a; ~**ous** a alborotado; (party) bullicioso; (uncontrolled) desenfrenado.

rip [rɪp] n rasgón m, rasgadura // vt rasgar, desgarrar // vi rasgarse, desgarrarse; ~**cord** n cabo de desgarre.

ripe [raɪp] a (fruit) maduro; ~**n** vt madurar // vi madurarse.

rip-off ['rɪpɔf] n (col): **it's a** ~! ¡es una estafa!

ripple ['rɪpl] n onda, rizo; (sound) murmullo m // vi rizarse // vt rizar.

rise [raɪz] n (slope) cuesta, pendiente f; (hill) altura; (increase: in wages: Brit) aumento; (: in prices, temperature) subida; (fig: to power etc) ascenso // vi (pt **rose**, pp **risen** ['rɪzn]) (gen) elevarse; (prices) subir; (waters) crecer; (river) nacer; (sun) salir; (person: from bed etc) levantarse; (also: ~ **up**: rebel) sublevarse; (in rank) ascender; **to give** ~ **to** dar lugar or origen a; **to** ~ **to the occasion** ponerse a la altura de las circunstancias; **rising** a (increasing: number) creciente; (: prices) en aumento or alza; (tide) creciente; (sun, moon) naciente // n (uprising) sublevación f.

risk [rɪsk] n riesgo, peligro // vt arriesgar; (run the ~ of) exponerse a; **to take** or **run the** ~ **of doing** correr el riesgo de hacer; **at** ~ en peligro; **at one's own** ~ bajo su propia responsabilidad; ~**y** a arriesgado, peligroso.

risqué ['rɪskeɪ] a (joke) subido de color.

rissole ['rɪsəul] n croqueta.

rite [raɪt] n rito; **last** ~**s** exequias fpl.

ritual ['rɪtjuəl] a ritual // n ritual m, rito.

rival ['raɪvl] n rival m/f; (in business) competidor(a) m/f // a rival, opuesto // vt competir con; ~**ry** n rivalidad f, competencia.

river ['rɪvə*] n río // cpd (port, fish) de río; (traffic) fluvial; **up/down** ~ río arriba/abajo; ~**bank** n orilla (del río); ~**bed** n lecho, cauce m.

rivet ['rɪvɪt] n roblón, remache m // vt remachar; (fig) captar.

Riviera [rɪvɪ'eərə] n: **the** (French) ~ la Costa Azul (francesa); **the Italian** ~ la Riviera italiana.

road [rəud] n (gen) camino; (motorway etc) carretera; (in town) calle f; **major/minor** ~ carretera principal/secundaria; ~**block** n barricada; ~**hog** n loco/a del volante; ~ **map**

n mapa m de carreteras; ~ **safety** n seguridad f vial; ~**side** n borde m (del camino) // cpd al lado de la carretera; ~**sign** n señal f de tráfico; ~ **user** n usuario/a de la vía pública; ~**way** n calzada; ~**works** npl obras fpl; ~**worthy** a (car) en buen estado para circular.

roam [rəum] vi vagar // vt vagar por.

roar [rɔː*] n (of animal) rugido, bramido; (of crowd) rugido; (of vehicle, storm) estruendo; (of laughter) carcajada // vi rugir, bramar; hacer estruendo; **to** ~ **with laughter** reírse a carcajadas; **to do a** ~**ing trade** hacer buen negocio.

roast [rəust] n carne f asada, asado // vt (meat) asar; (coffee) tostar; ~ **beef** n rosbif m.

rob [rɔb] vt robar; **to** ~ **sb of sth** robar algo a uno; (fig: deprive) quitar algo a uno; ~**ber** n ladrón/ona m/f; ~**bery** n robo.

robe [rəub] n (for ceremony etc) toga; (also: **bath** ~) bata.

robin ['rɔbɪn] n petirrojo.

robot ['rəubɔt] n robot m.

robust [rəu'bʌst] a robusto, fuerte.

rock [rɔk] n (gen) roca; (boulder) peña, peñasco; (Brit: sweet) ~ piruli // vt (swing gently: cradle) balancear, mecer; (: child) arrullar; (shake) sacudir // vi mecerse, balancearse; sacudirse; **on the** ~**s** (drink) con hielo; (marriage etc) en ruinas; ~ **and roll** n rocanrol m; ~**bottom** n (fig) punto más bajo // a: **at** ~-**bottom prices** a precios regalados; ~**ery** n cuadro alpino.

rocket ['rɔkɪt] n cohete m.

rocking ['rɔkɪŋ]: ~ **chair** n mecedora; ~ **horse** n caballo de balancín.

rocky ['rɔkɪ] a (gen) rocoso; (unsteady: table) inestable.

rod [rɔd] n vara, varilla; (TECH) barra; (also: **fishing** ~) caña.

rode [rəud] pt of **ride**.

rodent ['rəudnt] n roedor m.

roe [rəu] n (species: also: ~ **deer**) corzo; (of fish): **hard/soft** ~ hueva/

lecha.

rogue [rəug] *n* pícaro, pillo.

role [rəul] *n* papel *m*, rol *m*.

roll [rəul] *n* rollo; (*of bank notes*) fajo; (*also:* **bread ~**) panecillo; (*register*) lista, nómina; (*sound: of drums etc*) redoble *m*; (*movement: of ship*) balanceo // *vt* hacer rodar; (*also: ~ up: string*) enrollar; (: *sleeves*) arremangar; (*cigarettes*) liar; (*also: ~ out: pastry*) aplanar // *vi* (*gen*) rodar; (*drum*) redoblar; (*in walking*) bambolearse; (*ship*) balancearse; **to ~ about** *or* **around** *vi* (*person*) revolcarse; **to ~ by** *vi* (*time*) pasar; **to ~ in** *vi* (*mail, cash*) entrar a raudales; **to ~ over** *vi* dar una vuelta; **to ~ up** *vi* (*col: arrive*) aparecer // *vt* (*carpet*) enrollar; **~ call** *n*: **to take a ~ call** pasar lista; **~er** *n* rodillo; (*wheel*) rueda; **~er coaster** *n* montaña rusa; **~er skates** *npl* patines *mpl* de rueda.

rolling [ˈrəulɪŋ] *a* (*landscape*) ondulado; **~ pin** *n* rodillo (de cocina); **~ stock** *n* (*RAIL*) material *m* rodante.

ROM [rɔm] *n abbr* (= *read only memory*) ROM *f*.

Roman [ˈrəumən] *a, n* romano/a *m/f*; **~ Catholic** *a, n* católico/a *m/f* (romano/a).

romance [rəˈmæns] *n* (*love affair*) amor *m*; (*charm*) lo romántico; (*novel*) novela de amor.

Romania [ruːˈmeɪnɪə] *n* = **Rumania**.

Roman numeral *n* número romano.

romantic [rəˈmæntɪk] *a* romántico.

Rome [rəum] *n* Roma.

romp [rɔmp] *n* retozo, juego // *vi* (*also: ~ about*) jugar, brincar.

rompers [ˈrɔmpəz] *npl* pelele *m*.

roof [ruːf], *pl* **~s** *n* (*gen*) techo; (*of house*) techo, tejado; (*of car*) baca // *vt* techar, poner techo a; **the ~ of the mouth** el paladar; **~ing** *n* techumbre *f*; **~ rack** *n* (*AUT*) baca, portaequipajes *m inv*.

rook [ruk] *n* (*bird*) graja; (*CHESS*) torre *f*.

room [ruːm] *n* (*in house*) cuarto, habitación *f*, pieza (*esp LAm*); (*also:* **bed~**) dormitorio; (*in school etc*) sala; (*space*) sitio, cabida; **~s** *npl* (*lodging*) alojamiento *sg*; '**~s to let**', (*US*) '**~s for rent**' 'se alquilan pisos *or* cuartos'; **single/double ~** habitación individual/doble *or* para dos personas; **~ing house** *n* (*US*) pensión *f*; **~mate** *n* compañero/a de cuarto; **~ service** *n* servicio de habitaciones; **~y** *a* espacioso.

roost [ruːst] *n* percha // *vi* pasar la noche.

rooster [ˈruːstə*] *n* gallo.

root [ruːt] *n* (*BOT, MATH*) raíz *f* // *vi* (*plant, belief*) arraigarse; **to ~ about** *vi* (*fig*) buscar y rebuscar; **to ~ for** *vt fus* apoyar a; **to ~ out** *vt* desarraigar.

rope [rəup] *n* cuerda; (*NAUT*) cable *m* // *vt* (*box*) atar *or* amarrar con (una) cuerda; (*climbers: also:* **to ~ together**) encordarse; **to ~ sb in** (*fig*) persuadir a uno a tomar parte; **to know the ~s** (*fig*) conocer los trucos (del oficio); **~ ladder** *n* escala de cuerda.

rosary [ˈrəuzərɪ] *n* rosario.

rose [rəuz] *pt of* **rise** // *n* rosa; (*also:* **~bush**) rosal *m*; (*on watering can*) roseta *f* color de rosa.

rosé [ˈrəuzeɪ] *n* vino rosado.

rose: **~bud** *n* capullo de rosa; **~bush** *n* rosal *m*.

rosemary [ˈrəuzmərɪ] *n* romero.

rosette [rəuˈzet] *n* escarapela.

roster [ˈrɔstə*] *n*: **duty ~** lista de beres.

rostrum [ˈrɔstrəm] *n* tribuna.

rosy [ˈrəuzɪ] *a* rosado, sonrosado; **the future looks ~** el futuro parece prometedor.

rot [rɔt] *n* (*fig: pej*) tonterías *fpl* // *vt, vi* pudrirse; **it has ~** está podrido.

rota [ˈrəutə] *n* lista (de tandas).

rotary [ˈrəutərɪ] *a* rotativo.

rotate [rəuˈteɪt] *vt* (*revolve*) hacer

rote [rəʊt] *n*: **by ~** maquinalmente, de memoria.

rotten [ˈrɔtn] *a (decayed)* podrido; *(dishonest)* corrompido; *(col: bad)* pésimo; **to feel ~** *(ill)* sentirse muy mal.

rouge [ruːʒ] *n* colorete *m*.

rough [rʌf] *a (skin, surface)* áspero; *(terrain)* quebrado; *(road)* desigual; *(voice)* bronco; *(person, manner: coarse)* tosco, grosero; *(weather)* borrascoso; *(treatment)* brutal; *(sea)* bravo; *(cloth)* basto; *(plan)* preliminar; *(guess)* aproximado; *(violent)* violento // *n (GOLF)*: **in the ~** en las hierbas altas; **to ~ it** vivir sin comodidades; **to sleep ~** *(Brit)* pasar la noche al raso; **~age** *n* fibra(s) *f(pl)*; **~-and-ready** *a* improvisado; **~cast** *n* mezcla gruesa; *(copy n, ~ draft* *n* borrador *m*; **~en** *vt (a surface)* poner áspero; **~ly** *ad (handle)* torpemente; *(make)* toscamente; *(approximately)* aproximadamente.

roulette [ruːˈlet] *n* ruleta.

Roumania [ruːˈmeɪnɪə] *n* = **Rumania**.

round [raʊnd] *a* redondo // *n* círculo; *(Brit: of toast)* rodaja; *(of policeman)* ronda; *(of milkman)* recorrido; *(of doctor)* visitas *fpl*; *(game: of cards, in competition)* partida; *(of ammunition)* cartucho; *(BOXING)* asalto; *(of talks)* ronda // *vt (corner)* doblar // *prep* alrededor de // *ad*: **all ~** por todos lados; **the long way ~** por el camino menos directo; **all the year ~** durante todo el año; **it's just ~ the corner** *(fig)* está a la vuelta de la esquina; **~ the clock** *ad* las 24 horas; **to go ~ to sb's** *(house)* ir a casa de uno; **to go ~ the back** pasar por atrás; **to go ~ a house** visitar una casa; **enough to go ~** bastante (para todos); **to go the ~s**

(story) circular; **a ~ of applause** una salva de aplausos; **a ~ of drinks/sandwiches** una ronda de bebidas/bocadillos; **to ~ off** *vt (speech etc)* acabar, poner término a; **to ~ up** *vt (cattle)* acorralar; *(people)* reunir; *(prices)* redondear; **~about** *n (Brit: AUT)* isleta; *(: at fair)* tiovivo // *a (route, means)* indirecto; **~ers** *n (Brit: game)* juego similar al béisbol; **~ly** *ad (fig)* rotundamente; **~-shouldered** *a* cargado de espaldas; **~ trip** *n* viaje *m* de ida y vuelta; **~up** *n* rodeo; *(of criminals)* redada.

rouse [raʊz] *vt (wake up)* despertar; *(stir up)* suscitar; **rousing** *a (applause)* caluroso; *(speech)* conmovedor(a).

rout [raʊt] *n (MIL)* derrota.

route [ruːt] *n* ruta, camino; *(of bus)* recorrido; *(of shipping)* derrota; **~ map** *n (Brit: for journey)* mapa *m* de carreteras.

routine [ruːˈtiːn] *a (work)* rutinario // *n* rutina; *(THEATRE)* número.

roving [ˈrəʊvɪŋ] *a (wandering)* errante; *(salesman)* ambulante.

row [rəʊ] *n (line)* fila, hilera; *(KNITTING)* pasada; [raʊ] *(noise)* escándalo; *(dispute)* bronca, pelea; *(fuss)* jaleo; *(scolding)* regaño // *n (in boat)* remar; [raʊ] *vi/vt (boat)* conducir remando; **4 days in a ~** 4 días seguidos; **~boat** *n (US)* bote *m* de remos.

rowdy [ˈraʊdɪ] *a (person: noisy)* ruidoso; *(: quarrelsome)* pendenciero; *(occasion)* alborotado // *n* pendenciero.

row houses *(US)* casas *fpl* adosadas.

rowing [ˈrəʊɪŋ] *n* remo; **~ boat** *n (Brit)* bote *m* de remos.

royal [ˈrɔɪəl] *a* real; **R~ Air Force (RAF)** *n* Fuerzas Aéreas Británicas *fpl*; **~ty** *n (= persons)* familia real; *(payment to author)* derechos *mpl* de autor.

rpm *abbr* (= revs per minute) r.p.m.

R.S.V.P. *abbr* (= *répondez s'il vous plaît*) SRC.

Rt.Hon. *abbr* (*Brit*: = *Right Honourable*) título honorífico de diputado.

rub [rʌb] *vt* (*gen*) frotar; (*hard*) restregar // *n* (*gen*) frotamiento; (*touch*) roce *m*; **to ~ sb up** *or* (*US*) **~ sb the wrong way** entrarle uno por mal ojo; **to ~ off** *vi* borrarse; **to ~ off on** *vt fus* influir en; **to ~ out** *vt* borrar.

rubber [rʌbə*] *n* caucho, goma; (*Brit*: *eraser*) goma de borrar; **~ band** *n* goma, gomita; **~ plant** *n* ficus *m*; **~y** *a* elástico.

rubbish [rʌbɪʃ] *n* (*Brit*) (*from household*) basura; (*waste*) desperdicios *mpl*; (*fig*: *pej*) tonterías *fpl*; (*trash*) pacotilla; **~ bin** *n* cubo o bote *m* (*LAm*) de la basura; **~ dump** *n* (*in town*) vertedero, basurero.

rubble [rʌbl] *n* escombros *mpl*.

ruby [ru:bɪ] *n* rubí *m*.

rucksack [rʌksæk] *n* mochila.

ructions [rʌkʃənz] *npl* lío *sg*.

rudder [rʌdə*] *n* timón *m*.

ruddy [rʌdɪ] *a* (*face*) rubicundo; (*col*: *damned*) condenado.

rude [ru:d] *a* (*impolite*: *person*) mal educado; (: *word, manners*) grosero, (*indecent*) indecente.

rueful [ru:ful] *a* arrepentido.

ruffian [rʌfɪən] *n* matón *m*, criminal *m*.

ruffle [rʌfl] *vt* (*hair*) despeinar; (*clothes*) arrugar; **to get ~d** (*fig*: *person*) alterarse.

rug [rʌg] *n* alfombra; (*Brit*: *for knees*) manta.

rugby [rʌgbɪ] *n* (*also*: **~ football**) rugby *m*.

rugged [rʌgɪd] *a* (*landscape*) accidentado; (*features*) robusto.

rugger [rʌgə*] *n* (*Brit col*) rugby *m*.

ruin [ru:ɪn] *n* ruina // *vt* arruinar; (*spoil*) estropear; **~s** *npl* ruinas *fpl*, restos *mpl*.

rule [ru:l] *n* (*norm*) norma, costumbre *f*; (*regulation*) regla; (*govern-*

ment) dominio // *vt* (*country, person*) gobernar; (*decide*) disponer // *vi* gobernar; (*LAW*) fallar; **as a ~** por regla general; **to ~ out** *vt* excluir; **~d** *a* (*paper*) rayado; **~r** *n* (*sovereign*) soberano; (*for measuring*) regla; **ruling** *a* (*party*) gobernante; (*class*) dirigente // *n* (*LAW*) fallo, decisión *f*.

rum [rʌm] *n* ron *m*.

Rumania [ru:ˈmeɪnɪə] *n* Rumania; **~n** *a, n* rumano/a *m/f*.

rumble [rʌmbl] *vi* retumbar, hacer un ruido sordo; (*stomach, pipe*) sonar.

rummage [rʌmɪdʒ] *vi*: **to ~** (in *or* among) revolver (en).

rumour, (*US*) **rumor** [ru:mə*] *n* rumor *m* // *vt*: **it is ~ed that...** se rumorea que... .

rump [rʌmp] *n* (*of animal*) ancas *fpl*, grupa; **~ steak** *n* filete *m* de lomo.

rumpus [rʌmpəs] *n* (*col*) lío, jaleo; (*quarrel*) pelea, riña.

run [rʌn] *n* (*SPORT*) carrera; (*outing*) paseo, excursión *f*; (*distance travelled*) trayecto; (*series*) serie *f*; (*THEATRE*) temporada; (*SKI*) pista; (*in tights, stockings*) carrera; // *vb* (*pt* **ran**, *pp* **run**) *vt* (*operate*: *business*) dirigir; (: *competition, course*) organizar; (: *hotel, house*) administrar, llevar; (*COMPUT*) ejecutar; (*to pass*: *hand*) pasar; (*bath*): **to ~ a bath** llenar la bañera // *vi* (*gen*) correr; (*work*: *machine*) funcionar, marchar; (*bus, train*: *operate*) circular, ir; (: *travel*) ir; (*continue*: *play*) seguir; (: *contract*) ser válido; (*flow*: *river, bath*) fluir; (*colours, washing*) desteñirse; (*in election*) ser candidato; **there was a ~ on** (*meat, tickets*) hubo mucha demanda de; **in the long ~** a la larga; **on the ~** en fuga; **I'll ~ you to the station** te llevaré a la estación en coche; **to ~ a risk** correr un riesgo; **to ~ about** *or* **around** *vi* (*children*) correr por todos lados; **to ~ across** *vt fus* (*find*) dar o topar con; (*govern-*

away vi huir; **to ~ down** vi (clock) parar // vt (production) en reduciendo; (factory) ir restringiendo la producción en; (AUT) atropellar; (criticise) criticar; **to be ~ down** (person: tired) estar debilitado; **to ~ in** (Brit: car) rodar; **to ~ into** vt fus (meet: person, trouble) tropezar con; (collide with) chocar con; **to ~ off** vi (water) dejar correr // vi huir corriendo; **to ~ out** vi (person) salir corriendo; (liquid) irse; (lease) caducar, vencer; (money) acabarse; **to ~ out of** vt fus quedar sin; **to ~ over** vt (AUT) atropellar // vt fus (revise) repasar; **to ~ through** vt fus (instructions) repasar; **to ~ up** vt (debt) contraer; **to ~ up against** (difficulties) tropezar con; **~away** a (horse) desbocado; (truck) sin frenos; (inflation) galopante.

rung [rʌŋ] pp of **ring** // n (of ladder) escalón m, peldaño.

runner ['rʌnə*] n (in race: person) corredor(a) m/f; (: horse) caballo; (on sledge) patín m; (wheel) ruedecilla; **~ bean** n (Brit) judía escarlata; **~-up** n subcampeón/ona m/f.

running ['rʌnɪŋ] n (sport) atletismo; (race) carrera // a (water, costs) corriente; (commentary) continuo; **to be in/out of the ~ for sth** tener/no tener posibilidades de ganar algo; **6 days ~** 6 días seguidos.

runny ['rʌnɪ] a derretido.

run-of-the-mill ['rʌnəvðə'mɪl] a común y corriente.

runt [rʌnt] n (also pej) redrojo, enano.

run-up ['rʌnʌp] n: **~ to** (election etc) período previo a.

runway ['rʌnweɪ] n (AVIAT) pista de aterrizaje.

rupee [ru:'pi:] n rupia.

rupture ['rʌptʃə*] n (MED) hernia // vt: **to ~ o.s.** causarse una hernia.

rural ['ruərl] a rural.

ruse [ru:z] n ardid m.

rush [rʌʃ] n ímpetu m; (hurry)

prisa; (COMM) demanda repentina; (BOT) junco; (current) corriente f fuerte, ráfaga // vt apresurar; (work) hacer de prisa; (attack: town etc) asaltar // vi correr, precipitarse; **~ hour** n horas fpl punta.

rusk [rʌsk] n bizcocho tostado.

Russia ['rʌʃə] n Rusia; **~n** a, n ruso/a m/f.

rust [rʌst] n herrumbre f, moho // vi oxidarse.

rustic ['rʌstɪk] a rústico.

rustle ['rʌsl] vi susurrar // vt (paper) hacer crujir; (US: cattle) hurtar, robar.

rustproof ['rʌstpru:f] a inoxidable.

rusty ['rʌstɪ] a oxidado.

rut [rʌt] n surco; (ZOOL) celo; **to be in a ~** ser esclavo de la rutina.

ruthless ['ru:θlɪs] a despiadado.

rye [raɪ] n centeno; **~ bread** n pan de centeno.

S

sabbath ['sæbəθ] n domingo; (Jewish) sábado.

sabotage ['sæbətɑ:ʒ] n sabotaje // vt sabotear.

saccharin(e) ['sækərɪn] n sacarina.

sachet ['sæʃeɪ] n sobrecito.

sack [sæk] n (bag) saco, costal m // vt (dismiss) despedir; (plunder) saquear; **to get the ~** ser despedido; **~ing** n (material) arpillera.

sacred ['seɪkrɪd] a sagrado, santo.

sacrifice ['sækrɪfaɪs] n sacrificio // vt sacrificar.

sacrilege ['sækrɪlɪdʒ] n sacrilegio.

sacrosanct ['sækrəusæŋkt] a sacrosanto.

sad [sæd] a (unhappy) triste; (deplorable) lamentable.

saddle ['sædl] n silla (de montar); (of cycle) sillín m // vt (horse) ensillar; **to be ~d with sth** (col) quedar cargado con algo; **~bag** n alforja.

sadistic [sə'dɪstɪk] a sádico.

sadness ['sædnɪs] n tristeza.

s.a.e. *abbr* (= *stamped addressed envelope*) sobre con las propias señas de uno y con sello.

safari [sə'fɑːrɪ] *n* safari *m*.

safe [seɪf] *a* (*out of danger*) fuera de peligro; (*not dangerous, sure*) seguro; (*unharmed*) ileso; (*trustworthy*) digno de confianza // *n* caja de caudales, caja fuerte; **~ and sound** sano y salvo; (*just*) **to be on the ~ side** para mayor seguridad; **~ conduct** *n* salvoconducto; **~ deposit** *n* (*vault*) cámara acorazada; (*box*) caja de seguridad; **~guard** *n* protección *f*, garantía // *vt* proteger, defender; **~keeping** *n* custodia; **~ly** *ad* seguramente, con seguridad; **to arrive ~ly** llegar bien.

safety ['seɪftɪ] *n* seguridad *f* // *a* de seguridad; **~ first!** ¡precaución!; **~ belt** *n* cinturón *m* (de seguridad); **~ pin** *n* imperdible *m*, seguro (LAm).

saffron ['sæfrən] *n* azafrán *m*.

sag [sæg] *vi* aflojarse.

sage [seɪdʒ] *n* (*herb*) salvia; (*man*) sabio.

Sagittarius [sædʒɪ'tɛərɪəs] *n* Sagitario.

Sahara [sə'hɑːrə] *n*: **the ~ (Desert)** el (desierto del) Sáhara.

said [sed] *pt, pp* of **say.**

sail [seɪl] *n* (*on boat*) vela // *vt* (*boat*) gobernar // *vi* (*travel: ship*) navegar; (*: passenger*) pasear en barco; (*set off*) zarpar; **to go for a ~** dar un paseo en barco; **they ~ed into Copenhagen** arribaron a Copenhague; **to ~ through** *vt fus* (*exam*) no tener problemas para aprobar; **~boat** *n* (US) velero, barco de vela; **~ing** *n* (*SPORT*) balandrismo; **to go ~ing** salir en balandro; **~ing ship** *n* barco de vela; **~or** *n* marinero, marino.

saint [seɪnt] *n* santo; **~ly** *a* santo.

sake [seɪk] *n*: **for the ~ of** por.

salad ['sæləd] *n* ensalada; **~ bowl** *n* ensaladera; **~ cream** *n* (Brit) (especie de) mayonesa; **~ dressing** *n* aliño.

salary ['sælərɪ] *n* sueldo.

sale [seɪl] *n* venta; (*at reduced prices*) liquidación *f*, saldo; **'for ~'** 'se vende'; **on ~** en venta; **on ~ or return** (*goods*) venta por reposición; **~room** *n* sala de subastas; **~s assistant**, (US) **~s clerk** *n* dependiente/a *m/f*; **~sman/woman** *n* vendedor(a) *m/f*; (*in shop*) dependiente/a *m/f*; (*representative*) viajante *m/f*.

salient ['seɪlɪənt] *a* sobresaliente.

saliva [sə'laɪvə] *n* saliva.

sallow ['sæləu] *a* cetrino.

salmon ['sæmən] *n, pl inv* salmón *m*.

saloon [sə'luːn] *n* (US) bar *m*, taberna; (Brit AUT) (coche *m* de) turismo; (*ship's lounge*) cámara, salón *m*.

salt [sɔlt] *n* sal *f* // *vt* salar; (**put ~ on**) poner sal en; **to ~ away** *n* (*col: money*) ahorrar; **~ cellar** *n* salero; **~water** *a* de agua salada; **~y** *a* salado.

salutary ['sæljutərɪ] *a* saludable.

salute [sə'luːt] *n* saludo; (*of guns*) salva // *vt* saludar.

salvage ['sælvɪdʒ] *n* (*saving*) salvamento, recuperación *f*; (*things saved*) objetos *mpl* salvados // *vt* salvar.

salvation [sæl'veɪʃən] *n* salvación *f*; **S~ Army** *n* Ejército de Salvación.

same [seɪm] *a* mismo *a* // *pron*: **the ~** él/la mismo/a, los/las mismos/as; **the ~ book** as el mismo libro que; **at the ~ time** (*at the ~ moment*) al mismo tiempo; (*yet*) sin embargo; **all** *or* **just the ~** sin embargo, aun así; **to do the ~ (as sb)** hacer lo mismo (que uno); **the ~ to you!** ¡igualmente!

sample ['sɑːmpl] *n* muestra // *vt* (*food, wine*) probar.

sanatorium [sænə'tɔːrɪəm], *pl* **-ria** [-rɪə] *n* (Brit) sanatorio.

sanction ['sæŋkʃən] *n* sanción *f* // *vt* sancionar.

sanctity ['sæŋktɪtɪ] *n* (*gen*) santidad *f*; (*inviolability*) inviolabilidad *f*.

sanctuary ['sæŋktjuəri] n santuario; (*refuge*) asilo, refugio; (*for wild life*) reserva.

sand [sænd] n arena // vt (*also:* ~ **down**) lijar.

sandal ['sændl] n sandalia; ~**wood** n sándalo.

sand: ~**box** n (US) = ~**pit**; ~**castle** n castillo de arena; ~ **dune** n duna; ~**paper** n papel m de lija; ~**pit** n (*for children*) cajón m de arena; ~**stone** n piedra arenisca.

sandwich ['sændwitʃ] n bocadillo (Sp), sandwich m (LAm) // vt (*also:* ~ **in**) intercalar; ~**ed between** apretujado entre; **cheese/ham** ~ sandwich de queso/jamón; ~ **board** n cartelón m; ~ **course** n (Brit) curso de medio tiempo.

sandy ['sændi] a arenoso; (*colour*) rojizo.

sane [sein] a cuerdo, sensato.

sang [sæŋ] pt of **sing**.

sanitarium [sæni'tɛəriəm] n (US) = **sanatorium**.

sanitary ['sænitəri] a (*system, arrangements*) sanitario; (*clean*) higiénico; ~ **towel**, (US) ~ **napkin** n paño higiénico, compresa.

sanitation [sæni'teiʃən] n (*in house*) servicios mpl higiénicos; (*in town*) servicio de desinfección; ~ **department** n (US) departamento de limpieza y recogida de basuras.

sanity ['sæniti] n cordura; (*of judgment*) sensatez f.

sank [sæŋk] pt of **sink**.

Santa Claus [sæntə'klɔːz] n San Nicolás, Papá Noel.

sap [sæp] n (*of plants*) savia // vt (*strength*) minar, agotar.

sapling ['sæpliŋ] n árbol nuevo or joven.

sapphire ['sæfaiə*] n zafiro.

sarcasm ['sɑːkæzm] n sarcasmo.

sardine [sɑː'diːn] n sardina.

Sardinia [sɑː'diniə] n Cerdeña.

sash [sæʃ] n faja.

sat [sæt] pt, pp of **sit**.

Satan ['seitn] n Satanás m.

satchel ['sætʃl] n (*child's*) cartera, mochila (LAm).

sated ['seitid] a (*appetite, person*) saciado.

satellite ['sætəlait] n satélite m.

satin ['sætin] n raso // a de raso.

satire ['sætaiə*] n sátira.

satisfaction [sætis'fækʃən] n satisfacción f.

satisfactory [sætis'fæktəri] a satisfactorio.

satisfy ['sætisfai] vt satisfacer; (*convince*) convencer; ~**ing** a satisfactorio.

saturate ['sætʃəreit] vt: **to** ~ (**with**) empapar or saturar (de).

Saturday ['sætədi] n sábado.

sauce [sɔːs] n salsa; (*sweet*) crema; ~**pan** n cacerola, olla.

saucer ['sɔːsə*] n platillo.

saucy ['sɔːsi] a fresco, descarado.

Saudi ['saudi]: ~ **Arabia** n Arabia Saudí or Saudita; ~ **(Arabian)** a, n saudí m/f, saudita m/f.

sauna ['sɔːnə] n sauna.

saunter ['sɔːntə*] vi: **to** ~ **in/out** entrar/salir sin prisa.

sausage ['sɔsidʒ] n salchicha; ~ **roll** n empanadita de salchicha.

sautéed ['səuteid] a salteado.

savage ['sævidʒ] a (*cruel, fierce*) feroz, furioso; (*primitive*) salvaje // n salvaje m/f // vt (*attack*) embestir.

save [seiv] vt (*rescue*) salvar, rescatar; (*money, time*) ahorrar; (*put by*) guardar; (*COMPUT*) salvar y guardar; (*avoid: trouble*) evitar // vi (*also:* ~ **up**) ahorrar // n (*SPORT*) parada // prep salvo, excepto.

saving ['seiviŋ] n (*on price etc*) economía // a: **the** ~ **grace of** el único mérito de; ~**s** npl ahorros mpl; ~**s account** n cuenta de ahorros; ~**s bank** n caja de ahorros.

saviour, (US) **savior** ['seivjə*] n salvador(a) m/f.

savour, (US) **savor** ['seivə*] n sabor m, gusto // vt saborear; ~**y** a sabroso; (*dish: not sweet*) salado.

saw [sɔː] pt of **see** // n (*tool*) sierra //

vt (*pt* sawed, *pp* sawed *or* sawn)
serrar; **~dust** *n* (a)serrín *m*; **~mill**
n aserradero; **~n-off shotgun** *n* escopeta de cañones recortados.

saxophone ['sæksəfəʊn] *n* saxófono.

say [seɪ] *n*: to have one's ~ expresar su opinión; **to have a** *or* **some**
~ **in sth** tener voz *or* tener que ver
en algo // *vt* (*pt*, *pp* said) decir; to ~
yes/no decir que sí/no; that is to ~
es decir; that goes without ~ing ni
que decir tiene; **~ing** *n* dicho, refrán
m.

scab [skæb] *n* costra; (*pej*) esquirol
m.

scaffold ['skæfəʊld] *n* (*for execution*)
cadalso; **~ing** *n* andamio, andamiaje *m*.

scald [skɔːld] *n* escaldadura // *vt* escaldar.

scale [skeɪl] *n* (*gen*, *MUS*) escala; (*of
fish*) escama; (*of salaries, fees etc*)
escalafón *m* // *vi* (*mountain*) escalar;
(*tree*) trepar; **~s** *npl* (*small*) balanza *sg*; (*large*) báscula *sg*; **on a
large** ~ en gran escala; **~ of
charges** tarifa, lista de precios; **to
~ down** *vt* reducir a escala; **~
model** *n* modelo a escala.

scallop ['skɒləp] *n* (*ZOOL*) venera;
(*SEWING*) festón *m*.

scalp [skælp] *n* cabellera // *vt* escalpar.

scalpel ['skælpl] *n* bisturí *m*.

scamper ['skæmpə*] *vi*: to ~ away,
~ off ir corriendo.

scampi ['skæmpɪ] *npl* gambas *fpl*.

scan [skæn] *vt* (*examine*) escudriñar;
(*glance at quickly*) dar un vistazo a;
(*TV, RADAR*) explorar, registrar.

scandal ['skændl] *n* escándalo; (*gossip*) chismes *mpl*.

Scandinavia [skændɪ'neɪvɪə] *n* Escandinavia; **~n** *a, n* escandinavo/a
m/f.

scant [skænt] *a* escaso; **~y** *a* (*meal*)
insuficiente; (*clothes*) ligero.

scapegoat ['skeɪpgəʊt] *n* cabeza de
turco, chivo expiatorio.

scar [skɑː] *n* cicatriz *f*.

scarce [skɛəs] *a* escaso; **~ly** *ad* apenas; **scarcity** *n* escasez *f*.

scare [skɛə*] *n* susto, sobresalto;
(*panic*) pánico // *vt* asustar, espantar; **to** ~ **sb stiff** dar a uno un susto
de muerte; **bomb** ~ amenaza de
bomba; **~crow** *n* espantapájaros *m
inv*; **~d** *a*: **to be ~d** estar asustado.

scarf [skɑːf], *pl* **scarves** [skɑːvz] *n*
(*long*) bufanda; (*square*) pañuelo.

scarlet ['skɑːlɪt] *a* escarlata; ~ **fever** *n* escarlatina.

scarves [skɑːvz] *pl of* **scarf**.

scathing ['skeɪðɪŋ] *a* mordaz.

scatter ['skætə*] *vt* (*spread*) esparcir, desparramar; (*put to flight*) dispersar // *vi* desparramarse; dispersarse; **~brained** *a* ligero de cascos.

scavenger ['skævəndʒə*] *n* (*person*)
basurero/a; (*ZOOL: animal*) animal
m de carroña; (: *bird*) ave *f* de carroña.

scenario [sɪ'nɑːrɪəʊ] *n* (*THEATRE*)
argumento; (*CINEMA*) guión *m*; (*fig*)
escenario.

scene [siːn] *n* (*THEATRE*, *fig etc*) escena; (*of crime, accident*) escenario;
(*sight, view*) panorama *m*; (*fuss*) escándalo; **~ry** *n* (*THEATRE*) decorado; (*landscape*) paisaje *m*; **scenic** *a*
(*picturesque*) pintoresco.

scent [sɛnt] *n* perfume *m*, olor *m*;
(*fig: track*) rastro, pista; (*sense of
smell*) olfato.

sceptic, (*US*) **skeptic** ['skɛptɪk] *n*
escéptico/a; **~al** *a* escéptico; **~ism**
['skɛptɪsɪzm] *n* escepticismo.

sceptre, (*US*) **scepter** ['sɛptə*] *n*
cetro.

schedule ['ʃɛdjuːl] *n* (*of trains*) horario; (*of events*) programa *m*; (*list*)
lista // *vt* (*visit*) fijar la hora de; **to
arrive on** ~ llegar a la hora debida;
to be ahead of/behind ~ estar
adelantado/en retraso; **~d flight** *n*
vuelo regular.

schematic [skɪ'mætɪk] *a* (*diagram
etc*) esquemático.

scheme [skiːm] *n* (*plan*) plan *m*, proyecto; (*method*) esquema *m*; (*plot*) intriga; (*trick*) ardid *m*; (*arrangement*) disposición *f*; (*pension ~ etc*) sistema *m* // *vt* proyectar // *vi* (*plan*) hacer proyectos; (*intrigue*) intrigar; **scheming** *a* intrigante.

schism ['skɪzəm] *n* cisma *m*.

scholar ['skɔlə*] *n* (*learned person*) sabio/a, erudito/a; **~ly** *a* erudito; **~ship** *n* erudición *f*; (*grant*) beca.

school [sku:l] *n* (*gen*) escuela, colegio; (*in university*) facultad *f* // *vt* (*animal*) amaestrar; **~ age** *n* edad *f* escolar; **~book** *n* libro de texto; **~boy** *n* alumno; **~children** *npl* alumnos *mpl*; **~days** *npl* años *mpl* del colegio; **~girl** *n* alumna; **~ing** *n* enseñanza; **~master/mistress** *n* (*primary*) maestro/a; (*secondary*) profesor/a *m/f*; **~teacher** *n* (*primary*) maestro/a; (*secondary*) profesor(a) *m/f*.

schooner ['sku:nə*] *n* (*ship*) goleta.

sciatica [saɪ'ætɪkə] *n* ciática.

science ['saɪəns] *n* ciencia; **~ fiction** *n* ciencia-ficción *f*; **scientific** [-'tɪfɪk] *a* científico; **scientist** *n* científico/a.

scintillating ['sɪntɪleɪtɪŋ] *a* brillante, ingenioso.

scissors ['sɪzəz] *npl* tijeras *fpl*; **a pair of ~** unas tijeras.

scoff [skɔf] *vt* (*Brit col: eat*) engullir // *vi*: **to ~ (at)** (*mock*) mofarse (de).

scold [skəuld] *vt* regañar.

scone [skɔn] *n* pastel de pan.

scoop [sku:p] *n* cucharón *m*; (*for flour etc*) pala; (*PRESS*) exclusiva; **to ~ out** *vt* excavar; **to ~ up** *vt* recoger.

scooter ['sku:tə*] *n* (*motor cycle*) moto *f*; (*toy*) patinete *m*.

scope [skəup] *n* (*of plan, undertaking*) ámbito; (*reach*) alcance *m*; (*of person*) competencia; (*opportunity*) libertad *f* de acción.

scorch [skɔːtʃ] *vt* (*clothes*) chamuscar; (*earth, grass*) quemar, secar; **~ing** *a* abrasador(a).

score [skɔː*] *n* (*points etc*) puntua-

ción *f*; (*MUS*) partitura; (*reckoning*) cuenta; (*twenty*) veintena // *vt* (*goal, point*) ganar; (*mark*) rayar // *vi* marcar un tanto; (*FOOTBALL*) marcar (un) gol; (*keep score*) llevar el tanteo; **on that ~** en lo que se refiere a eso; **to ~ 6 out of 10** obtener una puntuación de 6 sobre 10; **to ~ out** *vt* tachar; **~board** *n* marcador *m*; **~r** *n* marcador *m*; (*keeping score*) tanteador(a) *m/f*.

scorn [skɔːn] *n* desprecio // *vt* despreciar; **~ful** *a* desdeñoso, despreciativo.

Scorpio ['skɔːpɪəu] *n* Escorpión *m*.

scorpion ['skɔːpɪən] *n* alacrán *m*.

Scot [skɔt] *n* escocés/esa *m/f*.

scotch [skɔtʃ] *vt* (*rumour*) desmentir; (*plan*) abandonar; **S~** *n* whisky *m* escocés; **S~ tape** *n* ® (*US*) cinta adhesiva, celo, scotch *m* (*LAm*).

scot-free [skɔt'friː] *ad*: **to get off ~** (*unpunished*) salir impune.

Scotland ['skɔtlənd] *n* Escocia.

Scots [skɔts] *a* escocés/esa; **~man/woman** *n* escocés/esa *m/f*; **Scottish** ['skɔtɪʃ] *a* escocés/esa.

scoundrel ['skaundrl] *n* canalla *m/f*, sinvergüenza *m/f*.

scour ['skauə*] *vt* (*clean*) fregar, estregar; (*search*) recorrer, registrar.

scourge [skɔːdʒ] *n* azote *m*.

scout [skaut] *n* (*MIL, also: boy ~*) explorador *m*; **to ~ around** *vi* reconocer el terreno.

scowl [skaul] *vi* fruncir el ceño; **to ~ at sb** mirar con ceño a uno.

scrabble ['skræbl] *vi* (*claw*): **to ~ (at)** arañar; (*also: to ~ around*: *search*) revolver todo buscando // *n*: **S~** ® Scrabble *m* ®.

scraggy ['skrægɪ] *a* flaco, descarnado.

scram [skræm] *vi* (*col*) largarse.

scramble ['skræmbl] *n* (*climb*) subida (difícil); (*struggle*) pelea // *vi*: **to ~ out/through** salir/abrirse paso con dificultad; **to ~** por pelear por; **~d eggs** *npl* huevos *mpl* revueltos.

scrap [skræp] *n* (*bit*) pedacito; (*fig*)

pizca; (fight) riña, bronca; (also: ~ iron) chatarra, hierro viejo // vi (discard) desechar, descartar // vi reñir, armar (una) bronca; ~s npl (waste) sobras fpl, desperdicios mpl; ~book n álbum m de recortes; ~ dealer n chatarrero/a.

scrape [skreɪp] n: to get into a ~ meterse en un lío // vt raspar; (skin etc) rasguñar; (~ against) rozar // vi: to ~ through (exam) aprobar por los pelos; ~r n raspador m.

scrap: ~ heap n (fig) to be on the ~ heap estar acabado; ~ merchant n (Brit) chatarrero/a; ~ paper n pedazos mpl de papel.

scratch [skrætʃ] n rasguño; (from claw) arañazo // a: ~ team equipo improvisado // vi (record) rayar; (with claw, nail) rasguñar, arañar // vi rascarse; to start from ~ partir de cero; to be up to ~ cumplir con los requisitos.

scrawl [skrɔːl] n garabatos mpl // vi hacer garabatos.

scrawny ['skrɔːnɪ] a (person, neck) flaco.

scream [skriːm] n chillido // vi chillar.

scree [skriː] n cono de desmoronamiento.

screech [skriːtʃ] vi chirriar.

screen [skriːn] n (CINEMA, TV) pantalla; (movable) biombo; (wall) tabique m; (also: wind~) parabrisas m inv // vt (conceal) tapar; (from the wind etc) proteger; (film) proyectar; (candidates etc) investigar a; ~ing n (MED) investigación f médica; ~play n guión m.

screw [skruː] n tornillo; (propeller) hélice f // vt atornillar; to ~ up vt (paper etc) arrugar; (col: ruin) fastidiar; to ~ up one's eyes arrugar el entrecejo; ~driver n destornillador m.

scribble ['skrɪbl] n garabatos mpl // vt escribir con prisa.

script [skrɪpt] n (CINEMA etc) guión m; (writing) escritura, letra.

Scripture ['skrɪptʃə*] n Sagrada Escritura.

scroll [skrəʊl] n rollo.

scrounge [skraʊndʒ] vt (col): to ~ sth or from sb obtener algo de uno de gorra // vi: to ~ on sb vivir a costa de uno; ~r n gorrón/ona m/f.

scrub [skrʌb] n (clean) fregado; (land) maleza // vt fregar, restregar; (reject) cancelar, anular.

scruff [skrʌf] n: by the ~ of the neck por el pescuezo.

scruffy ['skrʌfɪ] a desaliñado, piojoso.

scrum(mage) ['skrʌm(mɪdʒ)] n (RUGBY) melée f.

scruple ['skruːpl] n escrúpulo.

scrutinize ['skruːtɪnaɪz] vt escudriñar; (votes) escrutar.

scrutiny ['skruːtɪnɪ] n escrutinio, examen m.

scuff [skʌf] vt (shoes, floor) rayar.

scuffle ['skʌfl] n refriega.

scullery ['skʌlərɪ] n trascocina.

sculptor ['skʌlptə*] n escultor(a) m/f.

sculpture ['skʌlptʃə*] n escultura.

scum [skʌm] n (on liquid) espuma; (pej: person) canalla m.

scupper ['skʌpə*] vt (plans) dar al traste con.

scurrilous ['skʌrɪləs] a difamatorio, calumnioso.

scurry ['skʌrɪ] vi: to ~ off escabullirse.

scuttle ['skʌtl] n (also: coal ~) cubo, carbonera // vt (ship) barrenar // vi (scamper): to ~ away, ~ off escabullirse.

scythe [saɪð] n guadaña.

SDP n abbr (Brit) = Social Democratic Party.

sea [siː] n mar m // cpd de mar, marítimo; by ~ (travel) en barco; on the ~ (boat) en el mar; (town) junto al mar; to be all at ~ (fig) estar despistado; out to ~ or at ~ en alta mar; ~board n litoral m; ~ breeze n brisa de mar; ~food n mariscos mpl; ~ front n paseo marítimo; ~gull n gaviota.

seal [si:l] n (animal) foca; (stamp) sello // vt (close) cerrar; (: with ~) sellar; **to ~ off** vt (area) acordonar.

sea level n nivel m del mar.

seam [si:m] n costura; (of metal) juntura; (of coal) veta, filón m.

seaman ['si:mən] n marinero.

seamy ['si:mi] a sórdido.

seance ['seiɔns] n sesión f de espiritismo.

sea plane ['si:plein] n hidroavión m.

seaport ['si:pɔ:t] n puerto de mar.

search [sə:tʃ] n (for person, thing) busca, búsqueda; (of drawer, pockets) registro; (inspection) reconocimiento // vt (look in) buscar en; (examine) examinar; (person, place) registrar // vi: **to ~ for** buscar; **in ~ of** en busca de; **to ~ through** vt fus registrar; **~ing** a penetrante; **~light** n reflector m; **~ party** n pelotón m de salvamento; **~ warrant** n mandamiento (judicial).

sea: **~shore** n playa, orilla del mar; **~sick** a mareado; **~side** n playa, orilla del mar; **~side resort** n playa.

season ['si:zn] n (of year) estación f; (sporting etc) temporada; (gen) época, periodo // vt (food) sazonar; **~al** a estacional; **~ed** a (fig) experimentado; **~ing** n condimento, aderezo; **~ ticket** n abono.

seat [si:t] n (in bus, train: place) asiento; (chair) silla; (PARLIAMENT) escaño; (buttocks) culo, trasero; (of government) sede f // vt sentar; (have room for) tener cabida para; **to be ~ed** sentarse; **~ belt** n cinturón m de seguridad.

sea: **~ water** n agua del mar; **~weed** n alga marina; **~worthy** a en condiciones de navegar.

sec. abbr = **second(s)**.

secluded [si'klu:did] a retirado.

second ['sekənd] a segundo // ad (in race etc) en segundo lugar // n segundo; (AUT: also: **~ gear**) segunda; (COMM) artículo con algún

desperfecto // vt (motion) apoyar; **~ary** a secundario; **~ary school** n escuela secundaria; **~class** a de segunda clase // ad (RAIL) en segunda; **~hand** a de segunda mano, usado; **~ hand** n (on clock) segundero; **~ly** ad en segundo lugar; **~ment** [si'kɔndmənt] n (Brit) traslado temporal; **~rate** a de segunda categoría; **~ thoughts** npl: **to have ~ thoughts** cambiar de opinión; **on ~ thoughts** or (US) **thought** pensándolo bien.

secrecy ['si:krəsi] n secreto.

secret ['si:krit] a, n secreto; **in ~** ad en secreto.

secretarial [sekri'teəriəl] a de secretario.

secretary ['sekrətəri] n secretario/a; **S~ of State (for)** (Brit POL) Ministro (de).

secretion [si'kri:ʃən] n secreción f.

secretive ['si:krətiv] a reservado, sigiloso.

secretly ['si:kritli] ad en secreto.

sect [sekt] n secta; **~arian** [-'teəriən] a sectario.

section ['sekʃən] n sección f; (part) parte f; (of document) artículo; (of opinion) sector m.

sector ['sektə*] n sector m.

secular ['sekjulə*] a secular, seglar.

secure [si'kjuə*] a (free from anxiety) seguro; (firmly fixed) firme, fijo // vt (fix) asegurar, afianzar; (get) conseguir.

security [si'kjuəriti] n seguridad f; (for loan) fianza; (: collateral) prenda.

sedan [si'dæn] n (US AUT) sedán m.

sedate [si'deit] a tranquilo; // vt tratar con sedantes.

sedation [si'deiʃən] n (MED) sedación f.

sedative ['seditiv] n sedante m, sedativo.

seduce [si'dju:s] vt (gen) seducir; **seduction** [-'dʌkʃən] n seducción f; **seductive** [-'dʌktiv] a seductor(a).

see [si:] (pt **saw**, pp **seen**) vt (gen) ver; (understand) ver, comprender //

vi ver // *n* (arz)obispado; **to ~ sb to the door** acompañar a uno a la puerta; **to ~ that** (*ensure*) asegurar que; **~ you soon!** ¡hasta pronto!; **to ~ about** *vt fus* atender a, encargarse de; **to ~ off** *vt* despedir; **to ~ through** *vt fus* calar // *vt* (*plan*) llevar a cabo; **to ~ to** *vt fus* atender a, encargarse de.

seed [siːd] *n* semilla; (*in fruit*) pepita; (*fig*) germen *m*; (*TENNIS*) preseleccionado/a; **to go to ~** (*plant*) granar; (*fig*) descuidarse; **~ling** *n* planta de semillero; **~y** *a* (*shabby*) desaseado, raído.

seeing ['siːɪŋ] *conj*: **~ (that)** visto que, en vista de que.

seek [siːk], *pt, pp* **sought** *vt* (*gen*) buscar; (*post*) solicitar.

seem [siːm] *vi* parecer; **there seems to be...** parece que hay; **~ingly** *ad* aparentemente, según parece.

seen [siːn] *pp* of **see**.

seep [siːp] *vi* filtrarse.

seesaw ['siːsɔː] *n* balancín *m*, columpio.

seethe [siːð] *vi* hervir; **to ~ with anger** estar furioso.

see-through ['siːθruː] *a* transparente.

segregate ['sɛgrɪgeɪt] *vt* segregar.

seize [siːz] *vt* (*grasp*) agarrar, asir; (*take possession of*) secuestrar; (*territory*) apoderarse de; (*opportunity*) aprovecharse de; **to ~ (up)** *vi* (*TECH*) agarrotarse.

seizure ['siːʒə*] *n* (*MED*) ataque *m*; (*LAW*) incautación *f*.

seldom ['sɛldəm] *ad* rara vez.

select [sɪ'lɛkt] *a* selecto, escogido // *vt* escoger, elegir; (*SPORT*) seleccionar; **~ion** [-'lɛkʃən] *n* selección *f*, elección *f*; (*COMM*) surtido.

self [sɛlf] *n* (*pl* **selves**) uno mismo; **the ~** el yo // *pref* auto...; **~-assured** *a* seguro de sí mismo; **~-catering** *a* (*Brit*) con cocina; **~-centred**, (*US*) **~-centered** *a* egocéntrico; **~-coloured**, (*US*) **~-**

colored *a* de color natural; (*of one colour*) de un color; **~-confidence** *n* confianza en sí mismo; **~-conscious** *a* cohibido; **~-contained** *a* (*gen*) autónomo; (*Brit: flat*) con entrada particular; **~-control** *n* autodominio; **~-defence**, (*US*) **~-defense** *n* defensa propia; **~-discipline** *n* autodisciplina; **~-employed** *a* que trabaja por cuenta propia; **~-evident** *a* patente; **~-governing** *a* autónomo; **~-indulgent** *a* autocomplaciente; **~-interest** *n* egoísmo; **~-ish** *a* egoísta; **~-ishness** *n* egoísmo; **~-less** *a* desinteresado; **~-made** *a*: **~-made man** hombre *m* que se ha hecho a sí mismo; **~-pity** *n* lástima de sí mismo; **~-portrait** *n* autorretrato; **~-possessed** *a* sereno, dueño de sí mismo; **~-preservation** *n* propia conservación *f*; **~-reliant** *a* independiente, autosuficiente; **~-respect** *n* amor *m* propio; **~-righteous** *a* santurrón/ona; **~-sacrifice** *n* abnegación *f*; **~-satisfied** *a* satisfecho de sí mismo; **~-service** *a* de autoservicio; **~-sufficient** *a* autosuficiente; **~-taught** *a* autodidacta.

sell [sɛl], *pt, pp* **sold** *vt* vender // *vi* venderse; **to ~ at** or **for £10** venderse a 10 libros; **to ~ off** *vt* liquidar; **to ~ out** *vi* transigir, transar (*LAm*); **~-by date** *n* fecha de caducidad; **~er** *n* vendedor(a) *m/f*; **~ing price** *n* precio de venta.

sellotape ['sɛləʊteɪp] *n* ® (*Brit*) cinta adhesiva, celo, scotch (*LAm*).

sellout ['sɛlaʊt] *n* traición *f*; **it was a ~** (*THEATRE etc*) fue un éxito de taquilla.

selves [sɛlvz] *pl* of **self**.

semaphore ['sɛməfɔː*] *n* semáforo.

semblance ['sɛmbləns] *n* apariencia.

semen ['siːmən] *n* semen *m*.

semester [sɪ'mɛstə*] *n* (*US*) semestre *m*.

semi... [sɛmɪ] *pref* semi..., medio...; **~circle** *n* semicírculo; **~colon** *n* punto y coma; **~conductor** *n* semiconductor *m*; ~**detached (house)** *n* (casa) semiseparada; ~**final** *n* semi-final *m*.

seminar ['sɛmɪnɑ:*] *n* seminario.

seminary ['sɛmɪnərɪ] *n* (REL) seminario.

semiskilled ['sɛmɪskɪld] *a* (work, worker) semi-cualificado.

senate ['sɛnɪt] *n* senado; **senator** *n* senador(a) *m/f*.

send [sɛnd], *pt, pp* **sent** *vt* mandar, enviar; **to** ~ **away** *vt* (letter, goods) despachar; **to** ~ **away for** *vt fus* pedir; **to** ~ **back** *vt* devolver; **to** ~ **for** *vt fus* mandar traer; **to** ~ **off** *vt* (goods) despachar; (Brit SPORT: player) expulsar; **to** ~ **out** *vt* (invitation) mandar; (signal) emitir; **to** ~ **up** *vt* (person, price) hacer subir; (Brit: parody) parodiar; ~**er** *n* remitente *m/f*; ~**off** *n*: a good ~**off** una buena despedida.

senior ['si:nɪə*] *a* (older) mayor, más viejo; (: on staff) de más antigüedad; (of higher rank) superior // *n* mayor *m*; ~ **citizen** *n* persona de la tercera edad; ~**ity** [-'ɔrɪtɪ] *n* antigüedad *f*.

sensation [sɛn'seɪʃən] *n* sensación *f*; ~**al** *a* sensacional.

sense [sɛns] *n* (faculty, meaning) sentido; (feeling) sensación *f*; (good ~) sentido común, juicio // *vt* sentir, percibir; ~ **of humour** sentido del humor; **it makes** ~ tiene sentido; ~**less** *a* estúpido, insensato; (unconscious) sin conocimiento.

sensibility [sɛnsɪ'bɪlɪtɪ] *n* sensibilidad *f*; **sensibilities** *npl* susceptibilidades *fpl*.

sensible ['sɛnsɪbl] *a* sensato (reasonable) razonable, lógico.

sensitive ['sɛnsɪtɪv] *a* sensible; (touchy) susceptible.

sensual ['sɛnsjuəl] *a* sensual.

sensuous ['sɛnsjuəs] *a* sensual.

sent [sɛnt] *pt, pp of* **send**.

sentence ['sɛntns] *n* (LING) oración *f*; (LAW) sentencia, fallo // *vt*: **to** ~ **sb to death/to 5 years** condenar a

uno a muerte/a 5 años de cárcel.

sentiment ['sɛntɪmənt] *n* sentimiento; (opinion) opinión *f*; ~**al** [-'mɛntl] *a* sentimental.

sentry ['sɛntrɪ] *n* centinela *m*.

separate ['sɛprɪt] *a* separado; (distinct) distinto // *vb* ['sɛpəreɪt] *vt* separar; (part) dividir // *vi* separarse; ~**s** *npl* (clothes) coordinados *mpl*; ~**ly** *ad* por separado; **separation** [-'reɪʃən] *n* separación *f*.

September [sɛp'tɛmbə*] *n* se(p)tiembre *m*.

septic ['sɛptɪk] *a* séptico; ~ **tank** *n* fosa séptica.

sequel ['si:kwl] *n* consecuencia, resultado; (of story) continuación *f*.

sequence ['si:kwəns] *n* sucesión *f*, serie *f*; (CINEMA) secuencia.

serene [sɪ'ri:n] *a* sereno, tranquilo.

sergeant ['sɑ:dʒənt] *n* sargento.

serial ['sɪərɪəl] *n* (TV) telenovela, serie *f* televisiva; ~ **number** *n* número de serie.

series ['sɪərɪs] *n, pl inv* serie *f*.

serious ['sɪərɪəs] *a* serio; (grave) grave; ~**ly** *ad* en serio; (ill, wounded etc) gravemente; ~**ness** *n* seriedad *f*; gravedad *f*.

sermon ['sɜːmən] *n* sermón *m*.

serrated [sɪ'reɪtɪd] *a* serrado, dentellado.

serum ['sɪərəm] *n* suero.

servant ['sɜːvənt] *n* (gen) servidor/a *m/f*; (house ~) criado/a.

serve [sɜːv] *vt* servir; (customer) atender; (subj: train) pasar por; (apprenticeship) hacer; (prison term) cumplir // *vi* (also TENNIS) sacar; **to** ~ **as/for/to do** servir de/para/para hacer // *n* (TENNIS) saque *m*; **it** ~**s him right** se lo merece, se lo tiene merecido; **to** ~ **out, ~ up** *vt* (food) servir.

service ['sɜːvɪs] *n* (gen) servicio; (REL) misa; (AUT) mantenimiento; (of dishes) juego // *vt* (car, washing machine) mantener; (: repair) reparar; **the S~s** las fuerzas armadas; **to be of ~ to sb** ser útil a uno;

~able *a* servible, utilizable; **~ area** *n* (*on motorway*) servicios *mpl*; **~ charge** *n* (*Brit*) servicio; **~man** *n* militar *m*; **~ station** *n* estación *f* de servicio.

serviette [sɜːvɪ'ɛt] *n* (*Brit*) servilleta.

session ['sɛʃən] *n* (*sitting*) sesión *f*; to be in ~ estar en sesión.

set [sɛt] *n* juego; (*RADIO*) aparato, (*TV*) televisor *m*; (*of utensils*) batería; (*of cutlery*) cubierto; (*of books*) colección *f*; (*TENNIS*) set *m*; (*group of people*) grupo; (*CINEMA*) plató *m*; (*THEATRE*) decorado; (*HAIRDRESSING*) marcado // *a* (*fixed*) fijo; (*ready*) listo; (*resolved*) resuelto, decidido // *vb* (*pt, pp* set) *vt* (*place*) poner, colocar; (*fix*) fijar; (*adjust*) ajustar, arreglar; (*decide: rules etc*) establecer, decidir // *vi* (*sun*) ponerse; (*jam, jelly*) cuajarse; (*concrete*) fraguar; **to be ~ on doing sth** estar empeñado en hacer algo; **to ~ to music** poner música a; **to ~ on fire** incendiar, poner fuego a; **to ~ free** poner en libertad; **to ~ sth going** poner algo en marcha; **to ~ sail** zarpar, hacerse a la vela; **to ~ about** *vt fus*: **to ~ about doing sth** ponerse a hacer algo; **to ~ aside** *vt* poner aparte, dejar de lado; **to ~ back** *vt*: **to ~ back (by)** retrasar (por); **to ~ off** *vi* partir // *vt* (*bomb*) hacer estallar; (*cause to start*) poner en marcha; (*show up well*) hacer resaltar; **to ~ out** *vi*: **to ~ out to do sth** proponerse hacer algo // *vt* (*arrange*) disponer; (*state*) exponer; **to ~ up** *vt* (*organization*) establecer; **~back** *n* (*hitch*) revés *m*, contratiempo; **~ menu** *n* menú *m*.

settee [sɛ'tiː] *n* sofá *m*.

setting ['sɛtɪŋ] *n* (*scenery*) marco; (*of jewel*) engaste *m*, montadura.

settle ['sɛtl] *vt* (*argument, matter*) resolver; (*accounts*) ajustar, liquidar; (*land*) colonizar; (*MED: calm*) calmar, sosegar // *vi* (*dust etc*) depo-

sitarse; (*weather*) serenarse; (*also:* ~ **down**) instalarse; tranquilizarse; **to ~ for sth** convenir en aceptar algo; **to ~ on sth** decidirse por algo; **to ~ up with sb** ajustar cuentas con uno; **to ~ in** *vi* instalarse; **~ment** *n* (*payment*) liquidación *f*; (*agreement*) acuerdo, convenio; (*village etc*) pueblo; **~r** *n* colono/a, colonizador(a) *m/f*.

setup ['sɛtʌp] *n* sistema *m*.

seven ['sɛvn] *num* siete; **~teen** *num* diez y siete, diecisiete; **~th** *a* séptimo; **~ty** *num* setenta.

sever ['sɛvə*] *vt* cortar; (*relations*) romper.

several ['sɛvərl] *a, pron* varios/as *m/fpl*, algunos/as *m/fpl*; **~ of us** varios de nosotros.

severance ['sɛvərəns] *n* (*of relations*) ruptura; **~ pay** *n* pago de despedida.

severe [sɪ'vɪə*] *a* severo; (*serious*) grave; (*hard*) duro; (*pain*) intenso; **severity** [sɪ'vɛrɪtɪ] *n* severidad *f*; gravedad *f*; intensidad *f*.

sew [səu], *pt* sewed, *pp* sewn *vt, vi* coser; **to ~ up** *vt* coser, zurcir.

sewage ['suːɪdʒ] *n* aguas *fpl* residuales.

sewer ['suːə*] *n* alcantarilla, cloaca.

sewing ['səuɪŋ] *n* costura; **~ machine** *n* máquina de coser.

sewn [səun] *pp* of sew.

sex [sɛks] *n* sexo; **to have ~ with sb** tener relaciones (sexuales) con uno; **~ist** *a, n* sexista *m/f*.

sexual ['sɛksjuəl] *a* sexual.

sexy ['sɛksɪ] *a* sexy.

shabby ['ʃæbɪ] *a* (*person*) desharrapado; (*clothes*) raído, gastado.

shack [ʃæk] *n* choza, chabola.

shackles ['ʃæklz] *npl* grillos *mpl*, grilletes *mpl*.

shade [ʃeɪd] *n* sombra; (*for lamp*) pantalla; (*for eyes*) visera; (*of colour*) matiz *m*, tonalidad *f* // *vt* dar sombra a; **in the ~** a la sombra; **a ~ of** un poquito de; **a ~ smaller** un poquito menor.

shadow ['ʃædəu] n sombra // vt (follow) seguir y vigilar; ~ **cabinet** n (Brit POL) gabinete paralelo formado por el partido de la oposición; ~**y** a oscuro; (dim) indistinto.

shady ['ʃeɪdɪ] a sombreado; (fig: dishonest) sospechoso; (: deal) turbio.

shaft [ʃɑːft] n (of arrow, spear) astil m; (AUT, TECH) eje m, árbol m; (of mine) pozo; (of lift) hueco, caja; (of light) rayo.

shaggy ['ʃægɪ] a peludo.

shake [ʃeɪk] vb (pt **shook**, pp **shaken**) vt sacudir; (building) hacer temblar; (bottle, cocktail) agitar // vi (tremble) temblar // n (movement) sacudida; to ~ **one's head** (in refusal) negar con la cabeza; (in dismay) mover or menear la cabeza, incrédulo; to ~ **hands with sb** estrechar la mano a uno; to ~ **off** vt sacudirse; (fig) deshacerse de; to ~ **up** vt agitar; **shaky** a (hand, voice) trémulo; (building) inestable.

shall [ʃæl] auxiliary vb: I ~ **go** iré; ~ **I help you?** ¿quieres que te ayude?; **I'll buy three, ~ I?** compro tres, ¿no te parece?

shallow ['ʃæləu] a poco profundo; (fig) superficial.

sham [ʃæm] n fraude m, engaño // a falso, fingido // vt fingir, simular.

shambles ['ʃæmblz] n confusión f.

shame [ʃeɪm] n vergüenza; (pity) lástima // vt avergonzar; **it is a** ~ **that/to do es** una lástima que/hacer; **what a** ~! ¡qué lástima!; ~**faced** a avergonzado; ~**ful** a vergonzoso; ~**less** a descarado.

shampoo [ʃæm'puː] n champú m // vt lavar con champú; ~ **and set** n lavado y marcado.

shamrock ['ʃæmrɔk] n trébol m (emblema nacional irlandés).

shandy ['ʃændɪ], (US) **shandygaff** ['ʃændɪgæf] n mezcla de cerveza con gaseosa.

shan't [ʃɑːnt] = **shall not.**

shanty town ['ʃæntɪ-] n barrio de chabolas.

shape [ʃeɪp] n forma // vt formar, dar forma a; (sb's ideas) formar; (sb's life) determinar // vi (also: ~ **up**) (events) desarrollarse; (person) formarse; to **take** ~ tomar forma; ~**d** suffix: heart-~d en forma de corazón; ~**less** a informe, sin forma definida; ~**ly** a bien formado or proporcionado.

share [ʃeə*] n (part) parte f, porción f; (contribution) cuota; (COMM) acción f // vt dividir; (have in common) compartir; to ~ **out** (among or between) repartir (entre); ~**holder** n (Brit) accionista m/f.

shark [ʃɑːk] n tiburón m.

sharp [ʃɑːp] a (razor, knife) afilado; (point) puntiagudo; (outline) definido; (pain) intenso; (MUS) desafinado; (contrast) marcado; (voice) agudo; (person: quick-witted) astuto; (: dishonest) poco escrupuloso // n (MUS) sostenido // ad: **at 2 o'clock** ~ a las 2 en punto; ~**en** vt afilar; (pencil) sacar punta a; (fig) agudizar; ~**ener** n (also: **pencil** ~**ener**) sacapuntas m inv; ~**eyed** a de vista aguda; ~**ly** ad (turn, stop) bruscamente; (stand out, contrast) claramente; (criticize, retort) severamente.

shatter ['ʃætə*] vt hacer añicos or pedazos; (fig: ruin) destruir, acabar con // vi hacerse añicos.

shave [ʃeɪv] vb (pt **shaved**, pp **shaved** or **shaven**) vt afeitar, rasurar // vi afeitarse // n: to **have a** ~ afeitarse; ~**r** n (also: **electric** ~**r**) máquina de afeitar (eléctrica).

shaving ['ʃeɪvɪŋ] n (action) el afeitarse, rasurado; ~**s** npl (of wood etc) virutas fpl; ~ **brush** n brocha (de afeitar); ~ **cream** n crema (de afeitar).

shawl [ʃɔːl] n chal m.

she [ʃiː] pron ella; ~**cat** n gata; NB: for ships, countries follow the gender of your translation.

sheaf [ʃiːf], pl **sheaves** [ʃiːvz] n (of

corn) gavilla; (of arrows) haz m; (of papers) fajo.

shear [ʃɪə*] vb (pt **sheared**, pp **sheared** or **shorn**) vt esquilar, trasquilar; **~s** npl (for hedge) tijeras fpl de jardín; **to ~ off** vi romperse.

sheath [ʃiːθ] n vaina; (contraceptive) preservativo.

sheaves [ʃiːvz] pl of **sheaf**.

shed [ʃed] n cobertizo // vt (pt, pp **shed**) (skin) mudar; (tears) derramar.

she'd [ʃiːd] = **she had**; **she would**.

sheen [ʃiːn] n brillo, lustre m.

sheep [ʃiːp] n, pl inv oveja; **~dog** n perro pastor; **~ish** a tímido, vergonzoso; **~skin** n piel f de carnero.

sheer [ʃɪə*] a (utter) puro, completo; (steep) escarpado; (material) diáfano // ad verticalmente.

sheet [ʃiːt] n (on bed) sábana; (of paper) hoja; (of glass, metal) lámina.

sheik(h) [ʃeɪk] n jeque m.

shelf [ʃelf], pl **shelves** n estante m.

shell [ʃel] n (on beach) concha; (of egg, nut) cáscara; (explosive) proyectil m, obús m; (of building) armazón f // vt (peas) desenvainar; (MIL) bombardear.

she'll [ʃiːl] = **she will**; **she shall**.

shellfish [ʃelfɪʃ] n, pl inv crustáceo; (pl: as food) mariscos mpl.

shelter [ʃeltə*] n abrigo, refugio // vt (aid) amparar, proteger; (give lodging to) abrigar; (hide) esconder // vi abrigarse, refugiarse; **~ed** a (life) protegido; (spot) abrigado.

shelve [ʃelv] vt (fig) aplazar; **~s** pl of **shelf**.

shepherd [ʃepəd] n pastor m // vt (guide) guiar, conducir; **~'s pie** n pastel de carne y patatas.

sherry [ʃeri] n jerez m.

she's [ʃiːz] = **she is**; **she has**.

Shetland [ʃetlənd] n (also: **the ~s**, the **~ Isles**) las Islas de Zetlandia.

shield [ʃiːld] n escudo; (TECH) blindaje m // vt: **to ~ (from)** proteger (de).

shift [ʃɪft] n (change) cambio; (at work) turno // vt trasladar; (remove) quitar // vi moverse; (change place) cambiar de sitio; **~less** a (person) perezoso; **~ work** n (Brit) trabajo por turno; **~y** a tramposo; (eyes) furtivo.

shilling [ʃɪlɪŋ] n (Brit) chelín m.

shilly-shally [ʃɪlɪʃælɪ] vi titubear, vacilar.

shimmer [ʃɪmə*] n reflejo trémulo // vi relucir.

shin [ʃɪn] n espinilla.

shine [ʃaɪn] n brillo, lustre m // (vb: pt, pp **shone**) vi brillar, relucir // vt (shoes) lustrar, sacar brillo a; **to ~ a torch on sth** dirigir una linterna hacia algo.

shingle [ʃɪŋgl] n (on beach) guijarras fpl; **~s** n (MED) herpes mpl or fpl.

shiny [ʃaɪnɪ] a brillante, lustroso.

ship [ʃɪp] n buque m, barco // vt (goods) embarcar; (oars) desarmar; (send) transportar o enviar por vía marítima; **~building** n construcción f de buques; **~ment** n (act) embarque m; (goods) envío; **~per** n exportador/a m/f; **~ping** n (act) embarque m; (traffic) buques mpl; **~shape** a en buen orden; **~wreck** n naufragio // vt: **to be ~wrecked** naufragar; **~yard** n astillero.

shire [ʃaɪə*] n (Brit) condado.

shirk [ʃəːk] vt eludir, esquivar; (obligations) faltar a.

shirt [ʃəːt] n camisa; **in ~ sleeves** en mangas de camisa.

shit [ʃɪt] excl (col!) ¡mierda! (!)

shiver [ʃɪvə*] vi temblar, estremecerse; (with cold) tiritar.

shoal [ʃəʊl] n (of fish) banco.

shock [ʃɔk] n (impact) choque m; (ELEC) descarga (eléctrica); (emotional) conmoción f; (start) sobresalto, susto; (MED) postración f o nerviosa // vt dar un susto a; (offend) escandalizar; ~ **absorber** n amortiguador m; ~**ing** a (awful) espantoso; (improper) escandaloso.

shod [ʃɔd] pt, pp of **shoe**.

shoddy [ˈʃɔdɪ] a de pacotilla.

shoe [ʃuː] n (on branch, seedling) retoño, vástago // vt (pt, pp **shot**) (kill) matar a tiros; (execute) fusilar; (film) rodear, filmar // vi (FOOTBALL) chutar; ~ **(at)** tirar (a); **to ~ down** vt (plane) derribar; **to ~ in/out** vi entrar corriendo/salir disparado; **to ~ up** vi (prices) dispararse; ~ (shots) tiros mpl; (HUNTING) caza con escopeta; ~**ing star** n estrella fugaz.

shoe [ʃuː] n (for horse) herradura; (brake ~) zapata // vt (pt, pp **shod**) (horse) herrar; ~**brush** n cepillo para zapatos; ~**horn** n calzador m; ~**lace** n cordón m; ~**polish** n betún m; ~**shop** n zapatería; ~**string** n (fig): **on a ~string** con muy poco dinero.

shone [ʃɔn] pt, pp of **shine**.

shoo [ʃuː] excl ¡fuera!

shook [ʃuk] pt of **shake**.

shoot [ʃuːt] n (on branch, seedling) retoño, vástago // vt (pt, pp **shot**) (kill) matar a tiros; (execute) fusilar; (film) rodear, filmar // vi (FOOTBALL) chutar; ~ **(at)** tirar (a); **to ~ down** vt (plane) derribar; **to ~ in/out** vi entrar corriendo/salir disparado; **to ~ up** vi (prices) dispararse; ~ (shots) tiros mpl; (HUNTING) caza con escopeta; ~**ing star** n estrella fugaz.

shop [ʃɔp] n tienda; (workshop) taller m // vi (also: go ~**ping**) ir de compras; ~ **assistant** n (Brit) dependiente/a m/f; ~ **floor** n (Brit fig) taller m, fábrica; ~**keeper** n (Brit) tendero/a; ~**lifting** n mechería; ~**per** n comprador(a) m/f; ~**ping** n (goods) compras fpl; ~**ping bag** n bolsa (de compras); ~**ping centre**, (US) ~**ping center** n centro comercial; ~**soiled** a (Brit) usado; ~ **steward** n (Brit INDUSTRY) enlace m sindical; ~**window** n escaparate m, vidriera (LAm); ~**worn** a (US) usado.

shore [ʃɔː*] n (of sea, lake) orilla // vt: **to ~ (up)** reforzar.

shorn [ʃɔːn] pp of **shear**.

short [ʃɔːt] a (not long) corto; (in time) breve, de corta duración; (person) bajo; (curt) brusco, seco // n (also: ~ film) cortometraje m; (a

pair of) ~s (unos) pantalones mpl cortos; **to be ~ of sth** estar falto de algo; **in ~** en pocas palabras; **~ of doing...** fuera de hacer...; **everything ~ of...** todo menos...; **it is ~ for** es la forma abreviada de; **to cut ~** (speech, visit) interrumpir, terminar inesperadamente; **to fall ~ of** no alcanzar; **to stop ~** parar en seco; **to stop ~ of** detenerse antes de; ~**age** n escasez f, falta; ~**bread** n especie de mantecada; ~**change** vt no dar el cambio completo a; ~**circuit** n cortocircuito // vt poner en cortocircuito // vi ponerse en cortocircuito; ~**coming** n defecto, deficiencia; ~**(crust) pastry** n (Brit) pasta quebradiza; ~**cut** n atajo; ~**en** vt acortar; (visit) interrumpir; ~**fall** n déficit m; ~**hand** n (Brit) taquigrafía; ~**hand typist** n (Brit) taquimecanógrafo/a; ~ **list** n (Brit: for job) lista de candidatos escogidos; ~**ly** ad en breve, dentro de poco; ~**sighted** a (Brit) corto de vista, miope; (fig) imprudente; ~**staffed** a falto de personal; ~ **story** n cuento; ~**tempered** a enojadizo; ~**term** a (effect) a corto plazo; ~**wave** n (RADIO) onda corta.

shot [ʃɔt] pt, pp of **shoot** // n (sound) tiro, disparo; (person) tirador(a) m/f; (try) tentativa; (injection) inyección f; (PHOT) toma, fotografía; **like a ~** (without any delay) como un rayo; ~**gun** n escopeta.

should [ʃud] auxiliary vb: **I ~ go now** debo irme ahora; **he ~ be there now** debe de haber llegado (ya); **I ~ go if I were you** yo en tu lugar me iría; **I ~ like to** me gustaría.

shoulder [ˈʃəuldə*] n hombro; (Brit: of road): **hard ~** andén m // vt (fig) cargar con; ~ **blade** n omóplato; ~ **strap** n tirante m.

shouldn't [ˈʃudnt] = **should not**.

shout [ʃaut] n grito // vt gritar // vi gritar, dar voces; **to ~ down** vt hundir a gritos; ~**ing** n griterío.

shove [ʃʌv] n empujón m // vt empujar; (col: put): **to ~ sth in** meter algo a empellones; **to ~ off** vi (NAUT) alejarse del muelle; (fig: col) largarse.

shovel [ˈʃʌvl] n pala; (mechanical) excavadora // vt mover con pala.

show [ʃəu] n (of emotion) demostración f; (semblance) apariencia; (exhibition) exposición f; (THEATRE) función f, espectáculo // vb (pt **showed**, pp **shown**) vt mostrar, enseñar; (courage etc) mostrar, manifestar; (exhibit) exponer; (film) proyectar // vi mostrarse; (appear) aparecer; **on ~** (exhibits etc) expuesto; **to ~ in** (person) hacer pasar; **to ~ off** vi (pej) presumir // vt (display) lucir; (pej) hacer gala de; **to ~ out** vt: **to ~ sb out** acompañar a uno a la puerta; **to ~ up** vi (stand out) destacar; (col: turn up) aparecer // vt descubrir; (unmask) desenmascarar; **~ business** n el mundo del espectáculo; **~down** n enfrentamiento (final).

shower [ˈʃauə*] n (rain) chaparrón m, chubasco; (of stones etc) lluvia; (also: **~bath**) ducha, regadera (LAm) // vi llover // vt: **to ~ sb with sth** colmar a uno de algo; **~proof** a impermeable.

showing [ˈʃəuɪŋ] n (of film) proyección f.

show jumping n hipismo.

shown [ʃəun] pp of **show**.

show-: **~off** n (col: person) presumido/a m; **~piece** n (of exhibition etc) objeto cumbre; **~room** n sala de muestras.

shrank [ʃræŋk] pt of **shrink**.

shrapnel [ˈʃræpnl] n metralla.

shred [ʃred] n (gen pl) triza, jirón m // vt hacer trizas; (CULIN) desmenuzar; **~der** n (vegetable ~der) picadora; (document ~der) trituradora (de papel).

shrewd [ʃru:d] a astuto.

shriek [ʃri:k] n chillido // vt, vi chillar.

shrill [ʃril] a agudo, estridente.

shrimp [ʃrimp] n camarón m.

shrine [ʃrain] n santuario, sepulcro.

shrink [ʃriŋk] pt **shrank**, pp **shrunk** vi encogerse; (be reduced) reducirse // vt encoger; **to ~ from doing sth** no atreverse a hacer algo; **~age** n encogimiento; reducción f; **~wrap** vt empaquetar al vacío.

shrivel [ˈʃrivl] (also: **~ up**) vt (dry) secar; (crease) arrugar // vi secarse; arrugarse.

shroud [ʃraud] n sudario // vt: **~ed in mystery** envuelto en el misterio.

Shrove Tuesday [ˈʃrəuv-] n martes m de carnaval.

shrub [ʃrʌb] n arbusto; **~bery** n arbustos mpl.

shrug [ʃrʌg] n encogimiento de hombros // vt, vi: **to ~ (one's shoulders)** encogerse de hombros; **to ~ off** vt negar importancia a.

shrunk [ʃrʌŋk] pp of **shrink**.

shudder [ˈʃʌdə*] n estremecimiento, escalofrío // vi estremecerse.

shuffle [ˈʃʌfl] n (cards) barajar; **to ~ (one's feet)** arrastrar los pies.

shun [ʃʌn] vt rehuir, esquivar.

shunt [ʃʌnt] vt (RAIL) maniobrar.

shut [ʃʌt], pt, pp **shut** vt cerrar // vi cerrarse; **to ~ down** vt, vi cerrar; **to ~ off** vt (supply etc) interrumpir, cortar; **to ~ up** vi (keep quiet) callarse // vt (close) cerrar; (silence) callar; **~ter** n contraventana; (PHOT) obturador m.

shuttle [ˈʃʌtl] n lanzadera; (also: **~ service**: AVIAT) puente m aéreo.

shuttlecock [ˈʃʌtlkɔk] n volante m.

shy [ʃai] a tímido; **~ness** n timidez f.

sibling [ˈsiblɪŋ] n hermano/a.

Sicily [ˈsisili] n Sicilia.

sick [sik] a (ill) enfermo; (nauseated) mareado; (humour) negro; **to be ~** (Brit) vomitar; **to feel ~** tener náuseas; **to be ~ of** (fig) estar harto de; **~ bay** n enfermería // vi enfermar; dar asco a // vi enfermar; **~ening** a (fig) asqueroso.

sickle ['sɪkl] n hoz f.

sick: ~ **leave** n baja por enfermedad; ~**ly** a enfermizo; (taste) empalagoso; ~**ness** n enfermedad f, mal m; (vomiting) náuseas fpl; ~ **pay** n subsidio de enfermedad.

side [saɪd] n (gen) lado; (of body) costado; (of lake) orilla; (team) equipo; (of hill) ladera // cpd (door, entrance) lateral // vi: to ~ with sb tomar el partido de uno; by the ~ of al lado de; ~ by ~ juntos/as; from all ~s de todos lados; to take ~s (with) tomar partido (con); ~**board** n aparador m; ~**boards** (Brit), ~**burns** npl patillas fpl; ~ **effect** n efecto secundario; ~**light** n (AUT) luz f lateral; ~**line** n (SPORT) línea lateral; (fig) empleo suplementario; ~**long** a de soslayo; ~**saddle** ad a mujeriegas, a la inglesa; ~ **show** n (stall) caseta; ~**step** vt (fig) esquivar; ~ **street** n calle f lateral; ~**track** vt (fig) desviar (de su propósito); ~**walk** n (US) acera; ~**ways** ad de lado.

siding ['saɪdɪŋ] n (RAIL) apartadero, vía muerta.

sidle ['saɪdl] vi: to ~ **up** (to) acercarse furtivamente (a).

siege [siːdʒ] n cerco, sitio.

sieve [sɪv] n colador m // vt cribar.

sift [sɪft] vt cribar; (fig: information) escudriñar.

sigh [saɪ] n suspiro // vi suspirar.

sight [saɪt] n (faculty) vista; (spectacle) espectáculo; (on gun) mira, alza // vt divisar; **in** ~ a la vista; **out of** ~ fuera de (la) vista; ~**seeing** n excursionismo, turismo; **to go** ~**seeing** hacer turismo.

sign [saɪn] n (with hand) señal f, seña; (trace) huella, rastro; (notice) letrero; (written) signo // vt firmar; **to** ~ **sth over to sb** firmar el traspaso de algo a uno; **to** ~ **on** vi (MIL) alistarse; (as unemployed) registrarse como desempleado // vt (MIL) alistar; (employee) contratar; **to** ~ **up** vi (MIL) alistarse // vt

(contract) contratar.

signal ['sɪgnl] n señal f // vi (AUT) hacer señales // vt (person) hacer señas a; (message) comunicar por señales; ~**man** n (RAIL) guardavía m.

signature ['sɪgnətʃə*] n firma; ~ **tune** n sintonía de apertura de un programa.

signet ring ['sɪgnət-] n anillo de sello.

significance [sɪg'nɪfɪkəns] n significado; (importance) trascendencia.

significant [sɪg'nɪfɪkənt] a significativo; trascendente.

signify ['sɪgnɪfaɪ] vt significar.

signpost ['saɪnpəʊst] n indicador m.

silence ['saɪləns] n silencio // vt hacer callar; (guns) reducir al silencio; ~**r** n (on gun, Brit AUT) silenciador m.

silent ['saɪlənt] a (gen) silencioso; (not speaking) callado; (film) mudo; **to remain** ~ guardar silencio; ~ **partner** n (COMM) socio/a comanditario/a.

silhouette [sɪluː'et] n silueta.

silicon chip ['sɪlɪkən-] n plaqueta de silicio.

silk [sɪlk] n seda // cpd de seda; ~**y** a sedoso.

silly ['sɪlɪ] a (person) tonto; (idea) absurdo.

silo ['saɪləʊ] n silo.

silt [sɪlt] n sedimento.

silver ['sɪlvə*] n plata; (money) moneda suelta // cpd de plata; ~ **paper** n (Brit) papel m de plata; ~**plated** a plateado; ~**smith** n platero/a; ~**ware** n plata; ~**y** a plateado.

similar ['sɪmɪlə*] a: ~ **to** parecido or semejante a; ~**ly** ad del mismo modo.

simile ['sɪmɪlɪ] n símil m.

simmer ['sɪmə*] vi hervir a fuego lento.

simpering ['sɪmpərɪŋ] a afectado; (foolish) bobo.

simple ['sɪmpl] a (easy) sencillo; (foolish, COMM: interest) simple; **simplicity** [-'plɪsɪtɪ] n sencillez f;

simplify ['sɪmplɪfaɪ] vt simplificar.

simply ['sɪmplɪ] ad (live, talk) sencillamente; (just, merely) sólo.

simultaneous [sɪməl'teɪnɪəs] a simultáneo; ~**ly** ad simultáneamente.

sin [sɪn] n pecado // vi pecar.

since [sɪns] ad desde entonces, después // prep desde // conj (time) desde que; (because) ya que, puesto que; ~ **then** desde entonces.

sincere [sɪn'sɪə*] a sincero; ~**ly** ad: yours ~**ly**, (US) ~**ly yours** (in letters) le saluda atentamente; **sincerity** [-'serɪtɪ] n sinceridad f.

sinew ['sɪnjuː] n tendón m.

sinful ['sɪnful] a (thought) pecaminoso; (person) pecador(a).

sing [sɪŋ], pt **sang**, pp **sung** vt cantar // vi cantar.

Singapore [sɪŋə'pɔː*] n Singapur m.

singe [sɪndʒ] vt chamuscar.

singer ['sɪŋə*] n cantante m/f.

singing ['sɪŋɪŋ] n (gen) canto; (songs) canciones fpl.

single ['sɪŋgl] a único, solo; (unmarried) soltero; (not double) simple, sencillo // a (Brit: also: ~ **ticket**) billete m sencillo; (record) sencillo, single m; ~**s** npl (TENNIS) individual msg; ~ **out** vt (choose) escoger; ~ **bed** n cama individual; ~**-breasted** (a jacket, suit) recto; **single-file** n: **in** ~ **file** en fila de uno; ~**-handed** ad sin ayuda; ~**-minded** a resuelto, firme; ~ **room** n cuarto individual.

singlet ['sɪŋlɪt] n camiseta.

singly ['sɪŋglɪ] ad uno por uno.

singular ['sɪŋgjulə*] a (odd) raro, extraño; (LING) singular // n (LING) singular m.

sinister ['sɪnɪstə*] a siniestro.

sink [sɪŋk] n fregadero // vb (pt **sank**, pp **sunk**) vt (ship) hundir, echar a pique; (foundations) excavar; (piles etc): **to** ~ **sth into** hundir algo en // vi (gen) hundirse; **to** ~ **in** vi (fig) penetrar, calar.

sinner ['sɪnə*] n pecador(a) m/f.

sinus ['saɪnəs] n (ANAT) seno.

sip [sɪp] n sorbo // vt sorber, beber a sorbitos.

siphon ['saɪfən] n sifón m; **to** ~ **off** vt desviar.

sir [sə*] n señor m; S~ John Smith Sir John Smith; yes ~ sí, señor.

siren ['saɪərn] n sirena.

sirloin ['sɜːlɔɪn] n solomillo.

sissy ['sɪsɪ] n (col) marica m.

sister ['sɪstə*] n hermana; (Brit: nurse) enfermera jefe; ~**-in-law** n cuñada.

sit [sɪt], pt, pp **sat** vi sentarse; (be sitting) estar sentado; (assembly) reunirse // vt (exam) presentarse a; **to** ~ **down** vi sentarse; **to** ~ **in on** vt fus asistir a; **to** ~ **up** vi incorporarse; (not go to bed) velar.

sitcom ['sɪtkɔm] n abbr (= situation comedy) comedia de situación.

site [saɪt] n sitio; (also: **building** ~) solar m // vt situar.

sit-in ['sɪtɪn] n (demonstration) ocupación f.

sitting ['sɪtɪŋ] n (of assembly etc) sesión f; (in canteen) turno; ~ **room** n sala de estar.

situated ['sɪtjueɪtɪd] a situado.

situation [sɪtju'eɪʃən] n situación f; '~**s vacant**' (Brit) 'ofrecen trabajo'.

six [sɪks] num seis; ~**teen** num diez y seis, dieciséis; ~**th** a sexto; ~**ty** num sesenta.

size [saɪz] n (gen) tamaño; (extent) extensión f; (of clothing) talla; (of shoes) número; **to** ~ **up** vt formarse una idea de; ~**able** a importante, considerable.

sizzle ['sɪzl] vi crepitar.

skate [skeɪt] n patín m; (fish: pl inv) raya // vi patinar; ~**board** n monopatín m; ~**r** n patinador(a) m/f; **skating** n patinaje m; **skating rink** n pista de patinaje.

skeleton ['skelɪtn] n esqueleto; (TECH) armazón f; (outline) esquema m; ~ **key** n llave f maestra; ~ **staff** n personal m reducido.

skeptic ['skeptɪk] etc (US) = **sceptic**.

sketch [skɛtʃ] n (drawing) dibujo; (outline) esbozo, bosquejo; (THEATRE) sketch m // vt dibujar; esbozar; ~ **book** n libro de dibujos; ~**y** a incompleto.

skewer ['skjuːə*] n broqueta.

ski [skiː] n esquí m // vi esquiar; ~ **boot** n bota de esquí.

skid [skɪd] n patinazo // vi patinar.

ski-: ~**er** n esquiador(a) m/f; ~**ing** n esquí m; ~ **jump** n salto con esquís.

skilful [skɪlful] a diestro, experto.

ski lift n telesilla m, telesquí m.

skill [skɪl] n destreza, pericia; ~**ed** a hábil, diestro; (worker) cualificado.

skim [skɪm] vt (milk) desnatar; (glide over) rozar, rasar // vi: to ~ **through** (book) hojear; ~**med milk** n leche f desnatada.

skimp [skɪmp] vt (work) chapucear; (cloth etc) escatimar; ~**y** a (meagre) escaso; (skirt) muy corto.

skin [skɪn] n (gen) piel f; (complexion) cutis m // vt (fruit etc) pelar; (animal) despellejar; ~**-deep** a superficial; ~ **diving** n buceo; ~**ny** a flaco; ~**tight** a (dress etc) muy ajustado.

skip [skɪp] n brinco, salto; (container) cuba // vi brincar; (with rope) saltar a la comba // vt (pass over) omitir, saltar.

ski pants npl pantalones mpl de esquí.

ski pole n bastón m de esquiar.

skipper ['skɪpə*] n (NAUT, SPORT) capitán m.

skipping rope ['skɪpɪŋ-] n (Brit) cuerda de saltar.

skirmish ['skəːmɪʃ] n escaramuza.

skirt [skəːt] n falda, pollera (LAm) // vt (surround) ceñir, rodear; (go round) ladear.

ski suit n traje m de esquiar.

skit [skɪt] n sátira, parodia.

skittle ['skɪtl] n bolo; ~**s** n (game) boliche m.

skive [skaɪv] vi (Brit col) gandulear.

skulk [skʌlk] vi esconderse.

skull [skʌl] n calavera; (ANAT) cráneo.

skunk [skʌŋk] n mofeta.

sky [skaɪ] n cielo; ~**light** n tragaluz m, claraboya; ~**scraper** n rascacielos m inv.

slab [slæb] n (stone) bloque m; (flat) losa; (of cake) trozo.

slack [slæk] a (loose) flojo; (slow) de poca actividad; (careless) descuidado; ~**s** npl pantalones mpl; ~**en** (also: ~**en off**) vi aflojarse // vt aflojar; (speed) disminuir.

slag [slæg] n escoria, escombros mpl; ~ **heap** n escorial m, escombrera.

slain [sleɪn] pp of **slay**.

slam [slæm] vt (throw) arrojar (violentamente); **to** ~ **the door** dar un portazo // vi cerrarse de golpe.

slander ['slɑːndə*] n calumnia, difamación // vt calumniar, difamar.

slang [slæŋ] n argot m; (jargon) jerga.

slant [slɑːnt] n sesgo, inclinación f; (fig) interpretación f; ~**ed**, ~**ing** a inclinado.

slap [slæp] n palmada; (in face) bofetada // vt dar una palmada/bofetada a // ad (directly) exactamente, directamente; ~**dash** a descuidado; ~**stick** n: ~**stick comedy** comedia de golpe y porrazo; ~**up** a: a ~**up meal** (Brit) un banquetazo, una comilona.

slash [slæʃ] vt acuchillar; (fig: prices) quemar.

slat [slæt] n tablilla, listón m.

slate [sleɪt] n pizarra // vt (Brit: fig: criticize) criticar duramente.

slaughter ['slɔːtə*] n (of animals) matanza; (of people) carnicería // vt matar; ~**house** n matadero.

Slav [slɑːv] a eslavo.

slave [sleɪv] n esclavo/a // vi (also: ~ **away**) sudar tinta; ~**ry** n esclavitud f.

slay [sleɪ], pt **slew**, pp **slain** vt matar.

SLD n abbr = Social and Liberal Democrats.

sleazy ['sliːzɪ] a de mala fama.

sled [sled] n (US) trineo.

sledge [sledʒ] n (Brit) trineo; **~hammer** n mazo.

sleek [sliːk] a (shiny) lustroso.

sleep [sliːp] n sueño // vi (pt, pp slept) dormir; **to go to ~** quedarse dormido; **to ~ in** vi (oversleep) quedarse dormido; **~er** n (person) durmiente m/f; (Brit RAIL: on track) traviesa; (: train) coche-cama m; **~ing bag** n saco de dormir; **~ing car** n coche-cama m; **~ing pill** n somnífero; **~less** a: a **~less night** una noche en blanco; **~walker** n sonámbulo/a; **~y** a soñoliento.

sleet [sliːt] n nevisca.

sleeve [sliːv] n manga; (TECH) manguito.

sleigh [sleɪ] n trineo.

sleight [slaɪt] n: **~ of hand** escamoteo.

slender ['slendə*] a delgado; (means) escaso.

slept [slept] pt, pp of **sleep**.

slew [sluː] vi (veer) torcerse // pt of **slay**.

slice [slaɪs] n (of meat) tajada; (of bread) rebanada; (of lemon) rodaja; (utensil) pala // vt cortar (en tajos); rebanar.

slick [slɪk] a (skilful) hábil, diestro // n (also: oil **~**) marea negra.

slide [slaɪd] n (in playground) tobogán m; (PHOT) diapositiva; (Brit: also: hair **~**) pasador m // vb (pt, pp slid) vt correr, deslizar // vi (slip) resbalarse; (glide) deslizarse; **~ rule** n regla de cálculo; **sliding** a (door) corredizo; **sliding scale** n escala móvil.

slight [slaɪt] a (slim) delgado; (frail) delicado; (pain etc) leve; (trivial) insignificante; (small) pequeño // n desaire m // vt (offend) ofender; **not in the ~est** en absoluto; **~ly** ad ligeramente, un poco.

slim [slɪm] a delgado, esbelto // vi adelgazar.

slime [slaɪm] n limo, cieno.

slimming ['slɪmɪŋ] n adelgazamien-

to.

sling [slɪŋ] n (MED) cabestrillo; (weapon) honda // vt (pt, pp slung) tirar, arrojar.

slip [slɪp] n (slide) resbalón m; (mistake) descuido; (underskirt) combinación f; (of paper) papelito // vt (slide) deslizar // vi (slide) deslizarse; (stumble) resbalar(se); (decline) decaer; (move smoothly) meterse into/out of (room etc) introducirse en/salirse de; **to give sb the ~** eludir a uno; a **~ of the tongue** un lapsus; **to ~ sth on/off** ponerse/quitarse algo; **to ~ away** vi escabullirse; **to ~ in** vt meter // vi meterse; **to ~ out** vi (go out) salir (un momento); **~ped disc** n vértebra dislocada.

slipper ['slɪpə*] n zapatilla, pantufla.

slippery ['slɪpərɪ] a resbaladizo.

slip: **~road** n (Brit) carretera de acceso; **~shod** a descuidado; **~-up** n (error) desliz m; **~way** n grada, gradas fpl.

slit [slɪt] n raja; (cut) corte m // vt (pt, pp slit) rajar, cortar.

slither ['slɪðə*] vi deslizarse.

sliver ['slɪvə*] n (of glass, wood) astilla; (of cheese etc) raja.

slob [slɔb] n (col) patán/ana m/f.

slog [slɔg] (Brit) vi sudar tinta; it was a **~** costó trabajo (hacerlo).

slogan ['slɔugən] n eslogan m, lema m.

slop [slɔp] vi (also: **~ over**) derramarse, desbordarse // vt derramar, verter.

slope [sləup] n (up) cuesta, pendiente f; (down) declive m; (side of mountain) falda, vertiente m // vi: **to ~ down** estar en declive; **to ~ up** inclinarse; **sloping** a en pendiente, en declive.

sloppy ['slɔpɪ] a (work) descuidado; (appearance) desaliñado.

slot [slɔt] n ranura // vt: **to ~ into** encajar en.

sloth [sləuθ] n (laziness) pereza.

slot machine n (Brit: vending machine) aparato vendedor, distribuidor *m* automático; (*for gambling*) máquina tragaperras.

slouch [slautʃ] *vi*: **to ~ about** (*laze*) gandulear.

slovenly ['slʌvənlɪ] *a* (*dirty*) desaliñado, desaseado; (*careless*) descuidado.

slow [sləu] *a* lento; (*watch*): **to be ~** atrasarse // *ad* lentamente, despacio // *vt, vi* (*also*: **~ down**, **~ up**) retardar; '**~**' (*road sign*) 'disminuir velocidad'; **~ down** *m* (US) huelga de manos caídas; **~ly** *ad* lentamente, despacio; **slow motion** *n*: **in ~ motion** a cámara lenta.

sludge [slʌdʒ] *n* lodo, fango.

slug [slʌg] *n* babosa; (*bullet*) posta; **~gish** *a* (*slow*) lento; (*lazy*) perezoso.

sluice [sluːs] *n* (*gate*) esclusa; (*channel*) canal *m*.

slum [slʌm] *n* casucha.

slumber ['slʌmbə*] *n* sueño.

slump [slʌmp] *n* (*economic*) depresión // *vi* hundirse.

slung [slʌŋ] *pt, pp* of **sling**.

slur [sləː*] *n* calumnia // *vt* calumniar, difamar; (*word*) pronunciar mal.

slush [slʌʃ] *n* nieve *f* a medio derretir; **~ fund** *n* caja negra (*fondos para sobornar*).

slut [slʌt] *n* (*sloppy*) marrana.

sly [slaɪ] *a* astuto.

smack [smæk] *n* (*slap*) manotada; (*blow*) golpe *m* // *vt* dar una manotada a; golpear con la mano // *vi*: **to ~ of** saber a, oler a.

small [smɔːl] *a* pequeño; **~ ads** *npl* (*Brit*) anuncios *mpl* por palabras; **~ change** *n* suelto, cambio; **~holder** *n* (*Brit*) granjero/a, parcelero/a; **~ hours** *npl*: **in the ~ hours** en las altas horas de la noche); **~pox** *n* viruela; **~ talk** *n* cháchara.

smart [smɑːt] *a* elegante; (*clever*) listo, inteligente; (*quick*) rápido, vivo // *vi* escocer, picar; **to ~en up** *vi* arreglarse // *vt* arreglar.

smash [smæʃ] *n* (*also*: **~-up**) choque

m // *vt* (*break*) hacer pedazos; (*car etc*) estrellar; (*SPORT: record*) batir // *vi* hacerse pedazos; (*against wall etc*) estrellarse; **~ing** *a* (*col*) cojonudo.

smattering ['smætərɪŋ] *n*: **a ~ of Spanish** algo de español.

smear [smɪə*] *n* mancha; (*MED*) frotis *m* inv // *vt* untar; (*fig*) calumniar, difamar.

smell [smɛl] *n* olor *m*; (*sense*) olfato // (*pt, pp* **smelt** or **smelled**), *vt, vi* oler; **it ~s good/of garlic** huele bien/a ajo; **~y** *a* maloliente.

smile [smaɪl] *n* sonrisa // *vi* sonreír; **smiling** *a* sonriente.

smirk [sməːk] *n* sonrisa falsa or afectada.

smith [smɪθ] *n* herrero; **~y** ['smɪðɪ] *n* herrería.

smock [smɔk] *n* blusa; (*children's*) delantal *m*; (US: *overall*) guardapolvo.

smog [smɔg] *n* esmog *m*.

smoke [sməuk] *n* humo *m* // *vi* fumar; (*chimney*) echar humo // *vt* (*cigarettes*) fumar; **~d** *a* (*bacon, glass*) ahumado; **~r** *n* (*person*) fumador/a *m/f*; (*RAIL*) coche *m* fumador; **~ screen** *n* cortina de humo; **~ shop** *n* (US) estanco, tabaquería (*LAm*); **smoking** *n*: '**no smoking**' 'prohibido fumar'; **smoky** *a* (*room*) lleno de humo.

smolder ['sməuldə*] *vi* (US) = **smoulder**.

smooth [smuːð] *a* liso; (*sea*) tranquilo; (*flavour, movement*) suave; (*person: pej*) meloso // *vt* alisar; (*also*: **~ out**) *creases, difficulties* allanar.

smother ['smʌðə*] *vt* sofocar; (*repress*) contener.

smoulder,   (US)   **smolder** ['sməuldə*] *vi* arder sin llama.

smudge [smʌdʒ] *n* mancha // *vt* manchar.

smug [smʌg] *a* presumido.

smuggle ['smʌgl] *vt* pasar de contrabando; **~r** *n* contrabandista *m/f*;

smuggling n contrabando.

smutty ['smʌtɪ] a (fig) verde, obsceno.

snack [snæk] n bocado; ~ **bar** n cafetería.

snag [snæg] n problema m.

snail [sneɪl] n caracol m.

snake [sneɪk] n (gen) serpiente f; (harmless) culebra; (poisonous) víbora.

snap [snæp] n (sound) chasquido; golpe m seco; (photograph) foto f // a (decision) instantáneo // vt (fingers etc) castañetear; (break) quebrar; (photograph) tomar una foto de // vi (break) quebrarse; (fig: person) contestar bruscamente; **to ~ shut** cerrarse de golpe; **to ~ at** vt fus (subj: dog) intentar morder; **to ~ off** vi (break) partirse; **to ~ up** vt agarrar; ~ **fastener** n botón m de presión; ~**py** a (col: answer) instantáneo; (slogan) conciso; **make it ~py!** (hurry up) ¡date prisa!; ~**shot** n foto f (instantánea).

snare [snɛə*] n trampa // vt cazar con trampa; (fig) engañar.

snarl [snɑːl] n gruñido // vi gruñir.

snatch [snætʃ] n (fig) robo; ~es of trocitos mpl de // vt (~ away) arrebatar; (grasp) coger, agarrar.

sneak [sniːk] vi: **to ~ in/out** entrar/salir a hurtadillas // n (col) soplón/ona m/f; ~**ers** npl (US) zapatos mpl de lona; ~y a furtivo.

sneer [snɪə*] vi sonreír con desprecio.

sneeze [sniːz] vi estornudar.

sniff [snɪf] vi sorber (por la nariz) // vt husmear, oler.

snigger ['snɪgə*] vi reírse con disimulo.

snip [snɪp] n (piece) recorte m; (bargain) ganga // vt tijeretear.

sniper ['snaɪpə*] n francotirador(a) m/f.

snippet ['snɪpɪt] n retazo.

snivelling ['snɪvlɪŋ] a llorón/ona.

snob [snɒb] n (e)snob m/f; ~**bery** n (e)snobismo; ~**bish** a (e)snob.

snooker ['snuːkə*] n especie de billar.

snoop [snuːp] vi: **to ~ about** fisgonear.

snooty ['snuːtɪ] a (e)snob.

snooze [snuːz] n siesta // vi echar una siesta.

snore [snɔː*] vi roncar; **snoring** n ronquidos mpl.

snorkel ['snɔːkl] n (tubo) respirador m.

snort [snɔːt] n bufido // vi bufar.

snout [snaʊt] n hocico, morro.

snow [snəʊ] n nieve f // vi nevar; ~**ball** n bola de nieve; ~**bound** a bloqueado por la nieve; ~**drift** n ventisquero; ~**drop** n campanilla; ~**fall** n nevada; ~**flake** n copo de nieve; ~**man** n figura de nieve; ~**plough**, (US) ~**plow** n quitanieves m inv; ~**shoe** n raqueta (de nieve); ~**storm** n nevada, nevasca.

snub [snʌb] vt: **to ~ sb** desairar a alguien // n desaire m, repulsa; ~-**nosed** a chato.

snuff [snʌf] n rapé m.

snug [snʌg] a (cosy) cómodo; (fitted) ajustado.

snuggle ['snʌgl] vi: **to ~ up to sb** arrimarse a uno.

KEYWORD

so [səʊ] ♦ ad **1** (thus, likewise) así, de este modo; **if ~** de ser así; **I like swimming — ~ do I** a mí me gusta nadar — a mí también; **I've got work to do — ~ has Paul** tengo trabajo que hacer — Paul también; **it's 5 o'clock — ~ it is!** son las cinco — ¡pues es verdad!; **I hope/think ~** espero/creo que sí; **~ far** hasta ahora; (in past) hasta este momento
2 (in comparisons etc: to such a degree) tan; **~ quickly (that)** tan rápido (que); **~ big (that)** tan grande (que); **she's not ~ clever as her brother** no es tan lista como su hermano; **we were ~ worried** estábamos preocupadísimos
3: **~ much** a tanto/a // ad tanto;

many tantos/as

4 (*phrases*): **10 or** ~ unos 10, 10 o así; ~ **long!** (*col*: *goodbye*) ¡hasta luego!

◆ *conj* **1** (*expressing purpose*): ~ **as to do** para hacer; ~ **(that)** para que + *subjun*

2 (*expressing result*) así que; ~ **you see, I could have gone** así que ya ves, (yo) podría haber ido.

soak [səʊk] *a* (*drench*) empapar // (*put in water*) remojar // *vi* remojarse, estar a remojo; **to ~ in** *vi* penetrar; **to ~ up** *vt* absorber.

so-and-so ['səʊənsəʊ] *n* (*somebody*) fulano de tal.

soap [səʊp] *n* jabón *m*; **~flakes** *npl* escamas *fpl* de jabón; **~ opera** *n* telenovela; ~ **powder** *n* jabón *m* en polvo; **~y** *a* jabonoso.

soar [sɔː] *vi* (*on wings*) remontarse; (*building etc*) elevarse.

sob [sɔb] *n* sollozo // *vi* sollozar.

sober ['səʊbə*] *a* (*moderate*) moderado; (*not drunk*) sobrio; (*colour, style*) sobrio; **to ~ up** *vt* pasársele a uno la borrachera.

so-called ['səʊ'kɔːld] *a* así llamado.

soccer ['sɔkə*] *n* fútbol *m*.

social ['səʊʃl] *a* social // *n* velada, fiesta; ~ **club** *n* club *m*; ~**ism** *n* socialismo; ~ **ist** *a*, *n* socialista *m/f*; ~**ize** *vi*: **to ~ize** (**with**) alternar (con); ~**ly** *ad* socialmente; ~ **security** *n* seguridad *f* social; ~ **work** *n* asistencia social; ~ **worker** *n* asistente/a *m/f* social.

society [sə'saɪətɪ] *n* sociedad *f*; (*club*) asociación *f*; (*also*: **high ~**) buena sociedad.

sociologist [səʊsɪ'ɔlədʒɪst] *n* sociólogo/a.

sociology [səʊsɪ'ɔlədʒɪ] *n* sociología.

sock [sɔk] *n* calcetín *m*, media (*LAm*).

socket ['sɔkɪt] *n* (*ELEC*) enchufe *m*.

sod [sɔd] *n* (*of earth*) césped *m*; (*col!*) cabrón/ona *m/f* (!).

soda ['səʊdə] *n* (*CHEM*) sosa; (*also*:

~ **water**) soda; (*US*: *also*: ~ **pop**) gaseosa.

sodden ['sɔdn] *a* empapado.

sodium ['səʊdɪəm] *n* sodio.

sofa ['səʊfə] *n* sofá *m*.

soft [sɔft] *a* (*not hard, lenient*) blando; (*gentle, not loud*) suave; (*stupid*) bobo; ~ **drink** *n* bebida no alcohólica; **~en** ['sɔfn] *vt* ablandar; suavizar // *vi* ablandarse; suavizarse; **~ly** *ad* suavemente; (*gently*) delicadamente, con delicadeza; **~ness** *n* blandura; suavidad *f*; **~ware** *n* (*COMPUT*) software *m*.

soggy ['sɔgɪ] *a* empapado.

soil [sɔɪl] *n* (*earth*) tierra, suelo // *vt* ensuciar; **~ed** *a* sucio.

solace ['sɔlɪs] *n* consuelo.

sold [səʊld] *pt*, *pp* of **sell**; ~ **out** *a* (*COMM*) agotado.

solder ['səʊldə*] *vt* soldar // *n* soldadura.

soldier ['səʊldʒə*] *n* (*gen*) soldado; (*army man*) militar *m*.

sole [səʊl] *n* (*of foot*) planta; (*of shoe*) suela; (*fish*: *pl inv*) lenguado // *a* único.

solemn ['sɔləm] *a* solemne.

solicit [sə'lɪsɪt] *vt* (*request*) solicitar // *vi* (*prostitute*) importunar.

solicitor [sə'lɪsɪtə*] *n* (*Brit*: *for wills etc*) = notario/a; (: *in court*) = abogado/a.

solid ['sɔlɪd] *a* sólido; (*gold etc*) macizo // *n* sólido.

solidarity [sɔlɪ'dærɪtɪ] *n* solidaridad *f*.

solitaire [sɔlɪ'tɛə*] *n* (*game, gem*) solitario.

solitary ['sɔlɪtərɪ] *a* solitario, solo; ~ **confinement** *n* incomunicación *f*.

solitude ['sɔlɪtjuːd] *n* soledad *f*.

solo ['səʊləʊ] *n* solo; **~ist** *n* solista *m/f*.

solution [sə'luːʃən] *n* solución *f*.

solve [sɔlv] *vt* resolver, solucionar.

solvent ['sɔlvənt] *a* (*COMM*) solvente // *n* (*CHEM*) solvente *m*.

sombre, (*US*) **somber** ['sɔmbə*] *a* sombrío.

some [sʌm] ♦ a **1** (*a certain amount or number of*): ~ tea/water/biscuits té/agua/(unas) galletas; there's ~ milk in the fridge hay leche en el frigo; there were ~ people outside había algunas personas fuera; I've got ~ money, but not much tengo algo de dinero, pero no mucho

2 (*certain: in contrasts*) algunos/as; ~ people say that ... hay quien dice que ...; ~ films were excellent, but most were mediocre hubo películas excelentes, pero la mayoría fueron mediocres

3 (*unspecified*): ~ woman was asking for you una mujer estuvo preguntando por ti; he was asking for ~ book (or other) pedía un libro; ~ day algún día; ~ day next week un día de la semana que viene

♦ pron **1** (*a certain amount*): I've got ~ (*books etc*) tengo algunos/as

2 (*a certain amount*) algo; I've got ~ (*money, milk*) tengo algo; could I have ~ of that cheese? ¿me puede dar un poco de ese queso?; I've read ~ of the book he leído parte del libro

♦ ad: ~ **10** people unas 10 personas, una decena de personas

somebody ['sʌmbədɪ] pron = **someone.**

somehow ['sʌmhau] ad de alguna manera; (*for some reason*) por una u otra razón.

someone ['sʌmwʌn] pron alguien.

someplace ['sʌmpleɪs] ad (US) = **somewhere.**

somersault ['sʌməsɔ:lt] n (*deliberate*) salto mortal; (*accidental*) vuelco // vi dar un salto mortal; dar vuelcos.

something ['sʌmθɪŋ] pron algo; would you like ~ to eat/drink? ¿te gustaría cenar/tomar algo?

sometime ['sʌmtaɪm] ad (*in future*) algún día, en algún momento; ~ last

month durante el mes pasado.

sometimes ['sʌmtaɪmz] ad a veces.

somewhat ['sʌmwɔt] ad algo.

somewhere ['sʌmwɛə*] ad (*be*) en alguna parte; (*go*) a alguna parte; ~ else (*be*) en otra parte; (*go*) a otra parte.

son [sʌn] n hijo.

song [sɔŋ] n canción f.

sonic ['sɔnɪk] a (*boom*) sónico.

son-in-law ['sʌnɪnlɔ:] n yerno.

sonnet ['sɔnɪt] n soneto.

sonny ['sʌnɪ] n (*col*) hijo.

soon [su:n] ad pronto, dentro de poco; ~ afterwards poco después; see also **as;** ~**er** ad (*time*) antes, más temprano; I would ~er do that preferiría hacer eso; ~er or later tarde o temprano.

soot [sut] n hollín m.

soothe [su:ð] vt tranquilizar; (*pain*) aliviar.

sophisticated [sə'fɪstɪkeɪtɪd] a sofisticado.

sophomore ['sɔfəmɔ:*] n (US) estudiante m/f de segundo año.

soporific [sɔpə'rɪfɪk] a soporífero.

sopping ['sɔpɪŋ] a: ~ (**wet**) empapado.

soppy ['sɔpɪ] a (*pej*) bobo, tonto.

soprano [sə'prɑːnəu] n soprano f.

sorcerer ['sɔ:sərə*] n hechicero.

sore [sɔ:*] a (*painful*) doloroso, que duele; (*offended*) resentido // n llaga; ~ly ad: I am ~ly tempted to estoy muy tentado a.

sorrow ['sɔrəu] n pena, dolor m.

sorry ['sɔrɪ] a (*regretful*) arrepentido; (*condition, excuse*) lastimoso; ~! ¡perdón!, ¡perdone!; to feel ~ for sb tener lástima a uno; I feel ~ for him me da lástima.

sort [sɔ:t] n clase f, género, tipo // vt (*also*: ~ **out**: *papers*) clasificar; (: *problems*) arreglar, solucionar; ~**ing office** n sala de batalla.

SOS n abbr (= *save our souls*) SOS m.

so-so ['səusəu] ad regular, así así.

soufflé ['su:fleɪ] n suflé m.

sought [sɔːt] *pt, pp of* **seek.**

soul [saul] *n* alma *f*; **~-destroying** *a* (*work*) deprimente; **~ful** *a* lleno de sentimiento.

sound [saund] *a* (*healthy*) sano; (*safe, not damaged*) en buen estado; (*reliable: person*) digno de confianza; (*sensible*) sensato, razonable // *ad*: **~ asleep** profundamente dormido *p*; *n* (*noise*) sonido, ruido; (GEO) estrecho // *vt* (*alarm*) sonar; (*also*: **~ out: opinions*) consultar, sondear // *vi* sonar, resonar; (*fig: seem*) parecer; **~ like** sonar a; **~ barrier** *n* barrera del sonido; **~ effects** *npl* efectos *mpl* sonoros; **~ing** *n* (NAUT *etc*) sondeo; **~ly** *ad* (*sleep*) profundamente; (*beat*) completamente; **~proof** *a* insonorizado; **~track** *n* (*of film*) banda sonora.

soup [suːp] *n* (*thick*) sopa; (*thin*) caldo; **in the ~** (*fig*) en apuros; **~plate** *n* plato sopero; **~spoon** *n* cuchara sopera.

sour [ˈsauəˤ] *a* agrio; (*milk*) cortado; it's just ~ grapes! (*fig*) ¡están verdes!

source [sɔːs] *n* fuente *f*.

south [sauθ] *n* sur *m* // *a* del sur // *ad* al sur, hacia el sur; S**~ Africa** *n* África del Sur; S**~ African** *a*, *n* sudafricano/a; S**~ America** *n* América del Sur, Sudamérica; S**~ American** *a*, *n* sudamericano/a *m/f*; **~-east** *n* sudeste *m*; **~erly** ['sʌðəlɪ] *a* sur; (*from the ~*) del sur; **~ern** ['sʌðən] *a* del sur, meridional; S**~ Pole** *n* Polo Sur; **~ward(s)** *ad* hacia el sur; **~-west** *n* suroeste *m*.

souvenir [suːvəˈnɪəˤ] *n* recuerdo.

sovereign ['sɒvrɪn] *a*, *n* soberano/a *m/f*.

soviet ['səuvɪət] *a* soviético; **the** S**~ Union** la Unión Soviética.

sow [sau] *n* cerda, puerca // *vt* ([səu], *pt* **sowed**, *pp* **sown** [səun]) (*gen*) sembrar.

soya [ˈsɔɪə], (US) **soy** *n* soja.

spa [spaː] *n* balneario.

space [speɪs] *n* espacio; (*room*) sitio

// *vt* (*also*: ~ **out**) espaciar; **~craft** *n* nave *f* espacial; **~man/woman** *n* astronauta *m/f*, cosmonauta *m/f*; **~ship** *n* = **~craft**; **spacing** *n* espaciamiento.

spacious ['speɪʃəs] *a* amplio.

spade [speɪd] *n* (*tool*) pala, laya; **~s** *npl* (CARDS: *British*) picos *mpl*; (: *Spanish*) espadas *fpl*.

spaghetti [spəˈgetɪ] *n* espaguetis *mpl*, fideos *mpl*.

Spain [speɪn] *n* España.

span [spæn] *n* (*of bird, plane*) envergadura; (*of hand*) palmo; (*of arch*) luz *f*; (*in time*) lapso // *vt* extenderse sobre, cruzar; (*fig*) abarcar.

Spaniard ['spænjəd] *n* español/a *m/f*.

spaniel ['spænjəl] *n* perro de aguas.

Spanish ['spænɪʃ] *a* español(a) // *n* (LING) español *m*, castellano; **the ~** *npl* los españoles.

spank [spæŋk] *vt* zurrar.

spanner ['spænəˤ] *n* (*Brit*) llave *f* (inglesa).

spar [spaːˤ] *n* palo, verga // *vi* (BOXING) entrenarse.

spare [spɛəˤ] *a* de reserva; (*surplus*) sobrante, de más // *n* (*part*) pieza de repuesto // *vt* (*do without*) pasarse sin; (*afford to give*) tener de sobra; (*refrain from hurting*) perdonar; (*details etc*) ahorrar; **to ~** (*surplus*) sobrante, de sobra; **~ part** *n* pieza de repuesto; **~ time** *n* tiempo libre; **~ wheel** *n* (AUT) rueda de recambio.

sparing ['spɛərɪŋ] *a*: **to be ~ with** ser parco en; **~ly** *ad* poco; con moderación.

spark [spaːk] *n* chispa; **~ plug**, (*Brit*) **~ing plug** *n* bujía.

sparkle [spaːkl] *n* centelleo, destello // *vi* centellear; (*shine*) relucir, brillar; **sparkling** *a* centelleante; (*wine*) espumoso.

sparrow ['spærəu] *n* gorrión *m*.

sparse [spaːs] *a* esparcido, escaso.

spartan ['spaːtən] *a* (*fig*) espartano.

spasm ['spæzəm] *n* (MED) espasmo; (*fig*) arranque *m*, ataque *m*.

spastic ['spæstɪk] n espástico/a.

spat [spæt] pt, pp of **spit**.

spate [speɪt] n (fig): ~ of torrente m de; in ~ (river) crecido.

spatter ['spætə*] vt: to ~ with salpicar de.

spawn [spɔ:n] vi desovar, frezar // n huevas fpl.

speak [spi:k], pt **spoke**, pp **spoken** vt (language) hablar; (truth) decir // vi hablar; (make a speech) intervenir; to ~ to sb/of or about sth hablar con uno/de or sobre algo; ~ up! ¡habla fuerte!; ~er n (in public) orador(a) m/f; (also: loud~er) altavoz m; (for stereo etc) bafle m (pl); (POL): the S~er (Brit) el Presidente de la Cámara de los Comunes; (US) el Presidente del Congreso.

spear [spɪə*] n lanza; (for fishing) arpón m // vt alancear; arponear; ~head vt (attack etc) encabezar.

spec [spɛk] n (col): on ~ como especulación.

special ['spɛʃl] a especial; (edition etc) extraordinario; (delivery) urgente; ~ist n especialista m/f; ~ity [spɛʃɪ'ælɪtɪ] n (Brit) especialidad f; ~ize vi: to ~ize (in) especializarse en; ~ly ad sobre todo, en particular; ~ty n (US) = ~ity.

species ['spi:ʃi:z] n especie f.

specific [spə'sɪfɪk] a específico; ~ally ad específicamente.

specify ['spɛsɪfaɪ] vt, vi especificar, precisar.

specimen ['spɛsɪmən] n ejemplar m; (MED: of urine) espécimen m (: of blood) muestra.

speck [spɛk] n grano, mota.

speckled ['spɛkld] a moteado.

specs [spɛks] npl (col) gafas fpl (Sp), anteojos mpl.

spectacle ['spɛktəkl] n espectáculo; ~s npl (Brit) gafas fpl (Sp), anteojos mpl; **spectacular** [-'tækjulə*] a espectacular; (success) impresionante.

spectator [spɛk'teɪtə*] n espectador(a) m/f.

spectre, (US) **specter** ['spɛktə*] n

espectro, fantasma m.

spectrum ['spɛktrəm], pl **-tra** [-trə] n espectro.

speculation [spɛkju'leɪʃən] n especulación f.

speech [spi:tʃ] n (faculty) habla; (formal talk) discurso; (words) palabras fpl; (manner of speaking) forma de hablar; lenguaje m; ~less a mudo, estupefacto.

speed [spi:d] n velocidad f; (haste) prisa; (promptness) rapidez f; at full or top ~ a máxima velocidad; to ~ up vi acelerar // vt acelerar; ~boat n lancha motora; ~ily ad rápido, rápidamente; ~ing n (AUT) exceso de velocidad; ~ limit n límite m de velocidad, velocidad f máxima; ~ometer [spɪ'dɔmɪtə*] n velocímetro; ~way n (SPORT) pista de carrera; ~y a (fast) veloz, rápido; (prompt) pronto.

spell [spɛl] n (also: magic ~) encanto, hechizo; (period of time) rato, periodo; (turn) turno // vt (pt, pp spelt (Brit) or spelled (also: ~ out) deletrear; (fig) anunciar, presagiar; to cast a ~ on sb hechizar a uno; he can't ~ no sabe escribir bien, sabe poco de ortografía; ~bound a embelesado, hechizado; ~ing n ortografía.

spend [spɛnd], pt, pp **spent** [spɛnt] vt (money) gastar; (time) pasar; (life) dedicar; ~thrift n derrochador(a) m/f, pródigo/a.

sperm [spə:m] n esperma.

spew [spju:] vt vomitar, arrojar.

sphere [sfɪə*] n esfera.

spice [spaɪs] n especia.

spick-and-span ['spɪkən'spæn] a aseado, (bien) arreglado.

spider ['spaɪdə*] n araña.

spike [spaɪk] n (point) punta; (ZOOL) pincho, púa; (BOT) espiga.

spill [spɪl], pt, pp **spilt** or **spilled** vt derramar, verter // vi derramarse; to ~ over desbordarse.

spin [spɪn] n (revolution of wheel) vuelta, revolución f; (AVIAT) barre-

na; (trip in car) paseo (en coche) //
vb (pt, pp **spun**) vt (wool etc) hilar;
(wheel) girar // vi girar, dar vueltas;
to ~ out vt alargar, prolongar.

spinach ['spɪnɪtʃ] n espinaca; (as
food) espinacas fpl.

spinal ['spaɪnl] a espinal; **~ cord** n
columna vertebral.

spindly ['spɪndlɪ] a (leg) zanquivano.

spin-dryer [spɪn'draɪə*] n (Brit) secador m centrifugo.

spine [spaɪn] n espinazo, columna
vertebral; (thorn) espina.

spinning ['spɪnɪŋ] n (of thread) hila-
do; (art) hilandería; **~ top** n peonza; **~ wheel** n rueca, torno de hilar.

spin-off ['spɪnɔf] n derivado, producto secundario.

spinster ['spɪnstə*] n soltera.

spiral ['spaɪərl] n espiral f // a en espiral; **~ staircase** n escalera de caracol.

spire ['spaɪə*] n aguja, chapitel m.

spirit ['spɪrɪt] n (soul) alma f;
(ghost) fantasma m; (attitude) espíritu m; (courage) valor m, ánimo;
~s npl (drink) alcohol msg, bebidas
fpl alcohólicas; **in good ~s** alegre,
de buen ánimo; **~ed** a enérgico, vigoroso; **~ level** n nivel m de aire.

spiritual ['spɪrɪtjuəl] a espiritual.

spit [spɪt] n (for roasting) asador m,
espetón m // vi (pt, pp **spat**) escupir;
(sound) chisporrotear.

spite [spaɪt] n rencor m, ojeriza // vt
causar pena a, mortificar; **in ~ of** a
pesar de, pese a; **~ful** a rencoroso,
malévolo.

spittle ['spɪtl] n saliva, baba.

splash [splæʃ] n (sound) chapoteo;
(of colour) mancha // vt salpicar de //
vi (also: **~ about**) chapotear.

spleen [spli:n] n (ANAT) bazo.

splendid ['splendɪd] a espléndido.

splint [splɪnt] n tablilla.

splinter ['splɪntə*] n (of wood) astilla; (in finger) espigón m // vi asti-
llarse, hacer astillas.

split [splɪt] n hendedura, raja; (fig)
división f; (POL) escisión f // vb (pt,

pp **split**) vt partir, rajar; (party) dividir; (work, profits) repartir // vi
(divide) dividirse, escindirse; **to ~
up** vi (couple) separarse; (meeting)
acabarse.

splutter ['splʌtə*] vi chisporrotear;
(person) balbucear.

spoil [spɔɪl], pt, pp **spoilt** or **spoiled**
vt (damage) dañar; (ruin) estropear,
echar a perder; (child) mimar, consentir; **~s** npl despojo sg, botin msg;
~ed a (US: food: bad) pasado,
malo; (: milk) cortado; **~sport** n
aguafiestas m inv.

spoke [spəuk] pt of **speak** // n rayo,
radio.

spoken ['spəukn] pp of **speak**.

spokesman ['spəuksmən] n,
spokeswoman [-wumən] n vocero
m/f, portavoz m/f.

sponge [spʌndʒ] n esponja // vt
(wash) lavar con esponja // vi: **to ~
off or on sb** vivir a costa de uno; **~
bag** n (Brit) esponjera; **~ cake** n
bizcocho.

sponsor ['spɔnsə*] n (RADIO, TV)
patrocinador/a m/f; (for membership) padrino/madrina; (COMM) fia-
dor/a m/f // vt patrocinar; apadrinar; (idea etc) presentar, promover;
~ship n patrocinio.

spontaneous [spɔn'teɪnɪəs] a espontáneo.

spooky ['spu:kɪ] a espeluznante, horripilante.

spool [spu:l] n carrete m; (of sewing
machine) canilla.

spoon [spu:n] n cuchara; **~feed** vt
dar de comer con cuchara a; (fig)
tratar como un niño a; **~ful** n cucharada.

sport [spɔːt] n deporte m; (person):
to be a good ~ ser muy majo;
~ing a deportivo; **to give sb a
~ing chance** darle a uno una (buena) oportunidad; **~s car** n coche m
sport; **~s jacket**, (US) **~ jacket** n
chaqueta deportiva; **~sman** n deportista m; **~smanship** n deportivi-
dad f; **~swear** n trajes mpl de de-

porte *or* sport; **~swoman** *n* deportista; **~y** a deportivo.

spot [spɔt] *n* sitio, lugar *m*; (*dot: on pattern*) punto, mancha; (*pimple*) grano; (*small amount*): **a ~ of** un poquito de // *vt* (*notice*) notar, observar; **on the ~** en el acto, acto seguido; **~ check** *n* reconocimiento rápido; **~less** *a* perfectamente limpio; **~light** *n* foco, reflector *m*; (*AUT*) faro auxiliar; **~ted** a (*pattern*) de puntos; **~ty** a (*face*) con granos.

spouse [spauz] *n* cónyuge *m/f*.

spout [spaut] *n* (*of jug*) pico; (*pipe*) caño // *vi* chorrear.

sprain [spreɪn] *n* torcedura // *vt*: **to ~ one's ankle** torcerse el tobillo.

sprang [spræŋ] *pt of* **spring.**

sprawl [sprɔːl] *vi* tumbarse.

spray [spreɪ] *n* rociada; (*of sea*) espuma; (*container*) atomizador *m*; (*of paint*) pistola rociadora; (*of flowers*) ramita // *vt* rociar; (*crops*) regar.

spread [spred] *n* extensión *f*; (*of idea*) diseminación *f*; (*food*) pasta para untar // *vb* (*pt*, *pp* **spread**) *vt* extender; diseminar; (*butter*) untar; (*wings*, *sails*) desplegar; (*scatter*) esparcir // *vi* extenderse; diseminarse; untarse; desplegarse; esparcirse; **~-eagled** a a pata tendida; **~sheet** *n* (*COMPUT*) hoja electrónica *or* de cálculo.

spree [spriː] *n*: **to go on a ~** ir de juerga.

sprightly [ˈspraɪtlɪ] a vivo, enérgico.

spring [sprɪŋ] *n* (*season*) primavera; (*leap*) salto, brinco; (*coiled metal*) resorte *m*; (*of water*) fuente *f*, manantial *m* // *vi* (*pt* **sprang**, *pp* **sprung**) (*arise*) brotar, nacer; (*leap*) saltar, brincar; **to ~ up** *vi* (*problem*) surgir; **~board** *n* trampolín *m*; **~-clean** *n* (*also*: **~-cleaning**) limpieza general; **~time** *n* primavera; **~y** a elástico; (*grass*) muelle.

sprinkle [ˈsprɪŋkl] *vt* (*pour*) rociar; **to ~ water on**, **~ with water** *etc* rociar *o* salpicar de agua *etc*; **~r** *n* (*for lawn*) rociadera; (*to put*

out *fire*) aparato de rociadura automática.

sprint [sprɪnt] *n* esprint *m* // *vi* esprintar.

sprout [spraut] *vi* brotar, retoñar; **(Brussels) ~s** *npl* coles *fpl* de Bruselas.

spruce [spruːs] *n* (*BOT*) pícea // a aseado, pulcro.

sprung [sprʌŋ] *pp of* **spring.**

spry [spraɪ] a ágil, activo.

spun [spʌn] *pt*, *pp of* **spin.**

spur [spəː*] *n* espuela; (*fig*) estímulo, aguijón *m* // *vt* (*also*: **~ on**) estimular, incitar; **on the ~ of the moment** de improviso.

spurious [ˈspjuərɪəs] a falso.

spurn [spəːn] *vt* desdeñar, rechazar.

spurt [spəːt] *n* chorro; (*of energy*) arrebato // *vi* chorrear.

spy [spaɪ] *n* espía *m/f* // *vi*: **to ~ on** espiar a // *vt* (*see*) divisar, lograr ver; **~ing** *n* espionaje *m*.

sq. *abbr* = **square.**

squabble [ˈskwɔbl] *vi* reñir, pelear.

squad [skwɔd] *n* (*MIL*) pelotón *m*; (*POLICE*) brigada; (*SPORT*) equipo.

squadron [ˈskwɔdrn] *n* (*MIL*) escuadrón *m*; (*AVIAT*, *NAUT*) escuadra.

squalid [ˈskwɔlɪd] a vil, miserable.

squall [skwɔːl] *n* (*storm*) chubasco; (*wind*) ráfaga.

squalor [ˈskwɔlə*] *n* miseria.

squander [ˈskwɔndə*] *vt* (*money*) derrochar, despilfarrar; (*chances*) desperdiciar.

square [skwɛə*] *n* cuadro; (*in town*) plaza // a cuadrado; (*col*: *ideas*, *tastes*) trasnochado // *vt* (*arrange*) arreglar; (*MATH*) cuadrar // *vi* cuadrar, conformarse // a = igual(es); **to have a ~ meal** comer caliente; **2 metres ~** = 2 metros en cuadro; **a metre square** un metro cuadrado; **~ly** *ad* (*fully*) de lleno.

squash [skwɔʃ] *n* (*Brit*: *drink*): **lemon/orange ~** = zumo (*Sp*) *or* jugo (*LAm*) de limón/naranja; (*SPORT*) squash *m*, frontenis *m* // *vt* aplastar.

squat [skwɔt] a achaparrado // *vi*

agacharse, sentarse en cuclillas; ~**ter** *n* persona que ocupa ilegalmente una casa.

squawk [skwɔːk] *vi* graznar.

squeak [skwiːk] *vi* (*hinge, wheel*) chirriar, rechinar; (*shoe, wood*) crujir.

squeal [skwiːl] *vi* chillar, dar gritos agudos.

squeamish ['skwiːmɪʃ] *a* delicado, remilgado.

squeeze [skwiːz] *n* presión *f*; (*of hand*) apretón *m*; (*COMM*) restricción *f* // *vt* (*lemon etc*) exprimir; (*hand, arm*) apretar; **to ~ out** *vt* exprimir; (*fig*) excluir.

squelch [skweltʃ] *vi* chapotear.

squid [skwɪd] *n* calamar *m*.

squiggle ['skwɪgl] *n* garabato.

squint [skwɪnt] *vi* bizquear, ser bizco // *n* (*MED*) estrabismo; **to ~ at sth** mirar algo de soslayo.

squire ['skwaɪə*] *n* (*Brit*) terrateniente *m*.

squirm [skwəːm] *vi* retorcerse, revolverse.

squirrel ['skwɪrəl] *n* ardilla.

squirt [skwəːt] *vi* salir a chorros.

Sr *abbr* = **senior**.

St *abbr* = **saint; street.**

stab [stæb] *n* (*of pain*) pinchazo; **to have a ~ at** (*doing*) **sth** (*col*) intentar (hacer) algo // *vt* apuñalar.

stable ['steɪbl] *a* estable // *n* cuadra, caballeriza.

stack [stæk] *n* montón *m*, pila // *vt* amontonar, apilar.

stadium ['steɪdɪəm] *n* estadio.

staff [stɑːf] *n* (*work force*) personal *m*, plantilla; (*Brit SCOL*) cuerpo docente; (*stick*) bastón *m* // *vt* proveer de personal.

stag [stæg] *n* ciervo, venado.

stage [steɪdʒ] *n* escena; (*point*) etapa; (*platform*) plataforma; **the ~** el escenario, el teatro // *vt* (*play*) poner en escena, representar; (*organize*) montar, organizar; (*fig: perform: recovery etc*) efectuar; **in ~s** por etapas; **~coach** *n* diligencia; **~ door**

n entrada de artistas; **~ manager** *n* director(a) *mf* de escena.

stagger ['stægə*] *vi* tambalear // *vt* (*amaze*) asombrar; (*hours, holidays*) escalonar.

stagnant ['stægnənt] *a* estancado.

stagnate [stæg'neɪt] *vi* estancarse.

stag night, stag party *n* despedida de soltero.

staid [steɪd] *a* (*clothes*) serio, formal.

stain [steɪn] *n* mancha; (*colouring*) tintura // *vt* manchar; (*wood*) teñir; **~ed glass window** *n* vidriera de colores; **~less** *a* (*steel*) inoxidable; **~ remover** *n* quitamanchas *m inv*.

stair [stɛə*] *n* (*step*) peldaño, escalón *m*; **~s** *npl* escaleras *fpl*; **~case, ~way** *n* escalera.

stake [steɪk] *n* estaca, poste *m*; (*BETTING*) apuesta // *vt* apostar; **to be at ~** estar en juego.

stale [steɪl] *a* (*bread*) duro; (*food*) pasado.

stalemate ['steɪlmeɪt] *n* tablas *fpl* (por ahogado); **to reach ~** (*fig*) estancarse.

stalk [stɔːk] *n* tallo, caña // *vt* acechar, cazar al acecho; **to ~ off** irse airado.

stall [stɔːl] *n* (*in market*) puesto; (*in stable*) casilla (de establo) // *vt* (*AUT*) parar // *vi* (*AUT*) pararse; (*fig*) buscar evasivas; **~s** *npl* (*Brit: in cinema, theatre*) butacas *fpl*.

stallion ['stælɪən] *n* semental *m*.

stalwart ['stɔːlwət] *n* partidario/a incondicional.

stamina ['stæmɪnə] *n* resistencia.

stammer ['stæmə*] *n* tartamudeo // *vi* tartamudear.

stamp [stæmp] *n* sello, estampilla (*LAm*); (*mark, also fig*) marca, huella; (*on document*) timbre *m* // *vi* (*also*: **~ one's foot**) patear // *vt* (*letter*) poner sellos en; (*with rubber ~*) marcar con sello; (**~ album** *n* álbum *m* para sellos; **~ collecting** *n* filatelia.

stampede [stæm'piːd] *n* estampida.

stance [stæns] *n* postura.

stand [stænd] *n* (*attitude*) posición *f*, postura; (*for taxis*) parada; (*SPORT*) tribuna; (*at exhibition*) stand *m* // (*pt, pp stood*) *vi* (*be*) estar, encontrarse; (*be on foot*) estar de pie; (*rise*) levantarse; (*remain*) quedar en pie // *vt* (*place*) poner, colocar; (*tolerate, withstand*) aguantar, soportar; **to make a ~** resistir; **to ~ for parliament** (*Brit*) presentarse (como candidato) a las elecciones; **to ~ by** *vi* (*be ready*) estar listo // *vt fus* (*opinion*) aferrarse a; **to ~ down** *vi* (*withdraw*) ceder el puesto; **to ~ for** *vt fus* (*signify*) significar; (*tolerate*) aguantar, permitir; **to ~ in for** *vt fus* suplir a; **to ~ out** *vi* (*be prominent*) destacarse; **to ~ up** *vi* (*rise*) levantarse, ponerse de pie; **to ~ up for** *vt fus* defender; **to ~ up to** *vt fus* hacer frente a.

standard ['stændəd] *n* patrón *m*, norma; (*flag*) estandarte *m* // *a* (*size etc*) normal, corriente, estándar; **~s** *npl* (*morals*) valores *mpl* morales; **~ lamp** *n* (*Brit*) lámpara de pie; **~ of living** *n* nivel de vida.

stand-by ['stændbaɪ] *n* (*alert*) alerta, aviso; **to be on ~** estar sobre aviso; **~ ticket** *n* (*AVIAT*) (billete *m*) standby *m*.

stand-in ['stændɪn] *n* suplente *m/f*; (*CINEMA*) doble *m/f*.

standing ['stændɪŋ] *a* (*upright*) derecho; (*on foot*) de pie, en pie // *n* reputación *f*; (*of many years*) **~** que lleva muchos años; **~ order** *n* (*Brit: at bank*) orden *f* de pago permanente; **~ orders** *npl* (*MIL*) reglamento *sg* general; **~ room** *n* sitio para estar de pie.

stand: **~-offish** *a* reservado, poco afable; **~ point** *n* punto de vista; **~still** *n*: **at a ~still** (*industry, traffic*) paralizado; (*car*) parado; **to come to a ~still** quedar paralizado; pararse.

stank [stæŋk] *pt of* **stink.**

staple ['steɪpl] *n* (*for papers*) grapa // *a* (*food etc*) básico // *vt* engrapar; **~r** *n* grapadora.

star [stɑ:*] *n* estrella; (*celebrity*) estrella, astro // *vi*: **to ~ in** ser la estrella *or* el astro de.

starboard ['stɑ:bəd] *n* estribor *m*.

starch [stɑ:tʃ] *n* almidón *m*.

stardom ['stɑ:dəm] *n* estrellato.

stare [stɛə*] *n* mirada fija // *vi*: **to ~ at** mirar fijo.

starfish ['stɑ:fɪʃ] *n* estrella de mar.

stark [stɑ:k] *a* (*bleak*) severo, escueto // *ad*: **~ naked** en cueros.

starling ['stɑ:lɪŋ] *n* estornino.

starry ['stɑ:rɪ] *a* estrellado; **~-eyed** *a* (*innocent*) inocentón/ona, ingenuo.

start [stɑ:t] *n* (*beginning*) principio, comienzo; (*of race*) salida; (*sudden movement*) salto, sobresalto // *vt* empezar, comenzar; (*cause*) causar; (*found*) fundar; (*engine*) poner en marcha *vi* (*begin*) comenzar, empezar; (*with fright*) asustarse, sobresaltarse; (*train etc*) salir; **to ~ doing** *or* **to do sth** empezar a hacer algo; **to ~ off** *vi* empezar, comenzar; (*leave*) salir, ponerse en camino; **to ~ up** *vi* comenzar; (*car*) ponerse en marcha // *vt* comenzar; (*car*) poner en marcha; **~er** *n* (*AUT*) botón *m* de arranque; (*SPORT: official*) juez *m/f* de salida; (*: runner*) corredor(a) *m/f*; (*Brit CULIN*) entrada; **~ing point** *n* punto de partida.

startle ['stɑ:tl] *vt* asustar, sobrecoger; **startling** *a* alarmante.

starvation [stɑ:'veɪʃən] *n* hambre *f*.

starve [stɑ:v] *vi* pasar hambre; **to ~ to death** morir de hambre // *vt* hacer pasar hambre; (*fig*) privar de; **I'm starving** estoy muerto de hambre.

state [steɪt] *n* estado // *vt* (*say, declare*) afirmar; (*a case*) presentar, exponer; **to be in a ~** estar agitado; **the S~s** los Estados Unidos; **~ly** *a* majestuoso, imponente; **~ment** *n* afirmación *f*; (*LAW*) declaración *f*; **~sman** *n* estadista *m*.

static ['stætɪk] n (RADIO) parásitos mpl // a estático; **~ electricity** n estática.

station ['steɪʃən] n (gen) estación f; (RADIO) emisora; (rank) posición f social // vt colocar, situar; (MIL) apostar.

stationary ['steɪʃnərɪ] a estacionario, fijo.

stationer ['steɪʃənə*] n papelero/a; **~'s (shop)** n (Brit) papelería; **~y** [-nərɪ] n papel m de escribir, artículos mpl de escritorio.

station master n (RAIL) jefe m de estación.

station wagon n (US) furgoneta.

statistic [stə'tɪstɪk] n estadística; **~s** n (science) estadística; **~al** a estadístico.

statue ['stætjuː] n estatua.

status ['steɪtəs] n estado; (reputation) estatus m; **~ symbol** n símbolo de prestigio.

statute ['stætjuːt] n estatuto, ley f; **statutory** a estatutario.

staunch [stɔːntʃ] a leal, incondicional.

stave [steɪv] vt: **to ~ off** (attack) rechazar; (threat) evitar.

stay [steɪ] n (period of time) estancia // vi (remain) quedar(se); (as guest) hospedarse; **to ~ put** seguir en el mismo sitio; **to ~ the night/5 days** pasar la noche/estar 5 días; **to ~ behind** vi quedar atrás; **to ~ in** vi (at home) quedarse en casa; **to ~ on** vi quedarse; **to ~ out** vi (of house) no volver a casa; **to ~ up** vi (at night) velar, no acostarse; **~ing power** n aguante m.

stead [sted] n: **in sb's ~** en lugar de uno; **to stand sb in good ~** ser muy útil a uno.

steadfast ['stedfɑːst] a firme, resuelto.

steadily ['stedɪlɪ] ad (improve, grow) constantemente; (work) sin parar; (gaze) fijamente.

steady ['stedɪ] a (fixed) firme, fijo; (regular) regular; (person, charac-

ter) sensato, juicioso // vt (hold) mantener firme; (stabilize) estabilizar; (nerves) calmar; **to ~ o.s. on** or **against sth** afirmarse en algo.

steak [steɪk] n (gen) filete m; (beef) bistec m.

steal [stiːl], pt **stole**, pp **stolen** vt, vi robar.

stealth [stelθ] n: **by ~** a escondidas, sigilosamente; **~y** a cauteloso, sigiloso.

steam [stiːm] n vapor m; (mist) vaho, humo // vt (CULIN) cocer al vapor // vi echar vapor; (ship): **to ~ along** avanzar, ir avanzando; **to ~ up** vi empañarse; **~ engine** n máquina de vapor; **~er** n (buque m de) vapor m; **~roller** n apisonadora; **~ship** n = **~er**; **~y** a (room) lleno de vapor; (window) empañado.

steel [stiːl] n acero // cpd de acero; **~works** n acería.

steep [stiːp] a escarpado, abrupto; (stair) empinado; (price) exorbitante, excesivo // vt empapar, remojar.

steeple ['stiːpl] n aguja.

steer [stɪə*] vt (car) conducir (Sp), manejar (LAm); (person) dirigir // vi conducir; **~ing** n (AUT) dirección f; **~ing wheel** n volante m.

stem [stem] n (of plant) tallo; (of glass) pie m; (of pipe) cañón m // vt detener; (blood) restañar; **to ~ from** vt fus ser consecuencia de.

stench [stentʃ] n hedor m.

stencil ['stensl] n (typed) cliché m, clisé m; (lettering) plantilla // vt hacer un cliché de.

stenographer [ste'nɔɡrəfə*] n (US) taquígrafo/a.

step [step] n (also: sound) paso, pisada; (on stair) peldaño, escalón m // vi: **to ~ forward** dar un paso adelante; **~s** npl (Brit) = **ladder**; **to be in/out of ~ with** estar acorde con/estar en disonancia con; **to ~ down** vi (fig) retirarse; **to ~ off** vt fus bajar de; **to ~ up** vt (increase) aumentar; **~brother** n hermanastro; **~daughter** n hijastra;

~**father** n padrastro; ~**ladder** n escalera doble or de tijera; ~**mother** n madrastra; ~**ping stone** n pasadera; (fig) trampolín m; ~**sister** n hermanastra; ~**son** n hijastro.

stereo ['strərɪəʊ] n estéreo // a (also: ~**phonic**) estéreo, estereofónico.

sterile ['strɪraɪl] a estéril; **sterilize** ['strɪrɪlaɪz] vt esterilizar.

sterling ['stɜːlɪŋ] a (silver) de ley // n (ECON) (libras fpl) esterlinas fpl; a **pound** ~ una libra esterlina.

stern [stɜːn] a severo, austero // n (NAUT) popa.

stethoscope ['stɛθəskəʊp] n estetoscopio.

stew [stjuː] n cocido, estofado, guisado (LAm) // vt estofar, guisar; (fruit) cocer.

steward [stjuːəd] n (Brit: AVIAT, NAUT, RAIL) camarero; ~**ess** n azafata.

stick [stɪk] n palo; (as weapon) porra; (walking ~) bastón m // vb (pt, pp **stuck**) vt (glue) pegar; (col: put) meter; (: tolerate) aguantar, soportar // vi pegarse; (come to a stop) quedarse parado; to ~ **sth into** clavar or hincar algo en; to ~ **out**, to ~ **up** vi sobresalir; to ~ **up for** vt fus defender; ~**er** n (label) etiqueta engomada; (with slogan) pegatina; ~**ing plaster** n (Brit) esparadrapo.

stickler ['stɪklə*] n: to be a ~ **for** insistir mucho en.

stick-up ['stɪkʌp] n asalto, atraco.

sticky ['stɪkɪ] a pegajoso; (label) engomado; (fig) difícil.

stiff [stɪf] a rígido, tieso; (hard) duro; (difficult) difícil; (person) inflexible; (price) exorbitante; ~**en** vt hacer más rígido; (limb) entumecer // vi endurecerse; (grow stronger) fortalecerse; ~ **neck** n tortícolis m inv; ~**ness** n rigidez f, tiesura.

stifle ['staɪfl] vt ahogar, sofocar; **stifling** a (heat) sofocante, bochornoso.

stigma ['stɪgmə], pl (BOT, MED, REL) ~**ta** [-tə], (fig) ~**s** n estigma

m.

stile [staɪl] n escalera (para pasar una cerca).

stiletto [strˈlɛtəʊ] n (Brit: also: ~ **heel**) tacón m de aguja.

still [stɪl] a inmóvil, quieto // ad (up to this time) todavía; (even) aún; (nonetheless) sin embargo, aun así; ~**born** a nacido muerto; ~ **life** n naturaleza muerta.

stilt [stɪlt] n zanco; (pile) pilar m, soporte m.

stilted ['stɪltɪd] a afectado.

stimulate ['stɪmjuleɪt] vt estimular.

stimulus ['stɪmjuləs], pl -**li** [-laɪ] n estímulo, incentivo.

sting [stɪŋ] n (wound) picadura; (pain) escozor m, picazón f; (organ) aguijón m // vb (pt, pp **stung**) vt picar // vi picar, escocer.

stingy ['stɪndʒɪ] a tacaño.

stink [stɪŋk] n hedor m, tufo // vi (pt **stank**, pp **stunk**) heder, apestar; ~**ing** a hediondo, fétido; (fig: col) horrible.

stint [stɪnt] n tarea, destajo // vi: to ~ **on** escatimar; to do one's ~ hacer su parte.

stir [stɜː*] n (fig: agitation) conmoción f // vt (tea etc) remover; (move) agitar; (fig: emotions) provocar // vi moverse; to ~ **up** vt excitar; (trouble) fomentar.

stirrup ['stɪrəp] n estribo.

stitch [stɪtʃ] n (SEWING) puntada; (KNITTING) punto; (MED) punto (de sutura); (pain) punzada // vt coser; (MED) suturar.

stoat [stəʊt] n armiño.

stock [stɔk] n (COMM: reserves) existencias fpl, stock m; (: selection) surtido; (AGR) ganado, ganadería; (CULIN) caldo; (FINANCE) capital m; (: shares) acciones fpl // a (fig: reply etc) clásico // vt (have in stock) tener existencias de; (supply) proveer, abastecer; ~**s and** cepo sg; **in** ~ en existencia or almacén; **out of** ~ agotado; to **take** ~ **of** (fig) asesorar, examinar; ~**s and shares** acciones y valores; **to ~ up with** vt fus abastecerse de.

stockbroker ['stɔkbrəukə*] n agente m/f or corredor(a) m/f de bolsa.

stock cube n pastilla de caldo.

stock exchange n bolsa.

stocking ['stɔkiŋ] n media.

stock: **~holder** n (US) accionista m/f; **~ist** n (Brit) distribuidor(a) m/f; **~ market** n bolsa (de valores); **~ phrase** n cliché m; **~pile** n reserva // vt acumular, almacenar; **~taking** n (Brit COMM) inventario.

stocky ['stɔki] a (strong) robusto; (short) achaparrado.

stodgy ['stɔdʒi] a indigesto, pesado.

stoke [stəuk] vt atizar.

stole [stəul] pt of **steal** // n estola.

stolen ['stəuln] pp of **steal**.

stolid ['stɔlid] a (person) imperturbable, impasible.

stomach ['stʌmək] n (ANAT) estómago; (abdomen) vientre m // vt tragar, aguantar; **~ ache** n dolor m de estómago.

stone [stəun] n piedra; (in fruit) hueso; (Brit: weight) = 6.348kg; 14 pounds // cpd de piedra // vt apedrear; **~cold** a helado; **~deaf** a sordo como una tapia; **~work** n (art) cantería.

stood [stud] pt, pp of **stand**.

stool [stu:l] n taburete m.

stoop [stu:p] vi (also: have a ~) ser cargado de espaldas.

stop [stɔp] n parada, alto; (in punctuation) punto // vt parar, detener; (break off) suspender; (block) tapar, cerrar; (also: **put a ~ to**) poner término a // vi pararse, detenerse; (end) acabarse; **to ~ doing sth** dejar de hacer algo; **to ~ dead** pararse en seco; **to ~ off** vi interrumpir el viaje; **to ~ up** vt (hole) tapar; **~gap** n (person) interino/a, (thing) recurso m provisional; **~lights** npl (AUT) luces fpl de detención; **~over** n parada; (AVIAT) rescala.

stoppage ['stɔpidʒ] n (strike) paro; (temporary stop) interrupción f; (of pay) suspensión f; (blockage) obstrucción f.

stopper ['stɔpə*] n tapón m.

stop press n noticias fpl de última hora.

stopwatch ['stɔpwɔtʃ] n cronómetro.

storage ['stɔ:ridʒ] n almacenaje m; (COMPUT) almacenamiento; **~ heater** n acumulador m.

store [stɔ:*] n (stock) provisión f; (depot; large shop) almacén m; (US) tienda; (reserve) reserva, repuesto // vt almacenar; (keep) guardar; **~s** npl víveres mpl; **to ~ up** vt acumular; **~keeper** n (US) tendero/a; **~room** n despensa.

storey, (US) **story** ['stɔ:ri] n piso.

stork [stɔ:k] n cigüeña.

storm [stɔ:m] n tormenta; (wind) vendaval m // vi rabiar (fig) // vt tomar por asalto; **~y** a tempestuoso.

story ['stɔ:ri] n historia; (joke) cuento, chiste m; (US) = **storey**; **~book** n libro de cuentos; **~teller** n cuentista m/f.

stout [staut] a (strong) sólido; (fat) gordo, corpulento // n cerveza negra.

stove [stəuv] n (for cooking) cocina; (for heating) estufa.

stow [stəu] vt meter, poner; (NAUT) estibar; **~away** n polizón/ona m/f.

straddle ['strædl] vt montar a horcajadas.

straggle ['strægl] vi (lag behind) rezagarse; **~r** n rezagado.

straight [streit] a recto, derecho; (frank) franco, directo // ad derecho, directamente; (drink) sin mezcla; **to put** or **get sth ~** dejar algo en claro; **~ away**, **~ off** (at once) en seguida; **~en** vt (also: **~en out**) enderezar, poner derecho; **~faced** a serio; **~forward** a (simple) sencillo; (honest) honrado, franco.

strain [strein] n (gen) tensión f; (MED) torcedura // vt (back etc) torcerse; (tire) cansar; (stretch) estirar; (filter) filtrar // vi esforzarse; **~s** npl (MUS) son m; **~ed** a (laugh) forzado; (relations) tenso; **~er** n colador m.

strait [streit] n (GEO) estrecho; ~-
jacket n camisa de fuerza; ~-**laced**
a mojigato, gazmoño.

strand [strænd] n (of thread) hebra;
(of hair) trenza; ~**ed** a (person:
without money) desamparado;
(: transport) colgado.

strange [streindʒ] a (not known) desconocido; (odd) extraño, raro; ~**r** n
desconocido/a; (from another area)
forastero/a.

strangle ['stræŋgl] vt estrangular;
~**hold** n (fig): to have a ~**hold** on
sth dominar algo completamente.

strap [stræp] n correa; (of slip,
dress) tirante m // vt atar con correa.

strapping ['stræpiŋ] a robusto, fornido.

stratagem [strætidʒəm] n estratagema.

strategic [strə'ti:dʒik] a estratégico.

strategy ['strætidʒi] n estrategia.

straw [strɔ:] n paja; (drinking ~) caña, pajita; **that's the last ~!** ¡eso
es el colmo!

strawberry ['strɔ:bəri] n fresa, frutilla (LAm).

stray [strei] a (animal) extraviado;
(bullet) perdido // vi extraviarse, perderse.

streak [stri:k] n raya; (fig: of madness etc) vena // vt rayar // vi: to ~
past pasar como un rayo.

stream [stri:m] n riachuelo, arroyo;
(jet) chorro; (flow) corriente f; (of
people) oleada // vt (SCOL) dividir en
grupos por habilidad // vi correr,
fluir; to ~ in/out (people) entrar/
salir en tropel.

streamer ['stri:mə*] n serpentina.

streamlined ['stri:mlaind] a aerodi-
námico; (fig) racionalizado.

street [stri:t] n calle f // cpd callejero; ~-**car** n (US) tranvía m; ~-
lamp n farol m; ~-**plan** n plano;
~-**wise** a (col) que tiene mucha calle.

strength [streŋθ] n fuerza; (of girder, knot etc) resistencia; ~**en** vt fortalecer, reforzar.

strenuous ['strenjuəs] a (tough) arduo; (energetic) enérgico.

stress [stres] n (force, pressure) presión f; (mental strain) estrés m; (accent) acento; (TECH) tensión f, carga // vt subrayar, recalcar.

stretch [stretʃ] n (of sand etc) trecho; (of road) tramo // vi estirarse //
vt extender, estirar; (make demands
of) exigir el máximo esfuerzo a; to
~ to o as far as extenderse hasta;
to ~ out vi extenderse // vt (arm etc)
extender; (spread) estirar.

stretcher ['stretʃə*] n camilla.

strewn [stru:n] a: ~ **with** cubierto
or sembrado de.

stricken ['strikən] a (person) herido;
(city, industry etc) condenado; ~
with (disease) afligido por.

strict [strikt] a estricto; ~**ly** ad estrictamente; (totally) terminante-
mente.

stride [straid] n zancada, tranco //
(pt **strode**, pp **stridden** ['stridn]) dar
zancadas, andar a trancos.

strident ['straidnt] a estridente; (colour) chillón/ona.

strife [straif] n lucha.

strike [straik] n huelga; (of oil etc)
descubrimiento; (attack) ataque m;
(SPORT) golpe m // vb (pt, pp
struck) vt golpear, pegar; (oil etc)
descubrir; (obstacle) topar con // vi
declarar la huelga; (attack) atacar;
(clock) dar la hora; **on** ~ (workers)
en huelga; to ~ **a match** encender
un fósforo; to ~ **down** vt derribar;
to ~ **out** vt borrar, tachar; to ~
up vt (MUS) empezar a tocar; (conversation) entablar; (friendship) trabar; ~**r** n huelgista m/f; (SPORT)
delantero; **striking** a llamativo; (obvious: resemblance) notorio.

string [striŋ] n (gen) cuerda; (row)
hilera // vt (pt, pp **strung**) to ~ to-
gether ensartar; to ~ **out** extenderse; the ~**s** npl (MUS) los instrumentos de cuerda; **to pull** ~**s** (fig) mover palancas; ~-**bean** n judía verde,
habichuela; ~-**(ed) instrument** n

(MUS) instrumento de cuerda.

stringent ['strindʒənt] a riguroso, severo.

strip [strip] n tira; (of land) franja; (of metal) cinta, lámina // vt desnudar; (also: ~ **down**: machine) desmontar // vi desnudarse; ~ **cartoon** n tira cómica, historieta (LAm).

stripe [straip] n raya; (MIL) galón m; ~**d** a a rayas, rayado.

strip lighting n alumbrado fluorescente.

stripper ['stripə*] n artista m/f de striptease.

strive [straiv], pt **strove**, pp **striven** ['strivn] vi: **to** ~ **to do** sth esforzarse or luchar por hacer algo.

strode [straud] pt of **stride**.

stroke [strauk] n (blow) golpe m; (MED) apoplejía; (caress) caricia // vt acariciar; **at a** ~ de un solo golpe.

stroll [straul] n paseo, vuelta // vi dar un paseo or una vuelta; ~**er** n (US: for child) sillita de ruedas.

strong [strɔŋ] a fuerte; they are 50 ~ son 50; ~**box** n caja fuerte; ~**hold** n fortaleza; (fig) baluarte m; ~**ly** ad fuertemente, con fuerza; (believe) firmemente; ~**room** n cámara acorazada.

strove [strauv] pt of **strive**.

struck [strʌk] pt, pp of **strike**.

structure ['strʌktʃə*] n estructura; (building) construcción f.

struggle ['strʌgl] n lucha // vi luchar.

strum [strʌm] vt (guitar) rasguear.

strung [strʌŋ] pt, pp of **string**.

strut [strʌt] n puntal m // vi pavonearse.

stub [stʌb] n (of ticket etc) talón m; (of cigarette) colilla; **to** ~ **one's toe** dar con el dedo (del pie) contra algo; **to** ~ **out** vt apagar.

stubble ['stʌbl] n rastrojo; (on chin) barba (incipiente).

stubborn ['stʌbən] a terco, testarudo.

stucco ['stʌkəu] n estuco.

stuck [stʌk] pt, pp of **stick** // a (jam-

med) atascado; ~-**up** a engreído, presumido.

stud [stʌd] n (shirt ~) corchete m; (of boot) taco; (of horses) caballeriza; (also: ~ **horse**) caballo semental // vt (fig): ~**ded with** salpicado de.

student ['stju:dənt] n estudiante m/f // cpd estudiantil; ~ **driver** n (US AUT) aprendiz/a m/f.

studio ['stju:diəu] n estudio; (artist's) taller m; ~ **flat**, (US) ~ **apartment** n estudio.

studious ['stju:diəs] a estudioso; (studied) calculado; ~**ly** ad (carefully) con esmero.

study ['stʌdi] n estudio // vt estudiar; (examine) examinar, investigar // vi estudiar.

stuff [stʌf] n materia; (cloth) tela; (substance) material m, sustancia; (things, belongings) cosas fpl // vt llenar; (CULIN) rellenar; (animals) disecar; ~**ing** n relleno; ~**y** a (room) mal ventilado; (person) de miras estrechas.

stumble ['stʌmbl] vi tropezar, dar un traspié; **to** ~ **across** (fig) tropezar con; **stumbling block** n tropiezo, obstáculo.

stump [stʌmp] n (of tree) tocón m; (of limb) muñón m // vt: **to be** ~**ed for an answer** no saber qué contestar.

stun [stʌn] vt dejar sin sentido.

stung [stʌŋ] pt, pp of **sting**.

stunk [stʌŋk] pp of **stink**.

stunning ['stʌniŋ] a (news) pasmoso; (fabulous) sensacional.

stunt [stʌnt] n (AVIAT) vuelo acrobático; (publicity) ~ truco publicitario; ~**ed** a enano, achaparrado; ~**man** n especialista m.

stupefy ['stju:pifai] vt dejar estupefacto.

stupendous [stju:'pendəs] a estupendo, asombroso.

stupid ['stju:pid] a estúpido, tonto; ~**ity** [-'piditi] n estupidez f.

sturdy ['stə:di] a robusto, fuerte.

stutter ['stʌtə*] vi tartamudear.

sty [staɪ] n (*for pigs*) pocilga.

style [staɪl] n (*MED*) orzuelo.

style [staɪl] n estilo; (*fashion*) moda; **stylish** a elegante, a la moda; **stylist** n (*hair stylist*) peluquero/a.

stylus ['staɪləs] n (*of record player*) aguja.

suave [swɑːv] a cortés; (*pej*) zalamero.

sub... [sʌb] pref sub...; **~conscious** a subconsciente // n subconsciente; **~contract** vt subcontratar; **~divide** vt subdividir.

subdue [səb'djuː] vt sojuzgar; (*passions*) dominar; **~d** a (*light*) tenue; (*person*) sumiso, manso.

subject ['sʌbdʒɪkt] n súbdito; (*SCOL*) tema m, materia // vt [səb'dʒɛkt]: **to ~ sb to** sth someter a uno a algo; **to be ~ to** (*law*) estar sujeto a; (*subj: person*) ser propenso a; **~ive** [-'dʒɛktɪv] a subjetivo; **~ matter** n materia; (*content*) contenido.

subjunctive [səb'dʒʌŋktɪv] a, n subjuntivo.

sublet [sʌb'lɛt] vt subarrendar.

submachine gun ['sʌbmə'ʃiːn-] n metralleta.

submarine [sʌbmə'riːn] n submarino.

submerge [səb'məːdʒ] vt sumergir; (*flood*) inundar // vi sumergirse.

submissive [səb'mɪsɪv] a sumiso.

submit [səb'mɪt] vt someter // vi someterse.

subnormal [sʌb'nɔːməl] a subnormal.

subordinate [sə'bɔːdɪnət] a, n subordinado/a mf.

subpoena [səb'piːnə] n (*LAW*) citación f // vt citar.

subscribe [səb'skraɪb] vi suscribir; **to ~ to** (*opinion, fund*) suscribir, aprobar; (*newspaper*) suscribirse a; **~r** n (*to periodical, telephone*) abonado/a.

subscription [səb'skrɪpʃən] n (*to club*) abono; (*to magazine*) suscripción f.

subsequent ['sʌbsɪkwənt] a subsiguiente, posterior; **~ly** ad posteriormente, más tarde.

subside [səb'saɪd] vi hundirse; (*flood*) bajar; (*wind*) amainar; **~nce** [-'saɪdns] n hundimiento; (*in road*) socavón m.

subsidiary [səb'sɪdɪərɪ] n sucursal f, filial f.

subsidize ['sʌbsɪdaɪz] vt subvencionar.

subsidy ['sʌbsɪdɪ] n subvención f.

substance ['sʌbstəns] n sustancia; (*fig*) esencia.

substantial [səb'stænʃl] a sustancial, sustancioso; (*fig*) importante.

substantiate [səb'stænʃɪeɪt] vt comprobar.

substitute ['sʌbstɪtjuːt] n (*person*) suplente mf; (*thing*) sustituto // vt: **to ~ A for B** sustituir B por A, reemplazar A por B.

subtitle ['sʌbtaɪtl] n subtítulo.

subtle ['sʌtl] a sutil; **~ty** n sutileza.

subtract [səb'trækt] vt restar; sustraer; **~ion** [-'trækʃən] n resta; sustracción f.

suburb ['sʌbəːb] n suburbio; **the ~s** las afueras (de la ciudad); **~an** [sə'bəːbən] a suburbano; (*train etc*) de cercanías; **~ia** [sə'bəːbɪə] n barrios mpl residenciales.

subway ['sʌbweɪ] n (*Brit*) paso subterráneo or subterránea; (*US*) metro.

succeed [sək'siːd] vi (*person*) tener éxito; (*plan*) salir bien // vt suceder a; **to ~ in doing** lograr hacer; **~ing** a (*following*) sucesivo.

success [sək'sɛs] n éxito; **~ful** a (*venture, person*) exitoso; (*business*) próspero; **to be ~ful (in doing)** lograr (hacer); **~fully** ad con éxito.

succession [sək'sɛʃən] n sucesión f, serie f.

successive [sək'sɛsɪv] a sucesivo, consecutivo.

succinct [sək'sɪŋkt] a sucinto.

such [sʌtʃ] a tal, semejante; (*of that kind*): **~ a book** tal libro; (*so much*): **~ courage** tanto valor // ad tan; ~ **a long trip** un viaje tan largo; ~ **a lot of** tanto(s)/a(s); ~ **as** (like) tal como; **a noise** ~ **as** to un ruido tal que; **as** ~ **ad** como tal; ~ **and**~ *a* tal o cual.

suck [sʌk] *vt* chupar; (bottle) sorber; (breast) mamar; ~**er** *n* (BOT) serpollo; (ZOOL) ventosa; (col) bobo, primo.

suction ['sʌkʃən] *n* succión *f.*

Sudan [su'dæn] *n* Sudán *m.*

sudden ['sʌdn] *a* (rapid) repentino, súbito; (unexpected) imprevisto; **all of a** ~ *ad* de repente; ~**ly** *ad* de repente.

suds [sʌdz] *npl* espuma *sg* de jabón.

sue [su:] *vt* demandar.

suede [sweid] *n* ante *m*, gamuza (LAm).

suet ['suɪt] *n* sebo.

Suez ['su:ɪz] *n*: **the** ~ **Canal** el Canal de Suez.

suffer ['sʌfə*] *vt* sufrir, padecer; (tolerate) aguantar, soportar // *vi* sufrir; ~**er** *n* víctima; (MED) enfermo/a; ~**ing** *n* sufrimiento; (pain) dolor *m.*

suffice [sə'faɪs] *vi* bastar, ser suficiente.

sufficient [sə'fɪʃənt] *a* suficiente, bastante; ~**ly** *ad* suficientemente, bastante.

suffocate ['sʌfəkeɪt] *vi* ahogarse, asfixiarse.

suffrage ['sʌfrɪdʒ] *n* sufragio.

suffused [sə'fjuːzd] *a*: ~ **with** bañado de.

sugar ['ʃugə*] *n* azúcar *m* // *vt* echar azúcar a, azucarar; ~ **beet** *n* remolacha; ~ **cane** *n* caña de azúcar; ~**y** *a* azucarado.

suggest [sə'dʒɛst] *vt* sugerir; (recommend) aconsejar; ~**ion** [-'dʒɛstʃən] *n* sugerencia.

suicide ['suːɪsaɪd] *n* suicidio; (person) suicida *mf.*

suit [suːt] *n* (man's) traje *m*; (woman's) conjunto; (LAW) pleito; (CARDS) palo // *vt* convenir; (clothes) sentar a, ir bien a; (adapt):

to ~ **sth to** adaptar *or* ajustar algo a; **well** ~**ed** (well matched: couple) hechos el uno para el otro; ~**able** *a* conveniente; (apt) indicado; ~**ably** *ad* convenientemente; en forma debida.

suitcase ['suːtkeɪs] *n* maleta, valija (LAm).

suite [swiːt] *n* (of rooms, MUS) suite *f*; (furniture): **bedroom/dining room** ~ (juego de) dormitorio/comedor *m.*

suitor ['suːtə*] *n* pretendiente *m.*

sulfur ['sʌlfə*] *n* (US) = **sulphur.**

sulk [sʌlk] *vi* estar de mal humor; ~**y** *a* malhumorado.

sullen ['sʌlən] *a* hosco, malhumorado.

sulphur, (US) **sulfur** ['sʌlfə*] *n* azufre *m.*

sultana [sʌl'tɑːnə] *n* (fruit) pasa de Esmirna.

sultry ['sʌltrɪ] *a* (weather) bochornoso.

sum [sʌm] *n* suma; (total) total *m*; **to** ~ **up** *vt* resumir // *vi* hacer un resumen.

summarize ['sʌmeraɪz] *vt* resumir.

summary ['sʌmərɪ] *n* resumen *m* // *a* (justice) sumario.

summer ['sʌmə*] *n* verano // *cpd* de verano; ~**house** *n* (in garden) cenador *m*, glorieta; ~**time** *n* (season) verano; ~ **time** *n* (Brit: by clock) hora de verano.

summit ['sʌmɪt] *n* cima, cumbre *f*; ~ **(conference)** *n* (conferencia) cumbre *f.*

summon ['sʌmən] *vt* (person) llamar; (meeting) convocar; (LAW) citar; **to** ~ **up** *vt* (courage) armarse de; ~**s** *n* llamamiento, llamada // *vt* citar, emplazar.

sump [sʌmp] *n* (Brit AUT) cárter *m.*

sumptuous ['sʌmptjuəs] *a* suntuoso.

sun [sʌn] *n* sol *m.*

sunbathe ['sʌnbeɪð] *vi* tomar el sol.

sunburn ['sʌnbəːn] *n* (painful) quemadura; (tan) bronceado.

Sunday ['sʌndɪ] *n* domingo; ~

school n catequesis f dominical.
sundial ['sʌndaɪəl] n reloj m de sol.
sundown ['sʌndaʊn] n anochecer m.
sundry ['sʌndrɪ] a varios/as, diversos/as; all and ~ todos sin excepción; **sundries** npl géneros mpl diversos.
sunflower ['sʌnflaʊə*] n girasol m.
sung [sʌŋ] pp of **sing**.
sunglasses ['sʌnglɑːsɪz] npl gafas fpl or anteojos mpl (LAM) de sol.
sunk [sʌŋk] pp of **sink**.
sun: ~light n luz f del sol; ~lit a iluminado por el sol; ~ny a soleado; (day) de sol; (fig) alegre; ~rise n salida del sol; ~ roof n (AUT) techo corredizo; ~set n puesta del sol; ~shade n (over table) sombrilla; ~shine n sol m; ~stroke n insolación f; ~tan n bronceado; ~tan oil n aceite m bronceador.
super ['suːpə*] a (col) bárbaro.
superannuation [suːpərænjuˈeɪʃən] n cuota de jubilación.
superb [suːˈpəːb] a magnífico, espléndido.
supercilious [suːpəˈsɪlɪəs] a altanero.
superfluous [suˈpəːfluəs] a superfluo, de sobra.
superhuman [suːpəˈhjuːmən] a sobrehumano.
superimpose ['suːpərɪmˈpəʊz] vt sobreponer.
superintendent [suːpərɪnˈtendənt] n director(a) m/f; (police ~) subjefe/a m/f.
superior [suˈpɪərɪə*] a superior; (smug) desdeñoso // n superior; ~ity [-ˈɔrɪtɪ] n superioridad f; desdén m.
superlative [suˈpəːlətɪv] a, n superlativo.
superman ['suːpəmæn] n superhombre m.
supermarket ['suːpəmɑːkɪt] n supermercado.
supernatural [suːpəˈnætʃərəl] a sobrenatural.
superpower ['suːpəpaʊə*] n (POL)

superpotencia.
supersede [suːpəˈsiːd] vt suplantar.
supersonic ['suːpəˈsɔnɪk] a supersónico.
superstitious [suːpəˈstɪʃəs] a supersticioso.
supertanker ['suːpətæŋkə*] n superpetrolero.
supervise ['suːpəvaɪz] vt supervisar; **supervision** [-ˈvɪʒən] n supervisión f; **supervisor** n supervisor(a) m/f.
supper ['sʌpə*] n cena; to have ~ cenar.
supplant [səˈplɑːnt] vt suplantar.
supple ['sʌpl] a flexible.
supplement ['sʌplɪmənt] n suplemento // vt [sʌplɪˈment] suplir; ~ary [-ˈmentərɪ] a suplementario.
supplier [səˈplaɪə*] n suministrador(a) m/f; (COMM) distribuidor(a) m/f.
supply [səˈplaɪ] vt (provide) suministrar; (information) facilitar; (equip): to ~ (with) proveer (de) // n provisión f; (gas, water etc) suministro // cpd (Brit: teacher etc) suplente; **supplies** npl (food) víveres mpl; (MIL) pertrechos mpl.
support [səˈpɔːt] n (moral, financial etc) apoyo; (TECH) soporte m // vt apoyar; (financially) mantener; (uphold) sostener; ~er n (POL etc) partidario/a; (SPORT) aficionado/a.
suppose [səˈpəʊz] vt, vi suponer; (imagine) imaginarse; to be ~d to do sth deber hacer algo; ~dly [səˈpəʊzɪdlɪ] ad según cabe suponer; **supposing** conj en caso de que.
suppress [səˈpres] vt suprimir; (yawn) ahogar.
supreme [suˈpriːm] a supremo.
surcharge ['səːtʃɑːdʒ] n sobretasa, recargo.
sure [ʃuə*] a seguro; (definite, convinced) cierto; to make ~ of algo/asegurarse de algo/asegurar que; ~! (of course) ¡claro!, ¡por supuesto!; ~ enough efectivamente; ~ly ad (certainly) seguramente.
surety ['ʃuərətɪ] n fianza; (person)

fiador(a) m/f.

surf [sɜːf] n olas fpl.

surface ['sɜːfɪs] n superficie f // ut (road) revestir // vi salir a la superficie; ~ **mail** n vía terrestre.

surfboard ['sɜːfbɔːd] n plancha (de surf).

surfeit ['sɜːfɪt] n: a ~ of un exceso de.

surfing ['sɜːfɪŋ] n surf m.

surge [sɜːdʒ] n oleada, oleaje m // vi avanzar a tropel.

surgeon ['sɜːdʒən] n cirujano/a.

surgery ['sɜːdʒərɪ] n cirugía; (Brit: room) consultorio; **to undergo** ~ operarse; ~ **hours** npl (Brit) horas fpl de consulta.

surgical ['sɜːdʒɪkl] a quirúrgico; ~ **spirit** n (Brit) alcohol m de 90°.

surly ['sɜːlɪ] a hosco, malhumorado.

surmount [sɜː'maunt] ut superar, vencer.

surname ['sɜːneɪm] n apellido.

surpass [sɜː'pɑːs] ut superar, exceder.

surplus ['sɜːpləs] n excedente m; (COMM) superávit m // a excedente, sobrante.

surprise [sə'praɪz] n sorpresa // ut sorprender; **surprising** a sorprendente; **surprisingly** ad (easy, helpful) de modo sorprendente.

surrender [sə'rɛndə*] n rendición f, entrega // vi rendirse, entregarse.

surreptitious [sʌrɛp'tɪʃəs] a subrepticio.

surrogate ['sʌrəgɪt] n sucedáneo; ~ **mother** n madre f portadora.

surround [sə'raund] ut rodear, circundar; (MIL etc) cercar; ~**ing** a circundante; ~**ings** npl alrededores mpl, cercanías fpl.

surveillance [sɜː'veɪləns] n vigilancia.

survey ['sɜːveɪ] n inspección f, reconocimiento; (inquiry) encuesta f // ut [sɜː'veɪ] examinar, inspeccionar; (look at) mirar, sondear; (make inquiries about) hacer una encuesta de; ~**or** n (Brit) agrimensor(a) m/f.

survival [sə'vaɪvl] n supervivencia.

survive [sə'vaɪv] vi sobrevivir; (custom etc) perdurar // ut sobrevivir a; **survivor** n superviviente m/f.

susceptible [sə'sɛptɪbl] a: ~ (to) (disease) susceptible (a); (flattery) sensible (a).

suspect ['sʌspɛkt] a, n sospechoso/a m/f // ut [səs'pɛkt] sospechar.

suspend [səs'pɛnd] ut suspender; ~**ed sentence** n (LAW) libertad f condicional; ~**er belt** n portaligas m inv; ~**ers** npl (Brit) ligas fpl; (US) tirantes mpl.

suspense [səs'pɛns] n incertidumbre f, duda; (in film etc) suspense m.

suspension [səs'pɛnʃən] n (gen, AUT) suspensión f; (of driving licence) privación f; ~ **bridge** n puente m colgante.

suspicion [səs'pɪʃən] n sospecha; (distrust) recelo; (trace) traza; **suspicious** [-ʃəs] a (suspecting) receloso; (causing ~) sospechoso.

sustain [səs'teɪn] ut sostener, apoyar; (suffer) sufrir, padecer; ~**ed** a (effort) sostenido.

sustenance ['sʌstɪnəns] n sustento.

swab [swɔb] n (MED) algodón n; (for specimen) frotis m inv.

swagger ['swægə*] vi pavonearse.

swallow ['swɔləu] n (bird) golondrina // ut tragar; **to** ~ **up** ut (savings etc) consumir.

swam [swæm] pt of **swim**.

swamp [swɔmp] n pantano, ciénaga // ut: **to** ~ (**with**) abrumar (de), agobiar (de); ~**y** a pantanoso.

swan [swɔn] n cisne m.

swap [swɔp] ut: **to** ~ (**for**) canjear (por).

swarm [swɔːm] n (of bees) enjambre m; (fig) multitud f // vi: **to** ~ (**with**) pulular (de).

swarthy ['swɔːðɪ] a moreno.

swastika ['swɔstɪkə] n esvástica, cruz f gamada.

swat [swɔt] ut aplastar.

sway [sweɪ] vi mecerse, balancearse // ut (influence) mover, influir en.

swear [sweə*], *pt* **swore**, *pp* **sworn** *vi* jurar; **to ~ to** sth declarar algo bajo juramento; **~word** *n* palabrota.

sweat [swet] *n* sudor *m* // *vi* sudar.

sweater ['swetə*], **sweatshirt** ['swetʃə:t] *n* suéter *m*.

sweaty ['swetɪ] *a* sudoroso.

Swede [swi:d] *n* sueco/a.

swede [swi:d] *n* (*Brit*) nabo.

Sweden ['swi:dn] *n* Suecia.

Swedish ['swi:dɪʃ] *a* sueco // *n* (*LING*) sueco.

sweep [swi:p] *n* (*act*) barrido; (*of arm*) manotazo; (*curve*) curva, alcance *m*; (*also*: **chimney ~**) deshollinador/a] *m/f* // *vb* (*pt, pp* **swept**) *vt, vi* barrer; **to ~ away** *vt* barrer; (*rub out*) borrar; **to ~ past** *vt* pasar majestuosamente; **to ~ up** *vi* barrer; **~ing** (*gesture*) dramático; (*generalized*) generalizado.

sweet [swi:t] *n* (*candy*) dulce *m*, caramelo; (*Brit*: *pudding*) postre *m* // *a* dulce; (*sugary*) azucarado; (*fig*) dulce, amable; **~corn** *n* maíz *m*; **~en** *vt* endulzar; (*add sugar to*) poner azúcar a; **~heart** *n* novio/a; **~ness** *n* (*gen*) dulzura; **~ pea** *n* guisante *m* de olor.

swell [swel] *n* (*of sea*) marejada, oleaje *m* // *a* (*US*: *col*: *excellent*) estupendo, fenomenal // *vb* (*pt* **swelled**, *pp* **swollen** *or* **swelled**) *vt* hinchar, inflar // *vi* hincharse, inflarse; **~ing** *n* (*MED*) hinchazón *f*.

sweltering ['sweltərɪŋ] *a* sofocante, de mucho calor.

swept [swept] *pt, pp* of **sweep**.

swerve [swə:v] *vi* desviarse bruscamente.

swift [swift] *n* (*bird*) vencejo // *a* rápido, veloz; **~ly** *ad* rápidamente.

swig [swig] *n* (*col*: *drink*) trago.

swill [swil] *n* bazofia // *vt* (*also*: **~ out**, **~ down**) lavar, limpiar con agua.

swim [swim] *n*: **to go for a ~** ir a nadar *or* a bañarse // *vb* (*pt* **swam**, *pp* **swum**) *vi* nadar; (*head, room*)

dar vueltas // *vt* pasar *or* cruzar a nado; **~mer** *n* nadador(a) *m/f*; **~ming** *n* natación *f*; **~ming cap** *n* gorro de baño; **~ming costume** *n* bañador *m*, traje *m* de baño; **~ming pool** *n* piscina, alberca (*LAm*); **~suit** *n* = **~ming costume**.

swindle ['swindl] *n* estafa // *vt* estafar.

swine [swain] *n, pl inv* cerdos *mpl*, puercos *mpl*; (*col!*) canalla *sg* (!).

swing [swiŋ] *n* (*in playground*) columpio; (*movement*) balanceo, vaivén *m*; (*change of direction*) viraje *m*; (*rhythm*) ritmo // *vb* (*pt, pp* **swung**) *vt* balancear; (*on a ~*) columpiar; (*also*: **~ round**) voltear, girar // *vi* balancearse, columpiarse; (*also*: **~ round**) dar media vuelta; **to be in full ~** estar en plena marcha; **~ bridge** *n* puente *m* giratorio; **~ door**, (*US*) **~ing door** *n* puerta giratoria.

swingeing ['swindʒiŋ] *a* (*Brit*) abrumador(a).

swipe [swaip] *vt* (*hit*) golpear fuerte; (*col*: *steal*) guindar.

swirl [swə:l] *vi* arremolinarse.

swish [swiʃ] *a, n* (*col*: *smart*) elegante // *vi* chasquear.

Swiss [swis] *a, n, pl inv* suizo/a *m/f*.

switch [switʃ] *n* (*for light, radio etc*) interruptor *m*; (*change*) cambio // *vt* (*change*) cambiar de; **to ~ off** *vt* apagar; (*engine*) parar; **to ~ on** *vt* encender, prender (*LAm*); (*engine, machine*) arrancar; **~board** *n* (*TEL*) centralita (de teléfonos), conmutador *m* (*LAm*).

Switzerland ['switsələnd] *n* Suiza.

swivel ['swivl] *vi* (*also*: **~ round**) girar.

swollen ['swəulən] *pp* of **swell**.

swoon [swu:n] *vi* desmayarse.

swoop [swu:p] *n* (*by police etc*) redada // *vi* (*also*: **~ down**) calarse.

swop [swɔp] = **swap**.

sword [sɔ:d] *n* espada; **~fish** *n* pez *m* espada.

swore [swɔ:*] *pt* of **swear**.

sworn [swɔːn] *pp of* **swear**.

swot [swɒt] (*Brit*) *vt, vi* empollar.

swum [swʌm] *pp of* **swim**.

swung [swʌŋ] *pt, pp of* **swing**.

sycamore ['sɪkəmɔː*] *n* sicomoro.

syllable ['sɪləbl] *n* sílaba.

syllabus ['sɪləbəs] *n* programa *m* de estudios.

symbol ['sɪmbl] *n* símbolo.

symmetry ['sɪmɪtrɪ] *n* simetría.

sympathetic [sɪmpə'θetɪk] *a* compasivo; (*understanding*) comprensivo.

sympathize ['sɪmpəθaɪz] *vi:* to ~ with sb compadecerse de uno; ~r *n* (*POL*) simpatizante *m/f*.

sympathy ['sɪmpəθɪ] *n* (*pity*) compasión *f*; (*understanding*) comprensión *f*; with our deepest ~ nuestro más sentido pésame.

symphony ['sɪmfənɪ] *n* sinfonía.

symposium [sɪm'pəʊzɪəm] *n* simposio.

symptom ['sɪmptəm] *n* síntoma *m*, indicio.

synagogue ['sɪnəgɒg] *n* sinagoga.

syndicate ['sɪndɪkɪt] *n* (*gen*) sindicato; (*of newspapers*) agencia (de noticias).

syndrome ['sɪndrəʊm] *n* síndrome *m*.

synonym ['sɪnənɪm] *n* sinónimo.

synopsis [sɪ'nɒpsɪs], *pl* **-ses** [-siːz] *n* sinopsis *f inv*.

syntax ['sɪntæks] *n* sintaxis *f inv*.

synthesis ['sɪnθəsɪs], *pl* **-ses** [-siːz] *n* síntesis *f inv*.

synthetic [sɪn'θetɪk] *a* sintético.

syphilis ['sɪfɪlɪs] *n* sífilis *f*.

syphon ['saɪfən] = **siphon**.

Syria ['sɪrɪə] *n* Siria; ~n *a, n* sirio/a *m/f*.

syringe [sɪ'rɪndʒ] *n* jeringa.

syrup ['sɪrəp] *n* jarabe *m*, almíbar *m*.

system ['sɪstəm] *n* sistema *m*; (*ANAT*) organismo; ~atic [-'mætɪk] *a* sistemático; metódico; ~ disk *n* (*COMPUT*) disco del sistema; ~s analyst *n* analista *m/f* de sistemas.

T

ta [tɑː] *excl* (*Brit col*) ¡gracias!

tab [tæb] *n* lengüeta; (*label*) etiqueta; to keep ~s on (*fig*) vigilar.

tabby ['tæbɪ] *n* (*also:* ~ cat) gato atigrado.

table ['teɪbl] *n* (*of statistics etc*) cuadro, tabla // *vt* (*Brit: motion etc*) presentar; to lay or set the ~ poner la mesa; ~cloth *n* mantel *m*; ~ of contents *n* índice *m* de materias; ~ d'hôte [tɑːbl'dəʊt] *n* menú *m*; ~ lamp *n* lámpara de mesa; ~mat *n* salvamantel *m*; ~spoon *n* cuchara grande; (*also:* ~spoonful: *as measurement*) cucharada.

tablet ['tæblɪt] *n* (*MED*) pastilla, comprimido; (*for writing*) bloc *m*; (*of stone*) lápida.

table tennis *n* ping-pong *m*, tenis *m* de mesa.

table wine *n* vino de mesa.

tabloid ['tæblɔɪd] *n* periódico popular sensacionalista; the ~s la prensa amarilla.

tabulate ['tæbjuleɪt] *vt* disponer en tablas.

tacit ['tæsɪt] *a* tácito.

tack [tæk] *n* (*nail*) tachuela; (*stitch*) hilván *m*; (*NAUT*) bordada // *vt* (*nail*) clavar con tachuelas; (*stitch*) hilvanar // *vi* virar.

tackle ['tækl] *n* (*gear*) equipo; (*fishing* ~, *for lifting*) aparejo; (*RUGBY*) placaje *m* // *vt* (*difficulty*) enfrentar; (*grapple with*) agarrar; (*RUGBY*) placar.

tacky ['tækɪ] *a* pegajoso.

tact [tækt] *n* tacto, discreción *f*; ~ful *a* discreto, diplomático.

tactical ['tæktɪkl] *a* táctico.

tactics ['tæktɪks] *n, npl* táctica *sg*.

tactless ['tæktlɪs] *a* indiscreto.

tadpole ['tædpəʊl] *n* renacuajo.

taffy ['tæfɪ] *n* (*US*) melcocha.

tag [tæg] *n* (*label*) etiqueta; to ~ along with sb acompañar a uno.

tail [teɪl] n cola; (of shirt, coat) faldón m // vt seguir; **to ~ away**, **~ off** vi (in size, quality etc) ir disminuyendo; **~back** n (Brit AUT) cola; **~ coat** n frac m; **~ end** n cola, parte f final; **~gate** n (AUT) puerta trasera.

tailor ['teɪlə*] n sastre m; **~ing** n (cut) corte m; **~-made** a (also fig) hecho a la medida.

tailwind ['teɪlwɪnd] n viento de cola.

tainted ['teɪntɪd] a (water, air) contaminado; (fig) manchado.

take [teɪk], pt **took**, pp **taken** vt tomar; (grab) coger (Sp), agarrar (LAm); (gain: prize) ganar; (require: effort, courage) exigir; (support weight of: passengers etc) tener cabida para; (hold: passengers etc) tener cabida para; (accompany, bring, carry) llevar; (exam) presentarse a; **to ~ sth from** (drawer etc) sacar algo de; (person) coger (Sp) ou tomar (LAm) algo a; **I ~ it that...** supongo que...; **to ~ after** vt fus parecerse a; **to ~ apart** vt desmontar; **to ~ away** vt (remove) quitar; (carry off) llevar; **to ~ back** vt (return) devolver; (one's words) retractar; **to ~ down** vt (building) derribar; (letter etc) apuntar; **to ~ in** vt (Brit: deceive) engañar; (understand) entender; (include) abarcar; (lodger) acoger, recibir; **to ~ off** vi (AVIAT) despegar // vt (remove) quitar; (imitate) imitar; **to ~ on** vt (work) aceptar; (employee) contratar; (opponent) desafiar; **to ~ out** vt sacar; (remove) quitar; **to ~ over** vt (business) tomar posesión de // vi: **to ~ over from sb** reemplazar a uno; **to ~ to** vt fus (person) coger cariño a (Sp), encariñarse con (LAm); (activity) aficionarse a; **to ~ up** vt (a dress) acortar; (occupy: time, space) ocupar; (engage in) dedicarse a; **~away** a (Brit: food) para llevar; **~home pay** n salario neto; **~off** n (AVIAT) despegue m; **~over** n (COMM) absorción f.

takings ['teɪkɪŋz] npl (COMM) ingresos mpl.

talc [tælk] n (also: **~um powder**) talco.

tale [teɪl] n (story) cuento; (account) relación f; **to tell ~s** (fig) chismear.

talent ['tælnt] n talento; **~ed** a talentoso.

talk [tɔːk] n charla; (gossip) habladurías fpl, chismes mpl; (conversation) conversación f // vi (speak) hablar; (chatter) charlar; **~s** npl (POL etc) conversaciones fpl; **to ~ about** hablar de; **to ~ sb into doing sth** convencer a uno para que haga algo; **to ~ sb out of doing sth** disuadir a uno de que haga algo; **to ~ shop** hablar del trabajo; **to ~ over** vt discutir; **~ative** a hablador(a); **~ show** n programa m magazine.

tall [tɔːl] a alto; (tree) grande; **to be 6 feet ~** = medir 1 metro 80, tener 1 metro 80 de alto; **~boy** n (Brit) cómoda alta; **~ story** n cuento chino.

tally ['tælɪ] n cuenta // vi: **to ~ (with)** corresponder (con).

talon ['tælən] n garra.

tambourine [tæmbə'riːn] n pandereta.

tame [teɪm] a (mild) manso; (tamed) domesticado; (fig: story, style) mediocre.

tamper ['tæmpə*] vi: **to ~ with** tocar, andar con.

tampon ['tæmpɔn] n tampón m.

tan [tæn] n (also: **sun~**) bronceado // vt broncear // vi ponerse moreno // a (colour) marrón.

tang [tæŋ] n sabor m fuerte.

tangent ['tændʒənt] n (MATH) tangente f; **to go off at a ~** (fig) salirse por la tangente.

tangerine [tændʒə'riːn] n mandarina.

tangle ['tæŋgl] n enredo; **to get in(to) a ~** enredarse.

tank [tæŋk] n (water ~) depósito, tanque m; (for fish) acuario; (MIL) tanque m.

tanker ['tæŋkə*] n (ship) buque m cisterna; (truck) camión m cisterna.

tanned [tænd] a (skin) moreno, bronceado.

tantalizing ['tæntəlaızıŋ] a tentador(a).

tantamount ['tæntəmaunt] a: ~ to equivalente a.

tantrum ['tæntrəm] n rabieta.

tap [tæp] n (Brit: on sink etc) grifo, canilla (LAm); (gentle blow) golpecito; (gas ~) llave f // vt (table etc) tamborilear; (shoulder etc) palmear; (resources) utilizar, explotar; (telephone) intervenir; **on** ~ (fig: resources) a mano; ~**dancing** n zapateado.

tape [teıp] n cinta; (also: **magnetic** ~) cinta magnética; (sticky ~) cinta adhesiva // vt (record) grabar (en cinta); ~ **measure** n cinta métrica, metro.

taper ['teıpə*] n cirio // vi afilarse.

tape recorder n grabadora.

tapestry ['tæpıstrı] n (object) tapiz m; (art) tapicería.

tar [tɑː] n alquitrán m, brea.

target ['tɑːgıt] n (gen) blanco; ~ **practice** n tiro al blanco.

tariff ['tærıf] n tarifa.

tarmac ['tɑːmæk] n (Brit: on road) alquitranado; (AVIAT) pista (de aterrizaje).

tarnish ['tɑːnıʃ] vt deslustrar.

tarpaulin [tɑː'pɔːlın] n alquitranado.

tart [tɑːt] n (CULIN) tarta; (Brit col: pej: woman) puta // a (flavour) agrio, ácido; **to** ~ **up** n (room, building) dar tono a.

tartan ['tɑːtn] n tartán m, escocés m // a de tartán.

tartar ['tɑːtə*] n (on teeth) sarro; ~(**e**) **sauce** n salsa tártara.

task [tɑːsk] n tarea; **to take to** ~ reprender; ~ **force** n (MIL, POLICE) grupo de operaciones.

tassel ['tæsl] n borla.

taste [teıst] n sabor m, gusto; (also: **after**~) dejo; (sip) sorbo; (fig: glimpse, idea) muestra, idea // vt

probar // vi: **to** ~ **of** or **like** (fish etc) saber a; **you can** ~ **the** garlic (in it) se nota el sabor a ajo; **can I have a** ~ **of this wine**? ¿puedo probar este vino?; **to have a** ~ **for** sth ser aficionado a algo; **in good/bad** ~ de buen/mal gusto; ~**ful** a de buen gusto; ~**less** a (food) soso; (remark) de mal gusto; **tasty** a sabroso, rico.

tatters ['tætəz] npl: **in** ~ (also: tattered) hecho jirones.

tattoo [tə'tuː] n tatuaje m; (spectacle) espectáculo m militar // vt tatuar.

tatty ['tætı] a (Brit col) raído.

taught [tɔːt] pt, pp of **teach**.

taunt [tɔːnt] n burla // vt burlarse de.

Taurus ['tɔːrəs] n Tauro.

taut [tɔːt] a tirante, tenso.

tawdry ['tɔːdrı] a de mal gusto.

tax [tæks] n impuesto // vt gravar (con un impuesto); (fig: test) poner a prueba (: patience) agotar; ~**able** a (income) imponible; ~**ation** [-'seıʃən] n impuestos mpl; ~**avoidance** n evasión f de impuestos; ~ **collector** n recaudador(a) m/f; ~ **disc** n (Brit AUT) pegatina del impuesto de circulación; ~ **evasion** n evasión f fiscal; ~**free** a libre de impuestos.

taxi ['tæksı] n taxi m // vi (AVIAT) rodar por la pista; ~ **driver** n taxista m/f; (Brit) ~ **rank**, ~ **stand** n parada de taxis.

tax: ~ **payer** n contribuyente m/f; ~ **relief** n desgravación f fiscal; ~ **return** n declaración f de ingresos.

TB n abbr = **tuberculosis**.

tea [tiː] n té m; (Brit: snack) merienda; **high** ~ (Brit) merienda-cena; ~ **bag** n bolsita de té; ~ **break** n (Brit) descanso para el té.

teach [tiːtʃ], pt, pp taught vt: **to** ~ **sb sth**, ~ **sth to sb** enseñar algo a uno // vi enseñar; (be a teacher's) ser profesor(a); ~**er** n (in secondary school) profesor(a) m/f; (in primary school) maestro/a; ~**ing** n enseñanza.

tea cosy n cubretetera m.

teacup ['tiːkʌp] n taza para el té.

teak [tiːk] n (madera de) teca.

team [tiːm] n equipo; (of animals) pareja; ~**work** n trabajo en equipo.

teapot ['tiːpɔt] n tetera.

tear [teə*] n rasgón m, desgarrón m // n [tɪə*] lágrima f // vb (pt **tore**, pp **torn**) vt romper, rasgar // vi rasgarse; **in ~s** llorando; **to ~ along** vi (rush) precipitarse; **to ~ up** vt (sheet of paper etc) romper; ~**ful** a (sheet of paper etc) romper; ~**ful** a lloroso; ~ **gas** n gas m lacrimógeno.

tearoom ['tiːruːm] n salón m de té, cafetería.

tease [tiːz] n bromista m/f // vt tomar el pelo a.

tea: ~ **set** n servicio de té; ~**spoon** n cucharita; (also: ~**spoonful**: as measurement) cucharadita.

teat [tiːt] n (of bottle) tetina.

teatime ['tiːtaɪm] n hora del té.

tea towel n (Brit) paño de cocina.

technical ['tɛknɪkl] a técnico; ~**ity** [-'kælɪtɪ] n detalle m técnico.

technician [tɛk'nɪʃn] n técnico/a.

technique [tɛk'niːk] n técnica.

technological [tɛknə'lɔdʒɪkl] a tecnológico.

technology [tɛk'nɔlədʒɪ] n tecnología.

teddy (bear) ['tɛdɪ-] n osito de felpa.

tedious ['tiːdɪəs] a pesado, aburrido.

tee [tiː] n (GOLF) tee m.

teem [tiːm] vi: **to ~ with** rebosar de; **it is ~ing (with rain)** llueve a mares.

teenage ['tiːneɪdʒ] a (fashions etc) juvenil; ~**r** n adolescente m/f.

teens [tiːnz] npl: **to be in one's ~** ser adolescente.

tee-shirt ['tiːʃəːt] n = **T-shirt**.

teeter ['tiːtə*] vi balancearse.

teeth [tiːθ] npl of **tooth**.

teethe [tiːð] vi echar los dientes.

teething ['tiːðɪŋ]: ~ **ring** n mordedor m; ~ **troubles** npl (fig) dificultades fpl iniciales.

teetotal ['tiː'təutl] a (person) abstemio.

telegram ['tɛlɪgræm] n telegrama m.

telegraph ['tɛlɪgrɑːf] n telégrafo.

telepathy [tə'lɛpəθɪ] n telepatía.

telephone ['tɛlɪfəun] n teléfono // vt llamar por teléfono, telefonear; ~ **booth**, (Brit) ~ **box** n cabina telefónica; ~ **call** n llamada (telefónica); ~ **directory** n guía (telefónica); ~ **number** n número de teléfono; **telephonist** [tə'lɛfənɪst] n (Brit) telefonista m/f.

telephoto ['tɛlɪ'fəutəu] a: ~ **lens** teleobjetivo.

telescope ['tɛlɪskəup] n telescopio.

televise ['tɛlɪvaɪz] vt televisar.

television ['tɛlɪvɪʒən] n televisión f; ~ **set** n televisor m.

telex ['tɛlɛks] n télex m // vt, vi enviar un télex (a).

tell [tɛl], pt, pp **told** vt decir; (relate: story) contar; (distinguish): **to ~ sth from** distinguir algo de // vi (talk): **to ~ (of)** contar; (have effect) tener efecto; **to ~ sb to do sth** mandar a uno hacer algo; **to ~ off** vt: **to ~ sb off** regañar a uno; ~**er** n (in bank) cajero/a; ~**ing** a (remark, detail) revelador(a); ~**tale** a (sign) indicador(a).

telly ['tɛlɪ] n (Brit col) tele f.

temp [tɛmp] n abbr (Brit: = **temporary**) temporero/a // vi trabajar de interino/a.

temper ['tɛmpə*] n (mood) humor m; (bad ~) (mal) genio; (fit of anger) ira; (of child) rabieta // vt (moderate) moderar; **to be in a ~** estar furioso; **to lose one's ~** enfadarse, enojarse (LAm).

temperament ['tɛmprəmənt] n (nature) temperamento.

temperate ['tɛmprət] a moderado; (climate) templado.

temperature ['tɛmprətʃə*] n temperatura; **to have or run a ~** tener fiebre.

tempest ['tɛmpɪst] n tempestad f.

template ['tɛmplɪt] n plantilla.

temple ['templ] n (building) templo; (ANAT) sien f.

temporarily ['tempərərɪlɪ] ad temporalmente.

temporary ['tempərərɪ] a provisional, temporal; (passing) transitorio; (worker) temporero.

tempt [tempt] vt tentar; to ~ sb into doing sth tentar or inducir a uno a hacer algo; ~ation [-'teɪʃən] n tentación f; ~ing a tentador(a).

ten [ten] num diez.

tenable ['tɛnəbl] a sostenible.

tenacity [tə'næsɪtɪ] n tenacidad f.

tenancy ['tɛnənsɪ] n alquiler m; (of house) inquilinato.

tenant ['tɛnənt] n (rent-payer) inquilino/a; (occupant) habitante m/f.

tend [tend] vt cuidar // vi: to ~ to do sth tener tendencia a hacer algo.

tendency ['tɛndənsɪ] n tendencia.

tender ['tɛndə*] a (meat) tierno; (sore) sensible; (affectionate) tierno, cariñoso // n (COMM: offer) oferta; (money): legal ~ moneda de curso legal // vt ofrecer; ~ness n ternura; (of meat) blandura.

tenement ['tɛnəmənt] n casa de pisos or vecinos (Sp).

tenet ['tɛnət] n principio.

tennis ['tɛnɪs] n tenis m; ~ ball n pelota de tenis; ~ court n cancha de tenis; ~ player n tenista m/f; ~ racket n raqueta de tenis; ~ shoes npl zapatillas fpl de tenis.

tenor ['tɛnə*] n (MUS) tenor m.

tense [tɛns] a (moment, atmosphere) tenso; (stretched) tirante; (stiff) rígido, tieso; (person) nervioso // n (LING) tiempo.

tension ['tɛnʃən] n tensión f.

tent [tɛnt] n tienda (de campaña), carpa (LAm).

tentacle ['tɛntəkl] n tentáculo.

tenterhooks ['tɛntəhuks] npl: on ~ sobre ascuas.

tenth [tɛnθ] a décimo.

tent peg n clavija, estaca.

tent pole n mástil m.

tenuous ['tɛnjuəs] a tenue.

tenure ['tɛnjuə*] n (of land) tenencia; (of job: period) ejercicio.

tepid ['tɛpɪd] a tibio.

term [təːm] n (COMM: time limit) plazo; (word) término; (period) período; (SCOL) trimestre m // vt llamar; ~s npl (conditions) condiciones fpl; in the short/long ~ a corto/largo plazo; to be on good ~s with sb llevarse bien con uno; to come to ~s with (problem) adaptarse a.

terminal ['təːmɪnl] a (disease) mortal // n (ELEC) borne m; (COMPUT) terminal m; (also: air ~) terminal f; (Brit: also: coach ~) (estación f) terminal f.

terminate ['təːmɪneɪt] vt terminar // vi: to ~ in acabar en.

terminus ['təːmɪnəs], pl -mini [-mɪnaɪ] n término, (estación f) terminal f.

terrace ['tɛrəs] n terraza; (Brit: row of houses) hilera de casas adosadas; the ~s (Brit SPORT) las gradas fpl; ~d a (garden) colgante; (house) adosado.

terrain [tɛ'reɪn] n terreno.

terrible ['tɛrɪbl] a terrible, horrible; (fam) atroz; **terribly** ad terriblemente; (very badly) malísimamente.

terrier ['tɛrɪə*] n terrier m.

terrific [tə'rɪfɪk] a fantástico, fenomenal; (wonderful) maravilloso.

terrify ['tɛrɪfaɪ] vt aterrorizar.

territory ['tɛrɪtərɪ] n territorio.

terror ['tɛrə*] n terror m; ~ism n terrorismo; ~ist n terrorista m/f; ~ize vt aterrorizar.

terse [təːs] a (style) conciso; (reply) brusco.

Terylene ['tɛrɪliːn] n ® (Brit) terylene m ®.

test [tɛst] n (trial, check) prueba, ensayo; (: of goods in factory) control m; (of courage etc, CHEM) prueba; (MED) examen m; (exam) examen m, test m; (also: driving ~) examen m de conducir // vt probar, poner a prueba; (MED) examinar.

testament ['tɛstəmənt] n testamento; **the Old/New T~** el Antiguo/ Nuevo Testamento.

testicle ['tɛstɪkl] *n* testículo.

testify ['tɛstɪfaɪ] *vi* (*LAW*) prestar declaración; **to ~ to sth** atestiguar algo.

testimony ['tɛstɪmənɪ] *n* (*LAW*) testimonio, declaración *f*.

test: ~ **match** *n* (*CRICKET*, *RUGBY*) partido internacional; ~ **pilot** *n* piloto/mujer piloto *m/f* de pruebas; ~ **tube** *n* probeta; ~ **tube baby** *n* niño/a probeta.

tetanus ['tɛtənəs] *n* tétano.

tether ['tɛðə*] *vt* atar (con una cuerda) // *n*: **to be at the end of one's ~** no aguantar más.

text [tɛkst] *n* texto; **~book** *n* libro de texto.

textiles ['tɛkstaɪlz] *npl* textiles *mpl*, tejidos *mpl*.

texture ['tɛkstʃə*] *n* textura.

Thai [taɪ] *a*, *n* tailandés/esa *m/f*; **~land** *n* Tailandia.

Thames [tɛmz] *n*: **the ~** el (río) Támesis.

than [ðæn] *conj* (*in comparisons*): **more ~ 10/once** más de 10/una vez; **I have more/less ~ you/Paul** tengo más/menos que tú/Paul; **she is older ~ you think** es mayor de lo que piensas.

thank [θæŋk] *vt* dar las gracias a, agradecer; ~ **you (very much)** muchas gracias; **~s** *npl* gracias *fpl* // *excl* ¡gracias!; **~s to** *prep* gracias a; **~ful** *a*: **~ful (for)** agradecido (por); **~less** *a* ingrato; **T~sgiving (Day)** *n* día *m* de Acción de Gracias.

KEYWORD

that [ðæt] ◆ *a* (*demonstrative*: *pl* those) ese/a, *pl* esos/as; (*more remote*) aquel/aquella, *pl* aquellos/as; **leave those books on the table** deja esos libros sobre la mesa; ~ **one** ése/a; (*more remote*) aquél/ aquélla; ~ **one over there** ése/ésa de ahí; aquél/aquélla de allí

◆ *pron* 1 (*demonstrative*: *pl*

those) ése/a, *pl* ésos/as; (*neuter*) eso; (*more remote*) aquél/aquélla, *pl* aquéllos/as; (*neuter*) aquello; **what's ~?** ¿qué es eso (or aquello)?; **who's ~?** ¿quién es ése/a (or aquél/ aquélla)?; **is ~ you?** ¿eres tú?; **will you eat all ~?** ¿vas a comer todo eso?; **~'s my house** ésa es mi casa; **~'s what he said** eso es lo que dijo; ~ **is** (*to say*) es decir

2 (*relative*: *subject*, *object*) que; (*with preposition*) que *etc*, el/ la cual *etc*; **the book (~)** I read el libro que leí; **the books ~ are in the library** los libros que están en la biblioteca; **all (~)** I have todo lo que tengo; **the box (~)** I put it in la caja en la que *or* donde lo puse; **the people (~)** I spoke to la gente con la que hablé

3 (*relative*: *of time*) que; **the day (~)** he came el día (en) que vino

◆ *conj* que; **he thought ~ I was ill** creyó que estaba enfermo

◆ *ad* (*demonstrative*): **I can't work ~ much** no puedo trabajar tanto; **I didn't realise it was ~ bad** no creí que fuera tan malo; **~ high** así de alto.

---

thatched [θætʃt] *a* (*roof*) de paja; ~ **cottage** casita con tejado de paja.

thaw [θɔ:] *n* deshielo // *vi* (*ice*) derretirse; (*food*) descongelarse // *vt* (*food*) descongelar.

KEYWORD

the [ðiː, ðə] *definite article* 1 (*gen*) el, *f* la, *pl* los, *fpl* las (NB = **el** immediately before *f* noun beginning with stressed (h)*a*; **a** + **el** = **al**; **de** + **el** = **del**); ~ **boy/girl** el chico/la chica; ~ **books/flowers** los libros/las flores; **to ~ postman/from ~ drawer** al cartero/del cajón; **I haven't ~ time/money** no tengo tiempo/dinero 2 (+ *adjective to form noun*) lo; ~ **rich and ~ poor** los ricos y los pobres; **to attempt ~ impossible** intentar lo imposible

3 (in titles): Elizabeth ~ First Isabel primera; Peter ~ Great Pedro el Grande

4 (in comparisons): ~ **more he works** ~ **more he earns** cuanto más trabaja más gana.

theatre, (US) **theater** ['θɪətə*] n teatro; ~**goer** n aficionado/a al teatro.

theatrical [θɪ'ætrɪkl] a teatral.

theft [θɛft] n robo.

their [ðɛə*] a su; ~**s** pron (el) suyo/(la) suya etc; see also **my, mine.**

them [ðɛm, ðəm] pron (direct) los/las; (indirect) les; (stressed, after prep) ellos/ellas; see also **they.**

theme [θiːm] n tema m; ~ **song** n tema m (musical).

themselves [ðəm'sɛlvz] pl pron (subject) ellos mismos/ellas mismas; (complement) se; (after prep) sí (mismos/as); see also **oneself.**

then [ðɛn] ad (at that time) entonces; (next) pues; (later) luego, después; (and also) además // (therefore) en ese caso, entonces // a: **the** ~ **president** el entonces presidente; **from** ~ **on** desde entonces.

theology [θɪ'ɔlədʒɪ] n teología.

theoretical [θɪə'rɛtɪkl] a teórico.

theory ['θɪərɪ] n teoría.

therapist ['θɛrəpɪst] n terapeuta m/f.

therapy [θɛrəpɪ] n terapia.

KEYWORD

there ['ðɛə*] ad **1:** ~ **is,** ~ **are** hay; ~ **is** no-one here/no bread left no hay nadie aquí/no queda pan; ~ **has been an accident** ha habido un accidente

2 (referring to place) ahí; (distant) allí; **it's** ~ está ahí; **put it in/on up/down** ~ ponlo ahí dentro/encima/arriba/abajo; **I want that book** ~ quiero ese libro de ahí; ~ **he is!** ¡ahí está!

3: ~, ~, (esp to child) ea, ea.

there: ~**abouts** ad por ahí; ~**after** ad después; ~**by** ad así, de ese modo; ~**fore** ad por lo tanto; ~**'s** = ~ **is;** = ~ **has.**

thermal ['θəːml] a termal; (paper) térmico; ~ **printer** n termoimpresora.

thermometer [θə'mɔmɪtə*] n termómetro.

Thermos ['θəːməs] n ® (also: ~ **flask**) termo.

thermostat ['θəːməustæt] n termostato.

thesaurus [θɪ'sɔːrəs] n tesoro.

these [ðiːz] pl a estos/as // pl pron éstos/as.

thesis ['θiːsɪs], pl **-ses** [-siːz] n tesis f inv.

they [ðeɪ] pl pron ellos/ellas; (stressed) ellos (mismos)/ellas mismas); ~ **say that...** (it is said that) se dice que...; ~**'d = they had, they would;** ~**'ll = they shall, they will;** ~**'re = they are;** ~**'ve = they have.**

thick [θɪk] a (liquid, smoke) espeso; (wall, slice) grueso; (vegetation, beard) tupido; (stupid) torpe // n: **in the** ~ **of the battle** en lo más reñido de la batalla; **it's 20 cm** ~ tiene 20 cm de espesor; ~**en** vi espesarse // vt (sauce etc) espesar; ~**ness** n espesor m, grueso; ~**set** a fornido; ~**skinned** a (fig) insensible.

thief [θiːf], pl **thieves** [θiːvz] n ladrón/ona m/f.

thigh [θaɪ] n muslo.

thimble ['θɪmbl] n dedal m.

thin [θɪn] a (person, animal) flaco; (material) delgado; (liquid) poco denso; (soup) aguado; (fog) ligero; (crowd) escaso // vt: to ~ (**down**) (sauce, paint) diluir.

thing [θɪŋ] n cosa; (object) objeto, artículo; (contraption) chisme m; ~**s** npl (belongings) efectos mpl (personales); **the best** ~ **would be to...** lo mejor sería...; **how are** ~**s?** ¿qué tal?

think [θɪŋk], pt, pp **thought** vi pensar // vt pensar, creer; **what did you ~ of them?** ¿qué te parecieron?; **I'll ~ about it** lo pensaré; **to ~ of doing sth** pensar en hacer algo; **I ~ so/not** creo que sí/no; **to ~ well of sb** tener buen concepto de uno; **to ~ over** vt reflexionar sobre, meditar; **to ~ up** vt imaginar; **~ tank** n gabinete m de estrategia.

third [θɜːd] a tercer(a) // n tercero/a; (fraction) tercio; (Brit SCOL: degree) de tercera clase; **~ly** ad en tercer lugar; **~ party insurance** n (Brit) seguro contra terceros; **~rate** a (de calidad) mediocre; **the T~ World** el Tercer Mundo.

thirst [θɜːst] n sed f; **~y** a: **to be ~y** tener sed.

thirteen [ˈθɜːˈtiːn] num trece.

thirty [ˈθɜːtɪ] num treinta.

this [ðɪs] ◆ a (demonstrative: pl these) este/a; pl estos/as; (neuter) esto; **~ man/woman** este hombre/ esta mujer; **these children/flowers** estos chicos/estas flores; **~ one** (here) éste/a, esto (de aquí)
◆ pron (demonstrative: pl these) éste/a; pl éstos/as; (neuter) esto; **who is ~?** ¿quién es éste/ésta?; **what is ~?** ¿qué es esto?; **~ is where I live** aquí vivo; **~ is what he said** esto es lo que dijo; **~ is Mr Brown** (in introductions) le presento al Sr. Brown; (photo) éste es el Sr. Brown; (on telephone) habla el Sr. Brown
◆ ad (demonstrative): **~ high/long** etc así de alto/largo etc; **~ far** hasta aquí.

thistle [ˈθɪsl] n cardo.

thong [θɒŋ] n correa.

thorn [θɔːn] n espina.

thorough [ˈθʌrə] a (search) minucioso; (knowledge, research) profundo; **~bred** a (horse) de pura sangre; **~fare** n calle f; **'no ~fare'**

'prohibido el paso'; **~ly** ad minuciosamente; profundamente, a fondo.

those [ðəuz] pl pron ésos/ésas; (more remote) aquéllos/as // pl a esos/esas; aquellos/as.

though [ðəu] conj aunque // ad sin embargo.

thought [θɔːt] pt, pp of **think** // n pensamiento; (opinion) opinión f; (intention) intención f; **~ful** a pensativo; (considerate) atento; **~less** a desconsiderado.

thousand [ˈθauzənd] num mil; **two ~** dos mil; **~s of** miles de; **~th** a milésimo.

thrash [θræʃ] vt apalear; (defeat) derrotar; **to ~ about** vi revolcarse; **to ~ out** vt discutir a fondo.

thread [θred] n hilo; (of screw) rosca // vt (needle) enhebrar; **~bare** a raído.

threat [θret] n amenaza; **to ~ sb with sth/to do** amenazar a uno con algo/con hacer.

three [θriː] num tres; **~-dimensional** a tridimensional; **~-piece suit** n traje m de tres piezas; **~-piece suite** n tresillo; **~-ply** a (wool) triple; **~-wheeler** n (car) coche m china.

thresh [θreʃ] vt (AGR) trillar.

threshold [ˈθreʃhəuld] n umbral m.

threw [θruː] pt of **throw**.

thrifty [ˈθrɪftɪ] a económico.

thrill [θrɪl] n (excitement) emoción f // vt emocionar; **to be ~ed** (with gift etc) estar encantado; **~er** n película/novela de suspense.

thrilling [ˈθrɪlɪŋ] a emocionante.

thrive [θraɪv], pt **thrived** or **throve** [θrəuv], pp **thrived** or **thriven** [ˈθrɪvn] vi (grow) crecer; (do well) prosperar; **thriving** a próspero.

throat [θrəut] n garganta; **to have a sore ~** tener dolor de garganta.

throb [θrɒb] vi (heart) latir; (engine) vibrar; (with pain) dar punzadas.

throes [θrəuz] npl: **in the ~ of** en medio de.

throne [θrəʊn] n trono.

throng [θrɒŋ] n multitud f, muchedumbre f // vt agolparse en.

throttle [ˈθrɒtl] n (AUT) acelerador m // vt estrangular.

through [θruː] prep por, a través de; (time) durante; (by means of) por medio de, mediante; (owing to) gracias a // a (ticket, train) directo // ad completamente, de parte a parte; de principio a fin; **to put sb ~ to sb** (TEL) poner o pasar a uno con uno; **to be ~** (TEL) tener comunicación; (have finished) haber terminado; **'no ~ road'** (Brit) 'calle sin salida'; **~out** prep (place) por todas partes de, por todo; (time) durante todo // ad por o en todas partes.

throve [θrəʊv] pt of **thrive**.

throw [θrəʊ] n tiro; (SPORT) lanzamiento // vt (pt **threw**, pp **thrown**) tirar, echar; (SPORT) lanzar; (rider) derribar; (fig) desconcertar; **to ~ a party** dar una fiesta; **to ~ away** vt tirar; **to ~ off** vt deshacerse de; **to ~ out** vt tirar; **to ~ up** vi vomitar; **~away** a para tirar, desechable; **~-in** n (SPORT) saque m.

thru [θruː] (US) = **through**.

thrush [θrʌʃ] n zorzal m, tordo.

thrust [θrʌst] n (TECH) empuje m // vt (pt, pp **thrust**) empujar; (push in) introducir.

thud [θʌd] n golpe m sordo.

thug [θʌg] n gamberro/a.

thumb [θʌm] n (ANAT) pulgar m // vt: **to ~ a lift** hacer autostop; **to ~ through** vt fus (book) hojear; **~tack** n (US) chincheta, chinche m (LAm).

thump [θʌmp] n golpe m; (sound) ruido seco o sordo // vt, vi golpear.

thunder [ˈθʌndə*] n trueno; (of applause etc) estruendo // vi tronar; (train etc): **to ~ past** pasar como un trueno; **~bolt** n rayo; **~clap** n trueno; **~storm** n tormenta; **~y** a tormentoso.

Thursday [ˈθɜːzdɪ] n jueves m inv.

thus [ðʌs] ad así, de este modo.

thwart [θwɔːt] vt frustrar.

thyme [taɪm] n tomillo.

thyroid [ˈθaɪrɔɪd] n tiroides m inv.

tiara [tɪˈɑːrə] n tiara, diadema.

tic [tɪk] n tic m.

tick [tɪk] n (sound: of clock) tictac m; (mark) palomita; (ZOOL) garrapata; (Brit col): **in a ~** en un instante // vi hacer tictac // vt marcar; **to ~ off** vt marcar; (person) reñir; **to ~ over** vi (engine) girar en marcha lenta; (fig) ir tirando.

ticket [ˈtɪkɪt] n billete m, tíquet m, boleto (LAm); (for cinema etc) entrada, boleto (LAm); (in shop: on goods) etiqueta; (for library) tarjeta; **~ collector** n revisor/a m/f; **~ office** n (THEATRE) taquilla, boletería (LAm); (RAIL) despacho de billetes o boletos (LAm).

tickle [ˈtɪkl] n: **to give sb a ~** hacer cosquillas a uno // vt hacer cosquillas a; **ticklish** a (person) cosquilloso.

tidal [ˈtaɪdl] a de marea; **~ wave** n maremoto.

tidbit [ˈtɪdbɪt] (US) = **titbit**.

tiddlywinks [ˈtɪdlɪwɪŋks] n juego infantil de habilidad con fichas de plástico.

tide [taɪd] n marea; (fig: of events) curso, marcha; **high/low ~** marea alta/baja.

tidy [ˈtaɪdɪ] a (room) ordenado; (drawing, work) limpio; (person) (bien) arreglado // vt (also: **~ up**) poner en orden.

tie [taɪ] n (string etc) atadura; (Brit: neck~) corbata; (fig: link) vínculo, lazo; (SPORT: draw) empate m // vt atar // vi (SPORT) empatar; **to ~ in a bow** atar con un lazo; **to ~ a knot in sth** hacer un nudo en algo; **to ~ down** vt atar; (fig): **to ~ sb down** to obligar a uno a; **to ~ up** vt (parcel) envolver; (dog) atar; (boat) amarrar; (arrangements) concluir; **to be ~d up** (busy) estar ocupado.

tier [tɪə*] n grada; (of cake) piso.

tiger [ˈtaɪgə*] n tigre m.

tight [taɪt] a (rope) tirante; (clothes,

budget) ajustado; (*programme*) apretado; (*bend*) cerrado; (*col: drunk*) borracho // *ad* (*squeeze*) muy fuerte; (*shut*) herméticamente; **~s** *npl* (*Brit*) pantimedias *fpl*; **~en** *vt* (*rope*) estirar; (*screw*) apretar // *vi* apretarse; estirarse; **~-fisted** *a* tacaño; **~ly** *ad* (*grasp*) muy fuerte; **~rope** *n* cuerda floja.

tile [taɪl] *n* (*on roof*) teja; (*on floor*) baldosa; (*on wall*) azulejo; **~d** *a* embaldosado.

till [tɪl] *n* caja (registradora) // *vt* (*land*) cultivar // *prep, conj* = until.

tiller ['tɪlə*] *n* (*NAUT*) caña del timón.

tilt [tɪlt] *vt* inclinar // *vi* inclinarse.

timber ['tɪmbə*] *n* (*material*) madera; (*trees*) árboles *mpl*.

time [taɪm] *n* tiempo; (*epoch: often pl*) época; (*by clock*) hora; (*moment*) momento; (*occasion*) vez *f*; (*MUS*) compás *m* // *vt* calcular o medir el tiempo de; (*race*) cronometrar; (*remark etc*) elegir el momento para; **a long ~** mucho tiempo; **4 at a ~** 4 a la vez; **for the ~ being** de momento, por ahora; **from ~ to ~** de vez en cuando; **in ~** (*soon enough*) a tiempo; (*after some time*) con el tiempo; (*MUS*) al compás; **in a week's ~** dentro de una semana; **in no ~** en un abrir y cerrar de ojos; **any ~** cuando sea; **on ~** a la hora; **5 ~s 5** 5 por 5; **what ~ is it?** ¿qué hora es?; **to have a good ~** pasarlo bien, divertirse; **~ bomb** *n* bomba de efecto retardado; **~ lag** *n* desfase *m*; **~less** *a* eterno; **~ly** *a* oportuno; **~ off** *n* tiempo libre; **~r** *n* (~ *switch*) interruptor *m*; (*in kitchen etc*) programador *m* horario; **~ scale** *n* escala de tiempo; **~ switch** *n* (*Brit*) interruptor *m* (horario); **~table** *n* horario; **~ zone** *n* huso horario.

timid ['tɪmɪd] *a* tímido.

timing ['taɪmɪŋ] *n* (*SPORT*) cronometraje *m*; **the ~ of his resignation** el momento que eligió para dimitir.

timpani ['tɪmpənɪ] *npl* tímpanos *mpl*.

tin [tɪn] *n* estaño; (*also: ~ plate*) hojalata; (*Brit: can*) lata; **~foil** *n* papel *m* de estaño.

tinge [tɪndʒ] *n* matiz *m* // *vt:* **~d with** teñido de.

tingle ['tɪŋgl] *vi* sentir hormigueo.

tinker ['tɪŋkə*] *n* calderero/a; (*gipsy*) gitano/a; **to ~ with** *vi fus* jugar con, tocar.

tinkle ['tɪŋkl] *vi* tintinear.

tinned [tɪnd] *a* (*Brit: food*) en lata, en conserva.

tin opener [-əʊpnə*] *n* (*Brit*) abrelatas *m inv*.

tinsel ['tɪnsl] *n* oropel *m*.

tint [tɪnt] *n* matiz *m*; (*for hair*) tinte *m*; **~ed** *a* (*hair*) teñido; (*glass, spectacles*) ahumado.

tiny ['taɪnɪ] *a* minúsculo, pequeñito.

tip [tɪp] *n* (*end*) punta; (*gratuity*) propina; (*Brit: for rubbish*) vertedero; (*advice*) consejo // *vt* (*waiter*) dar una propina a; (*tilt*) inclinar; (*empty: also ~ out*) vaciar, echar; **to ~ over** *vt* volcar // *vi* volcarse; **~-off** *n* (*hint*) advertencia; **~ped** *a* (*Brit: cigarette*) con filtro.

tipsy ['tɪpsɪ] *a* alegre, mareado.

tiptoe ['tɪptəʊ] *n* (*Brit*): **on ~** de puntillas.

tiptop ['tɪp'tɒp] *a:* **in ~ condition** en perfectas condiciones.

tire ['taɪə*] *n* (*US*) = tyre // *vt* cansar // *vi* (*gen*) cansarse; (*become bored*) aburrirse; **~d** *a* cansado; **to be ~d of sth** estar harto de algo; **~less** *a* incansable; **~some** *a* aburrido; **tiring** *a* cansado.

tissue ['tɪʃu:] *n* tejido; (*paper handkerchief*) pañuelo de papel, kleenex *m* ®; **~ paper** *n* papel *m* de seda.

tit [tɪt] *n* (*bird*) herrerillo común; **to give ~ for tat** dar ojo por ojo.

titbit ['tɪtbɪt], (*US*) **tidbit** *n* (*food*) golosina; (*news*) pedazo.

titillate ['tɪtɪleɪt] *vt* estimular, excitar.

titivate ['tɪtɪveɪt] *vt* emperejilar.

title ['taɪtl] *n* título; **~ deed** *n*

(LAW) título de propiedad; ~ **role** n papel m principal.

titter ['tɪtə*] vi reírse entre dientes.

titular ['tɪtjʊlə*] a (in name only) nominal.

TM abbr (= trademark) marca de fábrica.

───────────────

┌──────────────────────┐
│ **KEYWORD** ◆ │
└──────────────────────┘

to [tuː, tə] ◆ prep 1 (direction) a; **to go ~ France/London/school/the station** ir a Francia/Londres/al colegio/a la estación; **to go ~ Claude's/the doctor's** ir a casa de Claude/al médico; **the road ~ Edinburgh** la carretera de Edimburgo

2 (as far as) hasta, a; **from here ~ London** de aquí a or hasta Londres; **to count ~ 10** contar hasta 10; **from 40 ~ 50 people** entre 40 y 50 personas

3 (with expressions of time): **a quarter/twenty ~ 5** las 5 menos cuarto/veinte

4 (for, of); **the key ~ the front door** la llave de la puerta principal; **she is secretary ~ the director** es la secretaria del director; **a letter ~ his wife** una carta a or para su mujer

5 (expressing indirect object) a; **to give sth ~ sb** darle algo a alguien; **to talk ~ sb** hablar con alguien; **to be a danger ~ sb** ser un peligro para alguien; **to carry out repairs ~ sth** hacer reparaciones en algo

6 (in relation to): **3 goals ~ 2** 3 goles a 2; **30 miles ~ the gallon** = 9,4 litros a cien (kms)

7 (purpose, result): **to come ~ sb's aid** venir en auxilio or ayuda de alguien; **to sentence sb ~ death** condenar a uno a muerte; **~ my great surprise** con gran sorpresa mía

◆ with vb 1 (simple infinitive): ~ go/eat ir/comer

2 (following another vb): **to want/try/start ~ do** querer/intentar/empezar a hacer; see also relevant verb

3 (with vb omitted): **I don't want ~** no quiero

4 (purpose, result) para; **I did it ~ help you** lo hice para ayudarte; **he came ~ see** see vino a verte

5 (equivalent to relative clause): **I have things ~ do** tengo cosas que hacer; **the main thing is ~ try** lo principal es intentarlo

6 (after adjective etc): **ready ~ go** listo para irse; **too old ~ ...** demasiado viejo (como) para ...

◆ ad: **pull/push the door ~** tirar de/empujar la puerta

───────────────

toad [təʊd] n sapo; **~stool** n hongo venenoso.

toast [təʊst] n (CULIN: also: piece of ~) tostada; (drink, speech) brindis m // vt (CULIN) tostar; (drink to) brindar; **~er** n tostador m.

tobacco [tə'bækəʊ] n tabaco; **~nist** n estanquero/a, tabaquero/a (LAm); **~nist's (shop)** (Brit) estanco, tabaquería (LAm); ~ **shop** n (US) = **~nist's (shop).**

toboggan [tə'bɒgən] n tobogán m.

today [tə'deɪ] ad, n (also: fig) hoy m.

toddler ['tɒdlə*] n niño/a (que empieza a andar).

toddy ['tɒdɪ] n ponche m.

to-do [tə'duː] n (fuss) lío.

toe [təʊ] n dedo (del pie); (of shoe) punta; to ~ the line (fig) conformarse; **~nail** n uña del pie.

toffee ['tɒfɪ] n caramelo.

together [tə'gɛðə*] ad juntos; (at same time) al mismo tiempo, a la vez; ~ **with** prep junto con.

toil [tɔɪl] n trabajo duro, labor f.

toilet ['tɔɪlət] n (Brit: lavatory) servicios mpl, wáter m, sanitario (LAm) // cpd (soap etc) de aseo; ~ **bag** n esponjera; ~ **bowl** n taza (de retrete); ~ **paper** n papel m higiénico; **~ries** npl artículos mpl de aseo; (make-up etc) artículos mpl de tocador; ~ **roll** n rollo de papel higiénico; ~ **water** n (agua de) colonia.

token ['təʊkən] n (sign) señal f,

muestra; (*souvenir*) recuerdo; (*voucher*) vale *m*; (*disc*) ficha; **book/record ~** (*Brit*) vale *m* para comprar libros/discos.

Tokyo ['təʊkjəʊ] *n* Tokio, Tokío.

told [təʊld] *pt, pp of* **tell**.

tolerable ['tɒlərəbl] *a* (*bearable*) soportable; (*fairly good*) pasable.

tolerance ['tɒlərns] *n* (*also: TECH*) tolerancia.

tolerant ['tɒlərnt] *a*: **~ of** tolerante con.

tolerate ['tɒləreɪt] *vt* tolerar.

toll [təʊl] *n* (*of casualties*) número de víctimas; (*tax, charge*) peaje *m* // *vi* (*bell*) doblar.

tomato [tə'mɑːtəʊ], *pl* **~es** *n* tomate *m*.

tomb [tuːm] *n* tumba.

tomboy ['tɒmbɔɪ] *n* marimacho.

tombstone ['tuːmstəʊn] *n* lápida.

tomcat ['tɒmkæt] *n* gato.

tomorrow [tə'mɒrəʊ] *ad, n* (*also: fig*) mañana; **the day after ~** pasado mañana; **~ morning** mañana por la mañana; **a week ~** de mañana en ocho (días).

ton [tʌn] *n* tonelada (*Brit* = 1016 kg; *US* = 907 kg); (*metric* **~**) tonelada métrica; **~s of** (*col*) montones de.

tone [təʊn] *n* tono // *vi* armonizar; **to ~ down** *vt* (*criticism*) suavizar; (*colour*) atenuar; **to ~ up** *vt* (*muscles*) tonificar; **~-deaf** *a* que no tiene oído musical.

tongs [tɒŋz] *npl* (*for coal*) tenazas *fpl*; (*for hair*) tenacillas *fpl*.

tongue [tʌŋ] *n* lengua; **~ in cheek** *ad* irónicamente; **~-tied** *a* (*fig*) mudo; **~-twister** *n* trabalenguas *m inv*.

tonic ['tɒnɪk] *n* (*MED*) tónico; (*MUS*) tónica; (*also:* **~ water**) (agua) tónica.

tonight [tə'naɪt] *ad, n* esta noche.

tonnage ['tʌnɪdʒ] *n* (*NAUT*) tonelaje *m*.

tonsil ['tɒnsl] *n* amígdala; **~litis** [-'laɪtɪs] *n* amigdalitis *f*.

too [tuː] *ad* (*excessively*) demasiado;

(*also*) también; **~ much** *ad*, *a* demasiado; **~ many** *a* demasiados/as; **~ bad!** ¡mala suerte!

took [tʊk] *pt of* **take**.

tool [tuːl] *n* herramienta; **~ box** *n* caja de herramientas.

toot [tuːt] *vi* (*with car horn*) tocar la bocina.

tooth [tuːθ], *pl* **teeth** *n* (*ANAT, TECH*) diente *m*; (*molar*) muela; **~ache** *n* dolor *m* de muelas; **~brush** *n* cepillo de dientes; **~paste** *n* pasta de dientes; **~pick** *n* palillo.

top [tɒp] *n* (*of mountain*) cumbre *f*, cima; (*of head*) coronilla; (*of ladder*) lo alto; (*of cupboard, table*) superficie *f*; (*lid: of box, jar*) tapa; (: *of bottle*) tapón *m*; (*of list etc*) cabeza; (*toy*) peonza // *a* de arriba; (*in rank*) principal, primero; (*best*) mejor // *vt* (*exceed*) exceder; (*be first in*) encabezar; **on ~ of** sobre, encima de; **from ~ to bottom** de pies a cabeza; **to ~ up**, (*US*) **to ~ off** *vt* llenar; **~ floor** *n* último piso; **~ hat** *n* sombrero de copa; **~-heavy** *a* (*object*) descompensado en la parte superior.

topic ['tɒpɪk] *n* tema *m*; **~al** *a* actual.

top: ~-less *a* (*bather etc*) topless; **~-level** *a* (*talks*) al más alto nivel; **~-most** *a* más alto.

topple ['tɒpl] *vt* volcar, derribar // *vi* caerse.

top-secret ['tɒp'siːkrɪt] *a* de alto secreto.

topsy-turvy ['tɒpsɪ'tɜːvɪ] *a, ad* patas arriba.

torch [tɔːtʃ] *n* antorcha; (*Brit: electric*) linterna.

tore [tɔː*] *pt of* **tear**.

torment ['tɔːment] *n* tormento // *vt* [tɔː'ment] atormentar; (*fig: annoy*) fastidiar.

torn [tɔːn] *pp of* **tear**.

torrent ['tɔrnt] *n* torrente *m*.

torrid ['tɒrɪd] *a* (*fig*) apasionado.

tortoise ['tɔːtəs] *n* tortuga; **~shell**

[ˈtɔːtəfəl] a de carey.

torture [ˈtɔːtʃəʳ] n tortura // vt torturar; (fig) atormentar.

Tory [ˈtɔːrɪ] a, n (Brit POL) conservador(a) m/f.

toss [tɔs] vt tirar, echar; (head) sacudir; **to ~ a coin** echar a cara o cruz; **to ~ up for sth** jugar a cara o cruz algo; **to ~ and turn** (in bed) dar vueltas.

tot [tɔt] n (Brit: drink) copita; (child) nene/a m/f.

total [ˈtəʊtl] a total, entero // n total m, suma f // vt (add up) sumar; (amount to) ascender a.

totalitarian [təʊtælɪˈtɛərɪən] a totalitario.

totally [ˈtəʊtəlɪ] ad totalmente.

totter [ˈtɔtəʳ] vi tambalearse.

touch [tʌtʃ] n tacto; (contact) contacto; (FOOTBALL): **to be in ~** estar fuera de juego // vt tocar; (emotionally) conmover; **a ~ of** (fig) una pizca or un poquito de; **to get in ~ with sb** ponerse en contacto con uno; **to lose ~** (friends) perder contacto; **to ~ on** vt fus (topic) aludir (brevemente) a; **to ~ up** vt (paint) retocar; **~-and-go** a arriesgado; **~down** n aterrizaje m; (on sea) amerizaje m; (US FOOTBALL) ensayo; **~ed** a conmovido; (col) chiflado; **~ing** a conmovedor(a); **~line** n (SPORT) línea de banda; **~y** a (person) quisquilloso.

tough [tʌf] a (meat) duro; (difficult) difícil; (resistant) resistente; (person) fuerte // n (gangster etc) gorila m; **~en** vt endurecer.

toupée [ˈtuːpeɪ] n peluca.

tour [tʊəʳ] n viaje m, vuelta; (also: **package ~**) viaje m todo comprendido; (of town, museum) visita // vt viajar por; **~ing** n viajes mpl turísticos, turismo.

tourism [ˈtʊərɪzm] n turismo.

tourist [ˈtʊərɪst] n turista m/f // cpd turístico; **~ office** n oficina de turismo.

tournament [ˈtʊənəmənt] n torneo.

tousled [ˈtaʊzld] a (hair) despeinado.

tout [taʊt] vi: **to ~ for business** solicitar clientes // n (also: **ticket ~**) revendedor/a m/f.

tow [taʊ] vt remolcar; **'on** or (US) **in ~'** (AUT) 'a remolque'.

toward(s) [təˈwɔːd(z)] prep hacia; (of attitude) respecto a, con; (of purpose) para.

towel [ˈtaʊəl] n toalla; **~ling** n (fabric) felpa; **~ rail**, (US) **~ rack** n toallero.

tower [ˈtaʊəʳ] n torre f; **~ block** n (Brit) torre f (de pisos); **~ing** a muy alto, imponente.

town [taʊn] n ciudad f; **to go to ~** ir a la ciudad; (fig) echar los botes por; **~ centre** n centro de la ciudad; **~ clerk** n secretario del ayuntamiento; **~ council** n ayuntamiento, consejo municipal; **~ hall** n ayuntamiento; **~ plan** n plano de la ciudad; **~ planning** n urbanismo.

towrope [ˈtaʊrəʊp] n cable m de remolque.

tow truck n (US) camión m grúa.

toy [tɔɪ] n juguete m; **to ~ with** vt fus jugar con; (idea) acariciar; **~shop** n juguetería.

trace [treɪs] n rastro // vt (draw) trazar, delinear; (locate) encontrar; **tracing paper** n papel m de calco.

track [træk] n (mark) huella, pista; (path: gen) camino, senda; (: of bullet etc) trayectoria; (: of suspect, animal) pista, rastro; (RAIL) vía; (SPORT) pista; (on record) canción f // vt seguir la pista de; **to keep ~ of** mantenerse al tanto de, seguir; **to ~ down** vt (person) localizar; (sth lost) encontrar; **~suit** n chándal m.

tract [trækt] n (GEO) región f; (pamphlet) folleto.

traction [ˈtrækʃən] n (AUT, power) tracción f; **in ~** (MED) en tracción.

tractor [ˈtræktəʳ] n tractor m.

trade [treɪd] n comercio; (skill, job) oficio // vi negociar, comerciar; **to ~ in sth** comerciar en algo; **to ~ in** vt (old car etc) ofrecer como parte del pago; ~ **fair** n feria comercial; ~**in price** se aplica a un objeto usado que se descuenta del precio de otro nuevo; ~**mark** n marca de fábrica; ~ **name** n marca registrada; ~**r** n comerciante m/f; ~**sman** n (shopkeeper) tendero; ~ **union** n sindicato; ~**unionist** n sindicalista m/f; **trading** n comercio; **trading estate** n (Brit) zona comercial.

tradition [tra'dɪʃən] n tradición f; ~**al** a tradicional.

traffic ['træfɪk] n (gen, AUT) tráfico, circulación f, tránsito (LAm); air ~ tránsito aéreo // vi: **to ~ in** (pej: liquor, drugs) traficar en; ~ **circle** n (US) glorieta de tráfico; ~ **jam** n embotellamiento; ~ **lights** npl semáforo sg; ~ **warden** n guardia m/f de tráfico.

tragedy ['trædʒədɪ] n tragedia.

tragic ['trædʒɪk] a trágico.

trail [treɪl] n (tracks) rastro, pista; (path) camino, sendero; (dust, smoke) estela // vt (drag) arrastrar; (follow) seguir la pista de; (follow closely) vigilar // vi arrastrarse; **to ~ behind** vi quedar a la zaga; ~**er** n (AUT) remolque m; (caravan) caravana; (CINEMA) trailer m, avance m; ~ **truck** n (US) trailer m.

train [treɪn] n tren m; (of dress) cola; (series) serie f // vt (educate) formar; (teach skills to) adiestrar; (sportsman) entrenar; (plant) hacer crecer; (point: gun etc): **to ~ on** apuntar a // vi (SPORT) entrenarse; (be educated) formarse; **one's ~ of thought** razonamiento de uno; ~**ed** a (worker) cualificado; (animal) amaestrado; ~**ee** [treɪ'niː] n aprendiz(a) m/f; ~**er** n (SPORT) entrenador a m/f; (of animals) domador(a) m/f; ~**ing** n formación f; entrenamiento; **to be in ~ing** (SPORT) estar entrenando; (: fit) estar en forma; ~**ing college** n (gen) colegio de formación profesional; (for teachers) escuela normal; ~**ing shoes** npl zapatillas fpl (de deporte).

traipse [treɪps] vi andar penosamente.

trait [treɪt] n rasgo.

traitor ['treɪtə*] n traidor(a) m/f.

tram [træm] n (Brit: also: ~**car**) tranvía m.

tramp [træmp] n (person) vagabundo/a; (col: offensive: woman) puta // vi andar con pasos pesados.

trample ['træmpl] vt: **to ~** (underfoot) pisotear.

trampoline ['træmpəliːn] n trampolín m.

tranquil ['træŋkwɪl] a tranquilo; ~**lizer** n (MED) tranquilizante m.

transact [træn'zækt] vt (business) tramitar; ~**ion** [-'zækʃən] n transacción f, operación f.

transcend [træn'sɛnd] vt rebasar.

transcript ['trænskrɪpt] n copia; ~**ion** [-'skrɪpʃən] n transcripción f.

transfer ['trænsfə*] n transferencia; (SPORT) traspaso; (picture, design) calcomanía // vt [træns'fəː*] trasladar, pasar; **to ~ the charges** (Brit TEL) llamar a cobro revertido.

transform [træns'fɔːm] vt transformar.

transfusion [træns'fjuːʒən] n transfusión f.

transient ['trænzɪənt] a transitorio.

transistor [træn'zɪstə*] n (ELEC) transistor m; ~ **radio** n transistor m.

transit ['trænzɪt] n: **in ~** en tránsito.

transitive ['trænzɪtɪv] a (LING) transitivo.

translate [trænz'leɪt] vt traducir; **translation** [-'leɪʃən] n traducción f; **translator** n traductor/a m/f.

transmission [trænz'mɪʃən] n transmisión f.

transmit [trænz'mɪt] vt transmitir; ~**ter** n transmisor m; (station) emisora.

transparency [træns'pɛərnsɪ] n (Brit PHOT) diapositiva.

transparent [træns'pærnt] a transparente.

transpire [træns'paɪə*] vi (turn out) resultar; (happen) ocurrir, suceder; it ~d that ... se supo que ...

transplant [træns'plɑ:nt] vt transplantar // n ['trænsplɑ:nt] (MED) transplante m.

transport [træns'pɔ:t] n transporte m // vt [-'pɔ:t] transportar; ~**ation** [-'teɪʃən] n transporte m; (of prisoners) deportación f; ~ **café** n (Brit) bar-restaurant m de carretera.

trap [træp] n (snare, trick) trampa; (carriage) cabriolé m // vt coger (Sp) or agarrar (LAm) en una trampa; (immobilize) bloquear; (jam) atascar; ~ **door** n escotilla.

trapeze [trə'pi:z] n trapecio.

trappings ['træpɪŋz] npl adornos mpl.

trash [træʃ] n (pej: goods) pacotilla; (: nonsense) tonterías fpl; ~ **can** n (US) cubo or balde m (LAm) de la basura.

travel ['trævl] n viaje m // vi viajar // vt (distance) recorrer; ~ **agency** n agencia de viajes; ~ **agent** n agente m/f de viajes; ~**ler**, (US) ~**er** n viajero/a; ~**ler's cheque**, (US) ~**er's check** n cheque m de viajero; ~**ling**, (US) ~**ing** n los viajes mpl, el viajar; ~ **sickness** n mareo.

travesty ['trævəstɪ] n parodia.

trawler ['trɔ:lə*] n pesquero de arrastre.

tray [treɪ] n (for carrying) bandeja; (on desk) cajón m.

treachery ['tretʃərɪ] n traición f.

treacle ['tri:kl] n (Brit) melaza.

tread [trɛd] n (step) paso, pisada; (sound) ruido de pasos; (of tyre) banda de rodadura // vi (pt trod, pp trodden) pisar; **to ~ on** vt fus pisar.

treason ['tri:zn] n traición f.

treasure ['trɛʒə*] n tesoro // vt (value) apreciar, valorar.

treasurer ['trɛʒərə*] n tesorero/a.

treasury ['trɛʒərɪ] n: **the T~**, (US) **the T~ Department** el Ministerio de Hacienda.

treat [tri:t] n (present) regalo; (pleasure) placer m // vt tratar; **to ~ sb to sth** invitar a uno a algo.

treatise ['tri:tɪz] n tratado.

treatment ['tri:tmənt] n tratamiento.

treaty ['tri:tɪ] n tratado.

treble ['trɛbl] a triple // vt triplicar // vi triplicarse; ~ **clef** n (MUS) clave f de sol.

tree [tri:] n árbol m.

trek [trɛk] n (long journey) expedición f; (tiring walk) caminata.

trellis ['trɛlɪs] n enrejado.

tremble ['trɛmbl] vi temblar.

tremendous [trɪ'mɛndəs] a tremendo; (enormous) enorme; (excellent) estupendo.

tremor ['trɛmə*] n temblor m; (also: **earth ~**) temblor m de tierra.

trench [trɛntʃ] n zanja; (MIL) trinchera.

trend [trɛnd] n (tendency) tendencia; (of events) curso; (fashion) moda; ~**y** a de moda.

trepidation [trɛpɪ'deɪʃən] n inquietud f.

trespass ['trɛspəs] vi: **to ~ on** entrar sin permiso en; **'no ~ing'** 'prohibido el paso'.

tress [trɛs] n trenza.

trestle ['trɛsl] n caballete m; ~ **table** n mesa de caballete.

trial ['traɪəl] n (LAW) juicio, proceso; (test: of machine etc) prueba; (hardship) desgracia; **by ~ and error** a fuerza de probar.

triangle ['traɪæŋgl] n (MATH, MUS) triángulo.

tribe [traɪb] n tribu f.

tribunal [traɪ'bju:nl] n tribunal m.

tributary ['trɪbjutərɪ] n (river) afluente m.

tribute ['trɪbju:t] n homenaje m, tributo; **to pay ~ to** rendir homenaje a.

trice [traɪs] n: **in a ~** en un santiamén.

trick [trɪk] n trampa; (conjuring ~, deceit) truco; (joke) broma; (CARDS) baza // vt engañar; **to play**

a ~ on sb gastar una broma a uno; **that should do the ~** a ver si funciona así; **~ery** n engaño.

trickle ['trɪkl] n (of water etc) chorrito // vi gotear.

tricky ['trɪkɪ] a difícil; delicado.

tricycle ['traɪsɪkl] n triciclo.

trifle ['traɪfl] n bagatela; (CULIN) dulce de bizcocho borracho, gelatina, fruta y natillas // ad: **a ~ long** un poquito largo; **trifling** a insignificante.

trigger ['trɪgə*] n (of gun) gatillo; **to ~ off** vt desencadenar.

trill [trɪl] n (of bird) gorjeo.

trim [trɪm] a (elegant) aseado; (house, garden) en buen estado; (figure) de talle esbelto // n (haircut etc) recorte m // vt (neaten) arreglar; (cut) recortar; (decorate) adornar; (NAUT: a sail) orientar; **~mings** npl (extras) accesorios mpl; (cuttings) recortes mpl.

trinket ['trɪŋkɪt] n chuchería, baratija.

trip [trɪp] n viaje m; (excursion) excursión f; (stumble) traspié m // vi (stumble) tropezar; (go lightly) andar a paso ligero; **on a ~** de viaje; **to ~ up** vi tropezar, caerse // vt hacer tropezar or caer.

tripe [traɪp] n (CULIN) callos mpl; (pej: rubbish) bobadas fpl.

triple ['trɪpl] a triple.

triplets ['trɪplɪts] npl trillizos/as m/fpl.

triplicate ['trɪplɪkət] n: **in ~** por triplicado.

tripod ['traɪpɔd] n trípode m.

trite [traɪt] a trillado.

triumph ['traɪʌmf] n triunfo // vi: **to ~ (over)** vencer.

trivia ['trɪvɪə] npl trivialidades fpl.

trivial ['trɪvɪəl] a insignificante, trivial.

trod [trɔd], **trodden** ['trɔdn] pt, pp of tread.

trolley ['trɔlɪ] n carrito.

trombone [trɔm'bəun] n trombón m.

troop [tru:p] n grupo, banda; **~s** npl

(MIL) tropas fpl; **to ~ in/out** vi entrar/salir en tropel; **~er** n (MIL) soldado (de caballería); **~ing the colour** n (ceremony) presentación f de la bandera.

trophy ['trəufɪ] n trofeo.

tropic ['trɔpɪk] n trópico; **~al** a tropical.

trot [trɔt] n trote m // vi trotar; **on the ~** (Brit fig) seguidos/as.

trouble ['trʌbl] n problema m, dificultad f; (worry) preocupación f; (bother, effort) molestia, esfuerzo; (unrest) inquietud f; (MED): stomach ~ problemas mpl gástricos // vt molestar; (worry) preocupar, inquietar // vi: **to ~ to do sth** molestarse en hacer algo; **~s** npl (POL etc) conflictos mpl; **to be in ~** estar en un apuro; **to go to the ~ of doing sth** tomarse la molestia de hacer algo; **what's the ~?** ¿qué pasa?; **~d** a (person) preocupado; (epoch, life) agitado; **~maker** n agitador(a) m/f; **~shooter** n (in conflict) conciliador(a) m/f; **~some** a molesto, inoportuno.

trough [trɔf] n (also: drinking ~) abrevadero; (also: feeding ~) comedero; (channel) canal m.

troupe [tru:p] n grupo.

trousers ['trauzəz] npl pantalones mpl; **short ~** pantalones mpl cortos.

trousseau ['tru:səu], pl **~x** or **~s** [-z] n ajuar m.

trout [traut] n, pl inv trucha.

trowel ['trauəl] n paleta.

truant ['truənt] n: **to play ~** (Brit) hacer novillos.

truce [tru:s] n tregua.

truck [trʌk] n (US) camión m; (RAIL) vagón m; **~ driver** n camionero; **~ farm** n (US) huerto de hortalizas.

truculent ['trʌkjulənt] a agresivo.

trudge [trʌdʒ] vi caminar penosamente.

true [tru:] a verdadero; (accurate) exacto; (genuine) auténtico; (faithful) fiel.

truffle ['trʌfl] n trufa.

truly ['truːlɪ] ad (genuinely, emphatic: very) realmente; (faithfully) fielmente.

trump [trʌmp] n triunfo; **~ed-up** a inventado.

trumpet ['trʌmpɪt] n trompeta.

truncheon ['trʌntʃən] n (Brit) porra.

trundle ['trʌndl] vt, vi: **to ~ along** rodar haciendo ruido.

trunk [trʌŋk] n (of tree, person) tronco; (of elephant) trompa; (case) baúl m; (US AUT) maletero; **~s** npl (also: **swimming ~s**) bañador m; **~ call** n (Brit TEL) llamada interurbana.

truss [trʌs] n (MED) braguero; **to ~ (up)** vt atar; (CULIN) espetar.

trust [trʌst] n confianza; (COMM) trust m; (LAW) fideicomiso // vt (rely on) tener confianza en; (entrust): **to ~ sth to sb** confiar algo a uno; **~ed** a de confianza; **~ee** [trʌs'tiː] n (LAW) fideicomisario m; (of school) patrono/a; **~ful, ~ing** a confiado; **~worthy** a digno de confianza.

truth [truːθ], pl **~s** [truːðz] n verdad f; **~ful** a (person) veraz.

try [traɪ] n tentativa, intento; (RUGBY) ensayo // vt (LAW) juzgar, procesar; (test: sth new) probar, someter a prueba; (attempt) intentar; (strain: patience) hacer perder // vi probar; **to ~ to do sth** intentar hacer algo; **to ~ on** vt (clothes) probarse; **to ~ out** vt probar, poner a prueba; **~ing** a cansado; (person) pesado.

T-shirt ['tiːʃəːt] n camiseta.

T-square ['tiːskweəˀ] n regla en T.

tub [tʌb] n cubo (Sp), balde m (LAm); (bath) tina, bañera.

tuba ['tjuːbə] n tuba.

tubby ['tʌbɪ] a regordete.

tube [tjuːb] n tubo; (Brit: underground) metro.

tuberculosis [tjubəːkjuˈləusɪs] n tuberculosis f inv.

tubing ['tjuːbɪŋ] n tubería (Sp), ca-

ñería; **a piece of ~** un trozo de tubo.

tubular ['tjuːbjuləˀ] a tubular.

TUC n abbr (Brit: = Trades Union Congress) federación nacional de sindicatos.

tuck [tʌk] n (SEWING) pliegue m // vt (put) poner; **to ~ away** vt esconder; **to ~ in** vt meter dentro; (child) arropar // vi (eat) comer con apetito; **to ~ up** vt (child) arropar; **~ shop** n (SCOL) tienda de golosinas.

Tuesday ['tjuːzdɪ] n martes m inv.

tuft [tʌft] n mechón m; (of grass etc) manojo.

tug [tʌg] n (ship) remolcador m // vt remolcar; **~-of-war** n lucha de tiro de cuerda.

tuition [tjuːˈɪʃən] n (Brit) enseñanza; (: private ~) clases fpl particulares; (US: school fees) matrícula.

tulip ['tjuːlɪp] n tulipán m.

tumble ['tʌmbl] n (fall) caída // vi caerse, tropezar; **to ~ to sth** (col) caer en la cuenta de algo; **~down** a destartalado; **~ dryer** n (Brit) secadora.

tumbler ['tʌmbləˀ] n vaso.

tummy ['tʌmɪ] n (col) barriga, vientre m.

tumour, (US) **tumor** ['tjuːməˀ] n tumor m.

tuna ['tjuːnə] n, pl inv (also: **~ fish**) atún m.

tune [tjuːn] n (melody) melodía // vt (MUS) afinar; (RADIO, TV, AUT) sintonizar; **to be in/out of ~** (instrument) estar afinado/desafinado; (singer) cantar afinadamente/desafinar; **to ~ in** (to) (RADIO, TV) sintonizar (con); **to ~ up** vi (musician) afinar (su instrumento); **~ful** a melodioso; **~r** n (radio set) sintonizador m; **piano ~r** n afinador(a) m/f de pianos.

tunic ['tjuːnɪk] n túnica.

tuning ['tjuːnɪŋ] n sintonización f; (MUS) afinación f; **~ fork** n diapasón m.

Tunisia [tjuːˈnɪzɪə] n Túnez m.

tunnel ['tʌnl] n túnel m; (in mine) galería // vi construir un túnel/una galería.

turban ['təːbən] n turbante m.

turbine ['təːbaɪn] n turbina.

turbulence ['təːbjuləns] n (AVIAT) turbulencia.

tureen [tə'riːn] n sopera.

turf [təːf] n césped m; (clod) tepe m // vt cubrir con césped; **to ~ out** vt (col) echar a la calle.

turgid ['təːdʒɪd] a (prose) pesado.

Turk [təːk] n turco/a.

Turkey ['təːkɪ] n Turquía.

turkey ['təːkɪ] n pavo.

Turkish ['təːkɪʃ] a turco.

turmoil ['təːmɔɪl] n desorden m, alboroto.

turn [təːn] n turno; (in road) curva; (THEATRE) número; (MED) ataque m // vt girar, volver; (collar, steak) dar la vuelta a; (change): **to ~ sth into** convertir algo en // vi volver; (person: look back) volverse; (reverse direction) dar la vuelta; (milk) cortarse; (change) cambiar; (become) convertirse en; **a good ~** un favor; **it gave me quite a ~** me dio un susto; **'no left ~'** (AUT) 'prohibido girar a la izquierda'; **it's your ~** te toca a ti; **in ~** por turnos; **by take ~s** turnarse; **to ~ away** vi apartar la vista; vt volver; **to ~ back** vi volverse atrás; **to ~ down** vt (refuse) rechazar; (reduce) bajar; (fold) doblar; **to ~ in** vi (col: go to bed) acostarse // vt (fold) doblar hacia dentro; **to ~ off** vi (from road) desviarse // vt (light, radio etc) apagar; (engine) parar; **to ~ on** vt (light, radio etc) encender, prender (LAm); (engine) poner en marcha; **to ~ out** vt (light, gas) apagar // vi: **to ~ out to be...** resultar ser...; **to ~ over** vi (person) volverse // vt (object) dar la vuelta a; (page) volver; **to ~ round** vi volverse; (rotate) girar; **to ~ up** vi (person) llegar, presentarse; (lost object) aparecer // vt (gen) subir; **~ing** n (in road)

vuelta; **~ing point** n (fig) momento decisivo.

turnip ['təːnɪp] n nabo.

turnout ['təːnaut] n concurrencia.

turnover ['təːnəuvəˀ] n (COMM: amount of money) facturación f; (: of goods) movimiento.

turnpike ['təːnpaɪk] n (US) autopista de peaje.

turnstile ['təːnstaɪl] n torniquete m.

turntable ['təːnteɪbl] n plato.

turn-up ['təːnʌp] n (Brit: on trousers) vuelta.

turpentine ['təːpəntaɪn] n (also: turps) trementina.

turquoise ['təːkwɔɪz] n (stone) turquesa // a color turquesa.

turret ['tʌrɪt] n torreón m.

turtle ['təːtl] n galápago; **~neck (sweater)** n (jersey m de) cuello cisne.

tusk [tʌsk] n colmillo.

tussle ['tʌsl] n lucha, pelea.

tutor ['tjuːtəˀ] n profesor(a) m/f; **~ial** [-'təːrɪəl] n (SCOL) seminario.

tuxedo [tʌk'siːdəu] n (US) smoking m.

TV [tiː'viː] n abbr (= television) tele f.

twang [twæŋ] n (of instrument) punteado; (of voice) timbre m nasal.

tweezers ['twiːzəz] npl pinzas fpl (de depilar).

twelfth [twelfθ] a duodécimo.

twelve [twelv] num doce; **at ~ o'clock** (midday) a mediodía; (midnight) a medianoche.

twentieth ['twentɪɪθ] a vigésimo.

twenty ['twentɪ] num veinte.

twice [twaɪs] ad dos veces; **~ as much** dos veces más.

twiddle ['twɪdl] vt, vi: **to ~ (with) sth** dar vueltas a algo; **to ~ one's thumbs** (fig) estar mano sobre mano.

twig [twɪg] n ramita // vi (col) caer en la cuenta.

twilight ['twaɪlaɪt] n crepúsculo.

twin [twɪn] a, n gemelo/a m/f // vt hermanar; **~-bedded room** n habitación f con camas gemelas.

twine [twaɪn] n bramante m // vi (plant) enroscarse.

twinge [twɪndʒ] n (of pain) punzada, (of conscience) remordimiento.

twinkle ['twɪŋkl] vi centellear; (eyes) parpadear.

twirl [twə:l] n giro // vt dar vueltas a // vi piruetear.

twist [twɪst] n (action) torsión f; (in road, coil) vuelta; (in wire, flex) doblez f; (in story) giro // vt torcer; torcer; (roll around) enrollar; (fig) deformar // vi serpentear.

twit [twɪt] n (col) tonto.

twitch [twɪtʃ] // vi moverse nerviosamente.

two [tu:] num dos; **to put ~ and ~ together** (fig) atar cabos; **~-door** a (AUT) de dos puertas; **~-faced** a (pej: person) falso; **~-fold** ad: **to increase ~fold** doblarse; **~-piece (suit)** n traje m de dos piezas; **~-piece (swimsuit)** n dos piezas m inv, bikini m; **~-seater plane/car** n avión m/coche m de dos plazas; **~some** n (people) pareja; **~-way** a: **~-way traffic** circulación f de dos sentidos.

tycoon [taɪ'ku:n] n: **(business) ~** magnate m/f.

type [taɪp] n (category) tipo, género; (model) modelo; (TYP) tipo, letra // vt (letter etc) escribir a máquina; **~-cast** (actor) encasillado; **~-face** n tipo; **~-script** n texto mecanografiado; **~-writer** n máquina de escribir; **~-written** a mecanografiado.

typhoid ['taɪfɔɪd] n tifoidea.

typical ['tɪpɪkl] a típico.

typing ['taɪpɪŋ] n mecanografía.

typist ['taɪpɪst] n mecanógrafo/a.

tyranny ['tɪrənɪ] n tiranía.

tyrant ['taɪərnt] n tirano/a.

tyre, (US) tire ['taɪə*] n neumático, llanta (LAm); **~ pressure** n presión f de los neumáticos.

U

U-bend ['ju:'bend] n (AUT, in pipe) recodo.

udder ['ʌdə*] n ubre f.

UFO ['ju:fəu] n abbr = (unidentified flying object) OVNI m.

ugh [ə:h] excl ¡uf!

ugly ['ʌglɪ] a feo; (dangerous) peligroso.

UK n abbr = **United Kingdom**.

ulcer ['ʌlsə*] n úlcera.

Ulster ['ʌlstə*] n Ulster m.

ulterior [ʌl'tɪərɪə*] a ulterior; **~ motive** segundas intenciones fpl.

ultimate ['ʌltɪmət] a último, final; (authority) más alto; **~-ly** ad (in the end) por último, al final; (fundamentally) a or en fin de cuentas.

ultrasound [ʌltrə'saund] n (MED) ultrasonido.

umbilical cord [ʌm'bɪlɪkl-] n cordón m umbilical.

umbrella [ʌm'brelə] n paraguas m inv.

umpire ['ʌmpaɪə*] n árbitro.

umpteen [ʌmp'ti:n] a enésimos/as; **for the ~th time** por enésima vez.

UN n abbr = **United Nations (Organization)**.

unable [ʌn'eɪbl] a: **to be ~ to do sth** no poder hacer algo.

unaccompanied [ʌnə'kʌmpənɪd] a no acompañado.

unaccountably [ʌnə'kauntəblɪ] ad inexplicablemente.

unaccustomed [ʌnə'kʌstəmd] a: **to be ~ to** no estar acostumbrado a.

unanimous [ju:'nænɪməs] a unánime; **~-ly** ad unánimemente.

unarmed [ʌn'ɑ:md] a desarmado.

unassuming [ʌnə'sju:mɪŋ] a modesto, sin pretensiones.

unattached [ʌnə'tætʃt] a (person) sin pareja; (part etc) suelto.

unattended [ʌnə'tendɪd] a (car, luggage) sin atender.

unauthorized [ʌn'ɔ:θəraɪzd] a no

autorizado.

unavoidable [ʌnə'vɔɪdəbl] a inevitable.

unaware [ʌnə'wɛə*] a: to be ~ of ignorar; ~s ad de improviso.

unbalanced [ʌn'bælənst] a desequilibrado; (mentally) trastornado.

unbearable [ʌn'bɛərəbl] a insoportable.

unbeknown(st) [ʌnbɪ'nəun(st)] ad: ~ to me sin saberlo yo.

unbelievable [ʌnbɪ'liːvəbl] a increíble.

unbend [ʌn'bɛnd] (irg: like bend) vi (fig: person) relajarse // vt (wire) enderezar.

unbiased [ʌn'baɪəst] a imparcial.

unborn [ʌn'bɔːn] a que va a nacer.

unbreakable [ʌn'breɪkəbl] a irrompible.

unbroken [ʌn'brəukən] a (seal) intacto; (series) continuo; (record) no batido; (spirit) indómito.

unbutton [ʌn'bʌtn] vt desabrochar.

uncalled-for [ʌn'kɔːldfɔː*] a gratuito, inmerecido.

uncanny [ʌn'kænɪ] a extraño, extraordinario.

unceasing [ʌn'siːsɪŋ] a incesante.

unceremonious ['ʌnsɛrɪ'məunɪəs] a (abrupt, rude) brusco, brusco.

uncertain [ʌn'sɜːtn] a incierto; (indecisive) indeciso; ~ty n incertidumbre f.

unchecked [ʌn'tʃɛkt] a desenfrenado.

uncivilized [ʌn'sɪvɪlaɪzd] a (gen) inculto; (fig: behaviour etc) bárbaro.

uncle [ʌŋkl] n tío.

uncomfortable [ʌn'kʌmfətəbl] a incómodo; (uneasy) inquieto.

uncommon [ʌn'kɔmən] a poco común, raro.

uncompromising [ʌn'kɔmprəmaɪzɪŋ] a intransigente.

unconcerned [ʌnkən'sɜːnd] a indiferente, despreocupado.

unconditional [ʌnkən'dɪʃənl] a incondicional.

unconscious [ʌn'kɔnʃəs] a sin senti-

do; (unaware) inconsciente // n: the ~ el inconsciente; ~ly ad inconscientemente.

uncontrollable [ʌnkən'trəuləbl] a (temper) indomable; (laughter) incontenible.

unconventional [ʌnkən'vɛnʃənl] a poco convencional.

uncouth [ʌn'kuːθ] a grosero, inculto.

uncover [ʌn'kʌvə*] vt (gen) descubrir; (take lid off) destapar.

undecided [ʌndɪ'saɪdɪd] a (character) indeciso; (question) no resuelto, pendiente.

under ['ʌndə*] prep debajo de; (less than) menos de; (according to) según, de acuerdo con // ad debajo, abajo; ~ there allí abajo; ~ construction bajo construcción.

under... ['ʌndə*] pref sub; ~ -age a menor de edad; ~**carriage** n (Brit AVIAT) tren m de aterrizaje; ~**charge** vt cobrar menos de la cuenta; ~**clothes** npl ropa sg interior or íntima (LAm); ~**coat** n (paint) primera mano; ~**cover** a clandestino; ~**current** n corriente f submarina; (fig) tendencia oculta; ~**cut** vt irg vender más barato que; ~**developed** a subdesarrollado; ~**dog** n desvalido/a; ~**done** a (CULIN) poco hecho; ~**estimate** vt subestimar; ~**exposed** a (PHOT) subexpuesto; ~**fed** a subalimentado; ~**foot** ad: it's wet ~foot el suelo está mojado; ~**go** vt irg sufrir; (treatment) recibir; ~**graduate** n estudiante m/f; ~**ground** n (Brit: railway) metro; (POL) movimiento clandestino // a subterráneo; ~**growth** n maleza; ~**hand(ed)** a (fig) socarrón; ~**lie** vt irg (fig) ser la razón fundamental de; ~**line** vt subrayar; ~**ling** ['ʌndəlɪŋ] n (pej) subalterno/a; ~**mine** vt socavar, minar; ~**neath** [ʌndə'niːθ] ad debajo // prep debajo de, bajo; ~**paid** a mal pagado; ~**pants** npl calzoncillos mpl; ~**pass** n (Brit) paso subterráneo; ~**privileged** a desvalido;

~**rate** vt menospreciar, subestimar; ~**shirt** n (US) camiseta; ~**shorts** npl (US) calzoncillos mpl; ~**side** n parte f inferior, revés m; ~**skirt** n (Brit) enaguas fpl.

understand [ʌndə'stænd] vt, vi entender, comprender; (assume) tener entendido; ~**able** a comprensible; ~**ing** a comprensivo // n comprensión f, entendimiento f; (agreement) acuerdo.

understatement ['ʌndəsteitmənt] n subestimación f; (modesty) modestia (excesiva).

understood [ʌndə'stud] pt, pp of understand // a entendido; (implied): **it is** ~ that se sobreentiende que.

understudy ['ʌndəstʌdɪ] n suplente m/f.

undertake [ʌndə'teɪk] (irg: like take) vt emprender; **to** ~ **to do sth** comprometerse a hacer algo.

undertaker ['ʌndəteɪkə*] n director(a) m/f de pompas fúnebres.

undertaking [ʌndə'teɪkɪŋ] n empresa; (promise) promesa.

undertone ['ʌndətəun] n: **in an** ~ en voz baja.

underwater [ʌndə'wɔ:tə*] ad bajo el agua // a submarino.

underwear ['ʌndəwɛə*] n ropa interior or íntima (LAm).

underworld ['ʌndəwə:ld] n (of crime) hampa, inframundo.

underwriter ['ʌndəraɪtə*] n (INSURANCE) asegurador(a) m/f.

undies ['ʌndɪz] npl (col) ropa interior or íntima (LAm).

undo [ʌn'du:] (irg: like do) vt deshacer; ~**ing** n ruina, perdición f.

undoubted [ʌn'dautɪd] a indudable; ~**ly** ad indudablemente, sin duda.

undress [ʌn'drɛs] vi desnudarse.

undue [ʌn'dju:] a indebido, excesivo.

undulating ['ʌndjuleɪtɪŋ] a ondulante.

unduly [ʌn'dju:lɪ] ad excesivamente, demasiado.

unearth [ʌn'ə:θ] vt desenterrar.

unearthly [ʌn'ə:θlɪ] a (hour) inverosímil.

uneasy [ʌn'i:zɪ] a intranquilo; (worried) preocupado.

uneducated [ʌn'ɛdjukeɪtɪd] a ignorante, inculto.

unemployed [ʌnɪm'plɔɪd] a parado, sin trabajo // n: **the** ~ los parados.

unemployment [ʌnɪm'plɔɪmənt] n paro, desempleo.

unending [ʌn'ɛndɪŋ] a interminable.

unerring [ʌn'ə:rɪŋ] a infalible.

uneven [ʌn'i:vn] a desigual; (road etc) quebrado.

unexpected [ʌnɪk'spɛktɪd] a inesperado; ~**ly** ad inesperadamente.

unfailing [ʌn'feɪlɪŋ] a (support) indefectible; (energy) inagotable.

unfair [ʌn'fɛə*] a: ~ **(to sb)** injusto (con uno).

unfaithful [ʌn'feɪθful] a infiel.

unfamiliar [ʌnfə'mɪlɪə*] a extraño, desconocido.

unfashionable [ʌn'fæʃnəbl] a pasado or fuera de moda.

unfasten [ʌn'fa:sn] vt desatar.

unfavourable, (US) **unfavorable** [ʌn'feɪvərəbl] a desfavorable.

unfeeling [ʌn'fi:lɪŋ] a insensible.

unfinished [ʌn'fɪnɪʃt] a inacabado, sin terminar.

unfit [ʌn'fɪt] a indispuesto, enfermo; (incompetent) incapaz; ~ **for work** no apto para trabajar.

unfold [ʌn'fəuld] vt desdoblar; (fig) revelar // vi abrirse; revelarse.

unforeseen ['ʌnfɔ:'si:n] a imprevisto.

unforgettable [ʌnfə'gɛtəbl] a inolvidable.

unforgivable [ʌnfə'gɪvəbl] a imperdonable.

unfortunate [ʌn'fɔ:tʃnət] a desgraciado; (event, remark) inoportuno; ~**ly** ad desgraciadamente.

unfounded [ʌn'faundɪd] a infundado.

unfriendly [ʌn'frɛndlɪ] a antipático.

ungainly [ʌn'geɪnlɪ] a (walk) desgarbado.

ungodly [ʌnˈgɔdlɪ] *a*: **at an ~ hour** a una hora inverosímil.

ungrateful [ʌnˈgreɪtful] *a* ingrato.

unhappiness [ʌnˈhæpɪnɪs] *n* tristeza.

unhappy [ʌnˈhæpɪ] *a* (*sad*) triste; (*unfortunate*) desgraciado; (*childhood*) infeliz; **~ with** (*arrangements etc*) poco contento con, descontento de.

unharmed [ʌnˈhɑːmd] *a* (*person*) ileso.

unhealthy [ʌnˈhelθɪ] *a* (*gen*) malsano; (*person*) enfermizo.

unheard-of [ʌnˈhɜːdɔv] *a* inaudito, sin precedente.

unhook [ʌnˈhuk] *vt* desenganchar; (*from wall*) descolgar; (*undo*) desabrochar.

unhurt [ʌnˈhɜːt] *a* ileso.

uniform [ˈjuːnɪfɔːm] *n* uniforme *m* // *a* uniforme; **~ity** [-ˈfɔːmɪtɪ] *n* uniformidad *f*.

unify [ˈjuːnɪfaɪ] *vt* unificar, unir.

uninhabited [ʌnɪnˈhæbɪtɪd] *a* desierto.

unintentional [ʌnɪnˈtenʃənəl] *a* involuntario.

union [ˈjuːnjən] *n* unión *f*; (*also*: **trade ~**) `sindicato // cpd` sindical; **U~ Jack** *n* bandera del Reino Unido.

unique [juːˈniːk] *a* único.

unison [ˈjuːnɪsn] *n*: **in ~** (*speak*, *reply*) al unísono; **in ~ with** junto con.

unit [ˈjuːnɪt] *n* unidad *f*; (*team*, *squad*) grupo; **kitchen ~** módulo de cocina.

unite [juːˈnaɪt] *vt* unir // *vi* unirse; **~d** *a* unido; **U~d Kingdom (UK)** *n* Reino Unido; **U~d Nations (Organization) (UN, UNO)** *n* Naciones *fpl* Unidas (ONU *f*); **U~d States (of America) (US, USA)** *n* Estados *mpl* Unidos (EE.UU.).

unit trust *n* (*Brit*) bono fiduciario.

unity [ˈjuːnɪtɪ] *n* unidad *f*.

universal [juːnɪˈvɜːsl] *a* universal.

universe [ˈjuːnɪvɜːs] *n* universo.

university [juːnɪˈvɜːsɪtɪ] *n* universidad *f*.

unjust [ʌnˈdʒʌst] *a* injusto.

unkempt [ʌnˈkempt] *a* descuidado; (*hair*) despeinado.

unkind [ʌnˈkaɪnd] *a* poco amable; (*comment etc*) cruel.

unknown [ʌnˈnəʊn] *a* desconocido.

unlawful [ʌnˈlɔːful] *a* ilegal, ilícito.

unleash [ʌnˈliːʃ] *vt* desatar.

unless [ʌnˈles] *conj* a menos que; **~ he comes** a menos que venga; **~ otherwise stated** salvo indicación contraria.

unlike [ʌnˈlaɪk] *a* distinto // *prep* a diferencia de.

unlikely [ʌnˈlaɪklɪ] *a* improbable.

unlisted [ʌnˈlɪstɪd] *a* (*US TEL*) que no consta en la guía.

unload [ʌnˈləʊd] *vt* descargar.

unlock [ʌnˈlɔk] *vt* abrir (con llave).

unlucky [ʌnˈlʌkɪ] *a* desgraciado; (*object*, *number*) que da mala suerte; **to be ~** tener mala suerte.

unmarried [ʌnˈmærɪd] *a* soltero.

unmistakable [ʌnmɪsˈteɪkəbl] *a* inconfundible.

unmitigated [ʌnˈmɪtɪgeɪtɪd] *a* rematado, absoluto.

unnatural [ʌnˈnætʃrəl] *a* (*gen*) antinatural; (*manner*) afectado; (*habit*) perverso.

unnecessary [ʌnˈnesəsərɪ] *a* innecesario, inútil.

unnoticed [ʌnˈnəʊtɪst] *a*: **to go ~** pasar desapercibido.

UNO [ˈjuːnəʊ] *n abbr* = **United Nations Organization**.

unobtainable [ʌnəbˈteɪnəbl] *a* inconseguible; (*TEL*) inexistente.

unobtrusive [ʌnəbˈtruːsɪv] *a* discreto.

unofficial [ʌnəˈfɪʃl] *a* no oficial.

unpack [ʌnˈpæk] *vi* deshacer las maletas, desempacar (*LAm*).

unpalatable [ʌnˈpælətəbl] *a* (*truth*) desagradable.

unparalleled [ʌnˈpærəleld] *a* (*unequalled*) sin par; (*unique*) sin precedentes.

unpleasant |ʌnˈpleznt| a (*disagreeable*) desagradable; (*person, manner*) antipático.

unplug |ʌnˈplʌg| vt desenchufar, desconectar.

unpopular |ʌnˈpɔpjuləˣ| a poco popular.

unprecedented |ʌnˈpresidəntid| a sin precedentes.

unpredictable |ʌnprɪˈdɪktəbl| a imprevisible.

unprofessional |ʌnprəˈfeʃənl| a: ~ conduct negligencia.

unqualified |ʌnˈkwɔlɪfaɪd| a sin título, no cualificado; (*success*) total, incondicional.

unquestionably |ʌnˈkwestʃənəblɪ| ad indiscutiblemente.

unravel |ʌnˈrævl| vt desenmarañar.

unreal |ʌnˈrɪəl| a irreal.

unrealistic |ʌnrɪəˈlɪstɪk| a poco realista.

unreasonable |ʌnˈriːznəbl| a irrazonable; (*demand*) excesivo.

unrelated |ʌnrɪˈleɪtɪd| a sin relación; (*family*) no emparentado.

unreliable |ʌnrɪˈlaɪəbl| a (*person*) informal; (*machine*) poco fiable.

unremitting |ʌnrɪˈmɪtɪŋ| a constante.

unreservedly |ʌnrɪˈzɜːvɪdlɪ| ad sin reserva.

unrest |ʌnˈrest| n inquietud f, malestar m; (*POL*) disturbios mpl.

unroll |ʌnˈrəul| vt desenrollar.

unruly |ʌnˈruːlɪ| a indisciplinado.

unsafe |ʌnˈseɪf| a peligroso.

unsaid |ʌnˈsed| a: to leave sth ~ dejar algo sin decir.

unsatisfactory |ˈʌnsætɪsˈfæktərɪ| a poco satisfactorio.

unsavoury, (*US*) **unsavory** |ʌnˈseɪvərɪ| a (*fig*) repugnante.

unscathed |ʌnˈskeɪðd| a ileso.

unscrew |ʌnˈskruː| vt destornillar.

unscrupulous |ʌnˈskruːpjuləs| a sin escrúpulos.

unsettled |ʌnˈsetld| a inquieto; (*situation*) inestable; (*weather*) variable.

unshaven |ʌnˈʃeɪvn| a sin afeitar.

unsightly |ʌnˈsaɪtlɪ| a feo.

unskilled |ʌnˈskɪld| a: ~ workers mano fsg de obra no cualificada.

unspeakable |ʌnˈspiːkəbl| a indecible; (*awful*) incalificable.

unstable |ʌnˈsteɪbl| a inestable.

unsteady |ʌnˈstedɪ| a inestable.

unstuck |ʌnˈstʌk| a: to come ~ despegarse; (*fig*) fracasar.

unsuccessful |ˈʌnsəkˈsesful| a (*attempt*) infructuoso; (*writer, proposal*) sin éxito; to be ~ (*in attempting sth*) no tener éxito, fracasar; **~ly** ad en vano, sin éxito.

unsuitable |ʌnˈsuːtəbl| a inapropiado; (*time*) inoportuno.

unsure |ʌnˈʃuəˣ| a inseguro, poco seguro.

unsympathetic |ˈʌnsɪmpəˈθetɪk| a poco comprensivo.

untapped |ʌnˈtæpt| a (*resources*) sin explotar.

unthinkable |ʌnˈθɪŋkəbl| a inconcebible, impensable.

untidy |ʌnˈtaɪdɪ| a (*room*) desordenado, en desorden; (*appearance*) desaliñado.

untie |ʌnˈtaɪ| vt desatar.

until |ʌnˈtɪl| prep hasta // conj hasta que; ~ he comes hasta que venga; ~ now hasta ahora; ~ then hasta entonces.

untimely |ʌnˈtaɪmlɪ| a inoportuno; (*death*) prematuro.

untold |ʌnˈtəuld| a (*story*) nunca contado; (*suffering*) indecible; (*wealth*) incalculable.

untoward |ʌntəˈwɔːd| a (*behaviour*) impropio; (*event*) adverso.

unused |ʌnˈjuːzd| a sin usar.

unusual |ʌnˈjuːʒuəl| a insólito, poco común.

unveil |ʌnˈveɪl| vt (*statue*) descubrir.

unwavering |ʌnˈweɪvərɪŋ| a inquebrantable.

unwelcome |ʌnˈwelkəm| a (*at a bad time*) inoportuno.

unwell |ʌnˈwel| a: to feel ~ estar indispuesto.

unwieldy |ʌnˈwiːldɪ| a difícil de manejar.

unwilling [ʌn'wɪlɪŋ] *a*: to be ~ to do sth estar poco dispuesto a hacer algo; **~ly** *ad* de mala gana.

unwind [ʌn'waɪnd] (*irg: like* wind) *vt* desenvolver // *vi* (*relax*) relajarse.

unwise [ʌn'waɪz] *a* imprudente.

unwitting [ʌn'wɪtɪŋ] *a* inconsciente.

unworkable [ʌn'wəːkəbl] *a* (*plan*) impráctico.

unworthy [ʌn'wəːðɪ] *a* indigno.

unwrap [ʌn'ræp] *vt* deshacer.

unwritten [ʌn'rɪtn] *a* (*agreement*) tácito; (*rules, law*) no escrito.

KEYWORD

up [ʌp] ♦ *prep*: to go/be ~ sth subir/estar subido en algo; he went ~ the stairs/the hill subió las escaleras/la colina; **we walked/climbed ~ the hill** subimos la colina; **they live further ~ the street** viven más arriba en la calle; go ~ that road and turn left sigue por esa calle y gira a la izquierda

♦ *ad* **1** (*upwards, higher*) más arriba; ~ **in the mountains** en lo alto (de la montaña); **put it a bit higher ~** ponlo un poco más arriba or alto; ~ **there** ahí or allí arriba; ~ **above** en lo alto, por encima, arriba

2: to be ~ (*out of bed*) estar levantado; (*prices, level*) haber subido

3: ~ to (*as far as*) hasta; ~ to now hasta ahora or la fecha

4: to be ~ to (*depending on*): it's ~ to you depende de ti; he's not ~ to it (*job, task etc*) no es capaz de hacerlo; his work is not ~ to the required standard su trabajo no da la talla; (*col: be doing*): what is he ~ to? ¿que estará tramando?

♦ *n*: ~s and downs altibajos *mpl*.

up-and-coming [ʌpənd'kʌmɪŋ] *a* prometedor(a).

upbringing [ʌp'brɪŋɪŋ] *n* educación *f*.

update [ʌp'deɪt] *vt* poner al día.

upheaval [ʌp'hiːvl] *n* trastornos

mpl; (*POL*) agitación *f*.

uphill [ʌp'hɪl] *a* cuesta arriba; (*fig: task*) penoso, difícil // *ad*: to go ~ ir cuesta arriba.

uphold [ʌp'həuld] (*irg: like* hold) *vt* sostener.

upholstery [ʌp'həulstərɪ] *n* tapicería.

upkeep [ʌpkiːp] *n* mantenimiento.

upon [ə'pɔn] *prep* sobre.

upper [ʌpə*] *a* superior, de arriba // *n* (*of shoe: also*: ~s) pala; **~-class** *a* de clase alta; **~ hand**: to have the ~ hand tener la sartén por el mango; **~most** *a* el más alto; **what was ~most in my mind** lo que me preocupaba más.

upright [ʌpraɪt] *a* vertical; (*fig*) honrado.

uprising [ʌp'raɪzɪŋ] *n* sublevación *f*.

uproar [ʌprɔː*] *n* tumulto, escándalo.

uproot [ʌp'ruːt] *vt* desarraigar.

upset [ʌpsɛt] *n* (*to plan etc*) revés *m*, contratiempo; (*MED*) trastorno // *vt* [ʌp'sɛt] (*irg: like* set) (*glass etc*) volcar; (*spill*) derramar; (*plan*) alterar; (*person*) molestar, perturbar // *a* [ʌp'sɛt] molesto, perturbado; (*stomach*) revuelto.

upshot [ʌpʃɔt] *n* resultado.

upside-down [ʌpsaɪd'daun] *ad* al revés.

upstairs [ʌp'stɛəz] *ad* arriba // *a* (*room*) de arriba // *n* el piso superior.

upstart [ʌpstɑːt] *n* advenedizo/a.

upstream [ʌp'striːm] *ad* río arriba.

uptake [ʌpteɪk] *n*: he is quick/slow on the ~ es muy listo/torpe.

uptight [ʌp'taɪt] *a* tenso, nervioso.

up-to-date [ʌptə'deɪt] *a* moderno, actual.

upturn [ʌptəːn] *n* (*in luck*) mejora; (*COMM: in market*) resurgimiento económico.

upward [ʌpwəd] *a* ascendente; **~(s)** *ad* hacia arriba.

urban [ʌːbən] *a* urbano.

urbane [əː'beɪn] *a* cortés, urbano.

urchin [ʌːtʃɪn] *n* pilluelo, golfillo.

urge [əːdʒ] *n (force)* impulso *m*; *(desire)* deseo // *vt*: to ~ sb to do sth animar a uno a hacer algo.

urgency ['əːdʒənsi] *n* urgencia.

urgent ['əːdʒənt] *a* urgente.

urinate ['juərineit] *vi* orinar.

urine ['juərin] *n* orina, orines *mpl*.

urn [əːn] *n* urna; *(also: tea ~) n* cacharro metálico grande para hacer té.

Uruguay ['juərəgwai] *n* el Uruguay; **~an** *a*, *n* uruguayo/a *m/f*.

us [ʌs] *pron* nos; *(after prep)* nosotros/as; see also me.

US, USA *n abbr* = **United States (of America)**.

usage ['juːzidʒ] *n (LING)* uso; *(utilization)* utilización *f*.

use [juːs] *n* uso, empleo; *(usefulness)* utilidad *f* // *vt* usar, emplear; she ~**d** to do it (ella) solía or acostumbraba hacerlo; **in** ~ en uso; out ~ en desuso; to be of ~ servir; it's no ~ *(pointless)* es inútil; *(not useful)* no sirve; to be ~**d** to estar acostumbrado a, acostumbrar; to ~ **up** *vt* agotar; ~**d** *a (car)* usado; ~**ful** *a* útil; ~**fulness** *n* utilidad; ~**less** *a* inútil; ~**r** *n* usuario/a; ~**r-friendly** *a (computer)* amistoso.

usher ['ʌʃə*] *n (at wedding)* ujier *m*; *(in cinema etc)* acomodador *m*; ~**ette** [-'rɛt] *n (in cinema)* acomodadora.

USSR *n abbr*: the ~ la URSS.

usual ['juːʒuəl] *a* normal, corriente; **as** ~ como de costumbre; ~**ly** *ad* normalmente.

utensil [juː'tɛnsl] *n* utensilio; **kitchen** ~**s** batería *sg* de cocina.

uterus ['juːtərəs] *n* útero.

utilitarian [juːtɪlɪ'tɛərɪən] *a* utilitario.

utility [juː'tɪlɪtɪ] *n* utilidad *f*; ~ **room** *n* trascocina.

utilize ['juːtɪlaɪz] *vt* utilizar.

utmost ['ʌtməust] *a* mayor // *n*: to do one's ~ hacer todo lo posible.

utter ['ʌtə*] *a* total, completo // *vt* pronunciar, proferir; ~**ance** *n* palabras *fpl*, declaración *f*; ~**ly** *ad* com-

pletamente, totalmente.

U-turn ['juː'təːn] *n* viraje *m* en U.

V

v. *abbr* = **verse**; **versus**; **volt**; (= *vide*) véase.

vacancy ['veikənsi] *n (Brit: job)* vacante *f*; *(room)* cuarto libro.

vacant ['veikənt] *a* desocupado, libre; *(expression)* distraído; ~ **lot** *n (US)* solar *m*.

vacate [və'keit] *vt (house, room)* desocupar; *(job)* dejar *(vacante)*.

vacation [və'keiʃən] *n* vacaciones *fpl*, ~**er** *n (US)* turista *m/f*.

vaccinate ['væksineit] *vt* vacunar.

vaccine ['væksiːn] *n* vacuna.

vacuum ['vækjum] *n* vacío; ~ **bottle** *n (US)* = **flask**; ~ **cleaner** *n* aspiradora; ~ **flask** *n (Brit)* termo; ~-**packed** *a* empaquetado al vacío.

vagina [və'dʒainə] *n* vagina.

vagrant ['veigrənt] *n* vagabundo/a.

vague [veig] *a* vago; *(blurred: memory)* borroso; *(ambiguous)* impreciso; *(person)* distraído; ~**ly** *ad* vagamente.

vain [vein] *a (conceited)* presumido; *(useless)* vano, inútil; **in** ~ en vano.

valentine ['væləntain] *n (also: ~ card)* tarjeta del Día de los Enamorados.

valet ['vælei] *n* ayuda *m* de cámara.

valiant ['væljənt] *a* valiente.

valid ['vælid] *a* válido; *(ticket)* valedero; *(law)* vigente.

valley ['væli] *n* valle *m*.

valour, *(US)* **valor** ['vælə*] *n* valor *m*, valentía.

valuable ['væljuəbl] *a (jewel)* de valor; *(time)* valioso; ~**s** *npl* objetos *mpl* de valor.

valuation [vælju'eiʃən] *n* tasación *f*, valuación *f*.

value ['væljuː] *n* valor *m*; *(importance)* importancia *f* // *vt (fix price of)* tasar, valorar; *(esteem)* apreciar; ~ **added tax (VAT)** *n (Brit)* impuesto

sobre el valor añadido (IVA *m*); ~**d**
a (*appreciated*) apreciado.

valve [vælv] *n* (*ANAT, TECH*) válvula.

van [væn] *n* (*AUT*) furgoneta, camioneta (*LAm*); (*Brit RAIL*) furgón *m*
(de equipajes).

vandal ['vændl] *n* vándalo/a; ~**ism** *n*
vandalismo; ~**ize** *vt* dañar, destruir.

vanilla [və'nilə] *n* vainilla.

vanish ['vænɪʃ] *vi* desaparecer, esfumarse.

vanity ['vænɪtɪ] *n* vanidad *f*; ~ **case**
n neceser *m*.

vantage point ['vɑ:ntɪdʒ-] *n* (*for
views*) punto panorámico.

vapour, (*US*) **vapor** ['veɪpə*] *n* vapor *m*; (*on breath, window*) vaho.

variable ['vɛərɪəbl] *a* variable; (*person*) voluble.

variance ['vɛərɪəns] *n*: to be at ~
(with) estar en desacuerdo (con).

variation [vɛərɪ'eɪʃən] *n* variación *f*.

varicose ['værɪkəʊs] *a*: ~ **veins** várices *fpl*.

varied ['vɛərɪd] *a* variado.

variety [və'raɪətɪ] *n* variedad *f*; ~
show *n* espectáculo de variedades.

various ['vɛərɪəs] *a* varios/as,
diversos/as.

varnish ['vɑ:nɪʃ] *n* barniz *m* // *vt* barnizar; (*nails*) pintar (con esmalte).

vary ['vɛərɪ] *vt* variar; (*change*)
cambiar // *vi* variar.

vase [vɑ:z] *n* florero.

Vaseline ['væsɪli:n] *n* ® Vaselina ®.

vast [vɑ:st] *a* enorme; (*success*)
abrumador(a).

VAT [væt] *n* (*Brit*) *abbr* = **value
added tax**.

vat [væt] *n* tina, tinaja.

Vatican ['vætɪkən] *n*: the ~ el Vaticano.

vault [vɔ:lt] *n* (*of roof*) bóveda;
(*tomb*) panteón *m*; (*in bank*) cámara
acorazada // *vt* (*also*: ~ **over**) saltar
(por encima de).

vaunted ['vɔ:ntɪd] *a*: **much** ~ cacareado, alardeada.

VCR *n abbr* = **video cassette re-**

corder.

VD *n abbr* = **venereal disease.**

VDU *n abbr* = **visual display unit.**

veal [vi:l] *n* ternera.

veer [vɪə*] *vi* (*ship*) virar.

vegetable ['vedʒtəbl] *n* (*BOT*) vegetal *m*; (*edible plant*) legumbre *f*, hortaliza // *a* vegetal; ~**s** *npl* (*cooked*)
verduras *fpl*.

vegetarian [vedʒɪ'tɛərɪən] *a, n*
vegetariano/a *m/f*.

vehement ['vi:mənt] *a* vehemente,
apasionado.

vehicle ['vi:ɪkl] *n* vehículo.

veil [veɪl] *n* velo // *vt* velar.

vein [veɪn] *n* vena; (*of ore etc*) veta.

velocity [vɪ'lɒsɪtɪ] *n* velocidad *f*.

velvet ['velvɪt] *n* terciopelo.

vending machine ['vendɪŋ-] *n* distribuidor *m* automático.

vendor ['vendə*] *n* vendedor(a) *m/f*.

veneer [və'nɪə*] *n* chapa, enchapado;
(*fig*) barniz *m*.

venereal [vɪ'nɪərɪəl] *a*: ~ **disease**
(**VD**) enfermedad *f* venérea.

Venetian blind [vɪ'ni:ʃən-] *n* persiana.

Venezuela [vɛnɪ'zweɪlə] *n* Venezuela; ~**n** *a, n* venezolano/a *m/f*.

vengeance ['vendʒəns] *n* venganza;
with a ~ (*fig*) con creces.

venison ['venɪsn] *n* carne *f* de venado.

venom ['venəm] *n* veneno.

vent [vent] *n* (*opening*) abertura;
(*air-hole*) respiradero; (*in wall*) rejilla (de ventilación) // *vt* (*fig: feelings*) desahogar.

ventilate ['ventɪleɪt] *vt* ventilar;
ventilator *n* ventilador *m*.

ventriloquist [ven'trɪləkwɪst] *n*
ventrílocuo/a.

venture ['ventʃə*] *n* empresa // *vt*
arriesgar; (*opinion*) ofrecer // *vi*
arriesgarse, lanzarse.

venue ['venju:] *n* lugar *m* de reunión.

veranda(h) [və'rændə] *n* terraza;
(*with glass*) galería.

verb [və:b] *n* verbo; ~**al** *a* verbal.

verbatim [və:'beɪtɪm] *a, ad* palabra

por palabra.

verbose [vəˈbəus] a prolijo.

verdict [ˈvəːdɪkt] n veredicto, fallo; (fig) opinión f, juicio.

verge [vəːdʒ] n (Brit) borde m; to be on the ~ of sth estar a punto de hacer algo; to ~ on vt fus rayar en.

verify [ˈvɛrɪfaɪ] vt comprobar, verificar.

veritable [ˈvɛrɪtəbl] a verdadero, auténtico.

vermin [ˈvəːmɪn] npl (animals) bichos mpl; (insects, fig) sabandijas fpl.

vermouth [ˈvəːməθ] n vermut m.

versatile [ˈvəːsətaɪl] a (person) polifacético; (machine, tool etc) versátil.

verse [vəːs] n versos mpl, poesía; (stanza) estrofa; (in bible) versículo.

versed [vəːst] a: (well-)~ in versado en.

version [ˈvəːʃən] n versión f.

versus [ˈvəːsəs] prep contra.

vertebra [ˈvəːtɪbrə], pl ~e [-briː] n vértebra.

vertical [ˈvəːtɪkl] a vertical.

vertigo [ˈvəːtɪgəu] n vértigo.

verve [vəːv] n brío.

very [ˈvɛrɪ] ad muy // a: the ~ book which el mismo libro que; the ~ last el último de todos; at the ~ least al menos; ~ much muchísimo.

vessel [ˈvɛsl] n (ANAT) vaso; (ship) barco; (container) vasija.

vest [vɛst] n (Brit) camiseta; (US: waistcoat) chaleco; ~ed interests npl (COMM) intereses mpl creados.

vestibule [ˈvɛstɪbjuːl] n vestíbulo.

vestige [ˈvɛstɪdʒ] n vestigio, rastro.

vestry [ˈvɛstrɪ] n sacristía.

vet [vɛt] n abbr = **veterinary surgeon** // vt repasar, revisar.

veteran [ˈvɛtərn] n veterano.

veterinary [ˈvɛtrɪnərɪ] a veterinario; ~ **surgeon**, (US) **veterinarian** n veterinario/a m/f.

veto [ˈviːtəu], pl ~es n veto // vt prohibir, vedar.

vex [vɛks] vt fastidiar; ~ed a (question) controvertido.

VHF abbr (= very high frequency) muy alta frecuencia.

via [ˈvaɪə] prep por, por vía de.

vibrate [vaɪˈbreɪt] vi vibrar.

vicar [ˈvɪkə*] n párroco (de la Iglesia Anglicana); ~**age** n parroquia.

vicarious [vɪˈkɛərɪəs] a indirecto.

vice [vaɪs] n (evil) vicio; (TECH) torno de banco.

vice- [vaɪs] pref vice-; ~**chairman** n vicepresidente m.

vice versa [ˈvaɪsɪˈvəːsə] ad viceversa.

vicinity [vɪˈsɪnɪtɪ] n vecindad f; in the ~ (of) cercano (a).

vicious [ˈvɪʃəs] a (remark) malicioso; (blow) fuerte; ~ **circle** n círculo vicioso.

victim [ˈvɪktɪm] n víctima; ~**ize** vt (strikers etc) tomar represalias contra.

victor [ˈvɪktə*] n vencedor(a) m/f.

victory [ˈvɪktərɪ] n victoria.

video [ˈvɪdɪəu] cpd video // n (~ film) videofilm m; (also: ~ cassette) videocassette f; (also: ~ cassette recorder) videograbadora; ~ **tape** n cinta de vídeo.

vie [vaɪ] vi: to ~ with competir con.

Vienna [vɪˈɛnə] n Viena.

Vietnam [ˈvjɛtˈnæm] n Vietnam m.

view [vjuː] n vista, perspectiva; (landscape) paisaje m; (opinion) opinión f, criterio // vt (look at) mirar; (examine) examinar; ~ (in museum etc) expuesto; in full ~ (of) en plena vista de; in ~ of the fact that en vista del hecho de que; ~**er** n (small projector) visionadora; (TV) televidente m/f; ~**finder** n visor m de imagen; ~**point** n punto de vista.

vigil [ˈvɪdʒɪl] n vigilia.

vigorous [ˈvɪgərəs] a enérgico, vigoroso.

vigour, (US) **vigor** [ˈvɪgə*] n energía, vigor m.

vile [vaɪl] a (action) vil, infame; (smell) asqueroso.

vilify [ˈvɪlɪfaɪ] vt vilipendiar.

villa ['vɪlə] n (country house) casa de campo; (suburban house) chalet m.

village ['vɪlɪdʒ] n aldea; **~r** n aldeano/a.

villain ['vɪlən] n (scoundrel) malvado/a; (criminal) maleante m/f.

vindicate ['vɪndɪkeɪt] vt vindicar, justificar.

vindictive [vɪn'dɪktɪv] a vengativo.

vine [vaɪn] n vid f.

vinegar ['vɪnɪɡə*] n vinagre m.

vineyard ['vɪnjɑːd] n viña, viñedo.

vintage ['vɪntɪdʒ] n (year) vendimia, cosecha; ~ **wine** n vino añejo.

vinyl ['vaɪnl] n vinilo.

viola [vɪ'əʊlə] n (MUS) viola.

violate ['vaɪəleɪt] vt violar.

violence ['vaɪələns] n violencia.

violent ['vaɪələnt] a (gen) violento; (pain) intenso.

violet ['vaɪələt] a violado, violeta // n (plant) violeta.

violin [vaɪə'lɪn] n violín m; ~**ist** n violinista m/f.

VIP n abbr (= very important person) VIP m.

viper ['vaɪpə*] n víbora.

virgin ['vɜːdʒɪn] n virgen f // a virgen.

Virgo ['vɜːɡəʊ] n Virgo.

virile ['vɪraɪl] a viril.

virtually ['vɜːtjʊəlɪ] ad prácticamente.

virtue ['vɜːtjuː] n virtud f; **by ~ of** en virtud de.

virtuous ['vɜːtjʊəs] a virtuoso.

virus ['vaɪərəs] n virus m.

visa ['viːzə] n visado, visa (LAm).

vis-à-vis [viːzə'viː] prep con respecto a.

visibility [vɪzɪ'bɪlɪtɪ] n visibilidad f.

visible ['vɪzəbl] a visible.

vision ['vɪʒən] n (sight) vista; (foresight, in dream) visión f.

visit ['vɪzɪt] n visita // vt (person) visitar, hacer una visita a; (place) ir a, (ir a) conocer; ~**ing hours** npl (in hospital etc) horas de visita; ~**or** n (in museum) visitante m/f; (tourist) turista m/f; **to have ~ors** (at

home) tener visita; ~**ors' book** n libro de visitas.

visor ['vaɪzə*] n visera.

vista ['vɪstə] n vista, panorama.

visual ['vɪzjʊəl] a visual; ~ **aid** n medio visual; ~ **display unit (VDU)** n unidad f de presentación visual (UPV); ~**ize** vt imaginarse; (foresee) prever.

vital ['vaɪtl] a (essential) esencial, imprescindible; (dynamic) dinámico; ~**ly** ad: ~**ly important** de primera importancia; ~ **statistics** npl (fig) medidas fpl vitales.

vitamin ['vɪtəmɪn] n vitamina.

vivacious [vɪ'veɪʃəs] a vivaz, alegre.

vivid ['vɪvɪd] a (account) gráfico; (light) intenso; (imagination) vivo; ~**ly** ad (describe) gráficamente; (remember) como si fuera hoy.

V-neck ['viːnek] n cuello de pico.

vocabulary [vəʊ'kæbjʊlərɪ] n vocabulario.

vocal ['vəʊkl] a vocal; (articulate) elocuente; ~ **chords** npl cuerdas fpl vocales.

vocation [vəʊ'keɪʃən] n vocación f; ~**al** a profesional.

vociferous [və'sɪfərəs] a vociferante.

vodka ['vɒdkə] n vodka m.

vogue [vəʊɡ] n boga, moda.

voice [vɔɪs] n voz f // vt (opinion) expresar.

void [vɔɪd] n vacío; (hole) hueco // a (invalid) nulo, inválido; (empty): ~ **of** carente o desprovisto de.

volatile ['vɒlətaɪl] a volátil.

volcano [vɒl'keɪnəʊ], pl **-es** n volcán m.

volition [və'lɪʃən] n: **of one's own ~** de su propia voluntad.

volley ['vɒlɪ] n (of gunfire) descarga; (of stones etc) lluvia; (TENNIS etc) ~**ball** n vol(e)ibol m.

volt [vəʊlt] n voltio; ~**age** n voltaje m.

voluble ['vɒljʊbl] a locuaz, hablador(a).

volume ['vɒljuːm] n (gen) volumen m; (book) tomo.

voluntarily [ˈvɒləntrɪlɪ] *ad* libremente, voluntariamente.

voluntary [ˈvɒləntərɪ] *a* voluntario; (*statement*) espontáneo.

volunteer [vɒlənˈtɪə*] *n* voluntario/a // *vi* ofrecerse (de voluntario); **to ~ to do** ofrecerse a hacer.

vomit [ˈvɒmɪt] *n* vómito // *vt, vi* vomitar.

vote [vəut] *n* voto; (*votes cast*) votación *f*; (*right to ~*) derecho de votar; (*franchise*) sufragio *f* // *vi* elegir // *vi* votar, ir a votar; **~ of chairman** *n* votante *m/f*; **~r** *n* votante *m/f*; **voting** *n* votación *f*.

vouch [vautʃ]: **to ~ for** *vt fus* garantizar, responder de.

voucher [ˈvautʃə*] *n* (*for meal, petrol*) vale *m*.

vow [vau] *n* voto // *vi* jurar.

vowel [ˈvauəl] *n* vocal *f*.

voyage [ˈvɔɪdʒ] *n* (*journey*) viaje *m*; (*crossing*) travesía.

vulgar [ˈvʌlgə*] *a* (*rude*) ordinario, grosero; (*in bad taste*) de mal gusto; **~ity** [ˈgærɪtɪ] *n* grosería; mal gusto.

vulnerable [ˈvʌlnərəbl] *a* vulnerable.

vulture [ˈvʌltʃə*] *n* buitre *m*.

W

wad [wɒd] *n* (*of cotton wool, paper*) bolita; (*of banknotes etc*) fajo.

waddle [ˈwɒdl] *vi* anadear.

wade [weid] *vi*: **to ~ through** (*water*) caminar por; (*fig: a book*) leer con dificultad; **wading pool** *n* (US) piscina para niños.

wafer [ˈweifə*] *n* (*biscuit*) galleta, barquillo; (*COMPUT, REL*) oblea.

waffle [ˈwɒfl] *n* (*CULIN*) gofre *m* // *vi* dar el rollo.

waft [wɒft] *vt* llevar por el aire // *vi* flotar.

wag [wæg] *vt* menear, agitar // *vi* moverse, menearse.

wage [weidʒ] *n* (*also*: **~s**) sueldo, salario // *vt*: **to ~ war** hacer la guerra; **~ earner** *n* asalariado/a;

packet *n* sobre *m* de paga.

wager [ˈweidʒə*] *n* apuesta // *vt* apostar.

waggle [ˈwægl] *vt* menear, mover.

wag(g)on [ˈwægən] *n* (*horse-drawn*) carro; (*Brit RAIL*) vagón *m*.

wail [weil] *n* gemido // *vi* gemir.

waist [weist] *n* cintura, talle *m*; **~coat** *n* (*Brit*) chaleco; **~line** *n* talle *m*.

wait [weit] *n* espera; (*interval*) pausa // *vi* esperar; **to lie in ~ for** acechar a; **I can't ~ to** (*fig*) estoy deseando; **to ~ for** esperar (a); **to ~ behind** *vi* quedarse; **to ~ on** *vt fus* servir a; **~er** *n* camarero; **~ing** *n*: **'no ~ing'** prohibido estacionarse'; **~ing list** *n* lista de espera; **~ing room** *n* sala de espera; **~ress** *n* camarera.

waive [weiv] *vt* suspender.

wake [weik] *vb* (*pt* **woke** *or* **waked**, *pp* **woken** *or* **waked**) *vt* (*also*: **~ up**) despertar // *vi* (*also*: **~ up**) despertarse // *n* (*for dead person*) vela, velatorio; (*NAUT*) estela; **~n** *vt, vi* = **wake**.

Wales [weilz] *n* País *m* de Gales.

walk [wɔːk] *n* (*stroll*) paseo; (*hike*) excursión *f* a pie, caminata; (*gait*) paso, andar *m*; (*in park etc*) paseo, alameda // *vi* andar, caminar; (*for pleasure, exercise*) pasearse // *vt* (*distance*) recorrer a pie, andar; (*dog*) pasear; **10 minutes' ~ from here** a 10 minutos de aquí andando; **people from all ~s of life** gente de todas las esferas; **to walk out on** *vt fus* (*col*) abandonar; **~er** *n* (*person*) paseante *m/f*, caminante *m/f*; **~ie-talkie** [ˈwɔːkiˈtɔːki] *n* walkie-talkie *m*; **~ing** *n* el andar; **~ing shoes** *npl* zapatos *mpl* para andar; **~ing stick** *n* bastón *m*; **~out** *n* (*of workers*) huelga; **~over** *n* (*col*) pan *m* comido; **~way** *n* paseo.

wall [wɔːl] *n* pared *f*; (*exterior*) muro; (*city ~ etc*) muralla; (*of a city*) amurallado; (*garden ~*) tapia.

wallet ['wɔlɪt] n cartera, billetera (LAm).

wallflower ['wɔːlflauə*] n alhelí m; to be a ~ (fig) comer pavo.

wallop ['wɔləp] vt (col) zurrar.

wallow ['wɔləu] vi revolcarse.

wallpaper ['wɔːlpeɪpə*] n papel m pintado.

wally ['wɔlɪ] n (Brit: col) palurdo/a.

walnut ['wɔːlnʌt] n nuez f; (tree) nogal m.

walrus ['wɔːlrəs], pl ~ or ~es n morsa.

waltz [wɔːlts] n vals m // vi bailar el vals.

wan |wɔn| a pálido.

wand [wɔnd] n (also: magic ~) varita (mágica).

wander ['wɔndə*] vi (person) vagar; deambular; (thoughts) divagar; (get lost) extraviarse // vt recorrer, vagar por.

wane [weɪn] vi menguar.

wangle ['wæŋgl] vt (Brit col): to ~ sth agenciarse algo.

want [wɔnt] vt (wish for) querer, desear; (need) necesitar; (lack) carecer de // n: for ~ of por falta de; ~s npl (needs) necesidades fpl; to ~ to do querer hacer; to ~ sb to do sth querer que uno haga algo; ~ing: to be found ~ing no estar a la altura de las circunstancias.

wanton ['wɔntn] a (playful) juguetón/ona; (licentious) lascivo.

war [wɔː*] n guerra; to make ~ hacer la guerra.

ward [wɔːd] n (in hospital) sala; (POL) distrito electoral; (LAW: child) pupilo/a; to ~ off (blow) desviar, parar; (attack) rechazar.

warden ['wɔːdn] n (Brit: of institution) director(a) m/f; (of park, game reserve) guardián/ana m/f; (Brit: also: traffic ~) guardia m/f.

warder ['wɔːdə*] n (Brit) guardián/ana m/f, carcelero/a.

wardrobe ['wɔːdrəub] n armario, guardarropa, ropero (esp LAm).

warehouse ['wɛəhaus] n almacén m, depósito.

wares [weəz] npl mercancías fpl.

warfare ['wɔːfɛə*] n guerra.

warhead ['wɔːhed] n cabeza armada.

warily ['wɛərɪlɪ] ad con cautela, cautelosamente.

warm [wɔːm] a caliente; (thanks) efusivo; (clothes etc) abrigado; (welcome, day) caluroso; it's ~ hace calor; I'm ~ tengo calor; to ~ up vi (room) calentarse; (person) entrar en calor; (athlete) hacer ejercicios de calentamiento; (discussion) acalorarse // vt calentar; ~-hearted a afectuoso; ~ly ad afectuosamente; ~th n calor m.

warn [wɔːn] vt avisar, advertir; ~ing n aviso, advertencia; ~ing light n luz f de advertencia; ~ing triangle n (AUT) triángulo señalizador.

warp [wɔːp] vi (wood) combarse // vt combar; (mind) pervertir.

warrant ['wɔrnt] n (LAW: to arrest) orden f de detención; (: to search) mandamiento de registro.

warranty ['wɔrəntɪ] n garantía.

warren ['wɔrən] n (of rabbits) madriguera; (fig) laberinto.

warrior ['wɔrɪə*] n guerrero/a.

Warsaw ['wɔːsɔː] n Varsovia.

warship ['wɔːʃɪp] n buque m o barco de guerra.

wart [wɔːt] n verruga.

wartime ['wɔːtaɪm] n: in ~ en tiempos de guerra, en la guerra.

wary ['wɛərɪ] a cauteloso.

was [wɔz] pt of be.

wash [wɔʃ] vt lavar // vi lavarse // n (clothes etc) lavado; (bath) baño; (of ship) estela; to have a ~ lavarse; to ~ away vt (stain) quitar lavando; (subj: river etc) llevarse; (fig) limpiar; to ~ off vt quitar lavando; to ~ up vi (Brit) fregar los platos; (US) lavarse; ~able a lavable; ~basin, (US) ~bowl n lavabo; ~cloth n (US) manopla; ~er n (TECH) arandela; ~ing n (dirty) ropa sucia; (clean) colada; ~**ing machine** n lavadora; ~**ing powder** n (Brit) detergente m (en polvo); ~**ing-up** n fregado, platos mpl (para fregar); ~**ing-up liquid** n líquido lavavajillas; ~**out** n (col) fracaso; ~**room** n servicios mpl.

wasn't ['wɔznt] = **was not**.

wasp [wɔsp] n avispa.

wastage ['weistidʒ] n desgaste m; (loss) pérdida; **natural** ~ desgaste natural.

waste [weist] n derroche m, despilfarro; (misuse) desgaste m; (of time) pérdida; (food) sobras fpl; (rubbish) basura, desperdicios mpl // a (material) de desecho; (left over) sobrante // vt (squander) malgastar, derrochar; (time) perder; (opportunity) desperdiciar; ~**s** npl (area of land) tierras fpl baldías; **to lay** ~ devastar, arrasar; **to** ~ **away** vi consumirse; ~ **disposal unit** n (Brit) triturador m de basura; ~**ful** a derrochador(a); (process) antieconómico; ~ **ground** n (Brit) terreno baldío; ~**paper basket** n papelera; ~ **pipe** n tubo de desagüe.

watch [wɔtʃ] n reloj m; (MIL: guard) centinela m; (: spell of duty) guardia // vt (look at) mirar, observar; (: match, programme) ver; (spy on, guard) vigilar; (be careful of) cuidarse de, tener cuidado de // vi ver, mirar; (keep guard) montar guardia; **to keep** ~ **on sb** mantener a uno bajo vigilancia; **to** ~ **out** vi cuidarse, tener cuidado; ~**dog** n perro guardián; ~**ful** a vigilante, sobre aviso; ~**maker** n relojero/a; ~**man** n guardián m; (also: **night** ~**man**) sereno, vigilante m (LAm); (in factory) vigilante nocturno; ~ **strap** n pulsera (de reloj).

water ['wɔ:tə*] n agua f // vt (plant) regar // vi (eyes) hacerse agua; **in British** ~**s** en aguas británicas; **to** ~ **down** vt (milk etc) aguar; ~ **closet** n wáter m; ~**colour** n acua-

rela; ~**cress** n berro; ~**fall** n cascada, salto de agua; ~ **heater** n calentador m de agua; ~**ing can** n regadera; ~ **level** n nivel m del agua; ~ **lily** n nenúfar m; ~ **line** n (NAUT) línea de flotación; ~**logged** a (boat) anegado; (ground) inundado; ~ **main** n cañería del agua; ~**mark** n (on paper) filigrana; ~**melon** n sandía; ~ **polo** n polo acuático; ~**proof** a impermeable; ~**shed** n (GEO) momento crítico; (fig) momento crítico; ~**skiing** n esquí m acuático; ~ **tank** n depósito de agua; ~**tight** a hermético; ~**way** n vía fluvial or navegable; ~**works** npl central f depuradora; ~**y** a (colour) desvaído; (coffee) aguado; (eyes) lloroso.

watt [wɔt] n vatio.

wave [weiv] n ola; (of hand) señal f con la mano; (RADIO, in hair) onda; (fig) oleada // vi agitar la mano; (flag) ondear // vt (handkerchief, gun) agitar; ~**length** n longitud f de onda.

waver ['weivə*] vi (flame etc) oscilar; (confidence) disminuir; (faith) flaquear.

wavy ['weivi] a ondulado.

wax [wæks] n cera // vt encerar // vi (moon) crecer; ~ **paper** n (US) papel apergaminado; ~**works** npl museo sg de cera.

way [wei] n camino; (distance) trayecto, recorrido; (direction) dirección f, sentido; (manner) modo, manera; (habit) costumbre f; **which** ~? – **this** ~ ¿por dónde?, ¿en qué dirección? – por aquí; **on the** ~ (en route) en (el) camino; **to be on one's** ~ estar en camino; **to be in the** ~ bloquear el camino; (fig) estorbar; **to go out of one's** ~ **to do sth** desvivirse por hacer algo; **to lose one's** ~ extraviarse; **in a** ~ en cierto modo or sentido; **by the** ~ a propósito; '~ **in**' (Brit) 'entrada'; '~ **out**' (Brit) 'salida'; **the** ~ **back** el camino de vuelta; **'give** ~' (Brit

AUT) 'ceda el paso'; **no** ~! (*col*) ¡ni pensarlo!

waylay [weɪ'leɪ] (*irg: like lay*) *vt*: I was **waylaid** (by) me entretuve (con).

wayward ['weɪwəd] *a* díscolo; caprichoso.

W.C. ['dʌblju:'si:] *n* (*Brit*) wáter *m*.

we [wi:] *pl pron* nosotros/as.

weak [wi:k] *a* débil, flojo; (*tea*) claro; ~**en** *vi* debilitarse; (*give way*) ceder // *vt* debilitar; ~**ling** *n* debilucho/a; ~**ness** *n* debilidad *f*; (*fault*) punto débil.

wealth [welθ] *n* (*money, resources*) riqueza; (*of details*) abundancia; ~**y** *a* rico.

wean [wi:n] *vt* destetar.

weapon ['wepən] *n* arma.

wear [wɛə*] *n* (*use*) uso; (*deterioration through use*) desgaste *m*; (*clothing*): **sports/baby**~ ropa de deportes/de niños // *vb* (*pt* **wore**, *pp* **worn**) *vt* (*clothes*) llevar; (*shoes*) calzar; (*damage: through use*) gastar, usar // *vi* (*last*) durar; (*rub through etc*) desgastarse; **evening** ~ (*man's*) traje *m* de etiqueta; (*woman's*) traje *m* de noche; **to** ~ **away** *vt* gastar // *vi* desgastarse; **to** ~ **down** *vt* gastar; (*strength*) agotar; **to** ~ **off** *vi* (*pain etc*) pasar, desaparecer; **to** ~ **out** *vt* desgastar; (*person, strength*) agotar; ~ **and tear** *n* desgaste *m*.

weary ['wɪərɪ] *a* (*tired*) cansado; (*dispirited*) abatido.

weasel ['wi:zl] *n* (*ZOOL*) comadreja.

weather ['wɛðə*] *n* tiempo // (*storm, crisis*) hacer frente a; **under the** ~ (*fig: ill*) indispuesto, pachucho; ~-**beaten** *a* curtido; ~**cock** *n* veleta; ~ **forecast** *n* boletín *m* meteorológico; ~ **vane** *n* = ~**cock**.

weave [wi:v], *pt* **wove**, *pp* **woven** *vt* (*cloth*) tejer; (*fig*) ~**r** *n* tejedor/a *m/f*.

web [web] *n* (*of spider*) telaraña; (*on foot*) membrana; (*network*) red *f*.

wed [wed], *pt*, *pp* **wedded** *vt* casar

// *vi* casarse.

we'd [wi:d] = **we had; we would**.

wedding ['wedɪŋ] *n* boda, casamiento; **silver/golden** ~ **anniversary** bodas *fpl* de plata/de oro; ~ **day** *n* día *m* de la boda; ~ **dress** *n* traje *m* de novia; ~ **present** *n* regalo de boda; ~ **ring** *n* alianza.

wedge [wedʒ] *n* (*of wood etc*) cuña; (*of cake*) trozo // *vt* acuñar; (*push*) apretar.

wedlock ['wedlɔk] *n* matrimonio.

Wednesday ['wednzdɪ] *n* miércoles *m inv*.

wee [wi:] *a* (*Scottish*) pequeñito.

weed [wi:d] *n* mala hierba, maleza // *vt* escardar, desherbar; ~**killer** *n* herbicida *m*; ~**y** *a* (*person*) debilucho.

week [wi:k] *n* semana; **a** ~ **today/ on Friday** de hoy/del viernes en ocho días; ~**day** *n* día *m* laborable; ~**end** *n* fin *m* de semana; ~**ly** *ad* semanalmente, cada semana // *a* semanal // *n* semanario.

weep [wi:p], *pt*, *pp* **wept** *vi*, *vt* llorar; ~**ing willow** *n* sauce *m* llorón.

weigh [weɪ] *vt*, *vi* pesar; **to** ~ **anchor** levar anclas; **to** ~ **down** *vt* sobrecargar; (*fig: with worry*) agobiar; **to** ~ **up** *vt* pesar.

weight [weɪt] *n* peso; (*metal* ~) pesa; **to lose/put on** ~ adelgazar/ engordar; ~**ing** *n* (*allowance*) (*London*) ~**ing** dietas *fpl* (*por residir en Londres*); ~ **lifter** *n* levantador(a) *m/f* de pesas; ~**y** *a* pesado.

weir [wɪə*] *n* presa.

weird [wɪəd] *a* raro, extraño.

welcome ['welkəm] *a* bienvenido // *n* bienvenida // *vt* dar la bienvenida a; (*be glad of*) alegrarse de; **thank you** — **you're** ~ gracias — de nada.

weld [weld] *n* soldadura // *vt* soldar.

welfare ['welfɛə*] *n* bienestar *m*; (*social aid*) asistencia social; **W**~ *n* (*US*) subsidio de paro; ~ **state** *n* estado del bienestar; ~ **work** *n* asistencia social.

well [wel] *n* fuente *f*, pozo // *ad* bien //

a: **to be** ~ estar bien (de salud) // *excl* ¡vaya!; ¡bueno!; **as** ~ también; **as** ~ **as** además de; ~ **done!** ¡bien hecho!; **get** ~ **soon!** ¡que te mejores pronto!; **to do** ~ (business) ir bien; (in exam) salir bien; **to** ~ **up** *vi* brotar.

we'll [wi:l] = **we will; we shall.**

well: ~-**behaved** *a* modoso; ~-**being** *n* bienestar *m*; ~-**built** *a* (person) fornido; ~-**deserved** *a* merecido; ~-**dressed** *a* bien vestido; ~-**heeled** *a* (col: wealthy) rico.

wellingtons ['wɛlɪŋtənz] *npl* (also: **wellington boots**) botas *fpl* de goma.

well: ~-**known** *a* (person) conocido; ~-**mannered** *a* educado; ~-**meaning** *a* bienintencionado; ~-**off** *a* acomodado; ~-**read** *a* leído; ~-**to-do** *a* acomodado; ~-**wisher** *n* admirador(a) *m/f*.

Welsh [wɛlʃ] *a* galés/esa // *n* (LING) galés *m*; **the** ~ *npl* los galeses; ~**man/woman** *n* galés/esa *m/f*; ~**rarebit** *n* pan *m* con queso tostado.

went [wɛnt] *pt of* **go.**

wept [wɛpt] *pt, pp of* **weep.**

were [wə:*] *pt of* **be.**

we're [wɪə*] = **we are.**

weren't [wə:nt] = **were not.**

west [wɛst] *n* oeste *m* // *a* occidental, del oeste // *ad* al or hacia el oeste; **the W~** *n* el Oeste, el Occidente; **the W~ Country** *n* (Brit) el suroeste de Inglaterra; ~**erly** *a* (wind) del oeste; ~**ern** *a* occidental // *n* (CINEMA) película del oeste; **W~ Germany** *n* Alemania Occidental; **W~ Indian** *a, n* antillano/a *m/f*; **W~ Indies** *npl* Antillas *fpl*; ~**ward(s)** *ad* hacia el oeste.

wet [wɛt] *a* (damp) húmedo; (~ through) mojado; (rainy) lluvioso; **to get** ~ mojarse; '~ **paint'** 'recién pintado'; ~ **blanket** *n*: **to be a** ~ **blanket** (fig) ser un/una aguafiestas; ~ **suit** *n* traje *m* de buzo.

we've [wi:v] = **we have.**

whack [wæk] *vt* dar un buen golpe a.

whale [weɪl] *n* (ZOOL) ballena.

wharf [wɔ:f], *pl* **wharves** [wɔ:vz] *n* muelle *m*.

---

what [wɔt] ◆ *a* **1** (in direct/indirect questions) qué; ~ **size is he?** ¿qué talla usa?; ~ **colour/shape is it?** ¿de qué color/forma es?

2 (in exclamations): ~ **a mess!** ¡qué desastre!; ~ **a fool I am!** ¡qué tonto soy!

◆ *pron* **1** (interrogative) qué; ~ **are you doing?** ¿qué haces or estás haciendo?; ~ **is happening?** ¿qué pasa or está pasando?; ~ **is it called?** ¿cómo se llama?; ~ **about me?** ¿y yo qué?; ~ **about doing** ...? ¿qué tal si hacemos ...?

2 (relative) lo que; **I saw** ~ **you did/was on the table** vi lo que hiciste/había en la mesa

◆ *excl* (disbelieving) ¡cómo!; ~, **no coffee!** ¡que no hay café!

whatever [wɔt'ɛvə*] *a*: ~ **book you choose** cualquier libro que elijas // *pron*: **do** ~ **is necessary** haga lo que sea necesario; **no reason** ~ or **whatsoever** ninguna razón sea la que sea; **nothing** ~ nada en absoluto.

wheat [wi:t] *n* trigo.

wheedle ['wi:dl] *vt*: **to** ~ **sb into doing sth** engatusar a uno para que haga algo; **to** ~ **sth out of sb** sonsacar algo a uno.

wheel [wi:l] *n* rueda; (AUT: also: **steering** ~) volante *m*; (NAUT) timón *m* // *vt* (pram etc) empujar // *vi* (also: ~ **round**) dar la vuelta, girar; ~**barrow** *n* carretilla; ~**chair** *n* silla de ruedas; ~ **clamp** *n* (AUT) cepo.

wheeze [wi:z] *vi* resollar.

---

when [wɛn] ◆ *ad* cuando; ~ **did it happen?** ¿cuándo ocurrió?; **I know** ~ **it happened** sé cuándo ocurrió

◆ conj 1 (at, during, after the time that) cuando; be careful ~ you cross the road ten cuidado al cruzar la calle; that was ~ I needed you fue entonces que le necesité
2 (on, at which): on the day ~ I met him el día en qué le conocí
3 (whereas) cuando.

whenever [wɛn'ɛvə*] conj cuando; (every time) cada vez que.

where [wɛə*] ad dónde // conj donde; this is ~ aquí es donde; ~abouts ad dónde // n: nobody knows his ~abouts nadie conoce su paradero; ~as conj visto que, mientras; ~by pron por lo cual; ~upon conj con lo cual, después de lo cual; ~ver [-'ɛvə*] ad dondequiera que; (interrogative) dónde; ~withal n recursos mpl.

whet [wɛt] vt estimular.

whether ['wɛðə*] conj si; I don't know ~ to accept or not no sé si aceptar o no; ~ you go or not vayas o no vayas.

KEYWORD
---

which [wɪtʃ] ◆ a 1 (interrogative: direct, indirect) qué; ~ picture(s) do you want? ¿qué cuadro(s) quieres?; ~ one? ¿cuál?
2: in ~ case en cuyo caso; we got there at 8 pm, by ~ time the cinema was full llegamos allí a las 8, cuando el cine estaba lleno
◆ pron 1 (interrogative) cual; I don't mind ~ el/la que sea
2 (relative: replacing noun) que; (: replacing clause) lo que; (: after preposition) (el/la) que etc, el/la cual etc; the apple ~ you ate/~ is on the table la manzana que comiste/ que está en la mesa; the chair on ~ you are sitting la silla en la que estás sentado; he said he knew, ~ is true/I feared dijo que lo sabía, lo cual or lo que es cierto/me temía.

whichever [wɪtʃ'ɛvə*] a: take ~

book you prefer coja el libro que prefiera; ~ book you take cualquier libro que coja.

whiff [wɪf] n bocanada.

while [waɪl] n rato, momento // conj durante; (whereas) mientras; (although) aunque; for a ~ durante algún tiempo; to ~ away the time pasar el rato.

whim [wɪm] n capricho.

whimper ['wɪmpə*] vi (weep) lloriquear; (moan) quejarse.

whimsical ['wɪmzɪkl] a (person) caprichoso.

whine [waɪn] vi (with pain) gemir; (engine) zumbar.

whip [wɪp] n látigo; (POL: person) encargado/a de la disciplina partidaria en el parlamento // vt azotar; (snatch) arrebatar; (US: CULIN) batir; ~ped cream n nata or crema montada; ~-round n (Brit) colecta.

whirl [wə:l] vt hacer girar, dar vueltas a // vi girar, dar vueltas; (leaves, water etc) arremolinarse; ~pool n remolino; ~wind n torbellino.

whirr [wə:*] vi zumbar.

whisk [wɪsk] n (Brit: CULIN) batidor m // vt (Brit: CULIN) batir; to ~ sb away or off llevar volando a uno.

whisker ['wɪskə*] n: ~s (of animal) bigotes mpl; (of man: side ~s) patillas fpl.

whisky, (US, Ireland) **whiskey** ['wɪskɪ] n whisky m.

whisper ['wɪspə*] vi cuchichear, hablar bajo // vt decir en voz muy baja.

whistle ['wɪsl] n (sound) silbido; (object) silbato // vi silbar.

white [waɪt] a blanco; (pale) pálido // n blanco; (of egg) clara; ~ coffee n (Brit) café m con leche; ~ collar worker n oficinista m/f; ~ elephant n (fig) maula; ~ lie n mentirilla; ~ness n blancura; ~ noise n sonido blanco; ~ paper n (POL) libro rojo; ~wash n (paint) jalbegue m, cal f // vt (also fig) encubrir.

whiting ['waɪtɪŋ] n, pl inv (fish) pescadilla.

Whitsun ['wɪtsn] *n* (*Brit*) pentecostés *m*.

whittle ['wɪtl] *vt*: to ~ **away**, ~ **down** ir reduciendo.

whizz [wɪz] *vi*: to ~ **past** *or* **by** pasar a toda velocidad; ~ **kid** *n* (*col*) prodigio.

---

who [huː] *pron* **1** (*interrogative*) quién; ~ **is it?**, ~ **'s there?** ¿quién es?; ~ **are you looking for?** ¿a quién buscas?; **I told her** ~ **I was** le dije quién era yo

2 (*relative*) que; **the man/woman** ~ **spoke to me** el hombre/la mujer que habló conmigo; **those** ~ **can swim** los que saben *or* sepan nadar.

---

whodun(n)it [huː'dʌnɪt] *n* (*col*) novela policíaca.

whoever [huː'ɛvə*] *pron*: ~ **finds it** cualquiera *or* quienquiera que lo encuentre; **ask** ~ **you like** pregunta a quien quieras; ~ **he marries** no importa con quién se case.

whole [həʊl] *a* (*not broken*) intacto; (*all*): **the** ~ **of the town** toda la ciudad, la ciudad entera // *n* (*total*) total *m*; (*sum*) conjunto; **on the** ~, **as a** ~ en general; ~**hearted** *a* sincero, cordial; ~**meal** *a* integral; ~**sale** *n* venta al por mayor // *a* al por mayor; (*destruction*) sistemático; ~**saler** *n* mayorista *m/f*; ~**some** *a* sano; ~**wheat** *a* = ~**meal**; **wholly** *ad* totalmente, enteramente.

---

whom [huːm] *pron* **1** (*interrogative*): ~ **did you see?** ¿a quién viste?; **to** ~ **did you give it?** ¿a quién se lo diste?; **tell me from** ~ **you received it** dígame de quién lo recibió

2 (*relative: direct object*) que: ~ **a quien(es)**; **of** ~ de quien(es), del/ de la que *etc*; **the man** ~ **I saw/to** ~ **I wrote** el hombre que vi/a quien escribí; **the lady about/with** ~ **I**

was talking la señora de/con quien *or* (la) que hablaba.

whooping cough ['huːpɪŋ-] *n* tos *f* ferina.

whore [hɔː*] *n* (*col: pej*) puta.

---

whose [huːz] ◆ *a* **1** (*possessive: interrogative*): ~ **book is this?**, ~ **is this book?** ¿de quién es este libro?; ~ **pencil have you taken?** ¿de quién es el lápiz que has cogido?; ~ **daughter are you?** ¿de quién eres hija?

2 (*possessive: relative*) cuyo/a, *pl* cuyos/as; **the man** ~ **son you rescued** el hombre cuyo hijo rescataste; **those** ~ **passports I have** aquellas personas cuyos pasaportes tengo; **the woman** ~ **car** was stolen la mujer a quien le robaron el coche

◆ *pron* de quién; ~ **is this?** ¿de quién es esto?; **I know** ~ **it is** sé de quién es.

---

why [waɪ] ◆ *ad* por qué; ~ **not?** ¿por qué no?; ~ **not do it now?** ¿por qué no lo haces (*or* hacemos *etc*) ahora?

◆ *conj*: **I wonder** ~ **he said that** me pregunto por qué dijo eso; **that's not** ~ **I'm here** no es por eso (por lo) que estoy aquí; **the reason** ~, **the reason** ~ la razón por la que

◆ *excl* (*expressing surprise, shock, annoyance*) ¡hombre!, ¡vaya! (*explaining*): ~, **it's you!** ¡hombre, eres tú!; ~, **that's impossible!** ¡pero sí eso es impossible!

---

wick [wɪk] *n* mecha.

wicked ['wɪkɪd] *a* malvado, cruel.

wicker ['wɪkə*] *n* (*also*: ~**work**) artículos *mpl* de mimbre // *cpd* de mimbre.

wicket ['wɪkɪt] *n* (*CRICKET*) palos *mpl*.

wide [waɪd] a ancho; (*area, knowledge*) vasto, grande; (*choice*) grande // ad: **to open** ~ abrir de par en par; **to shoot** ~ errar el tiro; ~**angle lens** n objetivo granangular; ~**awake** a bien despierto; ~**ly** ad (*differing*) muy; **it is** ~**ly believed that...** hay una convicción general de que...; ~**n** vt ensanchar; ~**open** a abierto de par en par; ~**spread** a (*belief etc*) extendido, general.

widow ['wɪdəu] n viuda; ~**ed** a viudo; ~**er** n viudo.

width [wɪdθ] n anchura; (*of cloth*) ancho.

wield [wiːld] vt (*sword*) manejar; (*power*) ejercer.

wife [waɪf], pl **wives** [waɪvz] n mujer f, esposa.

wig [wɪg] n peluca.

wiggle ['wɪgl] vt menear // vi menearse.

wild [waɪld] a (*animal*) salvaje; (*plant*) silvestre; (*rough*) furioso, violento; (*idea*) descabellado; ~**s** npl regiones fpl salvajes, tierras fpl vírgenes; ~**erness** ['wɪldənɪs] n desierto; ~**goose chase** n (*fig*) búsqueda inútil; ~**life** n fauna; ~**ly** ad (*roughly*) violentamente; (*foolishly*) locamente; (*rashly*) descabelladamente.

wilful ['wɪlful] a (*action*) deliberado; (*obstinate*) testarudo.

KEYWORD

will [wɪl] ♦ *auxiliary vb* **1** (*forming future tense*): **I** ~ **finish it tomorrow** lo terminaré or voy a terminar mañana; **I** ~ **have finished it by tomorrow** lo habré terminado para mañana; ~ **you do it?** — **yes I** ~/**no I won't** ¿lo harás? — sí/no
2 (*in conjectures, predictions*): **he** ~ **or he'll be there by now** ya habrá or debe (de) haber llegado; **that** ~ **be the postman** será or debe ser el cartero
3 (*in commands, requests, offers*): ~ **you be quiet!** ¡quieres callarte?;

you help me? ¿quieres ayudarme?; ~ **you have a cup of tea?** ¿te apetece un te?; **I won't put up with it!** ¡no lo soporto!
♦ vt (*pt, pp* willed): **to** ~ **sb to do sth** desear que alguien haga algo; **he** ~**ed himself to go on** con gran fuerza de voluntad, continuó
♦ n voluntad f; (*testament*) testamento.

willing ['wɪlɪŋ] a (*with goodwill*) de buena voluntad; complaciente; **he's** ~ **to do it** está dispuesto a hacerlo; ~**ly** ad con mucho gusto; ~**ness** n buena voluntad.

willow ['wɪləu] n sauce m.

will power n fuerza de voluntad.

willy-nilly [wɪlɪ'nɪlɪ] ad quiérase o no.

wilt [wɪlt] vi marchitarse.

wily ['waɪlɪ] a astuto.

win [wɪn] n (*in sports etc*) victoria, triunfo // vb (*pt, pp* **won**) vt ganar; (*obtain*) conseguir, lograr // vi ganar; **to** ~ **over**, (*Brit*) ~ **round** vt convencer a.

wince [wɪns] vi encogerse.

winch [wɪntʃ] n torno.

wind [wɪnd] n viento; (*MED*) gases mpl // vb [waɪnd] (*pt, pp* **wound**) vt enrollar; (*wrap*) envolver; (*clock, toy*) dar cuerda a // vi (*road, river*) serpentear // vt (*wind*) dejar sin aliento a; **to** ~ **up** vt (*clock*) dar cuerda a; (*debate*) concluir, terminar; ~**fall** n golpe m de suerte; ~**ing** a (*road*) tortuoso; ~ **instrument** n (*MUS*) instrumento de viento; ~**mill** n molino de viento.

window ['wɪndəu] n ventana; (*in car, train*) ventanilla; (*in shop etc*) escaparate m, vitrina (*LAm*), vidriera (*LAm*); ~ **box** n jardinera de ventana; ~ **cleaner** n (*person*) limpiacristales m inv; ~ **ledge** n alféizar m, repisa (*LAm*); ~ **pane** n cristal m; ~**sill** n alféizar m, repisa (*LAm*).

windpipe ['wɪndpaɪp] n tráquea.

windscreen ['wɪndskri:n],   (US) **windshield** ['wɪndʃi:ld] n parabrisas m inv; ~ **washer** n lavaparabrisas m inv; ~ **wiper** n limpiaparabrisas m inv.

windswept ['wɪndswept] a azotado por el viento.

windy ['wɪndɪ] a de mucho viento; it's ~ hace viento.

wine [waɪn] n vino; ~ **cellar** n bodega; ~ **glass** n copa (para vino); ~ **list** n lista de vinos; ~ **merchant** n vinatero; ~ **tasting** n degustación f de vinos; ~ **waiter** n escanciador m.

wing [wɪŋ] n ala; (Brit AUT) aleta; ~**s** npl (THEATRE) bastidores mpl; ~**er** n (SPORT) extremo.

wink [wɪŋk] n guiño, pestañeo f o guiñar, pestañear; (light etc) parpadear.

winner ['wɪnə*] n ganador(a) m/f.

winning ['wɪnɪŋ] a (team) ganador(a); (goal) decisivo; ~**s** npl ganancias fpl; ~ **post** n meta.

winter ['wɪntə*] n invierno // vi invernar; ~ **sports** npl deportes mpl de invierno.

wintry ['wɪntrɪ] a invernal.

wipe [waɪp] n: to give sth a ~ pasar un trapo sobre algo // vt limpiar; to ~ **off** vt limpiar con un trapo; to ~ **out** vt (debt) liquidar; (memory) borrar; (destroy) destruir; to ~ **up** vt limpiar.

wire ['waɪə*] n alambre m; (ELEC) cable m (eléctrico); (TEL) telegrama m // vt (house) instalar el alambrado en; (also: ~ **up**) conectar.

wireless ['waɪəlɪs] n (Brit) radio f.

wiring ['waɪərɪŋ] n alambrado.

wiry ['waɪərɪ] a enjuto y fuerte.

wisdom ['wɪzdəm] n sabiduría, saber m; (good sense) cordura; ~ **tooth** n muela del juicio.

wise [waɪz] a sabio; (sensible) juicioso.

...**wise** [waɪz] suffix: time~ en cuanto a or respecto al tiempo.

wisecrack ['waɪzkræk] n broma.

wish [wɪʃ] n (desire) deseo // vt desear; (want) desear; best ~**es** (on birthday etc) felicidades fpl; with best ~**es** (in letter) saludos mpl, recuerdos mpl; to ~ sb goodbye despedirse de uno; he ~ed me well me deseó mucha suerte; to ~ to do/sb to do sth querer hacer/que alguien haga algo; to ~ for desear; ~**ful** n: it's ~**ful** thinking eso sería soñar.

wishy-washy ['wɪʃɪwɔʃɪ] a (col: colour, ideas) desvaído.

wisp [wɪsp] n mechón m; (of smoke) voluta.

wistful ['wɪstful] a pensativo.

wit [wɪt] n (wittiness) ingenio, gracia; (intelligence: also: ~**s**) inteligencia; (person) chistoso/a.

witch [wɪtʃ] n bruja.

---

with [wɪð, wɪθ] prep **1** (accompanying, in the company of) con (con + mi, ti, si = conmigo, contigo, consigo); I was ~ him estaba con él; we stayed ~ friends nos hospedamos en casa de unos amigos; I'm (not) ~ you (understand) (no) te entiendo; to be ~ it (col: person: up-to-date) estar al tanto; (: alert) ser despabilado

2 (descriptive, indicating manner etc) de; a room ~ a view una habitación con vistas; the man ~ the grey hat/blue eyes el hombre del sombrero gris/de los ojos azules; red ~ anger rojo/a de ira; to shake ~ fear temblar de miedo; to fill sth ~ water llenar algo de agua.

---

withdraw [wɪθ'drɔ:] (irg: like draw) vt retirar, sacar // vi retirarse; (go back on promise) retractarse; to ~ **money** (from the bank) retirar fondos (del banco); ~**al** n retirada; ~**n** a (person) reservado, introvertido.

wither ['wɪðə*] vi marchitarse.

withhold [wɪθ'həʊld] vt (irg: like hold) vt (money) retener; (decision) aplazar; (*permission*) negar; (*information*) ocultar.

within [wɪð'ɪn] *prep* dentro de // *ad* dentro; ~ **reach** al alcance de la mano; ~ **sight** of a la vista de; ~ **the week** antes de acabar la semana.

without [wɪð'aut] *prep* sin.

withstand [wɪθ'stænd] (*irg: like* **stand**) *vt* resistir a.

witness ['wɪtnɪs] *n* (*person*) testigo *m/f*; (*evidence*) testimonio // *vt* (*event*) presenciar; (*document*) atestiguar la veracidad de // ~ **box**, (*US*) ~ **stand** *n* tribuna de los testigos.

witticism ['wɪtɪsɪzm] *n* occurencia.

witty ['wɪtɪ] *a* ingenioso.

wives [waɪvz] *npl of* **wife**.

wizard ['wɪzəd] *n* hechicero.

wk *abbr* = **week**.

wobble ['wɔbl] *vi* tambalearse; (*chair*) ser poco firme.

woe [wəu] *n* desgracia.

woke [wəuk], **woken** ['wəukən] *pt, pp of* **wake**.

wolf [wulf], *pl* **wolves** [wulvz] *n* lobo.

woman ['wumən], *pl* **women** *n* mujer *f*; ~ **doctor** *n* médica; **women's lib** *n* (*pej*) la liberación de la mujer; ~**ly** *a* femenino.

womb [wu:m] *n* (*ANAT*) matriz *f*, útero.

women ['wɪmɪn] *npl of* **woman**.

won [wʌn] *pt, pp of* **win**.

wonder ['wʌndə*] *n* maravilla, prodigio; (*feeling*) asombro // *vi*: to ~ **whether** preguntarse si; to ~ **at** asombrarse de; to ~ **about** pensar sobre *or* en; it's no ~ that no es de extrañarse que + *subjun*; ~**ful** *a* maravilloso; ~**fully** *ad* maravillosamente, estupendamente.

won't [wəunt] = **will not**.

woo [wu:] *vt* (*woman*) cortejar.

wood [wud] *n* (*timber*) madera; (*forest*) bosque *m*; ~ **alcohol** *n* (*US*) alcohol *m* desnaturalizado; ~ **carving** *n* tallado en madera; ~**ed** *a* arbolado; ~**en** *a* de madera; (*fig*)

inexpresivo; ~**pecker** *n* pájaro carpintero; ~**wind** *n* (*MUS*) instrumentos *mpl* de viento de madera; ~**work** *n* carpintería; ~**worm** *n* carcoma.

wool [wul] *n* lana; **to pull the** ~ **over sb's eyes** (*fig*) dar a uno gato por liebre; ~**len**, (*US*) ~**en** *a* de lana; ~**lens** *npl* géneros *mpl* de lana; ~**ly**, (*US*) ~**y** *a* lanudo, de lana; (*fig: ideas*) confuso.

word [wə:d] *n* palabra; (*news*) noticia; (*promise*) palabra (de honor) // *vt* redactar; **in other** ~**s** en otras palabras; **to break/keep one's** ~ faltar a la palabra/cumplir la promesa; ~**ing** *n* redacción *f*; ~ **processing** *n* proceso de textos; ~ **processor** *n* procesador *m* de palabras.

wore [wɔ:*] *pt of* **wear**.

work [wə:k] *n* trabajo; (*job*) empleo, trabajo; (*ART, LITERATURE*) obra // *vi* trabajar; (*mechanism*) funcionar, marchar; (*medicine*) ser eficaz, surtir efecto // *vt* (*shape*) trabajar; (*stone etc*) tallar; (*mine etc*) explotar; (*machine*) manejar, hacer funcionar; **to be out of** ~ estar parado, no tener trabajo; ~**s** *n* (*Brit: factory*) fábrica // *npl* (*of clock, machine*) mecanismo *sg*; **to** ~ **loose** *vi* (*part*) desprenderse; (*knot*) aflojarse; **to** ~ **on** *vt fus* trabajar en, dedicarse a; (*principle*) basarse en; **to** ~ **out** *vi* (*plans etc*) salir bien, funcionar // *vt* (*problem*) resolver; (*plan*) elaborar; **it** ~**s out at £100** suma 100 libras; **to** ~ **up** *vt*: to get ~**ed up** excitarse; ~**able** *a* (*solution*) práctico, factible; **workaholic** *n* trabajador(a) obsesivo/a *m/f*; ~**er** *n* trabajador(a) *m/f*, obrero/a; ~**force** *n* mano *f* de obra; ~**ing class** *n* clase *f* obrera; ~**ing-class** *a* obrero; ~**ing order** *n*: **in** ~**ing order** en funcionamiento; ~**man** *n* obrero; ~**manship** *n* (*art*) hechura, arte *m*; (*skill*) habilidad *f*, trabajo; ~**mate** *n* compañero/a de trabajo; ~**sheet** *n* hoja de trabajo; ~**shop** *n* taller m; ~ **station** n puesto or estación f de trabajo; ~-**to-rule** n (Brit) huelga de brazos caídos.

world [wə:ld] n mundo // cpd (champion) del mundo; (power, war) mundial; **to think the ~ of sb** (fig) tener un concepto muy alto de uno; ~**ly** a mundano; ~**-wide** a mundial, universal.

worm [wə:m] n gusano; (earth ~) lombriz f.

worn [wɔ:n] pp of **wear** // a usado; ~**-out** a (object) gastado; (person) rendido, agotado.

worried ['wʌrɪd] a preocupado.

worry ['wʌrɪ] n preocupación f // vt preocupar, inquietar // vi preocuparse; ~**ing** a inquietante.

worse [wə:s] a, ad peor // n lo peor; **a change for the ~** un empeoramiento; ~**n** vt, vi empeorar; ~ **off** a (fig): **you'll be ~ off this way** de esta forma estarás peor que nunca.

worship ['wə:ʃɪp] n (organized ~) culto; (act) adoración f // vt adorar; **Your W~** (Brit: to mayor) señor alcalde; (: to judge) señor juez.

worst [wə:st] a el/la peor // ad peor // n lo peor; **at ~** en lo peor de los casos.

worsted ['wustɪd] n: (wool) ~ estambre m.

worth [wə:θ] n valor m // a: **to be ~** valer; **it's ~ it** vale or merece la pena; **to be ~ one's while** (to do) merecer la pena (hacer); ~**less** a sin valor; (useless) inútil; ~**while** a (activity) que merece la pena; (cause) loable.

worthy ['wə:ðɪ] a (person) respetable; (motive) honesto; ~ **of** digno de.

---

would [wud] auxiliary vb **1** (conditional tense): **if you asked him he ~ do it** si se lo pidieras, lo haría; **if you had asked him he ~ have done it** si se lo hubieras pedido, lo habría or hubiera hecho

2 (in offers, invitations, requests): ~ **you like a biscuit?** ¿quiere(s) una galleta?; (formal) ¿querría una galleta?; ~ **you ask him to come in?** ¿quiere(s) hacerle pasar?; ~ **you open the window please?** ¿quiere or podría abrir la ventana, por favor?

3 (in indirect speech): **I said I ~ do it** dije que lo haría

4 (emphatic): **it WOULD have to snow today!** ¡tenía que nevar precisamente hoy!

5 (insistence): **she ~n't behave** no quiso comportarse bien

6 (conjecture): **it ~ have been midnight** sería medianoche; **it ~ seem so** parece ser que sí

7 (indicating habit): **he ~ go there on Mondays** iba allí los lunes.

would-be ['wudbi] a (pej) presunto.

wouldn't ['wudnt] = would not.

wound [waund] pt, pp of **wind** // [wu:nd] herida // vt herir.

wove [wəuv], **woven** ['wəuvən] pt, pp of **weave**.

wrangle ['ræŋgl] n riña // vi reñir.

wrap [ræp] n (stole) chal m // vt (also: ~ **up**) envolver; ~**per** n (Brit: of book) sobrecubierta; ~**ping paper** n papel m de envolver.

wrath [rɔθ] n cólera.

wreak [ri:k] vt: **to ~ havoc (on)** hacer estragos (en); **to ~ vengeance (on)** vengarse (de).

wreath [ri:θ], pl ~**s** [ri:ðz] n (funeral ~) corona; (of flowers) guirnalda.

wreck [rek] n (ship: destruction) naufragio; (: remains) restos mpl del barco; (pej: person) ruina // vt (ship) hundir; (fig) arruinar; ~**age** n (remains) restos mpl; (of building) escombros mpl.

wren [ren] n (ZOOL) reyezuelo.

wrench [rentʃ] n (TECH) llave f inglesa; (tug) tirón m // vt arrancar; **to ~ sth from sb** arrebatar algo violentamente a uno.

wrestle ['resl] vi: **to ~ (with sb)** lu-

char (con *or* contra uno); ~**r** in luchador(a) *m/f* (de lucha libre);
wrestling *n* lucha libre.
wretched ['rɛtʃɪd] *a* miserable.
wriggle ['rɪgl] *vi* serpentear.
wring [rɪŋ], *pt, pp* **wrung** *vt* torcer, retorcer; (*wet clothes*) escurrir; (*fig*): to ~ **sth out of sb** sacar algo por la fuerza a uno.
wrinkle ['rɪŋkl] *n* arruga // *vt* arrugar // *vi* arrugarse.
wrist [rɪst] *n* muñeca; ~ **watch** *n* reloj *m* de pulsera.
writ [rɪt] *n* mandato judicial.
write [raɪt], *pt* **wrote**, *pp* **written** *vt, vi* escribir; to ~ **down** *vt* escribir; (*note*) apuntar; to ~ **off** *vt* (*debt*) borrar (como incobrable); (*fig*) desechar por inútil; to ~ **out** *vt* escribir; to ~ **up** *vt* redactar; ~**off** *n* pérdida total; the car is a ~**off** el coche quedó para chatarra; ~**r** *n* escritor(a) *m/f*.
writhe [raɪð] *vi* retorcerse.
writing ['raɪtɪŋ] *n* escritura; (*hand~*) letra; (*of author*) obras *fpl*; in ~ por escrito; ~ **paper** *n* papel *m* de escribir.
written ['rɪtn] *pp* of **write**.
wrong [rɒŋ] *a* (*wicked*) malo; (*unfair*) injusto; (*incorrect*) equivocado, incorrecto; (*not suitable*) inoportuno, inconveniente // *ad* mal; you are ~ no tienes razón, estás equivocado; to be in the ~ no tener razón, tener la culpa; what's ~? ¿qué pasa?; to go ~ (*person*) equivocarse; (*plan*) salir mal; (*machine*) estropearse; ~**ful** *a* injusto; ~**ly** *ad* injustamente.
wrote [rəʊt] *pt* of **write**.
wrought [rɔːt] *a*: ~ **iron** hierro forjado.
wrung [rʌŋ], *pt, pp* of **wring**.
wry [raɪ] *a* irónico.
wt. *abbr* = **weight**.

X

Xmas ['ɛksməs] *n abbr* = **Christmas**.
X-ray [ɛks'reɪ] *n* radiografía; ~**s** *npl* rayos *mpl* X.
xylophone ['zaɪləfəʊn] *n* xilófono.

Y

yacht [jɒt] *n* yate *m*; ~**ing** *n* (*sport*) balandrismo; ~**sman/woman** *n* balandrista *m/f*.
Yank [jæŋk], **Yankee** ['jæŋkɪ] *n* (*pej*) yanqui *m/f*.
yap [jæp] *vi* (*dog*) aullar.
yard [jɑːd] *n* patio; (*measure*) yarda; ~**stick** *n* (*fig*) criterio, norma.
yarn [jɑːn] *n* hilo; (*tale*) cuento, historia.
yawn [jɔːn] *n* bostezo // *vi* bostezar; ~**ing** *a* (*gap*) muy abierto.
yd(s). *abbr* = **yard(s)**.
yeah [jɛə] *ad* (col) sí.
year [jɪə*] *n* año; to be 8 ~**s old** tener 8 años; an **eight-~-old child** un niño de ocho años (de edad); ~**ly** *a* anual // *ad* anualmente, cada año.
yearn [jɜːn] *vi*: to ~ **for sth** añorar algo, suspirar por algo; ~**ing** *n* ansia, añoranza.
yeast [jiːst] *n* levadura.
yell [jɛl] *n* grito, alarido // *vi* gritar.
yellow ['jɛləʊ] *a, n* amarillo.
yelp [jɛlp] *n* aullido // *vi* aullar.
yeoman ['jəʊmən] *n*: **Y~ of the Guard** alabardero de la Casa Real.
yes [jɛs] *ad, n* sí *m*; to **say/answer** ~ decir/contestar que sí.
yesterday ['jɛstədɪ] *ad, n* ayer *m*; ~ **morning/evening** ayer por la mañana/tarde; **all day** ~ todo el día de ayer.
yet [jɛt] *ad* todavía // *conj* sin embargo, a pesar de todo; **it is not finished** ~ todavía no está acabado; **the best** ~ el/la mejor hasta ahora;

as ~ hasta ahora, todavía.

yew [ju:] *n* tejo.

yield [ji:ld] *n* producción *f*; (*AGR*) cosecha; (*COMM*) rendimiento // *vt* producir, dar; (*profit*) rendir // *vi* rendirse, ceder; (*US AUT*) ceder el paso.

YMCA *n abbr* (= *Young Men's Christian Association*) Asociación *f* de Jóvenes Cristianos.

yoga ['jəugə] *n* yoga *m*.

yog(h)ourt, yog(h)urt ['jəugət] *n* yogur *m*.

yoke [jəuk] *n* yugo.

yolk [jəuk] *n* yema (de huevo).

yonder ['jɔndə*] *ad* allá (a lo lejos).

KEYWORD

you [ju:] *pron* **1** (*subject: familiar*) tú, *pl* vosotros/as (*Sp*), ustedes (*LAm*); (*polite*) usted, *pl* ustedes; ~ **are very kind** eres/es *etc* muy amable; ~ **French enjoy your food** a vosotros (*or* ustedes) los franceses os (*or* les) gusta la comida; ~ **and I will go** iremos tú y yo

2 (*object: direct: familiar*) te, *pl* os (*Sp*), les (*LAm*); (*polite*) le, *pl* les, *f* la, *pl* las; **I know** ~ te/le *etc* conozco

3 (*object: indirect: familiar*) te, *pl* os (*Sp*), les (*LAm*); (*polite*) le, *pl* les; **I gave the letter to** ~ **yesterday** te/os *etc* di la carta ayer

4 (*stressed*): **I told** you **to do it** te dije a ti que lo hicieras, era a ti a quien dije que lo hicieras; *see also* **3, 5**

5 (*after prep: NB:* con + ti = contigo: *familiar*) ti, *pl* vosotros/as (*Sp*), ustedes (*LAm*); (: *polite*) usted, *pl* ustedes; **it's for** ~ es para ti/ vosotros *etc*

6 (*comparisons: familiar*) tú, *pl* vosotros/as (*Sp*), ustedes (*LAm*); (: *polite*) usted, *pl* ustedes; **she's younger than** ~ es más joven que tú/ vosotros *etc*

7 (*impersonal: one*): **fresh air does** ~ **good** el aire puro (te) hace bien; ~ **never know** nunca se sabe; ~

can't do that! ¡eso no se hace!

you'd [ju:d] = **you had, you would.**

you'll [ju:l] = **you will, you shall.**

young [jʌŋ] *a* joven // *npl* (*of animal*) cría *sg*; (*people*): **the** ~ los jóvenes, la juventud *sg*; ~**er** *a* (*brother etc*) menor; ~**ster** *n* joven *m/f*.

your [jɔ:*] *a* tu; (*pl*) vuestro; (*formal*) su; *see also* **my.**

you're [juə*] = **you are.**

yours [jɔ:z] *pron* tuyo; (: *pl*) vuestro; (*formal*) suyo; *see also* **faithfully, mine, sincerely.**

yourself [jɔ:'sɛlf] *pron* (*reflexive*) tú mismo; (*complement*) te; (*after prep*) ti (mismo); (*formal*) usted mismo; (: *complement*) se; (: *after prep*) sí (mismo); **yourselves** *pl pron* vosotros mismos; (*after prep*) vosotros (mismos); (*formal*) ustedes (mismos); (: *complement*) se; (: *after prep*) sí mismos; *see also* **oneself.**

youth [ju:θ] *n* juventud *f*; (*young man: pl* ~**s** [ju:ðz]) joven *m*; ~ **club** *n* club *m* juvenil; ~**ful** *a* juvenil; ~ **hostel** *n* albergue *m* de juventud.

you've [ju:v] = **you have.**

YTS *n abbr* (*Brit*) = *Youth Training Scheme*) plan de inserción profesional juvenil.

Yugoslav ['ju:gəusla:v] *a, n* yugo(e)slavo/a *m/f.*

Yugoslavia [ju:gəu'sla:vɪə] *n* Yugoslavia.

yuppie ['jʌpɪ] (*col*) *a, n* yuppie *m/f.*

YWCA *n abbr* (= *Young Women's Christian Association*) Asociación *f* de Jóvenes Cristianas.

Z

zany ['zeɪnɪ] *a* estrafalario.
zap [zæp] *vt* (*COMPUT*) borrar.
zeal [ziːl] *n* celo, entusiasmo.
zebra ['ziːbrə] *n* cebra; ~ **crossing** *n* (*Brit*) paso de peatones.
zenith ['zenɪθ] *n* cénit *m*.
zero ['zɪərəu] *n* cero.
zest [zest] *n* ánimo, vivacidad *f*.
zigzag ['zɪgzæg] *n* zigzag *m*.
zinc [zɪŋk] *n* cinc *m*, zinc *m*.

zip [zɪp] *n* (*also*: ~ **fastener**, (*US*) ~**per**) cremallera, cierre *m* (*LAm*) // *vt* (*also*: ~ **up**) cerrar la cremallera de; ~ **code** *n* (*US*) código postal.
zodiac ['zəudɪæk] *n* zodíaco.
zone [zəun] *n* zona.
zoo [zuː] *n* (jardín *m*) zoológico.
zoologist [zuːˈɔlədʒɪst] *n* zoólogo/a.
zoology [zuːˈɔlədʒɪ] *n* zoología.
zoom [zuːm] *vi*: **to** ~ **past** pasar zumbando; ~ **lens** *n* zoom *m*.
zucchini [zuːˈkiːnɪ] *n* (*pl*) (*US*) calabacín(ines) *m* (*pl*).

SPANISH VERB TABLES

1 Gerund. *2* Imperative. *3* Present. *4* Preterite. *5* Future. *6* Present subjunctive. *7* Imperfect subjunctive. *8* Past participle. *9* Imperfect. *Etc* indicates that the irregular root is used for all persons of the tense, e.g. oír: *6* oiga, oigas, oigamos, oigáis, oigan.

acertar *2* acierta *3* acierto, aciertas, acierta, aciertan *6* acierte, aciertes, acierte, acierten

acordar *2* acuerda *3* acuerdo, acuerdas, acuerda, acuerdan *6* acuerde, acuerdes, acuerde, acuerden

advertir *1* advirtiendo *2* advierte *3* advierto, adviertes, advierte, advierten *4* advirtió, advirtieron *6* advierta, adviertas, advierta, advirtamos, advirtáis, adviertan *7* advirtiera *etc*

agradecer *3* agradezco *6* agradezca *etc*

aparecer *3* aparezco *6* aparezca *etc*

aprobar *2* aprueba *3* apruebo, apruebas, aprueba, aprueban *6* apruebe, apruebes, apruebe, aprueben

atravesar *2* atraviesa *3* atravieso, atraviesas, atraviesa, atraviesan *6* atraviese, atravieses, atraviese, atraviesen

caber *3* quepo *4* cupe, cupiste, cupo, cupimos, cupisteis, cupieron *5* cabré *etc* *6* quepa *etc* *7* cupiera *etc*

caer *1* cayendo *3* caigo *4* cayó, cayeron *6* caiga *etc* *7* cayera *etc*

calentar *2* calienta *3* caliento, calientas, calienta, calientan

6 caliente, calientes, caliente, calienten

cerrar *2* cierra *3* cierro, cierras, cierra, cierran *6* cierre, cierres, cierre, cierren

COMER *1* comiendo *2* come, comed *3* como, comes, come comemos, coméis, comen *4* comí, comiste, comió, comimos, comisteis, comieron *5* comeré, comerás, comerá, comeremos, comeréis, comerán *6* coma, comas, coma, comamos, comáis, coman *7* comiera, comieras, comiera, comiéramos, comierais, comieran *8* comido *9* comía, comías, comía, comíamos, comíais, comían

conocer *3* conozco *6* conozca *etc*

contar *2* cuenta *3* cuento, cuentas, cuenta, cuentan *6* cuente, cuentes, cuente, cuenten

costar *2* cuesta *3* cuesto, cuestas, cuesta, cuestan *6* cueste, cuestes, cueste, cuesten

dar *3* doy *4* di, diste, dio, dimos, disteis, dieron *7* diera *etc*

decir *2* di *3* digo *4* dije, dijiste, dijo, dijimos, dijisteis, dijeron *5* diré *etc* *6* diga *etc* *7* dijera *etc* *8* dicho

despertar *2* despierta *3* despierto, despiertas, despierta, despiertan *6* despierte, despiertes, despierte, despierten

divertir *1* divirtiendo *2* divierte *3* divierto, diviertes, divierte, divierten *4* divirtió, divirtieren *6* divierta, diviertas, divierta, divirtamos, divirtáis, diviertan *7* divirtiera *etc*

dormir *1* durmiendo *2* duerme *3* duermo, duermes, duerme, duermen *4* durmió, durmieron *6* duerma, duermas, duerma, durmamos, durmáis, duerman *7* durmiera *etc*

empezar *2* empieza *3* empiezo, empiezas, empieza, empiezan *4* empecé *6* empiece, empieces, empiece, empecemos, empecéis, empiecen

entender *2* entiende *3* entiendo, entiendes, entiende, entienden *6* entienda, entiendas, entienda, entiendan

ESTAR *2* está *3* estoy, estás, está, están *4* estuve, estuviste, estuvo, estuvimos, estuvisteis, estuvieron *6* esté, estés, esté, estén *7* estuviera *etc*

HABER *3* he, has, ha, hemos, han *4* hube, hubiste, hubo, hubimos, hubisteis, hubieron *5* habré *etc* *6* haya *etc* *7* hubiera *etc*

HABLAR *1* hablando *2* habla, hablad *3* hablo, hablas, habla, hablamos, habláis, hablan *4* hablé, hablaste, habló, hablamos, hablasteis, hablaron *5* hablaré, hablarás, hablará, hablaremos, hablaréis, hablarán *6* hable, hables, hable, hablemos, habléis, hablen *7* hablara, hablaras, hablara, habláramos, hablarais, hablaran *8* hablaba *9* hablaba, hablabas, hablaba, hablábamos, hablabais, hablaban

hacer *2* haz *3* hago *4* hice, hiciste, hizo, hicimos, hicisteis, hicieron *5* haré *etc* *6* haga *etc* *7* hiciera *etc* *8* hecho

instruir *1* instruyendo *2* instruye *3* instruyo, instruyes, instruye, instruyen *4* instruyó, instruyeron *6* instruya *etc* *7* instruyera *etc*

ir *1* yendo *2* ve *3* voy, vas, va, vamos, vais, van *4* fui, fuiste, fue, fuimos, fuisteis, fueron *6* vaya, vayas, vaya, vayamos, vayáis, vayan *7* fuera *etc* *8* iba, ibas, iba, íbamos, ibais, iban

jugar *2* juega *3* juego, juegas, juega, juegan *4* jugué *6* juegue *etc*

leer *1* leyendo *4* leyó, leyeron *7* leyera *etc*

morir *1* muriendo *2* muere *3* muero, mueres, muere, mueren *4* murió, murieron *6* muera, mueras, muera, muramos, muráis, mueran *7* muriera *etc* *8* muerto

mostrar *2* muestra *3* muestro, muestras, muestra, muestran *6* muestre, muestres, muestre, muestren

mover *2* mueve *3* muevo, mueves, mueve, mueven *6* mueva, muevas, mueva, muevan

negar *2* niega *3* niego, niegas, niega, niegan *4* negué *6* niegue, niegues, niegue, neguemos, neguéis, nieguen

ofrecer *3* ofrezco *6* ofrezca *etc*

oír *1* oyendo *2* oye *3* oigo, oyes, oye, oyen *4* oyó, oyeron *6* oiga *etc* *7* oyera *etc*

oler *2* huele *3* huelo, hueles, huele, huelen *6* huela, huelas, huela, huelan

318

parecer *3* parezco *6* parezca *etc*

pedir *1* pidiendo *2* pide *3* pido, pides, pide, piden *4* pidió, pidieron *6* pida *etc 7* pidiera *etc*

pensar *2* piensa *3* pienso, piensas, piensa, piensan *6* piense, pienses, piense, piensen

perder *2* pierde *3* pierdo, pierdes, pierde, pierden *6* pierda, pierdas, pierda, pierdan

poder *1* pudiendo *2* puede *3* puedo, puedes, puede, pueden *4* pude, pudiste, pudo, pudimos, pudisteis, pudieron *5* podré *etc 6* pueda, puedas, pueda, puedan *7* pudiera *etc*

poner *2* pon *3* pongo *4* puse, pusiste, puso, pusimos, pusisteis, pusieron *5* pondré *etc 6* ponga *etc 7* pusiera *etc 8* puesto

preferir *1* prefiriendo *2* prefiere *3* prefiero, prefieres, prefiere, prefieren *4* prefirió, prefirieron *6* prefiera, prefieras, prefiera, prefiramos, prefiráis, prefieran *7* prefiriera *etc*

querer *2* quiere *3* quiero, quieres, quiere, quieren *4* quise, quisiste, quiso, quisimos, quisisteis, quisieron *5* querré *etc 6* quiera, quieras, quiera, quieran *7* quisiera *etc*

reír *2* ríe *3* río, ríes, ríe, ríen *4* rio, rieron *6* ría, rías, ría, riamos, riáis, rían *7* riera *etc*

repetir *1* repitiendo *2* repite *3* repito, repites, repite, repiten *4* repitió, repitieron *6* repita *etc 7* repitiera *etc*

rogar *2* ruega *3* ruego, ruegas, ruega, ruegan *4* rogué *6*

ruegue, ruegues, ruegue, roguemos, roguéis, rueguen

saber *3* sé *4* supe, supiste, supo, supimos, supisteis, supieron *5* sabré *etc 6* sepa *etc 7* supiera *etc*

salir *2* sal *3* salgo *5* saldré *etc 6* salga *etc*

seguir *1* siguiendo *2* sigue *3* sigo, sigues, sigue, siguen *4* siguió, siguieron *6* siga *etc 7* siguiera *etc*

sentar *2* sienta *3* siento, sientas, sienta, sientan *6* siente, sientes, siente, sienten

sentir *1* sintiendo *2* siente *3* siento, sientes, siente, sienten *4* sintió, sintieron *6* sienta, sientas, sienta, sintamos, sintáis, sientan *7* sintiera *etc*

SER *2* sé *3* soy, eres, es, somos, sois, son *4* fui, fuiste, fue, fuimos, fuisteis, fueron *6* sea *etc 7* fuera *etc 9* era, eras, era, éramos, erais, eran

servir *1* sirviendo *2* sirve *3* sirvo, sirves, sirve, sirven *4* sirvió, sirvieron *6* sirva *etc 7* sirviera *etc*

soñar *2* sueña *3* sueño, sueñas, sueña, sueñan *6* sueñe, sueñes, sueñe, sueñen

tener *2* ten *3* tengo, tienes, tiene, tienen *4* tuve, tuviste, tuvo, tuvimos, tuvisteis, tuvieron *5* tendré *etc 6* tenga *etc 7* tuviera *etc*

traer *1* trayendo *3* traigo *4* traje, trajiste, trajo, trajimos, trajisteis, trajeron *6* traiga *etc 7* trajera *etc*

valer *2* val *3* valgo *5* valdré *etc 6* valga *etc*

venir *2* ven *3* vengo, vienes, viene, vienen *4* vine, viniste, vino, vinimos, vinisteis, vinieron *5* vendré *etc 6* venga *etc 7* viniera *etc*

ver *3* veo *6* vea *etc 8* visto *9* veía *etc*

vestir *1* vistiendo *2* viste *3* visto, vistes, viste, visten *4* vistió, vistieron *6* vista *etc 7* vistiera *etc*

VIVIR *1* viviendo *2* vive, vivid *3* vivo, vives, vive, vivimos, vivís, viven *4* viví, viviste, vivió, vivimos, vivisteis, vivieron *5* viviré, vivirás, vivirá, viviremos, viviréis, vivirán *6* viva, vivas, viva, vivamos, viváis, vivan *7* viviera, vivieras, viviera, viviéramos, vivierais, vivieran *8* vivido *9* vivía, vivías, vivía, vivíamos, vivías, vivían

volver *2* vuelve *3* vuelvo, vuelves, vuelve, vuelven *6* vuelva, vuelvas, vuelva, vuelvan *8* vuelto

VERBOS IRREGULARES EN INGLÉS

present	pt	pp	present	pt	pp
arise	arose	arisen	dig	dug	dug
awake	awoke	awaked	do (3rd	did	done
be (am, is,	was,	been	person;		
are;	were		he/she/it/		
being)			does)		
bear	bore	born(e)	draw	drew	drawn
beat	beat	beaten	dream	dreamed,	dreamed,
become	became	become		dreamt	dreamt
begin	began	begun	drink	drank	drunk
behold	beheld	beheld	drive	drove	driven
bend	bent	bent	dwell	dwelt	dwelt
beset	beset	beset	eat	ate	eaten
bet	bet,	bet,	fall	fell	fallen
	betted	betted	feed	fed	fed
bid	bid,	bid,	feel	felt	felt
	bade	bidden	fight	fought	fought
bind	bound	bound	find	found	found
bite	bit	bitten	flee	fled	fled
bleed	bled	bled	fling	flung	flung
blow	blew	blown	fly (flies)	flew	flown
break	broke	broken	forbid	forbade	forbidden
breed	bred	bred	forecast	forecast	forecast
bring	brought	brought	forget	forgot	forgotten
build	built	built	forgive	forgave	forgiven
burn	burnt,	burnt,	forsake	forsook	forsaken
	burned	burned	freeze	froze	frozen
burst	burst	burst	get	got	got, (US)
buy	bought	bought			gotten
can	could	(been	give	gave	given
		able)	go (goes)	went	gone
cast	cast	cast	grind	ground	ground
catch	caught	caught	grow	grew	grown
choose	chose	chosen	hang	hung,	hung,
cling	clung	clung		hanged	hanged
come	came	come	have (has;	had	had
cost	cost	cost	having)		
creep	crept	crept	hear	heard	heard
cut	cut	cut	hide	hid	hidden
deal	dealt	dealt	hit	hit	hit

321

present	pt	pp	present	pt	pp
hold	held	held	sell	sold	sold
hurt	hurt	hurt	send	sent	sent
keep	kept	kept	set	set	set
kneel	knelt,	knelt,	shake	shook	shaken
	kneeled	kneeled	shall	should	—
know	knew	known	shear	sheared	shorn,
lay	laid	laid			sheared
lead	led	led	shed	shed	shed
lean	leant,	leant,	shine	shone	shone
	leaned	leaned	shoot	shot	shot
leap	leapt,	leapt,	show	showed	shown
	leaped	leaped	shrink	shrank	shrunk
learn	learnt,	learnt,	shut	shut	shut
	learned	learned	sing	sang	sung
leave	left	left	sink	sank	sunk
lend	lent	lent	sit	sat	sat
let	let	let	slay	slew	slain
lie (lying)	lay	lain	sleep	slept	slept
light	lit,	lit,	slide	slid	slid
	lighted	lighted	sling	slung	slung
lose	lost	lost	slit	slit	slit
make	made	made	smell	smelt,	smelt,
may	might	—		smelled	smelled
mean	meant	meant	sow	sowed	sown,
meet	met	met			sowed
mistake	mistook	mistaken	speak	spoke	spoken
mow	mowed	mown,	speed	sped,	sped,
		mowed		speeded	speeded
must	(had to)	(had to)	spell	spelt,	spelt,
pay	paid	paid		spelled	spelled
put	put	put	spend	spent	spent
quit	quit,	quit,	spill	spilt,	spilt,
	quitted	quitted		spilled	spilled
read	read	read	spin	spun	spun
rid	rid	rid	spit	spat	spat
ride	rode	ridden	split	split	split
ring	rang	rung	spoil	spoiled,	spoiled,
rise	rose	risen		spoilt	spoilt
run	ran	run	spread	spread	spread
saw	sawed	sawn	spring	sprang	sprung
say	said	said	stand	stood	stood
see	saw	seen	steal	stole	stolen
seek	sought	sought	stick	stuck	stuck

present	pt	pp	present	pt	pp
sting	stung	stung	think	thought	thought
stink	stank	stunk	throw	threw	thrown
stride	strode	stridden	thrust	thrust	thrust
strike	struck	struck, stricken	tread	trod	trodden
			wake	woke, waked	woken, waked
strive	strove	striven			
swear	swore	sworn	wear	wore	worn
sweep	swept	swept	weave	wove, weaved	woven, weaved
swell	swelled	swollen, swelled	wed	wedded, wed	wedded, wed
swim	swam	swum			
swing	swung	swung	weep	wept	wept
take	took	taken	win	won	won
teach	taught	taught	wind	wound	wound
tear	tore	torn	wring	wrung	wrung
tell	told	told	write	wrote	written

LOS NÚMEROS

NUMBERS

un, uno(a)	1	one
dos	2	two
tres	3	three
cuatro	4	four
cinco	5	five
seis	6	six
siete	7	seven
ocho	8	eight
nueve	9	nine
diez	10	ten
once	11	eleven
doce	12	twelve
trece	13	thirteen
catorce	14	fourteen
quince	15	fifteen
dieciséis	16	sixteen
diecisiete	17	seventeen
dieciocho	18	eighteen
diecinueve	19	nineteen
veinte	20	twenty
veintiuno	21	twenty-one
veintidós	22	twenty-two
treinta	30	thirty
treinta y uno(a)	31	thirty-one
treinta y dos	32	thirty-two
cuarenta	40	forty
cuarenta y uno(a)	41	forty-one
cincuenta	50	fifty
sesenta	60	sixty
setenta	70	seventy
ochenta	80	eighty
noventa	90	ninety
cien, ciento	100	a hundred, one hundred
ciento uno(a)	101	a hundred and one
doscientos(as)	200	two hundred
doscientos(as) uno(a)	201	two hundred and one
trescientos(as)	300	three hundred
trescientos(as) uno(a)	301	three hundred and one
cuatrocientos(as)	400	four hundred
quiniento(as)	500	five hundred
seiscientos(as)	600	six hundred

LOS NÚMEROS

NUMBERS

setecientos(as)	700	seven hundred
ochocientos(as)	800	eight hundred
novecientos(as)	900	nine hundred
mil	1 000	a thousand
mil dos	1 002	a thousand and two
cinco mil	5 000	five thousand
un millón	1 000 000	a million

primer, primero(a), 1º, 1er (1ª, 1era)		first, 1st
segundo(a) 2º (2ª)		second, 2nd
tercer, tercero(a), 3º (3ª)		third, 3rd
cuarto(a), 4º (4ª)		fourth, 4th
quinto(a), 5º (5ª)		fifth, 5th
sexto(a), 6º (6ª)		sixth, 6th
séptimo(a)		seventh
octavo(a)		eighth
noveno(a)		ninth
décimo(a)		tenth
undécimo(a)		eleventh
duodécimo(a)		twelfth
decimotercio(a)		thirteenth
decimocuarto(a)		fourteenth
decimoquinto(a)		fifteenth
decimosexto(a)		sixteenth
decimoséptimo(a)		seventeenth
decimoctavo(a)		eighteenth
decimonoveno(a)		nineteenth
vigésimo(a)		twentieth
vigésimo(a) primero(a)		twenty-first
vigésimo(a) segundo(a)		twenty-second
trigésimo(a)		thirtieth
centésimo(a)		hundredth
centésimo(a) primero(a)		hundred-and-first
milésimo(a)		thousandth

LOS NÚMEROS

NUMBERS

Números Quebrados etc

Fractions etc

un medio	a half
un tercio	a third
dos tercios	two thirds
un cuarto	a quarter
un quinto	a fifth
cero coma cinco, 0,5	(nought) point five, 0.5
tres coma cuatro, 3,4	three point four, 3.4
diez por cien(to)	ten per cent
cien por cien	a hundred per cent

Ejemplos

Examples

va a llegar el 7 (de mayo)

he's arriving on the 7th (of May)

vive en el número 7

he lives at number 7

el capítulo/la página 7

chapter/page 7

llegó séptimo

he came in 7th

N.B. In Spanish the ordinal numbers from 1 to 10 are commonly used; from 11 to 20 rather less; above 21 they are rarely written and almost never heard in speech. The custom is to replace the forms for 21 and above by the cardinal number.

LA HORA	**THE TIME**
¿qué hora es?	*what time is it?*
es/son	*it's o it is*
medianoche, las doce (de la noche)	midnight, twelve p.m.
la una (de la madrugada)	one o'clock (in the morning), one (a.m.)
la una y cinco	five past one
la una y diez	ten past one
la una y cuarto *or* quince	a quarter past one, one fifteen
la una y veinticinco	twenty-five past one, one twenty-five
la una y media *or* treinta	half-past one, one thirty
las dos menos veinticinco, la una treinta y cinco	twenty-five to two, one thirty-five
las dos menos veinte, la una cuarenta	twenty to two, one forty
las dos menos cuarto, la una cuarenta y cinco	a quarter to two, one forty-five
las dos menos diez, la una cincuenta	ten to two, one fifty
mediodía, las doce (de la tarde)	twelve o'clock, midday, noon
la una (de la tarde)	one o'clock (in the afternoon), one (p.m.)
las siete (de la tarde)	seven o'clock (in the evening), seven (p.m.)
¿a qué hora?	*(at) what time?*
a medianoche	at midnight
a las siete	at seven o'clock
en veinte minutos	in twenty minutes
hace quince minutos	fifteen minutes ago